ΑΥΤΟΝ Ο ΜΕΝ ΕΠΕΣΕΝ ΠΑΡΑ ΤΗΝ Ο
ΔΟΝ ΚΑΙ ΚΑΤΕΠΑΤΗΘΗ ΚΑΙ ΑΠΕ
ΤΕΙΝΑΤΟ ΟΥ ΟΥΡΑΝΟΥ ΚΑΤΕΦΑΓΕΝ
ΑΥΤΑ ΚΑΙ ΕΤΕΡΟΝ ΚΑΤΕΠΕΣΕΝ ΕΠΙ
ΠΕΤΡΑΝ ΚΑΙ ΦΥΕΝ ΕΞΗΡΑΝΘΗ ΔΙ
Α ΤΟ ΜΗ ΕΧΕΙΝ ΙΚΜΑΔΑ ΚΑΙ ΕΤΕΡΟ
ΕΠΕΣΕΝ ΕΝ ΜΕΣΩ ΤΩΝ ΑΚΑΝΘΩΝ
ΚΑΙ ΣΥΜΦΥΙΣΑΙ ΑΙ ΑΚΑΝΘΑΙ ΑΠΕΠΝΙ
ΞΑΝ ΑΥΤΑ ΚΑΙ ΕΤΕΡΟΝ ΕΠΕΣΕΝ ΕΙΣ
ΤΗΝ ΓΗΝ ΤΗΝ ΑΓΑΘΗΝ ΚΑΙ ΦΥΕΝ
ΕΠΟΙΗΣΕΝ ΚΑΡΠΟΝ ΕΚΑΤΟΝΤΑΠΛΑΣΙ
ΟΝΑ ΤΑΥΤΑ ΛΕΓΩΝ ΕΦΩΝΕΙ Ο ΕΧΩ
Ω ΤΑ ΑΚΟΥΕΙΝ ΑΚΟΥΕΤΩ ΕΠΗΡΩΤΩ
ΔΕ ΑΥΤΟΝ ΟΙ ΜΑΘΗΤΑΙ ΑΥΤΟΥ ΤΙΣ ΕΑΥ
ΤΗ ΕΙΗ Η ΠΑΡΑΒΟΛΗ Ο ΔΕ ΕΙΠΕΝ ΥΜΙΝ
ΔΕΔΟΤΑΙ ΓΝΩΝΑΙ ΤΑ ΜΥΣΤΗΡΙΑ ΤΗΣ
ΒΑΣΙΛΕΙΑΣ ΤΟΥ ΘΥ ΤΟΙΣ ΔΕ ΛΟΙΠ
ΕΝ ΠΑΡΑΒΟΛΑΙΣ ΙΝΑ ΒΛΕΠΟΝΤ
ΜΗ ΒΛΕΠΩΣΙΝ ΚΑΙ ΑΚΟΥΟΝΤΕ
ΜΗ ΣΥΝΙΩΣΙΝ ΕΣΤΙΝ ΔΕ ΑΥΤΗ
ΠΑΡΑΒΟΛΗ Ο ΣΠΟΡΟΣ ΕΣΤΙΝ Ο
ΘΥ ΟΙ ΔΕ ΠΑΡΑ ΤΗΝ ΟΔΟΝ
ΑΚΟΥΣΑΝΤΕΣ ΕΙΤΑ ΕΡΧΕΤΑΙ Ο Δ
ΛΟΣ ΚΑΙ ΑΙΡΕΙ ΤΟΝ ΛΟΓΟΝ ΑΠΟ Τ
ΚΑΡΔΙΑΣ ΑΥΤΩΝ ΙΝΑ ΜΗ ΠΙΣΤΕ
ΣΑΝΤΕΣ ΣΩΘΩΣΙΝ ΟΙ ΔΕ ΕΠΙ ΤΗΣ
ΠΕΤΡΑΣ ΟΙ ΟΤΑΝ ΑΚΟΥΣΩΣΙΝ ΜΕΤΑ
ΧΑΡΑΣ ΔΕΧΟΝΤΑΙ ΤΟΝ ΛΟΓΟΝ ΚΑΙ ΟΥ
ΤΟΙ ΡΙΖΑΝ ΟΥΚ ΕΧΟΥΣΙΝ ΟΙ ΠΡΟΣ ΚΑΙ
ΡΟΝ ΠΙΣΤΕΥΟΥΣΙΝ ΚΑΙ ΕΝ ΚΑΙΡΩ
ΠΕΙΡΑΣΜΟΥ ΑΦΙΣΤΑΝΤΑΙ ΤΟ ΔΕ ΕΙΣ ΤΑΣ
ΑΚΑΝΘΑΣ ΠΕΣΟΝ ΟΥΤΟΙ ΕΙΣΙΝ ΟΙ ΑΚΟΥ
ΣΑΝΤΕΣ ΚΑΙ ΥΠΟ ΜΕΡΙΜΝΩΝ ΚΑΙ
ΠΛΟΥΤΟΥ ΚΑΙ ΗΔΟΝΩΝ ΤΟΥ ΒΙΟΥ
ΠΟΡΕΥΟΜΕΝΟΙ ΣΥΝΠΝΙΓΟΝΤΑΙ
ΚΑΙ ΟΥ ΤΕΛΕΣΦΟΡΟΥΣΙΝ ΤΟ ΔΕ ΕΝ ΤΗ
ΚΑΛΗ ΓΗ ΟΥΤΟΙ ΕΙΣΙΝ ΟΙΤΙΝΕΣ ΕΝ
ΚΑΡΔΙΑ ΚΑΛΗ ΚΑΙ ΑΓΑΘΗ ΑΚΟΥΣΑΝ
ΤΕΣ ΤΟΝ ΛΟΓΟΝ ΚΑΤΕΧΟΥΣΙΝ ΚΑΙ ΚΑΡ
ΠΟΦΟΡΟΥΣΙΝ ΕΝ ΥΠΟΜΟΝΗ ΟΥΔΕΙΣ
ΔΕ ΛΥΧΝΟΝ ΑΨΑΣ ΚΑΛΥΠΤΕΙ ΑΥΤΟΝ
ΣΚΕΥΕΙ Η ΥΠΟΚΑΤΩ ΚΛΕΙΝΗΣ ΤΙΘΗ

**Hermeneia
—A Critical
and Historical
Commentary
on the Bible**

Luke 1

A Commentary
on the Gospel of Luke 1:1–9:50
by François Bovon

Translation by
Christine M. Thomas

Edited by
Helmut Koester

**Fortress
Press**   Minneapolis

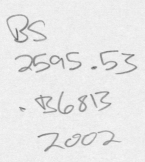

Luke 1
A Commentary
on the Gospel of Luke 1:1—9:50

Cover and interior design by Kenneth Hiebert
Typesetting and page composition by
The HK Scriptorium

Library of Congress Cataloging-in-Publication Data

Bovon, François.
     [Evangelium nach Lukas: 1. English]
     Luke 1 : a commentary on the Gospel of Luke
1:1-9:50 / by François Bovon ; translated by
  Christine M. Thomas.
        p. cm.
     Includes bibliographical references and index.
     ISBN 0-8006-6044-7 (alk. paper)
     1. Bible. N.T. Luke I, 1-IX, 50—Commentaries.
  I. Title: Luke one. II. Title.

BS 2595.53 .B6813 2002
226.4'077—dc21
                                        2001059786

The paper used in this publication meets the minimum requirements of American National Standard
for Information Sciences—Permanence of paper for
Printed Library Materials, ANSI Z329.48–1984.

Manufactured in the U.S.A.   AF 1-6044

06 05 04 03 02   1 2 3 4 5 6 7 8 9 10

The Author

François Bovon is Frothingham Professor of the History of Religion at Harvard Divinity School. He received his appointment to Harvard in 1993, where he was chair of the New Testament Department from 1993–98, resuming the chair again in 2001. A native of Switzerland, for twenty-six years he was Professor of New Testament and Christian Origins at the Divinity School of the University of Geneva, where he was also dean from 1976–79, and continues as an honorary professor.

He received his baccalaureate degree and licentiate in theology from the University of Lausanne, and his Th.D. from the University of Basel. He has also received an honorary doctorate from the University of Uppsala, Sweden.

His research has focused on the Gospel of Luke and Acts of the Apostles, as well as noncanonical Acts of the Apostles. His major publications include: *De Vocatione Gentium* (1967), *Exegesis: Problems of Method and Exercises in Reading* (editor, 1978), *Les Actes Apocryphes des Apôtres* (editor, 1981), *Luke the Theologian* (1987), *New Testament Traditions and Apocryphal Narratives* (1995), *Écrits apocryphes chrétiens I* (editor with Pierre Geoltrain, 1997), *Acta Philippi* (1999), and *The Apocryphal Acts of the Apostles* (editor, 1999). He is also interested in the history of interpretation and critical editions of new early Christian texts in Greek, traveling regularly to the Vatican Library and the monastery libraries on Mount Athos, Greece, for this research.

Endpapers

The endpapers display two fragments of the oldest preserved manuscript of the Gospel of Luke, namely the Papyrus Bodmer XIV-XV, which contains the Gospel of Luke and the Gospel of John. Known by scholars as Papyrus 75 ($\mathfrak{P}^{75}$), it dates to the third century CE. The two plates reproduced in this volume represent Luke 8:5-16 (the parable of the sower in particular) and Luke 24:51 to John 1:1-16 (the ascension of Jesus, the final title "Gospel of Luke," the initial title "Gospel of John," and the beginning of the Johannine prologue). The photographs of the manuscript are from *Papyrus Bodmer XIV-XV: Évangiles de Luc et Jean,* 2 vols., ed. Victor Martin and Rodolphe Kasser (Cologny-Genève: Bibliotheca Bodmeriana, 1961) and are reprinted with the permission of the Bodmer Foundation.

**Contents
Luke 1**

■ **Commentary**

The guiding principle of this translation is that it be optimally meaningful for nonspecialist readers of English. Though it follows Bovon's original in citing fully every ancient text that appears there, an English translation is regularly provided. The New Revised Standard Version forms the basis of all biblical quotations, including the Old Testament Apocrypha. Professor Bovon has created, however, a fresh translation of the Gospel of Luke in his German original, so, in this case, the NRSV translation was necessarily altered to reflect his exegetical and text-critical decisions. Additionally, this English translation reflects revisions the author has made since the German edition was published. Unless otherwise noted, translations of the Old Testament Pseudepigrapha have been taken from Charlesworth's edition, the Dead Sea Scrolls from Vermes's translation, the New Testament Apocrypha from Wilson's standard edition and translation of Hennecke and Schneemelcher's collection, and other ancient authors from the Loeb Classical Library. I have also striven to use easily accessible English translations of modern scholarly works in foreign languages; these are noted consistently throughout. When these were unavailable, I myself have translated the direct quotations of foreign-language authors.

It is a rare privilege for a scholar in my field to translate the work of a living and breathing author. François Bovon has graciously devoted countless hours to reading and evaluating this translation, rescuing me time and again from infelicity and incomprehension. What shortcomings remain reflect my own persistence in error, and where they appear, it is not for lack of correction or guidance.

I would also like to thank David Warren, erstwhile fellow doctoral student at Harvard, for his meticulous work on some of the bibliographic data for the second half of the book, and for his translation of the notes of the pericopes after 6:27. Not only his hard work but his encouraging presence made the last months of labor on the translation much lighter. I thank also the talented assistants at the University of California, Santa Barbara, who have helped me over the years: Sara Kviat, Rachel Bernson, and Michael Cox.

Those who believe in the dissemination of knowledge must also hold to the value of the labor of translation. While working on this, I have often wished that it had been finished already and made available for the students I was instructing at the time. Now it is, not only for them, but for many others.

Christine M. Thomas
University of California, Santa Barbara
July 21, 2000

The name *Hermeneia*, Greek ἑρμηνεία, has been chosen as the title of the commentary series to which this volume belongs. The word *Hermeneia* has a rich background in the history of biblical interpretation as a term used in the ancient Greek-speaking world for the detailed, systematic exposition of a scriptural work. It is hoped that the series, like its name, will carry forward this old and venerable tradition. A second, entirely practical reason for selecting the name lies in the desire to avoid a long descriptive title and its inevitable acronym, or worse, an unpronounceable abbreviation.

The series is designed to be a critical and historical commentary to the Bible without arbitrary limits in size or scope. It will utilize the full range of philological and historical tools, including textual criticism (often slighted in modern commentaries), the methods of the history of tradition (including genre and prosodic analysis), and the history of religion.

Hermeneia is designed for the serious student of the Bible. It will make full use of ancient Semitic and classical languages; at the same time, English translations of all comparative materials—Greek, Latin, Canaanite, or Akkadian—will be supplied alongside the citation of the source in its original language. Insofar as possible, the aim is to provide the student or scholar with full critical discussion of each problem of interpretation and with the primary data upon which the discussion is based.

Hermeneia is designed to be international and interconfessional in the selection of authors; its editorial boards were formed with this end in view. Occasionally the series will offer translations of distinguished commentaries which originally appeared in languages other than English. Published volumes of the series will be revised continually, and eventually, new commentaries will replace older works in order to preserve the currency of the series. Commentaries are also being assigned for important literary works in the categories of apocryphal and pseudepigraphical works relating to the Old and New Testaments, including some of Essene or Gnostic authorship.

The editors of *Hermeneia* impose no systematic-theological perspective upon the series (directly, or indirectly by selection of authors). It is expected that authors will struggle to lay bare the ancient meaning of a biblical work or pericope. In this way the text's human relevance should become transparent, as is always the case in competent historical discourse. However, the series eschews for itself homiletical translation of the Bible.

The editors are heavily indebted to Fortress Press for its energy and courage in taking up an expensive, long-term project, the rewards of which will accrue chiefly to the field of biblical scholarship.

The editor responsible for this volume is Helmut Koester of Harvard University.

Frank Moore Cross	*Helmut Koester*
For the Old Testament	For the New Testament
Editorial Board	Editorial Board

As Luke faced the history of early Christianity, so I, similarly, face Luke's work, with my experience and particular convictions. I wish to examine his Gospel with the sober reserve of a scholar and with the confidence of a believer. For I hope in this manner to arrive at genuine understanding. I also realize that this becomes possible only if God leads me to his Word.

As an interpreter, I never face the text alone. I am always accompanied by the long series of my predecessors, and by the still larger throng of Christian readers. I realize, as well, that both the interpretation and the reception of the text have their own history, which has come down to me only in fragments. When I read, the theologians and teachers of long ago, as well as students and colleagues of today, are enriching company. The sheer number of interpreters and the multitude of their publications intimidate me. I wish to consider these publications and their results with the seriousness they deserve, yet also to be able to relativize them by direct contact with the text itself, which should remain our common standard.

In my encounter with the scholarly works on Luke, the formal analyses of its pericopes and examinations of Jewish contributions to the Gospels have shed the most light. Older works (1800–1950), as well as the commentaries from the Middle Ages and the Reformation, have received in this first volume somewhat less attention in my reading than I would have wished. For the history of effects *(Wirkungsgeschichte)*, I have concentrated on a few works from the patristic era and the Reformation, and have depended on the results of essays and monographs in this field, which are, unfortunately, still not numerous. I hope to continue this dialogue with the interpretation and reception of Luke in the Christian past with greater intensity in the subsequent volumes.

Two recurring themes set the tone for my commentary. First, despite his interest in history, Luke remains in my opinion a theologian of God's Word. This word becomes audible, of course, only in concrete human situations, through human mediation. Second, Luke never develops his christology apart from a living relationship to Christ. The same applies to ecclesiology and ethics. According to Luke, it is only within the context of personal relationships that people participate in the church and remain loyal to the gospel. I am convinced that Luke intends to emphasize both this interrelation and the Word of God.

I wish to add a few words in regard to the completion of this volume. I thank my colleagues in the Evangelisch-katholischer Kommentar for repeatedly giving me fresh motivation and encouraging me to forge ahead in the face of all difficulties. Above all, because my native tongue is French, greater difficulties emerged than first expected precisely on the linguistic level; again and again, I required foreign assistance to correct my German. For this, I extend my thanks to all who supported me: to Reverend Peter Strauss and Elisabeth Hartmann, who did a first revision of the German of the manuscript, also to Dr. Emi Bätschmann, who polished its style, and to Prof. Eduard Schweizer, who helped to shorten an all-too-extensive work and to lend it greater economy. The notes, originally composed in

French, were translated, checked, and often supplemented, with extraordinary accuracy, by Albert Frey. He as well receives my thanks. For five years, I discussed various pericopes with my first assistants, Denise Jornod and Marcel Durrer; together with them I worked through the most important commentaries and the infinite expanse of secondary literature. Annegreth Bovon-Thurneysen directed my attention to the more recent interpretations and to the relevance of the biblical text for the present. Many suggestions came from students with whom I read Luke's Gospel. My later assistants Frédéric Amsler and Emi Bätschmann, then Isabelle Juillard and Eva Tobler shared with me the burden of preparing this volume, at last, for print, and the joy of faithfully continuing the remaining work, particularly the history of interpretation. This "Lukan" partnership with so many people has been valuable and stimulating. I would like to express my heartfelt thanks to all of them, even to those friends who have voiced their sometimes impatient hopes for the birth of this volume (especially of the French version). My thanks also extend to Neukirchener Verlag, and above all to Dr. Volker Hampel, who thoroughly proofread the manuscript and prepared it for press. I thank also Janine Cherix, my secretary for many years, and remember with gratitude the memory of Marie Molina-Bovon, who read the proofs.

I would like to add some lines to these slightly revised words written in Geneva in 1989. I am pleased that this commentary is now available in English, and I would like to thank my colleague and friend Prof. Christine M. Thomas, who brought this remarkable translation to completion. It has been a pleasure to read her drafts and installments over the years. I always admired her skill in English and her grasp of German. I would express also my gratitude to David Warren, a former doctoral student at Harvard and a friend, who spent many hours in the translation of the notes of several pericopes and the checking of bibliographical items. I would like to thank the editorial board of Hermeneia, particularly my colleagues and friends Helmut Koester, James Robinson, and Eldon Epp, who supported the publication of this volume. I warmly thank Helmut Koester for his work as editor of this volume.

Since the publication of this volume in German twelve years ago, I have published the exegesis of Luke 9:51—14:35 (in 1996) and 15:1—19:27 (in 2001). I was not able or willing to "look backward" (Luke 9:62!) to update this volume, for example, to take up a dialogue with Hans Dieter Betz's commentary on the Sermon on the Mount. It would have distracted my energy from my goal: to finish the commentary in the next few years. I hope that readers will understand my decision. With the help of another friend, Dr. Christopher R. Matthews, whom I also thank warmly, I have added some entries to the general bibliography and to the bibliographies of the pericopes.

Cambridge, Massachusetts
December 21, 2001

Reference Codes

1. Sources and Abbreviations

AAR	American Academy of Religion
AB	Anchor Bible
'Abot R. Nat.	*'Abot de Rabbi Nathan*
Acts John	*Acts of John*
Acts Phil.	*Acts of Philip*
Acts Pil.	*Acts of Pilate*
Acts Pet.	*Acts of Peter*
Aeschylus	
Prom.	*Prometheus vinctus*
AJBI	*Annual of the Japanese Biblical Institute*
ALBO	Analecta lovaniensia biblica et orientalia
AnBib	Analecta biblica
AnBoll	Analecta Bollandiana
ANF	Ante-Nicene Fathers
ANRW	*Aufstieg und Niedergang der römischen Welt*
Apoc. Elijah	*Apocalypse of Elijah*
Apoc. Pet.	*Apocalypse of Peter*
Aristotle	
Poet.	*Poetica*
Rhet.	*Rhetorica*
Arrian	
Anab.	*Anabasis*
ASB	Atti della settimana biblica
ASNU	Acta seminarii neotestamentici upsaliensis
AsSeign	*Assemblées du Seigneur*
AThANT	Abhandlungen zur Theologie des Alten und Neuen Testaments
ATLA	American Theological Libraries Association
ATR	*Anglican Theological Review*
Aug	*Augustinianum*
AUSS	*Andrews Univeristy Seminary Studies*
b.	Babylonian Talmud
B. Mesʿ.	*Baba Mesiʿa*
BA	*Biblical Archaeologist*
BAC	Biblioteca de autores cristianos
BAGB	*Bulletin de l'association Guillaume Budé*
BAGD	Walter Bauer, *A Greek-English Lexicon of the New Testament and Other Early Christian Literature* (trans. and ed. William F. Arndt and F. Wilbur Gingrich; rev. Gingrich and Friedrick W. Danker; 2d ed.; Chicago: University of Chicago Press, 1979)
1 Bar	1 Baruch (in OT Apocrypha)
2 Bar.	Syriac *Apocalypse of Baruch*
3 Bar.	Greek *Apocalypse of Baruch*
BARev	*Biblical Archaeology Review*
Barn.	*Barnabas*
BBB	Bonner biblische Beiträge
BDF	Friedrich Blass and Albert Debrunner, *A Greek Grammar of the New Testament and Other Early Christian Literature* (trans. and rev. Robert W. Funk; Chicago: University of Chicago Press, 1961)
BeO	*Bibbia e oriente*
Ber.	*Berakot*
BETL	Bibliotheca ephemeridum theologicarum lovaniensium
BEvTh	Beiträge zur evangelischen Theologie
BFCTh	Beiträge zur Forderung christlicher Theologie
BGBE	Beiträge zur Geschichte der biblischen Exegese
BHH	Bo Reicke and Leonhard Rost, eds., *Biblisch-Historisches Handwörterbuch: Landeskunde, Geschichte, Religion, Kultur, Literatur* (4 vols; Göttingen: Vandenhoeck & Ruprecht, 1962–79)
BHTh	Beiträge zur historischen Theologie
Bib	*Biblica*
Bib. Ant.	Pseudo-Philo, *Biblical Antiquities*
BibLeb	*Bibel und Leben*
BibRev	*Bible Review*
BibS (N)	Biblische Studien (Neukirchen, 1951–)
Bijdr	*Bijdragen: Tijdschrift voor filosofie en theologie*
BJRL	*Bulletin of the John Rylands University Library of Manchester*
BK	*Bibel und Kirche*
BKAT	Biblischer Kommentar: Altes Testament
BLit	*Bibel und Liturgie*
BN	*Biblische Notizen*
BSac	*Bibliotheca Sacra*
BT	*The Bible Translator*
BTB	*Biblical Theology Bulletin*
BU	Biblische Untersuchungen
BurH	*Buried History*
BVC	*Bible et vie chrétienne*
BWANT	Beiträge zur Wissenschaft vom Alten und Neuen Testament
BZ	*Biblische Zeitschrift*
BZAW	Beihefte zur *Zeitschrift für die alttestamentliche Wissenschaft*

BZNW	Beihefte zur *Zeitschrift für die neutestamentliche Wissenschaft*		Kommentar zum Neuen Testament Vorarbeiten
CBC:NEB	Cambridge Bible Commentary: New English Bible	*Emm*	*Emmanuel*
CBFV	*Cahiers bibliques de Foi et Vie*	1 *Enoch*	Ethiopic *Enoch*
CBQ	*Catholic Biblical Quarterly*	2 *Enoch*	Slavonic *Enoch*
CCSA	Corpus Christianorum Series Apocryphorum	3 *Enoch*	Hebrew *Enoch*
CCSL	Corpus Christianorum Series Latina	*Ep.*	*Epistle*
CD	Cairo (Genizah) text of the Damascus Document	*Ep. Arist.*	*Epistle of Aristeas*
		Epictetus	
CEA	Collection d'études anciennes	*Diss.*	*Dissertationes*, the *Discourses*
CEv	*Cahiers évangile*	*Ench.*	*Enchiridion*
Chrysostom	John Chrysostom	Epiphanius	
Hom. in Act.	*Homiliae in Acta apostolorum*	*Adv. haer.*	*Adversus haereses* (*Panarion*)
Cicero		1-2 *Esdr*	1-2 Esdras
Lig.	*Pro Ligario*	*EstBib*	*Estudios bíblicos*
CIL	*Corpus inscriptionum latinarum*	*EstEcl*	*Estudios eclesiásticos*
1–2 Clem.	*1–2 Clement*	EtB	Études bibliques
Clement of Alexandria		*EThL*	*Ephemerides theologicae lovanienses*
Exc. Theod.	*Excerpta ex Theodoto*	*EThR*	*Études théologiques et religieuses*
Strom.	*Stromateis*	EThSt	Erfurter theologische Studien
CNT	Commentaire du Nouveau Testament	Eunapius	
ConBNT	Coniectanea biblica, New Testament	*VS*	*Vitae Sophistarum*
		Euripides	
CRAIBL	*Comptes rendus de l'Académie des inscriptions et belles-lettres*	*Herac.*	*Heraclidae*
		Hipp.	*Hippolytus*
CRB	Cahiers de la *Revue biblique*	*Or.*	*Orestes*
CRINT	Compendia rerum iudicarum ad Novum Testamentum	Eusebius	Eusebius of Caesarea
		Comm. Ps.	*In Psalmos Commentarius*
		Hist. eccl.	*Historia ecclesiastica*
CSCO	Corpus scriptorum christiano-rum orientalium	*EvQ*	*Evangelical Quarterly*
		EvTh	*Evangelische Theologie*
CSEL	Corpus scriptorum ecclesiastico-rum latinorum	*ExpTim*	*Expository Times*
		FB	Forschung zur Bibel
CTh	Cahiers théologiques	FRLANT	Forschungen zur Religion und Literatur des Alten und Neuen Testaments
CurTM	*Currents in Theology and Mission*		
CV	*Communio Viatorum*	FTS	Frankfurter theologische Studien
Cyril	Cyril of Jerusalem	*FV*	*Foi et Vie*
Cat. Myst.	*Catecheses Mystagogicae*	GCS	Griechische christliche Schrift-steller der ersten drei Jahr-hunderte
DBSup	*Dictionnaire de la Bible, Supplément*		
Demosthenes			
De cor.	*De corona*	*Gos. Heb.*	*Gospel According to the Hebrews*
Did.	*Didache*	*Gos. Phil.*	*Gospel of Philip*
Dionysius of Halicarnassus		*Gos. Thom.*	*Gospel of Thomas*
Ant. Roma.	*Antiquitates Romanae*	*GrB*	*Grazer Beiträge*
Pomp.	*Epistula ad Pompeium*	*Greg*	*Gregorianum*
DissAb	*Dissertation Abstracts*	GThA	Göttinger theologische Arbeiten
EDNT	Horst Balz and Gerhard Schneider, eds., *Exegetical Dictionary of the New Testament* (3 vols.; Grand Rapids: Eerdmans, 1990–93)	HB	Hebrew Bible
		Hermas	*Shepherd of Hermas*
		Sim.	*Similitude*
		Vis.	*Vision*
		Hesiod	
EeT	*Église et théologie*	*Op.*	*Opera et dies*
EHS	Europäische Hochschulschriften	Hippolytus	
EKKNT	Evangelisch-katholischer Kommentar zum Neuen Testament	*Comm. Dan.*	*Commenarium in Danielem*
		Ref.	*Refutatio omnium haeresium*
		HNT	Handbuch zum Neuen Testament
EKKNTV	Evangelisch-katholischer		

HNTC	Harper's NT Commentaries	KEK	Kritisch-exegetischer Kommentar über das Neue Testament
Homer			
Il.	*Iliad*	KEKSup	KEK, Supplement
HThKNT	Herders theologischer Kommentar zum Neuen Testament	1-4 Kgdms	1-4 Kingdoms (LXX)
		LCL	Loeb Classical Library
		LD	Lectio divina
HTR	*Harvard Theological Review*	log.	logion, logia
HTS	Harvard Theological Studies	LPGL	G. W. H. Lampe, ed., *A Patristic Greek Lexicon* (Oxford: Clarendon, 1961)
HUCA	*Hebrew Union College Annual*		
IBS	*Irish Biblical Studies*		
ICC	International Critical Commentary	LSJ	Henry George Liddell and Robert Scott, *Greek-English Lexicon* (9th ed; 1940; rev. Henry Stuart Jones; reprint Oxford: Clarendon, 1961)
IDB	G. A. Buttrick, ed., *Interpreter's Dictionary of the Bible*		
IG	*Inscriptiones graecae*		
Ignatius		Lucian	Lucian of Samosata
Trall.	*Letter to the Trallians*	*De Merc. cond.*	*De Mercede conductis*
ILS	*Inscriptiones latinae selectae*	*Dial. deor.*	*Dialogi deorum*
Imm	*Immanuel: A Bulletin of Religious Thought and Research in Israel*	*Hist. conscr.*	*Quomodo historia conscribenda sit*
		LumVie	*Lumière et vie*
Int	*Interpretation*	LXX	Septuagint
Irenaeus		*m.*	Mishna
Adv. haer.	*Adversus haereses*	*Mar*	*Marianum*
ITQ	*Irish Theological Quarterly*	ms(s).	manuscript(s)
ITS	*Indian Theological Studies*	MT	Masoretic (Hebrew) text
JAC	Jahrbuch für Antike und Christentum	*MThZ*	*Münchener theologische Zeitschrift*
		n(n).	note(s)
JBL	*Journal of Biblical Literature*	NCB	New Century Bible
JBR	*Journal of Bible and Religion*	*NedThT*	*Nederlands theologisch tijdschrift*
Jerome		*Neot*	*Neotestamentica*
Ad. Pelag.	*Adversus Pelagium*	NHC	Nag Hammadi Codex
Comm. in Is.	*Commentarii in Isaiam prophetam*	NICNT	New International Commentary on the New Testament
Ep. ad Paulinum	*Epistula ad Paulinum*		
Vir. ill.	*De viris illustribus*	*NovT*	*Novum Testamentum*
JETS	*Journal of the Evangelical Theological Society*	NovTSup	*Novum Testamentum,* Supplements
JJS	*Journal of Jewish Studies*	*NRSV*	*New Revised Standard Version*
Jos. Asen.	*Joseph and Aseneth*	*NRTh*	*La nouvelle revue théologique*
Josephus	Flavius Josephus	n.s.	new series
Ant.	*Antiquitates Judaicae*	NT	New Testament
Ap.	*Contra Apionem*	NTAbh	Neutestamentliche Abhandlungen
Bell.	*Bellum Judaicum*		
JQR	*Jewish Quarterly Review*	NTD	Das Neue Testament Deutsch
JR	*Journal of Religion*	NTL	New Testament Library
JSHRZ	Jüdische Schriften aus hellenistisch-römischer Zeit	*NTS*	*New Testament Studies*
		NTT	*Norsk Teologisk Tidsskrift*
JSNT	*Journal for the Study of the New Testament*	OBO	Orbis biblicus et orientalis
		OBT	Overtures to Biblical Theology
JSNTSup	Supplement to *Journal for the Study of the New Testament*	*Odes Sol.*	*Odes of Solomon*
		OrChr	*Oriens christianus*
JSOTSup	Supplement to *Journal for the Study of the Old Testament*	Origen	
		Comm. in Joh.	*In Johannem Commentarius*
JTS	*Journal of Theological Studies*	*Comm. in Matt.*	*In Mattheum Commentarius*
Jub.	*Jubilees*	*Hom. in Luc.*	*Homiliae in Evangelium secundum Lucam*
Justin	Justin Martyr		
Apol.	*Apologia*	OT	Old Testament
Dial.	*Dialogus cum Tryphone*		
KBANT	Kommentare und Beiträge zum Alten und Neuen Testament		
KD	*Kerygma und Dogma*		

OTP	James H. Charlesworth, ed., *The Old Testament Pseudepigrapha* (2 vols.; Garden City, N.Y.: Doubleday, 1983–85)	PTMS	Pittsburgh/Princeton Theological Monograph Series
p(p).	page(s)	Q	The Sayings Gospel
P. Egerton	Papyrus Egerton	1QapGen	*Genesis Apocryphon* from Qumran Cave 1
P. Lond.	F. G. Kenyon et al., eds., *Greek Papyri in the British Museum* (5 vols.; London: British Museum, 1893–1917)	1QH	*Hôdayôt* (*Thanksgiving Hymns*) from Qumran Cave 1
		1QM	*Milḥamah* (*War Scroll*)
P. Oxy.	B. P. Grenfell and A. S. Hunt, eds., *The Oxyrhynchus Papyri* (15 vols.; London: Egypt Exploration Fund, 1898–1922)	1QpHab	*Pešer on Habbakuk* from Qumran Cave 1
		1QS	*Serekh* (*Rule of the Community, Manual of Discipline*)
par.	parallel(s)	1QSa	Appendix A (*Rule of the Congregation*) to 1QS
PG	J.-P. Migne, ed., *Patrologia graeca*	1QSb	Appendix B (*Blessings*) to 1QS
Philo	Philo of Alexandria	4QPsDanA[a]	pseudo-Danielic text in Aramaic from Qumran Cave 4
Abr.	*De Abrahamo*		
Agr.	*De agricultura*	4QTestim	*Testimonia* from Qumran Cave 4
Cher.	*De cherubim*	11QMelch	*Melchizedek* text from Qumran Cave 11
Flacc.	*In Flaccum*		
Mig.	*De migratione Abrahami*	*Rab.*	*Rabbah* (following the abbreviation of a biblical book)
Rer. div. her.	*Quis rerum divinarum heres*	*RAC*	*Reallexikon für Antike und Christentum*
Somn.	*De somniis*		
Spec.	*De specialibus legibus*	*RB*	*Revue biblique*
Virt.	*De virtutibus*	*RBén*	*Revue bénédictine*
Vit. cont.	*De vita contemplativa*	*RBR*	*Ricerche bibliche e religiose*
Vit. Mos.	*De vita Mosis*	RechBib	Recherches bibliques
Philostratus		*RechSR*	*Recherches de science religieuse*
Vit. Ap.	*Vita Apollonii*	*REG*	*Revue des études grecques*
Phrynichus		*ResQ*	*Restoration Quarterly*
Ecl.	*Eclogae nominum et verborum Atticorum*	*RevExp*	*Review and Expositor*
		RevistB	*Revista bíblica*
Pirqe R. El.	*Pirqe Rabbi Eliezer*	*RevQ*	*Revue de Qumrân*
PL	J.-P. Migne, ed., *Patrologia latina*	*RevScRel*	*Revue des sciences religieuses*
Plato		*RevThom*	*Revue thomiste*
Leg.	*Leges*	*RGG*	*Religion in Geschichte und Gegenwart*
Polit.	*Politicus*		
Resp.	*Respublica* (*The Republic*)	*RHPhR*	*Revue d'histoire et de philosophie religieuses*
Tim.	*Timaeus*		
Pliny		*RivB*	*Rivista biblica*
Nat. hist.	*Naturalis historia*	RNT	Regensburger Neues Testament
Plutarch		*RPh*	*Revue de philologie, de littérature et d'histoire anciennes*
Ages.	*De Agesilao* in *Parallel Lives*		
Caes.	*De Caesare* in *Parallel Lives*	*RSPhTh*	*Revue des sciences philosophiques et théologiques*
Is. et Os.	*De Iside et Osiride*		
Lib. Educ.	*De liberis educandis*	*RThL*	*Revue théologique de Louvain*
Numa	*De Numa Pompilio* in *Parallel Lives*	*RThPh*	*Revue de théologie et de philosophie*
Quaest. conv.	*Quaestiones convivales*	*RTR*	*Reformed Theological Review*
PNTC	Pelican New Testament Commentaries	*Šabb.*	*Šabbat*
		SANT	Studien zum Alten und Neuen Testament
Pollux	Julius Pollux		
Onom.	*Onomasticon*	SB	Sources bibliques
Polycarp		SBB	Stuttgarter biblische Beiträge
Phil.	*Epistle to the Philippians*	*SBFLA*	*Studii biblici franciscani liber annuus*
Prot. Jas.	*Protevangelium of James*		
Ps.-Clem.	*Pseudo-Clementine literature*	SBLDS	Society of Biblical Literature Dissertation Series
Rec.	*Recognitions*		
Ps. Sol.	*Psalms of Solomon*		

SBLMS	Society of Biblical Literature Monograph Series	*Syll.*[3]	Wilhelm Dittenberger, *Sylloge inscriptionum graecarum* (3d ed.; Leipzig: Hirzel, 1915–24)
SBLSBS	Society of Biblical Literature Sources for Biblical Study	Symm	Symmachus (Greek version of OT)
SBLSP	Society of Biblical Literature Seminar Papers	*t.*	Tosephta
SBLTT	Society of Biblical Literature Texts and Translations	*T. 12 Patr.*	*Testaments of the Twelve Patriarchs*
SBS	Stuttgarter Bibelstudien	*T. Abr.*	*Testament of Abraham*
SBT	Studies in Biblical Theology	*T. Ash.*	*Testament of Asher*
SBU	Symbolae biblicae upsalienses	*T. Benj.*	*Testament of Benjamin*
SC	Sources chrétiennes	*T. Gad*	*Testament of Gad*
ScEccl	*Sciences ecclésiastiques*	*T. Jos.*	*Testament of Joseph*
ScEs	*Science et esprit*	*T. Jud.*	*Testament of Judah*
SCHNT	Studia ad corpus hellenisticum Novi Testamenti	*T. Levi*	*Testament of Levi*
		T. Naph.	*Testament of Naphtali*
Sef	*Sefarad*	*T. Sim.*	*Testament of Simeon*
Sem	*Semitica*	*T. Zeb.*	*Testament of Zebulun*
SHAW.PH	Sitzungsberichte der Heidelberger Akademie der Wissenschaften: Philosophisch-historische Klasse	Tacitus	
		Ann.	*Annals*
Sib. Or.	*Sibylline Oracles*	*TBT*	*The Bible Today*
SJLA	Studies in Judaism in Late Antiquity	*TDNT*	Gerhard Kittel and Gerhard Friedrich, eds., *Theological Dictionary of the New Testament* (trans. and ed. Geoffrey W. Bromiley; 10 vols.; Grand Rapids: Eerdmans, 1964–76)
SJT	*Scottish Journal of Theology*		
SN	Studia neotestamentica		
SNTSMS	Society for New Testament Studies Monograph Series		
SNTU	Studien zum Neuen Testament und seiner Umwelt	*TDOT*	G. J. Botterweck et al., eds., Theological Dictionary of the Old Testament (trans. D. E. Green et al.; Grand Rapids: Eerdmans, 1974–)
Sophocles		Tertullian	
Ai.	*Aiax*	*Adv. Marc.*	*Adversus Marcionem*
Ant.	*Antigone*	*Bapt.*	*De baptismo*
SPAW	Sitzungsberichte der preussischen Akademie der Wissenschaften	*Tg. Neof.*	*Targum Neofiti I*
		Tg. Ps.-J.	*Targum Pseudo-Jonathan*
		Th	Theodotion (Greek version of OT)
SR	*Studies in Religion/Sciences religieuses*	*ThBei*	*Theologische Beiträge*
StEv	*Studia Evangelica*	ThBü	Theologische Bücherei
StNT	Studien zum Neuen Testament	ThF	Theologische Forschung
STö.H	Sammlung Töpelmann: Hilfsbücher	ThH	Théologie historique
		ThHKNT	Theologischer Handkommentar zum Neuen Testament
StPatr	Studia Patristica		
Str-B	Hermann Strack and Paul Billerbeck, *Kommentar zum Neuen Testament aus Talmud und Midrasch*, vols. 1–4 (5th ed.; Munich: Beck, 1969); vols. 5–6 and index (ed. Joachim Jeremias and K. Adolph; 3d ed.; Munich: Beck, 1963)	*ThLZ*	*Theologische Literaturzeitung*
		ThQ	*Theologische Quartalschrift*
		ThViat	*Theologia Viatorum*
		ThWNT	Gerhard Kittel and Gerhard Friedrich, eds., *Theologisches Wörterbuch zum Neuen Testament* (10 vols.; Stuttgart: Kohlhammer, 1932–79)
StTh	*Studia Theologica*	*ThZ*	*Theologische Zeitschrift*
StudNeot	Studia neotestamentica	*TLOT*	E. Jenni and C. Westermann, eds., *Theological Lexicon of the Old Testament* (trans. M. E. Biddle; 3 vols.; Peabody, Mass.: Hendrickson, 1997)
Suetonius			
Aug.	*Augustus (De vita Caesarum)*		
Sukk.	*Sukka*		
SUNT	Studien zur Umwelt des Neuen Testaments		

TOB	*Traduction œcuménique de la Bible* (Paris: Société biblique française, 1977)
TPQ	*Theologisch-praktische Quartalschrift*
TRE	*Theologische Realenzyklopädie*
TRev	*Theologische Revue*
TS	*Theological Studies*
TThZ	*Trierer theologische Zeitschrift*
TU	Texte und Untersuchungen
UUÅ	Uppsala universitetsårskrift
v(v).	verse(s)
VC	*Vigiliae christianae*
VD	*Verbum domini*
Virgil	
Ecl.	*Ecloge*
VF	*Verkündigung und Forschung*
VT	*Vetus Testamentum*
VTSup	*Vetus Testamentum*, Supplements
WD	*Wort und Dienst*
WdF	Wege der Forschung
WMANT	Wissenschaftliche Monographien zum Alten und Neuen Testament
WSAMA.T	Walberger Studien der Albertus-Magnus Akademie: Theologie
WUNT	Wissenschaftliche Untersuchungen zum Neuen Testament
Xenophon	
An.	*Anabasis*
Cyrop.	*Cyropaedia*
Hist. Graec.	*Historia Graeca*
Xenophon Ephesius	
Eph.	*Ephesiaca*
y.	Jerusalem Talmud
ZDPV	*Zeitschrift des deutschen Palästina-Vereins*
ZEE	*Zeitschrift für evangelische Ethik*
ZKTh	*Zeitschrift für katholische Theologie*
ZNW	*Zeitschrift für die neutestamentliche Wissenschaft*
ZRGG	*Zeitschrift für Religions- und Geistesgeschichte*
ZThK	*Zeitschrift für Theologie und Kirche*

2. Short Titles

À cause
F. Refoulé, ed., *À cause de l'Évangile: Études sur les Synoptiques et les Actes: Festschrift Jacques Dupont* (LD 123; Paris: Cerf, 1985).

Abel, *Grammaire*
Félix-Marie Abel, *Grammaire du grec biblique suivie d'un choix de papyrus* (2d ed.; EtB; Paris: Gabalda, 1927).

Achtemeier, "Lucan Perspective"
Paul J. Achtemeier, "The Lucan Perspective on the Miracles of Jesus: A Preliminary Sketch," *JBL* 94 (1975) 547–62, reprinted in C. H. Talbert, ed., *Perspectives on Luke-Acts* (Danville, Va.: Association of Baptist Professors of Religion, 1978) 153–67.

Achtemeier, "Miracles"
Paul J. Achtemeier, "Miracles and the Historical Jesus: A Study of Mk 9,14–29," *CBQ* 37 (1975) 471–91.

Agouridès, "Béatitudes"
Savas Agouridès, "La tradition des béatitudes chez Matthieu et Luc," in A. Descamps and A. de Halleux, eds., *Mélanges bibliques: Festschrift Béda Rigaux* (Gembloux: Duculot, 1970) 9–27.

Aland, *Synopsis*
K. Aland, ed., *Synopsis Quattuor Evangeliorum* (3d ed.; Stuttgart: Deutsche Bibel-Stiftung, 1966).

Alt, *Peace*
Franz Alt, *Peace Is Possible: The Politics of the Sermon on the Mount* (trans. J. Neugroschel; New York: Scribner, 1985).

Annen, *Heil*
Franz Annen, *Heil für die Heiden: Zur Bedeutung und Geschichte der Tradition vom besessenen Gerasener (Mk 5,1–20 parr.)* (FTS 20; Frankfurt am Main: Knecht, 1976).

Antoniadis, *Évangile*
Sophie Antoniadis, *L'Évangile de Luc: Esquisse de grammaire et de style* (Collection de l'Institut néo-héllenique de l'Université de Paris 7; Paris: Belles Lettres, 1930).

Audet, "Annonce"
Jean-Paul Audet, "L'annonce à Marie," *RB* 63 (1956) 346–74.

Auffret, "Note"
Pierre Auffret, "Note sur la structure littéraire de Lc 1, 68–79," *NTS* 24 (1977–78) 248–58.

Bailly, *Dictionnaire*
Anatole Bailly, *Dictionnaire grec-français . . .* (2 ed.; rev. E. Egger; Paris: Hachette, 1897).

Baldermann, *Gott des Friedens*
Ingo Baldermann, *Der Gott des Friedens und die Götter der Macht: Biblische Alternativen* (Wege des Lernens 1; Neukirchen-Vluyn: Neukirchener Verlag, 1983).

Baltensweiler, *Verklärung*
Heinrich Baltensweiler, *Die Verklärung Jesu: Historisches Ereignis und synoptische Berichte* (AThANT 33; Zurich: Zwingli-Verlag, 1959).

Bastin, "Annonce"
Marcel Bastin, "L'annonce de la passion et les critères de l'historicité," *RevScRel* 50 (1976) 289–329; 51 (1977) 187–213.

Benoit, "Annonciation"
Pierre Benoit, "L'annonciation," *AsSeign* 6 (1965) 40–57, reprinted in idem, *Exégèse et théologie* (4 vols.; Paris: Cerf, 1961–83) 3.197–215. Cited from the latter.

Benoit, "Enfance"
Pierre Benoit, "L'enfance de Jean-Baptiste selon Luc 1," *NTS* 3 (1956–57) 169–94, reprinted in idem, *Exégèse*, 3.165–96. Cited from the journal.

Benoit, "Épis"
Pierre Benoit, "Les épis arrachés (Mt 12,1–8 et par.)," *SBFLA* 13 (1962–63) 76–92, reprinted in idem, *Exégèse*, 3.228–50. Cited from the latter.

Benoit, "Et toi-même"
Pierre Benoit, "'Et toi-même, un glaive te transpercera l'âme!' (Luc 2,35)," *CBQ* 25 (1963) 251–61, reprinted in idem, *Exégèse*, 3.216–27. Cited from the latter.

Benoit, *Exégèse*
Pierre Benoit, *Exégèse et Théologie* (4 vols.; Paris: Cerf, 1961–83).

Benoit, "Non erat"
Pierre Benoit, "'Non erat eis locus in diversorio' (Lc 2,7)," in A. Descamps and A. de Halleux, eds., *Mélanges bibliques: Festschrift Béda Rigaux* (Gembloux: Duculot, 1970) 173–86, reprinted in Benoit, *Exégèse*, 4.95–111. Cited from the latter.

Benoit, "Quirinius"
Pierre Benoit, "Quirinius (Recensement de)," *DBSup* 9 (1977) 693–720.

Bertrand, *Baptême*
Daniel A. Bertrand, *Le baptême de Jésus: Histoire de l'exégèse aux deux premiers siècles* (BGBE 14; Tübingen: Mohr, 1973).

Betz, *Abraham*
O. Betz et al., eds., *Abraham unser Vater: Juden und Christen im Gespräch über die Bibel: Festschrift Otto Michel* (Leiden: Brill, 1963).

Betz, *Sermon on the Mount*
Hans-Dieter Betz, *The Sermon on the Mount: A Commentary on the Sermon on the Mount Including the Sermon on the Plain (Matthew 5:3–7:27 and Luke 6:20–49)* (Hermeneia; Minneapolis: Fortress Press, 1995).

Bieler, *ΘΕΙΟΣ ΑΝΗΡ*
Ludwig Bieler, *ΘΕΙΟΣ ΑΝΗΡ: Das Bild des "göttlichen Menschen" in Spätantike und Frühchristentum* (2 vols. in 1; Vienna: Oskar Höfels, 1935–36).

Billerbeck, "Tempelgottesdienst"
Paul Billerbeck, "Ein Tempelgottesdienst in Jesu Tagen," *ZNW* 55 (1964) 1–17.

Böcher, *Dämonenfurcht*
Otto Böcher, *Dämonenfurcht und Dämonenabwehr: Ein Beitrag zur Vorgeschichte der christlichen Taufe* (BWANT 90; Stuttgart: Kohlhammer, 1970).

Böcher, "Johannes"
Otto Böcher, "Aß Johannes der Täufer kein Brot (Luk. 7,33)?" *NTS* 18 (1971–72) 90–92.

Bornhäuser, *Sondergut*
Karl Bornhäuser, *Studien zum Sondergut des Lukas* (Gütersloh: Bertelsmann, 1934).

Bornkamm, "Πνεῦμα"
Günther Bornkamm, "Πνεῦμα ἄλαλον: Eine Studie zum Markusevangelium," in K. Gaiser, ed., *Das Altertum und jedes neue Gute: Festschrift W. Schadewaldt* (Stuttgart: Kohlhammer, 1970) 369–85, reprinted in Bornkamm, *Gesammelte Aufsätze*, vol. 4, *Geschichte und Glaube II* (BEvTh 53; Munich: Kaiser, 1971) 21–36. Cited from the latter.

Bossuyt-Radermakers
Philippe Bossuyt and Jean Radermakers, *Jésus, Parole de la grâce: Selon St. Luc* (2 vols.; Brussels: Institut d'études théologiques, 1981).

Bovon, *Actes apocryphes*
F. Bovon, ed., *Les Actes apocryphes des apôtres: Christianisme et monde païen* (Publications de la Faculté de théologie de l'Université de Genève 4; Geneva: Labor et Fides, 1981).

Bovon, *Lukas*
François Bovon, *Lukas in neuer Sicht: Gesammelte Aufsätze* (trans. E. Hartmann, A. Frey, and P. Strauss; Biblisch-theologische Studien 8; Neukirchen-Vluyn: Neukirchener Verlag, 1985).

Bovon, *Theologian*
François Bovon, *Luke the Theologian: Thirty-three Years of Research: 1950–1983* (trans. K. McKinney; PTMS 12; Allison Park, Pa.: Pickwick, 1987).

Braumann, *Lukas-Evangelium*
G. Braumann, ed., *Das Lukas-Evangelium: Die Redaktions- und Kompositionsgeschichtliche Forschung* (WdF 280; Darmstadt: Wissenschaftliche Buchgesellschaft, 1974).

Brown, *Antiquity*
Peter R. L. Brown, *The Making of Late Antiquity* (Carl Newell Jackson Lectures; Cambridge, Mass.: Harvard University Press, 1978).

Brown, *Birth*
Raymond E. Brown, *The Birth of the Messiah: A Commentary on the Infancy Narratives in Matthew and Luke* (New York: Doubleday; London: G. Chapman, 1977).

Brown, *Mary*
Raymond E. Brown et al., eds., *Mary in the New Testament* (Philadelphia: Fortress Press, 1978).

Brown, *Apostasy*
Schuyler Brown, *Apostasy and Perseverance in the Theology of Luke* (AnBib 36; Rome: Pontifical Biblical Institute Press, 1969).

Brunner-Traut, "Geburtsgeschichte"
Emma Brunner-Traut, "Die Geburtsgeschichte der Evangelien im Lichte ägyptologischer Forschungen," *ZRGG* 12 (1960) 97–111.

Bultmann, *History*
Rudolf Bultmann, *The History of the Synoptic Tradition* (trans. J. Marsh; rev. ed.; New York: Harper & Row, 1976).

Burchard, "Fußnoten"
Christoph Burchard, "Fußnoten zum neutestamentlichen Griechisch II," *ZNW* 69 (1978) 145–46.

Busse, *Nazareth-Manifest*
Ulrich Busse, *Das Nazareth-Manifest: Eine Einführung in das lukanische Jesusbild nach Lk 4,16–30* (SBS 91; Stuttgart: Katholisches Bibelwerk, 1978).

Busse, *Wunder*
Ulrich Busse, *Die Wunder des Propheten Jesus: Die Rezeption, Komposition, und Interpretation der Wundertradition im Evangelium des Lukas* (FB 24; Stuttgart: Katholisches Bibelwerk, 1977).

Cadbury, "Commentary"

Henry J. Cadbury, "Commentary on the Preface of Luke," in F. J. Foakes-Jackson and K. Lake, eds., *The Beginnings of Christianity*, part 1: *The Acts of the Apostles* (5 vols.; London: Macmillan, 1920–33), vol. 2: *Prolegomena II: Criticism*, 489–510.

Cadbury, *Style*

Henry J. Cadbury, *The Style and Literary Method of Luke* (1920; HTS 6; reprinted New York: Kraus Reprint, 1969).

Calvin, *Harmony*

Jean Calvin, *A Harmony of the Gospels Matthew, Mark and Luke* (trans. A. W. Morrison [vols. 1, 3], T. H. L. Parker [vol. 2]; 3 vols.; Calvin's Commentaries 1–3; Edinburgh: Oliver and Boyd, 1972).

Cambe, "Χάρις"

M. Cambe, "La χάρις chez Saint Luc," *RB* 70 (1963) 193–207.

Cerfaux, "Fructifiez"

Lucien Cerfaux, "Fructifiez en supportant (l'épreuve): À propos de Luc VIII,15," *RB* 64 (1957) 481–91, reprinted in idem, *Recueil Lucien Cerfaux: Études d'exégèse et d'histoire religieuse* (3 vols.; BETL 6–7, 18; Gembloux: Duculot, 1954–62) 3.111–22.

Christ, *Jesus Sophia*

Felix Christ, *Jesus Sophia: Die Sophia-Christologie bei den Synoptikern* (AThANT 57; Zurich: Zwingli-Verlag, 1970).

Conzelmann, *Theology*

Hans Conzelmann, *The Theology of St. Luke* (1961; trans. G. Buswell; reprinted Philadelphia: Fortress Press, 1982).

Couroyer, "Mesure"

Bernard Couroyer, "'De la mesure dont vous mesurez, il vous sera mesuré,'" *RB* 77 (1970) 366–70.

Crockett, "Jewish-Gentile"

Larrimore C. Crockett, "Luke 4:25–27 and the Jewish-Gentile Relations in Luke-Acts," *JBL* 88 (1969) 177–83.

Dautzenberg, *Leben*

Gerhard Dautzenberg, *Sein Leben bewahren: Ψυχή in den Herrenworten der Evangelien* (SANT 14; Munich: Kösel, 1966).

de Jonge, "Sonship"

Henk J. de Jonge, "Sonship, Wisdom, Infancy: Lk 2,41–51a," *NTS* 24 (1977–78) 317–54.

de Robert, *Berger*

Philippe de Robert, *Le Berger d'Israël: Essai sur le thème pastoral dans l'Ancien Testament* (CTh 57; Neuchâtel: Delachaux et Niestlé, 1968).

Delebecque

Edouard Delebecque, *Évangile de Luc: Texte traduit et annoté* (CEA; Paris: Belles Lettres, 1976).

Delebecque, *Études*

Edouard Delebecque, *Études grecques sur l'Évangile de Luc* (CEA; Paris: Belles Lettres, 1976).

Delebecque, "Moissonneurs"

Edouard Delebecque, "Les moissonneurs du sabbat (6,1)," in idem, *Études*, 71–84.

Delebecque, "Note"

Edouard Delebecque, "Note sur Lc 2,41–52," *BAGB* (1973) 75–83, reprinted in idem, *Études*, 39–51. Cited from the latter.

Delobel, "Onction"

Joël Delobel, "L'onction par la pécheresse: La composition littéraire de Lc 7,36–50," *EThL* 42 (1966) 415–75 (= ALBO 4.33).

Derrett, "Lamp"

J. Duncan M. Derrett, "The Lamp Which Must Not Be Hidden (Mk IV,21)," in idem, *Law in the New Testament* (London: Darton, Longman and Todd, 1970) 189–207.

Derrett, *Studies*

J. Duncan M. Derrett, *Studies in the New Testament* (6 vols.; Leiden: Brill, 1977–95).

Descamps and de Halleux, *Mélanges*

A. Descamps and A. de Halleux, eds., *Mélanges bibliques: Festschrift Béda Rigaux* (Gembloux: Duculot, 1970).

Dibelius, *Aufsätze*

Martin Dibelius, *Aufsätze zur Apostelgeschichte* (ed. H. Greeven; 4th ed.; FRLANT 60; Göttingen: Vandenhoeck & Ruprecht, 1961).

Dibelius, *Jungfrauensohn*

Martin Dibelius, *Jungfrauensohn und Krippenkind: Untersuchungen zur Geburtsgeschichte Jesu im Lukas-Evangelium* (SHAW.PH 1931–32; Heidelberg: Carl Winter, 1932), reprinted in idem, *Botschaft und Geschichte: Gesammelte Aufsätze* (ed. G. Bornkamm; 2 vols.; Tübingen: Mohr-Siebeck, 1953) 1.1–78. Cited from the latter.

Dibelius, *Tradition*

Martin Dibelius, *From Tradition to Gospel* (trans. B. L. Woolf; New York: Scribner, 1965).

Dietrich, *Petrusbild*

Wolfgang Dietrich, *Das Petrusbild der lukanischen Schriften* (BWANT 94; Stuttgart: Kohlhammer, 1972).

Dihle, *Regel*

Albrecht Dihle, *Die Goldene Regel: Eine Einführung in die Geschichte der antiken und frühchristlichen Vulgärethik* (Studienhefte zur Altertumswissenschaft 7; Göttingen: Vandenhoeck & Ruprecht, 1962).

Dinkler, *Zeit und Geschichte*

E. Dinkler, ed., *Zeit und Geschichte: Festschrift Rudolf Bultmann* (Tübingen: Mohr-Siebeck, 1964).

Dodd, "Translation"

C. H. Dodd, "New Testament Translation Problems II," *BT* 28 (1977) 104–10.

Dömer, *Heil*

Michael Dömer, *Das Heil Gottes: Studien zur Theologie des lukanischen Doppelwerkes* (BBB 51; Cologne/Bonn: Hanstein, 1978).

Drexler, "Sünderin"
 Hans Drexler, "Die große Sünderin Lucas 7,36–50," *ZNW* 59 (1968) 159–73.

du Plessis, "Once More"
 I. I. du Plessis, "Once More: The Purpose of Luke's Prologue (Lk I 1–4)," *NovT* 16 (1974) 259–71.

Dubois, "Elie"
 Jean-Daniel Dubois, "La figure d'Elie dans la perspective lucanienne," *RHPhR* 53 (1973) 155–76.

Dubois, "Jean-Baptiste"
 Jean-Daniel Dubois, "De Jean-Baptiste à Jésus: Essai sur la conception lucanienne de l'esprit à partir des premiers chapitres de l'évangile" (diss., Strasbourg, 1977).

Duplacy, "Disciple"
 Jean Duplacy, "Le véritable disciple: Un essai d'analyse sémantique de Luc 6,43–49," *RechSR* 69 (1981) 71–86.

Dupont, "Ambassade"
 Jacques Dupont, "L'ambassade de Jean-Baptiste (Matthieu 11,2–6; Luc 7,18–23)," *NRTh* 83 (1961) 805–21, 943–59.

Dupont, *Béatitudes*
 Jacques Dupont, *Les Béatitudes* (3 vols.; EtB; Paris: Gabalda, 1969–73).

Dupont, *Christologie*
 Jacques Dupont, et al., eds., *Jésus aux origines de la christologie* (BETL 40; Leuven/Gembloux: Leuven University Press, 1975).

Dupont, *Études*
 Jacques Dupont, *Études sur les Évangiles synoptiques* (ed. F. Neirynck; 2 vols.; BETL 70; Leuven: Leuven University Press and Peeters, 1985).

Dupont, "Jésus retrouvé"
 Jacques Dupont, "Jésus retrouvé au temple," *AsSeign* 11 (1970) 40–51.

Dupont, "Magnificat"
 Jacques Dupont, "Le Magnificat comme discours sur Dieu," *NRTh* 102 (1980) 321–43, rèprinted in idem, *Études*, 2.953–75. Cited from the journal.

Dupont, "Parfaits"
 Jacques Dupont, "'Soyez parfaits' (Mt V,48) 'Soyez miséricordieux' (Lc VI,36)," in J. Coppens, et al., eds., *Sacra Pagina* (2 vols.; BETL 12–13; Paris/Gembloux: Duculot, 1959) 2.150–62.

Dupont, "Pharisien"
 Jacques Dupont, "Le pharisien et la pécheresse (Lc 7,36–50)," *Communautés et Liturgies* 4 (1980) 260–68.

Dupont, "Semeur"
 Jacques Dupont, "La parabole du semeur dans la version de Luc," in W. Eltester and F. H. Kettler, eds., *Apophoreta: Festschrift Ernst Haenchen* (BZNW 30; Berlin: Töpelmann, 1964) 97–108, reprinted in Dupont, *Études*, 2.1019–31.

Dupont, *Tentations*
 Jacques Dupont, *Les tentations de Jésus au désert* (SN 4; Paris: Desclée de Brouwer, 1968).

Elliott, "Anointing"
 J. K. Elliott, "The Anointing of Jesus," *ExpTim* 85 (1973–74) 105–7.

Erdmann, *Vorgeschichten*
 Gottfried Erdmann, *Die Vorgeschichten des Lukas- und Matthäus-Evangeliums und Vergils vierte Ekloge* (FRLANT 48; Göttingen: Vandenhoeck & Ruprecht, 1932).

Ernst
 Josef Ernst, *Das Evangelium nach Lukas: Übersetzt und erklärt* (RNT 3; Regensburg: F. Pustet, 1977).

Escudero Freire, *Devolver*
 Carlos Escudero Freire, *Devolver el Evangelio a los pobres: A propósito de Lc 1–2* (Biblioteca de estudios bíblicos 19; Salamanca: Sígueme, 1978).

Farrer, "Loaves"
 Austin M. Farrer, "Loaves and Thousands," *JTS* n.s. 4 (1953) 1–14.

Farris, *Hymns*
 Stephen Farris, *The Hymns of Luke's Infancy Narratives: Their Origin, Meaning and Significance* (JSNTSup 9; Sheffield: JSOT Press, 1985).

Feuillet, "Épreuve"
 A. Feuillet, "L'épreuve prédite à Marie par le vieillard Siméon (Luc 2,35a)," in *À la rencontre de Dieu: Mémorial Albert Gelin* (Le Puy: X. Mappus, 1961) 243–63.

Feuillet, "Hommes"
 A. Feuillet, "Les hommes de bonne volonté ou les hommes que Dieu aime: Note sur la traduction de Luc 2,14b," *BAGB* (1974) 91–92.

Figueras, "Syméon"
 Pau Figueras, "Syméon et Anne ou le témoignage de la loi et des prophètes," *NovT* 20 (1978) 84–99.

Fitzmyer
 Joseph A. Fitzmyer, *The Gospel According to Luke: Introduction, Translation, and Notes* (2 vols.; AB 28–28A; Garden City, N.Y.: Doubleday, 1981–85).

Flender, *Heil*
 Helmut Flender, *Heil und Geschichte in der Theologie des Lukas* (BEvTh 41; Munich: Kaiser, 1965).

Flusser, "Notes"
 David Flusser, "Some Notes on the Beatitudes (Mt 5,3–12; Lc 6,20–26)," *Imm* 8 (1976) 37–47.

Gamba, "Senso"
 Guiseppe Gamba, "Senso e significato funzionale di Luca 9,43b–45," in idem, *Il messianismo* (ASB 18; Brescia: Paidea, 1966) 233–67.

Geninasca, "Pêcher"
 Jacques Geninasca, "Pêcher/prêcher: Récit et métaphore: Luc 5,1–11," in Groupe d'Entrevernes, *Signes et paraboles: Sémiotique et texte évangélique* (Paris: Seuil, 1977) 143–71.

George, "Disciple"
 Augustin George, "Le disciple fraternel et efficace," *AsSeign* 39 (1972) 68–77.

George, *Études*
 Augustin George, *Études sur l'œuvre de Luc* (SB; Paris: Gabalda, 1978).

George, "Miracle"
Augustin George, "Le miracle dans l'œuvre de Luc," in X. Léon-Dufour, ed., *Les miracles de Jésus selon le Nouveau Testament* (Parole de Dieu; Paris: Seuil, 1977) 249–68, reprinted in George, *Études*, 133–48.

George, "Parallèle"
Augustin George, "Le parallèle entre Jean-Baptiste et Jésus en Luc 1–2," in A. Descamps and A. de Halleux, eds., *Mélanges bibliques: Festschrift Béda Rigaux* (Gembloux: Duculot, 1970) 147–71, reprinted in George, *Études*, 43–65.

Gerhardsson, "Sower"
Birger Gerhardsson, "The Parable of the Sower and Its Interpretation," *NTS* 14 (1967–68) 165–93.

Gerhardsson, *Testing*
Birger Gerhardsson, *The Testing of God's Son (Matt 4:1–11 & Par.): An Analysis of an Early Christian Midrash* (ConBNT 2; Lund: Gleerup, 1966).

Gils, *Jésus prophète*
Félix Gils, *Jésus prophète d'après les évangiles synoptiques* (Orientalia et Biblica Lovaniensia 2; Louvain: Publications Universitaires, 1957).

Glöckner, *Verkündigung*
Richard Glöckner, *Die Verkündigung des Heils beim Evangelisten Lukas* (Walberger Studien der Albertus-Magnus-Akademie: Theologie 9; Mainz: Matthias Grünewald, 1975).

Glombitza, "Titel"
Otto Glombitza, "Die Titel διδάσκαλος und ἐπιστάτης für Jesus bei Lukas," *ZNW* 49 (1958) 275–78.

Gnilka, "Hymnus"
Joachim Gnilka, "Der Hymnus des Zacharias," *BZ* n.s. 6 (1962) 215–38.

Gnilka, *Markus*
Joachim Gnilka, *Das Evangelium nach Markus* (2d ed.; 2 vols.; EKKNT 2; Zurich: Benziger; Neukirchen-Vluyn: Neukirchener Verlag, 1986).

Gnilka, *Verstockung*
Joachim Gnilka, *Die Verstockung Israels: Isaias 6,9–10 in der Theologie der Synoptiker* (SANT 3; Munich: Kösel, 1961).

Godet
Frédéric Godet, *A Commentary on the Gospel of St. Luke* (trans. E. W. Shalders; 4th ed.; 2 vols.; Edinburgh: Clark, 1890).

Godet, *Commentaire*
Frédéric Godet, *Commentaire sur L'Évangile de Saint Luc* (4th ed.; 2 vols.; reprinted Neuchâtel: L.-A. Monnier, 1969).

Goulet, "Vies"
Richard Goulet, "Les Vies de philosophes dans l'Antiquité tardive et leur portée mystérique," in F. Bovon, ed., *Les Actes apocryphes des apôtres: Christianisme et monde païen* (Publications de la Faculté de théologie de l'Université de Genève 4; Geneva: Labor et Fides, 1981) 161–208.

Grässer, *Jesus in Nazareth*
Erich Grässer, ed., *Jesus in Nazareth* (BZNW 40; Berlin/New York: de Gruyter, 1972).

Gressmann, *Weihnachtsevangelium*
Hugo Gressmann, *Das Weihnachtsevangelium auf Ursprung und Geschichte untersucht* (Göttingen: Vandenhoeck & Ruprecht, 1914).

Grundmann
Walter Grundmann, *Das Evangelium nach Lukas* (2d ed.; ThHKNT 3; Berlin: Evangelische Verlagsanstalt, 1961).

Grundmann, *Markus*
Walter Grundmann, *Das Evangelium nach Markus* (ThHKNT 2; Berlin: Evangelische Verlagsanstalt, 1965).

Gueuret, *Engendrement*
Agnès Gueuret, *L'engendrement d'un récit: L'évangile de l'enfance selon saint Luc* (LD 113; Paris: Cerf, 1983).

Gunkel, "Lieder"
Hermann Gunkel, "Die Lieder in der Kindheitsgeschichte Jesu bei Lukas," in *Festgabe von Fachgenossen und Freunden . . . dargebracht: Festschrift Adolf von Harnack* (Tübingen: Mohr, 1921) 43–60.

Haenchen, *Weg*
Ernst Haenchen, *Der Weg Jesu: Eine Erklärung des Markus-Evangeliums und der kanonischen Parallelen* (STö.H 6; Berlin: de Gruyter, 1966).

Hahn, *Mission*
Ferdinand Hahn, *Mission in the New Testament* (trans. F. Clarke; SBT 1.47; Naperville, Ill.: Allenson, 1965).

Hahn, *Titles*
Ferdinand Hahn, *The Titles of Jesus in Christology: Their History in Early Christianity* (trans. H. Knight and G. Ogg; London: Lutterworth, 1969).

Hamel, "Magnificat"
Édouard Hamel, "Le Magnificat et le renversement des situations: Réflections théologico-bibliques (Lc 1,51–53)," *Greg* 60 (1979) 55–84.

Harbarth, "'Gott'"
Anita Harbarth, "'Gott hat sein Volk heimgesucht': Eine form- und redaktionsgeschichtliche Untersuchung zu Lk 7,11–17: 'Die Erweckung des Jünglings von Nain'" (diss., Heidelberg, 1977); see *TRev* 74 (1978) 510.

Hatch and Redpath
Edwin Hatch and Henry A. Redpath, *Concordance to the Septuagint and the Other Greek Versions of the Old Testament* (2 vols.; Graz: Akademische Druck und Verlagsanstalt, 1954).

Haulotte, *Vêtement*
Edgar Haulotte, *Symbolique du vêtement selon la Bible* (Théologie 65; Paris: Aubier, 1966).

Hebert, "Feeding"
Arthur G. Hebert, "History in the Feeding of the Five Thousand," *StEv* 2 (1964) 65–72 (= TU 87).

Heising, "Exegese"
Alkuin Heising, "Exegese und Theologie der alt- und neutestamentlichen Speisewunder," *ZKTh* 86 (1964) 80–96.

Hengel, *Charismatic Leader*
Martin Hengel, *The Charismatic Leader and His Followers* (trans. J. Greig; New York: Crossroad, 1981).

Hennecke-Schneemelcher
Edgar Hennecke, *New Testament Apocrypha* (ed. W. Schneemelcher; trans. and ed. R. McL. Wilson; 2d ed.; 2 vols.; Louisville: Westminster John Knox, 1991–92).

Henss, *Diatessaron*
Walter Henss, *Das Verhältnis zwischen Diatessaron, christlicher Gnosis und "Western Text": Erläutert an einer unkanonischen Version des Gleichnisses vom gnädigen Gläubiger: Materialien zur Geschichte der Perikope von der namenlosen Sünderin Lk 7,36–50* (BZNW 33; Berlin: Töpelmann, 1967).

Higgins, "Preface"
A. J. B. Higgins, "The Preface to Luke and the Kerygma in Acts," in W. W. Gasque and R. P. Martin, eds., *Apostolic History and the Gospel: Festschrift F. F. Bruce* (Grand Rapids: Eerdmans; Exeter: Paternoster, 1970) 78–91.

Hill, "Rejection"
David Hill, "The Rejection of Jesus at Nazareth (Luke IV 16–30)," *NovT* 13 (1971) 161–80.

Hoehner, *Herod*
Harald W. Hoehner, *Herod Antipas* (SNTSMS 17; Cambridge: Cambridge University Press, 1972).

Hoffmann, *Logienquelle*
Paul Hoffmann, *Studien zur Theologie der Logienquelle* (NTAbh n.s. 8; Münster: Aschendorff, 1972).

Hoffmann, *Orientierung*
P. Hoffmann et al., eds., *Orientierung an Jesus: Zur Theologie der Synoptiker: Festschrift Josef Schmid* (Freiburg: Herder, 1973).

Hooker, *Jesus and the Servant*
Morna D. Hooker, *Jesus and the Servant: The Influence of the Servant Concept of Deutero-Isaiah in the New Testament* (London: SPCK, 1959) 92–97.

Hubbard, "Commissioning"
B. J. Hubbard, "Commissioning Stories in Luke-Acts: A Study of their Antecedents, Form and Content," *Semeia* 8 (1977) 103–26.

Jacquemin, "Béatitudes"
Paul-Edmond Jacquemin, "Les béatitudes selon saint Luc: Lc 6,17.20–26," *AsSeign* 37 (1971) 80–91.

Jacquemin, "Visitation"
Paul-Edmond Jacquemin, "La visitation," *AsSeign* 8 (1972) 64–75.

Jeremias, *Gleichnisse*
Joachim Jeremias, *Die Gleichnisse Jesu* (5th ed.; Göttingen: Vandenhoeck & Ruprecht, 1958).

Jeremias, *Jerusalem*
Joachim Jeremias, *Jerusalem in the Time of Jesus: An Investigation into Economic and Social Conditions during the New Testament Period* (trans. F. H. and C. H. Cave; Philadelphia: Fortress Press, 1969).

Jeremias, *Parables*
Joachim Jeremias, *The Parables of Jesus* (trans. S. H. Hooke; London: SCM, 1954).

Jeremias, *Sprache*
Joachim Jeremias, *Die Sprache des Lukasevangeliums: Redaktion und Tradition im Nicht-Markusstoff des dritten Evangeliums* (KEKSup; Göttingen: Vandenhoeck & Ruprecht, 1980).

Jones, "Background"
Douglas Jones, "The Background and Character of the Lukan Psalms," *JTS* n.s. 19 (1968) 19–50.

Joüon, "Pécheresse"
Paul Joüon, "La pécheresse de Galilée et la parabole des deux débiteurs (Luc 7,36–50)," *RechSR* 29 (1939) 615–19.

Jülicher, *Gleichnisreden*
Adolf Jülicher, *Die Gleichnisreden Jesu* (2d ed.; 2 vols.; Tübingen: Mohr-Siebeck, 1910).

Junod and Kaestli, *Acta Iohannis*
Eric Junod and Jean-Daniel Kaestli, *Acta Iohannis* (CCSA 1–2; Turnhout: Brepols, 1983).

Keck and Martyn, *Studies*
Leander E. Keck and J. L. Martyn, eds., *Studies in Luke-Acts: Festschrift Paul Schubert* (2d ed.; Nashville: Abingdon, 1966).

Kertelge, *Wunder*
Karl Kertelge, *Die Wunder Jesu im Markusevangelium* (Munich: Kösel, 1970).

Kieffer, *Essais*
René Kieffer, *Essais de méthodologie néo-testamentaire* (ConBNT 4; Lund: Gleerup, 1972).

Klauck, *Allegorie*
Hans-Josef Klauck, *Allegorie und Allegorese in synoptischen Gleichnistexten* (NTAbh n.s. 13; Münster: Aschendorff, 1978).

Klein, "Programm"
Günter Klein, "Lukas 1,1–4 als theologisches Programm," in E. Dinkler, ed., *Zeit und Geschichte: Festschrift Rudolf Bultmann* (Tübingen: Mohr-Siebeck, 1964) 193–216, reprinted in idem, *Rekonstruktion und Interpretation: Gesammelte Aufsätze zum Neuen Testament* (BEvTh 50; Munich: Kaiser, 1969) 237–61, also reprinted in G. Braumann, ed., *Das Lukas-Evangelium: Die Redaktions- und Kompositionsgeschichtliche Forschung* (WdF 280; Darmstadt: Wissenschaftliche Buchgesellschaft, 1974) 170–203. Cited from the first.

Klostermann
Erich Klostermann, *Das Lukasevangelium: Erklärt* (3d ed.; HNT 5; Tübingen: Mohr-Siebeck, 1975).

Koch, *Growth*
Klaus Koch, *The Growth of the Biblical Tradition: The Form-Critical Method* (trans. S. M. Cupitt; New York: Scribner's, 1969).

Kopp, *Places*
Clemens Kopp, *The Holy Places of the Gospels* (trans. R. Walls; New York: Herder and Herder, 1963).

Krämer, "Hütet euch"
Michael Krämer, "Hütet euch vor den falschen Propheten: Eine überlieferungsgeschichtliche Untersuchung zu Mt 7,15–23 / Lk 6,43–46 / Mt 12,33–37," *Bib* 57 (1976) 349–77.

Kraus, *Psalmen*
Hans-Joachim Kraus, *Psalmen* (2 vols.; BKAT 15; Neukirchen: Neukirchener Verlag, 1960–61).

Kraus, *Psalms*
Hans-Joachim Kraus, *Psalms* (trans. H. C. Oswald; 2 vols.; Minneapolis: Augsburg, 1988–89).

Lagrange
M.-J. Lagrange, *Évangile selon Saint Luc* (4th ed.; EtB; Paris: Gabalda, 1927).

Lapide, "Bergpredigt"
Pinchas Lapide, "Die Bergpredigt—Theorie und Praxis," *ZEE* 17 (1973) 369–72.

Lattke, "Jungfrauengeburt"
G. Lattke, "Lukas 1 und die Jungfrauengeburt," in K. S. Frank, et al., eds., *Zum Thema Jungfrauengeburt* (Stuttgart: Katholisches Bibelwerk, 1970) 61–89.

Laurentin, *Jésus au temple*
René Laurentin, *Jésus au temple: Mystère de Pâques et foi de Marie en Luc 2,48–50* (EtB; Paris: Gabalda, 1966).

Laurentin, *Structure*
René Laurentin, *Structure et théologie de Luc I–II* (EtB; Paris: Librairie Lecoffre, Gabalda, 1957).

Laurentin, *Truth*
René Laurentin, *The Truth of Christmas Beyond the Myths: The Gospels of the Infancy of Christ* (trans. M. J. Wrenn et al.; Studies in Scripture; Petersham, Mass.: St. Bede's Publications, 1986).

Légasse, *Jésus et l'enfant*
Simon Légasse, *Jésus et l'enfant: 'Enfants,' 'Petits' et 'Simples' dans la tradition synoptique* (EtB; Paris: Gabalda, 1969) 27–32, 72–75.

Legrand, *Annonce*
Lucien Legrand, *L'annonce à Marie (Lc 1,26–38): Une apocalypse aux origines de l'Évangile* (LD 106; Paris: Cerf, 1981).

Legrand, "Arrière-plan"
Lucien Legrand, "L'arrière-plan néo-testamentaire de Lc 1,35," *RB* 70 (1963) 161–92.

Legrand, "Évangile aux Bergers"
Lucien Legrand, "L'Évangile aux Bergers: Essai sur le genre littéraire de Luc II,8–20," *RB* 75 (1968) 161–87.

Lentzen-Deis, *Taufe*
Fritzleo Lentzen-Deis, *Die Taufe Jesu nach den Synoptikern: Literarkritische und gattungsgeschichtliche Untersuchungen* (FTS 4; Frankfurt am Main: J. Knecht, 1970).

Léon-Dufour, "Épisode"
Xavier Léon-Dufour, "L'épisode de l'enfant épileptique," in J. Cambier et al., *La formation des Évangiles: Problème synoptique et Formgeschichte*
(Recherches bibliques 2; Bruges/Paris: Desclée de Brouwer, 1957) 85–115, reprinted in Léon-Dufour, *Études*, 183–227. Cited from the latter.

Léon-Dufour, *Études*
Xavier Léon-Dufour, *Études d'Évangile: Parole de Dieu* (Paris: Seuil, 1965).

Léon-Dufour, "Guérison"
Xavier Léon-Dufour, "La guérison de la belle-mère de Simon-Pierre," *EstBib* 24 (1965) 193–216, reprinted in idem, *Études*, 123–48. Cited from the latter.

Léon-Dufour, "Tempête"
Xavier Léon-Dufour, "La tempête apaisée," in idem, *Études*, 149–82.

Léon-Dufour, "Transfiguration"
Xavier Léon-Dufour, "La transfiguration de Jésus," in idem, *Études*, 83–122.

Lesky and Waszink, "Epilepsie"
Erna Lesky and Jan Hendrik Waszink, "Epilepsie," *RAC* 5 (Stuttgart: Hiersemann, 1962) 819–31.

Lindars, "Elijah"
Barnabas Lindars, "Elijah, Elisha and the Gospel Miracles," in C. F. D. Moule, ed., *Miracles: Cambridge Studies in Their Philosophy and History* (London: Mowbray, 1965) 63–79.

Lohfink, *Sammlung*
Gerhard Lohfink, *Die Sammlung Israels: Eine Untersuchung zur lukanischen Ekklesiologie* (SANT 39; Munich: Kösel, 1975).

Loisy
Alfred Loisy, *L'Évangile selon Luc* (Paris: Émile Nourry, 1924).

Lührmann, "Liebet"
Dieter Lührmann, "Liebet eure Feinde (Lk 6,27–36 / Mt 5,39–48)," *ZThK* 69 (1972) 412–38.

Lührmann, *Logienquelle*
Dieter Lührmann, *Die Redaktion der Logienquelle: Anhang: Zur weiteren Überlieferung der Logienquelle* (WMANT 33; Neukirchen-Vluyn: Neukirchener Verlag, 1969).

Luther, *Evangelien-Auslegung*
Christian G. Eberle, *Luthers Evangelien-Auslegung: Ein Kommentar zu den vier Evangelien* (2d ed.; Stuttgart: S. G. Liesching, 1877).

Luz, *Matthew*
Ulrich Luz, *Matthew 1–7: A Continental Commentary* (trans. W. C. Linss; Minneapolis: Fortress Press, 1989).

Lyonnet, "Annonciation"
S. Lyonnet, "L'annonciation et la mariologie biblique: Ce que l'exégèse conclut du récit lucanien de l'annonciation concernant la mariologie," in *Maria in Sacra Scriptura* (6 vols.; Rome: Pontificia Academia Mariana, 1967) 4.59–72.

Mahnke, *Versuchungsgeschichte*
Hermann Mahnke, *Die Versuchungsgeschichte im Rahmen der synoptischen Evangelien: Ein Beitrag zur frühen Christologie* (BEvTh 9; Frankfurt am Main: Lang, 1978).

Mánek, "On the Mount"
   Jindrich Mánek, "On the Mount—on the Plain (Mt
   v 1 – Lk vi 17)," *NovT* 9 (1967) 124-31.
Marguerat, *Jugement*
   Daniel Marguerat, *Le jugement dans l'Évangile de
   Matthieu* (Le Monde de la Bible 6; Geneva: Labor
   et Fides, 1981).
Maria in Sacra Scriptura
   Maria in Sacra Scriptura (6 vols.; Rome: Pontificia
   Academia Mariana, 1967).
Marshall
   I. Howard Marshall, *The Gospel of Luke: A
   Commentary on the Greek Text* (New International
   Greek Testament Commentary; Grand Rapids:
   Eerdmans; Exeter: Paternoster, 1978).
Marxsen, "Biblearbeit"
   Willi Marxsen, "Bibelarbeit über Mk 5,21-43 / Mt
   9,18-26," in idem, *Der Exeget als Theologe: Vorträge
   zum Neuen Testament* (Gütersloh: Mohn, 1968).
März, *Wort Gottes*
   Claus-Peter März, *Das Wort Gottes bei Lukas* (EThSt
   11; Leipzig: St. Benno, 1974).
Masson, *Vers les sources*
   Charles Masson, *Vers les sources d'eau vive: Études
   d'exégèse et de théologie du Nouveau Testament*
   (Lausanne: Librairie Payot, 1961).
May, "Power"
   Eric May, "'. . . For Power Went Forth from Him
   . . .' (Luke 6:19)," *CBQ* 14 (1952) 93-103.
McHugh, *Mother*
   John McHugh, *The Mother of Jesus in the New Testa-
   ment* (London: Darton, Longman and Todd, 1975).
McKnight, *Meaning*
   Edgar V. McKnight, *Meaning in Texts: The Histori-
   cal Shaping of a Narrative Hermeneutics* (Phila-
   delphia: Fortress Press, 1978).
Merkelbach, "Über eine Stelle"
   Reinhold Merkelbach, "Über eine Stelle im Evan-
   gelium des Lukas," *GrB* 1 (1973) 171-75.
Metzger, *Textual Commentary*
   Bruce M. Metzger, *A Textual Commentary on the
   Greek New Testament: A Companion Volume to the
   United Bible Societies' Greek New Testament* (1st ed.;
   London/New York: United Bible Societies, 1971).
Minear, "Audiences"
   Paul Sevier Minear, "Jesus' Audiences, According
   to Luke," *NovT* 16 (1974) 81-109.
Miquel, "Mystère"
   Pierre Miquel, "Le mystère de la Transfiguration,"
   Questions liturgiques et paroissiales 42 (1961)
   194-223.
Miyoshi, "Jesu Darstellung"
   Michi Miyoshi, "Jesu Darstellung oder Reinigung
   im Tempel unter Berücksichtigung von 'Nunc
   Dimittis' Lk 2,22-38," *AJBI* 4 (1978) 85-115.
Moltmann-Wendel, *Women*
   Elisabeth Moltmann-Wendel, *The Women Around
   Jesus* (trans. J. Bowden; New York: Crossroads,
   1982).

Monloubou, *Prière*
   Louis Monloubou, *La prière selon Saint Luc:
   Recherche d'une structure* (LD 89; Paris: Cerf, 1976).
Moulton and Milligan, *Vocabulary*
   James Hope Moulton and George Milligan, *The
   Vocabulary of the Greek New Testament: Illustrated
   from the Papyri and Other Non-Literary Sources* (1930;
   reprinted Grand Rapids: Eerdmans, 1963).
Mussner, "Kairos"
   Franz Mussner, "Der nicht erkannte Kairos (Mt
   11,16-19 = Lk 7,31-35)," *Bib* 40 (1959) 599-612.
Neirynck, *Évangile*
   Frans Neirynck, ed., *L'Évangile de Luc: Problèmes
   littéraires et théologiques: Mémorial Lucien Cerfaux*
   (BETL 32; Gembloux: Duculot, 1978).
Neirynck, "Minor Agreements"
   Frans Neirynck, "Minor Agreements: Matthew-
   Luke in the Transfiguration Story," in P. Hoff-
   mann et al., eds., *Orientierung an Jesus: Zur
   Theologie der Synoptiker: Festschrift Josef Schmid*
   (Freiburg: Herder, 1973) 253-66.
Nestle-Aland
   Eberhardt Nestle, ed., *Novum Testamentum Graece*
   (27th ed.; rev. Kurt Aland; Stuttgart: Württem-
   bergische Bibelgesellschaft, 1993).
New Testament in Greek
   The Gospel According to St. Luke (ed. American and
   British Committees of the International Greek
   New Testament Project; 2 vols.; The New
   Testament in Greek 3; Oxford: Clarendon,
   1984-87).
Norden, *Geburt*
   Eduard Norden, *Die Geburt des Kindes: Geschichte
   einer religiösen Idee* (Studien der Bibliothek
   Warburg 3; Leipzig/Berlin: Teubner, 1924).
Nützel, *Verklärungserzählung*
   Johannes M. Nützel, *Die Verklärungserzählung im
   Markusevangelium: Eine redaktionsgeschichtliche
   Untersuchung* (FB 6; Würzburg: Echter, 1973).
Orbe, *Cristología*
   Antonio Orbe, *Cristología gnóstica: Introducción a la
   soteriología de los siglos II y III* (2 vols.; BAC 384-85;
   Madrid: La Editorial Catolica, 1976).
Orbe, "Hijo del hombre"
   Antonio Orbe, "El Hijo del hombre come y bebe
   (Mt 11,19; Lc 7,34)," *Greg* 58 (1977) 523-55.
Patsch, "Abendmahlsterminologie"
   Hermann Patsch, "Abendmahlsterminologie außer-
   halb der Einsetzungsberichte: Erwägungen zur
   Traditionsgeschichte der Abendmahlsworte," *ZNW*
   62 (1971) 210-31.
Percy, *Botschaft*
   Ernst Percy, *Die Botschaft Jesu: Eine traditions-kriti-
   sche und exegetische Untersuchung* (Lund: Gleerup,
   1953).
Pernot, "Correction"
   Hubert Pernot, "Une correction à Luc VI,35,"
   CRAIBL (1929) 277-80.

Perrot, *Lecture*

Charles Perrot, *La lecture de la Bible dans la synagogue: Les anciennes lectures palestiniennes du Shabbat et des fêtes* (Hildesheim: Gerstenberg, 1973).

Perrot, "Récits"

Charles Perrot, "Les récits de l'enfance de Jésus: Matthieu 1–2: Luc 1–2," *CÉv* 18 (1976) 35–72.

Pesch, *Besessene*

Rudolf Pesch, *Der Besessene von Gerasa: Entstehung und Überlieferung einer Wundergeschichte* (SBS 56; Stuttgart: Katholisches Bibelwerk, 1972).

Pesch, "Weihnachtsevangelium"

Rudolf Pesch, "Das Weihnachtsevangelium (Lk 2,1–21): Literarische Kunst, politische Implikation," in idem, ed., *Zur Theologie der Kindheitsgeschichten: Der heutige Stand der Exegese* (Munich/Zurich: Schnell und Steiner, 1981) 97–118.

Petzke, "Historizität"

Gerd Petzke, "Historizität und Bedeutsamkeit von Wunderberichten: Möglichkeiten und Grenzen des religionsgeschichtlichen Vergleichs," in H. D. Betz and L. Schottroff, eds., *Neues Testament und christliche Existenz: Festschrift Herbert Braun* (Tübingen: Mohr-Siebeck, 1973) 367–85.

Piper, *Love*

John Piper, *"Love your enemies": Jesus' Love Command in the Synoptic Gospels and in the Early Christian Paraenesis: A History of the Tradition and Interpretation of Its Uses* (SNTSMS 38; Cambridge: Cambridge University Press, 1979).

Pirot, *Paraboles*

Jean Pirot, *Paraboles et allégories évangéliques: La pensée de Jésus, les commentaires patristiques* (Paris: P. Lethielleux, 1949).

Plummer

A. Plummer, *A Critical and Exegetical Commentary on the Gospel According to St. Luke* (5th ed.; ICC; New York: Scribner's Sons; Edinburgh: Clark, 1902).

Pokorný, "Core"

Petr Pokorný, "The Core of the Sermon on the Mount," *StEv* 6 (1973) 429–33 (= TU 112).

Ramaroson, "Structuram"

Leonardus Ramaroson, "Ad structuram cantici 'Magnificat,'" *VD* 46 (1968) 30–46.

Rehkopf, *Sonderquelle*

Friedrich Rehkopf, *Die lukanische Sonderquelle: Ihr Umfang und Sprachgebrauch* (WUNT 5; Tübingen: Mohr-Siebeck, 1959).

Reicke, "Fastenfrage"

Bo Reicke, "Die Fastenfrage nach Luk. 5,33–39," *ThZ* 30 (1974) 321–28.

Rengstorf, *Concordance*

Karl H. Rengstorf, ed., *A Complete Concordance to Flavius Josephus* (4 vols.; Leiden: Brill, 1973–83).

Rese, *Alttestamentliche Motive*

Martin Rese, *Alttestamentliche Motive in der Christologie des Lukas* (Gütersloh: Mohn, 1969).

Rese, "Forschungsbericht"

Martin Rese, "Das Lukas-Evangelium: Ein Forschungsbericht," *ANRW* 2.25.3 (1985) 2258–2328.

Riesenfeld, *Jésus transfiguré*

Harald Riesenfeld, *Jésus transfiguré: L'arrière plan du récit évangélique de la transfiguration de Notre-Seigneur* (ASNU 16; Copenhagen: E. Munksgaard, 1947).

Roloff, *Kerygma*

Jürgen Roloff, *Das Kerygma und der irdische Jesus: Historische Motive in den Jesus-Erzählungen der Evangelien* (2d ed.; Göttingen: Vandenhoeck & Ruprecht, 1973).

Rüger, "Maß"

Hans Peter Rüger, "'Mit welchem Maß ihr meßt, wird euch gemessen werden,'" *ZNW* 60 (1969) 174–82.

Rydbeck, *Fachprosa*

L. Rydbeck, *Fachprosa, vermeintliche Volkssprache und Neues Testament: Zur Beurteilung der sprachlichen Niveauunterschiede im nachklassischen Griechisch* (Acta Universitatis Upsaliensis: Studia Graeca Upsaliensia 5; Stockholm: Almqvist & Wiksell, 1967).

Sahlin, *Lukas-Stellen*

Harald Sahlin, *Zwei Lukas-Stellen. Lk 6,43–45; 18,7* (SBU 4; Uppsala: Wretmans, 1945).

Sahlin, *Messias*

Harald Sahlin, *Der Messias und das Gottesvolk: Studien zur protolukanischen Theologie* (ASNU 12; Uppsala: Almqvist & Wiksell, 1945).

Samain, "Discours-programme de Jésus"

Étienne Samain, "Le discours-programme de Jésus à la synagogue de Nazareth, Lc 4,16–30," *CBFV* 10 (1971) 25–43.

Samain, "Évangile"

Étienne Samain, "L'évangile de Luc: Un témoignage ecclésial et missionnaire: Lc 1,1–4; 4,14–15," *AsSeign* 34 (1973) 60–73.

Sanders, "From Isaiah"

James A. Sanders, "From Isaiah 61 to Luke 4," in J. Neusner, ed., *Christianity, Judaism, and Other Greco-Roman Cults: Festschrift Morton Smith* (4 vols.; SJLA 12; Leiden: Brill, 1975) 1.75–106.

Schenke, *Wundererzählungen*

Ludger Schenke, *Die Wundererzählungen des Markusevangeliums* (SBB; Stuttgart: Katholisches Bibelwerk, 1974).

Schnackenburg, "Mark"

Rudolf Schnackenburg, "Mk 9,33–50," in J. Schmid and A. Vögtle, eds., *Synoptische Studien: Festschrift A. Wikenhauser* (Munich: K. Zink, 1953) 184–206.

Schnackenburg, "Traditionsgeschichte"

Rudolf Schnackenburg, "Zur Traditionsgeschichte von Joh. 4,46–54," *BZ* n.s. 8 (1964) 58–88.

Schneider

Gerhard Schneider, *Das Evangelium nach Lukas* (2d ed.; 2 vols.; Ökumenischer Taschenbuchkommentar zum Neuen Testament 3.1–2; Gütersloh/Würzburg: Mohn, 1984).

Schneider, "Antworten"
Gerhard Schneider, "Jesu überraschende Antworten: Beobachtungen zu den Apophthegmen des dritten Evangeliums," *NTS* 29 (1983) 321–36.

Schneider, "Christusbekenntnis"
Gerhard Schneider, "Christusbekenntnis und christliches Handeln: Lk 6,46 und Mt 7,21 im Kontext der Evangelien," in R. Schnackenburg et al., eds., *Die Kirche des Anfangs: Festschrift Heinz Schürmann* (EThSt 38; Leipzig: St. Benno, 1977) 9–24.

Schneider, "Einheit"
Gerhard Schneider, "Lk 1, 34.35 als redaktionelle Einheit," *BZ* n.s. 15 (1971) 255–59.

Schnyder, "Leben"
C. Schnyder, "Zum Leben befreit: Jesus erweckt den einzigen Sohn einer Witwe vom Tode (Lukas 7,11–17): Eine Totenerweckung," in A. Steiner and V. Weymann, eds., *Wunder Jesu* (Bibelarbeit in der Gemeinde: Themen und Materialien 2; Zurich/Basel: Benzinger, 1978) 77–87.

Schottroff, "Magnificat"
Luise Schottroff, "Das Magnificat und die älteste Tradition über Jesus von Nazareth," *EvTh* 38 (1978) 298–312.

Schottroff, "Non-Violence"
Luise Schottroff, "Non-Violence and the Love of One's Enemies," in idem et al., *Essays on the Love Commandment* (trans. R. H. and I. Fuller; Philadelphia: Fortress Press, 1978) 9–39.

Schottroff and Stegemann, *Jesus*
Luise Schottroff and Wolfgang Stegemann, *Jesus and the Hope of the Poor* (trans. M. J. O'Connell; Maryknoll, N.Y.: Orbis, 1986).

Schrage, *Thomas-Evangelium*
Wolfgang Schrage, *Das Verhältnis des Thomas-Evangeliums zur synoptischen Tradition und zu den koptischen Evanglienübersetzungen* (BZNW 29; Berlin: Töpelmann, 1964).

Schramm, *Markus-Stoff*
Tim Schramm, *Der Markus-Stoff bei Lukas: Eine literarkritische und redaktionsgeschichtliche Untersuchung* (SNTSMS 14; Cambridge: Cambridge University Press, 1971).

Schulz, *Nachfolgen*
Anselm Schulz, *Nachfolgen und Nachahmen: Studien über das Verhältnis der neutestamentlichen Jüngerschaft zur urchristlichen Vorbildethik* (SANT 6; Munich: Kösel, 1962).

Schulz, *Q*
Siegfried Schulz, *Q: Die Spruchquelle der Evangelisten* (Zurich: Theologischer Verlag, 1972).

Schürmann
Heinz Schürmann, *Das Lukasevangelium*, part 1, *Kommentar zu Kap. 1,1–9,50* (2d ed.; HThKNT 3; Freiburg im Breisgau: Herder, 1982).

Schürmann, "Promesse"
Heinz Schürmann, "La promesse à Simon-Pierre: Lc 5,1–11," *AsSeign* 36 (1974) 63–70.

Schürmann, *Untersuchungen*
Heinz Schürmann, *Traditionsgeschichtliche Untersuchungen zu den synoptischen Evangelien: Beiträge* (KBANT; Düsseldorf: Patmos, 1968).

Schürmann, *Ursprung*
Heinz Schürmann, *Ursprung und Gestalt: Erörterungen und Besinnungen zum Neuen Testament* (KBANT; Düsseldorf: Patmos, 1970).

Schweizer
Eduard Schweizer, *Das Evangelium nach Lukas* (NTD 3; Göttingen: Vandenhoeck & Ruprecht, 1982).

Seitz, "Love"
Oscar J. F. Seitz, "Love Your Enemies: The Historical Setting of Matthew V.43f.; Luke VI.27f.," *NTS* 16 (1969–70) 39–54.

Sölle, "Meditation"
Dorothee Sölle, "Meditation on Luke 1," in idem, *Revolutionary Patience* (trans. R. and R. Kimber; rev. ed.; Maryknoll, N.Y.: Orbis, 1977) 51–52.

Spicq, *Agape*
Ceslas Spicq, *Agape in the New Testament* (trans. M. A. McNamara and M. H. Richter; 3 vols.; St. Louis/London: B. Herder, 1963–66).

Spicq, *Agapè*
Ceslas Spicq, *Agapè dans le Nouveau Testament: Analyse des textes* (3 vols.; Paris: Gabalda, 1958–59).

Spicq, *Lexicon*
Ceslas Spicq, *Theological Lexicon of the New Testament* (trans. and ed. J. D. Ernest; 3 vols.; Peabody, Mass.: Hendrickson, 1994).

Stock, "Berufung"
Klemens Stock, "Die Berufung Marias (Lk 1,26–38)," *Bib* 61 (1980) 457–91.

Strobel, "Gruss"
August Strobel, "Der Gruss an Maria (Lc 1,28): Eine philologische Betrachtung zu seinem Sinngehalt," *ZNW* 53 (1962) 86–110.

Strobel, *Verzögerung*
August Strobel, *Untersuchungen zum eschatologischen Verzögerungsproblem* (NovTSup 2; Leiden: Brill, 1961).

Taeger, *Mensch*
Jens W. Taeger, *Der Mensch und sein Heil: Studien zum Bild des Menschen und zur Sicht der Bekehrung bei Lukas* (StNT 14; Gütersloh: Mohn, 1982).

Talbert, *Luke-Acts*
C. H. Talbert, ed., *Luke-Acts: New Perspectives from the Society of Biblical Literature Seminar* (New York: Crossroad, 1984).

Talbert, *Patterns*
Charles H. Talbert, *Literary Patterns, Theological Themes, and the Genre of Luke-Acts* (SBLMS 20; Missoula, Mont.: Scholars Press, 1974).

Talbert, *Perspectives*
Charles H. Talbert, *Perspectives on Luke-Acts* (Danville, Va.: Association of Baptist Professors of Religion, 1978).

Tannehill, "Magnificat"

Robert C. Tannehill, "The Magnificat as Poem," *JBL* 93 (1974) 263–75.

Ternant, "Résurrection"

Paul Ternant, "La résurrection du fils de la veuve de Naïn," *AsSeign* 41 (1971) 69–79.

Theissen, *Miracle Stories*

Gerd Theissen, *Miracle Stories of the Early Christian Tradition* (trans. F. McDonagh; Philadelphia: Fortress Press, 1983).

Theissen, "Nonviolence"

Gerd Theissen, "Nonviolence and Love of Our Enemies (Matthew 5:38–48; Luke 6:27–38): The Social Background," in idem, *Social Reality and the Early Christians* (trans. M. Kohl; Minneapolis: Fortress Press, 1992) 115–56.

Trémel, "Signe"

B. Trémel, "Le signe du nouveau-né dans la mangeoire: À propos de Lc 2,1–20," in P. Casetti et al., eds., *Mélanges: Festschrift Dominique Barthélemy* (OBO 38; Fribourg: Éditions Universitaires; Göttingen: Vandenhoeck & Ruprecht, 1981) 593–612.

Vaganay, "Schématisme"

Léon Vaganay, "Le schématisme du discours communautaire," *RB* 60 (1953) 203–44, reprinted in idem, *Le problème synoptique: Une hypothèse de travail* (Bibliothèque de théologie 1; Tournai: Desclée, 1954) 361–404.

van Cangh, "Multiplication"

Jean-Marie van Cangh, "La multiplication des pains dans l'évangile de Marc: Essai d'exégèse globale," in M. Sabbe, ed., *L'Évangile selon Marc: Tradition et rédaction* (BETL 34; Gembloux: Duculot, 1974) 309–46.

van Cangh, "Thème"

Jean-Marie van Cangh, "Le thème des poissons dans les récits évangéliques de la multiplication des pains," *RB* 78 (1971) 71–83.

van der Loos, *Miracles*

Hendrik van der Loos, *The Miracles of Jesus* (trans. T. S. Preston; NovTSup 9; Leiden: Brill, 1965).

van Iersel, "Finding"

Bastiaan Martinus Franciscus van Iersel, "The Finding of Jesus in the Temple: Some Observations on the Original Form of Luke 2,41–51a," *NovT* 4 (1960) 161–73.

van Unnik, "Bedeutung"

W. C. van Unnik, "Die rechte Bedeutung des Wortes 'treffen': Lukas 2,19," in idem, *Sparsa Collecta*, 1.72–91.

van Unnik, "Motivierung"

W. C. van Unnik, "Die Motivierung der Feindesliebe in Lukas VI,32–35," *NovT* 8 (1966) 284–300, reprinted in idem, *Sparsa Collecta*, 1.111–26. Cited from the latter.

van Unnik, "Once More"

W. C. van Unnik, "Once More St. Luke's Prologue," *Neot* 7 (1973) 7–26.

van Unnik, "Remarks"

W. C. van Unnik, "Remarks on the Purpose of Luke's Historical Writing (Luke i 1–4)," in idem, *Sparsa Collecta*, 1.6–15.

van Unnik, *Sparsa Collecta*

W. C. van Unnik, *Sparsa Collecta: The Collected Essays of W. C. van Unnik* (3 vols.; NovTSup 29–31; Leiden: Brill, 1973–83).

Vanhoye, "Structure"

Albert Vanhoye, "Structure du Benedictus," *NTS* 12 (1965–66) 382–89.

Vermes, *Dead Sea Scrolls*

Geza Vermes, *The Dead Sea Scrolls in English* (2d ed.; New York: Penguin, 1975).

Vögtle, *Evangelium*

Anton Vögtle, *Das Evangelium und die Evangelien: Beiträge zur Evangelienforschung* (KBANT; Düsseldorf: Patmos, 1971).

Völkel, "Anfang"

Martin Völkel, "Der Anfang Jesu in Galiläa: Bemerkungen zum Gebrauch und zur Funktion Galiläas in den lukanischen Schriften," *ZNW* 64 (1973) 222–32.

Voss, *Christologie*

G. Voss, *Die Christologie der lukanischen Schriften in Grundzügen* (StudNeot 2; Bruges/Paris: Desclée de Brouwer, 1965).

Weber, *Jesus and the Children*

Hans Ruedi Weber, *Jesus and the Children: Biblical Resources for Study and Preaching* (Geneva: World Council of Churches, 1980) 34–51, 92–94.

Weder, *Gleichnisse*

Hans Weder, *Die Gleichnisse Jesu als Metaphern: Traditions- und redaktionsgeschichtliche Analysen und Interpretationen* (FRLANT 120; Göttingen: Vandenhoeck & Ruprecht, 1978).

Weiss, "Westliche Text"

Konrad Weiss, "Der westliche Text von Lc 7,46 und sein Wert," *ZNW* 46 (1955) 241–45.

Wenham, "Sower"

David Wenham, "The Interpretation of the Parable of the Sower," *NTS* 20 (1973–74) 299–319.

Wettstein

Johann Jakob Wettstein, *Η ΚΑΙΝΗ ΔΙΑΘΗΚΗ: Novum Testamentum Graecum* (2 vols.; Amsterdam: Ex officina Dommeriana, 1751–52).

Wilckens, "Vergebung"

Ulrich Wilckens, "Vergebung für die Sünderin (Lk 7,36–50)," in P. Hoffmann et al., eds., *Orientierung an Jesus: Zur Theologie der Synoptiker: Festschrift Josef Schmid* (Freiburg: Herder, 1973) 394–424.

Winandy, "Prophétie"

Jacques Winandy, "La prophétie de Syméon (Lc II,34–35)," *RB* 72 (1965) 321–51.

Wink, *John*

Walter Wink, *John the Baptist in the Gospel Tradition* (SNTSMS 7; Cambridge: Cambridge University Press, 1968).

Winter, "Magnificat"
Paul Winter, "Le Magnificat et le Bénédictus sont-ils des Psaumes macchabéens?" *RHPhR* 36 (1956) 1–17.

Winter, "Miszellen"
Paul Winter, "Lukanische Miszellen: I: Lk 1,17 und Ben Sira 48,10 Heb.; II a) Lc 1,68.72.73 und die Kriegsrolle; b) Lc 1,48–52 und Judiths Jubellied" *ZNW* 49 (1958) 65–67.

Witherington, "On the Road"
Ben Witherington III, "On the Road with Mary Magdalene, Joanna, Susanna, and Other Disciples—Lk 8,1–3," *ZNW* 70 (1979) 243–48.

Wrege, *Bergpredigt*
Hans-Theo Wrege, *Die Überlieferungsgeschichte der Bergpredigt* (WUNT 9; Tübingen: Mohr-Siebeck, 1968).

Zahn
Theodor Zahn, *Das Evangelium des Lukas: Ausgelegt* (1st–2d ed.; Kommentar zum Neuen Testament 3; Leipzig/Erlangen: Deichert, 1913).

Zeller, "Bildlogik"
Dieter Zeller, "Die Bildlogik des Gleichnisses Mt 11,16f / Lk 7,31f," *ZNW* 68 (1977) 252–57.

Ziener, "Brotwunder"
Georg Ziener, "Die Brotwunder im Markusevangelium," *BZ* n.s. 4 (1960) 282–85.

Zimmermann, *Methodenlehre*
Heinrich Zimmermann, *Neutestamentliche Methodenlehre: Darstellung der historisch-kritischen Methode* (Stuttgart: Katholisches Bibelwerk, 1967).

Zingg, *Wachsen*
Paul Zingg, *Das Wachsen der Kirche: Beiträge zur Frage der lukanischen Redaktion und Theologie* (OBO 3; Fribourg: Universitätsverlag; Göttingen: Vandenhoeck & Ruprecht, 1974).

3. Historical List of Commentaries on Luke

This compilation, created by the translator, attempts to be as complete as possible. Not all works were consulted in the composition of this volume.

253

Origen, *Homélies sur S. Luc: Texte latin et fragments grecs* (ed. H. Crouzel, F. Fournier, and P. Perichon; 2d ed.; SC 87; Paris: Cerf, 1998).

M. Rauer, ed., *Origenes Werke*, vol. 9: *Die Homilien zu Lukas in der Übersetzung des Hieronymus und die griechischen Reste der Homilien und Lukas-Kommentars* (2d ed.; GCS 49 [35]; Berlin: Akademie-Verlag, 1959).

378

J. von Sickenberger, ed., *Titus von Bostra: Studien zu dessen Lukashomilien* (TU 21.1; Leipzig: Hinrichs, 1901).

397

Ambrose, Bishop of Milan, *Expositio evangelii secundum Lucan* (ed. K. Schenkl; CSEL 32; Vienna: Tempsky; Leipzig: Freytag, 1902).

idem, *Traité sur l'évangile de S. Luc* (ed. and trans. G. Tissot; 2 vols.; SC 45, 52; Paris: Cerf, 1956–58).

430

Augustine, Bishop of Hippo, *Quaestiones Evangeliorum* (ed. A. Mutzenbecher; Corpus Christianorum Series Latina 44B; Turnholt: Brepols, 1980).

444

Cyril, Patriarch of Alexandria, *Commentarii in Lucam* (ed. I.-B. Chabot; CSCO 70, 140; Paris: Typographeum Reipublicae, 1912).

519

Philoxenus of Mabbug, Bishop of Hierapolis, *Fragments of the Commentary on Matthew and Luke* (ed. J. W. Watt; 2 vols.; CSCO 392–93; Louvain: Secretariat du Corpus SCO, 1978).

735

Bede Venerabilii, *In Lucae Evangelium expositio* (ed. D. Hurst; Corpus Christianorum Series Latina 120; Turnholt: Brepols, 1960).

11th century

J. Sickenberger, ed., *Die Lukaskatene des Niketas von Herakleia* (TU 22.4; Leipzig: Hinrichs, 1902).

J. Reuss, ed., *Lukas-Kommentare aus der griechischen Kirche aus Katenenhandschriften* (TU 130; Berlin: Akademie-Verlag, 1984).

1274

Bonaventure, *Opera omnia*, vol. 7: *Commentarius in Evangelium S. Lucae* (ed. R. P. Bernardini; Quaracchi: Collegium S. Bonaventurae, 1882–1902).

1523

Jacques Le Fèvre d'Etaples, *Commentarii initiatorii in qvatvor Evangelia* (Basel: Andreae Cratandri, 1523).

1537

Johannes Brenz, *In evangelii quod inscribitur, secundum Lucam* (Halae Sueuorum: Petri Brubachii, 1537–46).

1546

Heinrich Bullinger, *In luculentum et sacrosanctum Euangeliu[m] Domini Nostri Iesu* (Zurich: Christ. Froschovervs, 1546).

Martin Luther, *Evangelien-Auslegung*, part 3: *Markus- und Lukasevangelium* (ed. E. Mulhaupt; Göttingen: Vandenhoeck & Ruprecht, 1938–54).

1555

Jean Calvin, *Commentaires sur le Nouveau Testament,* vol. 1, *Sur la Concordance ou Harmonie composée de trois évangélistes asçavoir S. Matthieu, S. Marc, et S. Luc* (Geneva: Conrad Badius, 1561).

1600

Francisco de Toledo, *Commentarii in prima XII Capita . . . Evangelii secundam Lucam* (Venice: Ioannes Baptista Ciottus Senenses, 1600).

1612

Diego de Estella, *Didaci stellae: . . . examini verbi diuini concionatoris: in sacrosanctum Iesu Christi Domini nostri Euangelium secundum Lucam* (Antwerp: Petri Belleri, 1612).

1628

Balthasar Corder, *Catena sexaginta quinque Graecorum patrum in S. Lucam* (Antwerp: Oficina Plantiniana, 1628).

1675

John Lightfoot, *Horae Hebraicae et Talmudicae in quatuor evangelistas cum tractatibus chorographicis, singulis suo evangelistae praemissis* (Leipzig: Fridericus Lanckisius, Johannis Colerus, 1675).

1741

Reinier toe Laer, *Het H. Evangelium beschreven door Lucas: naar het oogmerk en deszelfs zamenhang verklaart* (Nymegen: Henrik Heymans, 1741–42).

1795

Samuel Friedrich Nathanael Morus, *Praelectiones in Lucae Evangelium* (ed. K. A. Donat; Leipzig: Sommer, 1795).

1817

Friedrich Schleiermacher, *Über die Schriften des Lucas: Ein kritischer Versuch* (Berlin: Reimer, 1817).

1830

Karl Wilhelm Stein, *Kommentar zu dem Evangelium des Lucas: Nebst einem Anhange über den Brief an die Läodiceer* (Halle: C. A. Schwetschte und Sohn, 1830).

1836

Wilhelm Martin Leberecht de Wette, *Kurze Erklärung der Evangelien des Lukas und Markus* (Kurzgefasstes exegetisches Handbuch zum Neuen Testament 1.2; Leipzig: Weidmannsche Buchhandlung, 1836).

1846

Heinrich August Wilhelm Meyer, *Kritisch exegetisches Handbuch über die Evangelien des Markus und Lukas* (2d ed.; KEK 1.2; Göttingen: Vandenhoeck & Ruprecht, 1846).

1852

John Clowes, *The Gospel According to Luke . . . Illustrated by Extracts from the Theological Writings of Emanuel Swedenborg* (London: J. S. Hodson, 1852).

1853

Melanchthon W. Jacobus, *Mark and Luke* (Philadelphia: Presbyterian Board of Publication, 1853).

1859

John J. Owen, *A Commentary, Critical, Expository and Practical, on the Gospel of Luke* (New York: Leavitt & Allen, 1859).

Johannes Jacobus van Oosterzee, *Das Evangelium nach Lukas* (Bielefeld: Velhagen und Klasing, 1859).

1866

James Stark, *Commentary on the Gospel According to Luke* (2 vols.; London: Longman, Green, Reader, and Dyer, 1866).

1871

Frédéric Godet, *Commentaire sur L'Évangile de Saint Luc* (2 vols.; Neuchâtel: Librairie Générale de Jules Sandoz, 1871).

1875

Arthur Carr, *The Gospel According to St. Luke* (London: Rivingtons, 1875).

1878

Lyman Abbott, *The Gospel According to Luke with Notes, Comments, Maps, and Illustrations* (New York: A. S. Barnes, 1878).

Bernhard Weiss, *Die Evangelien des Markus und Lukas* (6th ed.; KEK 1.2; Göttingen: Vandenhoeck & Ruprecht, 1878).

1879

Carl Friedrich Keil, *Commentar über die Evangelien des Markus und Lukas* (Leipzig: Dörffling und Franke, 1879).

1881

Matthew Brown Riddle, *The Gospel According to Luke* (New York: Charles Scribner, 1881).

1883

Paul Schanz, *Commentar über das Evangelium des heiligen Lucas* (Tübingen: F. Fues, 1883).

1884

George R. Bliss, *Commentary on the Gospel of Luke* (Philadelphia: American Baptist Publication Society, 1884).

Frederic William Farrar, *The Gospel According to Luke* (Cambridge: Cambridge University Press, 1884).

1887

August Dachsel, *St. Markus's og St. Lukas's Evangelier: med en i texten indskudt fortolkning: udførlige indholdsaugivelser og oplysende anmaerkninger* (ed. E. F. Eckhoff; Bergen: F. Beyer & H. Hansen, 1887).

1889

George Asbury McLaughlin, *A Commentary on the Gospel by St. Luke* (Boston: McDonald, Gill, 1889).

1890

Henry Burton, *The Gospel according to St. Luke* (London: Hodder & Stoughton, 1890).

1896

Henry Louis Baugher, *Annotations on the Gospel According to St. Luke* (Lutheran Commentary 4; New York: Christian Literature, 1896).

Joseph Knabenbauer, *Commentarius in quatuor S. Evangelia Domini N. Iesu Christi*, vol. 3, *Evangelium secundum Lucam* (Paris: P. Lethielleux, 1896).

Alfred Plummer, *A Critical and Exegetical Commentary on the Gospel According to St. Luke* (ICC; Edinburgh: T. & T. Clark, 1896).

1897

Friedrich Blass, *Evangelium secundum Lucam, sive Lucae ad Theopilum* (Leipzig: B. G. Teubner, 1897).

1898

Alexander Maclaren, *The Gospel of St. Luke* (2d ed.; London: Hodder & Stoughton, 1898).

Edwin Wilbur Rice, *Commentary on the Gospel According to Luke* (enlarged ed.; Philadelphia: Union Press, 1898).

Marie-Joseph Lagrange, *Évangile selon Saint Luc* (2d ed.; EtB; Paris: J. Gabalda, 1921).

1902

Jan van Andel, *Het evangelie naar de beschrijving van Lukas aan de gemeente toegelicht* (Leiden: Donner, 1902).

1904

Dewi Zephaniah Phillips, *Esboniad ar yr Efengyl yn ol Luc* (Caerdydd: Tom Roberts, 1904).

Julius Wellhausen, *Das Evangelium Lucae* (Berlin: Georg Reimer, 1904).

1908

Johannes Marinus Simon Baljon, *Commentaar op net Evangelie van Lukas* (Utrecht: J. Van Boekhoven, 1908).

1913

Theodor Zahn, *Das Evangelium des Lukas: Ausgelegt* (1st–2d ed.; Kommentar zum Neuen Testament 3; Leipzig/Erlangen: Deichert, 1913).

1917

Johannes de Zwaan, *Het evangelie van Lucas* (Groningen: J. B. Wolters, 1917).

1919

Erich Klostermann, *Das Lukasevangelium* (HNT 2.1; Tübingen: J. C. B. Mohr [Paul Siebeck], 1919).

1921

Charles R. Erdman, *The Gospel of Luke: An Exposition* (Philadelphia: Westminster, 1921).

1922

Lonsdale Ragg, *St. Luke: With Introduction and Notes* (Westminster Commentaries; London: Methuen, 1922).

Hermann Strack and Paul Billerbeck, *Kommentar zum Neuen Testament aus Talmud und Midrasch* (5 vols.; Munich: Beck, 1922–61) 2.55–301.

1924

Alfred Loisy, *L'Évangile selon Luc* (Paris: Émile Nourry, 1924).

1926

Burton S. Easton, *The Gospel According to Luke* (New York: Scribner's, 1926).

1930

H. Balmforth, *The Gospel According to Saint Luke in the Revised Version: With Introduction and Commentary* (Oxford: Clarendon, 1930).

John Martin Creed, ed., *The Gospel according to St. Luke: The Greek Text with Introduction, Notes, and Indices* (London: Macmillan, 1930).

William Manson, *The Gospel of Luke* (Moffatt New Testament Commentary; London: Hodder & Stoughton, 1930).

1931

George Campbell Morgan, *The Gospel According to Luke* (New York: Fleming H. Revell, 1931).

Adolf Schlatter, *Das Evangelium des Lukas: Aus seinen Quellen erklärt* (Stuttgart: Calwer, 1931).

1933

H. K. Luce, *The Gospel According to S. Luke: With Introduction and Notes* (Cambridge: Cambridge University Press, 1933).

1934

Friedrich Hauck, *Das Evangelium des Lukas (Synoptiker II)* (ThHKNT 3; Leipzig: A. Deichert, 1934).

1937

Wilhelm Bartelt, *Das Evangelium des hl. Lukas* (2d ed.; Herders Bibelkommentar 12; Freiburg: Herder, 1937).

Karl Heinrich Rengstorf and Friedrich Büchsel, *Das Evangelium nach Lukas und das Evangelium nach Johannes* (Göttingen: Vandenhoeck & Ruprecht, 1937).

1939

Josef Dillersberger, *Lukas: Das Evangelium des heiligen Lukas in theologischer und heilsgeschichtlicher Schau* (6 vols.; Salzburg: Otto Müller, 1939–49).

1940

Seakle Greijdanus, *Het heilig evangelie naar de beschrijving van Lucas* (2 vols.; Amsterdam: H. A. Van Bottenburg, 1940–41).

1951

Norval Geldenhuys, *Commentary on the Gospel of Luke* (NICNT; Grand Rapids: Eerdmans, 1951).

Ernest Fremont Tittle, *The Gospel According to Luke* (New York: Harper, 1951).

1955

Josef Schmid, *Das Evangelium nach Lukas* (3d ed.; RNT; Regensburg: F. Pustet, 1955).

1956

William Arndt, *Bible Commentary: The Gospel According to St. Luke* (Saint Louis: Concordia, 1956).

William Barclay, *The Gospel of Luke* (2d ed.; Philadelphia: Westminster, 1956).

1957

Jean-Samuel Javet, *L'Évangile de la Grâce: commentaire sur l'Évangile selon saint Luc* (Geneva: Labor et Fides, 1957).

C. C. Martindale, *The Gospel According to Saint Luke* (London: Longman, Green, 1957).

1958

A. R. C. Leaney, *A Commentary on the Gospel According to St. Luke* (HNTC; New York: Harper, 1958).

1959

Donald G. Miller, *The Gospel According to Luke* (Layman's Bible Commentary 18; Richmond, Va.: John Knox, 1959).

Fritz Rienecker, *Das Evangelium des Lukas* (Wuppertal: R. Brockhaus, 1959).

1960

Wilfrid Robert Francis Browning, *The Gospel According to Saint Luke* (Torch Bible Commentaries; New York: Macmillan, 1960).

1961

Walter Grundmann, *Das Evangelium nach Lukas* (2d ed.; ThHKNT 3; Berlin: Evangelische Verlagsanstalt, 1961).

1962

Dietrich Fischinger, *Das Lukasevangelium* (Stuttgart: Kreuz, 1962).

1963

George Bradford Caird, *The Gospel of St. Luke* (PNTC; Harmondsworth: Penguin, 1963).

Augustin George, *L'Annonce du salut de Dieu: Lecture de l'évangile de Luc* (Paris: Equipes Enseignantes, 1963).

1964

Alois Stöger, *Das Evangelium nach Lukas* (2 vols.; Düsseldorf: Patmos-Verlag, 1964–66).

1965

Walter Russell Bowie, *The Compassionate Christ: Reflections from the Gospel of Luke* (New York: Abingdon, 1965).

Lalsawma, *Chanchin tha Luka ziak: Thuthlung Thar hrilhfiahna* (Aijal: Synod Bookroom, 1965).

E. J. Tinsley, *The Gospel According to Luke* (CBC:NEB; Cambridge: Cambridge University Press, 1965).

1966

Edward Earle Ellis, *The Gospel of Luke* (2d ed.; NCB; 1966; reprinted Grand Rapids: Eerdmans, 1981).

1967

Douglas William Cleverley Ford, *A Reading of Saint Luke's Gospel* (London: Hodder & Stoughton, 1967).

Wilfrid J. Harrington, *The Gospel According to St. Luke: A Commentary* (Westminster, Md.: Newman, 1967).

1968

Henri Joseph Troadec, *Évangile selon saint Luc* (Tours: Mame, 1968).

1969

Heinz Schürmann, *Das Lukasevangelium,* part 1, *Kommentar zu Kap. 1,1– 9,50* (HThKNT 3; Freiburg im Breisgau: Herder, 1969).

1972

Anthony Lee Ash, *The Gospel According to Luke* (2 vols.; Austin: Sweet, 1972–73).

Frederick W. Danker, *Jesus and the New Age, According to St. Luke: A Commentary on the Third Gospel* (St. Louis: Clayton, 1972).

1973

John J. Coutts, *How the Christian Faith Began: A Commentary on the Gospel According to St. Luke and the Acts of the Apostles* (London: Longman, 1973).

John Rury, *Luke* (J. B. Phillips' Commentaries 3; New York: Macmillan, 1973).

1974

Feliks Gryglewicz, *Ewangelia wedug w. Lukasza: Wstep—Przekad z Oryginau—Komentarz* (Warsaw: Pallottinum, 1974).

Leon Morris, *The Gospel According to St. Luke: An Introduction and Commentary* (Tyndale New Testament Commentaries; Grand Rapids: Eerdmans, 1974).

1976

Mario Galizzi, *Vangelo secondo Luca* (3 vols.; Torino: Elle di Ci, 1976–79).

1977

Joan Casanas, *El Evangelio de Lucas* (8 vols.; Barcelona: Agermanament, 1977–79).

Josef Ernst, *Das Evangelium nach Lukas: Übersetzt und erklärt* (RNT 3; Regensburg: F. Pustet, 1977).

Robert J. Karris, *Invitation to Luke: A Commentary on the Gospel of Luke* (Garden City, N.Y.: Image Books, 1977).

Gerhard Schneider, *Das Evangelium nach Lukas* (2 vols.; Ökumenischer Taschenbuchkommentar zum Neuen Testament 3; Gütersloh: Mohn; Würzburg: Echter, 1977).

1978

I. Howard Marshall, *The Gospel of Luke: A Commentary on the Greek Text* (New International Greek Testament Commentary; Grand Rapids: Eerdmans; Exeter: Paternoster, 1978).

1979

Jan Tjeerd Nielsen, *Het Evangelie naar Lucas* (2 vols.; Nijkerk: Callenbach, 1979–83).

1980

Eugene LaVerdiere, *Luke* (Wilmington, Del.: Michael Glazier, 1980).

Walter Schmithals, *Das Evangelium nach Lukas* (Zürcher Bibelkommentare NT 3.1; Zurich: Theologischer Verlag, 1980).

1981

Philippe Bossuyt and Jean Radermakers, *Jésus, Parole de la grâce: Selon St. Luc* (2 vols.; Brussels: Institut d'études théologiques, 1981).

1981

Joseph A. Fitzmyer, *The Gospel According to Luke: Introduction, Translation, and Notes* (2 vols.; AB 28–28A; Garden City, N.Y.: Doubleday, 1981–85).

1982

Eduard Schweizer, *Das Evangelium nach Lukas* (NTD 3; Göttingen: Vandenhoeck & Ruprecht, 1982).

Charles H. Talbert, *Reading Luke: A Literary and Theological Commentary on the Third Gospel* (New York: Crossroad, 1982).

1983

Jerome Kodell, *The Gospel According to Luke* (Collegeville, Minn.: Liturgical, 1983).

Bruce Larson, *The Communicator's Commentary: Luke* (Waco: Word, 1983).

1985

Léopold Sabourin, *L'Évangile de Luc: Introduction et commentaire* (Rome: Gregorian University Press, 1985).

1986

Georges Gander, *L'Évangile pour les étrangers du monde: Commentaire de l'Évangile selon Luc* (Lausanne: 1986).

Charles L'Eplattenier, *Lecture de l'évangile de Luc* (Paris: Desclée, 1982).

Robert E. Obach, *A Commentary on the Gospel of Luke* (New York: Paulist, 1986).

1987

David Willoughby Gooding, *According to Luke: A New Exposition of the Third Gospel* (Grand Rapids: Eerdmans, 1987).

Samuel Tobias Lachs, *A Rabbinic Commentary on the New Testament: The Gospels of Matthew, Mark, and Luke* (Hoboken, N.J.: Ktav; New York: Anti-Defamation League of B'nai B'rith, 1987).

Claude Tresmontant, *Évangile de Luc* (Paris: O.E.I.L., 1987).

1988

John J. Kilgallen, *A Brief Commentary on the Gospel of Luke* (New York: Paulist, 1988).

Jacob Kremer, *Lukasevangelium* (Neue Echter Bibel, Neues Testament 3; Wurzburg: Echter, 1988).

Roland Meynet, *L'évangile selon Saint Luc: Analyse rhétorique* (2 vols.; Paris: Cerf, 1988).

David Lenz Tiede, *Luke* (Augsburg Commentary on the New Testament; Minneapolis: Augsburg, 1988).

Wolfgang Wiefel, *Das Evangelium nach Lukas* (ThHKNT 3; Berlin: Evangelische Verlagsanstalt, 1988).

1989

François Bovon, *Das Evangelium nach Lukas* (EKKNT 3.1–3; Zurich: Benziger; Neukirchener-Vluyn: Neukirchener Verlag, 1989–2000).

John Nolland, *Luke* (3 vols.; Word Biblical Commentary 35A-C; Dallas: Word, 1989–93).

1990

Christopher Francis Evans, *Saint Luke* (TPI New Testament Commentaries; Philadelphia: Trinity Press International, 1990).

Craig A. Evans, *Luke* (New International Biblical Commentary 3; Peabody, Mass.: Hendrickson, 1990).

1991

Luke Timothy Johnson, *The Gospel of Luke* (Sacra Pagina 3; Collegeville, Minn.: Liturgical Press, 1991).

Gerhard Maier, *Lukas-Evangelium* (2 vols.; Neuhausen-Stuttgart: Hanssler, 1991–92).

1992

Gerard Rosse, *Il Vangelo di Luca: commento esegetico e teologico* (Rome: Citta Nuova, 1992).

Robert H. Stein, *Luke* (New American Commentary 24; Nashville: Broadman, 1992).

1994

Darrell L. Bock, *Luke* (2 vols.; Baker Exegetical Commentary on the New Testament; Grand Rapids: Baker, 1994–96)

1995

Sharon H. Ringe, *Luke* (Louisville: Westminster John Knox, 1995).

1996

Herman Hendrickx, *The Third Gospel for the Third World* (vols. 1–; Collegeville, Minn.: Liturgical, 1996–).

Arthur A. Just, *Luke* (2 vols.; Concordia Commentary; St. Louis: Concordia, 1996–97).

Robert C. Tannehill, *Luke* (Abingdon New Testament Commentaries; Nashville: Abingdon, 1996).

Henry Wansbrough, *The Lion and the Bull: The Gospels of Mark and Luke* (London: Darton, Longman & Todd, 1996).

1997

Joel B. Green, *The Gospel of Luke* (NICNT; Grand Rapids: Eerdmans, 1997).

Judith Lieu, *The Gospel of Luke* (Epworth Commentaries; London: Epworth, 1997).

1998

Mazhar al-Malluhi, Amal al-Malluhi, *Al-Injil kama awhiy ila al-Qiddis Luqa: Qiraah sharqiyah* (Beirut: Dar al-Jil, 1998).

1. Text

Luke's two volumes are both a concrete and an abstract entity. As with all holy scriptures, they were revered down to their individual letters. But the accidents of history have not left the work untouched. Copyists in the second century worked on the text with the best of intents, but thus concealed the original shape of the text. Theologians attempted either to purify the work by abridgment (like Marcion) or to harmonize it with other Gospels (like Tatian). Even its reception into the Christian canon, which actually should have protected it from alterations, did not leave the Gospel untouched: precisely this led to the division of the two volumes and to their elevation to sacred status—presumably against Luke's intentions. From that point on, the Gospel of Luke and the book of Acts ceased to be two volumes of a single work circulating at the book markets. No single manuscript, not even the oldest, transmits Luke's two volumes according to their original form and intention. Thus text criticism is part of the history of interpretation, but at the same time also makes it possible for us still to hear Luke's voice for ourselves and to make out his words throughout the history of the text.

Despite numerous variants, the text is in relatively good condition. I do not share Marcion's opinion that the Gospel of Luke was adulterated by Judaizing interpolations, since Lukan idioms occur so regularly throughout the work. Marcion was perhaps still familiar with one or several of Luke's sources, and used this as a justification for his deletions and "extrapolations."

Three, possibly four, text types can be distinguished; these correspond more nearly to gradually evolving rather than one-time recensions. The Alexandrian text (esp. P^{75}, ℵ, B and C) developed in the second century. The Western text (D, some Old Latin witnesses, one Syriac version [the Curetonian], and citations by the church fathers) is about as old as the Alexandrian text. A third type from the fourth century is attested for the Gospels by A: the Byzantine text, which held sway for centuries (the textus receptus printed by Erasmus). Last, it is an open question whether one has to assume a fourth text type, the Caesarean text, as well.

The variant readings within the manuscript tradition have various causes: copyists' mistakes, the influence of oral tradition or of the other Gospels (esp. Matthew), recensions, and tendencies in theological development or ecclesiastical sensibilities. I would like to draw attention to at least a few of the principal problems in the textual criticism of the Gospel of Luke:[1]

1. What is the original formulation of the second petition of the Lord's Prayer: "Thy kingdom come," or "Your holy spirit come upon us and purify us" (11:2)?

2. Is Jesus' short address to the man working on the Sabbath apocryphal or genuine (6:4, in D alone)?

3. According to Luke, did Jesus send out seventy or seventy-two disciples (10:2)?

4. For the words of the institution of the Eucharist, should one prefer the long or the short text (without 22:19b–20)?

5. Should one include the appearance of the comforting angel at Gethsemane (22:43–44)?

6. Are the words "and he was taken up into heaven" a later accretion (24:51)?

Bibliography

Aland, Kurt, et al., eds., *The Greek New Testament* (3d ed.; Stuttgart: United Bible Societies, 1983).

Aland, Kurt, ed., *Synopsis of the Four Gospels: Greek-English Edition of Synopsis Quattuor Evangeliorum* (6th ed.; New York: United Bible Societies; Stuttgart: Biblia-Druck, 1983).

Amphoux, Christian Bernard, "Les premières éditions de Luc I: Le texte de Lc 5," *EThL* 67 (1991) 312–27.

idem, "Les premières éditions de Luc II: L'histoire du texte au IIe siècle," *EThL* 68 (1992) 38–48.

Boismard, M. E., and A. Lamouille, *Le texte occidental des Actes des Apôtres: Reconstitution et réhabilitation* (2 vols.; Synthèse 17; Éditions Recherche sur les civilisations).

Delebecque, Edouard, *Les deux Actes des Apôtres* (EtB n.s. 6; Paris: Gabalda, 1986).

Duplacy, J., "P75 (Pap. Bodmer XIV–XV) et les formes les plus anciennes du texte de Luc," in F. Neirynck, ed., *L'Évangile de Luc: Problèmes littéraires et théologiques: Mémorial Lucien Cerfaux* (BETL 32; Gembloux: Duculot, 1978) 111–28.

---

1 Cf. also Luke 5:39; 9:55; 10:20, 41–42; 11:8, 13, 41; 12:19, 21, 39; 16:9; 17:36; 19:25; 20:20; 21:35; 22:62, 68; 23:13, 15, 17, 35; 24:3, 6, 12, 17, 36, 40–42, 52.

Fitzmyer, Joseph A., *The Gospel According to Luke: Introduction, Translation, and Notes* (2 vols.; AB 28-28A; Garden City, N.Y.: Doubleday, 1981–85) 1.128–33.

Martini, C. M., *Il problema della recensionalità del codice B alla luce del papiro Bodmer XIV* (AnBib 26; Rome: Pontifical Biblical Institute, 1966).

Metzger, Bruce M., *A Textual Commentary on the Greek New Testament: A Companion Volume to the United Bible Societies' Greek New Testament* (3d ed.; London/New York: United Bible Societies, 1975) 129–93.

Nestle, Eberhard, ed., *Novum Testamentum Graece* (27th ed.; rev. Erwin Nestle and Kurt Aland; Stuttgart: Württembergische Bibelgesellschaft, 1979). *New Testament in Greek*.

Rice, George, "Western Non-Interpolations: A Defense of the Apostolate," in C. H. Talbert, ed., *Luke-Acts: New Perspectives from the Society of Biblical Literature Seminar* (New York: Crossroad, 1984) 1–16.

Vaganay, Léon, *Initiation à la critique textuelle du Nouveau Testament* (2d ed.; rev. C. B. Amphoux; Études annexes de la Bible de Jérusalem; Paris: Cerf, 1986).

2. Structure and Style

The work comprises two books of equal length, each one the average length of a book at that time, which was probably economically determined. The first describes the life of Jesus; the second illustrates the spread of the new message through a few primary witnesses.

Formally, the prologue (1:1–4) attempts to elevate gospel tradition to a literary level; its content indicates the author's method, purpose, and results. Following the prologue, Luke narrates, in unbalanced symmetry, the events surrounding the births of John and Jesus (1:5–2:52). Only then, introduced by an elaborate and solemn synchronism (3:1), begins the period of John's activity and—following directly upon it—Jesus' activity.

Luke divides the life of Jesus into three literary units. Jesus is active chiefly in Galilee (4:14–9:50), he then teaches and performs healings on the way to Jerusalem (9:51 probably to 19:27), and he finally concludes his saving activity in Jerusalem with a last series of teachings in the temple, and his suffering, death, resurrection, and ascension (19:28–24:53).

The parallelism between John and Jesus, so character-istic in the birth narrative, recedes at the time when both attain their calling. John is a figure on the threshold of two eras with one foot in prophecy (as the last prophet), and the other foot in its fulfillment (as the first preacher of the good news); he quickly fulfills his role. Luke, who does not intend to write parallel lives, promptly introduces, alongside and after John, the main character—Jesus. Until 4:13, we are still in the preparatory stages. Only then does Luke signal the beginning of Jesus' activity, in the more extensive scene of his first public appearance in Nazareth (4:14–30).

The picture of Jesus that Luke sketches in this first section is that of the healing (4:14–6:19) and teaching (6:20–49) Messiah, who travels through the cities of Galilee. The transfiguration (9:28–36) introduces the themes of the second unit, the travel account; the discussion between the three figures about the "exit" of Jesus (a euphemism for his death) makes the readers aware that Jesus' messianism is characterized by his suffering. According to the apologetic convictions of Luke, and of the Christians of his time, this suffering was part of God's plan (cf. Acts 2:23). Predictably, the triumphal entry of Jesus into Jerusalem opens the third unit of the narrative (Luke 19:28–44).

The points of reference for an outline of the travel account are, perhaps, the repeated allusions to Jesus' progress along the way to Jerusalem (esp. 13:22 and 17:11). One subdivision is thus marked off from 9:51 to 13:21. Here the author gives instruction for Christian existence according to the will of Jesus: What does it mean to become a disciple? What renunciations are prerequisite for this condition? How does one come to believe? How is the good news proclaimed? How has God expressed his love? The passage 13:22–17:10 forms a second subdivision; formally, it represents the midpoint of the Gospel. The theme of God's magnanimity toward the lost stands in the foreground, but the possible rejection of the offer by those addressed is not ignored; this is described contrastively in the dinner guests declining the invitation in the parable at 14:15–24, or by the older son at 15:25–32. This second subdivision presents greed as an obstacle to the acceptance of salvation (a sociological index for the composition of the community in Luke's era). Other obstacles are jealousy on the part of the chosen people, and the Christians' loss of zeal in view of the delay of the parousia. The third subdivision has a parabolic character throughout, with an eschatological orientation (17:11–19:27).

Luke combines longer passages with introductory and concluding frame verses, which provide a particular direction and interpretation to the narration; see, for example, Jesus' programmatic first sermon in Nazareth (4:16–30). But Luke is also effective at creating a climax at the center of these passages and units. The parable of the prodigal son, for example, appears exactly at the midpoint of the Gospel (15:11–32), just as the decisive council at Jerusalem forms the midpoint of the book of Acts (15:1–35). Such carefully considered and well-constructed episodes furnish the entire work with a sort of literary synopsis and hermeneutical key, something like the *mise en abîme* of recent French criticism.

Within the units and passages, Luke employs a simple narrative technique: he strings together smaller self-contained stories, which are intended to instruct and to elicit a response. This so-called episodic style was, of course, prescribed by the sources. But Luke does refine it; when possible, he inserts short summaries between the episodes; these summaries create transitions, allow the readers to pause, and, above all, effect a generalization of the events. Whereas the aorist is the logical choice for the individual episodes, the summaries are written in the imperfect; contrast Jesus' anointing by the sinful woman (Luke 7:36–50) with the description of the female disciples (8:1–3). As a rule, the pericopes are longer than the summaries.

Although Luke commands a broad and comprehensive education, simplicity is his aim. He abandons, for the most part, the persuasive techniques of rhetoric in order to conform his narrative technique to the biblical style of the historical books of the Hebrew Bible, so as to emphasize continuity between the LXX and his work. Alongside the books of prophecy, he places two books of fulfillment. Luke incorporates elements of biblical style into his sentence construction (the well-known introductory ἐγένετο δέ, "and it happened"), into his vocabulary (ἐν ταῖς ἡμέραις ἐκείναις, "in those days," 2:1), and in his episodic style. Less biblical is his concentration on a single holy individual, Jesus, as the representative of the divine will. Here Luke proves to be a transmitter of Christian tradition, which was influenced by the Hellenistic style of propaganda and by classical biography.

With each episode, Luke modifies his style accordingly. The thoughts and cares of Mary he expresses in motherly words; he sets the date of the Baptist's initial activity with solemnity; the failed fishing expedition is couched in trade language. The transfiguration is mysterious; Paul's confrontation with the Jews in Rome, polemical. The apostles' prayer and attitude after the ascension is painted in a hieratic fashion, like an icon. Jesus' encounter with Zacchaeus is vivid, moving, and almost naïve. Paul's dramatic shipwreck is novelistic, Peter's missionary sermon ecclesiastically kerygmatic, Paul's exegetical sermon in the synagogue, in its reasoning, Jewish. The various defense speeches of the apostles are presented with legal rhetoric. These variations in style should not be ascribed to the use of dissimilar sources, but are the sign of a gifted writer's technique.

It is not without reason that Luke has been imagined for centuries to have been a painter, since he plays up what is visible in the events. He immediately colors abstract speeches with an example or a parable. He illustrates the two great commandments first with the parable of the good Samaritan, then with the conversation with Martha and Mary (10:25–42). He brings difficult theological issues closer to the readers' comprehension through memorable dramatic settings, for example, the virgin birth through the vivid encounter between Mary and the angel, and their dialogue (1:26–38). Ethical decisions and ecclesiological questions are not justified or answered with intellectual arguments alone, but are supported with concrete cases; for example, the acceptance of Gentiles into the church is justified by the precedent-setting case of Cornelius, his family and friends (Acts 15:8, 9, 14).

Some claim that Luke suppresses emotions, particularly those of Jesus; this claim seems to me mistaken. Luke, indeed, does not speculate about feelings, but he does depict their expression. John, not yet born, leaps in his mother's womb (1:41); the sinful woman pours forth tears (7:38); Jesus stoops down over Peter's mother-in-law, who lies critically ill (4:39).

The structure and style of Luke's two volumes demonstrate his creative mastery, in both literary and theological respects. The manner in which Luke handles Greek confirms this observation.

Bibliography

On structure:

Bossuyt, Philippe, and Jean Radermakers, *Jésus, Parole de la grâce: Selon St. Luc* (2 vols.; Brussels: Institut d'études théologiques, 1981).

Conzelmann, Hans, *The Theology of St. Luke* (1961; trans. G. Buswell; reprint ed. Philadelphia: Fortress Press, 1982).

Fearghail, Fearghus Ó, *The Introduction to Luke-Acts: A Study of the Role of Luke 1,1–4,44 in the Composition of Luke's Two-Volume Work* (Rome: Pontifical Biblical Institute Press, 1991).

Fitzmyer, 1.91–97, bibliography 105–6.

George, Augustin, *Études sur l'œuvre de Luc* (SB; Paris: Gabalda, 1978) 15–41.

L'Epplatenier, Charles, *Lecture de l'Évangile de Luc* (Paris: Desclée, 1982).

Morgenthaler, Robert, *Die lukanische Geschichtsschreibung als Zeugnis: Gestalt und Gehalt der Kunst des Lukas* (2 vols.; AThANT 14–15; Zurich: Zwingli, 1948–49).

Radl, Walter, *Paulus und Jesus im lukanischen Doppelwerk: Untersuchungen zu Parallelmotiven im Lukasevangelium und in der Apostelgeschichte* (EHS Theologie 49; Frankfurt am Main/Bern: Lang, 1975).

Talbert, Charles H., *Literary Patterns, Theological Themes, and the Genre of Luke-Acts* (SBLMS 20; Missoula, Mont.: Scholars Press, 1974).

idem, *Reading Luke: A Literary and Theological Commentary on the Third Gospel* (1982; reprint ed. New York: Crossroad, 1986).

On style:

Cadbury, Henry J., *The Making of Luke-Acts* (2d ed.; London: SPCK, 1961).

idem, *Style.*

Fitzmyer, 1.107–27, bibliography 125–27.

Haenchen, Ernst, *The Acts of the Apostles: A Commentary* (trans. R. Mcl. Wilson et al.; 1965; Philadelphia: Westminster, 1971) 98–103.

Turner, Nigel, "The Style of Luke-Acts," in idem, *Style,* vol. 4 of James Hope Moulton et al., *A Grammar of New Testament Greek* (4 vols.; Edinburgh: Clark, 1908–76) 45–63.

van Unnik, W. C., "Éléments artistiques dans l'évangile de Luc," in Neirynck, *Évangile,* 129–40.

Vogel, Theodor, *Zur Charakteristik des Lukas nach Sprache und Stil: Eine philologische Laienstudie* (2d ed.; Leipzig: Dürr, 1899).

3. Language

Luke is a witness of the so-called Koine, the Greek of Hellenistic and Roman times, halfway between the Attic prose of classical antiquity and modern Greek. What Luke *writes* is not, of course, what one *spoke* then. Luke attempts to find a middle path between the vernacular, which one finds in Mark or nonliterary papyri, and the artificial Greek of the reform movements, such as the Atticizing fashion of the second century. The passages that contain what Luke considers to be his best-formulated language, such as the introduction, are in my opinion outdone by the straightforward narratives, which Luke builds to a climax with an unfailing intuition for language.

Luke attempts to improve on Mark's rough language. Mark's inelegant formulation, "and his disciples began to make their way, plucking ears of grain" (καὶ οἱ μαθηταὶ αὐτοῦ ἤρξαντο ὁδὸν ποιεῖν τίλλοντες τοὺς στάχυας, Mark 2:23), is rewritten by Luke: "his disciples plucked and ate some heads of grain, rubbing them in their hands" (καὶ ἔτιλλον οἱ μαθηταὶ αὐτοῦ καὶ ἤσθιον τοὺς στάχυας ψώχοντες ταῖς χερσίν, Luke 6:1). Luke refuses to describe as a "sea" (Mark 1:16–20; 4:1–2) that which is only a lake (Luke 5:1–2). Whatever sounds vulgar to the educated,[2] or irritates Christian sensibilities, Luke replaces.[3] With sexual vocabulary, as well, Luke exercises restraint, at the cost of an occasional loss of spontaneity and vividness: he deletes the word σπέρμα, "seed," as a term for progeny (20:29; cf. Mark 12:20), and does not risk the term πορνεία ("sexual sin"). Prudishly, he calls a prostitute "a sinful woman in the city" (7:37).

The question of the occurrence of Semitisms is a difficult one. On the one hand, Luke avoids many of the Semitisms from his source, Mark. On the other hand, Luke prefers a Semitic, or rather, biblical, tone in his narrative and employs Semitisms whenever he finds them tolerable, that is, when they appear legitimized by the usage of the LXX. The numerous sayings of Jesus, which Luke does not want to touch, also limit his modifications. Luke is in a situation similar to that of people in

---

2   Lists of such words to be avoided are transmitted by Phrynicus.

3   Compare Luke 18:25; 21:14; and 22:46 with their parallels in Mark.

advertising today, who must sacrifice some of their favorite slogans for the sake of general comprehensibility.[4]

In Lukan syntax it is clear that, as often as possible, this evangelist replaces Mark's monotonous parataxis with hypotaxis (subordinate clauses). Luke shows a preference for participial phrases.[5] As a historian, he likes to employ the aorist, with which he regularly replaces Mark's historical present. In contrast to other New Testament authors, Luke uses the tenses and moods correctly; he is one of the few Christian authors of his time who still dares and understands how to use the optative, though this occurs seldom (e.g., Luke 6:11). This cultivated writer also nearly always uses the correct terms. In the book of Acts, in which he is less dependent on written sources, he writes with greater ease and fluidity. His style, vocabulary, and tendencies emerge even more clearly there.

Bibliography

Argyle, A. W., "The Greek of Luke and Acts," *NTS* 20 (1973–74) 441–45.

Antoniadis, Sophie, *L'Évangile de Luc: Esquisse de grammaire et de style* (Collection de l'Institut néo-héllenique de l'Université de Paris 7; Paris: Belles Lettres, 1930).

Dawsey, James, "The Literary Unity of Luke-Acts: Questions of Style—A Task for Literary Critics," *NTS* 35 (1989) 48–66.

Delebecque, Édouard, *Études grecques sur l'Évangile de Luc* (CEA; Paris: Belles Lettres, 1976).

Fitzmyer, 1.107–27, bibliography 125–27.

Hawkins, John Caesar, *Horae Synopticae: Contributions to the Study of the Synoptic Problem* (2d ed.; Oxford: Clarendon, 1909).

Jeremias, Joachim, *Die Sprache des Lukasevangeliums: Redaktion und Tradition im Nicht-Markusstoff des dritten Evangeliums* (KEKSup; Göttingen: Vandenhoeck & Ruprecht, 1980).

Pernot, Hubert, *Études sur la langue des Évangiles* (Collection de l'Institut néo-hellénique de l'Université de Paris 6; Paris: Belles Lettres, 1927).

Turner, Nigel, "The Quality of the Greek of Luke-Acts," in J. K. Elliott, ed., *Studies in New Testament Language and Text: Essays in Honor of George D. Kilpatrick* (Leiden: Brill, 1976) 387–400.

Wilcox, Max, *The Semitisms of Acts* (Oxford: Clarendon, 1965).

4. Genre and Purpose

Whereas consensus reigns regarding the genres of the smaller units, there is debate about the genre of the work as a whole. The prologue shows significant interest for history; but Luke is not content with merely didactic ends. He would rather persuade than instruct. His work is more than a historical monograph and is reminiscent of Jewish historiography, which, though following in the footsteps of the writers of the Hebrew Bible, at the same time makes ample use of Hellenistic historiographic techniques. Yet Luke does not intend to describe the fate of a people or a city; in this, he remains bound to earliest Christian tradition. He wishes to set forth how God, through the agency of his son, accomplished the decisive act of deliverance, and how news of this event spread everywhere through its witnesses, with the help of the divine Spirit.

Understandably, Luke concentrates his attention on the person of Jesus in the first volume, in which he occasionally avails himself of the conventions of classical biography. For Luke, the tragedy of God's plan is that the people of Israel, the intended first recipients of God's εὐδοκία ("good favor"), react with noncomprehension. But this had always been so in Israel's history, and the Scriptures had even predicted this obduracy—these realizations dispel Luke's doubts, and those of his Chris-

---

4   This modified translation for English-speaking audiences differs slightly from the original, which reads, "people in advertising today, who, for the sake of comprehensibility, must sacrifice some English expressions that would evoke the coveted 'American Way of Life.'" *Trans.*

5   E.g., καὶ ὑποστρέψαντες . . . καὶ παραλαβὼν αὐτούς . . . οἱ δὲ ὄχλοι γνόντες . . . καὶ ἀποδεξάμενος, "and returning, they . . . and taking them along, he . . . but the crowd, realizing . . . and welcoming them, he . . ." (Luke 9:10–11).

tian readers. The Christians, troubled by the polemics of the Jews, yearn for an objective verification and theological justification of the facts. Thus, in his two volumes, Luke does not intend to proclaim God's salvation without reference to a tangible context, but to attest God's providential course in concrete history. For the Lukan community, danger arises not from the inside, in the form of dogmatic schisms or ethical controversies, but from outside the community.

Bibliography

Aune, David E., "The Problem of the Genre of the Gospels: A Critique of Charles H. Talbert's *What Is a Gospel?*" in R. T. France and D. Wenham, eds., *Gospel Perspectives*, vols. 1 and 2: *Studies of History and Tradition in the Four Gospels* (Sheffield: JSOT Press, 1981) 2.9–60.

Barr, David L., and Judith L. Wentling, "The Conventions of Classical Biography and the Genre of Luke-Acts: A Preliminary Study," in Talbert, *Luke-Acts*, 63–88.

Cancik, H., ed., *Markus-Philologie: Historische, literargeschichtliche und stilistische Untersuchungen zum zweiten Evangelium* (WUNT 33; Tübingen: Mohr-Siebeck, 1984).

Cantwell, Laurence, "The Gospels as Biographies," *SJT* 34 (1981) 193–200.

Dihle, Albrecht, "Die Evangelien und die biographischen Traditionen der Antike," *ZThK* 80 (1983) 33–49.

Drury, John, *Tradition and Design in Luke's Gospel: A Study in Early Christian Historiography* (London: Darton, Longman and Todd; Atlanta: John Knox, 1976).

Fusco, Vittorio, "Tradizione evangelica e modelli letterari: Riflessioni su due libri recenti," *BeO* 27 (1985) 77–103.

Houlden, J. L., "The Purpose of Luke," *JSNT* 21 (1984) 53–65.

Pokorný, Petr, "Die soziale Strategie in den lukanischen Schriften," *CV* 34 (1992) 9–19.

Stuhlmacher, P., ed., *The Gospel and the Gospels* (trans. J. Bowden and J. Vriend; Grand Rapids: Eerdmans, 1991).

Talbert, Charles H., *What Is a Gospel? The Genre of the Canonical Gospels* (Philadelphia: Fortress Press, 1977).

Vorster, Willem S., "Der Ort der Gattung Evangelium in der Literaturgeschichte," *VF* 29 (1984) 2–25.

5. Sources

Like every historian of classical antiquity, Luke had at hand a variety of written sources and miscellaneous information. Although he is dependent on the works of his predecessors (Luke 1:1), he reworks them to an extent that, within his entire composition, the sources rarely come to light in their original independent form.

The evaluation of the sources can be discussed only within the context of the Synoptic problem as a whole. Despite recent dissenting hypotheses, I advocate, now as ever, the priority of Mark and the existence of the sayings source, Q. Luke makes use of a form of Mark's Gospel that diverges only slightly from the canonical version. He does, however, inexplicably skip over Mark 6:45–8:26. Luke presumably also knows the sayings source in the form of a written exemplar. He preserves the order of the sayings of Jesus more clearly than does Matthew, but revises their grammatical form more decisively.

A comparison with Mark shows the following. Luke neither chops up the individual sources nor conflates them. He more often tends to alternate blocks from one source with blocks from another: Luke 3:1–4:30 is material from Q, Luke 4:31–6:20a is from Mark; Luke 6:20b–7:50 is Q, Luke 8:1–9:50, Mark. Thus Luke 3–9 contains almost all of the pericopes of Mark 1–9, with the above-mentioned exception (Mark 6:45–8:26, which would otherwise have had its place between Luke 9:17 and 9:18). The few short omissions can largely be explained on literary or theological grounds. Mark 1:1–20 is too similar to the Q material; Mark 6:1–6 was already incorporated into the pericope describing Jesus' first public appearance; Mark 6:17–29, the death of John, would have been too much of a deviation from the theme.

A few pericopes belong neither to Q nor to Mark: the Baptist's preaching to the classes, the genealogy of Jesus, his first preaching in Nazareth, the calling of Peter, the raising of the young man at Nain, and Jesus' anointing by the sinful woman.[6] Thus Luke possesses additional materials. Since he also has to insert these items at suitable points in his overall composition, he must occasionally suspend the pattern of alternation

---

6   Luke 3:10–14, 23–38; 4:16–30; 5:1–11; 7:11–17, 36–50.

between blocks of his two primary sources. The Baptist's instruction for the classes had to be integrated into the rest of his speech; other pericopes required specific localization within this Galilean period of Jesus' ministry.[7]

It is difficult to survey traditional elements in the travel account. Luke owes the idea of a journey from Galilee to Jerusalem, as such, to Mark 10 (par. Luke 18:15–43); but he expands it by developing it more extensively and adding a theological dimension. With the exception of Luke 9:52–56, all of the allusions to the journey are purely editorial.[8] Thus Luke, in the travel account, makes use of documents that were originally not necessarily located in this period of Jesus' life. Above all, the addresses, parables, and sayings were in all probability transmitted without local designations.

Between 9:51 and 19:39, Luke primarily follows Q's arrangement of materials, but inserts several pericopes from Mark and pericopes from his special source (L), as a look at a synopsis makes clear. From chap. 14 onward, however, Luke as a rule gives priority over Mark and Q to the special source, which shows greater literary refinement. To this source belong, for example, the parables of the prodigal son, the unjust steward, and the rich man and Lazarus.[9] Nonetheless, other parables within this context have their counterparts in Matthew, such as the invitation to the banquet (Luke 14:15–24) and the parable of the lost sheep (Luke 15:3–7). These parables either come from Q, where they appear in a different context, or they are from Luke's special source, where they were transmitted in a variant form from that in Q. Alongside these more substantial units in this subdivision, one also finds shorter sayings and discourses of Jesus, again either from Q or the special source: on salt, on the two masters, on the Law versus the kingdom of God, and bits of advice for disciples.[10]

In the third part of his Gospel, Luke returns to Mark's storyline, at least until the end of chap. 21, that is, from the triumphal entry to the apocalyptic discourse (Luke's second). In his account of the passion, however, Luke's divergence from Mark is considerable. Luke has either adapted Mark more radically than is usually the case, or he has used a competing account. Correspondences between Luke 22–23 and the Johannine account of the passion speak for the latter possibility.

The influence of Luke's special source is unmistakable at the close of the Gospel, as is evident in the stories of the appearances of the resurrected Christ on the road to Emmaus (Luke 24:13–35) and to the Eleven (24:36–49), as well as the ascension (24:50–53)—all of which have no parallels in Mark or Matthew.

In the birth narrative, Luke does not write without using sources. He uses a biographical legend about the birth of the Baptist, and several legends dealing with Jesus' birth and childhood: the annunciation of his birth to Mary (but without the eventual fulfillment of the prophecy: the birth in Nazareth), the tale about the shepherds, the presentation in the temple, and the pericope of the twelve-year-old Jesus in the temple. The scene in which Mary visits Elizabeth serves as the connecting link between the traditions about John and Jesus. It is difficult to determine whether Luke or an earlier writer is responsible for this rapprochement. The songs of the birth narrative do not originate with Luke himself, either, but are perhaps elements from the Baptist's movement (the Benedictus, 1:68–79), from Pharisaic spirituality (the Magnificat, 1:46–55), or the early church's treasury of prayers (the Nunc Dimittis, 2:29–32).

How did Luke obtain all these documents? As an evangelist, Luke received raw material through the course of church tradition, in particular through the churches of the Pauline mission, which, in turn, received their traditional materials from Antioch and the Hellenists. As a writer, Luke gathered additional information through his personal contacts and his own research. Was Luke aware of the sorts of Christian milieux from which these sources came, and of the kinds of interpretation of Christian faith they reflected? This is as difficult to assess as is the question of the extent to which Luke knew that Mark and Q originally represented two divergent types of Christianity. But from which milieu did his special source originate? We really do not know. At least in the case of the legends about Jesus' birth and child-

---

7   Luke 4:16–30 (localization in Nazareth); 5:1–11; 7:11–17 (Galilean ministry).

8   Luke 9:51; 10:38; 13:22, 33; 14:25; 17:11; 18:35; 19:28.

9   Luke 15:11–32; 16:1–9, 19–31.

10   Luke 14:34; 16:13, 14–18; 17:1–6.

hood, one can justifiably suppose that they came from Jewish Christian circles, perhaps from the community around James and the family of Jesus.

In conclusion, one must note that, despite all the fixation in writing, the stream of oral tradition did not immediately cease; Luke can have occasionally emended or augmented his written sources from the storehouse of oral tradition.

Bibliography

Brodie, Thomas L., "Greco-Roman Imitation of Texts as a Partial Guide to Luke's Use of Sources," in Talbert, *Luke-Acts,* 17–46.

Cadbury, Henry J., *The Style and Literary Method of Luke* (1920; HTS 6; reprinted New York: Kraus Reprint, 1969).

Farmer, William R., *The Synoptic Problem: A Critical Analysis* (2d ed.; Dillsboro, N.C.; Western North Carolina Press, 1976).

Fitzmyer, 1.63–106, bibliography, 97–106.

idem, "The Priority of Mark and the 'Q' Source in Luke," in D. G. Buttrick and D. G. Miller, eds., *Jesus and Man's Hope* (2 vols.; Pittsburgh: Pittsburgh Theological Seminary Press, 1970) 1.131–70, reprinted in Joseph A. Fitzmyer, *To Advance the Gospel: New Testament Studies* (New York: Crossroad, 1981) 3–40.

Hawkins, John Caesar, *Horae Synopticae: Contributions to the Study of the Synoptic Problem* (2d ed.; Oxford: Clarendon, 1909).

Jeremias, *Sprache.*

Neirynck, Frans, "La matière marcienne dans l'évangile de Luc," in idem, *Évangile,* 157–201.

Orchard, Bernard, and Thomas R. W. Longstaff, *J. J. Griesbach: Synoptic and Text-critical Studies 1776–1976* (SNTSMS 34; Cambridge/New York: Cambridge University Press, 1978).

Rehkopf, Friedrich, *Die lukanische Sonderquelle: Ihr Umfang und Sprachgebrauch* (WUNT 5; Tübingen: Mohr-Siebeck, 1959).

Rese, "Forschungsbericht," 2268–80, bibliography, 2320.

Schramm, Tim, *Der Markus-Stoff bei Lukas: Eine literarkritische und redaktionsgeschichtliche Untersuchung* (SNTSMS 14; Cambridge: Cambridge University Press, 1971).

Schweizer, Eduard, "Zur Frage der Quellenbenutzung durch Lukas," in idem, *Neues Testament und Christologie im Werden: Aufsätze* (Göttingen: Vandenhoeck & Ruprecht, 1982) 33–51.

Shellard, Barbara, "The Relationship of Luke and John: A Fresh Look at an Old Problem," *JTS* 46 (1995) 71–98.

Streeter, B. H., *The Four Gospels: A Study of Origins, Treating of the Manuscript Tradition, Sources, Authorship, and Dates* (rev. ed.; London: Macmillan, 1930).

Taylor, Vincent, *Behind the Third Gospel: A Study of the Proto-Luke Hypothesis* (Oxford: Clarendon, 1926).

Tyson, Joseph B., "Source Criticism of the Gospel of Luke," in C. H. Talbert, ed., *Perspectives on Luke-Acts* (Danville, Va.: Association of Baptist Professors of Religion, 1978) 24–39.

6. Author

The author communicates very little to us about himself and omits his name (the masculine participle in 1:3 makes it impossible for the author to be a woman). Nevertheless, in contrast to Mark and Matthew, the author expresses the motive for the work's composition in the prologue of the Gospel of Luke; there the author refers to himself twice in the first person. The cultivated language indicates that the author's roots are in one of the higher strata of society, and that the author had a good education encompassing Greek rhetoric as well as Jewish methods of exegesis. Luke was most likely a Greek by birth, who turned to Judaism early in life; he belongs to that circle of sympathizers whom one designates "God-fearers." In this environment, he heard the message of the gospel and became a Christian. As he himself emphasizes in the prologue (Luke 1:1–4), he belongs to the second or third generation of the church. He has had no immediate access or direct contact with the events that he narrates ($\pi\alpha\rho\alpha\kappa o\lambda o\upsilon\vartheta\acute{\epsilon}\omega$ means in 1:3 "to have followed in thought," rather than "to have taken part"). The "we" passages in the book of Acts are one of the artistic techniques he employs to substantiate the credibility of the story and to heighten its vividness. The occurrence of "we" for the first time in the description of the mission to the north Aegean, especially in relation to the appearance of the Macedonian man in Paul's dream (Acts 16:9–10), is, I think, an indication of the author's provenance. Luke may have been a Macedonian himself, with contacts in Troas; though he did not take part in the events he describes, he wishes to locate himself in this area, his native land. The copyists who secondarily inserted "we" as early as Acts 11 (11:28 D), in a story about Antioch, reacted and behaved similarly to the author of the two volumes of Luke by locating Luke's birthplace there, in Antioch, according to the

8

then-dominant opinion. Luke's precise knowledge of Macedonia, particularly of its Roman institutions, makes this region (Philippi?) a likely choice for his homeland.

After his conversion, Luke perhaps participated as a coworker on further missionary journeys and thus continued the Pauline mission. His interest applies more to the dissemination of the message than to the organization of the newly founded churches. The ancient church's prologues to the Gospels, as well as various church fathers, mention Luke's missionary activity. It is fairly certain that he composed his two volumes between 80 and 90 CE, after the death of Peter and Paul, and definitely after the fall of Jerusalem. Because of Luke's extensive travels, the matter of the place of composition is not a pressing concern. Rome still remains the next-best alternative.

Theophilus, to whom Luke dedicates his work, is not an abstraction, but a historical person (see commentary on 1:3). Luke expects his rich friend to circulate his two volumes to a broader readership. Among this readership, Luke, who writes with the care of a historian, the apologetic enthusiasm of a convert, and the earnest appeal of a missionary, envisages three target groups: educated Gentiles, Hellenistic Jews, and Christians unsettled by rumors (Luke 1:4; Acts 22:30).

Luke wants to attest to the truth of Christian faith and to quell Roman fears about the Christian mission. Luke is convinced that the gospel is politically innocuous; on the contrary, the ethical attitude of the Christians can only work to the advantage of their pagan neighbors. By emphasizing, with a mixture of naïveté and self-confidence, the interest of the authorities and upper classes for the message of Peter and, even more, of Paul, Luke advocates the social acceptance of the Christian church. He defends the church against Jewish polemic by claiming that the Christian communities are the legitimate heirs of the prophecies of Scripture. He defends the Pauline mission against Jewish Christian polemic, and emphasizes the harmonious cooperation between Peter and Paul, as well as the unbroken continuity from the Twelve in Jerusalem to the missionary activity of the Hellenists and especially of Paul.

Unfortunately, Papias's opinion (first half of the second century CE) about the Gospel of Luke has not come down to us. Neither Marcion nor Justin attests the name Luke. Not until a generation later does it appear, in Irenaeus: "Luke also, the companion of Paul, recorded in a book the gospel preached by Paul."[11] The Muratorian Canon was written at about the same time (text uncertain): "Tertium evangelii librum secundum Lucam, Lucas iste medicus, post ascensum Christi cum eum Paulus quasi ut iuris studiosum secundum [secum?] adsumpsisset, nomine suo ex opinione conscripsit, dominum tamen nec ipse videt in carne, et ideo prout assequi potuit ita et a nativitate Iohannis incipit dicere" ("The third book of the Gospel, that according to Luke, was compiled in his own name on Paul's authority by Luke the physician, when after Christ's ascension Paul had taken him to be with him like a legal expert. Yet neither did *he* see the Lord in the flesh; and he too, as he was able to ascertain events, begins his story from the birth of John").[12] The date of composition for the so-called Anti-Marcionite Prologues and Monarchian Prologues is uncertain. According to the former, Luke is from Antioch, a doctor, a student of the apostles and of Paul, single, childless; he died at the age of eighty-four in Boeotia, after writing the Gospel in Achaia and, following that, the book of Acts. The Monarchian Prologue contains similar information, except for the statement that Luke died at seventy-four in Bithynia.

Around 200 CE, the authorship of the Third Gospel and the book of Acts began to be ascribed with certainty to Luke (Clement and Tertullian), and thus it remains anchored in Christian consciousness. The oldest titles (superscriptions and subscriptions) in the manuscript tradition also date from the end of the second century CE.

Martin Hengel has posed the question whether perhaps the title κατὰ Λουκᾶν ("according to Luke") could come from Theophilus. I would rather ascribe this attribution to the tendency of the church fathers of this era to historicize apostolic origins. Papias (first half of the second century) uses the formula εὐαγγέλιον κατά ("gospel according to . . .") for Matthew. I believe that the original title of Luke's two-volume work, and with it perhaps the name of the author, have been lost in the

---

11   Irenaeus *Adv. haer.* 3.1.1; Greek text in Eusebius *Hist. eccl.* 5.8.3.

12   English translation from J. Stevenson, ed., *A New*

Eusebius (rev. ed.; rev. W. H. C. Frend; London: SPCK, 1987) 123. *Trans.*

process of canonization. *Εὐαγγέλιον κατὰ Λουκᾶν* ("Gospel according to Luke") is a harmonization with the other Gospels, and *Πράξεις Ἀποστόλων* ("Deeds of the Apostles"), a polemical formulation against the claims of the Apocryphal Acts, just developing at the time. Why anyone would happen upon the name Luke remains a riddle. Perhaps a student of Paul's was desired for this work. The names Titus and Timothy were already taken, if only as the addressees, and not the writers, of the Pastoral Epistles. Among the remaining frequently appearing names in the Pauline corpus, Luke all but jumped out.[13]

Bibliography

Aubineau, Michel, *Les homélies festales d'Hésychius de Jérusalem* (AnBoll: Subsidia Hagiographica 59; 2 vols.; Brussels: Société des bollandistes, 1980) 2.902–50.

Bovon, François, "Luc: Portrait et projet," *LumVie* 153–54 (1981) 9–18.

du Plooy, G. P. V., "The Author in Luke-Acts," *Scriptura* 32 (1990) 28–35.

Fitzmyer, 1.35–62, bibliography, 59–62.

Hengel, Martin, *Die Evangelienüberschriften.* (SHAW.PH 3; Heidelberg: C. Winter, 1984) 1–51.

Maddox, Robert, *The Purpose of Luke-Acts* (FRLANT 126; Göttingen: Vandenhoeck & Ruprecht, 1982).

Merkel, Helmut, *Die Pluralität der Evangelien als theologisches und exegetisches Problem in der alten Kirche* (Traditio Christiana 3; Bern/Las Vegas: P. Lang, 1978).

Rese, "Forschungsbericht," 2260–64, bibliography 2280–84.

7. Theology

According to Luke, the God of the Christians is the creator of whom the Scriptures speak, and the redeemer of Israel. From ages past, he has pursued his plan of salvation, which his chosen people have again and again resisted. Jesus' activity is the final and conclusive attempt of the benevolent God somehow still to win Israel for himself and, at the same time, to reach the Gentiles. All that the Messiah Jesus does, the Son, Lord, Savior, Teacher, and Physician, is on behalf of the one nation and, at the same time, the nations as a whole.

Because the synagogues have closed their doors to the Christian gospel in the evangelist's time, the Christian mission might well expect to find its success in the pagan world (see the conclusion of Acts, 28:28). The Christian message is universal, and it is free, according to Luke, from limitation to a particular national group (Acts 10:34–35).

Although Christians come from every nation and no longer obey the Law literally, especially in its ritual ordinances, they do not invalidate Israel's inheritance. On the contrary, Christians are the legitimate interpreters of the Scriptures. For the Scriptures, in the past inspired by the Holy Spirit, unveil themselves now through the will of the Lord Jesus and the help of the same Spirit: the Scriptures are found to be in harmony with the Christian message. Paul is in harmony with Isaiah. Joy and triumph are dominant in the christological interpretation of the Scriptures (see Acts 15:14–15; 28:25).

Luke is a witness for that Hellenistic form of Christianity, which, following Paul, placed itself beyond the strict adherence to the Law. If Luke nevertheless emphasizes that the apostles and other witnesses practiced the Jewish Law, this is the reaction of a historian emphasizing the historical roots of the Christian faith, not a theologian who demands such behavior from every Christian.

Fortunately, things have changed in the meantime. It is no longer the Law of Moses, but rather the dictates of the gospel, especially the two great commandments, that determine the Christian ethos. Luke desires Christians whose concern is with people, not laws, and whose self-identity is that of loyal, cheerful, free, uncalculating, socially aware, devout disciples of the Resurrected One. Luke's concern for women, children, and all the neglected, as well as his perspective on poverty and weakness, manifest a startlingly novel outlook in the world at that time. The radical asceticism and literal imitation of Jesus practiced by the Twelve can no longer be realized in the urban situation of the Lukan communities. Yet the attitude and the spirit behind and within this striking and provocative resolution should—must—

---

13   Cf. Col 4:14; 2 Tim 4:11; Jerome (*Vir. ill.* 7) identifies Luke with the unnamed "brother" in 2 Cor 8:18.

remain alive, now as ever, and must be actualized anew. This is Luke's ethical message.

Luke is a witness to a particular form of Pauline thought in the second or third generation. Because of his optimistic view of human nature (can one speak of his humanism?), he cannot comprehend Paul's conception of the enslavement of the human will, as it is found in the letter to the Romans. For this reason, the cross does not represent the unavoidable cursing of the Son but rather the consequence, predestined by God, of his obedience (cf. Acts 2:23); it is an expression of human sinfulness. Nevertheless, the shed blood of Jesus seals the new covenant of God with humankind (Luke 22:19–20) and the founding of the church (Acts 20:28).

In all of this, Luke is not precisely the one who, on his own, intends to overcome the traditional apocalyptic eschatological expectations with a salvation-historical perspective conceived by himself. Like the majority of his Christian contemporaries, Luke attempts far more to solve the problem of the delay of the parousia without betraying the original faith. In Acts 1:1–11 he expresses his own perspective on things: Christians should look toward the parousia with patience and levelheadedness. There is no room for partisan expectations in this. The main emphasis is no longer on the future but on the past, on the salvation of God already made manifest in Jesus' advent, death, and resurrection. From this backward glance arises every present hope for the future. Luke distinguishes not three salvation-historical eras (the time of prophecy, the time of Jesus as the midpoint, and the time of the church) but two: the time of prophecy and the time of fulfillment. The time of fulfillment is again divided into the time of Jesus and the time of his witnesses, and the latter again can be differentiated into the time of the eyewitnesses and the time after that, including the Lukan generation (Luke 1:1–4). At every point of transition from one era to the next, God provides individuals who maintain the necessary continuity; this is especially evident in the case of John the Baptist. The common life of the first community in Jerusalem, the missionary success of the apostles and witnesses, especially Paul, and the willingness to face martyrdom (Stephen) continue to be pledges for the coming of the kingdom of God.

In his ecclesiology, Luke consciously or unconsciously advocates a particular form of Christianity. Luke is interested in two groups: first, there is the circle of the Twelve, whose activity is, to Luke's mind, a bygone stage of initial organization, primarily in Jerusalem; then, there are the Hellenists, whom Luke admits to have the better chance of future success. It is they who pursue the more correct Christian practice in their ethics, which limit the function of the Law, and in their missionary activity, through their acceptance of the Gentiles without circumcision. Luke thus incorporates both the traditions of the Twelve and of the Seven. Peter and Paul are his main characters, for successful Christian expansion marches westward; for this reason, Luke passes over the beginnings of the church in eastern Syria and in Egypt. His church-historical horizon is thus geographically limited, but is nevertheless concerned with the regions in which the Christian faith enjoyed its greatest successes in the eras immediately to follow.

Bibliography

Bottini, Giovanni Claudio, *Introduzione all'opera di Luca* (Jerusalem: Franciscan Printing Press, 1992).

Bovon, François, *Lukas in neuer Sicht: Gesammelte Aufsätze* (trans. E. Hartmann, A. Frey, and P. Strauss; Biblisch-theologische Studien 8; Neukirchen-Vluyn: Neukirchener Verlag, 1985).

idem, *Luke the Theologian: Thirty-three Years of Research: 1950–1983* (trans. K. McKinney; PTMS 12; Allison Park, Pa.: Pickwick, 1987) (bibliography).

Conzelmann, *Theology*.

Dömer, Michael, *Das Heil Gottes: Studien zur Theologie des lukanischen Doppelwerkes* (BBB 51; Cologne/Bonn: Hanstein, 1978).

Fitzmyer, 1.143–270, bibliography 259–70.

Flender, Helmut, *Heil und Geschichte in der Theologie des Lukas* (BEvTh 41; Munich: Kaiser, 1965).

Green, Joel B., *Theology of the Gospel of Luke* (Cambridge: Cambridge University Press, 1995).

Jervell, Jacob, "God's Faithfulness to the Faithless People: Trends in Interpretation of Luke–Acts," *Word & World* 12 (1992) 29–36.

idem, *Luke and the People of God: A New Look at Luke-Acts* (Minneapolis: Augsburg, 1972).

Marguerat, Daniel, "Juifs et chrétiens selon Luc-Actes: Surmonter le conflit des lectures," *Bib* 75 (1994) 126–46.

Marshall, I. Howard, *Luke: Historian and Theologian* (Grand Rapids: Zondervan, 1970).

O'Toole, R. F., "Reflections on Luke's Treatment of Jews in Luke-Acts," *Bib* 74 (1993) 529–55.

Rasco, Emilio, *La Teología de Lucas: Origen, Desarollo, Orientaciones* (Analecta gregoriana 201 Series Facultatis Theologicae A.21; Rome: Università gregoriana, 1976) (bibliography).

Rese, Martin, "Das Lukas-Evangelium: Ein Forschungsbericht," *ANRW* 2.25.3 (1985) 2258–2328, esp. 2298–2312, bibliography 2320–25.

Schneider, Gerhard, *Lukas, Theologe der Heilsgeschichte: Aufsätze zum lukanischen Doppelwerk* (BBB 59; Königstein/Bonn: Hanstein, 1985).

Schweizer, Eduard, *Luke: A Challenge to Present Theology* (Atlanta: John Knox, 1982).

Strauss, Mark L., *The Davidic Messiah in Luke-Acts: The Promise and Its Fulfillment in Lukan Christology* (Sheffield: Sheffield Academic Press, 1995).

Talbert, Charles H., "The Place of the Resurrection in the Theology of Luke," *Int* 46 (1992) 19–30.

Wolter, Michael, "'Reich Gottes' bei Lukas," *NTS* 41 (1995) 541–63.

Luke 1

Commentary

The Prologue 1:1–4

Bibliography

Alexander, Loveday, "Luke's Preface in the Context of Greek Preface-Writing," *NovT* 28 (1986) 48–74.

idem, *The Preface to Luke's Gospel: Literary Convention and Social Context in 1:1–4 and Acts 1:1* (Cambridge: Cambridge University Press, 1993).

Bauer, J., "*ΠΟΛΛΟΙ*: Luk I,I," *NovT* 4 (1960) 263–66.

Cadbury, "Commentary."

Callan, Terence, "The Preface of Luke-Acts and Historiography," *NTS* 31 (1985) 576–81.

Delebecque, Édouard, "Le prologue de l'Évangile de S. Luc," *Itinéraires* 157 (1971) 278–85, reprinted in idem, *Études,* 1–14.

Dibelius, *Aufsätze,* 61, 79, 108–9, 118, 127–28.

Dillmann, Rainer, "Das Lukasevangelium als Tendenzschrift. Leserlenkung und Leseintention in Lk 1, 1-4," *BZ* 38 (1994) 86–93.

Dillon, Richard J., "Previewing Luke's Project from His Prologue (Luke 1:1-4)," *CBQ* 43 (1981) 205–27.

Dubois, J.-D., "Le prologue de Luc (Lc 1,1–4)," *EThR* 52 (1977) 542–47.

du Plessis, "Once More."

Dupont, Jacques, *Les sources du livre des Actes: État de la question* (Bruges: Desclée de Brouwer, 1960) 99–107.

Frankovic, Alexander, "Pieces to the Synoptic Puzzle: Papias and Luke 1:1-4," *Jerusalem Perspective* 40 (1993) 12–13.

Gese, Hartmut, "Natus ex virgine," in H. W. Wolff, ed., *Probleme biblischer Theologie: Festschrift Gerhard von Rad* (Munich: Kaiser, 1971) 73–89.

Gibbs, J. M., "Mark 1:1-15; Matthew 1:1–4:16; Luke 1:1–4:30; John 1:1-51: The Gospel Prologues and Their Function," *StEv* 6 (= TU 112) (1973) 154–88.

Glöckner, Richard, *Die Verkündigung des Heils beim Evangelisten Lukas* (Walberger Studien der Albertus-Magnus-Akademie: Theologie 9; Mainz: Matthias Grünewald, 1975) 3–41.

Goodman, F. W., "Ἐπειδήπερ πολλοὶ ἐπεχείρησαν (Luke 1,1): A Proposed Emendation," *StEv* 4 (= TU 102) (1968) 205–8.

Güttgemanns, Erhardt, "In welchem Sinne ist Lukas 'Historiker'? Die Beziehung von Lk 1,1–4 und Papias zur antiken Rhetorik," *Linguistica Biblica* 54 (1983) 7–26.

Higgins, "Preface."

Kahl, Brigitte, *Armenevangelium und Heidenevangelium: "Sola Scriptura" und die ökumenische Traditionsproblematik im Lichte von Väterkonflikt und Väterkonsens bei Lukas* (Berlin: Evangelische Verlagsanstalt, 1987) 25–85.

Klein, "Programm."

Kürzinger, J., "Lk 1,3: . . . ἀκριβῶς καθεξῆς σοι γράψαι," *BZ* n.s. 18 (1974) 249–55.

Minear, P. S., "Dear Theophilus: The Kerygmatic Intention and Claim of the Book of Acts," *Int* 27 (1973) 131–50.

Mußner, Franz, "Die Gemeinde des Lukasprologs," in SNTU A 6/7 (Linz: Albert Fuchs, 1981–82) 113–30.

idem, "Καθεξῆς im Lukasprolog," in E. E. Ellis and E. Gräßer, eds., *Jesus und Paulus: Festschrift Werner Georg Kümmel* (Göttingen: Vandenhoeck & Ruprecht, 1975) 253–55.

Nock, Arthur Darby, "Martin Dibelius: *Aufsätze zur Apostelgeschichte,*" *Gnomon* 25 (1953) 497–506.

Norden, Eduard, *Agnostos Theos: Untersuchungen zur Formengeschichte religiöser Rede* (1913. Darmstadt: Wissenschaftliche Buchgesellschaft, 1956).

Radaelli, A., "I racconti dell'infanzia nel contesto del prologo all'evangelo," *RBR* 15 (1980) 7–26, 199–227; 16 (1981) 292–330.

Robbins, Vernon K., "Prefaces in Greco-Roman Biography and Luke-Acts," *Perspectives in Religious Studies* 6 (1979) 94–108.

Samain, "Évangile."

Schneider, Gerhard, "Zur Bedeutung von καθεξῆς im lukanischen Doppelwerk," *ZNW* 68 (1977) 128–31.

Schulz, Siegfried, *Die Stunde der Botschaft: Einführung in die Theologie der vier Evangelisten* (Hamburg: Furche, 1967) 237–38, 243–50.

Schürmann, Heinz, "Evangelienschrift und kirchliche Unterweisung: Die repräsentative Funktion der Schrift nach Lk 1,1–4," in idem, *Untersuchungen,* 251–71, reprinted in G. Braumann, ed., *Das Lukas-Evangelium: Die Redaktions- und Kompositionsgeschichtliche Forschung* (WdF 280; Darmstadt: Wissenschaftliche Buchgesellschaft, 1974) 125–69.

Schwaiger, Georg, "'Diener des Wortes' (Lk 1,2) oder Größe und Grenze der Theologen," in W.-D. Hauschild et al., eds., *Kirchengemeinschaft: Anspruch und Wirklichkeit: Festschrift Georg Kretschmar* (Stuttgart: Calwer, 1986) 177–86.

Stein, Robert H., "Luke 1:1-4 and 'Traditionsgeschichte,'" *JETS* 26 (1983) 421–30.

Trocmé, Étienne, *Le "Livre des Actes" et l'histoire* (Paris: Presses Universitaires de France, 1957) 39–49, 78, 125–27.

van Unnik, "Once More."

idem, "Remarks."

Vögtle, Anton, "Was hatte die Widmung des lukanischen Doppelwerks an Theophilus zu bedeuten?" in idem, *Evangelium,* 31–42.

Völkel, Martin, "Exegetische Erwägungen zum Verständnis des Begriffs καθεξῆς im lukanischen Prolog," *NTS* 20 (1973–74) 289–99.

1 **Since many have undertaken to set down a narrative about the events that have been fulfilled among us, 2/ just as they were handed on to us by those who from the beginning had become eyewitnesses and servants of the word, 3/ it seemed right to me also, after investigating everything carefully from the very first, to write an orderly account for you, most excellent Theophilus, 4/ so that you may discern in their reliability the words about which you have been informed.**

Analysis

Luke is the only evangelist who sets forth in a prologue the motivation, purpose, and method of his work. In this, he takes a cue from Greek literature and lends his project the character of a literary creation for public distribution.[1] He attempts to elevate Christian traditions, until that time conveyed in vernacular style, to this higher plane.[2] Two difficulties confront him. First, given his intention, as historian and evangelist, to transmit the tradition faithfully—especially the words of Jesus—to what extent does he dare to intervene as a literary author? Second, does he possess sufficient training and natural ability for the completion of such a task? The first difficulty surfaces already in the course of the first chapter. After the elegantly balanced prologue (1:1–4), the first episode begins abruptly in vernacular style

(1:5–25). The close proximity of 1:1–4 and 1:5–25 must have surprised the Greek readers. Yet, because Luke imitated the style of the LXX, the strange Semitic locution was known to the literary world, accepted if not imitated.[3] The objections and criticisms leveled by the educated against the Gospels, criticisms that the church fathers feel compelled to deflect, do suggest that not even Luke suited the taste of his contemporaries. In a sense, Luke writes with an exaggerated artistry; the long sentence in 1:1–4 illustrates effort as much as ability.[4]

Ἐπειδήπερ ("since") should appear not at the beginning of a sentence, where one expects ἐπειδή, but after the main clause.[5] In the work of an author, the use of ἀνατάσσομαι ("to set down") is unusual; συντάσσομαι ("to compose") would be more customary. When the verb πληροφορέω ("to be fully accomplished") is used of events (πράγματα) that have taken place, instead of the usual πληρόω, this seems artificial. Καθώς appears where one would expect καθά ("just as").[6] The proximity of ἄνωθεν, ἀκριβῶς, and καθεξῆς ("from the very first," "carefully," and "in consecutive order") leaves the readers in a quandary, since they do not know to which verb they must assign these adverbs.[7] In comparison with other prologues, these couple of lines in 1:1–4 seem extraordinarily short.[8] This is not to place in question Luke's stylistic technique, but only to suggest that his

---

1   W. C. van Unnik mentions exegetes of the 18th century, G. Raphelius and J. J. Wettstein, who had already compared Luke's prologue with those of secular classical works ("Once More St. Luke's Prologue," *Neot* 7 [1973] 24 n. 62).

2   "By means of the dedication to Theophilus (repeated in Acts i I) the writer would have it known that he is conforming to the prevailing literary customs of his time and that he had a genuine book to offer; not a somewhat odd collection of pious stories" (W. C. van Unnik, "Remarks on the Purpose of Luke's Historical Writing [Luke i 1–4]," in idem, *Sparsa Collecta: The Collected Essays of W. C. van Unnik* [3 vols.; NovTSup 29–31; Leiden: Brill, 1973–83] 1.6–15, esp. 7).

3   See Henry J. Cadbury, "Commentary on the Preface of Luke," in F. J. Foakes-Jackson and K. Lake, eds., *The Beginnings of Christianity*, part 1: *The Acts of the Apostles* (5 vols.; London: Macmillan, 1920–33), vol. 2: *Prolegomena II: Criticism*, 489–510, esp. 490.

4   One should agree with Eduard Norden that Luke 1:1–4 represents the best-constructed sentence in the NT (*Agnostos Theos: Untersuchungen zur For-*

mengeschichte religiöser Rede [1913; reprinted Darmstadt: Wissenschaftliche Buchgesellschaft, 1956] 316 n.1). This does not necessarily mean that it appears particularly beautiful in comparison with those in classical prose. But one can sympathize with the author's efforts.

5   "Usually, however, like some other relatives in -περ, it occurs when it does not precede the main clause" (Cadbury, "Commentary," 492). According to BDF §456.3, a sentence introduced with this conjunction makes reference to something already known.

6   "Here is at least one word that the strictest Atticism condemns . . . Codex Bezae and Eusebius (*H.E.* iii.4.6; *Demon. Evang.* p. 120) correct it here to καθά, another post-classical word, which the Atticists recommend in its place (Phrynichus, edit. Rutherford, p. 495)" (Cadbury, "Commentary," 496–97).

7   See commentary on v. 3 below.

8   This is so, even if prologues were, as a rule, relatively short, as Cadbury remarks ("Commentary," 490). Van Unnik ("Once More," 8) is also surprised by the striking brevity of Luke's prologue.

artistry does not necessarily consist in his imitation of the style of contemporary authors. It is also the case that 1:1–4 is almost too good to be true.

The closest parallels to Luke's intention in the prologue are found in a few passages in the Johannine literature,[9] in which the author(s) reflect on their work at a metalinguistic level. In ancient literature, passages of this sort are usually located at the beginning or end of a book. Whereas John 20:30–31 expresses something about the writer's work and the function of the book, the conclusion of the supplemental chap. 21 (21:24–25) refers to the trustworthiness of the beloved disciple—he is both author and eyewitness—and to the reliability of his testimony: ἀληθὴς αὐτοῦ ἡ μαρτυρία ἐστίν ("his testimony is true"). The chronological and theological distance between John 20:31 and 21:24 corresponds to the transition from Mark to Luke, from the nonliterary testimony to a literary work: ταῦτα δὲ γέγραπται ἵνα πιστεύσητε ("but these are written so that you may come to believe . . . ," 20:31), versus οἴδαμεν ὅτι ἀληθὴς αὐτοῦ ἡ μαρτυρία ἐστίν ("we know that his testimony is true," John 21:24).

All exegetes agree that the author is making use of the literary forms of the time. Disagreement surfaces as soon as one asks to what end this appropriation took place. Should one see only the literary ambitions of the author, and his wish to arouse interest for the work and its subject? Or is a theological program implied in this conventional and literary prologue? Henry J. Cadbury and W. C. van Unnik can be counted advocates of the first interpretation, Günter Klein and Richard J. Dillon of the second.[10] On the one hand, above all, two considerations contradict a hasty theological exploitation of the prologue. First, except for the ambiguous term ὁ λόγος ("the word"), specifically theological concepts are absent; neither God nor Jesus is mentioned. Second, the content of the work is not concretely specified, surely because of Luke's conscious reticence; in contrast, consider Acts 1:1. On the other hand, both Luke's consciousness of his chronological distance from the facts and the function of the tradition as an attempt to bridge the gap between the generations are evidence against a literary trivialization of the prologue.

The prologue consists of a single sentence. It begins with a causal clause (which is in fact more of a concession) and a complementary infinitive (v. 1). Another dependent clause follows, subordinate to the first, which contains an important explanation (v. 2). After this protasis, Luke first notes down in the apodosis a solemn main clause, in which he himself emerges forcefully as the author (ἔδοξε κἀμοί, "it seemed . . . to me also"), while still remaining anonymous (v. 3), and then the conclusion of the sentence, a purpose clause (with ἵνα), which in turn incorporates a short relative clause (v. 4). Clearly, this sentence is the result of deliberate construction, and no other New Testament author has written with such dignity.

The structure and vocabulary show striking similarities to prologues of other ancient works, both historical and scholarly. Writing in the genre of a prologue,[11] ancient authors would typically mention their predecessors and give an assessment of their work; then they would emphasize the quality of their information (eyewitness observation and firsthand research) and the arrangement of the treatise; and last, they would make a few statements about their own person and literary purpose. A dedication was often added; this was not because authors expected commercial distribution of their work by the dedicatees, but rather because they felt obliged to these people and wished to express their friendship or gratitude, as well as their request that the dedicatees would introduce the work to their friends.[12] If a work was too extensive, the author would have to divide a book into various volumes; for reasons of production, distribution, taste, or convention, the average

---

9   John 20:30–31; 21:24–25; Rev 1:1–3; 22:18–19.

10   Cadbury, "Commentary"; van Unnik, "Once More"; Günter Klein, "Lukas 1,1–4 als theologisches Programm," in Dinkler, *Zeit und Geschichte*, 193–216, reprinted in Klein, *Rekonstruktion und Interpretation: Gesammelte Aufsätze zum Neuen Testament* (BEvTh 50; Munich: Kaiser, 1969) 237–61, also reprinted in Braumann, *Lukas-Evangelium*, 170–203 (cited from the first); Richard J. Dillon, "Previewing Luke's Project from His Prologue (Luke 1:1–4)," *CBQ* 43

(1981) 205–27.

11   See J.-D. Dubois, "Le prologue de Luc (Lc 1,1–4)," *EThR* 52 (1977) 542–47, esp. 543–44.

12   See Arthur Darby Nock (*Gnomon* 25 [1953] 497–506, esp. 501–2), who corrects Martin Dibelius on this point in his discussion of the German author's essays (*Aufsätze zur Apostelgeschichte* [ed. H. Greeven; FRLANT 60; Göttingen: Vandenhoeck & Ruprecht, 1951]).

length of a volume was not much greater than our longest Gospels. The prologue applied to the entire work, but each successive volume would also have a smaller, less pretentious prologue, which would make reference to the previous volume and specify the contents of the next. Here as well, Luke followed Greek conventions: the prologue of Acts corresponds to this genre (1:1).[13] Literary dependence cannot be demonstrated, but the force of the customs of that time is evident nonetheless.

As an example for a prologue to an entire book, I will cite Dioskourides, a Hellenistic physician from the first century CE:[14] "Although many reports have been made, not only in the past, but also recently, about the production, effects, and testing of medicines, I nevertheless intend to instruct you, dear Areios, about them; the decision to undertake such a thing is neither needless nor injudicious, for some of my predecessors have not completed [their works], and others have written most things down from hearsay."[15]

Two questions are often neglected in scholarship. First, the author is silent about his or her name and person in the prologue: is this surprising or not? Second, if the two-volume work, Luke-Acts, was intended as literature, what was its title?

The absence of the author's name in the prologue remains a riddle to me, despite the church's tradition of anonymity[16] and the possibility that the name was mentioned in the title of the work. The title would actually have had to be noted as a *subscriptio* at the end of the second volume, but was deleted when the Gospel and Acts were separated. The *subscriptio* at the end of Luke's Gospel in the oldest manuscript (P[75], 175–225 CE), left out of the apparatus in Nestle-Aland, reads εὐαγγέλιον κατὰ Λουκᾶν ("Gospel According to Luke");[17] it is much the same in the *inscriptio* of other manuscripts.[18] This was probably not original. The manuscripts of Acts also seem no longer to bear any remembrance of the original *subscriptio*.[19]

Commentary

Everyone who must write knows the difficulty of transposing one's thoughts into written form and of finding the right entrance. For this reason, one should pay close attention to how authors begin their texts.

---

13 With the peculiar feature that Luke manages in Acts 1:4–8, esp. in v. 8, to have the resurrected Christ express the content of his second volume. Josephus's *Contra Apionem* also contains a main prologue at the beginning of the first book, and a second prologue at the beginning of the second. See A. J. B. Higgins, "The Preface to Luke and the Kerygma in Acts," in W. W. Gasque and R. P. Martin, eds., *Apostolic History and the Gospel: Festschrift F. F. Bruce* (Grand Rapids: Eerdmans, 1970) 78–91, esp. 79.

14 See Étienne Samain, "L'évangile de Luc: Un témoignage ecclésial et missionnaire: Lc 1,1–4; 4,14–15," *AsSeign* 34 (1973) 60–73, esp. 64.

15 Περὶ ὕλης ἰατρικῆς 1.1 ("On the Subject of Medicine"). See van Unnik, "Remarks," 7–13. Cf. also, in the Latin domain, Livy's prologue to his Roman history *Ab urbe condita*.

16 Heinz Schürmann emphasizes in his commentary that it would have been superfluous to indicate the author of a work that addressed itself, among other things, to the church (*Das Lukasevangelium,* part I: *Kommentar zu Kap. 1,1–9,50* [2d ed.; HThKNT 3; Freiburg im Breisgau: Herder, 1982] 2 n. 8, toward the end). Van Unnik ("Once More," 8) points out that authors would generally give their names and, at the same time, explain what had led them to pick up the pen.

17 See V. Martin and R. Kasser, eds., *Papyrus Bodmer XIV–XV,* vol. 1: *Évangile de Luc* (2 vols.; Bibliotheca Bodmeriana; Cology-Genève: Bibliothèque Bodmer, 1961) 150 and plate 61. The title appears in the middle of the page and extends for three lines, i.e., it consists of three lines with one word per line.

18 See Nestle-Aland, 150. Cf. A. Plummer, *A Critical and Exegetical Commentary on the Gospel According to St. Luke* (5th ed.; ICC; New York: Scribner's Sons; Edinburgh: Clark, 1902) 1; Fitzmyer, 1.35–36; M.-J. Lagrange, *Évangile selon Saint Luc* (4th ed.; EtB; Paris: Gabalda, 1927) 1.

19 For publishing practices and distribution of books in antiquity see Henri Irénée Marrou, "La technique de l'édition à l'époque patristique," *VC* 3 (1949) 208–24 (reprinted in his *Patristique et humanisme: Mélanges* [Patristica Sorbonensia 9; Paris: Seuil, 1976] 239–52). To get some idea of how a book was produced in antiquity, read Roger Gryson, *Le recueil arien de Vérone . . . : Étude codicologique et paléographique* (Instrumenta Patristica 13; Steenbrugge: in Abbatia S. Petri; The Hague: Nijhoff, 1982).

■ **1** Luke begins with a reference to his predecessors (v. 1), but the manner in which he mentions them shows that he is, at the same time, more or less refuting them. But if he proceeds differently than they, this does not mean that he writes without analogies. On the contrary, he follows the "many" others.[20] The emphasis inherent in πολλοί ("many")[21] also corresponds to his literary models; aside from the authors of Mark, Q, and L (special source), there cannot have been "many" to whose works he could have had recourse.[22]

That "many" have "undertaken" (lit. "have laid their hand upon it")[23] means neither that they have been successful, nor that they have fallen short of their goal.[24] On the one hand, Luke classes himself among the "many";[25] on the other hand, he introduces his own product as better and more reliable.[26]

The "many" wished "to set down a narrative" (ἀνατάξασθαι διήγησιν).[27] Διήγησις designates an oral or written report longer than a χρεία ("anecdote") and presupposes a narrative development.[28] The word can also denote a historical account.[29] Ἀνατάσσομαι means, with emphasis on ἀνά, "to set in a series," in a metaphorical sense, "to repeat one after the other," "to retell a story." The word is unusual for the work of an author; if Luke does not intend it as an equivalent of συντάσσομαι ("to compose"),[30] one might conclude that

his predecessors have retold this story, possibly in the sense of a written adaptation of an oral account.

If Luke had been somewhat satisfied with the work of his predecessors, he would surely not have gone to the trouble of composing a new work. But his criticism is discreet and reticent. The faults he finds can only be determined from the analysis of his own performance. From this it is clear that the works of his predecessors neglected, first, the beginning (ἄνωθεν, "from the very first," v. 3) of the story of Jesus; neither Mark nor Q begins with the story of Jesus' birth. Second, they passed over the effect of the Resurrected One on later history, since their portrayal encompasses only the story of the earthly Jesus, and, to this extent, not the entire account (πᾶσιν, "everything," v. 3). Third, their work was not precise enough (ἀκριβῶς, "carefully," v. 3). Fourth, they did not pay enough heed to composition in their work (καθεξῆς, "orderly, " "in consecutive order," v. 3). Fifth and last, the style and character of their literature did not at all measure up to the canons of literary excellence.

With the words, "about the events that have been fulfilled among us," Luke nonetheless embraces the *content* both of these earlier works and of his own project; περί ("about, on") is the technical preposition for a work's title and contents.[31] Thus one expects neither a scholarly monograph nor a religious exposition, but an account of

---

20 On this, cf. the beginning of the first book of Josephus's *Jewish War* (*Bell.* 1.6.17): Ἐπειδήπερ καὶ Ἰουδαίων πολλοὶ πρὸ ἐμους τὰ τῶν προγόνων συνετάξαντο μετ' ἀκριβείας ("seeing that many Jews before me have accurately recorded the history of our ancestors . . .").

21 See J. Bauer, "ΠΟΛΛΟΙ: Luk I,I," *NovT* 4 (1960) 263–66.

22 Cadbury ("Commentary," 492–93) shows that πολύς often occurs at the beginning of a speech or work, but not always as a description of the predecessors. Cf. Acts 1:3 and Heb 1:1.

23 On ἐπιχειρέω see Lagrange (2), who cites a dedication to Nero, in which a doctor named Thessalos writes πολλῶν ἐπιχειρησάντων . . . παραδοῦναι ("many have undertaken . . . to pass [it] on").

24 Cadbury ("Commentary," 493–94) detects no criticism in this statement; whereas Klein ("Programm," 195–96) perceives an allusion to the inadequacy of these attempts.

25 Especially ἐπειδήπερ πολλοὶ . . . , ἔδοξε κἀμοί ("Since many . . . it seemed right to me also").

26 In its two other occurrences, Luke uses ἐπιχειρέω

27 See Klein, "Programm," 196.

28 See James Hope Moulton and George Milligan, *The Vocabulary of the Greek Testament: Illustrated from the Papyri and Other Non-Literary Sources* (1930; reprinted Grand Rapids: Eerdmans, 1963) s.v.

29 On διήγησις as a term for a historical account, cf. *Ep. Arist.* 8, 322; 2 Macc 2:32; 6:17; Diodorus Siculus 11.20.1; Lucian *Hist. conscr.* 55; Polybius 3.4.1; Dionysius of Halicarnassus *Ant. Roma.* 1.7.4; *Pomp.* 3. See van Unnik, "Once More," 12–15 (extensive notes).

30 A few older translations of the NT have translated the verb ἀνατάσσομαι with the same meaning as συντάσσομαι. See BAGD s.v.

31 For example, Origen's treatise Περὶ ἀρχῶν (*De Principiis*, "On the first things").

in a negative sense (Acts 9:29; 19:13).

events. The meaning of πράγμα is broad; it extends from "deed" and "thing," to "story" and "events." Πράγματα may be the Greek equivalent of the more strongly Semitic ῥήματα/דְּבָרִים ("things," Acts 5:32). In this sense it designates salvation-historical events in which, in the Lukan sense of the word, God collaborates with humans through his word and the mediation of his messengers.[32] But the term can also be understood by a non-Christian reader, although not in its entire fullness.[33] The Lukan formulation also encompasses the historical connotation of the word πράγμα, which the unbiased reader would understand correctly.

Πληροφορέω means here "to accomplish, complete, fulfill"; it can mean "to bring about full conviction" only when used of persons (cf. Col 4:12). In Luke's understanding, this long and uncommon verb,[34] which was by his time already used in a specifically Christian sense, implies a religious statement: the events spoken of here did not simply "happen," they "happened in fulfillment,"[35] as God willed it. If so secular a word as πράγμα ("events") can encompass the life, death, and resurrection of the Messiah, a verb such as πληροφορέω might allude to the harmony of the Scriptures, which promise, and history, which fulfills.[36]

"Among us" (ἐν ἡμῖν) is imprecise; some of the "events" lie far in the past (ἡμῖν in v. 2 is more exact, differentiating Luke's generation from the earlier generation of the apostles). But in comparison with world history, or rather with the ancient era of the patriarchs, these "events" are recent and indeed took place "among us"; they belong to the last stage of salvation history (Luke 16:16), which extends from the appearance of Jesus to the present. Livy also makes the founding of Rome seem nearer to the reader by stating that a single nation is the bearer of the story.[37] Chronological distance and personal proximity interrelate in both biblical and secular history. "Our" identity, even our existence, is conditioned by "the events that happened." Faith and recollection belong together in Israel.

■ **2** Verse 2, indicating interest above all for the transmission of the story, presupposes a well-considered consciousness of history. Luke belongs to a time in which recollection might already have been channeled and legitimized by tradition. The actual tradents and guarantors of the correctness of the tradition are not, indeed, the "many," but the more highly esteemed group of "those who from the beginning had become eyewitnesses and servants of the word." Παραδίδωμι in the sense of "hand down" (from teacher to students, from parents to the next generation) is deeply rooted in both the Greek and Jewish languages,[38] and in the church as well already in Luke's time. Laws, myths, instruction, and reports are transmitted in this manner, conscientiously and carefully. Even Paul already spoke of traditions—as do the Pastoral Epistles—but only in reference to liturgical, kerygmatic, and ethical materials.[39] In Luke's work, however, for the first time the entire story of Jesus and his apostles becomes the content of tradition. In Luke's use παραδίδωμι is primarily a literary term, rather than a dogmatic one.[40] He means by it an oral tradition;[41] and he emphasizes that the first witnesses have not merely passed on[42] the accounts, but

---

32   On this cooperation of God and humans in the development of πράγματα ("events"), see Bovon, *Lukas*, 75–97.

33   In the OT, in which the word is used both positively and negatively, cf. Isa 25:1 ἐποίησας θαυμαστὰ πράγματα ("you have done wonderful works"). In the NT cf. Heb 6:18; 10:1; 11:1. Luke also uses the term ἔργον ("work") to designate the plan of God that is realized by humans in history; cf. Acts 13:2.

34   See I. I. du Plessis, "Once More: The Purpose of Luke's Prologue (Lk I 1–4)," *NovT* 16 (1974) 259–71, esp. 263.

35   Against Klein ("Programm," 198), who states that one should avoid referring here to past events that have found their fulfillment today (on the basis of his artificial identification of the "we" in v. 1 with the "we" in v. 2). Klein's explanation seems too forced. To contradict it, one should point out the *perfect* participle of πληροφορέω: the events of the past have consequences for the present.

36   A thorough study of this verb can be found in Lagrange, 3–4. He notes the secular meaning of the word and speaks of a clearly defined historical event, the consequences of which are recognized. Cf. BAGD *s.v.* (with bibliography).

37   Preface, *Ab urbe condita*.

38   On the Greek use of this verb, see BAGD *s.v.*

39   Cf. 1 Cor 11:23; 15:1–3; 1 Thess 4:1–2. In Jewish literature cf. *Ep. Arist.* 148, 196.

40   On παραδίδωμι among the Christians, see Cadbury, "Commentary," 497.

41   See Frederick Godet, *A Commentary on the Gospel of St. Luke* (trans. E. W. Shalders; 4th ed.; 2 vols.; Edinburgh: Clark, 1890) 1.60–61.

42   Παρέδοσαν is the Attic form, more literary than παρέδωκαν, which is the usual word in the NT,

have also transmitted them correctly and appropriately. Behind "just as" (καθώς), then, lies the consciousness that false transmission is possible.

Just as Luke alluded to the saving events in v. 1 without naming God and Christ, he refers here to the apostles and witnesses without using the respective terms, probably to avoid alienating non-Christian readers and discouraging them with sectarian language.

Eyewitness testimony was of great importance for historiography in those times, since the saying went that it was better to have seen than to have heard.[43] For the faith of a one such as Luke, eyewitnesses are at the same time witnesses of God's saving activity in history, and not only witnesses of Jesus' resurrection, such as Paul (1 Cor 9:1; 15:3–9), but of the entire life of Jesus (cf. the program stated in Acts 1:22–23).[44] It is a special concern of Luke that their testimony begin at the beginning; only in this manner can one avoid a gap and attain certainty (v. 4).[45]

The "eyewitnesses" are the same as the "servants of the word"; since only one article (οἱ) appears in the text, it must refer to the same persons exercising two functions.[46] It is more difficult to determine whether γενόμενοι ("[who] had become") should be taken only with ὑπηρέται ("servants"), or if it also refers to αὐτόπται ("eyewitnesses"). Despite the placement of the participle, the latter seems the case:[47] the parallel passage in Acts 26:16 supports this reading (ὑπηρέτην καὶ μάρτυρα, "a servant and a witness"), as does customary Greek usage, in which one "becomes" an eyewitness. Before Luke's time, the transmitted "narrative" was limited to the life of Jesus, although for Luke, "the events" extended into the time of the apostles.

Like "eyewitness" (αὐτόπτης), ὑπηρέτης is a word that one can read in both a secular and a Christian sense. Originally a "rower," the ὑπηρέτης is a "servant, deputy," and "adjutant."[48] Luke has in mind the accountability of the apostles, who are not only subject to the word but have been commissioned with its proclamation as well.

"Word" (λόγος), without the following phrase, "of God" (τοῦ θεοῦ), is similarly ambiguous, and this double meaning is intended by Luke. "Word" means here both the word of God and the narrated story of his saving activity, which has been written down in two volumes, the first and second "words" (λόγος, Acts 1:1).

■ 3 The "I" of the author is an innovation in the early Christian transmission of the Gospels. The author speaks[49] with self-awareness and emphasizes that he himself is speaking (metalanguage). "It seemed right to me also" (ἔδοξε κἀμοί) is reminiscent of Acts 15:22, 25, and 28: a correct decision in agreement with God's will receives proud emphasis. It is Luke's idea "to write for you," that is, to write this work for Theophilus.

The καί in κἀμοί means that Luke "also" has the same purpose as the "many" before him. The effect is at the same time proud and humble as he describes the intent with which he has composed his two volumes (v. 4). He himself has pursued (παρακολουθηκότι) everything that he describes. The meaning of παρακολουθέω in this passage has been fiercely debated,[50] because one can understand this verb either literally or metaphorically: to "follow along," and "accompany"; or to "pursue" intellectually, to "investigate" a topic. The latter is more likely. First, the verb is in common usage in ancient historiography[51] and indicates thorough preparatory study by the author;[52] in his research, then, Luke has read all sources available to him. Second, in v. 2 Luke names the apostles, that is, the eyewitnesses, as mediators between

including Luke (see Luke 24:20, 42 [ἐπέδωκαν]; Acts 1:26 [ἔδωκαν]; 3:13; 15:30 [ἐπέδωκαν]). "The literary flavour of this form (παρέδωσαν) is unmistakable" (Cadbury, "Commentary," 497).

43 See van Unnik, "Once More," 13–14.

44 On eyewitness testimony, see Klein, "Programm," 201–2. Cf. Acts 10:41; 13:31.

45 Cf. John 15:27; see du Plessis, "Once More," 266.

46 Cadbury ("Commentary," 498) recalls the most fitting parallel passage: Acts 26:16.

47 Against Klein, "Programm," 204–5. Josephus (Ant. 18.9.5 §342; 19.1.15 §125) links γενόμενος with αὐτόπτης. See further passages in BAGD s.v. αὐτόπτης.

48 Aeschylus Prom. 954: ὑπηρέτης θεῶν ("the gods' servant").

49 A few Latin mss. add: et spiritui sancto ("and to the holy spirit"). Cf. Acts 15:28.

50 Higgins ("Preface," 79–83) advocates a double meaning: research for one portion of the material, and direct experience in the remaining portion (i.e., the end of Acts).

51 References are found in Cadbury, "Commentary," 501–2, e.g., Demosthenes De cor. 172. See van Unnik, "Once More," 17.

52 In his Vita (357), Josephus accuses his rival of distorting historical truth, because he cannot demon-

the events and "us." Perhaps he still wishes to suggest for himself a form of direct contact with them (as does Josephus)[53] that he does not admit for the "many." In one way or another, the reader gets the impression of correct information.

Πᾶσιν ("everything," "everyone"), if neuter, could refer to the "events," or, if masculine, to the people (the "many" or the "witnesses"). The neuter is, however, more likely, since τὰ πάντα or πάντα is often attested in Luke's summary passages.[54] For Luke the "events" are comprehensible only through knowledge not just of the traditions of the eyewitnesses, but also of the narratives of his predecessors.[55]

The first bearers of the tradition were content with receiving it. Luke attempts, beyond this, to verify and evaluate the varying traditions historically.[56] Luke intends not to replace apostolic tradition with historical observation, but to confirm it (cf. v. 4); but just as important to remember is the actual historical frame of reference of the Synoptic traditions themselves.

The words ἀπ' ἀρχῆς ("from the beginning") and ἄνωθεν ("from the very first") occur in a polished literary speech of Paul in Acts 26:4–5. Does Luke use both these words synonymously, or does he denote with ἀπ' ἀρχῆς the beginning of Jesus' public activity, and the beginning of his life as a whole with ἄνωθεν?[57] As is true of the first Christians, especially the "many," the ἀρχή ("beginning"; also, "dominion") of Jesus (cf. Mark 1:1) begins, for Luke too, with his baptism (Luke 3:21–23; Acts 1:22; 10:37). It seems too subtle an interpretation to say that Luke added an additional (ἄνωθεν) introduction

(chaps. 1, 2) to the traditional Synoptic "beginning."[58] It is an open question whether "carefully" (ἀκριβῶς) should be taken with the preceding verb (παρακολουθηκότι, "after investigating") or the following verb (γράψαι, "to write"). According to the sense, ἀκριβῶς fits better with conscientious research methodology, and would seem to justify the former;[59] but an adverb normally refers to the verb that follows it, so the syntax speaks for the latter possibility. Perhaps a reference to Lukan style solves this riddle; it is Luke's practice *simultaneously* to draw loose connections between a word and those words that both precede and follow it.[60]

"Orderly" (καθεξῆς) belongs to the language of a prologue.[61] The meaning varies from "in consecutive order" to "in the following." The allusion to the orderliness[62] of presentation refers to comprehensive scope, as well as to a chronologically or salvation-historically correct sequence, and also to balanced composition. In any case, the adverb alludes to the literary structure of the work, to the extent that one takes it with γράψαι ("to write").

Γράψαι[63] describes the art of a writer, and is emphatic here. Until far into the second century, Christian writers dared publish literary works only with apologies and reservations; in view of oral transmission and the nearness of the parousia, this seemed presumptuous.[64]

"Most Excellent Theophilus": κράτιστος ("most excellent")[65] occurs in the New Testament only here and in

---

strate the truth of his statements: he had not been present at the events himself, nor did he inform himself carefully (παρακολουθήσας), nor had he examined the actions and statements of other participants. See van Unnik, "Once More," 17.

53 Josephus *Vita* 357; *Ap.* 1.10.53–55. See Cadbury, "Commentary," 502.

54 Cf. Luke 3:19; 7:18; and above all, Acts 1:1, περὶ πάντων . . . ὦν ἤρξατο ὁ Ἰησοῦς . . . ("about all that Jesus began . . .").

55 Against Klein, "Programm," 206–7: Luke does not pass over the apostolic traditions. Rather, he supplements these and applies to them a method of historical investigation in order to verify them.

56 Cf. Klein, "Programm," 206–7: "Tendentiously, apostolic tradition is replaced with his own examination of the truth." This thesis is exaggerated; see n. 55 above.

57 An investigation of the word ἄνωθεν and references to ancient authors can be found in du Plessis, "Once More," 267–68.

58 Klein, "Programm," 208.

59 Cf. Dionysius of Haliccarnassus *Ant. Roma.* 1.6.1. See van Unnik, "Once More," 17; he also (18) uses a passage of Eunapius (*VS* 1.1.3) to illustrate the relationship between the conscientiousness of the investigation and the certainty resulting from it.

60 See Cadbury, "Commentary," 504.

61 Examples in Cadbury, "Commentary," 504–5.

62 Luke 8:1; Acts 3:24; 11:4; 18:23.

63 First, "to scratch, scrape"; then, "to carve marks for sketching or writing"; finally, "to write."

64 See Lukas Vischer, "Die Rechtfertigung der Schriftstellerei in der alten Kirche," *ThZ* 12 (1956) 320–36.

65 This is an elative; see Cadbury, "Commentary," 505.

the letters and addresses to officials in Acts, always in the vocative.[66] But the term often appears in the dedications of literary works, the dedicatees of which did not necessarily occupy an official position. The first usage corresponds to the Latin *egregius*; the second, to *optimus*. Thus the "most excellent" of Luke 1:3 does not constrain one to assume that Theophilus was a high-ranking official.[67]

Theophilus is a common first name; parents giving this name to a child were perhaps still aware of its original meaning.[68] Although of Greek origin, the name was also adopted by Jews. A questionable notice in the Pseudo-Clementines states that Theophilus resided in Antioch;[69] aside from this, we know nothing about him. Yet he is a historical figure, and not a symbolic representative "of all *amici* ['friends'] or *amatores dei* ['lovers of God'], as the church fathers would have it."[70] The literary use of "most excellent" does not prohibit the conclusion that Theophilus had already become a Christian.[71]

A brief note on the name "Luke," with which church tradition and especially the manuscripts identify the "I" of v. 3: the name is probably a short form of the Latin *praenomen* Lucius (Λούκιος).[72] One of Paul's loyal friends, a physician, bears this name.[73] Tradition has this man in view as the author of the two volumes.

■ **4** "So that" (ἵνα) introduces a dependent clause expressing the author's purpose; it is not his own fame, nor the apologetic defense of a nation, nor the analysis of human nature, but rather the ἐπιγινώσκω ("to discern") of the readers. Here ἐπιγινώσκω has the meaning "to perceive thoroughly,"[74] after one's attention is directed to (ἐπί) the person or thing; it is thus a conscious and acquired discernment, not complete knowledge.[75]

Ἡ ἀσφάλεια means "firmness" or, metaphorically, "reliability." The word is attested in works of history, in legal usage, and in the arena of political power as an expression of the reliability of information, or of a source, document, or report, sometimes connected with ἐπιγινώσκω ("to discern") or γράφω ("to write")[76] as in Acts 25:26: περὶ οὗ ἀσφαλές τι γράψαι τῷ κυρίῳ οὐκ ἔχω ("But I have nothing definite to write our sovereign [the emperor] about him"). Just as Paul in Acts 26 supplied information and evidence to Festus, so Luke now does for Theophilus.[77] The word "reliability" (ἀσφάλεια) is placed at the end of the sentence with intentional emphasis.[78]

Under Rudolf Bultmann's influence, Luke met with the reproach of replacing the truth of faith with historical knowledge, and the decision of faith with knowledge based on evidence. Indeed, in comparison with Mark or Q, Luke undertakes something new: he consciously introduces historical observation alongside proclamation. But this does not at all arise from doubt in the

---

66 Acts 23:26; 24:3; 26:25. Papyri and official documents illustrate this usage copiously. See Cadbury, "Commentary," 505–7.

67 "The word may be merely an illustration of conventionally formal, friendly or flattering speech (cf. Theophrastus *Characteres* 5)" (Cadbury, "Commentary," 507).

68 This follows from the 3d-century BCE inscription, Θεόφιλος Φιλοθέου Λαμπτρεύς ("Theophilos the son of Philotheos ['the one who loves God'], a Lamptrian"), *IG* II² 788.8.

69 *Ps.-Clem. Rec.* 10.71: "so that, Theophilos, who was more distinguished than all the men of the city, with fiery enthusiasm consecrated the large basilica of his house as a church."

70 Erich Klostermann, *Das Lukasevangelium: Erklärt* (3d ed.; HNT 5; Tübingen: Mohr-Siebeck, 1975) 3.

71 Against Theodor Zahn, *Das Evangelium des Lukas: Ausgelegt* (1st–2d ed.; Kommentar zum Neuen Testament 3; Leipzig/Erlangen: Deichert, 1913) 57–58; agreeing with Klostermann, 3.

72 Other possibilities are shortenings of the Latin names Lucilius (Λουκίλιος) or Lucanus (Λουκανός).

See the excursus by Zahn, 735–38.

73 Col 4:14; Phlm 24; 2 Tim 4:11.

74 Agreeing with Moulton and Milligan, *Vocabulary, s.v.* ἐπιγινώσκω.

75 Ἐπιγινώσκω can, of course, mean "to recognize (again)," "to acknowledge," or, without the emphasis on the preposition, can simply mean "to know, notice" (BAGD *s.v.*).

76 BAGD *s.v.* ἀσφαλής; Cadbury, "Commentary," 509.

77 Cf. Acts 2:36: Ἀσφαλῶς οὖν γινωσκέτω πᾶς οἶκος Ἰσραήλ ("Let all the house of Israel therefore know assuredly"). Luke produces historical facts to shore up his theological program. See du Plessis, "Once More," 270.

78 See Cadbury, "Commentary," 509.

kerygma, but from the perhaps optimistic conviction that genuine research can only confirm the truth of the gospel. For Luke there is only one truth and one world; evidence for him, as for his time (in contrast to our own scientific age), is always rhetorical argument[79] in the domain of persuasion, not objective evidence. The world and truth are not, as in present-day science, rationalistic and limited to the visible and tangible. God himself, of course, does not fall into the purview of the history that Luke researches with such industry and talent; but his voice, his word, and his mediated activity doubtless do.[80] Luke is thus not only a historian but also an evangelist and witness.[81]

The need for historical confirmation was surely awakened by the chronological distance and by contradictory rumors, discussions, and information about the Jesus movement, which finally precipitated into criticisms against the church and the Christian message (as is suggested by Acts 25:26). The "reliability" (ἀσφάλεια) of the Lukan reportage refers both to the theological and the secular realms, because salvation has happened in history. A reader such as Theophilus thus receives concrete historical information, but can also at the same time appropriate the content of faith personally. Through narrative, Luke wants not only to persuade but also to confirm and to defend.[82]

The grammatical attempts of exegetes to dissect the construction περὶ ὧν κατηχήθης λόγων τὴν ἀσφάλειαν ("so that you may discern in their reliability the words about which you have been informed") into its con-stituent elements sometimes seem awkward.[83] The root meaning of κατηχέω, "to let resound" (τὸ ἦχος, "the sound"), developed in various directions: "to report, inform" (passive, "to find out") on one hand, "to instruct, teach" on the other. Paul uses it already for Christian instruction.[84] As in Acts 21:21, 24, the weight is probably on the secular meaning, "to find out." The "words" (λόγοι) could mean various rumors, or also the proclaimed word of God as a whole (cf. Luke 1:2), or even Jesus' concrete sayings.[85] In view of Theophilus's uncertainty, which might correspond to a vacillation between church instruction and critical remarks or false rumors, Luke stresses less the truth of the λόγοι than their reliability.[86]

In regard to the two prologues of the two-volume work, the story of Jesus is beyond doubt more important than that of the apostles (Luke 1:2 confirms this). But the "events" (v. 1) extend beyond the ascension. The author also proposes to describe the first phase of the church as the period of the word's dissemination (v. 3). Thus the prologue in Luke 1:1–4 opens the entire work, and not merely the Gospel,[87] without stressing this *expressis verbis*. This demonstrates once again that Luke is a cultivated writer. According to the prologue of Acts, the Gospel is "the first book" of the entire work (Acts 1:1). The word "narrative" (διήγησις), which Luke uses in reference to the works of his predecessors, could probably come into consideration as a generic description for his own work, because "narrative" can also designate the written product of a historian. According to Acts 1:1,

---

79   Cf. the search for the basis of conviction in Aristotle *Rhet.* 1.1.1355 b.7–12, 25–26.

80   My theological position is close to that of du Plessis, "Once More," 271; and to Samain, "Évangile," 65. Samain emphasizes the theological affinity between Luke's program and the historiography of the OT and of Judaism: history does not prove God's existence, but it allows him to be recognized.

81   See Higgins, "Preface," 89–91.

82   Van Unnik ("Remarks," 13–15) lays stress on the substantiation of the truth and the correction of inaccuracies. Cadbury ("Commentary," 510) accentuates, on the other hand, the defense of Christianity for which Luke has prepared himself.

83   Godet already mentions three possible constructions (1.62–63). Acts 18:25 construes κατηχημένος ("having been instructed") with an accusative of respect, whereas 21:21 makes recourse to περί ("about"). Cf. BAGD s.v. κατηχέω.

84   1 Cor 14:19; Gal 6:6. Also in the Lukan works, Acts 18:25; later as a technical term for catechism, *2 Clem.* 17.1.

85   Cf. van Unnik, "Remarks," 13.

86   In agreement with van Unnik ("Remarks," 13–14), who, among other things, expounds the following hypothesis: Theophilus can find the already familiar truth in the earlier works of the πολλοί ("many").

87   According to Klein ("Programm," 215–16), Luke's recourse to historiography coincides with his invocation of the apostles, because the apostolate is, of course, evident in history. There is thus a theological connection between the prologue of Luke and the book of Acts.

this first volume encompasses the entire life of Jesus (ἤρξατο . . . ἄχρι, "[Jesus] began . . . until"), although in Acts 1:1 and 10:37, Luke marks the beginning with Jesus' baptism (ἤρξατο . . . ποίειν . . . "[Jesus] began to do"), in agreement with early Christian tradition. Jesus' life is characterized by the typical complementarity of word and deed, which extends, according to Luke, even to the sequence of events. In Acts 1:2 Luke sets great weight on the apostles, their selection and training; they bridge the gap between the time of Jesus and the time of the church and ensure the reliability of the message. Verses 3–8 allow insight into the book that follows, and in v. 8, the resurrected Christ himself circumscribes the contents of the book of Acts. For this theological advantage, Luke must indeed pay a high price in the literary aspects. For after a good stylistic beginning, a stylistically unsuitable continuation follows from v. 2 onward: the half-begun sentence is not continued, no δέ appears to correspond to the μέν of v. 1, and the syntax of vv. 2–3 is incorrect.

Conclusion

In the prologue of Luke 1:1–4, Luke openly states his literary, historical, and theological purpose. He brings clearly to expression the degree to which he is conscious of his temporal distance from the events he narrates. In this, his authorial autonomy comes into view at the same time.

Although Luke accepts the role of the eyewitnesses as mediators with approval and admiration, he shows more distance toward the first writers before him. He realizes

he is part of a series of πολλοί, he belongs among them, but he puts forth a claim to pass on something more, and also something better, that is, historically reliable information in a stylistically correct form.

In terms of content, Luke describes multidimensional events: the works that God performed through Jesus, including the testimonies of the apostles that carried them further, works that belong to history but also have significance for salvation. They concern the present-day Christians to such an extent that Luke can say that they happened "among us."

Just as the events portrayed have both historical (πράγματα, "events") and salvation-historical (πεπληρο-φορημένα, "[events] fulfilled," v. 1) significance, and just as the apostles are at once both eyewitnesses and witnesses to the truth (v. 2), so does knowledge accompany faith; that is, Luke's historiographical activity cooperates with the kerygmatic traditions of the church. In this way, readers who were informed about the Christian faith only halfway, or wrongly, will find out exactly what the historical state of affairs was, and what the existential consequences are.

Luke seems unpretentious when compared with the seer of Patmos, who received and proclaimed a new revelation. But Luke is ambitious in his drive for order, accuracy, good technique, and the theological arrangement of the course of time. For Luke's consciousness of the chronological distance from the events of that time is accompanied by his unconditional confidence that the church, the eyewitnesses, and the saving events are all part of a single story.

The Birth Narrative (1:5—2:52)

Bibliography

Anderson, Janice Capel, "Mary's Difference: Gender and Patriarchy in the Birth Narratives," *JR* 67 (1987) 183–202.

Beauduin, Armand, "The Infancy Narratives, a Confession of Faith (Texts from Lk 1)," *Lumen Vitae* 39 (1984) 167–77.

Beckwith, Roger T., "St. Luke, the Date of Christmas and the Priestly Courses at Qumran," *RevQ* 9 (1977–78) 73–94.

Brodie, L. T., "A New Temple and a New Law: The Unity and Chronicler-based Nature of Luke 1:1–4:22a," *JSNT* 5 (1979) 21–45.

Brown, *Birth*.

idem, "Gospel Infancy Narrative Research from 1976 to 1986: Part II (Luke)," *CBQ* 48 (1986) 660–80.

Brunner-Traut, Emma, "Die Geburtsgeschichte der Evangelien im Lichte ägyptologischer Forschungen," *ZRGG* 12 (1960) 97–111.

Cabaniss, A., "Christmas Echoes at Paschaltide," *NTS* 9 (1962–63) 67–69.

Coleridge, Mark, *The Birth of the Lukan Narrative: Narrative as Christology in Luke 1–2* (JSNTSup 88; Sheffield: JSOT Press, 1993).

Conybeare, F. C., "Ein Zeugnis Ephräms über das Fehlen von c. 1 und 2 im Texte des Lukas," *ZNW* 3 (1902) 192–97.

Craig-Faxon, Alicia, *Women and Jesus* (Philadelphia: United Church Press, 1973).

Davies, J. H., "The Lucan Prologue (1–3): An Attempt at Objective Redaction Criticism," *StEv* 6 (1973) 78–85 (= TU 112).

Derrett, J. Duncan M., "Further Light on the Narratives of the Nativity," *NovT* 17 (1975) 81–108, reprinted in idem, *Studies in the New Testament* (6 vols.; Leiden: Brill, 1978–95), vol. 2: *Midrash in Action*, 4–32.

Dibelius, *Jungfrauensohn*.

Díez Macho, Alejandro, "Deras y exégesis del Nuevo Testamento," *Sef* 35 (1975) 37–89.

Drewermann, Eugen, *Dein Name ist wie der Geschmack des Lebens: Tiefenpsychologische Deutung der Kindheitsgeschichte nach dem Lukasevangelium* (Freiburg im Breisgau: Herder, 1986).

Dubois, Jean-Daniel, "De Jean-Baptiste à Jésus: Essai sur la conception lucanienne de l'esprit à partir des premiers chapitres de l'évangile" (diss., Strasbourg, 1977).

Erdmann, Gottfried, *Die Vorgeschichten des Lukas- und Matthäus-Evangeliums und Vergils vierte Ekloge* (FRLANT 48; Göttingen: Vandenhoeck & Ruprecht, 1932).

Escudero Freire, Carlos, *Devolver el Evangelio a los pobres: A propósito de Lc 1–2* (Biblioteca de estudios bíblicos 19; Salamanca: Sígueme, 1978).

Farris, Stephen, *The Hymns of Luke's Infancy Narratives: Their Origin, Meaning and Significance* (JSNTSup 9; Sheffield: JSOT Press, 1985).

Feuillet, André, *Jésus et sa mère d'après les récits lucaniens de l'enfance et d'après S. Jean: Le rôle de la Vierge Marie dans l'histoire du salut et la place de la femme dans l'Eglise* (Paris: Gabalda, 1974).

idem, "Quelques observations sur les récits de l'enfance chez S. Luc," *L'Ami du Clergé* 82 (1972) 721–24.

Firpo, Giulio, *Il problema cronologico della nascita di Gesù: Con una nota di Fabrizio Fabbrini* (Biblioteca di cultura religiosa 42; Brescia: Paideia, 1983).

Ford, J. Massyngberde, "Zealotism and the Lukan Infancy Narratives," *NovT* 18 (1976) 280–92.

George, Augustin, "La mère de Jésus," in idem, *Études*, 429–63.

idem, "Parallèle."

Gibbs, J. M., "Mark 1:1–15; Matthew l:1–4:16; Luke 1:1–4:30; John 1:1–51: The Gospel Prologues and Their Function," *StEv* 6 (= TU 112) (1973) 154–88.

Globe, Alexander, "Some Doctrinal Variants in Matthew 1 and Luke 2, and the Authority of the Neutral Text," *CBQ* 42 (1980) 52–72.

Glöckner, *Verkündigung*, 68–124.

Goulder, M. D., and M. L. Sanderson, "St. Luke's Genesis," *JTS* n.s. 8 (1957)12–30.

Green, Joel B., "The Social Status of Mary in Luke 1:5–2:52: A Plea for Methodological Integration," *Bib* 73 (1992) 457–72.

Grelot, Pierre, "La naissance d'Isaac et celle de Jésus: Sur une interprétation 'mythologique' de la conception virginale," *NRTh* 94 (1972) 462–87, 561–85.

Gryglewicz, Feliks, "Die Herkunft der Hymnen des Kindheitsevangeliums des Lukas," *NTS* 21 (1974–75) 265–73.

Gueuret, *Engendrement*.

idem, "Luc I–II: Analyse sémiotique," *Sémiotique et Bible* 25 (1982) 35–42.

Gunkel, Hermann, "Die Lieder in der Kindheitsgeschichte Jesu bei Lukas," in *Festgabe von Fachgenossen und Freunden . . . dargebracht: Festschrift Adolf von Harnack* (Tübingen: Mohr-Siebeck, 1921) 43–60.

Higgins, A. J. B., "Luke 1–2 in Tatian's Diatessaron," *JBL* 103 (1984) 193–222.

Himmler, D. L., "History and Christology in the Lucan Infancy Narratives" (diss., Catholic University of America, 1971); see *DissAb* 32 (1971) 2177-A.

Horsley, Richard A., *The Liberation of Christmas: The Infancy Narratives in Social Context* (New York: Crossroad, 1989).

Isaacs, M. E., "Mary in the Lucan Infancy Narratives," *Way* Sup 25 (1975) 80–95.

Kassel, Maria, "Weibliche Aspekte im lukanischen Kindheitsevangelium," *Diakonia* 15 (1984) 391–97.

Kirchschläger, Walter, "Beobachtungen zur Struktur der lukanischen Vorgeschichten Lk 1–2," *BLit* 57 (1984) 244–51.

Krafft, Eva, "Die Vorgeschichten des Lukas: Eine Frage nach ihrer sachgemäßen Interpretation," in Dinkler, *Zeit und Geschichte,* 217–23.

Larson, Stan, "The 26th Edition of the Nestle-Aland Novum Testamentum Graece: A Limited Examination of Its Apparatus," *JSNT* 12 (1981) 53–58.

Laurentin, René, "Bulletin sur la Vierge Marie," *RSPhTh* 65 (1981) 123–54, 299–335.

idem, *Structure.*

idem, "Traces d'allusions étymologiques en Luc 1–2," *Bib* 37 (1956) 435–56; 38 (1957) 1–23.

idem, *Truth.*

idem, "Vérité des Évangiles de l'enfance," *NRTh* 105 (1983) 691–710.

Lauverjat, M., "Luc 2: Une simple approche," *Sémiotique et Bible* 27 (1982) 31–47.

Leaney, R., "The Birth Narratives in St Luke and St Matthew," *NTS* 8 (1961–62) 158–66.

idem, "Luc I–II," *Sémiotique et Bible* 3 (1976) 6–25.

Malet, André, *Les évangiles de Noël: Mythe ou réalité?* (Alethina l; Paris/Lausanne: Éditions l'Age d'Homme, 1970).

Mann, C. S., "The Historicity of the Birth Narratives," *SPCK Theological Colloquium* 6 (1965) 46–58.

Mather, P. B., "The Search for the Living Text of the Lukan Infancy Narrative," in D. E. Groh and R. Jewett, eds., *The Living Text: Festschrift Ernest W. Saunders* (New York/London/Lanham, Md.: University Press of America, 1985) 123–40.

McHugh, John, *The Mother of Jesus in the New Testament* (London: Darton, Longman and Todd, 1975).

Meagher, G., "The Prophetic Call Narratve," *ITQ* 39 (1972) 164–77.

Mees, M., "Lukas 1–9 in der Textgestalt des Codex Bezae: Literarische Formen im Dienste der Schrift," *Vetera Christianorum* 5 (1968) 89–110.

Meynet, Roland, *Quelle est donc cette parole? Lecture "rhétorique" de l'évangile de Luc (1–9; 22–24)* (LD 99; Paris: Cerf, 1979) 149–65.

Minear, P. S., "Luke's Use of the Birth Stories," in L. E. Keck and J. L. Martyn, eds., *Studies in Luke-Acts: Festschrift Paul Schubert* (2d ed.; Nashville: Abingdon, 1966) 111–30, reprinted as "Die Funktion der Kindheitsgeschichten im Werk des Lukas," in Braumann, *Lukas-Evangelium,* 204–35.

Moloney, F. J., "The Infancy Narratives: Another View of R. E. Brown's 'The Birth of the Messiah,'" *Clergy Review* 64 (1979) 161–66.

Muñoz Iglesias, Salvador, *Los Cánticos del Evangelio de la Infancia según San Lucas* (Madrid: Instituto Francisco Suárez, 1983).

idem, "Estructura y teología de Lucas I–II," *EstBib* 17 (1958) 101–7.

idem, "El evangelio de la infancia en S. Lucas y las infancias de los héroes bíblicos," *EstBib* 16 (1957) 329–82.

idem, *Los Evangelios de la Infancia,* vol. 3: *Nacimiento e infancia de Juan y de Jésus en Luca 1–2* (BAC 488; Madrid: Católica, 1987).

idem, "María y la Trinidad en Lucas 1–2," *Estudios Trinitarios* 19 (1985) 143–61.

idem, "Midrás y evangelios de la infancia," *EstBib* 47 (1972) 331–59.

Neirynck, Frans, *L'évangile de Noël selon S. Luc* (Paris/Brussels: La pensée catholique, 1960).

Norden, Eduard, *Die Geburt des Kindes: Geschichte einer religiösen Idee* (Studien der Bibliothek Warburg 3; Leipzig/Berlin: Teubner, 1924).

Oliver, H. H., "The Lucan Birth Stories and the Purpose of Luke-Acts," *NTS* 10 (1963–64) 202–26.

Panier, Louis, *La naissance du Fils de Dieu: Sémiotique et théologie discursive, lecture de Luc 1–2* (Paris: Cerf, 1991).

Perrot, "Récits."

Radl, Walter, *Der Ursprung Jesu: Traditionsgeschichtliche Untersuchungen zu Lukas 1–2* (New York: Herder, 1996).

Redford, J., "The Quest of the Historical Epiphany: Critical Remarks on R. E. Brown's 'The Birth of the Messiah,'" *Clergy Review* 64 (1979) 5–11.

Resch, Alfred, *Aussercanonische Paralleltexte zu den Evangelien,* part 5: *Das Kindheitsevangelium nach Lucas und Matthaeus unter Herbeiziehung der ausser-canonischen Paralleltexte quellenkritisch untersucht* (TU 10.5; Leipzig: Hinrichs, 1897).

Richard, L., "L'Évangile de l'enfance et le décret impérial," in *Mémorial J. Chaine* (Bibliothèque de la Faculté catholique de théologie de Lyon 5; Lyon: Facultés catholiques, 1950) 297–308.

Rossmiller, Celeste J., "Prophets and Disciples in Luke's Infancy Narrative," *TBT* 22 (1984) 361–65.

Ryoo, S. W., "The Lucan Birth Narratives and the Theological Unity and Purpose of Luke-Acts" (diss., Boston University, 1969); see *DissAb* 30 (1970) 4539-A.

Sahlin, Harald, *Der Messias und das Gottesvolk: Studien zur protolukanischen Theologie* (ASNU 12; Uppsala: Almquist and Wicksell, 1945).

Schaberg, Jane, *The Illegitimacy of Jesus: A Feminist Theological Interpretation of the Infancy Narratives* (Sheffield: Sheffield Academic Press, 1995).

Schürmann, Heinz, "Aufbau, Eigenart und Geschichtswert der Vorgeschichte Lk 1–2," *BK* 21 (1966) 106–11, reprinted in idem, *Traditionsgeschichtliche Untersuchungen zu den synoptischen*

Evangelien: Beiträge (KBANT; Düsseldorf: Patmos, 1968) 198–208.

Schweizer, Eduard, "Zum Aufbau von Lukas 1 und 2," in D. Y. Hadidian, ed., *Intergerini Parietis Septum (Eph. 2:14): Festschrift Markus Barth* (PTMS 33; Pittsburgh: Pickwick, 1980) 309–35, reprinted in Eduard Schweizer, *Neues Testament und Christologie im Werden: Aufsätze* (Göttingen: Vandenhoeck & Ruprecht, 1982) 11–32.

Silberman, Lou H., "A Model for the Lukan Infancy Narratives?" *JBL* 113 (1994) 491–94.

Stenger, Hermann, "Die Wiederentdeckung der Bilder: Überlegungen zu E. Drewermanns Deutung der lukanischen Kindheitsgeschichte," *Theologie der Gegenwart im Auswahl* 30 (1987) 232–41.

Tam, D. S., "The Literary and Theological Unity between Lk 1–2 and Lk 3–Acts 28" (diss., Duke University, 1978); see *DissAb* 39 (1978–79) 5663–64-A.

Tatum, W. Barnes, "The Epoch of Israel: Luke I–II and the Theological Plan of Luke-Acts," *NTS* 13 (1966–67) 184–95, reprinted as "Die Zeit Israels: Lukas 1–2 und die theologische Intention der lukanischen Schriften," in Braumann, *Lukas-Evangelium,* 317–36.

Tsuchiya, H., "The History and the Fiction in the Birth Stories of Jesus: An Observation on the Thought of Luke the Evangelist," *AJBI* 1 (1975) 73–90.

Tyson, Joseph B., "The Birth Narratives and the Beginning of Luke's Gospel," *Semeia* 52 (1990) 103–20.

Venetz, H. J., "Kindheitsgeschichten für Erwachsene: Zur Bedeutung der neueren Exegese für die Verkündigung," *Diakonia* 7 (1976) 390–407.

Vögtle, Anton, "Offene Fragen zur lukanischen Geburts- und Kindheitsgeschichte," *BibLeb* 11 (l970) 51–67, reprinted in idem, *Das Evangelium und die Evangelien: Beiträge zur Evangelienforschung* (KBANT; Düsseldorf: Patmos, 1971) 43–56.

Wilson, R. McL., "Some Recent Studies in the Lucan Infancy Narratives," *StEv* 1 (1959) 235–53 (= TU 73).

Winandy, Jacques, *Autour de la naissance de Jésus: Accomplissement et prophétie* (Lire la Bible 26; Paris: Cerf, 1970).

Wink, *John.*

Winter, Paul, "Some Observations on the Language in the Birth and Infancy Stories of the Third Gospel," *NTS* 1 (1954–55) 111–21.

Analysis

Luke 1:5–2:52 forms a unit. The short prologue (1:1–4), with its metalinguistic level, stands by itself; and the great synchronism (3:1) begins the Gospel in the traditional sense of Mark, with the Baptist's proclamation. The passage 1:5–2:52 exists independently, then, as a cycle of stories about the birth of the Baptist and of the Messiah. One and the same set of topics, the same genre, and a uniform style all characterize this unit.

The beginnings of a new intervention by God are set up by the miraculous births; this is the preliminary stage of the life and times of the Messiah. The genre of this section can be described as a midrash only with qualifications; for it is essential to midrash to apply an earlier revelation to the present situation. Here the narrative represents reports about events just now being brought about by the Word of God. Its authors want to enrich the previous written revelations with information about more recent events. Seen as a whole, the genre is Old Testament historiography (e.g., the genre of the book of Judges); the smaller units are biographical legends and hymns. Here we encounter the phenomenon of post-textuality.[1] The same tendency dominates the cycles in the book of Acts, which are often modeled on the Gospels and attempt to emulate them.

In addition to simpler methods of organizing these two chapters, such as by time, place, characters, and action, there are also stylistic and formal devices: the narratives are interspersed with hymns. Are the hymns the refrainlike hermeneutical keys to the whole (so Agnès Gueuret)?[2] Or were they, as other interpreters suppose, foreign elements artfully interpolated by the last author?[3] All readers have, of course, noted the strik-

---

[1]   I.e., the effect of earlier texts on later ones created in implicit analogy to them. *Trans.* See Gérard Genette, *Palimpsestes: La littérature au second degré* (Collection Poétique; Paris: Seuil, 1982) 11–12.

[2]   Agnès Gueuret, *L'engendrement d'un récit: L'évangile de l'enfance selon saint Luc* (LD 113; Paris: Cerf, 1983) 295.

[3]   See Raymond E. Brown, *The Birth of the Messiah: A Commentary on the Infancy Narratives in Matthew and Luke* (New York: Doubleday; London: G. Chapman, 1977) 244.

ing parallels between John and Jesus; but are they merely conceived as a symmetry in the sense of Plutarch's biographies?[4] Or is there a conscious asymmetry inherent in the parallels, in Jesus' favor?[5] The assessment of this parallelism depends not only on stylistic considerations, but also on the extent and nature of the sources. Luke 2:21–52 preserves individual elements that Luke by no means wants to lose. Although they disturb the literary balance, they do throw Jesus into sharper relief (cf. the addition of the supplemental chap. 21 in the Gospel of John); but disturbing the balance is not equivalent to disturbing the harmony.[6] In addition, the content of the annunciations, as a whole, and the portrayal of the births are not fully analogous. Luke has coordinated the materials that came down to him about the Baptist and Jesus' birth by means of the encounter between Mary and Elizabeth, which interrupts a homogeneous legend about the Baptist. Moreover, Luke has not narrated the two legends in simple succession, but has interwoven them so that the respective annunciation or birth runs parallel to the other. There are, then, two currents of symmetry (1:5–25 and 1:26–38; 1:57–80 and 2:1–40). The first is concluded with the encounter of the two mothers, the second, with the account of the superiority of the twelve-year-old Jesus in the temple (2:41–52). Walter Wink's outline, inspired by René Laurentin and Martin Dibelius, is arranged in twos with respect to *paradigm*, and in threes with respect to *syntax*. In consecutive order, then, there are six subunits arranged in pairs:

a. The annunciation of John the Baptist's birth (1:5–25)

a.' The annunciation of Jesus the Messiah's birth (1:26–38)

   b. The encounter of Mary and Elizabeth (1:39–56)

     c. The birth of John the Baptist (1:57–80)

       1. Birth (1:57–66)

       2. Greeting (1:67–80)

     c.' The birth of Jesus the Messiah (2:1–40)

       1. Birth (2:1–21)

       2. Greeting (2:22–40)

       d. Jesus in the temple (2:41–52)

The two chapters, on the basis of form-critical analysis, belong to the latest genres of Synoptic tradition. The length itself, but also the biographical interest, betray the style of a biographical legend. It is much too seldom taken into account that these units correspond to the cycles in the book of Acts. Luke 1:5–80, in particular, is structurally similar to the story of Cornelius:

1. A "pre-Christian" righteous person receives a divine message (Luke 1:5–25; Acts 10:1–8).
2. At approximately the same time, a "Christian" figure receives a divine message (Luke 1:26–38; Acts 10:9–23).
3. The two persons meet; the Christian kerygma appears (Luke 1:39–56; Acts 10:24–43).
4. That which was announced appears; the consequences are described (Luke 1:57–80; Acts 10:44—11:18).

What is significant is that Luke incorporates, into self-contained legends, traditions and texts that are independent in origin, such as the annunciation to Mary and her visitation, and, in the other account, Peter's vision. Even the prayers and speeches are padded with material from some other source, such as the Magnificat and the Benedictus, or Peter's two speeches (Acts 10:34–43; 11:5–17).

So we can divide Luke 1 into the following components ("decomposition"[7]): a biographical legend about the Baptist's birth, the annunciation to Mary, the encounter of Mary and Elizabeth, and two songs. The hermeneutical function of the speeches or the prayers gives no information about their origin; traditional materials such as the Magnificat or the Benedictus can easily assume a redactional function. The provenance of the angelic messages (1:13–17, 30–33, 35) will become clearer in the course of the exegesis.

---

4   Greek text and English translation in *Plutarch's Lives* (trans. Bernadotte Perrin; LCL; 11 vols.; Cambridge: Harvard University Press; London: Heinemann, 1914–26).

5   See Brown's outline, *Birth*, 248–49.

6   Walter Wink, *John the Baptist in the Gospel Tradition* (SNTSMS 7; Cambridge: Cambridge University Press, 1968) 59.

7   Martin Dibelius, *Jungfrauensohn und Krippenkind: Untersuchungen zur Geburtsgeschichte Jesu im Lukas-Evangelium* (SHAW.PH 1931–32; Heidelberg: Carl Winter, 1932), reprinted in idem, *Botschaft und Geschichte: Gesammelte Aufsätze* (ed. G. Bornkamm; 2 vols.; Tübingen: Mohr-Siebeck, 1953) 1.1–78, esp. 2.

In comparison with the parables, miracle stories, and apothegms, the legends in Luke 1 belong to a later phase of development. Their provenance is difficult to localize. The Semitisms,[8] noted again and again (and often only Septuagintisms), are interwoven with Lukan idioms to such an extent that Luke must be considered the actual author—the final author—of this chapter, and the birth narrative integrated into his theological plan.[9] There is no compelling reason to assume a previous Semitic version. Luke prefers to employ Greek sources, presumably already fixed in writing,[10] which have in any case already assumed a stable structure.

The language imitates that of the LXX. This indicates that the author intends to be counted among the legitimate successors of the Scriptures. The concern is not to bring a particular narrative up to date, but to continue sacred history by assuming its style; thence come the many "quotations" and motifs from birth accounts in the Old Testament.[11] Whereas the legends in Matthew are of Semitic origin, here they are Jewish traditions in Greek. Despite the objections of Benoit and Wink,[12] it is probable that they originated in the Baptist's movement, since the Baptist is not diminished at all in this legend and is more than a mere precursor.

On the basis of form-critical analysis, the two legends must be considered as two independent units, which Luke was the first to compose in a parallelism in the style of Plutarch. Though the Christian traces are minimal in the birth legend of the Baptist, the story of Jesus' birth is not merely a slavish imitation of John's. After all, John's followers and Jesus' disciples were competitors for some time. Luke has transformed this competition into *concordia*. What he later brilliantly accomplished with Peter and Paul, he is already attempting here with John and Jesus.[13]

It is difficult to determine the Christian movement out of which the accounts of the annunciation to Mary, the visitation, and the birth of Jesus originate. In any case, Luke follows in the wake of Paul and the Hellenists, whereas Matthew remains closer to the Petrine tradition. The Hellenists may have taken these traditions from the Jewish Christian circle of James, the Lord's brother. On the other hand, the hypothesis that the memoirs of Mary transmitted by Luke are to be attributed to the apostle John (John 19:25–27) is purely speculative and apologetic. Stylistically, the narratives in chaps. 1 and 2 come from the same phase as countless others from the special source in Luke and the cycles in Acts. For good reason, they have often been admired for their aesthetic beauty.

8   As Pierre Benoit supposes ("L'enfance de Jean-Baptiste selon Luc 1," *NTS* 3 [1956–57] 169–94, reprinted in idem, *Exégèse et Théologie* [4 vols.; Paris: Cerf, 1961–83] 3.165–96, esp. 171 n.4 [cited from journal]), these are probably Hebraisms rather than Aramaisms.

9   In agreement with Charles Perrot, "Les récits de l'enfance de Jésus: Matthieu 1–2: Luc 1–2," *Cahiers Évangile* 18 (1976) 35–72, esp. 35; Gueuret, *Engendrement*, 297; and Bovon, *Theologian*, 54–55, 260 n. 76.

10   "It was worth the trouble to enumerate the cases that challenge the hypothesis of a Hebrew original; these are decidedly more numerous than the cases that support the existence of such an original" (Benoit, "Enfance," 175).

11   See Benoit, "Enfance," 177. For actual citations, see Gueuret's compilation (*Engendrement*, 273–81), which compares five modern editions or translations.

12   A presentation and critique of this hypothesis can be found in Wink, *John*, 60–71.

13   See Augustin George, "Le parallèle entre Jean-Baptiste et Jésus en Luc 1–2," in A. Descamps and R. P. A. de Halleux, *Mélanges bibliques: Festschrift R. P. Béda Rigaux* (Gembloux: Duculot, 1970) 147–71, reprinted in George, *Études*, 43–65.

The Proclamation to Zechariah (1:5–25)

Bibliography

Balz, Horst, "λειτουργία, κτλ.," *EDNT* 2 (1991) 347–49.

Benoit, "Enfance."

Berger, Christoph, "Die literarische Eigenart von Lk 1,5–38: Zum Sprachstil der Evangelien" (diss., Jena, 1972); see *ThLZ* 98 (1973) 153–56.

Berlingieri, Giovanni, *Il lieto annuncio della nascita e del concepimento del precursore di Gesu (Lc 1:5–23, 24–25) nel quadro dell'opera lucana: uno studio tradizionale e redazionale* (Rome: Gregorian University Press, 1991).

Betz, Otto, "μέγας, κτλ.," *EDNT* 2 (1991) 399–401.

Brown, Raymond E., "The Annunciation to Zechariah, the Birth of the Baptist, and the Benedictus (Luke 1:5–25, 57–80)," *Worship* 62 (1988) 482–96.

idem, *Birth*, 1–38, 232–69.

Dibelius, *Jungfrauensohn*, 1–9.

Dömer, *Heil*, 15–42.

Dubois, Jean-Daniel, "La figure d'Elie dans la perspective lucanienne," *RHPhR* 53 (1973) 155–76.

idem, "Jean-Baptiste."

Escudero Freire, *Devolver*, 55–66.

Fearghail, Fearghus Ó, "The Literary Forms of Lc 1:5–25 and 1:26–38," *Mar* 43 (1981) 321–44.

Gen, Raymond M., "The Phenomena of Miracles and Divine Infliction in Luke-Acts: Their Theological Significance [Luke 1:5–25; Acts 5:1–14; 9:1–21; 12:20–23; 13:4–12]," *Pneuma* 11 (1989) 3–19.

George, "Parallèle."

Gueuret, *Engendrement*, 31–65.

Hahn, *Titles*, 365–66.

Hubbard, B. J., "Commissioning Stories in Luke-Acts: A Study of Their Antecedents, Form and Content," *Semeia* 8 (1977) 103–26.

Klaiber, Walter, "Eine lukanische Fassung des Sola Gratia: Beobachtungen zu Lk 1,5–56," in J. Friedrich, et al., eds., *Rechtfertigung: Festschrift Ernst Käsemann* (Tübingen: Mohr-Siebeck; Göttingen: Vandenhoeck & Ruprecht, 1976) 211–28.

Laurentin, *Structure*, 32–42.

idem, *The Truth of Christmas Beyond the Myths: The Gospels of the Infancy of Christ* (Studies in Scripture; Petersham, Mass.: St. Bede's Publications, 1986) 137–42 and passim.

Leaney, R., "The Birth Narratives in St Luke and St Matthew," *NTS* 8 (1961–62) 158–66.

Lohfink, *Sammlung*, 17–23.

Perrot, "Récits," 40–42.

Sahlin, *Messias*, 70–97.

Sussarellu, B., "De praevia sanctificatione praecursoris: Quaestio exegetica in Luc. 1,15.41–44," *SBFLA* 3 (1952–53) 37–110.

Wilckens, U., "Das christliche Heilsverständnis nach dem Lukasevangelium," in P. A. Potter, ed., *Das Heil der Welt heute* (Stuttgart/Berlin: Kreuz-Verlag, 1973) 65–74.

Wink, *John*, 58–86.

Winter, "Miszellen," 65–66.

idem, "Ὅτι recitativum in Lk I 25, 61, II 23," *HTR* (1955) 213–16.

5 It happened that in the days of Herod, king of Judea, there was a priest named Zechariah, who belonged to the priestly order of Abijah, and he had a wife from the daughters of Aaron, and her name was Elizabeth. 6/ Both of them were righteous before God, walking blamelessly according to all the commandments and regulations of the Lord. 7/ But they had no children, because Elizabeth was barren, and both were getting on in years.

8 Once when he was serving as priest before God and his section was on duty, 9/ he was chosen by lot, according to the custom of the priesthood, to enter the temple of the Lord and offer incense. 10/ Now at the hour of the incense offering, the whole multitude of the people was praying outside. 11/ Then there appeared to him an angel of the Lord, standing at the right side of the altar of incense. 12/ When Zechariah saw him, he was terrified, and fear fell upon him. 13/ But the angel said to him, "Do not be afraid, Zechariah, for your prayer has been heard, and your wife Elizabeth will bear you a son, and you will call his name John. 14/ And he will bring you joy and gladness, and many will rejoice at his birth. 15/ For he will become great before the Lord, and he will not drink wine or strong drink, and even from his mother's womb, he will be filled with holy spirit, 16/ and he will turn many of the people of Israel to the Lord their God. 17/ And in the spirit and power of Elijah he will go before him, to turn the hearts of parents to their children, and the disobedient to the wisdom of the righteous, to make ready for the Lord a people prepared." 18/ And Zechariah said to the angel, "How will I recognize this? For I am an old man, and my wife is getting on in years." 19/ And the angel answered and said to him, "I am Gabriel, who stands in the presence of God, and I have been sent to speak to you, and to bring you this good news. 20/ But now, because you did not believe my words, which will be fulfilled in their time, you will become mute and unable to speak, until the day that these things occur."

21 Meanwhile the people were waiting for Zechariah, and wondered at his delay in the temple. 22/ When he did come out, he could not speak to them, and they realized that he had seen a vision in the temple, and he kept motioning to them and remained mute. 23/ And it happened that when his time of service was ended, he went to his home. 24/ After those days his wife

Elizabeth became pregnant, and for five months she remained in seclusion, and she said, 25/ "This is what the Lord has done for me in the days when he looked favorably on me, to take away my disgrace among humankind."

Analysis

It should be pointed out that "the narrative of the proclamation to Zechariah and the birth of the Baptist has its own unique form and value, completeness, style, and significance"; both parts of the narrative (1:5–25 and 1:57–80) cohere and "form a genuine biographical legend, which presents the importance of its hero by the events surrounding his conception and birth."[1]

Luke transmits the Jewish context and the details of Jewish ceremonies almost faultlessly.[2] One perceives no criticism of the temple and the priesthood, as would be expected from an Essene account.[3] Renewed prophecy is what issues from the temple, as is characteristic of the Baptist's movement.

It is not out of the question that later Christian authors worked similarly to Luke, using older legends about the Baptist. Mark 6 is evidence that, as was the case with Jesus, a series of legends circulated about the Baptist—at least about his birth, baptizing, message, and death. Josephus and the existence of the sect of the Mandaeans also illustrate his impact. The guardians of these recollections, and those responsible for their further development, were, at first, the disciples of the Baptist.[4]

Here are the constituent elements of the legend. Verses 5–7: presentation of the parents, and the tension between their righteousness and their childlessness, which awakens the anticipation of a story.[5] Verses 8–12: beginning of the story. God makes use of an institutional encounter with Zechariah to reveal himself with signs and wonders. Despite Isaiah 6, the scene has no counterpart in the Hebrew Bible, but certainly does in rabbinic literature.[6] Verses 13–17: angelic message. Despite its rhythmic form, it should not be typographically arranged as poetry, as in Nestle-Aland. Verses 18–20: true to the Hebrew Bible, Zechariah demands a sign.[7] But because he asks in unbelief, the sign becomes a punishment (in contrast with the HB, a new state of affairs). Verses 21–23: the important role of the people (Gueuret),[8] and a recollection of vv. 9–10. Verses 24–25: Elizabeth now assumes importance. She expects a child and secludes herself. The temporal references (vv. 24, 26, 56–57) are principally links between the legend and the interpolation. Verses 57–58: birth of the Baptist, and the people's rejoicing. Verses 59–66: eight days later, at the liturgical ceremony of circumcision, John's name is given charismatically (a scene symmetric to 1:18–20). Luke passes over the etymology of the name, "God is merciful," either because it is obvious to Jews or, more likely, because it is incomprehensible to Greek-speakers.

In sum, Luke knows that John is the precursor. Luke borrows from the Baptist's movement a portrayal of John's birth corresponding to the birth narrative of Jesus; in the Greek method of parallel vitae, he then links it artfully with the developing traditions about Jesus' conception and birth. The meeting of the mothers is the narrative expression of a rapprochement between

1   Dibelius, *Jungfrauensohn*, 3.
2   According to Luke, there was one solemn moment during which the officiating priest stood alone in the "holy place" (the room in front of the holy of holies). Does this detail correspond to reality? See Paul Billerbeck, "Ein Tempelgottesdienst in Jesu Tagen," *ZNW* 55 (1964) 1–17.
3   One can very well spare oneself this detour into Qumran. The Essenes were not the only ones to withdraw into the wilderness. Cf. the Baptist's movement and Bannus (Josephus *Vita* §11).
4   Joachim Gnilka hesitates to ascribe Mark 6:14–29 to the Baptist's movement (*Das Evangelium nach Markus* [2d ed.; 2 vols.; EKKNT 2; Zurich: Benziger; Neukirchen-Vluyn: Neukirchener Verlag, 1986] 1.246); yet to call it a story circulating among the people is rather vague.
5   Perhaps this introductory tension can be under-

stood along the lines of the categories of the folk-tale, e.g., as a situation of lack. See V. Propp, *Morphology of the Folktale* (trans. Laurence Scott; 2d ed.; Publications of the American Folklore Society: Bibliographical and Special Series 9; Austin: University of Texas Press, 1968) 35–36.
6   *b. Yoma* 39b; *y. Yoma* 5.42c (compiled in Dibelius, *Jungfrauensohn*, 35).
7   Cf. Exod 4:1–9 (Moses); Judg 6:17–24 (Gideon).
8   Gueuret, *Engendrement*, 44–45, 54–55.
9   I. Howard Marshall summarizes neatly the various hypotheses on the origin of the accounts in 1:5–2:52 and names their advocates: (1) Luke is writing without sources; (2) Luke depends on a proto-Luke; (3) Luke uses various sources, etc. (*The Gospel of Luke: A Commentary on the Greek Text* [New International Greek Testament Commentary; Grand

the traditions. But a shift in emphasis exalts the later-born, the Messiah, who alone can call God his father (2:49). This issue belongs to a later stage of Synoptic tradition, in which the father-son relationship is projected back from the resurrection, through the baptism, to the birth itself.[9]

Commentary

■ **5–7** The context of the story[10] is given (v. 5): Palestine,[11] in the time of Herod the Great.[12] The ἐγένετο ("it happened that") without the connective δέ ("and") marks the beginning, which, after the Greek prologue, sounds strongly Semitic.[13] A married couple is introduced briefly and crisply, as will also be the case with Mary and Joseph (v. 27). Despite the *Protoevangelium of James*, Zechariah[14] is not the high priest, nor is

he from the high-priestly family; he is a simple priest.[15] Of the twenty-four classes of the priesthood, the division of Abijah is the eighth, not one of the more prestigious. The priests of a given division[16] officiate twice yearly in the temple for one week. For the rest of the year, Zechariah lives with his wife in the mountains of Judah, outside Jerusalem (1:23, 39).[17] Elizabeth is also of priestly origin[18] (the only regulation concerning a priest's wife is that she be of genuine Hebrew origin). The novel event, prophecy, thus emerges from a traditional sacral context.

In the same biblical tone, Luke describes (v. 6) the righteousness of both parents;[19] for Luke, God works together with those who love him. The description of their righteousness[20] is formulated in v. 6b in a strikingly symmetrical sentence construction.[21]

Rapids: Eerdmans; Exeter: Paternoster, 1978] 47–49).

10 The temporal reference (1:5) is not very exact. But this does not mean that Luke has betrayed his stated purpose (1:3), against Fitzmyer (1.321).

11 For the broad semantic range of Ἰουδαία ("Judea") in Hellenistic usage (although not in Jewish), see Benoit, "Enfance," 174.

12 "King of Judea" was the title granted Herod by the Roman senate at the request of Antony, Messala, and Atratinus (Josephus *Ant.* 14.14.4 §384); see Plummer, 8. About Herod, who ruled from 40 (really 37) to 4 BCE, see Godet, 1.71, and the Bible lexica. The mss. vary in the placement of the definite article before "king"; the LXX usually omits it in such cases.

13 Ἐγένετο with a personal subject is not Greek (Lagrange, 8; cf. John 1:6); the expression ἐν ταῖς ἡμέραις ("in the days") is Semitic (Plummer, 7; cf. Tob 1:16; Judg 1:1; see Fitzmyer, 1.322).

14 About Zechariah, whose name means "God has remembered," and about the traditions regarding him (his death is described at the end of *Protoevangelium of James*), see J.-D. Dubois, "L'apocryphe de Zacharie et sur les traditions concernant la mort de Zacharie" (diss., Oxford, 1979).

15 The high priest was not chosen by lot, and one would not describe him as ἱερεύς τις ("a [certain] priest").

16 Ἐφημερία ("order") denotes first the day of service, then the roster of the divisions of officiating priests, and finally the group subject to this sequence (Godet, 1.71). For the history of this institution, see Str-B 2.55–68; and Fitzmyer, 1.322. Cf. 1 Chr 23:6; 24:1–18; Ezra 2:36–39; 10:18–22; Neh

12:1–7; 13:30.

17 In 1:39 Luke adds the term πόλις ("city"), because for him everything takes place in an urban setting (cf. the commentary to Luke 4:43).

18 According to Marshall (52), the etymology suggested by Godet (*Commentaire sur L'Évangile de Saint Luc* [4th ed.; 2 vols.; reprinted Neuchâtel: L.-A. Monnier, 1969] 1.98) for Elizabeth, "God is my vow," is not certain. The commentators mention expressions parallel to "daughters of Aaron": "daughters of Dan" (2 Chr 2:14; see Fitzmyer, 1.322), and "daughter of Bilgas" (*b. Sukk.* 56b; cf. Str-B 2.71). But who are these "daughters of Aaron"? This expression is more likely a stylistic attempt to intensify the sense of historical reality than a recollection of a historical fact.

19 This verse mixes Lukan idioms with those of the LXX (Num 36:13; Deut 4:40; Gen 26:5). Benoit ("Enfance," 172) speaks of a miscarried imitation of the LXX.

20 The ms. tradition varies between ἐναντίον and ἐνώπιον ("in the presence of," "facing," 1:6). According to Marshall (52), ἐναντίον was replaced by the more usual ἐνώπιον. At the end of the verse, God is called ὁ κύριος ("the Lord"), as is often the case in the NT texts that most resemble HB texts (twenty-four or twenty-five times in Luke 1–2).

21 One should notice the "rhythmic breadth of the sentence" (1:6; Alfred Loisy, *L'Évangile selon Luc* [Paris: Émile Nourry, 1924] 77): πορευόμενοι ("walking") at the beginning, ἄμεμπτοι ("blameless") at the end, and in between the adverbial elements, which surely refer to both words. "To walk, travel" in an ethical sense is commonly used in the

As with Abraham[22] and Sarah (Gen 18:11),[23] sterility[24] and old age are the reasons for their childlessness; but their faith and obedience is a guarantee of their progeny—a paradoxical situation full of tension.[25]

■ **8–10** Luke's description of the temple officiant Zechariah is that of a Jewish writer, not of a liturgical expert.[26] Completeness takes a back seat to lively narration: Luke centers his description on one of many casts of the lot[27] and remains silent about the accompanying priests.[28] On this day, Zechariah is the chief officiant. Luke knows the sequence: the cast of the lot, entrance into the holy place, the offering.[29] He knows that the offering consists of incense,[30] and that the moment of offering is dangerous, because the priest in the holy place lingers near the presence of God, which resides in the Holy of Holies.[31] Luke also knows that the nation shares this moment's experience with particular attention (v. 10),[32] and thus he can narrate it suspensefully. Jewish ritual is presented vividly: v. 6 emphasizes the

obedience demanded by God in the Law; vv. 8–10, the cultic relationship with the divinity, granted by God and brought about by sacrifice. The people stand before God, their prayer accompanying the priest's ritual activity.[33] The priesthood, like the Law, plays a mediating role.

■ **11–12** In the midst of the performance of these ritual obligations, God takes the initiative and signals it with a revelation by an angel. To make this epiphany on the threshold of the new age comprehensible, Luke employs a common Jewish topos, the proclamation of an extraordinary birth to a childless couple,[34] the model for which is the theophany to Abraham. The proclamation of such births was, in the Hebrew Bible, always an expression of initiative on the part of the saving God; in each case the saving event happened for the good not only of individuals but of the whole nation.

Luke does not find it necessary to describe all the details: is the "hour of the incense offering" the morn-

HB, Acts, and Epistles (less in the Gospels). "Blameless" is an ideal of piety (Gen 17:1).

22 The classical καθότι ("because,"1:7) is a peculiarity of Luke; see Godet (1.72–73), who also examines the syntax of the concluding sentence in v. 7.

23 The ἐν (Luke1:7), missing in the LXX (Gen 18:11), does not mean that Luke is depending on a Hebrew text (in agreement with Benoit, "Enfance," 173); cf. Luke 1:5.

24 On barrenness in the HB, cf. Gen 17:17; Judg 13:2; 1 Sam (LXX 1 Kgdms) 1:2, 5, 11; 2:5; see Walter Grundmann, *Das Evangelium nach Lukas* (2d ed.; ThHKNT 3; Berlin: Evangelische Verlagsanstalt, 1961) 49. On fertility see Pss 127:3; 128:3.

25 Cf. John 9:3 (Marshall, 53).

26 Josephus also tries to make the Jewish priesthood and ritual comprehensible to his Gentile readers (e.g., *Bell.* 5.5.7 §§228–37).

27 Λαγχάνω ("to obtain by lot"), which is usually followed by an accusative or an infinitive, is here accompanied by an articular infinitive. Cf. BDF §400.3.

28 Cf. nn. 2 and 16 above.

29 The syntax of this verse (1:9) is, according to Loisy (79), not quite so strange or Semitic as many commentators assume. Κατὰ τὸ ἔθος ("according to the custom") can refer to what precedes or follows, but most likely, following Luke's preference, it refers to both.

30 See Billerbeck, "Tempelgottesdienst," on this bloodless offering (incense, etc.).

31 Ναός ("temple") denotes the building itself, ἱερόν

the entire sacred space. On the temple in Luke, see Marshall, 54; and Michael Bachmann, *Jerusalem und der Tempel: Die geographisch-theologischen Elemente in der lukanischen Sicht des jüdischen Kultzentrums* (BWANT 109; Stuttgart: Kohlhammer, 1980).

32 In moments decisive for salvation history, and for the individuals' lives, Luke often has them take up an attitude of prayer, as the people do here (1:10); see Louis Monloubou, *La prière selon Saint Luc: Recherche d'une structure* (LD 89; Paris: Cerf, 1976) 61. Worth noting is the strange or contrived formulation πᾶν τὸ πλῆθος ἦν τοῦ λαοῦ προσευχόμενον ("the whole multitude of the people was praying").

33 As in John 18:28–19:16, Luke plays on the categories "inside" and "outside."

34 Cf. Gen 18; further, Judg 13 and 1 Sam (LXX 1 Kgdms) 1. An angelophany (cf., e.g., Dan 8:15–18; 9:20–22; 10:9–11) is linked with the annunciation of a miraculous birth (cf., e.g., Judg 13:3; Luke 1:26–39). Cf. n. 37 below. For appearances by the altar of incense, cf. Josephus *Ant.* 13.10.3 §§282–83; and Grundmann, 50.

ing or evening offering?[35] Is "the right side of the altar of incense" seen from Zechariah's perspective or that of the divine presence?[36] The important point for Luke is that an angel of God appears.[37] There is no article; this angel has a name (v. 19), which differentiates him from others. But Luke does not expand on angelology. Ὤφϑη, found in the LXX and New Testament (esp. in the Easter appearances), has an active and intransitive meaning; "appeared" is the correct translation.[38] The angel is "standing" there,[39] as God's envoy.

The narrative sequence is suited to the topos, and conforms to the given models even in vocabulary. Zechariah is shaken by the appearance; "fear fell upon him." But the angel calms him with his words.[40]

■ **13–14** "For" (διότι) makes sense only if one presupposes that, "Do not be afraid, Zechariah, but believe, *for* . . . ," has been shortened. "Your prayer" (ἡ δέησίς σου) in the context of the narrative, can only mean Zechariah's personal intercession. The old man's barren wife—for this is how the biblical language characterizes the miracle—will give birth.[41] But this answer to personal

prayer converges with the "prayer" (προσευχή) of the nation, which, according to Luke, awaits redemption (1:68). For, with John the Baptist, the new age dawns for the entire nation (vv. 16–17).[42]

God not only gives the child, but also determines his name.[43] Its etymology, "YHWH is merciful," was probably still perceived during the first stage of the story's transmission (for other symbolic and prophetic names given to children, see Hos 1:2–9). For Luke, this no longer plays a role (because he did not understand, or did not want to?). Rabbinic literature[44] attests that biblical heroes received their names before birth.[45]

Verse 14 mentions the expected happiness of the father and the nation (both in future tense). The relatedness of the individual and the nation, and the election of an individual for the salvation of the community, is seldom so clearly expressed.[46] Happiness and rejoicing are not secular, but feelings of the believers while in God's presence.[47] "Many" (πολλοί) perhaps has an ecclesiological tone, as it does in the saying about "the ransom for many" (Mark 10:45),[48] and in the Qumran

---

35 The morning offering is suggested by the casting of lots and the announcement of a birth; the evening, by the parallel passage in Dan 9:21. See Godet, 1.73–74; Loisy, 79; and Marshall, 54.

36 The perspective must be God's; the angel is standing on the right side of the altar, i.e., left of the altar (from Zechariah's standpoint, who stands facing him). For divine appearances in the temple, cf. 1 Sam (LXX 1 Kgdms) 3; Isa 6; Josephus *Ant.* 13.10.3 §§282–83; see Marshall, 55.

37 Here I agree with Godet, 1.74–75. With the exception of the choir of angels (Luke 2:13–14), in Luke it is always the appearance of a single angel, sometimes called "an angel of the Lord" (Acts 5:19; 8:26; 12:7). Here the angel has a name, which distinguishes him from the others, whose existence is tacitly assumed. But Luke does not further develop his conception of angels. The angel is an instrument of God, through which, in his grace, he makes contact with his people, i.e., with the most attentive of his servants (excepting the religious leaders). See Godet, 1.75; Grundmann, 50; and Marshall, 55; see Ingo Broer, "ἄγγελος, κτλ.," *EDNT* 1 (1990) 13–16 (for bibliography also).

38 See G. B. Caird, "The Glory of God in the Fourth Gospel: An Exercise in Biblical Semantics," *NTS* 15 (1968–69) 265–77.

39 On the standing position (ἑστώς), which is not that of a judge, who sits, but of an envoy, defender, witness, or victor, all of whom come and take their

stand, cf. Acts 7:55 and Rev 5:6. See C. Kingsley Barrett, "Stephen and the Son of Man," in W. Eltester and F. H. Kettler, eds., *Apophoreta: Festschrift Ernst Haenchen* (BZNW 30; Berlin: Töpelmann, 1964) 32–38.

40 Cf. Luke 1:30; 2:10; Acts 18:9. Jesus uses the same expression in Luke 5:10 and 8:50. In the HB cf. Gen 15:1; Dan 10:12.

41 Γεννάω ("to beget, bring forth") instead of τίκτω ("to bring forth, bear"), though not unknown in the current linguistic usage, irritates one's stylistic sense; see Godet, 1.77.

42 Luke seems to presuppose that Zechariah has already prayed to God for a son before our account begins.

43 Καλέω τὸ ὄνομα ("call his name") is Semitic (cf. Gen 16:11). The father usually gives the child its name.

44 Plummer, 13.

45 The σοι ("[will bear] you [a son]") in v. 13 is lacking in some mss.

46 According to Godet (1.77), there will be nationwide rejoicing.

47 The subject of ἔσται ("will be") is χαρά ("joy"); see Lagrange, 66.

48 Cf. Luke 2:10 and Joachim Jeremias, "Das Lösegeld für viele (Mk 10,45)," *Judaica* 3 (1947) 249–64. According to Godet (*Commentaire*, 1.105), however, it means "the best." See Marshall, 57.

literature. The object of the rejoicing is not just any birth,[49] but that of a prophet.

■ **15** The prediction of the happiness and rejoicing at the birth is followed by predictions about the child's future (vv. 15–17). He will become great. Is the use of "great" ($\mu\acute{\epsilon}\gamma\alpha\varsigma$) as a title of divine sovereignty, of Hellenistic, Samaritan, or Jewish origin? And how does the term relate to the same designation of Jesus (1:32)? I understand the word in a Jewish sense. John will become great before the Lord,[50] that is, a great prophet. Similarly, Elijah is called this in Sir 48:22, and John in Luke 7:28, under the influence of the Elijah tradition.[51] Luke probably retained this word from the legend.[52] There, it had an eschatological significance: John, like Elijah, was the ultimate prophet, as one can also deduce from v. 17. In the angel's message to Mary, by contrast, Luke emphasizes with Christian exactness that Jesus, not John, is "great," in the absolute sense that, in the LXX, is the privilege of God alone. Nimrod (Gen 10:9) and Elijah (Sir 48:22) are only "great *before God*."[53]

The words about abstinence from wine are closer to Lev 10:9 than to Num 6:3; thus they are more reminiscent of the regulations for priests (and their children!) preparing for service than they are of the life of a Nazirite. The ban on haircutting does not appear in this passage; conversely, the account of Samson does not include the prohibition of alcohol.[54] Abstinence should

accordingly prepare and accompany effective service to God for the deliverance of the nation.

In tradition the eschatological figure of the prophet had perhaps been assimilated to the priestly Messiah; if *Testament of Levi* 17 and 18 are not completely Christian interpolations, various points of correspondence exist.[55] The priest of the first year of Jubilee "will be great" ($\epsilon\dot{\iota}\varsigma$ $\dot{\iota}\epsilon\rho\omega\sigma\acute{\nu}\nu\eta\nu$ $\mu\acute{\epsilon}\gamma\alpha\varsigma$ $\check{\epsilon}\sigma\tau\alpha\iota$, *T. Levi* 17.2); and the messianic priest of the last (eighth?) will receive the "spirit" ($\pi\nu\epsilon\hat{\upsilon}\mu\alpha$) of intelligence and of sanctification from above (*T. Levi* 18.7). This could explain why John's father had to be a priest. Along with the Qumran sect, the Baptist's movement would then be a reform movement of eschatological character, in which prophecy and the priesthood had moved closer together. Luke has restricted this as much as possible and has limited John to his prophetic function, though he is indeed placed at the beginning of the last phase of salvation history. The notion of the spirit's residence in the Baptist was probably traditional, but its expression is typically Lukan.[56] Luke conceives of it as a prophetic gift, as in the case of Elizabeth, Zechariah, and Simon.[57] Yet there is some tension, because, according to Luke,[58] only Jesus receives the eschatological gift of the Spirit, and his disciples will not partake of it until after the ascension.[59] The standing

---

49   The ms. tradition varies between $\gamma\acute{\epsilon}\nu\epsilon\sigma\iota\varsigma$ ("genesis, origin, birth") and $\gamma\acute{\epsilon}\nu\nu\eta\sigma\iota\varsigma$ ("conception, birth").

50   The text is not stable here; one can read $\dot{\epsilon}\nu\acute{\omega}\pi\iota\upsilon\nu$ $\kappa\upsilon\rho\acute{\iota}\upsilon\upsilon$, $\dot{\epsilon}\nu\acute{\omega}\pi\iota\upsilon\nu$ $\tau\upsilon\hat{\upsilon}$ $\kappa\upsilon\rho\acute{\iota}\upsilon\upsilon$, or $\dot{\epsilon}\nu\acute{\omega}\pi\iota\upsilon\nu$ $\tau\upsilon\hat{\upsilon}$ $\vartheta\epsilon\upsilon\hat{\upsilon}$ ("before the Lord" vs. "before God"). Because $\dot{\upsilon}$ $\kappa\acute{\upsilon}\rho\iota\upsilon\varsigma$ means "God" here, the variant readings do not alter the sense. According to Plummer (14), the prepositional use of $\dot{\epsilon}\nu\acute{\omega}\pi\iota\upsilon\nu$ is a Semitism.

51   Cf. below, commentary on 7:28.

52   See Dibelius (*Jungfrauensohn*, 4): "It is not conceivable that a Christian writing freely from his own inspiration would have described both the savior and his precursor with the same adjective. One perceives here nothing of inferiority, and thus no Christian perspective."

53   Agreeing with René Laurentin, *Structure et théologie de Luc I–II* (EtB; Paris: Librairie Lecoffre, Gabalda, 1957) 36–7. On $\mu\acute{\epsilon}\gamma\alpha\varsigma$ see Fitzmyer, 1.325; Otto Betz, "$M\acute{\epsilon}\gamma\alpha\varsigma$, $\kappa\tau\lambda$.," *EDNT* 2 (1991) 399–401; Ferdinand Hahn, *The Titles of Jesus in Christology: Their History in Early Christianity* (trans. H. Knight and G. Ogg; London: Lutterworth, 1969) 365 n. 111, 379. *T. Levi* 17.2 is a remarkable parallel (and a

Christian interpolation?). Cf. Luke 7:28.

54   The Israelites' fear of anything having to do with the vine comes clearly to expression in Num 6. According to Loisy (80–81), $\sigma\acute{\iota}\kappa\epsilon\rho\alpha$ ("strong drink") corresponds to the Hebrew שֵׁכָר, i.e., a fermented drink produced from grain or fruit. Cf. Judg 13:4, 7, 14.

55   On this text see A. Dupont-Sommer, "Le Testament de Lévi (XVII–XVIII) et la secte juive de l'Alliance," *Sem* 4 (1952) 33–53.

56   In the NT one finds $\pi\acute{\iota}\mu\pi\lambda\eta\mu\iota$ ("to fill") almost exclusively in Luke. He indicates with this word the presence of the Holy Spirit. See Benoit, "Enfance," 180 n. 1.

57   Luke 1:41, 67; 2:25–26.

58   Luke 1:35; 3:2; 4:18–21.

59   Luke 3:16; 24:49; Acts 1:4, 5, 8; 2:4. See Bovon, *Theologian*, 203–4.

expression, "even from his mother's womb," has its roots in the language of prophetic calling,[60] and had revived in the first century (see Gal 1:15). "Even" (ἔτι) clarifies "from" (ἐκ): John will receive the Spirit even before birth. Instead of the effects of alcohol, used in some of the pagan mantic practices, there is the welcome influence of the Spirit; Eph 5:18 expresses the same antithesis and emphasizes wisdom as the fruit of this sort of inspiration.

■ **16** The Baptist's mission is, first of all, not apocalyptic but prophetic; John shall lead the people back to their God.[61] "Many" first means, exclusively, "not all" (the notion of the hardening of hearts is implied), and, inclusively, "the multitude" of the nation. Typical of this period in Israelite theology is the concept of individual accountability. The expression lays the groundwork for the Baptist's instruction, which is directed to individuals. "Their God" does not mean that Luke is distancing himself from Jewish religion in a "Johannine" manner, but rather emphasizes the relationship between God and *his* people.

■ **17** Verse 17 explicitly mentions John's function as precursor[62] and the quickly approaching fulfillment of Mal 4:5 (MT/LXX 3:23). He is consequently the precursor of God. Here we come across traditional materials; for Luke, writing on his own, would have associated this function with the coming of the Messiah. "In the spirit and power of Elijah" is a curious expression;[63] is John Elijah *redivivus* ("renewed") or not? Yes, the tradition affirmed; but the redaction limits this statement; our text is the result of this compromise. It is well known how alive was the expectation of a last prophet in the reform movements of contemporaneous Judaism, whether it was a prophet such as Moses (Deut 18:15, 18), or a trailblazer (Isa 40:3), or a precursor and new Elijah (Mal 3:1; 4:5, 6 [MT/LXX 3:23–24]).[64]

In Malachi 3–4 the contrast between the sinful condition of the nation and its expected repentance is heightened. The prophet's message is the last chance for the nation in view of the coming day of the Lord with its consuming judgment (Mal 4:1, 5 [MT/LXX 3:19, 23]). Luke only alludes to it here by saying that the people will be prepared for something by John. The Baptist's future activity thus receives an eschatological apocalyptic significance. The Baptist tradition behind these verses reflects the prophetic consciousness of the historical Baptist (Luke 3:7–9); it is not merely Luke projecting the Synoptic portrayal of John back into the birth narrative.[65] The lack of any preliminary announcement of John's baptizing is surprising, but probably attributable to the absence of baptizing in the Hebrew Bible accounts of the prophets.

Like Jewish sages before him, Jesus refers to two commandments as a canon within a canon;[66] John also demands a twofold "turning back." The structure is the same as the two great commandments: the "turning back" first brings individuals back to God;[67] it then re-creates fellowship among these individuals. Verse 17b is a free citation of Mal 4:6 (MT/LXX 3:24), which depends on neither the LXX nor the MT (cf. Mal 3:7).

Malachi's expectation is that the fathers' hearts should first turn to their children. How does the legend, and then Luke, understand this? It is a sign of eschatological wisdom and penitence that the parents, against all expectations, should make the first step toward reconciliation. Perhaps Luke has in mind the deuteronomistic tradition of the sinful *fathers*[68] and the *younger* Christian generation that has heard the final message. More important than the father-to-son direction is the theological symbolism of disrupted family relationships, for apocalyptic tradition foresees terrible family conflicts in

---

60 Cf. Jer 1:4, 5; Judg 13:5–7 (LXX). See Benoit, "Enfance," 180. Benoit remarks (180 n. 1) that being filled with the Spirit is not a HB theme.

61 On the fixed LXX expression, κύριος ὁ θεός ("the Lord God"), see Gottfried Quell, "κύριος," TDNT 3 (1965) 1059.

62 The variant προσελεύσεται ("will go to") renders no sense and is a scribal error.

63 On this see Grundmann, 51; and Fitzmyer, 1.326–27. Πνεῦμα ("spirit") and δύναμις ("power") are closely related in Luke 1:35; 4:14; 1QH 7.61.

64 On this prophet see Hahn, *Titles*, 352–406.

65 As Benoit ("Enfance," 181, 194) and Wink (*John*, 79–82) suppose.

66 See the commentary on 10:25–29 (vol. 2).

67 For ἐπιστρέφω ("to turn around"), see Bovon, *Theologian*, 271–89.

68 Cf. Luke 11:47–48; Acts 7:52. Grundmann (52) suggests the Hasidic movement; it consisted of younger people who had broken ties with the older generation, which had become guilty. Cf. *Jub.* 23:26; *1 Enoch* 90:6–7.

the last days (Luke 21:16). The tradition present here looks even further into the future and hopes for an eschatological reconciliation following a joint effort.

We know several variants of "and the disobedient to the wisdom of the righteous, to make ready for the Lord a people prepared" (Luke 1:17, καὶ ἀπειθεῖς[69] . . . λαὸν κατεσκευασμένον):

Mal 4:6 (MT 3:24): "and the hearts of the children to their fathers"

Mal 4:6 (LXX 3:23): καὶ καρδίαν ἀνθρώπου πρὸς τὸν πλησίον αὐτοῦ ("and the heart of each to one's neighbor")

Sir 48:10: καὶ καταστῆσαι φυλὰς Ἰακώβ ("and to restore the tribe of Jacob")

Sir 48:10 (Hebrew): "and to lead the tr[ibes of Israe]l to understanding."[70]

Luke 1:17b is probably meant to bring together the fathers' inclination toward the sons (in line with Mal 4:6 [MT/LXX 3:23]) with an ecclesiological addition (in line with Sir 48:10).[71] It is important that Mal 4:6 represents the last message of the prophetic books; both the tradition and the redaction intend to create a close tie between the new covenant and the old by means of typology.[72]

By this time, the old ethic of *works* is no longer sufficient; repentance is a matter of the *heart*, and obedience begins with "wisdom" (φρόνησις). The righteous are

people who wait on God like the believers in the birth narrative.

The nation is not prepared for visitation by its God; it is now the responsibility and mission of the last prophet to prepare[73] its twofold repentance (vv. 16, 17). Its preparation (κατασκευάζω, "to prepare," used of a ship, city, or army)[74] is nothing other than repentance and righteousness. The continuity of the nation thus exists in God's continuing solicitude, although the people—beginning with the fathers—have disrupted their relationship with God and with each other again and again.[75]

■ **18** Nothing is said of Zechariah's state of mind in v. 18; only his uncertainty[76] and demand for a sign[77] are mentioned. In the Hebrew Bible such a sign is often given by an angel, but the demand for one occasionally betrays weak faith.[78]

In human terms Zechariah has good reason for skepticism; his own condition[79] and that of his wife recall v. 7 (with Luke's practiced care to avoid repetition). Zechariah politely and tactfully avoids mention of his wife's barrenness. From the angel's perspective, the situation looks completely different. Offended, he justifies his mission, which he has carried out in correct and dignified fashion. Gabriel—he now introduces himself—finds such unbelief truly unbelievable. The muteness has more than one significance; it is both a punishment and a sign that reverses Zechariah's unbelief.

---

69   Who are these ἀπειθεῖς? The young or the old? One can read the two middle phrases in v. 17 as either a parallel (ἀπειθεῖς = fathers) or a chiastic (ἀπειθεῖς = children) construction.

70   See Grundmann, 52; and Paul Winter, "Lukanische Miszellen: I: Lk 1,17 und Ben Sira 48,10 Heb.; II a) Lc 1,68.72.73 und die Kriegsrolle; b) Lc 1,48–52 und Judiths Jubellied," *ZNW* 49 (1958) 65–67, esp. 65.

71   Winter ("Miszellen," 65–66) remarks that the Hebrew text of Sirach also speaks of a return to understanding, and cites this as evidence of a Semitic source for Luke 1:17.

72   Marshall (60) mentions four different ways of interpreting v. 17.

73   On ἑτοιμάζω see Gerhard Lohfink, *Die Sammlung Israels: Eine Untersuchung zur lukanischen Ekklesiologie* (SANT 39; Munich: Kösel, 1975) 22–23, and the commentary below on Luke 2:31.

74   On κατασκευάζω ("prepare"), see Horst Balz,

"κατασκευάζω, κτλ.," *EDNT* 2 (1991) 268.

75   Lohfink, *Sammlung*. On λαός ("people," "nation") in Luke, see Hubert Frankemölle, "λαός, κτλ.," *EDNT* 2 (1991) 341–42.

76   On knowledge in Luke, see Bovon, *Lukas*, 112–14, and the commentary above on 1:4

77   On the concept σημεῖον ("sign") in Luke, see the commentary below on 2:12.

78   Cf. Gen 15:8; Exod 4:3, 6 (two unrequested signs); Judg 6:36–40 (Gideon realizes that he is asking too much); 1 Sam (LXX 1 Kgdms) 10:2–9; 2 Kgs (LXX 4 Kgdms) 20:8–11; Isa 7:11; 1 Cor 1:22.

79   The exegetes do not agree whether priests retired at a certain age. Levites may not exercise their office after fifty years of age; cf. Num 8:25. See Godet, *Commentaire*, 1.112.

■ **19** The angel's speech is strongly Lukan in character. Luke is well read and may recall Tob 12:15 or similar texts (perhaps apocalyptic texts, too).[80] Gabriel is attested and valued since Daniel,[81] as is his position before God[82] (although contemporaneous Judaism knew of seven such angels). Mission and proclamation are essential to angelic beings. Since this is good news, Luke uses the verb "to bring good news" (εὐαγγελίζομαι), although in Isaiah's sense and not yet the Christian sense.[83]

■ **20** In v. 20 the angel begins to speak about the near future with the words "but now." The positive "be mute" (σιωπῶν) and the negative "unable to speak" (μὴ δυνάμενος λαλῆσαι) are rhetorical redundancies, although the former concept perhaps implies deafness as well (cf. 1:62).[84]

Retribution is clearly expressed with "because" (ἀνθ᾽ ὧν). Only now is judgment rendered on Zechariah; according to Luke, the priest did not *believe*.[85] The speech of the angel consists of "words"[86] that, as prophecy, will be fulfilled.[87] All of this is Lukan, as is the conviction that God's plan possesses not only chronology but also "kairology."[88]

■ **21** Verse 21[89] describes more than the mere impatience of the people.[90] Every word should be accorded theological significance: the people chosen by God await the deliverance of Israel and are amazed at God's delay. I would also caution, however, against overinterpretation. What confronts us is the not-uncommon tension between the liturgical rite and the liturgical event. The Mishnah mentions the nation's anxiety if the high priest stays too long in the holy of holies on the Day of Atonement.[91] It is dangerous to be allowed to enjoy God's presence too closely and too long.

■ **22** Finally, the priest comes out. Luke neglects to mention that Zechariah was accompanied by other priests as he exited,[92] which, though historically imprecise, is narratively successful. The people notice the priest's muteness, since he should have now bestowed the blessing. It is logical for them to conclude that something numinous has happened in the temple (note the repetition of "in the temple" [ἐν τῷ ναῷ] in vv. 21, 22); to maintain the narrative tension, Luke interprets this immediately[93] with the clause "that he had seen a vision[94] in the temple."

---

80 See Loisy, 82.

81 On Gabriel cf. first of all Daniel (8:16; 9:21). Gabriel is the third of the seven angels who stand before God's presence. Cf. *1 Enoch* 40:9; Rev 4:5. See Grundmann, 52; and Fitzmyer, 1.327–28.

82 Cf. 1 Kgs (LXX 3 Kgdms) 10:8 (although not said of an angel).

83 Εὐαγγελίζομαι is attested about twenty times in the LXX; see, e.g., Isa 52:7.

84 Κωφός in v. 22 can mean either "deaf" or "mute" (cf. Luke 1:62). For Godet (1.84) μὴ δυνάμενος λαλῆσαι states the cause and σιωπῶν indicates the result. Cases of muteness in the HB are Ezek 3:26 (muteness as a sign) and 2 Macc 3:29 (muteness as a punishment). Cf. Dan 10:15–17.

85 On πίστις ("faith, belief") in Luke see the commentary below on 7:9. The Gospel of John will meditate on the transition from a faith based on signs to a faith without signs (John 20:29). Luke 1:20 is already headed in this direction; see Grundmann, 53.

86 On λόγοι ("words") cf. Luke 1:4. Οἵτινες instead of the simple relative οἵ is not only used in colloquial speech (as the NT grammarians suppose), but also in literature (with the exception of the Atticists). See L. Rydbeck, *Fachprosa, vermeintliche Volkssprache und Neues Testament: Zur Beurteilung der sprachlichen*

Niveauunterschiede im nachklassischen Griechisch (Acta Universitatis Upsaliensis: Studia Graeca Upsaliensia 5; Stockholm: Almqvist and Wicksell, 1967) 98–118.

87 On πληρόω ("to fill, fulfill, make full") in Luke, see Hans Hübner, "πληρόω, κτλ.," *EDNT* 3 (1993) 108–9.

88 On καιρός ("the proper time") and its meaning in salvation history, cf. Luke 12:56; 18:30; 19:44; 21:8, 24; Acts 1:7; 3:20; 17:26. See Fitzmyer, 1.328.

89 Nestle-Aland prefers the reading ἐν τῷ χρονίζειν ἐν τῷ ναῷ αὐτόν, but goes too far here with the principle of the *lectio difficilior*; ἐν τῷ χρονίζειν αὐτὸν ἐν τῷ ναῷ ("at his delay in the temple") is better in attestation and style.

90 The people are surely waiting for the Aaronic blessing (Num 6:24–26), which was given "from the top of the cornice which surrounded the altar of burnt offering in the temple forecourt" (Godet, *Commentaire*, 1.115). According to Loisy (83), five priests participated in this.

91 *m. Yoma* 5.1.

92 For the details see Billerbeck, "Tempelgottesdienst."

93 "Luke does not tell us how the crowd could have been so perceptive; but to ask how is to miss the point of his story" (Fitzmyer, 1.329).

94 On ὀπτασία ("vision") in Luke, see Otto Betz, "Die Vision des Paulus im Tempel von Jerusalem—Apg

Because Zechariah can tell nothing, the story actually does not end at all; instead of a conclusion, the readers encounter a description (v. 22b) that leaves them waiting for a continuation.[95]

■ **23** The period of service[96] lasted a week.[97] Then the priest would normally return home; v. 39 presupposes, as in this passage, that Zechariah did not live in Jerusalem, and speaks of a little town in the midst of the hill country (of Judah).

■ **24** After the time of his service, Zechariah remains at his place of residence. Luke leaves this miracle within the bounds of natural marital relations, differently than he does with the conception of Jesus.[98]

Why does Elizabeth hide[99] for five months? Perhaps she had stayed home before this because of her disgrace (her barrenness) and now lingers there until people can see that she is pregnant. But the number of months, as stated above,[100] also connects her story to the traditions about Mary. Mary should be the first to marvel at Elizabeth's pregnancy, significant as it is in salvation history.

■ **25** Ὅτι in v. 25 has the value of a colon.[101] It stands before Elizabeth's short Magnificat, which possesses a biblical and soteriological tone. In Luke, God's activity is connected either with the creation or with any type of redemption.[102] Childlessness was, in that time, the fault of the woman; for that reason the text reads "for me," not "for us." The relative clause ("when he looked favorably on me . . .") makes parallelism possible but is redundant, since it only explains the main clause.[103] In the perfect formulation "[the Lord] has done" ($\pi\epsilon\pi o\acute{\iota}\eta\kappa\epsilon\nu$), the result is central for *Elizabeth*; in the aorist "he looked favorably on [me]" ($\dot{\epsilon}\pi\epsilon\hat{\iota}\delta\epsilon\nu$), *God's* action alone is important (his saving glance; $\dot{\epsilon}\pi\acute{\iota}$, "upon," means here "for the benefit of").[104] "To take away" ($\dot{\alpha}\phi\epsilon\lambda\epsilon\hat{\iota}\nu$,[105] e.g., for forgiveness, Heb 10:4) shows that Elizabeth is speaking biblically and imitating Rachel at the birth of Joseph: "God has taken away my disgrace" ($\dot{\alpha}\phi\epsilon\hat{\iota}\lambda\epsilon\nu$ ὁ θεός μου τὸ ὄνειδος, Gen 30:23 LXX).[106]

Childlessness was felt to be a humiliation[107] in a society in which motherhood was the woman's raison d'être (e.g., the stories of Leah and Rachel); deliverance by God was perceived as a burden "taken away." Elizabeth is speaking both biblically and poetically, in two rhythmically constructed members. The lack of articles (κύριος, ὄνειδος, "Lord," "disgrace") confirms the poetic diction.[108]

22,17–21—als Beitrag zur Deutung des Damaskuserlebnisses," in O. Boecher and K. Haacker, eds., *Verborum Veritas: Festschrift Gustav Stählin* (Wuppertal: Brockhaus, 1970) 113–23.

95 Διανεύω and κατανεύω (Luke 5:7) indicate signals given with the head.

96 Λειτουργία ("service") appears only here in Luke; at Heb 9:21 it indicates, as here, the temple service (cf. the verb at Heb 10:11). The same term occurs in the LXX and Josephus. See Loisy, 84; Marshall, 61; Horst Balz, "λειτουργία, κτλ.," *EDNT* 2 (1991) 347–49.

97 In contrast to πληρόω (cf. n. 87 above), πίμπλημι (cf. n. 56 above) does not include the idea of the fulfillment of Scripture. This verb, frequent in Luke, can be associated with the category of time in Luke 1–2, in contrast to the rest of this Gospel. See Benoit, "Enfance," 175.

98 Συλλαμβάνω ("to become pregnant") describes the conception of a child in secular Greek and in the LXX, e.g., Gen 21:2.

99 Περικρύβω is a very rare neologism derived from the second aorist of the verb περικρύπτω (περιεκρύβην), itself rather rare and recent. It occurs neither in the LXX nor in Josephus. It means "to hide oneself on all sides," i.e., "to hide oneself carefully." Cf. BDF §73.

100 See above, Analysis of 1:5–2:52.

101 On this ὅτι see Paul Winter, "Ὅτι recitativum in Lk I 25, 61, II 23," *HTR* (1955) 213–16. See also Fitzmyer, 1.329.

102 On the "activity" of God in Luke, see Gerhard Lohfink, *The Work of God Goes On* (trans. L. M. Maloney; The Bible for Christian Life; Philadelphia: Fortress Press, 1987) 17–51.

103 Cf. Luke 1:49, 51; and Isa 48:3, 6, 11, 14 (LXX).

104 Ἐφοράω ("to look upon") occurs variously in the LXX to describe God's eye, which nothing eludes (Zech 9:1; cf. Ezek 8:12; 9:9) and which takes note of the lowly (Ps 138[LXX 137]:6).

105 Ἀφαιρέω: cf. BAGD *s.v.*

106 Ἐπεῖδεν ἀφελεῖν ("he looked on [me], to take away") is also reminiscent of Gen 30:22 (LXX): Ἐμνήσθη δὲ ὁ θεὸς τῆς Ῥαχήλ, καὶ ἐπήκουσεν αὐτῆς ὁ θεός ("Then God remembered Rachel and God listened to her").

107 On ὄνειδος – ὀνειδίζω ("reproach, to reproach"), cf. 1 Sam (LXX 1 Kgdms) 17:36 and Isa 25:8. See also Ceslas Spicq, *Theological Lexicon of the New Testament* (trans. and ed. J. D. Ernest; 3 vols.; Peabody, Mass.: Hendrickson, 1994) 2.585–87.

108 Godet (1.85) mentions various ways of interpreting 1:24–25. Loisy (84–85) looks at this text from the perspective of redaction history: Zechariah says

Conclusion

Within Judaism, within cultic ritual, something happens that is more than just prophecy: it is a new beginning from God. This God is the God of fulfillment, of days of old, the God of fathers (Abraham) and mothers (Hannah); he has already promised and granted many children. But "in these days" he has remained silent and inactive. Now he begins again for one last time. He hears the prayer of an individual and, through him—because he is a priest—the prayer of the nation. He takes away the disgrace of an individual and, through her, the disgrace of Israel. Through this example, the possibility of deliverance from the final wrath is offered; but the nation, every Israelite, must first accept this gift and appropriate it personally.

What God gives is not yet the fulfillment of salvation, but rather the word of salvation. John will preach repentance: a turning back to God and to one's neighbor. Thus will he prepare Israel for the last "visitation."

---

nothing; Elizabeth hides; God alone prepares everything and will inform Mary of his purpose through the angel Gabriel.

The Annunciation to Mary (1:26–38)

Bibliography

Audet, "Annonce."

Bardenhewer, O., *Mariae Verkündigung: Ein Kommentar zu Lukas 1, 26–38* (Freiburg im Breisgau: Herder, 1905).

Bauer, Johannes B., "Philologische Bemerkungen zu Lk 1,34," *Bib* 45 (1964) 535–40.

Bellet, Pauli, "Estructura i forma: Anunciació de naixement i forma d'elecció profètica (Lc 1,26–38)," *Revista Catalana de Theologiá* 7 (1982) 91–130.

Benoit, "Annonciation."

Berger, Christoph, "Die literarische Eigenart von Lk 1,5–38: Zum Sprachstil der Evangelien" (diss., Jena, 1972), see *ThLZ* 98 (1973) 153–56.

Boslooper, Thomas David, *The Virgin Birth* (Philadelphia: Westminster, 1962).

Bostock, Gerald, "Virgin Birth or Human Conception," *ExpTim* 98 (1987) 331–33.

Brock, Sebastian, "Passover, Annunciation and Epiclesis: Some Remarks on the Term *Aggen* in the Syriac Versions of Lk. 1:35," *NovT* 24 (1982) 222–33.

Brown, *Birth*, 286–341.

idem, "Luke's Description of the Virginal Conception," *TS* 35 (1974) 360–62.

idem, *Mary*, 105–34.

Brunner-Traut, "Geburtsgeschichte."

Buzzeti, Carlo, "Traducendo κεχαριτωμένη (Lc 1,28)," in *Testimonium Christi: Festschrift Jacques Dupont* (Brescia: Paideia, 1985) 111–16.

Cambe, M., "La χάρις chez Saint Luc," *RB* 70 (1963) 193–207.

de la Potterie, Ignace, "*Κεχαριτωμένη* en Lc 1,28: Étude philologique," *Bib* 68 (1987) 357–82.

Delebecque, Édouard, "Sur la salutation de Gabriel à Marie (Lc 1,28)," *Bib* 65 (1984) 352–55.

Dumermuth, Fritz, "Bemerkungen zu Jesu Menschwerdung," *ThZ* 20 (1964) 52–53.

Escudero Freire, Carlos, "Alcance cristológica y traducción de Lc 1,35: Aportación al estudio de los títulos Santo e Hijo de Dios en la obra lucana," *Communio* 8 (1975) 5–77.

idem, *Devolver*, 67–171.

Espinel, J. L., "Maria como discipula responsable y fiel en el Evangelio de San Lucas," *Ciencia Tomista* 112 (1985) 197–204.

Fitzmyer, Joseph A., "The Contribution of Qumran Aramaic to the Study of the New Testament," *NTS* 20 (1973–74) 382–407, esp. 391–94, reprinted in idem, *A Wandering Aramean: Collected Aramaic Essays* (SBLMS 25; Missoula, Mont.: Scholars Press, 1979) 85–113, esp. 90–94.

Fuller, Reginald H., "A Note on Luke 1:26 and 38," in W. C. Weinrich, ed., *The New Testament Age: Festschrift Bo Reicke* (2 vols.; Macon, Ga.: Mercer University Press, 1984) 1.201–6.

George, Augustin, "La royauté de Jésus," in idem, *Études*, 257–82.

Gese, Hartmut, "Natus ex virgine," in H. W. Wolff, ed., *Probleme biblischer Theologie: Festschrift Gerhard von Rad* (Munich: Kaiser, 1971) 73–89.

Gewiess, Josef, "Die Marienfrage, Lk 1, 34," *BZ* n.s. 5 (1961) 221–54.

Harnack, Adolf von, "Zu Lc I, 34.35," *ZNW* 2 (1901) 53–57.

Hubbard, "Commissioning."

Landry, David, "Narrative Logic in the Annunciation to Mary (Luke 1:26–38)," *JBL* 114 (1995) 65–79.

Lattke, "Jungfrauengeburt."

Laurentin, *Truth*, 143–54.

La Verdiere, E., "Be it done to me," *Emm* 90 (1984) 184–90, 196.

idem, "The Virgin's Name Was Mary," *Emm* 92 (1986) 185–89.

Legrand, *Annonce*.

idem, "Arrière-plan."

Lemmo, N., "Maria, 'Figlia di Sion,' a partire da Lc 1,26–38: Bilancio esegetico dal 1939 al 1982," *Mar* 45 (1983) 175–258.

Luke, K., "The Koranic Recension of Luke 1:34," *ITS* 22 (1985) 380–99.

Lyonnet, "Annonciation."

idem, "Χαῖρε, κεχαριτωμένη," *Bib* 20 (1939) 131–41.

McHugh, *Mother*, 37–67.

Meynet, Roland, "Dieu donne son Nom à Jésus: Analyse rhétorique de Lc 1,26–56 et de 1 Sam 2,1–10," *Bib* 66 (1985) 39–72.

Miyoshi, Michi, "Zur Entstehung des Glaubens an die jungfrauliche Geburt Jesu in Mt 1 und Lk 1," *AJBI* 10 (1984) 33–62.

Muñoz Iglesias, Salvador, "El anuncio del Angel y la objeción de Maria," *EstBib* 42 (1984) 315–62.

idem, "El procedimiento literario del annuncio previo en la Biblia," *EstBib* 42 (1984) 21–70.

Norden, *Geburt*.

Orsatti, Mauro, "Verso la decodificazione di una insolita espressione: Analisi filologica di ἄνδρα οὐ γινώσκω (Lc 1,34)," *RivB* 29 (1981) 343–57.

idem, "*Κεχαριτωμένη* en Lc 1,28: Étude exégétique et théologique," *Bib* 68 (1987) 480–508.

Nourry, Émile Dominique (pseudonym P. Saintyves), *Les vierges mères et les naissances miraculeuses* (Bibliothèque de critique religeuse; Paris: Librairie Critique, 1908).

Schneider, Gerhard, "Einheit."

idem, "Jesu geistgewirkte Empfängnis (Lk 1,34f): Zur Interpretation einer christologischen Aussage," *TPQ* 119 (1971) 105–16.

Schürmann, Heinz, "Die geistgewirkte Lebensentste-hung Jesu: Eine kritische Besinnung auf den Beitrag der Exegese zur Frage," in W. Ernst and K. Feiereis, eds., *Einheit in der Vielfalt: Festschrift Hugo Aufderbeck* (EThSt 32; Leipzig: St. Benno, 1974) 156–69.

Smith, D. M., "An Exposition of Luke 1:26–38," *Int* 29 (1975) 411–17.

Stock, "Berufung."

Strobel, "Gruss."

Talbert, Charles H., "Luke 1:26–31," *Int* 39 (1985) 288–91.

Topping, E. C., "The Annunciation in Byzantine Hymns," *Mar* 47 (1985) 443–69.

Vallauri, Emiliano, "L'annunciazione in Luca e la verginità di Maria: Una rassegna esegetica," *Laurentianum* 28 (1987) 286–327.

Verweyen, Hansjürgen, "Mariologie als Befreiung: Lk 1,26–45.56 im Kontext," *ZKTh* 105 (1983) 168–83.

Vicent, Antonio, "La presunta sustantivación τὸ γεννώμενον en Lc 11,35b [*sic;* read 1:35b]," *EstBib* 33 (1974) 265–73.

Vogels, Heinrich, "Zur Textgeschichte von Lc 1,34ff," *ZNW* 43 (1950–51) 256–60.

Vorster, W. S., "The Annunciation of the Birth of Jesus in the Protoevangelium of James," in J. H. Petzer and P. J. Hartin, eds., *A South African Perspective on the New Testament: Festschrift Bruce M. Metzger* (Leiden: Brill, 1986) 33–53.

Voss, G., *Die Christologie der lukanischen Schriften in Grundzügen* (StudNeot 2; Paris/Bruges: Desclée de Brouwer, 1965) 62–83.

Weis, Adolf, *Die Madonna Platytera: Entwurf für ein Christentum als Bildoffenbarung anhand der Geschichte eines Madonnenthemas* (ed. E. Weis; Die Blauen Bücher; Königstein: Langewiesche, 1985).

Winter, Urs, *Frau und Göttin: Exegetische und ikonographische Studien zum weiblichen Gottesbild im alten Israel und dessen Umwelt* (OBO 53; Freiburg: Universitätsverlag; Göttingen: Vandenhoeck & Ruprecht, 1983).

Zedda, Silverio, "Lc 1,35b, 'Colui che nascerà santo sarà chiamato Figlio di Dio,'" *RivB* 33 (1985) 29, 43, 165–89.

idem, "Il χαίρε di Lc 1,28 in Luce di un triplice contesto anticotestamentario," in C. C. Marcheselli, ed., *Parola e Spirito: Festschrift Settimio Cipriani* (2 vols.; Brescia: Paideia, 1982) 1.273–92.

Joseph, of the house of David, and the virgin's name was Mary. 28/ And when he came to her, he said, "Greetings, favored one, the Lord is with you." 29/ But she was much perplexed by his words, and she pondered what this greeting might mean. 30/ And the angel said to her, "Do not be afraid, Mary, for you have found favor with God. 31/ And now, you will become pregnant and bear a son, and you will call his name Jesus. 32/ He will be great, and will be called Son of the Most High, and the Lord God will give to him the throne of his ancestor David, 33/ and he will reign over the house of Jacob forever, and of his kingdom there will be no end." 34/ Mary said to the angel, "How will this happen, since I know no man?" 35/ And the angel answered and said to her, "Holy spirit will come upon you, and the power of the Most High will overshadow you; therefore the child to be born will be called holy, Son of God. 36/ And now, your relative Elizabeth in her old age has also become pregnant with a son; and this is the sixth month for her who was said to be barren. 37/ For from God, nothing is impossible." 38/ Then Mary said, "Here I am, the servant of the Lord; let it be with me according to your word." Then the angel departed from her.

Excursus: The Virgin Birth and the History of Religions

---

1. Genre of the Annunciation

The motif of the virgin birth, or, rather, of Mary's miraculous conception by the Holy Spirit, is embedded in an account the genre of which one can clearly define as that of "divine message to an individual."[1] Within this genre, it belongs to the subset, "the promise of a child,"[2] which possesses a particular structure in the Hebrew Bible:

　a. Appearance of the divine messenger

　b. Bewilderment of the person addressed

　c. Angel's message

　d. The addressed person's objection

　e. Confirmation of the message through a sign

With regard to this structure, the Lukan account displays a redundancy: v. 35 adds to the angel's message an answer to Mary's question, "How?" before the confirmatory sign (vv. 36–37), because Mary (v. 34) does not allude, as is usual, to old age or barrenness,

26 In the sixth month the angel Gabriel was sent by God to a city in Galilee called Nazareth, 27/ to a virgin engaged to a man whose name was

---

1　See Hubbard, "Commissioning," who, however, does not know of Dennis J. McCarthy's article ("An Installation Genre?" *JBL* 90 [1971] 31–41).

2　See Salvador Muñoz Iglesias, "El Evangelio de la Infancia en San Lucas y las infancias de los héroes bíblicos," *EstBib* 16 (1957) 329–82; Escudero Freire,

but to her virginity. The theme and form show a certain autonomy that transcends the genre.[3]

We thus read a *double* announcement in 1:26–38. Verses 30–33 prophesy the imminently approaching birth of the Son, and his glorious future; v. 35, his conception through the Spirit and power of God.

2. Motifs

The mother-to-be is introduced as $\pi\alpha\rho\vartheta\acute{\epsilon}\nu o\varsigma$ ("virgin," v. 27); Mary herself confirms this fact. In what follows, Mary's pregnancy and Jesus' birth are mentioned repeatedly, but never the end of Mary's virginity.

Pregnancy and birth are expressed with the usual vocabulary.[4] But after 1:35 God takes the place of the human father through the working of his spirit, so that "Son of the Most High" (v. 32) is now to be understood in the literal sense.

Thus, alongside the motif of virginity appear the motifs of God's fatherhood and the angel's promise. The description of the child's future nature and function is described in successive steps (vv. 32–33): the title is "Son," the function, "reigning"; the reign is indeed spatially limited, but temporally infinite. The title "Son" is repeated in v. 35 (connected with $\vartheta\epsilon o\hat{v}$ ["of God"] instead of $\dot{v}\psi\acute{\iota}\sigma\tau ov$ ["of the Most High," v. 32]), and the cultic $\ddot{\alpha}\gamma\iota ov$ ("holy") is added.

3. History of the Transmission of the Story

Although the paralleling of John and Jesus is, in my opinion, Luke's work, he employs the legends available to him for the birth of both the forerunner and the Messiah. Thus Luke did not conceive of the annunciation to Mary by analogy to the Zechariah pericope. But he also did not simply take it as he found it; he reworked it. Perceptible tensions within the narrative appear between vv. 35 and 36. Verses 34–35 should not, however, be considered secondary developments. It remains uncertain whether they originate with Luke. In any case, without a miracle—if the angel simply promised a child to a bride—the episode would have no raison d'être. In terms of the narrative, the mere prediction of the child's brilliant future would not have sufficed; so Mary's virginity is

indispensable within the legend. Moreover, v. 35 is not peculiarly Lukan in its language.[5] Despite this, the tension with v. 36 remains perceptible. Could v. 36 be a secondary, redactional allusion to the Baptist complex? If so, then in an earlier version, as in the Christmas story, the baby Jesus himself would have been the sign of his own future. But even with this, a dogmatic-historical development from the Davidic messianism of vv. 31–33 to the son's divine origin in v. 35 must be assumed; this development probably took place in the time before the legend's development, so that, from the start, the legend contained the virgin birth of the divine Messiah.[6]

4. Provenance of the Motifs

The provenance of the motifs is of considerable significance, because, in the rest of the New Testament, one encounters these themes only in Matt 1:18–25.[7] There, the themes are associated with Isa 7:14 (LXX); there, too, virginity and the fatherhood of God occur together.

We know the general development of christology in the early church. Shortly after Easter, Jesus was announced as the Messiah; the resurrection and ascension prove Jesus' attainment of that position. In the early community Davidic messianism was, on the one hand, universalized through the concept of the Son of Man and, on the other hand, bound up with the concept of the suffering messenger of God. Reflection soon concentrated on the "beginning" of Jesus: the christology of the Greek-speaking Christians applied the Sophia speculation of Hellenistic Judaism to the preexistent Messiah Jesus, while the christology of the Synoptic tradition projected the messiahship of Jesus—less speculatively—into the life of Jesus, first back to his baptism, then finally to his birth. The virgin birth is *at the end* of this development, as the form-critically late[8] legends in Matthew 1–2 and Luke 1–2 also attest.

Apologetic explanations tend to draw the recollections of Mary into their arguments at this point:[9] after a long silence, she finally lays open the treasure of her personal experiences. All that the earliest Synoptic traditions are able to report about Jesus' family

Devolver, 70–77; Jean-Paul Audet, "L'annonce à Marie," *RB* 63 (1956) 346–74.

3   Escudero Freire (*Devolver,* 70) even thinks that the narrative breaks the scheme of the genre.

4   Luke 1:31; 2:5–7, 11, 21, 23.

5   Despite all the arguments that Gerhard Schneider presents ("Lk 1, 34.35 als redaktionelle Einheit," *BZ* n.s. 15 [1971] 255–59, esp. 255–57).

6   After some hesitation, Fitzmyer also voices his assent to this general idea (1.338).

7   Brown (*Birth,* 518–21) points out the silence of the rest of the NT on this topic.

8   See Rudolf Bultmann, *The History of the Synoptic Tradition* (trans. J. Marsh; rev. ed.; New York: Harper & Row, 1976) 291–302; Martin Dibelius, *From Tradition to Gospel* (trans. B. L. Woolf; New York: Scribner, 1965) 123–24.

9   See, e.g., René Laurentin, "Bulletin sur la Vierge Marie," *RSPhTh* 58 (1974) 67–102, 277–328; idem,

clearly contradicts such a hypothesis (Mark 3:21, 31–35).

Of greater importance is the exegetical work of the early church. As Matt 1:18–25 proves, Isaiah 7 had been christologically interpreted in Jewish Christian circles, which probably acted as a stimulus for further reflection. The scene in Luke, too, is hard to understand without the Immanuel prophecy.[10] But this alone does not suffice as an explanation.

In works like the targums or Pseudo-Philo's *Biblical Antiquities,* postbiblical legends occur about miraculous births, such as those of Isaac or Moses.[11] The role of God was so decisive that the figure of the father was sometimes repressed.[12] In contrast, biblical marriages are sometimes spiritualized in the Hellenistic Judaism of Egypt, and the sexual vocabulary applied to the mystical union with God. In Philo it becomes clear that births like that of Isaac were regarded as virgin births; for Philo himself these are only an allegory of the ecstatic union of the soul with God.[13] This sort of exegesis was already provided for in the LXX.[14] The hope of a Davidic Messiah (Luke 1:32–33), on the other hand, suits the expectations of both the Pharisees and the Essenes.[15] The Hebrew Bible–like expressions in v. 35 are not far removed from 4Q243 (4Qps-DanAa). From Gen 6:4, Judaism knew of the possibility of the begetting of humans by angels (cf. 1QapGen 2.1), and perhaps even the begetting of the Messiah by God (1QSa 2.11–12).

Even in this, however, syncretistic influences do play a role. Norden has drawn particular attention to Egypt, the sun cult, and the Isis cult: "Helios takes over the reign on the day of the winter solstice; at this point, the birth of a boy and of a new age ensues on earth."[16] Despite all the current criticism of the history-of-religions school and the present openness to Judaism, one must hold to the realization that Judaism, even in Palestine, did not remain untouched by foreign influences. Astrology and sun symbolism had wide currency, as well as motifs such as the birth of an auspicious child. The polemic itself had led to the acceptance of foreign elements: Antiochus IV introduced a sun cult in Jerusalem, and after the Jews had purified and reopened the temple, they celebrated light[17] at the consecration festival[18] on the twenty-fifth of December. The Christian doctrine of the Messiah could not remain unaffected by these diffuse and widespread expectations of a human and divine deliverer. "The final age has come; the birth of a divine child approaches. The child is commissioned to cancel the old debt of sin and then renew humanity, for whom an age of peace and righteousness dawns. On this account, joy prevails throughout the whole world, in heaven as on earth."[19] This summary of *Eclogue* 4 of Virgil, an expression of political ideology, could just as well apply to the Lukan Christmas story.[20]

A few striking passages indicate that the ancient church was fighting against pagan solar festivals when it celebrated Christ's birth on the sixth of January or the twenty-fifth of December; sensitivity to the connotations of the birth narrative in the Gospels definitely plays a part in setting this date. In the night between the twenty-fourth and twenty-fifth of Decem-

"Bulletin sur Marie mère du seigneur," *RSPhTh* 60 (1976) 309–45, 451–500.

10 Agreeing with Gerhard Schneider, *Das Evangelium nach Lukas* (2d ed.; 2 vols.; Gütersloh/Würzburg: Mohn, 1984) 1.48–49. In contrast, Fitzmyer (1.336) rules out a dependence on Isa 7:14.

11 See Perrot, "Récits," 13–16; Gerhard Delling, "παρθένος," *TDNT* 5 (1967) 832–33.

12 One finds the same phenomenon in Virgil *Ecl.* 4.49: Pollio, the father, recedes behind Jupiter. See Hildebrecht Hommel, "Vergils 'messianisches' Gedicht," *ThViat* (Berlin) 2 (1950) 182–212, esp. 199–200 (reprinted in H. Oppermann, ed., *Wege zu Vergil: Drei Jahrzehnte Begegnungen in Dichtung und Wissenschaft* [WdF 19; Darmstadt: Wissenschaftlich Buchgesellschaft, 1963] 380–81).

13 *Cher.* 40–52; *Vit. cont.* 25; *Mig.* 33–35; *Somn.* 1.200. See Lucien Legrand, *L'annonce à Marie (Lc 1,26–38): Une apocalypse aux origines de l'Évangile* (LD 106; Paris: Cerf, 1981) 260–63.

14 Cf. the use of the word παρθένος ("virgin" or "young woman") in Isa 7:14. The LXX translator probably had a virgin birth in mind, but this cannot be claimed with absolute certainty. See Delling, "παρθένος," *TDNT* 5.832–33.

15 Legrand (*Annonce,* 262 n. 32) discusses two controversial texts: 1QSa 2.11 and *2 Enoch* 23.

16 Norden, *Geburt,* 22.

17 See Norden, *Geburt,* 141–42. Antony and Cleopatra also availed themselves of sun symbolism for the names of their children. See Adolf Weis, *Die Madonna Platytera: Entwurf für ein Christentum als Bildoffenbarung anhand der Geschichte eines Madonnenthemas* (ed. E. Weis; Die Blauen Bücher; Königstein: Langewiesche, 1985) 147.

18 According to Josephus, the festival is called τὰ φῶτα ("the lights," *Ant.* 12.7.7 §325). See Norden, *Geburt,* 26. Robert Hanhart ("Tempelweihfest," *BHH* 3 [1966] 1951) disagrees: "The connection of the festival of temple consecration with the festival of the winter solstice lacks historical basis."

19 Norden, *Geburt,* 3.

20 The history of research on the fourth *Eclogue* from Norden to 1963 is presented in Hommel, "Vergils Gedicht," 182–212 (pagination of journal article).

ber, a congregation assembled in Alexandria; as soon as the rays of the newborn sun fell on the believers, they broke forth with the cry, "The virgin has given birth, the light increases."[21] A parallel festival was celebrated in Alexandria on the night between the fifth and sixth of January for the birth of the aeon.[22] One saying claims, Ταύτῃ τῇ ὥρᾳ σήμερον ἡ κόρη ἐγέννησε τὸν Αἰῶνα ("Today, at this hour, the maiden has borne the aeon"; cf. Luke 2:11).[23] Such hopes were also bound up with the birth of the emperor Augustus in the Priene inscription.[24] The Assos inscription, which reports the accession of the emperor Gaius, describes the age that dawned with it as the era most pleasant for humanity: Ὡς ἂν τοῦ ἡδίστου ἀνθρώποις αἰῶνος νῦν ἐνεστῶτος ("as if the age most pleasant for humanity had commenced").[25] The attestation of an announcement to the young mother of the aeon has often been cited: a voice speaks to her, promising the birth of the child in the name of Helios.[26]

Conception by a divine father plays a significant role in Egyptian religion and in pharaonic ideology.[27] The sun god Amon-Re is the king's father, and the king receives the title "son." The record of an enthronement in three phases is similar to the structure of Luke 1:31–33 and several christological texts: (a) the son receives divine life; (b) he tarries with the gods; (c) he becomes a world ruler.[28] In the titulary not only sonship but also greatness is important (μέγας, "great," 1:32).[29] Further, the king is loved and selected as a son. The texts of Philo and Plutarch mentioned above, which speak of conception through the πνεῦμα ("spirit"), are surely influenced by this Egyptian theology. Theogamy, divine marriage, was thus spiritualized and, as such, made more tolerable.[30] In contrast, virginity as purity is, in Egypt, a late motif, the origin of which is to be sought in Greece.[31] The relationship of Isis and Horus, mother and son, should also be kept in mind. Horus (= Harpocrates) is "the child" (τὸ παιδίον) par excellence.[32]

Miracles also occurred at the birth of Zoroaster, Krishna, and the Buddha.[33] But one ought to remain in the Near East, particularly with the royal ideology of Egypt and Mesopotamia, which had already affected Davidic ideology in the Hebrew Bible.

---

21 ἡ παρθένος τέτοκεν, αὔξει φῶς, cited by Norden, *Geburt*, 25; and Karl Holl, "Der Ursprung des Epiphanienfestes," SPAW 1917.1, 427 n. 4 (reprinted in idem, *Gesammelte Aufsätze*, vol. 2: *Der Osten* [1928; reprinted Darmstadt: Wissenschaftliche Buchgesellschaft, 1964] 145 n. 3).

22 Details can be found in Wolfgang Fauth, "Aion (Αἰών)," in K. Ziegler and W. Sontheimer, eds., *Der kleine Pauly: Lexikon der Antike* (5 vols.; Stuttgart: Druckenmüller, 1964–75) 1.186. Fauth mentions that the festival of January 5 and 6 was perhaps dedicated to another divinity, i.e., Osiris/Adonis.

23 Epiphanius lists this saying (*Adv. haer.* 51.22.8). See Norden, *Geburt*, 28. A statement of the astrologer Hephaistion (4th century CE) should be added (cited in Norden, *Geburt*, 21 n. 1): "[He] will be sown from divine seed and will be great and worshiped with the gods, and he will be the ruler of the world, and everything will obey him."

24 The inscription is easily accessible in Gerhard Friedrich, "εὐαγγελίζομαι, κτλ.," *TDNT* 2 (1964) 724. He also translates it: "The birthday of the god was for the world the beginning of the joyful messages which have gone forth because of him."

25 See Norden, *Geburt*, 43 n. 2.

26 This text comes from the dialogue, "Discussions of religion at the court of Sassanids," mentioned in Hermann Karl Usener, *Das Weihnachtsfest* (3d ed.; Bonn: Bouvier, 1969) 32–38; and quoted in Norden, *Geburt*, 50. See in addition the text of Hippolytus (*Ref.* 5.8.45; appears as 5.3.45 in ANF) on the Naasenes (cited in Norden, *Geburt*, 51): "'This is the virgin who is pregnant and conceives and brings forth a son'—not earthly, not material, but a blessed aeon of aeons." The Greek text can be found in P. Wendland, ed., *Hippolytus Werke*, vol. 3: *Refutatio omnium haeresium* (GCS 26; Leipzig: Hinrichs, 1916).

27 Cf. Plutarch *Is. et Os.* 36; *Numa* 4; *Quaest. conv.* 8.1.717–18. See Norden, *Geburt*, 76–78.

28 See in addition the obelisk inscription cited by Norden (*Geburt*, 123), in which these three phases are clearly expressed: (1) ᾧ οἱ θεοὶ ζωῆς χρόνον ἐδωρήσαντο ("to whom the gods granted the span of life"); (2) ὃν οἱ θεοὶ ἐτίμησαν ("whom the gods honored"); (3) ὁ πάσης γῆς βασιλεύων ("who rules the whole earth"). See Adolf Erman, "Die Obeliskenübersetzung des Hermapion," SPAW 1914, 245–73, esp. 250.

29 E.g., the citation of Hephaiston in n. 23 above.

30 Cf. the instantaneous fertilization by the spirit in *Sib. Or.* 8.460–68. See Norden, *Geburt*, 81.

31 If the motif of divine fatherhood is to be located in Egypt, then, in contrast, the motif of virginity originated in Greece, according to Norden (*Geburt*, 81).

32 See Norden, *Geburt*, 73–76.

33 See Legrand, *Annonce*, 259 n. 23, where one can find bibliography. On Zoroaster see G. Lattke, "Lukas 1 und die Jungfrauengeburt," in Karl Suso Frank, et al., *Das Zeugnis der alten Kirche: Zum Thema Jungfrauengeburt* (Stuttgart: Katholisches Bibelwerk, 1970) 61–89, esp. 76.

5. Results

The following elements in Luke 1:26–38 can be better understood from this theological reflection: the virginity of the Messiah's mother (vv. 27, 34–35); the child's greatness (μέγας, "great," v. 32) and sonship (υἱός, vv. 32, 35); the title ὕψιστος for God ("the Most High," vv. 32, 35);[34] the eternal reign of the son of David (v. 33); and the child's conception by the Spirit (v. 35). An additional consideration is Mary's place of residence: Norden thinks that she is already living with Joseph, that is, that the motif of virginity is secondary to the Egyptian structure of the legend.[35] Also, the chronology works out so that Jesus is born six months after John, as the winter solstice follows the summer solstice by an interval of six months.[36] The three motifs in section 2 above thus belong together and demand a common solution.

Luke 1:26–38 and Matt 1:18–25 are not alien to New Testament christology. The conception of the Messiah through the divine Spirit is a development of Jewish messianism and earliest christology that, though subject to foreign influences, is not a foreign element.[37] The virgin birth, like the preexistence of the Messiah, is intended to attest, in a narrative manner, the divine origin of the Son. The terminology of both vv. 31–33 and 34–35 is thoroughly Jewish; but Jewish messianism—as can often be shown to be the case with minorities—expressed its identity polemically, in foreign categories. One should thus neither fear nor neglect the comparative study of religion.[38] The Lukan version is characterized, on the one hand, by the quickly developing christology, and on the other by the Hellenistic-Jewish doctrine of the Messiah, in which the effect of the Jewish congregation at Alexandria is especially perceptible. Of importance is not the nondemonstrable historicity of the events, but rather the theological significance of the acceptance and correction of the various motifs.

Analysis

Luke inherited a narrative of the annunciation to Mary. In terms of tradition history, this account has nothing to do with the legend about John into which Luke introduces it, thereby disrupting the legend. But in the redaction, Luke requires details about chronology and familial relationships (vv. 26–27, 36) to unite two independent accounts. It is strange that in the following pericopes, which deal with the fulfillment of the annunciation, Luke creates no connections to the scene of the prophecy itself (except for 2:21), and especially that he does not resume the idea of the virgin conception.[39]

The story itself unfolds according to the Hebrew Bible genre of the birth prophecy. Such legends are concerned with a certain individual who is sought out by a messenger of God; the latter determines the entire interaction and the course of the conversation.[40] The elements of the earlier legend are the following: the angel's arrival and greeting, Mary's shock, the angel's prophecy, the girl's question, an explanatory answer and sign from the angel, the faithful acceptance of the message by Mary, and the angel's disappearance. A fearful silence is the usual response to an angel's greeting (v. 29); "Do not be afraid" is the expected reassurance (v. 30). Doubt or questioning (as here) is the standard reaction to a divine message (v. 34). Appropriately for the style of the account, the angel promises a sign (v. 36) that is also an answer to the question. Mary's attitude at the conclusion (v. 38a) and the angel's departure (v. 38b) are also in typically biblical style.[41]

34 On this title see the commentary on 1:32, 35, 76 below.
35 *Geburt*, 81.
36 Norden (*Geburt*, 99–112) finally decides against a symbolic interpretation of these dates.
37 See Legrand, *Annonce*, 262 n. 32; and Fitzmyer, 1.339.
38 One can mention here the excurses of more recent commentators: Grundmann, 59–61; Josef Ernst, *Das Evangelium nach Lukas: Übersetzt und erklärt* (RNT 3; Regensburg: Pustet 1977) 75–80; Marshall, 72–77; Brown, *Birth*, 517–33; a few monographs: Émile Dominique Nourry (pseudonym P. Saintyves), *Les vierges mères et les naissances miraculeuses* (Bibliothèque de critique religieuse; Paris: Librairie Critique, 1908); Thomas David Boslooper, *The Virgin Birth* (Philadelphia: Westminster, 1962);

Legrand, *Annonce*; and some essays: Lattke, "Jungfrauengeburt"; Brunner-Traut, "Geburtsgeschichte." By and large, present-day research takes a reserved stand toward theses such as Norden's and seeks instead a Hebrew origin for the themes of God's fatherhood and the virgin birth.
39 See Dibelius, *Jungfrauensohn*, 9–10.
40 See the excursus above, "The Virgin Birth and the History of Religions"; Escudero Friere, *Devolver*, 70–77; Legrand, *Annonce*, 89–125 (with bibliography, 89 n. 1).
41 According to Lucien Legrand ("L'arrière-plan néotestamentaire de Lc 1,35," *RB* 70 [1963] 161–92), Luke supposedly adopts and adapts an apocalyptic perspective ("spirit" and "power" create the descendant).

Of course, after the prophecy of vv. 31–33, one expects a humble reaction ("Such a future for a child of *mine?*"), but not the answer that Mary gives, very surprising for a virgin approaching marriage (v. 34). Some have therefore suggested that vv. 34–35 are an addition by Luke or a later interpolator, who wanted to incorporate the virgin birth as presented in Matt 1:18–25.[42] But although the language of vv. 34–35a sounds Lukan, the content of v. 35b seems to be pre- and not post-Lukan.[43] Moreover, the concept of the virgin birth dominates the entire account of the annunciation, not only vv. 34–35; nor does the concept first appear there (cf. v. 27).[44] Finally, the manuscript tradition shows no trace of a later insertion of these two verses. Rather, the theological notion in v. 35, though it is the *conclusion* of a christological development, forms the *beginning* of the narrative. As with the resurrection or the descent into hell, a kerygmatic or hymnic expression (such as v. 35) precedes its narrative elaboration. In the virgin's question at v. 34, one hears the narrator, who knows in advance how the child will be conceived and arranges his account accordingly. Thus v. 35 is not an additional explanatory interpolation.[45]

No reader of chap. 1 can miss the exact congruence with the scene of Zechariah in the temple. But it is improbable that Luke himself has freshly composed the one scene by analogy to another scene prescribed for him by tradition.[46] Both stories have a past oral tradition: each is independent in narrative and theology, each influenced by Hebrew Bible models.[47] Also improbable is the hypothesis that an annunciation to *Elizabeth* is behind 1:26–38;[48] in its support, the proponents of this hypothesis point out that Elizabeth already knows John's name in v. 60, never doubts (in contrast to Zechariah), and perhaps originally spoke the Magnificat instead of Mary.[49] In this case the cycle of Baptist legends would be symmetrically balanced with two annunciations and two songs of praise. But these arguments are of unequal weight. The third is very hypothetical, and the first two ignore the rules of narrative economy: one divine annunciation is enough, and Elizabeth's role remains offstage. Luke must indeed have been familiar with the *Greek* genre of the double vision;[50] but, quite aside from the *Palestinian* provenance of the Baptist traditions, this genre serves to bring separated people into contact. Zechariah and Elizabeth, however, have lived together for years.

The legend of the annunciation developed in a Hellenistic-Jewish milieu, in which Christians were interested in the origin of the Messiah and wanted to retain his divine generation, his true sonship, and the virgin birth in one narrative unit. As a counterpart to it, they also likely told a birth narrative that differs from Luke 2:1–20 but has not been transmitted. Theologically, they were influenced by Egyptian Hellenistic Judaism, which in turn also depended on Egyptian concepts. The style of this narrative places it in the latest layer of Synoptic tradition; it is similar to the pericopes from Luke's special source, such as the Emmaus legend (24:13–35). It is not easy to find a *Sitz im Leben* within the Hellenistic-Jewish church either for the christological motifs or for the narrative itself.

Commentary

■ **26** The date ties into the preceding story. As Jesus follows John, so his prophetic mission follows that of his precursor. The church recalls that it is more recent than the Baptist's movement.

---

42 See Adolf von Harnack, "Zu Lc I, 34.35," *ZNW* 2 (1901) 53–57 (the verses were certainly added shortly after Luke); Schneider, "Einheit," 255–59 (Luke himself).

43 See the commentary on 1:35 below.

44 Agreeing with Dibelius, *Jungfrauensohn*, 3, 15–18; and Fitzmyer, 1.336–37.

45 I am, however, aware that Luke often likes to put new life into a story by means of an interpolated question. See Josef Gewiess, "Die Marienfrage, Lk 1, 34," *BZ* 5 (1961) 221–54, esp. 242–43; and Schneider, "Einheit," 255.

46 Whether the annunciation to Mary be based on that to Zechariah (so, with hesitation, Schürmann, 1.59) or the other way around (Benoit, "Enfance," 191).

47 Agreeing with Marshall, 63.

48 Grundmann (54) is not the first to advance it.

49 See the commentary on 1:46 below.

50 See Alfred Wikenhauser, "Doppelträume," *Bib* 29 (1948) 100–111.

The angel's name (cf. 1:19) is a further point of contact between the two annunciations. But the first account begins with a description of the situation (1:5–10), the second, directly with the story (1:26). In the first case, the sudden appearance of the angel is his first contact with the person and suffices as his greeting. In the second, the angel quietly approaches Mary and addresses her (1:28); the author even begins mythologically, with God sending Gabriel forth (1:26).[51] Mary's home (cf. 1:56) is Nazareth, a town in Galilee.[52] One can detect Luke's hand here: salvation history, like the Christian mission, proceeds from city to city. Judea, the Baptist's arena (1:39) and, later, the site of the passion (9:51; 13:22; etc.), is contrasted narratively and theologically to Galilee, the place of origin.

■ **27** With παρθένος ("virgin, girl"), the transmitters of the tradition surely mean to indicate virginity. In official Judaism it was neither morally nor mystically of value; but this is not official Judaism. The Essenes and the Therapeutae were pre-Christian ascetic movements advocating an ideal of chastity that probably had Greek roots.[53] Perhaps those recounting the annunciation belonged to one of these reform movements and had an interest in Mary's virginity as such. The readers of the LXX, and perhaps even the translators themselves, apparently understood from Isa 7:14 that a virgin would be the mother of the Messiah. Consistent methodology does not allow one to overlook those virgins who are positively evaluated in the New Testament.[54] Though discreet (cf. Luke 1:34), the text is nevertheless interested not only in the miracle of the divine begetting, but also in Mary's status as virgin. Of course, only the name of Jesus' mother and the family's residence in Nazareth are historical for certain.

In Judaism a girl reached a decisive phase in her life at twelve years of age. Between twelve and twelve and a half, according to the rabbinic tradition, she was called a נַעֲרָה ("little girl, marriageable girl"): she was still under her father's authority but was already considered responsible. At this age she could be promised in marriage. Later, she was called בֹּגֶרֶת ("a girl who has come of age"). Παρθένος presupposes that Mary was the age of a נַעֲרָה and was engaged to Joseph.[55] Engagement was a significant legal act. "At this point, the bride price, the compensation (*mohar*) that the fiancé was obliged to pay his father-in-law was discharged completely or in part. Through engagement, the fiancé was purchasing the proprietary right to the girl."[56] "During the period of time remaining before the wedding, which was determined by the particular conditions (age, dowry), the fiancée was further subject to her father's authority, but her legal status was that of a woman."[57]

According to Luke, Joseph is descended from David; the appearance of the husband in this complicated sentence is intended to prepare vv. 32–33, and is possibly a secondary addition from Luke. In this case the miracle of the virgin birth would be important for Luke, though not Mary's perpetual virginity; in chap. 2 Luke fully considers Mary[58] to be Joseph's wife, and he later speaks of the brothers of Jesus (Luke 8:19–21; Acts 1:14).

51 "By . . . to": most mss. read ὑπό ("by" or "from [God]").

52 On Galilee in Luke, see Conzelmann, *Theology*, 27–60; see the commentary on 4:14 below. Strangely, some mss. read "Judea" (although in an inclusive sense as at 4:44) instead of "Galilee." On Nazareth see Godet, 1.88–89; and Ernest W. Saunders, "Nazareth," *BHH* 2 (1964) 1291–92.

53 See Delling, "παρθένος," *TDNT* 5.826–37; and Aline Rousselle, who brings to light the reservations of ancient medicine regarding sexuality (*Porneia: On Desire and the Body in Antiquity* [trans. F. Pheasant; Oxford/New York: Blackwell, 1988]).

54 Cf. Acts 21:9; 1 Cor 7:25; Rev 14:4; also 2 Cor 11:1.

55 As a rule, engaged couples had no sexual relations during their engagement. Ἐμνηστευμένη and μεμνηστευμένη are two variants of the perfect passive participle of μνηστεύω ("to court; to promise in marriage," BDF §68) and usually designate "fiancée" or, exceptionally, "wife." See Pierre Benoit, "L'annonciation," *AsSeign* 6 (1965) 40–57, reprinted in idem, *Exégèse* 3.197–215, esp. 203. On the various types of rape of engaged girls and virgins, see Deut 22:23–29.

56 Stig Hanson ("Verlobung," *BHH* 3 [1966] 2091) lucidly outlines the significance of engagement in Israel. See also Angelo Tosato, *Il matrimonio israelitico: Una teoria generale* (AnBib 100; Rome: Biblical Institute Press, 1982).

57 August Strobel, "Braut, Bräutigam," *BHH* 1 (1962) 271.

58 On the various ways of spelling Mary's name, see Gerhard Schneider, "Μαρία, κτλ.," *EDNT* 2 (1991) 387; and François Bovon, "Le privilège pascal de Marie-Madeleine," *NTS* 30 (1984) 50–62, esp. 58–59 n. 1.

■ **28** Is χαῖρε ("greetings!") the angel's greeting,[59] a simple "good morning,"[60] or a genuine invitation to rejoice? Catholic exegetes have connected Mary with the daughter of Zion and understand the greeting as a call to eschatological joy.[61] Certainly the far-fetched vocative κεχαριτωμένη ("favored one") is a play on words; but v. 29 does understand v. 28 as a greeting. Thus, with Strobel, I would hold to the profane meaning, which, of course, could occasionally attain the original, more vivid sense of a call of joy. This is the case when the greeting, as here, is accompanied by further clauses.[62]

Κεχαριτωμένη is rare in profane Greek, but fairly frequently attested in biblical Greek.[63] The Vulgate translation *gratia plena* ("full of grace") is deceptive, because the word in Luke alludes to God's favor, not to the grace that makes humans holy.[64] Mary is first addressed by name in the angel's second speech (v. 30). Like Gideon long ago (Judg 6:12),[65] she receives here a divinely appointed, salvation-historical address. God has already expressed his favor to her in the mere fact of his visit.

"The Lord is with you" repeats the salutation and makes it more specific.[66] When God is "with" Israel or a chosen individual, this alludes not only to his protection but also to the task to come.[67]

■ **29** The many corrections in v. 29 suggest that the scribes were not completely satisfied with the rather affected language of this verse.[68] It is neither the unusual greeting nor the appearance of the angel that confuses the virgin and leads her to puzzle over it,[69] but rather the content of the message.

■ **30** Verse 30 repeats v. 28 in different words. The words of reassurance, "Do not be afraid," belong to the genre of the divine visitation.[70] To "find favor" is a Semitism that occurs with particular frequency in the LXX.[71] It does not at all describe the result of human activity, but rather expresses God's gracious election.

■ **31** Verse 31 can prophesy the miracle with everyday words, since divine action has preceded the three steps: conception, birth, and naming.[72] Καὶ ἰδού ("and now") is the signal of an event that is about to begin, here an event prophetically forecasted. Conception, birth, and naming are the human analogues of the divine purpose.

---

59   See esp. August Strobel,"Der Gruss an Maria (Lc 1,28): Eine philologische Betrachtung zu seinem Sinngehalt," *ZNW* 53 (1962) 86–110.

60   Cf. Matt 26:49; 27:29; 28:9. In addition to χαῖρε, one finds the elliptical χαίρειν and the distinguished χαίροις. Strobel vociferously advocates its meaning here as a simple greeting. As with every formula, the sense of χαῖρε could have faded, but could also return to its original meaning (a morning greeting to the light). Strobel believes that χαῖρε is employed here in this original sense (he sees a connection with the advent of the king, v. 32), but the sense is more Greek (a greeting) than Jewish (rejoicing).

61   See S. Lyonnet, "Χαῖρε κεχαριτωμένη," *Bib* 20 (1939) 131–41. He relies on four LXX texts: Zeph 3:14; Joel 2:21; Zech 9:9; Lam 4:21 (a special case). See also Laurentin, *Structure*, 64–65; and Klemens Stock, "Die Berufung Marias (Lk 1,26–38)," *Bib* 61 (1980) 457–91, esp. 468–71.

62   Strobel, "Gruss," 108.

63   In *Acts Phil.* 48, the author uses this participle for Ireus.

64   See Benoit, "Annonciation," 200; and Audet, "Annonce," 358–60, who suggests the translation *privilégiée* ("privileged").

65   See Audet, "Annonce," 352–55; Stock ("Berufung," 461–65) compares Judg 6:11–24 to Luke 1:26–38, but rejects the possibility of a literary form common to both.

66   For the Hebrews the name, especially when God gives it, determines the entire person. See S. Lyonnet, "L'annonciation et la mariologie biblique: Ce que l'exégèse conclut du récit lucanien de l'annonciation concernant la mariologie," in *Maria in Sacra Scriptura* (6 vols.; Rome: Pontificia Academia Mariana, 1967) 4.59–72, esp. 64.

67   A few scribes have added, surely under the influence of Tatian's *Diatesseron*, a third phrase at the end of v. 28, which they have taken from v. 42: "Blessed are you among all women." See Strobel, "Gruss," 108–9.

68   ῾H as a demonstrative pronoun is correct, but is still just as surprising as the διαλογίζομαι ("to debate") used for a single person. Ποταπός with optative (oblique, BDF §386.1), though rare in the NT, conforms completely to the rules of grammar.

69   Luke often uses διαλογίζομαι in a contemptuous sense; here it expresses Mary's confusion.

70   Cf. Luke 1:13. One encounters the formula "Do not fear" with a subsequent name in Gen 15:1 and Dan 10:12, two divine visitations.

71   מָצָא חֵן. Cf. Gen 6:8: Νῶε δὲ εὗρεν χάριν ἐναντίον κυρίου τοῦ θεοῦ ("But Noah found favor in the eyes of the Lord"). Cf. also 1 Sam (LXX 1 Kgdms) 1:18. Also with παρά, see Exod 33:16.

72   In Israel the father generally named the child. Cf. Luke 1:13, 62; Matt 1:21.

In contrast to Matt 1:22–23, no allusion is made to the etymology of the name "Jesus." But in the subtext of Luke's composition, one does sense a reverence for this name, as in the hymn of Phil 2:10.

■ **32–33** As is often the case with religious discourse, the text becomes ever broader at the conclusion. For this reason, it is not easy to determine the structure of the passage. At the end, in v. 33, we find *parallelismus membrorum*: twice, the eternal reign of Jesus is mentioned. Verse 32b speaks of its divine origin (the "throne of David"). Verse 32a portrays the Messiah's essence in a doubled rhythm; the titles are significant. Also important is the transition from v. 31, in which the mother is the subject (birth of the Messiah), to vv. 32–33, in which the son becomes significant (enthronement of the Messiah).[73]

Ideologically, the imagery is in the tradition of the Davidic Messiah-king,[74] and not that of the eschatological prophet or the messianic priest; the concepts of redemption and savior are also absent, as is the motif of victory over the enemy, and the title "Messiah." The foundation of this tradition is 2 Samuel (LXX 2 Kgdms) 7. It lives on in the Chronicles and in Jewish literature.[75] The explicit statements in this passage are astonishing in a time in which Jewish messianism concealed itself behind symbols and metaphors for reasons of political caution. The reason for the openness here is that Davidic messianism had been transcendentalized in the Jewish Hellenistic church of Luke's era. Also, the royal ideology of the Israelites, like the later Jewish Davidic messianism, was influenced from the beginning by both the Egyptian and the Mesopotamian conceptions of kingship. Thus it is no surprise that the elements of the enthronement ceremony are present here (albeit not as nicely structured as Norden thought):[76] (1) the Messiah receives life; (2) he is enthroned and obtains honor and a title; (3) he reigns.

A few points of detail: μέγας ("great") and υἱὸς ὑψίστου ("Son of the Most High") are not peculiar to the Davidic tradition, but belong to every religiously colored ideology of rulership[77] and can therefore also be understood by non-Jews.

God is named with his Hellenistic title: κύριος ὁ θεός ("the Lord God"). He appears as a father only from v. 35 onward. Here Jesus is described in terms of his human genealogy: David is his "ancestor." Although one cannot cite precise Hebrew Bible parallels (with the exception of 2 Sam [LXX 2 Kgdms] 7:14 par. 1 Chr 17:13), the prophecy in vv. 32–33 is a sort of scriptural anthology.[78]

■ **34** In the legend of Zechariah, the question "How will I recognize this?" (v. 18) is an expression of culpable unbelief (v. 20). In this passage Mary's words, "How will this happen?" (v. 34), express questioning belief and are therefore legitimate (v. 38). This contrast in itself points to the different origins of these traditions and reflects the varying evaluations of the request for a sign in the Hebrew Bible. The interiorization of ethics and faith in the New Testament era is evident in the comparison between Zechariah and Mary. Similar sentences, and similar actions, can be words of belief or unbelief, good or evil deeds, depending on the intent of the individual.

No one doubts that γινώσκω ("to learn, get to know"), in Semitic idiom, denotes intimate conjugal relations. In question is the meaning of the present tense: Does Mary simply mean to say that she has not had any sexual relations up to this point? But in this case, would one not expect the perfect? A few church fathers have concluded, under the influence of the ideal of virginity, that Mary took the vow never to "know" a man (progressive nuance of the present tense).[79] Although such vows are an anachronism in the early church, they were not in the Jewish reform movements.[80] We can know nothing

---

73 I do not believe that vv. 30b–33 were written in rhythmic prose. The typographical arrangement in Nestle-Aland is deceptive.

74 On Davidic messianism see Hahn, *Titles*, 136–48, 240–78.

75 If this text depends on a tradition—as I assume—it is strongly marked by Jewish Davidic messianism. But if the text is to be ascribed primarily to the author, he learned it from the Scriptures, which is also possible outside the Jewish homeland.

76 Norden, *Geburt*, 126–27.

77 See the excursus above, "The Virgin Birth and the History of Religions."

78 See Laurentin, *Structure*, 71–73.

79 Gregory of Nyssa and Augustine, and also medieval exegetes. See Legrand, *Annonce*, 238.

80 For example, the Essenes and Therapeutae. See Bernhard Lohse, *Askese und Mönchtum in der Antike und in der alten Kirche* (Religion und Kultur der alten Mittelmeerwelt in Parallelforschungen; Munich: Oldenbourg, 1969) 88–101.

certain about this aspect of the historical Mary. From the standpoint of Lukan redaction, the medieval hypothesis about the vow is certainly wrong. But one should not exclude the possibility that oral tradition still knew something of the ascetic ideals of the Hellenistic-Jewish movement from which the legends of the birth narratives originate.

■ **35** At v. 17 "spirit" and "power" have already been placed together.[81] When it appears without the article, πνεῦμα ἅγιον ("holy spirit") is the creative power of God. Luke uses ἐπέρχομαι ἐπί ("to come upon") for the gift of the Holy Spirit in Acts 1:8 (cf. Isa 32:15). The expression does not indicate the future essence of *Jesus*, but rather God's action with *Mary*. Ἐπισκιάζω means to "throw his shadow" or "overshadow."[82] Neither verb possesses an inherent sexual nuance, but here they explain how divine power will replace masculine begetting. Jewish scholars knew equally well how to use clever euphemisms. Ὕψιστος ("the Most High"), and not simply God, appears here because ὕψιστος was the common designation for God in Hellenistic Judaism. This designation expresses the preeminence of the divine father of Jesus.[83]

The last sentence in v. 35 is difficult.[84] Τὸ γεννώμενον[85] ("the child to be born") is the child developing in the mother's womb, not the child at birth, because, in contrast to Matt 1:20 (τὸ γεννηθέν), the participle is in the present tense. Should ἅγιον ("holy") be taken substantively as a subject in apposition to τὸ γεννώμενον, or as an adjective and attribute of υἱὸς θεοῦ ("Son of God")? Because ἅγιον κληθήσεται (with ἅγιον as an adjectival attribute, i.e., "[he] will be called holy") sounds like the Hebrew Bible (Isa 4:3) and corresponds to the promise πνεῦμα ἅγιον ἐπελεύσεται ἐπὶ σέ ("holy spirit will come upon you"), it should be taken as a pred-

icate adjective: "This child will be called holy"[86] (i.e., selected by and for God). Although ἅγιος belonged originally to the language of cult, it does not necessarily designate a priestly function. The prophet is also ἅγιος, as is here the future Messiah. Υἱὸς θεοῦ ("Son of God") occurs here for the first time in Luke's Gospel.[87] It seems like an afterthought and could be a clumsy addition of Luke's; what is bothersome is the transition from neuter to masculine. But this title probably always belonged to the content of the statement, since υἱὸς θεοῦ, like ἅγιον, is connected to δύναμις ὑψίστου ("power of the Most High") and πνεῦμα ἅγιον ("holy spirit"; cf. υἱὸς ὑψίστου, "Son of the Most High," v. 32). Jesus is called not only holy but also—in a different sense than Israel or the ancient kings—the Son of God.

Verse 35 interprets Jewish Davidic messianism in a Christian manner: the Messiah will not be a national ruler. Descent from David is spiritualized: Mary's son is engendered by God himself. Verse 35 is less corresponding to the structure of Rom 1:3–4 (son of David according to the flesh, Son of God according to the spirit) than it is interpreting vv. 31–33.[88] As the son of David, Jesus is the Son of God, just as the reign of David derives its true significance from the rulership of God. Of course, Jesus is still Mary's son, a human, but the theme of the verse concerns neither the two natures nor the two levels of christology, but the true nature of the Messiah and his reign. It is a topic pertaining to the polemics against Judaism, although the Christian position is itself influenced by Hellenistic Judaism.

■ **36** "And now" in this verse refers to the sign, whereas in v. 31 it refers to the prophecy; God is active in events, and is not merely present in thoughts and feelings. The rapprochement between the traditions creates a familial relationship between the two mothers. The allusion to a

---

81 Cf. Luke 4:14; Acts 1:8; 6:8; 10:38. See Legrand, "Arrière-plan," 164–69.

82 The word is used in Acts 5:15 of Peter's healing shadow, and in Luke 9:34, in HB style, "of the cloud that indicates the presence of God," as Bauer notes (BAGD, s.v. ἐπισκιάζω). Cf. Exod 40:35. Norden's portrayal, argued from the perspective of mysticism, is not very convincing (*Geburt*, 92–99).

83 See Georg Bertram, "ὕψιστος," *TDNT* 8 (1972) 618–19.

84 According to Legrand (*Annonce*, 243–48) the consecutive διὸ καί ("therefore") follows a christological logic.

85 See Antonio Vicent, "La presunta sustantivación τὸ γεννώμενον en Lc 11,35b [sic; read 1:35b]," *EstBib* 33 (1974) 265–73.

86 Instead of assuming ἔσται ("[he] will be") before ἅγιον, I prefer to place a comma after κληθήσεται.

87 On this title see Hahn, *Titles*, 279–346; and Martin Hengel, *The Son of God: The Origin of Christology and the History of Jewish-Hellenistic Religion* (trans. J. Bowden; Philadelphia: Fortress Press, 1976).

88 Legrand, "Arrière-plan," 177–83.

"relative"[89] forms a link without making it too precise. Even Elizabeth expects a child, despite her age.[90] Almost poetically the angel repeats with greater specificity, "and this is the sixth month[91] for her who was said to be barren."

■ **37** The angel cannot close his speech with so matter-of-fact a statement. Verse 37 rounds out the message theologically and piously with a citation from Gen 18:14. It is a Hebrew Bible credo that, for God, nothing is impossible.[92] The contrast is not between God and nature, but between the powerful God and powerless humanity. Ῥῆμα ("word, saying") here alludes rather to a promised *event* (as in Acts 10:37) than to mere *words*. The future tense[93] fits in the context of a theology of hope: God will soon realize the possible impossibility. One should prefer the reading παρὰ τοῦ θεοῦ ("from God")[94] instead of the static παρὰ τῷ θεῷ ("with God").

■ **38** Mary places herself at God's behest (cf. 16:13); she does not merely submit herself but demonstrates her agreement. Her human response appertains to history (ἰδού, "here") and not to an abstract ontology (εἰμί, "I am"). Like Jesus before the passion (22:42) or Paul in view of his fate (Acts 21:14), Mary awaits the fulfillment of God's will, a divine history written not in the letters of the Scriptures but in the life of the people.[95]

The message has been transmitted. The addressee not only received but accepted it. Now the angel can depart.

Conclusion

In narrative form Luke describes and pictures the renewed relationship between God and humanity. The faithful God will begin, again, with a birth. The long-awaited king will be not only protected by God but engendered by him. But the end will far surpass the beginning. The Spirit is the eschatological instrument of the end that is beginning, the instrument of the Son (1:35), and later of the people (Acts 1:8). The phrases "throne of David" and "house of Jacob" are provincially limited concepts (Luke 1:32), but the endlessness of his reign advocates its future extension to universality. Time and space become the property of the Son of God. In order to realize his plan, God chooses the humanly limited and overlooked, this time a girl of about twelve years (1:27), and long ago the young man Gideon (Judg 6:15). The impossible, which for God is possible (Luke 1:37), becomes evident by a comparison of the feeble means with the greatness of the result. But the feebleness is not weakness, for Mary possesses inner strength and trusting faith.[96] The first step over the threshold into God's future has been taken.

---

89   See Spicq, *Lexicon*, 3.306–7.

90   The more recent dative γήρει ("old age") often supplants γήρᾳ; cf. BDF §47.1.

91   Μήν here means "month" and is not a particle. Cf. 1:26.

92   In addition to Gen 18:14, cf. also Job 10:13 (LXX); 42:2; Zech 8:6 (LXX); 2 Chr 14:10; Jer 32:17 (39:17, Aquila and Symmachus); in the NT, Luke 18:27 par. and Mark 14:36.

93   In agreement with Plummer (25), οὐκ ("not") and ἀδυνατήσει ("is impossible") should be read together; οὐκ should not be connected with πᾶν ῥῆμα ("every thing").

94   Here I agree with Nestle-Aland.

95   The ῥῆμα ("word," "saying") of the angel (v. 38) corresponds to the ῥῆμα ("thing") of God (v. 37). For Luke ῥῆμα has the same semantic range that דָּבָר ("word") has in the HB: it is the word carried along by God's will, which can and shall realize his plan of salvation in the life of his people.

96   In none of the HB parallels does one find such an explicitly formulated assent as in this passage. See Lyonnet, "Annonciation," 62.

The Meeting of Mary and Elizabeth (1:39–56)

Bibliography

Bailey, Kenneth E., "The Song of Mary: Vision of a New Exodus (Lk 1:46–55)," *Theological Review* (Near East School of Theology) 2 (1979) 29–35.

Bemile, Paul, *The Magnificat Within the Context and Framework of Lukan Theology: An Exegetical Theological Study of Lk 1:46–55* (Regensburger Studien zur Theologie 34; Frankfurt am Main/Bern/New York: P. Lang, 1986).

Beverly, H. B., "An Exposition of Luke 1:39–45," *Int* 30 (1976) 396–400.

Bogaert, Pierre-Maurice, "Épisode de la controverse sur le 'Magnificat': À propos d'un article inédit de Donatien de Bruyne (1906)," *RBén* 94 (1984) 38–49.

Brown, *Birth*, 330–66.

Buth, Randall, "Hebrew Poetic Tenses and the Magnificat," *JSNT* 21(1984) 67–83.

Chappius-Juillard, Isabelle, *Le temps des rencontres: Quand Marie visite Elisabeth (Luc 1)* (Aubonne: Le Moulin, 1991).

Delorme, Jean, "Le Magnificat: La forme et le sens," in H. Cazelles, ed., *La vie de la Parole: De l'Ancien au Nouveau Testament: Festschrift Pierre Grelot* (Paris: Desclée, 1987) 175–94.

Dubois, "Jean-Baptiste," 94–99.

Dupont, Jacques, *Les Béatitudes* (3 vols.; EtB; Paris: Gabalda, 1969–73) 3.186–93.

idem, "Magnificat."

Eivers, A. M., "The Song and the Singer: Reflecting on Mary's Magnificat," *Emm* 100 (1994) 624–26.

Escudero Freire, *Devolver*, 173–221.

Farris, *Hymns*, 108–26.

Grigsby, Bruce, "Compositional Hypotheses for the Lucan 'Magnificat'—Tensions for the Evangelical," *EvQ* 56 (1984) 159–72.

Gryglewicz, Feliks, "Die Herkunft der Hymnen des Kindheitsevangeliums des Lukas," *NTS* 21 (1974–75) 265–73.

Gueuret, Agnès, "Sur Luc 1,46–55: Comment peut-on être amené à penser qu'Élisabeth est 'sémiotiquement' celle qui a prononcé le Cantique en Lc 1, 46?" *Centre protestant d'études et de documentation: Supplément* (April 1977) 3–11.

Gunkel, "Lieder."

Hamel, "Magnificat."

Horn, Friedrich Wilhelm, *Glaube und Handeln in der Theologie des Lukas* (GThA 26; Göttingen: Vandenhoeck & Ruprecht, 1983) 137–44, 181–83.

Irigoin, Jean, "La composition rythmique du magnificat (Luc I 46–55)," in *Zetesis: Festschrift Émile de Strycker* (Antwerp/Utrecht: Nederlandsche Boekhandel, 1973) 618–28.

Jacquemin, Paul-Edmond, "Le Magnificat Lc 1,46–55," *AsSeign* 66 (1973) 28–40.

idem, "Visitation."

Jones, "Background."

Joüon, Paul, "Notes de philologie évangélique: Luc 1, 54–55: Une difficulté grammaticale du Magnificat," *RechSR* 15 (1925) 440–41.

Karris, Robert J., "Mary's Magnificat and Recent Study," *Review for Religious* 42 (1983) 903–8.

Köbert, R., "Lk 1,28.42 in den Syrischen Evangelien," *Bib* 42 (1961) 229–30.

Laurentin, René, "Traces d'allusions étymologiques en Luc 1–2," *Bib* 38 (1957) 15–23.

Leivestad, Ragnar, "Ταπεινός-ταπεινόφρων," *NovT* 8 (1966) 36–47.

McHugh, *Mother*, 68–79.

Minguez, Dionisio, "Poética generativa del Magnificat," *Bib* 61 (1980) 55–77.

Monloubou, *Prière*, 219–39.

Muñoz Iglesias, Salvador, et al., "El Magnificat, teología y espiritualidad," *Ephemerides Mariologicae* 36 (1986) 9–147.

Obbard, Elizabeth Ruth, *Magnificat: The Journey and the Song* (New York: Paulist, 1985).

Perrot, "Récits," 47–48.

Ramaroson, "Structuram."

Rinaldi, Bonaventura, "Chiarificazioni sul Magnificat," *Ephemerides Mariologicae* 37 (1987) 201–5.

Rivera, Luis Fernando, "El concepto 'tapeinos' en el Magnificat (Lc. 1:48)," *RB* 20 (1958) 70–72.

Sahlin, *Messias*, 140–54.

Schoonheim, P. L., "Der alttestamentliche Boden der Vokabel ὑπερήφανος Lukas 1, 51," *NovT* 8 (1966) 235–46.

Schöpfer, J., "Der Christ steht vor Gott: Albertus Magnus und Martin Luther kommentieren das Magnificat," *GuL* 58 (1985) 460–66.

Schottroff, "Magnificat."

Tannehill, "Magnificat."

Thaidigsmann, Edgar, "Gottes schöpferisches Sehen: Elemente einer theologischen Sehschule im Anschluß an Luthers Auslegung des Magnificat," *Neue Zeitschrift für systematische Theologie* 29 (1987) 19–38.

Valentini, Alberto, "La controversia circa l'attribuzione del Magnificat," *Mar* 45 (1983) 55–93.

idem, "Il Magnificat e l'opera lucana," *RivB* 33 (1985) 395–423.

idem, *Il Magnificat: Genere letterario, struttura, esegesi* (RivBSup 16; Bologna: Edizioni Dehoniane, 1987).

idem, "Il Magnificat: Ricerche di struttura letteraria," *Mar* 48 (1986) 40–104.

Verweyen, Hansjürgen, "Mariologie als Befreiung: Lk 1,26–45.56 im Kontext," *ZKTh* 105 (1983) 168–83.

Vogels, T., "Le Magnificat, Marie et Israël," *EeT* 6 (1975) 279–96.

Winter, "Magnificat."

39 In those days Mary arose and went with haste into the hill country to a city of Judah, 40/ and entered the house of Zechariah and greeted Elizabeth. 41/ And it happened that when Elizabeth heard Mary's greeting, the child leaped in her womb, and Elizabeth was filled with holy spirit 42/ and exclaimed with a loud cry and said, "Blessed are you among all women, and blessed is the fruit of your womb. 43/ And why has this happened to me, that the mother of my Lord comes to me? 44/ For as soon as the sound of your greeting came to my ears, the child in my womb leaped for joy. 45/ And happy are you who believed that there would be a fulfillment of what was promised to her by the Lord." 46/ And Mary said, "My soul praises the greatness of the Lord, 47/ and my spirit rejoices in God, my Savior, 48/ for he has looked with favor on the lowliness of his servant. For see, from now on all generations will call me blessed; 49/ for the Mighty One has done great things for me, and holy is his name, 50/ and his mercy is from generation to generation for those who fear him. 51/ He has shown strength with his arm. He has scattered those who are proud in the thoughts of their hearts, 52/ he has brought down the powerful from their thrones, and lifted up the lowly; 53/ he has filled the hungry with good things, and sent the rich away empty. 54/ He has attended to his servant Israel, so that he remembers his mercy, 55/ as he foretold to our ancestors, as he has promised to Abraham and his descendants forever." 56/ And Mary remained with her about three months, and then returned to her home.

Analysis

The Narrative

In the meeting of Mary and Elizabeth, Luke links the Jesus traditions with those of John the Baptist. Already in the preceding pericope, he has prepared the scene by making Elizabeth's pregnancy a sign for Mary. The gravity that this scene has for Luke expresses itself in the forcefulness of the image he creates. The women's recognition of each other's pregnancy grants them a double honor. Because Mary seeks out Elizabeth, attention is first directed to what has happened with John's mother. But when John leaps in his mother's womb, showing himself already to be a prophet and precursor, the narrative turns toward Mary. The emphasis of the scene is on Jesus; this becomes explicit in that Elizabeth praises God for Mary and Jesus,[1] but not a word about Elizabeth or John is heard in the Magnificat.

It remains an open question whether Luke is writing on his own or referring to an isolated tradition. The Hebrew Bible evidences no actual genre of interpersonal encounters, although it tells of many visits.[2]

The progress of the narrative is halted in the women's two speeches. These speeches, formulated in Israel's prayer language, emphasize the fulfillment of the promised sign and the mothers' joyful faith.

The Magnificat

Mary's prayer is a hymn—or, more correctly, an individual's song of praise; an invitation to the congregation to join in is lacking—in which God is for the most part addressed not directly but in the third person. As appropriate to the genre, the hymn begins with a recapitulation of "the praise already sounded" (vv. 46–47).[3]

Israel has an uninterrupted tradition in the composition of hymns, psalms, and prayers;[4] the Magnificat can be compared[5] not only with the Hebrew Bible but with more recent texts, such as the hymns from Qumran, the Psalms of Solomon, or isolated songs of praise.[6]

The main body, as in every hymn, is constituted by the praise of God. The transition from the introduction

1   As Paul-Edmond Jacquemin notes ("La visitation," *AsSeign* 8 [1972] 64–75, esp. 70–71), vv. 42b–45 already demonstrate a fairly high degree of Christian reflection.

2   Cf. the meeting of Abraham and Melchizedek (Gen 14:17–24), with a word of blessing in the priest-king's mouth and an oath from Abraham to God. The final form of Gen 14 unambiguously exalts Abraham. See Claus Westermann, *Genesis: A Commentary* (trans. J. J. Scullion; 3 vols.; Minneapolis: Augsburg, 1984–86) 2.191–92.

3   Hans-Joachim Kraus, *Psalmen* (2 vols.; BKAT 15; Neukirchen: Neukirchener Verlag, 1960–61) 1.xli.

4   See Paul Winter, "Le Magnificat et le Bénédictus

sont-ils des Psaumes macchabéens?" *RHPhR* 36 (1956) 1–17, esp. 1–5. See also Perrot ("Récits," 48), who mentions the *piyyutim*, poems sung after the reading of the Scriptures.

5   Gunkel, "Lieder"; Hans-Joachim Kraus, *Psalms* (trans. H. C. Oswald; 2 vols.; Minneapolis: Augsburg, 1988–89) 1.38–62; Claus Westermann, *Praise and Lament in the Psalms* (Atlanta: John Knox, 1981) 115, 118, 124–25, 128, 129, 136. More bibliography on the Lukan hymns appears in Fitzmyer, 1.370–71, 390, 433.

6   Cf. 1 Chr 16:8–36; 1 Macc 2:7–13; 2 Esdr 10:20–24; 2 Bar 10:6–12:4; Rev 15:3b–4; 4:11; 11:17–18;

to the main body is signaled in Hebrew by כִּי ("for," "because"), and in Greek by ὅτι ("that," "because," "for"). Here we find ὅτι twice (vv. 48, 49), because in v. 48b a beatitude interrupts the song of praise. Missing is the usual short conclusion (coda), in which elements of the introduction are recapitulated, or wishes and requests are introduced. Nonetheless, v. 55 shifts attention from praise of God's saving act back to the ancient prophecy, which yields a good conclusion (with an almost doxological εἰς τὸν αἰῶνα ["forever"]).[7] Perhaps v. 54 should also be considered part of the conclusion.[8]

God is the subject of all the verbs with the exception of v. 48b. The verbs are in the aorist, because the main body of a hymn revolves on Yahweh's words and actions in creation and history.[9] Hymns also typically mention *characteristics* of God alongside *actions,* in predicate sentences such as vv. 49b and 50 (cf. Ps 111[LXX 110]:9, "Holy and awesome is his name!" and 145[LXX 144]:9), "his compassion is over all that he has made"). The recipient of God's salvific activity ("my, me" [μου, μοι, με]) is generalized to include "those who fear him," who are probably identical with "the lowly" and "the hungry," and even with Israel itself. The vague and general description of God's work is typical for a psalm, which can, in the same form, be spoken liturgically in prayer by various individuals.

Jacques Dupont has pointed out that the Magnificat makes many allusions to its context:[10] Ἠγαλλίασεν ("rejoices," v. 47) recalls ἐν ἀγαλλιάσει ("for joy," v. 44); the singer refers to herself as the "servant" (ἡ δούλη) of God (v. 48), which corresponds to v. 38 ("Behold, I am the servant of the Lord" [ἰδοὺ ἡ δούλη κυρίου]); and her beatification is presupposed (v. 48), as already in Elizabeth's mouth (v. 45). Ὁ δυνατός ("the Mighty One") could be recapitulating the content of v. 37. Despite this,

it remains probable that Luke has adopted and adapted an already extant song,[11] since it refers neither to a birth nor to a virgin birth. These correspondences with its context are redactional, or else Luke selected precisely this hymn because it suited the situation better than others. It is superfluous to the progress of the narrative,[12] but nonetheless has a hermeneutical function, as I shall demonstrate.

In contrast to the Qumran psalms, God is not praised as creator, and reflection is also lacking on the problems of persecution and death, as are any polemical arguments and messianic expectations. Formally, God is regularly addressed in the *Hodayot* in the second person, and the psalmist often uses metaphors and images for him- or herself and for others. In comparison with the *Psalms of Solomon*, the Magnificat is discreet in referring to its enemies, and reticent about the victory of the righteous, and sin and judgment. Rather than awakening hope, it emphasizes faith in God's historical activity.

The author doubtless knows Hannah's song after the birth of Samuel (1 Sam [LXX 1 Kgdms] 2:1–10) and makes use of it. But the compositional technique in the Magnificat is different: the poem is composed from excerpted fragments.[13] Nearly every expression has a Hebrew Bible parallel (cf. Nestle-Aland). But its proximity to the *Psalms of Solomon* should not be overlooked, either. First, there is the vocabulary: "those who fear him" (v. 50): *Ps. Sol.* 2:33; 3:12; 4:23; 15:13; "his/your servant Israel" (v. 54): *Ps. Sol.* 12:6; 17:21; "[Abraham's] posterity" (v. 55): *Ps. Sol.* 18:3; ὑπερηφανία ("arrogance, pride," v. 51): *Ps. Sol.* 2:1, 2, 31; 17:13, 23; the contrast between rich and poor (v. 53): *Ps. Sol.* 5:11 (although with the conviction that God is concerned about both groups); to "bring down the powerful" (v. 52): *Ps. Sol.* 11:4; God's mercy (v. 50): *Ps. Sol.* 10:3; the arm of God

---

12:12a; 19:1–2, 5b, 6b–8a. Philo recalls the use of hymns among the Therapeutae (*Vit. cont.* 79–80). In *Agr.* 79–80 he mentions two choirs: according to Exod 15:1–21, Moses leads the chorus of men, and Miriam that of the women. See Winter, "Magnificat," 1–5.

7 Gunkel elucidates the contrasts between vv. 49–54 and v. 55 with great sensitivity ("Lieder," 52).

8 So Brown, *Birth*, 356.

9 Kraus, *Psalms*, 1.45–46.

10 See Jacques Dupont, "Le Magnificat comme discours sur Dieu," *NRTh* 102 (1980) 321–43, esp. 324; reprinted in idem, *Études sur les Évangiles syn-*

optiques (ed. F. Neirynck; 2 vols.; BETL 70; Leuven: Leuven University Press and Peeters, 1985) 2.953–75.

11 Brown (*Birth*, 347) supports the following thesis: the Magnificat and Benedictus originated in a Jewish Christian movement of the "poor of God." Luke himself then inserted them here secondarily, after he had already written the birth narratives.

12 "Magnificat," 325 (according to the journal article). Against this, Schürmann writes (1.78), "the narrative cries out for a climax of this sort."

13 See Winter, "Magnificat," 6–7; Perrot, "Récits," 48.

(v. 51): *Ps. Sol.* 13:2; the strength of God (v. 51): *Ps. Sol.* 17:3; ἐπιβλέπω ("to look with favor on," v. 48): *Ps. Sol.* 18:2; ἀντιλαμβάνομαι ("to attend to," v. 54): *Ps. Sol.* 16:3, 5; μιμνήσκομαι (v. 54, "to remember"): *Ps. Sol.* 10:1, 4; λαλέω with the Semitic nuance of "promise" (v. 55): *Ps. Sol.* 11:7.

They also have in common two formal elements: Ἰδού ("and now") as an introductory word (v. 48; *Ps. Sol.* 8:25), and–this seems very significant–the frequent occurrence of beatitudes within the hymn itself (v. 48): *Ps. Sol.* 4:23; 5:16; 6:1; 10:1; 17:44; 18:6. For this reason, any attempt to view v. 48b as an interpolation is doomed.[14] Also notable is the indeterminate structure of the *Psalms of Solomon*,[15] in which context one should especially praise the brevity and solidity of the Magnificat, which the author achieved with excerpted fragments. The Pharisaic nature of the *Psalms of Solomon* is probable. Since Luke also shows sympathy for the Pharisees in the book of Acts, it is more likely that the Magnificat originated in this movement rather than in the Jewish Christian or the Baptist's movement.

The model of all songs of praise in Israel remains the hymn recounting the miraculous parting of the Red Sea (Exod 15), which was sung by a male choir, and then by the women under Miriam's direction.[16] Did this influence the doubling of the Magnificat in the hymn of Zechariah?

For exegesis, much depends on the interpretation of the aorists. Are they ordinary observations of past history, or gnomic attestations of God's usual conduct? Are they ingressive aorists, signaling the beginning of escha-tological events? Or are they influenced by the prophetic perfect in Hebrew, and thus pictures of the future? In sum, is this hymn a genuine praise to God for help granted, or a hidden prophecy of hoped-for salvation?

Structure: Metrical criteria show, from the arrangement of syllables and accents, a two-part composition (vv. 46b–50, 51–55), with three strophes apiece. In the first part, the second and third strophes correspond to each other (vv. 48b–49a, 49b–50), as do the first and third strophes of the second part (vv. 51–53, 54–55).[17]

The units of meaning suggest that the song can also be understood as a poem with two strophes. The conclusions of both strophes are given greater gravity by means of longer versification (vv. 49b–50, 54b–55). All the other lines begin with action verbs (excepting vv. 48b and 53).[18] I consider the Magnificat as a hymn and analyze it by the criteria of Jewish poetry.[19] One should consider the manner in which the most ancient manuscripts present such poetic texts, whether with or without division marks and structuring. Moreover, canonization should not be viewed as a guarantee of perfected external form[20] or profound theology.[21]

Commentary

■ **39–40** In contrast to Luke 2 and to Matthew 1–2, Joseph plays no role here. Mary sets out alone on a fairly long journey. "In those days" is an indefinite expression reminiscent of the Hebrew Bible.[22] Ἀναστάς ("arose," v. 39) is a Semitic idiom that, from its use in the LXX, has become a favorite expression of Luke. It does not

---

14 According to Leonardus Ramaroson ("Ad structuram cantici 'Magnificat,'" *VD* 46 [1968] 30–46, esp. 43–45) and McHugh (*Mother*, 74), v. 48b is a secondarily introduced parenthesis.

15 The *dispositio* ("structure, arrangement") is, according to Gunkel ("Lieder," 52), "the weak point of OT artistry."

16 See n. 6 above. Philo's interpretation of Exod 15 is allegorizing, whereas Luke's is realized in composing new stories.

17 Jean Irigoin, "La composition rythmique du Magnificat (Luc I 46–55)," in *Zetesis: Festschrift Émile de Strycker* (Antwerp/Utrecht: Nederlandsche Boekhandel, 1973) 618–28.

18 Robert C. Tannehill, "The Magnificat as Poem," *JBL* 93 (1974) 263–75.

19 According to Douglas Jones ("The Background and Character of the Lukan Psalms," *JTS* n.s. 19 [1968]

19–50), the hymn represents a hybrid form and indicates the dissolution of this genre after the exile. Schürmann (71) also considers it a hybrid: eschatological hymn and personal song of thanks.

20 Most evident in Ramarosan's article ("Structuram," 30): "*hymnus valde perfectus*" ("a quite perfect hymn"). Ramarosan divides the hymn into three strophes: vv. 46–50 describe God's treatment of Mary; vv. 51–53, of the lowly; and vv. 54–55, of Israel.

21 According to Tannehill ("Magnificat," 265), the hymn performs the function of an aria.

22 Plummer (39) remarks that Luke likes to use such expressions.

necessarily denote "standing up," but metaphorically describes the preparation or beginning of an action, sometimes pleonastically and formulaically.[23] Πορεύομαι ("to go, walk") has theological significance in the Gospel of Luke: Jesus, and here Mary, "walk" according to God's will and plan of salvation.[24] Μετὰ σπουδῆς ("with haste" or "eagerly") narratively confirms Mary's willingness, and the harmony between her faith and the divine purpose.[25] The people of the Bible often "run" as soon as divine activity is perceptible.[26] Like Mary on her journey, Luke wastes no time in describing what is surely a trip of several days.[27] Everything is directed toward arrival, as the thrice-repeated, almost exaggerated εἰς ("to, into") makes clear.[28] From the Hebrew Bible, Luke knows that the promised land consists of "hills" and "valleys."[29] Mary hikes from the lower ground of Galilee up into the hills of Judah.[30] After giving a general direction (e.g., a city), Luke often mentions a specific destination, such as a synagogue or house,[31] sometimes without καί ("and") between the two (Luke 2:4; 4:16). Εἰς τὴν ὀρεινήν ("into the hill country") and εἰς πόλιν Ἰούδα ("to a city of Judah"), then, should not be attributed to different sources.

Mary reaches her destination and greets Elizabeth.[32] Many people greet each other in this chapter (1:28–29, 40, 41, 44), since many encounters are narrated. God, actively intervening, brings people together. Salvation develops in the context of human relations. Here the greeting is the expression of an affectionate encounter, and is, like the births, the beginning of new life. In antiquity, and especially in the regions of Judaism and early Christianity, words of greeting had not yet acquired the formulaic quality that they possess today.[33] They are not a simple wish for the well-being of the person addressed, but, much more, they possess the power to effect it.[34] Luke does not give the content of Mary's greeting, because he is concerned above all with Elizabeth's reaction.

■ **41–42a** Verses 41–42a are awkward; "Elizabeth" occurs twice, and there is parataxis with a change of subject.[35] The child leaps[36] for joy in the mother's womb (vv. 41, 44), which here attains the nature of a sign. God makes use not only of words but also of body language. In antiquity, people made predictions about the future of children from the signs and wonders surrounding their birth.[37] Just as Esau and Jacob anticipate their future

---

23   In addition to the commentaries, see BDF §419.2, 5; §461 n. 1; and Felix-Marie Abel, *Grammaire du grec biblique suivie d'un choix de papyrus* (EtB; Paris: Gabalda, 1927) §74c.

24   See esp. in the case of travel 9:51; 13:22, etc.

25   Cf. Exod 12:11 (LXX).

26   David Daube, *The Sudden in the Scriptures* (Leiden: Brill, 1964). See Jacquemin, "Visitation," 68. Cf. Gen 18:2.

27   "Comfortably in four days" judges Lagrange (41), who knows the country.

28   Similarly in Acts 14:21; 21:1; 25:8.

29   See the commentary to Luke 6:17 below. On the hills of Judea, cf. Num 13:29 and Jdt 4:7.

30   Ἰούδας was the name of the patriarch and son of Jacob, then of the tribe descended from him, and finally of the region settled by this tribe (this region is also described with the substantivized adjective ἡ Ἰουδαία [sc. γῆ]). Cf. Matt 2:6. This Ἰούδας is not to be considered an incorrect city name. The commentators are very verbose and inventive here: see Godet, 1.96–97; Plummer, 41; and Marshall, 80.

31   Acts 13:14; 18:19; 21:8; cf. Luke 14:8.

32   The formulation, "to her [Mary's] home" (εἰς τὸν οἶκον αὐτῆς, v. 56), in contrast to the expression then customary, "the house of Zechariah" (v. 40),

hints at the extraordinary situation of Jesus' parents.

33   Cf. Rom 16:16; 1 Cor 16:19–20; 1 Pet 5:13–14.

34   Peter Trummer, "ἀσπάζομαι, κτλ.," *EDNT* 1 (1990) 173, with extensive bibliography.

35   Precisely the awkwardness of the sentence led scribes to improve the text; cf. the critical apparatus for v. 41 in Nestle-Aland. On ἐγένετο plus the aorist (ἐσκίρτησεν) without καί, see BDF §442 n. 5.

36   See Gottfried Fitzer, "σκιρτάω," *TDNT* 7 (1971) 401–2. The verb describes, essentially, the clumsy jumping and love of motion in young animals. "Two motifs control the use in Luke: the natural movement of the child in the womb, and eschatological joy at the coming of Christ. The former is prefigured in Gn. 25:22 . . . , the latter in Mal 4:2 . . . , where the comparison gives expression to joy at eschatological salvation."

37   For example, if a nursing babe could smile before the fortieth day. See Norden, *Geburt*, 59–72.

relationship already in their mother's womb (Gen 25:22–28),[38] the Baptist even now exercises his prophetic function as precursor.[39]

After this sign, Elizabeth is filled with the Holy Spirit[40] and utters a prophetic cry.[41] This joyful exclamation, like the leaping of the child, illustrates the new beginning in salvation history.

■ **42b** Verse 42b contains the poetic parallelism of two nominal sentences.[42] The implied verb (in the indicative) expresses a fact, not a wish. Εὐλογημένη and εὐλογημένος ("blessed") are divine passives. "Among all women" is the Semitic idiom for a superlative phrase.[43] God's blessing goes together with God's election. The Lord blesses *new* people on the fringes of Israel, and outside its body of officials. In the worldview of antiquity, a woman's son brought her dignity; the benediction finds its cause and goal in Mary's offspring. In the parallelism there is symmetry, not repetition. God's blessing is a word (εὐλογέω ["to bless," lit. "to say a good word"]), but as God's word it is also power. His blessing accompanies those who receive a mission from God, but does not exclude suffering (cf. 2:35).[44] The Gospel begins with the blessing of Mary and Jesus, and ends with the blessing of the disciples by the resurrected one (24:50).

■ **43–44** No answer follows the question πόθεν ("why . . . ?" not "from where") . . . τοῦτο (clarified with ἵνα),[45] since this is an exclamation[46] that plays on the difference between John's position of honor and that of Jesus. "My Lord" is Jewish rather than Christian (Phil 3:8; John 20:13, 28).

Luke has difficulty composing a coherent speech for Elizabeth. After the poetic blessing (v. 42), he switches abruptly to prose, and, after the rhetorical question (v. 43), to a summary (v. 44 repeats v. 41). The prophetically gifted mother gives one rather the impression of a surprised woman who does not really know what is happening. This incoherence could result from the lack of a fixed tradition or from an intention to express charged emotions. But in v. 45 inspiration comes again to the fore in a beautiful beatitude.

Elizabeth's speech proceeds in three waves: the middle one treats the meeting of the two mothers, the first, God's gift, and the third, Mary's faith.

■ **45** In v. 45 Luke, who branded Zechariah's lack of faith (1:20), repeats his praise of Mary's believing attitude (in 1:38) on a metanarrative level (ὅτι means "that," not "since").

Despite the Lukan scheme of prophecy and fulfillment, this passage contains the only occurrence of τελείωσις ("fulfillment")[47] in his works. His choice of λαλέω ("to speak") is skillful, with its Hebraic connotation of prophecy (as in 1:55), especially when the words are of divine origin (παρά, "from beside," which presupposes the angel's mediation, instead of ἀπό, "from").

---

38 Sahlin (*Messias*, 143 n. 1) refers to the Targum to Ps 68:27, "Praise God, you embryos in the womb, you seed of Israel!" and to *Odes Sol.* 28:2, "My heart continually refreshes itself and leaps for joy, like the babe who leaps for joy in his mother's womb" (translation from James H. Charlesworth, *The Odes of Solomon* [Oxford: Clarendon, 1973] 108).

39 Jacquemin ("Visitation," 70) assumes rightly that the tradition attested in Luke 1:15 has affected the composition of 1:41.

40 See Luke 1:15 and the commentary on it above. See Dubois, "Jean-Baptiste," 94–99.

41 Walter Grundmann, "κράζω, κτλ.," *TDNT* 3 (1965) 899 A.1 and 900 A.3. A few scribes preferred the Semitically tinged pleonasm, ἀνεφώνησεν φωνῇ μεγάλῃ, or the expression ἀνεβόησεν φωνῇ μεγάλῃ (cf. Gen 27:34 [LXX]: ἀνεβόησεν φωνὴν μεγάλην).

42 Cf. Jdt 13:18; Laurentin (*Structure*, 81–82), Brown (*Birth*, 347), and McHugh (*Mother*, 69–71) all refer to it. Along with Sahlin (*Messias*, 146 n. 1), one could add 2 *Bar.* 54.10 and Judg 5:24. Cf. in contrast

43 BDF §245.3; Fitzmyer, 1.364.

44 For bibliography on blessing in the Bible, see "εὐλογέω, κτλ.," *ThWNT* 10.2 (1979) 1089–90 (bibliography); and Hermann Patsch, "εὐλογέω, κτλ.," *EDNT* 2 (1991) 79–80.

45 See Anatole Bailly, *Dictionnaire grec-française . . .* (rev. E. Egger; 2d ed.; Paris: Hachette, 1897) s.v. πόθεν (3). One must supply γέγονεν.

46 Some exegetes, such as Laurentin (*Structure*, 79–81), Escudero Freire (*Devolver*, 182–83), and Ernst (83), compare Luke 1:43 with 2 Sam (LXX 2 Kgdms) 6:9, in which David is upset about the presence of the ark in Jerusalem. The comparison of Mary with the ark is, however, a bit far-fetched. See Fitzmyer, 1.364.

47 Gerhard Delling, "τελείωσις," *TDNT* 8 (1972) 84–86. Cf. Jdt 10:9, to which Sahlin refers (*Messias*, 148 n. 2): "and I will go out and accomplish the things about which you spoke with me" (καὶ ἐξελεύσομαι εἰς τελείωσιν τῶν λόγων, ὧν ἐλαλήσατε μετ᾽ ἐμοῦ).

2 Esdr 10:6, "You most foolish of women."

Despite the overriding atmosphere of fulfillment in this chapter, the future tense of ἔσται ("will be") is a discreet reminder that God's plan is not yet even close to being realized. The isolated beatitude is an earlier form than the series of beatitudes. Whereas in the Hebrew Bible beatitudes concerned concrete and present prosperity, this one signifies something inward and spiritualized.[48]

■ **46** A number of Latin manuscripts put the Magnificat in Elizabeth's mouth. Σὺν αὐτῇ ("with her [Elizabeth]") in v. 56 also seems to presuppose that she is the singer. One could hypothetically reconstruct two annunciations for the Baptist tradition—one to Zechariah, one to Elizabeth—and, correspondingly, two songs: one by Elizabeth, one by Zechariah. But all the Greek texts and ancient versions, with the noted exception, read "Mary." After Elizabeth's speech, one should also expect a reaction on the part of Mary. If Elizabeth continued to speak, a second introduction would be superfluous, or it should at least contain an indication that she again began to speak and spoke further. Nevertheless, how could Elizabeth have become the one who prays the Magnificat in these Latin manuscripts? Had the encounter of the two women perhaps been chosen as the liturgical reading for the (very ancient) festival of Zechariah and Elizabeth, and the song attributed to John's mother because of this?[49]

Mary does not really answer Elizabeth's question (v. 43); she reacts very independently with her joy over the sign's confirmation (v. 36): "My soul praises the greatness of the Lord." Hannah thanks God for Samuel's birth in a similar manner (1 Sam [LXX 1 Kgdms] 2:1);

but there is also a clear relationship to the Psalms, especially Ps 34:1–3 (LXX 33:2–4). "My soul" here means Mary's "I" in her consciousness and inner life. "The Lord" is the living God, the Father, who acts faithfully and kindly in the present generation. Μεγαλύνω ("to make great") means, as often in the Jews' religious language, "to praise, extol."[50] Recognizing God's greatness and declaring it in the form of a prayer also belong to the word's semantic range. The greatness for which God is praised is not that of a ruler who degrades, but that of a savior who applies his power on behalf of people.

■ **47** Verse 47 and v. 46b are symmetrical; but, in the Psalms' poetic language, the second statement of a parallelism is not a simple repetition of the first.[51] Here it interprets the content of the first line: the "Lord" (κύριος) is the Hebrew Bible God who delivers people. Ἀγαλλιάω ("to rejoice"), attested only in biblical and ecclesiastical usage, is a Hellenistic neologism based on ἀγάλλω;[52] the object of rejoicing is introduced with ἐπί. In the New Testament it occurs in proximity to χαίρω ("to rejoice") and εὐφραίνομαι ("to be happy") and receives an eschatological tone. The present praise (μεγαλύνει) draws on past joy (ἠγαλλίασεν, aorist).[53] "My spirit" (τὸ πνεῦμά μου) is a variation of "my soul" (ἡ ψυχή μου) and designates, in contrast to the intellectual νοῦς ("mind"), the affective faculty.[54] In v. 47 one can hardly miss the author's citation of Hab 3:18 (LXX), which in turn belongs to the liturgical language of Israel.

■ **48** In v. 48 the main body of the song begins. The reason for the praise is God's "regard." Ἐπιβλέπω ἐπί ("to regard, look upon") is reminiscent of ἐπελεύσεται ἐπὶ

---

48 On the Beatitudes in Luke, see the commentary on Luke 6:20 below. The controversy over whether Mary is praised for her faith, her personality, or her experience is often characterized by denominational prejudice.

49 This last hypothesis was suggested to me by my assistant, M. Durrer. On this great text-critical problem, see Metzger, *Textual Commentary*, 130–31; Brown, *Birth*, 334–36; Fitzmyer, 1.365–66; Gueuret, *Engendrement*, 75 n. 36, 85–100; idem, "Sur Luc 1,46–55: Comment peut-on être amené à penser qu'Élisabeth est 'sémiotiquement' celle qui a prononcé le cantique en Lc 1, 46?" *Centre protestant d'études et de documentation: Supplément* (April 1977) 3–11.

50 On μεγαλύνω in Luke (rare; see Acts 10:46; 19:17) and in the NT, see Spicq, *Lexicon*, 2.459–60.

51 Tannehill, "Magnificat," 266.

52 BAGD s.v.

53 Some commentators offer grammatical explanations of the aorist. Lagrange (46) believes that the καί before ἠγαλλίασεν corresponds to the Hebrew idiom and has a causal sense. Schürmann (1.73 n. 216) writes, "The aorist ἠγαλλίασεν perhaps betrays the change of tense in an earlier Hebrew version (waw plus imperfect)." Plummer (31–32) thinks that the aorist ἠγαλλίασεν is equivalent to the perfect here.

54 Τὸ πνεῦμά μου ("my spirit") occurs in the Psalms much less frequently than "my soul": 31:5 (LXX 30:6); 77:3, 6 (LXX 76:4, 7); 143(LXX 142):4, 7.

σέ ("will come upon you") and ἐπισκιάσει ("will over-shadow") in v. 35. If God looks upon people, he does not forget them (cf. 1 Sam [LXX 1 Kgdms] 1:11). His "regard" can either judge them or, as here, select or deliver them (Lev 26:9). The author here follows 1 Sam (LXX 1 Kgdms) 1:11: "If you will indeed look on the lowliness of your servant" (ἐὰν ἐπιβλέπων ἐπιβλέψῃς ἐπὶ τὴν ταπείνωσιν τῆς δούλης σου, but cf. 1 Sam [LXX 1 Kgdms] 9:16; Ps 102:17 [LXX 101:18]).[55] In the LXX and the New Testament, ταπεινός ("humble") and ταπείνωσις ("humility, lowliness") are to be understood metaphorically, according to Greek usage, in a social and economic sense.[56] Both the MT and the LXX differentiate between this meaning and the virtue of humility, which is expressed by ταπεινὸς τῇ καρδίᾳ ("humble in heart"), ταπεινόφρων ("lowly in mind"), and ταπεινοφροσύνη ("humility"). Only the context would indicate—particularly in wisdom literature—that the wretched are also humble. But even in secular prose, ταπεινός and ταπείνωσις can have a positive connotation.[57] Mary's ταπείνωσις expresses, in Luke's eyes, her distance from God ("servant") and her place among the socially poor of Israel.

In v. 48b the sense is the confident expectation of future benedictions.[58] The LXX shows the sociological *Sitz im Leben* of the beatitude on the occasion of a birth, victory, or festival, as well as the literary position which the promised beatification occupies in a speech.[59] In time, prophecy received the same value as the beatitude.[60] The author again takes from the story of Leah (Gen 30:13) and interprets this promise to mean

all generations.[61] In Balaam's beatitude, the Messiah's coming lay still in the future (καὶ οὐχὶ νῦν ["but not now"]; Num 24:17); in our passage, his present arrival is discreetly indicated (ἀπὸ τοῦ νῦν ["from now on"]).

■ **49a** Verse 49a is perhaps a citation from Deut 10:21, but could just as well be prayer language inspired by hymnic prose.[62] The Lord's great deeds[63] are the deliverances and victories that God achieves for nation or individual. The font of every praise in Israel remains the exodus from Egypt (cf. Deut 3:24). Ὁ δυνατός ("the Mighty One") in the LXX is an exalted title for the king, a hero, or—though not very frequently—God.[64] We do not know what the author intends. Luke certainly has divine engenderment in mind (cf. δύναμις ὑψίστου ["power of the Most High"], 1:35), and thinks of vv. 48a and 49a as synonymous.[65]

■ **49b–50** As v. 48b called the recipient blessed, vv. 49b–50 praise the giver. Thus both ὅτι-clauses (vv. 48a and 49a) have a following clause that describes divine activity. Verses 49b–50 recognize the attributes of God behind the deeds: the holiness of his name, and his eternal mercy. Like the psalmists before him, the poet is not reflecting philosophically about God's essence, but rather recalling that God's actions correspond to his essence, and that God does not remain self-isolated. Both concepts (ὄνομα, "name," and ἔλεος, "mercy") presuppose a relationship between God and his people. God delivers his people in faithfulness to his holy name, that is, to himself. Those delivered learn their deliverer's name in that they experience the effect of his mercy. Similar formulations are frequent in the Psalms,[66] for

---

55 Cf. 2 Esdr 9:45: "And after thirty years God heard your servant, and looked upon my low estate, and considered my distress, and gave me a son." The weeping woman stands for Zion.

56 Ragnar Leivestad, "Ταπεινός–ταπεινόφρων," *NovT* 8 (1966) 36–47.

57 Walter Grundmann, "ταπεινός, κτλ.," *TDNT* 8 (1972) 1–26. On this point, more recently, see Escudero Freire, *Devolver*, 204–7.

58 Ἰδοὺ γάρ ("and now") can make a speech more lively, wake one's attention, or introduce an example. See BAGD *s.v.* ἰδού (1).

59 Gen 30:13; Num 24:17 (LXX); Cant 6:9.

60 In addition to Gen 30:13, cf. also Job 29:11–12 (LXX 10–11).

61 Extension to "all nations" in Ps 72(LXX 71):17 and Mal 3:12.

62 LXX Ps 70(MT 71):18–19 is not, indeed, the model

for the Magnificat, but it has a similar tone.

63 More than a few mss. read μεγαλεῖα ("mighty works"; cf. Acts 2:11).

64 Ps 120(LXX 119):4; Zeph 3:17. Walter Grundmann, "δύναμαι, κτλ.," *TDNT* 2 (1964) 284–317.

65 For this reason the punctuation in Nestle-Aland at the end of v. 48a, as at the end of v. 49a, seems too strong (a low point). One should not place so long a pause until the end of the first strophe.

66 Gunkel, "Lieder," 49.

example, in Ps 111(LXX 110):9[67] and 103(LXX 102):17.[68]

With "those who fear him,"[69] the purview widens. In place of the first person singular, the third person plural appears. Those who fear God are the faithful members of the people of God. The text looks beyond the bounds of the Jewish people toward the pagans who will confess the gospel (cf. Acts 10:35).

■ **51** The second half of the prayer begins at v. 51. In the first half, a causal relation united the praise (vv. 46–47) with the personally experienced reason for it (vv. 48–50). The poet can do without ὅτι ("that," "for") here, since this part begins with a general description of God's work:[70] three small strophes appear in a series (vv. 51, 52–53, 54–55).

Verse 51a recapitulates thoughts from v. 49a (ἐποίησεν ["he has done"]). Instead of mentioning God's deed, the author stays with the two attributes of God, as in vv. 49b–50, and adds a third, strength (κράτος). This should probably be taken in a positive sense: the redemption of the believers is a foil for the punishment of the proud. The deliverance of one (v. 51a) means the defeat of the other (v. 51b).[71] The prototype of such a deed by God,

with his "arm," is the exodus from Egypt (cf. Acts 13:17).[72] The language is still hymnic. There are parallels in Ps 118(LXX 117):15–16 for v. 51a; in Prov 3:34 for v. 51a–b; and in Ps 89:10 (LXX 88:11) for v. 51b. But v. 51b has incorporated an additional concept in "the thoughts of their hearts" (διανοίᾳ καρδίας αὐτῶν). This dative can be taken with ὑπερηφάνους (the enemies are "proud in the thoughts of their hearts")[73] or with διεσκόρπισεν,[74] thus explaining the manner in which God punishes these people; in favor of the first construction, one must note that the LXX usually has a preposition (ἐν, εἰς, or ἐπί) for the second construction (cf. Rom 1:24).

■ **52–53** Verses 52–53, two sets of doubled antithetical sentences, are closely related. The symmetry is chiastic, with two rhymes (-ων and -ους): the punished are named in lines 1 and 4, and the protected in lines 2 and 3. The reversal of conditions is also a familiar topos in Greek literature;[75] there Zeus, the divine, or fate can be responsible for it. But v. 52 has its roots rather in the Hebrew Bible, for there one reads about both God's transcendence over rich and poor, and his active decision in favor of the little ones.[76] Both are components of the

---

67 Cf. Pss 8:1 (LXX 8:2); 76:1 (LXX 75:2); 113(LXX 112):3; 135(LXX 134):3, 13; 148:13; Isa 12:4; Jer 10:6.

68 Cf. Pss 89:1 (LXX 88:2); 100(LXX 99):5; 103(LXX 102):11, 13; 119(LXX 118):156; 145(LXX 144):9; Lam 3:22. Gunkel ("Lieder," 50) cites *Ps. Sol.* 2:33: "For the mercy of the Lord will be upon them that fear him, in the judgment." Cf. *Ps. Sol.* 10:3.

69 The same or similar expressions occur in Ps 103(LXX 102):11, 13, 17; and *Ps. Sol.* 2:33; 3:12.

70 A transition from the first to the third person is not uncommon in the Psalms. It makes it possible to juxtapose the salvation offered to the suppliant and the punishment of the unbelievers. Cf. *Ps. Sol.* 2:31.

71 I agree with Tannehill ("Magnificat," 266), who concludes that v. 51 is a synthetic parallelism.

72 Exod 6:6 (LXX): "I will redeem you with an out-stretched arm and with a great judgment." This is an odd turn of phrase, but it shows—like Luke 1:51—that the nation's salvation and the punishment of its enemies belong together. Cf. Deut 4:34 and Isa 51:9 (MT).

73 P. L. Schoonheim has examined the usage of the concept ὑπερήφανος ("arrogant") in the HB and divides into six categories the roughly one hundred passages in which this mostly religiously tinged word occurs: (1) special cases; (2) insolence and

presumption; (3) mockery and derision; (4) contempt of the Law; (5) impudence and intimidation; (6) rebellion against God. He concludes that it is a *theological* lapse with *human* elements, for which a horrible fall is foreseen ("Der alttestamentliche Boden der Vokabel ὑπερήφανος Lukas 1, 51," *NovT* 8 [1966] 235–46). See Georg Bertram, "ὑπερήφανος, κτλ.," *TDNT* 8 (1972) 525–29.

74 Διασκορπίζω ("to scatter") can be found quite frequently in the LXX. Mostly, God is scattering Israel's enemies, but he can also be punishing Israel by scattering them among the nations.

75 Hesiod *Op.* 5–8; Aristotle *Poet.* 9.11.1452a.23; Aesop, fable 20 (the two roosters and the eagle); Xenophon *An.* 3.2.10; *Hist. Graec.* 6.4.23; cf. Pliny the Younger *Ep.* 4.11.2. See Luise Schottroff, "Das Magnificat und die älteste Tradition über Jesus von Nazareth," *EvTh* 38 (1978) 298–312, esp. 298–300; and Édouard Hamel, "Le Magnificat et le renversement des situations: Réflexion théologico-biblique (Lc 1,51–53)," *Greg* 60 (1979) 55–84, esp. 58–60.

76 Cf. 1 Sam (LXX 1 Kgdms) 2:7–8; Isa 2:11–17; Ezek 21:26, 31; Ps 147(LXX 146):6; Job 12:14–25; Sir 10:14. See Hamel, "Magnificat," 60–64.

eschatological plan. Both Jesus' parables and Paul's theology of the cross attest this reversal of conditions.[77] The Magnificat fits into both Jewish tradition and Christian interpretation. Verse 52 speaks explicitly only of socioeconomic conditions, but, true to the Hebrew Bible, outer appearance is the mirror of inner attitudes. The song is not only about the dangers of power and possessions; no more does it demonize the political and economic world. God desires and carries out the overthrow because injustice prevails among people. When God inaugurates his reign, he necessarily shakes the mighty from their thrones and demands the money of the rich. If he did not do so, he would be neither just nor good, and thus not God. The child's birth signifies the end of many privileges and oppressions. It is not enough to say that rich and poor must live in the Gospel's spirit of poverty, nor to say that the old ways of thinking about power no longer have meaning.[78] The Magnificat corresponds to Hebrew wisdom and Hebrew lessons about retribution: "The Lord overthrows the thrones of rulers, and enthrones the lowly in their place" ($\vartheta\rho\acute{o}\nu o\upsilon\varsigma$ $\mathring{\alpha}\rho\chi\acute{o}\nu\tau\omega\nu$ $\kappa\alpha\vartheta\varepsilon\hat{\imath}\lambda\varepsilon\nu$ $\acute{o}$ $\kappa\acute{\upsilon}\rho\iota o\varsigma$ $\kappa\alpha\grave{\iota}$ $\mathring{\varepsilon}\kappa\acute{\alpha}\vartheta\iota\sigma\varepsilon$ $\pi\rho\alpha\varepsilon\hat{\iota}\varsigma$ $\mathring{\alpha}\nu\tau'$ $\alpha\mathring{\upsilon}\tau\hat{\omega}\nu$, Sir 10:14).[79]

In the chiasm, the song describes the social advancement and the "Wirtschaftswunder" (economic miracle) of God's elect. In line with Hebrew Bible symbolism, "to lift up" ($\mathring{\upsilon}\psi\acute{o}\omega$) and "good things" ($\mathring{\alpha}\gamma\alpha\vartheta\acute{\alpha}$) mean more than human status and consumer goods; recall the exaltation of Christ and the eschatological blessings (in Luke, the Holy Spirit).[80] In liturgical language $\tau\alpha\pi\varepsilon\iota\nu o\acute{\iota}$ ("the lowly") are, as believers, hungry also for God's word. They are also "those who fear him" ($\varphi o\beta o\acute{\upsilon}\mu\varepsilon\nu o\iota$ $\alpha\mathring{\upsilon}\tau\acute{o}\nu$, v. 50b).[81]

■ **54–55** Verses 54–55 seem rather ponderous after the artful vv. 52–53. This is a result of the literary principle of lengthening and slowing down a concluding sentence.[82] After "I" and "those who fear him," "Israel" occurs for the first time. The description of the singer as the handmaiden, and of Israel as the servant of God, are traditional expressions.[83] God has attended to his people; in the language of the Psalms, the verb is unambiguously soteriological.[84] The infinitive construction $\mu\nu\eta\sigma\vartheta\hat{\eta}\nu\alpha\iota$ $\mathring{\varepsilon}\lambda\acute{\varepsilon} o\upsilon\varsigma$ ("to remember mercy") is surprising: "so that he remembers his mercy" is an expression from the Hebrew Bible.[85] God remains true to his "mercy." This word, which emphasizes the affective, stands at the conclusion of the first half of the song (v. 50) and reappears at the end of the last half.

The infinitive has already interrupted the series of aorists. The $\kappa\alpha\vartheta\acute{\omega}\varsigma$ ("as") clause (v. 55) definitively breaks off the construction, thus making the conclusion possible. Israel's deliverance was promised to the fathers ($\pi\rho\acute{o}\varsigma$) and pledged to Abraham and his posterity (dative), if one takes this dative not with $\mu\nu\eta\sigma\vartheta\hat{\eta}\nu\alpha\iota$ ("to remember"), but with $\mathring{\varepsilon}\lambda\acute{\alpha}\lambda\eta\sigma\varepsilon\nu$ ("he spoke"),[86] and interprets this word Semitically as "to promise" (thus deleting the comma after $\mathring{\eta}\mu\hat{\omega}\nu$, "our"). On the other hand, Ps 98(LXX 97):3 does combine $\mu\nu\eta\sigma\vartheta\hat{\eta}\nu\alpha\iota$ $\mathring{\varepsilon}\lambda\acute{\varepsilon} o\upsilon\varsigma$ with $\tau\hat{\omega}$ $\mathring{\iota}\alpha\kappa\acute{\omega}\beta$ ("to Jacob"), which again favors understanding v. 55a as a parenthesis. Thus, depending on one's evaluation of the sentence structure, the song concludes with a reference either to God's eternal promise or to his everlasting faithfulness.

■ **56** Mary stays with Elizabeth[87] for approximately[88] three months. She is thus separated from Joseph long enough so that the readers cannot doubt the virgin

---

77 Luke 10:29–37; 15:11–32; 16:19–31; 18:9–14; 1 Cor 1:26–31; 2 Cor 8:9; Phil 2:6–11. See Hamel, "Magnificat," 65–70.

78 So Ernst, 87.

79 $\mathring{E}\xi\alpha\pi o\sigma\tau\acute{\varepsilon}\lambda\lambda\omega$ with $\kappa\varepsilon\nu\acute{o}\varsigma$ ("to send away empty") is a HB idiom: Gen 31:42; Deut 15:13; 1 Sam (LXX 1 Kgdms) 6:3; Job 22:9; cf. Ruth 1:21; 3:17; 1 Kgs (LXX 3 Kgdms) 6:13; Luke 20:11.

80 $\mathring{\Upsilon}\psi\acute{o}\omega$: cf. Acts 3:22 and John 3:14. $\mathring{A}\gamma\alpha\vartheta\acute{\alpha}$: cf. Matt 7:11.

81 Verse 53a adapts Ps 107(LXX 106):9b: $\kappa\alpha\grave{\iota}$ $\psi\upsilon\chi\grave{\eta}\nu$ $\pi\varepsilon\iota\nu\hat{\omega}\sigma\alpha\nu$ $\mathring{\varepsilon}\nu\acute{\varepsilon}\pi\lambda\eta\sigma\varepsilon\nu$ $\mathring{\alpha}\gamma\alpha\vartheta\hat{\omega}\nu$.

82 Cf. the conclusion of the Beatitudes (6:22).

83 ($\mathring{O}$) $\pi\alpha\hat{\iota}\varsigma$ $\mu o\upsilon$ ("my servant") as a designation for Israel: Isa 41:8–9 (where we also find the words $\sigma\pi\acute{\varepsilon}\rho\mu\alpha$ $\mathring{A}\beta\rho\alpha\acute{\alpha}\mu$ ["Abraham's seed"] and $\mathring{\alpha}\nu\tau\varepsilon$-

$\lambda\alpha\beta\acute{o}\mu\eta\nu$ ["to attend to"]); 42:1; 44:1; 45:4; 52:13.

84 Cf. Ps 118(LXX 117):13: "But the Lord helped me" ($\kappa\alpha\grave{\iota}$ $\acute{o}$ $\kappa\acute{\upsilon}\rho\iota o\varsigma$ $\mathring{\alpha}\nu\tau\varepsilon\lambda\acute{\alpha}\beta\varepsilon\tau\acute{o}$ $\mu o\upsilon$).

85 Ps 98(LXX 97):3. Cf. *Ps. Sol.* 10:4.

86 Paul Joüon, "Notes de philologie évangélique: Luc 1, 54–55: Une difficulté grammaticale du Magnificat," *RechSR* 15 (1925) 440–41.

87 Luke prefers $\sigma\acute{\upsilon}\nu$ to $\mu\varepsilon\tau\acute{\alpha}$ (both, "with") and avoids naming Elizabeth in v. 56 to prevent a repetition in v. 57, where her name is indispensable.

88 Luke occasionally uses $\acute{\omega}\varsigma$ before temporal designations either to indicate that they are approximate, or to let the readers know that they should not assign too much significance to them. Cf. BAGD s.v. $\acute{\omega}\varsigma$ (IV. 5).

birth. But she cannot stay too long, either, since she should leave the scene for John's birth.[89] In contrast to Elizabeth, who lives in Zechariah's house (v. 40), Mary returns to *her* house (v. 56); this detail does not demonstrate a biographical interest, but rather a theological interest in reference to Mary's virginity.

Conclusion

The scene of the meeting receives its character from the speech and the hymn that responds to it. The hymn seems to derive from an older psalm constructed from biblical citations and liturgical formulae.[90] The evangelist has Christianized the song only slightly, but, in adopting it, has annexed and reinterpreted it. Like the speeches in the book of Acts, he attaches a great importance to it: the hymn is intended to interpret the events theologically. This hermeneutical function helps one better understand the direction of Luke's new interpretation. The key to it, I believe, is the Lukan beatitude in v. 45, in which Mary is described as blessed and believing; she awaits the fulfillment of God's promise in faith.

In the earlier version of the Magnificat, the aorists[91] were completely suited to the genre. In the present version, however, they receive a new sense. Mary has already experienced God's attention, and v. 48a ($\dot{\epsilon}\pi\dot{\epsilon}\beta\lambda\epsilon\psi\epsilon\nu$ ["he has looked with favor upon"]) has been fulfilled in the annunciation. One could also say the same of v. 49, although, like Hannah's song (1 Sam 2:1–10), it would be more suitable *after* the birth. Verse 45 speaks of the fulfillment ($\tau\epsilon\lambda\epsilon\dot{\iota}\omega\sigma\iota\varsigma$) expected by Mary; so vv. 51–55, for Luke, also extol the eschatological fulfillment expected by faith. The evangelist knows how the prophets, especially Deutero-Isaiah, reinterpreted the genre of the hymn eschatologically.[92] The

Hebrew perfect tense was still retained even by the late prophets, so solidly rooted was their expectation. The prophetic function of the aorists is even more probable here, since Luke knows more than Mary and lives *after* Jesus' mission, cross, and resurrection. He knows how God *has* attended to his people Israel in Jesus Christ. But the tension remains; less than ever have the rich and the rulers lost their position of power today. The song's prerequisite—according to v. 45—is faith: Christians believe that the resurrected one reigns *now*, and they do sometimes see the oppressed gaining their dignity through God's action. The reversal of conditions has already begun in form of a sign. Thus Luke could also have understood the aorists as inchoate. To this extent we can find no final solution, but we can *pray* the Magnificat, in faith that a fulfillment of God's word should be expected, and that it has already begun.

The transition from the individual "I" to the plural describing the congregation is typical of the form. The individual believer here expresses his or her experience of God ecclesiologically. Luke adopts this perspective: for him, Mary is not the embodiment of the people of Israel, of the daughter of Zion, but rather of the small and hungry ones whom God particularly values and protects. "In its dynamic unity this text holds together the small and the great, the birth of a baby to an unimportant woman and the fulfillment of Israel's promise through the overturn of human society."[93]

The hymn does not explicitly mention the Messiah.[94] Luke wants to say something about *God* with the Magnificat. The song extols the threefold activity of God on the religious, sociopolitical, and ethnic levels. As Lord and God, he is transcendent, stands on the side of the poor, and applies his work to all of humanity through Israel.[95] I see in it the God who lays claim to the whole

---

89 According to Lagrange (51), Greek patristic tradition, in contrast to the Latins, displayed the conviction that Mary had already left Elizabeth when John the Baptist was born.

90 Schürmann (1.78 nn. 264–66) lists the advocates of the various hypotheses about the Magnificat's origin.

91 The various hypotheses (aorist of historical narrative, gnomic aorist, ingressive aorist, aorist corresponding to the Hebrew perfect) are presented by Plummer (33), Lagrange (48), Gunkel ("Lieder," 53), and Dupont ("Magnificat," 331–35). Dupont finally decides that the aorists are ingressive.

92 See Gunkel, "Lieder," 53–56.

93 Tannehill, "Magnificat," 275.

94 Escudero Freire (*Devolver*, 117–79) exaggerates the messianic character of the scene.

95 Cf. on this the title of Dupont's article itself: "Le Magnificat comme discours sur Dieu."

of a human life, and places his power in the service of his compassion. But as a consequence of human resistance (each person sits on his or her own throne), this power must result in judgment, in order to make the compassion *concrete*. "Thus God cannot place his power at the service of his compassion for the humble and weak, without it coming into conflict with that of the mighty of this world."[96]

History of Interpretation

From the Magnificat, a new power goes forth into our own time. The liberation that it announces is understood as a promise by all those who work for the liberation of individuals and peoples. Like all biblical texts, the Magnificat has been interpreted in both the literal and metaphorical senses in the course of history. Luise Schottroff objects with conviction to attempts to understand "poor" in only a spiritual sense.[97] According to her, the two senses must not be separated from each other. Because the poor possess nothing that binds their heart to this world, nothing hinders them from devoting themselves to the requirements of God's kingdom. For some theologians of the Third World, the sociological sense has become so essential that they occasionally see only the horizontal, forgetting the vertical. By contrast, Gustavo Gutiérrez sees in the Magnificat a new "spiritu-

ality of liberation," that is, a concrete manner in which to live the gospel: inspired by the Holy Spirit, and in solidarity with all people before the Lord.[98] In this sense the Magnificat is a pattern for every prayer, every praise of God; at the same time it is one of the New Testament texts with the most strongly political and liberating content. It calls on us to take the words totally concretely, and to fight against oppression in order to take seriously the Lord of history. Finally, Dorothee Sölle has transposed the Magnificat into poetic words for our time.[99] She calls us to reappropriate Mary's song for ourselves, and, by means of this song of joy, victory, and humility, to seek out our own place. She not only sings of God's overall victory, but also expresses her confidence about the freedom that is beginning, there where she applies the Magnificat to herself, and to the overlooked women shoved back into the shadows: "The empty faces of women will be filled with life."[100] And, like Mary, she visualizes the freedom to which she appeals, of which she dreams for all women, by extending her "I" to "we" and "all." It is a preliminary step toward universal freedom: "The great change that is taking place in us and through us,/ will reach all."[101]

---

96 Dupont, "Magnificat," 342.

97 Schottroff, "Magnificat," 311–12.

98 Gustavo Gutiérrez, *A Theology of Liberation: History, Politics, and Salvation* (1973; trans. and ed. C. Inda and J. Eagleson; Maryknoll, N.Y.: Orbis, 1988) 116–20.

99 Dorothee Sölle, "Meditation on Luke 1," in idem, *Revolutionary Patience* (trans. R. and R. Kimber; rev. ed.; Maryknoll, N.Y.: Orbis, 1977) 51.

100 Ibid.

101 Ibid. See Monika Stocker, "Dorothee Sölle: Eine Begegnung auf den vier Lebensfeldern der Dichterin," *Neue Wege* 79 (1985) 19–25.

The Birth of John (1:57-80)

Bibliography

Audet, Jean-Paul, "Esquisse historique du genre litté-raire de la 'bénédiction' juive et de l' 'eucharistie' chrétienne," *RB* 65 (1958) 371–99.

Auffret, "Note."

Benoit, "Enfance," 176, 182–91.

Bikerman, E., "Ἀνάδειξις," in *Mélanges: Festschrift Émile Boisacq* (2 vols.; Annuaire de l'Institut de philologie 5; Brussels: Secrétariat des éditions de l'Institut, 1937–38) 1.117–24.

Brown, *Birth*, 367–92.

Carter, Warren, "Zechariah and the Benedictus (Luke 1,68–79): Practising What He Preaches," *Bib* 69 (1988) 239–47.

Croatto, J. Severino, "El 'Benedictus' como memoria de la alianza (Estructura y teología de Lucas, 1,68–79)," *RevistB* 47 (1985) 207–19.

Dibelius, *Jungfrauensohn*, 1–9, 77–78.

Dubois, "Jean-Baptiste," 83–86, 99–101.

Erdmann, *Vorgeschichten*, 10–11, 37–38, 41–42.

Farris, *Hymns*, 127–42.

Funk, Robert W., "The Wilderness," *JBL* 78 (1959) 205–14.

George, "Parallèle."

Geyser, A. S., "The Youth of John the Baptist: A Deduction from the Break in the Parallel Account of the Lucan Infancy Story," *NovT* 1 (1956) 70–75.

Gnilka, Joachim, "Der Hymnus des Zacharias," *BZ* n.s. 6 (1962) 215–38.

Gunkel, "Lieder."

Jacoby, Adolf, "Ἀνατολὴ ἐξ ὕψους," *ZNW* 20 (1921) 205–14.

Jones, "Background."

Kaut, Thomas, *Befreier und befreites Volk: Traditions- und redaktionsgeschichtliche Untersuchung zu Mag- nifikat und Benedictus im Kontext der vorlukanischen Kindheitsgeschichte* (Frankfurt am Main: Hain, 1990).

Legrand, L., "L'Évangile aux bergers: Essai sur le genre littéraire de Luc II,8–20," *RB* 75 (1968) 161–87.

Mussies, Gerard, "Vernoemen in de antieke wereld: De historische achtergrond van Luk. 1,59–63," *NedThT* 42 (1988) 114–25.

Oro, María del Carmen, "Benedictus de Zacarias (Luc 1,68–79): Indicios de una cristología arcaica?" *RevistB* 45 (1983) 145–77.

Rousseau, François, "Les structures du Benedictus (Luc 1,68–79)," *NTS* 32 (1986) 268–82.

Sahlin, *Messias*, 153–59, 175–82, 288–306.

Vanhoye, "Structure."

van Kasteren, R. P., "Analecta exegetica—Luc 1,76s," *RB* 3 (1894) 54–56.

Vielhauer, Philipp, "Das Benedictus des Zacharias (Lk 1,68–79)," *ZThK* 49 (1952) 255–72, reprinted in idem, *Aufsätze zum Neuen Testament* (ThBü 31; Munich: Kaiser, 1965) 28–46.

Winter, "Magnificat."

idem, "Miszellen," 66–67.

57 The time was fulfilled for Elizabeth to give birth, and she bore a son. 58/ And her neighbors and relatives heard that the Lord had made great his compassion to her, and they rejoiced with her. 59/ And it happened on the eighth day that they came to circumcise the child, and they were going to name him after his father, Zechariah. 60/ But his mother answered and said, "No; he is to be called John." 61/ And they said to her, "None of your relatives is called by this name." 62/ And they motioned to his father, to find out what name he wanted to call him. 63/ And he asked for a writing tablet, and wrote, "His name is John." And all of them were amazed. 64/ Then immediately his mouth was opened and his tongue freed, and he spoke, praising God. 65/ And fear came over all their neighbors, and all these things were talked about throughout the entire hill country of Judea, 66/ and all who heard them pondered them in their hearts, and said, "What then will this child become?" For, indeed, the hand of the Lord was with him. 67/ And his father Zechariah was filled with holy spirit and prophesied, 68/ "Blessed be the Lord, the God of Israel, for he has visited his people and has brought about deliverance for his people, 69/ and he has raised up a horn of sal-vation for us in the house of David, his servant, 70/ as he spoke through the mouth of his holy prophets from of old, 71/ salvation from our enemies, and from the hand of all who hate us; 72/ to perform mercy to our ancestors and to remember his holy covenant, 73/ the oath that he swore to our father Abraham, and to grant us 74/ that we, without fear, being rescued from the hands of our enemies, might serve him 75/ in holiness and righteousness before him all our days. 76/ And you, child, will be called prophet of the Most High; for you will go before the Lord to prepare his ways, 77/ to give knowledge of sal-vation to his people in the forgiveness of their sins, 78/ by the compassionate heart of our God, who will visit us through the one arising from on high 79/ to appear to those who sit in darkness and in the shadow of death, to guide our feet into the way of peace." 80/ The child grew and became strong in spirit, and he was in the wil-derness until the day he appeared publicly in Israel.

Analysis

The fulfillment of the promise began already with the child's conception (vv. 24–25; see commentary there), but really takes place only in the birth itself (vv. 57–58). The symbolic muteness (vv. 18–20) must also find its conclusion (vv. 59–66a). The Benedictus does not belong to the original legend and was introduced by Luke into this passage. The two short summary passages (v. 66b, comparable to Acts 11:21; and v. 80, closely connected to Luke 2:40), which more or less skillfully insert a pause, are most probably also Lukan.

The Narrative

Although the birth is narrated in a sober and colorless manner, the following scene is particularly lively. Tension arises between Elizabeth and her relatives (vv. 59–61), who then question Zechariah, and this confirms the mother's opinion (vv. 62–63). After this miraculous unanimity, another wonder occurs: Zechariah's mouth is opened (v. 64). The report about the event spreads throughout the entire region, and everyone marvels at the future of a newborn child accompanied by such miracles (vv. 65–66a). Because of the form of the account and the nature of its subject, the people who ask the question (v. 66a) expect no answer. The relatively extensive birth legend of John—its complex structure suggests a late development—narrates various episodes and employs several smaller genres. In this passage there is an apothegm (vv. 59–66a), and earlier (vv. 8–20) an annunciation.

The Benedictus

1. *Form.* The song of Zechariah is a psalm in the Hebrew Bible tradition, a prayer of thanks that begins with a blessing (v. 68a) and then, in the form-critically appropriate manner, indicates the reason for thanksgiving (introduced with ὅτι, v. 68b). After three statements in the aorist (ἐπεσκέψατο, ἐποίησεν, and ἤγειρεν, "visited . . . brought . . . raised"), the prayer broadens its purview with a dependent clause (καθὼς ἐλάλησεν . . . , "as he spoke . . ."), as in the conclusion of the Magnificat (v. 55). It is more difficult to make out the structure of what

follows, since the sentence that has found its conclusion in v. 70 nevertheless continues. Similar to the Hebraic syntax of the Psalms, several unconnected constructions, which are introduced by an accusative (σωτηρίαν, "salvation," v. 71) or an infinitive (ποιῆσαι, "to perform," v. 72; τοῦ δοῦναι, "to grant," v. 73; λατρεύειν, "might serve," v. 74) appear until the end of v. 75. In v. 76 a new sentence begins, with a change of person (from the third, God, to the second, the child) and tense (from aorist to future).[1] As in the first half, the sentence begins better than it ends, for the two coordinated main sentences (connected with γάρ, "for") draw in their wake a series of subordinate clauses, the structure of which is less than lucid: v. 77 describes a purpose; v. 78b, a main event, but in a relative clause; and v. 79 contains two infinitive clauses. The poorly construed v. 78a and the uncoordinated infinitives in v. 79 have a disturbing effect. From a form-critical perspective, the second half of the Benedictus is no longer a song of praise to God, but a *genethliakon,* that is, the expression of a wish or oracle concerning a newborn child.[2] From beginning to end, the rhythm of the prose shows a structuring of small units. Nestle-Aland's division of it into lines is justified, although one could argue about the length and number of these lines, which have no symmetry: v. 69 is a single line and should be spoken in one breath; in contrast, v. 71 shows *parallelismus membrorum* and should be divided differently than in Nestle-Aland.

In my formal description of the prayer, I isolated two parts (vv. 68–75, 76–79), on the basis of the grammar. Albert Vanhoye devotes his attention to substantive correspondences within the poem (e.g., the "visit," vv. 68, 78; or the "enemies," vv. 71, 74) and works out a chiastic structure, with its center in vv. 72b–73a (the covenant and oath).[3] Hence the prayer articulates three themes: God's saving act, the deliverance of the people, and the word of God. It is theologically relevant that the child is

---

1 Benoit ("Enfance," 185) sees in the aorist ἐπεσκέψατο ("has visited us," one variant in v. 78) a reminiscence of the earlier version, and in the future ἐπισκέψεται ("will visit us," another variant, preferred by Nestle-Aland) Luke's editorial hand. He believes that Luke inserted vv. 76–77 and adjusted the tense of v. 78 to the two futures in the insertion.

2 On this genre see Erdmann, *Vorgeschichten,* 32, 41,

136–37; and Klaus Berger, *Formgeschichte des Neuen Testaments* (Heidelberg: Quelle und Meyer, 1984) 348.

3 "Structure."

not at the center: the Baptist will only be a witness (v. 76), like the prophets (v. 70). As Pierre Auffret notes, this outline overlooks the unmistakable caesura between vv. 75 and 76 and neglects other formal elements (e.g., the pronouns "he," "we," and "you").[4]

2. *Origin*. Purely Lukan authorship[5] is surely not the case; rather, this is a more or less radical rewriting of a Jewish or Jewish Christian original.

The Lukan idioms are inconsistently distributed. Verse 70 is in almost literal agreement with Acts 3:21b; the beginning of v. 76 forms a counterpart to 1:32. $\Sigma\omega\tau\eta\rho\iota\alpha$ ("salvation") and other expressions in these verses are Lukan. Should vv. 76–77 be taken as a Lukan insertion,[6] or as a common Christian tradition,[7] which alludes only indirectly (cf. Mark 1:2–3 par. Luke 3:4–5) to Mal 3:1 and Isa 40:3? The vocabulary and style of the remaining portions are not Lukan,[8] although themes such as "salvation" and "mercy" echo the evangelist's intention. I am of the opinion that Luke did not even completely interpolate vv. 70 and 76–77; one detects his hand, but it is the hand of an editor (the same is true of Acts 3:20–21; 3:21b repeats our v. 70).[9] In vv. 76–77 the words $\pi\rho\sigma\pi\sigma\rho\epsilon\dot{\upsilon}\sigma\mu\alpha\iota$ ("to go before") and $\gamma\nu\hat{\omega}\sigma\iota\varsigma$ $\sigma\omega\tau\eta\rho\iota\alpha\varsigma$ ("knowledge of salvation") are not specifically Lukan expressions.[10] Did Luke know only one model, or two? Hermann Gunkel and many others separate the thanksgiving (vv. 68–75) from the salutation (vv. 76–79), since, according to the genres, a prophecy is seldom found within such a song.[11] It must be taken into consideration that vv. 68–75 form a complete hymn in themselves, containing an invitation to praise, the reason for thanksgiving, and a conclusion; the broader style as well as the mention of many days is typical for a conclusion. If the aorists of vv. 68–69 describe God's concrete acts of salvation that have taken place recently, the poem is messianic and was thus composed by Christians. But v. 69 is not necessarily Christian and, on the basis of v. 70, it could be taken as the fulfillment of a prophecy, analogous to 1QM 11.5: "Our strength and the power of our hands accomplish no mighty deeds except by Thy power and by the might of Thy great valour. This Thou hast taught us from ancient times, saying 'A star shall come out of Jacob, and a sceptre shall rise out of Israel.'"[12] Israel, too, thanks God for individual, preliminary acts of deliverance. In 1QM 18–19 the army of the elect gives thanks, first, for an initial victory (as in our vv. 68–75), and then hopes for the final salvation (like our vv. 78b–79).[13] Thus there were mixed forms in Jewish literature as well.[14] As a song of thanksgiving, the Benedictus praises God for the beginning of salvation; as prophecy, it awaits the final victory. So Luke possessed only one model, which he altered just a little.

The place of origin is probably not Christian, but rather Jewish, although indeed not Pharisaic or Essene, since both milieux expect a *warrior* Messiah. Unlike the *Psalms of Solomon* and the songs of the *War Scroll*, the deliverance of the people in this passage is not effected by the power of weapons. Thus the Benedictus is not a Maccabean psalm,[15] but a poem of the Baptist's movement, though this does not mean that one must identify John with the Messiah.[16] The original version characterized the Baptist rather as a prophet and precursor of

4   "Note," 248.
5   Brown (*Birth*, 377) has listed the defenders of this hypothesis.
6   Brown, *Birth*, 379–80, 389. According to Gunkel ("Lieder," 57–60), the entire conclusion (i.e., vv. 76–79) is a Christian addition to a Jewish psalm.
7   Agreeing with Gnilka ("Hymnus," 232–34).
8   To mention only three examples: $\pi\sigma\iota\dot{\epsilon}\omega$ $\lambda\dot{\upsilon}\tau\rho\omega\sigma\iota\nu$ ("to bring about deliverance"), $\kappa\dot{\epsilon}\rho\alpha\varsigma$ $\sigma\omega\tau\eta\rho\iota\alpha\varsigma$ ("a horn of salvation"), and $\mu\nu\eta\sigma\vartheta\hat{\eta}\nu\alpha\iota$ $\delta\iota\alpha\vartheta\dot{\eta}\kappa\eta\varsigma$ ("to remember the covenant").
9   Against Gerhard Lohfink, "Christologie und Geschichtsbild in Apg 3,19–21," *BZ* n.s. 13 (1969) 223–41.
10 $\Pi\rho\sigma\pi\sigma\rho\epsilon\dot{\upsilon}\sigma\mu\alpha\iota$ occurs only once more in the Lukan writings, in Acts 7:40, a HB citation.
11 Gunkel, "Lieder," 53. Also Winter, "Magnificat," 8.
12 Geza Vermes, *The Dead Sea Scrolls in English* (2d ed.;

New York: Penguin, 1975) 138.
13 The parallelism could be drawn out even further, if the invocation (1QM 12.8–13; 19.2–5) did not address God himself, but rather the human instrument of divine salvation, as is the case in Luke 1:76–77.
14 As Gunkel writes ("Lieder," 59): "Indeed, a later poetic creation, which was no longer truly familiar with the genres, could mix up disparate elements in disorganized fashion."
15 Against Winter ("Magnificat"). In a further article ("Miszellen"), Winter calls attention to the *War Scroll*, particularly to the parallel in 1QM 14.4–5, to substantiate the warlike character of the Benedictus and the Magnificat.
16 Philip Vielhauer, "Das Benedictus des Zacharias (Lk 1, 68–79)" *ZThK* 49 (1952) 255–72, reprinted in

God, a description that conforms with the message of the Baptist himself (cf. Luke 3:7–9, 15–17). The original version thus belongs to an early period of the Baptist's movement, which did not yet view John as the Messiah. The author was inspired by the Psalms and assembled the text from borrowed fragments, although the borrowings are less transparent than in the Magnificat.[17] A certain proximity to the *Testaments of the Twelve Patriarchs*[18] is particularly evident in vv. 76–79: σπλάγχνα ἐλέους ("compassionate heart") is found in neither the Old Testament nor New Testament, but occurs in *T. Zeb.* 7.3 and 8.2, although in an anthropological sense; ἐπισκέπτομαι ("to visit"), which describes the divine act of salvation, occurs frequently in *Testaments of the Twelve Patriarchs*.[19]

3. *Function.* If the Benedictus were Christian in origin, would it have been a congregational hymn thanking God for the birth of Jesus, the Messiah (v. 76; vv. 76–77 or 76–79 would be considered a Lukan addition in this case)? In my opinion, it is a hymn and also a prophecy sung in regard to John's birth by his disciples. But I am aware of two difficulties. First, what concrete message did the Baptist's community wish to express in vv. 68–69? Second, could this prophecy have been sung independently of an account of the birth of John, or did the song already belong to the narrative in the tradition, as, for example, the song of Hannah in 1 Sam (LXX 1 Kgdms) 1–2?

Commentary

We often compare the Benedictus with the Magnificat, while forgetting that, according to Luke's arrangement, the believing Mary answers the unbelief of the mute Zechariah with the Magnificat, while the Benedictus, as a song of birth, corresponds to Simeon's Nunc Dimittis. Of course, this parallelism is not completely symmetrical; Zechariah sings because he has now begun to believe, and thus approximates Mary. On this second level, the Magnificat and the Benedictus would then be comparable. The present *function* of the Benedictus in Luke's composition should not, then, be neglected, especially since the prose and poetry together express the point of the narrative and thus have a hermeneutical function. The verbal constructions indicate the "when" and "where" of salvation.

God is the subject of most of the verbs, but he does not act alone. The child is ascribed the role of preparation, and the cryptic ἀνατολή ("the dawn," "the one arising") is given an executive function. The human agents cannot be separated from the ubiquitous "we." How do the acts of God unfold, and the relationship of the human "we" to him? Is not the song also, for this reason, a song of praise, since the history of a people is marked by life and movement: the almost-present Lord on his way and the wandering community on their path?

The Narrative

■ **57–58** Mary is off the stage. Elizabeth remains alone in her pregnancy. Readers accustomed to biblical language could understand "the time was fulfilled" as the fulfillment of divine prophecy (cf. 2:6).[20]

The angel's message (1:13) is fulfilled literally.[21] News spreads; Elizabeth, who at first withdrew because of her pregnancy (1:24, 56), now rejoices together with her neighbors and relatives. The crescendo from Elizabeth's reaction to that of her neighbors is an aesthetic component of the pericope, not a piece of historical information. The newborn child is introduced—in Hebraistic language—as the fruit of God's compassion[22] (1:58). Μεγαλύνω here takes its literal meaning: "to make great." A normal birth is usually associated with joy, let alone a birth so wondrous, destined by God. Joy is, in

idem, *Aufsätze zum Neuen Testament* (ThBü 31; Munich: Kaiser, 1965) 28–46.

17 Brown (*Birth*, 386–89) compiles the closest parallels. See the commentary on the Benedictus below.

18 Gnilka, "Hymnus," 235–37.

19 *T. Levi* 4:4; *T. Jud.* 23:5; *T. Ash.* 7:3.

20 Agreeing with Fitzmyer (1.373). Cf. Gen 25:24; Luke 1:23; 2:6.

21 In both places (Luke 1:13, 57), γεννάω υἱόν ("to bring forth a son") is used; in 2:6–7, on the other hand, the more correct τίκτω ("to bear, give birth") is employed.

22 The LXX chose the neuter τὸ ἔλεος to translate this concept, although in secular Greek it is the masculine ὁ ἔλεος that is used almost exclusively; see BAGD *s.v.* Does the LXX intend thereby to extol the special quality of this compassion?

Luke, a characteristic of faith that recognizes salvation history marching forward.[23] But v. 58 at first describes only the relevance of the event for the mother. The next episode broadens its significance in respect to the whole people.

This episode, a successful episode, creates problems only for scholars. Normal readers accept that things are told in this manner because something extraordinary has happened.

■ **59–66** At the circumcision, everything still runs as expected. The peculiar events begin only when the name is given: Elizabeth, along with Zechariah, is on the side of the divine plan. It should not be questioned how the mother learned of the prophesied name. Her knowledge is a sign of her election. Zechariah, unbelieving at that time, now shows by his written communication that he, for his part, finally believes the angel. Suddenly,[24] that is, miraculously, Zechariah can speak again. He understands this as the completion of the sign (1:18–20); the people see in it the divine origin of the unexpected name. After everyone's astonishment (v. 63), the fear of God descends (v. 65) and seizes the entire region (v. 65). In those times a child always awakened interest in its future. That is why the people discuss all of these events (v. 65)[25] and inquire about God's plan for this child (v. 66). Since Luke does not intend to return to John until chap. 3, he stresses, temporarily and with a Hebrew Bible expression that attests God's care and providence: "For, indeed, the hand of the Lord was with him" (v. 66).

Circumcision on the eighth day is based in the Scriptures[26] and belongs to common Jewish tradition.[27] The first difficulty is with the naming.[28] A son was usually named after his grandfather rather than his father.[29] Is Zechariah's grandfatherly age the reason for the exception suggested (v. 59)? Or did the customs change? Or is Luke misinformed? It could also be that *we* are misinformed. A father who was physically handicapped would give his son his own name, probably in order to compensate for the father's imperfection in the son.[30] Thus Matthias, Josephus's ancestor who stuttered, named his son Matthias.

Matthew, at home in Judaism, has the angel say to Joseph, "She will bear a son, and *you* [the father] are to name him Jesus" (1:21). But Luke leaves this responsibility to the mother in the angel's message to Mary (1:31). For here Zechariah is, of course, in no position to speak; and it is not clear that Elizabeth is speaking completely independently. On the contrary, the text seems rather to indicate harmonious accord between the spouses. Nevertheless, that Mary and Elizabeth name their children is probably exceptional to Luke.

Is Luke mistaken here that a child was not named until the eighth day? In the Hebrew Bible a child usually received its name at birth, and the inclusion of the naming in the ceremony of circumcision is unattested.[31] But in later Judaism these two important events became linked.[32] Perhaps this passage is one of the oldest testimonies of this tendency. Luke could, however, also be under the influence of Greek custom, according to which a child received its name only after seven or ten days.

---

23 Luke attaches great importance to this joy, which is personal and communal, bound to salvation history, and directed toward the kingdom; see Bovon, *Theologian*, 483–84 (the end of n. 118).

24 On παραχρῆμα see Luke 5:25 and the commentary on it below.

25 On ῥῆμα ("word") in Luke, see Luke 1:37–38 and the commentary on it above.

26 Gen 17:12; 21:4; Lev 12:3.

27 Luke 2:21; Acts 7:8; Phil 3:5. See Str-B 4.1.23–40.

28 Ἐκάλουν is a conative imperfect (see BDF §326): "they wanted to name him . . ." Καλέω ἐπὶ τῷ ὀνόματι ("to name him after") is an LXX expression, although somewhat rare. Cf. 2 Sam (LXX 2 Kgdms) 18:18 (Codex Alexandrinus); 1 Chr 6:50; 1 Esdr 5:38; 2 Esdr 2:61; 10:16 (Codices Alexandrinus and Sinaiticus).

29 Str-B (2.107–8), Fitzmyer (1.380), and Brown (*Birth*, 369) produce a few examples, despite all, of sons who are named after their fathers: e.g., Josephus *Vita* 1.4; *Ant.* 14.1.3 §10.

30 Under discussion is, then, what one calls "delegation" in systems theory (what one of the parents cannot attain is expected from the child). One can therefore understand why the neighbors, in view of the father, who has become unfit for service, wanted to give the child his name. Bodily ailments were particularly burdensome to priestly families, since they excluded the afflicted one from priestly service.

31 Gen 4:1; 25:25–26. But in Gen 21:3–4, the two ceremonies are very close. Cf. also Gen 17:5, 10–14.

32 For the example of Moses, see *Pirke R. El.* 48(27c), cited by Brown (*Birth*, 369).

In Hebrew, John's name means "YHWH is gracious."[33] "Grace" was regularly translated in the LXX by ἔλεος and χάρις. Ἔλεος appears in the narrative (1:58) as well as the Benedictus (1:72). Jewish ears would understand the meaning of John's name. But is this true of Luke? Does he fail to explain it because he does not like to use etymologies?

The designation of the child is τὸ παιδίον ("child") in 1:59, 66, as well as in 1:76, 80. But in 1:41 and 44 one reads βρέφος (an infant or small child), as for Jesus in 2:12, 16. This difference in terminology shows that the Jesus tradition (and also Lukan redaction?) prefers τὸ βρέφος, while the John tradition prefers τὸ παιδίον.

Zechariah is portrayed in vv. 62–63 as being not only mute but also deaf.[34] The indirect question addressed to him is expressed by means of an introductory article and a potential optative, in good Lukan idiom, and good Greek.[35] Πινακίδιον ("writing tablet") is a diminutive of πινακίς.[36] Λέγων serves formally as a colon, probably with a Semitic flavor (cf. 2 Kgs [LXX 4 Kgdms] 10:1, 6; Jdt 4:6–7).[37] Καὶ ἡ γλῶσσα αὐτοῦ ("and his tongue") appears without a verb in v. 64 because the readers supply it silently on the basis of the preceding sentence.[38] Does the allusion to "the hill country of Judea" (cf. 1:39) give a hint as to the tradition-historical locus of the legend?[39]

What is central in vv. 57–66 is not only the fulfillment of the prophecy in the guise of the child's birth, but also the giving of the name. Humanity lives not only biologically but also in social relationships: in the family and in the nation. A name makes it possible for a child to come into contact with others and, at the same time, to become certain of its own identity. In this passage there is a further component: the name puts the child in a relationship to God, because the angel prescribed it.

The child is a consolation to his parents, and also a sign of God's compassion. In the history of the transmission of the traditions, one can understand the development of the legend as an etiological account of the child's name. But more important than this diachronic observation is the synchronic realization that the legend develops, in a *narrative* manner, the significance of the name, and that the name is an *emblem* of the story. The network of relationships for this child is greater than its family, and the narrative more than just a family memory. It has its *Sitz im Leben* (functional setting) in a community, and so describes only the beginning of a life that has public significance.

■ **67** This is exactly what the father attests in his prayer. Just as Elizabeth possessed God-given insight (1:41–45), Zechariah, conditioned by the fullness of the Holy Spirit, can now also speak prophetically (v. 67).[40] According to Luke the religion of Israel, bound to history and the word of God, was as good as blocked off at that time. Both the experience of divine deliverance and the creative word of God lay in the past. It was the hour of the scribe. The hopes of the bravest were apocalyptic. Yet in John's circle, and finally with Jesus, salvation again begins to happen, and the word of God can be heard anew. But this fulfillment does not arrive immediately: on the contrary, one has to wait for growth; of this, the months of Elizabeth's pregnancy are a sign. Zechariah cannot yet announce the fulfillment, but must allude to it in prophetic manner. The Benedictus, too, characterizes this intermingling of fulfillment and trusting expectation, this "pregnancy" of salvation history, as we have noticed from the beginning of the legend of John. So one can see the hermeneutical side of the narrated ῥήματα ("words") in the poetic passages of the birth narrative.

---

33 See Luke 1:13 and the commentary on it. The name John was known at that time; see Neh 12:13, 42; 1 Macc 2:1–2; Luke 6:14; Rev 1:9.

34 In Luke 1:20 only muteness is indicated; but in Luke 1:22, κωφός ("deaf" and/or "mute") is ambiguous.

35 On the τό see BDF §267.2 and n. 2; and on the potential optative, §65 n. 2 and §385.1

36 Comparison of Ezek 9:2 (πινακίδιον) with 9:11 (πινακίς) in Symm shows that the diminutive was no longer considered as such. A wax tablet is surely meant. Wood is mentioned as a writing surface in Num 17:17; Ezek 37:16, 20; 2 Esdr 14:24. Cf. Str-B 2.108–10.

37 See Sahlin, *Messias,* 156. But one also finds a similar conjuction in classical Greek; cf. Thucydides 6.54.7.

38 On zeugma see BDF §479.2. A few mss. complete it and add ἐλύθη ("was loosed").

39 Schürmann, 1.83 n. 18.

40 Dubois, "Jean-Baptiste," 100.

The Benedictus

The first part of the Benedictus (v. 68a) is an example of the praise of God reported in v. 64.[41] In v. 66a the expectant question of the entire audience is, "What then will this child become?" The second part of the Benedictus, structurally well composed, answers this.

■ **68a** "Blessed be the Lord, the God of Israel" is, form-critically, a benediction.[42] In Luke's time this formula found its place in the prayers (e.g., the books of the Psalms or the Eighteen Blessings or Benedictions), at the end, in the middle, or at the beginning.[43] "Blessed be the God of Israel/ who keeps mercy toward His Covenant,/ and the appointed times of salvation/ with the people He has delivered!": so begins an Essene song.[44] The passive idiom εὐλογητός ("blessed") leaves the subject of the blessing in theological suspense.[45] Both the works of God themselves as well as the recipient or audience can express praise. The individual or congregation does not praise God adequately until they are included in the praise. In the last analysis, only God himself can praise God. The restriction to Israel (τοῦ Ἰσραήλ, "of Israel") attests not God's limitations but his will and his love. His universal purpose begins concretely.

■ **68b–69** The reason for praise is introduced in both beatitudes and songs of thanksgiving by a ὅτι-clause ("for"). The Lord,[46] the God of Israel, has "visited" his people. Ἐπισκέπτομαι ("to visit") means: God not only has oversight of his people, he also comes concretely to punish his congregation (Ps 89:33 [LXX 88:33]; Sir 2:14), or to deliver.[47] The expression (as verb or substantive) is attested in absolute usage in the Judaism of that time, as here, and designates the eschatological "visit."[48] Luke is familiar with this meaning.[49]

"He brought about deliverance for his people" sounds like the Hebrew Bible and is reminiscent of the exodus tradition. But the expression ποιέω λύτρωσιν ("to bring about deliverance") does not occur elsewhere in the Bible. In Ps 111(LXX 110):9 one does find something similar: λύτρωσιν ἀπέστειλεν τῷ λαῷ αὐτοῦ ("he has sent redemption to his people").[50] Λύτρωσις ("deliverance") means deliverance from one's enemies (vv. 71, 74), but the word is so stereotypical that a figurative meaning is also possible.

The perspective of the song is that of the people (τῷ λαῷ αὐτοῦ, "for his people"), and no longer that of the family (1:58).

"And he has raised up a horn of salvation for us in the house of his servant David": the tone and language continue to be biblical. The horn is a symbol of power (Deut 33:17), especially of military might. God himself or his servant, the king or Messiah, can be compared with this image.[51] Here the Davidic tradition is revised for the present time, and Luke interprets it in an unmis-

---

41 It would be wrongheaded to assume, because of the words ἐλάλει εὐλογῶν τὸν θεόν ("he spoke, praising God," Luke 1:64), that the Benedictus (1:68–79) immediately followed upon v. 64, and that vv. 65–67 were introduced later.

42 Cf. Gen 9:26; 1 Sam (LXX 1 Kgdms) 25:32; 1 Kgs (LXX 3 Kgdms) 1:48; frequently in the book of Tobit, e.g., 3:11; *Ps. Sol.* 2:37. See Jean-Paul Audet, "Esquisse historique du genre littéraire de la 'bénédiction' juive et de l' 'eucharistie' chrétienne," *RB* 65 (1958) 371–99. Should one supply an indicative (ἐστίν) or an optative (εἴη)?

43 Pss 41:13 (LXX 40:14); 72(LXX 71):18–19; 106(LXX 105):48; 144(LXX 143):1.

44 1QM 14.4–5. See Vermes, *Dead Sea Scrolls*, 142.

45 Usually, εὐλογητός is reserved for God (cf. Luke 1:68) and εὐλογημένος for the creatures (cf. 1:42).

46 Although the word is missing in some good witnesses, κύριος ("Lord") must be the original reading.

47 Gen 50:24–25; Exod 3:16; 4:31; 13:19; 30:12; Isa 23:17; Pss 80:14 (LXX 79:15); 106(LXX 105):4; Ruth 1:6.

48 Wis 3:7; *Ps. Sol.* 3:11; 10:4; 11:6; 15:12.

49 Luke 1:78; 7:16; 19:44; Acts 15:14. See Christian Abraham Wahl, *Clavis librorum Veteris Testamenti apocryphorum philologica* (1853; ed. J. B. Bauer; reprinted Graz: Akademische Druck und Verlagsanstalt, 1972) 229–30, 569, 615. For Qumran, cf. CD 1.7–11. See Joachim Rohde, "ἐπισκέπτομαι, κτλ.," *EDNT* 2 (1991) 33–34.

50 See Sahlin, *Messias*, 288. The word λύτρωσις occurs only once more in the Lukan writings, and there, as well, it is from tradition: Luke 2:38.

51 Κέρας σωτηρίας ("horn of salvation"); cf. 2 Sam (LXX 2 Kgdms) 22:3; Ps 18:2 (LXX 17:3); 1 Sam (LXX 1 Kgdms) 2:10 (about God's anointed); Ezek 29:21; Ps 132(LXX 131):17; 148:14. The expression occurs frequently in Daniel. About the horns of the messianic king, cf. 1QSb 5.26. Cf. Str-B 2.110–11; and Schürmann, 1.86 n. 33.

takably messianic fashion. Ἐγείρω means "to make to arise," "to awaken."[52] This first strophe expresses in the indicative what the fifteenth of the Eighteen Benedictions expresses with the imperative of intercession: "Let the shoot of David spring forth quickly, and may his horn raise itself up with your help. Praised be you, YHWH, who let help spring forth."[53]

The song speaks in metaphors: visit, deliverance, and horn are used figuratively, but instead of being metaphors that awaken the imagination, they are almost code words for the initiated, who find in them a truth already known.[54] But what can always be new in Judaism is the relating of confessional language with the history of the people; through these old metaphors, the voice of one gripped by eschatological reality speaks. When Luke unites himself with this voice and gives thanks for the coming of Jesus, the Davidic Messiah (1:31–33), the faded images bloom anew.

■ **70** The Benedictus has in common with the Magnificat that it speaks of a fulfillment of salvation that is, at the same time, a fulfillment of the prophetic word (cf. 1:55). This double fulfillment has its roots in the Hebrew Bible (2 Chr 36:22), and also explains the hermeneutic of the Qumran *Pesher on Habakkuk*. This aspect is happily adopted by the Christian community, and particularly by Luke.[55] The description of the prophets as "holy" is pious terminology[56] and presupposes the canonization of their writings (cf. 24:44). Ἀπ᾽ αἰῶνος does not mean "from the beginning," but rather "the entire time," "always."[57]

■ **71–73a** Verses 71–73a form a second strophe of four

lines, the first and last with an accusative at the beginning, the second and third with an infinitive. Grammatically, the entire portion stands free of syntactic connections. As *nomina actionis*, the substantives are not far removed from the infinitives, and the whole could be understood either as an apposition to the work of God indicated in vv. 68–69, or as the purpose of the divine will. The biblical Psalms employ the nominative as an apposition to the God who is being praised, for example, ἔλεός μου καὶ καταφυγή μου ("my steadfast love and my fortress," Ps 144[LXX 143]:2). One also finds accusatives at the beginning of a line before a verb of speaking (Ps 145[LXX 144]:5–7). Should one assume such a verb here? The structure of the first strophe supports, rather, an epexegetical apposition: the visitation of God, his deliverance of the people, and the introduction of the metaphor of the horn signify salvation from their enemies.

The formulation of v. 71 is consistent with Luke's preference for the vocabulary of salvation, but "our enemies" and "all who hate us" are expressions of the conventional language of the Psalms (cf. Ps 18:17 [LXX 17:18]). When Luke analyzes the tragedy of human captivity, the devil is usually the true enemy,[58] and very seldom are there human enemies, as here. Above all, nothing is said here about the human lack of contrition, which is otherwise important to Luke.[59] Since Luke is, at

52 Fitzmyer (1.383) points out that ἐγείρω in the LXX is not used with κέρας ("horn"), but with other concepts that denote an instrument of salvation: Judg 2:16, 18; 3:9, 15; cf. Acts 13:22.

53 German translation in Str-B 4.1.213; cf. 2.111. See Gnilka, "Hymnus," 223–24.

54 Paul Ricoeur has perhaps accorded the significance and function of the faded metaphor too little emphasis (*The Rule of Metaphor: Multi-disciplinary Studies of the Creation of Meaning in Language* [trans. R. Czerny; Toronto/Buffalo: University of Toronto Press, 1977]).

55 See chapter two of Bovon, *Theologian*, 78–108.

56 One finds the expression "holy prophets" only once more in the Lukan writings (Acts 3:21). In the singular, it occurs in Wis 11:1; in the plural, *2 Bar.* 85:1. I believe it is absent from Philo. In Josephus it is attested only in *Ant.* 12.10.6 §413 in a few mss.;

cf. K. H. Rengstorf, ed., *A Complete Concordance to Flavius Josephus* (4 vols.; Leiden: Brill, 1973–83) 3.588. A sentence similar to v. 70 can be found in 1QS 1.3 (Fitzmyer, 1.384).

57 Grundmann (72) writes: "Ἀπ᾽ αἰῶνος is used formulaically and does not mean 'from the beginning of world history,' but 'from of old.'"

58 Cf. Luke 13:16; Acts 10:38.

59 Cf. Luke 15:11–32. According to Jens W. Taeger, Luke is of the opinion that people manage well enough by their will and by repentance alone. Taeger thereby underestimates the role of the enemy (*Der Mensch und sein Heil: Studien zum Bild des Menschen und zur Sicht der Bekehrung bei Lukas* [StNT 14; Gütersloh: Mohn, 1982]).

the same time, interested in present salvation, and less in its origin or, indeed, in the converse of salvation, judgment,[60] v. 71 proves to be a *Hebrew Bible* formulation (in the language of the exodus) of a *New Testament* reality.

According to v. 72a, God has let his compassion become concrete (ποιεῖν, "to perform"); or, if one assumes a substantivized infinitive of result,[61] he has intended this. Ποιῆσαι ἔλεος μετά ("to perform mercy to") is common in the LXX.[62] Luke writes "to our ancestors," instead of "to us,"[63] probably because in the tradition vv. 68–75 alluded to a past, preliminary phase of redemption, while the second half (vv. 76–79) concentrates on "our" salvation. Luke accepts this slight tension. Perhaps he still has a dim notion of the promise to the patriarchs (v. 70; cf. Abraham, "our father," v. 73) and its present fulfillment (vv. 68–69).

Verse 72b draws the train of thought back to the prophecy or, here, to God's remembrance of it. The Lord remains faithful; he will not forget. His covenant is holy because it is *his* covenant (here, with Abraham).[64] The concept of covenant does not appear often in Luke; when it does, it is always connected to Abraham, despite the prevalent exodus typology.[65] The list of Hebrew Bible parallels for v. 72b is long.[66]

The Hebrew Bible link between covenant and oath, especially in the case of Abraham,[67] would suggest a parallelism between vv. 72b and 73a.[68] But the link between compassion and covenant is equally traditional (Deut 7:9; 1 Kgs [LXX 3 Kgdms] 8:23).[69] The three elements—covenant, oath,[70] and compassion—thus belong together (vv. 72–73a), and they are also, in turn, connected with redemption in the Hebrew Bible (vv. 68–69). The content of the oath, that is, numerous and blessed progeny, is not indicated; both are assumed to be well known. In Luke's era both nationalistic and universalistic expectations were possible.[71] Luke would have had in mind the church, composed of Jews and Gentiles, which the tradition was still interpreting in a Jewish manner: Israel will become great. The prerequisite for this growth was redemption (vv. 73b–74a).

■ **73b–74a** The fact that the liberation of the people, and not their expansion, has become the primary content of the promise to Abraham[72] reflects the miserable condition of the Jews in this era. One would speak of the covenant with Abraham (vv. 72–73) and recall the promises to David (v. 69), but one had to use the soteriological categories of the exodus. The syntax is less impressive than the train of thought: the juxtaposition of the dative (ἡμῖν, "us") and accusative (ῥυσθέντας, "rescued") for the same person is particularly bothersome, as is the semantic function of ἀφόβως ("without fear").[73] This can hardly be explained as inept translation, since no clear-cut Semitisms appear. Ἀφόβως should be understood anthropologically, and should not be construed with God, the subject of δοῦναι ("to grant"). A normal deliverance does not take place without fear. But here the hand of God is so active that the people are delivered from their enemies without fear.

---

60 See Bovon, *Lukas,* 67–69.

61 So Plummer, 41.

62 Gen 24:12; Judg 1:24; 8:35; Ruth 1:8; 1 Sam (LXX 1 Kgdms) 20:8 (Plummer, 41).

63 Sahlin (*Messias,* 289–90) sees this problem and considers the words "to our ancestors" to be a "marginal gloss that was introduced at the wrong point."

64 Gen 17:4, 7, 21; 22:18.

65 Luke 1:72; Acts 3:25; 7:8. Once, the word denotes the covenant through Jesus Christ (Luke 22:20).

66 E.g., Exod 2:24; Lev 26:42; Ps 106(LXX 105):45; Ezek 16:60. See Annie Jaubert, *La notion d'alliance dans le judaïsme aux abords de l'ère chrétienne* (Patristica Sorbonensia 6; Paris: Seuil, 1963) 30–31.

67 Gen 17:4; 22:16–17; cf. Ps 105(LXX 104):8–9.

68 Vanhoye, "Structure," 382–83. He cites a further employment of the link between covenant and oath in Ps 89:3, 34–35. Cf. Wis 12:21; 18:22.

69 Pierre Auffret, "Note sur la structure littéraire de Lc 1, 68–79," *NTS* 24 (1977–78) 248–58, esp. 250.

70 The accusative ὅρκον ("oath") creates difficulties. Is this the unusual case of the attraction of an antecedent to the relative pronoun? Or is it in series with σωτηρίαν ("salvation") in v. 71? But, in terms of the sense, it would be more natural to connect it with διαθήκης ("covenant," v. 72).

71 Acts 3:25 cites Gen 22:18 or 26:4. It is difficult to decipher which expectation Luke is reading out of the text from Genesis.

72 Τοῦ δοῦναι ("to grant") allows no doubt; this is precisely what God desires when he remembers.

73 Sahlin (*Messias,* 291) is of the opinion that Luke has translated poorly here; he sets about to improve it: τοῦ ποιεῖν ἡμᾶς ἄνευ φόβου, ἐκ χειρὸς ἐχθρῶν ῥυσθέντας ("to make us without fear, when we have been saved from the hand of the enemies").

They are both the recipients of the gift as well as the object of the deliverance, and are, to this extent, set free for a life with God (vv. 74b–75).[74]

■ **74b–75** Divine deliverance takes place in Israel in a concrete manner, that is, socially and politically, but in the sight of God (ἐνώπιον αὐτοῦ, "before him") in the performance of religious (ἐν ὁσιότητι, "in holiness") and collective life (καὶ δικαιοσύνῃ, "and in righteousness").[75] The goal of the promised exodus is a cultic existence in the Holy Land. Luke has faithfully and soberly preserved this Jewish perspective. He has neither universalized nor eschatologized it, but has definitely considered the soteriological effect of Jesus' life and its ultimate universal significance, and perhaps even conceives of holiness and righteousness as a summary of the two greatest commandments (cf. 10:26–28). Luke's ethic of daily perseverance shows itself in the mention of "all our days" (cf. 9:23).[76] The theological structure of the indicative and the imperative in vv. 73b–75 displays God's work as the foundation of all human life.

■ **76–77** Verses 76–77 describe the future of the Baptist in prophetic language. Luke intervenes more strongly here, because the oracle is more concrete than the hymnic language of vv. 68–75. The destiny of a *son* of the Most High has been promised to Mary's son (1:32); John, on the other hand, will be a *prophet* of the Most High. The role of forerunner, announced in Isa 40:3 and Mal 3:1, was interpreted by the Baptist's community in reference to God himself (ἐνώπιον κυρίου, "before the Lord"); the Christian community applied it to the *Messiah Jesus*. In 3:1–22 Luke, too, emphasizes less the bap-

tizing than the prophetic function of John. As a prophet, John has only one foot in the old covenant; the other is in the new. He is the last prophet, the forerunner. His birth and office are on the threshold between the two testaments.[77]

The Benedictus surprisingly conceals John's primary activity, his baptizing. But it appertains to the essence of a song of birth that the prophecy remains cryptic: in the words ἐν ἀφέσει ἁμαρτιῶν αὐτῶν ("in the forgiveness of their sins") the readers should probably recognize an allusion to baptism (3:3). The expression is not from the Hebrew Bible,[78] but, conversely, it is not necessarily Christian.[79] What Luke understands by it is clear from his entire corpus: the rite does not grant forgiveness, nor is forgiveness God's work alone; it is also a matter of the introspective human individual, who turns to God at the call of the prophetic or kerygmatic voice. That God gives atonement means, for Luke, that people should receive it as an invitation to an existential decision (Acts 5:31; 11:18).

Salvation begins only with Jesus (vv. 68–71). But the forerunner brings more than just its promise through the prophets. John will grant "knowledge of salvation." This is more than a mere intellectual knowledge, since it results from existentially experiencing forgiveness,[80] and emerges from a living relationship with God as the fruit of the preaching of repentance. The un-Lukan word γνῶσις[81] ("knowledge") should be understood in the Semitic sense, as practical knowledge, wisdom, faith, acknowledgment. Did the Hellenistic Jewish synagogue adopt elements of the Greek γνῶσις, such as theoretical

---

74   There is certainly a symmetry between v. 71 and vv. 73b–74a (deliverance from the enemy) and between v. 70 and vv. 72b–73a (faithfulness of God), but one must not forget the progress of the dominant thought: liberation leads to life with God (vv. 74b–75).

75   One finds these two concepts in connection in Wis 9:3; Eph 4:24; and in Philo *Abr.* 208 (holiness for God, righteousness for humanity).

76   See Bovon, *Theologian*, 384–90.

77   Against Conzelmann, *Theology*, 22–27. I am close to Emmeram Kränkl's position (*Jesus der Knecht Gottes: Die heilsgeschichtliche Stellung Jesu in den Reden der Apostelgeschichte* [BU 8; Regensburg: Pustet, 1972] 88–97, 211–12).

78   See Brown, *Birth*, 373.

79   The expression "forgiveness of sins" is also found in Philo *Vit. Mos.* 2:147; *Spec.* 1.190; cf. *Rer. div. her.* 20;

and Josephus *Ant.* 6.5.6 §92.

80   See Brown, *Birth*, 373. Brown also notes that the expression is not in the HB. According to Sahlin (*Messias*, 294), the expression originally denoted the confession of sins, whereas it now means that forgiveness offered by God reveals the knowledge of salvation. R. P. van Kasteren offers a penetrating paraphrase of vv. 76–77 and mentions the parallel in Acts 26:18 ("Analecta exegetica—Luc 1, 76s," *RB* 3 [1894] 54–56).

81   The word occurs again in Luke 11:52, in one of the words of woe from Luke's special source (L).

understanding and empirical knowledge, without renouncing the Hebrew Bible concept of acknowledgment?[82] In Luke the aspect of γνῶσις that includes humans and the perspective in it that unites them with God are central.[83] The people recognize their salvation only when they consider themselves, question their conception of God, and listen to the word of God.

■ **78–79** A strong expression ("by the compassionate heart of our God") connects the description of the forerunner (vv. 76–77) with the proclamation of the Messiah (vv. 78–79) and pertains to both. The work of the Baptist, like the visit of the ἀνατολή ("the one arising," "the dawn"), is comprehensible only as concrete results of God's compassion.[84] Ἐλέους ("compassionate") is a genitive of quality and describes the "bowels" of God, that is, the seat of emotions, in our idiom, "the heart."[85] Seldom has the compassion of God been declared in so personal and experiential a manner as the source and motive of salvation history. Luke, who understands εὐδοκία ("good favor") as the quintessence of the active God,[86] gladly adopts the expression in v. 78a of the Benedictus.[87]

After the two future verbs in v. 76 (κληθήσῃ "you . . . will be called," and προπορεύσῃ "you will go before"), one expects another future verb in v. 78b. So the future ἐπισκέψεται ("[he] will visit") is preferable to the equally well-attested aorist ἐπισκέψατο ("[he] visited").[88] For Luke and, I believe, for the earlier version, ἀνατολή ("the one arising," "the dawn") is the subject of ἐπισκέψεται ("[he] will visit") and is not identical with the Baptist. Otherwise it is incomprehensible whose way John could be preparing.

Ἐξ ὕψους ("from on high") alludes to God as ὕψιστος ("the highest"), but is not simply equivalent with him. In contrast to a visitor "from earth," it describes the "divine" Messiah (cf. 1:32, 35).

No one doubts that ἀνατολή ("the one arising," "the dawn") is a messianic metaphor; in the LXX it can translate צֶמַח ("branch, shoot"), one of the stereotypical messianic titles.[89] Ἐξ ὕψους ("from on high") gives it the necessary precision; the son of David "sprouts" not like others, from the earth, but out of heaven. But I am of the opinion that the author of the Benedictus, like the translators of the LXX, already had the same meaning in mind—which is nearer to the Greek—as in the Balaam oracle, important at Qumran:[90] ἀνατελεῖ ἄστρον ἐξ Ἰακώβ, καὶ ἀναστήσεται ἄνθρωπος ἐξ Ἰσραήλ ("A star shall rise out of Jacob, and a human being shall rise up out of Israel," Num 24:17 [LXX]).[91] Indeed, the "rising" of a star "out of" the heavens is unnatural, but this encoded language is determined by a theological purpose: ἀνατολή ("the one arising," "the dawn") denotes the appearing of the Messiah, ἐξ ὕψους ("from on high"), his origin. For Luke, even this tension is pregnant with content: Jesus will arise in the midst of humanity, within his people. Yet it will happen "from heaven" (cf. 1:35).[92]

The indicated purpose of this visit confirms the above meaning: the Messiah will bring divine light (ἐπιφᾶναι, "to appear").[93] Readers of v. 78 will think of Ps 107(LXX 106):10 and the beginning of the messianic oracle in Isa 9:2 (LXX 9:1). The eschatological light of the Messiah suddenly illumines the dark world of the dying. Ἐπιφᾶναι alludes first to the *life*-bringing light. "Those who sit in darkness and in the shadow of death" are not primarily the Gentiles, but "we" (v. 79). But Luke does also have in mind the Christian message, which leads also the Gentiles from blindness to sight, and from death to life (Acts 26:17–18).

The "epiphany" of the Messiah also requires the active behavior of those who see (v. 79b). The people who, until then, have sat, can stand up and go. Their steps will be straight (κατευθῦναι, "to guide"). Both Judaism and the early church adopted this Hebrew Bible

82   Walther Schmithals, "γινώσκω, κτλ.," *EDNT* 1 (1990) 249.

83   See Bovon, *Lukas,* 112–14.

84   On the meaning of διά plus the accusative in this passage, see BDF §222: "by someone's merit."

85   BAGD *s.v.* σπλάγχνον. The expression σπλάγχνα ἐλέους appears in *T. Zeb.* 7:3; 8:2, referring to the believers (Gnilka, "Hymnus," 235).

86   Cf. Bovon, *Lukas,* 106–8.

87   Ἐν οἷς refers to σπλάγχνα, which are in action at the coming of the Messiah.

88   On these variants see above, under the analysis of the Benedictus; and Metzger, *Textual Commentary,* 132.

89   Zech 3:8; 6:12.

90   1QM 11:6–7; CD 7:18–21. Cf. *T. Levi* 18:3–4.

91   Cf. Mal 4:2 (MT/LXX 3:20); Isa 4:2; Jer 23:4; 33:15.

92   See the important article by Adolf Jacoby, "Ἀνατολὴ ἐξ ὕψους," *ZNW* 20 (1921) 205–14.

93   One or two mss. insert an explicative φῶς ("light").

theme: obedience expresses itself by "going"; and life within the covenant and according to God's will takes place upon a "way."[94] Peace is the harmonious condition of a people delivered from their enemies and living in fellowship with God.[95]

The Summary Passage

■ **80** Already v. 66b attested, in a small summary passage, God's continual solicitude. Now the development of the child is discussed briefly ($\pi\alpha\iota\delta\acute{\iota}ov$, as in the narrative in vv. 57–66, and in the song in vv. 68–79). The anthropological context—despite biblical tradition—is the Greek differentiation between body and soul. Those expressions are biblical that record the physical development of the child and the strengthening of his $\pi\nu\epsilon\hat{v}\mu\alpha$ ("spirit," not his soul). In the summary passages that describe the growth of the congregation or of the word, one learns how Luke understands $\alpha\mathring{v}\xi\acute{\alpha}\nu\omega$ ("to grow") and $\kappa\rho\alpha\tau\alpha\iota\acute{o}\omega$ ("to become strong"). God is the author of this process.[96] Growth[97] is a sign of life and of blessing. Everything is fine with John; Jesus merits the reader's attention from now on.

John's place of residence, the "wilderness," is not his parent's city in the hills of Judea (1:39; cf. 1:23, 65), but probably a lonely spot in the wilderness of Judea.[98] The theological distance between the historical Baptist and the sect at Qumran seems too large to make a sojourn there probable.[99]

The "wilderness" denotes a phase of preparation, with trial, prayer, and asceticism, until the $\mathring{\alpha}\nu\acute{\alpha}\delta\epsilon\iota\xi\iota\varsigma$ ("public appearance")[100] of John to Israel. $\mathring{\mathnormal{A}}\nu\alpha\delta\epsilon\acute{\iota}\kappa\nu\upsilon\mu\iota$

means "to show," and describes the reemergence of a subterranean river, or the gesture of someone who lifts up an object or person and points to it. For example, after the death of a king, the potential successor is lifted up and presented on a pedestal. Therefore the verb took on the meaning of "to install in office." It is also used for the formal proclamation of a royal edict. The $\mathring{\alpha}\nu\acute{\alpha}\delta\epsilon\iota\xi\iota\varsigma$ ("public appearance"), a rare word, denotes the ceremony of investiture for a monarch or high official, or the presentation of a divinity, whose image is brought before the people in a ceremony. According to Luke 3, the word of God takes hold of John in the wilderness and calls him to public manifestation. This is *his* official $\mathring{\alpha}\nu\acute{\alpha}\delta\epsilon\iota\xi\iota\varsigma$, seen from God's perspective (the use in 10:1 supports this). But Luke could also have understood $\alpha\mathring{v}\tauo\hat{v}$ ("his") subjectively; Luke 3 also describes how the Baptist presented Jesus. $\mathring{\mathnormal{A}}\nu\acute{\alpha}\delta\epsilon\iota\xi\iota\varsigma$ ("public appearance") would then be the presentation of the royal prince *Jesus* by John.

Conclusion

In the Benedictus, salvation history is not only recounted but sung. The church well understood this when it adopted the Benedictus and the Magnificat into its liturgy, and it retains them to this day.[101] The meaning, however, was unavoidably altered by this practice: in this passage salvation then becomes spiritualized, and eschatology ecclesiastically domesticated. But the words of the

---

94 *T. Sim.* 5:2: $\mathring{\mathnormal{A}}\gamma\alpha\vartheta\acute{v}\nu\alpha\tau\epsilon$ $\tau\grave{\alpha}\varsigma$ $\kappa\alpha\rho\delta\acute{\iota}\alpha\varsigma$ $\acute{v}\mu\hat{\omega}\nu$ $\mathring{\epsilon}\nu\acute{\omega}\pi\iota o\nu$ $\kappa\upsilon\rho\acute{\iota}o\upsilon$, $\kappa\alpha\grave{\iota}$ $\epsilon\mathring{v}\vartheta\acute{v}\nu\alpha\tau\epsilon$ $\tau\grave{\alpha}\varsigma$ $\acute{o}\delta o\grave{v}\varsigma$ $\acute{v}\mu\hat{\omega}\nu$ $\mathring{\epsilon}\nu\acute{\omega}\pi\iota o\nu$ $\tau\hat{\omega}\nu$ $\mathring{\alpha}\nu\vartheta\rho\acute{\omega}\pi\omega\nu$ ("Make your hearts virtuous in the Lord's sight, make your paths straight before men"). See Sahlin, *Messias,* 298.

95 See J. Comblin, "La paix dans la théologie de Saint Luc," *EThL* 32 (1956) 439–60.

96 $\Pi\nu\epsilon\acute{v}\mu\alpha\tau\iota$ ("in spirit") is perhaps intentionally ambiguous, i.e., in his human spirit and in God's Spirit.

97 See Paul Zingg, who treats the growth of the congregation and of the word, rather than that of the individual (*Das Wachsen der Kirche: Beiträge zur Frage der lukanischen Redaktion und Theologie* [OBO 3; Fribourg: Universitätsverlag; Göttingen: Vandenhoeck & Ruprecht, 1974]).

98 The LXX and the NT usually speak of "wilderness" in the singular, so the plural is surprising here; see

Fitzmyer, 1.388. Cf. Luke 3:2, which has the singular.

99 Fitzmyer (1.388–89) considers a sojourn by the young John in Qumran entirely possible. He also lists the bibliography on this disputed issue.

100 This concept is thoroughly examined by E. Bikerman ("$\mathring{\mathnormal{A}}\nu\acute{\alpha}\delta\epsilon\iota\xi\iota\varsigma$," in *Mélanges: Festschrift Émile Boisacq* [2 vols.; Annuaire de l'Institut de philologie 5; Brussels: Secrétariat des éditions de l'Institut, 1937–38] 1.117–24).

101 In monasteries and convents of the West, every morning the Benedictus is sung at the lauds, and every evening the Magnificat at vespers. Have these hymns lost some of their life for the Protestants, who have abandoned this liturgical custom?

prayer nevertheless retain their life in this manner; in the course of church history they can receive back some of their salvation-historical significance.

The nature, locus, and time of salvation remain indeterminate in the Benedictus. Something has begun. There is reason to praise God. But who are our enemies? According to vv. 74b–75a, where is the locus of our liturgical life? Time stops. We stand between two visits, still in the time of prophecy (v. 76), but already in the hour of thanksgiving (v. 68). We look backward at the path of the forerunner, and in front of us to the path of our own decisions. Perhaps the song intends to evoke the mood of preparation through its artistry. Thus we comprehend the theological role of a forerunner not only cognitively but affectively. Forerunner and follower, John and the apostles—why are they indispensable? Does this depend on the nature of God's activity? God's deeds must be attested, beforehand by prophets and afterward by witnesses, because they have not the power of proof and depend on the venture of faith. Even in the middle of time, God acts neither directly nor alone. For this reason, the beginnings of John and of Jesus run parallel. Human beings are called to work along with God. The people of God receive not only salvation; the participation God expects of them is also an expression of his compassion. But its first expression is a child. God comes not in the loud voice of an avenging angel, but in the small voice of a prophet who promises.

The Birth of Jesus (2:1–21)

Bibliography

Aubineau, Michel, "Proclus de Constantinople, In illud: 'Et postquam consummati sunt dies octo' (Lc 2,21)," in E. Lucchesi and H. D. Saffrey, eds., *Mémorial André-Jean Festugière: Antiquité païenne et chrétienne* (Cahier d'orientalisme 10; Geneva: P. Cramer, 1984) 199–207.

Barnett, Paul W., "Ἀπογραφή and ἀπογράφεσθαι in Luke 2:1–4," *ExpTim* 85 (1973) 377–80.

Bellia, Giuseppe, "'Confrontando nel suo cuore': Custodia sapienziale di Maria in Lc 2,19b" *BeO* 25 (1983) 215–28.

Benoit, "'Non erat'."

idem, "Quirinius."

Berger, P.-R., "Lk 2,14: ἄνθρωποι εὐδοκίας: Die auf Gottes Weisung mit Wohlgefallen beschenkten Menschen," *ZNW* 74 (1983) 129–44.

idem, "Menschen ohne 'Gottes Wohlgefallen': Lk 2,14?" *ZNW* 76 (1985) 119–22.

Berief, Maria, "'Maria aber bewahrte alle diese Worte und erwog sie in ihrem Herzen' (Lk 2,19): Eine Meditation," *Diakonia* 16 (1985) 127–28.

Brindle, Wayne A., "The Census and Quirinius: Luke 2:2," *JETS* 27 (1984) 43–52.

Brown, *Birth*, 393–434.

Burchard, "Fußnoten."

idem, "A Note on Ῥῆμα in JosAs 17:1f.; Luke 2:15, 17; Acts 10:37," *NovT* 27 (1985) 281–95.

Craig-Faxon, Alicia, *Women and Jesus* (Philadelphia: United Church Press, 1973).

de Robert, *Berger*.

Derrett, J. Duncan M., "The Manger at Bethlehem: Light on St. Luke's Technique from Contemporary Jewish Religious Law," *StEv* 6 (= TU 112) (1973) 86–94.

idem, "The Manger: Ritual Law and Soteriology (Lk 2:7, 12, 16)," *Theology* 74 (1971) 566–71, reprinted in idem, *Studies*, vol. 2: *Midrash in Action*, 48–53.

Dibelius, *Jungfrauensohn*, 9–10, 53–77.

Dodd, "Translation."

Ellingworth, Paul, "Luke 2:17: Just Who Spoke to the Shepherds?" *BT* 31 (1980) 447.

Escudero Freire, *Devolver*, 241–329.

Eulenstein, Robert, "'. . . und den Menschen ein Wohlgefallen' (Lk 2,14): Ein Beispiel für Sinn und Umfang philologischer Arbeit am Neuen Testament," *WD* 18 (1985) 93–103.

Fatio, Nicole, "Marie, servante du Seigneur: Des images tenaces . . . un regard nouveau," in *Groupe "IBSO": Réflexions théologiques au féminin: Bulletin du centre protestant d'études* (Geneva) 35.5 (1983) 17–21.

Feuillet, "Hommes."

Fitzmyer, Joseph A., "'Peace upon Earth among Men of His Good Will' (Lk 2:14)," *TS* 19 (1958) 225–27, reprinted in idem, *Essays on the Semitic Background of the New Testament* (SBLSBS 5; Missoula, Mont.: Scholars Press, 1974) 101–4.

Flusser, David, "'Sanctus' und 'Gloria,'" in Betz, *Abraham*, 129–52; revised in Flusser, *Entdeckungen im Neuen Testament*, vol. 1: *Jesusworte und ihre Überlieferung* (ed. M. Majer; Neukirchen-Vluyn: Neukirchener Verlag, 1987) 226–44.

Ford, J. Massyngberde, "Zealotism and the Lucan Infancy Narratives," *NovT* 18 (1976) 280–92.

Fusco, Vittorio, "Il messagio e il segno: Riflessioni esegetiche sul racconto lucano della natività (Lc 2,1–20)," in C. C. Marcheselli, ed., *Parola e Spirito: Festschrift Settimio Cipriani* (2 vols.; Brescia: Paideia, 1982) 1.293–333.

George, Augustin, "'Il vous est né aujourd'hui un Sauveur': Lc 2,1–20," *AsSeign* 10 (1970) 50–67.

Giblin, Charles H., "Reflections on the Sign of the Manger," *CBQ* 29 (1967) 87–101.

Gressmann, *Weihnachtsevangelium*.

Gros Louis, Kenneth R., "Different Ways of Looking at the Birth of Jesus," *BibRev* 1 (1985) 33–40.

Gueuret, *Engendrement*, 101–19, 192–96, 215–23.

Haacker, Klaus, "Erst unter Quirinius? Ein Übersetzungsvorschlag zu Lk 2,2," *BN* 38–39 (1987) 39–43.

Hayles, D. J., "The Roman Census and Jesus' Birth: Was Luke Correct?" *BurH* 9 (1973) 113–32; 10 (1974) 16–31.

Hermaus, L., "Lucas Pastorale: Exegetische kenttekeningen bij Lucas 2:1–20," in J. J. A. Kahmann and H. G. Manders, eds., *De weg van het woord* (Hilversum: Gooi & Sticht, 1975) 16–43.

Hunzinger, Claus-Hunno, "Ein weiterer Beleg zu Lc 2,14 ἄνθρωποι εὐδοκίας," *ZNW* 49 (1958) 129–130.

idem, "Neues Licht auf Lc 2,14 ἄνθρωποι εὐδοκίας," *ZNW* 44 (1952–53) 85–90.

Jansen, John F., "An Exposition of Lk 2:4–52," *Int* 30 (1976) 400–404.

Jeremias, Joachim, "ἄνθρωποι εὐδοκίας (Lc 2,14)," *ZNW* 28 (1929) 13–20.

Kellermann, Ulrich, *Gottes neuer Mensch: Exegetische Meditation der Weihnachtsgeschichte Lk 2,1–20* (Neukirchen-Vluyn: Neukirchener Verlag, 1978).

Kilpatrick, Ross S., "The Greek Syntax of Luke 2:14," *NTS* 34 (1988) 472–75.

Kipgen, Kaikhohen, "Translating κατάλυμα in Luke 2:7," *BT* 34 (1983) 442–43.

Kirchschläger, Walter, "Die Geburt Jesu von Nazaret (Lk 2,1–20): Zur biblischen Verkündigung der Weihnachtsbotschaft," *TPQ* 131 (1983) 329–42.

Kleiner, Josef R., "'Sie gaben ihm den Namen Jesus' (Lk 2,21)," *GuL* 57 (1984) 456–58.

Laurentin, *Truth*, 25, 61, 99–100, 172–92.

La Verdiere, E., "At the Table of the Manger," *Emm* 92 (1986) 22–27.

idem, "Jesus the First-born," *Emm* 89 (1983) 544–48.

idem, "No Room for Them in the Inn," *Emm* 91 (1985) 552–57.

idem, "Wrapped in Swaddling Clothes," *Emm* 90 (1984) 542–46.

Legrand, "The Christmas Story in Lk 2,1–7," *ITS* 19 (1982) 289–317.

idem, "Évangile aux Bergers."

Loftus, Francis, "The Anti-Roman Revolts of the Jews and the Galileans," *JQR* 68 (1977–78) 78–98.

McHugh, *Mother*, 80–98.

Muñoz Nieto, Jesús María, *Tiempo de anuncio: Estudio de Lc 1:5–2:52* (Taipei: Facultas Theologica S. Roberti Bellarmino, 1994).

Must, Hildegard, "A Diatessaric Rendering in Luke 2:7," *NTS* 32 (1986) 136–43.

Pax, Elpidius, "'Denn sie fanden keinen Platz in der Herberge': Jüdisches und frühchristliches Herbergswesen," *BibLeb* 6 (1965) 285–98.

Perrot, Charles, *Jésus et l'histoire* (Paris: Desclée, 1979) 81–93.

Pesch, "Weihnachtsevangelium."

Prete, Benedetto, "'Oggi vi è nato . . . il Salvatore che è il Cristo Signore' (Lc 2,11)," *RivB* 34 (1986) 289–325.

Schmithals, Walter, "Die Weihnachtsgeschichte Lukas 2,1–20," in G. Ebeling et al., eds., *Festschrift für Ernst Fuchs* (Tübingen: Mohr-Siebeck, 1973) 281–97.

Schwarz, Günther, "'. . . ἄνθρωποι εὐδοκίας'? (Lk 2,14)," *ZNW* 75 (1984) 136–37.

Sherwin-White, A. N., *Roman Society and Roman Law in the New Testament* (2d ed.; Oxford: Clarendon, 1965) 162–71.

Smith, Robert, "Caesar's Decree (Luke 2,1–2): Puzzle or Key?" *CurTM* 7 (1980) 343–51.

Smyth, Kevin, "'Peace on Earth to Men . . .' (Lk 2,14)," *IBS* 9 (1987) 27–34.

Soderlund, S. K., "Christmas as the Shalom of God," *Crux* 16 (1980) 2–4.

Steffen, Uwe, *Die Weihnachtsgeschichte des Lukas* (Hamburg: Agentur des Rauhen Hauses, 1978).

Stern, M., "The Census of Quirinius," in S. Safrai and M. Stern, eds., *The Jewish People in the First Century* (CRINT 1.1–2; 2 vols.; Assen: Van Gorcum; Philadephia: Fortress Press, 1974) 1.372–74 .

Stramare, Tarcisio, "La circoncisione di Gesù: Significato esegetico et teologico," *BeO* 26 (1984) 193–203.

Sudbrack, Josef, "Die Geburt des Lichts: Zur Ikonographie von Weihnachten," *GuL* 57 (1984) 451–55.

Trémel, "Signe."

van Unnik, "Bedeutung."

Vattioni, Francesco, "Pax hominibus bonae voluntatis," *RivB* 7 (1959) 369–70.

Vogt, Ernest, "'Peace among Men of God's Good Pleasure': Lk 2:14," in K. Stendahl, ed., *The Scrolls and the New Testament* (New York: Harper and Bros., 1957) 114–17.

Vögtle, Anton, "Offene Fragen zur lukanischen Geburts- und Kindheitsgeschichte," *BibLeb* 11(1970) 51–67, reprinted in idem, *Evangelium*, 43–56.

idem, *Was Weihnachten bedeutet: Meditation zu Lk 2,1–20* (Freiburg im Breisgau: Herder, 1977).

Westermann, Claus, "Alttestamentliche Elemente in Lukas 2:1–20," in G. Jeremias et al., eds., *Tradition und Glaube: Festschrift Karl Georg Kuhn* (Göttingen: Vandenhoeck & Ruprecht, 1971) 317–27.

Wiseman, T. P., "'There went out a Decree from Caesar Augustus . . . ,'" *NTS* 33 (1987) 479–80.

1 And it happened that in those days a decree went out from Emperor Augustus that all the world should be registered. 2/ This was the first registration when Quirinius was governor of Syria. 3/ And all went to their own towns to be registered. 4/ So Joseph also went from Galilee, from the city of Nazareth, up to Judea, to the city of David called Bethlehem, because he was descended from the house and family of David, 5/ to be registered with Mary, to whom he was engaged and who was pregnant. 6/ And it happened that while they were there, the days were fulfilled for her to give birth. 7/ And she gave birth to her firstborn son and wrapped him in bands of cloth, and laid him in a manger, because there was no place for them in the inn.

8 And in that region there were shepherds living in the fields, keeping watch over their flock by night. 9/ Then an angel of the Lord stood before them, and the glory of the Lord shone around them, and they were filled with great fear. 10/ But the angel said to them, "Do not be afraid! For see, I am proclaiming to you good news, a great joy for all the people; 11/ for to you is born this day in the city of David the Savior, who is the Messiah, the Lord. 12/ This will be the sign for you: You will find a child wrapped in bands of cloth and lying in a manger." 13/ And suddenly there was with the angel a multitude of the heavenly host, praising God and saying, 14/ "Glory to God in the highest, and on earth peace among people of good pleasure!"

15 And it happened that when the angels had left them and gone into heaven, the shepherds said to one another, "Let us go now to Bethlehem and see this thing that has taken place there, which the Lord has told us." 16/ So they went with haste and found Mary and Joseph, and the child lying in the manger. 17/ When they saw this, they made known the saying that had been told them about this child; 18/ and all who heard it were amazed at what the shepherds told them. 19/ But Mary treasured all these words, and pondered them in her heart. 20/ And the shepherds returned, glorifying and praising God for all they had heard and seen, as it had been told them. 21/ And when the eight days had been fulfilled for his circumcision, his name was called Jesus, the name that had been pronounced by the angel before he was conceived in the womb.

Analysis

After the summary concluding verse about John (1:80), a new pericope about Mary and Joseph begins in 2:1, composed in the style of the Hebrew Bible. The repetition of ἐγένετο δέ ("and it happened") in v. 6 is striking and reminds one of the story of Zechariah. There, the first ἐγένετο (1:5) introduces the situation, and the second (1:8), the actual narrative. Similarly, 2:1–5 presupposes the narrative of 2:6–20. From a form-critical perspective, this episode ends in v. 20 with an acclamation; from the redaction-historical perspective, it ends in v. 21 with the circumcision and name giving.[1] The similarity between the first words of vv. 21 and 22 is curious.

Verse 25 commences with καὶ ἰδού ("and see," "now"); hence vv. 22–24 offer, like 1:5–7 or 2:1–5, an introductory description of the situation. Verse 21 thus stands isolated, connected (2:21b) only to the annunciation by the angel in 1:26–38. This verse is presumably part of a birth story, not otherwise known to us, which is essentially presupposed by the annunciation to Mary.

According to the history of the transmission of the traditions, the present birth narrative is not the original continuation of 1:26–38. Mary is introduced anew in v. 5. Despite the angel's message in 1:26–38, she understands the gravity of the event only after the shepherds'

visit. Not a word alludes either to the virgin birth or to the divine conception;[2] Mary and Joseph turn up as an ordinary married couple; in terms of christology, the stress is also different. Whereas 1:26–38 develop the Davidic kingship, 2:1–20 bear witness to Jesus' soteriological function (2:11).

The pericope of 2:1–20 has only *become* unified and appealing through Luke's artistry. Various indices point to the Lukan redaction: (1) Verse 7b limps a bit and gives the impression of an accommodation to the following story. In a homogeneous legend, one would have told about the housing arrangements *before* the event. (2) The census episode is not necessary to the narrative; the story could begin in v. 6 (with a more precise local designation, of course).[3] (3) In v. 8 an episode begins that must be distinguished form-critically from the rest of the chapter. It is a proclamation, not a birth narrative, the shepherds' story, not Jesus' story. According to the genre, it is an angelic message with soteriological content, which is accompanied by the promise of a sign. The first half, the message (vv. 8–12), corresponds to the second, the confirmation (vv. 15–20).[4] The transition between the two is the angels' hymn (vv. 13–14). The content of the hymn corroborates the main point of the story: the union of heaven and earth through the loving act of God.

Without some kind of an introduction for vv. 8–20, it would remain unclear who Mary and Joseph really are, and why the child is lying in a manger. Hugo Gressmann thought that the parents did not belong to the original story; their insertion into it obscured the original function of the shepherds.[5] He claims they were originally called upon by the angel to protect and raise the foundling. This Jewish messianic legend, dependent on the Egyptian legend of Osiris, was adopted and applied to Jesus.

1   Rudolf Pesch assigns v. 21 to the tradition behind vv. 1–21, which is only slightly reworked by Luke ("Das Weihnachtsevangelium [Lk 2,1–21]: Literarische Kunst: Politische Implikation," in idem, ed., *Zur Theologie der Kindheitsgeschichten: Der heutige Stand der Exegese* [Munich/Zurich: Schnell und Steiner, 1981]) 97–118, esp. 99).

2   Gressmann has already noted this (*Das Weihnachtsevangelium auf Ursprung und Geschichte untersucht* [Göttingen: Vandenhoeck & Ruprecht, 1914] 2).

3   "But if the motive for the journey drops out, the journey itself becomes questionable," according to

Gressmann (*Weihnachtsevangelium*, 9), who adds (12) that the census is not mentioned again after v. 8.

4   The literary unity is vividly portrayed by Eduard Schweizer, *Das Evangelium nach Lukas* (NTD 3; Göttingen: Vandenhoeck & Ruprecht, 1982) 31.

5   *Weihnachtsevangelium*, 2: "Hence the parents supplanted the shepherds."

In contrast, Martin Dibelius has pointed out that the motif of the child in swaddling cloths is already present in the tradition.[6] Nevertheless, a few of Gressmann's observations are still valid: (1) the birth narrative is originally a separately circulating story; (2) the birth narrative stands at the end of a christological development; (3) Mary was originally presented as a wife, not a fiancée; (4) the journey to Bethlehem is secondary; (5) the shepherds' function in the present Lukan version appears enigmatic.[7]

Dibelius himself explains further: first, the present census story destroyed the original beginning of the legend, which described how the parents found only a manger for the newborn child in a καταλυμα ("inn"); second, the shepherd motif is neither bucolic nor proletarian, but probably Davidic and biblical.[8]

More recent scholars, in particular René Laurentin and Raymond E. Brown,[9] emphasize Luke's midrash-like technique, and that the Hebrew Bible texts about Bethlehem[10] and מִגְדַּל עֵדֶר (Migdal Eder, "the tower of the flock")[11] stand in the background. Even the census episode could be traced back to the *Quinta* version of Ps 87(LXX 86):6.[12] Catholic exegesis also no longer attempts to salvage the historicity of the events, but rather their biblical character. I think it is time to rediscover the narrativity of the text by employing the aesthetic sensitivity of the first form critics. The Christmas story should not blind us to the literary achievement of the evangelist, even if he does not compose his work here in the absence of an influence from prior tradition.

The annunciation to Mary must have had a continuation in the tradition, which would have reported the birth, according to a prophecy-fulfillment scheme. Only a torso of this second part seems to have been preserved in Luke's version (vv. 6–7a, v. 21),[13] because the birth probably took place in Nazareth. By Luke's time, however, only Bethlehem could be considered as the birthplace of the Messiah. To bring about the necessary change of scene, Luke inserted the census episode (vv. 1–5), which also made possible the striking juxtaposition of the emperor, known to all, and the hidden Messiah. To complete it, Luke includes the tale of the shepherds, the beginning of which he shortens and adjusts to the contemporary situation. This tale was, first, a separately circulating legend with two poles, an apocalyptic prophecy and a historical fulfillment. In my opinion, the entire cycle of legends in Luke 2 is neither a wholly Lukan composition nor a unitary tradition accepted by Luke almost without change. Despite the varied origins of the material, Luke achieves a careful coherence in its composition and thus completes the parallelism between John and Jesus that he laid out in chap. 1.

In terms of the history of dogma, the birth narrative and the shepherds' story attempt to answer the question of the "beginning" of Jesus. In educated circles, christological reflection ran backward from the resurrection, with the help of Sophia speculation and the concept of preexistence; in another milieu or for another purpose, it also ran backward, but by means of narrative depiction of the birth of a "hero." It is difficult to say who was responsible for the first version of this narrative. One should not underestimate the power of popular storytelling, which intended to attest the messianic privilege of Jesus as well as his divine origin. The episode of the shepherds attempts less to *prove* something than to *bear witness* to a heavenly revelation that strengthens the Christian claim and the kerygmatic message; that is, the person of Jesus is less its concern than his soteriological significance. This is why the atmosphere has been so strongly infused with eschatological jubilation.

---

6   Dibelius, *Jungfrauensohn*, 61.
7   Gressmann, *Weihnachtsevangelium*, 1, 6, 8–9, 10–11, 13.
8   Dibelius, *Jungfrauensohn*, 64–66.
9   See Laurentin, *Structure*, 99–101; Brown (*Birth* 557–62) denies Luke 1–2 the character of a midrash, but concedes that the methods applied in the midrashim are put to full use in these two chapters.
10 Mic 5:2–6, above all.
11 Mic 4:8; Gen 35:19–21. See Brown, *Birth*, 422–23.
12 According to Eusebius *Comm. Ps.* (PG 23.1052c). The *Quinta* is the last of the five Greek columns that stood by the side of the two Hebrew columns in the Psalms of Origen's *Hexapla*. See Brown, *Birth*, 417–18.
13 Schweizer (31) conceives of vv. 4–7 as an introduction to 2:22–38.

Commentary

Under Caesar Augustus (vv. 1–5)

■ **1–3** The passage consists of two parts: first, the publication of the edict (vv. 1–2) and its execution (v. 3); second, the presentation of the concrete individual case of Mary and Joseph (vv. 4–5). Is the motif of the census a means of bringing the Galilean family to Bethlehem, a midrash that tells the fulfillment of a prophecy, or an opportunity to point out the juxtaposition of Jesus and Caesar—or is it simply a historical fact?

Luke has an affinity for dates, which he inserts while editing. In 3:1 he sets the date of the beginning of John's work impressively. In 1:5 he places the annunciation to Zechariah "in the days of Herod." There the perspective remains Jewish and bound to prophecy. Here in 2:1, in which the fulfillment begins, the horizon broadens to include the οἰκουμένη ("world," for Luke, the *imperium Romanum*). Against the backdrop of the imperial command,[14] the angels' message of the birth of the σωτήρ ("savior") and κύριος ("lord") receives its specific relevance. The dating as such alludes to the historicity of salvation, but also has a polemical point: the "political theology" of Augustus, supported particularly in the East by the religious worship of the ruler, is unmasked and invalidated by the christological claim.[15] At the same time, with the reference to the obedience of Mary and Joseph, Luke's polemic is directed against the Zealot movements. Luke is thus not pitting one political theology against another. The Gospel is a criticism of both the ruler cult and Zealot ideology.

Modern readers will easily miss the power claim behind a census in those times, by which a ruler wished to certify the number of his subjects in order to have them better in his grasp for military or financial service.

Since David, the Bible is aware of its temptation and danger:[16] the people belong to God, and even the chosen king should refrain from any census in order to depend on the power of God alone. God alone may institute a census (Num 1:26). Can it have been that Luke knew a messianic interpretation of Ps 87(LXX 86):6 that expected the birth of the Messiah during a universal census? In any case, the objection to any census in Israel had gained force. Did not, for this reason, the accommodation to Roman rule signify a betrayal of the only Lord, the God of Israel? The minds of people had become agitated and drifted apart over this question. According to Josephus, the beginnings of the Zealot movement were inseparably bound to a Roman census.[17]

But the ἀπογραφή should be distinguished from the ἀποτίμησις (both translate the Latin *census*). The ἀπογραφή is the official registration of every inhabitant (age, occupation, wife, children), in order to establish military service and head tax. The ἀποτίμησις, on the other hand, aimed at registration of goods and income.[18] Luke uses ἀπογραφή in the usual sense in vv. 1–5, and ἀπογράφεσθαι regularly, in the middle voice ("to register oneself").

Secular sources report that at various times Augustus ordered individual provinces to be counted, or his private property (including imperial provinces) to be estimated. A certain regularity (every fourteen years) seems to have prevailed for these censuses, at least in Egypt. But it never became a single, general decree.[19] Luke is mistaken in literal terms, but he does correctly capture the historical tendency of the time, and of the emperor, in narrative and popular terms.[20]

In v. 2 should the text critic read αὕτη ("this") or αὐτή ("it"), with or without the article, πρώτη ἐγένετο

---

14 *Τὸ δόγμα* means at root "opinion," but then denotes "instruction," "decree," "decretal," "edict," and, last, "didactic formula," "dogma."

15 See Pesch, "Weihnachtsevangelium"; and Walter Schmithals, "Die Weihnachtsgeschichte Lukas 2, 1–20," in G. Ebeling et al., eds., *Festschrift für Ernst Fuchs* (Tübingen: Mohr-Siebeck, 1973) 281–97, esp. 286–94. Hippolytus (*Comm. Dan.* 4.9.3) contrasts the imperial census with the census of the believers.

16 2 Sam (LXX 2 Kgdms) 24; 1 Chr 21.

17 *Bell.* 2.8.2 §118.

18 But the usage is not stable, and ἀπογραφή on occasion denotes the second operation.

19 On the sea of apologetic or critical publications about this decree, see Pierre Benoit, "Quirinius (Recensement de)," *DBSup* 9 (1977) 693–720.

20 Benoit ("Quirinius," 697) refers to Suetonius *Aug.* 28.1; Dio Cassius 53.30.2; Tacitus *Ann.* 1.11.7 on Augustus: "Among the documents that he left at his death figured a *Brevarium totius imperii*, which he had prepared as far back as 23 BCE." In this memorandum, all of the empire's sources of income are listed. According to Dio Cassius (54.35.1), Augustus also conducted an assessment of his property in 11–10 BCE.

("[this] was the first [registration]") or ἐγένετο πρώτη ("[this registration] happened first")? Moreover, should πρώτη be taken comparatively ("an earlier")? But the translation, "This census took place before that of the governor Quirinius," is, in any case, apologetic.[21] The traditional solution is probably the correct one: "This was the first registration"; the pronoun αὕτη ("this") without ἡ is the subject and is thus congruent with the predicate nominative.[22] Then ἡγεμονεύοντος . . . Κυρηνίου ("when Quirinius was governor") is understood as a genitive absolute.

According to Luke's chronology (cf. 1:5, 24, 26, 39, 56, 67), we are still in the days of Herod, or shortly after his death (4 BCE). But according to Josephus, Quirinius appears as a *legatus Augusti pro praetore* (governor of an imperial province) only in 6 CE; he was assigned to Syria to conduct the census in Syria and Palestine, and to liquidate the property of the recently deposed son of Herod, Archelaus, who had until then ruled over Judea.[23] All possible attempts have been undertaken to harmonize Josephus and Luke. Thus, for example, a fragmentary inscription, the *Titulus Tiburtinus*,[24] was assigned to Quirinius, who would then have been the governor of Syria twice (not impossible, but unusual). Others have argued that at the end of his life Herod was reproached by Augustus and was for that reason supposed to have demonstrated his loyalty to Roman power by an oath;[25] but an oath is no ἀπογραφή ("registration").[26]

Josephus is doubtless poorly informed about the era after Herod. Popular memory could have confused the

unrest after Herod's death with that which followed the removal of Archelaus. On both occasions, great, almost messianic expectations arose; and on both occasions not the divine but the imperial will won out. So Luke is writing of the time shortly after Herod's death and connecting it with the census under Quirinius after Archelaus.[27]

■ **4–5** The legal regulation in v. 3 is understood by Luke in v. 4 to be the occasion for a return to their hometown. But every census presupposes registration in the place of residence. The papyri, as well, expect travelers to return there, not to their hometown.[28]

Luke is probably aware of this legal injunction, but interprets it to serve his narrative and theological aims, so that he can bring Mary and Joseph from the historical Nazareth over to the messianic Bethlehem. "Bethlehem" is thus no more historically verifiable than the resurrection. It stands in the same relation to Nazareth as Easter to Good Friday. The novelistic solution that Bethlehem was Joseph's place of residence, and that he was only visiting his betrothed in Nazareth,[29] does not help (neither 2:4 nor 1:27 gives the explicit name of the place of residence). The flow of the narrative, however, clearly indicates Nazareth as the place of residence and Bethlehem as Joseph's hometown. Otherwise, Luke would have had to introduce him in 1:27 as an inhabitant of Bethlehem; and, at the latest in 2:39, he would have had to explain the move from Bethlehem to Nazareth; but he speaks there of Nazareth as "their city."

Thus Luke sees in the imperial census the reason for the journey and, in this context, also mentions the

---

21   Lagrange, 67.

22   See Adolf Kaegi, *Grammaire abrégée de la langue grecque* (rev. André Perrenoud; Paris/Neuchâtel: V. Attinger, 1949) §108.5; and BDF §132.1. So also Benoit, "Quirinius," 694.

23   Cf. Josephus *Ant.* 17.13.5 §355; 18.1.1 §1; 18.2.1 §26, cited by Benoit ("Quirinius," 707).

24   *CIL* 14:3613 and *ILS* 918; see Benoit, "Quirinius," 702–3.

25   Cf. Josephus *Ant.* 17.2.4 §42.

26   Quirinius could perhaps have been an extra-ordinary legate selected for this particular assignment, while Saturninus could have been the ordinary legate (9–6 BCE). Thus Tertullian's remarkable opinion that a census took place in Judea under Saturninus could be explained (*Adv. Marc.* 4.19.1). On the connection of Herod's oath of service with the ἀπογραφή, see Paul W. Barnett ("Ἀπογραφή and ἀπογράφεσθαι in Luke 2:1–4," *ExpTim* 85 [1973]

377–380); he does not place the census under Quirinius, since he interprets πρώτη ("first") in the sense of προτέρα ("earlier").

27   Luke also knew about the onset of Jewish resistance, particularly that of Judas the Galilean (Acts 5:37), who revolted against the census.

28   Cf. the edict of the prefect of Egypt, C. Vibius Maximinus (104 CE), often mentioned in this context. Benoit cites the text (P. Lond. 3.904, p. 125; Benoit, "Quirinius," 699).

29   Benoit judges this thesis more favorably in "Quirinius" (700) than in "'Non erat eis locus in diversorio' (Lc 2,7)," in A. Descamps and R. P. A. de Halleux, eds., *Mélanges Bibliques: Festschrift R. P. Béda Rigaux* (Gembloux: Duculot, 1970) 173–86, reprinted in Benoit, *Exégèse*, 4.95–111; see esp. 110–11.

regions and cities that will later be the scenes of Jesus' activity. Joseph, as the pater familias, takes the initiative. His Davidic lineage is noted redundantly.[30] Mary is mentioned discreetly, and for the first time, as pregnant.[31] It is shocking for the readers that a bride-to-be[32] is traveling with her fiancé and is, beyond this, pregnant. This is difficult to justify even by recourse to the nature of engagement, which legally constitutes marriage. A novelist could, in any case, postulate that Mary possessed real estate in Bethlehem that would require her personal presence in the city of David.[33] The shocking character of the pregnant bride-to-be who travels with her fiancé should not be smoothed over;[34] it is provoked by Luke.

The Birth of Jesus (vv. 6–7, 21)

■ **6–7a** Mary and Joseph are "there" (ἐκεῖ). Not only is it the right place, but also the time is "fulfilled." Already in 1:57, Luke let something of a fulfillment of the prophecy be heard in πληρόω ("to fulfill").[35] But what is being fulfilled here is not a biblical, liturgical, holy time (in connection with the messianic locus), but a natural, human phase of life. Mary experiences a normal birth. In contrast to later Mariology, which extends the miracle of virginity backward (immaculate conception) and forward (virginity *in partu et post partum*),[36] no further wonder is reported here. No divine intervention spares Mary the labor pains, or the fear of the unknown in a first

birth and her increasing weakness. Mariology in dogma and art has repressed this realism in the incarnation, and even Protestants are troubled by Kurt Marti's matter-of-fact verses:

> then
> when God
> in the cry of birth
> shattered the images of God
> and
> between Mary's thighs
> wrinkled red
> lay the child.[37]

Why does Luke write πρωτότοκος ("firstborn")? As such, the adjective πρωτότοκος could not furnish a decisive argument for the existence of brothers of Jesus according to the flesh. Does this adjective refer to the primordial will of God the creator, to whom Jesus belongs?[38] Or has it become a christological title that designates the Lord, in his incarnation and resurrection, as the firstborn of a new human race?[39] Luke does not, however, use this attribute in the context of the resurrection account or the kerygma. Although πρωτότοκος ("giving birth to the first child") is classical, πρωτότοκος ("firstborn") is very rare outside the Bible. The word is reminiscent of the birth of the patriarchs, or of the existence of Israel itself as the firstborn child of God.[40] In

---

30 Joseph is not only from the "house" of David, but also from the "family."

31 Ἔγκυος is ἐγκύμων, "pregnant," used of both women and animals.

32 On engagement see the commentary on 1:27 above.

33 "Her [Mary's] presence was not required for the census; the head of the family would register all of his household" (Benoit, "Quirinius," 700).

34 The text is, indeed, not stable. Along with the reading of Nestle-Aland, which I retain, there is the poorly attested variant "his wife," and the most widely attested harmonizing variant in Byzantine times, "the woman betrothed to him."

35 See the commentary on 1:57–58 above.

36 Already in the 2d century (*Prot. Jas.* 19–20; also 4–10), traditions about Mary's virginity *in partu et post partum*, and about her own birth and childhood, accompanied by miracles, prevailed.

37 The poem "Weihnacht" appeared in a volume of poetry of Kurt Marti (*Gedichte am Rand* [3d ed.; Teufen (Aargau): A. Niggli, 1974] 6).

38 Ἐμοί γὰρ πᾶν πρωτότοκον ("For all the firstborn

are mine [God's]"): Num 3:13; Exod 22:29 (LXX 22:28). Mosaic law is also concerned about the redemption of the firstborn (Num 18:15). The Levites are a substitute to God for every firstborn (Num 3:12).

39 Rom 8:29; Col 1:15, 18; Heb 1:6; Rev 1:5.

40 Πρωτότοκος ("firstborn") occurs frequently in the LXX, above all (1) in the stories of the patriarchs in Genesis; (2) in the account of the slaying of the firstborn in Exodus; (3) in the legislation regarding the firstborn, Exod 22:29-30 (primarily the neuter is used here, since it describes the firstborn of plants, animals, and people). Cf. Edwin Hatch and Henry A. Redpath, *Concordance to the Septuagint and the Other Greek Versions of the Old Testament* (2 vols.; Graz: Akademische Druck und Verlagsanstalt, 1954) *s.v.*; and Wilhelm Michaelis, "πρῶτος, κτλ.," *TDNT* 6 (1968) 871–76.

any case, Luke is placing Jesus in a privileged relationship to God, and not in a relationship with later sisters and brothers.[41]

■ **21** As in 2:6–7a and 1:26–38, Joseph fades into the background in v. 21. As in 2:6, the fulfillment of days is again mentioned, and the annunciation in 1:26–38 is fulfilled here. As a Jewish child, Jesus is enrolled in the people of the divine promise; he receives the sign of God's faithfulness and of his covenant with Israel. Luke mentions this event without interpreting it, because for him, a Gentile Christian, circumcision is no longer necessary for inclusion into the people of God. Luke cannot and will not deny that Jesus was a Jew and that his birth and childhood still belong to the old covenant. But his interest is directed toward the child's future, and thus toward the future of the people of God through him, in a time in which faith and baptism will replace circumcision. But Luke does not yet wish here to draw this conclusion explicitly. The controversy in Antioch (Acts 15) will give him the opportunity to present his own understanding—always in narrative style, of course.

The only comment on the naming remains strictly innertextual: Jesus receives the name pronounced by the angel (cf. 1:31). God wants him to be named Jesus and thereby to become what his name expresses. It is still surprising that, after 2:11, Luke does not allude to the etymology of the name ("YHWH saves").[42] Circumcision and etymology are as timidly and briefly treated as in the case of John the Baptist. Luke does not have anything comparable to the tense scene in 1:57–66 to narrate here. This does not upset him, because he has found something in the tradition more valuable in his eyes: the prophecy of the aged Simeon (2:24–35).

■ **7b** Κατάλυμα ("inn"), despite the Christian tradition about it, is no hostel in the modern sense, since Luke knows the word πανδοχεῖον for this (Luke 10:34). Κατάλυμα is a place where one can stop and unharness a mount or draught animal (and unload its burden? καταλύω, "to unharness"), a provisional place to spend

the night. The Semites became familiar with inns and hotels only rather late and probably under Greek influence. Until then, the traveler was dependent on the holy duty of hospitality.[43] In New Testament times there were private accommodations, boardinghouses of synagogues, cottages set up for the overnight stays of pilgrims, roadhouses; there were inns and caravanserais, as well as the *mutationes* (only for feeding and changing animals) and *mansiones* (for overnight stays, particularly in the cities). Here the word is used generally and vaguely.[44] I believe it means a room in a private house in which travelers could usually spend the night. It is highly unlikely that Luke has in mind Joseph's own house, in which the head of the family would have found no room upon his return.[45] It contradicts the text to say that the parents found no room only for the child and accordingly laid it in a manger; it says there was no room for *them*, not *him*.

The Shepherds (vv. 8–12)

It remains a riddle why Luke does not narrate Jesus' birth in greater detail. That he interrupts the tradition in v. 7 to make room for the shepherds' tale has a theological consequence: we are instructed less about the person of Jesus than about his effect.[46]

■ **8** The assessment of the shepherds is also a riddle. The rabbinic texts critical of shepherds[47] are not weighty enough to cancel out the positive evaluation of shepherds in biblical literature.[48] Israel understood themselves as a nation of shepherds in contrast to their neighbors, who are either city dwellers or settled farmers. As shepherds, they used the image of the shepherd both for their God[49] and for their king or Messiah.

In Ezekiel 34 there is first a criticism of the bad shepherds of Israel (vv. 1–10), and then the assembling of the people under God, its true shepherd (vv. 11–16), God's judgment of the sheep (the people), rams, and he-goats (the leaders, vv. 16–22), and last, the prophecy of the eschatological shepherd, "my servant David"

41   Here I agree with Schneider, 1.66.

42   See Gerhard Schneider, "Ἰησοῦς," *EDNT* 2 (1991) 180–81.

43   See Elpidius Pax, "'Denn sie fanden keinen Platz in der Herberge': Jüdisches und frühchristliches Herbergswesen," *BibLeb* 6 (1965) 285–98.

44   Cf. the many texts cited by Benoit ("Non erat").

45   See above, commentary on 2:4–5.

46   Philipp Melanchthon, "Loci communes" (1521), in R. Stupperich, ed., *Melanchthons Werke in Auswahl* (7 vols. to date; Gütersloh: Bertelsmann, 1951–), 2.1.7.

47   Str-B 2.113–14.

48   Philippe de Robert, *Le Berger d'Israël: Essai sur le thème pastoral dans l'Ancien Testament* (CTh 57; Neuchâtel: Delachaux et Niestlé, 1968).

49   See Philo *Agr.* 50: "Indeed, so good a thing is shep-

(23–24), and a description of the messianic age (vv. 25–31). In contrast to this text, there is no criticism of the shepherds in Luke 2:8–20. It is not surprising, in the city of David,[50] not far from the "Tower of the Flock," that shepherds, as representatives of the people, should be the first recipients of the good news. What was expected from Bethlehem since Micah 5 was, of course, not the birth of the Messiah among the shepherds, but the birth of a messianic shepherd.[51]

In the redaction, a Greek and Roman motif also plays a part: the discovery of the royal infant by shepherds.[52] With it, the narrative depicts the hiddenness of the new Messiah. The time of night affirms both the unexpected event and the dark predicament of the people of Israel.

The descriptive v. 8 portrays how the shepherds spend the night in the open[53] in the above-mentioned region.[54] Already Homer speaks of the "shepherds who live outside," ποιμένες ἄγραυλοι (Il. 18.162). The shepherds are discharging the night watch,[55] thus acting as shepherds must. The content of v. 8 is perhaps familiar and banal in order to accentuate the divine "ambush." Until now, only Mary has heard the message; now a larger circle will receive it (v. 18).

■ 9 The living relationship between God and his people ensues in the "sacramental" unity of res and verbum, in which the interpretation is added to the event.[56] God grants both at once. In v. 9 the third angelophany thus far is recorded. Thus God has something significant to tell to his people. The present introduction of the angels diverges here from the previous one, either because of the underlying source or to avoid monotony. Instead of the perfect ("to be there"), the aorist ἐπέστη ("stood before") depicts the emergence and self-presentation of the messengers. For the arrival of a heavenly being, this verb is common.[57] As in 1:11 (and the LXX)[58] the angel is called ἄγγελος κυρίου ("an angel of the Lord"); moreover, he should probably be equated with Gabriel.

After this signal of a divine intervention, Luke adds an unusual motif: the glory of God appears and surrounds the shepherds. The juxtaposition of night and light is composed as elegantly as in the messianic text of Isaiah (9:2 [MT 9:1]). This surpasses the time of preparation in Luke 1:11, 26. Now ("this day," v. 11) the day has dawned. It is remarkable, however, that the divine glory shines not around the manger but around the angels. Not history, but the Word of God has splendor. Only the Word of the Lord, which cannot be taken captive, can shine forth as *theologia gloriae*. The event itself is directed toward the mortally human, the cross. The crescendo of the δόξα κυρίου ("the glory of the Lord") plays up the eschatological relevance of the present happening, in contrast to the Hebrew Bible.[59]

In symmetry to this, the fear of God can only be great (v. 9); but Luke leaves no room for doubt. Though he

---

herding that it is justly ascribed not to kings only and wise men and perfectly cleansed souls, but also to God the All-Sovereign." Philo finds the proof text for his argument in Ps 23:1.

50 "Now, a scriptural relationship between Bethlehem and the Messiah seems to have been commonplace in first-century Judaism, if we can follow NT indications (Appendix III)" (Brown, *Birth*, 421). Cf. John 7:42.

51 Brown, *Birth*, 420–24. By contrast, Augustin George ("'Il vous est né aujourd'hui un Sauveur': Lc 2, 1–20," *AsSeign* 10 [1970] 50–67, esp. 55) is of the opinion that the text nowhere indicates that Luke is particularly predisposed to Davidic symbolism (1 Sam 16:11; 17:15; 2 Sam 7:8).

52 One thinks of Oedipus, Paris, and Romulus. See Gressmann, *Weihnachtsevangelium*, 18–19 (whose overall hypothesis, however, I reject); and de Robert, *Berger*, 19.

53 The periphrastic construction underscores the duration and sets into relief the contrast of the event that bursts upon them in v. 8.

54 I take τῇ αὐτῇ more in the sense of "the above-mentioned" (cf. LSJ s.v. αὐτός, 3) than in the sense of "the same" (cf. Bailly, *Dictionnaire, s.v.* αὐτός, 4). Verse 15 gives us to understand that the shepherds were not in Bethlehem itself.

55 Φυλάσσειν φυλακάς ("keeping watch"): cf. Xenophon *An.* 2.6.10; Plato *Leg.* 6.758D, etc. Cf. BDF §153.3.

56 See Paul Ricoeur, "Événement et sens," in E. Castelli, ed., *Révélation et histoire* (Paris: Aubier, 1971) 18–22.

57 Diodorus Siculus 1.25.5 (an angel); Lucian *Dial. deor.* 17:1 (Isis, in a dream); cf. *Syll.*³ 3.1168.37; Josephus *Ant.* 3.8.1 §188; 5.6.3 §215; Acts 12:7; 23:11; *Hermas* 9.6 (*Vis.* 3.1.6).

58 LXX Gen 16:7; 22:11, 15.

59 Jdt 9:8 presupposes that the name of the glory of God dwells in the temple, where it is threatened by desecration from unbelievers.

gives no definition of faith, he does describe the irrevocability of God's undertaking. Verse 9 serves as a sublime backdrop for the speech, but also as an anticipation of the angelic choir in vv. 13–14. The glory of God does not live in the absence of a heavenly court. God's glory has not disappeared, nor is it trapped in the temple. With unearthly life it shines forth here and now, in contradiction to every human or religious program. It is here, to express God's faithfulness, and now, to express God's freedom.[60]

The angel fulfills (vv. 10–12) his mission. True to style, its message is connected with the fear that the revelation has caused (cf. 1:13, 30). As in that passage, and in the Hebrew Bible genre of the angelophany, the messenger substantiates the word of encouragement with the content of its message, so that "do not be afraid" points both backward and forward. Even this is artfully emphasized through the juxtaposition of "great fear" (v. 9) and "great joy" (v. 10).

■ **10** In v. 10 the angel still has not unveiled the content of his message. On the metalinguistic level, the angel describes his own speech in advance as good news. Luke knows the Hebrew Bible roots of εὐαγγελίζομαι ("to proclaim good news"),[61] but he also knows its ideological significance for the Greeks, which here lends it an anti-imperial tone.

Joy has already suffused the first pages of Luke's Gospel,[62] but it is emphasized here in view of the main event. Since the hand of God is at work in the beginning and end of the Gospel, and the angels attest this activity (cf. 24:4), the people[63] experience peace (cf. 24:36) and great joy (cf. 24:52). The *inclusio* is not only a stylistic technique but, in its content, is also the fitting human appropriation of the birth of the Son, and his rebirth in the resurrection.

The mediating role of the shepherds is indicated ("you," "all the people"). The shepherds are rooted in the *New* Testament; the news is described with the vocabulary of the Christian mission, and Luke has in mind the apostolic work of the Christian missionaries.[64] Of course, "joy" should be understood metonymically. The good news for all the people is the birth of the son, not the shepherd's joy.

■ **11** While the shepherds learn of the good news in v. 11, the reader, who already knows about the event (vv. 6–7), learns its christological and soteriological significance,[65] the "to you."[66] The "this day" of the occurrence underscores both the fulfillment of prophecy and its present relevance. If God is acting for us, we should hear his voice today.[67] Neither the transitory nature of σήμερον ("this day")[68] nor its perennial present in the deuteronomistic sense should be stressed one-sidedly. It belongs to the past, because salvation history is history, but this past remains present for us when we keep salvation in our sight. Luke is both a historian and an evangelist; his identity as a historian is a means to accomplish his task as herald.[69]

With a title comprehensible to all, Jew and Greek, the angel announces the birth of the σωτήρ ("savior"). This title played a prominent role at that time, particularly in the ideology of the Hellenistic rulership. Luke lays claim to it for the Messiah, who is, particularly in the first chapters, a *healing* Messiah, and who thus proves his kindness palpably without thereby succumbing to the misconceptions of the political theology of the time. In the LXX the title describes the deliverer of Israel raised up by God (e.g., Judg 3:9, 15) or God himself, especially in the

---

60   The glory of God revealed itself during the exodus from Egypt (Exod 16:10), particularly to Moses (Exod 24:16–18; 33:18–23; 34:29–35). It fills the temple (2 Chr 7:1), but dwells, above all, in heaven (Tob 12:15). The angel departs from it in order to come to earth (Tob 3:16–17). See Gerhard von Rad, "δοκέω, κτλ.," *TDNT* 2 (1964) 238–42. For the Lukan περιλάμπω ("to shine around"), which does not appear in the LXX or the rest of the NT, see Acts 26:13.

61   See the commentary on 1:19 above, and on 4:20b–21 below.

62   See the commentary on 1:57–58 above.

63   See Lohfink, *Sammlung*, 28.

64   Legrand, "Évangile aux Bergers," 161.

65   Ἐτέχθη ("[he] is born," v. 11) takes up ἔτεκεν ("she gave birth," v. 7) and τοῦ τεκεῖν αὐτήν ("for her to give birth," v. 6).

66   One should note the emphasis: εὐαγγελίζομαι ὑμῖν ("I am proclaiming to you good news," v. 10), ἐτέχθη ὑμῖν ("to you is born," v. 11).

67   Cf. Heb 3:7–4:13.

68   Referring to Luke 4:21, Conzelmann (*Theology*, 103) writes, "the σήμερον of v. 21 is already thought of as belonging to past history."

69   See Martin Dibelius, "Der erste christliche His-

Psalms (e.g., 25[LXX 24]:5); it is less the title itself, but rather its emphatic placement before other titles that represents an accommodation to Hellenistic readers.[70]

Luke understands the birth "in the city of David" not only historically but biblically, as the fulfillment of the prophet's promise (Mic 5:2 [LXX 5:1]). It bestows on the savior a "messianic" character. The relative clause uses an attributive formula.[71] The absence of an article for the predicate is normal: the savior is the Messiah, not a messiah. But χριστὸς κύριος ("the Messiah, the Lord") is unusual. The LXX expresses the title "the anointed of God" as ὁ χριστὸς κυρίου.[72] By Luke's time the title has indeed become a component of christology, but these two titles never appear together elsewhere in the New Testament without articles and καί ("and"). Obviously, Luke wants to stress Jesus' dominion alongside his function as a savior. For Jewish readers ὁ χριστός ("the Messiah," "the anointed") was unambiguous in the context of Bethlehem; for Greek readers ὁ κύριος ("the Lord") fulfilled the same function. In Judaism the dominion of the Messiah was already an attribute of the "anointed" figure, and so perhaps too was the title κύριος in some places, although it is used almost exclusively of God in the LXX. Χριστὸς κύριος ("the Lord Messiah")[73] could have been a traditional title in Hellenistic Judaism (Lam 4:20; *Ps. Sol.* 17:32).

■ **12** The three components of the angel's speech treated thus far comprise a first half, the main message. Next is the unrequested offer of a sign.[74] Luke's appro-

priation of the traditional biblical function of the sign sheds light on his theology. The transcendence of the active God and the absolute independence of his action are respected when one depends on signs. It also proves (with the force of a rhetorical argument) that God works within the world. What is objectionable about this sign is its identity with the referent: Jesus is the sign of christology! Expressed differently, Jesus as a babe wrapped in swaddling cloths becomes the sign of Jesus as savior, Christ, and Lord. *Signum* and *res* are seldom compressed so closely in the Bible. Seldom, or never, has God come so close to us humans. But the contrast remains, narratively, between "manger" and "Lord," and, theologically, between the messianism lived by Jesus and the post-Easter christology. It is often said that Luke's birth narrative unfolds the christological *greatness* of Jesus backward. But this sign could just as well underscore, for example, the *lowliness* of Jesus. Just as the sign of Jonah is the only one that Jesus will concede to his contemporaries (Luke 11:29–30), this sign is the only opportunity to see God at work now. The manner of birth and of death correspond. Jesus the human is himself the sign that God promises to his people. But, as a sign, he also executes salvation: the resurrection (and ascension) relates to the birth, life, and death of Jesus as the referent does to the sign.

A newborn child in swaddling cloths is normal in Palestine, though not in Egypt.[75] What is unusual, and thus becomes a sign, is the φάτνη ("manger").[76] Its first

---

toriker," in idem, *Aufsätze,* 118. Since there was not yet a Christmas festival, it is wrong to ascribe to σήμερον ("this day") a liturgical value; see Brown, *Birth,* 402.

70   On σωτήρ ("savior") in Luke, see Voss, *Christologie,* 45–55; Glöckner, *Verkündigung,* 116–21; Bovon, *Theologian,* 152–53, 192.

71   On the various ways of interpreting these clauses (a formula of presentation, attribution, identification, or recognition) see Rudolf Bultmann, *The Gospel of John* (trans. and ed. G. R. Beasley Murray et al.; Philadelphia: Westminster, 1971) 225 n. 3.

72   Some Latin mss. (b, r¹) prefer this formulation in 2:11.

73   I agree with Sahlin (*Messias,* 214–18), who summarizes the opinions of various exegetes. But in contrast to Sahlin, I do not believe that one can retrovert from the Greek to a "Messiah-YHWH" formula.

74   On σημεῖον ("sign"), see B. Trémel ("Le signe du

nouveau-né dans la mangeoire: À propos de Lc 2,1–20," in P. Casetti et al., eds., *Mélanges: Festschrift Dominique Barthélemy* [OBO 38; Fribourg: Éditions Universitaires; Göttingen: Vandenhoeck & Ruprecht, 1981] 593–612, esp. 595): "The sign of a newborn lying in the manger is the 'signifier' (σημεῖον) of the message of salvation." Trémel emphasizes the three repetitions of the formula (vv. 7, 12, 16), which, in his opinion, determine the action completely (596): "The sign of the newborn lying in the manger is at once the destination of the shepherds' step of faith, and the point of departure for their message." See my commentary on Luke 11:29–30 (vol. 2).

75   See Gressmann (*Weihnachtsevangelium,* 23), who otherwise assumes Egyptian origin. Greek authors and the LXX (Job 38:9; Ezek 16:4) use σπαργανόω in the sense of "wrap (in bands of cloth)."

76   Against Ernst (105), who emphasizes the "banality" of the circumstances.

meaning, even before Homer, is "manger." The word could also mean the "stable" or, in Judea, the half-open "feeding place," sometimes located in a cave. Despite the contrast between κατάλυμα ("inn") and φάτνη ("manger"), the first meaning should probably be assumed;[77] following Luke, the manger should be imagined in a feeding place or stall; otherwise where it stood would have been indicated.[78] In large estates, farmers would build costly stables in caves; in farmhouses, "the feeding place for cattle would often be in the room where the family lived." Stables would also be located "in the ground-floor of the house or in annexes, or feeding-troughs outside, e.g., in the farm-yard."[79] The manger was probably made of stone (perhaps chiseled into the wall of a cave or the face of a rock) or of mud; wood was too expensive. Literarily significant is the thrice-repeated refrainlike occurrence of "child lying in a manger" (vv. 7, 12, 16).

The Angels' Song of Praise (vv. 13–14)

■ **13–14** As in Isa 6:1–2, the glory of the Lord (v. 9) corresponds to the host of angels (v. 13). "Suddenly" (this adverb emphasizes the miraculous element), the shepherds participate in the heavenly liturgy. The author's view, though, is directed not to the watching shepherds[80] but to the heavenly host, who surround God the king. Thus a heavenly vision is imagined already in 1 Kgs (LXX 3 Kgdms) 22:19. Πλῆθος στρατιᾶς οὐρανίου ("a multitude of the heavenly host") can denote the stars, which are, according to the ideas of certain Jewish scholars, moved by angels,[81] but this plays no role here. In the

history of the transmission of the traditions, the angel of YHWH who introduces an epiphany (God comes down to us) is a separate motif from the host of serving angels (they look up toward God).[82] The narrative unites both of them and assigns to each a different function. The revelatory character of the first is clear in vv. 10–12. The second serves as a liturgical commentary and choral finale. What the angels sing situates the christological revelation of vv. 10–12 in the broader context of God's covenant with his people: the acknowledgment of the distance between creator and creature, symbolized here by heaven and earth; and the liturgical worship of God "above" by the heavenly host, but also "below" by the believers. To know God is, for Luke, to praise God (v. 13) and to worship God (v. 14).

But the glory of God is so far from self-centered that it streams down to the shepherds (v. 9); God incorporates the glory into a movement toward human beings. The peace[83] that accompanies the glory is the condition desired by God for the covenant between him and his people (v. 14). It has now[84] been established by the Messiah's birth and the declaration of the word of God. Every human peace movement after this is linked to it, but cannot identify itself with it. It is the gift of God, and as such, like the Pauline δικαιοσύνη ("righteousness"), it is also both empowerment and requirement.

Structurally, the song falls into two parts,[85] as the καί ("and") demonstrates. It suits the Jewish style of prayer that the second is the longer part. Glory (A), highest (B), earth (B'), and peace (A') are juxtaposed chiastically. Symmetrically, God stands at the end of the first part,

77 Martin Hengel, "φάτνη," *TDNT* 9 (1974) 49–55; Trémel, "Signe."

78 On the formation of the legend (the cave), cf. *Prot. Jas.* 18; Justin *Dial.* 78; Jerome *Ep. ad Paulinum* 58.3. See Gressmann, *Weihnachtsevangelium*, 18–19; and Schürmann, 1.106.

79 Hengel, "φάτνη," 52–53.

80 As does *Prot. Jas.* (in this chap. 18, however, paragraphs 2 and 3 are not attested by the entire ms. tradition).

81 The worship of stars, characterized as idolatry, is also described as worship of the heavenly host. Cf. 2 Chr 33:3; Zeph 1:5; Jer 7:18 (LXX); Acts 7:42.

82 Claus Westermann, "Alttestamentliche Elemente in Lukas 2, 1–10," in G. Jeremias et al., eds., *Tradition und Glaube: Festschrift Karl Georg Kuhn* (Göttingen: Vandenhoeck & Ruprecht, 1971) 317–27, esp. 322–23.

83 On peace in Luke and his critique directed against imperial power, i.e., his political critique, see the commentary on 1:78–79 above (toward the end).

84 "Is" and not "may there be" should be supplied.

85 Against David Flusser ("'Sanctus' und 'Gloria,'" in O. Betz et al., eds., *Abraham unser Vater: Festschrift Otto Michel* [Leiden: Brill, 1963] 129–52, revised in Flusser, *Entdeckungen im Neuen Testament*, vol. 1: *Jesusworte und ihre Überlieferung* [ed. M. Majer; Neukirchen-Vluyn: Neukirchener Verlag, 1987] 226–44), who relates the Gloria to the Sanctus (Isa 6:3), of which it is to be the interpretive paraphrase, and who, for this reason, supports a three-part structure for it.

and humanity at the end of the second. The beauty of the song emerges from this "braided" composition.

Byzantine manuscripts, ancient translations, and some church fathers read ἐν ἀνθρώποις εὐδοκία ("among people, good pleasure") and thus presuppose a tripartite composition. But the most ancient Greek manuscripts and the Latin tradition read ἐν ἀνθρώποις εὐδοκίας ("among people of good pleasure"),[86] which is original, since the other variants attempt to improve on the ambiguous εὐδοκίας (if they cannot be explained palaeographically).

Supported by the imprecise Latin translation *hominibus bonae voluntatis* and the moralization of Christian faith in late antiquity, εὐδοκία ("good pleasure") was understood anthropologically: God's peace is for people of goodwill.

In Luke εὐδοκία and εὐδοκέω ("to be well pleased")[87] otherwise always denote the divine will to save. In 1QH 4.32–33 we find the corroborating expression, "the abundance of His mercies towards all the sons of His grace."[88] Like רָצוֹן,[89] εὐδοκία is, in Luke 2:14, God's good pleasure. C. H. Dodd has analyzed this concept thoroughly in the New Testament and notes its aspect of divine resolve and choice: "Essentially it is an act of will, not an expression of feeling," and "then εὐδοκία would indicate, not so much gratification or approval, but divine action, and the action in question is, characteristically, the predestinating act of grace which is the ultimate ground of our salvation."[90]

In Luke, at least, one should not play the will against the emotions. His concept of God is strongly affective.[91]

So he has in mind less a resolution than a loving movement of the entire person, which awaits love in return. Εὐδοκία thus has a relational quality; perhaps for this reason, there is no intensive pronoun ("his," αὐτοῦ):[92] the εὐδοκία of God sets in motion the εὐδοκία of people and waits impatiently for it. This is not synergism in the dogmatic sense, but rather mutual love and recognition.

The angels do not speak Jesus' name, but their prayer (v. 14) comments on his birth (vv. 6–7) and supplements the interpretation of his messianic function (vv. 10–11). Only this eschatological event, interpreted by the Word of God, makes possible the pure joy of the angels and the harmony between heavenly liturgy and earthly peace.

The angels sing their praise without a trace of jealousy, and they admit their own inability and feebleness. Their function is to help humans (Heb 1:14), but only deliverance through Jesus can bring salvation to humanity.[93]

The Visit of the Shepherds (vv. 15–20)

■ **15** The reader perceives an anticlimax in vv. 15–20. Each of the verses from 8 to 14 contains some astonishing event or a momentous announcement. Now the foreseen course of events develops itself in monotone. The vocabulary ceases to be vivid and confirms this negative impression. Wouldn't the reader have expected a glorious discovery of the sign? Luke has described the promise of a sign in a more polished manner than the reality to which it refers, but not for lack of creative

---

86 A portion of the Latin mss., however, omit the ἐν ("among"). On this problem see Metzger, *Commentary*, 133.

87 Εὐδοκία ("good pleasure"): Luke 10:21; εὐδοκέω ("to be well pleased"): Luke 3:22; 12:32. See Bovon, *Lukas*, 106–8.

88 Cf. 1QH 4.32–33; 11.9; 1QS 8.6; 8.10 (added on top of the line); 9.23. Extensive bibliography on these texts and their relation to Luke 2:14 can be found in Ernest Vogt, "'Peace among Men of God's Good Pleasure': Lk 2:14," in K. Stendahl, ed., *The Scrolls and the New Testament* (New York: Harper, 1957) 114–17; Joseph A. Fitzmyer, "'Peace upon Earth among Men of His Good Will' (Lk 2:14)," *TS* 19 (1958) 225–27, reprinted in idem, *Essays on the Semitic Background of the New Testament* (SBLSBS 5; Missoula, Mont.: Scholars Press, 1974) 101–4; Claus-Hunno Hunzinger, "Ein weiterer Beleg zu Lc 2, 14

ἄνθρωποι εὐδοκίας," *ZNW* 49 (1958) 129–30; Francesco Vattioni, "Pax hominibus bonae voluntatis," *RivB* 7 (1959) 369–70; A. Feuillet, "Les hommes de bonne volonté ou les hommes que Dieu aime: Note sur la traduction de Luc 2,14b," *BAGB* (1974) 91–92.

89 רָצָה is often rendered εὐδοκέω in the LXX.

90 C. H. Dodd, "New Testament Translation Problems II," *BT* 28 (1977) 106, 110.

91 See Bovon, *Lukas*, 98–119.

92 This suffix is noted in some Qumran texts and lacking in others. See Feuillet, "Les hommes," 91.

93 Origen *Hom. in Luc.* 13.1–3.

power. There is a reason: the angels' message is the most important, and the shepherds' visit less relevant, since the entire life of Jesus attests the good news, and not merely its first hours. Verses 15–20 form a transition; their colorless flow, especially the repetitions[94] and the abstract and formal vocabulary, serve as an invitation to read further in the Gospel.[95]

Let's follow the shepherds. In v. 15 we learn that the host of angels, according to Luke, really stepped down to earth, and that the shepherds did not merely see a vision. The shepherds (presented as individuals in *Prot. Jas.* 18:2–3) must first discuss the matter together.

As in Acts 9:38 and 11:19 (cf. 13:6), $\tilde{\epsilon}\omega\varsigma$ ("to") emphasizes the destination and $\delta\iota$- ("through") implies a distance.[96] "Even the haste in v. 16 . . . does not necessarily presuppose a short journey: see 1:39. A longer one suits Luke 1–2; journeys many and long are undertaken here."[97] The silence about the location of the manger would suggest, however, that its distance from the field was short; for a longer distance, the location would have been indicated, as the street in Damascus and the guest's name are in Acts 9:11.

The words of the shepherds sound very Lukan, and Luke speaks biblically. The angels' message comes from God ($\dot{o}$ $\kappa\dot{\nu}\rho\iota o\varsigma$, "the Lord") and has unveiled ($\gamma\nu\omega\rho\dot{\iota}\zeta\omega$, "to tell") a salvation-historical piece of news. The word of God accompanies his action, so that $\tau\dot{o}$ $\dot{\rho}\hat{\eta}\mu\alpha$ $\tau o\hat{\nu}\tau o$ ("this thing") can be seen (v. 15) as well as heard (vv. 17–18).

■ **16** Only this haste ($\sigma\pi\epsilon\dot{\nu}\sigma\alpha\nu\tau\epsilon\varsigma$, "with haste") gives the story a bit of tension. "Haste" is a literary instrument to express proximity to the God who directs history (cf. 1:39). The visit itself fills only a colorless half-verse

(16b): in contrast to $\epsilon\dot{\nu}\rho\dot{\iota}\sigma\kappa\omega$ ("to find"), $\dot{\alpha}\nu\epsilon\nu\rho\dot{\iota}\sigma\kappa\omega$ describes the moment of discovery.

■ **17–20** Verses 17–18 adopt a topos familiar from a few miracle stories (the healed person proclaims the news of his healing)[98] and may be redactional, since they stand in contradiction with v. 20, in which the end of the visit is actually first mentioned. The wonderment begins as an indirect reaction; the shepherds do not marvel, but their audience does.

The theological terms in this passage also have significance for Christian preaching; $\dot{\rho}\hat{\eta}\mu\alpha$ ("the word," "the saying")[99] denotes the event of salvation and its divine interpretation, and $\lambda\alpha\lambda\dot{\epsilon}\omega$ ("to say"),[100] not a usual speech act but the speech of preaching, which is self-involving and attempts to persuade. It is not strange that the shepherds, in the proleptic situation of faith, take up the song of the angels (v. 13) in v. 20.

Mary is in the same relation to the shepherds in v. 19 as Zechariah to his family and neighbors in 1:63–67. $\Sigma\nu\nu\tau\eta\rho\dot{\epsilon}\omega$ ("to treasure") and $\sigma\nu\mu\beta\dot{\alpha}\lambda\lambda\omega$ ("to ponder") are unusual for Luke.[101] They designate a highly positive attitude and activity. The first, not far removed from the Johannine $\tau\eta\rho\dot{\epsilon}\omega$, means the reception and retention of the event, as much the deed that one sees as the words one hears.[102] It is no melancholy reminiscence, but the living memory of the content of faith.

But it does not suffice to absorb these $\dot{\rho}\dot{\eta}\mu\alpha\tau\alpha$ ("words").[103] Mary, the paragon of faith, must understand them and interpret them correctly. $\Sigma\nu\mu\beta\dot{\alpha}\lambda\lambda o\nu\sigma\alpha$ designates the clear and correct interpretation of divine intervention.[104] Mary understands what she has seen and heard. As $\gamma\nu\omega\rho\dot{\iota}\zeta\omega$ ("to tell") does not denote any purely informational communication, $\sigma\nu\mu\beta\dot{\alpha}\lambda\lambda o\nu\sigma\alpha$ does not

---

94 $\Lambda\alpha\lambda\dot{\epsilon}\omega$ ("to say") four times, $\dot{\rho}\hat{\eta}\mu\alpha$ ("the word," "the thing," "the saying") three times, $\dot{o}\rho\dot{\alpha}\omega$ ("to see") three times, etc.

95 Similar to Brown's treatment (*Birth*, 429): the shepherds, as exemplars of faith, must step back, out of the field of vision, since the message of the apostles will not sound forth until later.

96 Christoph Burchard, "Fußnoten zum neutestamentlichen Griechisch II," *ZNW* 69 (1978) 145–46.

97 Ibid., 146.

98 Cf. Luke 8:39. It seems as though the entire city had assembled itself in the middle of the night to listen to them (Loisy, 117).

99 On $\dot{\rho}\hat{\eta}\mu\alpha$ ("the word," "the thing," "the saying") see the commentary on 1:37 above.

100 See Helmut Jaschke, "$\Lambda\alpha\lambda\epsilon\hat{\iota}\nu$ bei Lk," *BZ* n.s. 15 (1971) 109–14.

101 Zahn (147) points out the switch from the aorist (v. 18) to the imperfect (v. 19).

102 W. C. van Unnik examines the use of $\sigma\nu\nu\tau\eta\rho\dot{\epsilon}\omega$ ("Die rechte Bedeutung des Wortes treffen: Lukas 2,19," in idem, *Sparsa Collecta*, 1.72–91, esp. 88–89) and discusses Sir 39:2; Dan 7:28 (Th); and *T. Levi* 6:2.

103 Why this plural $\tau\dot{\alpha}$ $\dot{\rho}\dot{\eta}\mu\alpha\tau\alpha$ $\tau\alpha\hat{\nu}\tau\alpha$ ("these words"), strengthened all the more by $\pi\dot{\alpha}\nu\tau\alpha$ ("all")? Because of the consequences of these events since their proclamation.

104 See van Unnik, "Bedeutung." The most important texts supporting his exegesis: Josephus *Ant.* 2.5.3 §72 (though the text is unstable); *Bell.* 3.8.3 §352;

indicate a merely logical and intellectual interpretation of events. Thus the interpretation does not take place in her intellect ($\nu o \hat{\nu} \varsigma$), but in the seat of her will and emotion, her heart.

Conclusion

Just as the language of the Christmas story is Lukan, its content as well suits Luke's theological program. In Jesus, God's definitive act of salvation takes place; the birth story belongs to this phase of salvation history. Because miracles in Luke must ripen, the good news begins already with Jesus' childhood, and even with the Baptist's birth.

Typically Lukan is also the intertwining of glory and lowliness. Hosts of angels accompany a humble birth. Depending only on the point of view, this beginning, like the end of Jesus' life, stands under the mark of the cross, or of the resurrection. The child carries this double meaning: the present poverty and the potential future.

God and humanity meet in the events of Christmas. Luke knows how to make this encounter vivid. The visit does not take place in a sort of mystical unity, but in history (vv. 1–5), under the rubric of a sign (v. 12), which requires interpretation by the word (v. 14). A critique inheres in the eschatological significance: both imperial pretensions and religious fanaticism are repudiated by the Christmas story. The shepherds and especially Mary illustrate the attitude appropriate to God's act. It is not servility and blind obedience, but active faith. Mary is presented in the text not as a co-mediator of salvation or as an example of a submissive woman, but, like Abraham, as a model of the believer.[105] Her faith is active in two senses: she understands, and she experiences what she believes.

Luke narrates a story and cites divine voices. In this way he remains faithful to his theological and literary program. God acts through human situations, and he reveals those acts to the faithful through the word of his witnesses. Thus a complicated structure arises, in which events simultaneously become signs of God and stand in need of interpretation. Here the events must remain particularly ambiguous and hidden, since Luke can only hint at the role of Jesus. Luke knows the unfurling of salvation history too well to allow himself to disregard its stages. He resists depriving Jesus' baptism of its "canonical" relevance.

I see Luke in a dilemma: he would like to say more about Jesus' function, but he must wait until Jesus is grown. He wants to speak like the shepherds, but must still, like Mary, treasure "all these $\dot{\rho} \dot{\eta} \mu \alpha \tau \alpha$" in his heart. If one sees in the history of interpretation both a glorifying tendency and an abasing one, one can say that the history of interpretation has also run in the footsteps of the evangelist, or rather has limped.

History of Interpretation

Luther wrote a longer sermon for Christmas on Luke 2:1–14, and a shorter for the following Sunday[106] on 2:15–20. I cannot locate these typically Lutheran sermons historically, neither do I want to interpret them, but rather to communicate what impressed me in them. On the whole, it is striking that, despite the Reformation, the timbre of Christmas has remained surprisingly the same throughout church history, also in Luther's voice.

The first sermon divides the text (vv. 1–14) into two parts for substantive reasons; the story "described with great diligence" by Luke is in two parts, because the first half speaks "of the misery in the city of Bethlehem," and the second tells "the joy in heaven." There is a bifurcation, according to Luther, but not a literary one between the angels' proclamation (vv. 8–14) and the shepherds' visit (vv. 15–20), but rather a theological one between the incarnation, which carries misery and the cross, and the joyful word, which bears, for faith, a testimony of this birth. Luther thus strongly emphasizes earth and

---

Philo *Flacc.* §139; Xenophon Ephesius *Eph.* 1.7.1; Arrian *Anab.* 1.20.1; Dionysius of Halicarnassus *Ant. Roma.* 1.24.1; 1.34.5.

105 See N. Fatio, "Marie, servante du Seigneur: Des images tenaces . . . un regard nouveau," in *Groupe "IBSO": Réflexions théologiques au féminin, Bulletin du centre protestante d'études* (Geneva) 35.5 (1983) 17–21.

106 Christian G. Eberle, *Luthers Evangelien-Auslegung: Ein Kommentar zu den vier Evangelien* (2d ed.; Stuttgart: S. G. Liesching, 1877) 55–70.

heaven, history and the word, and event and interpretation.

This allows him first to disengage the dominion of Christ from every earthly government, "so that He shows that his kingdom should not be earthly, nor rule in an earthly manner over earthly dominions, so that He and His parents submit to the same." "But this angelic proclamation was very necessary; for if Christ had been born twenty times, it would have been in vain, had we not known anything of it." So the danger is great that people not pay attention to the story because they strive after greatness and wealth. For this reason, God provided that the angels, subsequent to it, gave the first Christian sermon immediately. Thus Luther illustrates the entire significance of the angels' message as a sermon, so that the shepherds—and we—do not believe only with the simple acknowledgment of the intellect, but with the faith of the heart.

For Luther, it is significant that the angel did not proclaim the good news generally, but to the shepherds personally ("to you"). Thus we are also addressed personally. And what we should do is not an act of reason, but of the affective heart: "Thus the evangelist, without a doubt, actually wanted to paint the story for us, who are otherwise so cold, to see if it could even warm our hearts a little, since our Savior was born so wretchedly on this earth." With faith are connected joy, confidence, and "tasting": "On this account, you should enter your heart and see whether these words also have a taste for us."

Luther shows with the example of the shepherds that this faith changes nothing about the outward person; they, though believing, still returned to their jobs and their daily lives. One detects the polemic against the monastic orders here, and also in the interpretation of εὐδοκία ("good pleasure"), for which Luther rejects a cheap grace just as violently as he rejects an exegesis according to the principle of good works.

In the second half (vv. 8–14), he introduces the Gloria thus: "A happy song belongs after a good sermon." The entire scene is dramatized so that the Christmas story becomes a Protestant worship service of the Reformation. To this end, the second sermon (on the shepherd's visit, vv. 15–20) becomes a lecture on faith and the Christian life. Where the patristic sermon of Leo the Great[107] projects the congregation back into the past of the first Christmas by means of the liturgical exegesis of "today," Luther's sermon draws the event into his own time. The reformer believes he has this right, since he respects the letter of the story (vv. 1–7) and understands the angels' sermon as a timeless and ever-present word of God. Are the two means of actualization so different, since both aim at a genuine encounter with the text, the word, and history?

---

107 *In nativitate Domini sermo* 1.1, in Léon le Grand, *Sermons*, vol. 1. (trans. René Dolle; 2d ed.; SC 22bis; Paris: Cerf, 1964) 66–67.

The Presentation at the Temple (2:22–40)

Bibliography

Benoit, "Et toi-même."

Berger, Klaus, "Das Canticum Simeonis (Lk 2,29–32)," *NovT* 27 (1985) 27–39.

Brown, *Birth*, 435–70.

Cutler, A., "Does Simeon of Luke 2 refer to Simeon the Son of Hillel?" *JBR* 34 (1966) 29–35.

Deug-Su, I., "La festa della purificazione in Occidente," *Studi Medievali* 15 (1975) 143–216.

Elliott, J. K., "Anna's Age (Luke 2:36–37)," *NovT* 30 (1988) 100–102.

Escudero Freire, *Devolver*, 332–63.

Feuillet, "Épreuve."

idem, "Le jugement messianique et la Vierge Marie dans la prophétie de Siméon (Lc 2,35)," in *Studia mediaevalia et mariologica: Festschrift Charles Balič* (Rome: Antonianum, 1971) 423–47.

Figueras, "Syméon."

Garofalo, S., "'Tuam ipsius animam pertransibit gladius' (Lc 2,35)," in *Maria in Sacra Scriptura*, 4.175–81.

George, Augustin, "La présentation de Jésus au temple," *AsSeign* 11 (1970) 29–39.

Grelot, Pierre, "Le Cantique de Siméon (Luc II,29–32)," *RB* 93 (1986) 481–509.

Gueuret, *Engendrement*, 119–46, 196–203.

Hatch, W. H. P., "The Text of Luke II,72," *HTR* 14 (1971) 377–81.

Jervell, Jacob, "Die Beschneidung des Messias," in A. Fuchs, ed., *Theologie aus dem Norden* (SNTU A.2; Linz: Albert Fuchs, 1976) 68–78.

John, Mathew P., "Lk 2:36–37: How Old Was Anna?" *BT* 26 (1975) 247.

Jones, "Background."

Jörgensen, P. H., "Das alte und das neue Israel: Der Lobgesang Simeons Lk 2,25–35," *Friede über Israel* 59 (1976) 147–59.

Joüon, Paul, "Notes philologiques sur les Évangiles: Lc 2,31," *RechSR* 18 (1928).

Kilpatrick, G. D., "ΛΑΟΙ at Luke II.31 and Acts IV.25,27," *JTS* n.s. 16 (1965) 127.

Knoch, Otto, and Rudolf Pesch, "Die Weissagung Simeons: Beiträge zu einem Text des Neuen Testaments (Lk 2,35)," *GuL* 57 (1984) 214–23.

Laurentin, *Truth*, 64, 67–68, 70–72, 73–4, 76–80, 193–207.

Legrand, Lucien, "On l'appela du nom de Jésus (Luc II,21)," *RB* 89 (1982) 481–91.

Mann, J., "Rabbinic Studies in the Synoptic Gospels, II: The Redemption of a First-Born Son and the Pilgrimages to Jerusalem," *HUCA* 1 (1924) 329–35.

Maria Alonso, J., "La espada de Simeón (Lc 2,35a) en la exégesis de los Padres," in *Maria in Sacra Scriptura*, 4.183–285.

Marquet, Claudette, *Femme et homme il les créa* (Paris: Les Bergers et les Mages, 1984) 159–63.

McHugh, *Mother*, 99–112.

Miyoshi, "Jesu Darstellung."

Prete, Benedetto, "Il senso della formula ἐν εἰρήνῃ in Lc 2,29," in G. Ghiberti, ed., *Chiesa per il mondo: Festschrift Michele Pellegrino* (2 vols.; Bologna: EDB, 1974) 1.39–60.

Scharfenberg, Joachim, *Den Widerspruch auf sich nehmen* (Schritte ins Offene 4; Zurich: Evangelischer Frauenbund der Schweiz, 1986) 28–29.

Schmaus, M., "De oblatione Iesu in templo (Lc 2,22–24)," in *Maria in Sacra Scriptura*, 4.287–95.

Simon Muñoz, Alfonso, *El Mesías y la Hija de Sión: Teología de la redencíon en Lc 2:29–35* (Studia Semitica Novi Testamenti 3; Madrid: Editorial Ciudad Nueva/Fundación San Justino, 1994).

Soards, M., "Luke 2:22–40," *Int* 44 (1990) 400–405.

Stramare, Tarcisio, "Compiuti i giorni della loro purificazione (Lc 2,22): Gli avvenimenti del Nuovo Testamento conclusivi di un disegno," *BeO* 24 (1982) 199–205.

idem, "La presentazione di Gesù al tempio (Lc 2,22–40): Eventi e parole intrinsecamente connessi," *BeO* 25 (1983) 63–71.

idem, "Sanctum Domino vocabitur (Lc 2,23): Il crocevia dei riti è la santità," *BeO* 25 (1983) 21–34.

Strickert, Frederick, "The Presentation of Jesus: The Gospel of Inclusion: Luke 2:22–40," *CurTM* 22 (1995) 33–37.

Varela, Alfredo Tepox, "Lk 2,36–37: Is Anna's Age What Is Really in Focus?" *BT* 27 (1976) 446.

Vincent, H., "Luc II,32," *RB* 9 (1900) 601–2.

Vogels, H. J., "Die 'Eltern' Jesu (Textkritisches zu Lk 2,23ff)," *BZ* 11 (1913) 33–43.

idem, "Lk 2,36 im Diatessaron," *BZ* 11 (1913) 168–71.

Winandy, "Prophétie."

Winter, Paul, "Lukanische Miszellen, IV: Lc 2,38 im Verhältnis zu 2,13.28.34a," *ZNW* 49 (1958) 76–77.

22 And when the days were fulfilled for their purification according to the Law of Moses, they went up to Jerusalem to present him to the Lord 23/ (as it is written in the Law of the Lord, "Every firstborn male shall be designated as holy to the Lord") 24/ and to offer a sacrifice according to what is stated in the Law of the Lord, "a pair of turtledoves or two young pigeons."

25 Now there was a man in Jerusalem whose name was Simeon; this man was righteous and devout, waiting for the consolation of Israel, and holy spirit was upon him. 26/ And it had been promised to him by the Holy Spirit that he would not see death before he had seen the

Lord's Messiah. 27/ Guided by the Spirit, Simeon came into the temple precinct. When the parents brought in the child Jesus, to do for him what was customary under the Law, 28/ he received him in his arms and praised God and said, 29/ "Master, now you are dismissing your servant in peace according to your word; 30/ for my eyes have seen your salvation, 31/ which you have prepared in the presence of all peoples, 32/ light for revelation for the peoples, and for glory to your people Israel." 33/ And his father and his mother were amazed at what was being said about him. 34/ Then Simeon blessed them and said to his mother Mary, "Behold, this child is destined for the falling and the rising of many in Israel, and for a sign of contradiction 35/ —and a sword will pierce your own soul too—so that the inner thoughts of many will be revealed."

36 There was also a prophetess, Anna the daughter of Phanuel, of the tribe of Asher. She was of a great age, having lived with her husband seven years after her marriage, 37/ and she was a widow to the age of eighty-four. She never left the temple precinct but worshiped God there night and day with fasting and prayer. 38/ At that moment she came and began to praise God, and to speak about him to all who were looking for the redemption of Jerusalem.

39 And when they had fulfilled everything required by the Law of the Lord, they returned to Galilee, to their own city of Nazareth.

40 And the child grew and became strong, filled with wisdom; and the favor of God was upon him.

Analysis

Verses 22–39 form a literary unit, whereas v. 21 stands by itself, and v. 40 rounds out the parallel to John's story (1:80). The action takes place in Jerusalem (vv. 22, 25, 38). In the context of the preceding pericope, one would expect that Jerusalem was one leg of the return trip from Bethlehem to Nazareth. But in this passage, Luke portrays the capital city as the destination required by the Law (vv. 22–24, 27, 39). With both the words "Jerusalem" and "Law," Luke signals an *inclusio* ("enclosure"), which underscores the unified character of vv.

22–39. Moreover, the theme of something that is fulfilled and carried out occurs both at the beginning and the end of the pericope (vv. 22a, 39a). On the one hand, Luke's literary technique neatly concludes the episode; on the other hand, it inserts the episode into a series to attest to the continuity of the story thus constructed. In 2:6 enough time has been fulfilled that Mary gives birth; in 2:21, that Jesus is circumcised; and in 2:22, that he is presented before the Lord. Only after this sequence does the summary statement in v. 40, composed in the imperfect, signal a break.

In Luke's account, the fulfillment of the Law remains the frame in which the extraordinary event, the last prophecy, is to be narrated. Like the circumcision, the prescriptions in vv. 22–24 are not described with any detail. They are either the purpose of the actions (vv. 22, 24, 27) or the duty fulfilled (v. 39), but never the content of the account.

Just as the Roman census (2:1–5) resulted in the journey to Bethlehem, so Jewish observance resulted in the journey to Jerusalem.[1] Luke mentions Jesus' presentation (vv. 22b–23) and the offering for his mother (v. 24) as two corollary requirements of the Law (vv. 23, 24b), which together effect "their" purification (v. 22, that of both mother and child),[2] although v. 22b names only Jesus.[3] Luke juxtaposes in this way the regulations[4] and their fulfillment, true to the Law.

With these verses (22–24), Luke ensures the family's presence at the temple. The story commences with a meeting that vv. 25–26 make possible. Verse 25 mentions a righteous man; v. 26, a prophecy by the Holy Spirit, the fulfillment of which becomes the content of the episode (vv. 27–35). Thus salvation history appears not simply out of a void, but from daily living true to the Law; it is also, however, not set into motion by human obedience. It is the frame, or the foundation, but movement results only through God's Spirit. After the three references to the Law (vv. 22–24), the word "Spirit" sounds forth three times as well. Law and Spirit are

---

1 Brown, *Birth*, 450.

2 The αὐτῶν ("their") presented the copyists with some problems. According to Lagrange (81–82), one minuscule connected καθαρισμός ("purification") to Lev 12, which describes the purification of women bearing children, and read αὐτῆς ("her"). A glance at the apparatus in Nestle-Aland shows that a few scribes had Christ in mind and wrote αὐτοῦ ("his"). Others again practiced caution and omitted the pronoun.

3 One must assume, with Lagrange (82), that the construction of the sentence is not the best.

4 These are, however, transmitted inaccurately (see commentary).

juxtaposed, but also at the same time intertwined, just as the old covenant (and the old man Simeon) is with the new (and the babe).

As often, the principal action begins with a nonverbal act,[5] with a gesture. The word follows it, a song of thanks in three strophes (the Nunc Dimittis, vv. 29–32).

It would be narratively successful for the miraculous action, directed by God, to end with the parents' reaction, a motif that concludes other miracle stories.[6] But to "be amazed" also implies a question; the text becomes exuberant, and Simeon's gaze, like that of the author, is directed toward the parents from this point on. The repetition of εὐλόγησεν ("he praised," "he blessed") does not express the same reality. After the prayer of thanks here (v. 28b), an action of blessing (v. 34) follows, which plays the narrative role of a nonverbal element and corresponds to the old man taking Jesus into his arms (v. 28a). The words directed to Mary (vv. 34b–35) are symmetrical to the song of thanks (vv. 29–32).

Even after the old man's twofold reaction, Luke still does not conclude this pericope. Anna is described in greater detail than Simeon (vv. 36–37). Her piety (v. 37b) explains her presence at the temple (v. 38). Like Simeon, she understands how to speak both to the Lord and to her peers. In comparison with vv. 28–35, the audience is broadened ("to all," v. 38). I consider Luke's linguistic economy here, however, to be a step backward: nothing is said of the content of the prayer or of Anna's proclamation. For this reason, I would attribute to the episode with the prophetess the function of an acclamation, since its significance lies in the miraculous encounter between the aged Simeon and the young Messiah.

From a form-critical perspective, this is a meeting directed by God, as in 1:39–56. There, and here, mother and child are received by a believing member of the expectant people of God. Simeon's panegyric, like Elizabeth's blessing (1:42; cf. 1:45), touches both son and mother. Though it is in different ways, God takes an active part in both encounters. But whereas the former takes place in the context of a family visit, this one is an almost official, sacral meeting in the center of the religious life of Judaism. Luke enjoys telling of such encounters directed by God.[7] The truth and significance of the story is indicated in narrative fashion by such providential elements. This genre, which should be classified as a novella, does not belong to the more ancient traditional materials. A further index of the late date are the redundancies listed above.

The motif of the old man who, late in life, still experiences something remarkable has roots in both Greek and Jewish literature. The two old servants of Odysseus, Eumaios the swineherd and Eurykleia the nurse, wait for their master for twenty years, and still have the chance to receive him back.[8] In the Hebrew Bible, the aged Joseph is allowed to see his son once again, and after that to explain, "I can die now, having seen for myself that you are still alive" (Gen 46:30). These are nearly the same words with which Anna, Tobit's wife, greets her son on his return (Tob 11:9), after which his father similarly sings a sort of Nunc Dimittis (Tob 11:14). Last, the dying Moses is allowed to "see" the promised land (Deut 32:49–50; 34:1–5). "The motif itself appears also in the legend of the Buddha, where it is said that the aged ascetic Asita, instructed by divine knowledge, came to the palace belonging to the father of the new-born child, and took the child into his arms and foretold the great role he would play, which he himself, nearing the end of his life, would not live to see."[9] Of course there are differences: in Luke 2:25–35 Simeon receives not his son but the Messiah, and, in contrast to Moses, the vision is not a punitive limitation. Nevertheless, there are familiar elements, which Luke artfully applies to prepare this significant transition.

After this synchronic analysis, we turn to the pre-Lukan tradition. According to Rudolf Bultmann,[10] in

---

5   Cf., e.g., Luke 7:14.

6   Gerd Theissen, *Miracle Stories of the Early Christian Tradition* (trans. F. McDonagh; Philadelphia: Fortress Press, 1983) 69–71.

7   Cf. the meeting of Paul and Ananias (Acts 9:10–18), and that of Peter and Cornelius (10:17–29).

8   In this context scholars often recall Alexander's visit to the temple of Ammon, whose oracle revealed the Macedonian man's descent from Zeus. This divine descent was confirmed by other oracles (Callisthenes in Strabo 17.1.43).

9   Bultmann, *History*, 299; he refers to the text edited by Johannes Aufhauser, *Buddha und Jesus in ihren Paralleltexten zusammengestellt* (Kleine Texte 157; Bonn: Marcus und Weber, 1926) 9–11.

10   *History*, 299–300. In the following, I twice cite from 299.

Luke 2:22–40 an originally independent single account was secondarily expanded, presumably by vv. 22d–24a (from παραστῆσαι ["to present"] to κληθήσεται, καί, ["'shall be designated as (holy to the Lord)' and . . ."]) since the journey is doubly motivated; and also by vv. 28b–34a, which contain a universalizing expansion. The stories about Simeon and Anna would accordingly be doublets, "which is made clear by the fact that there is really nothing for Anna to say after Simeon has spoken." The leading pre-Lukan motif, he believes, is "the prophecy of these two exemplars of piety about Jesus."

According to Raymond E. Brown, the Scriptures, in particular Mal 3:1, played an inspiring role in the development of the tale: "the Lord whom you seek will suddenly come to his temple."[11] But Luke would have composed a first version mostly by his own inspiration, without a written exemplar, making use of only one oracle (vv. 34b–35). Only in a second version of his work would he have inserted the poems not composed by himself, here the Nunc Dimittis. The same is true of the story of the twelve-year-old Jesus in the temple. In Luke's original version, the summary statement in 2:40 would have concluded the parallelism between John and Jesus, as well as the entire birth narrative. Like Bultmann, Brown perceives the interpolated character of the Nunc Dimittis, but he suggests a redaction-historical solution, and Bultmann a form-critical one.

The most thorough stylistic analysis, that of Michi Miyoshi,[12] recognizes Luke's formative hand throughout the entire unit, and thus presupposes no written exemplar, but rather a fixed oral tradition of Jewish Christian origin. Its roots in the Hebrew Bible are evident. Both parts of Simeon's blessing are influenced by Isaiah 51–52. The proximity to 1 Samuel (LXX 1 Kgdms) 1–2 does not pertain only to the narrative; in essence, as well, Jesus should be compared to the Nazirite Samuel. For this reason, the pericope describes the purification of the Nazirite Jesus according to Numbers 6 ("a pair of turtledoves or two young pigeons," thus the same offering as that for the purification of women giving birth, Lev 12). This explains the puzzling double purification of mother and son. "In the concluding sentence of the purification regulation in Numbers 6, the priestly bless-ing is also prescribed, and with the same words of peace and light that form the kernel of Simeon's blessing."[13]

According to Miyoshi, this is the connection between the presentation of Jesus and Simeon's blessing that scholars have heretofore missed. Jesus' purification is the preparation for his future role of being light for the nations. The redactional vv. 22–24 and 29–32 are symptomatic of Luke's theology. "Because of them, one might wonder whether the purification account had ever stood in the present context in pre-Lukan tradition, even if it were oral."[14] The traditional components would then be Simeon's prophecy (vv. 34–35) on the occasion of Jesus' circumcision (v. 21), without the localization in Jerusalem.

It seems to me improbable that the circumcision was part of the entire narrative unit; the tradition is inextricably connected to Jerusalem and the temple. The mention of Simeon and Anna probably points not to doublets but to complementary figures, like the aged parents of Tobias, or Eumaios and Eurykleia. They are components of the older tradition. Simeon's second intervention (vv. 34b–35) probably also belongs to the original version, and thus, similarly, the mother and her purification after the birth.

Luke gave this Jerusalem tradition a new twist by placing the stress on the Messiah's presentation in the temple, and by adding himself the Nunc Dimittis, which probably originally belonged to another tradition. Various texts from the Scriptures inform this account both narratively and theologically: 1 Samuel (LXX 1 Kgdms) 1–2 for the narrative, Exodus 13 for the consecration of the firstborn, Deutero-Isaiah for the Nunc Dimittis; from Deutero-Isaiah derives the expectation of redemption that infuses the entire pericope. A connection between Jesus' presentation in the temple and the content of the Nunc Dimittis by means of the concept of the Nazirite appears improbable.

Commentary

Should one follow the course of the narrative, that is, a meeting of the generations that looks like a farewell, and thus perform a narrative and affective exegesis? Or

11   Brown, *Birth*, 455–56, 469.
12   Michi Miyoshi, "Jesu Darstellung oder Reinigung im Tempel unter Berücksichtigung von 'Nunc Dimittis'

Lk 2,22–38," *AJBI* 4 (1978) 85–115.
13   Ibid., 111.
14   Ibid., 92.

should one focus on the paradigmatic structure of Simeon's blessing, which seems like a revelation, and thus attempt a theological and cognitive interpretation? Should one stress the parents' obedient behavior, or rather show its limitations because of the prophetic behavior of the old people? Should one consider this unit in form-critical isolation, or in its redactional context? These numerous possibilities explain the marked effect of this pericope in church history. To this passage, Origen dedicated no fewer than four sermons.[15] Egeria attests a festival forty days after Epiphany at the end of the fourth century.[16] Hesychius of Jerusalem (5th century CE) also composed two sermons for the occasion.[17] In Dionysius of Furna one can read how Byzantine painters must have fashioned the scene: "Next to him [Joseph] stands the prophetess Anna, who points to Christ and holds a tablet with this inscription: This baby created heaven and earth."[18]

The Purpose of the Trip to Jerusalem (vv. 22–24)

■ **22–24** According to v. 22, the time has come to complete the purification. Here Luke uses $καθαρισμός$ ("purification"), which is frequently attested in the LXX (Lev 12:4–6 [LXX] has $κάθαρσις$, which never occurs in the NT). The former is also used for "the ceremonies that a person who has been healed of leprosy undergoes"[19] (Luke 5:14; Lev 14:32). Despite the plural, "their purification," it is not a question of Jesus being defiled so that he would need ritual purification.[20] The expression is only to connect "purification" and "presentation." Luke brings these into the context of the redemption of the firstborn, as the citation from Exodus 13 indicates, surely because "purification" comes up in this context now and again, although not in Exodus 13. Although an inexact description both for the mother's purification (Lev 12) and for the son's redemption (Exod 13),

$καθαρισμός$ can be understood as such in a general sense, corresponding to the topic.

It is clear from two further details that Luke prefers the narrative quality over legal exactness: the child's presence was not necessary for the mother's purification, and the redemption of the firstborn was not connected to the temple. But the free citation from Exod 13:2, 12, 15 shows that Luke was thinking less of the redemption (the five shekels of Num 18:15–16 are not mentioned) than of the root meaning[21]—that each firstborn belongs to the Lord. Here we stumble into an ancient christological motif: Jesus is "something holy" (1:35). The free citation sanctions this designation ($κληθήσεται$, "shall be called," "shall be designated," as in 1:35). Luke gives this christological concept concrete expression in Jesus' presentation in the temple.[22] The portrayal corresponds less to that of the entrance of the Lord into the temple, as in Malachi 3 (the Lord is already in the temple), than to the dedication of Jesus to his Father as a sacrifice. But in connection with this, a devaluation of the temple occurs in the temple itself, for the holy, God's presence, shifts from the building to the person of Jesus.

The offering of Jesus to the Lord, "rendering to God the things that are God's" (Luke 20:25), is told in narrative imitation of the story of Samuel. For this reason, the second citation was cleverly chosen. A pair of turtledoves or young pigeons surely refers first to the mother (Lev 12:8); but a similar offering was required from the Nazirite in the case of defilement (Num 6:10), that is, from a man like Samuel (or Jesus) who was consecrated to the Lord. The present passage emphasizes the son rather than the mother. Luke's close attention to the Law does not stress observance as such, but prepares the next stage of salvation history: the transition from the Law to Christ.[23]

15 *Hom. in Luc.* 14–17.

16 *Itinerarium* 26.

17 Michel Aubineau provides text, commentary, and bibliography on this festival (*Les homélies festales d'Hésychius de Jérusalem* [Subsidia Hagiographica 59; Brussels: Société des bollandistes, 1978] 1–75; bibliography, 2 n. 1).

18 Dionysius de Fourna, *Manuel d'iconographie chrétienne* (ed. Athanasios Papadopoulos-Kerameus; St. Petersburg: B. Kirschenbaum, 1909) 87.

19 BAGD, *s.v.* The classical $καθαρμός$ appears in neither the LXX nor the NT. Philo seems not to know

$καθαρισμός$ and uses $κάθαρσις$.

20 Agreeing with Lagrange, 82.

21 $Διανοῖγον μήτραν$ ("to open the womb"): since Luke cites these words, he clearly has in mind a normal birth, not a *virginitas in partu*.

22 On standing "before the Lord," cf. Zech 6:5.

23 Detailed examinations of the vocabulary of vv. 22–24 can be found in Miyoshi, "Jesu Darstellung," 86, 89; and in Plummer (62–65): $καὶ ὅτε$ is Lukan (Luke 2:21, 42; 6:13; 22:14; 23:33); $κατὰ τὸν νόμον$ ("according to the Law," Acts 22:12; 24:6, 14) occurs already in the LXX (Deut 17:11; 2 Kgs [LXX

Simeon's Gesture (vv. 25–28)

■ **25** With the signal καὶ ἰδού ("now") begins the surprise within the ritual, the event within the institution. But since this divinely directed story is meant to be an encounter, the writer must first introduce the second party to it. This explains the slight tension between the eventful καὶ ἰδού and the description of the old man in the imperfect (ἦν, "there was").

Despite later hagiography, Simeon is not introduced as a priest, nor is his age given,[24] although his dignified place of residence is mentioned (Ἰερουσαλήμ in its sacral form), his name (is Luke aware of the etymology, "God has heard"?), and above all his piety. He is δίκαιος ("righteous," this occurs already at 1:6) and εὐλαβής ("devout"),[25] as are Zechariah and Elizabeth (1:6), in faithfulness to the divine Law. The similar introduction for Ananias, in Paul's description of his own conversion,[26] indicates that this is typically Lukan.[27]

Παράκλησις ("consolation") here has an unmistak-able eschatological tenor; its meaning in the context of religion is "consolation."[28] Like Anna the prophetess and her audience (v. 38), the layperson Simeon is a "waiting" figure.[29] He hopes in *God*, not for himself but for the people of *Israel*. Luke's message is striking in its simplicity: belief in Christ is the legitimate answer to the legitimate expectation of the Jews. According to Luke, the constant accompaniment of the Holy Spirit gives the Lord's guarantee to this expectant believer (cf. 1:41, 67).

■ **26** The description of Simeon is still insufficient. In v. 26 Luke reaches back into the past, to an old oracle given to Simeon.[30] Divine oracles in both Israel and Greece often concern death (Acts 21:11; Rom 14:8). Either lot, life or death, can have relevance for salvation history.

■ **27** The aorist ἦλθεν ("he came," v. 27) corresponds to the aorist ἀνήγαγον ("they went up," v. 22), and makes the encounter possible. The Holy Spirit, who sent forth the prophecy (v. 26), effects its fulfillment (v. 27).

---

4 Kgdms] 17:34): ἀνάγω ("to go up") is Lukan (e.g., Luke 4:5; Acts 9:39); δοῦναι θυσίαν ("to offer a sacrifice") is found neither in the LXX nor in the rest of the NT; on τὸ εἰρημένον ἐν τῷ νόμῳ ("what is stated in the Law"), cf. Acts 2:16; 13:40); Ἰεροσόλυμα ("Jerusalem") is the *Greek* form of the proper name (this example refutes Ignace de la Potterie's theory that Luke uses the Semitic form of the name for the solemn moments of salvation history; see "Les deux noms de Jérusalem dans l'évangile de Luc," in J. Delorme and J. Duplacy, eds., *La parole de grâce: Études lucaniennes à la mémoire d'Augustin George = RechSR* 69, nos. 1–2 [1981] 57–70, esp. 68).

24 According to *Prot. Jas.* 24.4, Simeon is chosen by lot to be high priest. In *Acts Pil.* 16.2, 6, he is a teacher, a rabbi (his name occurs also at 17.1). According to the Gospel of Pseudo-Matthew 15.2, he is 112 years old. A. Cutler cites further apocryphal passages, and suggests that Simeon may be the son of Hillel and father of Gamaliel ("Does Simeon of Luke 2 Refer to Simeon the Son of Hillel?" *JBR* 34 [1966] 29–35). Ms. B (Laurentianus, Goddiani 208), cited by Aurelio de Santos Otero (*Los Evangelios Apócrifos: Colección de textos griegos y latinos* [2d ed.; BAC 148; Madrid: BAC, 1963] 213 n.54), contains a remark-able addition. There, though the old man carries the child, it leads him; and Jesus, though only new-born, tells Simeon, to general astonishment, that his prayer has been answered.

25 In classical Greek this means "cautious," "guarded," sometimes "fearful"; in that of the LXX and the

Christians, it is "God-fearing," "law-abiding," "pious." Plato (*Polit.* 311AB) connects what is just (τὸ δίκαιον) with what is cautious (τὸ εὐλαβές), and from this derives the characteristics of the true ruler. The LXX uses the adjective εὐλαβής only three times (Lev 15:31; Sir 11:17 [in part of the ms. tradition]; Mic 7:2). In Josephus (7–8 occurrences), the word has the Greek meaning. See Rudolf Bultmann, "εὐλαβής, κτλ.," *TDNT* 2 (1964) 751–54; Plummer, 66.

26 Acts 22:12; cf. 2:5; 8:2.

27 As in many other passages (cf., e.g., Sir 11:17), the ms. tradition vacillates between εὐλαβής ("devout") and εὐσεβής ("pious").

28 On παράκλησις ("consolation"), see Plummer, 66.

29 In Luke προσδέχομαι more frequently has the meaning "to wait," "to expect" (Luke 2:25, 38; 12:36; 23:51; Acts 23:21) than "to receive," "to admit" (Luke 15:2; Acts 24:15).

30 Χρηματίζω in the passive means to be "instructed by divine guidance" (cf. Matt 2:22); also, "to carry a name," e.g., the name "Christians" (cf. Acts 11:26). Even if interpreted in a different way (John 21:23), Jesus' prediction about the beloved disciple (21:22) should be mentioned here. See Luke 9:27 and the commentary on it.

The stage is the temple precinct, that is, the building and its various courtyards (τὸ ἱερόν is the holy enclosure; the temple itself is ὁ ναός [1:21] or τὰ ἅγια).[31] After this digression into Simeon's past, Luke, like a reporter, introduces Jesus' parents (v. 27b). Cleverly and elegantly, he avoids any repetition and speedily brings the action to its climax: in v. 22 they set off for Jerusalem; in v. 27 they bring in the child (into the temple). The nomenclature of prophecy (ὁ χριστὸς κυρίου, "the Lord's Messiah")[32] and the person bringing fulfillment (τὸ παιδίον Ἰησοῦς, "the child Jesus") stand in closest proximity.

■ **28** The action is kept to essentials. Here the greeting is not important (in contrast to 1:40–41), but rather the contact between the old man and the child. Simeon does not "take" the child, but "receives" him into his arms, with the permission of the parents, one assumes. This motherly gesture is made vivid by the expression "in his arms."[33] The divine oracle is fulfilled not only by "seeing" (vv. 26, 30), but in "touching." The relationship between Simeon and Jesus is a microcosm of the relation between the messianic expectation of the people of Israel and its fulfillment. Simeon, at this point the stronger, carries Jesus, still weak for a brief interim. The former stands before death, the latter before life. Despite this, Simeon is happy, as his blessing attests. It is in this way that the Jewish people should receive the

Christian message in the time of the church. But already in 4:24 Jesus says, with the same verb, δέχομαι ("to receive"), that no prophet is welcome (δεκτός) in his own country. The themes of the reception of Jesus, of his message, and of his disciples are central in the third Gospel.[34] Jesus' reception by Simeon is a global behavior and attitude, in which the entire person of the old man, his body and inner self, his thoughts and feelings, become active.[35]

Simeon's Farewell Prayer (vv. 29–32)

■ **29** After the gesture follows a speech, a song of praise (εὐλόγησεν, "he praised").[36] Verses 29–32 can be read redaction-historically, with Luke's eyes, or form-critically for the purpose of the Jewish or early Christian tradition.

In the evangelist's view, the prayer introduces God as δεσπότης ("Master"),[37] as Lord and possessor of his δοῦλος ("servant"). This term recognizes the legal relationship between God and humans, but as the legal frame of this pericope (2:22–40) forms the entrance for the *Spirit*-caused event, something other than this hierarchical relationship develops between the Lord and Simeon: God can now let the old man depart *in peace*.

Ἀπολύω ("to let loose," "to dismiss") can describe death (euphemistically), or the liberation of a slave, or the release of an individual from service. Despite the

---

31   In Luke the temple stands in the center of Jerusalem, the holy city, by God's will. It becomes the site of revelation (Luke 2:46, 49) and of Jesus' teaching (19:45–47), and later, the first arena of activity for the Twelve (Acts 3:1, 11). After that, however, it loses its function in salvation history to Christ and the congregation, in a shift determined by providence. Bibliography on Luke's view of the temple is listed in Michael Bachmann, *Jerusalem und der Tempel: Die geographisch-theologischen Elemente in der lukanischen Sicht des jüdischen Kultzentrums* (BWANT 39; Stuttgart: Kohlhammer, 1979); and Francis D. Weinert, "The Meaning of the Temple in the Gospel of Luke" (Ph.D. diss., Fordham University, 1978–79).

32   This HB idiom occurs frequently in the LXX (e.g., 1 Sam [LXX 1 Kgdms] 24:7, 11; 26:9, 11, 16). It is also found in the intertestamental literature, e.g., *Ps. Sol.* 17:32.

33   Cf. Xenophon *Cyrop.* 7.5.50; Euripides *Or.* 464; 1 Kgs (LXX 3 Kgdms) 3:20; Esth 5:1e LXX; Josephus *Ant.* 8.2.2 §28; 11.6.9 §238. In general, ἀγκών ("elbow," "arm") is used in the singular, ἀγκάλη in

the plural. Str-B (2.138) write of Jewish children who are brought to be blessed by the elders.

34   Cf. Luke 8:13; 9:5, 48, 53; 10:8, 10; 18:17.

35   Origen (*Hom. Luc.* 15.3) uses the example of Simeon as a point of departure to emphasize both the role of the Holy Spirit as guide and our acts of service; we must be led by the Spirit into the temple of Jesus, his church.

36   The blessing (fifteen occurrences in Luke-Acts) goes in both directions, from God and Christ to the believers (Luke 24:51), and from their lips up to heaven (2:28). Words and their effect are the components of this relationship. See Claus Westermann, *Blessing in the Bible and in the Life of the Church* (trans. K. Crim; OBT; Philadelphia: Fortress Press, 1978).

37   The application of the title δεσπότης ("master") to God happens fairly late, both in the LXX (later, Hellenistic books) and in the NT (ten occurrences, four of them in Luke). This is an accommodation to the religious terminology of the Greeks. See Karl H. Rengstorf, "δεσπότης, κτλ.," *TDNT* 2 (1964)

proximity of δοῦλος to δεσπότης, the previous context (v. 26) and usage in the LXX and in classical Greek favor the first meaning.[38]

The present tense may emphasize that Simeon senses his impending death and is ready for it. The Nunc Dimittis is really a prayer, a conversation with God, at the moment of death. The accusative τὸν θεόν ("God") after εὐλόγησεν ("he praised," "he blessed," v. 28) is comprehensible when it is compared to αὐτούς ("them") in v. 34.

Νῦν ("now"), like σήμερον ("this day"), is a signal of the decisive phase of salvation history. God is active at the level of the world (v. 32), and at that of the individual (v. 29). He spoke[39] the prophecy and set in motion its fulfillment. God's means and end is peace,[40] both in the context of his covenant with his people, and, like here, in his relationship with an individual. In eschatological fulfillment, the death of an individual receives new meaning: Simeon can "see" this fulfillment (v. 26), not in his descendants (as in the HB),[41] but in the Messiah who brings salvation (as in the NT).

■ **30** The second part of the prayer begins in v. 30, introduced, as in the hymns, by ὅτι ("for"),[42] which indicates both the reason that death is now possible and the object of praise. God himself, of course, remains unseen, but his concrete action in history is manifest. Hebrew hymnody praises him for manifest victories (Ps 98 [LXX 97]); the hopes of the Jews expected them. Jesus already sees the fall of Satan (Luke 10:18), and describes his disciples' eyes as blessed (10:23–24, which, along with 3:6,

is the closest parallel to our passage). Verse 30 has been formulated in imitation of Hebrew Bible language.[43]

Seldom is it so clear that Luke's christology (τὸν χριστὸν κυρίου, "the Lord's Messiah," v. 26) is, above all, a soteriology (τὸ σωτήριόν σου, "your salvation," v. 30). God's eschatological deed is salvation, as liberation and well-being. Luke likes best to express the gospel's content with the root σαο- ("uninjured," "intact").[44] Salvation occurs independently of human striving; but the individual should react to this objective reality with subjective appropriation of it. Though objective, it is not readily available. Salvation is only visible as a sign. Σωτήριον stands between equivalent expressions such as παράκλησις τοῦ Ἰσραήλ ("consolation of Israel," v. 25) and λύτρωσις Ἰερουσαλήμ ("redemption of Jerusalem," v. 38).

■ **31** Verse 31 is not without its Hebrew Bible parallels. Even though, in the Bible, *humans* should prepare themselves for contact with God, not vice versa,[45] God has also prepared hidden works for his chosen ones, and for the last days (Isa 64:4; 1 Cor 2:9).[46] Simeon's blessing thanks God precisely for revelation, which his eyes have finally seen. Verses 30–31 transpose an apocalyptic tradition into a revelation, since the author is convinced that he lives in the last days. Of particular interest is Ps 31:19 (LXX 30:20), a parallel to Isa 64:4 (LXX 64:3), which praises the Lord's goodness "in the sight of the children of humankind," which corresponds to "in the presence of all peoples" in Luke 2:31. The rabbis, too,[47] interpret "in the sight of the children of this world" in contrast to the

---

44–49; and Günter Haufe, "δεσπότης, κτλ.," *EDNT* 1 (1990) 290–91.

38   Cf. Gen 15:2; Num 20:29; Tob 3:6, 13; 2 Macc 7:9; Sophocles *Ant.* 1268, 1314.

39   Cf. 1:38 and 5:5 (with ἐπί).

40   See Schürmann, 1.125 n. 101.

41   Cf. the example of Abraham (Gen 15:15): Σὺ δὲ ἀπελεύσῃ πρὸς τοὺς πατέρας σου μετ' εἰρήνης ("and you shall depart to your ancestors in peace").

42   Compare this ὅτι ("for") with the one in Luke 1:48, 68, and the commentary on these verses.

43   Cf. Ps 98(LXX 97):3; Isa 40:5 (LXX); Bar 4:24 (οὕτως ὄψονται ἐν τάχει τὴν παρὰ τοῦ θεοῦ ὑμῶν σωτηρίαν, "so they soon will see salvation from your God"). Further passages to be found in Jones, "Background," 41.

44   See Bovon, *Theologian*, 242–70 (statistics, 456 n. 3); idem, *Lukas*, 61–74.

45   Jones, "Background," 42.

46   See Michael E. Stone and John Strugnell, *The Books of Elijah, Parts 1–2* (SBLTT 18, Pseudepigrapha 8; Missoula, Mont.: Scholars Press, 1979) 41–73.

47   Oral teaching of Rabbi Levi (ca. 300), Midrash on Proverbs 13.25. Abbreviated citation in Str-B 3.329; fully in Stone and Strugnell, *Elijah*, 52–53. Rabbi Levi supports his statement that the benefits of the end times are already visible, even though they may not have been received (comment on Ps 31:20 [*NRSV* 31:19]). Rabbi Johanan refutes him and believes that the prophecies refer only to the messianic age, not the present world. In Luke, to see the eschatological treasures is somehow to possess them already.

believers, since the text does not say "among them."

The "preparation" is attested narratively in Luke 1–2 by the two pregnancies, and linguistically by the verbs κατασκευάζω ("to prepare," 1:17) and ἑτοιμάζω ("to make ready," "to prepare," 1:17, 76). The author intends to stress not the effort of preparation ("to plan," "to attempt," "to arrange"), but the revelation of the then-foreseen and now-established salvation. The use of Ps 31:19 (LXX 30:20) here creates a universalistic perspective that had been lacking up to this point.[48]

■ **32** Whereas the preparation happened *in the sight of the peoples*,[49] the fulfillment also takes place *for* them. This is expressed in v. 32, the third part of the song. Again, it is Hebrew Bible language, specifically Deutero-Isaiah.[50] The concept of a final revelation already can be heard in Isa 52:10 and 56:1, and is further developed in apocalyptic literature.[51]

There are three reasons for which ἐθνῶν ("for the peoples") should be taken with φῶς ("light") and not with ἀποκάλυψις ("revelation"): first, the Hebrew Bible parallels suggest this (see above); second, the genitive after ἀποκάλυψις specifies the author or content of the revelation, not the recipient; third, the parallelism with δόξαν λαοῦ σου Ἰσραήλ ("glory for your people Israel," v. 32b) shows that God not only reveals the hidden salvation but also bestows it.

The usual separation between Israel and the Gentiles is respected; but, surprisingly, the Gentiles are mentioned first, not second, perhaps because it is they who will accept the revelation (cf. Acts 28:28, "the Gentiles" contrasted with the stiff-necked λαός, "this people," v. 26).[52]

Eschatological salvation is conceived of as "light." We are not removed from history, suffering, and death, but we can understand our condition and future through the divine revelation.[53]

Δόξα ("glory") is primarily God's splendor, which, if Israel accepts it, will now reflect from Israel, as it once did from Moses' face.[54] For those who see it, it becomes the "glory" of Israel (in the sense of Isa 46:13). Nothing yet is said of the test that many in Israel will not pass; at the end of his two volumes, Luke has little hope left for the people of Israel.

Whereas vv. 30–31 allow christology to drift into soteriology, v. 32 indicates the inner connection between Christ and his church.

The Nunc Dimittis is regularly sung in the church at evening, before the night, so reminiscent of death (it is part of the daily liturgy of the complines). It could be a prayer that Luke adopts, perhaps even "an early Christian response to the problem of the death of a believer, at a time when the coming of the Lord was regarded as imminent (Acts 1.11)."[55] If this is so, the prayer would have retained its natural *Sitz im Leben*, the worship service, after a small detour into the Scriptures. The pre-Lukan origin of the other two hymns is probably Jewish, not Christian; but in this case, it is uncertain. (1) Simeon's situation, the content of salvation, and its recipients are described differently in the prayer and in its frame; but this could be attributed as easily to the author's technique as to differing origins. (2) The language of the Nunc Dimittis, although not its content, is related to the Christians' first prayer in Acts 4:24–30 (δοῦλος - δεσπότης, λαοί, "servant–master," "peoples");[56] both could, however, be traditional. (3) The Jewish distinction between "seeing prophetically" and "enjoying eschatologically" could indicate a pre-Christian origin, though this is improbable. (4) The emphasis on salvation and the universal perspective is typically Lukan. Thus I side with redactional origin. In this case the only speech in the pre-Lukan tradition would be vv. 34b–35, perhaps followed by the parents' surprise (v. 33).

---

48   Cf. Luke 1:17, 32–33, 54–55, 68–79; 2:10.

49   Paul Joüon suggests that κατὰ πρόσωπον ("in the presence of") is to be understood in the sense of לִפְנֵי, "at the disposal of"; cf. Gen 13:9; 24:51 ("Notes philologiques sur les Évangiles: Lc 2,31," *RechSR* 18 [1928] 352).

50   Isa 42:6; 49:6; 46:13; cf. 60:1–3.

51   Cf., e.g., *3 Bar.* 1–2; 11:7; 17:4 (substantive), and 4:13, 14 (verb). See Christian Abraham Wahl, *Clavis Librorum Veteris Testamenti Apocryphorum philologica* (1853; rev. Johannes Baptista Bauer; Graz: Akademischer Druck, 1972) 632.

52   On the extension to the nations which takes this verse as a point of departure, see Escudero Freire, *Devolver*, 345.

53   See Hans Conzelmann, "φῶς," *TDNT* 9 (1974) 334 n. 269.

54   Cf. Exod 34:29–35; 2 Cor 3:18, perhaps 6:15.

55   Jones, "Background," 48.

56   The plural λαοί ("peoples") is exceptional in Luke (only in this passage and Acts 4:25–27).

Simeon's Prophecy (vv. 33–35)

■ **33** Why does Luke choose to say (especially after 1:26–38) "his father," at which many scribes took offense?[57] In order not to repeat the word "parents" (v. 27), with "father" to be understood in a legal, not biological, sense? This is probably a trace of an earlier version, which, like other units in Luke 2, still did not presuppose the virgin birth. But both ϑαυμάζω with ἐπί ("to be amazed at") and τὰ λαλούμενα ("what was being said") are Lukan.[58]

■ **34** It is astonishing that Simeon never blesses the child. Is this from reverence for the Son of God, whom a mortal may not bless (but cf. 1:42)? Or was Jesus included by tradition in the αὐτούς ("them") of v. 34?

As in Zechariah's prayer, a personal section (2:34–35; 1:76–79) follows the general words of praise. The parallelism of mother and son (2:34–35), however, is reminiscent of Elizabeth's sayings (esp. 1:42). This probably indicates the evangelist's compositional technique.

Readers often miss the tension between the hymn (vv. 29–32) and its continuation, which is privately directed to Mary (vv. 34–35). In the one are peace and light; in the other, sword and suffering. I agree with Joachim Scharfenberg, who sees the old man discovering his inner contradictions in these two speeches and accepting them.[59] Only then can he "depart in peace," that is, achieve the resolution of opposites.

In the parallelism, "for the falling . . . for a sign," the second can act as the key to the first. Σημεῖον ("a sign") is not the confirmation of a message, but a divine action taking on concrete form (cf. 11:30).[60] Minds will be divided over him.[61] The structure of Luke's two volumes will confirm this oracle. The fall applies to the first, the rising to the second. Though Isa 8:14 is not cited, as often in these chapters it remains in the background. According to Isa 8:18, the prophet and his children will become signs and portents in Israel. Thus the image of falling and rising is also inspired by Isaiah 8; there (8:14) God himself reveals both through the sign of his prophets. In Luke, Jesus plays both the roles of the prophetic sign (Isa 8:18) and of the divinity himself (8:14).[62]

One cannot determine whether Luke 2:34 is nearer the Hebrew text of Isaiah than the Greek.[63] In Luke, as in Isaiah, the oracle opens onto a judgment (Luke 2:35b and Isa 8:15). Isaiah 8:14 and the vocabulary of Luke 2:34b conceive of Jesus as a holy stone, whom no one can sidestep. Κεῖται ("is laid," "is destined") can mean "to be appointed for" (cf. Phil 1:16; 1 Thess 3:3). Some stumble over the stone and fall; others find new strength in it, as in Isa 8:14—on the basis not of a double predestination, but of human decision in response to God's revelation. "In Israel" may be traditional, since Luke is thinking more universalistically here. But, to the end of the Acts, inner-Jewish discussion remains a constant theme in Lukan redaction, alongside the mission to the Gentiles (cf. Acts 28:19, 25). Ἀνάστασις ("rising") should not rashly be translated "resurrection," despite Luke's penchant for double meanings.[64]

---

57   Many copyists found the expression "his father" (v. 33) difficult and replaced it with the proper name "Joseph." A few also objected to the words "the parents" (v. 27) and "his parents" (vv. 41, 43), and corrected them. H. J. Vogels tries to demonstrate that these doctrinal corrections can be attributed to Tatian ("Die 'Eltern' Jesu [Textkritisches zu Lk 2,23ff]," *BZ* 11 [1913] 33–43).

58   Θαυμάζω ἐπί: Luke 4:22; 9:43; 20:26; Acts 3:12. Τὰ λαλούμενα: Luke 1:45; Acts 13:45; 16:14; cf. 17:19. With the exception of Mark 5:36 and 1 Cor 14:9, one finds this idiom in the NT only in Luke.

59   *Den Widerspruch auf sich nehmen* (Schritte ins Offene; Zurich: Evangelischer Frauenbund der Schweiz, 1986) 28–29.

60   Cf. Josh 4:6 LXX: εἰς σημεῖον κείμενον διὰ παντός.

61   Ἀντιλέγω: "to speak against, speak for one's part, contradict, oppose"; here, "to become a sign that produces opposition." Jacques Winandy ("La prophétie de Syméon [Lc II,34–35]," *RB* 72 [1965] 321–51, esp. 323–24) and A. Feuillet conceive of the expression differently (Feuillet, "L'épreuve prédite à Marie par le vieillard Siméon [Luc 2,35a]," in *À la rencontre de Dieu: Mémorial Albert Gelin* [Le Puy: X. Mappus, 1961] 243–63): "to be a sign that must be contradicted, i.e., rejected." Cf. Acts 13:45; 28:19, 22. Though infrequent, this verb occurs already in the LXX, directed toward Israel: Isa 65:2; Hos 4:4. See Miyoshi, "Jesu Darstellung," 88.

62   One could also think of the connection of Isa 28:16 with 8:14, which Rom 9:33 and 1 Pet 2:7–8 attest (Winandy, "Prophétie," 329).

63   Paul Winter, "Observations on the Language in the Birth and Infancy Stories of the Third Gospel," *NTS* 1 (1954–55) 111–21, esp. 118–19.

64   Winandy, "Prophétie," 323. In another sense see 332, 336.

■ **35a** Verse 35a poses difficult problems.[65] *Καὶ σοῦ δὲ αὐτῆς* ("and . . . your own [soul]") indicates an urgent address. *Ἡ ῥομφαία* ("a sword") denotes a large, straight, double-edged sword, differentiated from a curved *μάχαιρα* (with only one blade). In the LXX, however, both are used synonymously, even in metaphor, especially as an image of God's judgment.[66]

This prevalent image of punishment does not pertain to this passage (or in Luke at all). Nor is it an allusion to christological doubts in Mary's heart.[67] Next to the external trial (v. 34) is that from within (v. 35; cf. Pss 37:15; 22:20 [MT 22:21]). Judith 16:9 uses *διέρχομαι* ("pierce") for the motion of a weapon (cf. Jdt 6:6). The personal consequences of the dispute over Jesus' public works are discreetly but vividly announced. The Messiah, now present (vv. 26, 30), will be a suffering Messiah (Luke 9:22; Acts 26:23), and his mother will partake of his sorrows.[68] Thus the clause introduced with *ὅπως* ("so that") can only be dependent on v. 34b; v. 35a is a parenthesis.

With other Catholic exegetes,[69] Pierre Benoit considers Mary to be an embodiment of the daughter of Zion, that is, the nation of Israel. The "sword" would be, as in Ezek 14:17 (*διέρχομαι* also), a divine instrument for testing and refining his people. The Messiah's entire life, not his death alone, would set this process in motion. Thus v. 35a would be a parallel to v. 34b, not a parenthesis. Yet a collective understanding of Mary seems difficult.

Joseph A. Fitzmyer applies Ezek 14:17 to his interpretation of the passage, as does Benoit, but treats Mary as an individual.[70] He compares the sword with the word of God and interprets *διέρχομαι* as the way of proclamation. Within her family and in her own life, Mary will sense the discriminating action of God's word (cf. 8:21; 11:28).[71]

■ **35b** Just as divine preparation (v. 31) awaits that of mortals, in v. 35b the *ἀποκάλυψις* of human hearts is juxtaposed to the divine "revelation" (v. 32). *Διαλογισμοί* ("thoughts") elsewhere in Luke always has negative connotations. As in Isa 8:15, Luke probably means, here as elsewhere, the obduracy of the people. Jesus' activity forces Israel to seize the last chance, or miss out. The attitude of each individual would then become visible. This necessity, announced in advance, lends the literary work the grandeur and tension of a tragedy.[72]

The Prophetess Anna (vv. 36–38)

■ **36–37** Although symmetrical, the descriptions of Simeon and Anna are completely different and have separate functions. The man is determined by what he is. This view inward is juxtaposed to a view outward in the case of the woman. Anna receives her identity through her descent (v. 36a), age (v. 36b), and her social and religious position (vv. 36c–37). This literary distinction probably reflects the difference of status between men and women in contemporaneous Judaism. Is Luke's silence about the prophetess's words attributable to this?

"Anna" is the Greek form of חַנָּה (חֵן means "favor," "mercy") and brings to mind Samuel's mother and Tobit's wife.[73] Luke delights in her descent and under-

---

65 Bibliography to v. 35 in Pierre Benoit, "'Et toi-même, un glaive te transpercera l'âme!' (Luc 2,35)," *CBQ* 25 (1963) 251–61, reprinted in idem, *Exégèse*, 3.216–27; see esp. 216 n. 1.

66 Biblical passages in Benoit, "Et toi-même," 216–17.

67 Cf. Origen *Hom. in Luc.* 17.6.

68 Agreeing with Feuillet, "Épreuve," 249, even if the mariological conclusions that he draws from this interpretation should be criticized: "A genuine participation of the Savior's mother in the redemptive suffering."

69 Cf. esp. Laurentin, *Structure*, 148–63.

70 He cites Luke 11:28 and 8:21 (1.423).

71 Winandy ("Prophétie," 336–48) thinks of Zech 12:10 and 13:7, Christ's death, the fall of Jerusalem, and the suffering that resulted from it for Mary and the Christian community. S. Garofalo, on the other hand, doubts that Luke had any HB text in front of him when he wrote 2:35 ("'Tuam ipsius animam pertransibit gladius' [Lc 2,35]," in *Maria in Sacra Scriptura*, 4.175–81).

72 Without a change of sense, one can take *καρδιῶν* alone as a genitive attribute to *διαλογισμοί* ("thoughts"), or with *ἐκ πολλῶν*. The substantive use of *πολλῶν* in 2:34 and the sentence structure make the first possiblity seem more probable.

73 Cf. 1 Sam (LXX 1 Kgdms) 1–2; Tob 1:20; 2:1; 11:9. The name of the father of the prophetess, Phanuel, is attested in 1 Chr 4:4 (in Gen 32:31 and Judg 8:8, it is a place-name). Asher is a northern tribe. See Pau Figueras, "Syméon et Anne ou le témoignage de la loi et des prophètes," *NovT* 20 (1978) 84–99, esp. 96 n. 1. With these genealogical notices Luke intends to suggest Jewish descent and environment. Jdt 8:1–2, Tob 1:1–2, and Phil 3:5–6 show that, among the Jews, there was a customary form of introducing someone.

scores her age almost pleonastically.[74] Because of the ἕως plus the genitive, eighty-four is more likely her present age than the length of her widowhood. The three parts of her life should be distinguished precisely: virgin, wife,[75] widow. In Luke's eyes she lived piously and did well not to marry again. She corresponds to the ideal of the Jewish and Christian widow[76] (of course, she did not fast and pray every minute). Perhaps Luke thinks that she lived in the temple precinct, for whereas Simeon must enter (v. 27), she is already there.

Particularly interesting is the description of Anna as a prophetess. The Hebrew Bible knows only four such figures,[77] and the New Testament is rather reticent about the prophetic activity of women.[78] In Luke, Anna, like John and Simeon, stands on the threshold of the Testaments: all three are prophets, not yet witnesses, but they belong to the eschatological efflorescence of Spirit-directed prophecy (cf. Acts 2:17).

■ **38** The action finally begins in v. 38, parallel to v. 27 ("at that moment"). Anna does not remain a passive spectator; she prays to God. Ἀνθομολογέομαι ("to praise"), a hapax legomenon in the NT, means "to ratify an agreement," "to recognize something"; in the majority of isolated attestations in the LXX it means, in the absolute, "to thank God," "to praise" (the aspect of answering is still detectable because of the ἀντί).[79] After the prayer follows the prophetic message (v. 38b). Verse 38b is Lukan, with the exception of the word λύτρωσις

("redemption"). Even without the article, "redemption" is specific, and denotes eschatological liberation in its salvation-historical (exodus tradition), legal (Ruth 3:12–4:14), and liturgical (cultic *Sitz im Leben*) dimensions.[80] In Deutero-Isaiah[81] God effects the redemption, just as family members, following Lev 25:47–54, would intercede for their relatives as "redeemers." According to Luke, many in Jerusalem were awaiting such a "redemption," also attested in the Psalms. Jerusalem,[82] in synecdoche, represents the entire people (cf. 2:10).

The Journey Home (v. 39)

■ **39** Luke cannot or will not tell us more about Anna. After a formulaic conclusion (cf. 7:1; Acts 13:29), he leads the family home.

Jesus' Youth (v. 40)

■ **40** In a single verse, the twelve years of Jesus' youth are summarized (cf. 2:42). The language and symmetry with the story of John (1:80) are the author's work. After the next episode, Luke will write a similar summary statement (2:52). The source of inspiration is 1 Sam (LXX 1 Kgdms) 2:21c, 26. In variance from Luke 1:80, Jesus is said to be filled[83] with "wisdom" rather than "spirit" (as in 2:52), perhaps because πνεῦμα ("spirit") is associated with the virgin birth and Jesus' baptism.

The words "and the favor[84] of God was upon him" (cf. 2:25) underscore this divine aid.[85] God concerns

---

74 Mathew P. John believes that Anna was over a hundred years old ("How Old Was Anna?" *BT* 26 [1975] 247). Alfredo Tepox Varela allots the eighty-four years a symbolic value (7 × 12) and emphasizes the value of marriage and the still higher value of widowhood ("Lk 2:36–37: Is Anna's Age What Is Really in Focus?" *BT* 27 [1976] 446).

75 The reduction of the seven years to seven days in one part of the Syriac tradition is attributable to Tatian, according to H. J. Vogels ("Lk 2, 36 im Diatessaron," *BZ* 11 [1913] 168–71).

76 Jdt 8:4–6; 1 Tim 5:3–16; see Brown, *Birth*, 467.

77 Miriam (Exod 15:20), Deborah (Judg 4:4), Hulda (2 Kgs [LXX 4 Kgdms] 22:14), and Isaiah's wife (Isa 8:3).

78 Cf. Acts 21:9 and 1 Cor 11:5. In Rev 2:20 Jezebel calls herself a prophetess, and Acts 2:17 cites Joel's prophecy ("your daughters" will also prophesy).

79 Ps 79(LXX 78):13; 1 Esdr 8:91 (LXX 8:88); Dan 4:37, 37b (LXX). Twice in Josephus (*Ant.* 8.10.3 §257; 8.13.8 §362), both with the meaning "to

confess," in one case, "his sins," in the other, "his mistakes."

80 The word occurs in Heb 9:12; *1 Clem.* 12.7; *Did.* 4.6.

81 Isa 43:3–4; 45:14; 49:26; 54:1–8. The word group of λύτρωσις ("redemption") also occurs frequently in the Psalms: 49:7, 8, 15 (LXX 48:8, 9, 16); 130(LXX 129):8.

82 A few mss. read "the redemption in Jerusalem," not "the redemption of Jerusalem."

83 In Acts 6:8 Stephen is said to be "full of grace and power." In Acts 7:10 Joseph receives "favor" and "wisdom" from God. The present passive participle of πληρόω ("to fill," "to fulfill") also occurs in Eph 1:23; the perfect passive participle is more frequent.

84 See Cambe, "Χαρίς."

85 The formulation in Luke 2:40 (par. Acts 4:33) does not occur in the HB. It is even more abstract than the expression in Acts 11:21 ("and the hand of the Lord was with them"), but has the same meaning.

himself with the child not only because he loves him, but because he has a plan for him.[86] Thus supported, Jesus grows and becomes strong. More than this we (unfortunately?) do not know;[87] nor probably did Luke.

Conclusion

I close this exegesis with a few theses:

1. The Law is the context of prophecy and fulfillment.[88] In these parameters the living God creates the possibility of innovation.

2. The Spirit is, in Luke, a concept adequate for both prophecy and fulfillment; it is less an eschatological benefit (at the end of the end) than a salvation-historical one (at the beginning of the end).

3. In this scene the ancient faithfulness of God meets its new visible manifestation, for the same God stands behind both Simeon and Jesus. Luke narrates both the continuity of God's plan of salvation and the transition from the penultimate to the ultimate phase. Symptomatically, this "happens" in the form of a *human* encounter.

4. As "something holy," Jesus belongs to God. He has no need to be redeemed. Thus he can fulfill the λύτρωσις ("redemption") of Israel.

5. All believers can identify themselves with Simeon: all live in the penultimate time, but, in the light of revelation, they may look toward their death in peace.

6. In Christ, the history of the individual (2:29–30) and the history of the church (2:31–32) receive their meaning. Luke paints a microcosm, but indicates that it is the antitype of the macrocosmic plan of God.

---

86 The formulation, here referring to Jesus, should be connected with the words to Mary in Luke 1:30.

87 The apocryphal infancy Gospels, esp. that of Pseudo-Thomas, attempt to fill these gaps. See Stephen Gero, "The Infancy Gospel of Thomas: A Study of the Textual and Literary Problems," *NovT* 13 (1971) 46–80.

88 Figueras ("Syméon"), in juxtaposition to this, sees in Simeon an allegory of the Law, in Anna that of prophecy.

The Twelve-Year-Old Jesus in the Temple
(2:41–52)

Bibliography

Brown, *Birth,* 471–96.

Couroyer, B., "A propos de Lc II,52," *RB* 86 (1979) 92–101.

Delebecque, "Note."

Dupont, "Jésus retrouvé."

Elliott, J. K., "Does Luke 2:41–52 Anticipate the Resurrection?" *ExpTim* 83 (1971–72) 87–89.

Escudero Freire, *Devolver,* 365–418.

Glombitza, Otto, "Der Zwölfjährige Jesus: Lk 2,40–52: Ein Beitrag zur Exegese der lukanischen Vorgeschichte," *NovT* 5 (1962) 1–4.

Gray, John R., "Was Our Lord an Only Child? Luke 2:43–46," *ExpTim* 71 (1959–60) 53.

Gueuret, *Engendrement,* 145–73, 228–44.

Hastings, A. W., "Was Our Lord an Only Child: Luke 2:43–46?" *ExpTim* 71 (1959–60) 187.

van der Horst, P. W., "Notes on the Aramaic Background of Luke 2:41–52," *JSNT* 7 (1980) 61–66.

van Iersel, "Finding."

Jansen, John F., "An Exposition of Luke 2:41–52," *Int* 30 (1976) 400–404.

de Jonge, "Sonship."

Kilgallen, John J., "Luke 2,41–50: Foreshadowing of Jesus, Teacher," *Bib* 66 (1985) 553–59.

Laurentin, René, "Ce que le recouvrement (Lc 2:41–52) enseigne sur Marie," *Ephemerides Mariologicae* 43 (1993) 213–26.

idem, *Jésus au temple.*

idem, "'Non intellexerunt verbum quod locutus est ad eos' (Lc 2,50)," in *Maria in Sacra Scriptura,* 4.299–314.

idem, *Truth,* 80–89, 93–94.

Legrand, Lucien, "Deux voyages: Lc 2,41–50; 24,13–33," in F. Refoulé, ed., *À cause de l'Évangile: Études sur les Synoptiques et les Actes: Festschrift Jacques Dupont* (LD 123; Paris: Cerf, 1985) 409–29.

Lindemann, Friedrich-Wilhelm, "'Wisset ihr nicht, daß ich sein muß in dem, das meines Vaters ist?'" *Wege zum Menschen* 38 (1986) 70–77.

Manns, F., "Luc 2,41–50 témoin de la Bar Mitswa de Jésus," *Mar* 40 (1978) 344–49.

McHugh, *Mother,* 113–24.

Peretto, E., "La lettura origeniana di Lc 2,41–52," *Mar* 37 (1975) 336–57.

Pesch, Rudolf, "'Kind, warum hast du so an uns getan?' (Lk 2,48)," *BZ* n.s. 12 (1968) 245–48.

Schmahl, Günther, "Lk 2,41–52 und die Kindheitserzählung des Thomas 19,1–5: Ein Vergleich," *BibLeb* 15 (1974) 249–58.

Stock, Alex, "Der zwölfjährige Jesus in der Schulbibelillustration," *Katechetische Blätter* 112 (1987) 385–87.

Sylva, Dennis D., "The Cryptic Clause *en tois tou patros mou dei einai me* in Lk 2,49b," *ZNW* 78 (1987) 132–40.

Weinert, Francis D., "The Multiple Meanings of Luke 2:49 and Their Significance," *BTB* 13 (1983) 19–22.

Winter, Paul, "Luke 2,49 and Targum Yerushalmi," *ZNW* 45 (1954) 145–79.

idem, "Lk 2,49 and Targum Yerushalmi Again," *ZNW* 46 (1955) 140–41.

41 Now every year his parents went to Jerusalem for the festival of the Passover. 42/ And when he was twelve years old, they went up according to the custom of the festival. 43/ When the days had been fulfilled, and they started to return, the boy Jesus stayed behind in Jerusalem, but his parents did not know it. 44/ Assuming that he was in the group of travelers, they went a day's journey, then started to look for him among their relatives and friends; 45/ and when they did not find him, they returned to Jerusalem to search for him.

46 And it happened that after three days they found him in the temple precinct, sitting in the midst of the teachers, listening to them and asking them questions. 47/ And all who heard him were amazed at his understanding and his answers. 48/ And when they saw him they were astonished; and his mother said to him, "Child, why have you treated us like this? Look, your father and I have been searching for you in great anxiety." 49/ And he said to them, "Why were you searching for me? Did you not know that I must be in my Father's domain?" 50/ But they did not understand the saying that he spoke to them. 51/ Then he went down with them and came to Nazareth, and was obedient to them; and his mother treasured all these words in her heart. 52/ And Jesus made progress in wisdom and in years, and in divine and human favor.

Analysis

This pericope is framed by two summary passages (v. 40 and v. 52), both of which draw attention to wisdom and to grace. The author considers the episode an example; vv. 47 and 49 emphasize Jesus' cleverness on the one hand, and his attachment to his Father on the other.

At 2:40 the neatly balanced parallelism between John and Jesus has reached its conclusion; thus several exegetes consider the scene of the child Jesus in the temple to be a later accretion. The character of the language in 2:41–52 is undoubtedly Lukan. Is one to believe that Luke himself expanded his own text on second thought, or in a second edition?[1] Two considerations controvert this. First, the parallelism is nowhere perfectly balanced, because of the diversity of the traditions and the christological concerns of their redaction; the Messiah always receives the greater attention. Verses 41–51, of course, disturb the symmetry, but not the author's intention. Second, every significant transition contains a summary passage. The twelve years about which Luke tells nothing require such a passage (v. 40), just as the succeeding stage does (v. 52). That such summary passages in Luke resemble each other is natural. But each has its uniqueness: the first stresses growth during Jesus' childhood; the second, Jesus' progress into adulthood. The passage at 2:41–52 is therefore an original component of Jesus' birth narrative.

1. *Structure*. According to Henk J. de Jonge, this pericope is a paradigm of concentric symmetry.[2] The journey abroad (A; vv. 41–42) corresponds to the journey home (A'; v. 51a), Jesus' unnoticed tarrying (B; v. 43) to his uncomprehending reaction (B'; vv. 49–50), and the search and discovery by the anxious parents (C; vv. 44–46a) to their reproach of Jesus (C'; v. 48). The center of the pericope would then be Jesus' position among the scholars (X; vv. 46b–47). According to de Jonge, the word $\mu\acute{\epsilon}\sigma\omega$ ("in the midst") stands precisely in the middle, the eighty-fifth word of the 170 that compose the unit.[3]

This structural analysis does not do justice, however, to the movement of the narrative. Its dramatic tension arises through the contrary programs of parents and child: the will of the parents corresponds to the Law, the will of Jesus to the new revelation. The everyday character of the events is strongly emphasized at the beginning ($\kappa\alpha\tau$' $\acute{\epsilon}\tau o\varsigma$, "every year," v. 41; $\kappa\alpha\tau\grave{\alpha}$ $\tau\grave{o}$ $\acute{\epsilon}\vartheta o\varsigma$, "according to the custom," v. 42). Joseph and Mary are behaving as usual in vv. 41–42, like observant Jews. The unex-

pected appears for the first time in v. 43b: the boy stays in Jerusalem. Luke then skillfully leaves behind this salvation-historical *novum* to return to the theme of pious fulfillment of the Law (vv. 43c–44), which is broken off at v. 45a. After the long search (v. 45b), an unexpected vision meets the parents' eyes (vv. 46–47): Jesus in the midst of the teachers. This image is surely a high point in the narrative, but only the first. For a saying follows this picture, an explanation follows the sign, and an interpretation follows the event (vv. 48–49). After this climax, Luke brings the narrative to its conclusion (vv. 50–51) with the parents' final reaction (v. 50) and Jesus' behavior in response to it (v. 51). The parents remain closed to their son's program, while the son, for the time being, adapts himself to theirs.

According to de Jonge, v. 51a forms the conclusion, while v. 51b is linked to v. 52 and represents the final paragraph of the entire birth narrative. On the other hand, "*his* mother" alludes to the previous episode; thus Luke makes a progressive transition from the conclusion of the individual story to that of the entire birth narrative, maintaining a double interest for mother and son throughout.

2. *Tradition and Redaction*. Traditional material hides behind the final Lukan redaction.[4] First, the neatly rounded form suggests the possibility of an independently circulating story. Second, the birth narrative shows no influence on it; compare the virgin birth with Joseph's fatherhood here. Third, the "image" of the child's unusual wisdom is in tension with the "words" of the father-son relationship. Fourth, despite the acclamation in v. 47, the author failed to correct v. 48, so that the audience in v. 47 is actually still the subject.[5]

Luke has changed little of the gist of the narrative, but has rendered it in his own words.[6] With the supplementary v. 47, he gives the "image" (v. 46) equal weight

---

1   Brown (*Birth*, passim, e.g., 455) believes that Luke added the hymns (1:46–55, 68–79; 2:29–32) and this scene (2:41–52) later.

2   Henk J. de Jonge, "Sonship, Wisdom, Infancy: Lk 2,41–51a," *NTS* 24 (1977–78) 339.

3   de Jonge, "Sonship," 338 n. 5.

4   Bastiaan Martinus Franciscus Van Iersel ("The Finding of Jesus in the Temple: Some Observations on the Original Form of Luke 2,41–51a," *NovT* 4 [1960] 161–73, esp. 171) believes that v. 44 may also be a redactional addition, on the basis of its Lukan language and its "novelistic" style. Martin Dibelius

(*Tradition*, 106) is of the opinion that, in the tradition, Jesus' saying formed the conclusion of the episode.

5   The vocabulary of v. 47a is Lukan, as Acts 9:21 shows. See de Jonge, "Sonship," 344. The same cannot be claimed for v. 47b. Van Iersel does remark, however, that Luke 20:26—a statement of Luke's—is similar to v. 47 ("Finding," 170).

6   Van Iersel, "Finding," 166–67.

with the "words," and with the interpretation that he has embedded in the two summary passages (the theme of Jesus' wisdom). In the tradition the climax came at the end: Jesus' devastating retort (v. 49). Without any alteration of the formulation, Luke sees the father-son relationship in this from a higher christological perspective than the tradition. Luke and his readers would inevitably recall the conception by the Holy Spirit (1:35).

3. *Genre.* Is this not a biographical legend,[7] whereby the stress is on the ending in v. 49? If a legend, our pericope then would stand at the later end of the Jesus traditions; but as an apothegm, it would represent "the most reliable information about Jesus."[8] The *Sitz im Leben* would then be catechetical instruction.[9]

But the biographical nature of the tradition and its interest in Jesus' identity and life should not be overlooked. Moreover, the oldest apothegms are characterized not by the ontological christology we find here, but by a soteriological christology. In form, content, and tone, this account approximates the other episodes in the birth narrative. From a form-critical perspective, this should be counted among the anecdotes, like those beloved by ancient biographers, especially when they contained a bon mot. Such a biographical interest advocates a late date and a Jewish Christian milieu. The function of the anecdote is apologetic: to defuse the criticism of Jesus' humble human origin through his relationship to the heavenly Father.

The apocryphal infancy Gospel of Pseudo-Thomas (2d century) closes with this episode and emphasizes Jesus' miraculous wisdom, thus underscoring Luke's redactional tendency.[10] There, and even earlier in the *Epistula apostolorum*, one reads an anecdote that is form-critically and substantively comparable to ours. Jesus' parents have entrusted him to a teacher. When he expects Jesus to repeat the letter alpha, the child already

knows beta and demands an explanation of this second letter from his teacher.[11]

4. *Results of the Analysis.* Luke adopts and reworks an independent anecdote, and with it concludes the entire birth narrative. Inserted between two summary passages, it demonstrates Jesus' wisdom (vv. 46–47), although Jesus' saying (v. 49), which told something of the child's divine identity, originally formed the climax. The *Sitz im Leben* for this tradition was an inner-Jewish discussion, more specifically, an apologetic response of the Christians to Jewish aspersions about Jesus' miserable origins. It remains uncertain whether the conclusion of the narrative (v. 50 onward) is traditional or redactional, and where Luke begins the final summary passage (in v. 51b?).

Commentary

The Pilgrimage (vv. 41–45)

Only Luke tells anything about Jesus' youth. Is this scene the most important of the birth narrative, a sneak preview of the resurrection?[12] Or is it the beginning of the apocryphal accretions, the first sign of decline? Allusions of the resurrection are lacking; but the episode is important as the conclusion of the birth narrative, and as a transition between the Messiah's birth and his public appearance. Especially significant is the father-son relationship, which fits into a sequence with the annunciation to Mary (1:35) and Jesus' baptism (3:32). As always in Luke, theology is embedded in narrativity: v. 49 can serve as a theological description of Jesus' entire life, even if the sentence primarily portrays the matter-of-fact answer of a child to his mother.

■ **41–42** The account is neither pro- nor anti-Jewish.[13] Jesus' parents[14] are pious people, which is comprehensible and respectable to both Jews and pagans. The view

7   Dibelius, *Tradition*, 106–9.
8   So van Iersel, "Finding," 172–73.
9   René Laurentin shares this opinion (*Jésus au temple: Mystère de Pâques et foi de Marie en Luc 2,48–50* [EtB; Paris: Gabalda, 1966] 84, 143, 158–59).
10   A perceptive comparison of both texts is in Günther Schmahl, "Lk 2,41–52 und die Kindheitserzählung des Thomas 19,1–5: Ein Vergleich," *BibLeb* 15 (1974) 249–58.
11   This summarizes the oldest form of the scene, that of *Epistula apostolorum* 4 (15). The episode, further developed, appears twice in the Infancy Gospel of

Pseudo-Thomas (6, 14). Cf. the Gospel of Pseudo-Matthew 31.1–2; 38.1; the Arabic Infancy Gospel 48–49; the Armenian Infancy Gospel 20.1–7.
12   Laurentin, *Jésus au temple*, 8.
13   Whenever possible, Luke refrains from using foreign words. In 2:41, in which the word πάσχα ("Passover") is unavoidable, he clarifies it through the word "festival"; in 2:42 he omits it.
14   A few copyists replace this expression with "Joseph and Mary" in consideration of the virgin birth. See above, commentary on 2:33.

that the child became a "son of the Law" (בַּר מִצְוָה) at the festival at twelve years of age cannot yet be attested in this era.[15] Unlike a girl,[16] a twelve-year-old boy is not completely grown, but is indeed least a παῖς. Whoever places Jesus here at the stage of adulthood misses precisely the point: even as a child, Jesus possesses the wisdom of the great ones. Only later must he take the entire yoke of the Law upon himself, although, following the Mishnah, he participated in the pilgrimage to Jerusalem from the time he could go.[17] For text-critical considerations, "Jerusalem" in v. 42 should probably be stricken, since it occurs in both vv. 41 and 43.

In both Greek and Jewish biography, there is the topos of the gifted hero, who at twelve years demonstrates his superior intelligence: Cyrus, Cambyses, Alexander, and Epicurus—or Solomon, Samuel, and Daniel.[18] According to Josephus, Samuel began to prophesy as a twelve-year-old.[19] Thus Luke intends to describe Jesus' superiority by having him follow in the footsteps of the great heroes.

■ **43** In v. 43a Luke speaks as a writer, not as an expert on Jewish liturgy. It does not interest him whether the full seven days of the festival have been completed, or only the first two, which were prescribed for the pilgrims.[20]

Ἀναβαινόντων ("[they] went up")[21] and τελειωσάντων ("[the days] had been fulfilled") are not in the same tense. The first participle, in the present, attests duration; the second, in the aorist, summarizes a completed action, and begins the episode (see the translation above).[22] Moreover, from the beginning Luke neatly keeps parents and child separate: until v. 43b, only Mary and Joseph are active. Of course, Jesus has traveled with them, but he attracts attention as an individual only through his desire to stay in Jerusalem. His staying behind is placed in opposition to the "returning"[23] of the others through the compound verb ὑπομένω ("to stay behind"). Καὶ οὐκ ἔγνωσαν οἱ γονεῖς αὐτοῦ ("but his parents did not know") cannot refer to an earlier statement by Jesus (not transmitted by Luke), which would have announced to his parents that he must remain in Jerusalem.[24] Neither γινώσκω ("to know") nor its absolute usage is surprising.[25]

■ **44–45** In v. 44 the elegant syntax and choice of words are worth noting. When do the parents begin to seek the child?[26] As soon as they noticed that he was not with them, or only just in the evening, in the context of stopping for the night? The dramatization of the narrative supports the second possibility. A search first becomes necessary, when, at the end of the day's journey, anxious worries arise in their hearts.[27] "Among their relatives and friends" is reminiscent of similar Lukan expressions.[28] Verse 45 stands in antithetical parallelism to v. 43: when the parents "were returning," Jesus stayed in Jerusalem; when they did not find the child, they returned to Jerusalem. With the present participle (ἀναζητοῦντες, "to search for"),[29] Luke suggests that the parents inquired of every group they met.

The Image of the Wise Son (vv. 46–47)

■ **46–47** Καὶ ἐγένετο ("and it happened that") designates a new paragraph. After the seeking comes the

---

15 Most of the Talmudic texts cited by F. Manns set the majority of a boy at age thirteen ("Luc 2, 41–50 témoin de la Bar Mitswa de Jésus," *Mar* 40 [1978] 344–49). Manns does indeed mention a few passages in which the age is set at twelve (*b. Ber.* 24a; *Sifre Num* 22 [the ms. tradition here vacillates between twelve and thirteen years]). Further, he maintains that the Bar Mitzvah festival appears only in more recent texts.

16 See the commentary on 8:42 below.

17 *m. Hag.* 1.1. See de Jonge, "Sonship," 317–24.

18 De Jonge, "Sonship," 322–23.

19 Josephus *Ant.* 5.10.4 § 348.

20 See Plummer, 75; and Godet, 1.146. About the festival, cf. Exod 12:15, 16; Lev 23:6–8; Deut 16:3.

21 Since Jerusalem lies on a height, one says "go up to Jerusalem."

22 Édouard Delebecque, "Note sur Lc 2,41–52," *BAGB*

(1973) 75–83, reprinted in idem, *Études*, 39–51, esp. 45.

23 Cf. BAGD *s.v.*

24 Delebecque, "Note," 41–47.

25 Cf. Luke 9:11; 24:18; Acts 17:13.

26 In an effort to shield Mary and Joseph from the criticism that they did not pay close enough attention to Jesus, various authors have assumed that the men and women traveled to Jerusalem in separate groups. Lagrange (94) objects to this old hypothesis.

27 The syntax does not prevent the possibility that the search began while they were still on the road. Plummer (75) imagines that, during the whole day, they scoured the long train of pilgrims from the front to the rear, and from the rear to the front.

28 1:58; 14:12; 21:16; Acts 10:24.

29 One should not pass over the ἀνά of ἀναζητέω: "seek out."

finding (v. 46 contrasts with v. 45). Μετὰ ἡμέρας τρεῖς ("after three days") does not allude to the resurrection[30] (which is dated with τῇ τρίτῃ ἡμέρᾳ or τῇ ἡμέρᾳ τῇ τρίτῃ in Luke, "on the third day"),[31] but expresses an indefinite period, and should thus not be figured more exactly.[32]

The surprise is that the parents do not find their child just anywhere. For the second time, Jesus' "program" upsets his parents' expectations: he has installed himself in the temple. Because of this, the discussion that follows is full of misunderstandings. The parents ask about his remaining behind, while their son answers by asserting his place in the temple.

In the temple precincts (ἱερόν, not ναός), Jesus tarries "in the midst of the teachers"; this second specification makes the first more precise (as in 4:39). A synagogue in the Jerusalem temple is nowhere attested, but has nevertheless repeatedly been an object of conjecture since the seventeenth century. Since the place for instruction was the stoa (the portico, a covered hall of columns), Luke probably has in mind the portico of Solomon,[33] whose wisdom was, of course, well known to him (11:31); this is where he later localizes the apostles' place of instruction as well. Just as the gospel, through Paul, can encounter Greek philosophy only in Athens (Acts 17), Jesus' first discussion with the teachers of Israel should not take place in the village synagogue of Nazareth, but in the world-famous temple of the holy city, to which a religious occasion (Passover) brings him (cf. 2:1–5, 22).[34] The image is not of a classroom with a teacher, but of a learned assembly of wise men.[35] Regardless of whether Jewish rabbis ever met in such a manner, Luke employs the image of all the seated scholars, among whom Jesus is accepted with equal rank. He is not sitting like a disciple at the feet of these teachers (cf. Acts 22:3). His position is rather that of a teacher. The teachers' acceptance of him in this manner testifies to Jesus' wisdom, though this wisdom expresses itself in listening[36] and questioning.

Verse 47 allows the conjecture of an audience. This redactional verse also extends the wisdom of the child, who even knows how to answer difficult questions, which in this location are, of course, of a religious nature. Without rabbinic instruction, the child Jesus knows God's will. Behind this, and behind the apology of the "uneducated" apostles (Acts 4:13), there is a conflict with Jewish intellectuals, who derided the deficient education of Jesus, and also within the primitive community. "His understanding and his answers" is a hendiadys,[37] insofar as the understanding demonstrates itself in the answers. But with σύνεσις ("understanding") Luke intends to describe not only the answers but the person of Jesus.

Σύνεσις ("understanding") is the intellectual capacity to see connections and make judgments; it can be translated with "understanding," "judgment," "discernment," or "insight." In the LXX and especially in wisdom literature, the word frequently means the insight nourished by religious faith, often nearly synonymous with σοφία ("wisdom"). In biblical tradition, people possess this quality not in their worldly autonomy but in their union with God's will. But Hellenistic Judaism still presents itself more as a world of teaching and wisdom than as a world of revelation and prophecy, and this influences the later wisdom books in the LXX. Despite this, σύνεσις remains a religious and inspired power of insight, which is also true for Luke. Later in the Gospel, Jesus will appear as Messiah and miracle-worker. Here he is, even as a child, the model of pious wisdom.[38]

30   Against Laurentin, *Jésus au temple,* 101–2; and J. K. Elliot, "Does Luke 2:41–52 Anticipate the Resurrection?" *ExpTim* 83 (1971–72) 87–89.

31   9:22; 18:33; 24:7, 46; Acts 10:40.

32   Agreeing with de Jonge ("Sonship," 324–27), against the commentators who follow Grotius in counting one day for the return to Galilee, one day for the renewed trip to Jerusalem, and the day on which they find Jesus.

33   Acts 3:11; 5:12, 21, 25.

34   De Jonge, "Sonship," 330.

35   Luke designates the rabbis with διδασκάλων ("of the teachers") only here, and this is a hint that Luke has taken the passage from tradition.

36   In this case ἀκούω ("to listen") with the genitive of the person to whom one listens is the usual idiom. Cf. the discussion about ἀκούω with the genitive or the accusative in the accounts of Paul's conversion (Acts 9:7; 22:9).

37   BDF §442.16.

38   See Hans Conzelmann, "σύνεσις, κτλ.," *TDNT* 7 (1971) 888–96; and Horst Balz, "σύνεσις, κτλ.," *EDNT* 3 (1993) 305.

If one can speak of isotopy (semantic framework), the isotopy of knowledge controls this pericope. As often in Luke, the theme is not the antinomy of good and evil, knowledge and ignorance, but the choice between a good thing and a still higher value. At issue is the tension between Jewish wisdom, not yet enlightened, and the higher, Christian, revealed wisdom. Jesus' parents believe they know the Mosaic Law (v. 44), but exactly this is the issue (v. 49). It is still an open question whether they want to subscribe to the new thing manifested by Jesus (v. 51b) or not (v. 50). Depending on their decision, their partial knowledge can be either introductory or delusory. The stress, however, is not on this, but on Jesus' wisdom, which is first (vv. 46–47) that of the teachers, that is, knowledge of the Scriptures and past revelation, and then (in the saying, v. 49), the wisdom of a prophet, that is, knowledge of the eschatological and christological revelation.

One ancient interpretation of this passage goes in this direction. According to Irenaeus (*Adv. haer.* 1.20.2), heretics claimed that here Jesus had wanted to introduce his rather uninsightful parents to the unknown God. Origen, on the contrary, emphasized the parents' search for the son, and invited his audience to search the Scriptures and the Word with equal energy.[39] In addition, many of the church fathers remarked on the wordplay and emphasized that Jesus wishes to lead us to the true father.[40]

The Cryptic Explanation (vv. 48–49)

■ **48** Verse 48 depicts the shock[41] to the parents, quite understandable from a human point of view, and their pain. The mother, not the father, speaks, because of the Marianic perspective of the Lukan birth narrative, and because it is the author's literary purpose to make the opposition of the two fathers graphic in the dialogue.

The text indeed moves in the direction of a higher christology, but a serious acknowledgment of the incarnation forms its underpinnings. Is not Luke 1–2 also a recognition of Jesus' humanity, which is not only evident in the passion and Gethsemane? The twelve-year-old is also portrayed in his process of growing (cf. 2:40), and in his developing autonomy, which begins to assert itself (v. 43). He does not do what his parents expect; he does what they do not wish. This makes them suffer, and women, above all, can identify with Mary's question: "Child, why have you treated *us* ($\dot{\eta}\mu\hat{\iota}\nu$) like this?" Like an adolescent, Jesus does not give in. He asserts his opinion with absolute matter-of-factness. As often in generational conflicts, the parents do not understand their children at the close of the argument, and, as often in such cases, the father remains silent. In the memory of the Lukan community, Jesus appeared not only as the son of the divine Father, but also in complete humanity, as a maturing boy.

On the level of theological message, the narrative elements of this verse (v. 48) express the violent defense mechanisms of the half-initiated in the face of new perspectives from a new revelation. The residents of Nazareth react no differently, only more violently (4:16–30). The members of the congregation in Caesarea also react no differently when Paul sets himself to follow a higher standard (Acts 21:10–14). Knowledge of God is by no means only cognitive; strong feelings and impulses of emotion are pulled into the fray. Until the end of Acts, Luke will bring Jewish legal observance, which for him is incomplete knowledge, into the correct light of the final revelation (Acts 28:23–28).[42]

In the New Testament, $\tau\acute{\epsilon}\kappa\nu o\nu$ ("child," v. 48) occurs much more frequently than $\pi\alpha\hat{\iota}\varsigma$ ("boy," v. 43) in the vocative (only 8:54 contains an address that is grammatically in the nominative); the vocative $\mathring{\omega}$ $\pi\alpha\hat{\iota}$ became obsolete, and $\tau\acute{\epsilon}\kappa\nu o\nu$ still retains something of its etymological meaning ($\tau\acute{\iota}\kappa\tau\omega$, "give birth to"; cf. Gal 4:19). $T\acute{\iota}$ $\dot{\epsilon}\pi o\acute{\iota}\eta\sigma\alpha\varsigma$ $\dot{\eta}\mu\hat{\iota}\nu$ $o\ddot{\upsilon}\tau\omega\varsigma$ ("why have you treated us like

39   *Hom. in Luc.* 18.2–3; 19.4–5. See E. Peretto, "La lettura origeniana di Lc 2, 41–42," *Mar* 37 (1975) 336–57. Laurentin (*Jésus au temple*, 190) cites a further fragment, attributed to Origen (*Werke* 9 [GCS 49; Berlin: Akademie, 1959] 116.17–117.4).

40   See, e.g., the fragment of Titus of Bostra's commentary on Luke (Joseph Sickenberger, ed., *Titus von Bostra: Studien zu dessen Lukashomilien* [TU 21.1; Leipzig: Hinrichs, 1901] 152; cited by Laurentin, *Jésus au temple*, 190).

41   Jesus' parents (2:48) do not share the wonderment of the crowd. They are indignant that Jesus has left them, and are not at all impressed by their son's wisdom. The logic of the story prevents one from taking their side.

42   See the investigation of the various schemes in Jean Zumstein, "L'apôtre comme martyr dans les Actes de Luc: Essai de lecture globale," *RThPh* 112 (1980) 371–90.

this?") is a Hebrew Bible formulation.[43] It belongs "always in the context of a deception, out of which it is spoken; thus it is an expression of 'disillusionment' or 'disappointment.' In this sense, the idiom also suits perfectly the situation presupposed in Luke 2:48."[44] The postpositioned οὕτως ("like this"), which refers back to v. 43 and not to Jesus' last action (vv. 46–47), appears instead of the proleptic τοῦτο ("this"), which shows that Luke is consciously using this old formulation. Usually, "I" takes the first place in a coordinated formula ("I and Barnabas," 1 Cor 9:6).[45] Mary says here, "Your father and I." According to Augustine, Mary is following the *ordo conjugalis* (in Eph 5:23, the man is the head of the woman);[46] but Luke is rather trying to make the wordplay about the two fathers clearer (vv. 48, 49).

■ **49** Τί ὅτι ("how [is it] that," "why," v. 49) is infrequent (cf. Acts 5:4, 9)[47] and requires completion with an unexpressed verb (ἐστίν or γέγονεν, "is" or "has been"; cf. John 14:22). Luke uses ἀναζητέω ("to look for," "to search") in vv. 44 and 45,[48] because the parents are searching for their son on the way back (ἀνά); by contrast, in vv. 48–49, where they find themselves in Jerusalem, he writes the simple ζητέω. Οὐκ in a question (v. 49) anticipates a positive answer. According to the evangelist, the parents did not need to look for Jesus, for they should have known where he was staying. Ἐν τοῖς τοῦ πατρός μου δεῖ εἶναί με is an old *crux interpretum*, since various meanings are possible: (1) Since the scene takes place in the temple, one could assume a local meaning: to be "in my Father's domain," "at my Father's place";[49] (2) since τά with the genitive generally means "what belongs to one," and εἶναι ἐν means "to concern oneself with" in good Greek, one could translate, "to concern myself with my Father's business";[50] (3) since Luke values double meanings, the local antithesis (with

his heavenly, not his earthly, father) leads to the statement about Jesus' concern with that which is proper to his heavenly Father. Such an enigmatic response well suits the genre of the anecdote. The present tense of δεῖ ("must") alludes to a style of behavior that will last beyond this scene in the temple, which Jesus will soon conclude. His parents should have known of this enduring relationship with God. With this ambiguous answer,[51] Jesus gives his activity symbolic significance. His unexpected stay in the temple is a parable of the Messiah's constant activity, just as the unpretentious gesture of purification of the temple (19:45–46) also receives symbolic value.

In formal terms, the mother's double reaction (v. 48) is answered by her son with a double saying (v. 49). The construction shows both chiastic and parallel elements.[52]

In terms of content, the δεῖ ("must"),[53] so loved by Luke, describes the relationship between father and son as a salvation-historical one. Jesus' devotion to his Father corresponds to the Father's will for the Son. Their mutual relationship manifests itself in the economy of salvation, which should be considered neither purely functional nor abstractly ontological, but rather a personal *agape* relationship.

It is questionable that "my Father" possessed this broad christological connotation in the traditions, but it is improbable that every Jewish child could speak in this manner, since the addressing of God as "Abba" is part of the specific identity of the historical Jesus. But indeed, the midrashic literature demonstrates the oracular quality that Jews, pagans, and Christians liked to attribute to children's utterances.[54] Of particular interest is the addition to Exod 15:2 in the Fragment Targum: "From the breasts of [their] mothers, sucklings made signs with their fingers to their fathers and said to them: He is our

---

43   Gen 12:8; 20:9; 26:10; 29:25; Exod 14:11; Num 23:11; Judg 15:11.

44   Rudolf Pesch, "'Kind, warum hast du so an uns getan?' (Lk 2, 48)," *BZ* n.s. 12 (1968) 245–48.

45   Cf. 1 Cor 15:11; John 8:16; 10:30.

46   Augustine *Sermo* 11.18 (*PL* 38.343). See Laurentin (*Jésus au temple*, 217–18) and de Jonge ("Sonship," 330–31).

47   BDF §299.4; and Delebecque, "Note," 40–42.

48   In both occurrences the mss. alternate between the imperfect, which Nestle-Aland chooses, and the present.

49   See Laurentin, *Jésus au temple*, 68–72; idem, *Truth*,

212–13. He decides on the meaning "at my Father's place." Cf. the LXX: Job 18:19; Esth 7:9.

50   See Delebecque, "Note," 40–42.

51   See de Jonge, "Sonship," 331–37.

52   The subjects of the verbs are placed chiastically (son-parents in 2:48b, parents-son in 2:49); the two occurrences of τί that introduce the question are parallel, as are the mentions of the "father."

53   See de Jonge, "Sonship," 350–51; Jacques Dupont, "Jésus retrouvé au temple," *AsSeign* 11 (1970) 40–51, esp. 46–47.

54   One need think only of the *tolle, lege* of a child's voice, which Augustine interpreted as a command

father who gave us honey to suck out of the rock, and gave us oil from the flinty rock."[55]

The possibility of a historical memory cannot be dismissed; it is more important, however, to perceive the forces that gave rise to the transmission of such a story. First, there are the christological concerns of a community that presumed as much wisdom of its Lord as of other Jewish and pagan heroes. This competition explains the alien literary elements and thematic motifs.[56] The biblical accounts of Samuel (1 Sam [LXX 1 Kgdms] 2:18–26) and of Daniel have left their mark.[57] The second force at work is the memory of Jesus' human side. In v. 46 the child possesses no supernatural knowledge; he remains quite human throughout the course of the account. Jesus at twelve thus fits well with the christology of earliest Christianity: he is the Son of God, and a human being.

The Return to Normal Affairs (vv. 50–52)

■ **50–51** The door to the christological mystery[58] has briefly cracked open. Now Luke closes it and leaves off from the *novum*, in order to bring the family—including Jesus—back into the sphere of observant Judaism. Jesus' parents do not understand the ῥῆμα ("saying," refers probably to v. 49) and return to Nazareth. Jesus, true to the fifth commandment (Exod 20:12), remains obedient to them (the periphrastic form and the present participle emphasize duration).

Then Luke broadens his scope in the form of a summary statement. Mary retains the same attitude as twelve years before. The sentence recalls 2:19,[59] contextualized, but still a biblical formula.[60]

■ **52** The same is true of Jesus. Verse 52 seems like a refrain that the readers have already heard in 2:40, and it adapts 1 Sam (LXX 1 Kgdms) 2:26. But here the concern is less about the stage of growth (2:40) than about the stage of progress (προκόπτω, "to make progress"). But between σοφία ("wisdom") and χάρις ("favor," both in 2:40), ἡλικία ("stage in life," "bodily size")[61] is inserted. Χάρις is a term of relationship ("in divine and human favor") and should not be understood in a reified manner. God's favor and human recognition rest on the child as he develops.

Conclusion

Like a painter, Luke illustrates the miraculous wisdom of Jesus. Well versed in the Law, he is probably the wisest child in Israel—this was retold with pride. But in the striking response of the boy, the pericope contains a second pole: Jesus' will corresponds to God's new revelation and renders obsolete the lawful will of his earthly parents. This will has its legitimacy in the claim, now made explicit, of a son's relationship to his true father.

---

from heaven when he converted. See Augustine *Confessions* 8.12.

55 Translation from Paul Winter, "Luc 2:49 and Targum Yerushalmi," *ZNW* 45 (1954) 145–79, esp. 170–71.

56 Bultmann, *History*, 300–301; de Jonge, "Sonship," 339–42; Laurentin, *Jésus au temple*, 147–58.

57 According to various ancient witnesses, Daniel was twelve years old when he sat down with the elders and began to rule (according, e.g., to Harclensis, one of the Syrian translations in Brian Walton's Polyglot Bible [London: 1657] 4: *Historia Susannae, oratio Azariae cum cantico trium puerorum et historia Beli et draconis*, 8): cf. Sus 45 = Dan 13:45 (Th, Vulgate). See Dupont, "Jésus retrouvé," 45; and de Jonge, "Sonship," 323 n. 1. According to Josephus (*Ant.* 5.10.4 §348), Samuel was twelve when he began to prophesy (1 Sam [LXX 1 Kgdms] 2:26).

Finally, many LXX mss. mention that Solomon was twelve when he ascended to the throne (1 Kgs [3 Kgdms] 2:12).

58 See Laurentin, *Jésus au temple*, 84.

59 Πάντα τὰ ῥήματα ("all these words," text uncertain) goes beyond the episode at the temple and embraces the events in Luke 1 and 2. Διατηρέω ("to treasure") emphasizes keeping the memory, whereas in 2:19 συντηρέω stressed the retention of Mary's words, and συμβάλλω ("to ponder"), her interpreting them. The connotation of interpreting cannot be resumed here because, according to 2:50, neither Mary nor Joseph has comprehended Jesus' statement.

60 Cf. Gen 37:11 (*Tg. Ps.-J.* adds, "in his heart"); Dan 4:28 (LXX); 7:28 (Th); *T. Levi* 6:2.

61 See Dupont, "Jésus retrouvé," 43.

The Baptist's Ministry and the Baptism of Jesus
(Luke 3:1–22)

Bibliography

Alonso Diaz, J., "El Bautismo de fuego anunciado por el Bautista y su relación con la profecía de Malaquías," *EstBib* 23 (1964) 319–31.

Bernard, L. W., "Matt. III.11 / Luke III.16," *JTS* n.s. 8 (1957) 107.

Bertrand, *Baptême*.

idem, "*L'Évangile des Ebionites*: Une harmonie évangélique antérieure au *Diatessaron*," *NTS* 26 (1979–80) 548–63.

Best, Ernest, "Spirit-Baptism," *NovT* 4 (1960) 236–43.

Betz, Otto, "Die Proselytentaufe der Qumransekte und die Taufe im Neuen Testament," *RevQ* 1 (1958–59) 213–34.

Braun, Herbert, "Entscheidende Motive in den Berichten über die Taufe Jesu von Markus bis Justin," *ZThK* 50 (1953) 39–43.

Brown, S., "'Water-Baptism' and 'Spirit-Baptism' in Luke-Acts," *ATR* 59 (1977) 135–51.

Collins, R. F., "Luke 3:21–22: Baptism or Anointing," *TBT* 84 (1976) 821–31.

Conzelmann, *Theology*, 18–27.

Cronin, Hume S., "Abilene, the Jewish Herods and St Luke," *JTS* 18 (1917) 147–51.

de la Potterie, Ignace, "L'onction du Christ: Étude de théologie biblique," *NRTh* 80 (1958) 225–52.

Dennison, Charles G., "How Is Jesus the Son of God? Luke's Baptism Narrative and Christology," *Calvin Theological Journal* 17 (1982) 6–25.

Dieckmann, Hermann, "Das fünfzehnte Jahr des Caesar Tiberius," *Bib* 6 (1925) 63–67.

idem, "Das fünfzehnte Jahr des Tiberius (Lk 3,1)," *BZ* 16 (1922–24) 54–65.

Dunn, James D. G., *Baptism in the Holy Spirit: A Reexamination of the New Testament Teaching on the Gift of the Spirit in Relation to Pentecostalism Today* (SBT 2.15; Philadelphia: Westminster, 1970).

idem, *Jesus and the Spirit: A Study of the Religious and Charismatic Experience of Jesus and the first Christians as Reflected in the New Testament* (NTL; Philadelphia: Westminster, 1975).

idem, "Spirit-and-Fire Baptism," *NovT* 14 (1972) 81–92.

Feuillet, A., "Le baptême de Jésus," *RB* 71 (1964) 321–52.

idem, "Le symbolisme de la colombe dans les récits évangéliques du Baptême," *RechSR* 46 (1958) 524–44.

Fleddermann, Harry, "John and the Coming One (Matt 3:11–12 par. Luke 3:16–17)," in K. L. Richards, ed., SBLSP 23 (Chico, Calif.: Scholars Press, 1984), 377–84.

Garnet, Paul, "The Baptism of Jesus and the Son of Man Idea," *JSNT* 9 (1980) 49–65.

George, Augustin, "La venue du Seigneur," *AsSeign* 6 (1969) 70–79.

Gero, Stephen, "The Spirit as a Dove at the Baptism of Jesus," *NovT* 18 (1976) 16–35.

Geyser, A. S., "The Youth of John the Baptist: A Deduction from the Break in the Parallel Account of the Lucan Infancy Story," *NovT* 1 (1956) 70–75.

Glasson, T. Francis, "Water, Wind and Fire (Luke III.16) and Orphic Initiation," *NTS* 3 (1956–57) 69–71.

Gnilka, Joachim, "Die essenischen Tauchbäder und die Johannestaufe," *RevQ* 3 (1961–62) 185–207.

Goguel, Maurice, *Au seuil de l'évangile, Jean-Baptiste* (Paris: Payot, 1928).

Grant, Robert M., "The Occasion of Luke 3:1–2," *HTR* 33 (1940) 151–54.

Hoffmann, *Logienquelle*, 15–33.

Jacquemin, Paul-Edmond, "Le baptême du Christ," *AsSeign* 17 (1969) 48–66.

Jeremias, Joachim, "Der Ursprung der Johannestaufe," *ZNW* 28 (1929) 312–20.

Kazmierski, Carl R., "The Stones of Abraham: John the Baptist and the End of Torah (Matt 3:1–10 par. Luke 3:7–9)," *Bib* 68 (1987) 22–40.

Keck, Leander E., "The Spirit and the Dove," *NTS* 17 (1970–71) 41–67.

Kinman, Brent, "Luke's Exoneration of John the Baptist," *JTS* 44 (1993) 595–98.

Lentzen-Deis, Fritzleo, "The Gospel Between Myth and Historicity—as Demonstrated in the Accounts about the Baptism of Jesus," *Tantur Yearbook* (1980–81) 165–86.

idem, *Taufe*.

Rius-Camps, Josep, "¿Constituye Lc 3,21–38 un solo periodo? Propuesta de un cambio de puntuación," *Bib* 65 (1984) 189–209.

Robinson, John A. T., "The Baptism of John and the Qumran Community," *HTR* 50 (1957) 175–91, reprinted in idem, *Twelve New Testament Studies* (SBT 1.34; London: SCM, 1962) 11–27.

Sabbe, M., "Le baptême de Jésus: Étude sur les origines littéraires du récit des Évangiles synoptiques," in I. de la Potterie, ed., *De Jésus aux Évangiles: Tradition et Rédaction dans les Évangiles synoptiques* (BETL 25; Gembloux/Paris: Duculot, 1967) 184–211.

Sahlin, Harald, "Die Früchte der Umkehr: Die ethische Verkündigung Johannes des Taufers nach Lk 3,10–14," *StTh* 1 (1948) 54–68.

idem, *Studien zum dritten Kapitel des Lukasevangeliums* (UUÅ 2; Uppsala: Lundequistska bokhandeln, 1949).

Samain, Étienne, "La notion de ἀρχή dans l'œuvre lucanienne," in Neirynck, *Évangile*, 299–328.

Schottroff, Willy, "Die Ituräer," *ZDPV* 98 (1982) 125–52.

Schramm, *Markus-Stoff*, 34–36.

Schulz, *Q*, 366–78.

Schwarz, Günther, "τὸ δὲ ἄχυρον κατακαύσει," *ZNW* 72 (1981) 264–71.

Thompson, G. H. P., "Called—Proved—Obedient: A Study in the Baptism and Temptation Narratives of Matthew and Luke," *JTS* n.s. 11 (1960) 1–12.

Thyen, Hartwig, "Βάπτισμα μετανοίας εἰς ἄφεσιν ἁμαρτιῶν," in Dinkler, *Zeit und Geschichte*, 97–125.

Trilling, W., "Le message de Jean-Baptiste," *AsSeign* 7 (1969) 65–73.

Uprichard, R. E. H., "The Baptism of Jesus," *IBS* 3 (1981) 187–202.

Vögtle, Anton, *Die sogenannte Taufperikope Mk 1,9–11: Zur Problematik der Herkunft und des ursprünglichen Sinns* (EKKNTV 4; Zurich: Benziger, 1972) 105–39, revised and reprinted in idem, *Offenbarungsgeschehen und Wirkungsgeschichte: Neutestamentliche Beiträge* (Freiburg im Breisgau: Herder, 1985) 70–108.

von Baer, Heinrich, *Der Heilige Geist in den Lukasschriften* (Stuttgart: Kohlhammer, 1926).

Voss, *Christologie*, 83–94.

Williams, G. O., "The Baptism in Luke's Gospel," *JTS* 45 (1944) 31–38.

Wink, *John*, 42–58.

1 In the fifteenth year of the reign of Emperor Tiberius, when Pontius Pilate was governor of Judea and Herod was tetrarch of Galilee, and his brother Philip tetrarch of the region of Ituraea and Trachonitis, and Lysanias tetrarch of Abilene, **2/** during the high priesthood of Annas and Caiaphas, the word of God came to John son of Zechariah in the wilderness. **3/** And he went into all the region around the Jordan, proclaiming a baptism of repentance for the forgiveness of sins, **4/** as it is written in the book of the words of the prophet Isaiah, "The voice of one crying out in the wilderness: Prepare the way of the Lord, make his paths straight. **5/** Every valley shall be filled, and every mountain and hill shall be made low, and the crooked shall be made straight, and the rough ways made smooth; **6/** and all flesh shall see the salvation of God."

7 John said to the crowds that came out to be baptized by him, "You brood of vipers! Who warned you to flee from the wrath to come? **8/** Bear fruits worthy of repentance. And do not begin to say to yourselves, 'We have Abraham as our father'; for I tell you, God is able from these stones to raise up children to Abraham. **9/** Even now the ax is lying at the root of the trees; every tree therefore that does not bear good fruit is cut down and thrown into the fire."

10 And the crowds asked him, "What then should we do?" **11/** He answered and said to them, "Whoever has two coats must share with anyone who has none; and whoever has food must do likewise." **12/** Even tax collectors came to be baptized, and they asked him, "Teacher, what should we do?" **13/** And he said to them, "Collect no more than the amount prescribed for you." **14/** Soldiers also asked him and said, "And we, what should we do?" And he said to them, "Do not extort money from anyone by threats or false accusation, and be satisfied with your wages."

15 As the people were filled with expectation, and all were questioning in their hearts concerning John, whether he might be the Messiah, **16/** John answered and said to all, "I baptize you with water; but one who is more powerful than I is coming; I am not worthy even to untie the thong of his sandals. He will baptize you with holy spirit and fire. **17/** His winnowing fork is in his hand, to clear his threshing floor and to gather the wheat into his granary, but the chaff he will burn with unquenchable fire." **18/** So, with many other exhortations, he proclaimed the good news to the people.

19 But Herod the tetrarch, who had been rebuked by him because of Herodias, his brother's wife, and because of all the evil things that Herod had done, **20/** added to them all by shutting up John in prison.

21 Now it happened that, when all the people were being baptized, and when Jesus also had been baptized and was praying, the heaven opened, **22/** and holy spirit descended on him in bodily form like a dove, and a voice came from heaven, "You are my beloved Son; with you I am well pleased."

Analysis

Luke indicates the beginning of a new section stylistically with a comprehensive synchronism. By the call of God to John, and by the prophet's activity, initiated by God, a salvation-historical event is introduced. A scriptural proof text forms the conclusion (3:4–6).

The three paragraphs containing the typical content of John's preaching (3:7–9, 10–14, 15–17) are further expanded in a sort of summary (v. 18). The people addressed are "the crowds" (ὄχλοι, vv. 7, 10) and "the people" (λαός, vv. 15, 18)—these are probably synonymous—and thus neither, as in Mark, Judea and the Jerusalemites nor, as in Matthew, the Pharisees and Sadducees.

In the terse style of a historian, Luke reports the arrest of John (vv. 19–20)[1] and the (temporally earlier) baptism of Jesus (vv. 21–22). Ἐγένετο δέ ("now it happened that," v. 21) suggests a transition: the main concern shifts from John to Jesus, whose genealogy (vv. 23–38), "installation" (4:1–13), and first public activities (4:14–30) follow.

The abbreviated report about the Baptist's life and preaching pick up the thread of John's birth narrative (esp. 1:80), leaping over chap. 2. The reports about Jesus that follow serve as a literary counterweight to Luke 3. Thus both Luke 1–2 and 3–4 are dominated by a correspondence between these two figures—definitely weighted in Jesus' favor.

Luke has separated Jesus' words to, and about, John (7:18–35) from this section, and has transferred them into the narrative about Jesus' ministry. In addition, there are allusions to John in Acts.[2]

In terms of genre, Luke 3 belongs to historiography, with the peculiarity that the author places the words of the principal figure before the description of the events of his life; this is related to Hebrew Bible or Jewish historiography, with its divine intervention through the mouth of a prophet. The closest parallels are the beginnings of the prophetic books (esp. Hag 1:1) and Josephus, or Pseudo-Philo's *Biblical Antiquities*. Scriptural citations are not alien to the rest of Jewish historiography.[3] The brevity of the report about John should not be surprising. In Judges, as well in the accounts influenced by it in Josephus and Pseudo-Philo, a report about a prophet, judge, or king often does not exceed two pages, and only one or two characteristic events or typical utterances are selected from their lives.

Whence does the author derive this information? Many have solved the problem of the relationship between tradition and redaction by means of the hypothesis of Markan priority, since from this point Luke has a sequence of events similar to Mark (Baptist–baptism–temptation, etc.). Peculiarities not found in

Mark could be explained as the result of Luke's compositional technique. According to Hans Conzelmann, John still belongs among the prophets, and thus to the Hebrew Bible, since, in Luke, he has nothing to do with Judea or Galilee, the sites of Jesus' activity. To my mind, John is a figure on the threshold, both prophet and precursor. Since one also finds similar materials in Matthew, the present account probably has its basis in the tradition of the sayings source (Q). On the whole, this is true of the greater part of vv. 1–18,[4] that is, for the preaching of John. Whether John's preaching to the socioeconomic classes (vv. 10–14), which has no Matthean parallel, derives from a special source, or is a Lukan composition, remains unknown. Verses 19–20 (the arrest) are a literary excerpt from Mark 6:17–18 (Justin will summarize Mark 6 in a stylistically similar fashion).[5] The Lukan account of Jesus' baptism is very close to Mark. A minor agreement could point in the direction of a Q account: the verb ἀνοίγω ("to open," 3:21 par.). But since Luke follows Mark in v. 22 (σὺ εἶ, "you are"), dependence on Q is uncertain.

Similarities in structure and content between Luke and Matthew, however, support Q as the source for vv. 1–9 and 15–18: (1) In contrast to Mark (Luke 3:2–6 par.), the description of the event precedes the citation. (2) In Luke 3:4 par., only Isa 40:3 is cited (Mal 3:1 occurs later in Q, at Luke 7:27 par.). (3) Only Luke and Matthew recount the Baptist's preaching of repentance (Luke 3:7–9 par.). (4) Differently than in Mark, the saying about baptism with fire and water is interwoven with the saying about the one who is mightier (with fire appearing in apposition to spirit, a reading peculiar to Q, v. 16). (5) Luke 3:17–18 par. have no parallel in Mark.[6]

This does not mean that Luke completely ignores Mark. From Mark's volume—which Luke, as an educated historian, probably had lying open on his desk—he derived his summary of John's activity ("proclaiming a baptism of repentance for the forgiveness of sins," v. 3b), which seemed illuminating to him, since it stressed

1 Bossuyt-Radermakers (134) view Luke 3:1–20 as a unit and see the two mentions of Herod, in 3:1–2 and 3:19–20 as the brackets that enclose it.
2 Acts 1:5–22; 10:37; 11:16; 13:24–25; 19:3–4.
3 1 Macc 4:24; 7:17; 9:21, 41; 2 Macc 7:6.
4 Luke is probably following Q up to 4:15, and perhaps even as far as 4:30.
5 Justin *Dial.* 49.4–5.

6 Even the words πᾶσα ἡ περίχωρος τοῦ Ἰορδάνου (3:3a: "all the region around the Jordan"; cf. the parallel passage in Matt 3:5b; the expression already occurs in the LXX, Gen 13:10) might go back to Q. In Luke's redaction, these words are employed to describe a change of location on the part of *John*; in the Q tradition (cf. Matt 3:5b), they describe the movement of the *crowds* toward John.

John's preaching, not the ritual of baptism. What did Q have here, if Matt 3:2 (the call to repentance and nearness of kingdom of God) is redactional?[7]

Since Luke does not like to intertwine his various sources and would rather follow first one narrative sequence (here, until v. 18, Q), and then, from v. 19 onward, take up another (Mark), the description of John's costume and ascetic diet are lacking.

The extensive synchronism is clearly redactional, if not without its literary models. At this point, Luke opens the book of Isaiah (or of the Prophets). As in Q, he allows the word $\alpha\dot{\nu}\tau o\hat{\nu}$ ("his"; in the LXX, $\tau o\hat{\nu}\ \vartheta\epsilon o\hat{\nu}\ \dot{\eta}\mu\hat{\omega}\nu$, "of our God") to remain at the end of v. 4. But Luke is particularly interested in Isa 40:5 ("and all flesh shall see the salvation of God"—the word "salvation" is found only in the LXX).[8] Only then does he break off the citation. The reason for which Luke omits the words $\kappa\alpha\dot{\iota}\ \dot{o}\varphi\vartheta\dot{\eta}\sigma\epsilon\tau\alpha\iota\ \dot{\eta}\ \delta\dot{o}\xi\alpha\ \kappa\nu\rho\dot{\iota}o\nu$ ("and the glory of the Lord shall be revealed") from Isa 40:5 is a riddle (a few versions inserted the phrase later).[9]

On the basis of the language and a comparison with Matthew, it seems that v. 7a and the thrice-repeated "What should we do?" ($\tau\dot{\iota}\ \pi o\iota\dot{\eta}\sigma\omega\mu\epsilon\nu$), including their introductions (vv. 10, 12, 14a), are redactional. The participle $\sigma\tau\rho\alpha\tau\epsilon\nu\dot{o}\mu\epsilon\nu o\iota$ ("[those who are] soldiers") is noteworthy, because the command (v. 14b) could also be applied to other occupations.

In the introduction (v. 15) of the double saying (v. 16), the vocabulary and construction are typically Lukan,[10] although the content of the question is non-Lukan. As especially in the passion narrative, a tradition related to John the evangelist is evident here. John 1:24–27 also links a question about the messianic or prophetic identity of John the Baptist with the sayings about baptism and the one who is mightier (both extensively reworked

by John). It was in this tradition also known to John that Luke found the content of the question that serves as the introduction for the two Q sayings appearing after vv. 10–14.

The summary of v. 18 (generalizations in the imperfect) is, as always, redactional. Every word was written by Luke.[11]

Thus Luke precedes Jesus' activity with a fairly extensive section about his precursor. He uses the source Q in particular, but also draws from Mark, and knows still other traditions. All of these traditions have resulted from a long process of organizing still older materials. Above all, the passage contains sayings of the Baptist, information about his practices and arrest, and interpretation of his prophetic activity (with help from the Scriptures) and his person (in connection with the person of Jesus). It has its roots in the most ancient Christian kerygma (cf. Acts 10:37–38). Individual sayings could be attributed to the historical John, in which he probably spoke only of the fire of judgment, not of the fire of the Spirit, and meant God rather than the Messiah when he spoke of the one who is mightier.

Commentary

The Entrance of John (vv. 1–6)

■ **1–2** True to Hebrew Bible dating,[12] Luke now designates a time about a generation later than the first chronological indication in 1:5. The political situation has changed: a Roman governor rules Judea. Salvation-historical events belong even in a time of foreign rulers in Israel. Luke is well informed about these and familiar with official language, for $\dot{\eta}\gamma\epsilon\mu o\nu\epsilon\dot{\nu}\omega$ ("to govern") is customarily used of a Roman governor, especially of a *praefectus*, which is what Pontius Pilate was. The partici-

---

7 With Siegfried Schulz (*Q: Die Spruchquelle der Evangelisten* [Zurich: Theologischer Verlag, 1972] 368), I also assume that the words, "but one who is more powerful than I is coming" (Luke 3:16b), are drawn from Mark, whereas the parallel in Matt 3:11b reflects Q.

8 See Martin Rese, *Alttestamentliche Motive in der Christologie des Lukas* (Gütersloh: Mohn, 1969) 170.

9 Luke's text of the LXX is closely related to Codex Alexandrinus; cf. $\epsilon\dot{\iota}\varsigma\ \dot{o}\delta o\dot{\nu}\varsigma\ \lambda\epsilon\dot{\iota}\alpha\varsigma$ ("into smooth ways," v. 5). See Traugott Holtz, *Untersuchungen über die alttestamentliche Zitate bei Lukas* (TU 104; Berlin: Akademie, 1968) 39.

10 $\Pi\rho o\sigma\delta o\kappa\dot{\alpha}\omega$, $\lambda\alpha\dot{o}\varsigma$, $\delta\iota\alpha\lambda o\gamma\iota\zeta o\mu\dot{\epsilon}\nu\omega\nu\ \pi\dot{\alpha}\nu\tau\omega\nu\ \dot{\epsilon}\nu\ \tau\alpha\hat{\iota}\varsigma\ \kappa\alpha\rho\delta\dot{\iota}\alpha\iota\varsigma\ \alpha\dot{\nu}\tau\hat{\omega}\nu$ are all Lukan. See Schulz, *Q*, 368 nn. 300–301.

11 $\lambda\alpha\dot{o}\varsigma$, $\epsilon\dot{\nu}\alpha\gamma\gamma\epsilon\lambda\dot{\iota}\zeta o\mu\alpha\iota$; cf. $\dot{\epsilon}\tau\epsilon\rho\alpha\ \pi o\lambda\lambda\dot{\alpha}\ \beta\lambda\alpha\sigma\varphi\eta\mu o\hat{\nu}\nu\tau\epsilon\varsigma$ (Luke 22:65); $\pi\alpha\rho\alpha\kappa\alpha\lambda\dot{\epsilon}\sigma\alpha\varsigma\ \alpha\dot{\nu}\tau o\dot{\nu}\varsigma\ \lambda\dot{o}\gamma\omega\ \pi o\lambda\lambda\hat{\omega}$ (Acts 20:2); $\pi o\lambda\lambda\dot{\alpha}\ \kappa\alpha\dot{\iota}\ \beta\alpha\rho\dot{\epsilon}\alpha\ \alpha\dot{\iota}\tau\iota\dot{\omega}\mu\alpha\tau\alpha\ \kappa\alpha\tau\alpha\varphi\dot{\epsilon}\rho o\nu\tau\epsilon\varsigma$ (Acts 25:7).

12 Cf. Jer 1:2–3.

ple indicating the title "procurator" (Codex D: $\epsilon\pi\iota\tau\rho\sigma\pi\epsilon\upsilon\omega$) was only inserted later. In his will Herod had divided the extent of his kingdom among three sons: Archelaus, Herod Antipas, and Philip.[13] At the request of Jewish and Samaritan delegations, the Romans deposed Archelaus in 6 CE and installed a Roman *praefectus*. With Pontius Pilate in place of Archelaus, and Herod Antipas and Philip in addition, the entire realm of Herod the Great is circumscribed. Samaria, which otherwise concerns Luke, is not listed, because time rather than space is under consideration here; "Judea" can also mean the entire province including Samaria and Idumea, just as "Galilee" also includes regions like Perea.

Augustus recognized Herod's will, but Archelaus received from him not the anticipated title of king, but rather that of ethnarch, and Antipas and Philip that of tetrarch (originally a regent over a quarter of a region, "later, when the orig. sense was wholly lost, . . . title of a petty dependent prince, whose rank and authority were lower than those of a king."[14]). Perhaps Luke did not understand this, imagining a fourfold division and accordingly adding Lysanias, tetrarch of Abilene. But it is also possible that, by this, he intends to draw attention to the Gentile world, or has a particular interest in this region. Since Abilene was originally part of the Ituraean realm, and Caligula gave it, along with Philip's tetrarchy and the title of king, to Herod Agrippa I in 37 CE, Abilene may once have been part of Herod's united kingdom, and thus for Luke a Jewish region. At the time he wrote, it indeed still belonged to the Jewish king Agrippa II (53–100 CE). This all remains hypothetical; nothing certain can be found about Lysanias.

At any rate, the rulers of Israel can exercise their power only under the aegis of the emperor Tiberius; accordingly Luke begins the synchronism with his year of office. Since the exile, prophetic and apocalyptic writings—though surely not without certain qualms—had to reckon with foreign rulers, too, and not only for their dates. Here, as in 2:1, Luke seems to accept Roman rule, without hesitation, as the given framework of divine intervention. It is not known from what point Luke is reckoning—probably from the death of Augustus (14 CE), in which case the calling of John would have occurred in 28/29 CE.[15]

After the political rulers, Luke names two high priests. Annas occupied the office 6–15 CE, and Caiaphas, his stepson, 18–36 CE. Does Luke intend to indicate a fairly long period? When compared with the "political" section of the synchronism, this seems unlikely. If he had meant two high priests officiating at the same time, one would expect the plural $\dot{\alpha}\rho\chi\iota\epsilon\rho\dot{\epsilon}\omega\nu$ ("in the high priesthoods"). The only clear point is that Luke, like John the evangelist, connects Annas and Caiaphas with the story of Jesus, and considers both to be high priest.[16] Since other New Testament writings, as well as Josephus, often speak of the high priests in the plural, this probably describes the college of the highest religious authorities, in particular the officiating high priest and—so far as they are still living—his precursors.[17]

On a literary level, the synchronism first introduces a new section; but in a historical opus, it also introduces a new stage of the account. These elementary observations can be developed in two directions. On the one hand, through their relation to the great men of this world, the events of the Gospel are pulled out of the shadows: "for this was not done in a corner" (Acts 26:26). Through the synchronism, as well as through Luke's entire two volumes, Synoptic tradition experiences upward mobility: folk tradition is raised to the level of literature, reaches a higher standard, and is thereby confirmed.[18] But on the other hand, with the synchronism, Luke places himself in the train of prophetic literature. He structures the traditions about John into an account of prophetic calling, similar to the beginning of a prophetic book.

---

13 See Bo Reicke, *The New Testament Era* (trans. D. E. Green; Philadelphia: Fortress Press, 1968) 110–15.

14 BAGD, s.v. $\tau\epsilon\tau\rho\dot{\alpha}\rho\chi\eta\varsigma$.

15 For the debate over this date, as well as over the entire synchronism, in the 19th century (at the time of life-of-Jesus research)—by both critics and apologists—see Zahn, 175–88; and, more recently, Harald W. Hoehner, *Herod Antipas* (SNTSMS 17; Cambridge: Cambridge University Press, 1972) 307–12.

16 Acts 4:6; John 11:49; 18:13, 19.

17 See Albert Vanhoye, *Old Testament Priests and the New Priest According to the New Testament* (trans. B. Orchard; Petersham, Mass.: St. Bede's, 1986) 8.

18 Cf. the solemn introduction that was placed at the beginning of the martyrdom of Philip, when this part was separated from the context of the complete *Acts of Philip* (§§107–8).

■ **3** For this reason, the chronology is not followed by a sentence about the Baptist's activity, as in Matthew and Mark, but by God's intervention: "the word of God came to John." Through this, God's action reaches into the course of time. Is this as dangerous as Hans Conzelmann alleges? There are prophetic and apocalyptic precedents, and God's intervention occurs through the word. Luke is not claiming that God is directly effecting historical occurrences that would have in them salvific significance. His word indeed has consequences, both in private and public history. But these events are not filled with God's power or brilliance. If God speaks, it is through a messenger—here, John. What distinguishes him from other people as a concrete and historical figure does not have a visible or tangible quality. He walks through the country (v. 3a) like any other person. What is new, what God is bringing among people, is his message (v. 3b). It is neither an occupation of the earthly by the divine, nor a mere language event without historical consequences. God's word effects salvation history when people hear it, love it, and obey it.

Whether for theological reasons or literary requirements,[19] Luke, who seems here to follow Q, does not have "wilderness" and "Jordan" in the same sentence, as does Mark. The wilderness is the place of calling; the area around the Jordan, that of proclamation. The second expression is from the Hebrew Bible[20] and alludes to the region of Sodom and Gomorrah, ancestral home of sin, which is indeed connected to the sinful Dead Sea, according to Jewish tradition. Does Luke have Lot and Abraham in mind in separating John and Jesus? In the case of John, he develops the figure of the itinerant preacher (from Q; cf. Matt 3:1). Like Mark, he knows that people came out to John (ἐκπορευομένοις, "[those] that came out," v. 7).

The compact summary of John's message[21] is taken verbatim from Mark. But it receives a Lukan interpretation: the Baptist's water baptism seals a personal decision to accept that one's entire past life is under God's judgment, and to wait solely for his forgiveness.[22] The unique eschatological event is no longer the primary issue; the personal responsibility of the individual is underscored. This step leads to the construction of a new reality in thought, faith, and practice.

■ **4–6** The Scripture citation serves as proof text: the Baptist's preaching, later integrated by the Christians into their beliefs, was a genuine response to divine calling. John was the voice that cried in the wilderness. Luke has to put up with a slight tension:[23] when John is "crying," he is actually no longer located in the wilderness, but in the Jordan Valley. Perhaps Luke knows that the wilderness reaches almost to the Jordan. Luke separates the wilderness from the Jordan because, in his opinion, this latter luxuriant region is symbolically connected with sin.

The citation, however, does not refer only to the preaching of repentance and water baptism, but also to active anticipation of the Lord. The Essenes had already adopted Isa 40:3 for their purposes,[24] and now so do the Christians (Q, Mark), probably following the historical Baptist. Of course, for them, and especially for Luke, ὁ κύριος ("the Lord") indicates Jesus (for Isaiah, Qumran, and the Baptist, it still meant God); for this reason, τοῦ θεοῦ ἡμῶν ("of our God") is corrected to αὐτοῦ ("his [paths]") in Q and Mark.

The apocalyptic images, particularly the leveling of the path (v. 4), at which current attitudes toward the created world would take offense, convey prophetic proclamation. John prepares the people for Jesus the Messiah; they decorate and fix up the streets on which a prince or

19 See Conzelmann, *Theology*, 18–21; and the criticism of Conzelmann in Wink, *John*, 49–50.

20 Cf. Gen 13:10–11; 2 Chr 4:17.

21 Heralds (κῆρυξ, singular) perform an official function in Greece. They are subordinate to an authority, communicate a public message, and require attention from their audiences. The vocabulary of proclamation so prevalent in the NT appears already in the LXX: Gen 41:43; Dan 3:4; Sir 20:15. See Hermann Cremer, *Biblico-Theological Lexicon of New Testament Greek* (trans. W. Urwick; 4th ed.; New York: Scribner's, 1895) 355–56. It is true that one encounters the word κήρυγμα ("proclamation")

only once in Luke's two volumes (Luke 11:32, taken from Q), but the verb κηρύσσω ("to proclaim") occurs frequently (nine times in the Gospel, eight times in Acts). The proclamation of the witness—Jesus, or, as here, John the Baptist—is described with it. It comes close to the word "evangelize"; see Fitzmyer, 1.147.

22 On the forgiveness of sins see Fitzmyer, 1.459–60; and Herbert Leroy, "ἀφίημι, κτλ.," *EDNT* 1 (1990) 181–83.

23 See Conzelmann, *Theology*, 20.

24 Cf. 1QS 8.12–16.

king must walk when entering a city. The Lord's arrival (v. 4) affects not only Israel but all people. It brings them their salvation. To "see" something is, in Semitic idiom, the same as "having part in it."

The Preaching of Repentance (vv. 7–9)

■ **7** At v. 7 Luke returns to the Baptist's preaching (v. 3). In contrast to Mark, Luke is interested in John—as earlier in Q—more as a preacher than as a baptist. The form is that of the prophetic warning and prediction of judgment.[25] Against Siegfried Schulz, I do not view vv. 7–9 and 15–17 as a form-critical unit; likewise it does not seem apt to characterize vv. 7–9 as apothegms. The reaction of those addressed is not expressed in direct speech, but embedded in the Baptist's speech;[26] thus there is no dialogue. The verses are rather a chain of sayings with a brief introduction, which Luke has adopted from Q.[27] The crowd is addressed, and, later, the people (in contrast to Matthew). According to Luke, John, just like Jesus,[28] directs himself to the people of Israel, who have come out to him from city and country.

Luke considers these words to be a historical expression of the Baptist; he knows that, despite John's preaching and Jesus' message, the majority of the "crowd" of Israel did not bear the fruits of repentance. John's words of warning have become, by Luke's time, a sentence passed: the "wrath" is now inevitable,[29] and others, the Gentiles, are taking the place of the children of Abraham. The unrepentant children have become like unfruitful trees for Luke. No matter whether the judgment of Israel has already been fulfilled in the evangelist's opinion (e.g., with the fall of Jerusalem in 70 CE), or whether it is still pending, it is at least clear that Luke recognizes in the Baptist's preaching past warning and present judgment together, and, to this extent, prophecy fulfilled. This does not mean that Luke rejoices over it and legitimates the triumph of Gentile Christianity by gloating over others' misfortunes. It is possible that he transmits these words precisely to warn his addressees against "false security," and to protect them from a similar fate. The concepts "to flee from the wrath," and "fruits worthy of repentance" (the plural is Lukan, as Matt 3:8 shows) are part of Christian parenesis and missionary rhetoric.[30] The traditional words of John are thus not only understood historically, but were also made relevant for the community (in part already in Q).

The variety of means of expression is remarkable. A polemical address turns against Israel an imprecation otherwise used by Jews to describe the Gentiles, "brood of vipers"; then comes a rhetorical question in the style of the prophets.[31] John here assumes that the crowd has been seduced by false wisdom.

■ **8** The imperative that requires contrition juxtaposes the positive consequences ("fruits") of repentance with this seduction. The statement introduced by λέγω γὰρ ὑμῖν ("for I tell you"), a confession of God's creative and redemptive (ἐγεῖραι, "to raise up") power (δύναται, "[God] is able"), forestalls the anticipated objection ("We have Abraham as our father"). This is not far from the concept of election. But if it is true here that the children no longer enter into the posterity of Abraham through the flesh, neither does this take place by God's free choice, as in Paul, but rather through the responsible decision of the individual. Of course, the repentance now made available to all (Acts 11:18, "Then God has given even to the Gentiles the repentance that leads to life") is a response to the loving initiative of God, who is here, as in Acts 11:18, the subject. Far removed from

---

25   For Ernst Lohmeyer, "The words of the Baptist are a chain of proverbs, according to the genre of OT prophetic speech" (*Das Evangelium des Matthäus: Nachgelassene Ausarbeitungen und Entwürfe* [ed. W. Schmauch; KEKSup; Göttingen: Vandenhoeck & Ruprecht, 1967] 37). In particular, Matt 3:8–9 par. Luke 3:8 is a controversy speech, in his opinion.

26   See Schulz, *Q*, 366–69. Μὴ ἄρξησθε ("do not begin," Luke 3:8) is redactional, but compared with the μὴ δόξητε from the tradition ("do not presume," Matt 3:9), this is only a case of stylistic alteration.

27   See Schulz, *Q*, 367. He presents five arguments that support the thesis that these verses are a late composition from within the Hellenistic Christian Q community (*Q*, 371–72).

28   See Conzelmann, *Theology*, 20–21.

29   Just like the Christians, many Jews in those days believed that they could escape the wrath of God. See Schulz, *Q*, 374 n. 336.

30   See Acts 26:20: ἄξια τῆς μετανοίας ἔργα πράσσοντες ("do deeds consistent with . . . repentance") near τοῦ λαβεῖν αὐτοὺς ἄφεσιν ἁμαρτιῶν ("that they may receive forgiveness of sins") in v. 18.

31   Ὑποδείκνυμι occurs in Jewish wisdom literature with the meaning, "to prove," "to substantiate"; see Schulz, *Q*, 373.

every discussion of synergy, Luke can only understand salvation as a relational association, in which, as in human love, the mutual participation of both partners is necessary. Hearts hard as stone must first become flesh, that is, become living (Ezek 36:26; this is why we have the verb ἐγεῖραι in v. 8).[32]

But does the image of stones derive from Ezekiel, or from an Aramaic play on words between "stones" (אַבְנַיָּא) and "sons" (בְּנַיָּא), or from an allusion to Isa 51:1–2?[33] Joachim Jeremias understands ἐγείρω ἔκ τινος ("to raise up out of someone") as a Semitism: "Thus a striking figure is intentionally used: God can give stones the power to bring forth men. The strange image of stones which bring forth men is based on Is. 51:1–2, where Abraham is compared with a rock, and his descendants with stones hewn out of the rock."[34] But at least for Luke, the stones (λίθος means "stone," not "cliff, crag") are not the mothers of Abraham's future children but the Gentiles themselves, who can receive a new life, a resurrection (ἐγείρω ἐκ τῶν νεκρῶν, "to raise from the dead") through μετάνοια ("repentance"). To "raise up from these stones" (ἐκ τῶν λίθων τούτων ἐγεῖραι) can mean either that God will make "these stones" alive and create children for Abraham—the context would support this; or it can mean that God will select a few of these stones and bring them to life—the idiom itself would support this. Already in prophetic and apocalyptic writings, humans are compared with lifeless (not worthless) stones. In the Hebrew Bible, stones are positively valued in connection with the Jerusalem temple, but negatively in connection with Gentile sanctuaries. In the spiritualization of the cult common at the time, the stones become an image of humans: positively in Zech 9:16. In Luke 3:9 the stones are probably an image of the Gentiles in the negative sense. An allusion to Isa 51:1–2 is, at least on the redactional level, unlikely.[35]

■ **9** A prediction of judgment in the form of a simile (v. 9) constitutes the conclusion. "Even now" (ἤδη) the judgment dramatically draws near, the wrath of v. 7. The ax[36] is already laid at the root of the fruitless trees; its cutting into the trees should be expected. Deut 19:5 gives insight into the work of a lumberjack. Ps 74(LXX 73):6 uses the image of the ax for the work of the enemies, Jer 46:22 for the punishment of Egypt by the Assyrians (always ἀξίνη). The connection of tree and fruit is common in Jewish parenesis; Jesus and the Christians will adopt it.[37] Verse 9b par. might be a Christian gloss added to the traditional statement of the Baptist (v. 9a par.). Only in Matt 7:19 is a similar saying of Jesus transmitted, which saying, however, itself presumably developed out of the Baptist's sayings in the Q tradition (Matt 3:10 par. Luke 3:9). The responsibility of the trees is important; their essence is read from their fruits (cf. 6:43–44).

For Luke the ἤδη ("even now") is probably already in the past: the "ax" of the Romans, and with it, the "fire" of judgment (not of hell), has felled the "trees" of Jerusalem. But do not ax and fire threaten every community and all believers who bear no fruit?

The Preaching of the Baptist to the Estates (vv. 10–14)

After the variety of means of expression in vv. 3–9, the regular structure of questions and answers in Luke's special section is striking; and timeless ethical instruction follows upon the apocalyptic tension. Is this Christian parenesis from the Hellenistic congregation placed in the Baptist's mouth, or was it even composed by Luke himself?[38]

■ **10** The dialectical form with its stereotypical question, "What should we do?" (τί ποιήσωμεν, also in Acts 2:37),[39] points in this direction, as does the solid Lukan language. The evangelist probably views vv. 7–9 as John's first contact with the crowd. In vv. 15–18 he read the prophetic sayings of the Baptist. In between, he issues instruction for those who do penance. Of course, the instruction cannot yet lead into any sort of Christian confession of faith (in contrast to Acts 2:14–36).

---

32 On μετάνοια ("repentance") see Bovon, *Theologian,* 267–89; and Taeger, *Mensch,* 130–47.

33 See Schulz, *Q,* 375 n. 340.

34 Joachim Jeremias, "λίθος, κτλ.," *TDNT* 4 (1967) 270–71.

35 Despite Jeremias, "λίθος," 270–71, and Reinhard Kratz, "λίθος, κτλ.," *EDNT* 2 (1991) 352.

36 See Helga Weippert, "Axt," in K. Galling, ed., *Bibli-*

sches Reallexikon (2d ed.; Tübingen: Mohr, 1977) 23–26.

37 Cf. *Hermas* 53.4 (*Sim.* 4.4).

38 See Bultmann, *History,* 145.

39 In each of its three occurrences, Codex D writes out the entire question, "so that we will be saved," which would be correct, according to the sense; cf. Acts 16:30.

■ **11** The first command is for the "crowds" (ὄχλοι). Food and clothing are the most elementary of goods. Of these, the listener should retain only the most necessary. This is not a demand for an idealization of poverty, but rather the fulfillment of the command to love one's neighbor: no one in Israel should be in need (Deut 15:4; cf. later Zacchaeus in Luke 19:8).[40]

■ **12–13** Tax collectors and soldiers are exhorted; in contrast to the later church, there are at this point no forbidden occupations.[41] No one is excluded from repentance. People are neither defined by their external qualities nor evaluated by general socioeconomic conditions. Tax collectors[42] can and should be honest; that is the (only or first?)[43] fruit of their repentance. For us, this is a matter of course, but Cicero's *De signis* and his speeches against Verres show to what excesses power could lead at that time.

John is not only a prophet, but also a wise "teacher" (διδάσκαλε); the apocalyptic (vv. 7–9) and messianic (vv. 15–18) sections are appropriate for the prophet, and the wisdom sayings (vv. 10–14) for the teacher, which is typical for the flexible and implicit association between wisdom and Torah.

■ **14** Through repentance and baptism, access to God and to the fellowship of the church are granted to the new converts, to the tax collectors in the Jewish Christian congregations and the soldiers in the Hellenistic ones.[44] The additional καὶ ἡμεῖς ("And we, . . .") of the soldiers is a sign of the end of the sequence, or an expression of their fear of being left out.[45]

One comes across διασείω ("to extort") and συκοφαντέω ("to accuse falsely," "to slander," "to extort") in the papyri, also as substantives.[46] The root συκοφαντ- appears frequently in the LXX for various Hebrew verbs. Especially important is Lev 19:11 (οὐ συκοφαντήσει ἕκαστος τὸν πλησίον, "people shall not deal falsely with their neighbor").[47] This verse is in a chapter that Martin Noth describes thusly: "This chapter provides for everyone in Israel, for 'all the congregation of the people of Israel' (so the introductory formula in v. 2aα), a definite codex of regulations mostly concerned with daily life and its different circumstances and activities."[48]

The three expressions in v. 14b paraphrase a single danger: the misuse of the possession of weapons in order to gain money.[49] The situation is thus not one of war (neither plunder nor bloodshed is mentioned), but

---

40 See Luise Schottroff and Wolfgang Stegemann, *Jesus and the Hope of the Poor* (trans. M. J. O'Connell; Maryknoll, N.Y.: Orbis, 1986) 99.

41 Cf. Hippolytus of Rome *Apostolic Tradition* 16. On the occupations despised in Judaism, see Joachim Jeremias, *Jerusalem in the Time of Jesus: An Investigation into Economic and Social Conditions during the New Testament Period* (trans. F. H. and C. H. Cave; Philadelphia: Fortress Press, 1969) 303–12.

42 On tax collectors see Fritz Herrenbrück, *Jesus und die Zöllner: Historische und neutestamentlich-exegetische Untersuchungen* (WUNT 2.41; Tübingen: Mohr [Siebeck], 1990).

43 According to Harald Sahlin, the parenesis, i.e., the acts of love that John the Baptist requires in Luke 3:10–14, form, along with the kerygma and baptism, the fundamental aspects of his office, as it is introduced in 3:3b ("Die Früchte der Umkehr: Die ethische Verkündigung Johannes des Taufers nach Lk 3,10–14," *StTh* 1 [1948] 54–68, esp. 54, 66). In his opinion, this moral message corresponds to the ethics of the OT, of Jesus, and of the church, which is in the process of its formation. W. Trilling, on the other hand, believes that John, who refers to repentance, was more lenient than Jesus, who aims at faith ("Le message de Jean-Baptiste," *AsSeign* 7 [1969] 65–73, esp. 70).

44 In the historical imagination of Luke, these soldiers could be mercenaries of Herod Antipas, who ruled not only Galilee but also Perea (the whole region around the Jordan, v. 3). But it is not out of the question that the evangelist, in view of the future pagan Christian congregations, is thinking of Roman soldiers (Schneider [1.86–87] is of the opposite opinion).

45 See Zahn, 194–95; Marshall, 143.

46 See Moulton and Milligan, *Vocabulary, s.v.* A great number of examples of profane usages appears in Johann Jakob Wettstein, *Η ΚΑΙΝΗ ΔΙΑΘΗΚΗ: Novum Testamentum Graecum* (2 vols.; Amsterdam: Ex officina Dommeriana, 1751–52) 1.672.

47 Cf. Gen 43:18. Διασείω ("to extort") occurs only twice in the LXX: Job 4:14 (codices B and 68) and 3 Macc 7:21.

48 Martin Noth, *Leviticus: A Commentary* (trans. J. E. Anderson; rev. ed.; Old Testament Library; Philadelphia: Westminster, 1977) 138.

49 BAGD defines τὰ ὀψώνια (*s.v.*): "ration-(money) paid to a soldier, then pay, wages."

of peace, exactly the condition of the Roman Empire at the time of the evangelist. As in the answer to the tax collectors, Luke is concerned with an ethic of just earnings and just use of assets.

Luke has vividly arranged a general instruction to the people (vv. 10–11) and two extreme cases (vv. 12–14). To share—without becoming poor oneself (v. 11)—and to desire nothing beyond that which has been agreed upon: these form a sort of first and greatest commandment. For Luke the original sin is greed. Obedience along the lines of these instructions makes it possible to avert the wrath of God. John's message, for Luke, is nothing new, and not even specific; all together, it encompasses the requirements of wisdom, of the prophets, and finally of the Law of God. As a counterpart to it, Luke will develop the Christian requirements in Acts 2:37–47, at the end of the account of Pentecost.

Just as ethics and christology belong together as the content of a life of faith, christological doctrine—which develops from the juxtaposition of John and Jesus—follows moral instruction in this passage. In this manner, Luke creates the opportunity to transmit further traditional words of the Baptist in an appropriate framework.

The Proclamation of the Messiah (vv. 15–18)

In the redactional setting of v. 15, as in vv. 7 and 10, the Baptist's audience, and their hopes and questions, are introduced first, so that the sayings become answers. By means of the organization or transposition of numerous apothegms, Luke emphasizes the dialogical structure of teaching and preaching.[50]

■ **15** With $\pi\rho o\sigma\delta o\kappa\hat{\omega}\nu\tau o\varsigma$ ("[the people] were filled with expectation"), Luke again brings the future into view (cf. vv. 7–9), though not that of the wrath of God, but rather of the Messiah. "The crowds" ($\H{o}\chi\lambda o\iota$) was the

expression for the throngs in need of repentance, "the people" ($\lambda\alpha\acute{o}\varsigma$) for the people of Israel rightly waiting in expectation. For Luke the "heart" is the location of the will and of thought (more than of emotion). In it dwell both decisions and questions.

In the religious tradition of Judaism, one finds one's identity, in the final analysis, only on the basis of God's commission. It is fundamentally legitimate that the people inquire about John's theological identity. Their expectation is positively evaluated.

The Fourth Gospel is also aware of the question about the Baptist's messianic identity, as well as the response, the double saying about the thong of the sandal and the two baptisms.[51] This probably reflects a historical polemic between the Christians and the Baptist's disciples. The title "the anointed one," "the Messiah" ($\acute{o}$ $\chi\rho\iota\sigma\tau\acute{o}\varsigma$),[52] difficult for a Greek to comprehend, demonstrates that this is Jewish tradition. Q and Mark, which stand earlier in the transmission of the traditions, know only the Baptist's answer, not the question. Where the Fourth Gospel allows three possibilities (the Messiah, Elijah, the prophet, John 1:20–21, 25), Luke cites only the most important of them, the Messiah. He has simplified the dialogue to suit his own conviction.

■ **16** The answer is in principle directed toward all of Judaism ("to all," $\pi\hat{\alpha}\sigma\iota\nu$), but specifically toward the Baptist's group. Luke follows the rather complicated flow of Q, with traits from Mark.[53] He interprets it as a Christian, but believes that he is being true to the historical Baptist. The saying about the two baptisms and about the sandal thong had already been combined in tradition (Q, John). The $\mu\acute{e}\nu$ . . . $\delta\acute{e}$ ("on the one hand . . . on the other") juxtaposes John and the one who is more powerful, but, with its Christian tendency, it stresses hierarchy (superiority of the more powerful

---

50 On the apothegms in Luke, see Gerhard Schneider, "Jesu überraschende Antworten: Beobachtungen zu den Apophthegmen des dritten Evangeliums," *NTS* 29 (1983) 321–36. One should notice the *inclusio* formed by the word λαός (vv. 15, 18).

51 On the two baptisms see the works of James D. G. Dunn, *Baptism in the Holy Spirit: A Re-examination of the New Testament Teaching on the Gift of the Spirit in Relation to Pentecostalism Today* (SBT 2.15; Philadelphia: Westminster, 1970); idem, "Spirit-and-Fire Baptism," *NovT* 14 (1972) 81–92; and S. Brown, "'Water-Baptism' and 'Spirit-Baptism' in Luke-Acts," *ATR* 59 (1977) 135–51.

52 See the commentary on 2:11 above. Ulrich Luz believes, on the basis of v. 15, that Luke is arguing with the Baptist groups, who revere John the Baptist as the Messiah (*Matthew 1–7: A Continental Commentary* [trans. W. C. Linss; Minneapolis: Fortress Press, 1989] 174 n. 7).

53 See Schulz, *Q*, 368.

one) rather than analogy (two baptists). The "mighty one of Israel" is God himself in the Hebrew Bible, and the historical Baptist was probably awaiting God alone as "the one who is more powerful." But especially the messianically interpreted verb ἔρχεται ("he is coming") quickly led to a christological understanding—at the latest, when Christians adopted the sayings from the Baptist tradition for their own. In view of this state of affairs, the Christians' faithfulness to the figure and teaching of the Baptist is astounding.[54] John does not even dare, like a slave or a disciple, to unloosen the shoe of the one who is to come; in this, his distance is illustrated with excessive clarity.[55]

The two sayings were originally passed on separately. The first appears also in Acts 1:5 and 11:16, as a saying of Jesus. Luke intends to ratify the Baptist's teaching through the resurrected Lord and, accordingly, restructures it for his use (change of persons, a salvation-historical deletion of the first "you" [ὑμᾶς], christological reservation through use of the passive voice instead of an "I" saying). In 1:5 the saying is applied to the Jewish Christian community, in 11:16 to Cornelius and the Hellenistic Christians. The second saying (about the sandal thong) appears in Paul's speech in Antioch (Acts 13:24–25) as a saying of John at the end of his "course" (which the proximity of Luke 3:16 to 3:19–20 confirms). As in Luke 3:15–18 and John 1:24–28, the sentence is attributed to a false hope on the part of the people: "What do you suppose that I am?" (the neuter τί ["what"] in place of the word ὁ χριστός ["the Messiah"]; on μετ᾽ ἐμέ ["after me"], compare ὀπίσω μου ["after me"] in John 1:27 and Mark 1:7).

Verse 16b speaks only of John and Jesus, whereas v. 16a and c include the salvation-historical community with their statements about baptism ("you," ὑμᾶς,

twice). The present tense of John's baptism,[56] which for Luke stands in the past, is juxtaposed with the future tense—Luke's present—of Jesus' baptism. In the Scriptures the Spirit is promised; in the Gospel it pertains to Jesus alone; and after Easter and the Ascension (Acts 2:33), it is granted to the Christians.[57]

The baptism of the Holy Spirit cannot be completely separated from the Christian rite of baptism. Luke is not thinking exclusively in terms of charisma or of sacrament. The two occurrences in which the Spirit is granted independently of baptism (Acts 8 and 10) are exceptions in salvation history. According to Luke, the baptism of the church is fulfilled by means of the two gestures of water baptism (as a visible sign of repentance, the forgiveness of sins, and appeal to the name of Jesus) and the laying on of hands (as an effective sign of the granting of the Holy Spirit). "He will baptize you with holy spirit and fire" points ahead to the time of the church, the coming of the Holy Spirit upon the apostles at Pentecost, and the incorporation of believers into the community of the saved through baptism and the laying on of hands.

The mention of "fire" is from the original version of the Q saying;[58] the "holy spirit," on the other hand, probably derives from Christian interpretation. In the metaphorical language of the Hebrew Bible, fire is a symbol of judgment. The unrepentant sinner falls prey to it, as the next saying explains, for which "fire" is the catchword. But, unlike Q, Luke no longer has in mind the eschatological judgment, but the outpouring of the Holy Spirit expressed in graphic metaphor (Acts 2:3–4).

■ 17 The image of the farmer corresponds to an agrarian society, though one should not allow a sociological viewpoint to eclipse a literary one. The image of a harvest for the eschatological events had already been cur-

---

54 The earliest Christian communities laid claim to John the Baptist with a clear conscience. He had given expression to an eschatological expectation, according to which the end was just around the corner, and had baptized Jesus. The congregations had concluded from this that he had proclaimed the Messiah. In order to interpret the figure of the Baptist, they also made use of the Jewish model of the prophet as a precursor (cf. 11QMelch).

55 The adjective ἱκανός, so favored by Luke, which, according to his usage, is close to ἄξιος ("worthy," Rev 5:9), means here "competent," i.e., "able," "enabled."

56 The words εἰς μετάνοιαν ("for repentance," Matt 3:11) should probably be laid to the account of the Matthean redaction; see Schulz, Q, 368.

57 See Heinrich von Baer, Der Heilige Geist in den Lukasschriften (Stuttgart: Kohlhammer, 1926) 111–12; Bovon, Theologian, 204–7.

58 See Paul Hoffmann, Studien zur Theologie der Logienquelle (NTAbh n.s. 8; Münster: Aschendorff, 1972) 18–25.

rent for a long time. The sequential activities are portrayed in a compressed manner.[59] The threshing floor is a metonymy for the threshed kernels. The farmer uses the winnowing fork to separate the already threshed wheat from the chaff, then he collects it and brings it into the granary. Last, he burns the chaff.

῎Ασβεστος ("unquenchable") appears typically as the last word and the code word: it breaks the framework and forms the link from metaphor to allegory, thus inviting a Christian interpretation. Neither Matthew nor Luke has intensified the allegorization they found already in Q.[60]

The Baptist's last saying corresponds to his first, especially v. 9 (an *inclusio*): the images of tree and wheat field imply a call to repentance and a warning in the style and language of Hebrew Bible prophecy.

■ **18** On the redactional level, Luke emphasizes the glad and encouraging aspect of this message ($\pi \alpha \rho \alpha \kappa \alpha \lambda \hat{\omega} \nu$,[61] "with . . . exhortations"; $\epsilon \dot{\upsilon} \eta \gamma \gamma \epsilon \lambda \dot{\iota} \zeta \epsilon \tau o$, "he proclaimed the good news"). Luke thus does not view John as belonging exclusively to the stage of Hebrew Bible expectation, but as being on the threshold of the new era.[62] Through him, "the people" ($\dot{o} \lambda \alpha \dot{o} \varsigma$ again) come into contact with the good news. The image of John in the book of Acts corresponds to this: his preaching of repentance and messianic prophecy are the Baptist's two main characteristics in Luke.

The summary in v. 18 serves both as a conclusion ($\pi o \lambda \lambda \dot{\alpha} \ldots \kappa \alpha \dot{\iota} \ \ddot{\epsilon} \tau \epsilon \rho \alpha \ldots$, "many other [exhortations]") and as the beginning of a new section ($\mu \dot{\epsilon} \nu \ldots \delta \dot{\epsilon}$, "so . . . [he] . . . but [Herod]"). The author wants to make a transition from John's message to the two main events in his life: Jesus' baptism and his own arrest. But Luke's sequence runs opposite to the course of history. Is this a theological arrangement that separates the Bap-

tist as much as possible from Jesus, thus placing him in the old covenant?[63] Certainly, the message of the "kingdom" ($\beta \alpha \sigma \iota \lambda \epsilon \dot{\iota} \alpha$) and the presence of the Spirit enter history only with Jesus the Savior. But Luke's sequence does have a more immediate literary purpose: the evangelist does not want to turn to Jesus until he has finished his account of the Baptist. For him, Jesus' baptism belongs in the life of Jesus, no longer to the story of the Baptist.

John's Arrest (vv. 19–20)

■ **19** The source for the Baptist's arrest is Mark 6:17–18. Luke improves upon it logically and stylistically by following the historical sequence: found guilty by John, Herod Antipas reacts with repression. But the explicit charge (unlawful marriage) is missing in Luke. Only the additional words, "and because of all the evil things," qualifies the detail, "because of Herodias."

The length of the sentence forces Luke to repeat the subject—which is uncommon for him—although he repeats "Herod" without the title "tetrarch." Herod does evil, but the author stands on the side of the "good" Baptist. This simplification is more characteristic of folk literature than of the Hebrew Bible.[64]

■ **20** Luke's $\kappa \alpha \tau \alpha \kappa \lambda \epsilon \dot{\iota} \omega$ ("shut up"), instead of $\delta \dot{\epsilon} \omega$ ("to fetter") is more of a stylistic improvement than a clarification of the facts. The arrest of John, which is not explicitly mentioned in Mark, now appears strikingly as the apogee of this ruler's evil. The last word, "prison," has the emphasis again. Luke does not want to tell more about the Baptist's end, nor does he need to. All the interest is now directed toward the "more powerful one" announced by John: Jesus.

Luke may have omitted the account of the Baptist's death (Mark 6:19–29) because of aesthetic, historical, or

---

59   The infinitives ($\delta \iota \alpha \kappa \alpha \theta \hat{\alpha} \rho \alpha \iota$ and $\sigma \upsilon \nu \alpha \gamma \alpha \gamma \epsilon \hat{\iota} \nu$), as well as the $\alpha \dot{\upsilon} \tau o \hat{\upsilon}$, which is connected with $\dot{\alpha} \pi o \theta \dot{\eta} \kappa \eta$ and not $\sigma \hat{\iota} \tau o \nu$, are results of Luke's redactional activity.

60   Following the Midrash on the Song of Songs 7:3 (127a), Rabbi Abin, in a parable, compared Israel with the wheat and the Gentiles with the chaff (see Str-B 1.122).

61   In other passages $\pi \alpha \rho \alpha \kappa \alpha \lambda \dot{\epsilon} \omega$ means "to request," "to beseech" (Luke 7:4; 8:31, 32, 41; Acts 9:38; 13:42), or "to implore" someone to accept a message (Acts 2:40; 14:22). This second meaning fits here: John the Baptist is imploring the people with

further sentential sayings; see BAGD *s.v.* $\pi \alpha \rho \alpha \kappa \alpha \lambda \dot{\epsilon} \omega$, 2 (toward the end).

62   Against Conzelmann, *Theology*, 22–23. See Emmeram Kränkl, *Jesus der Knecht Gottes: Die heilsgeschichtliche Stellung Jesu in den Reden der Apostelgeschichten* (BU 8; Regensburg: Pustet, 1972) 88–97; Bovon, *Theologian*, 133–34.

63   See Conzelmann, *Theology*, 21.

64   On Herod in Luke, see the commentary on 9:7–9 below.

theological considerations (aversion to the Markan style of the account, knowledge of a divergent account such as that of Josephus, or to avoid competition with the martyr's death of the Messiah). But the number of possible reasons itself shows that we really do not know why he passes over this vivid story.

Jesus' Baptism (vv. 21–22)

■ **21** Luke uses Mark as the basis for relating the baptism of Jesus. The account serves the story of the Messiah more than that of the Baptist, whose name is not once mentioned, and who, for Luke, remains more a prophet and a preacher than a baptizer. As it was in the tradition, Jesus' baptism appears as a conclusion and a transition. The main event is not, however, Jesus' baptism itself, which is described in two words (see the weighty account in Mark 1:9); the baptism presented difficulties for the earliest community, for the sinless Jesus would hardly require repentance or a baptism for repentance.[65] Luke incorporates it into the general portrayal of the success of John's baptism, about which he knows from Q (Matt 3:5–6) and Mark 1:5. The ingathering of Israel thus found its beginning with the Baptist, but its real continuation occurred only in Jesus' activity, for which John's baptism was no more than a salvation-historical preparation. In all this, however, a tension cannot be denied between the structure, "Baptist's preaching of repentance–the people's repentance and baptism–final judgment," and the structure, "precursor–Messiah." This tension has its roots in the Scriptures themselves, for not all apocalyptic texts contain a messianic expectation.[66]

Luke has thought over this tension himself and resolved it in the Benedictus: with the Baptist and his forgiveness of sins, the people will receive knowledge of salvation (1:77)—no more, but no less.

Every important stage in God's time, and every communication between humans and their creator, is signaled literarily with a prayer. Prayer becomes the appropriate human response to God. Although the baptism is already finished (aorist participle), Jesus' supplication continues (present participle).[67]

In terms of genre, the account of Jesus' baptism,[68] because of the heavens opening, belongs together with apocalyptic literature.[69] But where Mark still works with a vision (εἶδεν, "he saw"), Luke historicizes the event, although not in the sense of a commissioning story, since there is no commission.

■ **22** The Spirit also descends concretely upon Jesus, even "in bodily form" (σωματικῷ εἴδει). A traditional apocalyptic vision in connection with an audition is transformed into a historical scene with a divine intervention.[70] But this miraculous event, the granting of the Spirit, is not the final word; at the conclusion, Luke has a voice from heaven ring out. He forgoes an acclamation on the part of the astonished onlookers, since Jesus, as the recipient of the voice, remains central. Thus Luke stands halfway between Mark, for whom the vision and voice from heaven are intended for Jesus alone, and Matthew, who imagines a public display.

Luke's addition of "in the last days" to the citation of Joel in the Pentecost account of Acts 2:17 shows that he was familiar with the eschatological significance of the

---

65 See the dialogue between John the Baptist and Jesus in Matt 3:14–15. Cf. the χωρὶς ἁμαρτίας ("without sin") in Heb 4:15.

66 Cf., e.g., the prophecies of Joel.

67 On Jesus in prayer, see Monloubou, *Prière*, 57.

68 This pericope has been viewed as a commissioning story, a legend, a myth, or a datum from the life of Jesus. With the aid of the Targums, especially those on the sacrifice of Isaac (Gen 22), and on the dream of Jacob (Gen 28), Fritzleo Lentzen-Deis has defined Jesus' baptism as an explanatory vision, as they are granted to an envoy and chosen individual of God at important points in time, so that the community may participate in this explanation (*Die Taufe Jesu nach den Synoptikern: Literarkritische und gattungsgeschichtliche Untersuchungen* [FTS 4; Frankfurt am Main: Knecht, 1970] 249–89). Lentzen-Deis thus finds a *Sitz im Leben* for this pericope in the

post-Easter Jewish Christian community.

69 Cf. Isa 63:19; *T. Levi* 18:6–7: "The heavens will be opened, and from the temple of glory sanctification will come upon him, with a fatherly voice, as from Abraham to Isaac. And the glory of the Most High shall burst forth upon him. And the spirit of understanding and sanctification shall rest upon him [in the water]." H. C. Kee, who translated this passage for *OTP* (1.795), views the text in brackets as a Christian interpolation.

70 The same tendency is evident in the ascension accounts (Luke 24:50–53; Acts 1:9–11), which historicize the kerygma of exaltation.

Spirit in the theology of contemporaneous Judaism. Luke thus ascribes both salvation-historical *and* eschatological significance to Jesus' baptism and God's action at the time. It is not certain that he is alluding to Isa 11:4; he has more likely been incited by the Jewish thesis of the absence of God's Spirit in the present time.[71]

The relationship between the outpouring of the Spirit and the virgin birth should be understood neither as a two-stage christology (Rom 1:3–4) nor as the later doctrine of two natures; it should only be construed on the basis of Lukan passages. The entire birth narrative proclaims that God's Spirit has become active again at the end of time. The Spirit has left its imprint on everyone, particularly Mary (1:35). Although God's Spirit had a part in Jesus' miraculous birth, for Luke this does not mean that the Messiah has been completely equipped. For his mission (more than for himself), he now receives the affirmation and the gift of divine power.

The cryptic "like a dove"[72] pertains to the style of an apocalyptic vision. It is supplemented by Luke's phrase, "in bodily form," which can be construed either as a description of the dove's appearance or as the bodily arrival of the Spirit. In the Pentecost account Luke uses other images, ones rooted in Jewish tradition: fire and tongues. In our passage, he is following his source, Mark, for whose image no one has yet found a direct parallel in Jewish literature.[73]

The text-critical attestation of the voice from heaven supports the text of Nestle-Aland, but internal criteria perhaps favor the Western text: "You are my son. Today I have begotten you" (Ps 2:7).[74] Although Luke does show interest in Ps 2:7 in Acts 13:33, and the accommodation to Mark could be attributed to scribes, the Nestle text should still be preferred: (1) a harmonization with Matthew, the chief Gospel of the church, would be more likely than with Mark; (2) Acts 13:33 means to attest Jesus' resurrection, not his baptism; (3) later scribes have also at times tried to bring mixed citations into line with the Hebrew Bible text.

The introduction ("and a voice came from heaven") is reminiscent of Gen 15:4, and Dan 4:28 and 31 in Theodotion; even so, because of the heavenly origin of the voice, the phrase is more likely apocalyptic than scriptural (although φωνή, "voice," is common in the LXX) or rabbinic. The rabbis conceive of the *bath qol*, the "daughter of a voice," "as the echo of a divine voice,"[75] whereas God speaks to his Son directly here.

The content of the voice from heaven is, on the one hand, a predication formula (alluding to Ps 2:7), and, on the other, an expression of the highest love (alluding to Isa 42:1). The origin of Ps 2:7 is royal ideology, with its appropriate *Sitz im Leben*, the enthronement liturgy. In Jewish interpretation of this, a shift occurred toward the hope for a future Messiah, so that Luke 3:22 expresses the fulfillment of this eschatological expectation. Since a predication formula is at issue here, the fulfillment does not remain abstract, vague, or general, but is bound up with the human figure of Jesus. Everything that Luke has so far written about Jesus serves to prove that he is God's Son. In view of 1:31–32,[76] the readers are not learning something completely new. What is new is only that Jesus is here now, receives the Spirit, and hears the voice himself (σύ, "you"). Luke thus does not understand the words in the sense of an adoption, but as the revelation of a truth, of a mystery.

Its content is not an abstract truth, but the recognition of a personal relationship by means of the metaphor of one of the closest human relationships, father and son. The affective aspect ("beloved," ὁ ἀγαπητός) accompanies the legal aspect ("my son," ὁ υἱός

---

71   See Max-Alain Chevallier, *Souffle de Dieu, le Saint-Esprit dans le Nouveau Testament* (Paris: Beauchesne, 1978) 48–49; cf. *t. Sota* 13.3; and 1 Macc 4:46; 9:27; 14:41.

72   On the riddle of the dove, see Str-B 1.123–25; Lentzen-Deis, *Taufe*, 170–83; Leander E. Keck, "The Spirit and the Dove," *NTS* 17 (1970–71) 41–67; Stephen Gero, "The Spirit as a Dove at the Baptism of Jesus," *NovT* 18 (1976) 16–35; Fitzmyer, 1.483–84.

73   See Gnilka, *Markus*, 1.52.

74   Nestle-Aland lists *D it Ju (Cl) Meth Hil Aug*, and gives two further readings influenced by the Matthean parallel passage. Metzger (*Textual Commentary*, 136) decides against the Western text. Augustin George, on the other hand, clearly inclines toward the Western text ("Jésus Fils de Dieu dans l'Évangile selon Saint Luc," *RB* 72 [1965] 185–209, reprinted in idem, *Études*, 215–36; see esp. 216–18 of the volume of collected essays).

75   See Gnilka, *Markus*, 1.52.

76   Cf. Luke 2:11.

$\mu o \upsilon$), and surpasses it at the end ("with you I am well pleased," $\dot{\epsilon} \nu$ $\sigma o \grave{\iota}$ $\epsilon \dot{\upsilon} \delta \acute{o} \kappa \eta \sigma \alpha$).

Augustin George described and sought to demonstrate that Jesus' baptism was his messianic installation into office, and his sermon in Nazareth his prophetic installation; the titles son and prophet, he claimed, were not interrelated until Jesus' transfiguration.[77] This interpretation seems too schematic, since the utterance of God also contains prophetic elements—at least if one takes the Nestle-Aland text as a basis, and not the Western variant, which refers only to Ps 2:7—and the sermon at Nazareth also has messianic aspects (cf. the reference to Isa 61:1–2). But it is true that Luke intends to present Jesus as both Messiah and prophet in these two accounts. Together they form the "beginning," the famous $\dot{\alpha} \rho \chi \acute{\eta}$ of the Gospel. In the first, Jesus, surrounded by the entire nation, receives the disclosure of his identity; in the second, he attempts to wake comprehension of it among his people through the Scriptures and interpretation. The disciples will truly understand this only after the resurrection; and only at the time of the transfiguration will the passion be introduced into the doctrine of the Messiah. The voice from heaven at Jesus' baptism develops the (interior) father-son relationship; the scriptural citation in the Nazareth scene develops his messianic and prophetic commission to those outside, to the people.

$\dot{A} \gamma \alpha \pi \eta \tau \acute{o} \varsigma$ can mean "beloved," "only beloved," and finally, "only,"[78] similarly to $\mu o \nu o \gamma \epsilon \nu \acute{\eta} \varsigma$ ("only begotten"). Its exclusivity, however, is transformed by the love of God into an integration of the community into the father-son relationship (10:21–22).

Since the connection $\upsilon \acute{\iota} \acute{o} \varsigma$-$\dot{\alpha} \gamma \alpha \pi \eta \tau \acute{o} \varsigma$[79] ("son-beloved") occurs several times in the scene of the sacrifice of Isaac (Gen 22 LXX), there could be an allusion to the עֲקֵדָה ("binding [of Isaac]," the Aqedah) typology (cf. Rom 8:32); then the shadow of the passion would already be visible here. But $\dot{\alpha} \gamma \alpha \pi \eta \tau \acute{o} \varsigma$ is more likely an expression of the Christian intensification of the father-

son relationship, which has its roots in Jewish messianism and prophecy (also added in the Targum to Ps 2:7).

Isaiah 42:1 is important for the connection between Jesus' baptism and Deutero-Isaiah, with its songs about the servant of God;[80] in it occur the I-you relationship, the servant's appurtenance to God, the father's affection, and the gift of the Spirit. This relationship indeed could only have arisen at the level of oral and Aramaic tradition, since the LXX diverges from Synoptic tradition in every respect. The most likely point of influence is, "with you I am well pleased" ($\dot{\epsilon} \nu$ $\sigma o \grave{\iota}$ $\epsilon \dot{\upsilon} \delta \acute{o} \kappa \eta \sigma \alpha$), since the concept of God's love for his prophets is traditional, and Jesus is also addressed as a prophet in Luke 3:22. Luke is consciously adopting the vocabulary of $\epsilon \dot{\upsilon} \delta o \kappa \acute{\iota} \alpha$ ("favor," "approval"), since God's loving affection for his son and for his children is the center of his own conception of faith.[81]

A connection between Jesus' baptism and death is, however, unlikely. Luke took the saying about his cross as a baptism (12:50) from his sources and did not construct it himself. The passion also does not enter the picture until after the transfiguration. Luke accords little significance to Jesus' water baptism as such. But as a conscientious historian and theologian, he does not wish to neglect transmitting the event as a historical occurrence, nor can he. For Luke, the significance of the action depends on God's double intervention through the Spirit and the word, as the summary in Acts 10:38 shows: "how God anointed Jesus of Nazareth with holy spirit and with power." Here the anointing ($\ddot{\epsilon} \chi \rho \iota \sigma \epsilon \nu$) is probably intended to make the christological title comprehensible, if the saying is redactional. Nevertheless, the baptism is neither adoption nor enthronement.

The scene of disclosure at the baptism inaugurates Jesus' messianic activity in Galilee. Correspondingly, the transfiguration leads into the second stage of Christ's commission.[82]

---

77 See George, "Jésus Fils de Dieu dans l'Évangile selon Saint Luc," *RB* 72 (1965) 185–209, esp. 217–18.

78 Thus Pollux can write, $K \alpha \lambda o \hat{\iota} \tau o$ $\ddot{\alpha} \nu$ $\upsilon \grave{\iota} o \varsigma$ $\dot{\alpha} \gamma \alpha \pi \eta \tau o \varsigma$ $\dot{o}$ $\mu \acute{o} \nu o \varsigma$ $\ddot{\omega} \nu$ $\pi \alpha \tau \rho \acute{\iota}$ ("he should be called the beloved son, who is the only one to the father," *Onom.* 3.19, cited in BAGD *s.v.*). On "son," see the commentary on Luke 1:32, 35 above.

79 See Gnilka, *Markus*, 1.53.

80 See Oscar Cullmann, *The Christology of the New Testament* (trans. S. C. Guthrie and C. A. M. Hall; rev. ed.; Philadelphia: Westminster, 1963) 66–67, 283–84.

81 See Bovon, *Lukas*, 105–8.

82 See Conzelmann, *Theology*, 57–59. G. O. Williams emphasizes that John is more important as witness

History of Interpretation[83]

In the second century, Jesus' baptism was discussed vehemently, as the large number of patristic and heretical references demonstrate;[84] before this, all was quiet. Ignatius concentrates his theological and soteriological considerations completely on the birth, cross, and resurrection of Jesus.[85] Only in Jewish Christian writings do certain texts give evidence of older traditions about Jesus' baptism, which diverge in three different directions:[86]

1. There is blatant embarrassment about a baptism for purification. Jesus, apparently pressured by his mother,[87] defends himself: "Wherein have I sinned that I should go and be baptized by him?"[88]

2. Jesus fulfills Isa 11:2 through his baptism. He is the prophet who sums up all prophets. Jesus is the preexistent son; he does not become God's son only through baptism, but is recognized as such here.[89]

3. The baptism is the moment at which Jesus becomes the Christ. God's Spirit unites with the human Jesus.[90] Thus Cerinthus believed that the divine Christ in the form of a dove descended upon the human Jesus at his baptism, and from then on, Jesus proclaimed the unknown Father.[91]

Other Christian authors see in Jesus' baptism the coming of the Spirit upon him (Isa 11:2), the beginning of Jesus' public life, or, in a combination of both motifs, the precise center of the pneumatic manifestations of all past and future time.[92]

For the church fathers,[93] Jesus' anointing had salvation-historical significance. But their opinions diverge when it is a matter of setting the moment of this anointing: is it the incarnation (thus Didymus, Hesychius, and Augustine, who was fighting against the subordinationists), or the baptism (Athanasius, Hilary of Poitiers, Cyril of Jerusalem, Theodore of Mopsuestia)? If one locates the commissioning of Jesus back at the virgin birth, or even in his preexistence, the meaning of the baptism becomes uncertain. For Augustine it had ecclesiastical, not christological, implications: the baptized Christ, united with the Spirit, symbolizes the church, which would also in turn be baptized with water and anointed with the Holy Spirit.

The later history of theology, especially the nineteenth century, shows radically diverging opinions. Some see in baptism a break with one's previous life and the act of entering into a new one. For others God has besmirched himself by contact with the human realm, just as one becomes impure by touching a corpse. Bap-

---

than as baptist, since the evangelist allows him to step out of the field of vision unobtrusively and leaves the matter unresolved, in order not to contradict Mark ("The Baptism in Luke's Gospel," *JTS* 45 [1944] 31–38).

83   I thank Denise Jornod, who compiled the section, "History of Interpretation."

84   Paul is not concerned about Jesus' baptism. The same is true of the Apostolic Fathers, who are more involved in pastoral questions than exegetical ones. In the Apologists one finds only a few references to the human activity of the earthly Jesus. For them the baptism of Jesus is more problematic than convincing. See Daniel A. Bertrand, *Le baptême de Jésus: Histoire de l'exégèse aux deux premiers siècles* (BGBE 14; Tübingen: Mohr-Siebeck, 1973) 134.

85   I owe these reflections in their essential outlines to Bertrand (*Baptême*, 134–36).

86   I rely here on the opinions of Eric Junod, which he communicated to me in a letter of 15 April 1985.

87   Cf. the *Praedicatio Pauli* in Ps.-Cyprian *De rebaptismate* 17 (CSEL 3.90).

88   The *Gospel of the Nazareans*, as cited by Jerome *Ad. Pelag.* 3.2 (*PL* 23.570B–571A); Eng. trans. from Edgar Hennecke, *New Testament Apocrypha* (ed. W.

Schneemelcher; trans. and ed. R. McL. Wilson; 2d ed.; 2 vols.; Louisville: Westminster John Knox, 1991–92) 1.160.

89   Cf. the *Gospel of the Hebrews,* as cited by Jerome in *Comm. in Is.* 4 (on Isa 11:2); see CCSL 73.148; Eng. trans. in Hennecke-Schneemelcher, 1.177; cf. *Ps.-Clem. Rec.* 1.48.3–6 (GCS 51.36).

90   Cf. the *Gospel of the Ebionites,* as cited by Epiphanius *Adv. haer.* 30.13.7–8 (GCS 25.350–51; Eng. trans. in Hennecke-Schneemelcher, 1.169).

91   Cf. Irenaeus *Adv. haer.* 1.26.1. According to Irenaeus, the Nicolaitans also advocate the same teaching (3.11.1). On the Ophites, cf. Irenaeus *Adv. haer.* 1.30.11–14; and on the Basilideans, Clement of Alexandria *Exc. Theod.* 16; *Strom.* 1.146.1–2; 2.36.1; 2.38.1–2.

92   See Bertrand, *Baptême,* 91–98.

93   See François Bovon, *De vocatione gentium: Histoire de l'interprétation d'Act. 10,1–11,18 dans les six premiers siècles* (BGBE 8; Tübingen: Mohr-Siebeck, 1967) 229, 245–46.

tism effects the necessary purification. For yet others, baptism is the condemnation of Jesus to death on behalf of humanity.[94] For Godet, Jesus is commissioned through his baptism.[95] That the Holy Spirit "descends" ($\kappa\alpha\tau\alpha\beta\hat{\eta}\nu\alpha\iota$, 3:22) contradicts every other interpretation. Luke 4:1 confirms this descent and emphasizes this aspect of newness. The son is thus not identical with the Messiah. His baptism is a moment of decision for Jesus. Here the mystery of his existence is disclosed to him. After his baptism, Jesus identifies himself with the Holy Spirit.

Karl Barth, too, understands it to mean that Jesus accepts his messianic commission at his baptism.[96] He sees above all the subjective aspect of baptism: it is the hinge between a turning point effected by God and the human decision that affirms this. In Jesus, the two aspects are one.

---

94 See Godet, 1.189–95, who is critically opposed to all this.
95 Ibid., 1.192–94.
96 See Karl Barth, *Church Dogmatics*, vol. 4: *The Doctrine of Reconciliation* (trans. G. W. Bromiley; ed. G. W. Bromiley and T. F. Torrance; Edinburgh: Clark, 1956) 4.58.

The Genealogy of Jesus (3:23–38)

Bibliography

Abel, E. L., "The Genealogies of Jesus Ο ΧΡΙΣΤΟΣ," NTS 20 (1973–74) 203–10.

Burger, Christoph, Jesus als Davidssohn: Eine traditionsgeschichtliche Untersuchung (FRLANT 98; Göttingen: Vandenhoeck & Ruprecht, 1970) 116–23.

Byskov, Martha, "Verus Deus—verus homo: Lc 3, 23–38," StTh 26 (1972) 25–32.

Hartl, V., "Zum Stammbaum Jesu nach Lukas," BZ 7 (1909) 156–73, 290–302.

Holtzmeister, U., "Ein Erklärungsversuch der Lk-Genealogie (3,23–38)," ZKTh 47 (1923) 184–218.

idem, "Geneaologia S. Lucae (Lc 3,23–38)," VD 23 (1943) 9–18.

Jeremias, Jerusalem, 213–16, 275–97.

Johnson, Marshall D., The Purpose of the Biblical Genealogies: With Special Reference to the Setting of the Genealogies of Jesus (SNTSMS 8; London: Cambridge University Press, 1969).

Kurz, William S., "Luke 3:23–38 and Greco-Roman and Biblical Genealogies," in Talbert, Luke-Acts, 169–87.

Lambertz, M., "Die Toledoth in Mt 1,1–17 und Lc 3,23bff," in H. Kusch, ed., Festschrift: Franz Dornseiff (Leipzig: Bibliographisches Institut, 1953) 201–25.

Lee, G. M., "Luke 3:23," ExpTim 79 (1967–68) 310.

Lerle, Ernst, "Die Ahnenverzeichnisse Jesu: Versuch einer christologischen Interpretation," ZNW 72 (1981) 112–17.

Nestle, Eberhard, "Sala, Salma, Salmon," ZNW 11 (1910) 242–43.

idem, "Salomo und Nathan in Mt 1 und Lc 3," ZNW 8 (1907) 72.

idem, "Zur Genealogie in Lukas 3," ZNW 4 (1903) 188–89.

Overstreet, R. L., "Difficulties of New Testament Genealogies," Grace Theological Journal 2 (1981) 303–26.

Plum, Karin F., "Genealogy as Theology," Scandinavian Journal of the Old Testament 3 (1989) 66–92.

Ramlot, Léon, "Les généalogies bibliques: Un genre littéraire oriental," BVC 60 (1964) 53–70.

Rius-Camps, Josep, "Constítuye Lc 3,21–28 un solo periodo? Propuesta de un cambio de punctuación," Bib 65 (1984) 189–209.

Seethaler, Paula, "Eine kleine Bemerkung zu den Stammbäumen Jesu nach Matthäus und Lukas," BZ n.s. 16 (1972) 256–57.

Siotis, Markos A., "Οἱ κατὰ σάρκα προπάτορες Ἰησοῦ Χριστοῦ," Theologia (Athens) 57 (1986) 127–54, 273–99.

da Spinetoli, O., "Les généalogies de Jésus et leur signification," AsSeign 9 (1974) 6–19.

Thompson, P. J., "The Infancy Gospels of St. Matthew and St. Luke Compared," StEv 1 (= TU 73) (1959) 217–22.

Throckmorton, Burton H., "Genealogy (Christ)," IDB 2.365–66.

Wilson, Robert R., Genealogy and History in the Old Testament (New Haven: Yale University Press, 1972).

idem, "The Old Testament Genealogies in Recent Research," JBL 94 (1975) 168–89.

Winandy, Jacques, Autour de la naissance de Jésus: Accomplissement et prophétie (Lire la Bible 26; Paris: Cerf, 1970) 15–31.

23 And he, Jesus, was about thirty years old when he began. He was considered to be the son of Joseph, son of Heli, 24/ son of Matthat, son of Levi, son of Melchi, son of Jannai, son of Joseph, 25/ son of Mattathias, son of Amos, son of Nahum, son of Esli, son of Naggai, 26/ son of Maath, son of Mattathias, son of Semein, son of Josech, son of Joda, 27/ son of Joanan, son of Rhesa, son of Zerubbabel, son of Shealtiel, son of Neri, 28/ son of Melchi, son of Addi, son of Cosam, son of Elmadam, son of Er, 29/ son of Joshua, son of Eliezer, son of Jorim, son of Matthat, son of Levi, 30/ son of Simeon, son of Judah, son of Joseph, son of Jonam, son of Eliakim, 31/ son of Melea, son of Menna, son of Mattatha, son of Natham, son of David, 32/ son of Jesse, son of Obed, son of Boaz, son of Sala, son of Nahshon, 33/ son of Amminadab, son of Admin, son of Arni, son of Hezron, son of Perez, son of Judah, 34/ son of Jacob, son of Isaac, son of Abraham, son of Terah, son of Nahor, 35/ son of Serug, son of Reu, son of Peleg, son of Eber, son of Shelah, 36/ son of Cainan, son of Arphaxad, son of Shem, son of Noah, son of Lamech, 37/ son of Methuselah, son of Enoch, son of Jared, son of Mahalaleel, son of Cainan, 38/ son of Enos, son of Seth, son of Adam, son of God.

Analysis

These days we find lists boring. But many older cultures treasure them.[1] Lists of ethnic groups or tribes can be

---

1   Bibliography in Fitzmyer, 1.504–5; see esp. Robert R. Wilson, "The Old Testament Genealogies in Recent Research," JBL 94 (1975) 168–89; and Marshall D. Johnson, The Purpose of the Biblical Genealogies: With Special Reference to the Setting of the Genealogies of Jesus (SNTSMS 8; London: Cambridge University Press, 1969).

expressions of the beginnings of scholarship and can demonstrate a desire for completeness and order. To this day, genealogies are still the pride of ancient families. Back then, they reflected the yearning for divine origins and legitimation. In addition to this, the Hebrew Bible genealogies gave the tribe or nation solidarity when this was threatened, and linked together separated periods of salvation history. Purity of bloodlines was especially important for the priestly families, and so precise genealogies were maintained. By its very essence, a genealogy encompasses a hyperindividual dimension of time and, in contrast to teacher-disciple traditions, attests the continuity of blood relations and family rather than of beliefs or knowledge. The presupposition is a claim to have inherited some aptitude or power. The idea of election can be expressed both by means of a charismatic individual and by means of natural posterity. In addition, a list without argumentation has an apodictic character; it tolerates neither doubt nor discussion and thus transmits a definite belief.

Ancient Jewish scholarship reveals hardly a trace of interest in the posterity of David and in the messianic expectations; but it was probably there, for various families in Judah made claims of royal, Davidic descent.[2] On the other hand, the concept of the hidden origins of the Messiah was probably also developing. Though it remains remarkable to us, the role of Jesus' family, considered to be messianic, in the earliest Christian community was typical of the sensibilities of that time. As late as Domitian, two relatives of Jesus were still known, and were denounced before the emperor because of their Davidic descent.[3]

Matthew 1:1–17 and Luke 3:23–38 are the most important testimonies of early Christian interest in Jesus' descent. Jesus' Davidic lineage is also claimed elsewhere without any attestation of it by a genealogy.[4] Although the evangelists certainly did not compose the lists themselves and did not use the same source, they employed their material with a distinct purpose.

After a transitional sentence about Jesus' age (v. 23), the Lukan list begins with what appears as a highly interesting exception, when compared with the succeeding stereotypical formula ("*x*, son of *x*"):[5] "he was considered to be the son of Joseph" (v. 23b). After Jesus and Joseph, seventy-five further names (seventy-six, if one includes God) are mentioned one after the other, in reverse order of biblical history.[6] The conclusion, in which Luke dares to make the link between the first man, Adam, to God himself, is perplexing: . . . τοῦ Ἀδὰμ τοῦ θεοῦ ("[son] of Adam, [son] of God"). In comparison with 3:22, this expresses a special manner of being God's son.

Most of the names mentioned are taken from the Bible. From Adam to Shem (vv. 36b–38), the list corresponds to Genesis 5, from Shem to Abraham (vv. 34–36a), to Gen 11:10–32.[7] For the time between Abraham and David, information has been taken from 1 Chronicles and Ruth. Since the canonicity of these two books was still not certain, a certain liberty was allowed. It is not known what sources or materials were available for the more recent times between David and Jesus.

Both Matthew and Luke concentrate on direct lines of descent through the men of the family. In the culture of that time, only this was conclusive, so that, despite the virgin birth, descent is reckoned through Joseph, not Mary. Both evangelists perceived this tension (one could hardly say that the previous versions had) and attempted to resolve it as well as possible. The similarity between the two lists for the time between Abraham and David is not surprising, given the authority of the Scriptures. Although Luke does not express a specific organization of the generations into groups, as does Matthew, it is not out of the question that he presupposes it.

But the differences are more weighty: in contrast to the custom represented by Matthew, Luke's genealogy runs in reverse. And where Matthew, favoring an Israelite perspective, begins only with Abraham, Luke forges ahead to Adam, thereby encompassing the entire human race. Even if this is based on diverging tradi-

---

2   See Jeremias, *Jerusalem*, 276–77.

3   Cf. Eusebius *Hist. eccl.* 2.19.1–20.7, who is quoting Hegesippus.

4   Cf. Rom 1:3; 2 Tim 2:8; Rev 5:5; 22:16; cf. also Heb 7:14.

5   See BDF §162, n. 2: τοῦ belongs to the preceding name; one must supply a υἱοῦ.

6   As often in such cases, the textual basis is not

entirely stable, so that the complete number of Jesus' ancestors can vary from one ms. to another; see Fitzmyer, 1.491–94.

7   This is according to the LXX, since the name Cainan (Καϊνάμ or Καϊνάν; in the LXX, Καϊνάν) is not found in the MT. See Marguerite Harl, *La Bible d'Alexandrie*, vol. 1: *La Genèse* (Paris: Cerf, 1986) 151.

tions, it still plays up their theological peculiarities: Matthew's perspective is dominated by the privileged status of Abraham's descendants; Luke shows a universalistic tendency.[8]

As for grammar, Matthew employs the verb γεννάω ("engender," "produce,"), as does 1 Chr 2:1–15, whereas Luke connects the son with his father by means of a genitive construction with an article. Although both genealogies contain no additional information about Jesus' ancestors, Matthew mentions the mother five times with ἐκ τῆς ("out of . . . ," "by . . ."). In the Hebrew Bible, genealogies are placed either at the beginning of an account (Abraham, Gen 11:10–16), or after a few initial episodes (Moses, Exod 6:14–20). The same liberty in composition is evident in Matthew and Luke. Matt 1:17 expressly divides the genealogy into three periods of equal length (fourteen generations each). Perhaps Luke—or, rather, his source—is counting seventy-seven generations, so that Jesus' activity starts at the end of the eleventh and the beginning of the twelfth (and last!) period of seven generations.[9]

In the period between David and Jesus, there are gaping differences in both the number of generations and the names of the ancestors. With twenty-eight names, the average length of Matthew's generations measures thirty-six years, but Luke comes up with forty-three names, which assumes an average length of twenty-five years. Even Jesus' grandfather is called Heli by Luke, and Jacob by Matthew. The despair of the scribes and theologians of the ancient church is quite comprehensible; in the Scriptures they held to be inerrant, they suddenly found contradictions. Codex D met the difficulty with a radical solution: in Luke's Gospel, in place of the Lukan genealogy, it copies the Matthean list in reverse order.[10]

For Julius Africanus (end of the 2d to beginning of the 3d century), both lists are canonical, and the Scriptures inerrant, since they make a distinction between φύσις ("nature") and νόμος ("custom"), between biological and legal paternity, which the custom of Levirate marriage shows to be scriptural.[11] His argumentation is indeed comprehensible only if one keeps in mind that his text of Luke was shorter than our Nestle-Aland text. The Matthean sequence Matthan–Jacob–*Joseph*, and the sequence of his Lukan text, Melchi–Heli–*Joseph*, are correct because in one case, father and grandfather are named according to nature, and in the other, according to the law. To demonstrate this, Julius tells the family history: Matthan (a descendant of Solomon) marries Estha, and they have a son, Jacob. After Matthan's early death, Estha contracts a second marriage with Melchi (a descendant of Natham), from the same tribe as Matthan; he must descend from Judah, but from another family. From this marriage between Estha and Melchi comes Heli. Jacob and Heli are thus half-brothers: "brothers" so that the regulations of Levirate marriage come into play for them, but "half" so that they descend from two different sons of David, Solomon and Natham. Since Heli dies without children, Jacob is obligated to provide descendants for his brother. Thus Joseph was born Jacob's son by nature and Heli's son by law.[12] For this reason, Matthew uses the word γεννάω ("to beget," "to engender") to describe biological descent, where Luke uses the genitive to emphasize the legal relationship. According to Julius, the archives of families had been maintained, but had been put to flame by Herod, so that only the records of a very few families, who had carefully made copies, remained intact (§§11–14). Only one conclusion is possible: "in any case the gospel speaks the truth" (τό γέ τοι εὐαγγέλιον πάντως ἀληθεύει, §15).

Eusebius, who transmits Julius's testimony, recognizes that Jesus is not Joseph's biological son. Thus Mary must also be Davidic,[13] so that Jesus can indeed be the son of David "according to the flesh" (κατὰ σαρκά, Rom 1:3).

Julius's solution is striking in its rationalism. Christian theology began very early to think logically. A similar rationalism, with the same dogma of the inerrancy of Scripture, holds sway among modern fundamentalists.

---

8   On Luke's universalism, see Bovon, *Lukas*, 121–27.

9   On this possible schematization of the family tree, see Metzger (*Textual Commentary*, 136 n. 1), as well as Schweizer (52), who seems to attribute this breakdown to tradition: "But Luke is no longer aware of this salvation-historical legitimization"; see the commentary on vv. 24–38 below.

10   See Schürmann, 1.200 n. 86.

11   Cf. Eusebius *Hist. eccl.* 1.7.1–16.

12   Eusebius *Hist. eccl.* 1.7.10.

13   Since every man in Israel was obligated to marry a woman out of the same tribe, Mary must have come from the same lineage as Joseph, according to Eusebius *Hist. eccl.* 1.7.17.

But, all the same, one can no longer apply this sort of a solution today, because, for starters, there is nothing about levirate marriage in Luke. We can bring into full consideration the meaning and function of these lists, which are both probably the result of the educated speculation of early Christians, only when we renounce artificial harmonization.

Commentary

■ **23** The baptism account, which breaks off sharply, is linked only loosely with the genealogy by v. 23. Αὐτός and Ἰησοῦς are the subject: "he," that is, "Jesus."[14] In ἦν Ἰησοῦς ἀρχόμενος ὡσεὶ ἐτῶν τριάκοντα ("Jesus was about thirty years old when he began"), ἦν ("was") has a double function: it forms a periphrastic construction with ἀρχόμενος ("when he began"), describing the period of beginning, and it also serves as the verb for the statements about Jesus' age (correctly, with the genitive). It is unclear whether the periphrastic construction indicates an ongoing period of time, or does not differ from the simple form.[15] It is also unclear to what degree Luke has been influenced in this by Semitic languages, which often use the periphrastic construction.

The "beginning" is always theologically significant for Luke (cf. Acts 10:37) as the start of a new stage in salvation history. God unites with his servants, here, with his son, in order to "begin," as Luke sometimes writes in the absolute.[16] The beginning of the church (Acts 11:15) will correspond to its beginning in Jesus (Acts 1:21–22). "Beginning" does not connote coming into being, but God's active participation in time. It thus aims at a completion, in which the reality that has just been sowed can develop. For this reason, Luke gives careful specifications about the direction in which this beginning is headed: from Galilee to Jerusalem, from the baptism to the ascension, from Pentecost to the parousia.[17]

According to Epiphanius, the Gospel of Matthew that the Ebionites used also has a statement about Jesus' thirtieth year: "There appeared a certain man named Jesus of about thirty years of age, who chose us" (Ἐγένετό τις ἀνὴρ ὀνόματι Ἰησοῦς, καὶ αὐτὸς ὡς ἐτῶν τριάκοντα ὃς ἐξελέξατο ἡμᾶς).[18] Statements about age pertain to the genre of biography. Thirty years was at the time a considerable age and described the prime of life (see David in 2 Sam [LXX 2 Kgdms] 5:4, and Joseph in Gen 41:46).[19] Despite this, these figures of the Hebrew Bible are not being used typologically.[20] Thirty was probably the correct age for the highest degrees of responsibility: at thirty, David was king, having still the strength of youth, and already the wisdom of age. Thus Luke shows biographical and narrative concerns. Luke frequently uses ὡσεί ("about") with figures to avoid seeming pedantic. The statement about age probably derives from Luke himself. The *Gospel of the Ebionites* probably found it in Luke.

As for grammar, ἐνομίζετο ("he was considered [to be]") can be read with two very different meanings: (1) "He was considered to be Joseph's biological son" (but I, Luke, know this is not true); (2) "He was rightfully declared to be Joseph's son" (and I, Luke, agree with this). The genealogy would tend to lose its significance if the first translation were chosen, and this detracts from its likelihood.[21] The last element ("of God," v. 38), which is most likely a redactional addition, shows that Luke is not merely copying down archaic materials. Although Luke is here substantiating Jesus' identity as the Son of God in a different manner than the virgin birth, he still believes that the genealogy, which places Jesus among the descendants of David through Joseph, is correct; it is so as a consequence of chaps. 1–2, on the basis of an adoption, which, then as now, granted the same rights as sonship. This legal relationship (ἐνομίζετο, "to be considered") holds only for

---

14 See BDF §277.3, with n. 5: Αὐτός can have the meaning of the demonstrative pronoun οὗτος or ἐκεῖνος, and extol the importance of the subject.

15 See BDF §353.1–3.

16 Cf. the participial form ἀρξάμενος in Luke 24:27; Acts 1:22; 8:35; 10:37; 11:4; see also Conzelmann, *Theology*, 22 n. 3. On the theme of "beginnings," see Bovon, *Theologian,* 76, 105.

17 See Etienne Samain, "La notion de ἀρχή dans l'œuvre lucanienne," in Neirynck, *Évangile,*

299–328.

18 Epiphanius *Adv. haer.* 30.13.2, cited in Aland, *Synopsis,* 30. Translation from Hennecke-Schneemelcher, 1.170.

19 Cf. Num 4:3; cf. *TOB* on Num 8:24, note h.

20 Agreeing with Fitzmyer, 1.499.

21 Cf. Luke 2:27, 41 (Mary and Joseph are called "the parents" and "his parents"), and Luke 2:48 (Joseph is called "your father" by Mary).

the relationship between Joseph and Jesus; from Adam to Joseph, Luke assumes normal descent. In this sense Jesus is the Son of God through God's creative work with Adam, through his promise to David,[22] and, in human mediation, through Joseph's legal fatherhood. In another sense, he is for Luke the Son of God through the conception by the Spirit, through the disclosure of his sonship at his baptism, and through the resurrection.

■ **24–38** The first authors of the genealogy probably lived in a Jewish Christian milieu, and intended this ad hoc genealogy as an apologetic strategy aimed at the Galileans, to introduce Jesus into the family tree of the descendants of David, who, necessarily, resided in Judea. The tendency behind this genealogy thus corresponds to the displacement of Jesus' parents from Nazareth to Bethlehem. At this point in time, no one yet knew of the virgin birth, and Joseph was considered as Jesus' father without reservations.

In addition, salvation history, from the creation (Adam) to redemption (Jesus), is strikingly articulated. According to an apocalyptic tendency to set human epochs at 3×7 generations after the exile, and 3×7 generations from David until the exile, Jesus stands at the beginning of the seventh period (the eschatological epoch). After counting 2×7 from Abraham to David, and 3×7 from Adam to Abraham, Jesus begins the twelfth epoch of world history, which, according to

2 Esdr 14:11, is the last. If this is correct, the first authors of this list were apocalyptically oriented Christians.[23]

The link between Luke and apocalyptic tradition becomes ever clearer these days. His salvation history is thus not a substitute for the earliest Christian eschatology. It does not deny its apocalyptic roots, even where Luke prefers other systems of classification.

Conclusion

An analysis of the numerous names,[24] their bearers, and their possible relationships is less interesting than the issue of their literary position between the baptism and temptation of Jesus. With this placement of the genealogy, Luke has loosened the tight connection between these two salvation-historical events, in contrast to Mark. After attesting Jesus' relationship to the divine sphere (3:22), Luke illustrates Jesus' human identity. This also allows the temptations of the Son of God, proclaimed as such by the voice of God, to become real, that is, dangerous.[25]

---

22 According to Luke 1:27 and 2:4, Joseph comes from the house of David.

23 See the comments of Metzger and Schweizer on the schematization of the genealogy, mentioned in n. 9 above.

24 On these names see the reflections by Fitzmyer, 1.492–94, 499–504.

25 According to Martha Byskov, Luke has given the family tree a kerygmatic value in the context in

which he places it, and in the place that he devotes it: he wants to testify to the connection between the divine and human life of Jesus ("Verus Deus—verus homo: Lc 3, 23–38," *StTh* 26 [1972] 25–32); see also Bossuyt-Radermakers (148), who conceive of the baptism, genealogy, and temptation of Jesus as a complete literary unit (Luke 3:21—4:15), which concentrates on the *identity* of Jesus, whereas Luke 4:16–44 extols his *mission* (143–44).

The Temptation of Jesus (4:1–13)

Bibliography

Achtemeier, Paul J., "It's the Little Things That Count (Mark 14:17–21; Luke 4:1–13; Matthew 18:10–14)," *BA* 46 (1983) 30–31.

Brown, *Apostasy*.

den Heyer, C. J., "Die Versuchungserzählung in den Evangelien," *Zeitschrift für dialektische Theologie* 2 (1986) 10–20.

Dupont, *Tentations*.

Duquoc, C., "La tentation du Christ," *LumVie* (Lyon) 53 (1961) 21–41.

Feuillet, A., "Le récit lucanien de la tentation (Lc 4,1–13)," *Bib* 40 (1959) 613–31.

Fridrichsen, Anton Johnson, *The Problem of Miracle in Primitive Christianity* (trans. R. A. Harrisville and J. S. Hanson; Minneapolis: Augsburg, 1972) 121–28.

Fuchs, Albert, "Versuchung Jesu," in idem, ed., SNTU A.9 (Linz: Albert Fuchs, 1984) 96–159.

Gerhardsson, *Testing*.

Hahn, *Titles*, 72, 158–59, 295.

Harsch, Helmut, "Psychologische Interpretation biblischer Texte?" *Wege zum Menschen* 20 (1968) 281–89, reprinted in Y. Spiegel, ed., *Psychoanalytische Interpretation biblischer Texte* (Munich: Kaiser, 1972) 49–59.

Hoffmann, Paul, "Die Versuchungsgeschichte in der Logienquelle: Zur Auseinandersetzung der Judenchristen mit dem politischen Messianismus," *BZ* n.s. 13 (1969) 207–23.

Humphrey, Hugh, "Temptation and Authority: Sapiential Narratives in Q," *BTB* 21 (1991) 43–50.

Köppen, Klaus-Peter, *Die Auslegung der Versuchungsgeschichte unter besonderer Berücksichtigung der Alten Kirche: Ein Beitrag zur Geschichte der Schriftauslegung* (BGBE 4; Tübingen: Mohr-Siebeck, 1961).

Mahnke, *Versuchungsgeschichte*.

Meynet, Roland, *Quelle est donc cette parole? Lecture 'rhétorique' de l'évangile de Luc (1–9, 22–24)* (LD 99; Paris: Cerf, 1979) 169–72.

Panier, Louis, *Récit et commentaires de la tentation de Jésus au désert: Approche sémiotique du discours interprétatif* (Paris: Cerf, 1984).

Pokorný, Petr, "The Temptation Stories and Their Intention," *NTS* 20 (1973–74) 115–27.

Rey, Bernard, *Les tentations et le choix de Jésus* (Lire la Bible 72; Paris: Cerf, 1986).

Riesenfeld, Harald, "Le caractère messianique de la tentation au désert," in E. Massaux et al., eds., *La venue du Messie* (RechBib 6; Bruges: Desclée de Brouwer, 1962) 51–63.

Schnackenburg, Rudolf, "Der Sinn der Versuchung Jesu bei den Synoptikern," *ThQ* 132 (1952) 297–326.

Schulz, *Q*, 177–90.

Smyth-Florentin, F., "Jésus, le Fils du Père, vainqueur de Satan," *AsSeign* 14 (1973) 56–75.

Steiner, M., *La tentation de Jésus dans l'interprétation patristique de Saint Justin à Origène* (EtB; Paris: Gabalda, 1962).

van Iersel, Bastiaan Martinus Franciscus, *"Der Sohn" in den synoptischen Jesusworten: Christusbezeichnung der Gemeinde oder Selbstbezeichnung Jesu?* (NovTSup 3; Leiden: Brill, 1961) 165–71.

Wengst, Klaus, "Anmerkungen zur Barthschen Auslegung der Versuchungsgeschichte aus heutiger exegetischer Perspektive," *Zeitschrift für dialektische Theologie* 2 (1986) 21–38.

Wilkens, Wilhelm, "Die Versuchungsgeschichte Luk. 4,1–13 und die Komposition des Evangeliums," *ThZ* 30 (1974) 267–72.

Zeller, D., "Die Versuchungen Jesu in der Logienquelle," *TThZ* 89 (1980) 61–73.

1 Then Jesus, full of holy spirit, returned from the Jordan and was led by the spirit in the wilderness, 2/ where for forty days he was tempted by the devil. He ate nothing during those days; and when they had ended, he was hungry. 3/ Then the devil said to him, "If you are the Son of God, command this stone to become a loaf of bread." 4/ And Jesus answered him, "It is written, 'One does not live by bread alone.'" 5/ Then the devil led him up and showed him in an instant all the kingdoms of the world. 6/ And the devil said to him, "To you I will give all their glory and authority; for to me it has been given, and I give it to anyone I please. 7/ If you, then, will worship me, it will all be yours." 8/ And Jesus answered and said to him, "It is written, 'You shall worship the Lord your God, and serve only him.'" 9/ But the devil took him to Jerusalem, and placed him on the pinnacle of the temple precinct, saying to him, "If you are the Son of God, throw yourself down from here, 10/ for it is written, 'He will command his angels concerning you, to protect you,' 11/ and 'On their hands they will bear you up, so that you will not dash your foot against a stone.'" 12/ Jesus answered and said to him, "It is said, 'You shall not put the Lord your God to the test.'" 13/ And when the devil had finished every temptation, he departed from him until an opportune time.

Analysis

Whereas Jesus has acted passively in 3:1–22 and 23–38 (he receives power and understanding after his baptism, and he is incorporated into a family genealogy), here he takes the initiative. Grammatically, he becomes the subject of the verbs. On the basis of what he has received and inherited from God, he begins to act.

Typically for Luke's episodic style, v. 13 establishes a definite conclusion. Since v. 1 clearly introduces the pericope, the boundaries in the text are distinct.[1]

Luke's chief reference in this passage is still the sayings source. Mark's influence is weak:[2] Matthew and Luke both call Jesus by name, read "the devil" (ὁ διάβολος) and not "Satan" (ὁ Σατανᾶς), use the passive voice (Luke: "was led" [ἤγετο]; Matthew: "was led up" [ἀνήχθη]), where Mark writes "the Spirit drove him out" (with ἐκβάλλει), and they both use the number forty after the word "days," and ignore the wild animals. Only Matthew repeats the motif of help from angels found in Mark. Traces of Markan influence in Luke are probably evident only in the difficult phrase ἐν τῇ ἐρήμῳ ("in the wilderness," directly after ἐν τῷ πνεύματι, "by the Spirit"), in the participle πειραζόμενος ("was tempted"), and in the sequence of wilderness—forty days—temptation.

The story of the temptation began in Q similarly as it does in Mark: Jesus, led and directed by the Spirit, is tempted for forty days. The devil's disappearance is mentioned in conclusion, rather than the angels and wild beasts.

Within this framework, Q narrates the temptation in the form of a dialogue. Matthew and Luke have recorded the second and third temptation in reverse order.[3] Matthew has probably preserved the original sequence.[4] Luke makes the transposition so that, first, Jesus' last temptation takes place in the temple, which will achieve salvation-historical significance in the course of the last stage of his life; second, the issue of political authority, awkward for Luke, does not take the final, that is, most important, position. This issue is one of the "things just before the end." The gradation of the three temptations shows that tempting God (4:12) is the most grave.

It is important for Luke that the devil clothes his greatest temptation in scriptural citations (vv. 10–11), and that, as in Jesus' life as a whole, the first temptation takes place in the wilderness, and the last in Jerusalem.

Thus the three stages in Jesus' active life correspond to the three temptations.[5] It is possible that Luke leaves the mountain (Matt 4:8) unmentioned because, in his account, no mountain plays a role in Jesus' life. The participle ἀναγαγὼν αὐτόν ("[the devil] led him up," v. 5) might even allude to the travel account, so that the devil would not then wait until 22:3 to become active again.[6]

Generally, this account arises from the conviction that people loved by God, such as Adam, Abraham,[7] Moses, David, and Job, all experienced temptation.[8] The attribution of it to Satan and not directly to God results

---

1   Roland Meynet suggests another division (*Quelle est donc cette parole? Lecture 'rhétorique' de l'évangile de Luc [1–9, 22–24]* [LD 99; Paris: Cerf, 1979] 169–72).

2   Others consider it to be greater; they say that Luke and Matthew have, to some extent, slipped the Q version over Mark 1:12–13 (Luke 4:1–2 would then be a reworking of the Markan version).

3   Hermann Mahnke has treated the question of the original sequence thoroughly (*Die Versuchungsgeschichte im Rahmen der synoptischen Evangelien: Ein Beitrag zur frühen Christologie* [BEvTh 9; Frankfurt am Main: Lang, 1978] 170–83).

4   Schulz (*Q*, 177) shares this opinion.

5   Wilhelm Wilkens sets forth this correspondence a bit too definitely ("Die Versuchungsgeschichte Luk. 4,1–13 und die Komposition des Evangeliums," *ThZ* 30 [1974] 267–72).

6   It is the thesis of Conzelmann that the life of Jesus between the final temptation (4:13) and the beginning of the passion narrative (22:3) is a "Satan-free

period," and that the devil waits until 22:3 to become active again (*Theology*, 16, 27–29, 80–81); cf. Luke 22:28.

7   Cf. the testing of Abraham in the furnace, after he refused to build the tower of Babel. This legend, which never made it into the Bible, is told in *Bib. Ant.* 6.

8   On this connection between temptation and the members of the covenant, see Birger Gerhardsson, *The Testing of God's Son (Matt 4:1–11 & Par.): An Analysis of an Early Christian Midrash* (ConBNT 2; Lund: Gleerup, 1966) 24. According to Gerhardsson, by withstanding temptation, Jesus loves God with his whole heart (bread), with his whole life (the pinnacle of the temple), and with all his strength, i.e., with all his possessions (all the riches of the world).

from the development of Jewish theology.[9] Even more generally, one could employ semiotics and say that, in the logic of the narrativity, the baptism account and the story of the temptation represent the two poles of the acquisition of competence. But the more important question can only be answered by specific exegesis: is this intended to defend Jesus against Jewish critique (that he is a charlatan or false messiah), or to offer Christians an encouraging example? Its development is best explained if the haggadic[10] and creative techniques of Christian readers are taken into account, which allows Scripture and memory, exegesis and art, to converge to form the final product. The dialogic and polemic form makes it probable that the *Sitz im Leben* is the controversy with Judaism, and that the theme is christology, not merely ethics.

Commentary

The threefold character of the temptations results from the following Jewish conceptualization: "Threefold performance of an action or the threefold occurrence of an event shows that it is complete, finished, definitive."[11] On top of this, according to the eastern standard, the greatest temptation occurs precisely in the last round of dialogue.[12] Perhaps Jewish legends about Moses exercised an influence: two of the temptations that the young Moses resists are the pleasures of the table and the exercise of political authority designated with the title "young king."[13]

■ **1–2a** The first half of this sentence (v. 1a) has a redactional character, as demonstrated by the use of $\pi\lambda\acute{\eta}\rho\eta\varsigma$ ("full") with the genitive, $\dot{\upsilon}\pi\acute{\epsilon}\sigma\tau\rho\epsilon\psi\epsilon\nu$ ("returned," see 4:14), and the geographical details. The lack of an article before "Jesus" is unusual for Luke (see 22:48, 52); this may have been conditioned by Luke's source. The second half (v. 1b) is more heavily traditional: "Although the three Synoptic evangelists differ markedly from one another in their introductions to the temptation story, and although an absolute use of $\tau\grave{o}\ \pi\nu\epsilon\hat{\upsilon}\mu\alpha$ ['the Spirit'] is quite rare in all of them, all three agree that an anaphoric article, which refers back to the baptism, belongs before the absolute use of $\pi\nu\epsilon\hat{\upsilon}\mu\alpha$ in the introduction to the temptation story (Mark 1:12, $\tau\grave{o}\ \pi\nu\epsilon\hat{\upsilon}\mu\alpha$ ['the Spirit']; Matt 4:1, $\dot{\upsilon}\pi\grave{o}\ \tau o\hat{\upsilon}\ \pi\nu\epsilon\acute{\upsilon}\mu\alpha\tau o\varsigma$ ['by the Spirit']; Luke 4:1, $\dot{\epsilon}\nu\ \tau\hat{\wp}\ \pi\nu\epsilon\acute{\upsilon}\mu\alpha\tau\iota$ ['by the Spirit']). This agreement among the Synoptic evangelists demonstrates that we have here very ancient traditions of the early church."[14]

Luke accepted this tradition with approval, and even developed it further. That Jesus has been filled with the Holy Spirit since his baptism alters the sense in which he is led by the Spirit. "By the Spirit" ($\dot{\epsilon}\nu\ \tau\hat{\wp}\ \pi\nu\epsilon\acute{\upsilon}\mu\alpha\tau\iota$) after "full of the Spirit" ($\pi\lambda\acute{\eta}\rho\eta\varsigma\ \pi\nu\epsilon\acute{\upsilon}\mu\alpha\tau o\varsigma$) cannot mean the subordination of Jesus, but rather the solidarity of the Messiah and the Spirit.

Jesus travels the same path as John (3:2–3), although in the opposite direction: from the Jordan into the wilderness. In the wilderness, the Baptist hears the call of God, but Jesus hears the voice of the devil. The symbolic value of the wilderness, then, is not fixed; it can have either positive or negative connotations. It is a disturbing place in which the individual (or the nation) can experience the divine or the monstrous.

The second account of the ascension (Acts 1:3) demonstrates the evangelist's interest in the traditional forty days. In that passage, the inner circle of witnesses to the resurrection were instructed and equipped during this period. The symbolic meaning of the forty days or years, common throughout the ancient East, related in Israel to the significant periods in the life of the servants of God, or of the entire nation. Moses spent forty days on Sinai during the making of the covenant (Exod 24:18; 34:28). In Jewish tradition, with which Luke is familiar, this is the standard length of time for receiving divine revelation.[15] Since forty years in the wilderness was also

---

9 Cf. the census that was displeasing to God, which David conducted, because, according to 2 Sam (LXX 2 Kgdms) 24:1, God provoked him; but according to the parallel passage (1 Chr 21:1), Satan did it.

10 Gerhardsson (*Testing*) considers both versions of the temptation of Jesus to be haggadic midrashim developed from Deut 6–8.

11 Gerhard Delling, "$\tau\rho\epsilon\hat{\iota}\varsigma,\ \kappa\tau\lambda.$," *TDNT* 8 (1972) 222.

12 Cf. Schulz, *Q*, 185; Mahnke, *Versuchungsgeschichte*, 377 n. 23.

13 Cf. Philo *Vit. Mos.* 1.28, 32.

14 Jeremias, *Sprache*, 115.

15 See Philippe Henri Menoud, "Pendant quarante jours (Actes 1,3)" in *Neotestamentica et Patristica: Festschrift Oscar Cullmann* (NovTSup 6; Leiden: Brill, 1962) 148–56, reprinted in English translation in Philippe Henri Menoud, *Jesus Christ and the Faith*

a time of punishment and testing for the nation (Deut 8:2),[16] Luke follows tradition in understanding this time in Jesus' life as one of temptation and testing, but also as a time of firsthand realization of the revelation mediated by the Spirit and in the Scriptures. The forty days should be linked with the imperfect tense ἤγετο ("was led") rather than with the participle πειραζόμενος ("was tempted").

Πειράζω is the intensive form ("to strive to tempt") of πειράω, and also the Ionic form of the Attic πειράω. In Hellenistic Judaism πειράω retained its secular meaning ("to tempt," "to put to the test"), whereas πειράζω, the form familiar from the LXX (translation of נָסָה), usually had a religious significance. The obedience of the nation or the believer is constantly threatened by temptation—whether by God or by Satan.[17] Conversely, people can also tempt God.[18] The issue at stake in temptation is less often a moral lapse than apostasy from God, although ethical components are perceptible in Hellenistic Judaism as a result of the influence of philosophy. In comparison with the current Jewish psychology of belief, the temptation account in the Gospels proves surprisingly realistic and theological.

The participle πειραζόμενος ("was tempted") seems to be a familiar expression for the believer in the language of the first Christians (Heb 2:18; Jas 1:13). The contention that πειρασμός in Luke means "apostasy," not "temptation," fails already at Luke 4:13.[19] But the word is not used in the book of Acts for the temptation of the first Christians, so the ethical component of Luke's account of Jesus' temptation should not be overemphasized.

In contrast to δοκιμάζω ("to test"), πειράζω has a connotation of hostile intent. Thus ὁ διάβολος ("the devil"), which for Luke is purely negative, is the author of the temptation (not the testing) of Jesus.

Excursus: The Devil

Luke employs ὁ διάβολος ("the devil," "the slanderer") seven times for the devil (esp. in 4:1–13, taken from Q) and ὁ Σατανᾶς ("Satan") seven times (five times in the Gospel[20] and twice in Acts). That Luke changed "Satan" (Mark 4:14) to "devil" (Luke 8:12) shows his preference for the Greek form. Although he has no developed demonology, he still has a few thoughts on the topic. After the failed attempt with Jesus, the devil leaves him "until an opportune time" (ἄχρι καιροῦ). The πειρασμός ("temptation," v. 13) of the passion episode is directed more at the disciples than at Jesus: the devil ambushes Judas (22:3) and "sifts" the disciples "like wheat" (22:31), and Jesus warns them of temptation in Gethsemane (22:40, 46). It is probably splitting hairs to say that Jesus, after the episode in the wilderness (4:1–13), is still put to the test, though no longer tempted.[21] It is clear, though, that the devil becomes active again at 22:3, and that Jesus in 4:1–13 is his first target. The period in between is not so much a "Satan-free time"[22] as a time in which Satan has taken the initiative against him. It is Luke's firm conviction that humans are afflicted by the devil and suffer from him.[23] This general power of the devil, which even encompasses the political realm (4:6), is not logically connected, but is narratively consistent with the sudden invasion of an individual by evil forces (13:16; 22:3). Both aspects stand side by side in Luke because every story must possess the quality of a unique

---

(trans. E. M. Paul; PTMS 18; Pittsburgh: Pickwick, 1978) 167–79, esp. 171; cf. Philo *Mos.* 2.71: during his time at the peak of Sinai, Moses was initiated into all of the activities of the priesthood.

16 Since a single individual cannot be tempted for forty years in the desert, it is understandable that, in transferring this motif from the people of the HB to Jesus, the number was retained, but the years were turned into days.

17 See Str-B 1.139–41, on the role of Satan as the tempter.

18 See Heinrich Seesemann, "πεῖρα, κτλ.," *TDNT* 6 (1968) 24.

19 See Schuyler Brown, *Apostasy and Perseverance in the Theology of Luke* (AnBib 36; Rome: Pontifical Biblical Institute Press, 1969); Bovon, *Theologian*, 387–88.

20 Of these five instances, one is taken from Mark (Luke 11:18), and four from Luke's special source (10:18; 13:16; 22:3, 31).

21 See Jacques Dupont, *Les tentations de Jésus au désert* (SN 4; Paris: Desclée de Brouwer, 1968) 70. On the differences of meaning between πειράζω and δοκιμάζω, see Richard Chenevix Trench, *Synonyms of the New Testament* (London: Kegan, Paul, Trench, Trübner, 1906) 260–63.

22 As Conzelmann would describe it (*Theology*, 27; see 16 and 80–81).

23 Luke 13:16; Acts 10:38, 26:18.

event, but even more because Luke does not consider the events he narrates to be exceptions, but rather visible signs of an invisible reality: when the devil takes possession of Judas, what was already a potentiality simply becomes evident. The time of Jesus is, nevertheless, a good period, because the Messiah's actions and God's power are attacking the devil and forcing him out of his strong position.[24] Yet the battle is to be fought until the parousia, and the victory is not yet final, for the devil, though he has fallen from heaven, is nevertheless active on the earth.[25] The Word of God and the Holy Spirit offer no guarantee that believers will not fall back into Satan's hands (Luke 8:12 par. Mark 4:15). Even after Easter, people must be transferred from the power of Satan to the hands of God (Acts 26:18).

Luke has accepted the mythological discourse about the devil, and for his part has not developed it further. It remains strictly tied to human beings; neither the creation nor history is demonized, but they are also not sacralized. This mythological language guards human existence from an overly irresponsible optimism. But Luke is also free of a defeatist attitude. "Repentance" ($\mu\epsilon\tau\acute{a}\nu o\iota\alpha$) calls people to ethical responsibility. Luke is aware of the power of supernatural forces that imprison humanity, but he knows far more about the power that can set the captives free.[26]

Is there anything left in Luke of an eschatological understanding of $\pi\epsilon\iota\rho\alpha\sigma\mu\acute{o}\varsigma$ ("temptation") and of victory over the devil?[27] The end of time is clearly delaying; the one period of testing has become a multitude. In this sense eschatology is being transformed into ethics. But, on the other hand, Luke does believe that the end of time has dawned with Jesus (Luke 16:16), and that nothing can stand in the way of its fulfillment. It is coming, even if not quickly.

■ **2b** Q already told about Jesus' hunger after the forty days, but at the same time, the Lukan redaction is manifest in the double negative (cf. 10:19 and Acts 4:12), the chronological information (cf. Luke 9:36), the genitive absolute, and $\sigma\upsilon\nu\tau\epsilon\lambda\acute{\epsilon}\omega$ ("to end"; cf. 4:13 and Acts 21:27 [as here, with "days"]). Matthew emphasizes typology by mentioning the nights as well, and he reads not $o\dot{\upsilon}\kappa\ \acute{\epsilon}\varphi\alpha\gamma\epsilon\nu$ ("he ate nothing"; cf. Exod 34:28 LXX), but

$\nu\eta\sigma\tau\epsilon\acute{\upsilon}\sigma\alpha\varsigma$ ("he fasted"). The interest of the New Testament community in fasting does not suffice as an explanation. Might not both $\nu\eta\sigma\tau\epsilon\acute{\upsilon}\sigma\alpha\varsigma$ ("he fasted," Matthew) and $o\dot{\upsilon}\kappa\ \acute{\epsilon}\varphi\alpha\gamma\epsilon\nu\ o\dot{\upsilon}\delta\acute{\epsilon}\nu$ ("he ate nothing," Luke) be redactional expansions of the sayings source, which spoke only of Jesus' hunger ($\dot{\epsilon}\pi\epsilon\acute{\iota}\nu\alpha\sigma\epsilon\nu$, "he was hungry," in both Matthew and Luke)?[28] In this case Luke would also have some sensitivity to the Moses-Jesus typology.[29] But one must admit that Moses' sojourn did not concern temptation, but the giving of the Law and the making of the covenant, and that Moses' face was made radiant at that time, which anticipates Jesus' transfiguration, not his temptation; and last, the event took place on a mountain, not in the wilderness.

This demonstrates the ingenious haggadic work of the first Christian teachers, who did not hesitate to unite various figures in Jesus: if Jesus bears Moses' characteristics, he also takes on the function of the nation loved by God, the "son of God," which was falling prey to temptation below in the wilderness[30] while Moses was waiting up on the mountain. Antinomy joins typology. As Paul elaborated sin and grace by means of the figures of Adam and Christ, the Q tradition uses Israel and Jesus for temptation and faith. They are not examples, but salvation-historical types from the two economies.

■ **3–4** After the description of the setting, the dialogue begins. The first command links the theme of miracles with the issue of nourishment. Jesus answers with a quotation from Deuteronomy 8. In v. 3 $\delta\acute{\epsilon}$ ("and," "but," "then") in Luke is secondary, in contrast to $\kappa\alpha\acute{\iota}$ ("and," Matthew). Matthew adds the suggestive movement of the devil ($\pi\rho o\sigma\epsilon\lambda\vartheta\acute{\omega}\nu$, "came," Matt 4:3), and replaces "the devil" ($\acute{o}\ \delta\iota\acute{a}\beta o\lambda o\varsigma$) with "the tempter" ($\acute{o}\ \pi\epsilon\iota\rho\acute{a}\zeta\omega\nu$). Luke improves $\epsilon\dot{\iota}\pi\grave{\epsilon}\ \acute{\iota}\nu\alpha$ ("speak so that") into $\epsilon\dot{\iota}\pi\grave{\epsilon}\ \tau\hat{\omega}\ \lambda\acute{\iota}\vartheta\omega\ \tau o\acute{\upsilon}\tau\omega\ \acute{\iota}\nu\alpha$ ("command this stone to"). It cannot be determined whether Q spoke of stone and bread in singular or plural. Matt 4:4 has extended the citation.[31]

According to Deuteronomy 8, God instructs his people in the wilderness and puts them to the test (esp.

---

24   Luke 10:18; 13:16; Acts 10:38.
25   1 Cor 7:5; Eph 6:11; Rev 13:1; 1 Pet 5:8; Jas 4:7, etc.
26   Acts 5:19; 12:7–10; 16:25–30.
27   See Bovon, *Theologian*, 12–14, 387–90.
28   See Schulz, *Q,* 179.
29   Various mss. allude to Exod 34:28 LXX ($\kappa\alpha\grave{\iota}\ \acute{\upsilon}\delta\omega\rho$ $o\dot{\upsilon}\kappa\ \acute{\epsilon}\pi\iota\epsilon\nu$) by adding $o\dot{\upsilon}\delta\grave{\epsilon}\ \acute{\epsilon}\pi\iota\epsilon\nu$ (cf. the apparatus to Luke 4:2 in Nestle-Aland).

30   Bultmann (*History*, 256–57) excludes the possibility of such a rapprochement.
31   Not a few copyists of the Gospel of Luke have also continued the citation, although somewhat differently than in Matthew; cf. the apparatus to Luke 4:4 in Nestle-Aland.

in the LXX, which follows targumic interpretation). From this chapter, Luke takes some phrases word for word (vv. 2–5).

In contrast to Israel, Jesus passes the test imposed on him. He rejects miracles, such as the miracle of manna, which were granted as concessions to Israel in the desert. Jesus proves himself to be an obedient Israelite, and, if one accepts the influence of Deuteronomy 8, his faith is linked with the "remembering" expressed in the scriptural citation. Following a well-known development in Israel,[32] God does not put one to the test, but rather the devil does. *Εἰ* ("if") should not be interpreted as hypothetical, but almost as causal. The devil is not in doubt; he believes that Jesus is the Son of God.

Jesus is more than a mere symbol of the new nation. He is the "Son of God." The absence of the article does not mean that *υἱός* ("son") is indefinite; predicate nouns typically lack the article if there is a copulative verb.[33] In connection with his baptism, Jesus is, at least for Luke, more than *a* son of God; he is *the* eschatological Son of God. Why does he not then perform the miracles of Moses? Will not a prophet like Moses arise in the last days (Deut 15:15, 18)? Jesus will indeed do miracles later, and even multiply bread (Luke 9:12–17). But he will do it for others, not for himself. If bread would have had priority over his relationship to the Father,[34] he would have succumbed to temptation. His messianic power would then have been destroyed.

Rudolf Bultmann rejected the messianic interpretation of the temptation, since, he claimed, Judaism did not recognize the figure of the Messiah as a wonderworker, and knew nothing of the temptation of the Messiah; the issue under discussion was the correct understanding of miracles.[35] Is the early Christian community then using the temptation story to defend Jesus against the accusation of sorcery, and his miracles as signs of the kingdom of God, and not diabolical magic?[36] It is clear that the title "Son of God" is not being defended as such, but rather the exercise of power associated with it; this power is, however, for Luke and probably already for Q, that of the Messiah. The original Semitic account was presumably defending the christological claims of the first community; in a Gentile environment, however, a caution against a false interpretation of the title "Son of God" was read into it.[37]

■ **5–8** Luke has transformed the Semitizing parataxis of Q into a hypotactic construction (v. 5), thereby improving it stylistically[38] and omitting the detail of the mountain.[39] The substitution of *ἡ οἰκουμένη* ("the [inhabited] world") for *ὁ κόσμος* ("the world") is also his work,[40] as is the addition of *ἐν στιγμῇ χρόνου* ("in an instant"). The extended version of v. 6 is also most likely redactional. The devil's double promise in vv. 6–7, as well as linguistic observations (*ἅπας*, "all," and *ἐνώπιον*, "[worship] before [me]"), are indications of this.

The phrase "all the kingdoms of the world" already touches on the theme of power. It shows the sorcery of the devil and the supernatural dimension of this event: a view of the entire world is possible in an "instant" (*ἐν στιγμῇ χρόνου*).

To "glory" (*δόξα*), Luke adds the "authority" (*ἐξουσία*) of these kingdoms, which strikes him as more important. Both are promised to the Son. Luke's expansion of the Q version of the saying becomes a linguistic parody of divine inspiration: the redactional addition is reminiscent of Dan 4:31 (LXX); 7:14; and Luke 10:22. In the words, "for to me it has been given" (*ὅτι ἐμοὶ*

---

32   See n. 9 above on David's census.

33   See BDF §273.

34   See Hahn, *Titles*, 295: "The Son of God may not misuse his power either in helping himself or in working a spectacular miracle, but must use it only in what he is commissioned to do. Thus divine sonship in the context of equipment with the wonderful power of the Spirit is stamped with the thought of obedience."

35   See Bultmann, *History*, 254–56.

36   See Luz, *Matthew*, 187–88. Luz refers to *Ps.-Clem. Rec.* 2.9.3; 3.47.2; and to *Acts Pet.* 31–32.

37   See Hahn, *Titles*, 294–95; and Petr Pokorný, "The

Temptation Stories and Their Intention," *NTS* 20 (1973–74) 115–27, esp. 125.

38   See Schulz, *Q*, 180–81.

39   Thus Conzelmann, *Theology*, 29. In the participle *ἀναγαγών* ("led him up," v. 5), a remnant of the mountain motif is hidden. Part of the textual tradition has reintroduced the "high mountain" under the influence of Matthew.

40   *Οἰκουμένη*: Luke 2:1; 4:5; 21:26; Acts 11:28; 17:6, 31; 19:27; 24:5. The use of this word reflects Luke's universalistic perspective; but universalistic, of course, means the civilized, i.e., inhabited, world, thus the space within the borders of the Roman

παραδέδοται), the devil is therefore saying that God has given him the political authority over the kingdoms of the world. Jesus does not address this claim. Thus the pessimistic view of the world that lies behind this statement may be peculiar to Luke. The devil further claims that he can grant this power to whom he pleases. This implies that the princes receive power and glory neither directly from God nor from the people, but from the devil, and that they therefore honor him, not God, or, in nonmythological language, that they exercise their power in their own interests, not in the service of others. This is the bondage of those who bring others into bondage. But the devil is also a liar, and Luke may well accept in a different context the Hebrew Bible belief in God as the source of political authority.

Luke is not writing a tractate on political theology, but telling a story; thus the condition attached to the promise is important. Προσκυνέω means here "to worship," not merely "to honor."[41] The devil demands nothing less than a change of command. Shortly after the establishment of the father-son relationship, he suggests another, perverted, bond. Does he hope that Jesus will simultaneously maintain both relationships, or that he will change camps? Again, Jesus answers with a text from Scripture.[42]

Luke knows that God demands exclusive service (16:13). The temptation to deny God in the realm of worldly power concerns money. Politics and economics thus become the locus of existential decisions of faith. Neither politics nor economics is attacked as such, only individuals who claim them for their own.

Jesus reacts not only as a pious Jew, but also—at least in the text as we have it—as the Christian Messiah and the Son of Man. Just as Jesus' miracles were suspected to be sorcery, the messianic claims of the first Christians with regard to Jesus were considered to be Satanic by Jewish sages. Jesus' answer, in the words of the first Christians, describes his life as service to God free from any demonic hopes for personal omnipotence. There is messianic omnipotence only in the future; in the interim, the pessimistic v. 6b is still valid. Only after the resurrection, and for Luke, only after the parousia, will Jesus Christ receive the "power and glory" of all the kingdoms of the earth. Thus this temptation is a parallel to the travel account, in which Jesus learns that precisely his identity as Son of God and Messiah will lead him into suffering.

■ 9–12 In the third phase of the temptation, the devil takes Jesus to Jerusalem, to the pediment of the temple precinct.[43] Here again Luke takes the Q tradition as his basis. As in v. 5, he avoids mentioning the devil expressly. "The holy city" (Matt 4:5), in place of "Jerusalem," should be attributed to Matthean redaction. Luke continues the quotation (Ps 91[LXX 90]:11) with the phrase τοῦ διαφυλάξαι σε ("to protect you"). The words "in all of your ways" (ἐν πάσαις ταῖς ὁδοῖς σου), at the end of LXX Ps 90:11, were, however, too general for Luke to quote in the context. The introduction of v. 12 may be traditional.[44] But "it is said" (εἴρηται) for a word from Scripture is Lukan (cf. Acts 2:16; 13:40).

The temptation takes place in the temple district. Is this a priestly temptation on the heels of a prophetic and a kingly temptation?[45] The devil brings Jesus to the location of greatest public visibility. The temptation is intended more to confirm the genuineness of the father-son relationship than to demonstrate Jesus' miraculous

---

Empire. Luke hardly ever refers to the world with the term ὁ κόσμος (cf. Luke 9:25; 11:50; 12:30; Acts 17:24). Luke 12:30 constitutes the only exception, if it should count at all, since the wording of these verses is traditional.

41   In Luke προσκυνέω always also has a religious sense. It is reserved for God and—after the resurrection (Luke 24:52)—for Jesus; it becomes idolatry if it is consciously performed before anyone other than God (Acts 7:43). When Cornelius honors Peter more than he is due, Peter corrects him (Acts 10:25–26). Jesus refuses to fall down before Satan (Luke 4:7–8). See Johannes M. Nützel, "προσκυνέω, κτλ.," EDNT 3 (1993) 173–75.

42   What is cited is Deut 6:13, or 10:20 according to the text of Alexandrinus. Other chief witnesses read φοβηθήσῃ ("you shall fear") in place of προσκυνή- σεις and overlook the important μόνῳ ("only"); see Traugott Holtz, Untersuchungen über die alttesta- mentliche Zitate bei Lukas (TU 104; Berlin: Akademie, 1968) 62–63.

43   On the πτερύγιον see Mahnke, Versuchungs- geschichte, 116–18: The πτερύγιον of the temple precinct (ἱερόν) is not part of the building (ναός) but a raised location in the surroundings that we can no longer identify, or the gable of one of the gates.

44   See Jeremias, Sprache, 117.

45   See Mahnke, Versuchungsgeschichte, 113–26; critically, Luz, Matthew, 185 n. 14.

144

strength. Why is it a temptation, if the citation from Psalm 91 (LXX 90) is correct? Because one would be tempting God, Jesus answers with another quotation: "You shall not put the Lord your God to the test" (Deut 6:16 LXX). Israel's temptation in that story consisted of their tempting God by demanding water from him. In all three temptations, then, Jesus wishes nothing for himself and thus will not put God to the test. The devil cites the Scriptures, but does not understand them. The hermeneutic of the Christians who placed Deut 6:16 in the mouth of Jesus consists in, first, their sensitivity to metaphor: Ps 91(LXX 90):11–12 should not be understood literally; second, their conviction that the help of God promised in this psalm is not automatic: the believer does not risk disaster to experience God. Salvation comes through suffering and death.

This biblical theology is not recited incidentally. It serves as the answer to a criticism, not of miracles, but of the cross of Jesus. Why did God not spare his son this death (Luke 23:35, 37, 39)? The Christian answer runs this way: It is because of faith, and not powerlessness, that Jesus did not save himself. Again, this is not only the answer of a believer, but also of the Messiah of the Christians, who is under attack.

■ **13** The devil possesses great power (v. 6), but is not capable of forcing the decisions of humans. Some, like Adam[46] and the people of God in the wilderness, succumb; others, like Job and Jesus, withstand. The devil employed all of his options, and now must signal his defeat somatically: he leaves Jesus, though a threat still lingers—until the next opportunity.

Conclusion

I have spoken of a controversy dialogue. That is, however, only one angle. Indeed, the devil and the Son argue with Bible texts like two rabbis. But the themes bring the account into relationship with narratives of another sort: with stories that tell of the temptation, sin, and fall of specific individuals, and with others that describe the resistance and triumph of believers.[47]

I know of only two form-critical parallels: Daniel 3 (the three men in the fiery furnace) and *Sipra* 22.32, 99d.[48] The latter passage transmits the legend of Emperor Trajan, who persecuted two Jews and said to them, "Are you not from the nation of Ananias, Misael, and Azariah [cf. Dan 3 LXX]? Let your God come and save you." The Jews answered, "Ananias, Misael, and Azariah were worthy, and Nebuchadnezzar merited to have a sign take place. We and you are not worthy of a miracle." Like the devil in Luke 4, the emperor argues on the basis of the Scriptures and the privileges of the people of God. Like Jesus, the two Jews repudiate their right to a miracle. Daniel 3 and *Sipra* 22.32, 99d draw our attention toward the issue of divine signs. As in Jewish and early Christian theology, Luke is persuaded that (1) God helps his servants in need with miracles and gives them signs; (2) only a false prophet capitalizes on a sign; and (3) only counterfeit believers fall into the temptation of demanding a miracle. This is also true of the passages in which Jesus refuses a sign (Luke 11:16, 29–30).

Though the *Sitz im Leben* of the temptation story is the polemic against the Jews, Jesus' discussion of divine signs with the Pharisees could represent the historical roots of Jesus' temptation. The New Testament is aware of other temptations of Jesus.[49] But this is not the point of the actual temptation story. On the contrary, the temptation stories result from a polemical discussion that the church—analogously to Jesus—had to carry on with Jewish sages.[50]

Luke takes pains to write correctly and to make the story verisimilar. Matthew puts greater emphasis on Jesus' answers, but Luke underscores the devil's

---

46 Agreeing with Fitzmyer, 1.512, and against A. Feuillet ("Le récit lucanien de la tentation [Lc 4,1–13]," *Bib* 40 [1959] 613–31), I consider the allusions to Adam in the temptations of Jesus to play a small role, and I decline to speak of a typology between Adam and Christ. According to Feuillet, Luke may be presenting Jesus, in his triumph over the devil, as an ethical model for baptized Christians in their fight against the tempter.

47 Cf. the Jewish stories of temptation, in which Satan transforms himself to lead people astray, listed in Str-B 1.140–41.

48 On *Sipra* 22.32, 99d see Joseph Bonsirven, *Textes rabbiniques des deux premiers siècles chrétiens* (Rome: Pontifical Biblical Institute Press, 1955) 45–46 §206.

49 Luke 22:28, 39–46; Heb 2:17; 4:15; 5:2; John 6:15, 26–34; 7:1–4. See C. Duquoc, "La tentation du Christ," *LumVie* 53 (1961) 21–41, esp. 32–33.

50 Here I agree with Fitzmyer, 1.508–12.

attacks.[51] Whereas the beginning is linked to the account of Jesus' baptism, the end connects with his passion. Jesus' path also leads from the wilderness to Jerusalem. In contrast with the sinful people of God in the desert, his attitude demonstrates faith in the one God, the creator and, above all, deliverer of Israel.[52] But by renouncing both signs and royal authority, he is also the Messiah who follows the path of service and obedient sonship. For this reason, he will achieve the sign of the resurrection and the honor of a kingdom, but only after his ministry in Galilee, his journey to Judea, and his passion in Jerusalem.[53] It is possible that the Messiah Jesus has prophetic and priestly characteristics in this pericope, but this is difficult to prove.[54]

History of Interpretation

The history of the exegesis of Luke 4:1–13 is extraordinarily instructive[55] because the life situations of the exegetes always influence their interpretation. For Ambrose, the ethical aspect is the central one. Jesus "allows himself to be tempted by the devil so that we all learn through him to triumph over him [the devil]." The "three most important spears of the devil" appear in the three temptations: gluttony, vanity, and ambition.[56] Origen sees the stones as heretical teachings that are offered to Christians instead of bread.[57]

Calvin, whose perception became especially keen toward the danger of setting too much emphasis on human works, objects to any comparison between Jesus'

temptation and ours. "Fasting brought Christ the distinction of divine glory."[58] Consequently, it would be mockery and detestable ridicule to imitate Christ. The temptation cannot be limited to gluttony, ambition, and avarice. All three temptations express a distancing of oneself from God: to withdraw from God (first temptation), to attribute to Satan an authority that God alone has (second temptation), to use God's power for one's own benefit (third temptation).

Karl Barth heads in the same direction as Calvin. If Jesus had succumbed to temptation, he would have committed a deed far graver than any offense or crime against morality or law, that is, the summit of all evil. "And in none of them [the three temptations] is the temptation a temptation to what we might call a breaking or failure to keep the Law on the moral or judicial plane. In all three we have to do 'only' with the counsel, the suggestion, that He should not be true to the way on which He entered in Jordan, that of a great sinner repenting; that he should take from now on a direction which will not need to have the cross as its end and goal."[59]

Certain contemporary theologians see in Jesus' temptation an example of not only an ethical but also a spiritual attitude. Jesus' conduct toward God during it is thus exemplary. According to Guy Lafon, Jesus renounces all possessions in each of the three temptations, "because being human is only guaranteed in us through the pres-

---

51 Agreeing with Dupont, *Tentations*, 70.
52 Adolf von Schlatter connects the first temptation (bread) with faith, the second (riches) with the love offered to God, and the third (jump from the pinnacle) with obedience (*Der Evangelist Matthäus: Seine Sprache, sein Ziel, seine Selbstständigkeit: Ein Kommentar zum ersten Evangelium* [7th ed.; Stuttgart: Calwer, 1982] 108). Thus Jesus becomes a pious Jew. Helmut Harsch interprets the temptations with the help of C. G. Jung's archetypes; e.g., he relates the bread to the Great Mother ("Psychologische Interpretation biblischer Texte?" *Wege zum Menschen* 20 [1968] 281–89, reprinted in Y. Spiegel, ed., *Psychoanalytische Interpretation biblischer Texte* [Munich: Kaiser, 1972] 49–59).
53 Dupont (*Tentations*, 70) emphasizes the relation of this passage with the passion narrative.
54 See Mahnke, *Versuchungsgeschichte*, 123.
55 See the monographs by Klaus-Peter Köppen, *Die*

Auslegung der Versuchungsgeschichte unter besonderer Berücksichtigung der Alten Kirche: Ein Beitrag zur Geschichte der Schriftauslegung (BGBE 4; Tübingen: Mohr-Siebeck, 1961); and M. Steiner, *La tentation de Jésus dans l'interprétation patristique de Saint Justin à Origène* (EtB; Paris: Gabalda, 1962).
56 Cf. Ambrose *Expositions in Luke* 4.4–42.
57 Cf. Origen *Hom. in Luc.* 29.3–5.
58 Jean Calvin, *A Harmony of the Gospels Matthew, Mark and Luke* (trans. A. W. Morrison [vols. 1, 3], Thomas Henry Louis Parker [vol. 2]; 3 vols.; Calvin's Commentaries 1–3; Grand Rapids: Eerdmans, 1972) 1.135.
59 *Church Dogmatics*, vol. 4: *The Doctrine of Reconciliation*, part 1 (trans. G. W. Bromiley; ed. G. W. Bromiley and T. F. Torrance; Edinburgh: Clark, 1956) 261.

ence of what is absent."[60] Neither bread nor power, offered in the first two temptations, will suffice to make human beings out of us. In the third temptation, Christ renounces the capacity to determine his death. "He lives from possessing nothing"—as do the Christians. In such a way, the two axes of temptation, the christological and the anthropological, are brought out clearly.

---

60 *Esquisses pour un christianisme* (Cogitatio fidei 96; Paris: Cerf, 1979) 13, 17.

The First Public Preaching in Nazareth (4:14–30)

Bibliography

del Agua Pérez, Agustín, "El cumplimiento del Reino de Dios en la misión de Jesús: Programa del Evangelio de Lucas (Lc 4,14–44)," *EstBib* 38 (1979–80) 269–94.

Albertz, Rainer, "Die 'Antrittspredigt' Jesu im Lukasevangelium auf ihrem alttestamentlichen Hintergrund," *ZNW* 74 (1983) 182–206.

Aletti, Jean-Noël, "Jésus à Nazareth (Lc 4,16–30): Prophétie, Écriture et typologie," in *À cause*, 431–51.

Anderson, Hugh, "Broadening Horizons: The Rejection of Nazareth Pericope of Lk 4:16–30 in Light of Recent Critical Trends," *Int* 18 (1964) 259–75.

Baarda, Tjitze, "'The Flying Jesus': Luke 4,29–30 in the Syrian Diatessaron," *VC* 40 (1986) 313–41.

idem, "Over de vaststelling van de tekst van Lukas 4,17 in het Diatessaron," *NedThT* 40 (1986) 199–208.

Baarlink, Heinrich, "Ein gnädiges Jahr des Herrn—und Tage der Vergeltung," *ZNW* 73 (1982) 204–20.

Bajard, J., "La structure de la péricope de Nazareth en Lc IV,16–30," *EThL* 45 (1969) 165–71.

Betz, Otto, "The Kerygma of Luke," *Int* 22 (1968) 131–46.

Blosser, Donald W., "Jesus and the Jubilee, Luke 4:16–30: The Significance of the Year of the Jubilee in the Gospel of Luke" (Ph.D. diss., University of St. Andrews [Scotland]), 1979).

Bornhäuser, Karl, *Studien zum Sondergut des Lukas* (Gütersloh: Bertelsmann, 1934) 20–33.

Busse, *Nazareth-Manifest.*

Chevalon, Maurice, "À propos de Nazareth," *Cahiers du cercle Ernest-Renan* 32 (1984) 75–76.

Combrink, H. J. B., "The Structure and Significance of Luke 4,16–30," *Neot* 7 (1973) 24–48.

Crockett, Larrimore, "Jewish-Gentile."

idem, "Luke 4:16–30 and the Jewish Lectionary Cycle: A Word of Caution," *JJS* 17 (1966) 13–46.

Delobel, J., "La rédaction de Lc. IV,14–16a et le 'Bericht vom Anfang'" in Neirynck, *Évangile*, 203–23.

Dupont, Jacques, "Le salut des Gentils et la signification théologique du livre des Actes," *NTS* 6 (1959–60) 141–46, reprinted in idem, *Études*, 404–9.

Eltester, Walter, "Israel im lukanischen Werk und die Nazareth-Perikope," in Grässer, *Jesus in Nazareth*, 76–147.

Escudero Freire, Carlos, "Jesús profeta, libertador del Hombre: Visión lucana de su ministerio terrestre," *EstEcl* 51 (1976) 463–95.

Fearghail, Fearghus Ó, "Rejection in Nazareth: Lk 4,22," *ZNW* 75 (1984) 60–72.

Finkel, Asher, "Jesus' Sermon at Nazareth (Luk. 4,16–30)," in Betz, *Abraham,* 106–15.

George, Augustin, "La prédication inaugurale de Jésus dans la synagogue de Nazareth: Luc 4,16–30," *BVC* 59 (1964) 17–29.

Haenchen, Ernst, "Historie und Verkündigung bei Markus und Lukas," in Braumann, *Lukas-Evangelium*, 287–316.

Hahn, *Titles*, 381–82.

Hill, "Rejection."

Horn, Friedrich Wilhelm, *Glaube und Handeln in der Theologie des Lukas* (GThA 26; Göttingen: Vandenhoeck & Ruprecht, 1983) 171–74.

Houston, Walter, "'Today in Your Very Hearing': Some Comments on the Christological Use of the Old Testament," in L. D. Hurst and N. T. Wright, *The Glory of Christ in the New Testament: Memorial George Bradford Caird* (Oxford: Clarendon, 1987) 37–47.

Jülicher, Adolf, *Die Gleichnisreden Jesu* (2d ed.; 2 vols.; Tübingen: Mohr-Siebeck, 1910) 2.171–74.

Kearney, S. M., "A Study of Principal Compositional Techniques in Luke-Acts Based on Luke 4:16–39 in Conjunction with Luke 7:18–23" (Ph.D. diss., Boston University, 1978); see *DissAb* 38 (1978) 7395-A.

Kenik, Helen A., "Messianic Fulfilment in Luke," *TBT* 18 (1980) 236–41.

Kirk, Andrew, "La conciencia mesiánica de Jesus en el sermon de Nazaret, Lc 4,16ss," *RevistB* 33 (1971) 127–37.

Kodell, Jerome, "Luke's Gospel in a Nutshell (Lk 4,16–20)," *BTB* 13 (1983) 16–18.

Koet, B.-J., "'Today this Scripture has been fulfilled in your ears': Jesus' explanation of Scripture," *Bijdr* 47 (1986) 368–94.

Mangatt, George, "The Acceptable Year of the Lord (Lk 4,16–30)," *Bible Bhashyam* 9 (1983) 179–86.

Masson, Charles, "Jésus à Nazareth (Marc 6,1–6a; Luc 4,16–30)," in idem, *Vers les sources d'eau vive: Études d'exégèse et de théologie du Nouveau Testament* (Lausanne: Librairie Payot, 1961) 38–69.

Menezes, Franklin, "The Mission of Jesus According to Lk 4,16–30," *Bible Bhashyam* 6 (1980) 249–64.

Miller, Donald G., "Luke 4:22–30," *Int* 40 (1986) 53–58.

Nolland, John L., "Words of Grace (Luke 4,22)," *Bib* 65 (1984) 44–60.

Oster, Richard E., "Supposed Anachronism in Luke-Acts' Use of Συναγωγῆ: A Rejoinder to H. C. Kee," *NTS* 39 (1993) 178–208.

Perrot, *Lecture.*

idem, "Luc 4,16–30 et la lecture biblique de l'ancienne synagogue," *RevScRel* 47 (1973) 324–40, reprinted in J.-E. Ménard, ed., *Exégèse biblique et judaisme* (Strasbourg: Faculté de Théologie catholique, 1973) 170–86.

Reicke, Bo, "Jesus in Nazareth—Lk 4,14–30," in H. Balz and S. Schulz, eds., *Das Wort und die Wörter: Festschrift Gerhard Friedrich* (Stuttgart: Kohlhammer, 1973) 47–55.

Reid, David P., "Jesus' Return to Nazareth," *TBT* 23 (1985) 39–43.

Rese, *Alttestamentliche Motive*, 143–54.

Rodgers, Margaret, "Luke 4,16–30—A Call for a Jubilee Year?" *RTR* 40 (1981) 72–82.

Samain, Étienne, "Aucun prophète n'est bien reçu dans sa patrie," *AsSeign* 35 (1973) 63–72.

idem, "Discours-programme de Jésus."

idem, "Le discours-programme de Nazareth," *AsSeign* 20 (1973) 17–27.

idem, "Évangile."

Sanders, "From Isaiah."

Schrage, *Thomas-Evangelium*, 75–77.

Schürmann, Heinz, "Der 'Bericht vom Anfang': Ein Rekonstruktionsversuch auf Grund von Lk 4,14–16," *StEv* 2 (1964) 242–58, reprinted in idem, *Untersuchungen*, 67–80.

idem, "Zur Traditionsgeschichte der Nazareth-Perikope Lk 4,16–30," in Descamps and de Halleux, *Mélanges*, 187–205.

Shin, Gabriel Kyo-Seon, *Die Ausrufung des endgültigen Jubeljahres durch Jesus in Nazaret: Eine historisch-kritische Studie zu Lk 4:16–30* (Bern: P. Lang, 1989).

Siker, Jeffrey S., "'First to the Gentiles': A Literary Analysis of Luke 4:16–30," *JBL* 111 (1992) 73–91.

Strobel, August, "Das apokalyptische Terminproblem in der sogenannte Antrittspredigt Jesu (Lk 4,16–30)," *ThLZ* 92 (1967) 251–54.

idem, "Die Ausrufung des Jobeljahres in der Nazarethpredigt Jesu: Zur apokalyptischen Tradition Lk 4,16–30," in Grässer, *Jesus in Nazareth*, 38–50.

Sturch, R. L., "'The Patris' of Jesus," *JTS* n.s. 28 (1977) 94–96.

Tannehill, Robert C., "The Mission of Jesus According to Luke IV 16–30," in Grässer, *Jesus in Nazareth*, 51–75.

Thiering, B. E., "The Three and a Half Years of Elijah," *NovT* 23 (1981) 41–55.

Völkel, Martin, "Der Anfang Jesu in Galiläa: Bemerkungen zum Gebrauch und zur Funktion Galiläas in den lukanischen Schriften," *ZNW* 64 (1973) 222–32.

Walker, T. Vaughn, "Luke 4,16–30," *RevExp* 85 (1988) 321–24.

14 **Then Jesus, in the power of the Spirit, returned to Galilee, and his renown spread through all the surrounding country, 15/ and he taught in their synagogues, and was praised by everyone.**

16/ And he came to Nazara, where he had been brought up, and went to the synagogue on the Sabbath day, as was his custom, and stood up to read. 17/ And the scroll of the prophet Isaiah was given to him. When he unrolled the scroll, he found the place where it was written: 18/ "The Spirit of the Lord is upon me, because he has anointed me. To bring good news to the poor he has sent me, to proclaim release to the captives and recovery of sight to the blind, to let the oppressed go free, 19/ to proclaim a welcome year of the Lord." 20/ And he rolled up the scroll, gave it back to the attendant, and sat down. And the eyes of all in the synagogue were fixed on him. 21/ Then he began to speak to them: "Today this scripture has been fulfilled in your hearing." 22/ And all spoke well of him, and were amazed at the gracious words that came from his mouth, and they said, "Is not this Joseph's son?" 23/ And he said to them, "Doubtless you will quote to me this proverb, 'Doctor, cure yourself! Do here also in your hometown the things that we have heard you did at Capernaum.'" 24/ And he said, "Truly I tell you, no prophet is welcome in the prophet's hometown. 25/ But I tell you the truth, there were many widows in Israel in the days of Elijah, when the heaven was shut up three years and six months, and there was a severe famine over all the land; 26/ yet Elijah was sent to none of them except to a widow at Zarephath in Sidon. 27/ There were also many lepers in Israel in the time of the prophet Elisha, and none of them was cleansed except Naaman the Syrian." 28/ When they heard this, all in the synagogue were filled with rage. 29/ They got up, drove him out of the city, and led him to the brow of the hill on which their city was built, so that they might hurl him off the cliff. 30/ But he passed through the midst of them and went on his way.

Analysis

Verses 14–15,[1] which point both forward and backward, form a transition. The formal similarity to 4:1 shows their introductory nature.

It is fiercely debated whether an earlier account of Jesus' beginning can be perceived behind 4:14–15.[2] Luke 4:14–44 and Matt 4:12–25 would then be reworking a variant of this tradition, and Mark 1:14–39 (plus 6:1–6?) would transmit another variant. This tradition (Q or proto-Luke?) would have contained two main blocks of material: (1) The Baptist, baptism, and Jesus' tempta-

---

1   See Fitzmyer, 1.521–24.

2   See Heinz Schürmann, "Der 'Bericht vom Anfang': Ein Rekonstruktionsversuch auf Grund von Lk 4,14–16," *StEv* 2 (1964) 242–58, reprinted in idem,

Traditionsgeschichtliche Untersuchungen zu den synoptischen Evangelien: Beiträge (KBANT; Düsseldorf: Patmos, 1968) 67–80.

tion; (2) the first preaching, first disciples, and first miracles. J. Delobel's detailed analysis, however, proves vv. 14–15 to be Lukan, so that one can hardly hypothesize any source other than Mark.[3]

Heinz Schürmann also includes vv. 16–30: "Luke had access to a variant of the Nazareth pericope also known to Mark (Mark 6:1–6). This pre-Lukan variant had already been heavily edited when Luke came upon it and expanded it with vv. 17–21 (23a) and vv. 25–27, in the interests of christology and universalism. The base text of the pre-Lukan pericope (behind Luke 4:16, 22, 23b, 24 [28ff.]) retains, in several places, an older version than Mark 6:1–6."[4]

Others presuppose a greater proportion of redaction: "Influenced by the sayings source, Mark 1:14–15 and 6:1–6, Luke composes his dramatic episode of Jesus' first public appearance in Nazareth in 4:16–30. From Q, Luke took the interpretation of Jesus' ministry according to Isa 61:1–2 that was already present there (cf. Luke 7:22 par. Matt 11:4–6), and that had been developed from the beatitudes of the Sermon on the Plain/Mount."[5] The deuteronomistic model of the violent fate of the prophet comes from Q, and Mark 6:1–6 lends the descriptive setting. Luke 3:21–4:14 is, nevertheless, a redactional expansion of Mark 1:14–15, but with the correction that Jesus, in his public manifestation, is not so much a fulfillment of time as a fulfillment of the Scriptures.

Some things are clear: first, that these verses have been recast redactionally in their language and conceptual framework; second, that heterogeneous elements are present (v. 15, "their" synagogues; v. 16, $N\alpha\zeta\alpha\rho\acute{\alpha}$ [same form as Matt 4:13]; $\tau\grave{o}\ \beta\iota\beta\lambda\acute{\iota}o\nu$ ["the scroll"] in vv. 17 and 20; the proleptic mention of the miracles in Capernaum in v. 23); third, that it is difficult to explain this as the result of Luke's use of Mark 6:1–6. The Markan passage is only distantly related to our pericope, and it appears in another context. Luke is familiar with it, but is probably not using it as his model here. But the similarities do allow one to determine the base form: Jesus is teaching in his town on the Sabbath. The audience expresses its astonishment with a question: Isn't he Joseph's son? Jesus answers with a proverb about a prophet not being understood in his own country. Then he leaves his hometown either out of anger or as banishment.

Could this be a conflation of two stories? "Because Luke's narrative is a conflation, there is, on the one hand, the fulfillment-story ending on the note of Jesus' success; on the other, there is the rejection-story."[6] The original account, however, developed in two different directions over the course of time. In the Markan variant, the emphasis is on the unbelief of the Nazarenes; in the later Lukan version, on the prophetic speech of Jesus. It is improbable that this developed from two originally independent units, that is, an isolated saying and a scene describing Jesus' success.[7] Both elements of the apothegm (the narrative context and the saying) probably belonged together from the beginning; the transmission of the narrative context was less fixed than that of the saying, though the latter is also transmitted in the *Gospel of Thomas* (Greek and Coptic) without a narrative

3   J. Delobel, "La rédaction de Lc. IV,14–16a et le 'Bericht vom Anfang'" in Neirynck, *Évangile*, 203–23.

4   "Zur Traditionsgeschichte der Nazareth-Perikope Lk 4,16–30," in Descamps and de Halleux, *Mélanges*, 187–205, esp. 205. A careful examination of the tradition and redaction history can be found in Robert C. Tannehill, "The Mission of Jesus According to Luke IV 16–30," in E. Grässer, ed., *Jesus in Nazareth* (BZNW 40; Berlin/New York: de Gruyter, 1972) 5–75. He argues that, in vv. 16–21, the non-Markan tradition is limited to Nazara and the contextual position of the narrative (between the temptation and Jesus' appearance in Capernaum); the rest is redactional; v. 22 is very Lukan; in vv. 23–24, there is non-Markan tradition especially in v. 23; vv. 25–27 are originally from an additional independent source; and in vv. 28–30, the rejection of Jesus

is traditional, and the evangelization of the Gentiles is redactional. Luke thus took the essential elements from Mark 6:1–6 but weakened their impact. The overall form of Luke 4:16–30 is redactional.

5   Ulrich Busse, *Das Nazareth-Manifest: Eine Einführung in das lukanische Jesusbild nach Lk 4,16–30* (SBS 91; Stuttgart: Katholisches Bibelwerk, 1978), 113.

6   Fitzmyer, 1.528.

7   As Bultmann hypothesizes (Bultmann, *History*, 31–32).

frame, but together with the proverb about the physician (cf. Mark 4:23). In Q, or more likely in Luke's special source, Luke found the saying in an expanded version, in which the Scripture citation and its interpretation already had their place, and perhaps also the Hebrew Bible examples (vv. 25–27), and the inhabitants' attack on Jesus the prophet (v. 29), though indeed in another formulation. It is precisely Luke's compositional technique, by which he reworks the source(s) so that the readers can no longer recognize them with certainty, that suggests the existence of a previous version. That is the recurrent paradox.

From a form-critical perspective, the pericope is an artful reworking of an already expanded apothegm. In the process, the weight shifted from the saying (v. 24) to the legitimization from the Scriptures (vv. 17–21), and from the simile about the physician (v. 23) to scriptural examples (vv. 25–27). Over time, through reflection on the Scriptures and history, the abortive encounter between Jesus and his hometown developed into an account laden with christology and ecclesiology. But in contrast to the theology of the New Testament letters, the pericope remained a narrative.

Commentary

■ **14** Jesus' return happens in two stages: the first leads him from the Jordan into the wilderness and to Jerusalem (4:1, 9), and the second, home (4:14; cf. 2:39). The temptation in the wilderness is a delay, but not a detour.

Jesus' relationship with the Spirit is expressed through the angel's annunciation to Mary (1:35), the descent of the Spirit at his baptism (3:22), and the statements in chap. 4 ("full of Holy Spirit," "by the Spirit," "in the power of the Spirit," "the Spirit of the Lord is upon me"; vv. 1, 14, 18). These repetitions are anything but literary clumsiness. Luke is trying to say that, in Jesus, God's power and justice have become active and perceptible again in the world and in history. It is surprising that Luke does not limit possession of the Spirit to Jesus alone; on the contrary, Zechariah (1:67), John (1:15), Elizabeth (1:41), Mary (1:35), and Simeon (2:25)

all partake of it, because the Spirit of prophecy and the Spirit of fulfillment are one in Luke. In this way, he illustrates that the turning point in time has come.

This apocalyptic turning point occurs concretely in time and space. Galilee is, for Luke, simultaneously a concrete region and a theological quantity: it is the historical, and salvation-historical, site of Jesus' first public activity.[8]

Luke mentions here for the first time Jesus' renown. Such a piece of information pertains to the genre of biography. In Greece the goal of many people was to become famous. Luke attests this fame of Jesus at various points and with several expressions: "And he found a response" (4:37, καὶ ἐξεπορεύετο ἦχος περὶ αὐτοῦ); "But now more than ever the word about him spread abroad" (5:15, διήρχετο δὲ μᾶλλον ὁ λόγος περὶ αὐτοῦ); "And this word about him spread . . ." (7:17, καὶ ἐξῆλθεν ὁ λόγος οὗτος . . . περὶ αὐτοῦ). Though Luke avoids repetition and alternates vocabulary, the structure of such notices remains the same: a verb of motion—a word for the praise and its consequences—the person of Jesus as the content of the speech ("about him," περὶ αὐτοῦ). In addition, the region through which the φήμη ("renown") is coursing is often mentioned. The meaning of the term φήμη is determined in each case by the context and by the proximity of δοξαζόμενος ("being praised") in 4:15. It does not mean only "reports of him"[9] or "Kunde von ihm,"[10] but, at the same time, "renown" or "fame." This is true of the first part of the Gospel. In the second and, above all, the third part, it is less Jesus' fame that is narrated than the attacks on him. Luke is also not the only Christian author who writes about Jesus' fame and success (cf. Mark 1:28, from which Luke possibly drew his formulation; and Matt 9:26, a redactional turn of phrase that is coincidentally very similar to Luke 4:14b).

The difference from the Greek tradition does not then lie in the consistent criticism of every panegyric, but in the rejection of self-exaltation. Christians do not seek glory for themselves, but they spread the renown of their Lord and their fellow believers.[11] Moreover, it is not superiority and victory, but rather right behavior and service that are praised. The roots of pride, indeed,

---

8   See the commentary on Luke 1:26 above.
9   Fitzmyer, 1.521.
10   *Einheitsübersetzung der Heiligen Schrift: Das Neue Tes-*

tament (4th ed.; Stuttgart: Katholische Bibelanstalt, 1973) 121.
11   Christian authors in patristic times adapted the lit-

are not thereby extirpated. Luke's Paul looks back on the beginnings of the gospel with pride: "For this was not done in a corner" (Acts 26:26). Perhaps one should distinguish between pride and (legitimate) honor, to which the Christians were absolutely amenable. In Luke 4:14, then, the widespread recognition of Jesus is attested, though Jesus, to this point, has not made a public appearance. Is Luke imagining that the temptation might not have remained unknown?

■ **15** In this verse the first general statement of Jesus' public activity, in which his teaching ability is given the highest prominence, follows in the form of a summary. Διδάσκω ("to teach") is the decisive term, which pre-Lukan tradition already applied to Jesus. The tradition, however, did not understand διδάσκω in the sense of the Greek scholastic tradition, but in terms of the Jewish interpretation of the Scriptures (Mark 1:21). In addition, for Luke, Jesus the teacher is at the same time the eschatological anointed one of Israel. Thus his teaching activity is the disclosure of christology and the fulfillment of prophecy. Luke uses διδάσκω as a comprehensive term for Jesus' public activity even into the book of Acts (1:1), but alongside it appears also the eschatological ποιέω ("to do"), which even at times appears in first place. Thus the temptation of Jesus, in which Luke describes Jesus as taking an active role, precedes his public teaching activity. The content of Jesus' teaching remains open in this verse, because Luke does not want to anticipate the representative sample of Jesus' teaching that follows, that is, his preaching in Nazareth, and thus diminish its effect.

Jesus' teaching activity, like the first proclamations of the Christians, was bound to the synagogues. The Jewish sermon, which was open to laypeople, gave the Christians the opportunity to proclaim their message (cf. Acts 13:15).

The reason that Luke emphasizes "their" synagogues is difficult to decide. In Acts he speaks often of "the synagogues of the Jews."[12] If he is doing the same thing here, it is either because he is shifting an expression taken from Mark further forward in the narrative, as he often does (Mark 1:23, ἐν τῇ συναγωγῇ αὐτῶν, "in their synagogue"), or he does not identify himself with the Jews (cf. "their city" in v. 29).

Jesus' fame is skillfully reiterated with varying words. The reason for this widespread admiration is Jesus' teaching, as was, before this, his victory over the devil (cf. the ποιεῖν, "to do," of Acts 1:1).

■ **16–20a** The tradition about Jesus in Nazareth was not originally connected with the beginning of his public activity (cf. Mark 6:1-6). But Luke wants to make a programmatic statement that precisely his hometown of Nazareth—which, in the final analysis, appears here representatively for all Israel—hears the good news (in the Pauline sense)[13] and resists it from the start. It was recognized of necessity in early Christianity that Jesus came from this insignificant town (cf. John 1:46); the weight of historical remembrance did not allow this fact to be suppressed.

Luke is familiar with the Greek tripartite chronology of birth, the first years at home (ἦν τεθραμμένος, "he had been brought up"), and the period of education at school (cf. Acts 22:3).[14] Jesus is presented as a pious Jew with a good upbringing; he regularly attends synagogue. Κατὰ τὸ εἰωθός with the dative ("as was [his] custom") is Lukan (Acts 17:2), as is "on the Sabbath day" (five times in the Gospel, three times in Acts). Standing up to read could describe the custom of the time. Luke does not tell us whether Jesus was requested in advance to take upon himself the reading and sermon, as would be usual. He seems to accept this; otherwise he surely would have emphasized Jesus' unusual initiative as just that.

erary form of the ἐγκώμιον (speech of praise, encomium) only after initial hesitation, and with changes. The encomium thereafter became one of the most often employed literary forms of hagiographic literature; see Auguste Piédnagel, *Jean Chrysostome: Panégyriques de S. Paul: Introduction, texte critique, traduction et notes* (SC 300: Paris: Cerf, 1982) 21–38.

12   Acts 13:5; 14:1; 17:1, 10.
13   Cf. Rom 1:16; 2:10.
14   See Willem Cornelius van Unnik, *Tarsus or Jerusalem: The City of Paul's Youth* (trans. G. Ogg;

London: Epworth, 1962), reprinted in *Sparsa Collecta*, 1.259–320; summarized and discussed in Bovon, *Theologian*, 354–55. In a biographical context τρέφω, like ἀνατρέφω, does not simply mean "to nourish a child," and also not merely "to raise a child"; these verbs rather describe the period of childhood that the child spends at home, and in which it is nourished, and initially raised, by its father and mother; cf. van Unnik, *Tarsus*, 33–34, 59–72 (in the monograph). Should one read ἀνατεθραμμένος, as in Acts 22:3, along with good witnesses?

Luke is at least describing in detailed fashion a synagogue service on the Sabbath,[15] in which, for understandable reasons, important elements such as the first part (with the Shema, prayer, and blessing) and the beginning of the second (such as the reading from the Torah) are lacking. Because he is narrating a special event within the usual run of things, he selects a moment in the middle of the second, more didactic, half of the service. He assumes that another person did the reading from the Torah. In Acts 13 Paul will begin even later, after the reading for the sermon. It is not certain that the portions of the Torah were already organized as a fixed cycle in the first century. It is probable that selection of the reading from the Prophets was still free. It is important that, despite the various types of homilies at the time, the preacher often interpreted the *seder* (selection from the Torah) with allusions to the *haphtara* (selection from the Prophets) and with the help of the so-called *petichtot* (chiefly citations from the Writings).[16]

In its Lukan description, the completeness of the composition of the first scene is striking: Jesus stands up, he is given the scroll, he opens it and finds the passage for which he is looking, he closes the scroll, gives it back, and sits down. Skillfully Luke, instead of saying that Jesus read aloud, implies it through the expression of his purpose and in the citation that follows (vv. 18–19). Ὑπηρέτης ("attendant") describes the *ḥazan*, the official from whom Jesus receives the scroll. Luke perhaps implies that Jesus selected the passage himself ("found"), but it is also possible that it was already prescribed for this day, or that it was apportioned to Jesus by lot.

Luke understands the citation as *haphtara*, even though the reading from the Prophets was normally longer: the usual pericope ran until v. 9. But Luke generally conserves space in citations, and "the day of vengeance" (Isa 61:2) would have been inappropriate. Moreover, he is citing the LXX, which suggests to him a play on words ("welcome," δεκτός, vv. 19, 24). Despite all this, the influence of synagogue practice on both tradition and redaction should not be underestimated.[17]

The manuscripts of Isaiah from Qumran attest that Isaiah 61 was read and commented on in schools and synagogues.[18] On the one hand, Isaiah 61 is associated with the beginning of the Year of Jubilee on Yom Kippur (cf. 11QMelch and its expectation of a priestly Messiah). On the other hand, Isaiah 61 probably served as the *haphtara* for the *seder* that begins at Gen 35:9 (God's blessing of Jacob, understood in oral tradition as a consolation). The Lukan text emphasizes neither the priestly perspective nor the explicit thought of consolation.

The citation agrees verbatim with the LXX; Luke only skips over the words, "to heal those who are downcast in their hearts," and adds the phrase, "to let the oppressed go free," from Isa 58:6. Did Luke intend to avoid connecting Jesus' miraculous healings to the Spirit,[19] or to concentrate only on the messianic interpretation, thus omitting, in opposition to Jewish trends of interpretation, the words of consolation?[20] Neither is convincing, but I have no better suggestion.[21] The addition of Isa 58:6 may have something to do with the technique of *haphtara*, and linking passages that share the same words (cf. Isa 58:4: σήμερον, "this day"; Isa 58:5: δεκτήν, "welcome").[22] Texts such as Isa 57:15—58:14 and Isa 61:1–11 became associated with each other on the occasion of the celebration of Yom Kippur, the first because of fasting and contrition, the second because of the beginning of the Year of Jubilee.[23]

■ **20b–21** The link between history and the Scriptures is redaction-historically significant. From the fulfillment

---

15 See Busse, *Nazareth-Manifest*, 107–12.
16 See Charles Perrot, *La lecture de la Bible dans la synagogue: Les anciennes lectures palestiniennes du Shabbat et des fêtes* (Hildesheim: Gerstenberg, 1973).
17 See ibid., 195–204.
18 See ibid., 197–99. In 11QMelch 14 and 1QH 18.14–15, an allusion to Isa 61:1–2 is made, and in one of the first Christian texts, *Barn.* 14.9, Isa 61:1–2 is cited. See James A. Sanders, "From Isaiah 61 to Luke 4," in J. Neusner, ed., *Christianity, Judaism, and Other Greco-Roman Cults: Festschrift Morton Smith* (4 vols.; SJLA 12; Leiden: Brill, 1975) 1.75–106, esp. 87–91.

19 See Eduard Schweizer, "πνεῦμα, κτλ.," *TDNT* 6 (1968) 407.
20 See Perrot, *Lecture*, 203.
21 Like Lagrange (138), Édouard Delebecque (*Évangile de Luc: Texte traduit et annoté* [CEA; Paris: Belles Lettres, 1976] 23) believes that Luke was citing from memory.
22 The addition of Isa 58:6c is perhaps no coincidence, suggests Étienne Samain ("Le discours-programme de Jésus à la synagogue de Nazareth, Lc 4,16–30," *CBFV* 10 [1971] 25–43, esp. 30), for Isa 58 seems to have been used rather extensively in the NT.
23 See Perrot, *Lecture*, 197–98.

after the baptism (3:22), it merges into the prophecy of the Messiah as the bearer of the Spirit (4:18).[24] Anointing with the Spirit justifies the title "Messiah" (2:11; cf. Acts 10:38). But Luke does not advocate a narrow royal messianism. His Christ is the son of David but also bears prophetic characteristics; much in the citation alludes to his message. The inherent qualities of this christology are, on one hand, evident in the σήμερον ("today," v. 21)—the Messiah is no longer only the object of expectation—and on the other, in the hostility of the fellow citizens (v. 29), which alludes to the passion. Εὐαγγελίσασθαι πτωχοῖς ("to bring good news to the poor") can be dependent on ἔχρισέν με ("he has anointed me"), or, closer to my opinion, on ἀπέσταλκέν με ("he has sent me"). Luke hardly understands the various categories of people in a merely literal sense. In any case, Jesus' offer—the good news; ἄφεσις ("release") and new sight, even when these can be perceived concretely—surpasses every human promise.[25] But the words should not be understood purely metaphorically for spiritual benefits, after death or the parousia. Jesus' speeches and miracles will show that salvation reaches the entire person even now. Jesus' offer will open the Year of Jubilee.[26] Κηρύξαι ("to proclaim") describes this salvation coming into power in the word, though indeed not yet completely in history. The "year," for Luke, is the eschatological turning point, which is announced by the prophetic resumption of the Year of Jubilee (Lev 25:8-54). Both the figure of the anointed one and the indication of time point toward the final fulfillment of God's will.

Verses 20b–21 mark the transition to the sermon, which was to be delivered sitting down. When the audience looks at Jesus, this emphasizes the person of Jesus more strongly than his words. Luke is dramatizing the

scene, and is already suggesting that, during this ordinary worship service, something extraordinary will happen. The first sentence (ἤρξατο, "he began") contains explosive material: today this biblical passage is fulfilled. Of course, for Luke this σήμερον ("today") already belongs in the past, but the composition of his work does not serve the interests of historicization, but rather the life of the contemporary church in the time of salvation, which had its beginning at that time.

"To fulfill" touches both the link from the Scriptures to history, as well as from prophecy to fulfillment.[27] Alongside the "eyes" (v. 20), the "ears" are now mentioned: the visible fulfillment of the Scriptures took place at Jesus' baptism; now comes the audible message of this fulfillment. Thus the scheme of prophecy and fulfillment is refined. This takes place in deed and word, in the event and its interpretation, in history and in preaching. All of this is reminiscent of Luke 1:1-2: the σήμερον becomes "today" for each hearer and reader to the extent that they rightly understand the proclamation.[28] When it is said that Mark proclaims the fulfillment of time (Mark 1:14-15), and Luke, the fulfillment of the Scriptures, this overlooks the fact that in Luke, fulfillment of the Scriptures simultaneously includes the fulfillment of time.

■ **22** Verses 22–30 describe: (1) the audience's reaction (v. 22); (2) the incremental answer of Jesus (vv. 23–27); (3) the wrath of the Nazarenes, and their attack on Jesus (vv. 28–29); (4) Jesus' departure (v. 30). Parts 1, 3, and 4 are short but emphatic, and Jesus' speech (2) is almost baroque.

As in v. 20, the audience is an undifferentiated mass ("all," πάντες, v. 20). They begin to appreciate and admire Jesus. Μαρτυρέω ("to speak well"), which occurs once in the Gospel and eleven times in Acts, often

---

24   See Rese, *Alttestamentliche Motive*, 148.

25   Samain ("Discours-programme de Jésus," 31 n. 9) shows that a spiritualized interpretation is already present in Isa 61 itself.

26   On performative speech see Emile Benveniste, *Problèmes de linguistique générale* (2 vols.; Paris: Gallimard, 1966) 1.269–76.

27   On πληρόω and the fulfillment of Scripture in Luke, see Hans Hübner, "πληρόω, κτλ.," *EDNT* 3 (1993) 108–9; and Bovon, *Theologian*, 84–90, 101–8.

28   The "today" of Deuteronomy is understood by Paul, Luke, and the author of the Epistle to the Hebrews in three different ways. But it is apparent that, for

all three, the same structure unites history with its actualization. Sanders ("From Isaiah") believes that the actualization of Isa 61:1 by means of the "today" in Luke 4:21 originates with Jesus himself, and that it surpasses all that Judaism dared to do and what the early church did, since Jesus, in fact, powerfully proclaimed forgiveness beyond the bounds of Israel, to the Gentiles. Sanders underestimates Luke's redactional work.

means "to give a good testimony," "to acclaim" (Acts 22:5).[29] Θαυμάζω ("to be amazed") is also an expression of positive marveling. The structure of this probably redactional sentence is strongly reminiscent of Acts 2:7;[30] and the following, and clearly Lukan, part of v. 22 is similar to Acts 14:3. God's word, for Luke, is embedded in human "words," and these words transmit God's favor, which is not only a feeling but, above all, the event that connects the individual to him. Χάρις ("grace") does not occur often in Luke, but it is not used unsympathetically: it is God's grace for Jesus (2:40), which, like wisdom, reflects around him and in him (2:52). Here it reaches others through his own words, and later through the words of his disciples (Acts 14:3; 20:24, 32).[31]

The reaction, "Is not this Joseph's son?" occurs in various traditions of the Gospels (Matt 13:55; John 6:42). Luke comments on it only indirectly in the speech of Jesus that follows. In his view such a reaction, though not incorrect, is only one aspect among others, and, moreover, is irrelevant here. Even in v. 21, Jesus did not introduce himself directly. Here, as well, the really relevant aspect—"I am the Son of God"—is not openly expressed. The audience has only gone halfway toward faith (v. 22), and has not completed the decisive second half. For this reason, Jesus puts them to the test (v. 23).

Luke is using traditional material here. The future tense of ἐρεῖτε ("you will quote"), and the mention of the miracles performed in Capernaum indicate that this episode, in its traditional setting, took place later in Jesus' life, as it does in Mark.

■ **23** The Lukan Jesus describes the people's reaction in a παραβολή ("parable"), which in Luke (6:39) and in the LXX (1 Sam [LXX 1 Kgdms] 1:12) can also mean "proverb." Jesus' reply is ironic. The metaphor of the physician is rare in Judaism and early Christian literature (cf. 5:31).[32] In *Gos. Thom.* 31 the metaphor of the physician appears alongside that of the prophet. It is uncertain whether this logion developed from the connection of v. 23b and v. 24, or whether this is a case of parallel traditions.[33]

The frequency of the verbs "to speak," "to say," "to tell" is remarkable: λέγειν (v. 21), ἔλεγον (v. 22), εἶπεν (v. 23), ἐρεῖτε (v. 23), εἶπεν (v. 24), λέγω (v. 24), λέγω (v. 25).[34] But the occurrences should not all be taken at equivalent value. The most important are, first, Luke's expressions for the prophetic speech of Jesus (vv. 21, 23, 24); and second, Jesus' statements in the first person: Ἀμὴν λέγω ὑμῖν ("Truly I tell you," v. 24) is understood, in the Semitic sense, as the beginning of an oracle,[35] and ἐπ' ἀληθείας δὲ λέγω ὑμῖν ("But I tell you the truth," v. 25) introduces its interpretation.

■ **24** It is no coincidence that the oracle in v. 24 is traditional (cf. Mark 6:4b, which does not have "Truly I tell you," and has ἄτιμος ["without honor"] instead of

29 See BAGD, s.v. Joachim Jeremias suggested understanding the verb here in the sense of "to testify against him," as in Hebrew and Aramaic; this would smooth over the tension between v. 22 and vv. 28–29 (*Jesus' Promise to the Nations* [trans. S. H. Hooke; reprinted Philadelphia: Fortress Press, 1982] 44–46). But this opinion has not won out. See Hugh Anderson, "Broadening Horizons: The Rejection of Nazareth Pericope of Lk 4:16–30 in Light of Recent Critical Trends," *Int* 18 (1964) 259–75, esp. 266–70; David Hill, "The Rejection of Jesus at Nazareth (Luke IV 16–30)," *NovT* 13 (1971) 161–80, esp. 163–65; Fitzmyer, 1.534. It is of course true that the dative αὐτῷ could be a *dativus incommodi* ("dative of disadvantage"; see BDF §188.1), but the rest of v. 22 shows that this is rather unlikely.

30 Samain ("Discours-programme de Jésus," 41) emphasizes Luke 4:22 and Acts 2:7.

31 See Cambe, "Χάρις."

32 See Wettstein, 1.681; Str-B 2.156; Lagrange, 142–43.

33 Wolfgang Schrage (*Das Verhältnis des Thomas-Evangeliums zur synoptischen Tradition und zu den kopti-*

schen Evanglienübersetzungen [BZNW 29; Berlin: Töpelmann, 1964] 75–77), in contrast to this, assumes that the logion in *Gospel of Thomas* is dependent on the Synoptics, esp. Luke.

34 The εἶπεν δέ of v. 24 resumes the εἶπεν of v. 23 in order to indicate unambiguously that it is no longer the inhabitants of Nazareth that are speaking. Ἔλεγον and ἐρεῖτε refer to the inhabitants.

35 See Heinz-Wolfgang Kuhn, "ἀμήν, κτλ.," *EDNT* 1 (1990) 70: "Ἀμήν occurs as an opening word in the Gospels only in the words of Jesus. There it has the character of an oath-formula or, possibly, an authority-formula: ἀμὴν (ἀμὴν) λέγω ὑμῖν / σοι . . . . The use of an opening nonresponsive use [sic] of 'Amen' has never been attested with certainty in ancient Judaism. . . . However, that Jesus himself already used 'âmên before his sayings is likewise unproven." See also Fitzmyer, 1.536–37.

οὐδείς . . . δεκτός, "no [prophet] . . . is welcome"). The proverb reveals the incipient tension between God's plan and the will of the people. Through Jesus, the welcome (δεκτόν) year of the Lord is proclaimed, but in his hometown the prophet is unwelcome (οὐδείς . . . δεκτός). The connection between the Year of Jubilee and the homeland in the LXX is usually forgotten. During this year of forgiveness (Lev 25:10 LXX)[36] and blessing (Lev 25:21 LXX), all people should return to their homeland: καὶ ἕκαστος εἰς τὴν πατρίδα αὐτοῦ ἀπελεύσεσθε ("and each should go off to his or her fatherland," Lev 25:10 LXX). Thus it is in accordance with the Scriptures that Jesus begins preaching the year of grace in his hometown. It is only that his call is not accepted there.[37]

■ **25–27** Verses 25–27 contain a Christian exegesis that adds a positive dimension to the negative judgment: even under the old covenant, prophets ministered outside Israel.[38] This points not so much to the mission to the Gentiles as it does to the fellowship between Jews and Gentiles;[39] here the passages from Acts (ἐπὶ πᾶσαν τὴν γῆν, "over all the land," v. 25; cf. Acts 11:28) are less illuminating than those concerning the Year of Jubilee in Leviticus 25, since "all the land" (originally the land of Israel) could be understood universalistically by Luke,[40] and, even before him, by Gentile Christians. Could one conclude from this that the church of Anti-

och is responsible for these expansions, since both examples concern Syria? Nothing more can be said than this: vv. 26–27 reflect a Christianity that has broken through its Jewish constraints.

■ **28–30** The conclusion diverges clearly from the Markan version. Jesus' words, instead of his miracles, and his audience's resistance, instead of the effect of his person, characterize the Lukan version. Jesus comes in the power of the Spirit (v. 14), but all of his hearers (corresponding to the Lukan tendency toward globalizing presentation) are seized by rage (v. 28). Luke does not explain their reason, merely their progress from admiration (v. 22) to indignation (v. 28). Even at the close of Acts, Luke does not, in the final analysis, understand the reason that Israel did not accept the good news. The precise and elegant description of the event and the geographical surroundings in v. 29 qualify for that which literary critics call the "effet de réel" (though it does not indeed correspond to the geographical setting of Nazareth).[41] Perhaps Luke intends to create a typological connection between Nazareth and Jerusalem, between the first and the last attempt at murder[42] "outside the city" (cf. Heb 13:12–13, as well as Acts 7:58 in the case of Stephen). But it still is not the time of the passion. So he (christological αὐτός) simply passes through the crowd, untouched and masterful. Πορεύομαι ("to go") is the "theological" verb for Jesus' journey from Galilee to

---

36 Διαβοήσετε ἄφεσιν ἐπὶ τῆς γῆς πᾶσιν τοῖς κατοικοῦσιν αὐτήν ("proclaim forgiveness in the land to all who inhabit it").

37 Fitzmyer (1.537) believes that in order to spare Mary, Luke, in contrast to Mark, does not name Jesus' family. This hypothesis would have some probability only if one assumes—and it is here that I am in doubt—that Luke is using and adapting Mark here.

38 Various details, such as the closed heavens and the forty-two months, are missing in the HB text but are attested in other Jewish and Christian texts: cf. Sir 48:3 and Jas 5:17; see Larrimore C. Crockett, "Luke 4:25–27 and the Jewish-Gentile Relations in Luke-Acts," *JBL* 88 (1969) 177–83.

39 See ibid. According to Crockett, this fellowship fulfills itself in various episodes of the Acts (11:28; 10:1–11:18).

40 "The example of Elijah and Elisha, bestowing the benefits of God to the Gentiles, allows one to foresee that, once refused by Israel as it had been by Jesus' contemporaries, the message of salvation will

pass on to the Gentiles. Thus the episode at Nazareth foretells what one will see take place at Pisidian Antioch and at Rome; and the manner in which Paul behaves in turning to the Gentiles is justified in advance because, already in their time, Elijah and Elisha had done this" (Jacques Dupont, "Le salut des Gentils et la signification théologique du livre des Actes," *NTS* 6 [1959–60] 141–46, reprinted in idem, *Études*, 404–9, esp. 406–7).

41 Ἡ ὀφρύς first describes the eyebrow, and then, in a metaphorical sense, the brow or ridge of a hill. Κατακρημνίζω means "to cast down from." Cf. 2 Chr 25:12: "The people of Judah captured another ten thousand alive, took them to the top of a rock and threw them down from the top of the rock, so that all of them were dashed to pieces." Thus the style of Luke 4:29 is influenced by the LXX (see also ἀναστάντες, "they rose up").

42 See Samain, "Discours-programme de Jésus," 37.

Jerusalem and for the salvation-historical course of his life (cf. 9:51 and 13:22).[43]

Conclusion

We stand here at the beginning: at the beginning of the new time (of the year of grace), of the proclamation of Jesus, of his office, and also of the human reaction to all of this. This beginning is anchored not only in time but in space. From this one location, it will unfurl itself throughout the entire earth. Jesus' word, which announces God's message and the intermediary role of the Messiah, is programmatic. Equally programmatic is the soteriological content and also, unfortunately, the human rejection.[44]

---

43 Luke is certainly not intending to tell a miracle, but, as in John 7:30; 8:59; 10:39; and 18:6, he is testifying to the omnipotence of Jesus. Nevertheless, we are not far removed from the motif of the miraculous journey of the saint or divine individual. Luke knows this motif (Acts 8:39–40). See Ludwig Bieler, *ΘΕΙΟΣ ANHP: Das Bild des "göttlichen Menschen" in Spätantike und Frühchristentum* (2 vols. in 1; Vienna: Oskar Höfels, 1935) 1.94–97. Perhaps one could also say that Jesus, at this point, could not be caught and held because—as in the Gospel of John (2:4; 7:30)—his hour had not yet come (cf. Luke 22:53). In P. Egerton 2, frg. 1, recto, lines 24–32, one finds a scene similar to Luke 4:28–30; after this comes the healing of a leper, a parallel text to Luke 5:12–14. See Aurelio de Santos Otero, *Los Evangelios Apócrifos: Colección de textos griegos y latinos* (2d ed.; BAC 148; Madrid: BAC, 1963) 98, and Hennecke-Schneemelcher, 1.98. See below, notes to the commentary on 5:15–16.

44 Hill ("Rejection") emphasizes the coherence of the Lukan composition: by proclaiming the year of the Lord's favor, Jesus evokes an approving amazement from the crowd; but by specifying that it will realize itself outside of Israel, he arouses angry rejection.

The First Public Activity in Galilee (4:31–44)

Bibliography

Busse, *Wunder*, 66–90.

Dietrich, Wolfgang, *Das Petrusbild der lukanischen Schriften* (BWANT 94; Stuttgart: Kohlhammer, 1972) 18–23.

Fuchs, Albert, "Entwicklungsgeschichtliche Studien zu Mk 1,29–31 par Mt 8,14–15 par Lk 4,38–39," in idem, SNTU A.6/7 (Linz: Albert Fuchs, 1981–82) 71–76.

Lamarche, Paul, "La guérison de la belle-mère de Pierre et le genre littéraire des évangiles," *NRTh* 87 (l965) 515–26.

Léon-Dufour, "Guérison."

Pesch, Rudolf, "Die Heilung der Schwiegermutter des Simon-Petrus: Ein Beispiel heutiger Synoptikerexegese," in idem, *Neuere Exegese: Verlust oder Gewinn?* (Freiburg im Breisgau: Herder, 1968) 143–75.

Rice, George E., "Luke 4:31–44: Release for the Captives," *AUSS* 20 (1982) 23–28.

Schramm, *Markus-Stoff*, 85–91.

Talbert, Charles H., "The Lukan Presentation of Jesus' Ministry in Galilee: Luke 4:31–9:50," *RevExp* 64 (1967) 485–97.

Völkel, "Anfang."

31 Then he went down to Capernaum, a city in Galilee, and taught them on the Sabbaths. 32/ They were astonished at his teaching, for his word was with authority. 33/ And in the synagogue there was a man who had the spirit of an unclean demon, and he cried out with a loud voice, 34/ "Ah! What have we to do with you, Jesus of Nazareth? You have come to destroy us. I know you, I know who you are, the Holy One of God." 35/ But Jesus rebuked him, saying, "Be silent, and come out of him!" And the demon threw him down in the midst of them and came out of him without having done him any harm. 36/ And terror overcame all of them, and they kept saying to one another, "What kind of word is this? For with authority and power he commands the unclean spirits, and out they come!" 37/ And he found a response in every place in the surrounding region.

38 After getting up and leaving the synagogue he entered Simon's house. Now Simon's mother-in-law was suffering from a high fever, and they asked him about her. 39/ And he bent down over her and rebuked the fever, and it left her. Immediately she got up and began to serve them. 40/ After sunset, all those who had any who were sick with various kinds of diseases brought them to him; and he laid his hands on each of them and cured them. 41/ Demons also came out of many, shouting, "You are the Son of God!" But he rebuked them and would not allow them to speak, because they knew that he was the Messiah. 42/ After daybreak he departed and went into a deserted place. And the crowds were looking for him; they reached him, and tried to hold him back from leaving them. 43/ But he said to them, "I must proclaim the good news of the kingdom of God to the other cities also; for I was sent for this purpose." 44/ So he continued proclaiming the message in the synagogues of Judea.

Analysis

From 4:31 through 6:19, Luke follows the Markan account. This return to Mark is easy to make, since Luke's earlier sequence, taken from Q, corresponded to Mark's: the Baptist, baptism, temptation, Jesus' teaching in the synagogues (v. 15). Luke introduces the account of the preaching in Nazareth only as a supplement, and, correspondingly, forgoes the account of the calling of the disciples (Mark 1:16–20), since he has at his disposal a calling scene that he finds more suitable (Luke 5:1–11). The soteriological activity of the Messiah in word (4:14–30) and deed (4:31–44) will precede the calling scene. Although Jesus' preaching in his hometown encountered resistance, his wonder-working was a great success, which the wonder-worker himself, however, limits (v. 43). Luke's dependence on Mark results in a change of locale. From now on, Jesus works in Capernaum, so that in Luke a juxtaposition of Nazareth–Capernaum develops.[1] As in 4:1 and 4:14, the account begins with a journey by Jesus and a summary passage (4:31–32; note the imperfect tense of the verbs). The transitional nature of such summaries becomes apparent in v. 44, which one can connect to either the preceding or the following pericope. Luke adopts several summary passages from Mark, but he is familiar with this compositional technique from his school days, and he employs these passages to stop for breath during the suspenseful narrative, or to create elegant transitions. Between these two summary passages (vv. 31–32 and v. 44) are four separate stories: two miracles concerning individuals with

---

1   According to M. D. Goulder, after the section "Nazareth" (Jesus' hometown), Luke created a section "Capernaum" (his home base), which extends from 4:31 to 8:1 (*Type and History in Acts* [London: SPCK, 1964] 125–37).

geographic indications (vv. 33, 38), and two encounters of Jesus with the crowd, at specified times (vv. 40, 42).

Corresponding to the rules of his craft, Luke says nothing about the above-mentioned switch of sources. From Mark—in the version known to us—he takes the gist of the events and even the sentences, as long as nothing significant is stylistically or conceptually objectionable to him.[2] Logical and grammatical corrections sometimes seem necessary to him, for example, the change to the singular in v. 31, since, according to Luke's portrayal, Jesus is still without disciples. Luke eliminates the various occurrences of εὐθύς ("immediately," Mark 1:21, 23, 28, 29, 30), since they seem monotonous and unliterary to him. Here and there he is more specific: the readers do not necessarily know that Capernaum is in Galilee (v. 31). Mark 1:22 is reformulated in v. 32, and gives a reason for the people's astonishment by understanding ὅτι ("for") as a causal conjunction. The comparison of Jesus to the scribes is missing. Does Luke mean to spare them from criticism? Or does he assume that his readers are not familiar with them? The favorite concept λόγος ("word"), theologically significant for Luke, appears in vv. 32 and 36. It is seldom recognized that Luke has read Mark in advance and often reworks later Markan elements into his account at an earlier point. For example, he is not using "their synagogues" (Mark 1:23) for the first time in v. 33; it already appears in the summary passage that precedes it (v. 15). In v. 38 ἀναστάς ("getting up") has no parallel in Mark 1:29, but may come from Mark 1:35. Then, in the parallel passages, Luke omits the Markan expressions that he has already used: αὐτῶν ("their") does not occur in Luke 4:33, nor does ἀναστάς in Luke 4:42. This state of affairs may explain why "Galilee" is missing in Luke 4:37: the evangelist already used it proleptically in v. 31.

Luke improves vv. 33–37 grammatically and theologically. The man carries "the spirit of an unclean demon"[3] in himself and screams "with a loud voice" (v. 33). Instead of saying that the demon convulses the man

(Mark 1:26), Luke speaks of a violent blow that does no harm (v. 35). It is uncertain whether Luke's preference for καὶ ἐγένετο ("and [terror] overcame"; elsewhere, "and it happened"), or rather the religious meaning of θάμβος ("terror"), plays a role in the reformulation of v. 36a; and the reason that Luke chooses parataxis (καὶ συνελάλουν, "and they kept saying to one another") instead of Mark's hypotaxis (Mark 1:27: ὥστε συζητεῖν, "so that they kept on asking") is also unclear. Luke's changes vis-à-vis Mark in Luke 4:36 are theologically significant: the insertion of ὁ λόγος ("the word"), a surprising designation for a miracle, and the omission of the allusion to the "new teaching" (Mark 1:27). It is not the "teaching" that disturbs Luke (vv. 15, 32), but perhaps its "newness" is suspect to him because of more recent, deceptive teachings, as the gloss in Luke 5:39 could attest, which confers on Jesus' words the dignity of age.

The omission of "and Andrew, with James and John" (Mark 1:29), may be coincidental, although the phrase is also not noted in Matt 8:14. Matthew tends to shorten miracle stories, and Luke for his part has not yet introduced the disciples. Stylistically, "suffering from a high fever" is more refined than πυρέσσουσα ("sick with a fever," Mark 1:30). In Mark Jesus' taking of the hand plays a role, and in Luke, Jesus' bending over the sick woman. Jesus' word (v. 39) alongside the gesture cannot be omitted in Luke. Since he does not want to lose the Markan allusion to new life, or even resurrection (Mark 1:31, ἤγειρεν, "[he] lifted her up"), despite the transposition of words, Luke adds ἀναστᾶσα ("she got up," v. 39). As is often the case, the miracle happens "immediately" (v. 39); the adverb suggests discreetly yet narratively the divine origin of an event.[4]

The healings in the evening (vv. 40–41) are a paradigmatic example of stylistic improvement. Out of the pleonastic temporal indications, Luke retains the men-

---

2 I see no better explanation for the relationship between Mark and Luke at the end of this chapter (Luke 4:31-44).

3 Luke introduces the word δαιμόνιον ("demon") for his Greek readers, since they are not familiar with the Semitic use of the word πνεῦμα ("spirit") in the sense of "demon"; see Fitzmyer, 1.544–45.

4 See Luke 1:64 and the commentary on Luke 1:39 above. Rydbeck has shown that παραχρῆμα ("immediately"), contrary to popular belief, does not belong to a higher level of language than εὐθέως (also "immediately"). As one can deduce from the papyri, παραχρῆμα is a word from government and business language (*Fachprosa*, 166–76, 184–85). See also Ulrich Busse, *Die Wunder des Propheten Jesus: Die Rezeption, Komposition, und Inter-*

tion of the sundown (Matthew, on the contrary, the evening). More consistently than Mark, Luke distinguishes between the sick (v. 40) and the demon-possessed (v. 41).[5] He avoids the popular expression, "those who were in a bad way," which clumsily occurs twice in Mark; and, about the sicknesses colorfully portrayed in Mark 1:34, he composes a refined sentence: ἅπαντες ὅσοι εἶχον ἀσθενοῦντας νόσοις ποικίλαις ("all those who had any who were sick with various kinds of diseases"). In the use of the unclassical construction, "to have" with a participle, lurks a trace of the Markan expression. The omission of the exaggerated description of the mass assembly in Mark 1:33 is not surprising. The augmentation from "all" who had sick people (v. 40a) to "each of them" who receives healing (v. 40b) is stylistically attractive, and the addition of laying on of hands (v. 40b), is substantively significant, since it is often attested in Luke as the effective gesture when used as a miraculous technique in the context of a healing (e.g., Acts 9:12, 17; 28:8). The mention of it could be explained on the basis of church practice in Luke's time,[6] but Paul's situation in Malta is strongly reminiscent of Jesus' situation here: in each case, a relative (mother/father) is healed in the house of a significant host (Simon/Publius), which attracts other sick people. Their healing happens thanks to the power of the man of God (Jesus/Paul) through the laying on of hands and prayer (Acts 28:8). In Luke the demons do not wait for Jesus' initiative (Mark 1:34): they flee before him "out of many" (Luke 4:41). As elsewhere, in this manner Luke makes otherwise fairly colorless traditional material more concrete. The command to the demons to remain silent interests him less than their christological knowl-

edge (Mark 1:34b). He took the title "the Holy One of God" from Mark 1:34. Luke is now using the opportunity to introduce his readers to the title. In the Lukan sense of christology, the demons call Jesus the Son of God (4:41a). In order to fill any gaps in this christological understanding, "Son of God" in v. 41b is equated with "Messiah." In this context, Luke succeeds in using many words from Mark: καί . . . οὐκ . . . λαλεῖν, ὅτι ᾔδεισαν . . . αὐτόν ("and . . . not . . . to speak, because they knew . . . he").[7]

Γενομένης δὲ ἡμέρας ("after daybreak," v. 42) is more correct than the three adverbs in Mark 1:35, and Luke expresses something different with his phrase. In Mark it is still dark, and the mysterious atmosphere is underscored by Jesus' prayer. Luke wants to avoid the impression of Jesus fleeing; so it is already daytime, and Jesus goes away—symmetrically to v. 30, with the same verb πορεύομαι—without hindrance. The reason that here Luke does not take from Mark the detail of Jesus praying, otherwise very important to him (cf. 3:21), is unclear; it is possible that he intends to create a summary passage around it later (5:16; in contrast to Mark 1:45). Mark distinguishes two groups: "Simon and his companions" and "everyone" (Mark 1:36–37). Luke, who has not yet narrated the calling of the disciples, simplifies this: he mentions only the redaction-historically significant crowd. This also changes the sequence of events: logically, the crowd searches for Jesus,[8] finds him,[9] and detains him with a request.[10] In Mark they look for him to request more miracles; in Luke they detain him in order not to lose him.[11]

---

pretation der Wundertradition im Evangelium des Lukas (FB; Stuttgart: Katholisches Bibelwerk, 1977) 75–76.

5   Contrary to the note on Luke 4:41 in *TOB*.

6   James 5:14 mentions prayer and anointing, but not the laying on of hands. Should these differences be attributed to differing conditions in the various congregations?

7   But Luke reads εἴα ("to allow ") instead of Mark's ἤφιεν ("to permit"). The difference in meaning is minimal, but εἴα is more appropriate for a granting of permission.

8   Luke was inspired to write the expression οἱ ὄχλοι ἐπεζήτουν αὐτόν ("the crowds were looking for him," v. 42b) by the statement of Peter and the disciples in Mark 1:37, πάντες ζητοῦσίν σε ("'everyone

is searching for you'"). That Luke uses the verb ἐπιζητέω indicates his preference for composite verbs. By contrast, he omits the verb καταδιώκω from the parallel passage in Mark 1:36, since this verb signifies persecution to him.

9   To respond to the possible impression that Jesus had fled, Luke substitutes "they reached him" (v. 42) for "they found him" (Mark 1:37).

10 Κατέχω, with its semantic field rich with nuances, must be translated here "to detain," "to hold back," "to hold fast." Cf. *TOB* on Luke 4:42; and Delebecque, 26.

11 On this motif see the bibliographic references in the notes to the commentary on 4:42 below.

If one is a Christian reader and knows what it is to "proclaim," then one can write as Mark does: ἵνα καὶ ἐκεῖ κηρύξω ("that I may proclaim the message there also," Mark 1:38). Luke names the content of this proclamation for his readership, part of which has not experienced Christian education. In doing so, he improves the entire sentence grammatically: an aorist (εἶπεν, "he said"), instead of a historical present (λέγει, "he says"), "the other cities" instead of the strange "neighboring towns." The goal is determined no longer with ἵνα ("in order that"), but with the theologically significant δεῖ ("must"). "To proclaim the good news" appears as an echo of the quotation from Isaiah (Luke 4:18). The content of the preaching is the kingdom of God. Luke thus makes up for what he omitted from Mark 1:14. The phrase, "I was sent for this purpose," instead of the odd, "that is what I came out to do" (Mark 1:38), may also derive from Isa 61:1, but at the same time it gives insight into the author's understanding of the faith: what is decided in Mark 1:38 by an independent "I" is decided by the will of God in Luke (εὐαγγελίσασθαί με δεῖ, "I must proclaim the good news"; ἐπὶ τοῦτο ἀπεστάλην, "I was sent for this purpose"). Jesus' complete harmony with the will of God proves itself in his refusal to stay (v. 43) and his ministry in Judea (v. 44). Verse 43 is thus not an expression of the resignation of servile obedience.

The Lukan expression "the other cities also" (v. 43) leads to the peculiar geographical destination, Judea; the name Judea makes more concrete the salvation-historical will of God and of Jesus to go elsewhere. Luke omits the exorcism in Mark 1:39, since Jesus' preaching is more important to him here.

The linguistic, stylistic, and theological tendencies of the redaction have become clear. There is thus no reason to suppose the existence of an additional source for this passage.[12]

Commentary

In the Synagogue at Capernaum (vv. 31–32)

■ **31–32** The teaching Messiah is a traveling preacher. Leaving Nazareth forever, he goes down to Capernaum.[13] Luke fills these traditional names with new content. On the one hand, Nazareth symbolizes for him the beginning, in which the Messiah is manifested, and in a prophetic speech he interprets both the Scriptures and history; but with this beginning, the murderous rejection of Jesus also occurs. On the other hand, Capernaum[14] is the place in which the fulfillment of the Scriptures is not only proclaimed, as in Nazareth, but is also experienced. Luke takes the exorcisms from the sources he has before him, but they do illuminate, in more specific fashion, the Lukan interpretation of Isa 61:1, as well as his understanding of human tragedy as demonic oppression (see earlier, Luke 4:6).[15] Capernaum, already known in the tradition as the scene of Jesus' miraculous activity (see 4:23), is the place of the first liberation from evil. Jesus' teaching immediately precipitates corresponding actions,[16] and the spectators marvel at them[17] (cf. v. 32). The ἐξουσία ("authority") of Jesus, a concept prescribed for Luke from tradition (particularly Mark), is integrated by Luke into his own christology, and even used independently—above all, in connection with Jesus' conferring forgiveness (5:24) and his activity as a miracle-worker (4:36). Jesus' supreme authority comes from God, as it is expressed in the granting of the Spirit (3:22; 4:14, 18), and is exercised legitimately by him. In the Lukan concept of ἐξουσία, then, inhere the components both of power and of justice.[18] Luke also employs ἐξουσία with a polemical and an ecclesiological meaning: polemically, when he contrasts Jesus' unique and supreme authority with the power of the devil;[19] and ecclesiologically, when he speaks of the transfer of Jesus'

---

12 In agreement with Busse, *Wunder*, 74; and Schramm, *Markus-Stoff*, 85–91.
13 "And he went down": Luke seems to be aware that the road from Nazareth to the lakeshore on which Capernaum is situated leads downhill. According to Conzelmann (*Theology*, 38–39), however, Luke never assumes that Capernaum is located on a lakeshore.
14 Influenced by the parallel passage in Matt 4:13, Codex D adds, "which lies on the lake in the region of Zebulon and Naphtali."
15 See Busse, *Wunder*, 65.
16 For v. 36 Fitzmyer (1.546–47) refers to 2 Sam (LXX 2 Kgdms) 1:4; Acts 8:21; and 15:6, in which λόγος, like דָּבָר, can mean "event," "matter." Correctly, he here prefers the meaning "word," i.e., effective word.
17 On astonishment (ἐξεπλήσσοντο, "they were astonished") see 9:43.
18 On the proximity between ἐξουσία ("authority") and δύναμις ("power") see 4:36; 9:1.
19 See Luke 4:6; 22:53; Acts 26:18.

ἐξουσία to the Twelve (9:1) and to the seventy(-two) (10:19). Would Luke also have disciples of the devil in mind, when he brings particular holders of political power into association with the devil?[20] For example, the alliance between Herod and Pilate stands under the sign of the devil according to Acts 4:27, though both officials were not presented as being subject to the devil from the beginning. One could maintain on this basis that, within Luke's two volumes, at one point or another, a dualistic worldview comes to light.

Here Jesus' power is expressly connected to his word. It is thus not a purely supernatural power that overcomes human beings, but proves to be a force that creates an interpersonal relationship, like a call from one person to another, which expects a response.[21]

The Healing of the Possessed Man (vv. 33–37)

■ **33** Whereas ὁ δαίμων meant, for the Greeks, the divinity and the numinous, τὸ δαιμόνιον (here, "demon") could describe, abstractly, the divine, or concretely, an intermediate being. The LXX uses δαιμόνιον in a disparaging sense, and contemporaneous Jewish literature followed suit. It also evidences a developed belief in demons. A dualistic doctrine of good and evil spirits became widespread at that time in the Greek world as well.[22] Δαιμόνιον occurs only a single time in Luke in the Greek sense, as a description of the divinity (Acts 17:18). For him, as for contemporaneous Judaism, the demons stood in the service of the devil, and in opposition to God and his angels.[23] They bring injury and destruction, but Luke does not reflect either on their origin or their dominion. For him, the most important aspect is the oppression that they bring upon human beings. Lukan demonology draws from early Christian tradition, particularly from Mark. Although he does not develop it further, he does emphasize the Messiah's eschatological victory over the demons,[24] which, in his anthropological orientation, is understood as a gift and a liberation of humanity.

Ἀκάθαρτον ("unclean") after δαιμόνιον ("demon") would seem pleonastic to a Jew, but this detail from Mark makes an understanding of δαιμόνιον in the positive sense impossible. It seems as if it is only the spirit of the demon that is ruling the person, but after vv. 35–36, πνεῦμα ("spirit") and δαιμόνιον occur almost synonymously.[25]

■ **34** The demon complains and attacks Jesus. The τί ἡμῖν καὶ σοί ("what have we to do with you?") means, to Semitic ears, "Why are you getting mixed up in our affairs?" But a Greek reader would probably understand it as, "What do we have in common?" Luke adds an ἔα ("ah!"), that is, a scream or a sigh,[26] perhaps to communicate the correct Semitic meaning. The following verse removes all doubt: "You have come to destroy us."[27] After this soteriologically and eschatologically unobjectionable diagnosis comes an equally correct formula of christological identification. The title ὁ ἅγιος τοῦ θεοῦ ("the Holy One of God"), rooted in the Hebrew Bible, is an archaic designation for Jesus.[28] The expression here does not indicate a priestly mission.[29] It illustrates Jesus' relationship to God and the prophetic mission conferred by God. Luke accepts this title.

---

20   See Luke 4:6; 20:20; 23:7. See the commentary to Luke 4:5–8 above.

21   See the commentary to Luke 4:16–30 above.

22   See BAGD *s.v.*; and Otto Böcher, "δαιμόνιον, κτλ.," *EDNT* 1 (1990) 271–74.

23   Contrary to this, Fitzmyer (1.545) believes that Luke is not making a connection between the demons and the devil. But Luke 13:11, 16 show that he is mistaken on this point. In addition to this, the knowledge that Jesus is the Son of God, which the demons bring to light (Luke 4:41), is on the same level as the devil's knowledge in Luke 4:3, 9.

24   See Otto Böcher, "δαιμόνιον, κτλ.," *EDNT* 1 (1990) 272: "Early Jewish eschatology expected the defeat of the devil and his demons in the end time (1QS 3:24f.; 4:20–22; 1QH 3:18; 1QM 1:10f.; 7:6; 12:7ff.)."

25   The genitive δαιμονίου ἀκαθάρτου can thus be understood as an elucidation of the word πνεῦμα (epexegetical genitive).

26   On ἔα see Fitzmyer (1.545): "It expresses displeasure or surprise."

27   The plural "we" is meant to indicate the world of the demons, and not the demon and the possessed individual.

28   Cf. Judg 13:7; 16:7 (LXX, Codex B: for Samson); and Ps 106(LXX 105):16 (for Aaron); Mark 1:24; John 6:69.

29   Despite the scholarly study of Gerhard Friedrich, "Beobachtungen zur messianischen Hohenpriestererwartung in den Synoptikern," *ZThK* 53 (1956) 265–311.

■ **35** Jesus' powerful word bids the demon be silent and announces the exorcism. Ἐπιτιμάω ("rebuke," "scold") and its Hebrew and Aramaic equivalents could attain a technical sense in Jewish literature and thus describe the word that God or his messenger pronounced in order to subdue evil spirits.[30] The redundancy of ἐξέρχομαι ("to come out," thrice in these verses) is neither coincidental nor artless: each occurrence has its narrative function, and its repetition underscores, as in Mark, the significance of Jesus' exorcisms for human beings, and thus for the readers of Luke's Gospel. About the exorcism itself, Luke tells that the demon openly admits defeat by throwing the liberated man into the midst of the crowd as it leaves him, and by doing this without hurting the man.

■ **36–37** Not only admiration but religious θάμβος ("terror")[31] fills all the spectators. Jesus' word conquers the demonic worlds, because it is filled with power and might. Like the widening circles in the water after a stone is thrown into it, Jesus' authoritative λόγος ("word") effects the miracle, then the θάμβος of the spectators, and finally a positive ἦχος ("sound," "echo," "response") in the entire region. Luke loves such generalizing details.

From a form-critical perspective, Luke remains true to Mark's miracle story,[32] because at each point in it he can introduce and develop his own concerns. He will only wait until later (4:41) to comment on the christological title, "Holy One of God." The command of silence, with which Mark is so concerned, is perhaps for Luke no more than a sign of Jesus' victory and of the defeat of the demons; φιμόω ("to silence") means "to shut the

mouth with a muzzle." It is unclear to me whether the figurative meaning, "to make to be quiet," is on a more vulgar linguistic level. The use of "binding" or overpowering by means of incantations is well attested for ancient magic.[33]

The Healing of Peter's Stepmother (vv. 38–39)

■ **38** As Luke later distinguishes (vv. 40–41) between sickness and exorcism, he now lets a healing follow an exorcism, and the liberation of a woman follow that of a man.[34] The short account begins with a change of scene from the synagogue to a house (correspondingly, the synagogue and the house of a new convert are places of missionary activity in the book of Acts and in the life of the Christians). Because the calling of the disciples has not yet taken place, Luke cannot correctly introduce the host, Simon Peter, nor even explain why it is that Jesus enters precisely this house.[35] He emphasizes the seriousness of the illness: the mother-in-law's[36] fever is high. This is the occasion of the request for help that Simon, and probably his wife, make to Jesus.

■ **39** Jesus' reaction proceeds in a different manner than in Mark. Ἐπιστάς hardly means only "to come toward,"[37] but, next to ἐπάνω αὐτῆς ("above her"), probably means that Jesus bent down over her (as Paul does in Acts 20:10 over Eutychus). The actions of Jesus that follow are first nonverbal, and then verbal. The nonverbal actions demonstrate Jesus' might and superiority, as they do in the case of Elisha (1 Kgs [LXX 3 Kgdms] 17:21), and perhaps also his nearness, from which he can breathe into the woman his healing breath (the LXX understood Elijah's gesture in this way).[38] The

30 See Howard Clark Kee, "The Terminology of Mark's Exorcism Stories," *NTS* 14 (1967–68) 232–46. Kee offers a good examination of the verb ἐπιτιμάω ("to rebuke") and the corresponding Semitic root נער (e.g., in the exorcism that Abraham accomplishes by means of prayer and the laying on of hands in 1QapGen 20.16–32).

31 See Georg Bertram, "θάμβος, κτλ.," *TDNT* 3 (1965) 6: "Expressions of fear and astonishment . . . serve to emphasise the revelatory content and christological significance of many incidents in the Synoptic Gospels."

32 According to Bultmann (*History*, 209–10) and Fitzmyer (1.542), the original story showed the typical features of an exorcism. Agreeing with Theissen (*Miracle Stories*, 85–94), one must differentiate between exorcisms and healings.

33 See BAGD *s.v.;* and, above all, Moulton and Milligan, *Vocabulary, s.v.*

34 See Flender, *Heil*, 15 n. 8.

35 The use of the article betrays Luke's embarrassment: in v. 38a the article is lacking ("into the house of a certain Simon"), but in v. 38b it is used ("Simon's mother-in-law").

36 Aside from references to Naomi, Ruth's mother-in-law (called πενθερά eleven times in the book of Ruth), the LXX uses this word only in Deut 27:23 and Mic 7:6; see Hatch and Redpath, *s.v.* Josephus uses the word four times in all, three of these occurrences for Naomi; see Rengstorf, *Concordance, s.v.*

37 See Delebecque, 25 (note on v. 39).

38 It is noteworthy that the posture is no longer given in the LXX; the LXX speaks only of breathing on the individual. Xavier Léon-Dufour interprets Jesus'

verbal action expresses Jesus' word, so important for Luke. Ἐπιτιμάω ("to rebuke") becomes a typical expression for the healing Messiah in Luke (see 4:35, 41). The fever is thereby personified and is drawn into proximity with the demon of the preceding verses. Jesus' success is told in a twofold manner: the fever disappears, and the woman can go back to work. This takes place miraculously swiftly, so that the recovery seems like a new life (ἀναστᾶσα, "she got up"). The obliging hospitality of the mother-in-law is a confirmation of the miracle, but at the same time also a sign that liberation is reflected in a new obligation. In Luke discipleship to Jesus for a woman expresses itself primarily in a ministry of service. This is reflected not only in practical work but also in financial support (cf. 8:3).

With these two stories, Luke narrates the liberation of the people of God, their λύτρωσις ("redemption," 2:38), by means of typical examples. It is not only the might of Jesus and the omnipotence of God that stand in the foreground, but also the goodness of the saving Messiah (cf. 19:44). This image of Jesus in the programmatic Capernaum episode corresponds to the redactional description of Jesus in Acts (10:38).[39]

The Healings in the Evening (vv. 40–41)

■ **40** Luke took the chronological arrangement, which assigns the events to the course of one day, from Mark. He himself is not particularly interested in it; the beginning of the day noted in Mark 1:21 becomes an indefinite period of time in the Lukan summary passage at 4:31. The evening, however, is important, since transport of the sick was allowed only after sundown on a Sabbath. But for Luke, only the healings and the exorcisms (chiastically recounted in comparison with 4:33–37 and 38–39) are pertinent. The kindhearted Messiah takes upon himself the tasks of the Hellenistic doctor.[40] But they are also the gestures of the Christian missionary, so that

Christian practice, itself influenced by Jesus' example, is affecting the portrayal of Jesus in Luke's Gospel. Mark's summary passage suits Luke's generalizing tendencies remarkably well: the exorcism (4:33–37)[41] and the healing (4:38–39) are only examples of more extensive activity (4:40–41).

■ **41** On the hermeneutical function of the christological titles, see the commentary on 3:22 and 4:3–4 above. What the devil knows (4:3, 9), the demons know too. The screams with which they express it (κραυγάζω or κράζω; cf. ἀνακράζω, 4:33, "to shout") indicate terror or religious tension rather than noise. The command to be silent, as in 4:35, scarcely has the Markan significance. It is also not included in order to emphasize that confession without accompanying belief is empty formula. The issue is much more that the demons know God and shudder before his might (cf. Jas 2:19); for this reason they employ their confession as a defensive tactic to awaken the impression that "We *are* orthodox and are thus not vulnerable to you, Jesus." The Messiah, who knows their hearts, confounds this stratagem and conquers them by first forcing them into silence.

Jesus Leaves Capernaum (vv. 42–43)

■ **42** Ἐπεζήτουν ("were looking") and κατεῖχον ("tried to hold back") hardly describe the crowd as aggressive,[42] but rather thus: they feel abandoned and so begin anxiously looking for their shepherd; they wish to detain him so that he might protect them forever. The congregation in Caesarea similarly clings to Paul, when he intends to leave them (Acts 21:8–14). This is an understandable reaction, anchored in affection. But there is a higher standard: that the Messiah is also there for others and must for this reason continue his mission. Jesus' word (v. 43), like Paul's voice in Acts 21, contains no criticism, only instruction. Further missionary work is more important than the desired time together. Other cities

---

gesture ("to bend down over") as an expression of his kindness ("La guérison de la belle-mère de Simon-Pierre," *EstBib* 24 [1965] 193-216, reprinted in idem, *Études d'Évangile: Parole de Dieu* [Paris: Seuil, 1965] 123–48).

39   Léon-Dufour ("Guérison," 139–40) writes as though citing Acts 10:38—without saying so: "Jesus appears with the characteristics of the Savior who goes around doing good, and liberating those who have fallen under the power of the devil."

40   Bibliography on doctors in antiquity is in Bovon (*Lukas*, 206 n. 7).

41   On ἐξέρχομαι ("to come out") see the commentary on 4:35 above; on ἐπιτιμάω ("to rebuke"), see n. 30 above.

42   See Busse, *Wunder*, 74 n. 1; on p. 78 he gives a less negative judgment.

must likewise hear the good news. To express this human, and also ecclesiological, tension, Luke employs a Greek topos that is known as early as the *Iliad* (dialogue between Andromache and Hector).[43] For this interpretation, the words "from leaving them" are decisive.

■ **43** The term $\pi \acute{o} \lambda \iota \varsigma$ ("city," 4:43; 5:21) has sociological significance. Nazareth (4:29), Capernaum (4:31), and Nain (7:11) are cities for Luke. He speaks of villages less frequently.[44] God's dominion is proclaimed in cities (as it is later, in the book of Acts). Here again the historical situation of the urban Christianity of Luke's time has been retrojected into Jesus' time.

The psychological significance of Jesus' reply for these people is that his departure brings frustration, but also the possibility to become mature. It is also true that Jesus was not sent from God for Capernaum alone, but that others should hear the message of salvation. There is no better summarization of Jesus' mission and message in Luke: the salvation-historical $\delta \epsilon \hat{\iota}$ ("it is necessary," "I must"), Christian mission ($\mathring{\alpha}\pi \epsilon \sigma \tau \acute{\alpha} \lambda \eta \nu$, "I was sent") through the redeeming word ($\epsilon \mathring{\upsilon}\alpha \gamma \gamma \epsilon \lambda \acute{\iota}\sigma \alpha \sigma \vartheta \alpha \iota$, "to proclaim the good news"), and, as content of the proclamation, God's dominion, the essence of which is more important that its nearness.

The Second Summary Passage (v. 44)

■ **44** Verse 44 was prescribed by Mark, and is accepted and corrected by Luke as a useful conclusion: the exorcisms are deleted, and Jesus' geographical sphere of activity is here Judea. By "Judea" Luke seems to mean not only the southern part but the entire country.

Conclusion

This section gives us a good glimpse of Luke's working procedures. As an ancient historian, he uses a source

without expressly mentioning it. He places his confidence in it, but still adjusts it literarily and theologically to his personal intention. What, in Mark, is a day in the life of Jesus the missionary and his disciples is transformed by Luke into the second half of the "visitation" of Israel by the healing Messiah. Thus the episodes in Nazareth and Capernaum form a programmatic diptych.

Mark cobbles together the "day in Capernaum" from older materials (independent episodes), influenced by missionary practice in his time (the role of the synagogue, the significance of a house, preaching and miracles, itinerant missionaries accompanied by assistants, etc.). The elements in Luke that mirror his own time are: a distancing from Judaism (cf. 4:32 with Mark 1:22), the effort to be understood by the Greeks (cf. 4:31 with Mark 1:21), the semi-liturgical healing technique of Jesus (4:40), the christological interest (Christ as a "benefactor," but also as a prophetic Messiah), the city as the location of mission and church, and the telling of Jesus' words and wonders as a means of spreading the message (4:37).

This is not to say that there are not older, and partially reliable, accounts behind Luke and Mark, although they are not indeed recollections of Peter, as is sometimes claimed, but important individual episodes that were recounted among the first Christians. But the historical issue in exegesis is not only the question of the historical Jesus, but also, and perhaps above all, the question of Luke's historical situation. Luke 4:43 is surely correct in stating that Jesus preached the kingdom of God; but as it stands, the verse says more about Lukan theology than it does about that of Jesus.

---

43   Cf. Homer *Il.*6.405–502; Bovon, *Lukas*, 181–95. The inhabitants want Jesus to stay on as the "town prophet"; see Völkel, "Anfang," 225.

44   5:17; 8:1; 9:52–56; 10:38; 13:22; 17:12.

Peter's Catch of Fish (5:1–11)

Bibliography

Abogunrin, S. O., "The Three Variant Accounts of Peter's Call: A Critical and Theological Examination of the Texts," *NTS* 31 (1985) 587–602.

Betz, Otto, "Donnersöhne, Menschenfischer und der davidische Messias," *RevQ* 3 (1961–62) 41–70.

Bornhäuser, *Sondergut*, 34–51.

Coulot, Claude, "Les figures du maître et de ses disciples dans les premières communautés chrétiennes (Mc 1:16–20; Lc 5:1–11; Jn 1:35–51)," *RevScRel* 59.1 (1985) 1–11.

Delorme, Jean, "Luc V.1–11: Analyse structurale et histoire de la rédaction," *NTS* 18 (1971–72) 331–50.

Deltombe, François, "Désormais tu rendras la vie à des hommes (Luc V,10)," *RB* 89 (1982) 492–97.

Derrett, J. Duncan M., "James and John as Co-Rescuers from Peril (Lk 5,10)," *NovT* 22 (1980) 299–303.

idem, "ἦσαν γὰρ ἁλιεῖς (Mk 1,16): Jesus' Fishermen and the Parable of the Net," *NovT* 22 (1980) 108–37, esp. 121–25.

Dietrich, *Petrusbild*, 23–81.

Geninasca, "Pêcher."

Grollenberg, L., "Mensen 'vangen' (Lk. 5,10): Het redden van de dood," *Tijdschrift voor theologie* 5 (1965) 330–36.

Jeremias, *Sprache*, 129–37.

Klein, Günther, "Die Berufung des Petrus," *ZNW* 58 (1967) 1–44, reprinted in idem, *Rekonstruktion und Interpretation: Gesammelte Aufsätze zum Neuen Testament* (BEvTh 50; Munich: Kaiser, 1969) 7–48.

Mánek, Jindrich, "Fishers of Men," *NovT* 2 (1957) 138–41.

McKnight, *Meaning*, 290–95.

Pesch, Rudolf, "La rédaction lucanienne du logion des pêcheurs d'homme (Lc. V,10c)," *EThL* 46 (1970) 413–32, reprinted in Neirynck, *Évangile*, 225–44.

idem, *Der reiche Fischfang: Lk 5,1–11/Jo 21,1–14: Wundergeschichte, Berufungserzählung, Erscheinungsbericht* (KBANT 6; Düsseldorf: Patmos, 1969).

Polich, James C., "The Call of the First Disciples: A Literary and Redactional Study of Luke 5:1–11" (Diss., Fordham University, 1985).

Rice, George E., "Luke's Thematic Use of the Call to Discipleship," *AUSS* 19 (1981) 51–58.

Schlichting, Wolfhart, "'Auf dein Wort hin' (Lukas 5,1–11)," *ThBei* 17 (1986) 113–18.

Schürmann, "Promesse."

idem, "Die Verheißung an Simon Petrus: Auslegung von Lk 5,1–11," *BibLeb* 5 (1964) 18–24, reprinted in idem, *Ursprung und Gestalt: Erörterungen und Besinnungen zum Neuen Testament* (KBANT; Düsseldorf: Patmos, 1970) 268–73.

Theobald, Michael, "Die Anfänge der Kirche: Zur Struktur von Lk 5,16.19," *NTS* 30 (1984) 91–108.

Wuellner, Wilhelm H., *The Meaning of "Fishers of Men"* (Philadelphia: Westminster, 1967).

Zillessen, Klaus, "Das Schiff des Petrus und die Gefährten vom anderen Schiff," *ZNW* 57 (1966) 137–39.

1 **And it happened that while the crowd was pressing in on him and hearing the word of God, he was standing beside the Lake of Gennesaret, 2/ and he saw two boats there at the shore of the lake; the fishermen had gone out of them and were washing their nets. 3/ He got into one of the boats, the one belonging to Simon, and asked him to put out a little way from the shore. Then he sat down and taught the crowds from the boat. 4/ But when he had finished speaking, he said to Simon, "Put out into the deep water and let down your nets for a catch." 5/ Simon answered and said, "Master, we have worked all night long but have caught nothing! Yet at your word I will let down the nets." 6/ And when they had done this, they caught so many fish that their nets were beginning to break. 7/ So they signaled their partners in the other boat to come and help them. And they came and filled both boats, so that they began to sink. 8/ But when Simon Peter saw it, he fell down at Jesus' knees, saying, "Go away from me, Lord, for I am a sinful man!" 9/ For a terrified astonishment at the catch of fish that they had taken had overcome him, and all that were with him, 10/ and also James and John, the sons of Zebedee, who were partners with Simon. Then Jesus said to Simon, "Do not be afraid; from now on you will be catching people alive." 11/ And they brought their boats to shore, left everything, and followed him.**

Analysis

Luke introduces the first disciples immediately after the twofold presentation of the Messiah (4:16–30 and 4:31–44). Acts 1:21–22 teaches us that Luke bases the office of apostle on the fact that these individuals followed the Lord from the beginning. Mark, Luke's source for the preceding and following pericopes (Mark 1:21–39, 40–45), presents the calling of the first disciples earlier in the narrative (Mark 1:16–20). Luke catches up with it only at this point because he wanted to present the Messiah beforehand in his two aspects: in teaching (Luke 4:16–30) and in action (4:31–44).

The calling of the disciples in Luke is significantly more than a mere reworking of Mark 1:16–20, despite the reuse of some of the details. Moreover, Mark 4:1–2 and perhaps also Mark 2:13 help Luke to compose an introductory setting: Jesus boards a boat as a successful teacher. The setting of the telling of the parables (Mark 4) is thus shifted forward in the narrative, like other transpositions of the Markan material.[1] This also explains the lack of a boat in Luke 8:4, the passage parallel to Mark 4:1–2.

The "frame" of Luke 5:1–11 is thus formed both artificially and artfully from elements of the Gospel of Mark. The center, the "picture" itself, contains the story of a miraculous catch of fish, which is also familiar from the supplementary chapter of the Gospel of John (21:1–11). Important structural elements are common to both accounts: the juxtaposition of Jesus and Simon; the first, unsuccessful fishing expedition; Jesus' command to undertake a new attempt; the trusting obedience of the fishermen; the miraculous catch of fish; a gesture from Simon expressing his faith; and probably a prophecy.

Most of the accounts in the Gospels circulated "context free" for a time. Luke connected this story with a scene of calling, and the Gospel of John connected it with an Easter appearance. The tendencies in these Gospels are not all that different, since the central importance of the disciples remains as a point of connection between the account of the calling and the account of the post-Easter appearances. The earliest community, then, told about the great catch of fish[2] from an ecclesiological perspective, which is embodied in Luke in a calling, and in John in an installation account. Easter was something like a renewed calling. A miracle story with a prophecy about Simon probably stands at the beginning of the tradition, since discipleship has the effect of something distant and secondary in Luke, as does the theme of mission in John. The motif of discipleship as a response to Jesus' call lags behind in Luke, and arises only through combination with Mark 1:16–20. Jesus' call itself (Mark 1:17: δεῦτε ὀπίσω μου, "follow me") remains unspoken in Luke. Only in v. 11 do we find out that the fishermen have become disciples, since they leave everything and follow Jesus.

Luke's redactional work seems to be more creative here than in the previous and following pericopes (Luke 4:31–44; 5:12–6:19). Contrary to his usual practice, he unites elements here from several sources. The literary caesurae between vv. 3 and 4, and vv. 9 and 10, as well as the Markan parallels for vv. 1–3 and large parts of vv. 10–11, make it unlikely that the entire unit *as such* derives from Luke's special source. This is, however, possible for the miracle itself and for the prophecy, that is, for the tradition behind vv. 4–9, 10b. The style supports this assumption. But it is also possible that Luke is here anchoring an individual tradition that circulated independently.

Commentary

■ **1** Ἐγένετο δέ and καὶ ἐγένετο ("and it happened that") are among the favorite expressions of the evangelist.[3] He uses them with various constructions, here with two infinitives coordinated with καί ("and") and introduced by ἐν τῷ ("while") plus an indicative. The Lukan ἐγένετο is reminiscent of the biblical style of the LXX, even when adjusted to Greek syntax after the model of the constructions with συνέβη ("it happened," Acts 21:35). With this, Luke is subtly telling the readers on what level they should read his stories. These sentences also have a narrative function. In a script that knows neither paragraphs nor punctuation marks, these expressions usually appear at the beginning as a sort of signal for a new paragraph (cf. 5:1, 12, 17, in which the ἐγένετο helps the readers to structure the text). The Lukan narrative thus begins with a notice about Jesus' success, to which Luke likes to refer in the first pericopes.[4] Here the crowd is thronging him closely (ἐπικεῖσθαι, "to press in on" with the dative). Chapter 4 spoke variously of the word of *Jesus* (4:22, 32, 36, 43–44). But what the people are awaiting, and what gives the word its prophetic power, is the word of *God*. This is emphasized in 5:1 concisely, but clearly.

---

1   On such transpositions see Cadbury, *Style*, 78–79, who does not, however, treat Luke 5:1–11.

2   See Schneider, 1.122. Rudolf Pesch notes correctly that this is a particular type of miracle: a multiplication or gift miracle (*Simon Petrus: Geschichte und geschichtliche Bedeutung des ersten Jüngers Jesu Christi*

[*Päpste und Papsttum* 15; Stuttgart: A. Hiersemann, 1980] 36).

3   See Plummer, 45; Cadbury, *Style*, 132; J. Reiling, "The Use and Translation of 'and it happened' in the New Testament," *BT* 16 (1965) 153–63.

4   4:14–15, 22, 32, 37, etc.

Excursus: The Word of God

Ὁ λόγος τοῦ θεοῦ ("the word of God") occurs here for the first time, although Luke already alluded to ὁ λόγος ("the word") in the preface (1:2). The expression is familiar, yet cryptic, like the face of a beloved individual or the picture of a famous painter; to comment on it is difficult. To begin with, there is nothing new about it; Luke adopts ὁ λόγος τοῦ θεοῦ from Christian tradition (cf. Mark 7:13 and 4:13–20 with Luke 8:12–15, in which a constant play on words is made with "word"). The language of mission, especially the Pauline mission, seems more important here than Synoptic tradition.[5] This means that, for Luke, the work of Christian preachers stands in continuity with the work of Jesus.

Jesus' proclamation is of a quite particular kind. Luke 4 speaks of Jesus' word, but chap. 5 shows that Jesus has spoken as a delegate; God speaks through him. To be a carrier of a message is a well-known phenomenon. But today individuals often disappear behind their roles as delegates, diplomats, or politicians. For this reason we want to know what they *themselves* actually mean and believe, but we often do not find this out, so that we have developed a great distrust toward every public message. Jesus speaks in the name of God, as do the witnesses later in the book of Acts. That people trust him, and that he for his part has attentive hearers, does not mean that no delegation is taking place here. The process of delegation is, however, specifically Christian, in that Jesus, as a prophet, is the bearer of the word of God, and yet remains himself at the same time. The publicly appearing persona (the officeholder) is one with the private individual. The word is not only the vehicle of another person, but is, in every respect, in cognitive and emotional harmony with the word of God. The radiant power and the truth value of Jesus' word and of Christian preaching cannot be measured objectively. They depend on the personal relationship between father and son, between God and his children. We do not know the precious word of God directly. The circuitous route of perceiving it only in the mouth of a prophet does signify a deficiency, but leads to the discovery of a living and exemplary relationship between the prophet and his or her God. The relational aspect is constitutive of the word of God for Luke, but probably even before him for the church and for the Scriptures. For this reason, λόγος and ῥῆμα mean both word and deed, expression and effect, simultaneously. God is not only present in his word but also integrates the hearers in the process of communication: Jesus as the hearer of God and carrier of the word, and then, correspondingly, Jesus' hearers. Thus when the word resounds, it not only offers a verbal *hope* for life, but effects even now the new life in us, because each one experiences in it the grace of God's vindication, the weight of responsibility, the freedom from the deadly effect of guilt and limitation. Now we understand the reason that the masses thronged about Jesus. Humanity does not live by bread alone, but neither from the word of God wrongly understood, that is, in an abstractly formulated Christian doctrine that runs in only one direction.

In Acts Luke uses ὁ λόγος τοῦ θεοῦ to describe the post-Easter kerygma, and in the Gospel to describe the proclamation of Jesus.[6] The "word of God"[7] in Luke is, then, the locus in which God manifests himself outwardly as the living and gracious God. Because this God remains true to himself, the word is not exclusively bound to the person of Jesus. It has resounded in the Hebrew Bible as the promise of salvation in Christ, and it remains living in the time of the church as a soteriological proclamation. Acts 6:7, 12:24, and 19:20 are specifically Lukan, and describe an "advancing" or "growing" of the word of God. The word of God is not only effective but also living and dynamic. It shows its growth in the rise and development of the Christian congregation.[8]

After the introduction of the attentive crowd, Luke allows Jesus to enter. Καὶ αὐτός ("and he") is redactional and typical for Luke, who thereby expresses his veneration of Jesus.[9] Jesus first *stands*, because the crowd presses around him to such an degree that he cannot share the word of God. In this way, the need for a place to sit down is created narratively, and the episode with the boat is prepared. The people stand on the beach as in an auditorium. The speaker has only the surface of the lake[10] as his podium. In v. 2, after the description of

---

5   Ὁ λόγος τοῦ θεοῦ in the Acts: 4:31; 6:2, 7; 8:14; 11:1; etc. In Paul: Rom 9:6; 1 Cor 14:36; 2 Cor 2:17; 4:2; 1 Thess 2:13.

6   See Jeremias, *Sprache*, 129.

7   See Claus-Peter März, *Das Wort Gottes bei Lukas* (EThSt 11; Leipzig: St. Benno, 1974); Zingg, *Wachsen*, 69–73.

8   Acts 2:41, 47; 4:4; 5:14. See Zingg, *Wachsen*, 19–60.

9   See Jeremias, *Sprache*, 37–38; W. Michaelis, "Das unbetonte καὶ αὐτός bei Lukas," *StTh* 4 (1950) 86–93.

10   Luke knows enough to differentiate between a lake and a sea; he speaks of the "lake of Genessaret," as does Josephus. See Rengstorf, *Concordance*, vol. 2, *s.v.* θάλασσα; and vol. 3, *s.v.* λίμνη.

the setting, the action begins. Jesus sees two boats lying on the shore (ἑστῶτα παρὰ τὴν λίμην ["there at the shore"] after ἑστὼς παρὰ τὴν λίμην ["he was standing beside the lake"] is a clumsy repetition without deeper significance).

■ **2** Everything begins with the "glance of Jesus," just as it is decisive at the beginning of the two calls to discipleship in Mark 1:16 and 19. That Mark 1:16–20 distinguishes between two pairs of fishermen probably explains the presence of two boats here, in contrast to Mark 4:1–2. Luke varies the "mending" of the nets in Mark 1:19 with "washing" them in Luke 5:2. The influence of Mark 1:16–20 is important not only for source criticism but also for exegesis, since Luke will later allude to the metaphorical significance of the catch of fish (5:10). In *re*reading the account—which is, in any case, the beginning of every "allegorization"—the readers should stumble upon the ecclesiological relevance of the fishermen's work. Jesus' summoning glance lies between the neediness of the crowd and the readiness of the fishermen.

■ **3** The ἐμβάς ("he got into") creates the possibility for Jesus to express his request.[11] In Luke's time and place, however, Jesus' request can only be understood as a command,[12] which is directed so unconditionally at a positive response that its result is mentioned immediately: the boat now has a little distance from the shore, and Jesus can finally teach. Jesus' seated position is doubly appropriate: theologically, because it is the position of a preacher, and narratively, because one can only remain in a boat for an extended period of time if in a seated position.

The episode is inspired by Mark 4:1–2, but other authors in antiquity recounted similar situations. Josephus tells of a speech that he held from a boat, though,

indeed, under different conditions.[13] This did not become a proper literary topos, but the readers would understand that the amazing hero, despite a difficult situation, prevailed in his intention to convey a message or speech. Similarly, in Acts 21:35–36 and 40, Paul, pressed by the crowd, must use the steps of a temple to be able to hold an important speech.

■ **4** In v. 4 Jesus' sermon is already over.[14] With the durative imperfect tense, Luke intends only to allude to Jesus' instruction in general, since he does not want to reproduce a speech here, but rather a miracle plus a prophecy that results in discipleship. The crowd slips into the background, so that one does not know to what extent they are aware of the course of events.

Simon was already polite and cooperative in the boat episode, though also discreet and silent. Now he is addressed in direct speech. Jesus expresses himself elegantly. Luke has both of them speak in a refined manner, with precise yet not pedantic expressions: "to put out a little way from the shore" (v. 3), "to let down your nets" (v. 4), "for a catch" (said of both hunters and fisherman). The switch from singular (for Peter) to plural (for the crew) is also noteworthy.[15] But did Jesus stay on board after the conclusion of the instruction? Where did Simon's prostration of himself before Jesus (v. 8) take place, in the boat or on the shore? This lack of specificity is perhaps meaningful for the present metaphor of Christ's presence in the "boat" of his church.

■ **5** In vv. 4–5 Jesus and Simon come into dialogue. Simon's answer to Jesus' summons sounds hesitant: on one hand, like the answer of a fisherman, on the other, like that of a disciple. As a fisherman, he really has nothing to learn from a man of his age who only knows his way around on dry land. He quickly expresses this: it is actually nonsense to go fishing in the heat of the day if

11 Ἐπαναγαγεῖν: "to travel away," "to put out (to sea)." The expression is correct and appropriate.

12 Ἐρωτάω: "to request to learn or receive something," i.e., also "to ask," or, as here, "to entreat." See Heinrich Greeven, "ἐρωτάω, κτλ.," *TDNT* 2 (1964) 685–87 ("a genuine request which is humble or courteous," 687).

13 See Josephus *Vita* 33 §167: "On nearing Tiberias, I ordered the pilots to cast anchor at some distance from the land, in order to conceal from the Tiberians the absence of any marine force on board the vessels. I myself approached the shore with one ship and severely reprimanded the people for their

folly." In contrast to Jesus, Josephus came in from the water when he spoke to the crowd.

14 On this sermon (v. 3b) of Jesus, the almighty Lord, which gives weight to v. 10b that follows later, see Heinz Schürmann, "La promesse à Simon-Pierre: Lc 5,1–11," *AsSeign* 36 (1974) 63–70, esp. 65.

15 Jeremias (*Sprache*, 131) observed the following redactional idioms: ὡς δέ, ἐπαύσατο with a predicative participle (λαλῶν), and εἶπεν πρός.

one has caught nothing in the more favorable hours of the night; moreover, the crew is tired. But, at the same time, he stands firm: "yet at your word I will let down the nets." On one hand, a fisherman; on the other, almost a disciple already—his address to Jesus is ἐπιστάτα ("master"). In the secular context of the fishermen, it fits well, if one disregards the fact that, as the owner of the boat, Simon does not really need to allow Jesus to say anything. Here it becomes apparent how the account gradually makes a transition from one signification into another. In that Simon recognizes the human Jesus as ἐπιστάτης, he is beginning to articulate his faith, which then expresses itself in the beautiful, "yet at your word." It is true that the title ἐπιστάτης had found no application within the ancient systems of education, but it nevertheless expresses the higher rank and authority of the one so addressed. For this reason, it is used, above all, by disciples of Jesus for their Lord.[16]

■ **6–7** Fishermen from the region of the Mediterranean help us to read the vivid scene in vv. 6–7 correctly. The nets not only catch the fish, but enclose them first: συνέκλεισαν ("they caught," "they encircled") testifies of a particular kind of fishing, in which the fish are surrounded from various sides by the nets, which often fails when there is only one boat. The most difficult task is drawing the nets out so as to prevent loss of fish or damage to the nets. Thus one can understand διερρήσσετο to mean that the nets were in danger of breaking.[17] Only this way is the "signaling"[18] of the other boat comprehensible. A "calling over" would lessen the catch of fish or even cause it to fail, since the fish *hear* the danger. As soon as Simon and his crew realize that the catch of fish is so abundant that the nets threaten to tear apart, they leave the circle of the full nets in the water and wait for the second boat. Its crew would first find a place across from them so as to encircle the fish.[19] The catch is so large that both boats almost sink (βυθός is attested fre-

quently in the LXX as a description of the depth of the sea that threatens the believers).[20]

■ **8–11** The glance of the Lord (5:2) organizes the church; the glance of the believer launches a confession. When Simon becomes conscious of the success of his expedition, he throws himself down before Jesus; whether this is in the boat or on the shore (as in John 21:4) is not said. Simon's reaction, like that of Jesus in 4:39, is simultaneously verbal and nonverbal. The nonverbal prostration is religious behavior before the divine: on one hand, an homage; and on the other, a question of survival. The appearance of the numinous uncovers the sins of human beings and becomes dangerous for them. Simon's reaction corresponds to the Hebrew Bible theophanies: one cannot see God without dying. In the style of a revelatory scene, the divine response resounds: "Do not be afraid!" (v. 10b), which picks up from vv. 9–10a in again addressing Simon alone. Luke thus does not want to say with "Go away from me" that Peter wishes to break off his relationship with Jesus, nor with "for I am a sinful man" that Peter is guilty in a particular way. To the contrary, the entire story stands at the service of a pro-Petrine perspective: Simon Peter, like Moses and Isaiah, partakes of the honor of a divine revelation or prophecy in a miracle of nature.

With the one correct answer, he has confessed his human limitation and has pled for compassion. And just as appropriately, the Lord (whom Simon has addressed correctly with κύριε, "Lord," v. 8) has concluded his revelation with a commission in the form of a prophecy or a promise. "From now on you will be catching people alive" (v. 10c: ἀπὸ τοῦ νῦν ἀνθρώπους ἔσῃ ζωγρῶν) is a

---

16   The title ἐπιστάτης ("Master") appears in Luke 5:5; 8:24; 9:33, 49; 17:13 (in 17:13, exceptionally, people other than the disciples use this title); see Otto Glombitza, "Die Titel διδάσκαλος und ἐπιστάτης für Jesus bei Lukas," *ZNW* 49 (1958) 275–78; and Bovon, *Theologian*, 179.

17   The translators of the *Einheitsübersetzung* have understood this quite correctly: "daß ihre Netze zu reißen drohten" (*Einheitsübersetzung der Heiligen Schrift: Das Neue Testament* [4th ed.; Stuttgart:

Katholische Bibelanstalt, 1973] 123).

18   See Bornhäuser, *Sondergut*, 40.

19   On traditional methods of fishing in Greece, see Giorgios Leukadites, *Τὸ ψάρεμα στὰ ἑλλενικὰ ἀκρογιάλια, τὰ σύνεργα, οἱ τρόποι, τὰ ψάρια* (Athens: Estia, 1941), with woodcuts by Spiros Vassiliou.

20   Cf. 2 Macc 12:4: the Gentiles from Joppa behave blasphemously by drowning two hundred Jews (the verb is here used actively).

redactional use not only of Mark 1:17, but also of a traditional logion circulating parallel to it.[21] Although Luke creates a first conclusion in v. 9 by means of a generalizing notice in the imperfect (the religious ϑάμβος ["terrified astonishment"], much-loved by Luke, spreads around), and although he is reworking material from Mark 1:16–20 in vv. 10a and 11, I still believe that the tradition of the catch of fish found its form-critical conclusion and punch line in the prophecy to Simon, which alludes to the metaphorical significance of the catch.

Mark 1:16–20 and Luke 5:1–11 are nearer the tradition than is John: the saying about the "catch of fish" is at home in a revelatory scene, not in an Easter appearance. Johannine redaction must shift the entire unit into the time after Easter, since John 21 could be incorporated only as an epilogue, not as an interpolation at the beginning of the Gospel.

The miracle story can best be described as a midrash or further development of the existing traditional saying. In comparison to it, Mark 1:16–20 seems pale and pedestrian. Even the logion has a more considered effect than in Mark, who emphasizes: they were fishermen, and now they will fish for people. Luke stresses: you were a fisherman, you will catch people *alive*.[22] The allegory becomes operative here, and covers over the limits of the image of the catch of fish. Another secondary element is the address in the singular, which singles out Simon; this also explains the disappearance of Andrew (Mark 1:16).

Luke takes up the sons of Zebedee as well as he can, but in a rather clumsy narrative fashion, by means of the insertion of v. 10a after the summary in v. 9, which also serves as a transitional link. Behind vv. 10a and 11 there is no other tradition save Mark 1:16–20. Surprisingly, Luke also transmits the decision of the disciples (without an actual call to discipleship)[23] to leave everything and follow Jesus, again in the plural. The detail that the first disciples left behind *everything* that they possessed is Lukan.[24]

Conclusion

Modern exegetes take various aspects of the text as central:[25] Peter's preeminence[26] and the missionary responsibility of the apostles; the apostolic office, which depends only on the gracious call of Christ, not on the ethical character of the apostles; doubt and belief, forgiveness and the power of Christ, about which every Christian who is set to be a fisher of people knows; the opening of the church not only to Jews but also to Gentiles.

For me, the metaphor of the catch of fish and the responsibility of proclamation are central. The example of Jesus preaching from a ship helps the readers to see this correspondence. Jesus is the first fisher of people; his catch is immense. In the center of this pericope, however, is the other, material, and nevertheless miraculous catch of fish. That Simon, who is henceforth called Peter, is the first but not the only fisherman is conditioned by his leading role in the Jerusalem congregation. His prominence here is intended to honor the first leader of the earliest community and to legitimate at the same time the church as such; but it serves less, or hardly at all, to highlight his office, or indeed to establish an apostolic succession. That two boats are needed for this fishing expedition may have something to do, in

21 Rudolf Pesch, on the other hand, intends to demonstrate the redactional character of v. 10c ("La rédaction lucanienne du logion des pêcheurs d'homme [Lc. V,10c]," *EThL* 46 [1970] 413–32, reprinted in Neirynck, *Évangile*, 225–44).

22 See François Deltombe, who emphasizes that the verb has not only the sense "to catch alive" but also "to bring to life" or "to bring back to life" ("Désormais tu rendras la vie à des hommes [Luc V,10]," *RB* 89 [1982] 492–97).

23 On ἀκολουθέω ("to follow") see the commentary on Luke 5:27 below.

24 On this Lukan radicalism see 9:2; 12:33; 14:26, 33.

25 See Edgar V. McKnight, *Meaning in Texts: The Historical Shaping of a Narrative Hermeneutics* (Philadelphia: Fortress Press, 1978) 293.

26 See Pesch, *Simon Petrus: Geschichte und geschichtliche Bedeutung des ersten Jüngers Jesu Christi* (Päpste und Papsttum 15; Stuttgart: A. Hiersemann, 1980) 16–17. For Schürmann ("Promesse," 64) the main stress of the Lukan account is on Peter: Luke is concerned to anchor the mission and authority of the apostles in a pre-Easter indication of Jesus' intent. Michael Theobald is of the opinion that Luke 4:14–44 is concentrating on Jesus (christological orientation), where Luke 5:1–6:19, in which the apostles are introduced, maintains an ecclesiological interest ("Die Anfänge der Kirche: Zur Struktur von Lk 5,16.19," *NTS* 30 [1984] 91–108).

Luke's presentation, with the twofold character of the Christian church as Jewish and Gentile. But Luke does not draw any explicit allegorical parallels between the boats and the church.

It is often overlooked that there is no talk of an apostolic commission here. It is rather a prophecy and a promise that are expressed,[27] and this compels us to understand the miracle as metaphor. In this way the paradoxical message of the pericope is explained: this time, Jesus' preaching is on the sidelines, and Peter's catch of fish in the center, but the miracle serves as a parable and points to the proclamation of the Word, which, seen from the united perspective of both of Luke's volumes, stands at the center.[28]

It remains unclear where Jesus keeps himself during the course of the miracle.[29] Thus he is, in a manner of speaking, both present and absent, as also in the ship of the church today.

---

27 As McKnight remarks correctly (*Meaning*, 290), "The mandate is accepted, but not yet finally accomplished."

28 Jacques Geninasca emphasizes the parallelism between the work of a fisher and that of a preacher, as the title of his article indicates ("Pêcher/prêcher: Récit et métaphore: Luc 5,1–11," in Groupe d'Entrevernes, *Signes et paraboles: Sémiotique et texte évangélique* [Paris: Seuil, 1977] 143–71).

29 Geninasca ("Pêcher," 164) underscores, with perspicacity, the functions that Jesus has in the three sections of the story (vv. 1–2, 3–7, and 8–11). In the second section Jesus assumes the function of the factitive, i.e., the subject that effects the action.

The Healing of a Leper (5:12–16)

Bibliography

Betz, Hans Dieter, "The Cleansing of the Ten Lepers (Luke 17:11–19)," *JBL* 90 (1971) 314–28.

Boismard, Marie-Émile, "La guérison du lépreux (Mc 1,40–45 et par.)," *Salmanticensis* 28 (1981) 283–91.

Busse, *Wunder*, 103–14.

Crossan, John Dominic, "Jesus and the Leper," *Forum* 8 (1992) 177–90.

Elliott, J. K., "The Healing of the Leper in the Synoptic Parallels," *ThZ* 34 (1978) 175–76.

Masson, Charles, "La guérison du lépreux (Marc 1,40–45)," *RThPh* n.s. 25 (1938) 287–95, reprinted in idem, *Vers les sources*, 11–19.

Mussner, Franz, *Die Wunder Jesu: Eine Hinführung* (Munich: Kösel, 1967) 34–42.

Neirynck, Frans, "Papyrus Egerton 2 and the Healing of the Leper," *EThL* 61 (1985) 153–60.

Paul, André, "La guérison d'un lépreux: Approche d'un récit de Marc (1,40–45)," *NRTh* 92 (1970) 592–604.

Pesch, Rudolf, *Jesu ureigene Taten? Ein Beitrag zur Wunderfrage* (Quaestiones disputatae 52; Freiburg im Breisgau: Herder, 1970) 98–113.

Schramm, *Markus-Stoff*, 91–99.

Theissen, *Miracle Stories*, 44–45, 141, 145–46, 185–86.

Zimmermann, *Methodenlehre*, 237–42.

12 **And it happened when he was in one of the cities, just then there was a man covered with leprosy. When he saw Jesus, he bowed with his face to the ground and begged him, "Lord, if you choose, you can make me clean." 13/ Then he stretched out his hand, touched him, and said, "I do choose. Be made clean." Immediately the leprosy left him. 14/ And he ordered him to tell no one. "Go," he said, "and show yourself to the priest, and, as Moses commanded, make an offering for your cleansing, for a testimony to them." 15/ But now more than ever the word about him spread abroad; and many crowds would gather to hear him and to be cured of their diseases. 16/ But he would withdraw to deserted places and pray.**

Analysis

After the insertion of Luke 5:1–11, Luke again resumes the train of Mark's story, which he has followed since 4:31. It is true that minor agreements with Matthew could allow one to suspect another tradition;[1] but Matthew and Luke had similar reactions and correspondingly reworked their source, independently of one another.[2]

Verse 12a skips over 5:1–11 to make reference to 4:43–44: Jesus must do his work in other cities also. Verses 15–16 diverge strikingly from Mark 1:45, a verse that also bothered Matthew. In place of the inappropriate proclamation by the healed man (Mark 1:45), Luke mentions first the spread of Jesus' fame (5:15a), which, as in 4:43–44, brings about the gathering of a crowd, and then Jesus' retreat into the desert (5:15b–16). This conclusion also serves to introduce 5:17–39.[3] The generalizing notice in v. 16, in the imperfect tense, is thus both a finishing touch and a caesura.

Lukan elements are the favorite words καὶ ἐγένετο ἐν τῷ with the infinitive ("and it happened when . . ."), and καὶ ἰδού ("just then") as an introduction formula, as well as the deletion of the recitative ὅτι (Mark 1:40), the ἀνὴρ πλήρης with the genitive ("a man covered with . . ."), and the substitution of a second, coordinated verb with a participial phrase (v. 13: λέγων, "and said"; v. 14: ἀπελθών, "go and"). The sequence of words is adapted to the Greek language in v. 13 (placement of αὐτοῦ, "him"). Ἐδεήθη ("begged [him]") suits the situation better than the Markan παρακαλῶν ("begging [him]," "encouraging [him]"), just as πεσὼν ἐπὶ πρόσωπον ("he bowed with his face to the ground") is perhaps more literary than γονυπετῶν ("kneeling"). Εὐθύς naturally becomes εὐθέως in Luke (both mean "immediately," v. 13). Παραγγέλλω with the infinitive ("to order

---

1   See Schramm, *Markus-Stoff*, 91–99.
2   So also Schürmann, 1.278 n. 39; Busse, *Wunder*, 103–10; Fitzmyer, 1.571, 574.
3   According to Heinrich Zimmermann (*Neutestamentliche Methodenlehre: Darstellung der historisch-kritischen Methode* [Stuttgart: Katholisches Bibelwerk, 1967] 237–42), Luke alters the accompanying circumstances of the Markan episode at the beginning and the end. Mark's paradigm becomes simplified in the extreme: everything that is not absolutely necessary is omitted. Only the words of Jesus are left basically unchanged. Luke lays the theological stress on the introduction and conclusion.

[him]," v. 14), διέρχομαι ("to go through," "to spread abroad," v. 15), μᾶλλον ("more than ever," in the additive or alternative sense), συνέρχομαι ("to gather"), θεραπεύω ("to cure"), and ὑποχωρέω ("to withdraw") are part of Luke's vocabulary.[4]

The style and composition of this pericope reworked by Luke make it into one of the gems in Luke's chain of individual vignettes. Luke employs his so-called episodic style[5] and "manifestly writes history in individual stories."[6] Better framed than it is in Mark, the narrative can be recognized as an independent unit, for the miraculous action (vv. 12b–14) follows a short exposition (v. 12a) and ends with the reaction of the inhabitants (v. 15), and a counterreaction by Jesus (v. 16). The beginning, which is in the style of the LXX, strikes up a suspenseful tone and rhythm:[7] the Messiah—Luke, on his own, adds κύριε ("Lord," v. 12) and καὶ αὐτός ("then he")[8]—meets the next test and passes it too.

The story was perhaps originally set in a house. Since it is forbidden for a leper to enter a house, Jesus becomes angry (Mark 1:41) and sends the man away immediately (Mark 1:43).[9] In this way, Jesus' mixture of wrath and compassion is comprehensible, and perhaps also the command to silence (Mark 1:44). It is a disputed point whether this first version of the tradition reflects a historical reminiscence or Mark's redactional assumptions.[10] More important is the reason that the first Christians loved and retold this story, and this in the form of a miracle story.

The repetitions in Mark's account have led to various exegetical solutions: Mark 1:40–45 may have conflated two stories, the first of which portrayed Jesus' wrath and ended with the command to silence, while the second depicted his compassion, ending with the proclamation; the middle of the story was the same in both cases.[11] Or, again, the story was expanded over time,[12] or an explanation of the story circulated parallel to it.[13] In any case, it is recognized that Luke intervened. The propagandistic portrayal of Jesus as a wonder-worker was not the most important element; the earliest community understood the healings, particularly those of lepers, as the work of the Messiah, and a legitimating sign of him (cf. 7:22).[14] Since the leper, after the healing, is immediately reintegrated into the people of God, the Christians also recognized their own soteriological existence in this story. The same is true of the healing of the lame man (vv. 17–26), the functional setting (*Sitz im Leben*) of which should be sought in the life of the earliest community, perhaps even in its baptismal instruction (the theme of forgiveness). It is out of the question that Luke failed to recognize this christological feature and this ecclesiological component.[15]

Commentary

■ **12** As announced (4:43), Jesus works from city to city. The phrase "in one of the cities" (not simply, "in a city") emphasizes his extended sphere of activity. The expression καὶ ἰδού ("just then") brings the story into motion.

4   On this see Busse, *Wunder*, 106–7.
5   On this style of Luke's see Ernst Haenchen, "The Book of Acts as Source Material for the History of Early Christianity," in Keck and Martyn, *Studies*, 260.
6   Busse, *Wunder*, 109–10.
7   See ibid., 109. Busse here speaks of concentric structure, without further explanation.
8   On καὶ αὐτός see the commentary on Luke 5:1 above.
9   So Charles Masson, "La guérison du lépreux (Marc 1,40–45)," *RThPh* n.s. 25 (1938) 287–95, reprinted in idem, *Vers les sources*, 11–19.
10   See Gnilka, *Markus*, 1.94.
11   See Grundmann, *Markus*, 50.
12   See Bultmann, *History*, 212.
13   See Theissen, *Miracle Stories*, 145.

14   See Schürmann (1.276), who attributes this claim to Jesus himself.
15   One should compare this healing of a leper with the healing of the ten lepers in Luke 17:11–19. The direction of the impact of these two healing accounts is different, since Luke 17 is concerned with the faith and the gratitude of a stranger. As for the healing itself, the one in 17:12–14 follows the structure of the one in 5:12–14 with a single exception: after the encounter between Jesus and the lepers, and the request for help, the command to show themselves to the priest precedes the healing, which is fulfilled only on the way to the temple. By means of this transposition, the further development of the story connects more logically (the leper must return to Jesus to thank him and praise God), and it becomes possible for Luke to emphasize the faith of

It remains unclear whether Luke is personifying leprosy,[16] as he did earlier the fever (4:38–39). But he has no doubt that this disease separates the afflicted from fellowship with God, and causes people to suffer and die. The realm of leprosy is thus not far from that of death and of the devil.

In Hebrew literature the term "leprosy" includes various severe skin diseases.[17] Leviticus 13 describes two types: the symptoms of the first involve the hairs becoming white and the skin deteriorating, along with skin eruptions, swellings, tumors, and light spots (13:2–3); the second consists of shiny, spreading spots on the skin (13:4–8). If these symptoms are recognized, the priest must declare the diseased individual to be a leper, and separate him or her from the rest of the people (13:45–46). These individuals must live in isolation and give notice of their illness by their clothing, and verbally as well. For the community, these people are as though dead, and the ritual of separation is reminiscent of that of mourning. The priest is neither doctor nor wonder-worker. He is familiar with the Scriptures, and on the basis of what he sees he passes his priestly sentence, which does not represent a medical diagnosis. Correspondingly, he also decides whether a leper has become healthy again. The Torah is astonishingly optimistic on this point: it takes into account a possible recovery, but indeed without any indication of how this can be made possible. Thus a ritual is prescribed for the purification of a diseased individual who has been healed (Lev 14), even separate ones for the rich and for the poor, since the disease does not erase class distinctions. Through the ritual the healed individual is declared to be pure (in the sight of God) and is "resocialized" into the community. Like one who has risen from the dead, the individual lives again.

Because the leper knows of Jesus' good reputation (Luke 4:37), and has not yet given up the hope that the Scriptures do not rule out, he calls on Jesus. To manifest his freedom and his faith, he throws himself to the ground in front of Jesus. His behavior and his words, in their confession and supplication,[18] are reminiscent of the language of the psalmist.

The conversation that follows is skillfully formulated with the words "if you choose," which express the confidence of the sick man. There is thus both a potential and an actual messianic capacity. Jesus' will (emphasized in 5:12–13) leads from the one level to the other. By this means, the general messianic power becomes a force that saves "me" ($\delta \acute{v} \nu \alpha \sigma \alpha \acute{\iota} \ \mu \epsilon \ \kappa \alpha \theta \alpha \rho \acute{\iota} \sigma \alpha \iota$, "you can make me clean").

■ **13** The aim of this narrative is to show how the will of Jesus decides, and how, behind this willingness, there genuinely is a corresponding ability. Jesus' emotions are not expressed. Luke either did not understand, or could not tolerate, the detail about Jesus' wrath (Mark 1:41), and he expunged it; Matthew did likewise. As in the request, Luke describes both the nonverbal and verbal aspects of the response. Like Mark, Luke demonstrates Jesus' courage and superiority in reaching forth his hand, which is in the LXX a soteriological category; in their distress threatened human beings need a hand that will pull them out, and the Lord has stretched out this hand to his people. Here help becomes concrete in touching.

Every culture, generation, and individual understands something different by "touching." The signification and perception depend on the contact and the type of gesture. One touches people to arouse their attention, to make a request that they move, to care for them, and to express love. The analysis of such elementary actions is decisive. Luke intends to say: Jesus took a risk, he came into direct contact with the individual, not in the attitude of a doctor, but in that of a divine helper. His gesture says to the eyes what his voice says to the ears: "I do choose. Be made clean" (v. 13). It is reminiscent of the laying on of his hand in 4:40.

Like $\pi \alpha \rho \alpha \chi \rho \hat{\eta} \mu \alpha$ ("on the spot," "immediately") in 4:39, $\epsilon \mathring{v} \vartheta \acute{\epsilon} \omega \varsigma$ ("straightway," "immediately") underscores

the person healed of leprosy. See Hans Dieter Betz, "The Cleansing of the Ten Lepers (Luke 17:11–19)," *JBL* 90 (1971) 314–28.

16   See Busse, *Wunder*, 110, 112.

17   As Donald Deer has brought to my attention, the skin disease mentioned in Lev 13:2 is not what we now call leprosy (Hansen's disease). See André Paul, "La guérison d'un lépreux: Approche d'un récit de Marc (1,40–45)," *NRTh* 92 (1970) 592–604; and Gnilka, *Markus*, 1.92, with bibliography in n. 12. Cf. also the description of the epidemic in Athens in Thucydides 2.47–52.

18   Cf. Busse, *Wunder*, 107: "Luke again replaces the colorless $\lambda \acute{\epsilon} \gamma \omega$ with his preferred word, $\delta \acute{\epsilon} o \mu \alpha \iota$, an idiom of Hellenistic petition formula."

the miracle, which is described in the brief words, "immediately the leprosy left him." It is uncertain whether Luke understood this disease as a demon, and the recovery as an exorcism.[19] In 4:40–41 Luke distinguishes the sick from the possessed. In 5:15 he speaks of the healing of diseases, to which the leprosy of v. 12 belongs.

■ **14** Luke replaces the banal λέγει ("he says") with παρήγγειλεν ("he ordered"). In the papyri this word is a technical term for officially spoken instructions and demands.[20] In colloquial language it means "to direct," "to request," "to command," "to order" (from all types of people of respect, from worldly dignitaries, etc.).[21] The καὶ αὐτός ("and he"), then, emphasizes the command of a person who possesses authority.

In contrast to Mark, Luke makes note of the less important first request—the command to silence—in indirect speech, possibly because he did not understand its significance in Mark.[22] For Luke the second request, put forth in direct speech, is the important one. The recovery has no effect as long as the society does not recognize it as a purification. The individual only "lives" again when he is accepted anew into the community. From a form-critical perspective, this command also serves as the confirmation of the miracle.

Καθαρίζω ("to purify," "make clean") occurs six times in Luke's Gospel in cases of healing from leprosy,[23] and once in the case of ritual purification according to the Law of Moses (11:39), thus, in all cases, in its Jewish meaning. In addition to this, the term appears in Acts 10:15; 11:9; and 15:9 in a Christian, spiritualized meaning: God declares the unclean animals of Leviticus 11, as well as the hearts of Gentiles and Jews, to be pure. Thus two variations of the meaning should be distin-

guished: a Jewish one that is understood ritually by Luke, and a Christian one, understood personally. It is important that at this stage of the Christian faith, its identity can only be expressed in a new understanding of its Jewish mother tongue.

It is up for discussion whether Luke is merely representing the Jewish background of 5:12–16 in a purely historical manner, or whether he is letting something of the new Christian interpretation of holiness be heard through these Jewish expressions. On one hand, he alters practically nothing of the Markan account in this respect,[24] but on the other, he does not understand the story of Jesus in a purely historicizing sense. In association with 4:27, the healing of the leper is a component of Jesus' messianic mission. As a physical miracle and a social reintegration simultaneously, it is, like the miraculous catch of fish (5:1–11), a sign of the divine economy and incorporation into the church.[25] In respect to his understanding of the Law, Luke wants neither to portray Jesus as especially observant nor to devalue legal purification vis-à-vis Christian healing.

■ **15–16** In contrast to Mark's Gospel, in which the healed leper manifestly transgresses Jesus' command not to tell anyone, the command is not even mentioned again in Luke.[26] Like Mark, Luke also does not report how the leper showed himself to the priest, probably to avoid unnecessary length. Luke adopts the term λόγος ("word," "report") from Mark, but this missionary word proclaimed by the healed man becomes, in Luke, the word about "him" (probably about Jesus rather than about the healed individual).[27]

Then the summary proceeds with the usual twofold content: the crowds gather[28] in order to hear (the Christ-

---

19 See ibid., 110–14.
20 See Moulton and Milligan, *Vocabulary, s.v.* παραγγέλλω.
21 See BAGD *s.v.* παραγγέλλω.
22 This command to be silent is interpreted in various ways. The concern may be: (1) to hide the miracle (historicizing perspective); (2) to wait for the inspection by the priests (harmonizing exegesis); (3) to conceal the messianity of Jesus (dogmatic perspective of biblical theology); (4) to construct an aura of mystery around the thaumaturg (perspective of comparative religion); (5) to keep Jesus' identity as the Christ quiet, out of consideration for the Jews (sociological orientation).

23 Luke 4:27; 5:12, 13; 7:22; 17:14, 17.
24 To replace ἅ with καθώς (v. 14) is a stylistic peculiarity of the LXX, to which Luke tends to revert.
25 The words εἰς μαρτύριον αὐτοῖς ("for a testimony to them") are notoriously hard to understand. The concern is not yet to offer a proof to the priests of Jesus' obedience to the Law, but rather to authenticate the healing officially; see Schürmann, 1.277.
26 Codex D regrets this change, and introduces the parallel passage from Mark 1:45—2:1a after Luke 5:14.
27 Luke 5:15a is similar to 7:17.
28 As Schürmann observes correctly (1.278 n. 33), Luke (συνήρχοντο ὄχλοι πολλοί, "many crowds

ian absolute $\dot{\alpha}\kappa o\acute{v}\epsilon\iota\nu$) and to be healed.[29] Nothing is said of a positive answer from Jesus. To the contrary, Jesus retreats, probably for the same reason as in 4:42–43—although this is not explicitly said. The wilderness is no longer a place of gathering, as it is in Mark 1:45, but a region in which Jesus tends his relationship with God through prayer.[30] One would like to know how, exactly, Luke visualizes this $\dot{v}\pi o\chi\omega\rho\acute{\epsilon}\omega$ ("to withdraw") of Jesus, but this may become clearer at 9:10.[31]

Conclusion

In this pericope Jesus acts as a wonder-worker. His power, but also his love, are expressed in his words of promise ("I do choose. Be made clean," v. 13b), and in the risk-taking gesture of direct contact ("then he stretched out his hand, [and] touched him," v. 13a). Above all, Jesus appears as a healing Messiah, who brings about the well-being of an individual within the chosen people. According to Jewish sensibilities, the recovery from leprosy would seem to be an eschatological victory.

Luke invites us to read the episode first historically, within Jewish categories. But as Christian readers we are led onward to a second reading, in which we learn to understand recovery and healing as allusions to redemption in Christ and to the obedience of faith.

---

would gather") is being inspired by the words in a later passage from Mark (Mark 2:2, $\sigma\upsilon\nu\acute{\eta}\chi\vartheta\eta\sigma\alpha\nu$ $\pi o\lambda\lambda o\acute{\iota}$, "many gathered around").

29 See Luke 4:40–44 and 9:11.

30 See Luke 4:42 and Monloubou, *Prière*, 57.

31 The fragment of an apocryphal Gospel in P. Egerton 2, frg. 1 (recto), lines 32–42, narrates the same (or an analogous) miracle. One should note (1) the two lines preceding it (lines 30–31, in which Jesus escapes his enemies), which are reminiscent of Luke 4:30; (2) the exactness with which the origin of the disease is described (contact with other lepers); (3) the lack of a command to silence (unless this was located in the lacuna after the command to show himself to the priests). See also Aurelio de Santos Otero, *Los Evangelios Apócrifos: Colección de textos griegos y latinos* (2d ed.; BAC 148; Madrid: BAC, 1963) 98; and Hennecke-Schneemelcher, 1.98; and the notes to the commentary on 4:28–30 above.

The Healing of a Paralytic (5:17–26)

Bibliography

Bultmann, *History*, 382.

Busse, *Wunder*, 115–34.

Dupont, Jacques, "Le paralytique pardonné (Mt 9,1–8)," *NRTh* 92 (1960) 940–58.

Feuillet, A., "L'ἐξουσία du Fils de l'homme (d'après Mc. II,10–28 et par.)," *RechSR* 42 (1954) 161–92.

Fuchs, Albert, "Offene Probleme der Synoptiker-forschung: Zur Geschichte der Perikope Mk 2:1–12 par Mt 9:1–8 par Lk 5:17–26," in SNTU 15 (Linz: Albert Fuchs, 1990) 73–99.

Jülicher, *Gleichnisreden*, 2.174–202.

Kertelge, Karl, "Die Vollmacht des Menschensohnes zur Sündenvergebung (Mk 2,10)," in P. Hoffmann et al., eds., *Orientierung an Jesus: Zur Theologie der Synoptiker: Festschrift Josef Schmid* (Freiburg: Herder, 1973) 205–13.

Klauck, Hans-Josef, "Die Frage der Sündenvergebung in der Perikope von der Heilung des Gelähmten (Mk 2,1–12 parr)," *BZ* n.s. 25 (1981) 223–48.

van der Loos, Hendrik, *The Miracles of Jesus* (trans. T. S. Preston; NovTSup 9; Leiden: Brill, 1965) 440–49.

Maisch, Ingrid, *Die Heilung des Gelähmten: Eine exegetisch-traditionsgeschichtliche Untersuchung zu Mk 2,1–12* (SBS 52; Stuttgart: Katholisches Bibelwerk, 1971).

May, "Power."

Mead, R. T., "The Healing of the Paralytic—a Unit?" *JBL* 80 (1961) 348–54.

Neirynck, Frans, "Les accords mineurs et la rédaction des évangiles: L'épisode du paralytique (Mt IX,1–8 / Lc V,17–26 par. Mc II,1–12)," *EThL* 50 (1974) 215–30.

Schramm, *Markus-Stoff*, 99–103.

17 **And it happened on one of these days while he was teaching, Pharisees and teachers of the Law were sitting nearby (they had come from every village of Galilee and Judea and from Jerusalem); and the power of the Lord was with him to heal. 18/ Just then some men came, carrying a paralyzed man on a bed, and they were trying to bring him in and lay him before him; 19/ but finding no way to bring him in because of the crowd, they went up on the roof and let him down with his stretcher through the tiles down into the middle of the crowd in front of Jesus. 20/ When he saw their faith, he said, "Friend, your sins are forgiven you." 21/ Then the scribes and the Pharisees began to discuss it: "Who is this who is speaking blasphemies? Who can forgive sins but God alone?" 22/ But Jesus perceived their questionings, answered and said to them, "Why do you raise such questions in your hearts? 23/ Which is easier, to say, 'Your sins are forgiven you,' or to say: 'Stand up and walk'? 24/ But so that you may know that the Son of Man has authority on earth to forgive sins"—he said to the one who was paralyzed—"I say to you, stand up and take your bed and go to your home." 25/ And immediately he stood up before them, took what he had been lying on, and went to his home, glorifying God. 26/ Amazement seized all of them, and they glorified God and were filled with awe, saying, "We have seen strange things today."**

Analysis

Luke follows Mark 2:1–12 with the same respect that he otherwise brings to his sources. There is a first redactional intervention in καὶ ἐγένετο ἐν μιᾷ τῶν ἡμερῶν ("And it happened on one of these days").[1] Also, the real action does not begin immediately (as it does in 5:12), but—similar to 5:1—only after a summary passage (5:17). Luke deletes the detail about returning to Capernaum (Mark 2:1), since, according to him, Jesus has left this city forever (4:42–44). Full of authority (καὶ αὐτός), Jesus fulfills his teaching activity. Luke leaves out mention of the crowd at the door (but see also v. 18b [redactional] and v. 19a = Mark 2:4a). He juxtaposes Jesus to the Pharisees and the legal experts, introduced for the first time and playing the role of his audience, with a sentence that occurs at a later point in Mark (2:6), which mentions only the legal experts. Luke presupposes the familiarity of his readers with the Pharisees. In v. 21 he will use the word γραμματεῖς ("scribes"), but here he names them with the more comprehensible νομοδιδάσκαλοι ("teachers of the Law"), which is otherwise unattested before Luke, perhaps because, in Greek, γραμματεῖς are scribes, not teachers. Luke's introduction of these future antagonists this early in the story has its logic: they are the front-row spectators. Luke adds that they come from everywhere, that is, from the three most important settings of Jesus' activity: Galilee, Judea, and Jerusalem. Since Luke considers the *city* to be Jesus' environment, and later that of the church, it is perhaps a sign of contempt that he situates the enemy party in the

---

1   Cf. Luke 5:12: καὶ ἐγένετο . . . ἐν μιᾷ τῶν πόλεων ("and it happened . . . in one of the cities").

villages.[2] The view that it is *here* that the opposition to Jesus organizes itself is taken from Mark; and Luke makes note of this, surprisingly, between the first sentence of the brief summary passage, concerning Jesus' teaching activity, and the final sentence, concerning Jesus' healing activity.[3] This concluding sentence is added by the redactor to bring together the words and deeds of the Messiah, and to introduce the miracle story. In comparison to Mark, Luke has thus smoothed out the introduction stylistically.[4]

In v. 18 Luke already mentions the bed, as does Matt 9:2;[5] in v. 19 with the diminutive κλινίδιον he will specify that it is a stretcher. He avoids there the vulgar κράβαττον ("pallet")[6] of Mark 2:4. He calls the sick individual ἄνθρωπος ὃς ἦν παραλελυμένος ("a man who was paralyzed") instead of παραλυτικός ("paralytic"), which he senses to be unliterary. Verse 18b becomes the redactional substitution for Mark 2:2.[7] Luke, like Matthew, considers the detail that it is four men to be not worthy of mention.

Verse 19 says exactly the same thing as Mark 2:4, though Luke has, almost without exception, used different words than Mark.[8] The result is not necessarily more beautiful than the original version: in comparison with Mark, the description of the opening of the roof and the letting down of the stretcher has forfeited some vividness, since the concrete χαλάω ("to loosen," "to let down"), which is used in Luke 5:4–5 for the nets, is replaced by the colorless καθίημι ("to let down"). Mark thinks that the carriers dig a hole through a roof made of branches and mud-and-straw bricks. Luke makes explicit the climb up to the roof that is only assumed in Mark, and, as a city dweller, he imagines that the roof[9] was covered with κέραμοι, which describe tiles or stone slabs, easier to lift up and remove.[10] Εἰς τὸ μέσον ("into the middle"), perhaps taken proleptically from Mark 3:3, dramatizes the situation. By ἔμπροσθεν τοῦ Ἰησοῦ ("in front of Jesus"), the decisive request is spoken nonverbally (cf. Luke 4:40).

Τέκνον ("friend," Mark 2:5) probably does not mean a child, but a man viewed in a fatherly way by Jesus. Luke prefers the vocative. More important is the change from ἀφίενται ("they are [being] forgiven," present) to ἀφέωνται ("they are forgiven," perfect). Does Luke mean to say that forgiveness has already been granted before the brave conduct of the people (see below, commentary to v. 20)?

In v. 21 Luke the historian and artist tries to make the invisible world of thoughts and feelings narratively visible, as he does so often.[11] The "interior dialogues" of Mark (2:6) begin to become[12] audible discussions

---

2 On this differentiation between city and village, see the commentary on Luke 4:43 above.

3 I.e., between v. 17a and 17c. The formulation at the end of v. 17c, εἰς τὸ ἰᾶσθαι αὐτόν ("to heal"), is not unambiguous, because αὐτόν can grammatically be either the accusative object or the subject of the verb. Not a few copyists thought that it was the accusative object and replaced the singular with a plural (αὐτούς), "to heal them."

4 Agreeing with Bultmann, *History*, 66; and with Ernst Haenchen, *Der Weg Jesu: Eine Erklärung des Markus-Evangeliums und der kanonischen Parallelen* (STö.H 6; Berlin: de Gruyter, 1966) 105 n. 6; and with Schramm, *Markus-Stoff*, 100.

5 Καὶ ἰδού ("just then") and ἐπὶ κλίνης ("on a bed") are two minor agreements between Luke and Matthew. Schramm (*Markus-Stoff*, 99–100) sees in these some traces of a source parallel to Mark.

6 Phrynichus (*Ecl.* 41) recommends not using this word. Despite this, Luke uses it, although probably under the influence of his sources, in Acts 5:15 and 9:33.

7 The vocabulary and syntax of v. 18 are Lukan: ἐζήτουν with the infinitive, ἐνώπιον.

8 After ποίας ("which") one must supply ὁδοῦ ("way"). Here I translate "no way."

9 Στέγη (Mark) describes something that covers, or is covered: a roof or a house. Δῶμα (Luke) describes something that is built, a building, a house, or a room, and then the top of a house, the roof (in the LXX the flat roof that served as a terrace, e.g., 1 Sam [LXX 1 Kgdms] 9:25–26; the word is used in the same sense in Luke 17:31).

10 See Lagrange, 166–67.

11 He handles heavenly and divine realities in the same way. Cf., e.g., the image of the dove for the descent of the Holy Spirit (Luke 3:22), or the tactile vividness of the ascension (Luke 24:50–53; Acts 1:9–11) in comparison with the kerygma of exaltation. See Gerhard Lohfink, *Die Himmelfahrt Jesu: Untersuchungen zu den Himmelfahrts- und Erhöhungstexten bei Lukas* (SANT 26; Munich: Kösel, 1971) 276–83; and Bovon, *Theologian*, 176–77.

12 It is a commonplace that Luke has a preference for the verb "to begin" (ἄρχομαι). On the opponents or enemies of Jesus, see 7:49; 11:53.

here.[13] With the word βλασφημία ("blasphemy"),[14] we are somewhere between the Greek meaning ("slander") and the specific rabbinic one (to utter the name of God slanderously). In Hellenistic Jewish literature, as in Hellenistic literature in general, βλασφημία describes every calumny against the divinity.[15] Luke replaces the Markan phrase εἷς ὁ θεός ("God is one") with μόνος ὁ θεός ("God alone"), though he uses the Markan phrase in 18:19.

In v. 22, despite his strong tendency for visible manifestations, Luke retains Mark's mention of the hearts, in that Jesus perceives the innermost motives of human behavior.[16] Luke passes over τῷ πνεύματι αὐτοῦ ("in his spirit") either because it was not in his copy of Mark, or because Mark was speaking of the human spirit, not the Holy Spirit. Jesus can hear without his supernatural spirit having to be mentioned.[17] Like v. 23, Matt 9:5 also omits the word "paralytic," as well as the phrase "take your bed." Were both of them independently avoiding colloquial expressions?[18]

Luke follows his source more closely in respect to the words of Jesus than he does for the actions and descriptions. Thus v. 24 is practically identical with Mark 2:10.[19]

The παραχρῆμα ("immediately") in v. 25 is the typical signal of a miracle in Luke's redaction. The glorification of God by the healed individual, inspired by Mark 2:12b, also proves to be Lukan.[20] As in the dialogue (v. 22), Luke also replaces a verb (Mark) with a noun in v. 26: ἔκστασις ("amazement"). The motif of fear, common to Matthew and Luke but absent from Mark, is striking; the "today" of salvation is quite Lukan, as is the extraordinary quality (παράδοξα, "strange things") of divine action through Jesus.[21]

Except for the improbable hypothesis of another written source, the minor agreements between Matthew and Luke against Mark, if they are not coincidental, can be explained only by the possibility of common oral tradition, since Markan priority is beyond question and Luke's knowledge of Matthew is unlikely.

From a form-critical perspective, this pericope is a miracle story expanded in the direction of a controversy story. Traces of the miracle story can be found at the beginning of the versions of Mark and Matthew, and at the end of all the Synoptic versions. Indices of the mixed form are the double issues of recovery and forgiveness, and the seam between the narration of the

---

13 One finds the same phenomenon in v. 22a (vis-à-vis Mark 2:8a).

14 Τί οὗτος οὕτως λαλεῖ; βλασφημεῖ ("Why does this fellow speak in this way? It is blasphemy!" Mark 2:7) is particularly graceless. Luke improves it with τίς ἐστιν οὗτος ὃς λαλεῖ βλασφημίας; ("Who is this who is speaking blasphemies?" Luke 5:21). See Schürmann, 1.282 n. 24.

15 In the books of the Maccabees, blasphemy is forbidden by oath; cf., e.g., in the prayer at 2 Macc 15:24: "By the might of your arm may these blasphemers who come against your holy people be struck down." See Otfried Hofius, "βλασφημία, κτλ.," *EDNT* 1 (1990) 219–21.

16 Matthew responds similarly in 9:4 with τὰς ἐνθυμήσεις αὐτῶν ("their thoughts").

17 Further alterations of minor details in v. 22: (1) Luke inserts a δέ; (2) he prefers εἶπεν ("he said") with πρός to the present tense with the dative; (3) he writes the substantive (τοὺς διαλογισμοὺς αὐτῶν, "their questionings") rather than the verb with a following ὅτι (by means of this, the sentence becomes more fluid); (4) he introduces an ἀποκριθείς ("answered"), which is necessary, since the scribes and Pharisees are now giving spoken expression to their feelings; (5) the ταῦτα ("these things") in Mark is omitted (in the version of Luke

in Codex D, it is replaced by a πονηρά ["evil things"]).

18 In contrast, Matthew let stand the word "paralytic" in 9:2, 6.

19 Doubtless under the influence of oral tradition (for Matthew does the same), Luke transposes the order of the words "on earth" and "to forgive sins" vis-à-vis his source, Mark. He also substitutes the participle "paralyzed" for the substantive "paralytic," and κλινίδιον for κράβαττον. Both of these—in his opinion—are improvements.

20 Three remarks on details in v. 25: (1) ἐνώπιον αὐτῶν ("before them," Luke) characterizes the event as a controversy dialogue; the ἔμπροσθεν πάντων ("before them all") in Mark 2:12 corresponds to the conclusion of a miracle story; (2) Luke avoids the word κράβαττον again, this time by rewriting (ἐφ᾽ ὃ κατέκειτο, "what he had been lying on"); (3) finally, one finds a surprising minor agreement with Matt 9:7 in ἀπῆλθεν εἰς τὸν οἶκον αὐτοῦ ("[he] went to his home")—influence of oral tradition?

21 Luke often uses ἅπας (here, in v. 26) rather than πᾶς (Mark 2:12; both mean "all"); see Cadbury, *Style*, 195–96.

miracle and the question of forgiveness (cf. 5:20, 24b). The functional setting (*Sitz im Leben*) can be assumed to be the missionary or homiletic activities of the church, which would be illustrating the healing power of Jesus Christ by means of this story. The polemic against the synagogues of the time, in which the controversy over forgiveness arose, is the second functional setting. Mark already found the mixed form in his sources, and Luke underlined the second theme with the help of an oral tradition also known to Matthew; but Luke is less concerned with deepening the meaning of forgiveness than with bearing witness to the incipient relationship between Jesus and the people he addresses.

Commentary

■ **17–19** The exposition leads one to expect a disputation. Teachers from everywhere are sitting there as Jesus' audience. They test and (v. 21) threaten Jesus—and thus the church. Like the other evangelists, Luke does not understand that Pharisaism is a movement, but the position of the Scripture expert is an institution.[22] This can be explained by the fact that the educational system in Israel was not as official as, for example, the Jewish priestly organization. Also, in Luke's time, after the Jewish war it was the Pharisaic scriptural experts who led the Jewish people and carried the standard of anti-Christian polemic. The Pharisees have two characteristics in Luke. First, they oppose Jesus only during the first two stages of his life, not during the trial. Their jurisdiction stays within the limits of teaching and practice: the violent polemic between them and Jesus concerns the Law, and the doctrine of God and the Messiah. Second, in the book of Acts the aggressiveness of the Pharisees diminishes, since the belief in the resurrection unites both parties. Beyond that, Luke is also hoping for the conversion of these Pharisaic opponents.

The two main traits of the Messiah who stands in opposition to the Pharisees are neither royal nor priestly: Jesus teaches and heals. This presupposes both the ignorance and the sickness of the people. As the expression of the eschatological εὐδοκία ("good favor") of God, Jesus is no ordinary teacher and doctor. His teaching is characterized by "authority" (4:32), and his healing art by the "power of the Lord" (5:17).[23] Divine commission and the possession of the Spirit make this messianic activity possible.

■ **20** The event narrated in v. 18 is brought about by another, non-Pharisaic group, whose action is described in v. 20a by the momentous word πίστις ("faith"). They represent life, trust, and faith. Their πίστις is described not theoretically but narratively: it is decision, action, penetrating force, solidarity, and acclamation all in one. Astonishingly, none of the evangelists states explicitly that this faith is also the faith of the paralyzed individual. This individual is logically included in the αὐτῶν ("their [faith]"), though none of the evangelists specifically mentions the individual's faith.

Luke imagines the procedure to be that the carriers use the outside stairs and remove a couple of stones from the flat roof (δῶμα)[24] in order to let the paralytic down into the center of the humble house.[25]

---

22 On the Pharisees in Luke, see Martin Rese, "Einige Überlegungen zu Lukas 13,31–33," in J. Dupont et al., eds., *Jésus aux origines de la christologie* (BETL 40; Leuven: Leuven University Press, 1975) 201–25; J. A. Ziesler, "Luke and the Pharisees," *NTS* 25 (1978–79) 146–57; Jack T. Sanders, "The Pharisees in Luke-Acts," in D. E. Groh and R. Jewett, eds., *The Living Text: Festschrift Ernest W. Saunders* (Lanham, Md.: University Press of America, 1985) 141–88; John T. Carroll, "Luke's Portrayal of the Pharisees," *CBQ* 50 (1988) 604–21.

23 God is the origin and source of δύναμις ("power"). He transfers it to his Son (Luke 1:35; 5:17) in the form of the Holy Spirit (4:14). Jesus, in turn, is also a source of δύναμις (8:46), and can give it to his coworkers, the disciples (9:1; 24:49). The competition, such as Simon (Acts 8:10), can only be viewed erroneously as "the power of God, which is called

great." There are powers over the creation, though they are ruled by God, and will begin to totter at the end of time (Luke 21:26), when the Son comes in great power (21:27). To my knowledge, there is no satisfactory study of the concept δύναμις in Luke (25 times in Luke's two volumes, 119 times in the NT as a whole). The study by Eric May is outdated, but has the virtue of reporting the positions of theologians from antiquity and the Middle Ages ("'. . . For Power Went Forth from Him . . .' [Luke 6:19]," *CBQ* 14 [1952] 93–103).

24 It was certainly the same type of roof as the one onto which Peter ascended (Acts 10:9) in order to pray.

25 Probably a house without a gate (πυλών, Matt 26:71) and without a courtyard (προαύλιον, Mark 14:68); cf. Xavier Léon-Dufour, *Dictionary of the New Testament* (trans. F. Prendergast; New York: Harper & Row, 1980) 53.

Excursus: The Forgiveness of Sins

The readers expect a miracle and hear a saying about forgiveness (v. 20b).[26] This is surprising but not entirely extraordinary, since Luke inserts an "aside" in several miracle stories between the request and the miracle, often a sentence from Jesus about the faith of the one making the request (e.g., 7:9). This form-critical possibility was already used in the tradition to introduce the dialogue about forgiveness here. According to Luke,[27] the forgiveness of sins is linked to the work of Jesus Christ. Through the resurrection and exaltation of the suffering Messiah, God has promised reconciliation to humanity (Acts 5:31; 26:18). But forgiveness is also very closely related to repentance and baptism (Acts 2:38; 13:38). On the one hand, God has opened up the way to forgiveness through Jesus; on the other hand, the individual shows his or her intention to turn to God—indeed, not through observance of the Law (Acts 13:38) but through a personal and living relationship, which incorporates faith and love. Thus for Luke the forgiveness of sins is not realized once for all time on the cross, for it is a question of a *relationship,* and the human decision for a renewed relationship with God is constitutive of this. For this reason Luke can write that the forgiveness of sins is *announced* "through this man [Jesus Christ]" (Acts 13:38) but is simultaneously *given* (Acts 5:31). Without the salvation-historical work of Jesus Christ, forgiveness is impossible, but without the human μετάνοια ("repentance"), it cannot be realized. Luke knows that this relationship with God is an eschatological one: the gracious year of the Lord is upon us (Luke 4:19), which John has prepared (cf. 1:77 and 3:3), and Jesus inaugurates even before his passion. Forgiveness thus does not depend exclusively on the blood of Christ, but on the entire commission, effect, and work of the Son. One could say that the forgiveness of sins is for the individual what the kingdom of God is for the people.

What the sins are here is not precisely stated. Luke does not have in mind primarily moral lapses, but a broken relationship to God, which, of course, brings ethical consequences in tow. The anthropology of the human being before forgiveness is that of a slave to the devil (see the images of the prisoners and the blind in Luke 4:18 and Acts 26:18). Forgiveness is

God's affair, as the passive ἀφέωνται shows ("they are forgiven," v. 20); but it is nevertheless promised by Jesus in the name of God, and is put into effect by this "performative speech-act."[28] There is an anteriority of God, as the preaching of the Baptist and the sending of the Son demonstrate. But God does not save us without a response from us. Jesus pronounces forgiveness here, because human individuals have already given this response on the basis of their faith. The perfect tense of ἀφέωνται should not be understood in the Pauline sense of the exclusive grace of God, but as a recognition of the restored relationship between God and human individuals. In its ultimate sense it has no other meaning than the present ἀφίενται ("they are [being] forgiven"). This was understood by Mark in an aorist sense, but could be understood incorrectly as a "durative" present tense. With the perfect, Luke has expressed both what has already begun and its present reality.

The violent reaction (v. 21) is comprehensible from the perspective of the *Jewish* faith, but it is transmitted here by a *Christian.* Although Jesus did not say "*ego* te absolvo" ("*I* absolve you"), and thus respects the prerogative of God by means of the passive construction, he still takes upon himself the right to pronounce the forgiveness of God *hic et nunc* (here and now). Does the blasphemy inhere in Jesus' doing something that Judaism never expected from the Messiah?[29] It is probably rather that the Judaism of that time claimed to possess already the institutions responsible for the forgiveness of sins: ritual activity and its legal piety. Jesus is attacked so vehemently because he plainly ignores both of these and mediates God's forgiveness of sins in a completely new manner. Of course, forgiveness, after all, depends on God, but the question is, how do we experience it, and through what means do we receive it? The early Christian answer,[30] as is still visible from Synoptic tradition and in Synoptic redaction, is given in the Son of Man, who now (ἔχει, "he has," present tense) possesses the authority to forgive "on earth," that is, *hic et nunc.*

■ **21–24** For the first time Luke uses the christological title, "Son of Man" (v. 24). It is unclear what awareness of this he expects on the part of his readers. From the logic of the sentence alone, they would not understand

---

26 Ἀφίημι can mean, "to allow to go," "to leave out," "to send away," "to send out," "to exclude," "to omit," "to release," "to expel," "to cancel (a debt)," "to forgive," "to let have one's way," "to admit," "to consent," "to leave behind," "to abandon."

27 See Taeger, *Mensch,* 32–33; Bovon, *Theologian,* 121–22, 245–46, 249–50, 285.

28 On performative speech see the notes to the

commentary on 4:21 above.

29 Cf. Str-B 1.495: "In contrast to this, we know of no passage in which the Messiah, on the strength of his personal authority, grants a person the forgiveness of sins."

30 One must note that Jesus is not without motive in his behavior (v. 22b): he has recognized the situation (ἐπιγνοὺς . . . τοὺς διαλογισμοὺς αὐτῶν,

exactly what the expression means, except that it described Jesus. And for the issues at hand, that sufficed.[31] The ability of Jesus, the Son of Man, to forgive sins is based on an "authority." This authority was already mentioned in 4:32, but there, like here, without explanation. From biblical tradition and from the christological passages of chaps. 1–3, one can determine: first, that it is not granted from below, from human individuals, but from above, from God; second, that it is not mere permission but a right, and thus at the same time a power.[32] From Luke's silence about theology, we can conclude that his account is not an attempt to replace "catechetical instruction," but to accompany it (cf. 1:4).

The answer to the question of how one receives the Messiah Jesus' mediation of the forgiveness of sins in the age of the church, that is, the age of Christ's physical absence, is, according to Luke: through the apostolic proclamation of the word[33] and of the new possibility ($\mu\epsilon\tau\acute{\alpha}\nu\text{o}\iota\alpha$, "repentance") for people to live with God (cf. Acts 13:38, an extremely important passage in this respect). Luke 5:21–24 testifies to the Christian claim to have been entrusted with the administration of God's forgiveness now, at the end of time. This pericope, then, reflects power relations and the possibility of conflict, since the first Christians were probably excluded from religious offices in their Jewish homeland, so that in their perception their relationship to God had been

"confiscated" by the Pharisaic authorities; thus they had to struggle for something highly important to them. The official Jewish reaction, for its part, could only develop into a battle for the institutions.

The first Christians were motivated through *Jesus'* reformatory and prophetic attitude and their conviction that they possessed the *Spirit* of God. Luke 5:24a sounds archaic, and perhaps represents an authentic saying of Jesus, originally transmitted as an isolated saying, then redactionally rearranged, and finally inserted into its present place. In this development the miracle did not merely retain its significance as a sign of the dawning age of salvation, but became an actual symbol of Christian authority to confer, and thereby realize, the forgiveness of God in this age.

Verses 23–24 are not saying that the forgiveness is easier than the miracle. On the contrary, it is much more weighty than the miracle, which is only illustrating the deeper reality. The text only says, "Which is easier, to *say* ($\epsilon\grave{\iota}\pi\epsilon\hat{\iota}\nu$): 'Your sins are forgiven you,' or to say: 'Stand up and walk'?" (v. 23), because a sign is inherently visible and subject to verification. The entire discussion about forgiveness erupted between Jesus and the scriptural experts, and then between the earliest Christians and the synagogue, because forgiveness is not tangible. The drive toward legitimating signs so important for the young Christian movement explains, in part, the

---

"perceived their questionings," v. 22a). Thus, in the eyes of Luke, his critical question is justified. For the evangelist, the $\delta\iota\alpha\lambda\text{o}\gamma\iota\sigma\mu\text{o}\acute{\iota}$ are usually culpable thoughts, since they spring from sinful hearts; cf. Bovon, *Lukas*, 89–90.

31 The Son of Man, for Luke, is primarily an apocalyptic figure, the authoritative judge (Luke 9:26; 12:8; 18:8; 21:36), whose coming (12:40; 17:24; 21:27) opens the final phase of salvation history (17:22, 26, 30). It is certain that he is coming, but the exact time of his arrival is not calculable. One should not expect him too soon (17:22), but should also not, in view of the delay of his coming, sit around with idle hands (18:8). One must remain ready (12:40). The Son of Man can appear to a martyr in the form of an individual epiphany (Acts 7:55–56). Since Luke—like the sum total of the Synoptic traditions—identifies Jesus with the Son of Man, the earthly lot of Jesus is the same as that of the Son of Man: Jesus is the Son of Man, the Savior and Redeemer (Luke 19:10); he is free (7:34), unprotected (9:58), like Jonah (11:30), and called to suffer (Luke empha-

sizes especially that the Son of Man was betrayed [22:48] and persecuted [9:22, 44; 18:31; 22:22; 24:7]). Believers are united with him, place themselves at his service, and are prepared to suffer for him (9:26; 12:8; 6:22). The Son of Man is redeeming them even now by offering them forgiveness (5:24), and leading them in their behavior (6:5); cf. 12:10. See, in general, Marshall, 215–16 (who offers a good overview of the most important historical questions that the issue of the Son of Man raises); Gerhard Schneider, "'Der Menschensohn' in der lukanischen Christologie," in R. Pesch and R. Schnackenburg, eds., *Jesus und der Menschensohn: Festschrift Anton Vögtle* (Freiburg im Breisgau: Herder, 1975) 267–82; Bovon, *Theologian*, 155–56, 181.

32 See the commentary on Luke 4:32 above.

33 The Matthean version of Mark 2:12 is indicative of this human responsibility: "they glorified God, who had given such authority to *human beings*."

role and significance of miracle stories in Synoptic tradition.

Verse 24 seems like the result of Jesus' speech,[34] but instead of the expected "I say to you," the unexpected phrase, "he said to the one who was paralyzed," appears in v. 24b first. It is unlikely that this anacolouthon taken from Mark should be understood in Luke in the same sense as in Mark, where it is an incidental remark and an aid to understanding for the readers (cf. similarly Mark 13:23).[35] The second person plural in v. 22 of Luke is clearly an address to the Pharisees, not to the readers. A sudden switch here would be just as clumsy as the anacolouthon. Thus in v. 24 the speech merges with narrative. This is not entirely smooth, but it lends the story a certain liveliness. In any case this peculiarity of Mark's diction did not compel either Luke or Matthew to correct it.

■ **25–26** In a theological vein, it should be added that forgiveness[36] concerns not only the past of the individual but, above all, the present and future. The view toward the past does not even play the leading role. Acts 26:18 beautifully unites forgiveness with one's eschatological condition ("so that they may receive forgiveness of sins and a place among those who are sanctified by faith in me"). The miracle story was able to portray this strikingly in its narrative manner: the healing shows how forgiveness faces forward, oriented toward the dynamic of Christian existence. Standing up, running, going home, and praising God (v. 25) testify to the healed existence, that is, to the existence that has received forgiveness, and is from now on determined by the relationship between God and the human individual. The faith at the beginning (v. 20) finds its expression in the praising of God (v. 25). Verse 26 speaks of the messianic effect of forgiveness and faith. When Christ brings into being the new relationship between God and individuals, and sets it in motion, something of it becomes visible, so that the spectators are astonished and can praise God and have awe before the $\pi\alpha\rho\acute{\alpha}\delta o\xi\alpha$ ("strange things"). According to Luke, exactly that became reality at this time in the life of Jesus. The past, considered at that time to be the eschatological "today" ($\sigma\acute{\eta}\mu\epsilon\rho o\nu$), becomes the saving time of the reader's encounter with God.

Conclusion

Sin and suffering stand in relationship to one another, although Luke does not say that the one who suffers much has sinned much (cf. 13:1–5). Sickness and mishaps are signs of the destruction into which humanity has been led by rebellion against God. Because injustice now rules, it is forbidden to make a direct connection between the guilt and the suffering of an individual. In Luke, Jesus does not inquire about the origins of suffering and sin,[37] but launches hope: resurrection, as the final conquest of suffering, is still a future benefit, but the possibility of forgiveness is offered even now (5:24). Though the refusal of $\mu\epsilon\tau\acute{\alpha}\nu o\iota\alpha$ ("repentance") leads to death (13:1–5), the forgiveness of sins will lead to the restoration of life. For this reason, a healing can allude theologically to the forgiveness of sins. If the analogy is correct, then in Luke's eyes the Pharisees and scriptural experts are the paralytics who must be called to repentance.

---

34 Ἵνα δὲ εἰδῆτε ("but so that you may know") can—as usual—be a final clause, but it can also have an imperative meaning; see C. F. D. Moule, *An Idiom Book of New Testament Greek* (2d ed.: Cambridge: Cambridge University Press, 1963) 144–45.

35 So Gnilka, *Markus*, 1.97.

36 On the forgiveness of sins see the excursus above and the commentary on 7:47 below.

37 See Grundmann, *Markus*, 59.

The Calling and Dinner Pary of Levi (5:27–39)

Bibliography

Arbesmann, Rudolf, "Fasttage," *RAC* 7 (1969) 500–524, esp. 509–10.

Beckwith, Roger T., "The Feast of New Wine and the Question of Fasting," *ExpTim* 95 (1984) 334–35.

Brooke, G., "The Feast of New Wine and the Question of Fasting," *ExpTim* 95 (1984) 175–76.

Cousar, Charles B., "Luke 5:29–35," *Int* 40 (1986) 58–63.

Cremer, F. G., "Lukanisches Sondergut zum Fastenstreitgespräch: Lk 5,33–39 im Urteil der patristischen und scholastischen Exegese," *TThZ* 76 (1967) 129–54.

Dupont, Jacques, "Vin vieux, vin nouveau (Luc 5,39)," *CBQ* 25 (1963) 286–304.

Feuillet, A., "La controverse sur le jeûne (Mc 2,18–20; Mt 9,14–15; Lc 5,33–35)," *NRTh* 90 (1968) 113–36, 252–77.

Flusser, David, "'Do you prefer new wine?'" *Imm* 9 (1979) 26–31.

Good, R. S., "Jesus, Protagonist of the Old, in Lk 5:33–39," *NovT* 25 (1983) 19–36.

Hahn, Ferdinand, "Die Bildworte vom neuen Flicken und vom jungen Wein," *EvTh* 31 (1971) 357–75.

Hengel, *Charismatic Leader*, 5, 19.

Herrenbrück, Fritz, *Jesus und die Zöllner: Historische und neutestamentlich-exegetische Untersuchungen* (WUNT 2.41; Tübingen: Mohr-Siebeck, 1990).

idem, "Steuerpacht und Moral: Zur Beurteilung des τελώνης in der Umwelt des Neuen Testaments," in *ANRW* 2.26.3 (1996) 2221–97.

idem, "Wer waren die 'Zöllner'?" *ZNW* 72 (1981) 178–94.

idem, "Zum Vorwurf der Kollaboration des Zöllners mit Rom," *ZNW* 78 (1987) 186–99.

van Iersel, Bastiaan Martinus Franciscus, "La vocation de Lévi (Mc., II,13–17; Mt., IX,9–13; Lc., V,27–32): Traditions et rédactions," in I. de la Potterie, ed., *De Jésus aux Évangiles: Tradition et rédaction dans les Évangiles synoptiques* (BETL 25.2; Gembloux/Paris: Duculot, 1967) 212–32.

Kee, Alistair, "The Old Coat and the New Wine: A Parable of Repentance," *NovT* 12 (1970) 13–21.

idem, "The Question about Fasting," *NovT* 11 (1969) 161–73.

Lapide, Pinchas, *Er wandelte nicht auf dem Meer: Ein jüdischer Theologe liest die Evangelien* (Gütersloh: Mohn, 1984) 7–15.

Mead, A. H., "Old and New Wine: St Luke 5:39," *ExpTim* 99 (1988) 234–35.

Mouson, J., "'Non veni vocare iustos, sed peccatores' (Mt IX,13 = Mc II,17 = Lc V, 32)," *Collectanea Mechliniensia* n.s. 28 (1958) 134–39.

Pesch, Rudolf, "Levi-Matthäus (Mc 2,14 / Mt 9,9; 10,3)," *ZNW* 59 (1968) 40–56.

idem, "Das Zöllnergastmahl (Mk 2,15–17)," in Descamps and de Halleux, eds., *Mélanges*, 63–87.

Quispel, Gilles, "The Gospel of Thomas and the New Testament," *VC* 11 (1957) 194–95.

Reicke, "Fastenfrage."

Rice, George E., "Luke 5:33–6:11: Release from Cultic Tradition," *AUSS* 20 (1982) 127–32.

Riley, Gregory J., "Influence of Thomas Christianity on Luke 12:14 and 5:39," *HTR* 88 (1995) 229.

Rolland, Philippe, "Les prédécesseurs de Marc: Les sources présynoptiques de Marc II,18–22 et parallèles," *RB* 89 (1982) 370–405.

Schrage, *Thomas-Evangelium*, 109–16.

Schramm, *Markus-Stoff*, 104–11.

Schulz, *Nachfolgen*, 97–116.

Steinhauser, Michael G., *Doppelbildworte in den synoptischen Evangelien* (Würzburg: Echter, 1983) 47–69.

Wibbing, Siegfried, "Das Zöllnergastmahl," in idem, Hans Stock, and Klaus Wegenast, eds., *Streitgespräche* (Gütersloh: Mohn, 1968) 84–107.

Ziesler, J. A., "The Removal of the Bridegroom: A Note on Mark II,18–22 and Parallels," *NTS* 19 (1972–73) 190–94.

Zimmermann, *Methodenlehre*, 90–104, 177–80.

27 And after this he went out and saw a tax collector named Levi, sitting at the tax booth; and he said to him, "Follow me." 28/ And he got up, left everything, and followed him. 29/ Then Levi gave a great banquet for him in his house; and there was a large crowd of tax collectors and others reclining at the table with them. 30/ And Pharisees and their scribes were grumbling to the disciples, saying, "Why do you eat and drink with tax collectors and sinners?" 31/ And Jesus answered and said to them, "Those who are well have no need of a physician, but those who are sick; 32/ I am here to call not the righteous but sinners to repentance." 33/ Then they said to him, "John's disciples frequently fast and pray, and so do the disciples of the Pharisees, but yours eat and drink." 34/ But Jesus said to them, "You cannot make wedding guests fast while the bridegroom is with them. 35/ The days will come, and when the bridegroom is taken away from them, then they will fast in those days." 36/ And he also told them a parable: "No one tears a patch from a new garment and sews it on an old garment; otherwise, the new will be torn, and the piece from the new will not match the old. 37/ And no one puts fresh wine into old wineskins; otherwise, the fresh wine will burst the skins and will be spilled, and the skins will be destroyed. 38/ But fresh wine must be put into new wineskins. 39/ And no one after drinking old wine desires new wine, but says, "The old is good to drink."

Analysis

The figure of Levi is the link that unites into a single unit this short scene of commissioning (5:27–28) and the dinner party (5:29–39) that he gives for Jesus. A separation between 5:32 and 33 would make sense only in Mark, who has different conversational participants (Mark 2:18) ask the question about fasting (Mark 2:18–22 par. Luke 5:33–39). In Luke a continuous conversation takes place between the same participants. Though he is bound to the original Markan version, Luke does form two seemingly independent passages into a continuous literary context. Out of this results a symposium (dinner party scene), a genre that has its roots in Greek history and that Luke particularly appreciates (cf. 7:36–50 and 14:1–24). Sociologically and literary-historically, Greek dinner parties fostered extemporaneous speeches. As in 7:37 and 14:2, an unexpected event—such as the appearance of an uninvited guest—often started the discussion. Here the uncomfortable γογγύζω ("to grumble") of the Pharisees and scribes leads to an argument. The theme corresponds to the frame story: With whom may one eat? With whom does Jesus wish to associate? When may one celebrate and when should one fast? It is not only his Greek education that raises these questions for Luke, but also the historical situation of his church. It is composed of former sinners who, in a religious sense, "follow" Jesus, "leave everything," and are requested by the community to place their house at the disposal of the church. This church, inspired by Jesus, wants to continue to accept sinners. In contrast to any sort of segregation, Luke remembers Jesus' open attitude toward sinners (v. 32). Of course, this is valid only if they repent, so Luke adds εἰς μετάνοιαν ("to repentance").

The question of who is invited is decisive for Luke. Alongside Simon Peter and those with him (5:8–11), there are also sinners like Levi (5:27–28), after whose example the Gentile Christians also feel themselves invited. All of them are sinners (even Simon Peter in 5:8), all are invited by God through Jesus to conversion and forgiveness of their sins. The distinction between the people of God and the heathen remains, but it has shifted: the people of God are those who convert, wherever they come from. Not until the book of Acts are the Gentiles explicitly numbered among them, but their inclusion is already symbolically prepared in the Gospel. In this respect the Law of Moses is also reinterpreted. The same is true of the question of fasting. Verses 33–39 give a nuanced answer: on one hand, a criticism of Pharisaic practice in the name of eschatological freedom, and on the other, a new regulation in the name of the eschatological delay.

For Luke, it is appropriate that the opponents remain outside, thus spying on Jesus and his disciples through the doors and windows (if there were such). One can thus only speak of a symposium with a grain of salt. This ironic frame story fits in with Luke's time, in which the Christian community is criticized from outside by its Jewish "neighbors."

Relationship of the Passage to Mark

The Lukan tendency to make a unit at this point was prepared by Mark, and even by pre-Markan tradition. It is evident that the verses about Levi, as well as those about fasting, are a conglomeration of originally independent units. Levi's name does not yet appear in the Markan version of the dinner party (Mark 2:15): "his house" could designate the house in which Jesus was living at the time. The scene of commissioning and the dinner conversation do not necessarily belong together form-critically. The same is true of the question about fasting, which is stylistically an apothegm and is concluded by the image of the wedding. The two parables that follow, linked together on the basis of the catchwords "old" and "new," were connected at the very latest by Mark, without any transition between them.[1] The authentic saying in Mark 2:19a was softened by the early

---

1   *Gos. Thom.* 104 corresponds to Mark 2:18–20 par. Luke 5:33–35. On the other hand, Mark 2:21–22 par. Luke 5:36–39 has its parallel in *Gos. Thom.* 47. This indicates that the two pericopes were originally transmitted independently of one another. Alistair Kee argues for the original unity of Mark 2:19a and 2:19b–20, and is of the opinion that the issue addressed therein reflects the concerns of the earliest community, not those of Jesus ("The Question about Fasting," *NovT* 11 [1969] 161–73).

church because of its new practice of fasting (Mark 2:19b–20). Thus tradition is understood anew in each new situation of the church and is modified accordingly.

Luke senses the redactional frame in Mark 2:13, and feels free effectively to eliminate it.[2] What is left is the καὶ . . . ἐξῆλθεν ("and . . . he went out," taken from Mark) and the transitional phrase μετὰ ταῦτα ("after this"). Luke deletes the motif of the sea and the reference to the teaching of the multitudes, since both have been mentioned already (see 4:31–32; 5:1–3, etc.). It is unclear whether Luke replaces εἶδεν ("he saw") with ἐθεάσατο (also "he saw") for stylistic reasons, or whether he wants to justify the selection of Levi theologically through a well-considered decision by Jesus. Luke omits the name of the father (Alphaeus) to avoid confusion with the Alphaeus, father of James, who appears in 6:15. But the repetition of the same addition that appeared at 5:11 is more significant: the commitment of the first disciples required the abandonment of every possession (v. 28), since Luke understands discipleship not as a first action (aorist in Mark) but as a continuing practice (imperfect tense).[3] The colorless sitting together in Mark 2:15 becomes, in Luke, a large dinner party thrown by Levi.[4] Doubts about the owner of the house are no longer possible. As guests, "a large crowd of tax collectors and others" (v. 29) recline at table "with them" (instead of "with Jesus and his disciples"). With "crowd," a favorite word of his for Jesus' audience, Luke avoids the word "sinner," which he does use in v. 30.

Luke could not well integrate Mark 2:15c: the mention of discipleship suits the scene well theologically, but it forms a poor image in a scene in which people are lying together at table. "The Pharisees" now describes Jesus' opponents as a whole (as in Matthew), not merely part of them (Mark 2:16), but out of faithfulness to his source Luke adds "and their scribes." Instead of merely repeating the dramatic situation (Mark 2:16a), he describes the feelings of the spectators with "grumble." Γογγύζω and διαγογγύζω are redactional idioms that

Luke derived from the LXX (cf. 15:2; 19:7). After the verb of speaking, Luke prefers πρός with the accusative to the dative (vv. 30–31). The criticism is aimed not only at Jesus (Mark and Matthew have ἐσθίει, "he eats"), but also at the disciples who are being addressed. Does Luke have the time of the church in mind more than Mark does? The Greek expression "eating and drinking" occurs frequently in Jewish authors in place of Hebrew idioms.[5]

As in 5:22, ἀποκριθεὶς . . . εἶπεν in v. 31 ("[Jesus] answered and said") proves to be redactional. Οἱ ὑγιαίνοντες ("those who are well") suits Luke better than οἱ ἰσχύοντες ("those who are strong," Mark 2:17). In Luke ἰσχύω means only "to have the power to bring something to completion." The perfect tense of ἐλήλυθα (v. 32, "I am here") expresses a completed event with present consequences better than the aorist ἦλθον ("I came," in Mark and Matthew). Luke emphasizes that the call is a call to repentance.[6]

Since v. 33 is the answer of the *Pharisees* (see above), the second example ("so do the disciples of the Pharisees") is shifted toward the end of the sentence; otherwise he would have to write "our disciples," in direct speech. To it he appends to the issue of fasting the reference to prayer in a less than logical manner.[7] As in Judaism and in Matt 6:1–18, fasting does not occur without prayer in Luke, either (cf. also Acts 13:2–3). In Luke 18:12 fasting and tithing belong together. In order not to use μαθηταί ("disciples") and νηστεύω ("to fast") too often, Luke uses a formulation similar to v. 30: οἱ δὲ σοὶ ἐσθίουσιν καὶ πίνουσιν ("but yours eat and drink"). He thereby makes a connection between vv. 27–32 and 33–39. Does Luke have in mind the saying about the Son of Man in 7:34?

In v. 34 the name Ἰησοῦς ("Jesus") is missing in many manuscripts, but the sense is not ambiguous: the singular εἶπεν ("he said") can only have Jesus as subject. More significant is the ease with which Luke alters the sense: "You cannot make wedding guests fast . . ." makes an

---

2   In this verse (Luke 5:27), Codex D also contains a very free version of the text, which seems to connect with Mark 2:13–14a.

3   The variant ἠκολούθησεν (aorist) is well attested, but has surely been taken from the parallel passages in Mark and Matthew.

4   In v. 29 one finds a few variants that seem—at least in part—to be influenced by the parallel passages in

Mark and Matthew, e.g., καὶ ἁμαρτωλῶν ("and sinners," instead of καὶ ἄλλων, "and others") and μετ᾿ αὐτοῦ ("with him," instead of μετ᾿ αὐτῶν, "with them").

5   Cf. BAGD *s.v.* πίνω.

6   See Bovon, *Theologian*, 281, 285–86.

7   The question of prayer is not brought up again in what follows; cf. Fitzmyer, 1.594.

allegory out of the parable, and explicitly casts the Pharisees as opponents. Luke, like Matthew, deletes Mark 2:19b because it is a repetition of Mark 2:19a. In v. 35 Luke transposes the καί ("and") and thereby lends the words "the days will come" an independent significance. The peculiar Markan switch from plural (ἡμέραι, "days") to singular (ἐν ἐκείνῃ τῇ ἡμέρᾳ, "on that day") disappears; there is thus only one era—though it is longer—for the Christian practice of fasting, that is, the time of the church.

Luke senses in v. 36 that some transition between the metaphors is necessary (vv. 34–35 and 36–39). His supplement, ἔλεγεν δὲ καὶ παραβολὴν πρὸς αὐτούς ("and he also told them a parable"), shows his conceptualization of παραβολή ("parable"; see the commentary on v. 36 below). Luke improves the language and content of the less than intelligible saying in Mark 2:21 as best he can. In the process an additional thought is developed: the new material is ruined by cutting off a piece of it.[8]

Verses 37–38 are practically identical to Mark 2:22.[9] The unexpected v. 39, related to the themes of "old" and "new," is still surprising. The saying is also found in *Gos. Thom.* 47, which gives the content of Luke 5:36–39 in reverse order and precedes it with an otherwise unknown saying about the individual who cannot ride two horses or draw two bows, and the saying about the two masters (Luke 16:13). It is true that the sayings have, in part, a different meaning there. Since, in comparison to Luke, they do not necessarily appear to be form-critically secondary, they may derive from a different tradition; the saying about the wine and the wineskins is more symmetrical and may reflect an older version. To support the independence of *Gos. Thom.* 47,[10] one could cite the verb ἐπιθυμεῖν ("to long for," in contrast to θελεῖν, "to desire," in Luke 5:39), in addition to the different sequence of the sayings.[11] Moreover, the *parallelismus membrorum* evident there is older. For the saying about the garments, *Gos. Thom.* 47 is closer to Luke than to Mark or Matthew.[12]

Commentary

The Calling of Levi (vv. 27–28)

■ **27–28** From a form-critical perspective, one can distinguish two types of commissioning.[13] Whereas the disciples in the first type are well-known personalities identified by name, those of the second type remain anonymous. In the first type Jesus takes the initiative; in the second, the individual asks to be enlisted. Though Jesus' call finds immediate success in the first type, in the second type the answer remains unknown. The sociological functional setting of the first type of commissioning would be a Christian congregation looking back on the conversion of its first leaders. The second

---

8   Luke replaces εἰ δὲ μή ("otherwise," Mark 2:21, 22) with εἰ δὲ μή γε ("otherwise," vv. 36, 37). The addition of γε does not alter the sense (Antoniadis, *Évangile*, 290).

9   The only differences are: in the second occurrence of the word, "wine" (v. 37b), ὁ νέος ("new") is added; the third occurrence of οἶνος ("wine," v. 37c) is replaced with αὐτός ("it"), and the verb, "to be spilled," (ἐκχυθήσεται) is added; at the end, the verbal adjective (which expresses a necessity; see Kaegi, *Grammaire*, §202.2) βλητέον ("must be put") is added, which makes more explicit the meaning already present in Mark. The minor agreements with Matthew are not sufficient to strengthen the thesis that another version, parallel to Mark, influenced Matthew and Luke (against Schramm, *Markus-Stoff*, 104–11): ἐπιβάλλει (v. 36), εἰ δὲ μή γε (vv. 36, 37); cf. the ἐκχεῖται of Matthew with the ἐκχυθήσεται of Luke.

10   The sequence wine-garment, which reverses the order of the Synoptics, can be found not only in *Gos. Thom.* 47 but also in other early sources, even if rarely, such as Marcion, Shenute, and further passages; see Schrage, *Thomas-Evangelium*, 114. This confirms the hypothesis of transmission as independent sayings.

11   Schrage (*Thomas-Evangelium*, 109–16) attempts to show that *Gos. Thom.* 47 is secondary to the Synoptic version. But according to Gilles Quispel, *Gos. Thom.* 47 corresponds to a Jewish Christian source, the *Gospel of the Hebrews*, which has remained untouched by the Gentile Christian traditions of the canonical Gospels ("The Gospel of Thomas and the New Testament," *VC* 11 [1957] 189–207, esp. 194–95).

12   Agreeing with Schrage, *Thomas-Evangelium*, 112; and Bertil Gärtner, *The Theology of the Gospel According to Thomas* (New York: Harper, 1961) 66–68.

13   See Anselm Schulz, *Nachfolgen und Nachahmen: Studien über das Verhältnis der neutestamentlichen Jüngerschaft zur urchristlichen Vorbildethik* (SANT 6; Munich: Kösel, 1962) 97–110. The first type of calling narrative belongs to the three Synoptic Gospels, the second, to the Q tradition.

type is of a missionary and parenetical character: by means of its anonymity and open-endedness, the preacher can call the audience to decision and discipleship. In this passage the structural elements of the first type of commissioning are evident, and Luke has faithfully preserved them. He does not insist that Jesus be in transit, but attends to his gaze: "The verb ϑεᾶσϑαι, rare in the New Testament, . . . indicates an intent gaze, an observance charged with thought; cf. 7:24 and above all, 23:55."[14] What does Luke find in the gaze of Jesus? Probably his compassion toward a sinner—the next word is "tax collector," which is underscored by "tax booth"— and his confidence that the sinner will follow him.

Luke accepts the paradigmatic significance of the tax collector. In addition to the direct tax, various types of tolls on slaves and merchandise were levied at the borders of countries, at bridges, in harbors, and in important cities. In Galilee and Judea they were levied not by officials but by free enterprisers, tax farmers. The chief tax collectors would have paid to lease the taxes of a city or region, and, because of this, would be fairly free to earn their profits several times over through their subordinates (thus the moral criticism of the Pharisees). In Galilee the proceeds of the tax leases ended up in Herod's cash box, and in Judea and Samaria, in that of the Roman fisc. The tax collectors, whose work was probably perceived as pro-Roman in Judea, attracted the hatred of the Jews because of their exploitation.[15] Since fear and mistrust of tax collectors was widespread in the Roman Empire, Luke could vividly illustrate Jesus' compassion for sinners, taken from Mark, with the calling of a tax collector.

Ἀκολουϑέω ("to follow") had already extended its meaning in secular Greek in the direction of a metaphor-ical, moral, or religious sense: to follow with the intellect, to follow an example, a leader, or the laws, or to follow the divinity. For a religious attitude, ἕπομαι (also, "to follow") is, however, more frequently attested. So Epictetus would write, "It is the goal to follow the gods."[16] Following *God* is avoided in the New Testament because of his transcendence. Since the Twelve always remain disciples of Jesus, the book of Acts also does not speak of new disciples following the apostles. Everything is concentrated on following Jesus. In the Hebrew Bible, the secular expression "to go along behind someone" (הָלַךְ אַחֲרֵי) achieves a religious sense, frequently, "to follow idols," but it is seldom used in reference to God.[17] In contemporaneous Judaism, there was discipleship of a sort, in that the students followed the rabbi, as also—in apocalyptic literature—the people follow the charismatic leader.[18]

That the initiative extends from Jesus suggests the charismatic leader. That discipleship consists in obedience, not enthusiastic participation in the benefits of salvation, is reminiscent of the rabbi. Alongside the Greek language and the Jewish conceptual world, however, the uniquely Christian aspect is important. Discipleship is strictly christologically determined, and as such is discipleship along the path of Jesus' suffering—before any participation in his glorification (cf. 9:23–24).

For Luke, discipleship is a matter of the intellect, the will, and the emotions, and, above all, one's concrete daily life, not only an eschatological decision but a salvation-historical course of life in the dawning of the last times.[19] The disciples leave all; they "get up" (ἀναστάς in v. 28, contrasting with καϑήμενον, "sitting," in v. 27), and no longer look behind themselves. This Christian

---

14 Delebecque, 30, on v. 27.

15 See Str-B 1.377–80; Gnilka, *Markus*, 1.105–6; Fritz Herrenbrück, "Wer waren die 'Zöllner'?" *ZNW* 72 (1981) 178–94. According to Herrenbrück, the NT tax collectors were neither the major contractors of the Roman period (*publicani*) nor their employees (*portitores*), but rather the local contractors of the Hellenistic period.

16 Τέλος ἐστὶ τὸ ἕπεσϑαι ϑεοῖς (*Diss.* 1.20.15).

17 In the LXX ἀκολουϑέω ("to follow") occurs only fourteen times; cf., e. g., Ruth 1:15 (LXX 14, Ruth follows Naomi); Jdt 15:13 (the Israelites follow the triumphant Judith); Isa 45:14 (defeated foreign nations will follow Israel); 2 Macc 8:36 (follow the Law). It is never said that one "follows (ἀκολουϑέω) God." In contrast, the idiom "go/run behind" (ὀπίσω) is well attested; cf., e.g., 1 Sam (LXX 1 Kgdms) 12:14 (to follow the Lord).

18 See Schulz, *Nachfolgen*, 19–32; Martin Hengel, *The Charismatic Leader and His Followers* (trans. J. Greig; New York: Crossroad, 1981) 18–33.

19 See Gerhard Schneider, "ἀκολουϑέω, κτλ.," *EDNT* 1 (1990) 51; Schneider notes that Luke eliminates Mark's ἀκολουϑέω eight times. Literary considerations and an effort to effect historical credibility can be cited as reasons for Luke's avoidance of the term. Luke's concern is the christological content of

existence, which can also be called "being my disciple" (14:27, 33) or "becoming my followers" (9:23), leads to participation in the βασιλεία ("kingdom"); this is emphatically expressed in 9:61–62.

Thus Luke has narrated two commissionings in 5:1–11 and 5:27–28, separated by a miracle story, which perhaps anticipate the two faces of the church: the Jewish Christian community and the Gentile Christian community, which consists of sinners.

With Whom to Eat? (vv. 29–32)

■ **29–32** It does not disturb Luke that Levi, who has left everything, still possesses a house and can throw a dinner party. According to Luke's ethical code, confirmed in Acts, Christians do not abandon everything in the literal sense, but place everything at the disposal of the church. Nevertheless, he idealistically sets the disciples into relief in 12:33 and 14:33 as those who sell everything and give the proceeds to the poor.[20] The tension between the radicalism of the redaction and the traditional feast cannot be completely overlooked.

The critical thoughts (διαλογισμοί) of the Pharisees were already mentioned (5:21–22). Here only their grumbling (γογγύζω) is at issue. Luke emphasizes how much the Pharisees want to retain their old privileges and continue practicing the old interpretation of the Law, and how they cannot understand the latest and

final initiative of God in the Messiah. For these reasons, their reaction is grumbling. The attitude of the people of God in the desert is comparable.[21] What they do not understand is that God is granting his grace to sinners, of which table fellowship is the visible expression. The criticism appears in Luke 7:34 par. and is very old.

The image of the doctor is original here, because medicine attained significance in Israel only relatively late. Wisdom literature can view the act of calling in a doctor as a lapse of faith, and his activity as divine aid.[22] The metaphor, if anything, irritated Jesus' audience, but it gives the Hellenistic author no cause for worry. On the contrary, he is attempting to portray Jesus as the teacher and doctor of the people.[23]

Are there any "well" (v. 31) and "righteous" (v. 32) people? Are not all people in Israel in need of conversion? Are not the "righteous" "self-righteous"? Only in 15:7 is an answer given to these questions. Here the emphasis is only that there are sick people, that is, sinners, and that Jesus (cf. the christological and messianic "I") has come to heal them, that is, to call them to repentance. Verse 32 is probably the interpretation of Jesus' metaphor.[24] The verb ἔρχομαι ("I have come," "I am here") has messianic significance[25] here and, in the

---

20 discipleship, the ramifications of which he spells out; see Bovon, *Theologian*, 483 n. 118.

20 See Bovon, *Theologian*, 390–96. At v. 30 we encounter the term "disciple" for the first time in this Gospel. Although in Greece the word was applied to the students of the philosophers and teachers of rhetoric, in Israel it served to designate the students of a rabbi. The Hebrew term תַּלְמִיד ("disciple," "student") is fairly recent, since in Israel, in contrast to Greece, there was no indigenous "school culture." In Christian usage the term means exclusive devotion to a master, to whom one always remains bound as a disciple, and with whom one never achieves equal rank, because he is the master. See Karl Heinrich Rengstorf, "μανθάνω, κτλ.," *TDNT* 4 (1967) 390–412.

21 Γογγύζω ("to grumble") occurs about fifteen times in the LXX; cf. esp. Exod 16:7 (LXX, Codex Alexandrinus); 17:3; Num 11:1; 14:27–29.

22 Doctors are mentioned in Isa 3:7 and Jer 8:22. 2 Chr 16:12 criticizes the practice of availing one-

self of a doctor. Jesus, the son of Sirach, is amazed by the practice of medicine (Sir 10:10; 38:1–15). See Karl Karner, "Arzt," *BHH* 1 (1963) 133. See also the bibliography on doctors in antiquity in the notes to the commentary on 4:40 above.

23 This is the second time that a doctor appears in a proverb; see Luke 4:23 (the proverb directed at Jesus by the crowd). Cadbury (*Style*, 39–72) has proven, contrary to W. K. Hobart, Adolf von Harnack, and Theodor Zahn, that Luke's vocabulary does not betray any professional knowledge of medicine. The language of Luke is no more specialized than that of any other author of his time; cf., e.g., Lucian of Samosata. The author of Luke's two volumes, then, was not necessarily a doctor.

24 The logion in v. 32 was extremely popular in both oral and written transmission; cf. *Barn.* 5.9; P. Oxy. 1224; *2 Clem.* 2.4; Justin *1 Apol.* 15.8 (cited in Aland, *Synopsis*, 63–64).

25 In Judaism the word ἔρχομαι ("to come") can be used to describe the coming of the Messiah, but also

aorist (Mark, Matthew) as well as the perfect (Luke), looks back over the entire life of Jesus.[26] In v. 31 the help of the doctor is only hoped for; here it is proclaimed and carried out.

When and Why to Fast (vv. 33–35)

■ **33–35** The second round begins in v. 33. Fasting and prayer are essential to the disciples of the Baptist and of the Pharisees. The pious members of these reform movements fasted not only at the obligatory occasions (on the Day of Atonement, and for catastrophes), but also voluntarily.[27] The Pharisees of Luke 18:9–14 fast twice a week. By individual fasting one would attempt to atone for a sin, accompany a dedication, penance, or prayer, or secure one's merit.[28] Fasting in the Pharisaic reform movement had collective significance and was to protect the land and contribute to the well-being of the nation. "Because of the expiatory significance of fasting, the accusation of failing in the national duty of the people of God stands behind this reproach."[29] Concretely, fasting means to eat no bread, to ingest no nourishment. Exod 34:28 and Deut 9:9 emphasize that Moses did not even drink water for forty days. It is not known whether only alcoholic drinks were forbidden, or water, too. Externally, fasting manifests itself in sackcloth and ashes (Dan 9:3). We know of the Baptist's ascetic behavior from Mark 1:6. It fits well with this that he also taught his disciples to fast; Luke probably adds prayer[30] because of the question of Jesus' disciples in 11:1.

Jesus answers with a rhetorical question. The image of the wedding is understandable in the context of that time;[31] during the festivities people had not only the permission, but almost the duty to break their fast. Thus the rabbinic tractate *Megillat Ta'anit* presents a list of the days in the year on which fasting was forbidden, so that people could devote themselves to the joy of the festival and the remembrance of God's action in history on behalf of his nation.[32] The day of a wedding was given the same status, on which a teacher even had to cease his instruction in the Law. Although weddings were not cultic events, they did symbolize God's history with his people (Hos 1–2; Ezek 20). Even more than today, the accent was on rejoicing.

Usually, νυμφών means the bridal chamber (Tob 6:14, 17). It cannot be definitely determined whether the wedding hall is meant here, as in Matt 22:10 (some mss. read γάμος, "marriage"). "The sons τοῦ νυμφῶνος" are, at any rate, participants in the wedding, not specifically the groomsmen (John 3:29). They cannot fast as long as[33] the groom is still with them. For Jesus, the time of his presence is a wedding day, without him identifying himself directly with the groom. But the evangelists could do nothing other than equate Jesus with the groom. The process of allegorical interpretation did not develop here in the direction of the married couple (Christ and his church),[34] but has in view the groom and his attendants, as in Matt 25:1–13. It follows that the symbolism is that of absence within the semantic field of friendship, rather than within that of married faithfulness or love.[35] This is still in the territory of Judaism, where "bridegroom" is not a messianic title. Later, within Gentile Christianity, the image would develop of

---

for everything having to do with the end of time; see Hahn, *Titles*, 380. Among the Christians in Luke's time, the word doubtless had messianic overtones.

26 See Bultmann, *History*, 155–56.

27 One encounters occasional voluntary fasting from the HB era: 2 Sam (LXX 2 Kgdms) 12:16; Ps 35(LXX 34):13; Dan 9:3 (LXX only). Πυκνός ("frequently") is found three times in the NT: once as an adjective (1 Tim 5:23), and twice as an adverb (here, and in Acts 24:26 in the comparative). In addition, there is an important variant in Mark 7:3 (cf. BAGD *s.v.* πυγμή and πυκνός). One finds πυκνά as a modal adverb "already in Homer, and it is still used today" (Antoniadis, *Évangile*, 72).

28 Day of Atonement: Lev 16:29–31. Penance: 1 Kgs (LXX 3 Kgdms) 21:27; Joel 1:14; 2:15–27; Isa 58:1–9. Mourning: Esth 4:3. This list is taken from Fitzmyer, 1.596.

29 See Grundmann, *Markus*, 65.

30 Δέησις ("request," "petition"). See Monloubou, *Prière*, 100–102. It is literally a need (δέομαι) brought to utterance.

31 On marriage and its symbolism in Israel, see Str-B 1.500–18; and Joachim Jeremias, "νύμφη, κτλ.," *TDNT* 4 (1967) 1103–4.

32 On this tractate see Hermann L. Strack and Günther Stemberger, *Introduction to the Talmud and Midrash*, trans. M. Bockmuehl (Minneapolis: Fortress Press, 1991) 34, 112.

33 Ἐν ᾧ: one must supply an antecedent such as ὁ χρόνος. One could actually anticipate an "as long as" (ἐφ᾽ ὅσον), as Matthew has written (9:15).

34 2 Cor 11:2; Eph 5:25; Rev 21:2, 9; 22:17.

35 Fitzmyer (1.599) agrees with Jeremias ("νύμφη," *TDNT* 4.1103–4) and disagrees with William H. Brownlee ("Messianic Motifs of Qumran and the

the *unio mystica* of the soul with the divine bridegroom in the bridal chamber.[36] Here we are still within the sober confines of an interpersonal relationship, which does not involve becoming one, in which one's own personality flows into that of the other. But the juxtaposition of the clearly separate individuals is still a happy experience of being together. The groom has a unique status: the wedding is *his* celebration, and the others are neither subordinate nor equal to him. The image of friendship for the relationship between Christ and Christians seldom occurs, but here, as in John 5:15, it is operative. In Acts Luke uses it for the relationship of Christians among themselves (with an adaptation of the Greek proverb: "everything is common to friends").[37]

In Luke another group appears in addition: the Pharisees. Their presence alone signifies a threat, or at least it reminds one of the reality principle, which prohibits carefree joy. In v. 34 the readers encounter a sort of summary of the entire Lukan scene of vv. 29–39: Jesus and his disciples (the groom and his friends) are observed from outside, though still from nearby, and thus the critics are the Pharisees. Luke does not understand Jesus' response in the sense of: "You could not imagine them fasting,"[38] but rather thus: "You could not force them to fast." Behind Luke's redaction, then, is the *Christian* community's critique of *Jewish* practice.

Ἀπαρθῇ ("[he] is taken away") in v. 35 should not be overinterpreted: Luke does not have in mind the allegorical meaning only of the cross or of the ascension (cf. Acts 1:9, Codex D). In a more general sense, the time of the church is envisioned, in which Christ is no longer "with them." This time of the church will again be a time of fasting (Acts 13:2–3; Matt 6:16–18). The Christians early on reintroduced days of fasting, although only on Wednesdays and Fridays, so that this practice would not be confused with Jewish or Judaizing practice (Mondays and Thursdays).[39] Is Christian fasting only a relapse, which forgets the joy and freedom of Jesus? Or did the practice of fasting attain a new significance, so that the time of Jesus separates the two periods? The following vv. 36–39, as well as the book of Acts, allow the conjecture that the Christian practice has a new, eschatological understanding in Luke. Like prayer, fasting becomes part of the Christian liturgy, in which Christ's presence can be experienced and Christians are responsive to the Spirit (Acts 13:2). During the lifetime of Jesus, the presence of salvation was indicated by not fasting; now, in the time of the church, it is indicated through fasting, which thereby receives a new meaning from top to bottom, and depends on rejoicing over the present salvation.[40] It is true that the practice of fasting

New Testament," *NTS* 3 [1956–57] 12–30, 195–210) in holding that the logion does not identify the bridegroom with the Messiah.

36   Cf. *Gos. Phil.* (NHC 2.3) 64.31–65.26 (the mystery of marriage); 67.27–30 (the bridal chamber); 69.1–4 (the bridal chamber is for the free individuals and virgins); 69.14–70.4 (the bridal chamber); 70.9–34 (Adam and Eve); 71.3–21 (the birth of Adam and the birth of Christ); 72.17–29 (rest and contemplation is offered to the children of the bridal chamber); 74.21–22 (the true Christian receives the gift of the Father in the bridal chamber); 75.25–76.9 (conception); 78.13–24 (children resemble their parents); 78.26–79.13 (human beings have intercourse with human beings); 81.28–82.26 (the spiritual marriage); 84.22–23 (the still-hidden bridal chamber); 85.32–86.7 (the promised entrance into the bridal chamber). In the editions of Walter C. Till (*Das Evangelium nach Philippos* [Berlin: de Gruyter, 1963]) and Jacques E. Ménard (*L'Évangile selon Philippe: Introduction, Texte, Traduction* [Paris: Letouzey et Ané, 1967]), the numeration of the

lines is higher by two: 64.31= 66.31. The text is also divided into paragraphs. The line numbers of this note correspond to paragraphs 60–61; 68; 73; 76; 78–80; 82–83; 87–88; 95; 102–4; 112; 113; 121–22; 125; 126–27.

37   See Jacques Dupont, "La communauté de biens aux premiers jours de l'Église," in idem, *Études sur les Actes des apôtres* (LD 45; Paris: Cerf, 1967) 503–19.

38   As Delebecque suggests (*Études*, 30).

39   Cf. *Did.* 8.1. Fasting is also mentioned in *Did.* 1.3 and 7.4. See Willy Rordorf and André Tuilier, *La Doctrine des apôtres (Didachè)* (SC 248; Paris: Cerf, 1978) 36–38. Bo Reicke sketches the development of Christian practices of fasting from the 1st to the 6th centuries ("Die Fastenfrage nach Luk. 5,33–39," *ThZ* 30 [1974] 321–28).

40   Just the opposite, then, of what Jörg Baumgarten writes in "καινός, κτλ.," *EDNT* 2 (1991) 229: "Thus fasting is an expression of sorrow in the time of the bridegroom's absence." Reicke emphasizes correctly the new meaning that fasting takes on among the Christians ("Fastenfrage"). According to Reicke,

in the church was quickly connected to the concept of penance: Wednesday as the day of the death sentence by the Sanhedrin, and Friday as the day of Jesus' death.[41]

Three Parables (vv. 36–39)

■ **36–39** The wisdom saying in v. 36 is parabolic;[42] οὐδείς ("no one") expresses its generality. Where Mark speaks of an unshrunk piece of material, Luke introduces a patch[43] torn from a new garment; "the foolishness of the action is increased."[44] Now a new and an old garment are juxtaposed to each other. The result of this is a complete reinterpretation of the difficult sentence in Mark 2:21b, so that damage to the new garment is added to the unsuitable patch on the old garment.[45]

For Luke, old and new practices stand opposed to one another. Above all, the new practice should remain untouched. The image is not very clear, because the practice of fasting required by the Pharisees seems to be the old piece that should not be patched onto the new Christian garment (in the sense of Gal 2:18). Or does Luke see an insufficiently radical renewal of the old religion in the fasting reform of the Baptist and the Pharisees, as Mark and the oral tradition do? Probably for Luke, the way of life introduced by Jesus is so new that one cannot simultaneously live as a Jew and as a Christian.

What is new (καινός appears three times in v. 36) is also the issue in vv. 37–38, in which νέος ("new") appears three times (for the wine) next to καινός (also "new," for the wineskins).[46] For wine, νέος ("fresh," "young") is the correct word. In classical Greek, καινός indicates qualitative newness, whether this be positive or negative, although here and in v. 36 it indicates something that has not been used, for which νέος would better fill the bill. But in Koine, καινός and νέος are used indiscriminately, it is true, and neither is a priori positive, which Luke, as a Greek author, probably knows. He does use the traditional saying about the new covenant (22:20), but otherwise never uses this adjective in an eschatological context. In Acts 17:19 and 21, καινός is, in accordance with the Greek sense, something with which one is not yet familiar. Here, on the other hand, Luke uses καινός and νέος in a purely positive sense for the Christian truth, on the basis of what the tradition prescribed for him. He himself believes that what is uniquely Christian is ancient and in conformity with the creation (see the commentary below on v. 39).

Despite the conceptual pair "new-old," vv. 37–38 have a meaning independent from v. 36. The wisdom in question comes this time from the sphere of the viticulturists. Only wineskins that are well broken in and in good condition have the necessary resilience to withstand fermenting wine. Thus one must pour fresh wine into new wineskins.

One could ask whether Jesus, Synoptic tradition, and the Gospel writers perceived here the symbolism of the eschatological feast, and thus introduced an easy allegorical interpretation of the wine: comparable to the wine, the joy of the kingdom of God, which one can already

---

41   Cf. *Constitutiones apostolorum* 5.14.20; 7.23.2, etc.
42   On the concept of the παραβολή ("parable") see the commentary on 8:4 below. The beginnings of a history of interpretation of v. 36 can be found in F. G. Cremer, "Lukanisches Sondergut zum Fastenstreitgespräch: Lk 5,33–39 im Urteil der patristischen und scholastischen Exegese," *TThZ* 76 (1967) 129–54. Cremer distinguishes among four types of interpretation, of which I mention two: first, Augustine *De consensu* 27.63 (CSEL 43.167): the disciples are like old garments, whom a new patch of cloth (fasting alone) from an entire new garment (the complete practice of asceticism) suits ill; second, Cyril of Alexandria *In Lucam Commentarius* 5.36 (*PG* 72.573C): No one can sew an old piece of cloth (the old Law) onto a new garment (believers

fasting was spiritualized, above all, in the meditative theology of the ancient church.

who have been renewed through the Spirit). The same interpretation is applied to the wineskin in Fragment 26, published by Joseph Reuss, *Lukas-Kommentare aus der griechischen Kirche: Aus Katenen-handschriften gesammelt und herausgegeben* (TU 130; Berlin: Akademie-Verlag, 1984) 65.
43   Ἐπίβλημα ("patch") is a vague description. As the etymology suggests, the word designates something that is laid or thrown over another object: "lid," "head scarf," "cover," "wrap," "carpet," etc. See LSJ *s.v.* Under consideration here is a "patch (placed upon something)"; see BAGD *s.v.*, who refers to this passage.
44   Klostermann, 73–74.
45   See Klostermann, 74; BDF §444.3
46   Many witnesses take the words καὶ ἀμφότεροι συντηροῦνται ("and so both are preserved") from Matt 9:17 and add them at the end of v. 38.

enjoy now, can be received only by new individuals.[47] If Luke perceived this, his echo of it remained muted.[48]

The fundamental meaning of the parable is that individuals should receive the gift of God with wisdom sufficient for it. In the context of the issue of fasting, Pharisaic practice no longer has the correct attitude of faith. Trust and joy should replace expiation and justification by works. But it is essential to faith and joy that one cannot demand or command them. The parable has the function of provoking individuals, leading them to a decision, and thus pulling them away from dead ends.

Verse 39 was not composed by Luke.[49] If one looks at it in isolation, its sense is clear: old wine is better.[50] Whoever has begun drinking the old wine will not put up with the new.[51] Such wisdom is also familiar in Judaism and in Greece.[52] In Luke the old wine can mean, first, negatively, the Jewish practice of fasting, which can attract people—even Christians—and lead them astray; second, positively, the Christian way of life, because on one hand what is new in the Gospel is also ancient (older than the Law; cf. Gal 3:17, 19), and on the other because it is now, at the end of the first century, an old tradition in comparison to the more recent doctrinal

deviations. If the second is correct, then Luke, like the author of First John, understands the Christian message as simultaneously new (vv. 36–38) and old (v. 39).[53]

Conclusion

1. With Luke 5:27–39, the second polemical section of Luke's Gospel comes to an end. The first (5:17–26) is christologically concentrated on the authority of the Son of Man to forgive sins, and the second, ecclesiologically on the Christian way of life.[54]

2. For Luke the Christian life is an existence threatened from the outside. Every type of euphoric enthusiasm is out of the question, because, in the reality of life, every form of escapism is out of the question.

3. The attitude of faith is determined by the community and by eschatological joy. What is eschatologically new places old religious practice in the shadows.

4. Living as a Christian does not mean living in disobedience to the Law: beyond the Law, but also prior to the Law, there is a kind of wisdom that Jesus revives through his parables and with which he has confronted and invited human beings.

---

47 On the theme of new wine, see Paul Lebeau, *Le vin nouveau du Royaume: Étude exégétique et patristique sur la parole eschatologique de Jésus à la Cène* (Museum Lessianum section biblique 5; Paris/Bruges: Desclée de Brouwer, 1966).

48 Cf. Jülicher, *Gleichnisreden*, 2.200: "And in Luke as well, who has more aptitude for embroidery than unequivocal statements, I perceive nothing that would support another meaning."

49 V. 39 is missing in some Greek and Latin mss. (D it) and in some ancient authors (Marcion, Irenaeus, Eusebius).

50 In this passage χρηστός ("good") has the sense of a comparative (as various mss. and versions, which read or translate χρηστότερος, have understood) or a superlative; see Klostermann, 74.

51 As John 2:10 shows, in those days, in contrast to today, hosts served the good wine first, since there

was a good possibility that the guests would not be able to appreciate it at the end of the evening.

52 Cf. Sir 9:10b; *m. 'Abot.* 4.20; *b.Ber.* 51a; Lucian *De merc. cond.* 26; further parallels in Wettstein, 689–90.

53 For the beginnings of a history of interpretation on v. 39 see Jacques Dupont, "Vin vieux, vin nouveau (Luc 5,39)," *CBQ* 25 (1963) 286–304.

54 Whereas Mark 2:16 still has a christological focus (*Jesus* is attacked), the parallel in Luke clearly shows an ecclesiological dimension (the *disciples* are addressed).

The Plucking of Grain on the Sabbath (6:1–5)

Bibliography

Aichinger, H., "Quellenkritische Untersuchungen der Perikope vom Ährenraufen am Sabbat: Mk 2,23–28 par, Mt 12,1–8 par Lk 6,1–5," in A. Fuchs, ed., *Jesus in der Verkündigung der Kirche* (SNTU A.1; Linz: Albert Fuchs, 1976) 110–53.

Audet, Jean-Paul, "Jésus et le 'calendrier sacerdotal ancien:' Autour d'une variante de Luc 6:1," *ScEccl* 10 (1958) 361–83.

Bammel, Ernst, "The Cambridge Pericope: The Addition to Luke 6:4 in Codex Bezae," *NTS* 32 (1986) 404–26.

Baumgarten, Joseph M., "The Counting of the Sabbath in Ancient Sources," *VT* 16 (1966) 277–86.

Beare, Francis Wright, "'The Sabbath Was Made for Man?'" *JBL* 79 (1960) 130–36.

Benoit, "Épis."

Buchanan, George Wesley, and Charles Wolfe, "The 'Second-First Sabbath' (Luke 6:1)," *JBL* 97 (1978) 259–62.

Bultmann, *History*, 16–17, 383.

Daube, David, "Responsibilities of Master and Disciples in the Gospels," *NTS* 19 (1972–73) 1–15, esp. 4–8.

Delebecque, "Moissonneurs."

idem, "Sur un certain Sabbat," *RPh* 48 (1974) 26–29.

Delobel, Joël, "Luke 6:5 in Codex Bezae: The Man Who Worked on the Sabbath," in *À cause,* 453–77.

Duprez, Antoine, "Deux affrontements un jour de sabbat (Mc 2:23–3:6)," *AsSeign* 40 (1972) 43–53.

Grassi, Joseph A., "The Five Loaves of the High Priest (Mt xii:1–8; Mk ii:23–28; Lk vi:1–7; 1 Sam xxi:1–6)," *NovT* 7 (1964–65) 119–22.

Hay, Lewis S., "The Son of Man in Mark 2:10 and 2:28," *JBL* 89 (1970) 69–75.

Hinz, Christoph, "Jesus und der Sabbat," *KD* 19 (1973) 91–108.

Hultgren, Arland J., "The Formation of the Sabbath Pericope in Mark 2:23–28," *JBL* 91 (1972) 38–43.

Isaac, Ephraim, "Another Note on Luke 6:1," *JBL* 100 (1981) 96–97.

Käser, Walter, "Exegetische Erwägungen zur Seligpreisung des Sabbatarbeiters Lk 6:5 D," *ZThK* 65 (1968) 414–30.

Kuhn, Heinz Wolfgang, *Ältere Sammlungen im Markusevangelium* (SUNT 8; Göttingen: Vandenhoeck & Ruprecht, 1971) 61–81.

Lapide, Pinchas, *Er predigte in ihren Synagogen: Jüdische Evangelienauslegung* (4th ed.; Gütersloh: Mohn, 1985) 56–76.

Lindemann, Andreas, "'Der Sabbat ist um des Menschen willen geworden . . .': Historische und theologische Erwägungen zur Traditionsgeschichte der Sabbatperikope Mk 2:23–28 par.," *WD* 15 (1979) 79–105.

Lohse, Eduard, "Jesu Worte über den Sabbat," in W. Eltester, ed., *Judentum, Urchristentum, Kirche: Festschrift Joachim Jeremias* (BZNW 26; Berlin: Töpelmann, 1960) 79–89.

Mezger, Edgar, "Le sabbat 'second-premier' de Luc," *ThZ* 32 (1976) 138–43.

Murmelstein, Benjamin, "Jesu Gang durch die Saatfelder," *Angelos* 3 (1930) 111–20.

Neirynck, Frans, "Jesus and the Sabbath: Some Observations on Mark II:27," in Dupont, *Christologie,* 227–70.

Pfättisch, Johannes Maria, "Der Herr des Sabbats," *BZ* 6 (1908) 172–78.

Roloff, *Kerygma,* 52–62.

Safrai, Samuel, "Sabbath Breakers?" *Jerusalem Perspective* 3 (1990) 3–5.

Schramm, *Markus-Stoff,* 111–12.

Skeat, Theodore Cressy, "The 'Second-First' Sabbath (Luke 6:1): The Final Solution," *NovT* 30 (1988) 103–6.

Staudinger, Ferdinand, "Die Sabbatkonflikte bei Lukas" (Diss., Graz, 1964).

Vogt, Ernst, "Sabbatum 'deuteróprôton' in Lc 6,1 et antiquum kalendarium sacerdotale," *Bib* 40 (1959) 102–5.

idem, "Hat 'šabbât' im A.T. den Sinn von 'Woche'?" *Bib* 40 (1959) 1008–11.

Wegenast, Klaus, "Das Ährenausraufen am Sabbat (Mk 2:23–28; vgl. Mt 12:1–8; Lk 6:1–5)," in idem, Hans Stock, and Siegfried Wibbing, eds., *Streitgespräche* (Gütersloh: Mohn, 1968) 27–37.

1 It happened that early on the second Sabbath while he was going through the grainfields, his disciples plucked some heads of grain, rubbed them in their hands, and ate them. 2/ But some of the Pharisees said, "Why are you doing what is not lawful on the Sabbath?" 3/ And Jesus answered and said to them, "Have you never read what David did when he and his companions were hungry? 4/ How he entered the house of God and took and ate the bread of the Presence, which it is not lawful to eat for anyone but the priests alone, and gave some to his companions?" 5/ Then he said to them, "The Son of Man is lord of the Sabbath."

Analysis

The text for this pericope is particularly unstable, and it is worthwhile to spend a little more time for once with the question of the form of the text.[1] Even textual variants that express the same basic sense allow insight into the work of the scribes, who were often under the influence of the other Gospels (esp. Matthew), who sat before slightly diverging manuscripts, and who consciously or unconsciously adjusted the Lukan language to their own habits of speech here and there as they were copying.

Many manuscripts read ἐν σαββάτῳ δευτεροπρώτῳ instead of "on the Sabbath" (the Nestle-Aland text). This variant has been a crux since Jerome,[2] since the adjective δευτερόπρωτος simply does not exist elsewhere during the time of Luke. Should δευτεροπρώτῳ still be considered the original reading because of the principle of the *lectio difficilior* ("the more difficult reading")? The attestation in the manuscripts Alexandrinus (A), Ephraemi rescriptus (C), and Codex Bezae (D) is impressive, and it is possible that other manuscripts simply omitted the puzzling word. Could it have been formed by analogy to δευτερέσχατος ("second to the last")[3] (cf. Epiphanius, who understands it in the sense of the "second after the first Sabbath,"[4] or a Latin ms. that reads *in sabbato secundo a primo*[5])? Eustratius (6th century) calls the first Sunday after Easter Sunday ἡ δευτεροπρώτη κυριακή.[6]

Or can the strange word be derived from Jewish practice, in which some (e.g., the Essenes) defended the old priestly calendar, and others (e.g., the Pharisees) the new? The dating of Pentecost according to the confusing passage in Lev 23:15 was especially difficult in this controversy. In this context the adjective could mean, "on the second Sabbath after Easter, which is the first Sabbath after the festival of loaves."[7] Or is this simply an error? But then one must be able to explain its origin. The best suggestion is that of Bruce M. Metzger: a scribe wrote πρώτῳ because of the next Sabbath in 6:6, and this word was in turn corrected to δευτέρῳ by another scribe because of the Sabbath in 4:31; this was transmitted as δευτεροπρώτῳ by a third scribe, who did not notice the points under the line (as signs of omission).[8] As for other suggestions, it is rather fantastic to suggest to read the line as ἐγένετο δὲ ἐν σαββάτῳ βίᾳ πορεύεσθαι αὐτόν ("and it happened that on the Sabbath he was forced to walk"), and to explain that Jesus was forced to go through the fields in order not to make too many steps on the Sabbath.[9] If Jesus respected the Sabbath to this extent, why did he not forbid the actions of his disciples? It can more cautiously be asked whether one should read ἐν σαββάτῳ δευτέρῳ πρωΐ (so the Latin witness e: *sabbato mane*), thus "on the second Sabbath, early in the morning" (which would explain their hunger).[10] None of the solutions is completely convinc-

---

1   In this section and in its notes, the following studies have been taken into account: Joseph Baumgarten, "The Counting of the Sabbath in Ancient Sources," *VT* 16 (1966) 277–86 (second Sabbath of the first month); George Wesley Buchanan and Charles Wolfe, "The 'Second-First Sabbath' (Luke 6:1)," *JBL* 97 (1978) 259–62 (a marginal note that entered the text); See Edouard Delebecque, "Les moissonneurs du sabbat (6,1)," in idem, *Études*, 71–84 (see the summary in the text); Edgar Mezger, "Le sabbat 'second-premier' de Luc," *ThZ* 32 (1976) 138–43 (second Sabbath of the first month, Nisan, i.e., Saturday, 29 March 32!); Ernst Vogt, "Sabbatum 'deuteróprôton' in Lc 6:1 et antiquum kalendarium sacerdotale," *Bib* 40 (1959) 102–5 (a very ancient marginal gloss influenced by an early liturgical calendar).

2   In one of his letters, Jerome tells of asking Gregory of Nazianzus about the meaning of δευτερόπρωτος (*Ep.* 52.8); Gregory's humorous response, he believes, nevertheless did not answer the question, but more likely meant that he also did not know.

3   As Klostermann believes (74). Moulton and Milligan argue against such a development (*Vocabulary, s.v.*).

4   Cf. Epiphanius *Adv. haer.* 51.31 (GCS 31.304).

5   This is in the hand of the original scribe of ms. f; see Klostermann, 75.

6   Cf. Eustratius *Vita Eutychii* 10.96 (*PG* 86.2381); Klostermann, 75.

7   See Fitzmyer (1.607–8), who mentions this hypothesis but does not accept it.

8   See Metzger, *Textual Commentary*, 139. Moulton and Milligan offer another clever suggestion (*Vocabulary, s.v.*): since the letters have numerical values (α= 1, β= 2), the strange δευτεροπρώτῳ was formed thus: "the βα of σαββάτῳ was repeated at the beginning of a new line, and then βατω expanded as δευτερο-πρώτῳ."

9   See Delebecque, "Moissonneurs," 72–75: A βίᾳ was misread as β΄ α΄, which, because of its numerical value, led to δευτερόπρωτος.

10   The disadvantage of this hypothesis is that Luke does not like to use πρωΐ ("early in the morning," only once, Acts 28:23), and avoids it when he finds

ing, but the authority of the Bible does not depend on the letters alone.

More interesting are two decisions in Codex Bezae (D): like Marcion, and thus perhaps under the influence of a Marcionite manuscript, D shifts the entire v. 5 to the point between vv. 10 and 11. In its place D introduces a short apothegm at the end of v. 4, which is largely considered to be apocryphal,[11] because its existential distance from the Sabbath regulations and the Law is only understandable from the perspective of a later time: "On the same day, he saw someone working on the Sabbath and said to him, 'Fellow, if you know what you are doing, you are blessed; but if you do not know it, you are accursed, and a transgressor of the Law.'"[12]

Smaller instabilities in the text involve: (1) the sequence of the words (twice in v. 1, once in v. 3); (2) the presence of a word, "to do," after "what is not lawful" in v. 2 (even without the verb, the thought is, of course, there implicitly); (3) "his companions" in v. 3; (4) "also" before "companions" in v. 4; (5) "that" at the beginning of Jesus' saying (v. 5); (6) variations in the conjunctions ($\H{o}\tau\epsilon$ or $\H{o}\pi\tau\epsilon$ in v. 3; $\H{\omega}\varsigma$ or $\pi\H{\omega}\varsigma$ or nothing at the beginning of v. 4) or in the syntax ($\lambda\alpha\beta\grave{\omega}\nu$ $\check{\epsilon}\varphi\alpha\gamma\epsilon\nu$ or the parataxis $\check{\epsilon}\lambda\alpha\beta\epsilon\nu$ $\kappa\alpha\grave{\iota}$ $\check{\epsilon}\varphi\alpha\gamma\epsilon\nu$ in v. 4).

In v. 5 the manuscripts vary between the Markan ("Son of Man" before "Sabbath") and the Matthean ("Sabbath" before "Son of Man") versions. In the second case, that is, presupposing the Matthean sequence of words (which Nestle-Aland chooses), Luke and Matthew agree against Mark, a detail that may be of significance, since both of them also do not transmit the Markan verse 2:27.

The similarities between Matthew and Luke, on the whole, are striking. In contrast to Mark, the first and third evangelists specify that the disciples eat the grains;

this is a fact that Mark, of course, presupposes, but he does not explicate it. Both delete the Latinism $\hat{o}\delta\grave{o}\nu$ $\pi o\iota\acute{\epsilon}\omega$ (*iter facere*, "to make a road") from Mark 2:23, the words $\chi\rho\epsilon\acute{\iota}\alpha\nu$ $\check{\epsilon}\sigma\chi\epsilon\nu$ ("he was in need [of food]") from Mark 2:25, the erroneous mention of the high priest Abiathar (Mark 2:26), the entire verse Mark 2:27, in addition to the word sequence "Sabbath–Son of Man," mentioned above (Luke 6:5 par. Matt 12:8).

The only real problem—and, with this, we are already in the tradition history of this pericope—is the nonacceptance of Mark 2:27.[13] Does Luke know of another traditional source in addition to his Markan source?[14] Or was 2:27 not contained in the version of Mark that Luke had?[15] The supplementary introduction with $\kappa\alpha\grave{\iota}$ $\check{\epsilon}\lambda\epsilon\gamma\epsilon\nu$ $\alpha\check{\upsilon}\tau o\hat{\iota}\varsigma$ ("then he said to them," Mark 2:27a par. Luke 6:5a) is, rather, an indication that the two sayings (Mark 2:27–28) were not part of the original episode. Matthew and Luke still knew this from oral tradition, and so omitted Mark 2:27. It is probably an authentic word of Jesus that well suited Jesus' battle for the original intention of God, evident in the creation, against a debased later interpretation of the Law,[16] and was probably added as a commentary at a pre-Markan level. Later, it seemed to be a rather skimpy christological conclusion, and it was interpreted by v. 28. The omission of v. 27 in Matthew and Luke indicates a further christological development, in which the earthly Jesus threatens to fade away before the exalted Christ. But the anecdote itself remains the same in all stages. In this faithfulness to the tradition, dependence on Jesus and love of Christ work together.[17]

Almost all elements of the redaction bear signs of the literary tendencies of the author, who specifies that the disciples "rubbed them [the grains] in their hands" (v. 1), and also formulates the dialogue (v. 2) more

it in Mark (Mark 1:35; 16:2).

11 A different opinion in Joachim Jeremias, *Unknown Sayings of Jesus* (trans. R. H. Fuller; New York: Macmillan, 1957) 7, 49–54.

12 Cited in Klostermann, 75. On this text see Walter Käser, "Exegetische Erwägungen zur Seligpreisung des Sabbatarbeiters Lk 6:5 D," *ZThK* 65 (1968) 414–30; and Ernst Bammel, "The Cambridge Pericope: The Addition to Luke 6:4 in Codex Bezae," *NTS* 32 (1986) 404–26.

13 See Fitzmyer, 1.605–6.

14 See Schramm, *Markus-Stoff*, 111–12.

15 See Pierre Benoit, "Les épis arrachés (Mt 12,1–8 et

par.)," *SBFLA* 13 (1962–63) 76–92, reprinted in idem, *Exégèse*, 3.228–50, esp. 235.

16 The commentators cite the rabbinic parallel in *Mekilta de Rabbi Yishmael* 31.14 (109b) to the point of weariness: "The Sabbath is given to you; you are not given to the Sabbath"; cf. *b.Yoma* 85b: "It [the Sabbath] is given into your hands; you are not given into the hands of the Sabbath."

17 The literature on the prior history of this text is boundless. The ones consulted here: H. Aichinger, "Quellenkritische Untersuchungen der Perikope vom Ährenraufen am Sabbat Mk 2:23–28 par., Mt 12:1–8 par., Lk 6:1–5," in A. Fuchs, ed., *Jesus in der*

vividly with a direct address to the disciples. This results, however, in a certain tension, since the answer to the question—in the usual way that students are defended by their teachers in Israel—comes from Jesus the teacher.[18]

From a form-critical perspective, the anecdote is "a paradigmatic example of an individual narrative that is not geographically or temporally fixed."[19] No biographical interest is apparent; only the minimum is said to make the story comprehensible. The entire situation is described at the beginning, with the mention of the Sabbath, grainfields, Jesus, and his group of disciples. The Pharisees are introduced only as critics; in the last analysis, nothing is said about their sudden appearance. One thinks immediately of the post-Easter situation of the disciples, who are spied upon by them. The short unit is both an apothegm and a controversy story at once: Jesus answers the Pharisaic criticism with authority, and thereby justifies the actions of his disciples. Their freedom is thus legitimized *post eventum* in a polemical context. The unit reflects an ecclesiastical situation in which the Christians fall back on the Jesus traditions available to them by making them relevant and applying them to their own situation. There is no reason to bring into question the antiquity or even the historicity of the event itself. As often in the dialogues with the Pharisees, the story remains within the sphere of Jewish tradition, in which the legitimacy of customs or beliefs is discussed

by having Jesus and the Pharisees playing God off against God. At issue is a *querelle des interprétations* ("dispute over interpretation"). Jesus argues on the basis of the Hebrew Bible. David's freedom and royal authority legitimate the attitude of the disciples toward the Sabbath. That the interpretation is a bit forced, because the example does not take place on a Sabbath, is a sign of its antiquity. Because Jesus' answer is not entirely satisfying, the first Christians tried, by adding the sayings one after the other, to concentrate the discussion on the Sabbath (Mark 2:27) and to find the solution in christology (Mark 2:28 par. Luke 6:5). Throughout, it seems as though it is not the Sabbath as such that is being criticized, but its understanding and regulation in Pharisaic tradition.

Commentary

Plucking grains bears the same relation to harvesting as anger does to murder (Matt 5:21–22). In one case, Jesus is more liberal than the Law, and in the other, more radical. Why is he always swimming against the stream? Because he places individuals and the people of God on center stage (cf. 6:8: $\epsilon\grave{\iota}\varsigma$ $\tau\grave{o}$ $\mu\acute{\epsilon}\sigma o\nu$, "in the middle"), and not obedience as such (i.e., Law as law).

■ **1–2** Here what is presupposed is the relationship of Jesus to his disciples as a teacher to his students. He is responsible for their actions. Also presupposed is the

---

Verkündigung der Kirche (SNTU A.1; Linz: Albert Fuchs, 1976) 110–53 (Aichinger holds to the two-source theory, but believes that Matthew and Luke depend on a secondary version of Mark); Francis Wright Beare, "'The Sabbath Was Made for Man?'" *JBL* 79 (1960) 130–36 (everything takes place in a post-Easter context; Mark 2:27–28 is the point of departure; the anecdote in Mark 2:23–24 is added to these two verses, and later the proof text Mark 2:25–26); Benoit, "Épis" (Matthew and Luke use Mark as a source, but they also depend on another tradition, which derives from an Aramaic version of Matthew and is often more reliable than Mark); Antoine Duprez, "Deux affrontements un jour de sabbat (Mc 2:23–3:6)," *AsSeign* 40 (1972) 43–53 (Mark 2:27 is redactional; the note in Matthew and Luke that the disciples eat is older than what Mark narrates; it was Jesus who cited the example of David); Arland J. Hultgren, "The Formation of the Sabbath Pericope in Mark 2:23–28," *JBL* 91 (1972) 38–43 (Mark 2:27 is authentic; vv. 23–24, and later vv. 25–26, 28, were added afterward); Heinz Wolf-

gang Kuhn, *Ältere Sammlungen im Markusevangelium* (SUNT 8; Göttingen: Vandenhoeck & Ruprecht, 1971) 61–81 (Mark 2:23–24, 27 is an old apothegm, v. 28 was inserted into the pre-Markan collection, and vv. 25–26 are Markan); Jürgen Roloff, *Das Kerygma und der irdische Jesus: Historische Motive in den Jesus-Erzählungen der Evangelien* (2d ed.; Göttingen: Vandenhoeck & Ruprecht, 1973) 52ff. (Mark 2:23–26 is a unit that goes back to Jesus; vv. 27–28 are also authentic, but were originally transmitted separately from vv. 23–26).

18   See David Daube, "Responsibilities of Master and Disciples in the Gospels," *NTS* 19 (1972–73) 1–15, esp. 4–8.

19   Karl L. Schmidt, *Der Rahmen der Geschichte Jesu: Literarkritische Untersuchungen zur ältesten Jesusüberlieferung* (Berlin: Trowitzsch, 1919; reprinted Darmstadt: Wissenschaftliche Buchgesellschaft, 1964), 89.

agreement of the will of the disciples with that of their teacher. Then the new obedience of Jesus and his disciples will be contrasted to the old obedience of the Pharisees (as in 5:30–32, 33–35). Jewish observance of the Law had its own logic and took human failings into account: to prevent harvesting on a Sabbath, even the plucking of individual grains was prohibited.[20] At issue is daily life. Jesus' disciples, and for Luke, the Christians with them, eat *differently*. They share their table with others (5:30), they fast differently or not at all (5:33–35), and they respect a different interpretation of the Sabbath commandment. Sociologically and theologically, a different set of ethics is defended: the attitude of a minority within Judaism, who, supported by their teacher, dare to live differently. In this there is, of course, some polemic against the usual way of life. Thus the aggressiveness of the Pharisees is not an *initiative*, but a *reaction*. For Jesus, and also in the earliest traditions, the nearness of the kingdom and the relationship of the Sabbath to God's will at creation are the theological basis of their freedom, and of the new attitude.

■ **3–4** Jesus responds with the weapon of the Pharisees,[21] that is, with the Scriptures. He defends a specific case[22] with a biblical exception recounted very freely.[23] Exceptions and individual cases are important for every storyteller—rules are boring—but behind them is a more general set of issues. The sociological *Sitz im Leben* (functional setting) of this pericope is the discussion about the correct understanding of the Sabbath. The themes, taken from Mark, run parallel to those of Luke's special source (cf. Luke 13:10–17; 14:1–6): in a situation of danger or affliction, one can intervene on behalf of life, one's own or that of others. Here the disciples (v. 1) eat because they are hungry. Hunger (v. 3) is an emergency that relativizes the command (vv. 2 and 4). What is permissible is to be measured by the standard of life, which is the reflection of the eschatological life. To live differently means to live *finally* and *already now* according to the will of God at creation, and according to the ethics of the kingdom. To say that, and to say it to the majority, who believe themselves to be in the right, costs a lot: the distance between polemic against certain attitudes and polemic against individuals is not far (cf. v. 11). It could, of course, be the case that Jesus is not so much polemicizing as he is defending his disciples and teaching the Pharisees.[24] The disciples, like David, were hungry and thus inculpable, and the Pharisees are invited to consider anew their obedience by means of the reference to Scripture.

Luke received this story, with its Sabbath motifs, from the Gospel of Mark in the context of his community. He himself does not like to be in the minority: all people should become Christians (see the book of Acts). The gospel lifestyle and the Christian message of faith can reach and persuade every individual. They are generally valid. Thus Luke reads the story in Mark with a Christian consciousness and with a critical superiority toward what he considers the parochial and outmoded Jewish set of ethics. This does not mean that the Scriptures, with their Sabbath commandment, have become out-of-date. In Luke's opinion, Jesus rediscovered the correct meaning of the Sabbath.

20   See Fitzmyer, 1.608. On the plucking of grains, cf. Deut 23:25 (LXX 23:26).

21   In the formulation τινὲς δὲ τῶν Φαρισαίων ("some of the Pharisees"), Luke employs language that is less colloquial than Mark's (who writes οἱ Φαρισαῖοι, "the Pharisees"), and perhaps also more polemic; cf. the contemptuous τινές ("some") in the polemic of the letters (1 Cor 15:12; Gal 1:7).

22   The addition in Luke 6:1 (ψώχοντες ταῖς χερσίν, "rubbed in their hands") describes what the disciples are doing, separating the grain from the chaff. The verb ψώχω ("to rub") is very rare; see BAGD *s.v.*; and Moulton and Milligan, *Vocabulary, s.v.* Τὰ σπόριμα ("grainfields") describes the sown field(s). Τίλλω means "pick," "pluck," "pull out."

23   On the relationship with 1 Sam 21, see Fitzmyer, 1.608–9. Joseph A. Grassi believes that this passage reflects a catechesis for the Eucharist based on a Christian interpretation of 1 Sam 21:1–6. He supports this hypothesis by citing the exegesis of the church fathers ("The Five Loaves of the High Priest [Mt xii:1–8; Mk ii:23–28; Lk vi:1–7; 1 Sam xxi:1–6]," *NovT* 7 [1964–65] 119–22).

24   In Jesus' response Luke uses οὐδέ ("not by any chance," "Have you not by chance read ...") where Mark has placed οὐδέποτε ("never") in Jesus' mouth. Luke's phrase is clearly ironic; it is difficult to judge to what extent this is intended in Mark.

■ **5** For this reason, he is the Lord, that is, not merely the hermeneut, of the Sabbath.[25] According to Luke, Jesus revoked the Pharasaic narrowness toward the Sabbath, and reconferred its meaning as a time for goodness (v. 9), liberation (13:16), and healing (14:3) of people, in remembrance of the rest after creation, and in anticipation of the rest of the kingdom of God.

Can one go a step further and say: as Lord of the Sabbath and of the temple, Jesus, like David, dares to nourish his disciples? Perhaps Luke is reading David's gesture from a eucharistic perspective: from the old temple comes forth the new Christian meal. Λαβὼν ἔφαγεν καὶ ἔδωκεν ("took and ate . . . and . . . gave," v. 4) sounds liturgical; the old restriction, "the priests alone," has been lifted, and it is now permissible to eat the bread.[26]

Conclusion

Luke discusses the theme of the Sabbath only in the passages he has taken from other sources. In Acts the apostles, and even Paul, still observe Jewish customs and festivals,[27] but reference is never made to the Sabbath. The issue of the Sabbath does not come up in Luke's church, or in the Pauline communities either: (1) *no longer*, because Jewish observance of the Law has become irrelevant; or (2) *not yet*, because Sunday has not yet attained its position.[28] The Christians may perhaps still have respected the Sabbath, but in its new Christian meaning, and little affected by the Jews, with whom they had broken off contact: as the day before the day on which they celebrated the resurrection of their Lord in the night or early morning.

---

25 See Busse, *Wunder*, 139: "In contrast to Mark, Luke limits human eschatological freedom over the Sabbath in v. 5 [by omitting Mark 2:27], in that he has Jesus emphasize the *kyriotes* ['lordship'] of the Son of Man."

26 On the bread of the Presence, see Fitzmyer, 1.609. According to Lev 24:5–9, every Sabbath, twelve freshly baked loaves would be laid out in two rows on the table before the Holy of Holies, and eaten by the priests in a holy place afterward.

27 Cf. Acts 2:46; 3:1; 16:3; 20:16.

28 Cf. Acts 20:7, a passage that may indeed already hint at Sunday worship.

The Healing of the Withered Hand (6:6–11)

Bibliography

Bultmann, *History*, 12, 382.

Busse, *Wunder*, 135–41.

Dautzenberg, *Leben*, 154–60.

Geoltrain, Pierre, "La violation du sabbat: Une lecture de Marc 3:1–6," *CBVF* 9 (1970) 70–90.

Hübner, Hans, *Das Gesetz in der synoptischen Tradition* (Witten: Luther-Verlag, 1973) 128–36.

Roloff, *Kerygma*, 63–66.

Schramm, *Markus-Stoff*, 112.

Trautmann, Maria, *Zeichenhafte Handlungen Jesu: Ein Beitrag zur Frage nach dem geschichtlichen Jesus* (FB 37; Würzburg: Echter, 1980) 293–308.

van der Loos, *Miracles*, 436–40.

van Unnik, "Motivierung."

6 It happened that on another Sabbath he entered the synagogue and taught, and there was a person there whose right hand was withered. 7/ But the scribes and the Pharisees watched him to see whether he would cure on the Sabbath, so that they might find a reason to accuse him. 8/ Even though he himself knew what they were thinking, he said to the man who had the withered hand, "Get up and stand here in the middle." And he got up and stood there. 9/ Then Jesus said to them, "I ask you, is it lawful to do good or to do harm on the Sabbath, to save life or to destroy it?" 10/ After looking around at all of them, he said to him, "Stretch out your hand." And he did so, and his hand was restored. 11/ But they were filled with blind fury and discussed with one another what they might do to Jesus.

Analysis

Luke continues to follow his copy of Mark. The small agreements with Matthew are insignificant:[1] ξηρά ("withered," Luke 6:6 par. Matt 12:10), and the omission of αὐτόν ("him") after θεραπεύει ("he would cure," Luke 6:7 par. Matt 12:10).

Characteristic of Luke's manner of redaction are the beginning in v. 6 with his favorite expression ἐγένετο δέ ("it happened that") with the infinitive (here, there are two);[2] the dating "on another Sabbath";[3] the mention of *the* synagogue," although we do not know which is meant concretely;[4] and the reminder of Jesus' primary mission (διδάσκειν, "taught"). After v. 6 Jesus continues his messianic activity. Verse 6 emphasizes the simple detail ξηρά ("withered"),[5] but describes the hand, novelistically, as the "right."[6] What is implicitly assumed by Mark becomes explicit in Luke (v. 7): the critical spectators are the Pharisees (cf. Mark 2:24), but in Luke, they have been jointly active with the scribes since 5:17 (cf. 5:21, 30; differently, 6:2). The deletion of αὐτόν ("him") after θεραπεύει ("he would heal") is important (v. 7):[7] the opponents are observing not this individual case but the overall behavior of Jesus. Luke shows a preference for the verb εὑρίσκω ("to find"); here he introduces it, and even dares to give it an infinitive object.[8] One should describe this as a tendency to use the infinitive, rather than as Aramaisms.[9] The infinitive in question

---

1   Even Schramm admits this (*Markus-Stoff*, 112).

2   See Busse, *Wunder*, 137 n.3.

3   Luke prefers the singular σάββατον ("Sabbath"), in contrast to Mark 3:4.

4   Busse believes that Jesus is here continuing his "Lukan" travels from city to city as itinerant preacher and miracle worker (*Wunder*, 135). Luke probably has in mind here, however, the synagogue of the neighboring city closest to the grainfield of the preceding pericope.

5   Mark 3:1 uses the more vivid passive participle.

6   The text of Codex D is influenced by the parallel passage in Matthew, and even more, in Mark. The novelistic tendency that can be perceived in Luke's mention that it was the *right* hand becomes even more marked in the fragment of the "Gospel which the Nazarenes and Ebionites use . . . and which is called by most people the authentic (Gospel) of Matthew" cited in Jerome's commentary on Matthew (on 12:13): "I [the man with the withered hand] was a mason and earned (my) living with

(my) hands; I beseech thee, Jesus, to restore to me my health that I may not with ignominy have to beg for my bread" (trans. P. Vielhauer and G. Strecker, in Hennecke-Schneemelcher, 1.160; Latin text in Aland, *Synopsis*, 158).

7   Many mss. also omit the αὐτόν after παρετηροῦντο δέ ("[they] watched"). A few, influenced by Mark, choose the future tense, θεραπεύσει.

8   The use of εὑρίσκω ("to find") with the infinitive already occurs in classical Greek (cf. LSJ *s.v.* εὑρίσκω II.2); it means "to find the opportunity," "to have the possibility," "to be able."

9   On the excessive use of the infinitive in Luke, see Antoniadis, *Évangile*, 174–75.

here has almost attained the meaning of a substantive, which numerous manuscripts have noted in writing κατηγορίαν ("accusation") instead.[10] In v. 8 he adds the words, "he knew what they were thinking," to the Markan text, which he takes from a later point in Mark (3:5).[11]

It is true that he tones down both Jesus' emotions (Mark 3:5: μετ᾽ ὀργῆς, συλλυπούμενος; "with anger, he was grieved")[12] and the condition of the audience's souls (ἡ πώρωσις, "hardness," a Markan word that Luke prefers to avoid, like the verb πωρόω [Mark 6:52 and 8:17]). But the inner thoughts (διαλογισμοί) are indeed negatively evaluated as being characterized by sin.[13] It is not surprising that Luke changes the word ἄνθρωπος ("person"), which is already in v. 6, to ἀνήρ ("man"). In the rewriting of v. 8, this man achieves independent significance; Luke adds a "get up" from Jesus. His careful obedience ("and he got up and stood there") is an additional characteristic that emphasizes the relationship of the sick individual to Jesus in the context of the miracle story.

Does Jesus seem more arrogant in v. 9 than in Mark? Should the supplemental "I ask you" be understood ironically?[14] Why does Luke leave out the opponent's silence (Mark 3:5)?[15] Is this an index of the shift of interest from the Sabbath to the healing? From v. 10 onward, the rewriting is more considerable. The Lukan tendency toward generalization is evident in πάντας ("all [of them]").[16] The transmission of the text is uncertain here; some manuscripts add "like the other [hand]," or "healthy like the other." For reasons of content, v. 11 has

been completely reformulated (in the same style as 4:28; 5:26; Acts 3:10).[17]

The unit is a composite form, as it is already in Mark: a miracle story serves as the argument in a controversy story. Verses 6 and 7 are devoted to describing the situation, which results from a diagnosis (in the imperfect tense).[18] Then, as the main character and sole speaker in this dialogue, Jesus talks successively to the sick man, to his opponents, and again to the sick man (5:17–26 are very similar in form). On a nonverbal level, however, the sick man does give a response through his trusting motion. This successful communication (the sick man is now standing in the midst of them, v. 8) leads first to the healing (v. 10) and finally to a reaction among the circle of opponents (cf. περιβλεψάμενος, "after looking around," in v. 10; and cf. v. 11). Jesus' disciples remain unmentioned. The conclusion is not formed, as would be typical, by Jesus' victory, but rather by the aggressivity against him, which points beyond the bounds of the form-critical unit: the future significance of Jesus' activities comes into view.

Luke remains faithful to the structure of his source and balances out the relationship between the opponents and the sick man through attention to the latter's person. He thus places a positive relationship alongside a negative one. Jesus' concern is as important to the Lukan redaction as the pre-Markan anti-Pharisaic attitude. Verse 9, in its expanded form, is equivalent to a similar question in a parallel miracle story (Luke 14:1–6).

---

10   Thus the textus receptus. Some mss. read κατ᾽ αὐτοῦ in v. 7, instead of the simply and wholly correct αὐτοῦ.

11   Εἶπεν δέ ("he said") in v. 8 is a stylistic improvement over καὶ λέγει in Mark 3:3.

12   Some mss. correct this by adding "with anger," or "angrily," following Mark's formulation. Albert Huck and Heinrich Greeven have the most extensive apparatus to this passage (*Synopse der drei ersten Evangelien/Synopsis of the First Three Gospels* [13th ed.; Tübingen: Mohr-Siebeck, 1981] 67). Luke could not admit that Jesus showed anger; see Metzger, *Textual Commentary*, 140.

13   See the commentary on 5:22 above.

14   Improvements in v. 9: Εἶπεν δὲ ὁ Ἰησοῦς πρὸς αὐτούς ("Then Jesus said to them"; Mark 3:4 has καὶ λέγει αὐτοῖς). In Mark the name of Jesus does

not occur once in the entire pericope. Luke also substitutes ἀπολέσαι ("to destroy") for ἀποκτεῖναι ("to kill"), since he notes that the problem is moral rather than physical.

15   Here too, as in Luke 6:9, a few witnesses have inserted Mark's more extensive text (οἱ δὲ ἐσιώπων, "but they were silent").

16   The changes in v. 10 include εἶπεν αὐτῷ ("he said to him," instead of λέγει τῷ ἀνθρώπῳ, Mark 3:5); addition of σου ("your") to τὴν χεῖρα ("hand"); and substitution of the usual ἐποίησεν with ἐξέτεινεν ("to stretch out," to avoid a repetition?).

17   See Busse, *Wunder*, 137; and the commentary on v. 11 below.

18   Busse detects the influence of an earlier pericope (Luke 5:17–26) here (*Wunder*, 136–38).

Commentary

■ **6–7** Like the Christian missionaries in the book of Acts,[19] the Lukan Jesus makes use of synagogue and Sabbath to preach, which, in Luke's language, is "to teach" (cf. 4:43–44 and 5:17). In a popular style, like Mark's, Luke confronts Jesus with a man with a withered hand, whereby ξηρός expresses the meaning "dry" (cf. Heb 11:29; Matt 23:15); this also appears in John 5:3 for "consumptives" in a list of sick people. Medically considered, the man's hand is probably paralyzed.[20] No one requests healing, not even the man. The scribes and Pharisees know of this case and wait to see whether Jesus will be incited to perform a healing. A sick or lame individual was not, in those times, a tragic isolated case, but rather a problem for the entire community. The society that was chosen in the wilderness, as well as the eschatological society, should really be a healthy society, since sickness and sin belong together. As contemporary family therapy has recently discovered anew, society is sick "with the individual,"[21] but here the healing of an individual causes the "sickness" (ἄνοια, "blind fury," v. 11) of others—and that is the tragedy. The healing itself is not the controversial issue, but rather the date: because of the Sabbath commandment. Παρατηρέω ("to watch") is an important verb in Lukan redaction. In the LXX it describes the evil people who lie in wait for a righteous individual to stumble.[22] It is manifest that the scribes and Pharisees, *on the Sabbath*, are not acting on the basis of the attitude of love commanded in the Law.[23] Luke 13:10–17; 14:1–5; John 5:9–16; and 9:14 also testify of a healing on the Sabbath being used as an argument against Jesus.

■ **8–9** In the first step Jesus authoritatively orders the man to stand up in their midst. According to Luke, he obeys immediately. The "case," which is for Luke a person, is handled by Jesus. The main question is asked again: Is it lawful to heal on the Sabbath? The question is cleverly posed by Jesus, almost too cleverly, because the alternative is obscured. To heal or not to heal is not the same as to heal or to destroy (v. 9). Now the Pharisees can neither answer that the Sabbath exists to do evil and to cast people[24] into destruction, nor that it is time to heal (because only the most pressing emergency aid is allowed on the Sabbath[25]). Their aggressivity at Jesus' provocation (v. 11) is understandable. Of course, with his glance and his word, Jesus intends the best not only for the sick man but also for them. Jesus is concerned not with his right to differ (6:1–5), but with the desire to practice love in every case. This itself should lead the Pharisees and scribes to reflect on themselves and the will of God. Luke teaches an ethical understanding of the Sabbath[26] that has its roots in the christology of Jesus as Deliverer (σῶσαι, "to save"). He is the Lord of the Sabbath (6:5) in delivering the one (the sick need the doctor, 5:31) and shaking up the others.

Jesus is not satisfied with the mere healing of the sick man, because the attention of his opponents is an expression of a counterfeit faithfulness to the Law:[27] an observance of the Sabbath that incites people to wait for their neighbor to stumble is no longer obedience to the will of God.[28] Luke wants the Sabbath to be the occasion

---

19 See, e.g., Acts 14:1; 17:1–2.

20 See van der Loos, *Miracles*, 438–39.

21 See, e.g., Michael Wirsching and Helm Stierlin, *Krankheit und Familie: Konzepte, Forschungsergebnisse, Therapie* (Stuttgart: Klett-Cotta, 1982) 50–62.

22 Cf. Ps 37(LXX 36):12: Παρατηρήσεται ὁ ἁμαρτωλὸς τὸν δίκαιον ("The sinner lies in wait for the righteous individual"). See also Schürmann, 1.306.

23 So Busse (*Wunder*, 140): "For Jesus, it is an evil deed when an act of rescue is left undone."

24 On the use of ψυχή in the sense of "person," see Gerhard Dautzenberg, *Sein Leben bewahren: Ψυχή in den Herrenworten der Evangelien* (SANT 14; Munich: Kösel, 1966) 154, 158–60. Luke is familiar with this usage: Acts 2:41, 43; 7:14; 27:37. See Schürmann, 1.307 n. 60.

25 On the suspension of the Sabbath regulations in the case of danger of life and limb, cf. Luke 14:5; see Str-B 1.623–29.

26 On Mark 3:4 par. Luke 6:9, Dibelius writes: "it [the narrative] proclaims the new righteousness under whose rule there is no limitation for doing good" (*Tradition*, 55).

27 See Vincent Taylor, *The Gospel According to St. Mark: The Greek Text with Introduction, Notes, and Indexes* (2d ed.; London: Macmillan, 1959) 222.

28 Schürmann rejects (in my opinion, wrongly) an intentional conceptual connection between the evil action of the scribes and Pharisees and the words κακοποιῆσαι ("to do harm") and ἀπολέσαι ("to destroy") in Jesus' saying.

and the reason for ἀγαθοποιῆσαι ("to do good") and σῶσαι ("to save"), because Jesus has experienced this with God's approval. This is the new interpretation of the Law.

A theological encomium of the hand can be inserted here.[29] The hand can hold, sense, love, and be creative; in it the analogy between the Creator and the Redeemer is most evident. The symbolism of the hand thus has deep roots in the Hebrew Bible and refers anthropologically to every aspect of human existence. The hand is important for this reason, because it can become, in its universality, a sign of the delivering Christ. With his hand Jesus heals (8:54), and with the finger of God he drives out demons (11:20).[30]

■ **10** "The restoration of the crippled hand demonstrates the new and superior economy of salvation in the coming of Jesus, and the dawning of the eschatological age of salvation, which reinstates the deeper sense of the Sabbath commandment: to *restore* human individuals to the integrity to which they were created."[31] It is no coincidence that the recovery is expressed by the theologically pregnant word ἀποκαθίστημι ("to restore"). In the LXX this word has "the specific meaning of the eschatological restoration of Israel from the Diaspora."[32] In this new definition of the kind action, Luke remains in dialogue not only with Jewish tradition but probably also with popular Hellenistic ethical traditions and with political benefactors.[33]

■ **11** In v. 11 Luke deletes from Mark 3:6 the political participation of the Herodians and avoids the word συμβούλιον, which could lead to misunderstanding, since it can mean both "deliberation" and "council meeting." According to Luke, the death sentence is leveled against Jesus only after the Galilean phase of his activity; and when it comes to pass, it is not through the Pharisees but through the leaders of the people in Jerusalem. Jesus' lot is not vested in human decision, but in God's providence and in Jesus' own explicit foreknowledge. So Luke replaces the Markan verse with a rather long dialogue (in the imperfect tense),[34] in which διαλαλέω ("to discuss"; cf. v. 11a) shows the same negative connotation as διαλογισμοί ("thoughts") in v. 8.

In Luke only the "being filled" (used since Homer for the inner life of the individual) with ἄνοια[35] ("blind fury") remains from the murder plot in Mark. The derivation of the word is clear (ἀνοέω, "not to discern," "not to think"), but its meaning varies from "madness" to "ignorance" (Plato: δύο ᾗ ἀνοίας γένη, τὸ μὲν μανίαν, τὸ δ᾽ ἀμαθίαν, "of folly there are two kinds, the one of which is madness, the other, ignorance"[36]). Since Luke expresses "ignorance" with ἄγνοια in Acts,[37] he probably has in mind here the meaning "madness." A few modern translations read accordingly: "Sie aber wurden voll blinder Wut,"[38] "they were filled with fury,"[39] "beside themselves with fury,"[40] "eux furent remplis de fureur."[41]

Conclusion

When individuals are once seized by an overpowering rage, in the final analysis they are no longer themselves; the madness of Ajax is the classical example of such a

---

29 See the praise of the hand in the appendix to Henri Focillon, *Vie des formes* (Bibliothèque de philosophie contemporaine; Paris: F. Alcan, 1947) 99–121.

30 See Eduard Lohse, "χείρ, κτλ.," *TDNT* 9 (1973) 424–37. One could wonder whether the word χείρ here means only the hand, or perhaps, like the χέρι of modern Greek, the whole arm.

31 Paul-Gerd Müller, "ἀποκαθίστημι, κτλ.," *EDNT* 1 (1990) 129–30.

32 Müller, "ἀποκαθίστημι," 129, who also adds a series of biblical references.

33 See W. C. van Unnik, "Die Motivierung der Feindesliebe in Lukas VI,32–35," *NovT* 8 (1966) 284–300, reprinted in idem, *Sparsa Collecta*, 1.111–26; and the commentaries on Acts 10:38, where Jesus is presented as "being a benefactor" (εὐεργετῶν).

34 On τί ἂν ποιήσαιεν ("what they might do"): Luke is using the optative, which was considered to be literary in his time. This is an oblique optative, as it would be used in an indirect question, though it appears here with ἄν, as would be expected for a direct question in the potential; see BDF §386.1.

35 The old Attic accentuation was ἀνοία, just as the old accentuation of ἄγνοια was ἀγνοία. See Bailly, *Dictionnaire, s.v.;* and LSJ *s.v.*

36 *Tim.* 86B.

37 See Acts 3:17; 17:30.

38 Klostermann, 76.

39 BAGD *s.v.*

40 Fitzmyer, 1.604.

41 *TOB*.

condition.[42] There is something tragic in the mission of Jesus, which should serve to heal the individual in both body and mind[43] but at the same time causes senseless fury, as it does here. The preaching of the kingdom and of the cross belong together, like the ἄγνοια ("ignorance") and ἄνοια ("blind fury") of the opponents. This ἄνοια is contagious, and the leaders of the people will persecute Jesus in ἄγνοια. He himself will intercede for them until the end: "Father, forgive them; for they *do not know* what they *are doing*" (Luke 23:34).

---

42   See the three studies that Jean Starobinski dedicates to the Ajax of Sophocles, the possessed man in Mark 5, and the "Nightmare" of the painter J.-H. Füssli: *Trois fureurs* (Le Chemin; Paris: Gallimard, 1974).

43   As is the case of the Gerasene demoniac, who is rescued (ἐσώθη, Luke 8:36), and comes into his right mind (σωφρονοῦντα, Luke 8:35).

The Choosing of the Twelve (6:12–16)

Bibliography

Barrett, Charles Kingsley, *The Signs of an Apostle: The Cato Lecture 1969* (London: Epworth, 1970).

Bovon, *Theologian*, 359–67, 403–5, 476–77.

Bühner, Jan-Adolf, "ἀπόστολος, κτλ.," *EDNT* 1 (1990) 142–46.

Dietrich, *Petrusbild*, 82–94.

Dupont, Jacques, "Le nom d'apôtre a-t-il été donné aux Douze par Jésus?" *Orient Syrien* 1 (1956) 267–90, 425–44, reprinted in idem, *Études*, 2.976–1018.

Giblet, Jean, et al., "The Twelve: History and Theology," in idem et al., *The Birth of the Church* (trans. C. U. Quinn; Staten Island: Alba House, 1968) 65–81.

Jeremias, Joachim, "Perikopen-Umstellungen bei Lukas?" *NTS* 4 (1957–58) 114–19, reprinted in idem, *Abba* (Göttingen: Vandenhoeck & Ruprecht, 1966) 93–97.

Klauck, Hans-Josef, *Judas: Ein Jünger des Herrn* (Quaestiones Disputatae 111; Freiburg im Breisgau: Herder, 1987).

Klein, Günter, *Die zwölf Apostel: Ursprung und Gestalt einer Idee* (FRLANT 77; Göttingen: Vandenhoeck & Ruprecht, 1961).

Kredel, Elmar Maria, "Der Apostelbegriff in der neueren Exegese: Historisch-kritische Darstellung," *ZKTh* 78 (1956) 169–93, 257–305.

Leidig, Edeltraud, "Natanael, ein Sohn des Tholomäus," *ThZ* 36 (1980) 374–75.

Lohfink, *Sammlung*, 63–83.

Meier, John P., "The Circle of the Twelve: Did It Exist During Jesus' Public Ministry?" *JBL* 116 (1997) 635–72.

Rigaux, Béda, "Die 'Zwölf' in Geschichte und Kerygma," in H. Ristow and K. Matthiae, eds., *Der historische Jesus und der kerygmatische Christus: Beiträge zum Christusverständnis in Forschung und Verkündigung* (Berlin: Evangelische Verlaganstalt, 1960) 468–86.

Roloff, Jürgen, *Apostolat, Verkündigung, Kirche: Ursprung, Inhalt, und Funktion des kirchlichen Apostelamtes nach Paulus, Lukas, und den Pastoralbriefen* (Gütersloh: Mohn, 1965) 169–235.

idem, "Apostel, Apostolat, Apostolizität, I. Neues Testament," *TRE* 3 (1973) 430–45.

Schramm, *Markus-Stoff*, 113–14.

Trilling, Wolfgang, "Zur Entstehung des Zwölferkreises: Eine geschichtskritische Überlegung," in R. Schnackenburg, et al., eds., *Die Kirche des Anfangs: Festschrift Heinz Schürmann* (EThSt 38; Leipzig: St. Benno-Verlag, 1977) 201–22.

von Campenhausen, Hans, "Der urchristliche Apostelbegriff," *StTh* 1 (1947) 96–130.

12 Now it happened that during those days he went up the mountain to pray; and he spent the whole night in prayer with God. 13/ And when day came, he addressed his disciples and chose twelve of them, whom he also named apostles; 14/ Simon, whom he named Peter, and his brother Andrew, and James, and John, and Philip, and Bartholomew, 15/ and Matthew, and Thomas, and James son of Alphaeus, and Simon who was called the Zealot, 16/ and Judas son of James, and Judas Iscariot, who became a traitor.

Analysis

In Luke 6:12–19 Luke transposes Mark 3:7–12 and 13–19 to provide for the insertion of texts from Q and Luke's special source (Luke 6:20 onward): after a night of prayer on the mountain (6:12), Jesus calls his disciples, from which circle he selects the twelve apostles (6:13). The list of names follows (6:14–16 par. Mark 3:13–19). Jesus then descends "with them" (probably the Twelve) to "a level place," where he stands together with the crowd of his disciples and the people (6:17). A summary passage follows (6:18–19 par. Mark 3:7–12), and after that, the Sermon on the Plain begins.

In the Sermon Luke seems to distinguish among various categories of listeners (6:20, 27, 39; 7:1). This also, in part, explains the transposition: Jesus first chooses his closest fellow workers from among his circle of disciples before he speaks to them and to the people. Elements of the Q tradition may already be evident behind 6:12–13a, since Matt 5:1 also introduces the Sermon on the Mount with a description of the scene (the place, i.e., a mountain, and the presence of the disciples). Since both Matthew (4:24–5:1) and Luke (6:17–19) use the same passage from Mark (3:7–12) to frame the Sermon on the Mount/Plain,[1] one could hypothetically assume a parallel pericope for the summary passage, and even a parallel pericope for the choosing of the Twelve, but for this

---

1   See Schramm, *Markus-Stoff*, 113; earlier, Burton S. Easton, *The Gospel According to Luke* (New York: Scribner's, 1926) 81.

supposition there is hardly sufficient basis.[2] The lists of the Twelve each have their own tradition, as Acts 1:13 shows, and the agreements between Matt 10:24 and Luke 6:14–16 are slight.[3]

Luke's freedom with regard to Mark 3:13–19 is surprising. In 6:12 he creates a redactional summary, with a reference to Jesus' prayer, and in 6:13 he recasts his Markan source in a stylistically and logically superior form. The word ἀπόστολοι ("apostles") occurs here because, first, it is suggested in his Markan source (ἵνα ἀποστέλλῃ αὐτούς . . . , "to send them out"); second, it probably stood at the beginning of the list of the Twelve circulating alongside Mark; third, it anchors the circle of the Twelve securely in the life of Jesus, which is a theological concern for Luke. In 6:14–16 Luke places Andrew second, as does Matthew, and he deletes the new name of the sons of Zebedee. In agreement with Mark, Matthew appears before Thomas, and without his occupation as tax collector. From Philip to James the son of Alphaeus, the list of Luke and Mark are the same. Peculiar to Luke are the absence of any indication of kinship between James and John (v. 14), the absence of Thaddaeus, the inclusion of Judas the son of James, and the correct translation of κανανc̄αιος with ζηλωτής ("zealot," v. 15). This is the state of affairs also in the list in Acts 1:13, although it does differ from the one in Luke 6:14–15 in five small peculiarities: (1) any indication of kinship disappears (striking in the case of Peter and Andrew); (2) John appears before James, and both appear before Andrew; (3) the sequence "Thomas, Bartholomew, Matthew"; (4) a two-by-two grouping results from the presence or absence of καί ("and");[4] (5) Judas Iscariot no longer belongs on the list. In Luke, then, the names are the same in both the Gospel and Acts, excluding the above-mentioned absence of Judas

Iscariot in the second list of disciples. But Luke is aware of at least two lists, which he has adjusted to his own concerns and to the predilections of his congregation.

One encounters three different genres in Luke 6:12–16: (1) a summary passage, which serves as the introduction of the next unit; (2) the terse story of the selection, with a calling, choosing, and conferring of a title; (3) a list.

The last two genres are important in the life of every community. They guarantee the social existence and the constitution of a congregation.[5] The Lukan church, like the earlier congregation of the Hellenists and the mother community in Jerusalem, asserts the legitimacy of the apostles by means of the calling and the listing of their names, although the church does not transmit much about the majority of these apostles. Nonetheless, there is an implicit criticism in such a list of any Christian movement that would base itself on other apostles.[6]

Commentary

Up to this point, the interest of the author, like that of the traditions that preceded him, lay in the person of Jesus, his installment in his office, his early ministry, the first calling of disciples, and the first controversies. Soon he will transmit Jesus' teaching. Like the biographers of his time, especially those of the philosophers, Luke is seeking to achieve a pleasant balance for his readers between narration and teaching.[7]

Chapter 5 told of growing resistance and the core group of future discipleship but—because of the traditions—not about what had become of these first disciples. Following Mark, Luke will now narrate, briefly and to the point, the second stage of the life of the Twelve.

---

2 Against Schramm, *Markus-Stoff*, 113.

3 See the common use of the word "apostle": οὓς καὶ ἀποστόλους ὠνόμασεν ("whom he also named apostles," Luke 6:13b) and τῶν δὲ δώδεκα ἀπο-στόλων ("of the twelve apostles," Matt 10:2). See Schürmann, 1.318 n. 55. Metzger (*Textual Commentary*, 80) and Nestle-Aland are indecisive.

4 The only departure from the pattern: the καί before "James son of Zebedee" in Acts 1:13.

5 In ancient Mediterranean societies, a social group based its right to exist in narratives—stories of commissioning, accounts of the foundation of a city, or a miraculous birth—or with lists of ancestors or kings.

Cf. the beginning of *Pirqe 'Abot*, the διαδοχαί ("successions") of the philosophical schools, and the lists of bishops.

6 See Bovon, *Lukas*, 212–13.

7 See Talbert (*Patterns*, 89–99, 125–29), who emphasizes the balance between living and thinking; see also Richard Goulet, "Les Vies de philosophes dans l'Antiquité tardive et leur portée mystérique," in Bovon, *Actes apocryphes*, 161–208.

One wonders whether Luke might be following the "establishment" of Israel on Sinai as a model in his portrayal of this phase.[8] In Philo's *Life of Moses*, this event plays no great role. For Philo, Moses' forty days of fasting and the revelation of the mystery, particularly that of the priesthood and the sanctuary, are of central significance.[9] But the following similarities of selection are still evident: (1) the twelve scouts, one from every tribe, each according to his virtue; (2) the priests (Aaron and his sons); and later, (3) the Levites, which selection Philo considers to be an extraordinary event.[10] Preparation by praying is important for the selection of the priests, but, unlike the Lukan Jesus, Moses is accompanied by his brother and the other priests.[11]

We are perhaps more on the right track with the *Biblical Antiquities* of Pseudo-Philo. After the first direct revelation of God's eternal law (11), and after the apostasy of the nation (12), Moses again climbs the mountain and *prays* (12.8) for the forgiveness and renewal of the nation, instead of its extermination. God answers his prayer and gives commands for ritual observance, that is, for a renewed life after the fall. Only a little later (15), the commissioning of the Twelve takes place, with a list of their names.[12] This shows how people were reading the biblical account in the first century CE. From Exodus to Deuteronomy, the structure of fall and forgiveness had been developed by means of Moses' intercession and a new giving of the Law. Luke 6:12–16 should be compared not with the Hebrew Bible account of the revelation on Sinai, but with this second giving of the Law. Only here are the motifs of the mountain and prayer connected, and only here is the holy state of the nation not a presupposition. The deuteronomistic tradition also emphasizes divine grace in the selection of leaders, whereas Jewish exegesis is otherwise concerned with the individual merit of the emissaries, priests, or Levites.

■ **12** "During those days," that is, in this time of unrepentance, Jesus climbs up the mountain to pray, as Moses did before him (Exod 32:30; 34:2). In Luke, Jesus prays before or during the most important events of his life. In this way the divine origin and nature of the event are indicated, as is the fellowship of the mediator with God. According to Luke, structural elements of Jesus' prayer are the expression of his relationship to God (i.e., worship), then requests and intercession not for secular goods but for the unfolding of the plan of salvation by means of obedient faith in response to the revealed Word of God.[13] This structure is also crucial for the prayer life of Christians, for the individual (Luke 11:5–13; 18:1–14; etc.) as well as the congregation (e.g., Acts 1:14, 4:24–31).[14] Of course, the times at which Jesus prays are again and again connected to a decisive stage of the new age of salvation;[15] in the prayers of the Christians, the issue is usually the role of the individual or the congregation in the history initiated by God through Christ. For them, prayer means not to lose faith, to endure, not to surrender to temptation, and so on. In the case of Jesus, the salvation-historical issues predominate in prayer; but for the Christians, it is the ethical issues.

Here Luke is describing the adaptation of Jesus' will to God's will, and his persistent action (periphrastic construction). Jesus prays the whole night through. This is not emphasizing Jesus' asceticism, but his total concentration on the one thing that is needful. He remains awake to the voice of God before this important event. He brings before God the condition of the nation and, implicitly, the lack of understanding among the theologians of his day (6:11). His intercession is linked with a daring resolve: Jesus does not hope for the sudden conversion of the Scripture experts and Pharisees, but intends to reach them indirectly through the selection of

---

8   Schürmann answers affirmatively (1.113 n. 7); Schweizer disagrees (75). See Exod 3:12; 24:1, 9; cf. 19:3, 20; 24:9–18; 34:29.

9   See Philo *Vit. Mos.* 2.70–71.

10 See, respectively, Philo *Vit. Mos.* 1.220–26; 2.141–42, 159–60.

11 See Philo *Vit. Mos.* 2.153.

12 See the edition of Daniel J. Harrington, *Pseudo-Philon: Les Antiquités Bibliques* (trans. J. Cazeaux; 2 vols.; SC 229–30; Paris: Cerf, 1976), commentary by Charles Perrot. See also the annotated translation

of Christian Dietzfelbinger, *Pseudo-Philo: Antiquitates Biblicae* (JSHRZ 2.2; Gütersloh: Mohn, 1975).

13 On prayer in Luke, see, in addition to the literature summarized in Bovon, *Theologian*, 400–403, José Caba, *La oración de petición: Estudio exegético sobre los evangelios sinópticos y los escritos joaneos* (AnBib 62; Rome: Pontifical Biblical Institute Press, 1974); and George, "La prière," in *Études*, 395–427. More literature cited in Fitzmyer, 1.268–69.

14 See Monloubou, *Prière*, 99.

15 See ibid., 98.

the Twelve. He is primarily concerned with the salvation and well-being of the nation; salvation-historically, according to Luke, Jesus is initiating a *new* leadership for the nation with the agreement of the *old* God of the fathers, in which neither expert knowledge of the Scriptures nor righteousness by works but rather messianic selection is decisive.

The unique phrase ἐν τῇ προσευχῇ τοῦ θεοῦ ("in prayer with God") deserves mention. If the scene has been modeled after the Hebrew Bible parallel suggested above, the prayer of Jesus to God is meant here. He speaks to God not for the sake of talking but to listen. Authentic communication, like true prayer, unites speaking and listening in a lively exchange. The expression encompasses not only Jesus' address but also his silence, the listening, and the answer of God. This takes place on the mountain, the place of the individual's encounter with God.[16] In the *night* (v. 12) Jesus comes before God alone, and the account dramatizes these hours as suspenseful ones. On the next *day* (v. 13) Jesus is in the middle of his community of followers, and the lively communication between them grants the narrative a sense of peacefulness.

■ **13** Προσφωνέω ("to address") is not a synonym of προσκαλέομαι ("to call," Mark 3:13). This poetic verb,[17] which entered into Koine prose, is rare, occurring a single time in Josephus.[18] It means "to address" (probably the sense here) and "to call by name (or title)." The meaning "to call over" is uncertain, and seems rather to have been read into the text of Luke by comparison with Mark (προσκαλέομαι, Mark 3:13; cf. Acts 6:2). In any case the scene does not begin with a call to repentance and faith, since those addressed are already disciples.

Luke separates the larger group of disciples from the inner circle of the Twelve more clearly than do Mark and Matthew; this is relevant for his ecclesiology. Although there will be no congregation without leaders,

these do not stand *before* the congregation but are appointed out of it by Christ. On the other hand, there is no talk of any conditions (education, merit, ability). The title of ἀπόστολος ("apostle") indicates a function, not an honor; a service, not a position of power. The genre of the list, and the first chapters of Acts, lead one to speculate that the first officials of the church arose out of the circle of the Twelve. There, of course, they are missionaries and preachers; but in Luke's time, after their death, they acquired the additional roles of founders and pillars.

Ἐκλέγομαι[19] ("to choose") describes a concrete, pragmatic selection of functionaries, not divine election in the dogmatic sense. The calling by name indicates new responsibility, which is not only a limited function but a permanent office.

Ἐκλέγομαι ("to choose") is frequently attested in Luke, both for Jesus (the beloved son, the "Chosen" [9:35]), and for the Twelve (Acts 1:2; cf. 15:7), for the additional apostles (1:24), and for other church officials (6:5; 15:22, 25). Whereas the Seven and the other officials were chosen by the apostles and the entire community, the choice of the Twelve remains the privilege of the Lord alone. The selection of the Seven in Acts 6:1–5 is similar in the separation of the Twelve from the group of assembled disciples, and in the listing of names, but it differs in the manner of selection (involving the participation of the community and its authorities), in the condition mentioned in 6:3, and in the lack of titles conferred.[20]

The title of apostle during the lifetime of Jesus is an anachronism. Their investiture is less important to Luke than their presence with Jesus, in view of their future role as witnesses (Acts 1:22–23). They are tested and equipped for service shortly before Jesus' death, during his passion, and after Easter.[21] Even beforehand they will fulfill a first mission (Luke 9:1–6); but only after Pente-

---

16   Cf. Mark 6:46; John 6:15.

17   See Moulton and Milligan, *Vocabulary*, s.v.

18   Cf. Josephus *Ant.* 7.4 §156; Rengstorf, *Concordance*, s.v.

19   See Jost Eckert, "ἐκλέγομαι, κτλ.," *EDNT* 1 (1990) 416–17. Recent literature in *ThWNT* 10.2 (1979) 1160–61. Dietrich is of the opinion that the verb ὀνομάζω does not have the same meaning in both occurrences (vv. 13, 14); in v. 13 it means "to give a title ('apostle')," in v. 14, "to give a name"

(*Petrusbild*, 90–91).

20   On Acts 6:1–6 see Bovon, *Theologian*, 346–50, 372; and Alfons Weiser, *Die Apostelgeschichte* (2 vols.; Ökumenischer Taschenbuchkommentar vom Neuen Testament 5.1–2; Gütersloh: Mohn; Würzburg: Echter, 1981–85) 1.163–64.

21   See Jürgen Roloff, *Apostolat, Verkündigung, Kirche: Ursprung, Inhalt, und Funktion des kirchlichen Apostelamtes nach Paulus, Lukas, und den Pastoralbriefen* (Gütersloh: Mohn, 1965) 192 and passim.

cost, and their receipt of the Holy Spirit, will they become apostles in the full sense. Luke sees in them great historical figures of the past. He limits their number to the Twelve, and anchors them in the life of Jesus. He is thinking institutionally here, but not in the sense of early Catholicism. As great figures in salvation history,[22] they are the first eyewitnesses of the resurrection (and, retrospectively, of the life and death of Jesus), the first leaders of the mother church, the representatives of the twelve tribes of the renewed Israel, and missionaries among the Jews.[23] Although the Twelve illustrate the restoration of Israel for the earliest level of oral tradition, they serve Luke as a portrayal of the coming into being of the people of God, that is, the church. If Pentecost is the date of birth for the church, then the calling of the disciples and the selection of the Twelve is part of the phase of its conception and pregnancy.[24]

■ **14** The first and the last places in the list[25] are important: Simon,[26] whom the readers already know (4:38), and whose calling they long since know about (5:1–11), takes the first place.[27] He is the only one to receive a new name. Luke views him as the spokesperson and

leader of the Jerusalem congregation, and probably also as the first witness of the resurrection (24:34). Along with the Jewish Christian church, Luke understands Peter to be the *rock*, that is, the foundation of the church.[28] But his church is not Petrine. Luke lays claim to the Petrine inheritance, but expands it by means of the Pauline inheritance. In v. 13 ὀνομάζω ("to name") is connected with a collective title, but here, with a proper name; this alludes to both the collective and the personal, but not transferable, responsibility of Peter.

In the last place is Judas Iscariot.[29] Christian readers know whom he betrayed,[30] but non-Christians are left on the edges of their seats waiting for the corresponding answer. Is "Iscariot"—otherwise not attested as a name[31]— a nickname ("man of falsity"), or an epithet ("man from Carioth," or *sicarius*, "cutthroat")? One cannot determine how Luke understood the name; it is only clear that he used it to distinguish him from Judas the son of James.

With James and John, the father's name is lacking (in contrast to Mark 3:17; Matt 10:2); this was probably no longer necessary after 5:10.[32] In Acts 1:13 John stands

---

22 Hans von Campenhausen has been able to distinguish clearly between the Lukan concept of the apostolate and that of Paul ("Der urchristliche Apostelbegriff," *StTh* 1 [1947] 96–130): for Luke, only the Twelve are apostles, and to be an apostle it does not suffice to have "seen" the risen Jesus—one must have accompanied him as well during the course of his earthly life.

23 On the position of Günter Klein (*Die zwölf Apostel: Ursprung und Gestalt einer Idee* [FRLANT 77; Göttingen: Vandenhoeck & Ruprecht, 1961]) see Bovon, *Theologian*, 360, 363–65. Jacques Dupont investigates Luke 6:13 ("Le nom d'apôtre a-t-il été donné aux Douze par Jésus?" *Orient Syrien* 1 [1956] 267–90, 425–44). According to him, Luke intends to say that the men whom Jesus chose at that time are the same as those known today as the "apostles." Luke 6:13 does not mean, then, that Jesus officially bestowed on the Twelve the title of "apostle."

24 Lohfink summarizes his own position (*Sammlung*, 93–99): Jesus did not "found" the church, but he did mark the decisive beginning of the eschatological gathering. This gathering is carried out in phases.

25 The ms. tradition tends toward grouping the Twelve in pairs with καί ("and"), under the influence of Acts 1:13 and of the missionary directive, "two by two" (Luke 10:2).

26 Luke knows of a number of people with the name Simon: Simon the Zealot (Luke 6:15; Acts 1:13), Simon the Pharisee (Luke 7:40), Simon of Cyrene (Luke 23:26), Simon the magician (Acts 8:9), and Simon the tanner (Acts 9:43). From this point on, Luke always calls this most important apostle by his new name, "Peter"—except in Luke 22:31 and 24:34 (two sayings from tradition), as in Acts 10:5, 18, 32, and 11:13 (here he makes clear that Peter is meant).

27 Codex D emphasizes the superior position of Peter, as the added πρῶτον ("first") shows in this passage. See Philippe Henri Menoud, "The Western Text and the Theology of Acts," in idem, *Jesus Christ and the Faith* (trans. E. M. Paul; PTMS 18; Pittsburgh: Pickwick, 1978) 61–83; as well as Eldon J. Epp, *The Theological Tendency of Codex Bezae Cantabrigiensis in Acts* (SNTSMS 3; Cambridge: Cambridge University Press, 1966) 154–64.

28 See Oscar Cullmann, *Peter: Disciple, Apostle, Martyr: A Historical and Theological Study* (trans. F. V. Filson; 2d ed.; London: SCM, 1962) 19–27.

29 Many mss. hellenize the name: Ἰσκαριώτην.

30 On προδότης ("traitor"), see BAGD *s.v.*

31 See Gnilka, *Markus*, 1.141; and Meinrad Limbeck, "Ἰσκαριώθ, κτλ.," *EDNT* 2 (1991) 200–201.

32 Two Syriac translations specify "the sons of Zebedee." Codex D and an Old Latin ms. (ff² with a

---

210

next to Peter and before James; other passages in Luke also speak of John's collaboration *with* Peter (and in Peter's shadow).[33] Luke reports the death of James in Acts 12:1–2. In Luke 9:54 he mentions the wrong reaction of James and John, but not—in contrast to Mark and Matthew—in 22:24.[34] In two important passages, he names Peter, James, and John as the disciples closest to Jesus (8:51; 9:28).

Luke knows as little to report about Philip, who should be distinguished from Philip the Hellenist,[35] as about Bartholomew, Matthew (for Luke, not identical with the Levi of 5:27), Thomas,[36] James the son of Alphaeus, Simon the Zealot,[37] and Judas son (rather than brother) of James.[38] The names at the end of the list are made more specific in order to prevent misunderstanding.

■ **15–16** Aside from Simon Peter and Judas Iscariot, Luke mentions very little about the pre- and post-Easter activities of the Twelve. He does possess the theologically significant list of names, but he cannot and will not do biographical research on the bearers of the names. Even in the few utterances in the form of questions or reactions of one or another, their personalities play no role. The listing of the names serves solely to make the story more lively and to strengthen its credibility. Anything more that the readers learn about these names exists strictly to portray Jesus and his message.

Conclusion

(1) The mediating role of the church was prepared by Jesus. (2) The apostles, the witnesses of Jesus, are chosen and named by himself. (3) The "eyewitnesses and servants of the word" (1:2) do not remain anonymous, a fact that stabilizes certainty (1:4) regarding the message and secures the fellowship of the church. (4) The leading role of Peter in the earliest post-Easter years is indicated by his position, as is Judas's responsibility for the betrayal at the end. Jesus alone is the envoy of God, the one anointed by the Spirit of God (4:18), who can announce the year of God's favor and initiate it. But just as the book of Acts follows the Gospel, the disciples will be installed in a mediating role after the earthly life of the Messiah. In themselves they are capable of nothing, and they work indirectly in history. But the history of the Word of God still needs people to carry on the work of Jesus.

few small differences) add after the name John, "his brother, [whom] he called Boanerges, which means, 'sons of thunder.'"

33 Luke 22:8; Acts 3:1, 11; 4:13, 19; 8:14.

34 Is the James in Luke 24:10 the same person? There it reads that the wife or mother of a certain James had been at the empty grave.

35 Martin Hengel does not deny the possibility of their identity ("Between Jesus and Paul: The 'Hellenists,' the 'Seven,' and Stephen," in *Between Jesus and Paul: Studies in the Earliest History of Christianity* [trans. J. Bowden; Philadelphia: Fortress Press, 1983] 14, 145 n. 95).

36 Codex D gives more specific information after John 11:16: "the one also named Didymus."

37 Luke is correctly translating the Semitic word καναναῖος with ζηλώτης. On the Zealot move- ment, see the literature cited in *ThWNT* 10.2 (1979) 1096–97. The term "zealot" (though not what it stands for) may be an anachronism in Jesus' time, but certainly not in Luke's era; see Marshall, 240.

38 This James is not the son of Zebedee, or the brother of the Lord, or the son of Alphaeus. Some harmonize by identifying him with Thaddaeus (Matt 10:3; Mark 3:18). Thaddaeus would then be his Greek name (and Lebbaus [Matt 10:3 D, Mark 3:18 D] his Aramaic name). I share the doubts expressed by Schürmann (1.317 n. 49).

The Healings before the Sermon on the Plain (6:17–19)

Bibliography

Egger, Wilhelm, "Die Verborgenheit Jesu in Mk 3,7–12," *Bib* 50 (1969) 466–90.

Keck, Leander E., "Mark 3:7–12 and Mark's Christology," *JBL* 84 (1964) 341–58.

Mánek, "On the Mount."

May, "Power."

Schramm, *Markus-Stoff*, 113–14.

17   **He came down with them and stopped at a level place, with a great crowd of his disciples and a great multitude of people from all Judea, Jerusalem, and the coast of Tyre and Sidon. 18/ They had come to hear him and to be healed of their diseases; and those who were troubled with unclean spirits were cured. 19/ And the whole crowd was trying to touch him, for a power came out from him and healed everyone.**

Analysis

The question presents itself whether Luke used Q as a source alongside Mark 3:7–12 in this introduction to the Sermon on the Plain.[1] Q seems to have contained, aside from the mountain and the disciples, also the crowd (cf. Luke 7:1 and Matt 7:28), and perhaps even a short description of Jesus' miraculous deeds.[2] This tradition parallel to Mark 3:7–12 may explain why Matthew and Luke position the Sermon on the Mount/Plain in the same place in the Markan sequence.

There are, however, no further agreements, and Matt 4:23–25 (except for 4:23b) is a mosaic of elements from Mark. Luke otherwise composes summary passages fairly independently of his sources. At any rate, the main source for Luke 6:17–19 remains Mark.

Because of the Sinai typology, Luke dispenses with the Markan motifs of the sea and the ship. He does take

from Mark: (1) the accompanying disciples; (2) the confluence of the masses both from Judea and Syria; (3) the crowd's desire to see and touch him; (4) the exorcisms (but, because of their mention in 4:41, in a shortened form); and (5) the healing of the sick through physical contact with Jesus. But Luke has largely reformulated most of these bits of information from Mark.[3]

In terms of genre, we have a transitional piece here, which leads from the selection of the Twelve to Jesus' first long public address. It begins in narrative (v. 17a), but quickly transforms into a summary (vv. 17b–19).

According to Jewish tradition, the nation born anew on Sinai lived for a time in an ideal state. In this period there were neither poor nor sick people.[4] This belief could have incited Matthew and Luke to move a healing ceremony into proximity with the mountain scene and Jesus' sermon (in Matthew, before these two items; in Luke, in between). Perhaps it can even be said that God, after the exodus from Egypt and every rebellion of Israel in the wilderness, first punished them by illness and then renewed them through healing.[5] The ascent up the mountain and the long prayer open a new age (6:12), at the beginning of which stand the naming of the Twelve (6:13–16) and the healings (6:17–19).

Commentary

■ **17** In the book of Exodus, ascent and descent symbolically stand for encountering God and then communicating the divine will to the people.[6] The LXX uses $\pi\epsilon\delta(\epsilon)\iota\nu\acute{o}\varsigma$ ("level") together with $\acute{o}\rho\epsilon\iota\nu\acute{o}\varsigma$ ("mountainous") as adjectives describing the promised land.[7] Luke might have symbolically combined both.

---

1   Various exegetes share this opinion, among them Schürmann (1.323) and Schramm (*Markus-Stoff*, 113–14).

2   See the analysis of 6:12–16 above.

3   Cf. in v. 17: $\mu\epsilon\tau\acute{\alpha}$, $\pi\lambda\hat{\eta}\vartheta\circ\varsigma$ $\pi\circ\lambda\acute{\upsilon}$, $\grave{\alpha}\pi\grave{\circ}$ . . . $\tau\hat{\eta}\varsigma$ $\grave{I}\circ\upsilon\delta\alpha\acute{\iota}\alpha\varsigma$ $\kappa\alpha\grave{\iota}$ $\grave{I}\epsilon\rho\circ\upsilon\sigma\alpha\lambda\acute{\eta}\mu$ (Mark repeats the preposition $\grave{\alpha}\pi\acute{\circ}$ and writes the hellenized form of the name of Jerusalem); in v. 18: $\hat{\eta}\lambda\vartheta\circ\nu$, $\grave{\alpha}\kappa\circ\acute{\upsilon}\omega$, $\pi\nu\epsilon\acute{\upsilon}\mu\alpha\tau\alpha$ $\grave{\alpha}\kappa\acute{\alpha}\vartheta\alpha\rho\tau\alpha$ (this has a doubled article in Mark), $\vartheta\epsilon\rho\alpha\pi\epsilon\acute{\upsilon}\omega$; in v. 19: $\ddot{\alpha}\pi\tau\epsilon\sigma\vartheta\alpha\iota$.

4   Cf. Deut 15:4 and Acts 4:34.

5   Cf. Ps 106 (LXX 105), which recounts unfaithfulness, punishment, and finally God's compassion.

6   This is characteristic of all of Exod 19. According to Jindrich Mánek ("On the Mount—on the Plain [Mt. v 1–Lk. vi 17]," *NovT* 9 [1967] 124–31), Matthew emphasizes the mountain as an eschatological locus, whereas Luke—like the prophets—expects the leveling of all mountains in the last days. This would explain why Matthew localized the sermon on a mountain, and Luke in a plain.

7   Cf., in the LXX, Deut 11:11; Josh 11:16; Zech 7:7; Jer 17:26. The expression $\grave{\epsilon}\pi$ $\ddot{\circ}\rho\circ\upsilon\varsigma$ $\pi\epsilon\delta\iota\nu\circ\hat{\upsilon}$ in Isa 13:2 ("on the mountains of the plain," LXX) seems strange.

At the foot of the mountain, then, Jesus stands along with three groups: the apostles, the band of disciples, and the people. Luke, of course, is primarily thinking historically and narratively here;[8] but the same relationships are repeated in the primitive community, and perhaps in Luke's time, as well: the church, led by the Lord, gathers disciples from the entire nation, under the direction of the Twelve. Up to this point, Luke has not yet written so dramatically about Jesus' success; in doing this, he distinguishes between two groups: those from Jewish territory ("all Judea" includes Galilee, as in 4:44), whose center is Jerusalem,[9] and those from the Gentile coast of Tyre and Sidon.[10] Thus the future of the church is presaged, as in Luke 14:21–23. Its development is a progressive and eschatological gathering of Israel.[11] Though ὄχλος ("crowd") and πλῆθος ("multitude") have prosaic connotations, λαός ("people") rings theological; it is not yet the time of the Gentiles (ἔθνη, "nations").

■ **18a** The salvific event takes place outside Jerusalem. Luke thereby criticizes any identification with the historical nation and the geographical extent of Israel. The Christian message is in continuity with the revelation of Sinai ("mountain" and "level place") but also in discontinuity (6:11).[12] Fortunately, there are enough people in the nation who want to hear the news and *come out* to meet Jesus. From the time of Abraham, contact with God has been connected with an exodus, according to Luke. For this reason, the Baptist is very important to him (3:7). The coming of Christ (5:32) is juxtaposed with the coming of the crowds (6:18). A new relationship with God develops by means of this.

It is characteristic of the worldview of late antiquity that the locus of *religio* (as a relationship to the divine) shifts, and is manifested progressively less often in temples than in called men and women.[13] This played to the advantage of christology and mission; the Gospels are the first witnesses of this.

The expectation of the people is stereotypical: they want to hear Jesus and to be healed by him (v. 18a, in contrast to Mark 3:8b, in which only "hearing" is mentioned). This is exactly what Luke's messianic prophet and doctor has to offer.

■ **18b** Luke adds the answer by word (vv. 20–49) to the answer by deed (vv. 18b–19). The exorcisms in v. 18b are thus a bit unconnected, since Luke differentiates them from the healings.[14] In comparison with 4:41, the attention is here directed toward the possessed individuals, not the demons. These ἐνοχλούμενοι, that is, the "troubled," "oppressed," "plagued," perhaps "sick,"[15] are healed through exorcism.[16]

■ **19** Without inhibition, Luke shares his conviction that a healing power (δύναμις)[17] exudes from Jesus. It suffices just to touch (ἅπτεσθαι) Jesus in order to be

---

8   Marshall emphasizes this aspect (242).

9   Ignace de la Potterie ascribes a theological significance to the two ways of writing the name of Jerusalem ("Les deux noms de Jérusalem dans l'évangile de Luc," in J. Delorme and J. Duplacy, eds., *La parole de grâce: Études lucaniennes à la mémoire d'Augustin George* = RechSR 69, nos. 1–2 [1981] 57–70): the Hebrew form is used for the outstanding events of salvation history, and the Greek form in the accounts in which the city plays a worldly or even sinful role.

10 One finds in Greek ἡ παράλιος, for ἡ παράλιος χώρα, or ἡ παραλία. Ἡ παραλία (without further specification) also occurs describing the coast of the Mediterranean in Isa 8:23 (LXX).

11 See Lohfink, *Sammlung*.

12 See Bovon, *Lukas*, 128–33.

13 See Peter R. L. Brown, *The Making of Late Antiquity* (Carl Newell Jackson Lectures; Cambridge: Harvard University Press, 1978), 1–26.

14 See the commentary on 4:40–41 above. The verb θεραπεύω ("to heal") suggested itself to Luke because of the parallel in Mark 3:10.

15 Moulton and Milligan name the Flinders Petrie Papyri 2.25 a12 as an example (*Vocabulary, s.v.*): εἰς ἵππον ἐνοχλούμενον ("for a sick horse").

16 Luke is perhaps using ἀπό ("with") consciously with a double sense: they are driven around by spirits (ἀπό in the sense of ὑπό, "by," "with"), and freed from them (ἀπό in the usual sense, "from"). As is his habit, Luke relates ἀπὸ πνευμάτων ἀκαθάρτων ("with unclean spirits") both to what precedes and what follows; see Plummer, 176.

17 See the commentary on Luke 5:17 above.

healed. Divine power went out as radiance already from Moses (Exod 34:29–35). The healing power of the divine was claimed in antiquity by various cultures as propaganda or apologetic. Here it is demonstrated: God is with Jesus; his will, his power, corresponds to the hopes of the crowd. But as already in 4:42–44, the speech that follows shows that people cannot live from this power alone, but from the word of God transmitted by Jesus. In Israel and in Greece, an elite struggled in vain against the success of "divine physicians." Luke knew no such inhibitions.[18]

Conclusion

The summary passage portrays the encounter of the physician and prophet, endowed by God, with the various groups within the chosen people. The divine condescension meets the human quest. The people, who have taken upon themselves the risk of this encounter, are first made capable of hearing by the healing of all (v. 19). Only then can the messianic "he" (αὐτός) address his disciples (v. 20a).

18   See Augustin George, "Le miracle dans l'œuvre de Luc," in Xavier Léon-Dufour, ed., *Les miracles de Jésus selon le Nouveau Testament* (Parole de Dieu; Paris: Seuil, 1977) 249–68, reprinted in George, *Études,* 133–48, esp. 102–3.

The Sermon on the Plain (6:20–49)

Bibliography

Barth, Gerhard, and Tor Aukrust, "Bergpredigt," *TRE* 5 (1979) 603–26.

Bartsch, Hans-Werner, "Feldrede und Bergpredigt. Redaktionsarbeit in Luk. 6," *ThZ* 16 (1960) 5–18.

Betz, Hans Dieter, *Essays on the Sermon on the Mount* (Philadelphia: Fortress Press, 1984).

idem, *The Sermon on the Mount: A Commentary on the Sermon on the Mount Including the Sermon on the Plain (Matthew 5:3—7:27 and Luke 6:20–49)* (Hermeneia; Minneapolis: Fortress Press, 1995).

Bonnard, Pierre, "Le Sermon sur la montagne," *RThPh* 3, 3d series (1953) 233–46, reprinted in idem, *Anamnesis: Recherches sur le Nouveau Testament* (Cahiers de la *RThPh* 3; Lausanne: Revue de théologie et de philosophie, 1980) 81–92.

Bornhäuser, Karl, *Die Bergpredigt: Versuch einer zeitgenössischen Auslegung* (BFCTh 2.7; Gütersloh: Bertelsmann, 1923).

Bornkamm, Günther, "Der Aufbau der Bergpredigt," *NTS* 24 (1977–78) 419–32.

Davies, William D., *The Setting of the Sermon on the Mount* (Cambridge: Cambridge University Press, 1964).

idem, *The Sermon on the Mount* (Cambridge: Cambridge University Press, 1966).

Eichholz, Georg, *Auslegung der Bergpredigt* (BibS[N]; Neukirchen-Vluyn: Neukirchener Verlag, 1965).

Frankemölle, Hubert, "Neue Literatur zur Bergpredigt," *TRev* 79 (1983) 177–98.

Grundmann, Walter, "Die Bergpredigt nach der Lukasfassung," *StEv* 1 (1959) 180–89 (= TU 73).

Jeremias, *Sprache*, 138–51.

Kahlefeld, Heinrich, *Der Jünger: Eine Auslegung der Rede Lk 6,20–49* (Frankfurt: J. Knecht, 1962).

Kennedy, George A., *New Testament Interpretation Through Rhetorical Criticism* (Chapel Hill: University of North Carolina Press, 1984) 63–67.

Kieffer, *Essais*, 26–50.

Kissinger, Warren S., *The Sermon on the Mount: A History of Interpretation and Bibliography* (ATLA Bibliographic Series 3; Metuchen, N.J.: Scarecrow, 1975).

Lambrecht, Jan, *The Sermon on the Mount: Proclamation and Exhortation* (Wilmington, Del.: Glazier, 1985).

Lührmann, Dieter, *Die Redaktion der Logienquelle: Anhang: Zur weiteren Überlieferung der Logienquelle* (WMANT 33; Neukirchen-Vluyn: Neukirchener Verlag, 1969) 53–56.

Luz, Ulrich, "Sermon on the Mount/Plain: Reconstruction of QMt and QLk," in K. H. Richards, ed., SBLSP 22 (Chico, Calif.: Scholars Press, 1983) 473–79.

Mánek, "On the Mount."

Menestrina, Giovanni, "Matteo 5–7 e Luca 6:20–49 nell'Evangelo di Tommaso," *BeO* 18 (1976) 65–67.

Minear, "Audiences."

Robinson, James M., "The Sermon on the Mount/Plain: Work Sheets for the Reconstruction of Q," in Richards, SBLSP 22, 451–54.

Schürmann, Heinz, "Die Warnung des Lukas vor der Falschlehre in der 'Predigt am Berge,' Lk 6:20–49," *BZ* n.s. 10 (1966) 57–81, reprinted in idem, *Untersuchungen*, 290–309 (cited from the collected essays).

Stevens, B. L., "Understanding the Sermon on the Mount, Its Rabbinic and New Testament Context," *Theological Educator* (1992) 83–95.

Strecker, Georg, *The Sermon on the Mount: An Exegetical Commentary* (trans. O. C. Dean Jr.; Nashville: Abingdon, 1988).

Topel, L. John, "The Lukan Version of the Lord's Sermon," *BTB* 11 (1981) 48–53.

Weder, Hans, *Die "Rede der Reden": Eine Auslegung der Bergpredigt heute* (Zurich: Theologischer Verlag, 1985).

Windisch, Hans, *Der Sinn der Bergpredigt: Ein Beitrag zum geschichtlichen Verständnis der Evangelien und zum Problem der richtigen Exegese* (2d ed.; Leipzig: Hinrichs, 1937).

Worden, Ronald D., "A Philological Analysis of Luke 6:20b–49" (Ph.D. diss., Princeton Theological Seminary, 1973).

idem, "The Q Sermon on the Mount/Plain: Variants and Reconstruction," in Richards, SBLSP 22, 455–71.

Wrege, *Bergpredigt*.

Analysis

In both scholarship and the church, the Matthean Sermon on the Mount has crowded out the Lukan Sermon on the Plain, which must be heard in its own guise.[1] Up to this point in the Gospel of Luke, Jesus has spoken only in isolated sayings (2:49; 4:4, 8, 12, etc.). Even the programmatic sermon in Nazareth (4:16–40) has remained a dialogue in structure. Now that he has called

---

1   Both *RGG* (3d ed.) and *TRE* devote an article to the Sermon on the Mount, but not to the Sermon on the Plain.

his disciples (5:1–11, 27–28) and has chosen the Twelve (6:12–16), the readers await some instruction.

According to Luke, Jesus' first great discourse, now to follow, is intended not only for the disciples (church) or the Twelve (the church officers),[2] but also for the nation. It is not an esoteric teaching, nor is it intended only for inner-church use. Alongside the disciples stand those sympathizing with Jesus. They come from both Judaism and paganism. They have all come along "to hear him" (6:18). Luke's two volumes are intended for both groups.

The introduction of the Sermon on the Plain in 6:20, and the back reference to it in 7:1, show that Luke considers 6:20–49 to be a self-contained speech of Jesus. Within this unit, however, there are two resumptions of the discourse: in v. 27 (signaled by Jesus himself) and in v. 39 (in the form of an incidental remark). Thus the beatitudes and the woes form a first part (vv. 20–26). Then follows a series of imperative sentences, which forms a second part (vv. 27–38), and then a chain of metaphors and parables—again departing stylistically from what precedes it—rounds out a third part (vv. 39–49).

In v. 20 only the disciples are explicitly addressed (v. 20a), but in the second and third parts, the crowd is included (vv. 27a, 39a). One should not overestimate these distinctions, since the resumption in v. 27, in addition to structuring the discourse, also performs a further function: after the series of woes[3] at the end of the first part, the listeners[4] who are open to Jesus' teaching must be drawn back into the action.

Luke scarcely offers any hints for divining the structure and process of thought in the speech. There is only a chain of sayings, which, because of his reverence for the words of the Lord, Luke interprets only slightly. In comparison with the words of Jesus transmitted previously in isolated sayings, the improvement here consists only of their collection into the speech before us.[5] Matthew has intervened more profoundly as a redactor,

but without actually leaving behind the genre of the sayings collection.

1. (6:17–19): the frame of the discourse

Part one

2. (6:20–23): the beatitudes
3. (6:24–26): the woes

Part two

4. (6:27–28): love of enemies (four imperatives in the second person plural)
5. (6:29–30): on not resisting (four imperatives in the second person singular)
6. (6:31): the Golden Rule
7. (6:32–34): a supporting argument (three examples)
8. (6:35a): love of enemies (three imperatives in the second person plural)
9. (6:35b): a double promise with justification
10. (6:36): reciprocity formula
11. (6:37–38a): on not judging; on giving (four imperatives in the second person plural)
12. (6:38b): the good measure as a reward
13. (6:38c): the measure as challenge

Part three

14. (6:39): the blind leader
15. (6:40): the master and his students
16. (6:41–42): the splinter and the beam
17. (6:43–44): the tree
18. (6:45): the individual
19. (6:46): Lord, Lord
20. (6:47–49): the two houses

21. (7:1): conclusion and transition

Even at this point, some features are striking: (1) The juxtaposition of those who are blessed and those who are warned at the beginning corresponds, at the end, to a repeated "teaching of the two ways" (from v. 39

---

2   The Twelve next appear as a group in 8:1.
3   The opponents present in 6:1–11 have since disappeared. They reappear only in 7:20, and there again, in a speech by Jesus.
4   Paul Sevier Minear lays great weight on the change of audience ("Jesus' Audiences, According to Luke," *NovT* 16 [1974] 81–109): in vv. 20–26 Jesus is speaking to those who have been won over by his mes-

sage, and in vv. 27–49 to those still hesitating. Dupont, on the other hand, is of the opinion that Luke is returning to the audience of v. 20 after addressing the rich (= unbelieving Jews) in vv. 24–26 (*Béatitudes*, 3.21–40). My position lies between these two extremes.
5   The same situation is present in Q and the *Gospel of Thomas*.

onward). In the first and third parts, then, a dualistic view of life is predominant, as it is in wisdom writings in the Hebrew Bible. (2) The middle part is chiefly concerned with the command to love one's enemy, found before and after the Golden Rule. Verses 36–38 do not exactly fit the context for this reason: v. 36 connects thematically with v. 35 (the kindness of God), while the concept of reward may explain the proximity of vv. 37–38 to v. 35. (3) Catchword association is especially evident in v. 38b–c ($\mu \acute{\epsilon} \tau \rho o \nu$, "measure"), where the sayings have little commonality of content.

In comparison with the Sermon on the Mount in Matthew, the Lukan Sermon on the Plain has a more missionary effect, particularly in its second part; in view of the audience here presupposed, this is hardly surprising.[6] With respect to the audience, one could perhaps even speak of a chiasm:[7] in vv. 12–16 the apostles are addressed; in vv. 17–19, the disciples; in 20–38, the disciples again; and in 39–49, correspondingly, the apostles. The Beatitudes, with their eschatological promise, are thereby directed toward the disciples (indicative), while the apostles are addressed from three angles (imperative, vv. 39–49).[8] Just as Matthew structures his Sermon on the Mount according to his anti-Pharisaic perspective, Luke interprets his Sermon on the Plain and makes it relevant with a view to his own situation and environment.

Heinz Schürmann emphasizes that the Lukan Sermon on the Plain appeals to believers, to those who have long been Christians; in vv. 20–26 they are reminded of their baptism and the origin of their faith, while vv. 27–38 sharpen the love commandment anew, and vv. 39–49 warn of false leaders. This would correspond (indeed, only in the case of vv. 27–49) to Eph 4:25–5:14 and the *Didache*. Thus the mountain/plain scenario would mean that the church stands before its Lord just as Israel stood before its intermediary, come down from Sinai: "The word of Jesus should further resound in the church and through the church as a living kerygma."[9]

As in rhetorical theory, one can also differentiate the exordium from the peroration (conclusion), both of which constitute the frame for two parts (love of enemies, and the love commandment).[10]

History of Transmission

The only elements from Mark are the summary passage (Luke 6:17–20a), which Luke uses as the setting and introduction, and the second saying about the measure (Luke 6:38c). At the same time, most of the words in the Sermon on the Plain can be found in Matthew's Sermon on the Mount (except Luke 6:27–28, 35a). Two further sayings (Luke 6:39, 40) are transmitted in Matthew in another context (Matt 15:14; 10:24–25a). Luke's doubling of the saying about love for enemies is worth noting (Luke 6:27–28, 35a).

The common tradition used in both the Sermon on the Mount/Plain also seems to have had largely the same sequence.[11] It is only in the paragraph about love of enemies (Matt 5:38–47) that the numbers of my outline appear in this order: 5, 4, 9, 7; the Golden Rule also appears much later in Matthew (7:12). Only two actual

---

6 See Minear, "Audiences," 104–9. On the composition of the audience, see n. 4 above.

7 See Walter Grundmann, "Die Bergpredigt nach der Lukasfassung," *StEv* 1 (1959) 180–89 (= TU 73).

8 Bartsch argues that the sermon, because of the "you" (in the singular and plural), has the character of an *eschatological* discourse directed at the entire population (aside from the Beatitudes, which are aimed only at the disciples). Within vv. 27–47, only vv. 27–31 and 37–38 are parenetic and not kerygmatic.

9 Heinz Schürmann, "Die Warnung des Lukas vor der Falschlehre in der 'Predigt am Berge,' Lk 6:20–49," in idem, *Untersuchungen,* 290–309, esp. 292.

10 See Lagrange (p. 183) and Dupont (*Béatitudes,* 1.200). They divide the sermon into the following units: Lagrange: vv. 20b–26, vv. 27–38, vv. 39–45, vv. 46–49; Dupont: vv. 20b–26 (exordium), vv. 27–36 (I), vv. 37–42 (II), vv. 43–49 (peroration). Their opinions, of course, diverge along the manner in which they divide the verses. See also Savas Agouridès, "La tradition des béatitudes chez Matthieu et Luc," in Descamps and de Halleux, *Mélanges,* 9–27, esp. 16.

11 Jacques Dupont vehemently reminds us in his Italian discussion of Hans-Theo Wrege's monograph (*Die Überlieferungsgeschichte der Bergpredigt* [WUNT 9; Tübingen: Mohr-Siebeck, 1968]), countering Wrege's position: "The same elements grouped together in Luke 6:20–49 are found again in Matt 5–7 *in the same order* (author's emphasis)" (*Rivista di storia e letteratura religiosa* 4 [1968] 560).

transpositions occur: 5/4 and 9/7. There is no question that the Sermon on the Mount also includes a whole host of sayings that Luke either does not know[12] or that he transmits elsewhere,[13] often in shortened form.[14]

The degree of literal agreement in the parallel passages varies greatly. The similarities are especially evident in a few of the parabolic sayings (Luke 6:41–42, 44, 45, 47–49). The more important the sayings were (the Beatitudes and love of enemies), the more vividly they were transmitted, and the more violent the debate over them in the early communities.

The literary relationship of the two discourses has been the object of countless studies.[15] Whereas Augustine[16] assumed a common source, an orthodox exegete[17] will still today try to defend the hypothesis of speeches given on two different occasions. Of the fifteen theoretical solutions tabulated by René Kieffer,[18] the most important are (1) Matthew and Luke used the same source, which each supplements and adapts; (2) both possess different sources; (3) one, probably Luke, knows the other, Matthew. The rediscovery of the significance of oral transmission has refined methods of research. By this means we know that orally transmitted sayings are

preserved with veneration in various constellations. Written activity, then, did not interrupt the continued life of the oral tradition.[19] Whoever used a written source still remained simultaneously under the influence of the oral tradition of the church. Several patristic citations do not originate in the Sermon on the Mount or the Plain, but in oral tradition.[20] Redaction history has also taught us to recognize the freedom and coherence of each evangelist.

The Griesbach hypothesis, whereby Luke would have known and reworked the first Gospel, for example, striking every allusion to the Law of Moses, is untenable.[21] The hypothesis of a Lukan special source is no more probable.[22] The same sequence in both discourses militates against it. Behind both texts there is likely a single Greek, probably written source, namely Q, which might approximately agree with Luke's version (on the woes, see below).

In Q, as in both Gospels, the discourse seems to have been an inaugural speech. Matthew, however, wants to construct a first large collection of Jesus' sayings; so he also includes here such sayings as Luke transmits elsewhere. Matthew also formulates sayings from his cate-

---

12   Matt 5:33–37: on swearing; 6:1–4: on giving alms; 6:16–18: on fasting; 6:22–23: the eye as lamp of the body; 7:6: pearls.

13   Matt 5:13: salt of the earth (Luke 14:34); 5:14–16: light of the world (Luke 8:16); 5:17–20: on the Law (Luke 16:16–17); 5:21–26: on the way to the judge (Luke 12:57–59); 5:27–32: cut off the hand, and divorce (Luke 9:43–48; 16:8); 6:5–15: prayer (Luke 11:1–4); 6:19–21: on gathering treasure (Luke 12:33–34); 6:24: two lords (Luke 16:13); 6:25–34: on cares (Luke 12:22–32); 7:7–11: on answers to requests (Luke 11:9–13); 7:13–14: two ways (Luke 13:23–24); 7:22–23: rejection (Luke 13:25–27).

14   The conclusion of the Sermon on the Mount is reminiscent, in its first section (Matt 7:28a), of the conclusion of the Sermon on the Plain (Luke 7:1, my number 21); but in the second section of the conclusion, Matthew modifies a passage from Mark (1:21–22) to suit his own needs.

15   See the literature cited in Gerhard Barth and Tor Aukrust, "Bergpredigt," *TRE* 5 (1979) 603–26, esp. 616–18, 626; see also Luz, *Matthew*, 209–11.

16   Cf. Augustine *De consensu evangelistarum* 2.19.44–47 (CSEL 43.144–48). See Lagrange, 185–86.

17   See Agouridès, "Béatitudes," 26.

18   See René Kieffer, *Essais de méthodologie néo-testamentaire* (ConBNT 4; Lund: Gleerup, 1972) 31–32.

19   On the relationship between oral tradition and its reduction to writing, see Erhardt Güttgemanns, *Candid Questions Concerning Gospel Form Criticism* (trans. W. G. Doty; PTMS 26; Pittsburgh: Pickwick, 1979) 191–215, 223–33.

20   Cf. the patristic citations listed after each pericope of the Sermon on the Plain in Aland, *Synopsis*.

21   See Johann Jakob Griesbach, *Synoptic and Text-Critical Studies 1776–1976* (SNTSMS 34; ed. B. Orchard and T. R. W. Longstaff; Cambridge: Cambridge University Press, 1978). See also Christopher M. Tuckett, *The Revival of the Griesbach Hypothesis: An Analysis and Appraisal* (Cambridge: Cambridge University Press, 1983).

22   According to Wrege (*Bergpredigt*), Matthew and Luke are dependent not on Q but on separate catechetical traditions (against this view, see Jacques Dupont in his discussion of Wrege's monograph in *Rivista di storia e letteratura religiosa* 4 [1968] 558–60).

chetical experience, which he understands as sayings of Jesus, and introduces others in the form of antitheses, opposing them to Scripture citations.

Luke's redaction is less artistic and creative, but we have already ascertained his logical and theological purpose, which will be confirmed in the specific exegesis. The traditional connection between the Beatitudes and love of enemies is his chief concern, but he interprets these by means of the Golden Rule (v. 31). In the same manner, he adds a kerygmatic counterpoint to the parenetic base of many individual sayings: the ethics of his Sermon on the Plain would be falsely understood if not theologically grounded in the love of God (God as χρηστός, "kind," and οἰκτίρμων, "merciful," in vv. 35–36).

The Sermon on the Plain I: Blessings and Woes (6:20–26)

Bibliography

Agouridès, "Béatitudes."

Betz, Hans Dieter, "Die Makarismen der Bergpredigt (Mt 5,3–12): Beobachtungen zur literarischen Form und theologischen Bedeutung," *ZThK* 75 (1978) 3–19.

idem, *Sermon on the Mount,* ad loc.

Broer, Ingo, *Die Seligpreisungen der Bergpredigt: Studien zu ihrer Überlieferung und Interpretation* (BBB 61; Bonn: Hanstein, 1986).

Brown, Raymond E., "The Beatitudes according to St. Luke," in idem, *New Testament Essays* (Milwaukee: Bruce, 1965) 334–41.

Catchpole, D. R., "Jesus and the Community of Israel—the Inaugural Discourse in Q," *BJRL* 68 (1986) 296–316.

Degenhardt, Hans-Joachim, *Lukas, Evangelist der Armen: Besitz und Besitzverzicht in den lukanischen Schriften: Eine traditions- und rekaktionsgeschichtliche Untersuchung* (Stuttgart: Katholisches Bibelwerk, 1965) 43–53.

Dupont, Jacques, "'Béatitudes' égyptiennes," *Bib* 47 (1966) 185–222.

idem, *Béatitudes,* 1.265–98; 3.19–206.

idem, "Introduction aux Béatitudes," *NRTh* 98 (1976) 97–108.

idem, "Le message des Béatitudes," *CEv* 24 (1978) 24–37.

Flusser, D., "Notes."

Frankemölle, Hubert, "Die Makarismen (Mt 5,1–12; Lk 6,20–23): Motive und Umfang der redaktionellen Komposition," *BZ* n.s. 15 (1971) 52–75.

George, Augustin, "La 'forme' des béatitudes jusqu'à Jésus," in *Mélanges bibliques rédigés en honneur d'André Robert* (Paris: Bloud et Gay, 1957) 398–403.

Jacquemin, "Béatitudes."

Jeremias, *Sprache,* 138–40.

Kähler, G. Christoph, "Studien zur Form- und Traditionsgeschichte der biblischen Makarismen" (diss.; Jena, 1974); see *ThLZ* 101 (1976) 77–80.

Karris, Robert J., "Poor and Rich: The Lukan Sitz im Leben," in Talbert, *Perspectives,* 112–25.

Kieffer, *Essais,* 26–50.

idem, "Weisheit und Segen als Grundmotive der Seligpreisungen bei Matthäus und Lukas," in A. Fuchs, ed., *Theologie aus dem Norden* (SNTU A.2; Linz: Albert Fuchs, 1977) 29–43.

Klein, Peter, "Die lukanischen Weherufe Lk 6,24–26," *ZNW* 71 (1980) 150–59.

Kloppenborg, John S., "Blessing and Marginality: The 'Persecution Beatitude' in Q, Thomas & Early Christianity," *Forum* 2 (1986) 36–56.

Koch, *Growth,* 6–8, 16–18, 28–29, 39–44, 59–62.

Lachs, Samuel T., "Some Textual Observations on the Sermon on the Mount," *JQR* 69 (1978–79) 98–111.

Lapide, "Bergpredigt."

Lührmann, *Logienquelle,* 53–56.

Manson, Thomas W., *The Sayings of Jesus* (3rd ed.; London: SCM, 1950) 47–49.

McEleney, Neil J., "The Beatitudes of the Sermon on the Mount/Plain," *CBQ* 43 (1981) 1–13.

Nickelsburg, George W. E., "Riches, the Rich, and God's Judgment in I Enoch 92–105 and the Gospel according to Luke," *NTS* 25 (1978–79) 324–44.

Percy, Ernst, *Botschaft,* 40–108.

Pokorný, "Core."

Rehkopf, *Sonderquelle,* 8–11, 19–20, 96.

Schottroff, Luise, "Selig die Armen—wehe den Reichen," *Entschluß* 8–9 (1977) 8–11, 19–20, 96.

idem and Stegemann, *Jesus,* 89–153.

Schulz, *Q,* 76–84.

Schwarz, Günther, "Lk 6,22a.23c.26: Emendation, Rückübersetzung, Interpretation," *ZNW* 66 (1975) 269–74.

Schweizer, Eduard, "Formgeschichtliches zu den Seligpreisungen Jesu," *NTS* 19 (1972/1973) 121–26.

Smith, P., "Beatitudes and Woes," *Journal of Spiritual Formation* 15 (1994) 35–45.

Steinhauser, Michael G., "The Beatitudes and Eschatology: Announcing the Kingdom," *Living Light* 19 (1982) 121–29.

Stenger, Werner, "Die Seligpreisung der Geschmähten (Mt 5,11–12; Lk 6,22–23)," *Kairos* 28 (1986) 33–60.

Stramare, P. Tarcisio, "Le beatitudini e la critica letteraria," *RivB* 13 (1965) 31–39.

Strecker, Georg, "Die Makarismen der Bergpredigt," *NTS* 17 (1970–71) 255–75.

Tiede, David L., "Luke 6,17–26," *Int* 40 (1986) 63–68.

Tuckett, Christopher M., "The Beatitudes: A Source-Critical Study: With a Reply by M. D. Goulder," *NovT* 25 (1983) 193–216.

Waitz, Hans, "Eine Parallele zu den Seligpreisungen aus einem außerkanonischen Evangelium," *ZNW* 4 (1903) 335–40.

20 Then he turned his eyes to his disciples and said: "Blessed are you who are poor, for yours is the kingdom of God. **21/** Blessed are you who are hungry now, for you will be filled. Blessed are you who weep now, for you will laugh. **22/** Blessed are you when people hate you, and when they exclude you, revile you, and cast out your name as evil on account of the Son of Man. **23/** Rejoice in that day and leap, for surely your reward is great in heaven; for that is what their ancestors did to the prophets. **24/** But woe to you who are rich, for you have already received your consolation. 25/ Woe to you who are full now, for you will be hungry. Woe to you who are laughing now, for you will mourn and weep. 26/ Woe to you when all speak well of you, for that is what their ancestors did to the false prophets."

Analysis

History of Transmission
Four early Christian texts contain beatitudes that display similarities: the Sermon on the Mount (Matt 5:1–12), the Sermon on the Plain (Luke 6:20–26), the *Gospel of Thomas* (log. 54, 68–69; cf. 58), and the *Acts of Paul and Thecla* (chaps. 5–6).[1]

The *Acts of Paul and Thecla* quote two beatitudes, which are probably taken from Matt 5:8 and 5:7. The rest are composed by the authors from passages in Paul's letters and from their own encratic perspective. These beatitudes do not date back to a time prior to Matthew or Luke. In the *Gospel of Thomas*, two of the beatitudes are isolated (log. 54 corresponds to Luke 6:20; log. 58 is similar to Matt 5:10), and three others appear as a unit.[2] The author thus knows at least three of the four Lukan beatitudes; but only the first (*Gos. Thom.* 54) is identical to the Lukan version. The last (*Gos. Thom.* 69b) is closer to Luke than to Matthew, but is not without its differences.[3] The additional beatitudes in Matthew and the woes in Luke are entirely absent.[4] The author knows the beatitude about persecution in two, or even three, forms (*Gos. Thom.* 58, 68, and perhaps 69a). Is *Thomas* dependent on Q and oral tradition? The earliest quotations in 1 Pet 4:14 and Polycarp *Phil.* 2.3 show that the early Christians used Jesus' beatitudes in free citation.

The first three Lukan beatitudes, transmitted as a unit, presumably go back to Jesus himself, but so also may the fourth, which is longer and was composed in a different style, and was first transmitted as a separate saying. These four beatitudes appear in immediate proximity as early as Q, although the fourth at this point still also circulated independently.[5] The three additional sayings (about the meek, the pure in heart, and the peacemakers) were possibly composed by means of exegetical work in the time between Q and Matthew, in an "intermediate stage."[6] Matthew attempts to form a complete collection: he collates Q, the exegetical additions, and the isolated beatitude about the persecuted, and composes a further one about the "merciful." Luke uses Q, but he, or an intermediary tradent, expands them with the woes. The very limited traces of these in patristic literature suggest a late date for their origin.

In terms of tradition history, the *Gospel of Thomas* has an earlier feel than Matthew and Luke. Its author knows only of Q and the isolated beatitude about the persecuted; by contrast, for the Lukan collection Tertullian is one of the oldest witnesses. The *Acts of Philip*, from the fourth century, shows the Christian love of composition. In a newly discovered portion, I have found these additional beatitudes: "Blessed are the upright in Jesus' word, for they will inherit the earth. Blessed are those who have hated the glory of this world, for they will be glorified. Blessed are those who have received the word of God, for they will inherit incorruptibility."[7]

Genre
One finds beatitudes in antiquity in various cultural matrixes, for example, in Egypt and Greece.[8] In Israel

1 The case of the *Kerygmata Petrou* is interesting; see Hans Waitz, "Eine Parallele zu den Seligpreisungen aus einem außerkanonischen Evangelium," *ZNW* 4 (1903) 335–40.
2 Log. 68 corresponds to Luke 6:22 par. Matt 5:11; log. 69a has no direct NT parallels, but could be a variant of Luke 6:21b; log. 69b corresponds to Luke 6:21a.
3 In log. 69b the third person appears instead of the second, there is no "now," and the saying has a different conclusion (". . . him who desires").
4 *Did.* 1.5 knows of the juxtaposition of a beatitude and a woe.
5 As can be seen in 1 Pet 4:14; Jas 1:12; Matt 5:10; *Hermas* 105.6–8 (*Sim.* 9.28.6–8).
6 See Klaus Koch, *The Growth of the Biblical Tradition:*

The Form-Critical Method (trans. S. M. Cupitt; New York: Scribner's, 1969) 41–42.
7 *Act. Phil.* 5.25(63) (according to the ms. Athous, Xenonphontos 32, folio 58 *recto*). See François Bovon, Betrand Bouvier, and Frédéric Amsler, *Acta Philippi* (CCSA 11; Turnhout: Brepols, 1999) 171.
8 See Jacques Dupont, "'Béatitudes' égyptiennes," *Bib* 47 (1966) 185–222. In Egypt beatitudes were cultic language, and they were employed to praise those who walked in the way of the god. On Greece see Koch, *Growth*, 18. Above all, the words $\mu\acute{\alpha}\kappa\alpha\rho$, $\acute{o}\lambda\beta\iota\sigma\varsigma$, and $\epsilon\grave{v}\delta\alpha\acute{\iota}\mu\omega\nu$ are used. It seems that justifications for the designation were not given. The gods themselves could be the addressees of the beatitudes: how could they not be blessed?

they occur in cultic and wisdom literature, usually at the beginning (Ps 1:1) or at the end (Prov 8:32–36) of an exposition.[9] The content of the promise is earthly prosperity, and later, especially in apocalyptic literature, eschatological salvation (Dan 12:12),[10] which explains the characteristic of happiness (Tob 13:15–16).

Formally, along with the isolated beatitude, small collections of them develop (Sir 25:7–11; *2 Enoch* 42.6–12); and exclamations of woes also occur in contrast to them (Tob 13:12; *2 Enoch* 52). The New Testament reflects the contemporary situation within the history of this genre at that time, that is, a broad spectrum of possibilities: isolated beatitudes (Luke 14:15), series such as at that at the beginning of the Sermon on the Mount (Matt 5:3–12), and juxtapositions with woes (Luke 6:20–26).[11] Some beatitudes give a justification, others do not. Happiness is usually, though not always, future-oriented and eschatological. It can depend on God or stem from human action.[12] In its typical format, the statement is usually composed in the third person (but cf. Deut 33:29; Ps 128[LXX 127]:2; Eccl 10:17, all in second person).

The question of the functional setting (*Sitz im Leben*) is difficult. In later times the cultic was, in any case, not the only possible setting; both family life, with its happy occurrences, and the schools, in which the happiness of the observant was praised, gave rise to beatitudes. It was even part of good form to open speeches on the most varied occasions with a beatitude (like the first speech of Jesus in Q, Matthew, and Luke), or to close with one. This was also true of rhetoric put down in writing. For this reason, the workroom of the Jewish authors is perhaps the primary functional setting of beatitudes.

Matthew and Luke

The first three beatitudes in Luke are found among the first four in Matthew (in which there is an addition at Matt 5:5, and a different sequence). Until v. 10, Matthew maintains the third person appropriate to the genre,

where Luke has the second person throughout. It is important to Matthew to continue to portray the pious nature of the blessed in the additional beatitudes at 5:5, 7–10. In Luke the blessed are distinguished by their condition: poverty, hunger, and mourning. Luke, for his part, shows an interest in contrasting the present with the future ($\nu\hat{\upsilon}\nu$, "now," appears twice in 6:21).

Three arguments support the third person as the original form of the beatitudes: (1) the genre itself; (2) the first part of the formula, $\mu\alpha\kappa\acute{\alpha}\rho\iota\iota\iota\iota\iota\iota\iota\iota\pi\tau\omega\chi o\acute{\iota}$ ("blessed [are] the poor"), which leaves no reason to expect the second person; (3) the possible influence of the fourth beatitude ("blessed are you . . .") on Luke. Against these reasons, one could object: (1) Jesus adapted the formula to his kerygmatic purpose (poetic license on Jesus' part); (2) Matthew shows the tendency to harmonize formulaic statements with their traditional style. The decision is a difficult one; I consider the third person to be original.

The evaluation of the other divergent elements is easier: secondary touches include $\tau\hat{\wp}\ \pi\nu\epsilon\acute{\upsilon}\mu\alpha\tau\iota$ ("in spirit," Matt 5:3) and $\kappa\alpha\grave{\iota}\ \delta\iota\psi\hat{\omega}\nu\tau\epsilon\varsigma\ \tau\grave{\eta}\nu\ \delta\iota\kappa\alpha\iota o\sigma\acute{\upsilon}\nu\eta\nu$ ("and thirst for righteousness," Matt 5:6), as well as $\dot{\eta}\ \beta\alpha\sigma\iota-\lambda\epsilon\acute{\iota}\alpha\ \tau\hat{\omega}\nu\ o\dot{\upsilon}\rho\alpha\nu\hat{\omega}\nu$ ("the kingdom of heaven," Matt 5:3) compared with $\dot{\eta}\ \beta\alpha\sigma\iota\lambda\epsilon\acute{\iota}\alpha\ \tauo\hat{\upsilon}\ \vartheta\epsilono\hat{\upsilon}$ ("the kingdom of God," Luke 6:20). Both occurrences of $\nu\hat{\upsilon}\nu$ ("now," Luke 6:21) are Lukan additions. The differences in composition between $o\acute{\iota}\ \pi\epsilon\nu\vartheta o\hat{\upsilon}\nu\tau\epsilon\varsigma$ ("those who mourn," Matthew) and $o\acute{\iota}\ \kappa\lambda\alpha\acute{\iota}o\nu\tau\epsilon\varsigma$ ("you who weep now," Luke), as between $\pi\alpha\rho\alpha\kappa\lambda\eta\vartheta\acute{\eta}\sigma o\nu\tau\alpha\iota$ ("they will be comforted," Matthew) and $\gamma\epsilon\lambda\acute{\alpha}\sigma\epsilon\tau\epsilon$ ("you will laugh," Luke), can be explained by assuming that Matthew found the vocabulary of Q too prosaic and altered it. Of course, the related forms $\pi\alpha\rho\acute{\alpha}\kappa\lambda\eta\sigma\iota\varsigma$ ("consolation," Luke 6: 24) and $\pi\epsilon\nu\vartheta\acute{\eta}\sigma\epsilon\tau\epsilon$ ("you will mourn," Luke 6:25) occur in the Lukan woes. Was it that Matthew drew his corrections from the woes, of which he was aware, though he did not use them? The $\alpha\dot{\upsilon}\tauo\acute{\iota}$ ("they") in the second half of the Matthean beatitudes are probably

---

9   אַשְׁרֵי (plural, *status constructus*): the meaning is "hail to the one who . . . ," "happy is the one. . . ."

10   Rabbinic literature contains few beatitudes; when they occur, they have no apocalyptic valence.

11   In Revelation seven beatitudes appear scattered through the text (1:3; 14:13; 16:15; 19:9; 20:6; 22:7, 14), as well as seven woes (8:13; 9:12; 11:14; 12:12; 18:10, 16, 19).

12   See G. Christoph Kähler, "Studien zur Form- und Traditionsgeschichte der biblischen Makarismen" (diss.; Jena, 1974); see *ThLZ* 101 (1976) 77–80.

redactional, and the Lukan sequence (the poor, the hungry, the mourning) is likely the original one.[13]

In Luke's fourth and last beatitude, the situation (v. 22b), which is noted in the first three by a single word, is painted in detail. The temporal clause (ὅταν, "when") forces the author to introduce ἐστέ ("are you"), which was absent in the first three beatitudes. The beatitude itself is then repeated with a double imperative (v. 23a). Then follows the reason for joy (ἰδοὺ γάρ . . . , "for surely," v. 23b), and a comparison with the past (κατὰ τὰ αὐτὰ γάρ . . . , "for that is what," v. 23c). This complicated structure is traditional, and known to both evangelists. But the tradition might itself be the result of a long process of development. The differences in vocabulary between Luke and Matthew are hard to evaluate. Are these two translations of a single original? The otherwise clearly Greek character of Q refutes this. This particular beatitude is in last place because, consistent with the well-known rule of composition for collections of sayings, one tries to achieve a good conclusion by means of a longer sentence.

Are the woes the product of tradition or redaction? Their secondary character as a colorless negative image of the beatitudes is manifest. In support of their pre-Lukan origin are these considerations: (1) their possible influence on Matthew;[14] (2) idioms untypical of Luke (ἀπέχω, "to receive," with the accusative; πενθέω, "to mourn");[15] (3) the common Jewish literary juxtaposition of blessings and woes. But the weightier arguments advocate Lukan composition: (1) Luke is familiar with the genre of woes;[16] (2) the contrast of rich and poor is typically Lukan (cf. 16:19–31); (3) πεινάω, "to be hungry," also appears next to ἐμπίμπλημι, "to fill," in the Magnificat (1:53); (4) καλῶς λέγω, "to speak well of," is Lukan (cf. Acts 28:25), as is πάντες οἱ ἄνθρωποι ("all"), πλήν ("but"), etc.; (5) the second person plural of the woes fits in with the Lukan beatitudes.[17]

Commentary

How can I, a well-off exegete, dare to interpret the Beatitudes in a world of poverty? In no wise could I style myself an intermediary. My only possible orientation is not on the side of Jesus, but rather on that of the listeners. I may only hear blessings and woes. This seems also to have been Luke's position. It is not even certain that Luke counted the disciples among the poor. Jesus indeed looks at them, but after ἔλεγεν ("[he] said") Luke places no pronoun (in contrast to v. 27). The "you" of the blessings and woes drifts beyond the audience present and describes, almost apocalyptically, the truly blessed and truly accursed. But everyone should feel themselves addressed. According to Luke, Jesus' diagnosis is irrevocable, for Jesus, like Moses, comes from the place of revelation, from the mountain, and conveys, like Moses, the "living word" (Acts 7:38).

Church history stands between us and the Beatitudes. Accordingly, we must, for the time being, ascetically renounce the riches of the history of interpretation in order to hear these sayings in their historical context. Thus the Jewish exegetes are welcome voices.[18] Also especially important is the relationship to the Scriptures (Isa 61:1–2; 29:18–19; 40:29–31), the apocalyptic framework (*T. Jud.* 25:4; 1QH 18.14–15),[19] and the observa-

---

13 Here I am close to the position of Schulz (*Q,* 76–78).

14 See the beginning of this section.

15 Following Rehkopf (*Sonderquelle,* 8–11, 19–20, 96), Jeremias (*Sprache,* 139) understands πλήν ("but") and παράκλησις ("consolation") in an eschatological sense, and declares κατὰ τὰ αὐτά ("that is what," "according to the same") as non-Lukan.

16 10:13; 11:42–52; 17:1; 21:23; 22:22.

17 Dupont (*Béatitudes,* 1.299–342) and Paul-Edmond Jacquemin ("Les béatitudes selon saint Luc: Lc 6,17.20–26," *AsSeign* 37 [1971] 80–91) believe that the woes are redactional. For Lührmann (*Logienquelle,* 54), they are traditional, but not from Q. According to Schürmann (1.336, 339), Schneider (1.151), and Hubert Frankemölle ("Die Makarismen [Mt 5,1–12; Lk 6,20–23]: Motive und Umfang der redaktionellen Komposition," *BZ* n.s. 15 [1971] 52–75, esp. 64–66), they are traditional and unquestionably from Q: Matthew knew them, but did not transmit them.

18 I have consulted David Flusser, "Some Notes on the Beatitudes (Mt 5,3–12; Lc 6,20–26)," *Imm* 8 (1976) 37–47; Pinchas Lapide, "Die Bergpredigt—Theorie und Praxis," *ZEE* 17 (1973) 369–72; and Samuel T. Lachs, "Some Textual Observations on the Sermon on the Mount," *JQR* 69 (1978–79) 98–111.

19 Cf. *T. Jud.* 25:4: "And those who died in sorrow shall be raised in joy; and those who died in poverty for the Lord's sake shall be made rich; those who

tion that, "in Jesus' Hebrew words both the spiritual and the social aspect were present."[20]

But the Gospel of Luke is a Christian text, and a bit of church history already stands between Jesus and his editors. Luke wants to hear Jesus and let him be heard, but his literary and exegetical abilities did not remain idle. Just as a photo often tells more about the photographer than the person photographed, Luke's text, at first analysis, characterizes its author.[21]

Rich and Poor (vv. 20, 24)

■ **20, 24** Luke is happy that tradition puts the poor in first place. Although Jewish Christian tradition still holds to the double connotation of πτωχός ("poor"), Luke understands the word concretely.[22] Throughout his Gospel he draws a portrait of the disciple as a person who is poor, or has become so. This image, however, is replaced in Acts with that of sharing. The word πτωχός disappears there.

One can schematize contemporary interpretations as follows: (1) Luke transmits an Ebionite tradition, which had its origin in Jesus, for whom property and the kingdom of God were irreconcilable (Ernst Percy); (2) a literally understood command of poverty applied only to the elite, the officials of the congregation (Hans-Joachim Degenhardt), or to the Christians who have progressed in their faith (in the sense of the Catholic distinction

between *consilia* and *praecepta* in the Gospels); (3) poverty is an ideal (Pierre Grelot); (4) Luke requires only the inner willingness to leave everything (Jacques Dupont); (5) he sketches a graphic portrait of poor disciples, but in his time, with its bourgeois conditions, literal poverty is not his literary aim. Its image should merely encourage generosity (Luise Schottroff).[23]

The following observations are pertinent. First, in sociological terms, Luke, his community, and his potential readership have established themselves in one of the higher classes. They are not exactly poor, and for this reason, they struggle fiercely with the problem of possessions.[24] Second, Luke has been influenced theologically by a tradition of apocalyptic judgment of the rich and the poor.[25] Third, whereas πορνεία ("prostitution") is the Hebrew Bible metaphor that illustrated a strained relationship to God, in Luke the attitude of people toward their possessions has become the test of their commitment to the faith. The issue of rich and poor is thus both a highly concrete affair and, simultaneously, a test case for Christian commitment.[26] The poor are the *concrete* heirs of the kingdom, but likewise a symbol of those who, like Luke, resemble them. And the property owners who wish to be like the poor no longer enjoy their possessions, their παράκλησις ("consolation," v. 24), but achieve the παράκλησις of others through their beneficence. A few summary passages in Acts

---

died on account of the Lord shall be wakened to life" (trans. H. C. Kee, "Testaments of the Twelve Patriarchs," in *OTP* 1.775–828, esp. 802). Cf. also 1QH 18.14–15: "that to the humble he might bring glad tidings of thy great mercy, [. . .] from out of the fountain [. . . contrite] of spirit, and everlasting joy to those who mourn."

20 Flusser, "Notes," 43.

21 One should not forget that we ourselves have no direct access to Luke. Between him and us stand a series of copyists who displayed definite creativity. It suffices to bring to mind how a few of them attempted to harmonize the Lukan text with that of Matthew by adding τῷ πνεύματι ("in spirit") in v. 20, by transposing it into the third person, and by omitting νῦν ("now").

22 Πτωχός means lit. "the one who cowers," "the one who hides himself," and then, "the poor," "the lowly." The situation of neediness is expressed with ἐνδεής, i.e., "the one in a situation of need," "the one who suffers lack" (cf. Acts 4:34). Πένης describes a person who struggles just to live, the

poor or needy. The concept of poverty underwent a clear development in the HB: from punishment to nearness to God. On the piety of the poor, see Pss 40:17 (LXX 39:18); 69(LXX 68):30–34. By the time of the Seleucids, the equation of poverty and piety gained general currency: *Ps. Sol.* 10:6; 1QM 14.6–7; *T. Jud.* 25:4. On the approximation of poor to holy cf. the Talmud, *b. Ber.* 6b; and Jas 1:9; 2:5; 5:1–6 in the NT.

23 These positions are summarized in Bovon, *Theologian*, 390–96, 481–82 (except for Schottroff and Stegemann, *Jesus*, 67–120); see also Bovon, *Lukas*, 51–52, 54 n. 42.

24 See Robert Karris, "Poor and Rich: The Lukan Sitz im Leben," in Talbert, *Perspectives*, 112–25.

25 See George W. E. Nickelsburg, "Riches, the Rich, and God's Judgment in I Enoch 92–105 and the Gospel according to Luke," *NTS* 25 (1978–79) 324–44.

26 See Bovon, *Lukas*, 110–12.

(2:44–45; 4:32, 34–35) show, within the church, the concrete outworking envisaged by Luke of these metaphorical beatitudes.

The structure has a very ordinary series of clauses: first a nominal clause ("Blessed are [you] poor," μακάριοι οἱ πτωχοί), and then a causal clause (introduced with ὅτι, "for"). But the hearers will perceive in the short main clause an unbearable tension: how can anyone view the poor as blessed? Something of the rhetorical flair and the theological power of Jesus inheres in this paradox. The dependent clause, which, not without justification, stands *after* the main clause, releases the tension: "for yours is the kingdom of God." Thus the dependent clause has a hermeneutical function. It is not because of their poverty that the poor are happy! On the contrary: Jesus and Luke are in agreement with the Hebrew Bible that poverty is neither a happy condition nor an ideal. But in their poverty the πτωχοί ("poor") can indeed be happy, because they know that the kingdom of God is there for them. What does that mean? God will soon rule and will enforce his justice,[27] which will signify a complete social rehabilitation for the poor. Ἐστίν ("is") designates three things for Luke: a future[28] collective expectation of the kingdom of God ἐν δυνάμει ("in power"); a present ecclesiological beginning of the community of goods among Christians in the sense of the summary passages in Acts; and a future individual source of consolation for the poor in the afterlife (in the sense of Luke's individual eschatology).[29]

Jesus is uniting the wisdom tradition of present happiness with the apocalyptic vision of future salvation. The kingdom of God has already come in hidden fashion through his person, message, and ministry. Neither the situation of the poor nor their virtue is the reason for their happiness, but rather God, who will bring about the just condition of his covenant.[30] In Jesus' mouth, μακάριοι ("blessed") is both an observation and a statement of trust. In relation to the poor, the welfare promised them is a subjective condition, a feeling of contentment that corresponds to an objective situation. From the perspective of God, it is the salvation of the blessed, willed by him and foreordained for the time of the eschaton.[31]

In v. 24 πλήν ("but") marks a change in addressee. Οὐαί could be a Latinism (*vae*): not a curse, but a strong expression for a misfortune, or a lamentation. The formulation ὅτι ἀπέχετε τὴν παράκλησιν ὑμῶν is worth comment. I have translated it thus: "for you have already received your consolation." That means: your happiness is limited to your possessions. Ἀπέχω ("to receive") is a technical term in business jargon: you have been paid in full, you have received your eschatological wages and have issued a receipt for it.[32]

Hunger and Satiety (vv. 21a, 25a)

■ **21a, 25a** Positively, satiety[33] in the Hebrew Bible can describe abundance as a gift of God (e.g., in the image of the eschatological banquet), and, negatively, the sinful satisfaction of desires (e.g., as the longing for the fleshpots of Egypt).[34] The foundation of happiness is neither physical hunger[35] nor the virtue of religious aspiration,

---

27 This is already the hope of the psalmist (whom I cite from the LXX): Ἔγνων ὅτι ποιήσει κύριος τὴν κρίσιν τοῦ πτωχοῦ καὶ τὴν δίκην τῶν πενήτων ("I know that the Lord will exercise judgment for the poor man, and justice for the needy," Ps 140:12 [LXX 139:13]).

28 Luke lets this present tense stand out of respect for the tradition; but if one observes how sharply he differentiates between now (νῦν) and the future, to assume that Luke interprets the Beatitudes in the sense of an imminent eschatological fulfillment is clearly wrong.

29 See Jacquemin, "Béatitudes," 84.

30 On this reversal of situations, see the Magnificat (Luke 1:52–53). Mark 10:29–30 has a similar structure that shows that the existence of believers waiting for the end consists of both joy and privation.

31 In contrast to the profane use of the word in Acts

26:2.

32 On ἀπέχω see BAGD *s.v.* ἀπέχω (1).

33 See Jan Nicolaas Sevenster, "Hungersnot," *BHH* 2 (1964) 753–54.

34 Χορτάζω means, first, "to feed an animal"; see Plato *Resp.* 2.372D; 9.586B. In the NT the verb is no longer used for animals and has no derogatory tone (see Plummer, 180). In Luke cf. 9:17; 15:16; 16:21. In the HB, with the meaning "to be sated," see Ps 37(LXX 36):19. This psalm calls to mind the HB theme of the God who sustains and satisfies the poor; cf. Ps 132(LXX 131):15.

35 Πεινάω means "to be hungry," and designates both the lack of nutrition and the desire for it.

but only the coming intervention of God. In contrast to Matthew, Luke remains at a literal understanding of the proverb. Only in the addition of νῦν ("now") does one detect his hand. With this little word, he attains various purposes: chronological distance until the fulfillment, a limitation of suffering, and a sharpening of the present paradox.

Neither Jesus, Q, nor Luke intends to list a catalogue of misery, but rather to announce the present and final salvific acts of God by means of three typical conditions. The selection corresponds both to present conditions and to the symbolic universe of the Scriptures. Isaiah 61:1–2 was interpreted christologically at Jesus' first public appearance in Nazareth (Luke 4:16–30). Of the recipients of salvation mentioned there, we find only the poor in the Beatitudes. But the same types are envisaged both here and there.[36] In Luke, Jesus' pronouncement of the Beatitudes (6:20a) lends them a kerygmatic scope, whereas Matthew is more concerned with the ethical situation of the believer.

Even more than in the case of the first beatitude, Luke presupposes for the second and third a reversal of present relations (cf. commentary on 1:52-53). The beatitudes *and* the woes yield the same message as the Magnificat: (1) present misery is not hopeless; (2) God intends to restore the justice of his convenant; (3) for the believer, the kerygmatic presentation of the divine will contain the tremendous ethical requirement neither to resign oneself nor to worry about the future;[37] (4) it is not enough to speak of material or spiritual compensation, for the promise concerns a new relationship to God and his people for the benefit of the new creation.[38]

Crying and Laughing (vv. 21b, 25b)

■ **21b, 25b** Κλαίω ("to cry") and γελάω ("to laugh") designate not only feelings but also their outwardly percep-

tible expressions. Crying and laughing are messages for others; people see and hear both.[39] Κλαίω is more general than the Matthean πενθέω ("to mourn") and includes, in the ancient Near East, screaming as well.

In the background of this third beatitude is the Hebrew Bible theology of the comforting God.[40] The quintessential experience of mourning was the exile in Babylon (Ps 137[LXX 136]:1), just as the return became the symbol of greatest joy (Jer 31:7–14). The first three beatitudes sound like prophecies of salvation (Isa 66:10).

In the joy of the saved, especially in their laughter, a certain gloating, or even a feeling of revenge, can also be detected.[41] But here the saved, first, do not hope for misfortune for their present rulers (quite different from Ps 137[LXX 136]:9). Second, any partisan or nationalistic outbursts are completely absent. In Jesus' perspective the μακάριοι ("blessed") were probably Jews, but the universalizing Luke has interpreted Jesus' silence in his own fashion.[42] Third, no ethical judgment is rendered: the small circle of the poor is not identified as the cluster of the pious over against the crowd of the godless (Ps 37 [LXX 36]). Even if the μακάριοι are, for Luke, also believers, the eschatological act of God remains the decisive element, rather than human initiative.

In lamentation, mourning is mentioned alongside tears.[43] In the LXX the unfortunate also mourn about themselves (Isa 3:26; 24:4).

Persecution (vv. 22–23, 26)

■ **22–23, 26** In the beatitude for the despised, Jesus continues the Hebrew Bible tradition of the persecuted prophets (cf. 13:34–35). It is transmitted both in Q and as an independent saying. Matthew received them both, and Luke uses only the Q version. In the course of time, the reason for persecution was given, in Christianizing fashion (as in 9:24 with ἕνεκεν ἐμοῦ, "for my sake"); in

---

36   See Jacques Dupont, "Introduction aux Béatitudes," *NRTh* 98 (1976) 97–108, esp. 99: "One has good reason to think that Jesus formulated his beatitudes by echoing this oracle."

37   The commentaries list a huge number of HB passages, e.g., Ps 107(LXX 106):9: "For he satisfies the thirsty, and the hungry he fills with good things"; Isa 35:10; 49:10, 13; 65:19; Ezek 34:29; cf. Sir 24:21. In the NT see Rev 19:1–8; 21:4.

38   Cf. Luke 9:17 (satiation in the church) and 14:15 (satiation in the kingdom of God).

39   Plummer, 180.

40   Drying tears: Isa 25:8. The God who consoles: Isa 40:1, 29, 31; 41:17; Jer 33:6. Joy over the return from exile: Ps 126 (LXX 127). The God who leads back the exiled: Jer 31:7–14; Zech 2:10–17.

41   Γελάω ("to laugh") can be used in a negative sense (Lam 1:7), i.e., the laughter of the contemptuous; cf. Marshall, 256. Here the word has a positive meaning.

42   The theme of the eschatological gathering of all peoples is lacking in the Beatitudes.

43   The Attic future of κλαίω ("to weep") would be κλαύσομαι, but the Koine tends to give the future

Luke 6:22 it is probably in the original Q form ("on account of the Son of Man").[44]

The reference to the present differs here from its previous occurrences, for the blessed condition depends now on the onset of persecution.[45] This fourth beatitude stands in the same relationship to the first three as casuistic law to apodeictic law. As soon as one examines the various cases, a host of possibilities arise: three verbs plus a participle in Matthew, and in Luke four verbs that occur in two waves (cf. the two ὅταν, "when"). The last verb, as in Matthew, is connected to a ponderous expression.

Luke describes the persecutors generally as οἱ ἄνθρωποι ("people"),[46] without using the technical early Christian term, "to persecute." It is unclear whether Luke has various cases of persecution in mind, or only makes a list for stylistic reasons.[47] Μισέω ("to hate") is not only the feeling of hate but also its effective expression and the manner in which the persecuted experience it.[48] Ἀφορίζω ("to exclude") means a separation, more probably religious excommunication from the synagogue than social discrimination.[49] Ὀνειδίζω ("to revile") means that the honor of the Christians is defamed (cf. 1 Pet 4:14; and Luke 1:25, the "reproach" of the childless Elizabeth).[50] The last verb is unclear: Matthew speaks of invective, and Luke of a cursing of the name of the Christians by their enemies. This could

be explained by the existence of two different translations.[51] Τὸ ὄνομα ὑμῶν ("your name") is more probably their individual names than the common description "Christian" (cf. 1 Pet 4:16).[52] Matthew has in mind a magical cursing, and Luke, an equally dangerous slander, which, in his time, perhaps had legal consequences.[53] Ἕνεκα τοῦ υἱοῦ τοῦ ἀνθρώπου ("on account of the Son of Man") specifies that the contempt is not the result of bad behavior on the part of the Christians, and that the relationship between the Christians and the Son of Man is so close that they suffer the same lot, in which the lord is the cause for the condemnation of his servants.

Verse 23a repeats v. 22 in altered form; the symmetry of the two imperatives alludes to the style of the psalmists and prophets. Verse 23b corresponds to the ὅτι-clauses of the other beatitudes. Since I do not interpret ἐν ἐκείνῃ τῇ ἡμέρᾳ ("in that day") eschatologically, as the last time, but historically, as the time of persecution (only thus is the ἰδοὺ γάρ ["for surely"] of the last verse comprehensible), the switch from the present to the aorist imperative is only a stylistic improvement.[54]

Σκιρτάω ("leap") is likely to be traditional. If the original had read ἀγαλλιᾶσθε ("be glad") as in Matthew, Luke would hardly have altered it, as Acts 2:46 shows.[55] Jubilation is part of the prophetic message of salvation,

---

in active voice a corresponding active (rather than deponent) form (cf. BDF §77).

44 Agreeing with Schulz, Q, 453. Luke does not add "Son of Man" to his sources.

45 Ὅταν here with the aorist subjunctive with the meaning, "if it happens that" (close to the hypothetical ἐάν).

46 These words are his own.

47 It is difficult to reconstruct the source Q here. How many verbs does Q list? And which ones?

48 Cf. μισέω in Ps 68:5 (LXX).

49 In Judaism there existed various forms of "excommunication"; see Gösta Lindeskog, "Ausschließung," BHH 1 (1963) 168; cf. John 9:22; 12:42; 16:2. Tannaitic religion provided for exclusion from the synagogue service, especially from active participation in it, but not for exclusion from the social community, as Lawrence H. Schiffmann has demonstrated ("At the Crossroads: Tannaitic Perspectives on the Jewish-Christian Schism," in E. P. Sanders, ed., Jewish and Christian Self-Definition, vol. 2, Aspects of Judaism in the Graeco-Roman Period [Philadelphia: Fortress Press, 1980] 114–56, esp. 149–53). See also

Gøran Forkman, The Limits of the Religious Community (ConBNT 5; Lund: Gleerup, 1972) 92–105.

50 For these insults see Ps 69(LXX 68):10; Rom 15:3; Heb 11:26; Luke 1:25 (with the commentary on this passage above).

51 See Marshall, 253. Lagrange (188) comes out against this hypothesis.

52 Cf. Acts 5:41; Jas 2:7; 1 Pet 4:14–16; and Pliny the Younger Ep. 10.96, "I am not a little uncertain whether the Name in itself is punishable, even if it is free of misdeeds, or whether it is the misdeeds connected with the Name."

53 Luke is concerned with more than being stricken from the list of names in the synagogue.

54 Agreeing with Adolf von Harnack, New Testament Studies, vol. 2, The Sayings of Jesus (trans. J. R. Wilkinson; New York: Putnam, 1908) 39; and against Schulz, Q, 453 n. 380.

55 According to Schulz (Q, 454), on the other hand, who considers the two imperatives to be eschatological imperatives, the change is from ἀγαλλιᾶσθε (Matthew) to σκιρτήσατε (Luke).

and the term is also familiar already from Luke 1:41, 44. It describes joyful movement of the body, while ἀγαλλιάω refers to the joy of the heart and mouth. In this sense the Lukan text is coherent, for it describes the outward manifestation of the Christian life, not the feelings of the believers. The reason for it all, which up to that point was lacking, is added, perhaps in a time in which beatitudes and love of enemies have already been connected. With little originality but with great faithfulness to Jesus, the Christians took this over from the pericope about love of enemies (6:35). The perspective is thereby altered: suffering Christians, not merely suffering people, are blessed. Their eschatological happiness is no longer a theocentric expression of God's justice, but an anthropocentric reward[56] for their suffering. The expression "their ancestors" could be redactional (cf. Acts 7:52),[57] but hardly the banal language in v. 23c (κατὰ τὰ αὐτά, "that is what," and ἐποίουν, "[they] did").[58] The Q community clarifies its self-understanding in v. 23c: its role within Israel is a prophetic one, and its persecution confirms this understanding.

Despite the formal differences between this beatitude and the first three, the theological perspective remains unaltered; the historical experience of suffering can be understood as a happy one because of its eschatological result. This perspective does not correspond precisely to the time of Luke, since the prophets were in the minority by then. But Luke is still in agreement with the main idea, since in Acts 14:22 as well the promise of participating in the kingdom of God results from the inevitable suffering. The length of the sentence can be explained by Semitic rhetoric: the concluding phrase is marked by a longer sentence.[59] The more weighty content is also reserved for the conclusion (cf. the prospects of persecution at the end of the Gospel, Mark 13, and at the end of the Lord's Prayer).

The fourth woe is a clever imitation of the fourth beatitude. Of the four parts in vv. 22–23, only the first and the last are used, and of the four verbs, only the fourth is used, though in a form (καλῶς . . . εἴπωσιν, "speak well of," v. 26) that sounds more Matthean (εἴπωσιν πᾶν πονηρόν, "utter all kinds of evil," Matt 5:11) than Lukan (ἐκβάλωσιν τὸ ὄνομα ὑμῶν ὡς πονηρόν, "cast out your name as evil," v. 22).[60] Accolades from human beings are otherwise understood positively (Matt 5:16; Phil 2:15), though it becomes suspicious if unanimous[61] (hence πάντες, "all"). The author finds a new point of comparison in the false prophets (also in Acts 13:6).

Conclusion

Neither the introduction (v. 20a) nor the πλήν ("but," v. 24a) demands the triumphalistic conclusion that the twelve apostles are to be equated with the blessed. The Lukan Jesus addresses both the disciples and the world, and the audience learns of two categories, without knowing in advance to which they belong. Luke leaves the text open and does not bar the way to its *parenetic* aspect.

The two-part composition is, however, *kerygmatically* laden. For those who want to hear, μακάριοι ("blessed") sounds joyful, for this happiness is neither earned nor

---

56 The concept of μισθός ("reward"), over which Protestants often stumble, does not have here the meaning that it has received in traditional Catholic theology—despite the assertions of Lagrange (189), for whom the individual who does good achieves a right to a reward. The word designates a payback, a compensation, a reward, and here the eschatological restitution proclaimed already in the other beatitudes (this is against the background of an ethic of obedience; see Ernst, 220). But there is something else in addition: just as this beatitude connects suffering with devotion to Christ, the happiness to come is bound up with this decision for Christ. Luke does not expunge the idea of reward, but connects it with grace.

57 "Their ancestors" relates to the "people" of v. 22.

58 One should note the imperfect ἐποίουν (vv. 23, 26):

an iterative imperfect to designate habitual action. See Godet, 1.316.

59 See David Daube, *The New Testament and Rabbinic Judaism* (London: Athlone Press, 1956) 196–201.

60 In other parts of his work, Luke nevertheless uses καλῶς εἶπεν ("he has spoken well," Luke 20:39) and καλῶς ἐλάλησεν ("he was right to say," Acts 28:25).

61 Although it is true that this means public opinion and not—mathematically—*all* people (Lagrange, 191), this does not mean that the πάντες does not correspond to a theological necessity. It is not merely a word that Luke enjoys, but, as Plummer writes (183): "Plutarch [Phoc 8.5] says that Phocion, when his speech was received with universal applause, asked his friends whether he had inadvertently said anything wrong."

expected. The Christian image of God, which designates God as a person, as a father, makes this cry of joy possible. The Son of Man, who is the reason for the persecution (v. 22), is also the proclaimer of this God (v. 20). His voice (ἔλεγεν, "he kept saying," not merely εἶπεν, "he said") can resound again in the church through the mouths and pens of Christians. Thus people may proleptically take part in the eschatological joy even now, in the midst of a dramatic situation. The voice of the Son of Man, his word today, and the kingdom of God all stand on the same plane, the plane of God's faithfulness.

Jesus himself knew neither riches nor recognition his whole life through, and from his birth had no part of the cultural and economic prosperity of the upper class. In the early church the situation was no different; only in the time of Luke does it change, though it does not lead to a compromise of the message, as one might have feared. On the contrary, a second strophe was added that reiterated for the rich the happiness of the poor.

But Jesus and the early Christians also experience the other side of the present situation: they partook of the eschatological joy. Neediness taught them to discover other riches, and to look to the unseen. In the situation that unjustly befell them, they found a hint of the kingdom of God already in the community. That the Beatitudes do not address a singular "you" but the entirety of the community (plural "you") is a sign of the close connection of believers with one another, and of the unity of the church.

The Sermon on the Plain II: Love of Enemies and Other Matters (6:27–38)

Bibliography

Bartsch, Hans-Werner, "Traditionsgeschichtliches zur 'Goldenen Regel' und zum Aposteldekret," *ZNW* 75 (1984) 128–32.

Betz, *Sermon on the Mount,* ad loc.

Black, *Aramaic Approach,* 179–81.

Couroyer, "Mesure."

Dihle, *Regel.*

Dupont, Jacques, "L'appel à imiter Dieu en Matthieu 5,48 et Luc 6,36," *RivB* 14 (1966) 137–58, reprinted in idem, *Études,* 2.539–50.

idem, *Béatitudes.*

idem, "Parfaits."

Ford, Josephine Massyngberde, *My Enemy Is My Guest: Jesus and Violence in Luke* (Maryknoll, N.Y.: Orbis, 1984).

Gill, D., "Socrates and Jesus on Non-Retaliation and Love of Enemies," *Horizons* 18 (1991) 246–62.

Heim, N. J., and Joachim Jeremias, "Goldene Regel," *RGG* (3d ed., 1958) 2.1687–89.

Klassen, William, *Love of Enemies: The Way to Peace* (Philadelphia: Fortress Press, 1984).

Lapide, "Bergpredigt."

Linsksens, John, "A Pacifist Interpretation of Peace in the Sermon on the Mount?" *Concilium: Religion in the Seventies/Eighties* 164 (1983) 16–25.

Lohfink, Gerhard, "Der ekklesiale Sitz im Leben der Aufforderung Jesu zum Gewaltverzicht (Mt 5,39b–42 / Lk 6,29f)," *ThQ* 162 (1982) 236–53.

Lührmann, "Liebet."

Mees, Michael, *Außerkanonische Parallelstellen zu den Herrenworten und ihre Bedeutung* (Quaderni di "Vetera Christianorum" 10; Bari: Istituto di letteratura cristiana antica, 1975).

Merkelbach, "Über eine Stelle."

Minear, Paul Sevier, "Jesus' Audiences, According to Luke," *NovT* 16 (1974) 81–109.

Neugebauer, Fritz, "Die dargebotene Wange und Jesu Gebot der Feindesliebe," *ThLZ* 110 (1985) 865–76.

Neuhäusler, Engelbert, "Mit welchem Maßstab mißt Gott die Menschen? Deutung zweier Jesussprüche," *BibLeb* 11 (1970) 104–13.

Percy, *Botschaft.*

Pernot, "Correction."

Piper, *Love,* 49–63, 153–170.

Pokorný, "Core."

Reinach, Théodore, "Mutuum date, nihil inde sperantes," *REG* 7 (1894) 57–58.

Rüger, "Maß."

Sauer, Jürgen, "Traditionsgeschichtliche Erwägungen zu den synoptischen und paulinischen Aussagen über Feindesliebe und Wiedervergeltungsverzicht," *ZNW* 76 (1985) 1–28.

Schneider, Günther, "Die Neuheit der christlichen Nächstenliebe," *TThZ* 82 (1973) 257–75.

Schottroff, "Non-Violence."

Schulz, *Q,* 127–39.

Schwarz, Günther, "Ἀγαπᾶτε τοὺς ἐχθροὺς ὑμῶν: Mt 5,44a / Lk 6,27a (35a): Jesu Forderung kat' exochèn," *BN* 12 (1980) 32–34.

idem, "Μηδὲν ἀπελπίζοντες," *ZNW* 71 (1980) 133–35.

Seitz, "Love."

Sladek, Paulus Friedrich, "'Liebet eure Feinde' (Mt 5,44): Ein moralpsychologischer Vortrag," in K. Reiss and H. Schütz, eds., *Kirche, Recht und Land: Festschrift Adolf Kindermann* (Königstein im Taunus: Das südetendeutsche Priesterwerk; Munich: Ackermann-Gemeinde 1969) 30–48.

Spicq, *Agape,* 1.77–125.

idem, *Agapè,* 1.98–116.

Strecker, Georg, "Compliance: Love of One's Enemy (Mt 5, 38–48): The Golden Rule (Mt 7, 12)," *Australian Biblical Review* 29 (1981) 38–46.

Theissen, "Nonviolence," 115–56.

van Unnik, "Motivierung."

Wittmann, Dieter, *Die Auslegung der Friedensweisungen der Bergpredigt in der Predigt der evangelischen Kirche im 20. Jahrhundert* (Frankfurt: Peter Lang, 1984).

Wolbert, Werner, "Die Liebe zum Nächsten, zum Feind und zum Sünder," *Theologie und Glaube* 74 (1984) 262–82.

27 "But I say to you that hear, Love your enemies, do good to those who hate you, 28/ bless those who curse you, pray for those who abuse you. 29/ To the one who strikes you on the cheek, offer the other also; and from the one who steals your overgarment, do not withhold even your undergarment. 30/ Give to every one who asks from you; and of the one who takes away what is yours, do not ask for it back. 31/ And as you wish that people would do to you, do so to them. 32/ And if you love those who love you, what return is that for you? For even sinners love those who love them. 33/ And if you do good to those who do good to you, what return is that for you? For even sinners do the same. 34/ And if you lend to those from whom you hope to receive, what return is that for you? Even sinners lend to sinners, to receive as much again. 35/ But love your enemies, and do good, and lend, without doubting at all, and your reward will be great, and you will be children of the Most High; for he is kind to the ungrateful and the evil. 36/ Become merciful, even as your Father is merciful. 37/ And judge not, and you will not be judged, and condemn not, and you will not be condemned. Forgive, and you will be forgiven; 38/ Give, and it will be given to you; good measure, pressed down, shaken together, running over, will be put into your lap; for with the measure with which you measure, it will be measured for you."

Analysis

Form

After a resumptive (1) introduction (v. 27a), Luke begins (2) a call to love one's enemies: four present imperatives (durative or iterative),[1] which are two pairs of synonymous expressions in the second person plural (vv. 27b–28). Then follow (3) a call to renounce resistance: four imperatives in the second person singular,[2] the first and third of which have a formal correspondence, likewise the second and fourth (vv. 29–30); and (4) the Golden Rule: after a dependent clause containing a comparison, a present imperative in the second person plural (v. 31). Appended to this is (5) the comparison with sinners, three symmetrical sentences, each of which contains two parts: a rhetorical question introduced by a dependent clause expressing a hypothetical situation, and a statement that gives the reasoning (vv. 32–34). After that comes (6) the reference to the defining characteristic of Jesus' disciples,[3] the love of enemies, which is set forth by means of three present imperatives (second person plural). These three positive possibilities correspond to the three negative cases in vv. 32–34. A double promise (of reward and sonship) is justified by a causal clause (God's kindness) at the end of this long verse (v. 35). Finally, there is (7) the call to compassion: a present imperative in the second person plural with a comparison (v. 36), which is formally related to the Golden Rule (v. 31); and (8) on not judging: two formulas of reciprocity with negative present imperatives in the second person plural, in which a passive statement is answered with an intensifying negation (v. 37ab); and (9) on giving: two formulas of reciprocity with positive present imperatives that confirm a passive statement (vv. 37c–38a). A transitional sentence about rewards (v. 38b) illustrates the passive idiom that immediately precedes it ($\delta o\vartheta\acute{\eta}\sigma\epsilon\tau\alpha\iota$ $\acute{\upsilon}\mu\hat{\iota}\nu$, "it will be given to you"), and is occasioned by the formal connection to the key word $\mu\acute{\epsilon}\tau\rho o\nu$ ("measure") in the next saying (v. 38c). (10) This proverb

about measuring forms the conclusion: a last formula of reciprocity, which is not an imperative but fulfills rather an explanatory function ($\gamma\acute{\alpha}\rho$, "for," v. 38c).

Despite the variety in the origin of the materials, the formal structure of this pericope is well planned. The reader perceives the symmetry between (2) and (3), and between (8) and (9). After the reasoned argument in (5), there is a repetition of the command (2) in (6). The Golden Rule (4) and the call to compassion (7) belong together formally. But what is their literary function: introductory or concluding? Both (6) and (9) develop the concept of reward at the conclusion, and (10) shares with (8) and (9) the form of reciprocity.

(2) and (3) are apodictic commands. (6), (8), (9), and (10) connect the desired behavior with its results. The two commands in (4) and (7) are justified with a comparison. The comparison with one's fellow human beings introduced in (4) is further developed in (5) and (6), while the comparison with God in (7) is expanded in (8), (9), and (10) in the concept of reciprocity.

I would outline the formal structure as follows:

1. Introduction (v. 27a)
2. Love of enemies (vv. 27b–28)
3. Renunciation of resistance (vv. 29–30)
4. The Golden Rule (v. 31)
5. Comparison with sinners (vv. 32–34)
6. The peculiar characteristic of Christians (v. 35)
7. The call to compassion (v. 36)
8. Not judging (v. 37ab)
9. Giving (vv. 37c–38b)
10. Measuring (v. 38c)

Genre

Part of the material is also attested elsewhere: in Matthew's Sermon on the Mount (5:38–48; 7:12; 7:1–2) and in a saying in Mark's Gospel (4:24b). Parallels, especially to Luke 6:29–30,[4] could derive from oral

---

1   See BDF §335: "The result of this distinction is that in general precepts (also to an individual) concerning attitudes and conduct there is a preference for the present."

2   The first and the third imperatives occur in the present tense, and are used positively; the second and fourth are negative. The second takes the form of a $\mu\acute{\eta}$ with the aorist subjunctive ($\mu\grave{\eta}$ $\kappa\omega\lambda\acute{\upsilon}\sigma\eta\varsigma$, "do

not try to hinder his actions"), and the fourth, a $\mu\acute{\eta}$ with the present imperative ($\mu\grave{\eta}$ $\grave{\alpha}\pi\alpha\acute{\iota}\tau\epsilon\iota$, "remain in the attitude of one who demands nothing").

3   Notice the sharp $\pi\lambda\acute{\eta}\nu$ ("but," "except"), which contrasts the attitude of Christians who live like pagans (vv. 32–34) with that of those who live like God (v. 35).

4   See Michael Mees, *Parallelstellen zu den Herrenworten*

tradition[5] or represent a free citation of the Gospels. The ethical content of the Sermon on the Mount/Plain was, of course, developed in the parenesis of the early church.[6] In this, the Synoptic tradition respects the historical voice of the Lord better than did the parenetic tradition, which had another aim, adapting the words of Jesus, as found in the Synoptic sayings, to the contemporary situation.[7]

The countless formal differences are just as striking as the content that is identical. As an example, here are three parallels to Luke 6:27–28:

Rom. 12:14	Did. 1.3	Justin 1 Apol. 15.9
εὐλογεῖτε τοὺς διώκοντας [ὑμᾶς],	εὐλογεῖτε τοὺς καταρωμένους ὑμῖν καὶ προσεύχεσθε ὑπὲρ τῶν ἐχθρῶν,	εὔχεσθε ὑπὲρ τῶν ἐχθρῶν ὑμῶν καὶ ἀγαπᾶτε τοὺς μισοῦντας ὑμᾶς
εὐλογεῖτε	νηστεύετε δὲ ὑπὲρ τῶν διωκόντων ὑμᾶς	καὶ εὐλογεῖτε τοὺς καταρωμένους ὑμῖν
καὶ μὴ καταρᾶσθε		καὶ εὔχεσθε ὑπὲρ τῶν ἐπηρεαζόντων ὑμᾶς.

The variations are no greater than those between Luke and Matthew. The evangelists simply had a different goal from the authors cited here, and not primarily a parenetic one. They intended to present the basic content of Jesus' teaching within the context of his mission and his life. For this task, they had at their disposal only individual sayings of the Lord, or occasionally a chain of such sayings. These were transmitted orally for various goals or occasions, in direct citation or applied interpretation. The multiplicity of forms shows that the use of these sayings varied, and that it exercised an influence on their form; the substantive message of these sayings was more determinative of their transmission than their external form.

Extended parallels to this pericope can be found only in Matthew, the *Didache*, and Justin Martyr:[8]

	Luke	Matthew	Didache	Justin
Introduction	1		*4*	
Love of enemies	2	*3*	2	5
No resistance	3	2	5	2
Golden Rule	4	6	*6*	3
Comparison with sinners	5	5	3	5
Characteristic: love of enemies	6	*7*		
Call to compassion	7	8		
Not judging	8	*10*		
Giving	9	4		
Measuring	10			

The following becomes clear from the table:

The historical Jesus pronounced the command to love one's enemies and connected it with the promise of adoption, and the justification of the command in God's lovingkindness (2 and 6). On another occasion he taught that one must renounce resistance (3), practice compassion (7), not pass judgment (8), and measure well (10).

The earliest tradition: In oral tradition love of enemies (2) was early associated with the renunciation of resistance (3), and was at the same time (6) explained by the comparison with sinners (5). The summonses not to judge (8) and to measure well (10) became connected early, but only later were they made part of a larger composition. The same is true of the call to compassion (7). The Golden Rule (4) was adopted not by Jesus but first by the early Christians,[9] though its position was not fixed. Q, Justin Martyr, and the *Didache* are witnesses of this oral tradition.

---

und ihre Bedeutung (Bari: Istituto di litteratura cristiana antica, 1975) 109–27.

5 See Aland, *Synopsis*, 106, 108. The columns on p. 84 contain an additional text, a parallel to Matt 5:45b, which is taken from the *Gospel of the Naasenes*.

6 Above all in Rom 12:14, 17–20; 1 Thess 5:15; 1 Pet 3:9; *Did.* 1.2–5.

7 See John Piper, *"Love your enemies": Jesus' Love Command in the Synoptic Gospels and in the Early Christian Paraenesis: A History of the Tradition and Interpretation of Its Uses* (SNTSMS 38; Cambridge: Cambridge University Press, 1979) 4–18, 100–133.

8 Cf. *Did.* 1.3–5; Justin 1 Apol. 15.9–10; also 14.3;

16.1. In this table the numbers refer to the units of text in the Lukan order. The sequence is given according to the individual authors. The numbers in italics mark those sections that I have rearranged for display. In their respective authors, they are not directly connected with the sections that precede and follow them in this table.

9 See Dieter Lührmann, "Liebet eure Feinde (Lk 6,27–36 / Mt 5,39–48)," *ZThK* 69 (1972) 412–38, esp. 427: One cannot tell at what stage of the transmission this reinterpretation took place.

The sayings source (Q): Either in the oral tradition, or first in Q, the Beatitudes and the command to love one's enemies were attached. Q is a witness, then, of the association of the love of enemies (2) with the renunciation of resistance (3),[10] as well as of the love of enemies (6) and the comparision with sinners (5). By means of an individual saying (7, the call to compassion), Q legitimizes the love of enemies. The source then integrates the sayings about not judging (8) and measuring (10). The Matthean structure of the antitheses is a redactional adaptation of Q.

Luke: The compositional skill of the evangelist leads to the addition of the Golden Rule (4) after the love of enemies (2) and the renunciation of resistance (3), thus juxtaposing it to the call to compassion (7). In Luke the comparision with sinners (5) comes *before* a repetition of the command to love one's enemies (6); the latter was taken from tradition. But such repeated injunctions are also a redactional feature, for example, in the love of enemies (2), where Luke makes a transition from two to four imperatives (2); and in the comparison with sinners (5), in which he supplements the two examples with a third ("greet" is replaced with "do good," and the short sentence about lending is added); and in the command not to judge (8), which he doubles. From another source Luke adds four imperatives about giving (beginning of 9), and a free saying as a promise (end of 9).

Functional Setting (*Sitz im Leben*)

The communities that transmitted these sayings were many and varied. A Palestinian context is still evident in isolated sayings (Matt 5:46–47, "to greet," and "tax collectors"). This context is characterized by the predominance of the Law (both Matthew and the *Didache* perceive a connection between love of enemies and love of neighbors). Matt 5:41 probably concerns compulsory labor for the Roman occupying forces.[11] Love of enemies can be directed toward both Zealots and Romans.[12] The carriers of the Q traditions before the Jewish War may have been itinerant Christian preachers, and the Matthean version of it probably reflects the dramatic situation of Judaism after the defeat of 70 CE.[13] Q shows that it was an important early concern to understand Jesus' teaching as ethical or salvific. The Matthean structure of the antitheses is redactional, but, even before Matthew, the sayings of Jesus were understood as a new teaching or as an eschatological interpretation of the Law. They were also employed in a missionary fashion, and their citation in the apologetic works of the second century points to a similar usage. The Lukan version adapts itself to another situation: it "translates" the tradition for a Greek audience (see the Lukan version of the sayings about love of enemies, 6:27–28 [2]), in which Christians are supposed to express their love in charity and lending money (see the extra comparison in Luke 6:34 [5]). The uniqueness of Jesus' message is no longer seen against the backdrop of the Law of Moses, but in the context of the Greek way of life (Luke 6:32–35 [5 and 6]).[14]

Results: The Sermon on the Plain summarizes the message of Jesus by integrating the Beatitudes with the command to love one's enemies. The pericope concerning love of enemies was formed into a tight composition by Luke himself out of materials from Q and other sayings. Two main themes that stand in reciprocal tension have contributed to this: the redactional concern to make the message understood, and the theological effort to make distinctively Christian teaching come alive. The concept of the feasibility of Christian ethics is resident in the first concern, and the perspective of persecution and the separation of Christians from the world, in the second. The text is to aid the Lukan congregations in treading the dangerous path of Christian ethics, between comfortable accommodation and excessive resistance.

---

10   See Lührmann, "Liebet," 417.

11   See Gerd Theissen, "Nonviolence and Love of the Enemies (Matthew 5:38–48; Luke 6:27–38): The Social Background," in *Social Reality and the Early Christians* (trans. M. Kohl; Minneapolis: Fortress Press, 1992) 115–56, esp. 133.

12   The Romans accused the Christians of a "a hatred of the human race" (the expression comes from Tacitus *Ann.* 15.44: *odium humani generis*).

13   See Theissen, "Nonviolence," 142–49.

14   See van Unnik, "Motivierung," 124–26; and Theissen, "Nonviolence," 137–41.

Commentary

The interpreter faces two difficulties with this text. First, the pericope is filled with smaller philological or text-critical problems. Second, it treats issues that are key to living: can one love one's enemies? Is it humane to give in on every occasion? Doesn't the Golden Rule contradict the love of enemies?[15] The interpreter must keep the entirety of the text in mind and should not get bogged down in details.

Love of Enemies (vv. 27–28, 32–35)

■ **27–28, 32–35** Church fathers in the second century, especially Justin, sensed that the command to love one's enemies was the new element in Christian ethics, and Justin pronounced this with pride.[16] A twentieth-century Jewish scholar can write: "Gloating, hatred of enemies, and returning evil for evil are thus forbidden, while generosity and loving deeds toward the enemy in need are commanded—but Judaism does not have the love of enemies as a moral principle. This imperative is probably the only one in all the three chapters of the Sermon on the Mount that lacks a clear parallel or analogy in rabbinic literature. It is, in the terminology of theologians, material specific to Jesus."[17] This uniqueness of the Christians should not, however, be understood ahistorically.

The parable of the good Samaritan (Luke 10:25–37) makes clear that the Jews and Christians of that time were arguing over the correct interpretation of the command to love one's neighbor. Matt 5:43–44 describes loving one's enemies as an intensification of loving one's neighbor (as also the Golden Rule), and *Did.* 1.2–4, as its correct interpretation. "Hating one's neighbor" (Matt 5:43) is unquestionably un-Jewish, but how far the compassion of the chosen people should extend was an existential question. In terms of individual ethics, the valid practice was, "If your enemy is hungry, feed the person bread, and if he or she is thirsty, give water to drink" (Prov 25:21).[18] But what may be appropriate for a weak enemy (compassion) is not necessarily desirable for a conqueror and his occupying forces. There were varying ethical responses toward Israel's political enemies: (1) completely traitorous collaboration; (2) defense of God's glory, and cleansing of the land by force of weapons;[19] (3) physical distancing from the enemy, along with apocalyptic dualism and hatred; (4) separation of political and religious spheres, along with pragmatic adaptation and a strong consciousness of their own status of election that expresses itself in a preference for one's brothers and sisters. In the time of the Gospel writers, these options were simplified and internalized. Jesus' behavior, and later that of the earliest Christians, takes place in the context of these ethical controversies. The command to love one's enemies was a vital element in the continuity of Christian identity during the first decades, as its multiple attestation demonstrates. In the view of Christians, Jesus interrupted the Hebrew Bible trajectory of the hatred of God for evil humanity,[20] and prohibited hallowing the name of the Lord by means of the mistreatment of Israel's enemies.[21] The exclusive ethnocentrism of Deut 30:7 is no longer appropriate: "And the

---

15 The tension between these two commandments is perceived very well by Dihle (*Regel*, 112) and Reinhold Merkelbach, "Über eine Stelle im Evangelium des Lukas," *GrB* 1 (1973) 171–75, esp. 171.

16 Justin *Apol.* 1.15.9–10 describes this Christian attitude as "new." See additional citations in van Unnik, "Motivierung," 111–13.

17 Lapide, "Bergpredigt," 371.

18 Cf. Prov 24:17; Exod 23:4–5; Josephus *Ap.* 2.28 §§209–10; *'Abot R. Nat.* 23 (for these references I am indebted to Lapide, "Bergpredigt," 370–71). Despite these literary parallels, Ernst Percy (*Botschaft*, 156–63) comes to the conclusion that this command of Jesus is something new. Piper (*Love*, 27–49) cites the following Jewish texts as closely related to the commandment to love one's enemies: *Ep. Arist.* 227; 2 *Enoch* 50:3; *Jos. Asen.* 23:9; 28:14; 29:3; Philo *Virt.* 116–18; *T. Benj.* 4:2–3; *T. Jos.* 18:2;

T. Gad 6:4–7.

19 This zealous attitude can be justified by a biblical precedent: In his zeal for YHWH, the Israelite Phinehas slew his fellow Israelite Zimri, who brought a Midianite woman into his tent (Num 25). The chapter closes with the commandment of God to repay violence with violence (Num 25:17). For various Jewish interpretations of the case involving Phinehas, see Esther Starobinski-Safran, "Les zélotes à Jérusalem," *Rencontre chrétiens et juifs* 14 (1980) 282–93, esp. 290–91.

20 Pss 5:5; 26(LXX 25):5; 119(LXX 118):113–115; 139(LXX 138):19–22; 2 Chr 19:2.

21 At the end of his investigation into the history behind the good Samaritan, Oscar J. F. Seitz draws the following conclusion ("Love Your Enemies: The Historical Setting of Matthew V.43f.; Luke VI.27f.," *NTS* 16 [1969–70] 47): "Loving is thus a matter of

234

LORD your God will put all these curses upon your foes and enemies who persecuted you." Jesus overcomes the principle of reciprocity and retribution.[22] He thus stands in opposition to the Essenes, who, in their concern for cultic purity, demanded every member of the sect to take an oath to hate the evil ones,[23] because they wanted in this manner to prepare for the eschatological battle.

Behavior toward one's enemy was also no new issue for Hellenism. Though the gap between theory and practice was often immensely wide, the price of human life low, and the mighty often ruling without pity, various ethical solutions were alive in public opinion. While living together in the same house, one would consider the situation of the suffering slaves, for whom hatred toward their master was forbidden. In the case of the conquered "enemy," wise teachers tried, by means of ethical counsels, to convince the conqueror and ruler of the value of compassion. Blind rage was improper for an educated master. In a third context, philosophers, who knew from the experience of their predecessors that they were often unwelcome in their own city, declared that both hatred and silent accommodation were prohibited responses to this injustice; the wise individuals should not fear the consequences of suffering and should, despite all rejection, continue to express their convictions.[24] But even in the case of the greatest possible approximation of the command to love one's ene-

mies, a bit of utilitarianism remains. This confirms the opinion "that the principle of reciprocity formed one of the foundations of social intercourse among the Greeks."[25]

Despite the various traditions, Jesus' call has remained constant: love of enemies is no general rule of society but an attitude characteristic of Jesus' disciples. Up to the point of Luke, their location in society has not been protected or dominating, but precarious and painful. This becomes clear in the parallel imperative in Q (the fourth imperative in Luke): the disciples should "pray" for their persecutors. So the enemies are stronger, and the only loving gesture that remains for the persecuted is prayer. Luke, who likes to illustrate Jesus' commands with narrative, portrays Jesus (23:34) and Stephen (Acts 7:60) in prayer for their enemies.[26] The presence of the kingdom of God does not suppress the dangers of suffering. In place of values such as success, prosperity, and happiness, the preaching of the kingdom brings with it a sorrowful tension that the Christians must bear, and for which they must justify themselves theologically.

Matthew 5:44 has the words, "pray for those who persecute you" (as in the Beatitudes). But Luke reads, "pray for[27] those who abuse you" (6:28b). Ἐπηρεάζω is rare and means "to threaten," "to mistreat," "to abuse," "to scold,"[28] that is, to mistreat by word or deed. Which

---

'doing mercy,' which is to stop at no frontiers, levelling all barriers erected by national and even religious hostility."

22 Albrecht Dihle (*Regel*) and Reinhold Merkelbach ("Über eine Stelle") have correctly recognized this point.

23 According to Josephus (*Bell.* 2.8.7 §139), this oath consists in μισήσειν δ᾿ ἀεὶ τοὺς ἀδίκους καὶ συναγωνιεῖσθαι τοῖς δικαίοις. See 1QS 1.3–4, 9–11; and Seitz, "Love," 49–51.

24 See Luise Schottroff, "Non-Violence and the Love of One's Enemies," in idem et al., *Essays on the Love Commandment* (trans. R. H. and I. Fuller; Philadelphia: Fortress Press, 1978) 9–39, esp. 15–22. See also Seneca *De otio* 1.4 (on helping one's enemies); *De beneficiis* 4.26; *De ira* 2.32.1–34.7 (on not repaying evil with evil); Epictetus *Ench.* 42; *Diss.* 3.13.11, 13; 3.22.54; 3.22.81–82.

25 Hendrik Bolkenstein, *Wohltätigkeit und Armenpflege im vorchristlichen Altertum* (Utrecht: International Institute of Social History, 1939) 158, quoted in van Unnik, "Motivierung," 118.

26 According to Hegesippus (quoted in Eusebius *Hist.*

eccl. 2.23.16), James the brother of the Lord, when he was in the throes of death, begged that God might forgive his tormentors. According to Clement of Alexandria (quoted in Eusebius *Hist. eccl.* 2.9.2–3), James the son of Zebedee forgave the one who had brought him before the court; through James's testimony, this man also became a Christian and was beheaded together with him.

27 After the verb προσεύχομαι, Luke (here and in Acts 8:15), Heb 13:18, as well as Paul and his school (1 Thess 5:25; Col 1:3; 2 Thess 1:11; 3:1) use the preposition περί. Matt 5:44 uses ὑπέρ.

28 BAGD *s.v.;* Moulton and Milligan, *Vocabulary, s.v.;* and LSJ *s.v.* distinguish between "speaking evil of someone" with the accusative and "doing evil to someone" with the dative, though they also mention exceptions to this rule. Luke 6:28 has the accusative. It is likely that Luke—like the author of 1 Pet 3:16, who knows the same tradition—is thinking more of aggressive words than of aggressive actions. According to Ceslas Spicq (*Agapè*, 1.101

reading is original? Luke has paraphrased the two imperatives from Q chiastically: before the command to pray (6:28b), he has added as commentary, "bless those who curse you" (6:28a). Rom 12:14 has a form[29] that is between Matt 5:44b and Luke 6:28a: "Bless [Lukan] those who persecute you [Matthean]." In Paul there is also a repetition, so that one can infer from the Lukan redundancy (Luke 6:28a) that it was used parenetically in the Greek-speaking churches. According to Q, the danger is less that of persecution (Paul and Q/Matthew) than of malicious gossip (Luke and 1 Pet 3:16). Ἐπηρεάζω in Luke 6:28b could thus be an alteration. Luke 6:28a juxtaposes blessing and cursing.[30] The vocabulary is convincingly Hellenistic Jewish, and is in the Hebrew Bible trajectory of ethical dualism (Deut 30:19). Ps 109(LXX 108):6–19 gives the content of a possible curse: the enemies wish for the rupture of any relationship of the accursed psalmist with God, family, and friends, for the end of his life and his goods, and for the obliteration of any remembrance of him. In contrast to this is the hope for God's blessing (Ps 109[LXX 108]:28)—differently than in the command to love one's enemies. In Jewish and Christian linguistic usage, εὐλογέω ("bless") is more than mere human speech; it achieves its weightiness by means of its religious component. In a time in which people spoke less frequently than they do today, and in which words were ontologically bound to their objects, cursing and blessing were serious acts, the unavoidable consequences of which were illustrated with a gesture. The weight of these words has remained conscious to the Greeks to this day. They greet a monk differently than they do ordinary people: εὐλογεῖτε, πάτερ ("bless, father"). In humility he responds, ὁ κύριος ("the Lord," i.e., "the Lord alone can bless").

The reiteration of the command to love one's enemies in 6:27b, as well as the third example in 6:34, and the synonymous expression in 6:35 show an altered situation vis-à-vis the Q community. The danger of Jewish persecution is less in Luke, and people from a higher class have become Christians. Their attitude to their fellow members of society is influenced by their social standing and their means. They are no longer persecuted (Q), but abused (Luke). Their practical response can also exceed a prayer, as the Lukan paraphrases underscore: they can also do good[31] (6:27b, 35a) and support others financially (6:34c, 35a). This social situation also explains the commands peculiar to Luke (9) about giving (6:37c–38a). The Lukan community, or Luke himself, is thus daring to make an unprecedented application and adaptation of the command to love one's enemies.[32] Last, the Lukan Christians all speak Greek, and need some good instruction in Semitic categories, beginning with the main verb of Christian ethics, ἀγαπάω, "to love."[33]

The LXX translated אהב ("to love") with ἀγαπάω, since στέργω ("to treasure") seemed too emotional, φιλέω confined love to one group, that is, one's friends, and ἐράω too strongly implied irrational and passionate love (though not exclusively in an erotic sense). Thus an unimportant verb was purposely selected. Like the oldest translations of Jesus' words, the LXX also allows the following connotations when it uses ἀγαπάω: (1) the anticipatory and unselfish initiative of the one who loves; (2) a hopeful awaiting of the response of the loved one in the love relationship that develops; (3) the cognitive aspect of love, which always accompanies the emotion;[34] (4) the recognition of the other person in her or his individuality (and when the other person is God, ἀγαπάω includes worship).[35] The imperative that only Luke attests, "Do good to those who hate you," is an

---

n. 2), the verb ἐπηρεάζω contains "the twin concepts of evil and insolence."

29   See above under Analysis of Genre. Note the parallel in P. Oxy. 1224 (fol. 2r, col. 1, p. 176): "And pray for your enemies. For he who is not against you is for you. He who today is far off—tomorrow will be near to you" (as translated in Hennecke-Schneemelcher, 1.100).

30   The mss. vary between the accusative and the dative after the verb καταράομαι in v. 28.

31   See Spicq, Agapè, 1.102 n. 1.

32   For the connection between the love of one's enemy

and the handling of one's possessions, see Piper, Love, 158.

33   See Spicq, Lexicon, 1.8–22.

34   Thus Christian love is not blind.

35   In this section I am in many respects indebted to Spicq, Lexicon, 1.8–22.

explanatory paraphrase for Greek listeners, who did not well understand the originally Semitic idiom.[36]

The comparison with an ethic of exact reciprocity (Luke 6:32–34) was still, in Q, conceptualized in Palestinian terms: Christian behavior presented itself as the correct interpretation of God's Law. True to Judaism, a strong self-identity and self-justification toward the Gentiles were at home in this environment. But Luke lives in a Hellenistic milieu. To speak of evil tax collectors and alien Gentiles would be senseless. For this reason, he speaks of "sinners," a word that all Gentile Christians would know. He also adjusts the examples in the comparison to his current situation: "to love," because of its broadly general meaning, can be left where it is, but "to greet" (Q and Matt 5:47) no longer reflects current customs and obligations and must be replaced (cf. Luke 10:4).[37] As in 6:27b, Luke interprets the first example with the second: "to love" thus means a concrete and active attitude, which one can translate as "to do good."[38] Luke adds the third example because of the social situation of the members of his community. This example may have been taken from among the stock pieces of philosophical instruction.[39]

In this context χάρις carries no theological connotation and should not be translated as "grace."[40] The word often occurs in Hellenistic Jewish texts, in which it describes the fruits of a reciprocal beneficence or retaliation.[41] Luke has thus correctly translated the Semitic μισθός ("reward") from Q (Matt 5:46) with a Greek concept.[42] The promise a bit later, καὶ ἔσται ὁ μισθὸς ὑμῶν πολύς ("and your reward will be great"), shows

that Luke did not intend to correct Q by substituting this word. Neither Q nor Luke ultimately overcomes the principle of reciprocity, shifting it as they do from inter-human reciprocity to the relationship between God and humans. For this reason, ποία ("what, what type") is quite apt here: what type of reward are you receiving? Usually, only a small, limited, and temporary one. The rupture with calculating reciprocity in the love of enemies opens, on the other hand, a promising response and return from God: a χάρις ("favor") of a completely different kind (the readers should also perceive the theological meaning), a great (when compared with the small human gift) "reward," divine adoption. Christian "reciprocity" is, then, simultaneously antithetical and analogous to human reciprocity; the Christian God remains kind toward ungrateful and evil people (v. 35). His love is considerate, lasting, and selfless. The Christians' behavior toward their enemies is also like this. In this inheres the vehement practical criticism of Hellenistic or utilitarian Jewish ethics by Christian ethics. But, like the Greeks and the Jews, the Christians also hope for a living reciprocal relationship, a joyful response. This is natural for the human creature, but a break with calculating reciprocity is nevertheless justified in soteriology and christology.

What does τὰ ἴσα ("as much")[43] mean in v. 34, which treats the subject of lending?[44] People who lend money want to receive more, not exactly the same, in return. Five explanations are possible. (1) According to the Scriptures,[45] Jews who lend money cannot demand interest from their fellow Jews; they can thus only expect the

---

36 See van Unnik, "Motivierung," 124–26.
37 Note also the variation in the mss. at v. 33: Should a γάρ be placed at the beginning of this verse (καὶ γὰρ ἐὰν ἀγαθοποιῆτε . . .) or does one belong before the second half of the verse (καὶ γὰρ οἱ ἁμαρτωλοί . . .)?
38 The meaning of ἀγαθοποιέω is clearly understandable, though it is hardly ever used by Greeks. The verb is also conspicuous due to the fact that it hardly ever occurs in the parenetic vocabulary of the early Christians (but cf. 1 Pet 2:15, 20; 3:6, 17; Hermas 13.4 [Vis. 3.5.4]; 17.5 [Vis. 3.9.5]; 95.1–2 [Sim. 9.18.1]). Also in the LXX, the verb is only seldom encountered (six or seven times, e.g., 1 Macc 11:33). The verb can be used either absolutely or (as it is here) transitively.
39 See Seneca De beneficiis 4.16; Piper, Love, 21.
40 Van Unnik ("Motivierung," 120 n. 1) is relying on

Bolkenstein, Wohltätigkeit, esp. 159–60: "It is instructive that the Greek (as well as the Latin) uses the same word for both service and reciprocal service, χάρις; the mutuality and the reciprocality inherent in χαρίζεσθαι is expressed in this fact."
41 E.g., Sir 12:1.
42 Zahn, 292 n. 62. The literature on μισθός is immense; see ThWNT 10.2 (1979) 1179; Wilhelm Pesch, s.v., EDNT 2 (1991) 432–33; and Piper, Love, 162–70 (concerning Luke): "Lk never asks a man to act against his own best interests" (166–67).
43 D it sys do not read (i.e., do not translate) the words τὰ ἴσα since they regard them as problematic.
44 In the active voice δαν(ε)ίζω means "to lend" (originally "to lend to others rather than to one's friends with interest"), in the middle "to borrow."
45 See Exod 22:24 (LXX 22:25); Lev 25:35–37. According to Deut 23:21 (LXX 23:20), to loan something

same sum. (2) τὰ ἴσα means the sum of money lent out, plus interest. (3) The comparison is not concerned with the issue of interest, but instead contrasts "lending" with "giving": people usually lend money, but Christians give it freely. (4) τὰ ἴσα does not mean, concretely, the same sum, but, abstractly, the same service in return.[46] (5) The additional example has a double point by mentioning a financial problem while also criticizing reciprocity (ἵνα ἀπολάβωσιν τὰ ἴσα, "to receive as much again"): human χάρις ("favor," or τὸ ἀνταπόδομα, "repayment"). If one assumes this metaphorical meaning, one understands the vivid τὰ ἴσα. Luke is content to pay the price of inexactness in his portrayal of lending (interest or not) in order to allude graphically to the general phenomenon of reciprocity. I prefer this last explanation.

In conjunction with v. 34, one would like to translate v. 35, "Lend,[47] even when you can expect nothing for it." Unfortunately, ἀπελπίζω does not mean "to hope for" or "from" something, but "to lose hope," "to doubt." The following explanations are possible: (1) The Aramaic text had פסק, a verb that can mean either "to doubt" or "to clap one's hands." The translator chose the wrong meaning. The original text read, "Give, and do not clap your hands (in refusal)."[48] (2) The text must be emended to ἀντελπίζοντες or ἐπελπίζοντες ("to hope for in return").[49] (3) With support from John Chrysostom and the Vulgate (nihil inde sperantes, "hoping nothing from it"), the meaning "to hope from it" could be assumed already for Luke's time.[50] (4) Subtly translated, it reads, "in no way doubting," not in receiv-

ing the lent money, but in the future of the person thus supported.[51] I have chosen this translation.

How should the love of enemies be understood hermeneutically? Three models of interpretation present themselves:

1. The existential model (Rudolf Bultmann):[52] Jesus' command governs close relationships,[53] the I-thou relationship.[54] Love of enemies is an existential and individual attitude that adapts and makes concrete the love of one's neighbor by deepening and extending the concept of neighbor. In practical terms this radicalization of the love of one's neighbor leads to cosmopolitical philanthropy.

2. The social model (Luise Schottroff):[55] Jesus' command becomes meaningful only in a concrete social and political situation. It dictates the nonviolent struggle of Jesus' disciples against the power of the enemies. Love of one's enemies is not a feeling but a behavior. Its proximity to a renunciation of resistance is not accidental, since this was, at that time, an appropriate interpretation, and a specific criticism directed toward the Zealots. In the time of the Jewish revolt, love of one's enemies was the Christian manner of defending God's honor and the integrity of the people of God.

3. The systemic model makes possible the integration of both close and distant relationships, of contacts with both proximus and socius, for the mechanisms of love and hate function analogously among individuals, social groups, and even nations. The command to love one's enemies is a practicable alternative to the other systems,

---

with interest to a foreigner is permissible; see Str-B 1.346–53; 2.159.

46   So Marshall, 263.

47   Spicq (Agapè, 1.111 n. 2) points out that the imperatives in v. 35 are in the present tense. Perhaps δανείζετε must accordingly be translated as "Be in the habit of loaning. . . ."

48   So Gerhard Schwarz, "Μηδὲν ἀπελπίζοντες," ZNW 71 (1980) 133–35.

49   Théodore Reinach ("Mutuum date, nihil inde sperantes," REG 7 [1894] 57–58) makes the case for ἀντελπίζοντες, while Hubert Pernot argues for ἐπελπίζοντες, citing the LXX and esp. Euripides Hipp. 1010–11 ("Une correction à Luc VI,35," CRAIBL [1929] 277–80).

50   So Zahn, 292 n. 63; and BAGD s.v. On the other hand, Pernot ("Correction") considers this meaning impossible.

51   The reading μηδένα for μηδέν can be understood

either as dittography (originating from μηδένα-πελπιζοντες) or as an effort to make sense out of the text (μηδένα ἀπελπίζοντες meaning "without disappointing someone"). Even though this variant is well attested, it is secondary.

52   See Bultmann, Jesus and the Word (New York: Scribner, 1958) 103–5; Schottroff, "Non-Violence," 9–12.

53   Paul Ricœur, "The Socius and the Neighbor," in idem, History and Truth (trans. C. A. Kelbley; Evanston: Northwestern University Press, 1965) 98–109.

54   Martin Buber, I and Thou (trans. R. Gregor Smith; New York: Scribner, 1970).

55   Schottroff, "Non-Violence."

which again and again end with power and oppression. How can one describe it?

a. According to the most ancient traditions (Luke 6:35c; Matt 5:45b), Jesus justified the command to love one's enemies with a theocentric statement ($\H{o}\tau\iota$ . . . , "because . . ."). This is not along the lines of imitating God, but is in the context of a reciprocal relationship. The disciples who are addressed can rely on the initiative of the God who loved first, who loves us, his enemies.[56] This very important remark situates the prescriptive in second place, after the primary performance of God. The indicative precedes the imperative. God is more than an example of a person who loves his enemies. His initiative grants us the possibility and the power to apply Jesus' command.[57] Without his love, the command would be just as weak and powerless as the Law is, according to Paul. The *imitatio Dei* is the consequence of this initiative on God's part (Luke 6:36; Matt 5:48).

b. The person in the background, the subject of $\hat{v}\mu\hat{\iota}\nu$ $\lambda\acute{e}\gamma\omega$ ("I say to you," Luke 6:27; Matt 5:44), is neither anonymous nor apathetic. Jesus has himself done what he demands. Discipleship and imitation are based on his life. "To love one's enemies" does not mean to stand alone, but to follow in the footsteps of the one who, in his agony, prayed for his persecutors (Luke 23:34).

c. The command is also connected with a promise, indeed the highest that humans can hope for: to become children of God (Luke 6:35b; Matt 5:45). God thus wants to grant life to those who love, but love of one's enemies does not function in a closed system of individual reward. In the act of loving their enemies, Christians act *on behalf of* the future of their enemies. Like the bearers of tradition and the evangelists, Jesus hopes that the new attitude will give the enemies the opportunity and ability themselves to step out of their enmity. In the behavior of the Christians, the enemies will discover someone facing them in love, where they expected an opponent.[58] The New Testament Scriptures want to win

over their opponents for the gospel.[59] Love of one's enemies is thus not a passive resignation.

This correct understanding of the love of enemies can be contrasted with a false one, for one that has only two poles, the enemies and us, is not sufficient. Jesus would then be demanding something impossible: a sick preference for being hated. Thus we definitely need a third pole, to which the other two must be related: Jesus, the giver of this command, who stands behind it with his person.

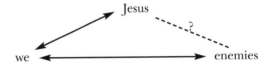

If we hear a law in Jesus' voice, we remain in the above-mentioned wrong understanding. But if we enter into a vital relationship with him, we can—because we receive much emotional support from Christ and from God—even love our enemies. In this way we can step out of the deadly, closed system of reciprocity, and we make possible a changing relationship of others to us and to Jesus (thus the hopeful question mark in the diagram above). If we love our enemies, then they are no longer our enemies. Then the hope cannot be excluded that we, too, will no longer be enemies in their eyes.

Renouncing Violent Resistance (vv. 29–30)

■ **29–30** Matt 5:39–42 and *Did.* 1.4–5 are parallels, despite differences of form and content: *Did.* 1.4a (slap on the face, miles, and shirt) is closer to Matthew, but *Did.* 1.4b–5 (your property) to Luke. It is thus hardly possible that all the texts stem from a single Greek translation: (1) Matthew and the *Didache* mention the right cheek[60] and reflect a Jewish sensitivity for a crescendo of humiliating punishments. (2) Matthew has in mind the situation of a Jewish court of law ($\sigma o\grave{\iota}$ $\kappa\rho\iota\vartheta\hat{\eta}\nu\alpha\iota$, "to sue you"), in which the judge may confiscate only the under-

---

56 See Piper, *Love*, 173. In my opinion this corresponds to what Paul says about the righteousness of God.

57 See Pokorný, "Core," who bases his argument on the connection between the Beatitudes and the command to love. Piper (*Love*, 76–85) views this command in relation to the good news of the kingdom of God.

58 See *m. 'Abot* 1.12; and Seitz, "Love," 43.

59 See 1 Pet 3:1; 1 Cor 9:19; also Rom 12:14, 21; 1 Cor 4:12; Luke 23:34; Acts 7:60.

60 $\Sigma\iota\alpha\gamma\acute{\omega}\nu$ primarily means "jaw" (usually $\gamma\nu\acute{\alpha}\vartheta o\varsigma$ or the poetic form $\gamma\nu\alpha\vartheta\mu\acute{o}\varsigma$). Then the word could also be used for "cheek" (the "cheek" was normally called $\pi\alpha\rho\epsilon\iota\acute{\alpha}$). $K\acute{o}\rho\rho\eta$ signifies the "temple," but in the wider sense also refers to the "cheek." Here, however, $\sigma\iota\alpha\gamma\acute{\omega}\nu$ is probably to be preferred over

garment, because the coat (used at night), for reason of divine care, remains the property of the condemned individual. Luke and the *Didache*, on the other hand, are thinking of thieves (cf. Luke 10:30), who naturally steal the first thing they can reach, namely, the coat.[61] The switch in external conditions requires an alteration of the image. (3) In the twofold final case, Luke and the *Didache* are united in their content: if someone "asks"[62] or "takes away," the Christian should give in (the *Didache* has reversed the order). In Matthew the person "asks" in both cases, to receive something as a gift or a loan.

Despite the multifarious examples and expressions, Jesus' command is, in the last analysis, understood in the same way by all the earliest witnesses. The disciples, seen here in their individuality and confronted with their personal responsibility, should in every case give in. The linking of this series of commands with the command to love one's enemies means that the latter receives a concrete expression of nonresistance. This again demonstrates that, sociologically, the situation of the earliest Christians was that of the unprotected and persecuted. This was not necessarily the condition of Jesus' audience. But his sayings regain in Luke's time some of their original relevance, since property owners, and even rich people, now belong to the congregation of Christians (cf. Jas 2).

Jesus' proverb about the "other" cheek, which states

that his disciples may not return evil for evil,[63] perhaps implies an anti-Zealot jibe. Unless the exaggeration is rhetorical, one must assume that Jesus is recommending a provocative attitude in order to unmask the complete aggressivity of the other, and thus to emphasize the dynamic momentum of the renunciation of violent resistance in the sense of a Gandhi or a Martin Luther King. But is this not anachronistic for the time of Jesus?

The Golden Rule (v. 31)

■ **31** Some philologists recognize an absolute criticism of every form of reciprocity in Jesus' ethics. They claim either that the Golden Rule was taken up only later by Christian ethics,[64] or that the original version of the Sermon on the Plain directly negates its content; this latter hypothesis is, however, only possible with the acceptance of an emendation of the text.[65]

The break with a law of rigorously equivalent behavior is not in contradiction to a reciprocal relationship between God and the human individual. Because of this, the earliest Christians (rather than Jesus himself) could adopt the Golden Rule in both its positive (Luke 6:31; Matt 7:12) and negative (Acts 15:29, *v. l.*) versions. This wisdom teaching originated outside Israel; it was transmitted to Judaism through Hellenistic popular philosophy.[66] Hillel knows the rule in its negative version as the heart of the Law.[67] The Christians did not invent the

---

παρειά, because παρειά is mostly used in the plural. When Matthew speaks of the *right* cheek, he is thinking either of a slap with the left hand, which is surely not very natural, since most people at that time were right-handed (indeed, the Jews perceived left-handedness as all the more degrading) or of a blow that is executed with the backside of the right hand; see Str-B 1.342; Dieter Lührmann, "Liebet," 418; Spicq, *Agapè*, 1.102 n. 7; Luz, *Matthew*, 325 n. 14.

61 Matthew has in mind a different situation than does Luke: Matthew is thinking of a lawsuit, Luke has in mind a robbery.

62 Note the precision in the vocabulary used: the opponent can request or demand (αἰτέω), the owner, on the other hand, can demand it back (ἀπαιτέω).

63 Concerning this ethical demand in Judaism, see Piper, *Love*, 35–39; and Percy, *Botschaft*, 150–52.

64 See in this regard Merkelbach, "Über eine Stelle." Dihle comments: "The Golden Rule thus shows two faces: although its formulation presupposes a rational analysis of interhuman relations that can only be

expected at a relatively late date, the traditional manner of judgment that operates within it has its roots in an extremely ancient system of compensation" (*Regel*, 12). According to Dihle, the Golden Rule belongs to a tradition of folk wisdom that was only gradually taken over by philosophers in order to substantiate the universality of their specific ethical teaching. Concerning the unexplained origin of the designation "Golden Rule" (which dates at least to the 16th century), see Spicq, *Agapè*, 1.105 n. 3.

65 So Merkelbach ("Über eine Stelle," 172), who proposes, through subordination and modification of the punctuation, to join v. 31 to the following verse: Καὶ <γὰρ ἐὰν> καθὼς θέλετε ἵνα ποιῶσιν ὑμῖν οἱ ἄνθρωποι, ποι<ῆ>τε αὐτοῖς ὁμοίως καὶ [εἰ] ἀγαπᾶτε τοὺς ἀγαπῶντας ὑμᾶς, ποία ὑμῖν χάρις ἐστίν; ("For if you do to others what you would have them do to you, and if you love those who love you, what credit do you gain for it?").

66 Diogenes Laertius 1.36, about Thales.

67 See *b. Šabb.* 31a; J. Jeremias and N. J. Heim, *RGG* 2 (3d ed. 1958) *s.v.* "Goldene Regel," esp. 1688.

positive version, for one finds already in Homer a corresponding example, which values active participation more highly than passive caution.[68]

The Golden Rule has its counterpart in the call to compassion (v. 36). The love of enemies (2) and renunciation of resistance (3), on the one hand (vv. 27b–30), and not judging (8) and giving (9) on the other, are rendered completely comprehensible, according to Luke, only by means of a twofold analogy (4 and 7). The disciples take the initiative, as does a loving God toward human beings (6:36). Whether they are poor and can offer only their prayers, or rich and can demonstrate their magnanimity, Christian ethics in Luke aim at a new form of reciprocity, with its roots in God (6:31 [4]).

The Call to Compassion (v. 36)

■ **36** Luke speaks of compassion, Matthew of perfection. Both versions hint at the rare Hebrew Bible theologoumenon of the *imitatio Dei* (Lev 19:2).[69] But in Lev 19:2 the determining quality of God is holiness ($\H{\alpha}\gamma\iota o\varsigma$, "holy"). Though the saying has a parenetic function in Matthew, in Luke it receives the role of a theological justification, which was already prepared in v. 35b.

In the LXX $o\dot{\iota}\kappa\tau\dot{\iota}\rho\mu\omega\nu$ ("sympathetic," "compassionate") is used thirteen times for God, and only three or four times for human beings. *Tg. Ps.-J.* Lev 22:28 reads: "My people, children of Israel, just as your father in heaven is compassionate, so be compassionate on the earth."[70] Of the two main attributes of God, his compassion and his holiness, Luke chooses compassion as the fount of Christian behavior. One can also detect this tendency in the concept of $\epsilon\dot{\upsilon}\delta o\kappa\dot{\iota}\alpha$ ("good favor"), as well as in the composition of Luke 15: the redaction of the parable of the lost sheep (15:4–7) expresses Jesus' loving initiative toward sinners (15:1–3), and, beyond that, God's accommodation toward human beings (with the goal of rehabilitating them as children, cf. 6:35 and 15:11–32); in Matthew, however, the same parable is meant parenetically for the leaders of the congregation (Matt 18:12–14).[71]

Not Judging, and Giving (vv. 37–38)

■ **37–38** Verse 37a comes from Q,[72] but v. 37b is a redactional paraphrase that removes any misunderstanding of the sense of $\kappa\rho\dot{\iota}\nu\omega$ ("to sentence," "to judge," "to condemn," v. 37a).[73] Verse 37c is a further instruction from Luke that restates the preceding prohibition in the positive.[74] Verse 38a is symmetrical to v. 37c, and takes up a pressing Lukan concern: generosity. In line with v. 37a–b, v. 37c demands kind behavior in the matter of persons, and v. 38a in the matter of material goods. The saying in 6:38c is attested in Q[75] and in Mark 4:24 (not duplicated in Luke 8:18, the parallel passage in Luke). Christians have brought eschatological reward into this context, as becomes unequivocally clear from the Markan addition $\kappa\alpha\dot{\iota}\ \pi\rho o\sigma\tau\epsilon\vartheta\dot{\eta}\sigma\epsilon\tau\alpha\iota\ \dot{\upsilon}\mu\hat{\iota}\nu$ ("will be given you," Mark 4:24), and the Lukan insertion in

---

68 See Homer *Od.* 5.188–91; Kalypso speaking to Odysseus (trans. R. Lattimore):
"But I am thinking and planning for you just as I would do it
"for my own self, if such needs as yours were to come upon me;
"for the mind in me is reasonable, and I have no spirit
"of iron inside my heart. Rather, it is compassionate. . . ."
The word "compassionate" translates $\dot{\epsilon}\lambda\epsilon\dot{\eta}\mu\omega\nu$ in the Greek. The text is cited in Spicq, *Agape*, 1.83; idem, *Agapè*, 1.107.

69 Jacques Dupont, "'Soyez parfaits' (Mt V,48) 'Soyez miséricordieux' (Lc VI,36)," in Joseph Coppens et al., eds., *Sacra Pagina* (2 vols.; BETL 12–13; Paris/Gembloux: Duculot, 1959) 2.150–62.

70 Ibid., 155.

71 Ibid., 158–59.

72 $K\alpha\dot{\iota}\ \mu\dot{\eta}\ \kappa\rho\dot{\iota}\nu\epsilon\tau\epsilon$ is a negated present imperative,

and $\kappa\alpha\dot{\iota}\ o\dot{\upsilon}\ \mu\dot{\eta}\ \kappa\rho\iota\vartheta\hat{\eta}\tau\epsilon$ is a negated aorist subjunctive with future meaning and without an imperatival sense (the aorist imperative would be $\kappa\rho\dot{\iota}\vartheta\eta\tau\epsilon$). Schulz (*Q,* 146) is of the opinion that the more graphic expression of Matthew (7:1, $\dot{\iota}\nu\alpha\ \mu\dot{\eta}$) is original. He goes on to say further that, since Matt 7:2a is constructed after the pattern of 7:2b, v. 7:2a must have been present in Q—which I doubt—and that Luke has omitted it.

73 $K\alpha\tau\alpha\delta\iota\kappa\dot{\alpha}\zeta\omega$: "to pronounce a judgment against someone," "to condemn."

74 $\mathrm{'}A\pi o\lambda\dot{\upsilon}\epsilon\tau\epsilon$ from $\dot{\alpha}\pi o\lambda\dot{\upsilon}\omega$, which means "to let loose," "to release," "to liberate," "to set free," "to dismiss," "to remit," "to acquit."

75 The form of Matt 7:2b (with $\kappa\alpha\dot{\iota}$ at the beginning and the simple verb $\mu\epsilon\tau\rho\eta\vartheta\dot{\eta}\sigma\epsilon\tau\alpha\iota$) is certainly the form of Q. Luke has a predilection for $\gamma\dot{\alpha}\rho$ and compound verbs ($\dot{\alpha}\nu\tau\iota\mu\epsilon\tau\rho\eta\vartheta\dot{\eta}\sigma\epsilon\tau\alpha\iota$). Also the simple verb occurs in Mark 4:24.

6:38b. Luke has thus interfered rather strongly with his source, and has created an artful small composition: two negative imperatives, two positive imperatives, a promise, and a statement.

The call to compassion (7) takes a transitional role, for it lends the command to love one's enemies a conclusion, while appropriately introducing the next unit (8 and 9). The Jesus of Luke demands, first, that we do not judge, that is, pass a definitive sentence about other people, and neither place a label on them nor fit them into hierarchical categories. If κρίνω ("to judge")[76] in v. 37a may still have had a double meaning, this now becomes impossible because of καταδικάζω ("to condemn") in v. 37b. If we judge other people, we put ourselves in God's place. We, indeed, can and must represent our Christian convictions, but must leave the others free to act (ἀπολύετε, "forgive"), and leave their decision to them. For Christians, who live by principles, this attitude is sometimes difficult. It is paradigmatically portrayed in Jesus' attitude toward outsiders (Luke 15:1–3). We know our neighbors, and often also their weaknesses, but we also know that God will judge us all. Both individually and in the context of human justice, one must distinguish between judgment of deeds on the one hand and of persons on the other. Jesus is not demanding that we simply accept everything blindly. He has no objections to a correct assessment of people and facts. Paul understood this when he said that the believer, enlightened by the Holy Spirit, knows how to assess everything (1 Cor 2:15; there he uses ἀνακρίνει, "to examine," not κρίνει or κατακρίνει, "to judge" or "to condemn"). Luke 6:37 summarizes the attitude of a *pastor*, and 1 Cor 2:15 that of a *preacher*.

Like Luke 6:36, 6:37 again puts giving and forgiving in first place. Historically, the order "Judge not" was in Jesus' mouth aimed polemically at the leaders of Israel, who placed religious and social life under the dominating category of the Law. Luke well understood Jesus' rediscovery of the love of God as the basis of the Law, and he gladly adopted it: the disciples should forgive (ἀπολύετε), not *in order* egoistically to secure forgiveness on the last day, but *because* forgiveness has entered into their lives through the message of Jesus. If they behave thus freely and selflessly, they will be accepted and set free by God eschatologically (ἀπολυθήσεσθε, "you will be forgiven"). It is uncertain whether Luke has only forgiveness in mind with all of this, or whether he also means debts that Christians pay on behalf of others, or from which they release the debtors, or even the manumission of slaves. What is certain is this: just as God is χρηστός ("kind," 6:35) toward humans, the disciples should also prove their love by their giving (δίδοτε, "give," 6:38a). Righteousness and forgiveness are, in the rediscovered economy of salvation, consequences of the divine initiative of love.

The image of reward (6:38b) originates in business practice. Customers stow away the bought or lent item in the folds of their garment (εἰς τὸν κόλπον ὑμῶν, "into your lap").[77] The merchant is so generous that he or she first fills the grain into the measuring cup (πιέζω, "to press down"), then shakes it (σαλεύω), and finally lets it flow over the rim.[78] Just as God, in the beginning, allows mercy to triumph over judgment, in the end he will not practice a meticulously exact return payment, but will instead allow his incalculable kindness to beam forth.[79]

After this promise, v. 38c causes some surprise, for the saying is enclosed in a wisdom formula that aims at strict reciprocity.[80] Luke probably understood it not didactically as a description of the eschaton, but parenetically as a warning for the present. In Luke the eschatological perspective of salvation never obscures the seriousness of the present decision.

---

76 Luke knows two uses for κρίνω: 7:43 and 12:57 are concerned with making a right judgment, 19:22 with condemnation.

77 Κόλπος originally signified the "bosom" (the shape of the bosom). The word is still used today in modern Greek for the "bosom of the sea" or "gulf" (a word that itself derives from the Greek κόλπος). Here the word signifies the fold of a garment. From ancient Israelite times, the expression εἰς τὸν κόλπον with the genitive was used metaphorically in a context involving compensation (Isa 65:6; Jer 32[LXX 39]:18; Ps 79[LXX 78]:12; etc.; see Str-B 2.160).

78 In Egyptian loan contracts for grain, "it is clearly specified that the measure, whatever be its exact volume, should be full but without surplus, and the grain should be leveled against the upper rim with a rod" (Bernard Couroyer, "'De la mesure dont vous mesurez, il vous sera mesuré,'" *RB* 77 [1970] 366–70, esp. 370). The word σκυτάλη refers to this rod (369 n. 23). When Luke speaks of an overflowing measure, he does not mean to say that the grain is flowing out over the brim of a basket or out of

History of Interpretation

Thomas Aquinas wonders whether war is always sin.[81] He mentions *ad primum* ("at first") four arguments that seem to answer this question in the positive. The second of them is the renunciation of resistance required by Jesus (Matt 5:39a) and Paul (Rom 12:19). But then (*sed contra*) he cites Augustine,[82] who invokes Luke 3:14: if the Scriptures require soldiers to be content with their wages, and do not command them to throw down their weapons, then they do not condemn all wars. In what follows (*respondeo*), Thomas analyzes the three requirements for a just war. First, a war cannot be declared by a private individual, but only by the current ruler (Rom 13:4). Second, a just cause is required (*Secundo, requiritur causa iusta*). Third, the people waging the war must have an upright purpose. In the last part of this first *articulus*, he is able to dismantle the four arguments with which he began. The instruction of the Gospels to renounce resistance concerns, according to Augustine, an inner readiness, while we must sometimes behave differently externally "because of the general good." To resist opponents with gentle firmness is often in their own best interest. Nothing is more unholy than the unpunished happiness of sinners.

Things are not much different in Calvin, who also defends the idea of just war.[83] He represents the position of the rulers, and supports his arguments from nature and the Scriptures. Without explicitly naming them, he attempts to refute the Anabaptists. If apostolic teaching contains no explicit statement on this, the reason lies in the separation of the two kingdoms. But allusions in the New Testament do help one understand that military service and just war are not sinful. Augustine and the narrow foundation of Luke 3:14 occur here again. Then he enumerates the conditions of a just war.

The command to love one's enemies and to renounce resistance play an astonishingly small role in both theologians. The Sermon on the Mount is cited by the opponents whom they must refute. In this, Augustine, Romans 13, and Luke 3:14 are the chief authorities. In Calvin's exegesis of the Sermon on the Mount, his discomfort can be detected in various places.[84] He is silent about war, since Jesus' commands regulate the private lives of Christians, not the destiny of kingdoms. But even so, he still cannot read the Scriptures literally in this passage—which is against his habit; he is of the opinion that individuals may defend themselves against injustice, so long as they can do this peaceably and according to civil law. He also does not reject charging interest.[85]

I stand in the same tradition. I see its exegetical weaknesses, but as a historian I can conclude that the first Christian congregations very early advocated an accommodation that is theologically not much different from the trajectory observed here from Augustine to Thomas to Calvin. Indeed, at that time the issue of military service was not relevant. Soldiers could become Christians, and Christians were not obligated to become soldiers. Already in Corinth, Paul could not enforce the commands of the Sermon on the Mount, but had to concede: if two Christians do not want to renounce their right to justice, one should institute a court of law in the

---

the lap of one's clothes, and perhaps falling onto the ground. Rather, he means that the measure has not been leveled with the σκυτάλη, which had precise legal specifications.

79   The plural δώσουσιν is either a *pluralis maiestatis* for God or, perhaps more likely, a plural that alludes to the eschatological coworkers of God, i.e., the angels.

80   The numerous Jewish parallels are examined by Hans Peter Rüger ("'Mit welchem Maß ihr meßt, wird euch gemessen werden,'" *ZNW* 60 [1969] 174–82). As a rule, they are based on three HB texts: Isa 27:8; Exod 18:11; and Gen 37:32 (par. 38:25). Rüger refers to a form of the Palestinian Targum at Gen 38:26 (25): "With what measure a man uses, it will be measured to him, be it a good measure or a bad measure." Rüger concludes: "That means, however, that the common opinion, that the

rabbinic statute in *Sota* 1.7 par. was first transformed into an eschatological meaning in Matt 7:2, can hardly be justified" (182). Couroyer ("Mesure" 370) offers precedents in Demotic and Greek contracts for grain loans: "In Egypt, in grain loans, in those since the reign of Chabaka (715 BCE), one would specify the measure that would be used to repay the loan."

81   See Thomas Aquinas *Sum. theol.* 2.q40.a1.
82   Augustine *Ep.* 138.
83   See John Calvin, *Institutes* 4.20.10–12.
84   Calvin, *Harmony*, 193–200.
85   See Andre Biéler, *La pensée économique de Jean Calvin* (Geneva: Georg, 1961) 453–76.

church (1 Cor 6:1–11). The ethics of the Pastoral Epistles and the later writings of the New Testament show that earliest Christianity could not come to terms with the radical message of Jesus.

But the practical and literal application of the Sermon on the Mount has, nevertheless, been demanded again and again, and rightly so, since it offers us a model for overcoming human power and the injustice of every human order. Especially since the mid-1980s, in which the munitions industry and the technology of destruction reached a climax, the Sermon on the Mount has again become *the* New Testament text. Christians should, by means of it, live exemplary lives. But as soon as I write this sentence, I am convinced of our inability to be Christians. Not only can one not demand of the state an orientation based on the Sermon on the Mount; even more, each individual among us is unable to live incessantly in the perfection of Christian ethics. As soon as we are assigned public responsibility in our profession or in politics, the difficult path for human justice between the gospel and sin becomes evident. The early Christians, Paul, and later the church fathers and the theologians of a Christian society all understood this. As a theologian, I do not, for example, want to question the value of a democracy achieved with such difficulty, only because it is imperfect when compared to the Sermon on the Mount. We have learned from the Greeks to distinguish levels of goodness. An imperfect democracy is still at a higher level than a dictatorship or anarchy.

In 1582 the Council of Geneva (the political authority) submitted to the *Compagnie des pasteurs* (the religious authority) an inquiry as to whether it should defend the city with weapons against the threat of troops from Savoy. Part of the answer read:

There is not a single person, unless they be completely unnatural, that does not have a horror of war, as much because of the effects that must naturally follow from it, such as the shedding of blood and destruction of all kinds, as of those things that result accidentally from it, such as pillaging, violence, blasphemies, impious acts, and other dreadful deeds by the military license, which is extremely unrestrained and untameable because of the laxness that is mostly customary on the part of those who carry arms. But to conclude, because of this, that it is never admissable to wage war would be to draw a conclusion that would be proved false as much by the express words of God, confirmed by numberless examples, as by common sense and all equity and reason, in this conformed to the sacred Scriptures, since magistrates are ordained by God with the sword not only to punish crimes committed within their jurisdiction by certain disrupters of the piety and honesty of which they are guardians, but also to defend, as fathers of the commonweal, the people who are committed to them against the violence of those from without. One must then find in this matter some well-structured middle way, which we ascertain in two parts, namely, that war must be both just and necessary.[86]

In view of our current situation,[87] countless synods, conferences of bishops and other church leaders have introduced balloting on resolutions on the question of armaments.[88] Exegetes and social ethicists, as well as involved laity, have authored essays and books.[89] Only in the year 1982–83, and in Germany alone, I can count, without any particular research, nine volumes in which the words "Sermon on the Mount" occur in the title or content of the book.[90] For exegetes it does not lack a certain tragic sense—in view of their identity in communicating with the biblical message—that they must sometimes conclude that the Sermon on the Mount is irrelevant for today's social, political, and human issues.[91]

---

86   O. Labarthe and B. Lescaze, eds., *Registre de la Compagnie des pasteurs de Genève 4 , 1575–1582* (Geneva: Droz, 1974) 434.

87   See Dieter Wittmann, *Die Auslegung der Friedensweisungen der Bergpredigt in der Predigt der evangelischen Kirche im 20. Jahrhundert* (Frankfurt: Peter Lang, 1984); Eberhardt Arnold, *Salz und Licht: Über die Bergpredigt* (Moers: Brendow, 1982).

88   Various texts in I. Baldermann, *Der Gott des Friedens und die Götter der Macht: Biblische Alternativen* (Wege des Lernens 1; Neukirchen-Vluyn: Neukirchener Verlag, 1983) 138–66.

89   References to these polemics in Baldermann, *Gott*, 63–64; and in Franz Alt, *Peace Is Possible: The Politics of the Sermon on the Mount* (trans. J. Neugroschel; New York: Scribner, 1985) 6–7.

90   Literature cited in Franz Alt, *Frieden ist möglich: Die Politik der Bergpredigt* (14th ed.; Serie Piper 284; Munich: Piper, 1983) 118–19 (not in the Eng. trans.).

91   See Baldermann, *Gott*, 62–68.

Many violently resist reading the Sermon on the Mount as the result of our failure: "Should the Sermon on the Mount have nothing else to say, except to convict us of our inability to do good, so that we must then console ourselves with a vague, 'It may well be' from the Holy Spirit?"[92] It should now much more be high time simply to read the words of Jesus, and to comprehend them just as they appear on the page. Above all, we should try to live according to the Sermon on the Mount.

As an example, I choose the small volume of Franz Alt[93] (of which, in October 1983, more than 500,000 copies were sold): religion and politics can no longer be separated (p. 112), since we are faced with possible global destruction (p. 31). The Sermon on the Mount is the only solution here. Now there is no more "on the one hand . . . on the other"; today there is only "either . . . or" (p. 28). One section is entitled, "The Sermon on the Mount or the End of History." Jesus preached the Sermon on the Mount in order that it be fulfilled. We must take the first step and take the initiative of unilateral disarmament. It is a matter of will. And also a matter of knowledge: through voluntary (p. 12) self-knowledge (p. 80), the author hopes for improvement (p. 79). Our repentance (p. 78) should achieve what two thousand years of Christianity have been unable to accomplish: the application of the Sermon on the Mount,[94] the only means today to avoid the destruction of the world.

Conclusion

What should one do, if one does not share the optimistic anthropology like that of this author? Resign oneself? Correct this clichéd diagnosis? The pedagogy of peace teaches an approximation of the fulfillment of the command to love one's enemies. On the basis of individual psychological mechanisms and of public opinion, we can learn to deconstruct our developing images of enemies. This may be the contribution of our century to the interpretation of the command to love one's enemies. We also are today aware of the connection between fear and aggressivity, so that all who, on the basis of this realization, take the initiative of giving in will subdue the fears of their enemy and find a way out of the spiral of escalation. They will not thereby weaken their own position, and they will make dialogue possible. This would be our current interpretation of the Golden Rule, which emphasizes reciprocity less than it does the challenge to take the first step.[95]

---

92 See ibid., 65.
93 See above, n. 89.
94 Alt, *Peace*, 15: "The history of the Sermon on the Mount has not taken place. It is the story of the repression of its demands."

95 I have before me a list (written in English) of 198 nonviolent tactics collected by Gene Sharp (facts of publication unknown).

The Sermon on the Plain III: The Parables
(6:39–49)

Bibliography

Abou-Chaar, Komal, "The Two Builders: A Study of
the Parable in Luke 6:47–49," *The Near East School
of Theology Theological Review* 5 (April 1982)
44–58.

Bouttier, Michel, "Les paraboles du maître dans la
tradition synoptique," *EThR* 48 (1973) 175–95.

Derrett, J. Duncan M., "Christ and Reproof (Mt 7,1–5
par. Lk 6,37–42)," *NTS* 34 (1988) 271–81.

Duplacy, "Disciple."

George, "Disciple."

Hahn, *Titles*, 76–77, 91–92, 123 n. 158.

Jeremias, Joachim, *The Parables of Jesus* (trans. S. H.
Hooke; London: SCM, 1954) 30 n. 3 (v. 39),
124–25 (vv. 39, 41–42, 43–44), 136 (vv. 47–49).

Jülicher, *Gleichnisreden*, 2.50–54 (v. 39), 44–50 (v. 40),
49, 51 (vv. 41–42), 116–26 (vv. 43–46), 22, 259–69
(vv. 47–49).

Krämer, "Hütet euch."

Marguerat, *Jugement*, 183–211.

Meynet, Roland, "Histoire de l'‘analyse rhétorique'
en exégèse biblique," *Rhetorica* 8 (1990) 291–320.

Pirot, *Paraboles*, 50–61.

Sahlin, *Lukas-Stellen*.

Schneider, "Christusbekenntnis."

Schrage, *Thomas-Evangelium*, 85–88 (v. 39), 71–74 (vv.
41–42), 100–106 (vv. 43–45).

Schulz, *Q*, 472–74 (v. 39), 449–51 (v. 40), 146–49 (vv.
41–42), 316–20 (vv. 43–45), 427–30 (v. 46),
312–16 (vv. 47–49).

Spicq, *Lexicon*, 2.18–20, 271–74.

Vielhauer, Philipp, *Oikodome: Das Bild vom Bau in der
christlichen Literatur vom Neuen Testament bis
Clemens Alexandrinus* (Karlsruhe-Durlach: Tron,
1939) 58–59 (reprinted in idem, *Oikodome: Aufsätze
zum Neuen Testament* II [ed. G. Klein; ThBü 65;
Munich: Kaiser, 1979] 59).

39   He told them a further parable: "Can a blind person lead a blind person? Will they not both fall into a pit? 40/ A disciple is not above the master; when fully taught, the disciple will be like the master. 41/ Why do you see the splinter that is in your brother's eye, but do not notice the log that is in your own eye? 42/ How can you say to your brother, 'Brother, let me take out the splinter that is in your eye,' when you do not see the log that is in your own eye? You hypocrite, first take the log out of your own eye, and then you will see clearly to take out the splinter that is in your brother's eye. 43/ For there is no good tree that bears bad fruit, nor again is there a bad tree that bears good fruit; 44/ for each tree is known by its own fruit. For figs are not gathered from a thicket of thorns, nor are grapes picked from a bramble bush. 45/ The good person produces good out of the good treasure of his or her heart, and the evil person produces evil out of his or hers; for out of the abundance of the heart the mouth speaks. 46/ Why do you call me, 'Lord, Lord,' and not do what I say? 47/ Every one who comes to me and hears my words and does them, I will show you who he is like: 48/ he is like a person building a house, who dug deep, and sunk a shaft, and laid the foundation on rock; and when a flood arose, the stream beat against that house, and could not shake it, because it had been well built. 49/ But whoever hears and does not do them is like a person who built a house on the ground without a foundation; against which the floods broke, and immediately it collapsed, and the ruin of that house was great."

Analysis

Form

As the third and last section of the Sermon on the Plain,[1] Luke presents a series of metaphors that he entitles a "parable" ($\pi\alpha\rho\alpha\beta o\lambda\acute{\eta}$, 6:39). (1) After the new introduction (v. 39a), he begins with (2) the proverb about the blind (v. 39b), which has taken the form of a repeated question. Without even a transitional particle, (3) the saying about the disciple and the master (v. 40) follows. To this is joined (4) the more extensive proverb about the splinter and the log (vv. 41–42): two rhetorical questions, an imperative, and a conclusion in the future. (5) The metaphor about the trees and their fruits (two repeated wisdom sayings in the negative [vv. 43 and 44b]) frames the general rule, which is positively expressed (v. 44a); the statements about the fruits of people consist of an antithetical *parallelismus membrorum* (v. 45a), which is rounded out with a wisdom saying (v. 45b). (6) Then follows an accusation, embedded in a rhetorical question (v. 46). After a redactional introduction placed in the mouth of Jesus (v. 47), (7) the parable of the two houses (vv. 48–49) concludes the entire composition.[2]

Everywhere, except in vv. 44b and 46, the number

---

1   Godet (1.329) does not recognize a caesura between
vv. 38 and 39, but is of the opinion that vv. 37–42
formed a continuous whole, which expresses an
objection to the condemnatory judgment of others.

Jülicher makes the case for a caesura (*Gleichnisreden*,
2.50).

2   Grundmann (151–52) perceives four parts in accordance with the fourfold structure that, in his opin-

two is emphasized: the two blind people (v. 39b), the disciple and master (v. 40), the two brothers (vv. 41–42), the two trees (vv. 43–44), the good and the evil persons (v. 45), the two houses (vv. 47–49). Often, but not everywhere, this duality makes possible a juxtaposition of good and evil. Following fine biblical tradition, the evangelist remembers the importance of the two ways.[3] This ethical dualism is, however, explicitly stated only in v. 43, because vv. 41 and 42 are closer in their content to the command not to judge (v. 37). The reason that Luke interrupts this logical sequence with the image of the blind people (v. 39b) is unclear, although Judaism connects this metaphor with the role of the teacher (v. 40).

From the rhetoric of his day, Luke is familiar with the difference between literal and figurative speech,[4] and he collects here sayings of Jesus that have a metaphorical nature. This means neither that each of these proverbs is metaphorical, nor that all of the images have the same function. Thus v. 39b is taken metaphorically in v. 40, but it is not inherently a metaphor. The exaggerations of "splinter" and "log" in the ironic vv. 41–42 suggest a metaphorical interpretation of their own, so that an interpretation in literal speech is unnecessary. Verses 43–44, like v. 39b, are wisdom sayings, and as such are not metaphors. Only their traditional usage and the application in v. 45 lend the sayings a metaphorical significance. Although the images of the blind people and the tree are hackneyed[5] and point in the direction of allegorization, the image of the splinter and the log seems fresh and lively. After humankind and nature, the house now appears as a third instance of comparison. The images and metaphors are drawn from the most

basic spheres of life. Luke himself understands vv. 48–49 not as metaphors but as comparisons ($\tau i \nu \iota \ \dot{\epsilon} \sigma \tau \grave{\iota} \nu$ $\ddot{o}\mu o\iota o\varsigma \cdot \ddot{o}\mu o\iota \acute{o}\varsigma \ \dot{\epsilon}\sigma\tau\iota\nu \ldots$, "whom he is like . . . he is like").

Genre and Tradition History

All of these proverbs are known from Matthew. Aside from Matt 15:14 (the blind people), 10:24–25 (the disciple and the master), and 12:33–35 (the tree and the person), they stand in the same sequence in the Sermon on the Mount,[6] so that we can hypothesize a common source in Q. It is difficult to decide whether the exceptions (Luke 6:39, 40, 45) were in the same location already in Q.

The *Gospel of Thomas* transmits half of these logia, but scattered and in different contexts.[7] Logion 45 is particularly interesting, since it contains the Lukan unit in a form that is independent of Luke, whereas Matthew distributes the entire unit between two different locations (Matt 7:15–20; 12:33–35).[8]

Christian authors of the second century still know a few of these proverbs from oral tradition, but in a form that is definitely more reminiscent of Matthew than of Luke. Only in three cases is the proximity to Luke greater: the logion of Jesus in P. Oxy. 1.1 cites the Lukan form (6:42) of the proverb about the splinter and the log; an extracanonical saying of Jesus in P. Egerton 2 uses the Lukan form of the logion "Lord, Lord!" (Luke 6:46); and Justin (*1 Apol.* 16.10) depends rather on Luke 6:47 than on Matt 7:24.[9]

---

ion, organizes the entire Sermon on the Plain.

3   A terrifying conclusion in the opinion of Augustine *De sermone Domini in monte* 2.25.82 (CCL 35.186), cited in Jean Pirot, *Paraboles et allégories évangéliques: La pensée de Jésus: Les commentaires patristiques* (Paris: P. Lethielleux, 1949) 57.

4   This does not mean that for him the pictorial language can be reduced to a simple statement without a loss in meaning. See further Hans Weder, *Die Gleichnisse Jesu als Metaphern: Traditions- und redaktionsgeschichtliche Analysen und Interpretationen* (FRLANT 120; Göttingen: Vandenhoeck & Ruprecht, 1978) 63–67.

5   On worn-out metaphors see Paul Ricœur, *The Rule of Metaphor* (trans. R. Czerny et al.; Toronto/Buffalo: University of Toronto Press, 1977) 285–95.

6   The connection between the "Do not judge!" (Luke 6:37–38) and the "splinter and the beam" (Luke 6:41–42) can also be observed in Matthew (7:1–2, 3–5).

7   See Schrage, *Thomas-Evangelium*, 85–88 (on *Gos. Thom.* 34), 71–74 (on *Gos. Thom.* 26), and 100–106 (on *Gos. Thom.* 45).

8   *Gos. Thom.* 45 consists of: (1) a text that is nearer to Matt 7:16b than to Luke 6:44b; (2) the words "because they bear no fruit," which can just as well summarize Matt 7:17–19 as they can Luke 6:43; and (3) a parallel passage to Luke 6:45 (in a lesser degree to Matt 12:34b–35).

9   See Edouard Massaux, *The Influence of the Gospel of Saint Matthew on Christian Literature before Saint Irenaeus* (trans. N. J. Belval and S. Hecht; ed. A. J. Bellinzoni; Louvain: Peeters; Macon, Ga.: Mercer University Press, 1990) 686 (the index refers to the

Commentary

Blindness and Instruction (vv. 39–40)

■ **39** Verse 39a is redactional.[10] Παραβολή can mean "speech in parables" in Luke (cf. 15:3).[11] The audience is the same as in 6:27, that is, a circle larger than the disciples (6:20), namely, the crowd (6:17–18). Καί after δέ means "yet," "another"; the whole speech is not yet finished. Verse 39b is traditional; here Luke has retained the Q version better than has Matthew,[12] and has probably adopted the location that it had there, since the association with the splinter and log (to be blind—to be able to see) was operative in the Semitic milieu.[13] The antithetical symmetry of the two questions is attractive. The first, with μήτι, expects a negative answer; and the second, with οὐχί, a positive.

Three interpretations can be defended on the basis of the content: (1) As in Matt 15:12–14 and Rom 2:19, an anti-Pharasaic polemic is at work. (2) In the context of the next parable (Luke 6:40), Luke is here already attacking leaders of the Christian congregation who arrogate to themselves a superior position.[14] (3) Within the Sermon on the Plain, believers as a whole are being addressed: as long as they themselves are blind, they may not advise others.[15]

The last interpretation seems to fit together harmoniously with the proverb about the splinter and the log. Nothing indicates a differentiation between the congregation as a whole and its leadership. It is not disciplinary leadership but intellectual leadership that is being illustrated. The proverb is not denying all responsibility for one's fellow, but is rather requiring the instruction and spiritual maturation of every Christian (see v. 40b). The anthropological presuppositions are pessimistic: despite the light of the Law and of natural revelation, human individuals are still like blind people. According to Luke, becoming a Christian means coming forth from the darkness and constructing a new reality with new eyes (cf. Acts 26:17–18).[16] Even the eyes of the disciples must be opened when the resurrection of Jesus occurs (24:31).[17] Despite the symbolism of light and shadow, sight and blindness, one should not allegorize too much within the parable.[18] The argument that risky leadership can lead one into a worse situation than before is what is significant. The blind person that is being led not only remains blind but falls into the pit along with the teacher.[19] Luke is thus afraid of tensions in the community between the believers in general and those who fancy themselves to be spiritually more mature and think, on this basis, that they ought to teach the others. He perhaps has in mind situations reminiscent of the spiritual enthusiasm in Corinth.[20]

---

pages on which the various patristic texts are discussed). Most of these texts are reproduced in Aland, *Synopsis*, 108–10, at the end of each pericope.

10 Εἶπεν δέ occurs frequently in Luke (Schulz, *Q*, 473 n. 539). The accusative object (here παραβολήν) is also often furnished in Luke after *verba dicendi* (Luke 5:36; 20:9; 21:29). And in spite of his preference for πρός with the accusative, Luke at times employs the dative after these verbs (as he does here, αὐτοῖς).

11 On the use and meaning of παραβολή in Luke, see the commentary on 8:4 below.

12 However, πεσοῦνται in Matt 15:14 appears to belong to the tradition, because Luke likes to use compound verbs (here ἐμπεσοῦνται).

13 See Augustin George, "Le disciple fraternel et efficace," *AsSeign* 39 (1972) 68–77, esp. 70.

14 So Schürmann, 1.365–66, concerning the conclusion of the sermon.

15 Ὁδηγέω ("to show the way") can also include the concepts of "correction" and of "guidance," or "instruction" (see Godet, 1.330). In the LXX the verb was used either in its original sense, as when God leads his people through the desert (e.g., Deut 1:33), or in the figurative sense of instruction in righteousness and in faith (e.g., Ps 86[LXX 85]:11).

16 See Bovon, *Theologian*, 289.

17 On the theme of opening the eyes or Scripture, see Gerhard Delling, "'. . . als er uns die Schrift aufschloß.' Zur lukanischen Terminologie der Auslegung des Alten Testaments," in H. Balz and S. Schulz, eds., *Das Wort und die Wörter: Festschrift G. Friedrich* (Stuttgart: Kohlhammer, 1973) 75–83.

18 Jülicher (*Gleichnisreden*, 2.51) calls attention to the fact that the word βόθυνος in patristic exegesis was readily interpreted in a figurative sense, particularly in reference to "hell."

19 Βόθυνος signifies here more likely a pit than a ditch (I agree with Plummer, 190). Lagrange (198–99) mentions the cisterns and grain pits along the roads. Ἐμπεσοῦνται is, according to Jülicher (*Gleichnisreden*, 2.50), a "future of a necessary consequence."

20 On Luke 6:39 and the meaning that Luke gives to this proverb, Jülicher (*Gleichnisreden*, 2.54) cites 2 Tim 3:13, where one finds the words πλανῶντες καὶ πλανώμενοι.

Here are three concluding remarks: First, the image of the blind person leading another blind person was adopted from the Greeks by the Jews.[21] Second, the image of the pit alludes to a Hebrew Bible proverb about the inescapability of God's judgment.[22] Third, the elder Pieter Breughel portrays the tragedy of human existence in two paintings for which this proverb is the basis: each is in the form of a line of blind people who are all about to fall into the pit together.[23]

■ **40a** "The first part of the proverb [disciple–teacher] agrees literally in Matthew and Luke (v. 40a)."[24] The traditional attestation of the second part of the Matthean proverb (slave–master) in John 13:16 and 15:20a as well as redactional tendencies allow us to assume that Luke deleted it.[25] In the second proverb (v. 40b), Luke apparently deleted the second parallelism (slave–master) again and reformulated the remaining sentence in better literary style,[26] whereas the Matthean version is reminiscent of rabbinic proverbs.[27] The original logion was transmitted independently, but the Q tradition already divested it of its parabolic character by using it as a commentary for the proverb about the blind people. While Matthew inserts the proverb into a statement about a persecution of the disciples that would be comparable to the passion of their Lord, in Luke the proverb is placed, with v. 39, between statements about judging (vv. 37–38, 41–42). The logion, which is originally a proverbial observation, becomes in this manner a community rule: the disciple is neither above the teacher nor above other disciples; and, just as the Lord did not judge, no disciple should judge a fellow disciple. Otherwise, the disciple proves him- or herself to be blind and uninstructed.

■ **40b** Verse 40b can either mean that the disciple will be completely educated like the teacher,[28] or that everyone will be educated like his or her teacher. Καταρτίζω,

especially attested in the language of mariners, politicians, and doctors, can mean "to bring into order," "to supplement," "to educate," or also "to reestablish." Here "education" in the Christian faith is the issue, which encompasses both teaching and life.[29]

The goal of instruction for a disciple in Judaism consisted in becoming like his or her teacher in order eventually to become a teacher himself or herself. Luke surely does not go so far. For him, only the analogy with the ethical behavior of Jesus is important. But there is also no exemplary christology without a soteriological christology. To become like Jesus the teacher is possible only through the work of Christ and a relationship of faith with him. For this reason to become like him means to enter into service for those who suffer.

Seeing and Education (vv. 41–42)

■ **41–42** Matthew and Luke agree here to such an extent that only a Greek version of Q can be considered as a source for this passage. The differences can be explained as the stylistic work of Luke.[30] The proverbs are constructed out of two rhetorical questions, an ethical imperative, and an expression of permission in the future tense. In both cases after the question, which is introduced by an interrogatory particle, comes a restriction in the second part (cf. δέ in the first question, and αὐτός . . . οὐ βλέπων in the second), which begins in each case with the exaggerated image of the log in the eye. Attentive readers can sense a progressing irritation between the first question ("why do you see . . . ?") and the second ("how can you say . . . ?"). Both are formed neatly into an *inclusio* through the verb βλέπω ("to see"). After this critical diagnosis, the imperative formulates the task to be done. The final sentence draws a logical conclusion and allows again the right to criticize.

---

21 See Plato *Resp.* 8.554b; Philo *Virt.* 7; Jülicher, *Gleichnisreden*, 2.51–52; Wolfgang Schrage, "τυφλός, κτλ.," *TDNT* 8 (1972) 270–75.

22 This proverb is found in both Isa 24:17–18 and Jer 48(LXX 31):43–44 (the LXX has βόθυνος).

23 One hangs in the Louvre in Paris, the other in the National Museum in Naples.

24 Schulz, *Q*, 449.

25 Luke sometimes destroys parallelisms (see Schulz, *Q*, 449 n. 337). He does it here in order to maintain the semantic framework of the teaching.

26 In view of the syntax as well as the vocabulary (καταρτίζω).

27 See Str-B 1.577–78.

28 In this case κατηρτισμένος . . . πᾶς is used predicatively (on the predicative use of the postpositive πᾶς see Abel, *Grammaire*, §32c, remark I).

29 The NT letters (1 Cor 1:10; 2 Cor 13:11; 1 Thess 3:10; Heb 13:21) attest that καταρτίζω can be used for Christian instruction; see Spicq, *Lexicon*, 2.271–74; Gerhard Delling, "ἄρτιος, κτλ.," *TDNT* 1 (1964) 475–76.

30 In Luke 6:41 two differences are to be ascribed to the redactional work of Luke: (1) the position of δοκός and the repetition of the article (τήν), and (2) ἴδιος as a possessive pronoun (BAGD *s.v.* ἴδιος

Oral parenesis expresses itself in the second person singular. The manner in which it is expressed by the wise teacher possesses authority, addresses the accused as ὑποκριτής ("hypocrite"), plays with irony, and employs, as often the case with Semitic teachers, extreme examples that draw their force from the exaggeration. The teacher tries, by means of ethical instruction, to bring order to the interpersonal life within a community. It is for this reason that these originally independent proverbs attached themselves relatively early to the words about judging. In terms of their genre, they belong to Jewish wisdom traditions; they reflect no apocalyptic concerns.

In contrast to the cases governed by the *lex talionis* (Matt 5:38–39), the "you" who is reproached takes the initiative here, and the issue is not a misdeed. The situation is interpersonal, although we do not know whether it is a tense one. The "you" begins with a movement toward the other, with a look. An individual's blindness concerning him- or herself corresponds to it. The "you" believes that his or her look is well meaning, or at least fair. This is accompanied by words and motivated by an intention to help. But in his or her self-blindness, the look and the words become damaging and have a one-sided, judgmental effect. In the search for imperfection, the other disappears as a person. The behavior of this "you" is that of an inauthentic person, a hypocrite, although not a conscious one, but in the sense of unconscious self-deception. The "you" intends to do good, but actually accomplishes evil by pointing out another's weakness with an oversensitive instinct for order. In its understanding of anthropology, Jesus' accusation is saying that our image of other people is distorted by our own projections, and that our image of ourselves is occluded by our defensiveness. The resistance becomes stronger, the more we are attacked. So the other person will close up when the "you," in blindness toward him- or herself, tries to wash the splinter out of "his" or "her" eye. The relationship then falls into jeopardy.

Does not Jesus himself fall prey to the problem about which he is warning us? Does he have no log in his own eye? The concern of Jesus for us is a different kind than that of the "you" about his or her brother or sister. The problem that he notes is not a mere splinter, but a log, a very serious disturbance of interpersonal relations. In addition, Jesus is not judging us in order to condemn us, but to lay open a hope and a future for us. He is thus concerned about human individuals in a loving way. He neither judges nor gives up hope. Instead of only suggesting a renewal of the Law, he gives us ethical instruction. According to him, the chief task is to become conscious of one's own hypocrisy and to work on oneself. But for this, one needs an untroubled relationship to one's fellows, for it is impossible to emerge from blindness on one's own. The originality of Jesus' instruction is that he takes the initiative for this relationship to us. Only then will it be possible for us to overcome our hypocrisy. The five steps of Jesus' pedagogy, as ecclesiologically understood by Luke, are (1) the renunciation of the right to exercise authority over others as a judge; (2) openness to the words of Jesus, who addresses me with love and hope; (3) the recognition of my serious mistakes ("logs," not "splinters"); (4) the readiness to become a different person (removal of the "log"); only then (5) can I become like Jesus (v. 40b) and become a master (because already a brother or sister!) for others. Only as a renewed person can I suggest—and not prescribe—a minimal change ("splinter," v. 42b).

Luke understands the word "brother, sister" in the Christian sense, and addresses inner-congregational relations, as normative for all members of the community in their relationships to one another, and not only exclusively for the relationship of the leaders of the congregation to the congregation as a whole.

The Test of the Tree (vv. 43–45)

■ **43** The hypothesis that Jesus' sayings were orally transmitted in polemical situations[31] is interesting methodologically. "Apparently, only the two metaphors [the two trees and their fruits] were originally joined

---

[2]). In Luke 6:42 there are a greater number of differences (see Schulz, *Q,* 147; and Schürmann, 1.371) that stem from the redactional pen of Luke. Important for the context is the vocative "brother," which Luke adds to this verse.

31   See Michael Krämer, "Hütet euch vor den falschen Propheten: Eine überlieferungsgeschichtliche Untersuchung zu Mt 7,15–23 / Lk 6,43–46 / Mt 12,33–37," *Bib* 57 (1976) 349–77.

together, and they represented a reproach that was still quite mild. As the argument heated up, the 'Lord, Lord' saying seems to have been added in the camps of the rigorists, in order to achieve a more directed admonition. In the camps of the antinomians, the proverb about the treasure of the heart seems to have enriched the chain of sayings for the same purpose."[32] Thus the two strands of traditional material reflect the opinions of the two parties: "The rigorists reproached their opponents for not doing the will of God because they did not follow the Torah; the antinomians, for their part, reproached them for not doing the will of God, because they set up a law other than the law of Christ."[33] Both parties sensed the difficulty in constructing the traditions into a "Jesus Torah." The Sermon on the Mount and the Sermon on the Plain are later echoes of the "Jesus Torah" of both parties, which developed in a different context. Luke adopts the version of the Pauline, antinomian circle: "The warning against false teachings, as it reads there, can be applied to any sort of false teaching at all."[34] The redactional significance of 6:43–46 would then be: whoever would intend to introduce a law other than the command of love (6:27–28) is a bad tree that bears bad fruit (6:43–44), an evil person who brings forth evil from the treasures of his or her heart (6:45). Such a false teacher cannot be allowed to call upon Jesus (6:46).

The form of the logion in 6:43–45 and its Lukan interpretation are interesting. Verse 44a was either attached by tradition as the conclusion of the proverb about the two trees (6:43; cf. Matt 12:33) or used as an introduction of the metaphor about the various fruits (Luke 6:44b; cf. Matt 7:16). In one phase of the tradition, probably in Q (cf. Matt 7:15–20), both of the two-part sayings (Luke 6:43, 44b) became, with the saying in 6:44a, a group of three, as Luke cites them.[35]

It is not certain that the two-part saying in v. 45 originally belonged here. Matthew introduces it into chap. 12, probably following Q, in connection with a variant version of the two-trees saying (12:33) and in (probably secondary) transposed order (Matt 12:34b–35). Luke, who usually avoids doublets, took the two-part saying from Q, and, like the tradition (cf. Matt 12:33–35), plays on the theme of good and evil[36] and the comparison between tree and human being. Not a single word of the text concerns false teachers. Luke—and the tradition before him—has the believers in general much more in mind.

The particle γάρ ("for") introduces a vague logical connection by means of a comparison known from the Hebrew Bible.[37] If the person continues to behave like a hypocrite (v. 42), his or her rotten fruit[38] shows that the person is like a bad tree. What is important is not what Christians think or say,[39] but what they do (see the two ποιοῦν, "to do").[40] Καλός in this context does not mean "beautiful," but "good," just as σαπρός does not correspond to "rotten," but to "bad."[41] Luke, along with the tradition, understands this simple rule of farmers' wisdom metaphorically, above all because, as a city boy, he has some distance from nature. Already Jeremiah lamented in the name of the Lord, "Yet I planted you a choice vine, wholly of pure seed. How then have you turned degenerate and become a wild vine?" (Jer 2:21). Jeremiah and Jesus remain rhetorically in the realm of

---

32 See ibid., 373.

33 See ibid.

34 See ibid., 375.

35 The oldest form of this verse can be reconstructed only with much difficulty; see the attempts by Krämer, "Hütet euch," 355–56; and Schulz, Q, 316–17. In my opinion Luke 6:43 par. Matt 7:17–18 and Matt 12:33a all derive from the same logion.

36 Καλός–σαπρός (v. 43) and ἀγαθός–πονηρός (v. 45): the meaning of both word pairs is nearly the same; the difference in the choice of words expresses an aesthetic decision.

37 There are several γάρ in these verses, even though not all of them appear to be text-critically sound. Nestle-Aland (27th ed.) has one γάρ in v. 43, two in v. 44, and one in v. 45b. Every sentence (except v. 45a) is accompanied, therefore, by a γάρ. According to Harald Sahlin (Zwei Lukas-Stellen. Lk

6,43–45;18,7 [SBU 4; Uppsala: Wretmans, 1945] 3–4), both γάρ in v. 44 hardly make logical sense, though perhaps the γάρ of v. 43, which justifies its religious and moral demand by an appeal to nature, is consistent with a teaching method that is habitual for Jesus.

38 The singular καρπόν (Luke 6:43) must also have been traditional (cf. Matt 12:33). Matt 7:17–18 has made it into a plural.

39 The thought approaches Luke 6:46.

40 The periphrastic form ἐστὶν . . . ποιοῦν was certainly traditional. Matthew improves it and writes ποιεῖ (Matt 7:17) and δύναται . . . ποιεῖν (Matt 7:18). He does the same with the first καλός and the first σαπρός (in Matt 7:17–18 he uses ἀγαθός twice to describe the tree and πονηρός twice to describe the fruit).

41 This applies to the fruit in every case. In regard to

nature, even if human decisions in the realm of faith and ethics elude its determinism. With the image of "rottenness" Luke is surely attacking not the nomians but rather socially respectable Christians, who, either from enthusiasm or convenience, would like to believe but do not want to realize their faith concretely.

■ **44** Verse 44a first repeats v. 43, but then also has a person in mind with γινώσκεται ("to know"),[42] namely, the farmer. Is ἕκαστος ("each") here being used, as often in Hellenistic Greek, for ἑκάτερος ("each of two"), a form that had become obsolete?[43] Verse 43, indeed, speaks only of two trees, but it introduces v. 44b, in which several types of trees are juxtaposed, so that the meaning "each," and not "each of two," actually fits.[44]

Despite their formal similarity (οὐ γάρ . . . οὐδέ), vv. 44b and 43 do not mean the same thing. The more concrete v. 44b, which contrasts two edible fruits with two fruitless trees, runs parallel in content only to the second half of v. 43.[45] The uselessness of the bad tree is to be demonstrated, accusingly, by its lack of fruit. Are the ἄκανθαι supposed to be "wild fig trees that bear only bad and hardly edible fruits," and βάτος, "a bush with wild grapes,"[46] since, at least in Matt 7:16b, there is an allusion to Isa 5:2 LXX: καὶ ἔμεινα τοῦ ποιῆσαι σταφυλήν, ἐποίησεν δὲ ἀκάνθας ("and I waited for it to produce grapes, but it produced thorns")? But if this were the case, it seems that Luke would have connected grapes and thorns, as in Isa 5:2. For him the rhetorical effect derives from the very difference between a fig tree and a thicket of thorns, not from their similarity. Since no reasonable farmer will look for fruit where it cannot grow, God also will inquire only about the fruits of believers. Luke's statements do not teach an ontological dualism: these examples from nature are only to encourage Christians parenetically to live out their relationship to Christ in their daily life (cf. v. 47).[47]

■ **45** In v. 45 Luke makes a transition from image to subject:[48] everything is decided in the heart. According to Luke, as long as the heart does not hear and accept the Word of God, it remains as though handicapped. Out of it, nothing good will come. But those who believe are called to bring forth goodness continuously[49] from the treasure[50] of their hearts.

---

the tree, σαπρός could have the meaning "rotten," "decayed," "worm-eaten," "decomposed." To the Greeks, σαπρός implies excess: "too ripe," "too old," "too soft."

42 The active compound verb in the second person plural of the future tense ἐπιγνώσεσθε in Matt 7:16 and 20 is secondary; the simple verb γινώσκεται in the third person singular of the passive present tense, in Luke 6:44, is original.

43 See Sahlin, *Lukas-Stellen*, 5, esp. n. 5.

44 The words ἕκαστον and ἴδιον are redactional according to Schulz, who nevertheless argues the point with some caution (*Q*, 317).

45 In Matt 7:16 the grapes are coupled with the thornbushes, and the figs with the thistles. In Luke 6:44, on the other hand, first there are the figs with the thornbushes, and then the grapes with the thistles. For other minor differences see Schulz, *Q*, 316–17. Both evangelists are attempting, each in his own way, to avoid repeating the verb συλλέγω: Matthew follows with an elliptical sentence, while Luke uses a synonym, τρυγάω, which means "to harvest grapes." It is entirely possible, however, that Luke substitutes grapes for figs on account of the verb and thus has deviated from Q (and from Matthew). Ἥ or ὁ βάτος (or even τὸ βάτον) signifies the "thornbush," the wild "bramblebush."

46 So Sahlin, *Lukas-Stellen*, 6–7.

47 See Jean Duplacy ("Le véritable disciple: Un essai d'analyse sémantique de Luc 6,43–49," *RechSR* 69 [1981] 74–75): "As for the apparent truism enunciated in v. 44, its role seems to be to emphasize to the point of absurdity that the relationship between the 'thusness' of the fruit and the 'thusness' of the tree is essentially nothing more than an aspect of a relationship situated, more fundamentally, on the level of being as such."

48 See Duplacy, "Disciple," 75.

49 Can the gnomic present προφέρει be interpreted perhaps in such a way as to include the idea of a continuous obligation on the part of the believer? In any case, this is the way Augustin George understands it. He argues ("Disciple," 74) that Luke here calls for a complete turnaround in one's life that must be demonstrated in a concrete way.

50 In the LXX θησαυρός is used according to its basic meaning, the temple treasure and the royal treasure, and in its figurative meaning to denote divine treasures (e.g., the heavens and their rain, Deut 28:12), and the spiritual possessions of the believer (for this use in wisdom literature, see Prov 2:4; 8:21; 21:20; Wis 7:14). Sir 29:11 straddles the literal and the figurative meanings: "Lay up your treasure according to the commandments of the Most High,

If one keeps in view the relationship of this saying to what precedes it, one sees that the ethical requirement extends to both the words and deeds of the believer. These two possibilities of realization are expressed with particular emphasis in the Lukan version of the command to love one's enemy (6:27–28). For this reason, Luke is able to take into account the not always logical tradition: in vv. 39–45a the *deed* of love is in the foreground, and in v. 45b, the *word*.[51]

Verse 45b plays upon a metaphor. What people say comes out of themselves: they are responsible for their speech.[52] The heart is thus like a fountain, and the mouth can but direct the words like a water pipe. The saying does not differentiate between honesty and hypocrisy, as in v. 46; in conformity with v. 45a, it says inexorably that the quality of words depends exclusively on the quality of one's heart. The mouth is capable of influencing the speech of people as little as the water pipes or basin can influence the water of a fountain or spring. In a time in which we often speak without saying anything, we are astonished at this old piece of wisdom, according to which one only speaks when too much lies upon one's heart.[53] Here there is no contrast between word and deed; what is decisive is the juxtaposition between the interior life of a person and its expression. The saying is about speech, but it can also be applied to people's deeds.[54]

Words, Words (v. 46)

■ **46** Is the Lukan version original (Heinz Schürmann, Gerhard Schneider), or is it the result of a later abbreviation (Ferdinand Hahn)?[55] Since Luke sometimes avoids sayings in the form of a question, it is probably original here. The absence of the probably Matthean addition, "shall not enter into the kingdom of heaven," does not mean that the eschatological perspective is lacking. Since Matthew "loves the figure of speech in which an ἀλλά follows a negation,"[56] the καὶ οὐ ποιεῖτε ("you do not do") may also be traditional. But Luke emphasizes the relationship to the person of Jesus at the end of the Sermon on the Plain (v. 47), so ἃ λέγω ("what I say") should probably be attributed to the redaction. But Matthew has transmitted the Q version no more faithfully, since the address "Lord!" requires a relationship to the words of Jesus, and not, as in Matthew, to the will of the Father. In Q the saying already began the parable of the two houses. It is difficult to evaluate its authenticity: the historical Jesus could have meant "Lord, Lord!" unchristologically or metaphorically, or even ironically. But it is more probable that it developed after Easter in a direction that was, from the beginning, christological.

Differently than the preceding saying, v. 46 presupposes that the will does not always follow the intention, and behavior is often untrue to an expressed promise (cf. Matt 21:30b). With the doubled[57] address, Luke has

---

and it will profit you more than gold." See Dieter Zeller, "θησαυρός, κτλ.," *EDNT* 2 (1991) 149–51.

51   Verse 46 will specify that speaking—even the correct declaration of faith—is nothing without doing, nothing without obeying the will of Christ.

52   In contrast to Matthew, whose version (without αὐτοῦ) is more reminiscent of a proverb and probably corresponds to Q, Luke inserts an αὐτοῦ after τὸ στόμα in v. 45b. Luke can be more specific since he has already introduced the ἄνθρωπος in v. 45a, while Matthew writes about the overflow of the heart (Matt 12:34b) before he mentions the person (Matt 12:35).

53   See Duplacy ("Disciple," 77): "Nothing is accessible to human individuals except what issues forth from that hidden zone: the 'product,' the 'overflow,' the word. In my opinion, v. 45 probably carries an *unexpressed* that one might express in this fashion: it is the 'thusness' of an apparent being that reveals a 'thusness' that is, in itself, inaccessible. It may be that even the *unexpressed* is the reason for the existence of that which is *expressed*."

54   Duplacy, "Disciple," 75–76, 78.

55   According to Schneider the Matthean revision of the logion corresponds to that of the Beatitudes ("Christusbekenntnis und christliches Handeln: Lk 6,46 und Mt 7,21 im Kontext der Evangelien," in R. Schnackenburg, et al., eds., *Die Kirche des Anfangs: Festschrift Heinz Schürmann* [EThSt 38; Leipzig: St. Benno, 1977] 9–24). In his opinion the original logion cannot derive from Jesus, since the christological title "Lord" is used. See also Schürmann, 1.379–80. Hahn (*Titles*, 91) defends his position: "For, on the one hand, Luke has deprived the saying of its eschatological bearing; on the other, instead of its being a question of doing the will of God, it is a question of carrying out the words of Jesus." Krämer ("Hütet euch," 373) locates in the camp of the rigorists any Christian interest in this saying of Jesus and its development.

56   Schneider, "Christusbekenntnis," 11.

57   The doubling of a vocative is common in Judaism (see Str-B 1.943; 2.258). It can express reverence or affection. Thus, for instance, in the case of the lat-

in mind prayer[58] rather than confession. The address κύριε ("Lord!") was used at that time both in private devotion and public liturgy. Κύριος was no longer only God the father, but also the risen Lord, whom one thanked for his saving work, whose presence one invoked, and whose return one awaited.[59]

The question and the observation are only indirectly parenetic. First, a diagnosis is offered: those addressed recognize in their prayers that Jesus has become Lord over their entire existence, but they are living as though this has no relevance outside the devotional sphere.[60] So this saying, like the Hebrew Bible accusations from YHWH in the mouth of a prophet,[61] is a painful lamentation on the part of Jesus. But threats and an announcement of punishment are missing here. With ἃ λέγω ("what I say") Luke has in mind the entire teaching of Jesus, which he is attempting to retain in his book. Luke thinks holistically, and this short proverb, like the two-part love command (10:25–29), requires not so much word or deed,[62] but rather an authentic relationship of the believer toward the divine, and, analogically, to fellow human beings.[63]

Building Well and Poorly (vv. 47–49)

After an introduction (v. 47), a symmetrical, two-part proverb compares the good disciple to a person who builds well (v. 48), and the evil disciple to a person building poorly (v. 49). The dualism that is in the background is reminiscent of the contrasts in the wisdom sayings at 6:43 and 6:45, as well as the parables about the parousia in 12:41–46 and 19:11–27. Formally, as well, this parable is in the Hebrew Bible tradition of dualistic wisdom (cf. Psalm 1, a wisdom psalm), and in the tradition of the blessings and curses (cf. Deut 30:15–20; and, later, the teaching of the two ways in *Did.* 1.2–5.2). The influence of wisdom dominates the content. The context (the conclusion of the Sermon on the Plain) and the allegorical possibilities in the image of the flood increase the apocalyptic perspective.

As in Luke, the parable in Matthew (7:24–27) follows the metaphor of the trees (7:15–20) and the "Lord, Lord" saying (7:21–23). These three units seem to have formed the conclusion of the Sermon on the Mount already in Q. Q, Matthew, and Luke are here, with a very serious parting shot, emphasizing the highest degree of human accountability and the final relevance, no longer of the Law of Moses, but of the words of Jesus.[64]

■ **47** In v. 47 one finds in Luke both stylistic improvements and a theologically significant addition ("who comes to me").[65] Common to both Matthew and Luke are the pair "hearing" and "doing," as well as the normative "words" of Jesus.

■ **48** In v. 48 Luke explains the careful building techniques used for a foundation. It is not enough for him to

ter sense one finds "Martha, Martha" (Luke 10:41), and "Simon, Simon" (22:31). Does the doubling of "Lord" occur elsewhere? In John 13:13 one finds "Master and Lord." For Oscar Cullmann (*The Christology of the New Testament* [trans. S. C. Guthrie and C. A. M. Hall; rev. ed.; Philadelphia: Westminster, 1963] 209–10) it is possible that this saying is authentic inasmuch as κύριος would have originally meant "master."

58   Agreeing with Hahn, *Titles*, 91–92.

59   To grasp the pervading climate, see Luke 13:25. On the use of κύριος in Luke, see Fitzmyer, 1.200–204; and Bovon, *Theologian*, 189–92.

60   See Ernst, 235 (with a question mark).

61   See Claus Westermann, *Basic Forms of Prophetic Speech* (trans. H. C. White; Philadelphia: Westminster, 1967) 142–49, 182–86. Cf. Mal 1:6.

62   Schneider ("Christusbekenntnis," 14) writes: "Practice is not being juxtaposed to theory here, but rather what is demanded is a complete confession of the Lord." Lukan texts pointing in the same direction are 6:27, 47–49; 8:21; 10:25–42; 11:28; 13:24a. According to Michel Bouttier ("Les

paraboles du maître dans la tradition synoptique," *EThR* 48 [1973] 175–95, esp. 179), the text of the Gospel reproaches Christians for not understanding what it means when they call Jesus their Lord, namely, that the Lord on whom they call and for whom they wait is not there, and that they as believers are encouraged through him to be watchful and responsible. "High" christology and "worldly" expectation belong together.

63   There is an apocryphal variant to Luke 6:46 in P. Egerton 2, frag. 2 recto, lines 52–54, cited in Aland, *Synopsis*, 111, and translated in Hennecke-Schneemelcher, 1.98–99.

64   See Daniel Marguerat, *Le jugement dans l'Évangile de Matthieu* (Le Monde de la Bible 6; Geneva: Labor et Fides, 1981) 207.

65   Luke avoids πᾶς οὖν ὅστις, uses present participles, and prefers the expression "I will show you what he is like" over the passive ὁμοιωθήσεται ("will become like"). For this reason the text appears in a different light than in Matthew: the future is directly imminent; the concept, however, is no longer apocalyptic.

say, as Matthew does, that the house was built on a rock. He describes what is involved in "building" with three verbs, which actually encompass only two phases: one must first "dig," even "dig deeply," and "excavate,"[66] in order then "to lay the foundation." Luke's attention is concentrated on the foundation.[67] This probably illustrates, for Luke, the decisive first burst of faith, μετάνοια ("repentance"),[68] and is symmetrically related to the Sermon on the Plain, which is the foundation of the new message. About the construction itself, he remains silent for the rhetorical purpose of brevity, as does Q before him.

The testing through the storm (v. 48b) begins with an adversative δέ. Whereas Matthew mentions rain, floods, and wind (7:25), Luke speaks only of an inundation, although in two phases. First he describes the rising of the flood. The redactional πλήμμυρα (also in the form πλήμυρα, classically πλημ[μ]υρίς)[69] is a literary term, which originally means the sea tide, then any tide, an inundation; in medical language also the excessive concentration of bodily fluids; thus in general it means "high tide" or "flood." Next, the text describes the power of the flood: the waves of water cast themselves against the house, but they lose their force against it,[70] and, as Luke consistently continues, they cannot "shake" it (one runs across σαλεύω in apocalyptic descriptions and theophanies; cf. Heb 12:27).[71] Matthew's description is probably closer to the text of Q, since it corresponds to Palestinian weather conditions.[72] Luke's image is reminiscent of floods that suddenly break out in the south during rainy season. At the end of v. 48, Luke avoids the repetition in Q and uses the hypotaxis διὰ τὸ καλῶς οἰκοδομῆσθαι αὐτήν ("because it had been well built"). In Luke's time καλῶς ("well") plays a theological role. The adverb describes Christian identity, whether it be in the realm of scriptural interpretation (Acts 28:25) or also—as here—in the realm of ethics. The "good" Christian has come to Jesus (v. 47a), has not only heard

Jesus' words (v. 47b), but has accepted them wholeheartedly (v. 47c). This Christian's believing existence is securely anchored (cf. Heb 2:1–4).

■ **49** In Luke the contrast is not between stone and sand, as in Matthew, but between stone and earth, and, above all, between the absence and presence of a foundation. Since this foundation is the result of intensive work, one can conclude that Luke is underscoring the participation of human beings. But he is not weighing the contributions of God and human beings against one another. He is not in a judicial frame of reference but in an interpersonal one, concerned with individual initiative. The similarity with v. 46 is great: the Christian confession loses any value if it is not embodied in active application and the corresponding behavior.

In the case of the absent foundation, the tide "breaks" against the house (the same expression as in v. 48), but this time the house "breaks" too, as Luke states with the wordplay of ῥήγνυμι–ῥῆγμα. "Immediately" (a Lukan overdramatization), the building collapses (συμπίπτω—Luke loves composita).

The Semitic background is apparent. "Hearing" and "doing" form a unit; in order to illustrate this necessary combination, Jewish teachers had already before this employed trees or houses in parables. Of course, from a Jewish standpoint, the Synoptic Gospels prove themselves to be unequivocally heretical writings, for the words that are to be heard and followed are not the commands of the Law but the new teaching of Jesus. In these last verses of the Sermon on the Plain, a strong christological claim is advanced, which becomes clear from the repeated occurrence of the first person singular (ἃ λέγω, "what I say," v. 46; πρός με, μου τῶν λόγων, "to me," "my words," v. 47). Is the type of obedience required thus "essentially"[73] different because of this? That depends on one's understanding of the nature of Jewish law: there were certainly pious Jews at that time who obeyed a lawbook in a utilitarian manner

---

66 Βαθύνω forms its aorist as ἐβάθυνα. Thus three aorists follow one another.

67 Luke "is probably explaining in detail the urban construction of his milieu" (Marguerat, *Jugement*, 204 n. 131); Marguerat then mentions still another possibility—a doctrinal concern, namely, that the active participation of the person is required for her or his salvation.

68 On μετάνοια see Bovon, *Theologian*, 267–89; and

Taeger, *Mensch*, 105–224.

69 See BDF §43.1. In both cases the spelling with one μ is the more ancient.

70 On the relationship between προσρήσσω and προσρήγνυμι, see BAGD *s.v.*

71 Σαλεύω is used in 6:38; on this verb see Horst Balz, "σαλεύω," *EDNT* 3 (1993) 224.

72 See Schulz, *Q*, 313 (although with some hesitation).

73 See Marguerat, *Jugement*, 206.

and were subject to Jesus' anti-Pharisaic criticism. But there was also a different type of Jewish obedience, one expressed in selfless love. This is exactly the expectation that Jesus has of his disciples, and it is rooted in authentic biblical tradition. For him, and then for Christian tradition as well, no contradiction existed between the Law and the new teaching, but there was a contradiction between right and wrong obedience, between a superficial and an authentic relationship to Christ. The issues are not anti-Jewish, but inner-Christian: with this parable, a series of church leaders (from Q through Matthew and Luke) are trying with all their might to direct the attention of the members of the congregation to their own accountability, and to instruct them and "build them up" for the final right decision.

Conclusion

All believers stand before a choice. Jesus' words should help them to choose the right path with unclouded vision, and should give them the strength to behave rightly on this path toward their Lord and teacher, and their brother and sister. But the nature of a believer discloses itself only in practical life. The goodness of their being, which is nourished by the goodness of their Creator and Savior, originates in the innermost part of their personality, the location at which $\mu\epsilon\tau\acute{\alpha}\nu o\iota\alpha$ ("repentance") has occurred. The more deeply that faith has renewed the heart, the more decisively the ethical consequences of this decision come to light.

The Centurion from Capernaum (7:1–10)

Bibliography

Aubineau, Michel, *Un traité inédit de christologie de Sévérien de Gabala in Centurionem et contra Manichaeos et Apollinaristas: Exploitation par Sévère d'Antioche (519) et le Synode du Latran (649)* (Cahiers d'Orientalisme 5; Geneva: P. Cramer, 1983).

Boismard, Marie-Émile, "Guérison du fils d'un fonctionnaire royal," *AsSeign* (I) 75 (1965) 26–37.

idem, "Saint Luc et la rédaction du quatrième évangile," *RB* 69 (1962) 185–211.

Busse, *Wunder*, 141–60.

Derrett, J. Duncan M., "Law in the New Testament: The Syro-Phoenician Woman and the Centurion of Capernaum," *NovT* 15 (1973) 161–86, reprinted in idem, *Studies*, 1.143–69.

Dodd, Charles Harold, *Historical Tradition in the Fourth Gospel* (Cambridge: Cambridge University Press, 1963) 188–95.

Gagnon, Robert A. J., "Luke's Motives for Redaction in the Account of the Double Delegation in Luke 7:1–10," *NovT* 36 (1994) 122–45.

George, Augustin, "Guérison de l'esclave d'un centurion," *AsSeign* 40 (1972) 66–77.

Haapa, Esko, "Zur Selbsteinschätzung des Hauptmanns von Kapharnaum im Lukasevangelium," in J. Kiilunen, V. Reikkinen, and H. Räisänen, eds., *Glaube und Gerechtigkeit: In Memoriam Rafael Gyllenberg* (Helsinki: Suomen Ekesegeettisen Seuran, 1983) 69–76.

Haenchen, Ernst, "Faith and Miracle," *StEv* 1 (1959) 495–98 (= TU 73).

idem, "Johanneische Probleme," *ZThK* 56 (1959) 19–54, esp. 23–31.

Haslam, J. A. G., "The Centurion at Capernaum: Luke 7:1–10," *ExpTim* 96 (1985) 109–10.

Jeremias, Joachim, *Jesus' Promise to the Nations* (trans. S. H. Hooke; SBT 1.24; Naperville, Ill.: Allenson; London: SCM, 1958) 29–31, 34.

Joüon, Paul, "Notes philologiques sur les Évangiles: Luc 7:9," *RechSR* 19 (1928) 352.

Kleist, James A., "'Axios' in the Gospels," *CBQ* 6 (1944) 342–46.

Martin, Ralph P., "The Pericope of the Healing of the Centurion's Servant/Son (Matt 8:5–13 par. Luke 7:1–10): Some Exegetical Notes," in R. A. Guelich, ed., *Unity and Diversity in New Testament Theology: Festschrift George E. Ladd* (Grand Rapids: Eerdmans, 1978) 14–22.

Mouson, J., "De sanatione pueri Centurionis (Mt 8,5–13)," *Collectanea Mechliniensia* 44 (1959) 633–39.

Schnackenburg, "Traditionsgeschichte," esp. 69–76.

Schnider, Franz, and Werner Stenger, *Johannes und die Synoptiker: Vergleich ihrer Parallelen* (Biblische Handbibliothek 9; Munich: Kösel, 1971) 54–88.

Schniewind, Julius, *Die Parallelperikopen bei Lukas und Johannes* (1914; reprinted Darmstadt: Wissenschaftliche Buchgesellschaft, 1970) 16–21.

Schramm, *Markus-Stoff*, 40–43.

Schulz, *Q*, 236–46.

Theissen, *Miracle Stories*, 182–83.

Wegner, Uwe, *Der Hauptmann von Kafarnaum (Mt 7,28a; 8,5–10.13 par Lk 7,1–10): Ein Beitrag zur Q-Forschung* (WUNT 2.14; Tübingen: Mohr-Siebeck, 1985).

1 When he had completed all these sayings for the ears of the people, he went to Capernaum. **2/** But a centurion's slave, whom he valued highly, was ill and close to death. **3/** When he heard about Jesus, he sent some Jewish elders to him and asked him to come to save his slave. **4/** And when they reached Jesus, they appealed to him ernestly, saying, "He is worthy to have you grant this to him, **5/** for he loves our people, and he built the synagogue for us." **6/** And Jesus went with them. When he was not far from the house, the centurion sent friends to say to him, "Lord, do not trouble yourself, for I am not worthy to have you come under my roof; **7/** therefore I did not presume myself worthy to come to you. But only speak a word, and my young slave will be healed. **8/** For I also am a person set under authority, with soldiers under me; and I say to one, 'Go,' and he goes; and to another, 'Come,' and he comes; and to my slave, 'Do this,' and he does it." **9/** When Jesus heard this he was amazed at him, turned to the crowd that followed him and said, "I tell you, not even in Israel have I found such great faith." **10/** And when those who had been sent returned to the house, they found the slave in good health.

Analysis

Form

After the Sermon on the Plain, Jesus goes directly to Capernaum (7:1), the city that he had left in 4:42–44, without there being any discussion of his return. Luke thus does not give the impression that Capernaum was Jesus' most important place of residence; also, contrary to his usual habit, Luke does not compose a transitional summary passage here.[1] The first half of 7:1 lends a conclusion to the preceding speech of Jesus, where the second half already begins the narrative that follows. The Matthean (8:5–13) and Johannine (4:46–54) parallels lead one to postulate a miracle story. But the importance of the dialogue, and the fact that the healing itself is presented almost as an addendum, disrupt the generic structure of the miracle story.[2]

Verse 2 describes the dramatic situation tersely. Immediately following this, the text tells of the first strategic move of the centurion (v. 3). After just being sent (v. 3), the legates have already reached Jesus (v. 4a). Surprisingly, their speech to Jesus (vv. 4b–5) does not correspond to their commission (v. 3). The readers expect a cry for help, and instead hear a panegyric. In Luke's conceptualization, however, this, like the legation, was itself a component of the strategy; and by breaking off the speech before it reaches the actual concern of the legates, he avoids repetition (the readers already know what is desired). Only then, and for a short period, does Jesus become active by accompanying the legates (v. 6a). But he does not even reach his destination, for the centurion ambushes him with a second legation (v. 6b), which transmits the exact words of its commissioner (even in the first person singular). It is a relatively long speech (vv. 6c–8), in which the centurion expresses a lot about himself through the mouths of his friends. He wants: (1) to spare Jesus; (2) to express his unworthiness, in order to keep Jesus away from his house and, at the same time, to excuse his own absence; (3) to ask Jesus to heal from afar; (4) to show his trust in Jesus' abilities by pointing to his own, which depend on his position within the military hierarchy. In all of this, the centurion is so much the center of attention that Luke does not consider it necessary to let us hear Jesus' healing word of power. Jesus finally begins to speak, but he neither gives a specific answer to the centurion's friends, nor speaks the expected healing word. In his answer, he includes far more: the crowd that accompanies him, in order to tell them, too, something about the true hero of this story (v. 9). This is the climax of the story. The last verse connects to the preceding ones like a prosaic consequence, like a return home from the theater after the curtain has fallen.

The sequence of the story can thus be presented in the following manner:

Jesus enters Capernaum.
The centurion has a dying slave.
He sends a first legation.
　　They reach Jesus and praise the centurion.
　　　Jesus follows them.
The centurion sends a second legation.
　　They present a long speech in his name.
　　　Jesus addresses the crowd, recognizing the centurion.
　　Return of *the legations* and the healing of the slave.

From this initial formal analysis, the following become evident: (1) the leading role of the centurion, who never himself appears, and his faith, praised in v. 9; (2) the juxtaposition of him and Israel (cf. the "crowd" behind Jesus in v. 9); (3) the significance of the distances: the centurion first begs for Jesus' nearness, but then refuses direct contact; (4) connected to this, the reciprocal role of the presence and absence of the major characters; (5) likewise, the function of the intercessors (the legates, the word of Jesus); (6) related to this, the relevance of worthiness: the centurion is ἄξιος ("worthy," v. 4), but denies being such (vv. 6–7), although in v. 8 he claims a limited but real authority; (7) the slave is healed at the end, but his external fate is only a foil to the inner attitude of the centurion.

Genre

This story belongs to those rare pieces of narrative that Matthew and Luke know independently of Mark. Its position in both Gospels immediately after the Sermon on the Mount/Plain[3] and the similarity of the dialogue

---

1　It is not necessary, since here he is not proceeding from one episode to another, but from a speech to a narrative.

2　Augustin George ("Guérison de l'esclave d'un centurion," *AsSeign* 40 [1972] 66–77, esp. 76) points out that in Luke the faith of the Gentile stands at the center of the narrative.

3　Between the end of the Sermon on the Mount (Matt 7:28–29) and the episode of the centurion (Matt 8:5–13), Matthew inserts Markan tradition (Mark 1:40–45 = Matt 8:1–4, the healing of a leper).

(7:6b–9 par. Matt 8:8b–10) strongly suggest that it belongs to Q.[4]

Both the Synoptic and Johannine versions probably derive from one and the same event,[5] as the existing commonalities make clear: (1) the sick individual lives in Capernaum; (2) the centurion is in the service of Herod Antipas;[6] (3) the sick individual belongs to the household of the centurion; (4) the officer takes the initiative (ἐρωτάω, "to ask," Luke 7:3; John 4:47); (5) faith plays a significant role; (6) the slave is on the point of dying (Luke 7:2; John 4:47); (7) Matt 8:13 and John 4:52–53a indicate the hour of the healing.[7]

The most important differences concern the point of the story: in the Synoptic Gospels, the centurion emphasizes his unworthiness and begs for a healing from afar through Jesus' word, while in John the "royal" man or official runs up to Jesus as he comes, and the word from afar is spoken directly by Jesus. But the first dialogue (John 4:48–49) is probably a redactional addition,[8] and this again would show that the two versions are very similar.

Both traditions, Q and John, thus reflect the same memory, but were transmitted independently thereafter with the result that the direction of the versions now diverge from one another.[9]

In Matthew, distance plays such a minor role that the centurion encounters Jesus immediately at the beginning. Matthew often simplifies the scenes of the miracle stories; thus the two legations are not necessarily attributable only to Lukan redaction.[10] Yet the speech of the second legation is introduced so clumsily in Luke that I

consider it to be a redactional addition.[11] Through it, Luke avoids direct contact between Jesus and a Gentile. Matt 8:11–13 clearly represents a Matthean expansion in the form of a saying of Jesus that was initially transmitted separately, which Luke, hardly by chance, records in another context (13:28–29).

A comparison with Acts 10:1–11:18 suggests that Luke reworked the passage. There, as well, the subject of the story is a pagan but pious centurion, who has been particularly kind to the Jewish population; similarly, a legation is sent to him, and something takes place shortly before the bearer of the divine message crosses the threshold. Jesus, however, does not meet the centurion, nor does he enter his house. Despite the Lukan formulation, the first legation is probably traditional. It is also possible that Luke knows two variants: the one in Q, and another. In John a memory of the legation remains, albeit with a different function (4:51).

The situation of the sick man in Capernaum is also part of the basic structure of the account in Q, as are the centurion's cry for help (perhaps by mediation of the legation), the centurion's long speech, Jesus' admiration, and the healing itself. It is uncertain whether Jesus hesitates, neglecting to come immediately, thereby motivating the centurion's speech (Q and Matthew), or whether the centurion rushes over only just before Jesus arrives and delivers his speech in this context (pre-Lukan tradition). In the second case, the first legation would be traditional.[12]

4   The dialogues in the present pericope favor their incorporation in Q, or their incorporation in Q led to their transformation in the direction of a "speech."

5   In 1964 Rudolf Schnackenburg remarked that nearly all modern Protestant commentaries favor the view that both narratives have the same origin, whereas this was not the case for Catholic commentaries ("Zur Traditionsgeschichte von Joh. 4,46–54," *BZ* n.s. 8 [1964] 58–88, esp. 70). Since that time, there has been some change among the ranks of the latter: see Schürmann, 1.397; Schneider, 1.165; Fitzmyer, 1.648, all of whom start with the premise that behind the different versions lies a single incident.

6   Under Herod Antipas, no Roman troops appear to have been stationed in Galilee. Βασιλικός ("royal," John 4:46b) can designate an official or officer in the service of a prince such as Antipas. In Josephus the plural is frequently found as a designation for the troops, the palace, officials, or officers (see Rengstorf, *Concordance*, 1.315–17).

7   This list of similarities is based on Schnackenburg, "Traditionsgeschichte," 71–72.

8   See ibid., 65–67.

9   Further differences between Q and John can be noted, especially that John does not note the Gentile status of the royal officer. See ibid., 73–75.

10   Nevertheless, Schulz (*Q*, 238 n. 410) shows that the vocabulary of vv. 3–6a is very Lukan.

11   If one compares Luke 7:6b–8 with Matt 8:8, it is clear that these words were traditionally spoken by the centurion, who has approached Jesus, as still preserved by Matthew, who also has nothing about the return of the legates (Matt 8:13; cf. Luke 7:10).

12   See Schulz, *Q*, 236–40; Schramm, *Markus-Stoff*, 40–43; Busse, *Wunder*, 142 n. 3.

Commentary

The Request (vv. 1–6a)

■ **1** Πληρόω ("to fulfill," "to complete") indicates not only the end of the Sermon on the Plain (see Matt 7:28: τελέω, "to bring to an end"), but also the fullness of Jesus' words:[13] Jesus has said everything that he intended at this time.[14] Τὰ ῥήματα αὐτοῦ ("all these sayings") is probably synonymous with μου τῶν λόγων ("my words," 6:47), but sounds more elevated and Semitic. The reference to the "people" is important, because it refers back to the audience of Jesus' message,[15] and forward to the people accompanying Jesus and to the encounter with the centurion's household (7:9). Εἰσῆλθεν means "he entered Capernaum" (the aorist cannot take an ingressive meaning here).[16]

■ **2–6a** Luke considers the centurion[17] to be a non-Jew. Since, in Jesus' time under Antipas, no Roman troops were normally stationed in Galilee, the *centurio* could only have belonged to the militia of Antipas himself, who also conscripted non-Jewish troops.[18] Whether Luke actually devoted any thought to this issue is unclear.

In addition to his profession, the text indicates the attitude of the man[19] to Judaism. "He loves our people"[20] sounds like an application (ironic?) of, if not love of one's enemies, then at least love of strangers. Ἀγαπάω ("to love," 7:5) is also suggested in the Sermon on the Plain. The alien nature of the man surfaces in the words of the elders: τὸ ἔθνος ἡμῶν ("our people").[21] This love has taken the concrete form of his donation[22] of a synagogue.[23] Dedicatory inscriptions demonstrate that, at that time, foreigners indeed paid for a few synagogues.[24] Sociologically, we are encountering here the category of the "God-fearers," who played an important role in the history of the earliest Christian mission. Although attracted to Judaism, its monotheism, and its ethical teachings, such men avoided the final step of circumcision, to avoid betraying their race and homeland. They did, however, attend Jewish liturgical services, knew the Law, and kept its major commands. The Christian mission enjoyed quick success with these people. Luke himself was probably one of them, and for this reason, has a particular interest in them.[25] According to Luke, the Christian message would make it possible for them to become members of the people (λαός, 7:1) of God, but by faith, not by circumcision.

---

13 Indeed, Luke frequently uses the word πληρόω, but nowhere else for the end of a speech; cf. Acts 13:25, where it is used for the end of one's life, which is compared to a race. Does he avoid τελέω (Matt 7:28) because of the following τελευτᾶν in Luke 7:2?

14 Ἐπειδή ("when"): Luke uses this conjunction in a temporal sense only here (elsewhere, it is always causal).

15 First of all, ἀκοή signifies the sense of "hearing," then it indicates the "ear," "listening," and finally "that which is heard" (see Acts 17:20; Sophocles *Ai.* 147). There is no question of a Semitism here.

16 On the ingressive aorist see BDF §331. I wonder whether it were not a question of such an aorist since, if Jesus has already entered Capernaum, where then would the centurion and his sick servant be located? Luke must nevertheless be following the tradition (see Matt 8:5; John 4:46b), according to which they are likewise located in Capernaum. According to Luke, then, the messengers do not have to travel a very long way.

17 On ἑκατοντάρχης (Luke) and ἑκατόνταρχος (Matthew), see BAGD, *s.v.*

18 Lagrange (205) thinks that a Roman officer could be meant, one who in addition to his regular duties oversees excavations at a mine.

19 In contrast to a Cornelius, Jairus, or Zacchaeus, this man has not yet received a name.

20 See Josephus *Ap.* 2.4 §43, who cites in his argument that Alexander was in favor of giving civil rights to the Alexandrian Jews, ἐτίμα γὰρ ἡμῶν τὸ ἔθνος ("for he honored our nation").

21 For Luke these are not scribes but prominent men.

22 On gifts and donations in the Roman Empire, see Paul Veyne, *Bread and Circuses: Historical Sociology and Political Philosophy* (London: A. Lane, 1990). The motif of contributing to a building is taken up in Christianity: In *Acts Phil.* 7(87–93) two men are competing to see which one could endow a church.

23 On the history of the word συναγωγή, see Wolfgang Schrage, "συναγωγή," *TDNT* 7 (1971) 798–808.

24 See Baruch Lifshitz, *Donateurs et fondateurs dans les synagogues juives: Répertoire des dédicaces grecques relatives à la construction et à la réfection des synagogues* (CRB 7; Paris: Gabalda, 1967).

25 Agreeing with Schweizer, 4. On the "God-fearers" see the excursus by Kirsopp Lake, in idem and F. J. Foakes-Jackson, eds., *The Beginnings of Christianity*, vol. 1: *The Acts of the Apostles* (5 vols.; London: Macmillan, 1920–33) 5.74–96; and more recently Thomas M. Finn, "The God-fearers Reconsidered," *CBQ* 47 (1985) 75–84.

The first legation[26] expresses the centurion's request for help[27] and quietly indicates that the officer respects the separation of Jews from non-Jews required by the Law (cf. Acts 10:28). The elders first give a moral justification: the centurion is worthy (ἄξιος) of Jesus' help.[28] Of course, this man, as well as Cornelius, provided the Pelagians and Semi-Pelagians with an argument against the theology of Augustine in respect to the *initium fidei*. Actually, Luke is simply describing the service of the centurion without any further motive. His concern is a loving, personal relationship between God and humans; when individuals love one another, to ask, "Who began it?" is nonsensical.

The centurion has a servant[29] who is sick,[30] in fact, at death's door.[31] The threat of death is all the more tragic in that the servant is "valuable" to his master. According to the legal concept of slavery in antiquity, this could be understood financially. Luke intends to describe, however, a threatened interpersonal relationship (cf. the friends in v. 6). The officer loves not only the alien people of Israel but also his neighbor (10:25–37). His high estimation of his servant shows that he considers him not only in his function but also as a person. Jesus' love, which reaches both the nearest and the farthest, responds to this double affection. Faith and love achieve an exemplary unity in the centurion.

The Faith of the Centurion (vv. 6b–10)

■ **6b–7a** The structure of the narrative follows this request with more than a mere answer. The request (vv.

2–6a) develops, far more, into a voluntary self-test. The centurion freely forgoes the nearness of Jesus. Jesus understands the trial and simultaneous request as an expression of πίστις ("faith"). According to Luke, the Gentiles trust that they will receive the benefits of salvation without personally having met Jesus. The evangelist thereby explains to the Gentiles of his own time that they are not inferior to the Jews or to the first generation of Christians. Neither physical proximity nor chronological immediacy decides salvation, but only personal attitude, love toward others, and faith in the Lord.

The redactional construction of the second legation intends to correspond to the rhythm of salvation history. The actual call to the Gentiles must wait for the saving event (Luke 22–24), the coming of Pentecost (Acts 2), and a further revelation (Acts 10:9–16), until the divine purpose has finally achieved full maturity. During the preparatory stage of Jesus' lifetime, Gentiles do not come into direct contact with the Lord. Luke thus achieves two goals: he qualifies the faith of the centurion with distance,[32] and indicates by this distance the unfulfilled character of the realization of salvation. Individual existence and the saving event are here intertwined.

Luke dramatizes the story: when Jesus is already (ἤδη) near the house,[33] the centurion sends his friends. With the word φίλοι ("friends"), rare in the New Testament, as well as with the kind relationship between master and slave, Luke suggests a harmonious atmosphere in the hospitable house of the centurion.

---

26 The legation is obviously introduced for the non-Jewish reader (cf. "the elders of the Jews," v. 3, and "our nation," v. 5).

27 The verb παρακαλέω (v. 4) also occurs in Matt 8:5; it belongs to the tradition. The tense of the verb (imperfect) as well as the adverb σπουδαίως underscores the urgency of the request made by the leading men. The adverb has three shades of meaning: diligence, earnestness, and urgency. The meaning of διασῴζω probably differs hardly at all from that of the simple σῴζω. Perhaps the δια- indicates that the salvation extends beyond the mere recovery from the sickness.

28 Of course, the speech is not a literal quotation but entirely tailored for the reader. The reader immediately grasps that παρέξῃ τοῦτο has in view the healing of the servant. In contrast to the active παρέχω ("to furnish"), the middle παρέχομαι ("to personally furnish something for oneself") under-

scores the personal concern that the messengers expected from Jesus.

29 The tradition read παῖς (Matt 8:6), which was interpreted by John as "son" (υἱός, John 4:46) and by Luke as "servant" (δοῦλος, Luke 7:2). Luke avails himself of the word δοῦλος as an *inclusio* for his narrative; it appears twice at the beginning (vv. 2–3) and once at the end (v. 10). The traditional παῖς survived where little would have changed—in the discourse (v. 7).

30 Matthew, who has a predilection for the paralyzed, altered the tradition transmitted by Luke (cf. John 4:46). The vernacular expression κακῶς ἔχων is not Lukan (see Marshall, 279).

31 The parallel passage in John 4:47 proves that this remark came from the tradition.

32 However, he also understands that the centurion overcomes the separation.

33 Wettstein (1.698) cites various possibilities of uses

Μὴ σκύλλου ("do not trouble yourself")[34] sounds colloquial, but the verb had already lost much of its coarseness (lit. "to flay," "to skin").[35] The centurion believes himself *οὐ γὰρ ἱκανός* ("not sufficient," "not large, strong, rich enough," or "not good enough" or "worthy").[36] Alongside the centurion's need for healing and the objective honesty is a note of a subjective feeling of insufficiency. Luke understands this existential lack ("we are unworthy servants," 17:10), and readers may recall the theology of *ἱκανότης* ("sufficiency") in 2 Corinthians (3:5–6: only God can enable us to serve). This is rooted in a strong awareness of human character. The story nevertheless emphasizes that the man becomes worthy by believing that he is not (cf. 9:24)—in Pauline language, that he becomes strong when he is weak (2 Cor 12:9). The repetition of the theme of unworthiness in v. 7a (not in Matthew or Q) suggests that the Gentile also considers himself unworthy with regard to the Law of God.

■ **7b** After this negative and yet very positive part of the speech, the centurion makes a suggestion. He trusts Jesus to such an extent that he believes that his mere word will suffice to heal his servant. The distinction is thus between word and deed, not between one word and many (accordingly, the phrase should not be translated, as so often, with "say only a single word," which is oriented toward the liturgy of the Matthean Last Supper). It is important to remember that, in antiquity, miraculous healings were thought to be possible only through direct contact (cf. Luke 5:17 and 6:19). The centurion, however, believes in the divine efficacy of Jesus' word, a conception of language not impossible in antiquity. It is not so much the difference in the transmission of divine power (language instead of action) that amazes Jesus, but the fundamental trust in the power of *Jesus* in

word.[37] In the faith of the centurion, the christological aspect is the deciding factor.

■ **8** The centurion concludes his second request with the well-known comparison with military discipline. This has nothing to do with the issue of the loyalty of Christians to the state. The most one can say is that Luke has no aversion here to the representatives of the army, quite the contrary. Indeed, the centurion does not begin with his authority, but stresses his subordination to others. This comparison can be understood either as an incomplete argument of the type "how much more," or as a strict analogical syllogism. In the first case, the centurion is saying, "Although I am under authority, I have the power to issue commands. How much more you. . . ." In the second case, God emerges behind Jesus: "As I am under authority, you are under the Father's authority, and precisely for this reason, your word has divine efficacy." I would argue for the first interpretation, but not necessarily for the concessive sense of *τασσόμενος* ("[although I am] set under authority"), because in military organizations (and this is the point of comparison), the power of the commanding officer is completely delegated to the subordinate.

■ **9** Jesus the teller of parables himself perceives the parable here. What he hears comes from the personal experience of the believer and displays a highly insightful understanding of Jesus' authority. To believe means to recognize one's responsibility not only psychologically but also in the social realm, to value not only the person of Jesus but also his position, and to distinguish the analogies and the differences between human reality and the divine sphere. The structure of the word of command is analogous, but the application is without analogy: no human being can cure a sick person with a word by him- or herself.[38] Despite his position of author-

---

for the words *οὐ μακρὰν ἀπέχω* (e.g., Dionysius of Halicarnassus *Ant. Roma.* 4.27).

34 Schramm (*Markus-Stoff*, 42) is of the opinion that Luke has adopted this expression from the story of Jairus's daughter (Mark 5:35 par. Luke 8:49). Yet the circumstances there are entirely different, since the messenger who notifies the father of his daughter's death is the one who bids the father not to trouble the master further (see Loisy, 217).

35 See Plummer, 196.

36 Do the words "that you come under my roof" involve a trite expression? In any case, the same expression occurs in Codex Alexandrinus Gen 19:8.

37 The vocabulary remains in the area of physical health: *ἰάομαι* (v. 7) and *ὑγιαίνω* (v. 10). But to the Christian ear, perhaps only *διασῴζω* (v. 3) can suggest a rescue that transcends recovery from bodily sickness.

38 Luke here sets himself in complete opposition to the magical view of faith current in his time. He believes in the *δύναμις* of Jesus, but not in its acquisition through magical formula or human rites and practices.

ity, the centurion stands over his servant (the same word as in the comparison in v. 8) wordless and powerless.

The aspect that probably disturbs us now may have been, in those days, the punch line of the comparison: the obedient soldier or servant could have no will of his own. The power of the healing Messiah to help is as effective, believes the centurion, as the word of a commanding officer.[39]

The centurion remains the main figure. Jesus does not act independently in v. 9, but merely reacts, as a spectator ($\dot{\epsilon}\vartheta\alpha\dot{\nu}\mu\alpha\sigma\epsilon\nu$, "he was amazed")[40] like the other spectators.[41] But his word transforms itself like lightning from a remark to a binding judgment. He authoritatively ($\lambda\dot{\epsilon}\gamma\omega$ $\dot{\nu}\mu\hat{\iota}\nu$, "I tell you") compares the faith of the alien with that "in Israel."[42] With this, the weight shifts from the centurion to Jesus, and the people now take the role of spectator.

Although Matthew writes "in no one in Israel," Luke has "not even ($o\dot{\nu}\delta\dot{\epsilon}$) in Israel."[43] In Luke's formulation, the criticism of Israel is much more reserved than in Matthew; nevertheless, it is still a prophetic reproach of Jesus toward his people, as the positive and contrasting description of the alien makes clear. The story was originally told in the sense of a complaint against Israel, later as an example of faith, and finally as a joyful endorsement of the inclusion of the Gentiles in the Christian church.

■ **10** The actual pronouncement of the expected words of healing ($\dot{\alpha}\lambda\lambda\dot{\alpha}$ $\dot{\epsilon}\dot{\iota}\pi\dot{\epsilon}$ $\lambda\dot{o}\gamma\omega$, "but only speak a word," v.

7) is purposely not recounted, so that the readers ascribe the healing, above all, to the centurion's faith. The effect of his faith[44] follows its assessment. It remains uncertain who the returning messengers are, perhaps a sign that the original version contained only one legation. When they return home, the messengers find the servant healthy, a state of affairs that should not be interpreted allegorically.[45]

History of Interpretation

The interpretation of the Valentinians transmitted by Irenaeus is striking: the centurion is identified with the Demiurge, who admits his lack of knowledge when the Savior appears. What he learns from him has the effect that he, along with his forces, comes over to the side of the Savior. He fulfills the economy of the world for the predetermined time, both because of the church, which is his responsibility, and because of his promised reward (his promotion to the "place of the mother"). Irenaeus's summary continues with a distinction between the three categories of human beings.[46]

Such a distinction occurs three hundred years later in a sermon of Severian of Gabala, published only in 1983. This opponent of Chrysostom begins with an exegesis of the Synoptic account,[47] then describes the true believer, the semi-believer, and the unbeliever, employing the account of the stilling of the storm (with the disciples' lack of faith)[48] extensively for this purpose, in order

---

39 The examples in v. 8 are well chosen: a soldier is commanded to move along; a slave is commanded to do something.

40 Throughout the history of exegesis, Christian readers have asked themselves over and over again how Jesus, the Son of God, could "be surprised" (see Calvin, *Harmony*, 249).

41 According to Joüon ("Notes," 352), the dative $\tau\hat{\omega}$ $\dot{\alpha}\kappa o\lambda o\upsilon\vartheta o\hat{\upsilon}\nu\tau\iota$ $\alpha\dot{\upsilon}\tau\hat{\omega}$ $\ddot{o}\chi\lambda\omega$ is not dependent on $\sigma\tau\rho\alpha\varphi\epsilon\dot{\iota}\varsigma$, which should be followed by $\pi\rho\dot{o}\varsigma$ or $\epsilon\dot{\iota}\varsigma$, but on $\epsilon\dot{\iota}\pi\epsilon\nu$: "And after he had turned himself around, he said to the crowd that was following him. . . ." However, the wording in Matt 5:39 is $\sigma\tau\rho\dot{\epsilon}\psi o\nu$ $\alpha\dot{\upsilon}\tau\hat{\omega}$ $\kappa\alpha\dot{\iota}$ $\tau\dot{\eta}\nu$ $\ddot{\alpha}\lambda\lambda\eta\nu$.

42 $To\sigma o\hat{\upsilon}\tau o\varsigma$ indicates the size or the quantity. Here—in a figurative sense—it is the size that is indicated: "also, *so great* (in rank, skill, or character)" (LSJ *s.v.*). Thus its meaning is close to that of $\tau o\iota o\hat{\upsilon}\tau o\varsigma$.

43 Even though other meanings are possible, $o\dot{\nu}\delta\dot{\epsilon}$ probably has the meaning I give it here. That is also

how Ambrose understood the Greek text long ago (*Expositiones in Lucam* 5.6.87).

44 Luke can indeed avoid the passive construction that is in Q ($\dot{\iota}\dot{\alpha}\vartheta\eta$, Matt 8:13), yet he does so only at the cost of an unfortunate repetition of $\epsilon\hat{\upsilon}\rho o\nu$ (third person plural, Luke 7:10; cf. the first person singular in 7:9).

45 Of course, the vocabulary of health used in Luke's day was also employed metaphorically by Christians to describe their instruction (Titus 1:9) or the life of faith (Titus 1:13).

46 Irenaeus *Adv. haer.* 1.7.4–5.

47 In *De centurione* Severian of Gabala refers to the accounts in both Matthew and Luke (Michel Aubineau, *Un traité inédit de christologie de Sévérien de Gabala in Centurionem et contra Manichaeos et Apollinaristas: Exploitation par Sévère d'Antioche [519] et le Synode du Latran [649]* [Cahiers d'Orientalisme 5; Geneva: P. Cramer, 1983]).

48 See Severian of Gabala *De centurione* 1–13. Luther

finally to denounce the Manichaeans and their conception of the evil σάρξ ("flesh").[49] There seems to have been an exegetical tradition that connected the centurion with believers. The orthodox variant of this would be the distinction that we find in Severian among believers, those of little faith, and nonbelievers. According to Severian, the centurion recognized the position of the Savior, which many heretics did not comprehend in subordinating him to the Father.[50] The lack of faith among the Jews (Luke 7:3) contrasts with the faith of the centurion, who does not demand the physical proximity of Jesus.[51] "Only speak a word" shows that the centurion understands the power of God's word both in the creation and in the miracles: Λόγον χρήζω παρὰ τοῦ θεοῦ λόγου ("I need a word from God, the Word").[52]

Both Luther and Calvin recognize the centurion's faith and his virtue, but expressly attribute this to the preexisting grace of God.[53] According to Luther, one component of his faith is his humility (7:6) toward Jesus, striking in consideration of the Jews' contempt for him.[54] Calvin also admires the centurion's love of God and of the Law in a time when the pagans hated the Jews.[55] Both of these Reformation figures believe (according to medieval interpretation?) that the centurion cannot yet recognize Jesus' two natures, but can see the power of God in the person of Christ, and this suffices for faith.[56] In the comparison to military discipline (7:8), both Luther and Calvin see the contrast between the centurion and the Lord, and they draw their conclusion using the analogy *a minore ad majus* (from lesser to greater).[57] About v. 9 Luther writes, "Interpreters have

devoted care to the fact that the mother of God and the apostles should not seem inferior to this centurion." Then he himself admits that Jesus is speaking here "of the great masses" and not of his most immediate followers. Nevertheless, we should not "bend Christ's words to our interpretation." Then follows a protestant exegesis of the saints, who are what they are through God's grace.[58] Since Luther takes into consideration two miracles,[59] the faith of the centurion and the word of Christ, he comes to the conclusion, "Here both his faith and the heart of Christ agree perfectly."[60]

Conclusion

This pericope grants insight into the social origins of some Christians: the Christian message found a strong response among Gentiles in Galilee and Syria who felt drawn to Judaism because of their religious needs and moral sensibilities, but did not dare take the plunge of truly converting. They belonged to the middle and upper classes.

From a form-critical perspective, the pericope appears between a miracle story (like the Jairus pericope, 8:40–56) and a biographical legend (like the story of Cornelius, Acts 10:1—11:18). The main character is the officer, and his faith forms the center of the story, with the healing of his servant rather on the fringe. By such a faith in Christ, together with obedience to the ethical requirements of the Law of God, such a person would belong fully to the people of God. Circumcision and ritual requirements are a thing of the past. Luke's

---

attests that a Christian could conscientiously ask the question: Did this officer have more faith than the apostle and Mary? (*Evangelien-Auslegung*, 367).

49 With *De centurione* 24, Severian of Gabala distances himself from the Apollinarians, who maintained that the divine Word had dwelt in a human body that indeed possessed a soul but not an intellect (νοῦς).

50 *De centurione* 2.

51 *De centurione* 2–3.

52 *De centurione* 4. Ambrosius (*Expositiones in Lucam* 5.6.83) understands the healing of the servant as an example of experiencing love for one's enemies.

53 See Luther, *Evangelien-Auslegung*, 364: "But God had rather arranged it thus. . . ." Calvin (*Harmony*, 247): "So before Christ healed his servant, he himself had been healed by the Lord."

54 Luther, *Evangelien-Auslegung*, 365.

55 Calvin, *Harmony*, 247.

56 Luther, *Evangelien-Auslegung*, 365; Calvin, *Harmony*, 249.

57 See Luther, *Evangelien-Auslegung*, 366; Calvin, *Harmony*, 249. "The pagan soldier becomes a theologian, and begins to dispute in so fine and Christian a manner, that it would have sufficed for someone who had already been a doctor four years" (Luther, *Evangelien-Auslegung*, 365).

58 Luther, *Evangelien-Auslegung*, 367.

59 Ibid., 366: "a double miracle."

60 Ibid., 369.

redactional work achieves a paradox: the centurion is the main character, but never personally appears on stage. The evangelist thereby shows that the Gentiles have been predestined by God as the chief recipients of the Christian message (cf. Acts 28:28), but will only achieve this goal in due course of the economy of salvation, that is, after Pentecost (cf. the story of Cornelius, in which this is treated explicitly, Acts 10:1–11:18). In connection with this, the text illustrates the essence of faith for today's audience. Faith means trust, and more concretely, to trust without having seen (cf. John 20:29),[61] to hold fast, and above all to enter into a personal relationship with Jesus Christ.

---

61 Luther has a keen sense for this power of the word, even when Christ himself is absent (see ibid., 366).

The Young Man at Nain (7:11–17)

Bibliography

Abel, Félix-Marie, *Géographie de la Palestine* (1933–1938; 2 vols.; EtB; reprinted Paris: Gabalda, 1967) 2.394–95.

Achtemeier, Paul J., "The Lucan Perspective on the Miracles of Jesus: A Preliminary Sketch," *JBL* 94 (1975) 547–62.

Bornhäuser, *Sondergut*, 52–64.

Brodie, Thomas Louis, "Toward Unravelling Luke's Use of the Old Testament: Luke 7:11–17 as an *Imitatio* of I Kings 17:17–24," *NTS* 32 (1986) 247–67.

Bultmann, *History*, 215, 424.

Busse, *Wunder*, 161–79.

Dibelius, *Tradition*, 75–76, 80, 82, 86, 165.

Dubois, "Elie."

Fuller, Reginald Horace, *Interpreting the Miracles* (Philadelphia: Westminster, 1963) 64.

George, "Miracle."

Gils, *Jésus prophète.*

Harbarth, "'Gott.'"

Jeremias, *Sprache*, 156–60.

Kopp, *Places*, 236–41.

Lindars, "Elijah."

Petzke, "Historizität."

idem, *Die Traditionen über Apollonius von Tyana und das Neue Testament* (Leiden: Brill, 1970) passim, esp. 129–30, 135–37.

Richardson, Alan, *The Miracle Stories of the Gospels* (London: SCM; New York: Harper, 1959) 113–14.

Sabugal, Santos, "'¡Joven, te lo digo, levántate!' (Lc 7:11–17): Análisis histórico-tradicional," *Estudio Agustiniano* 23 (1988) 469–82.

Schnyder, "Leben."

Ternant, "Résurrection."

Theissen, *Miracle Stories*, 161, 277.

van der Loos, *Miracles*, 573–76.

Vogels, Walter, "A Semiotic Study of Luke 7:11–17," *EeT* (Ottawa) 14 (1983) 273–92.

11   **And it happened that afterward he went to a town called Nain, and his disciples and a large crowd went with him. 12/ As he approached the gate of the town, just then someone who had died was being carried out, his mother's only son, and she was a widow; and with her was a large crowd from the town. 13/ When the Lord saw her, he** had compassion for her and said to her, "Do not weep." 14/ Then he came forward and touched the bier, and the bearers stood still. And he said, "Young man, I say to you, awake!" 15/ And the dead man sat up and began to speak, and Jesus gave him to his mother. 16/ Fear seized all of them; and they glorified God, saying, "A great prophet had risen among us!" and "God has visited his people!" 17/ This word about his work spread throughout Judea and all the surrounding country.

Analysis

The pericope in 7:11–17 has no parallel in the other Gospels. Although it is transmitted in one of Luke's Q passages (6:20—7:10; 7:18–35), it did not originate in Q. If Matthew had known this account, he would surely have not omitted it.[1]

Alongside the many Lukanisms, the narrative also contains non-Lukan elements: Nain (v. 11), ἐκκομίζω ("to carry out"), τεθνηκώς ("someone who had died," v. 12), possibly σπλαγχνίζομαι ("to have compassion," v. 13), and μὴ κλαῖε ("do not weep," v. 13), the touching of the bier, the verb ἐγείρω ("to wake up," "to rise up," v. 14), ἀνακαθίζω ("to sit up," v. 15) and προφήτης μέγας ("a great prophet," v. 16).[2] Luke was then probably using a written source in Greek from his special source. Although, as a rule, Luke alternates long passages from Mark and Q, he generally takes smaller individual accounts from his special material and inserts them into whatever passage from Mark or Q he is currently following: for example, the calling of Peter (5:1–11) is inserted into a longer passage from Mark, and the present pericope into a passage from Q.

The reason for including vv. 11–17 at precisely this point is obvious: Jesus is about to emphasize to the disciples of John, who will arrive in 7:22, that the dead are raised. Since Luke has not yet described any resurrections from the dead, he is now filling this lacuna, as 7:21 shows, a verse summarizing the healing activity of Jesus.

---

1   Thanks to Anita Harbarth, "'Gott hat sein Volk heimgesucht': Eine form- und redaktionsgeschichtliche Untersuchung zu Lk 7,11–17: 'Die Erweckung des Jünglings von Nain'" (diss., Heidelberg, 1977) 17–79 (the most important work on this pericope); and to Jeremias, *Sprache*, 156–60, we can now identify the Lukanisms in this section: e.g., ἐγένετο, ἑξῆς, πορεύομαι εἰς, πόλις, καλέω, συμπορεύομαι, μαθηταί, ὄχλος πολύς (v. 11), ὡς δέ, ἐγγίζω, καὶ ἰδού, ὄχλος . . . ἱκανός (v. 12), etc.

2   The language is examined in Harbarth, "'Gott,'" 17–79; Busse, *Wunder*, 165–70; and Jeremias, *Sprache*, 156–60.

If one tallies together the healing of the paralyzed individual (5:17–26), the recovery of the leper (5:12–16), our pericope (7:11–17), the Beatitudes (6:20–22), and the summary passage (7:21), it is clear that the evangelist consistently accounts for all parts of Jesus' answer to the Baptist (7:22) with the reality of his messianic activities.[3]

Luke has reworked his source so completely that it is nearly impossible to reconstruct the earlier tradition exactly. By means of a long analysis employing philological, stylistic, and tradition-historical criteria, Anita Harbarth managed a skeletal reconstruction of the tradition so close to that of Ulrich Busse that one can be safe in assuming that this structure and its elements belong to Luke's source.[4] What Luke actually possessed was, of course, more extensive than these meager data; but he would have omitted or replaced many of the traditional elements.

Presumably, Luke respected the obvious structure of the narrative in his source:

1. The introduction, with the motif of the coming of the miracle-worker (vv. 11–12a).

2. The exposition, with the depiction of the situation of need and the appearance of the person in need (the young man), his representative (the widow), and the crowd (v. 12b; καὶ ἰδού, "just then").

3. The middle of the narrative, with the miracle grounded in the compassion of the miracle-worker: on the one hand, this consists of the intiative of the miracle-worker with his two addresses (to the mother, and to the dead son), and an inserted gesture (touching the bier); on the other hand, it includes the reaction of the young man (his sitting up and speaking attests the miracle, vv. 13–15, καὶ ἰδών, "and seeing").

4. The conclusion, with the reaction of the crowd and its acclamation (vv. 16–17).[5]

Two peculiarities are noteworthy in contrast to the usual structure of such miracle stories:[6] first, the story describes a meeting between a parade of life (Jesus and his disciples) and a parade of death (the dead man, his mother, and the grieving crowd);[7] second, the behavior of the miracle-worker stands clearly at the beginning of the central section (middle), not at the end of the exposition.

Two further characteristics correspond to the typical structure of miracle stories: first, the middle section with the authoritative initiative of the miracle-worker is clearly the most important, this in vivid contrast to the story of the centurion that immediately precedes it (7:1–10); second, attention is turned to both mother *and* son (again in contrast to 7:1–10).[8]

After this resuscitation of a dead young man[9] comes the story of the daughter of Jairus; after mother and son come father and daughter. In the case of both Peter and Paul a similar great deed is also recorded (Tabitha, Acts 9:36–42; Eutychus, Acts 20:7–12).[10] All these cases concern young people, whose deaths are especially tragic. The Messiah or his most important disciples are always the miracle-workers. The tendencies of these accounts sometimes diverge because of the differing nature of the traditions: an atmosphere of mystery envelops the story of Jairus, as the closed doors illustrate; the obvious sovereign power of the "great prophet" in the present peri-

3   Of the healings enumerated in Luke 7:22, only the healing of deaf people has not yet been introduced in a narrative, though later an episode (Luke 11:14) does confirm the statement.

4   See Harbarth, "'Gott,'" 111; Busse, *Wunder*, 169 n. 3.

5   The pericope is structured somewhat differently by C. Schnyder ("Zum Leben befreit: Jesus erweckt den einzigen Sohn einer Witwe vom Tode (Lukas 7,11–17): Eine Totenerweckung," in A. Steiner and V. Weymann, eds., *Wunder Jesu* [Bibelarbeit in der Gemeinde: Themen und Materialien 2; Zurich: Benzinger, 1978] 77–87, esp. 80): (1) introduction (vv. 11–12a); (2) exposition (vv. 12b–13); (3) miracle (v. 14); and (4) reactions (vv. 15–17). The difference is in the treatment of v. 15, which Schnyder regards as a "demonstration"—in accordance with the distinction between recognition and demonstration in Theissen (*Miracle Stories*, 65–67)—thus placing it in

the conclusion of the narrative. However, that *Jesus* is again the subject of the last verb in v. 15 compels me to assign this verse to the middle section of the narrative.

6   See Schnyder, "Leben," 82–83.

7   Recognition of this double expression is found in not a few commentaries (e.g., Grundmann, 159).

8   See Harbarth, "'Gott,'" 121–25.

9   As Barnabas Lindars has correctly observed ("Elijah, Elisha and the Gospel Miracles," in C. F. D. Moule, ed., *Miracles: Cambridge Studies in Their Philosophy and History* [London: Mowbray, 1965] 63–79, esp. 63, 76), the resurrection of Jesus does not belong to the same literary form. It is a foundational story (like the story of the exodus) in which God alone acts.

10   Even though it is not a resuscitation, one can—as Harbarth does ("'Gott,'" 85–91, 107)—draw on the

cope is in contrast with this. The story of Tabitha resembles in part a biographical legend (the actions of the young woman are important, rather than her family). Tabitha is also already a disciple. The situation of mourning (Acts 9:39) is comparable to Luke 7:11–17. But whereas the apostle must implore God to send power (Acts 9:40), Jesus already possesses it in himself. The physical contact of the weaker Peter is more intense (ἐπιστρέψας πρὸς τὸ σῶμα, "he turned to the body," Acts 9:40) than that of Jesus, in whose case it suffices to touch the bier. In both cases the resuscitation is described as "sitting up" (ἀνεκάθισεν, Luke 7:15; Acts 9:40). In Luke 7:15 the young man's speaking confirms the miracle, and in Acts 9:40, the opening of the woman's eyes. As with Tabitha, the resuscitation of Eutychus is connected with the meeting place of the Christians, the upper room. Like Peter, Paul illustrates the transferral of life through a concrete gesture (ἐπέπεσεν αὐτῷ, "he fell upon him," Acts 20:10). The nighttime atmosphere as well as the spatial relations (above–below, inside–outside) in Acts 20 create a liturgical ambience that easily leads to an allegorization of the event, in the sense of new life through faith (Eph 5:14). Such a Christian meaning is still remote from Luke 7:11–17.

The style, structure, and genre of all four accounts bear close relationships to Hebrew Bible and extrabiblical accounts. From Scripture Christian tradition knew two resurrection accounts, that of the son of the widow of Zarephath and the more extensive parallel account of Shunem (1 Kgs [LXX 3 Kgdms] 17; 2 Kgs [LXX 4 Kgdms] 4). The circle of Elisha's disciples attributed to their master a miracle similar to the miracle of Elijah.

The influence of both accounts on a Jewish Christian circle that perceived Jesus as a great prophetic figure (Luke 7:16) is discernible, probably at a pre-Lukan level.[11] Luke has developed this still further.[12] (1) The account concerns a son[13] of a widow who has just died (1 Kgs 17:9, 17; 2 Kgs 4); (2) the miracle-worker reaches the city gate (1 Kgs 17:10); (3) after the miracle, the prophet gives the son back to his mother (cf. the editorial quotation of 1 Kgs 17:23–24 in Luke 9:42); (4) the miracle-worker is recognized as God's messenger (1 Kgs 17:24); (5) Nain and Shunem are not far from one other.[14] The account of Elijah (1 Kgs 17) is more likely the model for this narrative, since, in the mind of Israel, he was the most important prophet of the past and the prophet expected to appear in the last days (Mal 3:23–24 [MT 4:5–6]). His example would probably also explain the concision of the Gospel miracle, which distinguishes itself, like 1 Kings 17, from the baroque detail of the other composition in 2 Kings 4.

Luke 7:11–17 is, however, more than a pale imitation of 1 Kings 17. The discreet attempt to surpass the earlier account is clear: (1) The time elapsed between the death of the young man and the intervention of the miracle-worker becomes longer (cf. 1 Kgs 17:17–18 and 2 Kgs 4:18–21; (2) Jesus takes the initiative, whereas in 1 Kgs 17:18 and 2 Kgs 4:22, the widow turns to the prophet for help; (3) the resurrection occurs more spontaneously (cf. 1 Kgs 17:19–22 and 2 Kgs 4:31–35); (4) in the Lukan account, an additional acclamation by the crowd follows the account (7:16).[15] "There is something here which corresponds to the substance of the OT parallels and yet is *greater*."[16]

---

healing of the epileptic child (Luke 9:37–43a) for a comparison.

11 See Harbarth, "'Gott,'" esp. 80–110.

12 See ibid., 109; Félix Gils, *Jésus prophète d'après les évangiles synoptiques* (Orientalia et Biblica Lovaniensia 2; Louvain: Publications Universitaires, 1957) 26–27, 45, 164; Dubois, "Elie," 168.

13 The widow in 1 Kgs (LXX 3 Kgdms) 17:15, 17 apparently has other children (τέκνα) besides her son (υἱός). By contrast, the son of the widow from Shunem (2 Kgs [LXX 4 Kgdms] 4:8–37) is an only child. Moreover, the woman had remained childless up to that time and only became pregnant through the intervention of the prophet. In the LXX the son in 1 Kgs (LXX 3 Kgdms) 17 is called a υἱός and παιδάριον, while the one in 2 Kings (LXX 4 Kingdoms) is called a παιδάριον. In neither passage

does the LXX use the adjective μονογενής ("only"), which here in 7:12 is a Lukan addition, as it is also at 8:42 and 9:38.

14 Just as the two stories are near to one another, so are the two villages, but they are not identical. Shunem lies about 5 km. from Afula at the foot of Jebel Dahi, i.e., Little Hermon. See Hans Wildberger, "Sunem," *BHH* 3 (1966) 1895. See the beginning of the next section, on the location of Nain.

15 See Harbarth, "'Gott,'" 209.

16 Leonard Goppelt, *Typos: The Typological Interpretation of the Old Testament in the New* (trans. D. H. Madvig; Grand Rapids: Eerdmans, 1982) 199; see Harbarth, "'Gott,'" 210; see further Goppelt, *Typos*, 200–201.

The ephiphanic character of the Lukan account is important: the widow merely receives the miracle and does not fight against fate for her son. The reason for the deed is rooted in the compassion and power of the divine messenger. The christological title ὁ κύριος ("the Lord," v. 13) is as important as μέγας ("great") next to the word προφήτης ("prophet," v. 16). In the last pericope (7:1–10) the believer stood at the center of the account; here, the almighty Lord rules over death.

In the first century, such a claim by the Christians would be understood not only as typological in a Jewish context, but as polemical in an intercultural dialogue. In the various pantheons and colorful cult sites, figures of healing gods were prominent,[17] especially Asclepios and Serapis. Recollections, inscriptions, and accounts attested the healing power of these figures. In the Serapeion from Kanope, one could look at books called ἀρεταλόγοι ("aretalogies," "accounts of virtues"), which narrated, in honor of the deity, dreams and healings.[18] Of the various types of pagan miracles, one interesting for our account appears already in the fourth century BCE in Epidauros: Asclepios "along the way" comes upon "a mortally ill man being carried on a stretcher. He ordered them to put the stretcher down, and healed the sick man."[19] This motif is attested several times, especially for dead people.[20] The classic example is in Philostratus:

A girl seemed to have died at the very hour of her wedding, and the groom followed the bier and lamented much over the unfinished wedding; and with him, Rome lamented, for the girl was from one of the consular families. When Apollonius met up with this funeral procession, he said, 'Set the bier down, for I want to set you free from tears over this girl,' and at the same time, he asked what her name was. And the crowd believed that he was about to offer a speech, one of those speeches that is usual for burials and that stir up lamentation; but he did nothing of the sort, but he touched her, said something indistinct and awakened the girl from her apparent death; and the girl let her voice be heard and returned to her father's house, like Alkestis, who was revived by Herakles. When the relatives of the girl offered him 150,000 denarii, he said that he would give it to the girl as a dowry. Whether he found in her a spark of life that had remained hidden from those who cared for her—for it was said that Zeus allowed it to rain, and vapor arose from her face—or whether he rekindled her extinguished life and retrieved it, that remains mysterious to my comprehension, but also to those who were there.[21]

The expansion of this motif from the healing God to the wise man is interesting, as is the transfer from the divine to the human sphere (although indeed to a divine man).[22] The structure remains surprisingly constant. Luke 7:11–17 does not show a mere appropriation of this miracle form,[23] although its influence is undeniable:[24] (1) the miracle happens outside and is public; (2) it is the last moment before burial; (3) an encounter takes place; (4) the miracle-worker takes the intiative on his own; (5) he heals by both word and touch. As differences, one can list: (1) the gender and

---

17 See Antoine Duprez, *Jésus et les dieux guérisseurs: A propos de Jean V* (CRB 12; Paris: Gabalda, 1970) 57–85.

18 See Strabo 17.1.17; Artemidorus *Onirocriticus* 2.44.

19 Summarized in Harbarth, "'Gott,'" 132. The text is *IG* 4.952.27–35.

20 See Apuleius of Madaurus *Florida* 19; Iamblichus the Syrian *Babyloniaca* 6; Artemidorus *Onirocriticus* 4.82.

21 *Life of Apollonius of Tyana* 4.45 (2d century). See Gerd Petzke ("Historizität und Bedeutsamkeit von Wunderberichten: Möglichkeiten und Grenzen des religionsgeschichtlichen Vergleichs," in H. D. Betz and L. Schottroff, eds., *Neues Testament und christliche Existenz: Festschrift Herbert Braun* [Tübingen: Mohr-Siebeck, 1973] 367–85), who compares Luke 7:11–17 with the story of Philostratus. Diogenes Laertius (8.60) relates that Empedokles resurrected a dead woman.

22 The holy power that for a long time was connected only with the sanctuary has by now been transferred to the holy man. See Brown, *Antiquity*, who focuses his attention on the 3d century CE. In my opinion this tendency had already begun in the 1st century CE.

23 So says Harbarth, "'Gott,'" 178–81; and H.-J. Schütz, "Beiträge zur Formgeschichte der synoptischen Wundererzählungen, dargestellt an der Vita Apollonii des Philostratus" (diss., Jena, 1953).

24 The story of Philostratus is more recent than the Gospels and so could be a pagan resumption of this theme as a polemic directed against the holy books of the Christians. The motif, however, is older than Christianity. For that reason, I speak of an influence by means of the motif or form, and not by means of the story of Philostratus itself.

269

social class of the person in need; (2) Apollonius's use of secret formulas; (3) the absence of any title for Apollonius (there is no concluding acclamation).[25]

In view of the syncretistic tendencies in Galilee at that time, one can localize the tradition used by Luke in a primitive Christian milieu there, in which the typology of Jesus and Elijah was assimilated to the type of divine power demonstrated by nonindigenous healing figures. Such an extraordinary deed was ascribed to Jesus, the man of God, without further deliberation. The scholarly study of history can, of course, render no verdict on the historicity of this event.[26] The convictions of the tradents of the story, however, are historically tangible; they recognize Jesus as the eschatological prophet (v. 16) and omnipotent Lord (v. 13), and express with such a narrative their hope for the transformation from mortal existence into new life.[27] The function of these accounts was oriented toward missionary activity, for something of the gospel message of salvation issues forth narratively from such an anecdote: the compassion of the Lord for mortal existence, the initiative of the divine

messenger, and life within the Christian community. At the same time, this narrative strengthened the Christian community in its beliefs, and gave them some ethical motivation. Like Jesus, the Christians should concern themselves with the widows and the dying, so that these, along with the orphans, might have hope within the community.[28]

Commentary

The Introduction (vv. 11–12a)

■ **11–12a** The chronological ($\dot{\epsilon}\nu\ \tau\hat{\omega}\ \dot{\epsilon}\xi\hat{\eta}\varsigma$, "afterward")[29] and temporal notices make clear that a new episode has begun. The city of Nain lies south of Mount Tabor at the northern foot of the mountain Jebel Dahi[30] on the road that leads from the Lake of Gennesaret up into the plains of Jezreel.[31] The spot is not mentioned in the Hebrew Bible, but does probably appear in *Bereshit Rabbah* 98.12 (62a)[32] with the name of נָעִים ("lovely"). Eusebius and Jerome know the city.[33] The first evidence of a church there commemorating the miracle dates

25 One should remember the version of the story of Alkestis in which she accepts death in place of her husband, and is then rescued from Hades by Herakles.

26 Various authors have examined the question of miracles in Luke's work: Paul J. Achtemeier, "The Lucan Perspective on the Miracles of Jesus: A Preliminary Sketch," *JBL* 94 (1974) 547–62; Busse, *Wunder;* George, "Miracle" (Luke is following the rules of literary form; Jesus here is like Elijah, but he is much more than Elijah; the miracle is a work of God that is a sign to call people to faith); Lindars, "Elijah"; Frans Neirynck, "The Miracle Stories in the Acts of the Apostles: An Introduction," in J. Kremer, ed., *Les Actes des apôtres: Traditions, rédaction, théologie* (BETL 48; Gembloux: Duculot; Leuven: Leuven University Press, 1979) 169–213. Petzke ("Historizität," 385) concludes: "The miracle accounts, which from a scientific standpoint are unhistorical, are, from the perspective of the sociology of knowledge, evidence of ancient understandings of reality." Such miraculous accounts were used by ancient authors to draw attention to their teachings or theology (see van der Loos, *Miracles*).

27 According to Calvin (*Harmony,* 252), "This young man, whom Christ raised from the dead, is an example of the life of the Spirit to which he has restored us." On the issue of literal and spiritual interpretation of the miracles, see Reginald Horace Fuller, *Interpreting the Miracles* (2d ed.; London:

SCM, 1966) 124–25.

28 The literary form of the miracle of resuscitation lives on in the apocryphal and hagiographic literature; cf. *Acts Pet.* 26–27; and *Acts Phil.* 1.1–5(1–5); 6.16–21(80–85).

29 The text alternates between the masculine (supplementing χρόνῳ) and the feminine (supplementing ἡμέρᾳ).

30 Perhaps to be identified with the Mount Moreh (Judg 7:1). The description "Little Hermon" can be traced back to a misguided medieval identification of this mountain with Mount Hermon, which is based on an interpretation of the Psalms (42:6 [LXX 41:7]; 89:12 [LXX 88:13]). Mount Moreh is 515 m. high (Clemens Kopp, *The Holy Places of the Gospels* [trans. R. Walls; New York: Herder and Herder, 1963] 237–38).

31 The Greek mss. read Ναΐν. Only the family of Greek mss. f¹, and with minor differences, the minuscule 579, have Ναΐμ. In agreement with f¹, part of the Latin ms. tradition, among them the Vulgate, reads Naim. This Nain is to be distinguished from the Ναΐν mentioned by Josephus in *Bell.* 4.9.4–5 §§513–14. See Flavius Josephus, *De Bello Judaico* 2.1 (ed. O. Michel and O. Bauernfeind; Munich: Kösel, 1962) 229 n. 161; Str-B 2.161; and Ernest W. Saunders, "Nain," *BHH* 2 (1964) 1283–84.

32 See Str-B 2.161. *Midrash Rabbah, Genesis* 2 (3d ed.; trans. H. Freedman; London: Soncino, 1961) 961.

from the tenth century.[34] In the Middle Ages the pious discovered and revered the rock-cut grave in which the widow was intending to inter her son; Jesus was believed to have eaten not far from there, on the mountain Jebel Dahi or its slopes (in commemoration of the plucking of grain by the disciples, Luke 6:1 par.). The testimonies of medieval travelers are vague and infrequent, since the pilgrims often saw Nain only from a distance.[35] Today the city is a village inhabited by around two hundred Muslims (Nein, pronounced Nên). Since there have been no excavations to date, the gate mentioned by Luke (but see 1 Kgs [LXX 3 Kgdms] 17:10!) has not been found.

The funeral procession is exiting the city by the gate. Jesus, the Messiah, whom Luke portrays as an itinerant teacher and doctor, is coming toward the city with the accompaniment of his disciples and the crowd. Jesus' travel in the dangerous marginal zone between areas of human habitation[36] has salvation-historical significance for Luke.[37] Jesus is both on *his* way to Jerusalem (cf. 9:51; 13:22) and on the way of his *people,* whom he is to help. In the roles of teacher, of the accompanying disciples, and of the crowd, the various relationships in the church in Luke's own time become transparent, in that the exalted teacher and his congregation attract a large number of sympathizers. Christology and ecclesiology stand in the background of this scene.

The Exposition (v. 12b)

■ **12b** Verse 12a belongs syntactically to the following sentence in v. 12b. It repeats and specifies v. 11, and relates both to what precedes and follows. *Καὶ ἰδού*

("just then," v. 12b), is a textual signal that introduces an event worthy of notice among the habitual activities.[38]

In few words a situation of need is sketched dramatically: a deceased (τεϑνηκώς–the perfect participle is nearly a substantive) only son, and his widowed mother,[39] a cumulation of unhappy circumstances. The Christian message in it: Jesus, the healing Messiah, is master of every situation, since he did not avoid this one. Psychoanalysis and systemics have taught us the constitutive meaning of the relationship between mother and son, as well as its possible pathological side effects. The preunderstanding of those times is also important here, since this relationship, the quintessential example of close personal ties, was also oriented to the future. A son was the only possession of a poor widow, and her expected source of support in her old age. Luke has in mind not only the particular situation in the book of Kings (1 Kgs [LXX 3 Kgdms] 17 and 2 Kgs [LXX 4 Kgdms] 4), but also, known from wisdom tradition, the generally tragic situation of the loss of an only child.[40]

The Middle of the Miracle Story (vv. 13–15)

■ **13–15** In Luke's story Jesus, as the Lord (v. 13), takes the matter in hand. As in the commissioning accounts (cf. 5:27), the whole story begins with the gaze of Jesus, who turns his attention to the mother, rather than the son. His gaze expresses or accompanies[41] an emotion, his compassion. Luke does not shy from expressing

---

33 Eusebius *Onomasticon* 140–41; Jerome *Ep.* 46.13; 108.13, although the former places it too far (12 mi.) from Tabor, and the latter, in his Latin translation of Eusebius's *Onomasticon*, places it too near (2 mi.). In reality Nain lies about 4 mi. south of Mount Tabor. See Kopp, *Places*, 237–38.

34 In the patriarch Eutychios (d. 940); see Kopp, *Places*, 240.

35 See Kopp, *Places*, 298.

36 See Maurice Aymard, "Espaces," in F. Braudel, ed., *La Méditerranée: L'espace et l'histoire* (Paris: Arts et métiers graphiques, 1977) 179–218.

37 See William Childs Robinson, *Der Weg des Herrn: Studien zur Geschichte und Eschatologie im Lukas-Evangelium* (ThF 36; Hamburg-Bergstedt: H. Reich, 1964) 39–43.

38 On *καὶ ἰδού* ("and behold," "just then,"), see 1:20, 36, etc.

39 The ms. tradition vacillates in v. 12 between αὕτη ("this") and αὐτή (which one must understand as a Hellenistic form for αὕτη here; see BAGD *s.v.* αὐτός [2]).

40 See Harbarth, "'Gott,'" 37 n. 104: "'Weeping for an only son' is, moreover, a stock motif in the HB for expressing deep grief. See Amos 8:10; Jer 6:26; Zech 12:10." Of the approximately 10 passages where the LXX uses μονογενής ("only"), the following may be mentioned: Tob 3:15; 6:15 (Sinaiticus); 8:17; Ps 21(MT 22):21; 24(MT 25):16; 34(MT 35):17.

41 The aorist participle ἰδών ("when he saw") must here denote a time antecedent to that of the main verb ἐσπλαγχνίσϑη ("he had compassion"). The combination of "seeing" and "having compassion" is frequent in the Synoptics (see Matt 9:36; Mark 6:34; Luke 10:33).

Jesus' emotions and emphasizes Jesus' magnificent love.[42] His avoidance of σπλαγχνίζομαι ("to have compassion") elsewhere might be for philological rather than theological reasons.[43]

As in 10:33 and 15:20, the verb here was probably already in the source. Luke uses it with his theological approval.[44] Just as God is compassionate (6:36), so is the healing Messiah, who here shows great sympathy.[45] He not only possesses this emotional capacity, but also has the power to change fate. For this reason the otherwise intolerable, "Do not weep," is acceptable. The source of consolation can be found only in God, who resurrects the dead. Jesus shows his purpose and his intention not by a further word, but by a gesture. The significance of this nonverbal communication, the touching of the bier, did not remain the same in the course of the transmission. An antimagical rationalism has taken effect: now Jesus' action has the prosaic purpose of stopping the procession (the redactional consequence is, "And the

bearers stood still," v. 14). As in other miracle stories, this touch probably meant originally the transfer of divine, life-giving power.[46] By this antimagical reformulation, Luke transfers the emphasis to the word of Jesus. The second command, indeed, is addressed not to the mother but to the son. Already at the beginning of v. 14, Jesus had turned from her to him. The consolation of the mother results from the fate of her son.

The words, "Young man, I say to you" (v. 14b), sound formal.[47] At last comes the decisive command: ἐγέρθητι ("Arise"). The most immediate meaning is, "Wake up!"[48] But—and an English translation cannot capture this—this command also connotes a call to resurrection. The ambiguity can be made specific with the words ἐγέρθητι ἐξ ὕπνου ("wake up from your sleep") or ἐγέρθητι ἐκ νεκρῶν ("wake up from the dead").[49]

The success of the man of God is not only instantaneous but effortless. The text sounds simple and naive, but it is a refined, secondary terseness. At the moment

---

42 Agreeing with Dibelius (*Tradition*, 75) against George ("Miracle," 254) and Paul Ternant ("La résurrection du fils de la veuve de Naïn," *AsSeign* 41 [1971] 69–79, esp. 74).

43 This occurs five times in Matthew, four in Mark, and three in Luke (here about Jesus, in 10:33 about the good Samaritan, and in 15:20 about the father of the prodigal son—in each case at an important juncture in the narrative). Σπλαγχνεύω occurs in classical Greek, from which the later form σπλαγχνίζω derives. In the active voice the verb signifies "to eat the insides of a sacrificial animal" or "to evaluate them," "inspect them" (in order to foretell the future). In Hellenistic times σπλάγχνα and the verbs derived from it acquired a figurative sense because the entrails were regarded as the seat of intense emotions, just as the καρδία ("heart") was the seat of higher feelings. In the LXX σπλαγχνίζω occurs only twice, once in its literal sense (2 Macc 6:8; cf. the use of σπλαγχνισμός in this book—2 Macc 6:7, 21; 7:42—for the designation of a pagan ritual meal), and the other in its figurative sense: "but he who has compassion shall be shown mercy" (Prov 17:5 Codex A; B and S read ἐπισπλαγχνό-μενος). See further the wisdom literature (see Prov 12:10), which prepared the way for the NT usage, esp. the *Testaments of the Twelve Patriarchs*, in particular *T. Zeb.* 8:1: Καὶ ὑμεῖς οὖν, τέκνα μου, ἔχετε εὐσπλαγχνίαν κατὰ πάντος ἀνθρώπου ἐν ἐλέει ἵνα καὶ ὁ κύριος εἰς ὑμᾶς σπλαγχνισθεὶς ἐλε-ήσῃ ὑμᾶς ("And you then, my children, have compassion toward every person in mercy so that the

Lord may have compassion on you and show mercy to you"). For a complete discussion of the word, see Helmut Koester, "σπλάγχνον, κτλ.," *TDNT* 7 (1971) 551–52. In some Hellenistic Jewish texts, such as the *Testaments of the Twelve Patriarchs* (but not in Philo and Josephus), the words from the roots σπλαγχν- and οἰκτιρ- (Hebrew רחם) are synonymous.

44 On the verb in the Synoptic tradition, Koester states: "It is much more a theological characterization of Jesus as the Messiah, in whom divine compassion is present." He then specifically mentions that this is also true of Luke ("σπλάγχνον, κτλ.," *TDNT* 7 [1971] 554–55).

45 Ternant, "Résurrection," 73.

46 Cf. Luke 5:17; 6:19; 8:46; Acts 19:11–12; as well as Acts 5:15.

47 Some mss. construct the scene even more solemnly by repeating the vocative νεανίσκε ("young man").

48 The primary meaning for ἐγείρω is "to wake" (intransitive, "to awaken"), and then "to raise" (intransitive, "to rise"). The logic of the story invokes the image of waking/awakening.

49 The aorist passive imperative emphasizes less the passivity of the young man in contrast to, let us say, the action of God, than the fact that the subject—the young man—realizes and manifests his awakening. On this deponent use of the aorist passive, see G. B. Caird, "The Glory of God in the Fourth Gospel: An Exercise in Biblical Semantics," *NTS* 15 (1968–69) 268.

272

in which the person addressed begins to live again, he is no longer called "young man" (v. 14b), but "the dead man" (ὁ νεκρός, v. 15). In the word ἀνεκάθισεν ("sat up") the attentive reader hears the ἀνα- ("up," or "again"). "He sat up"[50] signifies his "awakening"; "he began" means to begin a new life. He began "to speak": language here appears as an index of human life.[51] The relationship broken off by death is reestablished. The son is "given" back to his mother. It is not that the static relationship of mother to son is lengthened beyond death, but that, by an analogical interpretation, a potential experience of faith is demonstrated. Just as Jesus has led the young man back to his mother, he can give us a new life in faith in the name of God.

Conclusion (vv. 16–17)

■ **16–17** The conclusion, which describes the impression that the miracle makes on the audience (v. 16) and on the people in the region (v. 17), has a broader perspective. Verse 17 may be Lukan, since it skillfully anticipates the question of the Baptist (7:19), thus fulfilling a transitional function. The vocabulary, style, and content are typically Lukan.[52]

Verse 16 was intensively rewritten by Luke. The phrase "they glorified God" and the mention of divine visitation are stereotypical. The acclamation accords with the expectations of the readers. The expression of

awe before the divine and the recognition of the presence of a great prophet (not a Lukan christological title at all) are probably traditional. Luke uses both elements, and expands the original conclusion.[53]

The fear of "all of them"[54] emphasizes the greatness of the event. It is not only a psychological but also a religious reaction. Thus it expresses itself in a hymn of praise. Since, in the statement about the great prophet from the tradition, one hears the faith that discovers the divine ambassador in the worker of miracles, the historicizing recognition ("has arisen," ἠγέρθη in the aorist) sounds like a confession of faith. Event (ἠγέρθη) and interpretation (προφήτης μέγας, "a great prophet") accompany each other in a self-involving (ἐν ὑμῖν, "among us") statement.[55] It is a sign producing faith in the arising (ἐγείρω, v. 16; also v. 14) of a great prophet. Through προφήτης μέγας ("great prophet"), which follows a miracle reminiscent of 1 Kings (LXX 3 Kgdms) 17, a connection to Elijah is, of course, created. But the definite article is lacking. The audience recognizes God's hand and his activity in his human emissary, but does not explicitly identify him with Elijah redivivus. But μέγας ("great")[56] does show the special position of this prophet, and ἐγείρω ("to arise") signifies not only his appearance but perhaps also his resurrection. In brief, the author allows the audience to express a not yet complete confession of faith, but also implies that, according

---

50 Delebecque (39): "The position can be explained because, according to custom, the bier has no lid."

51 In Acts 9:40 the ability to see plays this role: "and she suddenly opened her eyes." In a comparable apocryphal passage, *Acts Phil.* 1.4, the awakened young man begins to tell of his experiences in the realm of the dead until the moment of his awakening. In an expanded version of this same story in the ms. from Athos, *Xenophontos* 32, the young man describes in detail the chastisements that he has seen in Hades; see Bertrand Bouvier and François Bovon, "Actes de Philippe, I, d'après un manuscrit inédit," in D. Papandreou, W. A. Bienert, and K. Schäferdiek, eds., *Oecumenica et Patristica: Festschrift für Wilhelm Schneemelcher* (Chambésy, Switzerland: Metropolie der Schweiz, 1989) 367–94.

52 On the expression "all Judea" (cf. 1:65), i.e., all Palestine, including Galilee; cf. 1:5 and 4:44. On "the surrounding countryside" (περί with the genitive after a verb of saying), cf. 4:14; see also Jeremias, *Sprache*, 159–60.

53 A comparison with the attempted reconstruction mentioned above in the Analysis of this passage

shows that my own analysis concurs with those attempted by Anita Harbarth and Ulrich Busse—with one exception: agreeing with Busse against Harbarth, I hold that the mention of praise to God (v. 16) is redactional. The redactional character of ἐδόξαζον τὸν θεόν ("they glorified God") is highlighted by the reaction of the crowd that was in Luke's source, "a great prophet has arisen among us!"—this reaction does not actually constitute praise to God.

54 Similar expressions in 1:65; 5:26; 8:37; Acts 2:43; 5:5, 11; 19:17.

55 By "self-involving," I mean those statements whose validity is inseparably bound with the existence of the one speaking. The classic example is the confession of faith: "I believe that. . . ." Note here especially the phrase "among us."

56 See the commentary on 1:15 and 1:32 above.

to his own opinion, Jesus is the eschatological prophet (Deut 18:15) and Elijah redivivus (Mal 4:5-6 [LXX 3:23–24]).[57]

By means of a redactional addition (καὶ ὅτι . . . , "and," v. 16c), Luke develops the effects of the event in three directions: (1) Soteriologically, the arising of a prophet represents a salvific visitation (ἐπεσκέψατο, "God has visited"),[58] not in the sense of judgment, but in the sense of a necessary rescue.[59] That this does not bring some cheap grace in its train is well expressed in the audience's confession of faith. Like them, believers should recognize and confess the salvation-historical significance of the event. (2) Ecclesiologically, Jesus' action is valid for the entire people of God, who experience and recognize in the saving of one of its members the recovery of the whole. (3) Christologically, Luke makes explicit with the subject ὁ θεός ("God") the connection between the work of Jesus and the work of God. What Jesus does is nothing less than the fulfillment of God's will; indeed, in the final analysis, it is God's personal action. This identification exalts Jesus into the divine sphere, but it also abases him to the function of an obedient mediator.[60]

Although the reader can easily understand the general sense of v. 17, the precise meaning of ὁ λόγος οὗτος is difficult to grasp.[61] If one takes περὶ αὐτοῦ ("about him") together with λόγος ("word"), "this word" refers to the previous statement by the audience (v. 16b).[62] The comparable occurrences in Luke 5:5 and Acts 11:22, which are preceded only by events worthy of the telling, nevertheless show that ὁ λόγος οὗτος probably refers instead to the christologically interpreted event (in contrast to numerous translations).[63]

By the words "throughout Judea" Luke means Pales-tine. This phrase does not necessarily indicate the evangelist's poor knowledge of Palestinian geography.[64] For Luke, Judea is the land of the Jews, and Galilee belongs to it. But even this specification does not suffice for him. He adds the "surrounding country" to it, elegantly separated by the words περὶ αὐτοῦ ("about him"). With this he is anticipating the book of Acts, in which the word of God will spread outside Palestine through its witnesses. Luke is speaking "biblically," since ἡ περίχωρος (sc. γῆ, "the surrounding country") occurs especially frequently in the LXX: Lot chooses the rich περίχωρος of the Jordan, while Abraham is satisfied with Canaan. But God promises him both regions for his offspring. The combined view of a poor but holy land (Judea) and a rich but heathen neighboring region is, according to Luke, already attested in Scripture (Gen 13:5–18).

Conclusion

The narrative shows that the restored happiness of those who need help spreads Jesus' evangelistic summons. By giving the son back to his mother, he proves himself to be Lord over life and death, and a prophet of the highest God. This relational theology also brings people together: what Jesus achieves with this mother is a new, redeemed relationship between parents and children (cf. John 19:26–27). For this reason, the evangelist interprets the individual case as a general redemption ("God has visited his people").

An interpersonal relationship also appears on the divine level: Jesus' compassion is vividly illustrated, and his personal engagement is the consequence of this personal reaction. *He* takes action. Yet at the conclusion Luke interprets the event as the word of *God*. Both

---

57   On Jesus the prophet see Gils, *Jésus prophète*; Fitzmyer, 1.213–15; Bovon, *Theologian*, 177–79.

58   On ἐπισκέπτομαι see the commentary on 1:68.

59   In Luke 1:68 one finds alongside ἐπεσκέψατο ("he has visited") the mention of the redemption that has already been obtained for the benefit of the people: ἐποίησεν λύτρωσιν ("he has redeemed"). On the soteriology of Luke, see Dömer, *Heil;* and Bovon, *Theologian*, 239–66.

60   Fitzmyer (1.660) correctly rejects the notion of identifying the words "a great prophet" with the messianic function of Jesus. This is not about a figure who has been anointed. This observation holds true for the tradition, but at the redactional level it loses

its validity, since Luke links this pericope with the question that John the Baptist directs to Jesus and with Jesus' reply. According to the evangelist, the crowd holds Jesus to be a great prophet, whereas in truth, of course, he is the new Elijah and the Messiah.

61   On λόγος see BAGD *s.v.* λόγος (1a β.γ.ε).

62   Περὶ αὐτοῦ (v. 17) grammatically could refer back to the subject of the last verb in v. 16, viz., God, but this would not produce any satisfactory sense.

63   E.g., see *TOB* and the translation of Delebecque, 39.

64   Pace Conzelmann, *Theology*, 46 n. 1. See the commentary on 4:44.

274

programmatically and iconically, the evangelist attests, on the one hand, the harmony of feeling, kind intentions, and deed between the Father and the Son, and, on the other hand, as a gift freely received, the restored relationship between people within the Christian community.[65]

History of Interpretation

A single citation should suffice as an example of the sometimes disastrous history of interpretation. It demonstrates how a new understanding can grow out of a complete reinterpretation:

> It was one ninth of September, the birthday of Grand Duke Frederick I of Baden. I went with my brother to the special service of worship. I mention this fact, because that which we experienced there was so unbelievable that one is tempted to call to mind the phrase, "All things should be established on the testimony of two or three people." Even the text surprised us greatly, for there was no prescribed text for such a service of worship. The preacher read the story of the resurrection of the young man at Nain. We could not believe our ears when the sermon went on thus: if, anywhere in Baden, a woman sighs and cries in deep sorrow, then our Grand Duchess will come and say to her, "Woman, do not cry!" And if, anywhere in Baden, a man collapses under the weight of his predicament, then our Grand Duke comes and says, "Young man, I say to you, rise up!" Must one not then ask, How is such a thing possible? For it is understandable that it is not easy to preach about this story, if one cannot accept it.[66]

---

65 Various authors have examined the question of miracles in Luke's work: Paul J. Achtemeier, "The Lucan Perspective on the Miracles of Jesus: A Preliminary Sketch," *JBL* 94 (1974) 547–62; Busse, *Wunder*; George, "Miracle" (Luke is following the rules of literary form. Jesus here is like Elijah, but he is much more than Elijah. The miracle is a work of God which is a sign to call men to faith). Also Lindars, "Elijah"; Frans Neirynck, "The Miracle Stories in the Acts of the Apostles: An Introduction," in J. Kremer, ed., *Les Actes des apôtres: Traditions, rédaction, théologie* (BETL 48; Gembloux: J. Duculot; Louvain: Leuven University, 1979) 169–213. Petzke ("Historizität," 385) reaches the conclusion: "The miracle accounts, which from a scientific standpoint are unhistorical, are, from the perspective of the sociology of knowledge, evidence of ancient understandings of reality." Such miraculous accounts were used by ancient authors to draw attention to their teachings or theology (see van der Loos, *Miracles*).

66 Bornhäuser, *Sondergut*, 52.

The Testimony of Jesus about the Baptist
(7:18–35)

Bibliography

Bammel, Ernst, "The Baptist in Early Christian Tradition," *NTS* 18 (1971–72) 95–128.

Böcher, "Johannes."

Bultmann, *History*, 23–24, 384–85.

Busse, *Wunder*, 176–85.

Cameron, Ron, "'What Have You Come Out to See?' Characterizations of John and Jesus in the Gospels," *Semeia* 49 (1990) 35–69.

Christ, *Jesus Sophia*, 63–80.

Cotter, W. J., "The Parable of the Children in the Marketplace, Q (Lk) 7:31–35: An Examination of the Parable's Image and Significance," *NovT* 29 (1987) 289–304.

Craghan, John F., "A Redactional Study of Lk 7,21 in the Light of Dt 19,15," *CBQ* 29 (1967) 353–67.

Daniel, Constantin, "Les Esséniens et 'ceux qui sont dans les maisons des rois' (Matthieu 11,7–8 et Luc 7,24–25)," *RevQ* 6 (1967) 261–77.

Davies, S. L., "John the Baptist and Essene Kashruth," *NTS* 29 (1983) 569–71.

Dupont, "Ambassade."

idem, "Jésus annonce la bonne nouvelle aux pauvres," in B. Antonini, ed., *Evangelizare pauperibus* (Brescia: Paideia, 1978) 127–89.

Gander, Georges, "Notule sur Luc 7,29–30," *VC* 5 (1951) 141–44.

Grundmann, Walter, "Weisheit im Horizont des Reiches Gottes: Eine Studie zur Verkündigung Jesu nach der Spruchüberlieferung Q," in R. Schnackenburg et al., eds., *Die Kirche des Anfangs: Festschrift Heinz Schürmann* (Leipzig: St. Benno; Freiburg im Breisgau: Herder, 1977) 175–99.

Hoffmann, *Logienquelle*, 190–233.

Jacobson, Arland Dean, "Wisdom Christology in Q" (Ph.D. diss., Claremont Graduate School, 1978); see *DissAb* 39 (1978) 3653-A.

idem, *The First Gospel: An Introduction to Q* (Sonoma, Calif.: Polebridge, 1992).

Jeremias, *Parables*, 120–22.

idem, *Sprache*, 160–68.

Jülicher, *Gleichnisreden*, 2.23–36.

Kearney, Suzanne Marie, "A Study of Principal Compositional Techniques in Luke-Acts based on Lk 4:16–30 in Conjunction with Lk 7:18–23" (Ph.D. diss., Boston University, 1978); see *DissAb* 38 (1978) 7395-A.

Kilgallen, John J., "John the Baptist, the Sinful Woman, and the Pharisee," *JBL* 104 (1985) 675–79.

Kümmel, Werner Georg, *Jesu Antwort an Johannes den Täufer: Ein Beispiel zum Methodenproblem der Jesusforschung* (Sitzungsberichte der Wissenschaftlichen Gesellschaft an der Johann Wolfgang Goethe-Universität, Frankfurt am Main, 11.4; Wiesbaden: Franz Steiner, 1974) 129–59 (= idem, *Heilsgeschehen und Geschichte: Gesammelte Aufsätze 1965–76* [ed. E. Gräßer, O. Merk, and A. Fritz; 2 vols.; Marburg: Elwert, 1965–78] 2.177–200).

Linton, Olof, "The Parable of the Children's Game: Baptist and Son of Man (Matt. xi.16–19 = Luke vii.31–35): A Synoptic Text-Critical, Structural and Exegetical Investigation," *NTS* 22 (1975–76) 159–79.

Mattill, Andrew Jacob, *Luke and the Last Things: A Perspective for the Understanding of Lukan Thought* (Dillsboro, N.C.: Western North Carolina Press, 1979).

Mearns, Chris, "Realized Eschatology in Q? A Consideration of the Sayings in Luke 7.22;11.20 and 16.16," *SJT* 40 (1987) 189–210.

Mitton, Charles Leslie, "Uncomfortable Words IX: Stumbling-block Characteristics in Jesus," *ExpTim* 82 (1970–71) 168–72.

Moessner, David P., "The 'Leaven of the Pharisees' and 'This Generation': Israel's Rejection of Jesus According to Luke," *JSNT* 34 (1988) 21–46.

Mussner, "Kairos."

Orbe, "Hijo del hombre."

Peretto, Elio, "*Evangelizare pauperibus* (Lc 4,18; 7,22–23) nella lettura patristica dei secoli II–III," *Aug* 17 (1977) 71–100.

Pirot, *Paraboles*, 62–70.

Sabugal, Santo, *La embajada mesiánica de Juan Bautista (Mt 11,2–6 = Lc 7,18–23): Historia, exégesis teológica, hermenéutica* (Madrid: Systeco, 1980).

idem, "La embajada mesiánica del Bautista (Mt 11,2–6 = Lc 7,18–23): Análisis histórico-tradicional," *Aug* 13 (1973) 215–78; 14 (1974) 5–39; 17 (1977) 395–424, 511–39.

Schlosser, Jacques, *Les logia du règne: Étude sur le vocable "basileia tou theou" dans la prédication de Jésus* (Lille, France: Université de Lille III, 1982) 71–83, passim.

Schmid, Josef, *Matthäus und Lukas: Eine Untersuchung des Verhältnisses ihrer Evangelien* (Freiburg im Breisgau: Herder, 1930) 282–86.

Schrage, *Thomas-Evangelium*, 107–9, 160–64.

Schulz, *Q*, 190–203, 229–36, 379–86.

Siburt, Charles, "The Game of Rejecting God: Luke 7:31–35," *ResQ* 19 (1976) 207–10.

Strobel, *Verzögerung*.

Suggs, M. Jack, *Wisdom, Christology, and Law in Matthew's Gospel* (Cambridge: Harvard University Press, 1970) 33–61.

Testa, Emmanuele, "Un ostrakon sull'elogio funebre e Mt 11,16ss e paralleli," *RivB* 16 (1968) 539–46.

Vögtle, Anton, "Wunder und Wort in urchristlicher Glaubenswerbung (Mt 11,2–5; Lk 7,18–23)," in idem, *Evangelium*, 219–42.

Völkel, Martin, "Anmerkungen zur lukanischen

Fassung der Täuferanfrage Lk 7,18–23," in W.
Dietrich and H. Schreckenberg, eds., *Theokratia II:
Festschrift K. H. Rengstorf* (Leiden: Brill, 1973)
166–73.
Wink, *John*, 42–58, 82–86.
Zeller, "Bildlogik."

18 The disciples of John reported all these things to
him, and John summoned two of his disciples
19/ and sent them to the Lord and said, "Are you
the one who is to come, or are we to wait for
another?" 20/ When the men reached him, they
said, "John the Baptist has sent us to you and
says, 'Are you the one who is to come, or are we
to wait for another?'" 21/ In that hour Jesus had
cured many people of diseases, plagues, and evil
spirits, and had given sight to many who were
blind. 22/ And he answered and said to them,
"Go and tell John what you have seen and heard:
the blind see, the lame walk, the lepers are
cleansed, the deaf hear, the dead are raised, the
poor have good news brought to them, 23/ and
blessed is anyone who takes no offense at me."

24 When John's messengers had gone away, he
began to speak to the crowds about John:
"What did you go out into the wilderness to look
at? A reed shaken by the wind? 25/ What then
did you go out to see? Someone dressed in soft
robes? Look, those who put on fine clothing and
live in luxury are in royal palaces. 26/ What then
did you go out to see? A prophet? Yes, I tell you,
and more than a prophet. 27/ This is the one
about whom it is written, 'See, I am sending my
messenger before your face, who will prepare
your way before you.' 28/ I tell you, among those
born of women no one is greater than John. Yet
the least in the kingdom of God is greater than
he." 29/ (And all the people who had listened,
and the tax collectors, had acknowledged the
justice of God and had been baptized with
John's baptism. 30/ The Pharisees and the
experts in the Law had rejected God's purpose
for themselves and had not allowed themselves
to be baptized by him.) 31/ "To whom then will I
compare the people of this generation, and who
are they like? 32/ They are like children sitting in
the marketplace who call to one another, 'We
played the flute for you, and you did not dance;
we wailed, and you did not weep.' 33/ For John
the Baptist has come eating no bread and drinking no wine, and you say, 'He has a demon.'
34/ The Son of Man has come eating and drinking, and you say, 'Look, a glutton and a drunkard, a friend of tax collectors and sinners!'
35/ And wisdom was vindicated by all her
children."

Analysis

Between two stories from Luke's special source (7:11–17,
36–50), Luke includes a three-part excerpt from Q
(7:18–35), which may have immediately followed the
story of the centurion (7:1–10). It is difficult to determine whether the author of Q wished to conclude one
of the sections of the work with it.[1] The sequence and
the language render certain the origin of this segment
in Q.

Up to this point, Luke has alternated between Q and
Mark. From 8:1 through 9:50, it will be Mark's turn to
tell the story. But what is the situation in chap. 7, with
the bits from the special source worked into the material
from Q? Did the special material consist of a single
source text, or a number of individual documents? The
stylistic similarities of many of the individual narratives
would tend to favor a single document, which does not
exclude the possibility of some individual paragraphs
from other sources. If the passages from Q (7:1–10,
18–35) were already combined with the passages from
Luke's special source (7:11–17, 36–50), Luke would have
handled them as he did Mark and Q. What the prologue
of the Gospel would seem to indicate, then, would be a
simple dividing up and new arrangement of the various
sources, in which both faithful transmission and a certain freedom on the part of the author played a part. In
placing the legation from John after the narration of a
few miracles, however, Luke's work becomes clearer in
its structured alternation of words (6:20–49; 7:18–35;
8:4–18) with deeds (7:1–17, 36–50), which he explicitly
emphasizes in the second prologue in Acts 1:1.

The Legation (vv. 18–23)

Both Matthew and Luke leave Jesus' response (vv. 22–23
par.) almost unaltered. The only difference is the
sequence of the words "to see" and "to hear" (v. 22b
par.) and the respective tenses.[2] The order chosen by
Luke could be Luke's editorial intervention, since his
Messiah begins with deeds (cf. Acts 1:1),[3] in contrast to
Matthew (cf. Matt 5–7, 8–9). The use of the aorist is
Lukan and results in a grammatically preferable

---

1   By employing the stylistic device of the *inclusio*:
    John the Baptist is the subject for both the begin-
    ning of Q and the end of this pericope.

2   According to Schulz (Q, 192), Luke has deleted the

words ὁ Ἰησοῦς ("Jesus") in the introduction to his
reply in v. 22, because they are unnecessary after
the statements in vv. 20–21.

3   Conzelmann, *Theology*, 192.

sequence of tenses. In the question of the Baptist, the only difference is the use of ἄλλον in Luke versus ἕτερον ("another") in Matthew, probably used synonymously, as was usual at the time.[4]

In the introduction[5] and the setting, however, the two evangelists have left their imprint. Matthew begins abruptly with the mention of imprisonment and the "works of the Messiah." In Luke we read in vv. 18–19 of the Baptist's decision to ask for news through his disciples, and in v. 20, of his execution of the decision through two of his disciples sent as messengers. It is probably not the case here that Matthew is simplifying the setting (as often happens), but that Luke has expanded Q. He enjoys illustrating a scene and everywhere emphasizes the role of the witness (here there are two, as is appropriate). The monotony in vv. 18b–20 is intentional,[6] for it is fitting of messengers that they obey at a word. The Lukan title for Jesus, "the Lord," is noteworthy here (v. 19a).[7]

The greatest editorial intervention is in v. 21: Luke inserts a report of the various miracles of Jesus between the question and the answer. Vocabulary and syntax are Lukan. The aorist[8] shows that this is not a summary passage, but rather that Jesus decides right at this moment to perform healings, so that the disciples of the Baptist can take back a substantiation of the answer of Jesus that follows. The healing miracles find their justification not

in Jesus' compassion but in his messianic program and his proof of his status. But could the aorist not also mean, like the pluperfect, a given situation at the moment of the arrival of the messengers?

Verses 18–23 belonged originally to the genre of the apothegm. It is impossible to isolate the Baptist's question from Jesus' answer and consider them as individual sayings. The beatitude (v. 23) was certainly distinct from the apothegm. In the course of transmission, it was added as a generalizing interpretation, perhaps an early Christian prophetic saying. In contrast to the implicit christology of Jesus' answer with its allusion to Scripture (no citation), which implicitness probably indicates the authenticity of the conversation, ἐν ἐμοί ("at me") contains an explicit christology. Whether the Baptist's eschatological expectation of a messiah distinct from God is original and agrees with the expectation of God in the other sayings of John, which sound more archaic, is a point of debate[9] (see below on ὁ ἐρχόμενος, "the one who is to come").

Jesus' Testimony about the Baptist (vv. 24–28)

Luke and Matthew again remain true to their source.[10] They are reticent about adding to the words of Jesus, though Luke tries to make v. 25 more comprehensible. He expands ἐν μαλακοῖς ("in soft") with ἱματίοις ("robes"), and also employs a descriptive phrase ("that

---

4 Several mss. assimilate their text to Matthew and read ἕτερον in vv. 19–20. Ἕτερος can mean (1) "the other of two," i.e., of a pair of the same kind; (2) "of another kind"; or (3) "the other" in the usual meaning of ἄλλος. Among these various possible meanings of ἕτερος (which were in his source, Q), Luke—through his choice of ἄλλος—has decided on that which is the most common and, for our context, the most appropriate.

5 D has a different text in v. 18. It connects this pericope in a different way with the previous one. See Hans-Werner Bartsch, *Codex Bezae versus Codex Sinaiticus im Lukasevangelium* (Hildesheim: Olms, 1984) 64.

6 Luke substitutes ἀποστέλλω for πέμπω, and ἄνδρες ("men") for μαθηταί ("disciples"). Conscientiously he specifies that the John who sends these messengers is John the Baptist. Then he adds something necessary for the sequence of the narrative—that the messengers have reached Jesus.

7 Oddly, Jeremias (*Sprache*, 161) describes the title ὁ κύριος ("the Lord") as having been in Luke's

source. Furthermore, one notes that many mss. read πρὸς τὸν Ἰησοῦν ("to Jesus").

8 For that reason, Delebecque (40) chooses the historic perfect in his translation: "Sur l'heure, il guérit. . . ."

9 See Jacques Dupont, "L'ambassade de Jean-Baptiste (Matthieu 11,2–6; Luc 7,18–23)," *NRTh* 83 (1961) 805–21, 943–59; Werner Georg Kümmel, *Jesu Antwort an Johannes den Täufer: Ein Beispiel zum Methodenproblem der Jesusforschung* (Wiesbaden: Franz Steiner, 1974) 129–59; Anton Vögtle, "Wunder und Wort in urchristlicher Glaubenswerbung (Mt 11,2–5; Lk 7,18–23)," in idem, *Evangelium*, 219–42.

10 A parallel to the first two questions and answers is found in *Gos. Thom.* 78. See Schrage, *Thomas-Evangelium*, 160–64.

put on fine clothing and live in luxury").[11] In the mixed citation (v. 27), Matthew corrects it according to Scripture and adds ἐγώ ("I"). Luke simplifies the saying in v. 28: he omits the foreign expression ἀμήν[12] and replaces the ambiguous ἐγήγερται ("has arisen") with the simple ἐστίν ("is"). In the narrative introduction (v. 24a par.), the divergences are greater: Matthew is probably closer to Q, for it is Luke that insists here (τῶν ἀγγέλων Ἰωάννου, "the messengers of John"), as in vv. 18 and 20, on the messengers.[13]

Matthew transmits the famous saying about the position of the Baptist within salvation history (Matt 11:12–15) before the next parable (vv. 31–35; Matt 11:16–19). Luke knows of a similar saying (16:16; see ad loc.). Either Matthew and Luke have each used an isolated saying in a context that suited them, or it was in Q at the place where Matthew reads it, and in Luke's special source where he preserves it. Since Luke, as is usual in ancient literary practice, avoids doublets, he probably intentionally omitted it here. In view of the emphasis on Jesus' power, the saying might have seemed questionable to him in this context.

From a form-critical perspective, vv. 24b–26 belong together. The first two questions form one part of the unit and both demand a negative answer,[14] and the third forms the other part. They receive two answers: the first is that of the crowds ("a prophet"), the second affirms and cryptically completes the first ("more than a prophet"). The rhetoric of this question suits the historical Jesus and his public speeches. The concern with the Scriptures that appears in v. 27 has another functional setting, that of early Christian instruction. The use of Exod 23:20 and Mal 3:1 for the Baptist is familiar to us from Mark 1:2. The antithetical and temperamental proverb in v. 28 par. belongs, again, to another situation.

It is a prophetic statement that gives an almost retrospective view of the Baptist and his position on the threshold of the two ages. Such a saying might have originated in the cultic activity of an early Christian prophet. Of course, one cannot exclude the possibility that it is authentic. The collocation of the three sayings, however, is certainly secondary and the result of a progressive development: the cryptic answer of Jesus was "Christianized," that is, made clearer through Scripture (v. 27), and expanded with an additional saying (v. 28). In this, the intense interest of the Christian community for the figure of the Baptist is apparent. It is not certain that there is a polemical motivation behind this. At the most, there is concern over a right assessment of the Baptist.

The Parable of the Unwilling Children (vv. 29–35)

Just as Luke interrupted the conversation between John and Jesus with a sentence of narrative (v. 21), he here inserts an intermediate comment about the relative success of the Baptist (vv. 29–30). Two things are clear: first, whoever decided to follow the Baptist at that time was on God's side (δικαιόω, "acknowledge the justice," in v. 29 was suggested to Luke from v. 35, which he knew already); second, these followers were not the religious leaders of Israel but the people, indeed, the more dubious individuals. The division of Israel had already begun even at that time and has continued since then (cf. Acts 28:24). The Lukan character of both the language and content of these two verses is obvious,[15] although the sayings of Jesus that are transmitted in Matt 21:31–32 could stand behind them.

The linguistic differences between Matthew and Luke in the following vv. 31–35 are small. In the parable itself (vv. 31–32), Luke probably makes the Q version more specific by adding τοὺς ἀνθρώπους. It is uncertain

---

11   Here I agree with Schulz, Q, 229. Luke probably has improved on ἐν τοῖς οἴκοις τῶν βασιλέων with ἐν τοῖς βασιλείοις. But who preserves the original location of ἰδεῖν in v. 26? Presumably Matthew does, since Luke has shifted ἰδεῖν in order that the first part of this third question parallels the structure of the first two questions (vv. 24 and 25).

12   Schulz (Q, 230) holds a different opinion. However, I agree with Schulz on the explicative addition of "the Baptist," and on the Matthean nature of "kingdom of heaven" (instead of "kingdom of God").

13   Either πορεύομαι (Matthew) or ἀπέρχομαι (Luke) is equally likely to have been the Q version. But

πρός with the accusative after a verb of saying is Lukan. Matthew preserves the dative that was in Q.

14   The same division of three examples into two groups can be found in the parable of the ten minas in Luke 19:16–23.

15   Note the signs of Lukan revision in vv. 29–30: πᾶς ὁ λαός, ἀκούω, ἡ βουλὴ τοῦ θεοῦ.

whether the double question can also be laid to his account. The *parallelismus membrorum* would rather indicate a Semitic tradition.[16] In smoothing the style with ἀλλήλοις ("to one another"), Luke changes the rules of the children's game, perhaps without being aware of this.[17] He overlooks or does not want to understand the ritual lamentation (κόπτομαι, "to lament," in Q and Matthew). He prefers the more general κλαίω ("to weep").

The parable is interpreted in direct speech (vv. 33–34; see γάρ). Luke probably imports "bread" and "wine" from 1:15.[18] Aside from a change in tense and in person, and an inversion,[19] these sayings of Jesus, so important for early Christianity, are transmitted identically in Luke and Matthew.

As a conclusion we find the saying about wisdom with its famous divergence (ἔργα, "deeds," Matthew; τέκνα, "children," Luke). The Matthean version is determined by an *inclusio* with its redactional introduction (τὰ ἔργα τοῦ Χριστοῦ, "the deeds of Christ," Matt 11:2) and is thus secondary.[20] The expansion with πάντων ("all") is Lukan, however (see below).

From a form-critical perspective, Luke creates a third episode with vv. 29–30. The aorists (ἐδικαίωσαν, "had acknowledged the justice," and ἠθέτησαν, "had rejected") indicate the prior nature of the division,[21] but, like a pluperfect, also describe the condition of the current audience of Jesus and indicate the situation. The parable that follows (vv. 31–32) pertains only to the obdurate and unrepentant (v. 30). Its interpretation (vv. 33–34) suits Luke's point well: people have not recognized God's plan and its phases in the activity of the Baptist and the Son of Man.[22] Luke closes the pericope with the final saying that he found in his source (v. 35).

The history of the transmission of vv. 29–35 is similar to that of the preceding unit (vv. 24–28): early Christian prophets gave a first interpretation (vv. 33–34) to a parable of the historical Jesus (vv. 31–32), which interpretation linked the two situations (missed opportunity for joy and tears) to the chief figures of the early religious movement.[23] The isolated saying about wisdom (v. 35), now linked with the unit, gave it a conclusion.[24] This composition was then incorporated by Q into a longer unit about the Baptist. Luke made it part of the narrative with the introduction in vv. 29–30.

---

16   Thus Schulz, *Q*, 379.

17   See the commentary on v. 32 below. Luke correctly puts the verb in the singular (λέγει) after the neuter plural subject ἅ (= τὰ παιδία). The paratactic wording καθημένοις καὶ προσφωνοῦσιν is more elegant than Matthew's participle προσφωνοῦντα in apposition to the subject. Also the singular "the marketplace" (ἀγορά) is to be preferred over the plural in Matthew; the singular was apparently in Q, since Matthew here generalizes (see below), whereas Luke normally uses this word with the article (see Jeremias, *Sprache*, 166).

18   Perhaps Luke bases his statement on Mark (1:6), whose narrative thread he dropped in 3:1–6 to follow Q. The secondary character of the words "bread" and "wine" is confirmed by their absence in v. 34, a verse that is identical in both Matthew and Luke (pace Otto Böcher, "Aß Johannes der Täufer kein Brot [Luk. 7,33]?" *NTS* 18 [1971–72] 90–92, esp. 92, who argues that both substantives were in the tradition and proposes that behind the ἄρτον ["bread"] one should see a Hebrew לֶחֶם, which should have been translated with κρέας ["meat"]).

19   Compared to ἦλθεν (Matthew = Q), the perfect ἐλήλυθεν in Luke is more appropriate in reference to the entire phenomenon of the appearances of the two main figures and is certainly redactional.

Likewise the second person plural καὶ λέγετε (vv. 33, 34) is to be ascribed to Luke, while the elegant word order τελωνῶν φίλος καὶ ἁμαρτωλῶν (Matt 11:19) is Matthew's.

20   The term "works" is better suited to the context of justification than that of "children." For that reason, "works" probably represents a redactional improvement. See Schulz (*Q*, 380 n. 18), who cites a number of authorities.

21   Perhaps the same phenomenon occurs in v. 21.

22   Cf. the well-chosen title of the article by Franz Mussner, "Der nicht erkannte Kairos" ["the unrecognized Kairos"] (Mt 11,16–19 = Lk 7,31–35)," *Bib* 40 (1959) 599–612.

23   The transposition of the sequence makes it obvious that vv. 33–34 have been redacted: in the proverbial saying joy is mentioned first, followed by sorrow (v. 32). But in the interpretation of the saying this order is reversed: John the Baptist is mentioned first, then Jesus (vv. 34–35).

24   Does the saying have its origin in Jewish wisdom literature or does it go back to the historical Jesus?

The evangelist thus presents the reader with three successive scenes, each beginning with an indication of the situation (vv. 18–19, 24a, 29–30) and climaxing in a chain of valuable sayings of the Lord (vv. 22–23, 24b–28, 31–35). All three have to do with the Baptist: the first with his disciples, the second with the positive response he garnered, and the third with the negative response of many to his message. The significance of Jesus is relevant in each of these issues: he belongs to the eschatological expectation of the Baptist (vv. 18–23), indicates John's salvation-historical function (vv. 24–28), and stands on his side, in regard to both God's saving purpose and the human rejection of God's messengers (vv. 29–35).

Commentary

The Legation (vv. 18–23)

■ **18–23** After Luke introduces the Baptist and grants him a salvation-historical role on the threshold of both ages (1:5–80; 3:1–20), he concentrates on the activities of Jesus, especially on his mission and healing abilities in Galilee (4:14ff.). Even at that time, astonished or polemical voices raise themselves against Jesus (4:32; 5:21). Later, questions about Jesus' identity and opinions about it are expressed (9:7–9, 18–21). Thus it is not surprising that the evangelist adopts the Baptist's question here (7:19–20).

The readers learn about the relationship between the Baptist and the Messiah from Luke's reworking of the traditional birth narratives. John receives the function of the preparer of the way and the forerunner (1:17, 76). His way runs parallel to that of Jesus, but one step ahead; his prophetic voice should lead the nation to contrition and repentance in preparation for the final phase, and thus make level the path of the Messiah. Here Luke portrays the forerunner as one who turns around and asks the famous question, "Are you the one that is to come, or are we to wait for another?" (7:19–20).

Historically, this episode reflects the uncertainty of the Baptist's community toward the newborn Christian movement after Easter. Luke adopts the narrative depiction of this experience from Q. Two things are clear to him in doing so: first, the hastening of salvation history, for until now a prophet could never become the contemporary of the fulfillment of his own prophecy; second, the lack of rational unambiguity in prophecy and fulfillment. Luke redactionally emphasizes the cryptic nature of every prophecy[25] and gives the expression ὁ ἐρχόμενος ("the one who is to come") the mysterious appearance of genuine prophecy. Jesus' answer likewise avoids concrete unambiguity. The editorial work explains the important mediating role of an appointed and well-instructed witness between the events and John, whose personal faith is being addressed.[26] John wavers on the edge of a decision.

The end of the story, or rather the absence of the expected conclusion, that is, a clear affirmation of Jesus by the Baptist, expresses dramatically that the majority of John's disciples remained aloof from the Jesus movement and did not overcome the stumbling block. Narratively, however, the story ends in an uncertainty that is symmetrical to that at its outset. Already in the tradition, the beatitude (v. 23) formed a generalizing conclusion. Thus the historical story of the Baptist has been transferred into the contemporary sphere of the hearers and readers.

The similarity and differences in both formal structure and theological import between this episode and the story of doubting Thomas in John 20:24–29 have seldom been recognized. What is true there of the resurrected Jesus is here true of the "messianic" Jesus. Someone doubts; to defuse the tension in the situation, Jesus decides to act. But from there the narrative strategies diverge: in the Gospel of John, Jesus decides on unmediated and compelling revelation, whereas in Q, Matthew, and Luke, he chooses mediation through witnesses and free decision. But the point of both beatitudes (John 20:29; Luke 7:53) is the same, and reflects the same call to belief from a distance.

From these general premises, I will attempt to answer a few special questions and interpret the redactional passages.

1. What John is seeking is a confirmation of the reports and the revelation of their significance (in the

---

25 Cf. 2:35, 49; 24:49; Acts 21:11.

26 On v. 21 see John F. Craghan, "A Redactional Study of Lk 7,21 in the Light of Dt 19,15," *CBQ* 29 (1967) 353–67: the verse is redactional; it stands at the center of the pericope (7:18–24a); it has been influenced by the law in Deuteronomy concerning the giving of testimony (Deut 19:15); the two messen-

281

sense of the $\dot{\alpha}\sigma\varphi\dot{\alpha}\lambda\varepsilon\iota\alpha$, "reliability," that Luke offers to Theophilus, 1:3–4).[27] Two Jewish theologoumena illuminate the passage: (a) The theory of the two phases of revelation, as is present at Qumran: "And God told Habakkuk to write down that which would happen to the final generation, but He did not make known to him when time would come to an end. And as for that which He said, *That he who reads may read it speedily*: interpreted this concerns the Teacher of Righteousness, to whom God made known all the mysteries of the words of His servants the Prophets."[28] The relationship between the Baptist and Jesus is symmetrical to that between Habakkuk and the Teacher of Righteousness. (b) The idea of the prophet desirous of knowledge (cf. 1 Pet 1:10–11). John, like the prophets, wants exact knowledge about the end and eschatological salvation.

2. Whether $\dot{o}$ $\dot{\varepsilon}\rho\chi\acute{o}\mu\varepsilon\nu o\varsigma$ ("the one who is to come") is common or unusual is a point of debate. In Hab 2:3, according to the text of Aquila, the expression alludes to a messianic figure (not necessarily and exclusively a royal one):[29] $\pi\rho o\sigma\delta\acute{\varepsilon}\chi o\upsilon$ $\alpha\dot{\upsilon}\tau\acute{o}\nu$, $\ddot{o}\tau\iota$ $\dot{\varepsilon}\rho\chi\acute{o}\mu\varepsilon\nu o\varsigma$ $\ddot{\eta}\xi\varepsilon\iota$ ("receive him, for the one who is to come shall come"). "'Coming' means all that stands in association with the time of salvation."[30]

3. In the fulfillment of the command in v. 20 and the healing activity of Jesus, seldom narrated so obviously as in v. 21, Luke achieves a dramatization: the messianic figure is outlined in the question (v. 20), the messianic deed in the situation described in v. 21.[31] The only thing missing is Jesus' interpretive statement to hold the two together.

4. "The legation to the Baptist presents in its present form a collection of 'messianic' verses from Isaiah in a simple poetic structure: Isa 26:19 (dead), 29:18–19 (deaf, blind, poor), 35:5–6 (blind, deaf, lame, dumb), and, above all, 61:1 (message to the poor, blind; additionally, words such as 'heal' and 'preach')."[32]

5. Jesus' answer, which interprets his own deeds, emphasizes the kindly, healing Messiah,[33] not the bellicose and judgmental figure of some Jewish expectations.[34]

6. The $\sigma\kappa\acute{\alpha}\nu\delta\alpha\lambda o\nu$ ("offense," v. 23) of the Synoptics is not identical with that in Paul. It is not the decision for or against the crucified one that is central, but that for or against the earthly Jesus in his greatness and his limitation.

John's disciples return with Jesus' answer.[35] They will tell their teacher not only about the healings, as in v. 18, but also about their eschatological interpretation through Jesus' word. What John will learn in addition is the conformity of Jesus' healing deeds to Scripture. Jesus' interpretation of them is an actualization of prophecy through the schema of prophecy–fulfillment. In content, this corresponds to the *pesher* exegesis of the

---

gers will report what they have heard, give their understanding of the events, and so assume the function of witnesses. In this way Luke expresses his theology of testimony.

27 John sent out his disciples in order to find confirmation; only later do they become witnesses. There exists only a limited correspondence with the sending of the Twelve or the seventy.

28 1QpHab 7.1–5. Translation in Vermes, *Dead Sea Scrolls*, 286.

29 August Strobel emphasizes that the wording of the question is not "Are you the one who was supposed to come or not?" but rather—with an ethical nuance—"Are you the one who was supposed to come or should we wait for another?" (*Untersuchungen zum eschatologischen Verzögerungsproblem* [NovTSup 2; Leiden: Brill, 1961] 265–77).

30 Hahn (*Titles*, 380). In Dan 7:13 Theodotion associates the word $\dot{\varepsilon}\rho\chi\acute{o}\mu\varepsilon\nu o\varsigma$ with the title "Son of Man."

31 *Nóσοι* are chronic diseases, and $\mu\acute{\alpha}\sigma\tau\iota\gamma\varepsilon\varsigma$ are attacks of infectious diseases (lit. "scourges"). Luke distinguishes between demonic possession and

disease, even though both appear in the same list of sufferings. Finally, blindness—set off formally from the others—is singled out as an especially terrible misfortune.

32 Strobel, *Verzögerung*, 274.

33 On $\mu\alpha\kappa\acute{\alpha}\rho\iota o\varsigma$ ("blessed") and the literary genre of the Beatitudes, see the commentary on 1:45 and esp. on 6:20.

34 Dupont ("Ambassade") has in mind how unpleasant the surprise was for John the Baptist when he had been announcing the day of judgment and the coming of an avenging judge, only now to learn that the Messiah is full of compassion. Jesus' reply thus embarrasses John the Baptist, as he stands there just as do the Christians before the offense of the cross. This also explains the call not to be led to stumble on account of Jesus (v. 23).

35 Though $\ddot{\alpha}\gamma\gamma\varepsilon\lambda o\varsigma$ frequently means "angel," it sometimes retains its original signification of "emissary," "messenger," as it does here in Luke 7:24 and in 9:52.

Qumran community. Jesus' answer takes the promise of Scripture seriously and applies it to current events. Thus Jesus answers the Baptist's question with a yes, without specifically going into its personal aspect.

Jesus' Evaluation of John (vv. 24–28)

■ **24–26** The return of the messengers begins a paragraph and rounds off the pericope through its substantive and formal similarity to v. 18.[36] Too often, only the contrast between the forerunner and the Messiah is taken into account. Yet already in v. 22, Jesus appeals to his audience for cooperation.[37] Again, the question sounds not abstract but exhortative, for $\tau\acute{\iota}\ \grave{\epsilon}\xi\acute{\eta}\lambda\vartheta\alpha\tau\epsilon$ . . . $\vartheta\epsilon\acute{\alpha}\sigma\alpha\sigma\vartheta\alpha\iota$ (" what did you go out to see?") places at the midpoint not the theoretical identity of the Baptist but the relationship of the crowd to him. Just as Jesus' work belongs together with the participation of the witnesses (v. 22), the person of the Baptist cannot be isolated from the attraction of the crowds to him. The truth of the gospel exists only in the relationship of faith: the experience of the disciples of the Baptist and that of the crowds invite one to see a similar relationship to the Word and the Scriptures.

It is presupposed that John is active in the wilderness,[38] indicating the charismatic nature of his office. Luke probably shares with his sources the symbol-ism of the wilderness as the place of contrition and eschatological new beginning.

The two negative examples are hard for us to understand.[39] The comparison of a swaying or fragile person to a reed is attested in antiquity.[40] For the crowds, John was just the opposite.[41] Everyone also knew about the ascetic lifestyle of the Baptist, so that the second rhetorical question, like the first, demanded a negative answer.[42] $M\alpha\lambda\alpha\kappa\acute{o}\varsigma$ was often used for "soft" clothing, here in the negative sense of "effeminate," "womanish."[43] In contrast to the first, an answer follows the second question: one meets wealthy people not in the wilderness but in palaces. In the redactional repetition (v. 25b), Luke expands on the beauty of the clothing[44] with the luxuriousness ($\tau\rho\upsilon\varphi\acute{\eta}$) of the lifestyle (cf. 8:14). After the third rhetorical question comes the right answer ($\nu\alpha\grave{\iota}\ \lambda\acute{\epsilon}\gamma\omega\ \grave{\upsilon}\mu\hat{\iota}\nu$, "Yes, I tell you . . ."). Prophets are people whom God has called and sent out. One should listen to them and hurry to see them. Typical of the style of Jesus is a revelation in the form of a riddle: "and more than a prophet" (cf. similarly Luke 11:31–32).

■ **27–28** Between the prophet and the Messiah, there is only one position open: that of the eschatological last prophet, the prophet like Moses.[45] This early Christian interpretation of Jesus' riddle can be seen in the mixed citation from tradition.[46] The tradition behind Mark 1:2

---

36 See $\grave{\alpha}\pi\acute{\eta}\gamma\gamma\epsilon\iota\lambda\alpha\nu$ (v. 18) and $\grave{\alpha}\pi\epsilon\lambda\vartheta\acute{o}\nu\tau\omega\nu\ \delta\grave{\epsilon}\ \tau\hat{\omega}\nu\ \grave{\alpha}\gamma\gamma\acute{\epsilon}\lambda\omega\nu$ (v. 24) as well as the name of John here in v. 24 and in v. 18.

37 $\mathbf{\mathring{A}}\pi\alpha\gamma\gamma\epsilon\acute{\iota}\lambda\alpha\tau\epsilon\ \mathring{I}\omega\acute{\alpha}\nu\nu\eta\ \hat{\alpha}\ \epsilon\emph{\"{\iota}}\delta\epsilon\tau\epsilon\ \kappa\alpha\grave{\iota}\ \mathring{\eta}\kappa\omicron\acute{\upsilon}\sigma\alpha\tau\epsilon$ ("Go and tell John what you have seen and heard").

38 See 1:80; 3:2, 4, 7.

39 See Constantin Daniel, "Les Esséniens et 'ceux qui sont dans les maisons des rois' (Matthieu 11,7–8 et Luc 7,24–25)," *RevQ* 6 (1967) 261–77, esp. 262–68. In his opinion, when Jesus compares them to reeds (Hebrew קָנֶה) moving back and forth in the wind, he is portraying the weakness of the Zealots (Hebrew קַנָּא) in the face of the Romans. With his question about John's clothing, he is making a criticism of the Essenes, who set too much value on their attire.

40 See, e.g., Lucian of Samosata *Hermotimus* 68 (cited in BAGD *s.v.*). Rhetorically, the contrast between the desert wilderness and the reed (which suggests the image of water) is striking.

41 Cf. the fearless behavior of John in the face of Herod (Mark 6:18).

42 One could move the punctuation and thereby ask the rhetorical questions differently. If the question mark is placed before the infinitive ($\vartheta\epsilon\acute{\alpha}\sigma\alpha\sigma\vartheta\alpha\iota$,

$\grave{\iota}\delta\epsilon\hat{\iota}\nu$), one must translate the three $\tau\acute{\iota}$ as "why": "Why have you come out to the wilderness? To see a reed . . . ?" Nevertheless, I prefer to retain the punctuation of Nestle-Aland.

43 *Ad malam partem*, $\mu\alpha\lambda\alpha\kappa\acute{o}\varsigma$ can signify an effeminate person or a male prostitute.

44 For variety he says here in $\grave{\epsilon}\nu\delta\acute{o}\xi\omega$ attire," i.e., in "magnificent," "luxuriant," "brilliant," even "glittering" or "glistening" attire.

45 On the prophet as a forerunner in Jewish messianic expectation, see Hahn, *Titles*, 352–65; see in addition 11QMelch 2.18–20 (Marinus de Jonge and Adam S. van der Woude, "11Q Melchizedek and the New Testament," *NTS* 12 [1965–66] 301–26).

46 On this citation see Fitzmyer, 1.674. The beginning corresponds to Mal 3:1, but also to Exod 23:20. "Before your face" is taken from Exod 23:20, since Mal 3:1 reads "before my face." "Who will prepare . . ." is closer to the Hebrew than to the Greek text of Mal 3:1 and is far from Exod 23:20. Therefore, it involves a mixed citation of a Semitic original that

knows this, too, except that ἔμπροσθέν σου ("before you," v. 27b) completes the parallelism (cf. πρὸ προσώπου σου, "before your face," in v. 27a). The hope of an eschatological prophet was also alive in other reform movements, as the Qumran texts demonstrate.[47] According to Jewish expectation, however, Elijah *redivivus* was the forerunner not of the Messiah but of God himself.[48] Like Q, Luke sees in John the last prophet, who also belongs already to the age of fulfillment. In contrast to Mark, however, he uses the typology of Elijah for Jesus himself, because it is Jesus who opens the way for God's advent, and has healing power.

Verse 27 explains the cryptic identity of the Baptist (v. 26). The "more" of prophethood is illustrated by the mixed citation from Exod 23:20 and Mal 3:1. According to Luke, as the last prophet, John is the first companion of the Messiah, better said, the salvation-historical forerunner. Since he is the first to break the path into the eschatological fulfillment, he can be considered the greatest among humankind (v. 28a). But since he also has one foot in the old age, any full member of the kingdom of God is greater than he. The metaphorical comparison ("greater" and "smaller")[49] refers to persons not as individuals but as members of a community: humanity (ἐν γεννητοῖς γυναικῶν, "among those born of women") versus the reign of God, in which they have found their new home and their new identity. This double citizenship is expanded upon in vv. 29–30. Everyone belongs to the first circle, to humanity. In order to enter the second, an answer is necessary (to hear and acknowledge, v. 29a).[50]

The Division of Israel (vv. 29–35)

A redactional summary (vv. 29–30)[51] narratively prepares a prophetic accusation (vv. 31–35) of the hard-heartedness of the leaders of Israel. In the background, then, is the deuteronomistic motif of obduracy.[52]

■ **29–30** Not everyone in Israel, however, closes their ears and their hearts, but only the leaders of the nation: the Pharisees and experts in the Law.[53] Thus, at the beginning of the last phase of salvation history, there is a division among the people of Israel.[54] The people[55] hear and do what God expects of them. Seldom is Christian identity so sharply defined by hearing.[56] It is clear

---

had already been assimilated to the LXX—although only partially—at the redactional stage of Q. For Christians, it is *God* speaking in these words to his *Son* about *John* the Baptist.

47 In addition to 11QMelchizedek (mentioned above), see further 1QS 9.10–11 and 4QTestimonia.

48 See Fitzmyer, 1.671–72.

49 The meaning of ὁ μικρότερος is disputed. Does it involve a genuine comparative (one "lesser") or a comparative with a superlative sense ("the least")? I lean toward the superlative (see BDF §60). Various authors, even from ancient times (see here Fitzmyer, 1.675), identified "the lesser one" (understood as a comparative) with Jesus.

50 See *Gos. Thom.* 46: "Jesus said, 'Among those born of women, from Adam until John the Baptist, there is no one so superior to John the Baptist that his eyes should not be lowered (before him). Yet I have said, whichever one of you comes to be a child will be acquainted with the kingdom and will become superior to John'" (trans. T. O. Lambdin in J. M. Robinson, ed., *The Nag Hammadi Library* [rev. ed.; San Francisco: Harper & Row, 1988] 131). See Schrage, *Thomas-Evangelium,* 107–9.

51 Various commentators (e.g., Schürmann, 1.421–22; Schneider, 1.172) wrongly regard vv. 29–30 as part of Jesus' speech.

52 See Deut 10:16; Exod 32:9; 33:3, 5; Acts 7:51–53. See Odil Hannes Steck, *Israel und das gewaltsame Geschick der Propheten: Untersuchungen zur Überlieferung des deuteronomistischen Geschichtsbildes im Alten Testament* (WMANT 23; Neukirchen-Vluyn: Neukirchener Verlag, 1967).

53 For the literature on the Pharisees in Luke, see the notes to the commentary on 5:17 above. The word νομικός, popularized by Luke (6 occurrences), corresponds to the γραμματεύς of the Synoptic tradition: "a scribe," "a specialist in the Jewish Law." See Hans Hübner, "νομικός, κτλ.," *EDNT* 2 (1991) 470–71, who holds that νομικός in classical Greek is an adjective, but in later Greek it became a substantive signifying "a lawyer," "an attorney."

54 See Jacob Jervell, "Das gespaltene Israel und die Heidenvölker: Zur Motivierung der Heidenmission in der Apostelgeschichte," *StTh* 19 (1965) 68–96; available in English as *Luke and the People of God: A New Look at Luke-Acts* (Minneapolis: Augsburg, 1972) 41–74.

55 See Jacques Dupont, "Un peuple d'entre les nations (Actes 15,14)," *NTS* 31 (1985) 321–35.

56 Cf. the πίστις ἐξ ἀκοῆς ("faith from hearing") in Rom 10:17.

from the loaded term "tax collector"[57] that this hearing implies contrition; that it is more than an inner condition is clear from the mention of the visible seal, baptism. In Acts 19:4 Paul voices a Lukan understanding of the role of the Baptist. The words and rituals of the Baptist were meant to awaken contrition and faith, and to lead to Jesus. Both messengers, only slightly separated by chronology, belong to the same divine plan of salvation (v. 30). In refusing baptism (v. 30b), the leaders of Israel have failed to recognize the salvation-historical moment, an eschatological one for them. The sayings that follow (vv. 31–35) are intended to illustrate exactly this missed chance, these missed καιροί ("times," "moments in time").[58]

The historicizing prose of Luke reaches even further back, for the refusal of John's baptism means the rejection (ἀθετέω is hard to translate)[59] of the will of God.

The word βουλή, which means literally "what one wants," that is, "purpose," "counsel," "project," "plan,"[60] attested outside Luke only three times in the New Testament, appears here for the first time in Luke. It also occurs in nine further passages, especially in the book of Acts. Βουλή usually means, in the theological sense, God's plan (esp. Acts 2:23; 20:27).[61] The death of Jesus corresponds to the purpose of God (2:23; 4:28), but it also extends backward into the time of promise (13:36: the time of David), as it does forward into the time of

judgment (without βουλή, but with the verb ὁρίζω, "to ordain," 10:42). The God who carries out his plan is no blind fate, but rather a wonderful person who is open for conversation, who sees in the denial of the leaders of Israel a way in which humans can accomplish his plan. The specification εἰς ἑαυτούς ("for themselves"), however, shows the limits of human power: the Pharisees and the scribes have set at naught the will of God (cf. Acts 20:27) only as far as it concerns them.[62] Despite this, God has as much suffering as anger after this failure. He has never forced anyone to follow him.

The obedient and contrite remnant of Israel has justified (ἐδικαίωσαν) God. This verb, unusual for Luke, was probably suggested to him by the last saying of the unit (v. 35). Here it means that the believers have approved God's desire and have consented to his plan. In the initiative of his benevolence God has thus shown himself righteous not in the sense of distributive justice, but in the sense of a dynamic readiness to save that is precisely not "just" according to the rules of *aequitas*.[63]

■ **31** Verse 31 is linked to the tragic realization in v. 30. The parable,[64] introduced by a rhetorical question, describes, accuses, and addresses the resistant ones. There is, however, an undeniable tension between the generalization of the redaction (v. 29: the people accept the message) and that of the tradition (v. 31: the majority of this generation is against it). More important than

---

57 On the tax collectors, see the notes to the commentary on 3:12–13 and 5:27–28 above. The connection between the baptism of John and contrition appears also in Acts 19:4.

58 See the analysis above.

59 Ἀθετέω means "to remove," "to throw away," "to reject," "to break (an agreement, an alliance, or a law)," "to set aside." See Meinrad Limbeck, "ἀθετέω," *EDNT* 1 (1990) 35.

60 Βουλή is a product of the will (θέλημα), as is evident from Eph 1:11: "according to the βουλή of his θέλημα."

61 See Conzelmann, *Theology,* 151–52; Jacques Dupont, *Paulus an die Seelsorger: Das Vermächtnis von Milet (Acts 20:18–36)* (Düsseldorf: Patmos, 1966) 85–90; Felix Christ, *Jesus Sophia: Die Sophia-Christologie bei den Synoptikern* (AThANT 57; Zurich: Zwingli-Verlag,1970) 78; Fitzmyer, 1.179.

62 Although missing in ℵ and D, the difficult words εἰς ἑαυτούς ("for themselves," v. 30) must be retained. The dispute among exegetes as to whether these words are to be taken with the verb ἀθετέω

or with the substantive βουλή τοῦ θεοῦ is an idle question, since Luke has the (bad?) habit of constructing sentences that admit more than one interpretation. Georges Gander ("Notule sur Luc 7,29–30," *VC* 5 [1951] 141–44, summarized and critically examined in Fitzmyer, 1.676) sees the phrase as a misunderstanding of an Aramaism. That is unlikely, however, in a verse so heavily redacted as this one.

63 Δικαιόω occurs 7 times in Luke (5 times in the Gospel and 2 times in Acts), 2 times in Matthew, but not found a single time in Mark. In Luke, except for here and in v. 35, it always concerns the justification of human beings.

64 The same question introduced by τίνι is found in Luke 13:18, 20.

this is the consciously constructed division of Israel. The rejection embedded in stubborn, willful, and hardened hearts is juxtaposed to the success rooted in God's messengers. In the related situation at the end of Acts, the leaders of the Jews are also split (Acts 28:25). Both here and there, this division leads to warnings of judgment against the opposers.

■ **32** It is difficult to visualize the playing children,[65] since this game is otherwise unattested.[66] Despite the editorial phrase προσφωνοῦσιν ἀλλήλοις ("call to one another"), Luke does not have two groups in mind, each of which would speak one part of the rhyme.[67] Luke's "solution" in vv. 33–34 divides the saying differently: "we" are the messengers of God (and those hearers that accept the message), "you" are the antagonists. The game breaks down because the seated participants, that is, the resistant children, reject both of the suggestions (to dance as at a wedding, or to cry as at a burial) by the initiators, namely the musicians. The difficulty is in the phrase ἀλλήλοις ἃ λέγει,[68] according to which the rhyme, which clearly presupposes that the musicians say it, comes from the mouths of the seated children.[69]

The "we" develops two complementary reproaches. They have "played the flute," that is, invited them to a dance, to a party (usually understood as a wedding).[70] And the children[71] invited to play have not responded to this call. "We" then have summoned "you" to a show of lament,[72] and "you" have also turned this down.

Despite the bad reputation of dancing and flute playing, Jesus dares to use such parabolic elements. In it he is indicating the qualities of joy, liberation, and festival in his message, by alluding in reverse to the prophets, who characterized the time of apocalyptic urgency by the silencing of songs.[73] An eschatological setting similar to a dance, however, does not forbid one from recognizing the seriousness of the situation. It is right to cry and lament over sin. What makes a unity of the two parts of the saying is the attitude of the addressees. They do not

---

65   On τὰ παιδία ("children") see Delebecque 42.

66   J. Huizinga offers some valuable insights in *Homo Ludens: A Study of the Play-Element in Culture* (London: Routledge and Kegan Paul, 1949).

67   Agreeing with Jülicher, *Gleichnisreden*, 2.26. On the various ways in which the game in Matthew and in Luke can be envisioned, see Mussner, "Kairos," 599–601 (finally, Mussner defends the hypothesis involving two groups, which I reject); and Zeller, "Bildlogik."

68   The ms. tradition attests to the difficulties caused by ἃ λέγει (v. 32).

69   The novel interpretation offered by Olof Linton ("The Parable of the Children's Game: Baptist and Son of Man [Matt. xi.16–19 = Luke vii.31–35]: A Synoptic Text-Critical, Structural and Exegetical Investigation," *NTS* 22 [1975–76] 159–79, esp. 175) is noteworthy: It is not that the children who sit in the marketplace are simply responsive. On the contrary, they are taking the initiative. It is *they* who are speaking and reproaching Jesus and John the Baptist for not dancing and mourning, i.e., for not living in accordance with the Jewish liturgical year and holidays.

70   See Jülicher, *Gleichnisreden*, 2.26–27: "The flute-playing fisherman in Aesop (fab. 27, ed. Halm) shouts a saying similar to this one to the fish: ὅτε μὲν ηὔλουν, οὐκ ὠρχεῖσθε ['when I played the flute, you did not dance'], a fable already applied by Cyrus to the Ionians, according to Hdt. 1.141." See Zeller, "Bildlogik," 253. In *Acts John* 95, surrounded by his disciples, Christ sings a hymn in which he

begins to play—literally speaking—with our text: "I will pipe,/Dance, all of you." "-Amen."/"I will mourn,/Beat all your breasts." "-Amen!" See also the comments by Eric Junod and Jean-Daniel Kaestli in *Acta Iohannis* (2 vols.; CCSA 2; Turnhout: Brepols, 1983) 2.598–99.

71   Must one think—with Jeremias (*Parables*, 120–21)—of only the boys doing the dancing and the girls doing the lamenting, as is the case with adults? I do not believe so. According to Gerhard Wallis ("Tanz," *BHH* 3 [1966] 1931–32), the two most important forms of group dancing were the procession dance and the round dance. The latter is probably intended. On the various kinds of flute see Gerhard Wallis, "Musik usw.," *BHH* 2 (1964) 1258–62.

72   Must one place a ὑμῖν after ἐθρηνήσαμεν? The external evidence weighs against it (see Nestle-Aland), but the internal evidence of the parallel ὑμῖν in the previous line seems to demand a ὑμῖν here. Luke uses the image of tears (κλαίω), and Matthew thinks of the gesture of mourning (κόπτομαι, "to beat one's breast").

73   See the list provided by Gerhard Wallis in "Musik usw.," *BHH* 2 (1964) 1261: Isa 16:10; Jer 7:34; 16:9; 25:10; 48:33; Ezek 26:13.

74   See Acts 7:51–53. Zeller ("Bildlogik," 255–56) stresses the proverbial character of v. 32b and cites Eccl 3:4b ("a time to mourn, and a time to dance") and several rabbinical proverbs, esp.: "No matter

want to play along. Thus the saying is finally a prophetic accusation[74] against proud rejection or resigned passivity. The sequence is surprising, a sign of the authenticity of the saying, because the salvation-historical sequence from John to Jesus is reversed. This is brought into correct order again in the interpretation of the parable (vv. 33–34).

■ **33–34** The prophetic commissioning is expressed by the theologically charged verb "to come."[75] In the background is the scheme of the two successive divine messengers.[76] Each of them receives an epithet: John as the Baptist, and Jesus as the Son of Man.

More important than the name "Baptist"[77] is the description of his lifestyle. In the second century one would expect that an Encratite would eat no meat and drink no wine. So $\mu\grave{\eta}\ \dot{\epsilon}\sigma\theta\acute{\iota}\omega\nu\ \ddot{\alpha}\rho\tau\sigma\nu$ ("eating no *bread*") is astonishing.[78] If $\ddot{\alpha}\rho\tau\sigma\varsigma$ does not simply mean food (thus indicating sparing intake), as often in the Hebrew Bible, then it means that John, as Mark 1 intimates, eats only raw foods unprepared by human hands. His dietary intake was in any case more ascetic than the Law of Moses commanded, so that his lifestyle[79] attracted criticism: "He has a demon."[80] Jesus "ate and drank," which meant for the crowds another extreme, a libertine (cf. the hedonistic proverb criticized by Paul in 1 Cor 15:32).

Jesus' conversation partners pass judgment from a moral standpoint (criticism of excess) no less than does wisdom literature (Prov 31:4–7) or Christian parenesis (Eph 5:18).[81]

Luke accepts the formulation from Q with its remarkable association of tax collectors (a profession) and sinners (a moral or ethical category). The term "tax collectors" here has a parabolic aspect and stands for the "sinners" addressed first by John, then by Jesus (v. 29; cf. 5:27–28 and 15:1). Jesus' friendship with them (he is their $\varphi\acute{\iota}\lambda\sigma\varsigma$) expresses vividly God's $\epsilon\dot{\upsilon}\delta\sigma\kappa\acute{\iota}\alpha$ ("goodwill") for them (cf. Luke 15:1–2, 3–32).

■ **35** The originally independently circulating saying in v. 35 is added as the conclusion of the traditional unit. Perhaps the concept "child" ($\pi\alpha\iota\delta\acute{\iota}\sigma\nu$, $\tau\acute{\epsilon}\kappa\nu\sigma\nu$) plays a role as a linking word. The saying is one of the few so-called wisdom sayings of Jesus.[82] "Wisdom" is here to be identified not with Jesus, but probably with a personified attribute of God. She here stands for divinity in its concern with humanity, particularly with the chosen people, and she receives her due through her loyal dependents, her "children." In the course of salvation, and perdition, history, she has been recognized, proclaimed, and to this extent justified again and again by these few "children."[83] Tradition and redaction number

what song one sings, it never enters the ears of those dancing. No matter what song one sings, the hardheaded son does not hear it" (12th preface to the Midrash on Lamentations).

75 Matthew uses the aorist twice, and Luke the perfect twice. The perfect tense has the theological advantage of combining the action of the past (the event) with the meaning for today.

76 See Günther Bornkamm, "Der Paraklet im Johannes-Evangelium," in idem, *Gesammelte Aufsätze*, vol. 3, *Geschichte und Glaube I* (BEvTh 48; Munich: Kaiser, 1968) 68–76.

77 The only other passages where ὁ βαπτιστής ("the Baptist") is used in Luke's two-volume work are Luke 7:20 and 9:19. Outside Christian literature, the word occurs only in Josephus *Ant.* 18.5.2 §116, where it also describes this same John. However, BAGD *s.v.* cites Epictetus *Diss.* 2.9.21, which reads ἡμεῖς παραβαπτισταί.

78 On the unlikely hypothesis of Böcher, "Johannes," see the notes to the analysis of vv. 29–35 above.

79 Bernhard Lohse (*Askese und Mönchtum in der Antike und in der alten Kirche* [Religion und Kultur der alten Mittelmeerwelt in Parallelforschungen; Munich: Oldenbourg, 1969] 112) denies any influ-

ence from Greek asceticism, since the body-soul dualism is lacking here: "The continent lifestyle of the Baptist may possibly be seen in the context of his message of the imminent judgment of God. It is more probable, however, that it is an asceticism of purity, similar to the Essenes and Therapeutae."

80 "He has a demon" is also found in John 10:20–21, again applied to Jesus.

81 The meaning of φάγος as "glutton" or "pig" seems rather obivous, even though it is a rare and recent word (note that, except for Luke 7:34 and Matt 11:19, LSJ *s.v.* cites only Zenobius Paroemiographus 1.73, a writer from the 2d century CE). However, the meaning of οἰνοπότης as "drinker" or "drunkard" appears to have been more common (see LSJ *s.v.*; Marshall, 302).

82 Christ, *Jesus Sophia*, 63–80; and M. Jack Suggs, *Wisdom, Christology, and Law in Matthew's Gospel* (Cambridge: Harvard University Press, 1970) 33–61.

83 Ἀπό here has the same meaning as ὑπό after a passive (see Christ, *Jesus Sophia*, 64). Although Matthew puts "works" in the place of "children," he did not intend to say anything fundamentally different.

among her "children" both the Baptist and Jesus. With the aorist of ἐδικαιώθη ("was vindicated,")[84] the Christian movement looks back to its beginnings, which it places under the aegis of divine Wisdom.[85]

History of Interpretation

In the second and third centuries, the statement that Jesus ate and drank raised great controversy. Neither the moral aspect of excess nor the ritual aspect of the Law was the cause of the excitement, but rather the claim of Jesus' corporality. The Christian movement had begun to address the issue of the incarnation. Would not the divine nature of Jesus be compromised if the Son of God was said to have eaten and drunk? Between the two extremes of Ignatius, who emphasized that Jesus had

truly eaten and drunk,[86] and Marcion, who spoke only of appearance,[87] the middle way had much greater currency: Jesus ate and drank, but before he digested the food and drink, a burning spirit took away the physical elements and burned them like a whole burnt offering. Theologians like Clement of Alexandria and a few docetic Gnostics came to this or a similar solution.[88] Such answers were drawing on Jewish theology that used the same explanation for the visit of the angels at Mamre (Gen 17).[89] What they were trying to avoid was the assumption that stools would be formed in the body of the incarnate Logos.[90] Irenaeus, for whom the fact of eating and drinking was an important proof of the humanity of Jesus, used the same theory, although applying it to the resurrected Christ.[91]

---

84 The aorist has been interpreted either as a gnomic aorist or as the translation of a Hebraic "prophetic perfect" (with a future sense). See Christ, *Jesus Sophia*, 64.

85 This is wisdom tradition: Wisdom—personified—calls out, draws near, is rejected, and then chooses a faithful few. See Christ, *Jesus Sophia*, 67. On the hypostatization of wisdom, see Ulrich Wilckens, "σοφία," *TDNT* 7 (1971) 496–514; and François Bovon, "Le Christ, la foi et la Sagesse dans l'épître aux Hébreux," *RThPh* 101 (1968) 130–44. In contrast to Christ (*Jesus Sophia*, 73, 79), in Luke 7:35 I cannot detect any identification of Jesus with Wisdom.

86 Ignatius *Trall.* 9.1. See *T. Ash.* 7:3. Acts 10:40–41 has also been drawn into the argument.

87 See Tertullian *Adv. Marc.* 3.8.4. Perhaps Marcion also omitted these verses from his Gospel (see Antonio Orbe, "El Hijo del hombre come y bebe [Mt 11,19; Lc 7,34]," *Greg* 58 [1977] 523–55, esp. 524).

88 Clement of Alexandria *Strom.* 6.9.71.1–2. In 3.6.52.3–6.53.2 he cites Luke 7:34 in a passage directed against the Encratites. On the docetic Gnostics see 3.7.59.3.

89 See *T. Abr.* A 4. Origen also tackled this problem. See Pamphilus, *Apologia pro Origene*, V *Responsio ad quartam criminationem* (*PG* 17.586A–88A = *PG* 14.1295D–98A).

90 See Orbe, "Hijo del hombre," 552. In this section on the history of interpretation, I am greatly indebted to Orbe for his article.

91 See *Adv. haer.* 4.31.2; 5.12.2.

Jesus and the Sinful Woman (7:36–50)

Bibliography

Bouwman, G., "La pécheresse hospitalière (Lc 7,36–50)," *EThL* 45 (1969) 172–79.

Braumann, Georg, "Die Schuldner und die Sünderin Luk. 7,36–50," *NTS* 10 (1963–64) 487–93.

Brodie, Thomas L., "Luke 7,36–50 as an Internalization of 2 Kings 4,1–37: A Study in Luke's Use of Rhetorical Imitation," *Bib* 64 (1983) 457–85.

Bultmann, *History*, 20–21, 384.

Charpentier, Étienne, "Le prophète, ami des pécheurs," *AsSeign* 42 (1970) 80–94.

Delobel, Joël, "Encore la pécheresse: Quelques réflexions critiques," *EThL* 45 (1969) 180–83.

idem, "Onction."

Derrett, J. Duncan M., "The Anointing at Bethany and the Story of Zacchaeus," *StEv* 2 (1964) 174–82 (= TU 87 = idem, *Law in the New Testament* [London: Darton, Longman and Todd, 1970] 266–85).

Drexler, "Sünderin."

Dupont, "Pharisien."

Elliott, "Anointing."

Feuillet, A., "Les deux onctions faites sur Jésus, et Marie Madeleine: Contribution à l'étude des rapports entre les Synoptiques et le quatrième évangile," *RevThom* 75 (1975) 357–94.

Frei, Reinhard Clemens, "Die Salbung Jesu durch die Sünderin: Eine redaktionskritische Untersuchung zu Lk 7,36–50" (diss., Mainz, 1978; see *TRev* 74 [1978] 510).

Heutger, Nicolaus, "Münzen im Lukasevangelium," *BZ* n.s. 27 (1983) 97–101.

Henss, *Diatessaron*.

Jeremias, "Lukas 7,45: *ΕΙΣΗΛΘΟΝ*," *ZNW* 51 (1960) 131.

idem, *Parables*, 101–2, 119–20.

Joüon, Paul, "Notes philologiques sur les Évangiles: Luc 7,44," *RechSR* 18 (1928) 353.

idem, "Pécheresse."

Kilgallen, John J., "John the Baptist, the Sinful Woman, and the Pharisee," *JBL* 104 (1985) 675–79.

idem, "A Proposal for Interpreting Luke 7:36–50," *Bib* 72 (1991) 305–30.

Korenhof-Scharffenorth, Miecke, "Und siehe eine Frau," in idem et al., eds., *"Aus dem Brunnen schöpfen . . .": Geschichten aus der hebräischen Bibel und dem Neuen Testament, von Frauen erzählt und ausgelegt* (Neukirchen-Vluyn: Neukirchener Verlag, 1986) 31–37.

Legaré, Clément, "Jésus et la pécheresse: Analyse sémiotique d'un fragment de l'évangile de Luc 7,36–50," *Sémiotique et Bible* 29 (1983) 19–45.

Legault, André, "An Application of the Form-Critique Method to the Anointings in Galilee (Lk 7,36–50) and Bethany (Mt 26,6–13; Mk 14,3–9;

Jn 12,1–8)," *CBQ* 16 (1954) 131–45.

Leroy, Herbert, "Vergebung und Gemeinde nach Lk 7,36–50," in H. Feld and J. Nolte, eds., *Wort Gottes in der Zeit: Festschrift Karl Hermann Schelkle* (Düsseldorf: Patmos-Verlag, 1973) 85–94.

idem, *Zur Vergebung der Sünden* (SBS 73: Stuttgart: Katholisches Bibelwerk, 1974) 1–81.

Löning, Karl, "Ein Platz für die Verlorenen: Zur Formkritik zweier neutestamentlicher Legenden (Lk 7,36–50; 19,1–10)," *BibLeb* 12 (1971) 198–208.

Manns, Frédéric, "Luc 7,47 et les traditions juives sur Rahab," *RevScRel* 61 (1981) 1–16.

März, Claus-Peter, "Zur Traditionsgeschichte von Mk 14,3–9 und Parallelen," in SNTU A.6–7 (Linz: Albert Fuchs, 1981–82) 98–112.

Orchard, Ronald Kenneth, "On the Composition of Luke vii, 36–50," *JTS* 38 (1937) 243–45.

Platt, Elizabeth E., "The Ministry of Mary of Bethany," *Theology Today* 34 (1977) 32–35.

Ramaroson, Léonard, "Le premier, c'est l'amour (Lc 7,47a)," *ScEs* 39 (1987) 319–29.

Ravens, D. A. S., "The Setting of Luke's Account of the Anointing: Luke 7.2–8.3," *NTS* 34 (1988) 282–92.

Roloff, *Kerygma*, 161–63.

Schäfer, Klaus, *Zu Gast bei Simon: Eine biblische Geschichte langsam gelesen* (Düsseldorf: Patmos-Verlag, 1973).

Spicq, *Agape*, 1.95–108.

idem, *Agapè*, 1.120–37.

Steiner, Anton, "Une rencontre inattendue: Jésus dans la maison de Simon, Lc 7,36–50," in idem and V. Weymann, eds., *Rencontres de Jésus* (Lausanne: Évangile et Culture, 1978) 23–35.

Taeger, *Mensch*, 34–43.

Thibeaux, Evelyn R., "The Narrative Rhetoric of Luke 7:36–50: A Study of Context, Text, and Interpretation" (diss., Graduate Theological Union, Berkeley, Calif., 1990).

de Urrutia, J. L., "La parábola de los dos dendores, Lc 7,39–50," *EstEcl* 38 (1963) 459–82.

Völkel, Martin, "Freund der Zöllner und Sünder," *ZNW* 69 (1978) 1–10.

Weiss, "Westliche Text."

Wilckens, "Vergebung."

36 One of the Pharisees asked Jesus to eat with him. And when he went into the Pharisee's house, he reclined at the table. 37/ And look, a woman who was a sinner in the city, having learned that he was reclining at table in the Pharisee's house, brought an alabaster jar of ointment, 38/ stood behind him at his feet, weeping, and began to sprinkle his feet with her tears, and she dried them with her hair and kept kissing his feet and anointed them with the ointment. 39/ Now when the Pharisee who had invited him saw it, he said within himself, "If this man were a prophet, he would have known who and what kind of woman this is who is touching him—she is a sinner." 40/ And Jesus replied and said to him, "Simon, I have something to say to you." "Teacher," he replied, "speak." 41/ "A certain creditor had two debtors; one owed five hundred denarii, and the other fifty. 42/ When they could not pay, he cancelled the debts for both of them. Now which of them will love him more?" 43/ Simon answered, "I suppose the one for whom he cancelled the greater debt." And Jesus said to him, "You have judged rightly." 44/ Then turning toward the woman, he said to Simon, "Do you see this woman? I entered your house; you gave me no water for my feet, but she has sprinkled my feet with her tears and dried them with her hair. 45/ You gave me no kiss, but from the time I came in she has not stopped kissing my feet. 46/ You did not anoint my head with oil, but she has anointed my feet with ointment. 47/ Therefore, I tell you, her sins, which were many, have been forgiven; hence she has shown great love. But the one of whom little is forgiven, loves little." 48/ Then he said to her, "Your sins are forgiven." 49/ But those who were at the table with him began to say among themselves, "Who is this who forgives sins?" 50/ And he said to the woman, "Your faith has saved you; go in peace."

Analysis

The story of the sinful woman is impressive in its aesthetic self-enclosed nature. Its "simplicity," however, is anything but easy, as the violent disputes about its meaning show.[1]

Should one follow the text of D in v. 46,[2] which tells nothing of an anointing of Jesus' feet?[3] Since the beginning of its interpretation, v. 47 has led to dogmatic debates over the question of whether the love of the woman described here is the cause or the consequence of divine forgiveness, with each side interpreting the grammar of the sentence according to its position.

With an almost boring repetitiveness, exegetes have compared the two anointings, in Bethany (Mark 14:3–9)

and here. Are the differences between the two, if they have their roots in a single event, to be traced to variants within oral tradition, or to a conscious and theologically motivated composition by its tradents or the evangelists? Does the parable belong together with the anointing from the start? In addition, why does the pericope not end at v. 47? Knowledge of normal social relations at the time also forms part of the correct understanding of the passage. The position of women in society, the norms of hospitality, and the custom of anointing have been investigated both by experts in the Middle East and by sociologists. The genre of the pericope (apothegm, legend, or table talk) and its placement in the Gospel (at the end of the Lukan composition of 6:19–8:3) have also been topics of discussion. But, first and last, the question is: does the Lukan text concern the woman, the Pharisee, or Jesus?

After the Sermon on the Plain (6:20–49), Luke took materials from his special source and from Q (7:1–35). This pericope stands at the end of this passage, before the evangelist reattaches to his Markan source (8:4ff.), after a brief transition (8:1–3). The overarching theme of chap. 7 is the saving visitation of God, and also the identity of the mediating messengers (cf. 7:49). Whereas chaps. 6 and 8 transmit Jesus' message, chap. 7 treats this double theme with the help of short narratives.

Jesus' invitation by a Pharisee serves as an introduction and gives the text the character of a symposium (v. 36). As often, an extraordinary incident (the behavior of the woman, vv. 37–38) fuels the conversation. Indeed, the incident is so significant that the author will return to it (vv. 48–50). It concludes with the reaction of the Pharisee (v. 39), who condemns Jesus in his thoughts, expects no further conversation, and perhaps regrets the invitation. But what appears to be the end for some becomes the beginning for others. Jesus' behavior shows a prophetic knowledge of people's hearts (v. 40a).

In our narrative the various agendas of the three people, expressed both in word and deed, collide. Jesus

1   On the state of research see Joël Delobel, "L'onction par la pécheresse: La composition littéraire de Lc 7,36–50," *EThL* 42 (1966) (= ALBO 4.33) 415–75 , esp. 415–21.

2   More exactly D W 079 b q arm.

3   See Konrad Weiss, "Der westliche Text von Lc 7,46 und sein Wert," *ZNW* 46 (1955) 241–45: John has changed the anointing into an anointing of the feet.

This version has influenced the majority of the ms. witnesses of the Lukan text.

tells a short story (vv. 41–42a) that seems at first blush to have no relation to the situation initiated by the woman; he thus uses the medium of a story within a story. That Jesus is also following his own agenda comes to light in the concluding question. While the verdict of the Pharisee (v. 39) is "sin" (for the woman) and "not-prophet" (for Jesus),[4] Jesus proposes for discussion the maieutic question about active love (v. 42b). The teacher, now become a student, must give the single correct answer almost against his will (ὑπολαμβάνω, "I suppose"). The disputed prophet of v. 39 now dares take on the role of teacher (διδάσκαλε, "teacher," v. 40), and assesses (ὀρθῶς ἔκρινας, "you have judged rightly") the judgment of his Pharisaic student positively. As the host must descend from the position of teacher (in the first scene) to student (in the second),[5] Jesus gradually gains back his contested authority. But he has not yet arrived at his desired destination. In the third scene (vv. 44–47), Luke has him make two connections: first between the woman and Simon, this by means of the astonishing statements that Jesus devotes to the woman in order to address the man (v. 44a); and second, between the first two scenes of the story, the deed of the woman and the words of Jesus. The result of the comparison is not: she did what you did not do, but rather, she did *more* than that which you did *not* do. Simon thus descends one level further. He has nothing more to say, and thus Luke has him stand speechless at this verdict (cf. vv. 29–30). By contrast, Jesus continues in a serious vein and legitimates (v. 47a) not only the woman's action but his own actions that preceded it, before he expresses a heavy verdict (v. 47b). The Pharisee who passed judgment in v. 39 should now feel himself under judgment, although the statement is nothing more than a wisdom saying, even in its form.

After this conversation with Simon that, though hard, was filled with a loving desire to persuade him, Jesus owes the woman an answer. Thus he continues with a word of forgiveness (v. 48), and we understand why Luke included this story after the pericope about the Baptist—not only because Jesus eats and drinks with sinners, as is written in v. 34, but also because the course of the narrative illustrates the dramatic division within Israel (vv. 29–30). Both at the time of the Baptist and of Jesus or the church, it was unexpectedly the sinners who listened to the message of liberation and believed (v. 29), while the so-called righteous excepted themselves from it (v. 30).[6]

At the end, one sees a fourth agenda: that of the unexpected guests (οἱ συνανακείμενοι, "those who were at the table with him"). With a question (v. 49), they underscore the subdued christological statement of Jesus (vv. 47–48) and relate him, as a person, to the forgiveness promised by him. Their answer to the question remains unexpressed, as does Jesus' reaction to it. They, as well, stand before a decision, the response of faith. But the story must end with the woman. Although she entered the house, she should not remain there. Jesus sends her away kindly (εἰς εἰρήνην, "in peace") by revealing to her the reason for her being forgiven with terminology not yet employed (belief and salvation), without talking about his own person (v. 50). Thus the narrative ends in a rather colorless fashion, but with a distinct doctrinal accent.

Despite arguments to the contrary, I understand all four accounts (Mark 14:3–9; Matt 26:6–13; John 12:1–8; Luke 7:36–50) as written fixations of a single gospel memory.[7] The same narrative scheme is employed in each version: (1) Jesus is invited to a meal; (2) a woman comes in and anoints Jesus; (3) this gesture evokes a negative reaction; (4) Jesus defends the accused woman; and

---

4   For Étienne Charpentier the main focus of interest in this pericope lies in the question of the prophetic office of Jesus ("Le prophète, ami des pécheurs," *AsSeign* 42 [1970] 80–94, esp. 86).

5   The conspicuous absence of the name of the Pharisee in v. 36 can be explained as follows: in the first verses (vv. 37–39) Luke describes the Pharisee as the one that the Pharisee believes himself to be: lord and master. Subsequently, however, he becomes a disciple, a student, and he receives with his name (v. 40) also this implicit designation.

6   Up to this point my own structuring of this scene

corresponds with that of Karl Löning ("Ein Platz für die Verlorenen: Zur Formkritik zweier neutestamentlicher Legenden [Lk 7,36–50; 19,1–10]," *BibLeb* 12 [1971] 198–208, esp. 200), which is adopted also by Jacques Dupont,"Le pharisien et la pécheresse (Lc 7,36–50)," *Communautés et Liturgies* 4 (1980) 260–68, esp. 262–63.

7   In this I agree with J. K. Elliott, "The Anointing of Jesus," *ExpTim* 85 (1973–74) 105–7. Cf. André Legault ("An Application of the Form-Critique Method to the Anointings in Galilee [Lk 7,36–50] and Bethany [Mt 26,6–13; Mk 14,3–9; Jn 12,1–8],"

(5) he recognizes her action as worthy of praise.[8] Moreover, there are verbal correspondances: ἀλάβαστρον μύρου ("alabaster jar," Mark, Matthew, Luke); Σίμων ("Simon") as the host (Mark, Matthew, Luke); her anointing the feet and drying them with her hair (Luke, John). In addition, there is the question about money either in the criticism of the audience (Mark, Matthew, John) or in Jesus' parable (Luke), expressed with the word δηνάρια ("denarii"), even when the sum is not the same (Mark, John, Luke)—something that is not often enough commented on. Last, Luke ignores the anointing in Bethany (22:2–3), because he equates it with the previous episode.

The conventions of oral tradition and hagiography demonstrate how an individual episode can be applied differently. The Markan tradition read the anointing christologically. The second evangelist combined it with his theology of the cross; the messianic anointing of the head (Mark 14:3) becomes for him an anticipation of death ritual (Mark 14:8), because he inserts it into the context of the passion narrative that was originally foreign to it.[9] In the pre-Lukan tradition, the story was intended anthropologically as a legend, that is, as a narrative about the unusual gesture of a woman, including the discussion about her love for Jesus, and less about the love of Jesus for her. The narrative juxtaposition between the respectable host and the woman who disturbs his guests makes possible a *theological* interpretation that finally leads to a comparison of loving "more" or "less," and to the otherwise banal simile that results from this comparison.[10] This process, in any case, took place during oral transmission. The simile stands in some tension with the narrative, since it expresses not

the original sense of the story but the interpretation that was realized in the course of transmission. At that point the spontaneous gesture of the despised woman was interpreted as the expression of human contrition and divine forgiveness. The action of the story is thereby doctrinalized, probably for catechetical reasons: one was to reflect on divine initiative and the greatness of divine grace, a thought foreign to the original story. At the same time, love becomes quantified and brought into relationship with the burden of sin. Where v. 47a, with its double meaning, belongs more to the story of the woman, v. 47b interprets the simile and sets forth its catechetical meaning.[11] The secondary interpretation is paradoxical because it places divine forgiveness first, but nevertheless moralizes the salvific act (cf. the two occurrences of both ὀλίγον and πλεῖον, "little" and "much," which are hard to interpret in vv. 42 and 43).

The functional setting of this development was a congregation that could not separate the instruction of its members from polemic against the synagogue. The polemical undercurrents cannot be ignored: the host has become a Pharisee (in Mark it is a leper, and in John the beloved Lazarus), and the greater love of the woman is not without reference to the calling of the Gentiles. Behind the ἀμφότεροι ("both of them") in v. 42, every new convert saw on the one hand the Jews, who have sinned little, and on the other side the Gentile Christians, who have loved much.

In this fashion the narrative achieved a first literary form, which then found its way into Luke's special source.[12] It shares the form typical of the special source with other Lukan pericopes, in addition to characteristics such as proper names and the interest in Jesus' con-

---

CBQ 16 [1954] 131–45), who assumes two events, one of which took place in Judea (Matthew, Mark, and John) and the other in Galilee (Luke). In the course of transmission each report has mutually influenced the other (see before him already Zahn, 334).

8   This fifth element is missing in John. On this scheme see Delobel, "Onction," 467.

9   See Elliott, "Anointing," 106.

10   The creator of this parable has certainly been inspired by some other parables of Jesus: the parable of the unmerciful servant (Matt 18:23–35) and the parable of the dishonest steward (Luke 16:1–9). Ulrich Wilckens, however, is of the opinion that the story and the parable belonged together from the

beginning, forming an apothegm that had its origin in a baptismal sermon ("Vergebung für die Sünderin [Lk 7,36–50]," in Hoffmann, *Orientierung*, 394–424); here he agrees with Georg Braumann, "Die Schuldner und die Sünderin Luk. 7,36–50," *NTS* 10 (1963–64) 487–93, esp. 490.

11   This theology of balance can be found in many of the early Christian writings in which God's merciful love stands side by side with the genuine repentance of the human being.

12   See Delobel, "Onction," 422–44. Actually, however, the vocabulary, which the advocates of this hypothesis attribute to proto-Luke, is much more likely Lukan: ἐρωτάω, ἁμαρτωλός, κλαίω, παρὰ τοὺς πόδας, ἄρχομαι, εἶπεν πρός, compound verbs,

versation partners. The final form owes its language and vocabulary to the Lukan redaction, which also reworked the conclusion of the narrative.[13] In harmony with preceding pericopes (esp. 5:20–24), Luke directs attention to the christological roots of the forgiveness of sins[14] and ends with a pious formula (v. 50 is an anticipation of 8:48). The repeated introductory formulas (vv. 48 and 50 after v. 44) already betray the redactional expansion of the conclusion.[15]

Commentary

First Scene (vv. 36–39)

■ **36** The invitation (v. 36a) and acceptance (v. 36b)[16] are mentioned in a single breath. Whereas the first half attests un-Lukan, perhaps even un-Greek, elements (ἵνα after ἐρωτάω, ἐσθίω μετά),[17] the second half displays the style of the evangelist.[18] Luke thus did not invent the narrative frame of the banquet, but gladly took it over

from his source, as the great composition in chap. 14 attests; because of his education, he appreciated such scenes, which follow particular guidelines,[19] for the communication of philosophical or religious messages. The Jews had taken over the Hellenistic custom of reclining[20] (v. 38: παρὰ τοὺς πόδας αὐτοῦ, "at his feet"; v. 49: συνανακείμενοι, "those who were at the table with him").[21] The literary genre of the symposium often employs interruptions, here the entrance of a woman (v. 37), as the point of departure for a conversation. The repetition of the word "Pharisee" is a preparation for the hard words that ensue (cf. 15:1–2).

■ **37** Luke has no illusions about the woman. Her "sin" is a social one. That he takes her to be a prostitute is clear in the expression ἐν τῇ πόλει ("in the city").[22] The unexpected nature of her presence is signaled by the beloved καὶ ἰδού ("and look").[23] The nuance of

---

the repetition of the preposition after compound verbs, etc.

13 The Lukan vocabulary is perceptible throughout the whole pericope: δέ (v. 36); καὶ ἰδού, ἥτις, πόλις (v. 37); ἰδών, καλέω, Jesus as προφήτης (v. 39); ἀποκριθείς . . . εἶπεν, ἔχω with the infinitive (v. 40), etc. Ἔχω with the infinitive is found, for example, in Luke 12:4, 5; 14:14; Acts 4:14; 23:17, 18, 19; 25:26; 28:19.

14 See Herbert Leroy, "Vergebung und Gemeinde nach Lk 7,36–50," in H. Feld and J. Nolte, eds., *Wort Gottes in der Zeit: Festschrift Karl Hermann Schelkle* (Düsseldorf: Patmos-Verlag, 1973) 85–94; idem, *Zur Vergebung der Sünden* (SBS 73: Stuttgart: Katholisches Bibelwerk, 1974) 1–81.

15 See Bultmann, *History*, 20–21. His analysis reaches a conclusion essentially different from my own: he is of the opinion that parts of the anointing at Bethany (Mark 14:3–9) have been added to an original tradition that consisted of the parable and its interpretation, the beginning of which has been revised. I agree with Bultmann, however, that vv. 48–50 are secondary. On the various hypotheses explaining the relationship between tradition and redaction, see Grundmann, 169–70; Marshall, 304–7; Bultmann, *History*, 384.

16 See Luke 11:37 (a somewhat more pleasing expression) and 14:1.

17 See Delobel, "Onction," 458–62. The partitive genitive ("one of the Pharisees"), however, is correct. At that time the partitive genitive was in the process of disappearing and was being replaced by preposi-

tional expressions (see Abel, *Grammaire*, §44d). The expression "to eat with" is found in the LXX in 1 Sam [LXX 1 Kgdms] 1:18 and Prov 23:8; it is a Semitism. On φάγομαι, which is labeled as "barbaric" by Phrynichus (*The New Phrynichus, Being a Revised Text of the Ecloga of the Grammarian Phrynichus* [ed. W. G. Rutherford; London: Macmillan, 1881] 376), see Antoniadis, *Évangile*, 116.

18 On the use of the imperfect with verbs that indicate an action which actually takes place later, see BDF §328. Ἐρωτάω was used at that time for invitations (e.g., for an invitation to a cultic meal in honor of Serapis; see G. H. R. Horsley, *New Documents Illustrating Early Christianity* [8 vols. to date; North Ryde, Australia: Macquarie University, 1981–] 1.5).

19 See Bo Reicke, "Tisch 4," *BHH* 3 (1966) 1993. For a critique of the historical reconstruction proposed by Jeremias (*Parables*, 101: after the sermon, Jesus is invited to the Sabbath meal), see Hans Drexler, "Die große Sünderin Lucas 7,36–50," *ZNW* 59 (1968) 159–73, esp. 161.

20 Nestle-Aland has κατεκλίθη (from κατακλίνομαι, "to recline at table," "to lie down"; κατάκειμαι [v. 37] "to lie at table"). The text is not certain, though Luke prefers to use κατακλίνομαι (two times) over ἀνακλίνομαι.

21 See Ronald Kenneth Orchard, "On the Composition of Luke vii, 36–50," *JTS* 38 (1937) 243–45, esp. 244 n. 1.

22 Her entering into the house is not mentioned. See the discussion of v. 45 below (εἰσῆλθον).

23 Καὶ ἰδοὺ γυνὴ . . . καί with a participle is redac-

$\dot{\epsilon}\pi\iota\gamma\nuο\hat{\upsilon}\sigma\alpha$ is hard to determine: "to observe," "to know," "to recognize," "to notice," "to learn."[24] The transition from $οἶκος$ (v. 36) to $οἰκία$ (v. 37) perhaps betrays the seam between redaction and tradition.

The use of the $καί$ and the relationship between the present and aorist participles is not completely clear. With $κομίσασα$ ("to bring") (nicer in this context than the Johannine $λαβοῦσα$ or the Markan and Matthean $ἔχουσα$), the woman has made the transition from mere recognition to actual deed. Ὁ $ἀλάβαστρος$ or τὸ $ἀλάβαστρον$ usually designates a handleless perfume container of alabaster, not merely a glass flask the neck of which would be broken off to open it.[25] In contrast to the other three evangelists, Luke does not mention the price of the perfume. The intensity of the relationship consists for him not in the price but in the humility of attitude. Nevertheless, the elegant formulation indicates the value of the perfume ($κομίσασα$ $ἀλάβαστρον$ $μύρου$). In antiquity it was not alcohol but oil that was the medium for perfume. For this reason, $μύρον$ is often translated as "perfume oil"; it was in any case fluid ($ἤλειφεν$, "anoint").

■ **38** As the story continues, the woman then approaches Jesus, and from behind. The $ὀπίσω$ ("behind") perhaps manifests the surprise, after the narrative silence about her entrance, that one suddenly notes that she is standing there ($στᾶσα$, "she stood").[26]

She is crying so much (the present participle implies a durative mode) that her tears (which relate to $βρέχω$; cf. v. 44) sprinkle Jesus' feet.[27] The narrative understands these tears as a replacement for the washing of guests' feet, which was customary at the time (v. 44). A theatrical substitution for the towel is the woman's hair.[28] In the word $ἐκμάσσω$ an ancient reader would understand first the motion of wiping, and only then the result of being dried.[29] After this the evangelist mentions Jesus' feet a third time, which the woman now kisses for a long time (imperfect tense). Only then does she perform the act of anointing already prepared in v. 37b. In Israel, kings, priests, and prophets were ritually anointed, whereas anointing of the body was part of both the customs of hospitality and everyday care of the body.[30] But as in John 12:3, Luke clearly indicates an anointing of the feet,[31] which "in and of itself would be an unusual, indeed unheard-of action in antiquity."[32] Wettstein, however, shows that anointing the feet also has "its place either in the everyday care of a man by his wife or daughter" or "in the lives of libertines and sissies."[33] It is because something unusual happened, an anointing of the feet, that this recollection remained alive among the early Christians.[34] One could even make this more pre-

---

tional. On the displacement of $ἤ$ by $ἤτις$ at that time—and not just in popular literature—see Rydbeck, *Fachprosa*, 98–118, esp. 100–101, 110, 113. At any rate, thanks to the $ἤτις$, the hiatus of $ἤ$ $ἤν$ is avoided.

24 See Moulton and Milligan, *Vocabulary, s.v.* (with examples).

25 See Georg Fohrer, "Glas," *BHH* 1 (1963) 574–75. The commentators (see Fitzmyer, 1.689; BAGD *s.v.;* and the literature they cite), however, are fond of quoting Pliny the Elder: "unguenta optime servantur in alabastris" ("ointments keep best in alabaster," *Nat. hist.* 13.3.19).

26 The accusative after $παρά$ (v. 38) does not necessarily mean that the woman moves (see BAGD *s.v.* $παρά$ III.1). $Στᾶσα$: she stands there.

27 Following his normal practice, Luke states that she "begins" ($ἤρξατο$) to wet his feet. Why? In order to indicate that something important is beginning? On $ἄρχομαι$ see the commentary on 3:23 above. For $βρέχω$ LSJ *s.v.* cites a Greek inscription (*IG* 14.1422): $δακρύοισιν$ $ἔβρεξαν$ $ὅλον$ $τάφον$ ("they

made the tomb wet with tears"). $Βρέχω$ means first of all "to make wet (through immersion or flooding)" and then "to rain" or "to cause to rain."

28 Since $θρίξ$ can also mean "the hide of an animal," "fur," the words $τῆς$ $κεφαλῆς$ are not entirely superfluous. Αἱ $τρίχες$ $τῆς$ $κεφαλῆς$ with the genitive is even a common expression (Luke 12:7); see BAGD *s.v.*

29 To the best of my knowledge, there is no study of $ἐκμάσσω$ ("to wipe dry"); see BAGD *s.v.* The ms. tradition varies between the imperfect (Nestle-Aland) and the aorist.

30 See Eric Segelberg, "Salbung," *BHH* 3 (1966) 1646–47.

31 Unless one follows the D text, as does Weiss, "Westliche Text."

32 Weiss, "Westliche Text," 242.

33 Wettstein, 1.702–3. Cf. Weiss, "Westliche Text," 243.

34 An alteration from anointing the feet to anointing the head can be explained more easily than the reverse, since, for the pre-Markan tradition, the

cise by saying that this woman could find nothing better to express her love than a gesture of erotic love. In this one should not of course see an erotic scene, for the woman is crying,[35] but rather inappropriate behavior by the standards of that time. The woman comes into the midst of a dinner reserved for men, carries a bottle of perfume, unlooses her hair (a particularly erotic action for Jewish perceptions), repeatedly kisses Jesus' feet,[36] and finally in the presence of all the guests does something that belongs in the realm of intimate behavior or even of perverse practices: she anoints his feet. Jesus, however, interprets the entire sequence differently than does the Pharisee and does not reject these gestures. The Pharisee is outraged that Jesus allows himself to be "touched" by such a woman (v. 39), a fact that has been drawn into consideration far too seldom. Jesus reinterprets the gestures that are, according to the clichés of that time, erotic, because the woman's tears reveal the true meaning of her actions, although this is expressed, in a completely external sense, in a manner that is determined by her past.

■ **39** By recalling the invitation (καλέσας, "who had invited"),[37] Luke heightens the degree of outrage on the part of the Pharisee, who promptly reacts to the events in the form of an interior dialogue.[38] The Pharisee is interested not in the woman but only in Jesus, who (οὗτος is used in a derogatory fashion), after all this, cannot be a prophet,[39] otherwise he would know:[40] who

(τίς) this woman is (personal identity) and what kind of a woman (ποταπή)[41] she is (social category), that is, a sinner (ἁμαρτωλός as a label). Thus the woman knows about Jesus (ἐπιγνοῦσα, "having learned," v. 37), and the Pharisee similarly knows (v. 39) that Jesus knows nothing about the woman (ἐγίνωσκεν ἄν, "he would have known"). Jesus' maieutics intend to lead the Pharisee from a pseudo-knowledge to real knowledge, and to confirm the woman's knowledge and his own. Luke ironically contrasts in v. 40 Jesus' prophetic knowledge[42] to the mistaken judgment of the Pharisee (v. 39).

Second Scene (vv. 40–43)

■ **40** Jesus, until this point passive and silent, now takes the initiative. Ἔχω σοί τι εἰπεῖν ("I have something to say to you") is hardly oriental politeness asking to have the floor, but rather underscores the authority of the teacher demanding attention. Διδάσκαλε ("teacher") and Σίμων ("Simon") illustrate this new pedagogical relationship.[43]

■ **41–42** Jesus tells a story that suits the occasion, as once Nathan did to David.[44] In this manner he succeeds in maintaining the conversation and effecting conviction, where direct speech would have failed this objective. The story, as a parable, opens a new reality to Simon, but the tragic fact is that this reality has *already* been revealed to him in the relationship between Jesus and the sinful woman, and he remained blind to it.

---

anointing of the head meant the anointing of a king.

35 The woman weeps for herself and not for Jesus; her tears are tears of remorse and not tears of mourning.

36 One should not forget the HB euphemism; see Exod 4:25; Isa 6:2; 7:20; Richard Hentschke, "Fuß," *BHH* 1 (1963) 505–6.

37 Καλέω here means "to invite"; see Luke 14:7–14; and BAGD s.v. καλέω (1b).

38 Luke is aware of the inner dialogue that one has with oneself (Luke 15:17). Sometimes he tries to transfer these inner processes to the outside (cf. Luke 5:21–22 with Mark 2:8). On the redundant expression εἶπεν . . . λέγων as originating from the LXX, see Fitzmyer, 1.115.

39 Ὁ προφήτης (i.e. the [eschatological] prophet) is not as well attested as the anarthrous noun. Like the crowd (7:16) and the disciples on the road to Emmaus (24:19), the Pharisee is thinking of *a* prophet. See the notes to the commentary on

7:16–17 above.

40 V. 39b represents a correctly worded conditional sentence: it is a contrary-to-fact condition in the present tense (see Kaegi, *Grammaire*, §187).

41 Ποταπός: "of what sort," "of what kind"; see BAGD s.v., which translates the expression τίς καὶ ποταπὴ ἡ γυνή as "who and what kind of woman."

42 On such miraculous knowledge see Bieler, ΘΕΙΟΣ ANHP, 87–90.

43 See in addition Gen 24:33–34, where one finds the same sequence: one person announces that he has something to say, and the other person invites him to speak, and so the first person speaks.

44 See 2 Sam (LXX 2 Kgdms) 12.

Because parabolic language has a less direct effect, Jesus can thereby carefully persuade him.[45] Stories of debtors and lenders were often employed by Jewish teachers as examples, proverbs, or parables.[46] "The parable is almost colorless and omits all concrete references, so that all listeners, with their individual situations, can be included. Only one thing presents itself inescapably: the unusual aspect of the metaphor, that a moneylender would completely erase the debt of his borrower. Already here the real issue, the new fact, moves forward into view: God's eschatological act of forgiveness."[47]

Χαρίζομαι means first "to do something beneficial to someone," then, "to give as a gift." To use the word as a description of a release from financial debt is unusual, though it does occur in Philo in the context of ritual forgiveness of debts. Philo makes an ethical argument for generosity (χάρις) and violently rejects loans for interest.[48]

Luke's Jesus expects that, as a reaction to this story that reveals the theological origin of love, the Pharisee will see positively the woman's action and value it even higher than his own. This leads to the comparative πλεῖον ("more," v. 42). The aspect of thankfulness in the parable is expressed in ἀγαπάω ("love"),[49] but it is directed toward the true issue, and thus ἀγαπάω invites a semantic transfer.

■ **43** The Pharisee unwillingly admits (ὑπολαμβάνω, "I assume, I am of the opinion") that the greatest debtor would feel the greatest gratitude. "Correct," concludes Jesus, with nearly the same words as Socrates.[50]

History of Interpretation

It is very likely that Tatian, in his *Diatessaron* version of v. 42b, read "*whom* of them would *he* love most," rather than "*who* of them would love *him* the most."[51] Thus it is no longer the woman's grateful action, but God's election, or rather his favor, that is decisive for Tatian. The hypothetical reconstruction of the gnostic interpretation of this verse is closely related; like Tatian, it emphasizes the Savior's divine favor for this woman, who is identified by them with Mary Magdalene and understood as a symbol of the fallen Sophia.[52]

Commentary

Third Scene (vv. 44–47)

■ **44–46** The Pharisee now casts a fresh look at the woman (βλέπεις, "do you see," v. 44; cf. ἰδών in v. 39). The woman's three actions are supposed to make his own behavior more evident by contrast. He did not properly receive Jesus, as he would have been able to do. This lack of a gesture of hospitality reserved for select guests and special occasions[53] reflects a hidden con-

45 See P. Paul Watzlawick, Janet H. Beavin, and Don D. Jackson, *Pragmatics of Human Communication: A Study of Interactional Patterns, Pathologies, and Paradoxes* (New York: Norton, 1967) 50–66; Josef Kopperschmidt, *Allgemeine Rhetorik: Einführung in die Theorie der persuasiven Kommunikation* (Stuttgart: Kohlhammer, 1973).

46 See Str-B 2.163; and Grundmann, 171. The reason for this comparison certainly lies in the ambiguity of the Aramaic word חוֹבָה, which means "debt" as well as "sin." See Paul Joüon, "La pécheresse de Galilée et la parabole des deux Débiteurs (Luc 7,36–50)," *RechSR* 29 (1939) 615–19, esp. 616.

47 Schürmann, 1.434.

48 See Philo *Spec.* 2.39.71–78. Χαρίζομαι occurs frequently in Philo; see Günter Mayer, *Index Philoneus* (Berlin: de Gruyter, 1974) 303.

49 See Joüon, "Pécheresse," 616; Jeremias, *Parables*, 102. The reason given for this choice of wording is that there is no verb in either Aramaic or Hebrew to express one's gratitude. Fitzmyer (1.690) points out that the Greek verb ἀγαπάω can also have this nuance.

50 Ὀρθῶς ἔκρινας reminds one of πάνυ ὀρθῶς, which in the dialogues of Plato is used by Socrates whenever one of his disciples answers a question correctly (see Godet, 1.359).

51 See the learned book by Walter Henss, *Das Verhältnis zwischen Diatessaron, christlicher Gnosis und "Western Text": Erläutert an einer unkanonischen Version des Gleichnisses vom gnädigen Gläubiger: Materialien zur Geschichte der Perikope von der namenlosen Sünderin Lk 7,36–50* (BZNW 33; Berlin: Töpelmann, 1967).

52 See ibid., 39–45. Incidentally, Papias also states (as quoted in Eusebius *Hist. eccl.* 3.39.17) that the *Gospel of the Hebrews* contained a story about a woman who was sued by her husband for her many sins (see Henss, *Diatessaron*, 55). But the allusion could simply be a parallel to the story of the adulteress in John 7:53–8:11.

53 Jülicher (*Gleichnisreden*, 2.296–97) shows that such was done in the Judaism of that time; likewise Schürmann, 1.435 nn. 31–34.

54 "The defenders of the first person are promoting . . . worship for what is corrupt," writes Drexler ("Sünderin," 163), who considers the restoration of

tempt or doubt about Jesus' greatness (cf. v. 39). If one accepts (v. 45) the first person ($\epsilon\dot{\iota}\sigma\hat{\eta}\lambda\vartheta o\nu$) instead of the more comprehensible third person ($\epsilon\dot{\iota}\sigma\hat{\eta}\lambda\vartheta\epsilon\nu$),[54] one must assume that the woman's intervention took place shortly after Jesus' arrival, and that the guests cannot explain her sudden appearance.

■ **47** The most obvious sense of v. 47a (forgiveness on account of one's love) is immediately refuted by v. 47b (love as a consequence of forgiveness).[55] A possible solution is that it is the causation not of the actions but of the recognition that is in question here. Then $\mathring{o}\tau\iota$ would not mean "because," but "in recognition that" ("evidenced by the fact that")[56] and would be dependent on $\lambda\acute{\epsilon}\gamma\omega\ \sigma o\iota$ ("I tell you"). Her love would be a proof of the forgiveness of her sins. The exegetical discussion of this since the Reformation has been overloaded with doctrinal polemics.[57] But Luke is not posing the theological question of the *initium fidei*. For him, both God and humans are active in reconciliation. Even if God's love remains the center of Luke's message, he repeatedly pushes human responsibility into the foreground. There is no divine love without reciprocity. The logical and chronological first step of God is not the subject of debate, but the question of which of the two (the woman or Simon) has a reciprocal love relationship to Jesus and to God. In this sense the woman's actions are simultaneously indications of and reasons for her forgiveness. This seems to me Luke's solution of the problem, which is the result of a long period of transmission. The episode first narrated, without parable, the loving behavior of the woman, and then it was told, after the introduction of the parable, for the purpose of the catechetical understanding of forgiveness and ethics. The content of v. 47a belongs to the first stage of transmission, v. 47b to the second. Luke himself stands in the third stage, and leaves the tension in v. 47 as it is.[58]

Fourth Scene (vv. 48–50)

■ **48** Quite apart from the opinion of the Pharisee, Luke himself describes the woman as a sinner (v. 37). For this reason, in v. 48 Jesus can promise her the certainty of forgiveness, again independently of Simon. Luke is not interested in the exact moment that the forgiveness occurs. As in 5:20, he prefers the perfect ($\mathring{\alpha}\varphi\acute{\epsilon}\omega\nu\tau\alpha\iota$) to the present ($\mathring{\alpha}\varphi\acute{\iota}\epsilon\nu\tau\alpha\iota$, Mark 2:5 and Matt 9:2). In this he expresses both the roots of forgiveness in God and its anthropological realization.[59] The woman's joy over this is not stated, probably because it is obvious. The christo-

---

the original third person unavoidable. The hypothesis of an Aramaic original, where the same verb form could mean both "I came" as well as "she came" (so Joachim Jeremias, "Lukas 7,45: *EIΣ-HΛΘON*," *ZNW* 51 [1960] 131), is called into question by Fitzmyer (1.691).

55 The question has been raised whether $o\mathring{\hat{v}}\ \chi\acute{\alpha}\rho\iota\nu$ might not refer beyond $\lambda\acute{\epsilon}\gamma\omega\ \sigma o\iota$ also to the forgiveness, and thus reinforce the connection between the cause (love) and the effect (forgiveness). I believe, however, that both of these words are to be construed with $\lambda\acute{\epsilon}\gamma\omega\ \sigma o\iota$: Jesus is drawing a conclusion.

56 The grammars (see the list in Marshall, 313) allow this meaning; see C. F. D. Moule, *An Idiom Book of New Testament Greek* (2d ed.: Cambridge: Cambridge University Press, 1963) 147.

57 Traditional Catholic exegesis (Lagrange, 230–31, can be classified as a representative) sees in this verse a confirmation of the view that love precedes and leads to forgiveness (with the emphasis on v. 47a). Many Protestants are of the opinion that this verse cannot be interpreted without taking into consideration the overall meaning of the parable: forgiveness receives first place (with the emphasis therefore on v. 47b; so Marshall, 313; Wilckens,

"Vergebung," 404–11). For his part, Dupont ("Pharisien," 261) represents the opinion that what is important is not the causal relationship, since love and forgiveness are inextricably bound together. For a basic understanding of the historical impact of v. 47 in the 16th century, see Wilckens, "Vergebung," 394.

58 V. 47b could be misconstrued for understandable reasons. Thus, e.g., with the support of Rom 3:8 and 6:1, the church fathers had to object to an unrestrained interpretation (let us sin even more so that we may receive an even greater forgiveness!). See Henss (*Diatessaron*, 33–34), who cites, among others, Augustine *Sermo* 99.4–6 (*PL* 38.597–98). Henss (*Diatessaron*, 24–31) has also shown that an agraphon circulated in ancient Christianity, which John Chrysostom (*Hom. in Act.* 30.4 [*PG* 60.225]) quotes as follows: $\mathring{\hat{\omega}}\ \gamma\grave{\alpha}\rho\ \pi\lambda\epsilon\hat{\iota}o\nu\ \mathring{\alpha}\varphi\acute{\epsilon}\vartheta\eta\ \pi\lambda\epsilon\hat{\iota}o\nu\ \mathring{\alpha}\gamma\alpha\pi\acute{\eta}\sigma\epsilon\iota$ ("For the one who is forgiven of more will love more").

59 See the commentary on 5:20 as well as the excursus there on the forgiveness of sins. The rule of forgiveness is not the same here (7:47–48) as it is there (5:20, 23), though in both cases Luke prefers the perfect tense over the present (cf. Mark 2:5, 9).

logical roots of forgiveness are evident in the guests' astonished question.

■ **49** Both vv. 49 and 48 are reminiscent of the parable of the paralyzed individual: both verses are nearly copies of 5:20–21, and are narrative elements that allow a dignified though slightly formulaic and banal conclusion to the episode. Their christological interest is hardly superficial, however. The audience's reaction is repeated from 5:21 with urgency, thus foreshadowing Herod's question (9:7–9), the opinions of the people (9:18–19), Peter's confession (9:20), and Jesus' first prediction of the passion (9:22).

■ **50** The pericope, however, goes on. Luke does not want to conclude it with Jesus' response. The matter remains open (until 9:20, 22), and the woman herself receives a further concluding word from Jesus. Luke again contents himself with a formula (v. 50) that is this time taken from the material that follows (Mark 5:34 par. Luke 8:48). But it might also be a stock phrase. Love for Jesus and forgiveness are now expressed with different words, as "faith" and "salvation." Luke uses these concepts interchangeably. Thus the statement "your faith has saved you" is not to be interpreted in either a Pauline or a Pelagian sense.[60] The reader should become aware, rather, of the double movement, from sin to salvation (ἡ πίστις σου σέσωκέν σε, "your faith has saved you") and from salvation to Christian life (πορεύου εἰς εἰρήνην, "go in peace").[61]

classes, from drug addicts to bankers), and self-examination (where does my sin lie?) in the *individual* occur not in the legal investigation of inability and in the application of written rules, but in an *encounter*.[62] It is not enough to say that the woman (instead of Simon) properly received Jesus as a guest. She comes to him and wishes to follow him. This is illustrated in her action, in which the body becomes a means of expression not only of faith (v. 50) but also of love (v. 47a). Such close fellowship with Jesus is otherwise seldom narrated. Everywhere in this pericope one reads the verb "to love" where one would otherwise find "to hear" or "to believe." Ἀγαπάω ("to love") here demonstrates that, for Luke, salvation arises from God's free decision, from his χαρίζομαι ("to cancel" or "forgive" the debt, v. 42) and from a movement of human beings toward God (vv. 37–38) that is not motivated by self-interest. According to Luke, Jesus both preached this during his life and made this possible through his death. The resulting salvation is not, however, a passive, infantile, and euphoric union of believers with God. They are meant to return to concrete life (πορεύου, "go"), although not alone this time. To go "in peace" means that they are called to fellowship, and that Christ, even in his absence, does not abandon those who are his.

Conclusion

The overcoming of sin, or better, the removal of destructive prejudices in *society* (the cliques that exist in all

---

60 See the commentary on 8:48 below.
61 The verb of motion calls for an accusative. The peace does not just appear at the end of the way, as one perhaps would think; the believer already lives in restored peace.

62 Dupont ("Pharisien," 267–68) concludes his study by differentiating between two understandings of God: that of the Pharisee and that of Jesus.

The Discipleship of Women (8:1–3)

Bibliography

Bovon, "Le privilège pascal de Marie-Madeleine," *NTS* 30 (1984) 50–62."

Cassidy, Richard J., *Jesus, Politics and Society: A Study of Luke's Gospel* (Maryknoll, N.Y.: Orbis, 1978) 35–37.

Conzelmann, *Theology*, 46-48.

Daillez, Laurent, *Les Saintes Maries de la Mer: Mythes ou légendes* (Nice: Alpes-Méditerranée édition, 1978).

D'Angelo, Mary Rose, "Women in Luke-Acts: A Redactional View," *JBL* 109 (1990) 441–61.

Dumont, Louis, *La Tarasque: Essai de description d'un fait local d'un point de vue ethnographique* (L'Espèce Humaine 8; Paris: Gallimard, 1951).

Guillaume, Paul-Marie, "Marie-Madeleine (sainte)," *Dictionnaire de spiritualité* 10 (1980) 559–75.

Hastings, Adrian, *Prophet and Witness in Jerusalem: A Study of the Teaching of St. Luke* (London/New York: Longmans, Green, 1958) 38–49.

Hengel, Martin, "Maria Magdalena und die Frauen als Zeugen," in Betz, *Abraham*, 243–56.

Moltmann-Wendel, *Women*, 61–90, 131–44.

Mosco, Marilena, ed., *La Maddalena tra Sacro e Profano: Da Giotto a De Chirico: Centro Mostre di Firenze* (Milan: A. Mondadori, 1986).

Ryan, Rosalie, "The Women from Galilee and Discipleship in Luke," *BTB* 15 (1985) 56–59.

Saxer, Victor, "Marie-Madeleine (sainte)," *Catholicisme: Hier, aujord'hui, demain* 8 (1979) 631–38.

van Cangh, Jean M., "La femme dans l'évangile de Luc: Comparaison des passages narratifs propres à Luc avec la situation de la femme dans le judaïsme," *RThL* 24 (1993) 297–324.

Witherington, "On the Road."

1 **And it happened that afterward he went on from city to city and from village to village, proclaiming and presenting the kingdom of God as good news. The twelve were with him, 2/ as well as some women who had been cured of evil spirits and sicknesses: Mary, called Magdalene, from whom seven demons had gone out; 3/ and Joanna, the wife of Herod's steward Chuza; and Susanna; and many others, who provided for them out of their resources.**

Analysis

This is the end of the so-called Lesser Insertion, a portion of the text that Luke composed by alternating between Q and his special source (6:20–7:50). With a graceful transition, he resumes his place in Mark (8:4ff.). Verse 1 introduces a new paragraph with almost the same words as in 5:1 and 7:11, and vv. 2–3 summarize the earlier activity of Jesus. These verses, which describe conditions or continuing activities with the imperfect tense, belong to the genre of the summary passage.[1] Here as elsewhere the redactor's contribution is decisive.[2] Within this passage, Luke's reworking is concentrated in v. 1. The list of women is traditional, although the description of their healing (v. 2a) and of their participation in the ministry (v. 3b) contains redactional elements.[3] The hypothesis that vv. 1–3 originate in Q and are part of a unit in that text that especially stresses women (with 7:1–17, 36–50) is unlikely.[4]

The list is form-critically comparable to the lists of male disciples.[5] Both here and there the subject is the disciples and coworkers of Jesus. Some early Christian communities found in these lists the justification of their twofold ministry within society. The men spread the message outside the community, and the women strengthened the community from within by their "service." The individual names show that the question of authority was solved by *personal* responsibility. The women's service had its roots in miraculous healings, whereas the men's preaching was legitimated by their

---

1 On the Lukan summary passages, see the commentary on 4:31–44 above.

2 Several phrases here have near parallels elsewhere in Luke's Gospel: cf. καὶ ἐγένετο ἐν τῷ . . . καὶ αὐτός with the similar phrase in 5:1; cf. also καὶ ἐγένετο ἐν τῷ καθεξῆς with 7:11; διώδευεν κατὰ πόλιν καὶ κώμην with 13:22; and κηρύσσων καὶ εὐαγγελιζόμενος τὴν βασιλείαν τοῦ θεοῦ with 4:43–44. Like a good writer, Luke avoids verbatim repetitions.

3 E.g., ἀσθένειαι ("illnesses") in v. 2a and τὰ ὑπάρχοντα ("resources") in v. 3b.

4 Schürmann (1.447–48), who recognizes some redactional elements in v. 1, connects vv. 1–3 with Matt 9:35 and 11:1. I share the reservations of Schneider (1.179–80). Adolf Schlatter thinks: "These statements did not stand in a saying collection but in that gospel which closed with the Passion and Easter story reproduced by L. [Luke]" (*Das Evangelium des Lukas: Aus seinen Quellen erklärt* [Stuttgart: Calwer, 1931] 267).

5 See Luke 6:12–16; Acts 1:13; Mark 3:13–19; Matt 10:1–4.

calling. The respective numbers of men and women are also not accidental: the three women here recall the inner group of the circle of the Twelve. Mary Magdalene leads the list. Just as the first Christians kept the memory of Peter's exceptional destiny (betrayal and repentance), in the case of Mary Magdalene they remembered an exceptional exorcism. The post-Easter activities of the community in preaching and service needed to find their development in the pre-Easter period. This explains a pericope such as the present one. One unfortunately cannot determine any more precisely the functional setting and function in preaching for this passage.[6]

We meet three women again at the empty tomb (Luke 24:10), of whom two have the same names as the women here.[7] In 23:55–56, where the names are omitted, the text speaks of the women who came along with Jesus from Galilee. Just as with the Lukan office of apostle, an institution at Easter is not sufficient. In order to justify the ecclesiastical service of women, its development in the *pre-Easter,* Galilean period of Jesus' life is necessary.

For contemporary sensibilities, Jesus' willingness to accept female disciples was unheard-of, as was the freedom of these women, who left their homes to enter Jesus' band of disciples.[8] The limitation of their ministries to service probably has its origins in the tendencies of some early churches, rather than in Jesus' intention. The historical Mary Magdalene was certainly a witness of the resurrection, which role was gradually taken away from her with the passage of time;[9] in Luke, she is allowed to participate only in practical terms.[10] Women stood on the fringes of society at that time. Although this neglect was, for the historical Jesus, an impetus to include them, this positive attitude was retained by the early Christian communities only apologetically or hagiographically. At least for Luke these female disciples belonged to "good" society.[11]

Commentary

■ **1** True to his episodic style, Luke describes in v. 1 both a caesura and a transition. He uses favorite expressions[12] to describe Jesus' typical activities: he continually (imperfect tense) travels from place to place[13] (until now it was cities, here it is also villages).[14] The travel back and forth across Galilee is set off distinctly from the goal-oriented journey to Jerusalem (9:51ff.).[15] Here Jesus wishes to reach the entire nation, there he will fulfill his destiny. His travel serves the proclamation: $\kappa\eta\rho\acute{\upsilon}\sigma\sigma\omega$ ("to proclaim") indicates its sounding forth, $\epsilon\grave{\upsilon}\alpha\gamma\gamma\epsilon\lambda\acute{\iota}\zeta o\mu\alpha\iota$ ("to present . . . as good news"), its content.[16] The fact that God rules or will rule does not cause anxiety, but rather is liberating and joyful ($\epsilon\grave{\upsilon}$-). $\Sigma\acute{\upsilon}\nu$ ("in company with") is not the same as $\mu\epsilon\tau\acute{\alpha}$ ("with");[17] thus the Twelve are not yet (cf. 9:1–6) coworkers here, but companions.

---

6   On the normative authority of this list of women, see Martin Hengel, "Maria Magdalena und die Frauen als Zeugen," in Betz, *Abraham,* 243–56, esp. 247–51; and François Bovon, "Le privilège pascal de Marie-Madeleine," *NTS* 30 (1984) 51.

7   Cf. Luke 24:1 (no names), Mark 16:1 (three names), and Matt 28:1 (two names). See the enumerations of the women who watch the crucifixion from afar (Mark 15:40 and Matt 27:55–56 with three names, Luke 23:49 with no mention of names) and of those who watch the tomb (Mark 15:47 and Matt 27:61 with two names, Luke 23:55–56 with no mention of names).

8   See Ben Witherington III, "On the Road with Mary Magdalene, Joanna, Susanna, and Other Disciples—Lk 8,1–3," *ZNW* 70 (1979) 243–48, esp. 244–45; and Richard J. Cassidy, *Jesus, Politics and Society: A Study of Luke's Gospel* (Maryknoll, N.Y.: Orbis, 1978) 35–37.

9   See Bovon, "Privilège," 50–52.

10   In Acts 6:1–6 even this ministry seems to have been withheld from women.

11   A similar tendency appears in Acts; see Acts 17:4

and Ernst Haenchen, *The Acts of the Apostles: A Commentary* (trans. R. McL. Wilson et al.; Philadelphia: Westminster, 1971) 488.

12   See the notes to the analysis of the passage above.

13    $K\alpha\tau\acute{\alpha}$ with accusative is used distributively here as in Luke 8:4 (BDF §224.3): from city to city, from village to village. These words are to be connected with the verb $\delta\iota o\delta\epsilon\acute{\upsilon}\omega$ ("to travel through").

14   Cf. Luke 4:43. In fact, there is mention of villages in Luke 5:17, though here the purpose is to show that the scribes and Pharisees go out from the villages to meet Jesus.

15   See Conzelmann, *Theology,* 46–47. $\Delta\iota o\delta\epsilon\acute{\upsilon}\omega$ occurs in the NT only here and in Acts 17:1. The verb is found in the LXX (more than twenty times, e.g., Gen 12:6), in Polybius (e.g., 2.15.5), in Plutarch (e.g., *Ages.* 17.4) and in Josephus (about three to five times; e.g., *Bell.* 2.15.2 §340; 5.1.1 §1).

16   On $\kappa\eta\rho\acute{\upsilon}\sigma\sigma\omega$ ("to proclaim") and $\epsilon\grave{\upsilon}\alpha\gamma\gamma\epsilon\lambda\acute{\iota}\zeta o\mu\alpha\iota$ ("to present as good news") in Luke, see the commentary on 3:3 and 1:19 above.

17   See Plummer, 215.

■ **2** Verse 2 introduces some other and unexpected companions of Jesus: a few women presented as having been healed (doubtless by Jesus, though it is unexpressed). A single word expresses their rehabilitation, but two words their past conditions: possession and sickness.[18] In the background one can sense the christology of the physician developed during the Galilean period.[19]

Mary,[20] of the village of Magdala on the west shore of the Lake of Gennesaret, not far from Tiberias, is the first of the three women. The apposition Μαγδαληνή ("Magdalene") is necessitated by the commonness of her name. Possession by seven demons would be for Jesus,[21] and also for the rest of the Jews, an especially bad situation (the secondary ending of the Gospel of Mark [16:9] probably depends on this passage). This description of Mary makes her identification with the sinful woman of Luke 7:36–50 impossible.

■ **3** Only Luke knows of a Joanna, whom he mentions along with Mary Magdalene (also 24:10). The name Joanna is rare.[22] The Aramaic name of her husband Chuza is known from Nabatean inscriptions.[23] An ἐπίτροπος ("steward") is an administrator, overseer, governor.[24] Was his responsibility economic or political? Was he active in the private estates of the princes or in one of the districts? The first assumption seems the most probable.[25] "This special interest of Luke's in the

family of Herod and the note that Joanna came from the court society must be seen together. The radical decision of Joanna to leave her husband and the court and to follow Jesus stands in contrast with the half sympathy [of Herod] which turns from laxity and indecision into the opposition which forces the execution of Jesus. And Joanna is not just the one who provides prosperity and care. For Luke she is a member of the group of women from Galilee present at the crucifixion, and he makes special mention of her name in the resurrection scene."[26] Susanna, a rare personal name, means "lily" in Hebrew. We otherwise hear nothing of her in the New Testament. About the "many others"[27] one knows only that, like the three women already mentioned, they support the community with that which they possess.

Διακονέω ("to provide") is a general expression for various services both in Luke and in early Christian literature, in the case of women usually hospitality and the leadership of the household (as with Peter's mother-in-law in 4:39).[28] It does not signify only financial support. The Lukan usage is so consistent that one must visualize "service." These women are responsible for providing for Jesus' community and dip into their own resources to do so. Both willingness to serve and generosity are being expressed.[29] As in the book of Acts, it is not a legal com-

---

18 On ἀσθένεια meaning "sickness," see 5:15; 13:11–12; Acts 28:9. On the conscious separation of both phenomena, see the commentary on 4:40–41 above.

19 See the commentary on 4:40–41 above.

20 On the form Μαρία, which has been influenced by Latin, the Semitic form Μαριάμ, and the influence of social milieu on their usage, see Bovon, "Privilège," 58 n. 1.

21 Cf. Luke 11:26.

22 See Lagrange, 235. Interpreted etymologically from Hebrew, the name Joanna would mean "God is merciful."

23 See Hoehner, *Herod*, 303 n. 2.

24 Lagrange (p. 235) considers an official position more likely than employment as a personal steward. In Josephus the word usually signifies a Roman governor (see Rengstorf, *Concordance, s.v.*), though the Jewish historian also knows of other uses for the term (see Hoehner, *Herod*, 303–4).

25 On this person and his wife, see Hoehner, *Herod*, 120–21, 303–5, 317 n. 4.

26 Elisabeth Moltmann-Wendel, *The Women Around Jesus* (trans. J. Bowden; New York: Crossroad, 1982) 139.

27 On ἕτερος, α, ον ("other") see the commentary on 7:19–20 above. One encounters the expression καὶ ἕτεροι πολλοί ("and many others") especially at the end of an enumeration; see BAGD *s.v.* ἕτερος (1bβ). For Luke's usage, see Acts 15:35 and (in the neuter) Luke 22:65.

28 See Luke 10:40; 12:37; 17:8; 22:26–27; Acts 6:2. All of these instances deal primarily with "waiting on tables." According to Witherington ("On the Road," 246–47), the women do not abandon their traditional role but now fulfill their service for others. According to him, Luke preserves the old and the new in the role that the Christian women receive.

29 The ms. tradition varies between διηκόνουν αὐτοῖς ("to provide for them") and διηκόνουν αὐτῷ ("to provide for him"). The plural αὐτοῖς is probably the original. The correction into the singular, which had already taken place in the 2d century, can be explained as an expression of reverence for Christ, according to Metzger (*Textual Commentary*, 144): "The singular (compare Mt 27.55; Mk 15.41) appears to be a Christocentric correction, due perhaps to Marcion."

munity of goods that is presupposed here, but the charitable availability of possessions.[30]

Conclusion

In this summary Luke confirms the picture of Jesus that he has successively developed. In this first period of his ministry, he is the traveling Messiah, who persuades through his word. His activities are successful because the Messiah is simultaneously a doctor. The result of his activity is a community of disciples that accompanies him. Not only men but women, and even women from the best society, appear in this movement.[31] The unheard-of newness of a common life so deeply characterized by the content of the preaching (the kingdom of God) will necessarily encounter strong resistance. One will again hear about both the male and female disciples in the context of the passion, which is already foreshadowed here.[32]

---

30 See Bovon, *Theologian*, 390–96.

31 Witherington ("On the Road," 244) sees in Luke 8:1–3 a microcosm of Lukan themes.

32 In recent years a number of theologians have dealt with the topic of women in the Gospel, esp. Luke 8:1–3. See Moltmann-Wendel, *Women*, 61–90 (Maria Magdalena) and 131–44 (Joanna).

The Parable of the Sower and Other Teachings (8:4–21)

Bibliography

On Luke 8:4–15

Bovon, François, "'How Well the Holy Spirit Spoke Through the Prophet Isaiah to Your Ancestors!' (Acts 28:25)," in idem, *New Testament Traditions and Apocryphal Narratives* (trans. J. Happiseva-Hunter; PTMS 36; Allison Park, Pa.: Pickwick, 1995) 43–50.

Brown, *Apostasy*, 5–34.

Carlston, Charles E., *The Parables of the Triple Tradition* (Philadelphia: Fortress Press, 1975) 70–76.

Cerfaux, "Fructifiez."

Courthial, Pierre, "Du texte au sermon, 17: La parabole du semeur en Luc 8,5–15," *EThR* 47 (1972) 397–420.

Crossan, John Dominic, "The Seed Parables of Jesus," *JBL* 92 (1973) 244–66 (reworked in idem, *In Parables: The Challenge of the Historical Jesus* [New York: Harper & Row, 1973] 37–52).

Dietzfelbinger, Christian, "Das Gleichnis vom ausgestreuten Samen," in E. Lohse with C. Burchard and B. Schaller, eds., *Der Ruf Jesu und die Antwort der Gemeinde: Exegetische Untersuchungen: Joachim Jeremias zum 70 Geburtstag* (Göttingen: Vandenhoeck & Ruprecht, 1970) 80–93.

Dodd, Charles Harold, *The Parables of the Kingdom* (rev. ed.; New York: Scribner, 1961) 14–15, 135–36.

Dumézil, Georges, "La parabole du Semeur et la parabole de l'Allumeur de feu," in E. Lucchesi and H. D. Saffrey, eds., *Mémorial André-Jean Festugière: Antiquité païenne et chrétienne* (Cahiers d'Orientalisme 10; Geneva: P. Cramer, 1984) 107–12.

Dupont, Jacques, "Le chapitre des paraboles," *NRTh* 89 (1967) 800–820.

idem, "Semeur."

Fusco, Vittorio, *Parola e Regno: La sezione delle Parabole (Mc. 4,1–34) nella prospettiva marciana* (Aloisiana 13; Brescia: Morcelliana, 1980) 307–39.

Gerhardsson, "Sower."

Gervais, J., "Les épines étouffantes (Lc 8,14–15)," *EeT* 4 (1973) 5–39.

Gnilka, *Verstockung*, 119–54.

Hahn, Ferdinand, "Das Gleichnis von der ausgestreuten Saat und seine Deutung (Mk 4,3–8.14–20)," in E. Best and R. McL. Wilson, eds., *Text and Interpretation: Festschrift Matthew Black* (Cambridge: Cambridge University Press, 1979) 133–42.

Houston, Tom, "Preaching to the People of Luke's Time Today," *Christianity Today* 25 (1981) 731–34.

Jeremias, *Gleichnisse*, 5–12, 65–67, 130–31.

idem, "Palästinakundliches zum Gleichnis vom Säemann (Mc 4,3–8 par.)," *NTS* 13 (1966–67) 48–53.

idem, *Parables*, 9–16, 61–62, 92.

Jülicher, *Gleichnisreden*, 2.514–38.

Klauck, *Allegorie*, 185–209.

Köster, Helmut, "Three Thomas Parables," in A. H. B. Logan and A. J. M. Wedderburn, eds., *The New Testament and Gnosis: Festschrift Robert McLean Wilson* (Edinburgh: Clark, 1983) 195–203.

Krämer, Michael, *Die Gleichnisrede in den synoptischen Evangelien: Eine synoptische Studie zu Mt 13:1–52; Mk 4:1–34; Lk 8:4–21* (Egelsbach: Hansel-Hohenhausen, 1993).

idem, "Die Parabelrede in den synoptischen Evangelien: Eine überlieferungsgeschichtliche Untersuchung der parallelen Stellen Mt 13,1–53—Mk 4,1–34—Lk 8,4–18," in A. Bodem and A. M. Kothgasser, eds., *Theologie und Leben: Festschrift Georg Söll* (Rome: LAS, 1983) 31–53.

Léon-Dufour, Xavier, "La parabole du semeur," in idem, *Études*, 255–301.

Lindemann, Andreas, "Zur Gleichnisinterpretation im Thomas-Evangelium," *ZNW* 71 (1980) 214–43.

Lohfink, Gerhard, "Das Gleichnis vom Sämann (Mk 4,3–9)," *BZ* n.s. 30 (1986) 36–69.

idem, "Die Metaphorik der Aussaat im Gleichnis vom Sämann (Mk 4,3–9)," in *À cause*, 211–28.

Marshall, I. H., "Tradition and Theology in Luke (Luke 8:5–15)," *Tyndale Bulletin* 20 (1969) 56–75.

März, *Wort Gottes*, 57–59, 67–69.

Miguens, Manuel, "La predicazione di Gesù in parabole (Mc 4; Lc 8,4–18; Mt 13)," *BeO* 1 (1959) 35–40.

Moule, C. F. D., "Mark 4:1–20 Yet Once More," in E. E. Ellis and M. Wilcox, eds., *Neotestamentica et Semitica: Festschrift Matthew Black* (Edinburgh: Clark, 1969) 95–113.

Neil, William, "Expounding the Parables, II: The Sower (Mk 4:3–8)," *ExpTim* 77 (1965–66) 74–77.

Quispel, Gilles, "Some Remarks on the Gospel of Thomas," *NTS* 5 (1958–59) 277–78.

Robinson, William Childs, "On Preaching the Word of God (Luke 8:4–21)," in Keck and Martyn, *Studies*, 131–38.

Schrage, *Thomas-Evangelium*, 42–48.

Schramm, *Markus-Stoff*, 114–23.

Schürmann, Heinz, "Lukanische Reflexionen über die Wortverkündigung in Lk 8,4–21," in L. Scheffczyk et al., eds., *Wahrheit und Verkündigung: Festschrift Michael Schmaus* (2 vols.; Munich: Paderborn; Vienna: Schoningh, 1967) 1.213–28 (= idem, *Ursprung*, 29–41).

Siegman, Edward F., "Teaching in Parables (Mk 4:10–12; Lk 8:9–10; Mt 13:10–15)," *CBQ* 23 (1961) 161–81.

Vogels, Heinrich Joseph, "Lk 8,8 im Diatessaron," *BZ* 18 (1928–29) 83–84.

Weder, *Gleichnisse*, 99–117.

Wenham, "Sower."

Wilder, Amos Niven, "The Parable of the Sower: Naïveté and Method in Interpretation," *Semeia* 2 (1974) 134–51.

Zingg, *Wachsen*, 76–100.

On Luke 8:16–18

Derrett, "Lamp."

Dupont, Jacques, "La lampe sur le lampadaire dans l'évangile de saint Luc (VIII,16; XI,33)," in *Au service de la Parole de Dieu: Festschrift André-Marie Charue* (Gembloux: Duculot, 1969) 43–59 (= Dupont, *Études*, 2.1032–48).

idem, "La transmission des paroles de Jésus sur la lampe et la mesure dans Marc 4,21–25 et dans la tradition de Q," in J. Delobel, T. Baarta et al., eds., *Logia: Les paroles de Jésus–The Sayings of Jesus: Mémorial Joseph Coppens* (BETL 59; Leuven: Leuven University Press, 1982) 201–36 (= Dupont, *Études*, 1.259–94).

Fusco, Vittorio, *Parola e Regno: La sezione delle parabole (Mc. 4,1–34) nella prospettiva marciana* (Alosiana 13; Brescia: Morcelliana, 1980) 99–104, 279–304.

Jeremias, Joachim, "Die Lampe unter dem Scheffel," *ZNW* 39 (1940) 237–40 (reprinted in idem, *Abba: Studien zur neutestamentlichen Theologie und Zeitgeschichte* [Göttingen: Vandenhoeck & Ruprecht, 1966] 99–102).

Jülicher, *Gleichnisreden*, 2.79–88.

Kennedy, Harry Angus Alexander, "The Composition of Mark 4:21–25: A Study in the Synoptic Problem," *ExpTim* 25 (1913–14) 301–5.

Krämer, Michael, "Ihr seid das Salz der Erde . . . Ihr seid das Licht der Welt," *MThZ* 28 (1977) 143–47.

Laufen, Rudolf, *Die Doppelüberlieferung der Logienquelle und des Markusevangeliums* (BBB 54: Königstein/Bonn: Peter Hanstein, 1980) 165–73, 463–69.

Lindeskog, Gösta, "Logia-Studien," *StTh* 4 (1950) 129–89.

Schneider, Gerhard, "Das Bildwort von der Lampe: Zur Traditionsgeschichte eines Jesus-Wortes," *ZNW* 61 (1970) 183–209.

Schrage, *Thomas-Evangelium*, 81–85, 34–37, 96–98.

Schramm, *Markus-Stoff*, 23–26.

Schürmann, Heinz, "Lukanische Reflexionen über die Wortverkündigung in Lk 8,4–21," in L. Scheffczyk et al., eds., *Wahrheit und Verkündigung: Festschrift Michael Schmaus* (2 vols.; Vienna: Schöningh, 1967) 1.213–28 (= Schürmann, *Ursprung*, 29–41).

Steinhauer, Michael G., *Doppelbildworte in den synoptischen Evangelien: Eine form- und traditionskritische Studie* (FB 44; Würzburg: Echter, 1981) 384–404.

Zimmermann, *Methodenlehre*, 181–91.

On Luke 8:19–21

Blinzler, Josef, *Die Brüder und Schwestern Jesu* (SBS 21; Stuttgart: Katholisches Bibelwerk, 1967) 88.

Brown, *Mary*, 167–70.

Conzelmann, *Theology*, 34–35, 48–49.

Dibelius, *Tradition*, 46–47, 49–50.

März, *Wort Gottes*, 67–68.

Oberlinner, Lorenz, *Historische Überlieferung und christologische Aussage: Zur Frage der "Brüder Jesu" in der Synopse* (FB 19; Stuttgart: Katholisches Bibelwerk, 1975).

Schneider, "Antworten."

Schramm, *Markus-Stoff*, 123–24.

4 When a great crowd gathered and people from town after town came to him, he said by means of a parable: 5/ "The one who sows went out to sow his seed; and as he sowed, some fell on the side of the path and was trampled on, and the birds of the heaven ate it up. 6/ Some fell on the rock; and as it grew up, it withered, for it had no moisture. 7/ Some fell among thorns, and the thorns grew with it and choked it. 8/ Some fell into good soil, and when it grew, it produced a hundredfold." As he said this, he called out, "Let anyone with ears to hear listen!" 9/ But his disciples asked him what this parable meant. 10/ And he said, "To you it has been given to know the secrets of the kingdom of God; but to the others I speak in parables, for they should see and yet not see, hear and not yet understand. 11/ Now the parable means this: The seed is the word of God. 12/ The ones on the path are those who have heard; then the devil comes and takes away the word from their hearts, so that they may not believe and be saved. 13/ The ones on the rock are those who, when they hear the word, receive it with joy. But these have no root; they believe only for a while and in a time of testing fall away. 14/ As for what fell among the thorns, these are the ones who hear; but as they go on their way, they are choked by the cares and riches and pleasures of life, and their fruit does not mature. 15/ But as for that in the good soil, these are the ones who, when they hear the word, hold it fast in an honest and good heart, and bear fruit with patient endurance. 16/ No one who has lit a lamp hides it under a jar, or puts it under a bed, but puts it on a lampstand, so that those who enter may see the light. 17/ For nothing is hidden that will not be disclosed, nor is anything secret that will not become known and come to light. 18/ Then pay attention to how you listen; for to those who have, will be given; and from those who do not have, even what they think they have will be taken away." 19/ Then his mother and his brothers came to him, but they could not meet with him because of the crowd. 20/ And he was told,

"Your mother and your brothers are standing outside and want to see you." 21/ But he answered and said to them, "My mother and my brothers are these, who hear the word of God and do it."

Analysis

Until v. 21, Luke is developing the single theme of the "word of God." Even though the episode concerning the family of Jesus (vv. 19–21) is a form-critically complete unit, it still belongs, redaction-critically, with the parable of the sower (vv. 4–15) and with the three proverbs (vv. 16–18) to a larger pericope.[1] After a long interruption, Luke turns back to his source, Mark. In 6:12–19 he took from it the choosing of the disciples (Mark 3:13–19) and a summary passage (Mark 3:7–12). Here (8:4ff.) he returns to Mark, although he does not use the very next story (Mark 3:20), but skips over to the parable of the sower. He ignores the saying about the relatives of Jesus (Mark 3:20–21), which is offensive to him, just as he does the pericope about Beelzebul (Mark 3:22–30).[2] As in 6:12–19, he transposes the order of the units in his source: the paragraph about Jesus' true family (Mark 3:31–35) is placed at 8:19–21, after the parable, its interpretation (Luke 8:4–15), and the three proverbs (8:16–18). The reason for this is obvious: one can only define a right relationship with the word of God (8:19–21) after reflecting on the nature of the word (8:4–18). The desire to make a unified whole out of these elements is perceptible in the omission of the Markan transitional markers. Luke reduces to a single question from a disciple (8:9) the extended private instruction about the function of parables and the meaning of this particular one, as it appears in Mark (4:10). Where Mark introduces new discourse (4:13, 21), Luke omits the introductory formulas. Jesus' dramatic position on a boat (Mark 4:1) was already mentioned in Luke (5:1). Thus in v. 4 he mentions only that the audience runs together from various locations.

Lucien Cerfaux and Tim Schramm argue for the presence of a special source in the parable itself, though not with respect to its interpretation.[3] In the introduction, which diverges from Mark, not all of the expressions are redactional (such as σύνειμι ["to gather"], ἐπιπορεύομαι ["to come to"], and λέγω διὰ παραβολῆς ["to say in a parable"]). The agreements with Matthew are, for example, τοῦ σπεῖραι ("[in order] to sow") and καὶ ἐν τῷ σπείρειν αὐτόν ("and as he sowed") in 8:5; ἀπέπνιξαν ("they choked [it]"; the καὶ καρπὸν οὐκ ἔδωκεν ["and it yielded no grain"] of Mark is lacking) in 8:7; the hundredfold (in Matthew, this information is placed at the beginning, and in Luke it is the only figure mentioned) in 8:8; the οἱ μαθηταί ("the disciples"; καὶ ὅτε ἐγένετο κατὰ μόνας, "when he was alone" as in Mark is missing) in 8:9; and ὑμῖν δέδοται γνῶναι τὰ μυστήρια τῆς βασιλείας ("to you it has been given to know the secrets of the kingdom of God"; the Markan ending of the citation is missing) in 8:10.[4] "In Luke, precisely those elements are lacking that in Matthew and Mark underscore the meaning in preparation for its interpretation, and that push the parable itself far into the realm of allegory."[5] Καὶ κατεπατήθη ("[it] was trampled on," 8:5) is not included in the interpretation. The Lukan version of 8:6 corresponds to its interpretation (8:13) with less felicity than in Mark 4:5–6. The occurrence of ἰκμάς ("moisture," 8:6), where

1   See William Childs Robinson, "On Preaching the Word of God (Luke 8:4–21)," in Keck and Martyn, *Studies*, 131–38, esp. 131–33; and Jacques Dupont, "La parabole du semeur dans la version de Luc," in W. Eltester and F. H. Kettler, eds., *Apophoreta: Festschrift Ernst Haenchen* (BZNW 30; Berlin: Töpelmann, 1964) 97–108, reprinted in Dupont, *Études*, 2.1019–31, esp. 97–99 (cited according to the *Festschrift*).

2   Luke 11:14–23 corresponds to Mark 3:22–30, though the passage could have come from Q. In this case Luke, following his usual practice, would be omitting Mark 3:22–30 in order to avoid a doublet.

3   See Lucien Cerfaux, "Fructifiez en supportant (l'épreuve): A propos de Luc VIII,15," *RB* 64 (1957)

481–91, reprinted in idem, *Recueil Lucien Cerfaux: Études d'exégèse et d'histoire religieuse de Monseigneur Cerfaux . . .* (3 vols.; BETL 6–7, 18; Gembloux: Duculot, 1954–62) 3.111–22, esp. 111 n. 2; and Schramm, *Markus-Stoff*, 114–23, who is fully aware (p. 123 n. 1) that his hypothesis precludes that of Birger Gerhardsson, "The Parable of the Sower and Its Interpretation," *NTS* 14 (1967–68) 165–93, who champions the original unity of the parable and its interpretation.

4   See Schramm, *Markus-Stoff*, 114–16.

5   Ibid., 118.

both Mark 4:6 and its interpretation (8:13) speak of ῥίζα ("roots"), is surprising.

Most interpreters, however, explain the Lukan peculiarities of both parable and interpretation as indications of the literary and theological intentions of the redactor. The unusual διὰ παραβολῆς ("in a parable") in 8:4 is an expression of Luke's surprise at a parable accompanied by an interpretation;[6] κατεπατήθη ("[it] was trampled on") in 8:5 is a rather clumsy ornamentation evoked by the "path."[7] The shortening in 8:6 is the result of Luke's literary taste and his urban character.[8] In 8:7 there are literary reasons, and in 8:8 theological, that explain Luke's version of the parable.[9]

According to another hypothesis,[10] the three Synoptic authors attest a pre-Markan version of the *interpretation* of the parable, to which Matthew has remained particularly true. The main arguments for this are the agreements between Matthew and Luke even in the interpretation (e.g., the mention of the heart in Luke 8:12 and Matt 13:19). "In this pericope the situation appears to be this: each evangelist was familiar with a primitive tradition of the interpretation, likely enough an oral tradition; in addition, Mark knew Matthew, and Luke knew Mark."[11]

Luke most probably used Mark as his only written source both for the parable and its interpretation. The deviations can be explained from oral tradition, as well as from the theological individuality of each of the evangelists. One perceives the oral tradition especially in the parable itself, which is significantly older than its interpretation.[12] This can be seen in the *Gospel of Thomas*, which still transmits the parable without its interpretation.[13]

As for genre, one first encounters a genuine parable: an everyday occurrence is used to engage the audience and bring them to a decision. The parable mentions three failures and then an astounding success. This is thus a parable of contrast, which concentrates its entire emphasis on its last part. The implicit personal address of the parable becomes explicit with the probably secondary command in v. 8b, where ἀκούω means not only "to hear" but also "to accept (what one hears)," "to obey."[14]

An early Christian interpretation of the parable begins in v. 9. The functional setting would be Christian instruction. As soon as a parable is heard for the second time, it loses its surprise, and repetition begins the process of interpretation and allegorization.[15] Under Mark's influence, the interpretation does not directly follow the disciples' question (8:9). This creates a space for an aside about those who receive the mysteries of the kingdom of God (8:10). After this concession to Markan redaction, Luke develops the interpretation (8:11–15),

6   See Dupont, "Semeur," 100 n. 8, with the comment that διὰ παραβολῆς ("in a parable") signifies the use of a parable and not the content of a parable; likewise Charles E. Carlston (*The Parables of the Triple Tradition* [Philadelphia: Fortress Press, 1975] 70–76), who criticizes the hypothesis of Schramm (*Markus-Stoff*, 70 n. 1).

7   See Dupont ("Semeur," 100), who follows Lagrange (237).

8   See Dupont, "Semeur," 103.

9   See ibid., 104, 106.

10 See David Wenham, "The Interpretation of the Parable of the Sower," *NTS* 20 (1973–74) 299–319.

11 Ibid., 318 n. 4.

12 Against Gerhardsson ("Sower"), who argues for (1) the inner cohesion of parable and its interpretation; (2) the presence of both parts in the original version; and (3) the influence of Israel's Shema on the parable.

13 See *Gos. Thom.* 9. Some scholars are of the opinion that *Gos. Thom.* 9 reflects a tradition independent of the Synoptics (e.g., Gilles Quispel, "Some Remarks on the Gospel of Thomas," *NTS* 5 [1958–59] 277–78; and Helmut Köster, "Three Thomas Parables," in A. H. B. Logan and A. J. M. Wedderburn, eds., *The New Testament and Gnosis: Festschrift Robert McLean Wilson* [Edinburgh: Clark, 1983] 195–203, esp. 195–97). Others maintain that *Gos. Thom.* 9 has been influenced by the Synoptics and not (as one might suppose) by a pre-Synoptic tradition (e.g., Schrage, *Thomas-Evangelium*, 42–48). *1 Clem.* 24.5 furnishes evidence that the parable was known to the author—in my opinion, through oral tradition.

14 See Weder, *Gleichnisse*, 108–11.

15 Hans-Josef Klauck stresses that it is an allegorization, not in the sense of Greek interpretation of myths, but of the kind found in Jewish apocalyptic tradition, the interpretation of dreams and visions (*Allegorie und Allegorese in synoptischen Gleichnistexten* [NTAbh n.s. 13; Münster: Aschendorff, 1978] 201). This tendency in interpretation can be seen in the parable itself: as it is retold over and over again, the simile (*Gleichnis*) eventually becomes a *parable* (*Parabel*). See Klauck, *Allegorie*, 191.

that is, the illustration of human responses toward the word of God.

Faithful to his source, Luke then transmits three proverbs (8:16–18). The first two are parallel, and underscore in the style of a wisdom saying the responsibility of the preacher (8:16) and the unconcealable radiance of the word of God (8:17). The third proverb (8:18b), in the form of a paradox, is introduced by an imperative (8:18a). What concerns Luke is the *how* of hearing and no longer the *what*, as in Mark. The admonition (8:18a) and taking stock (8:18b) apply to the audience.

The verses that follow (8:19–21) transmit an apothegm[16] that describes the ones who listen well, and relate them to Jesus himself. This unit about the word of God thus closes with an ecclesiological perspective (the category of family) and with a point of orientation in Christ (μου, "my").

Commentary

The Frame (v. 4)

■ **4** At the beginning (8:4), Luke sets the stage with a model of communication that is followed through in the process of thought behind Jesus' speech (esp. 8:10, 18,

21): the encounter of Jesus and his audience can be actualized in the encounter between human beings and the Word. This coming together is hopeful, but also dangerous. A crowd has collected and has come out from every city to Jesus. He speaks in parables.[17] What will they understand through them, and how will they hear them (v. 18a)? In 8:5 the parable begins rather abruptly (ἐξῆλθεν, "[he] went out"), with the sower[18] going out to the field. The alliteration (ὁ σπείρων τοῦ σπεῖραι τὸν σπόρον αὐτοῦ, "a sower went out to sow his seed") is reminiscent of the repetition of the sower's arm motions in sowing. The style and the theme reinforce one another.

The Decisive Beginning (vv. 5a, 9, 11)

■ **5a, 9, 11** In contrast to the tradition, and to Mark 4:14, Luke places not the sower but the seed (ὁ σπόρος) at the center of the story (8:11). Since he lays no christological emphasis on ἐξέρχομαι ("to go out"),[19] he is apparently less concerned with the initiative of Jesus than with the gesture of God in sending forth his word (Isa 55), especially in the age of the church.

In terms of redaction criticism, the parable can be interpreted at the same time as its interpretation.[20] Verse 11 gives the interpretation of v. 5a: (1) since v. 11a

---

16 Schneider ("Antworten," 323) points to an indication of the literary form: It is found in the circumstance that Jesus here gives an answer: ὁ δὲ ἀποκριθεὶς εἶπεν πρὸς αὐτούς (8:21, "but he answered and said to them").

17 A parable does not have to illustrate a truth. It is an indirect means of communication and persuasion. By using metaphors the speaker attempts to enter into dialogue with his opponents. Moreover, the figurative mode of expression does not make listeners feel that they are being attacked, and so does not put them on the defensive. A parable is often told when the situation appears to get bogged down, and the usual means of communication prove to be ineffective. Moreover, the imagery of the parable with its appeal to daily life and nature and with its many cultural allusions (and in the case of Jesus also to biblical figures and symbols) says much more than can be said in a didactic style . The parable addresses itself to the whole person. Luke uses the word παραβολή ("parable") 18 times. For him, the term means either a parable or an allegory. He prefers the expression "he told a parable" (13 times). The expression "he spoke by means of a parable" (8:4) is an exception with Luke, because it

signifies the manner of speaking and not the parable itself. The question of the type of speech is taken up again in vv. 9–10, where the concern is about the effects of telling a parable. On the nature of the parable, see John Dominic Crossan, "The Seed Parables of Jesus," *JBL* 92 (1973) 244–66 (reworked in idem, *In Parables: The Challenge of the Historical Jesus* [New York: Harper & Row, 1973] 37–52); Jacques Dupont, "Le chapitre des paraboles," *NRTh* 89 (1967) 800–820; Klauck, *Allegorie*; Weder, *Gleichnisse*; and Wolfgang Harnisch, *Die Gleichniserzählungen Jesu* (Göttingen: Vandenhoeck & Ruprecht, 1985).

18 Σπείρων is not a noun but a substantivized present participle; in connection with the article it means: "the one who sows," "that one whose occupation is sowing" (see Plummer, 218). The expression is Semitic, for a Greek would call the sower ὁ σπορεύς or ὁ σπορευτής, though (in my opinion) these words do not occur frequently.

19 Luke has corrected Mark's εἰς τοῦτο γὰρ ἐξῆλθον ("for that is what I came out to do," 1:38) to ἐπὶ τοῦτο ἀπεστάλην ("for I was sent for this purpose," Luke 4:43).

20 Agreeing with Dupont, "Semeur."

responds to v. 9, αὕτη (v. 11a) is an adjective rather than a pronoun,[21] and αὕτη ἡ παραβολή (v. 11a) is the subject of ἔστιν; (2) ἔστιν as well as ἐστίν belong to the terminology of Jewish exegesis, whether it be the *pesher* of the prophets or the interpretation of the apodictic visions of dreams,[22] and they should be translated with "to mean";[23] (3) in neither of the other Synoptic Gospels is the identification with the Word of God so clear, and the shift from the sower to the seed so obvious.[24] This probably means that Luke is thinking less of the historical preaching of Jesus than of the kerygmatic preaching of the church. He finds the license to update the parable in this way from the nature of parable itself, and transfers the accent from the original eschatological emphasis toward the Word of God that is always realized anew in history.

The metaphor of seed for the word occurs frequently in antiquity. For example, Pseudo-Plutarch compares education with agriculture: "The soil [= predisposition] must be good, the farmer [= teacher] skillful, and the seed [= lesson of the teacher] viable."[25] Within Judaism, the illustration of sowing occurs in various metaphors. For example, in 2 Esdras (4 Ezra) one reads that God

has sown his law in the heart of the fathers so that it might bear fruit.[26]

The Unbelieving (vv. 5b, 12)

■ **5b, 12** There is much discussion about whether plowing took place before or after sowing in Palestine at the time. In the first case, the text would be a parable, and in the second, a parabolic narrative.[27] Luke seems to understand it as a parabolic narrative. The aorists that he uses indicate not a *custom* but an *event*. For him, the incident is not foolish but tragic. The sower cannot change the soil and cannot prevent the failure.

Part[28] of the seed falls[29] on the side of the path (παρὰ τὴν ὁδόν means neither on the path nor along the path). People passing by step on[30] the grains; the birds[31] easily find them and snatch them up.

The interpretation (v. 12) does not completely correspond to the parable. The people (οἱ) are identified neither with the seed nor with the soil. But the situation provides an analogy: there are people who listen to the word (ἀκούω, "to listen," is central in the interpretation), but an enemy comes, such as the birds in the parable. Luke knows him, the διάβολος ("the devil")[32] who steals

---

21 Marshall (324) and Fitzmyer (1.713), on the other hand, understand αὕτη as the predicate of "parable," which, while grammatically possible, ignores the connection with v. 9.

22 See Klauck, *Allegorie*, 88 n. 273.

23 See Delebecque (*Études*, 47): "Nothing is any longer confusing and everything becomes logical again, once one gives to the verb εἰμί (from v. 9 on) the meaning 'to signify'."

24 See Dupont, "Semeur," 97–99.

25 Klauck, *Allegorie*, 192 n. 38, who summarizes Ps.-Plutarch *Lib. Educ.* 4 (2b). Also helpful in this regard is Klauck, *Allegorie*, 192–96. See further Gottfried Quell and Siegfried Schulz, "σπέρμα, κτλ.," *TDNT* 7 (1971) 536–47. Of course, one must not forget Plato *Phaidros* 276B–277A.

26 See 2 Esdr 9:31; Klauck, *Allegorie*, 193. See also 2 Esdr 8:41: "For just as the farmer sows many seeds in the ground and plants a multitude of seedlings, and yet not all that have been sown will come up in due season, and not all that were planted will take root; so also those who have been sown in the world will not all be saved."

27 As is well known, Jeremias (*Parables*, 9–10) has been emphatic to point out that the field work was undertaken after the sowing, and so in the parable the everyday wisdom of the sower's procedure is

emphasized. Klauck (*Allegorie*, 189–91), who holds the opposite opinion without particular emphasis, presents the whole problem clearly. Ancient Jewish texts that attest that sowing precedes plowing are *Jub.* 11:11 and b. *Šabb.* 73b.

28 Should one read in v. 5 the masculine article ὁ or the neuter relative pronoun ὅ? In either case, the word has the "original" meaning of a demonstrative pronoun. The neuter αὐτό at the end of the verse speaks in favor of the relative pronoun. Some mss. read ἅ (neuter relative pronoun in the plural). The absence of δέ following the μέν (v. 5) is a mistake in style that Luke has reproduced from Mark.

29 Πίπτω ("to fall") gives to the parable a uniformity by appearing four times (once in the form καταπίπτω).

30 Κατεπατήθη (from καταπατέω, "to tread upon") occurs in the NT only in Luke. See, however, Plato *Leg.* 714A: "to tread on the laws."

31 Luke adds τοῦ οὐρανοῦ ("of the heaven") no doubt to give his language a more biblical-sounding tone (e.g., cf. Gen 1:26, 28, 30 LXX).

32 In Luke's two-volume work one reads ὁ διάβολος ("the devil") seven times and ὁ Σατανᾶς ("Satan") seven times (once without the article). The equal number of occurrences, however, may obscure the fact that Luke—as in this instance—tries to replace

away the word. Luke localizes the event in the heart,[33] which is visited first by God and then the devil. One *gives*, the other *robs*. This is not far from the two "drives" of rabbinic literature.[34] It is the goal of the devil to prevent belief and salvation, that is, his own defeat.[35]

The Weak (vv. 6 and 13)

■ **6, 13** For the second case (8:6), Luke shortens the repetitions in Mark.[36] Other grains fall on stony soil.[37] Luke is not describing stupid behavior on the part of the sower, but rather the irregular condition of natural soil. As soon as the seed springs up,[38] it withers immediately from lack of water.[39] Is Luke replacing the defect in the seed (no roots) with a defect in the soil (no moisture) out of respect for the word of God, and in order to direct attention toward its recipient?

The interpretation (8:13) is reminiscent of the Markan version of the parable and its interpretation (Mark 4:6, 17; cf. ῥίζα, "root," in v. 13 instead of ἰκμάς,

"moisture," in v. 6).[40] There is a shift that one also finds in the Markan version: the fate of these grains is not connected with the fate of the word of God, but with the fate of its weak hearers.

"On the rock"—these are the people that hear the word and receive it with joy (up to this point Mark and Luke are very similar), but "they have no roots": they believe only temporarily and do not stand up to testing. Luke is more precise about the ambivalent πρόσκαιροι ("for a while") of Mark, and shows that it concerns faith. He replaces the apocalyptic terminology (ϑλῖψις, "trouble," and διωγμός, "persecution") with ethical terminology (πειρασμός, "testing," in the Lukan sense).

Although the danger in Mark is specifically tied to the mission (Mark 4:17), the word πειρασμός ("testing") in Luke has a broader spectrum. It is the constant[41] temptation to betray one's faith within society. The result is the irresistible apostasy of this person.[42]

---

the Semitic word "Satan" with the Greek word "devil" (with the exception of Luke 22:3, "Satan" always appears in the speech of Jesus or the apostles, i.e., in those passages that Luke avoids altering out of respect). See the excursus on the devil at Luke 4:1–13 above.

33   The image of the seed sown into the heart of the human being is familiar in Judaism; see Klauck, *Allegorie*, 192–96.

34   See W. Harnisch, *Verhängnis und Verheißung der Geschichte: Untersuchungen zum Zeit- und Geschichtsverständnis im 4. Buch Esra und in der syr. Baruchapokalypse* (FRLANT 97; Göttingen: Vandenhoeck & Ruprecht, 1969) 167–69 on 2 Esdr 4:28–32 (the implanting of evil into the heart of the human being).

35   Luke here indicates the purpose of the devil (ἵνα μὴ πιστεύσαντες σωθῶσιν, "so that they may not believe and be saved"), no doubt from the influence of Mark 4:12b, though his own text at the point where he follows Mark 4:12b (Luke 8:10b) omits it.

36   Mark 4:5–6 mentions "earth" twice, "not having" twice, and ἐξανέτειλεν and ἀνέτειλεν one after the other. See further under Analysis above.

37   Why does Luke avoid τὸ πετρῶδες (Mark 4:5) in favor of τὴν πέτραν? One also observes the alliterations in κατεπατήθη, καὶ τὰ πετεινὰ . . . κατέφαγεν . . . καὶ ἕτερον κατέπεσεν (vv. 5–6).

38   Φυέν (in classical Greek, φύν) is an aorist participle with an intransitive meaning from the verb φύω ("to grow," "to bring forth"); cf. the present active participle φύουσα in Heb 12:15 (Deut 29:17); see BAGD *s.v.*

39   Ἡ ἰκμάς: "moisture," "moisture from the earth," "secretion," "body fluids." In his description of the miraculous spring near Jericho, Josephus praises the warmth of the air and the quality of the water (*Bell* 4.8.3 §471): The moisture (ἰκμάς) enables plants to grow and become strong so that they can withstand the heat of the summer (see Rengstorf, *Concordance*, *s.v.*).

40   Some grammatical and stylistic remarks on v. 13: (1) in 8:13a and 8:13b an ἐστίν (= "means") must be understood; (2) ὅταν with the aorist subjunctive is correct; (3) Luke's δέχομαι is more elegant and more refined than Mark's λαμβάνω; (4) by transposing Marks's τὸν λόγον ("the word"), Luke makes it the accusative object of both ἀκούσωσιν ("to hear") and δέχομαι ("to receive"), thus making the αὐτόν superfluous; (5) Mark's phrase ἐν ἑαυτοῖς is quite vivid, but awkward, and thus Luke deletes it; (6) οὗτοι resumes the οἱ at the beginning of the verse; (7) the repetition of καιρός ("a time") in v. 13b is most likely a deficiency in style rather than a theological device, and is thus not intentional.

41   See the additional "every day" in Luke 9:23.

42   See Mark 4:17: σκανδαλίζονται; Luke 8:13: ἀφίστανται. The verb has the intransitive meaning "to withdraw oneself," "abandon," "leave." On (religious) apostasy, see Jer 3:14 (LXX); Deut 9:9 (LXX and Th); Heb 3:12 and passim in *Hermas*; e.g., *Hermas* 7 = *Vis.* 2.3.2 and *Hermas* 75 = *Sim.* 8.9.1. See BAGD *s.v.*

The Strangled (vv. 7 and 14)

■ **7, 14** Luke improves his source (Mark 4:7) formally in the description of the third case (8:7).[43] He remains true to the content, however: the seed falls among thorns,[44] first grows up together with these, and is finally choked. Luke rewrites the interpretation (8:14), although he respects the content of Mark 4:18–19.[45] This group also hears the word (ἀκούω),[46] but (an adversative καί) they are not only slowed up but choked[47] in their life, which resembles a race (πορευόμενοι, "as they go on their way").[48]

Like Mark, Luke distinguishes among three main dangers: first, egocentric concerns (μέριμναι, "cares," seldom indicate justified worries in early Christian literature);[49] second, wealth, which Luke indicates both before this (6:24) and afterward (e.g., 18:24) as dangerous to salvation; third, enjoyment of earthly life (Luke avoids the Markan ἐπιθυμίαι, "desire," which is usually evaluated positively in the Greek language). What he means by this, he explains in passages such as 7:25, 12:19, and 16:19. One has "cares" when one's "possessions" are threatened, and "enjoyment" is not possible without wealth. With this third group, Luke has in mind above all the dangers of possessions, and not only material ones. These people indeed first react positively (οἱ ἀκούσαντες, "the ones who hear") to the activity that God begins with his word, but then, because of these three sins, they react so negatively that none of the fruit can mature and ripen.[50] They finish nothing and bring nothing to completion (cf. τέλος, "end," in τελεσφορέω, "to mature"). The Lukan expression insists on the process of ripening, while Mark 4:19 only indicates the unsuccessful result (ἄκαρπος, "[it] yields nothing").

While the first group loses its treasure *immediately*, the third group suffers from a temptation dangerous in Luke's time, prosperity. And where the second group *suddenly* (ἐν καιρῷ πειρασμοῦ, "in a time of testing") separates after a joyful "honeymoon," the third gradually falls away. They start out (πορευόμενοι, "as they go their way"), but do not reach the goal set by God. Their faith does not become complete, because they do not persevere, precisely in the realm of ethics.

Luke is seldom as personal as he is here, and seldom as representative of his own time. The primary dangers that he brands are discussed again and again, particularly in the *Shepherd of Hermas*.[51] But where that author is concerned with the ethical consequences of faith, Luke is dealing with faith itself, which he understands as nothing less than a global reality: perseverance and testimony are its two main characteristics, which he now illustrates in the fourth group.

---

43 Improvements include: (1) Luke again prefers ἕτερον here (Mark 4:7 has ἄλλο); (2) "amid the thorns" (Luke has a predilection for ἐν μέσῳ) instead of "in the thorns" (Mark 4:7); (3) "to come up with it" (Luke) is more precise than the uncertain "to grow up" (Mark 4:7). Finally, one observes the two minor agreements with Matthew, which can be explained by the influence of oral tradition: ἀποπνίγω (Mark 4:7 has συμπνίγω) as well as the words "and it bore no fruit," which Mark (4:7) does not transmit.

44 If ἄκανθα is translated as "thorn bush," then συμφυεῖσαι cannot be given the meaning "simultaneously sprouting forth from the earth," though it is possible to think of young shoots as "growing together." The thorn bush is, of course, a perennial plant. The phrase ἐν μέσῳ seems to point to the possibility that Luke has in mind "thorns," which were visible from the moment of sowing. On the other hand, Lagrange (238) translates ἄκανθα as "thistle" and has in mind the annual *notobasis syriaca*, a species well-known in Galilee, under whose sprawling leaves everything suffocates.

45 The "deceitfulness" (ἀπάτη) of wealth (Mark 4:19)

is missing in Luke; see Dupont, *Béatitudes*, 3.44 n. 1.

46 Ἀκούω ("to hear") occurs nine times in Luke 8:4–21!

47 The ὑπό construed with three genitives is here dependent on συμπνίγονται ("to choke") and not, as it is sometimes assumed, on πορευόμενοι ("to go").

48 This verb entered Luke's text through the parallel passage in Mark, although he uses it with an entirely different intention; see Dupont, "Semeur," 104 n. 26. The absolute use of πορεύομαι is a special case in the NT, though it does call to mind the "way" of Jesus (Luke 9:51; 13:22).

49 Cf. Luke 21:34. The verb μεριμνάω ("to worry") appears in Luke 10:41; 12:11, 22, 25, 26; Matt 6:25–34; 1 Cor 7:32–34. Both the verb and the noun occur in a positive sense in 2 Cor 11:28. One observes the role that Ps 54 (MT 55):23 (ἐπίρριψον ἐπὶ κύριον τὴν μέριμνάν σου, "cast your care upon the Lord") plays in the parenesis of *Hermas* 19 (= *Vis.* 3.11.3) and 23 (= *Vis.* 4.2.4–5).

50 On τελεσφορέω ("to mature"), see LSJ *s.v.* In contrast, v. 15 has καρποφορέω ("to yield grain").

51 See *Hermas* 19 (= *Vis.* 3.11.3), 23 (= *Vis.* 4.2.4–5), 51

The Successful (vv. 8 and 15)

■ **8, 15** This long series of failures leads one to expect the contrast of a happy conclusion. Luke (8:8a) omits everything peripheral in Mark (e.g., the increase in the harvest).[52] The event hits human beings in their hearts, that is, there where they are most themselves, not in the sense of a religion of the individual, or of a deeply interior pietism, but in the sense of a personal and responsible faith within the community desired by God (the plural οἵτινες, v. 15, and not simple οἱ, vv. 12, 13, 14). In order to make comprehensible the special character of Christian existence, Luke uses the Greek concept of ideal existence, καλοκἀγαθία ("noble goodness").[53]

The word genuinely falls into the heart. The prepositions are varied artfully: παρά ("on the side of," v. 5), ἐπί ("on," v. 6), ἐν μέσῳ ("among," v. 7), and here εἰς ("into," v. 8) and ἐν ("in," v. 15). This field is good earth[54] and thus stands for people who not only hear but also persevere in the word and bring forth fruit.

A hundredfold yield[55] indicates a miraculous harvest (8:8), and no miracle occurs without God's participation. But this evangelist always favors the anthropological side; thus the continuous responsibility of human beings (8:15) plays the main role (ὑπομονή is not only passive patience, but perseverance).[56] This consists in loyalty

to the divine transmission of the christological word (ἀκούω, "to listen," and κατέχω, "to hold fast") and in the bearing of fruit (καρποφορέω, "to bear fruit"), which is understood in an ethical sense. The eschatological reward only stands in the background. Where the most sharply condemned attitude was a false security in possessions (8:14), the sufficient definition of being a Christian here is to hold on to the Word. The concrete meaning of this is not developed, but can be visualized in the concept of discipleship (9:23).

In the parenetical addendum (8:8b), it is redundantly noted that Jesus speaks (λέγων, "to say"), indeed, that he speaks loudly (ἐφώνει, "he called out"), and that the one who can hear (ὁ ἔχων ὦτα ἀκούειν) should listen (ἀκουέτω). In this fashion the evangelist places us in the situation of decision of the long-ago audience of Jesus (8:4–8), which corresponds to the situation of every hearer of the Word of God (8:11–14).[57]

The Division of Israel (vv. 9–10)

■ **9–10** In the Lukan version the concern is not, as in Mark, the problem of parables, but rather, concretely, the meaning of this (αὕτη) parable (8:9).[58] This lends a

---

(= *Sim.* 2.5–7), 74 (= *Sim.* 8.8.5), 75 (= *Sim.* 8.9.4). In two passages this author appropriates elements from the parable and its interpretation: *Hermas* 15 (= *Vis.* 3.7.3) and 97 (= *Sim.* 9.20.1–2).

52 And thus transmission does not always signify expansion. A. R. C. Leaney (*A Commentary on the Gospel According to St. Luke* [HNTC; New York: Harper, 1958] 151) is of the opinion that Luke has deleted the growth for anti-gnostic reasons. Schürmann (1.465) is somewhat more cautious; he believes that Luke refuses to recognize various degrees of piety among Christians. The deviations from Mark are, with one exception, insignificant. Luke omits ἀναβαίνοντα καὶ αὐξανόμενα ("growing up and increasing," Mark 4:8), which is surprising since the idea of the growth is dear to him (see Zingg, *Wachsen*). Here perhaps oral tradition has had a decisive influence.

53 See Dupont, "Semeur," 107; and Ernst, 269. The expression had already penetrated Judaism (see Tob 5:14–15; 7:7–8; 9:6–7; 2 Macc 15:12; 4 Macc 4:1. Walter Grundmann ("καλός," *TDNT* 3 [1965] 538–40) discerns two different meanings for the expression καλὸς κἀγαθός as it was used in the Greek language: one is a sociopolitical meaning and

the other an ethical-spiritual one (introduced by Socrates).

54 In 8:8 Luke uses ἀγαθή rather than καλή (Mark 4:8) in describing the quality of the soil. In 8:15, however, he retains the adjective καλή from Mark 4:20. One observes how he plays with the article: in 8:8 he writes two articles ("the soil, namely the good one"), but in 8:15 he writes only one, since the quality of the ground is now known ("the good soil"). According to Heinrich Joseph Vogels ("Lk 8,8 im Diatessaron," *BZ* 18 [1928–29] 83–84), the Syriac Diatessaron contained the expression "the good and fat earth."

55 See Klauck, *Allegorie*, 191. Gen 26:12 says of Isaac's harvest that it equaled a hundredfold of his seed, thus conveying an image of the subsequently mentioned divine blessing.

56 On Luke's addition of ὑπομονή ("patient endurance"), see Cerfaux, "Fructifiez."

57 This saying is found again in Luke 14:35, and also in some mss. at Luke 12:21 and 21:4; cf. the parallel passages in the other NT books that are cited by Nestle-Aland at Matt 11:15 and Rev 2:7.

58 Luke likes to use compound verbs (ἐπηρώτων) and the optative (εἴη).

greater coherence to the pericope 8:4–21, but it creates some tension with the answer of Jesus that Luke knows from tradition (8:10),[59] although, indeed, the disciples receive an answer to their question in the interpretation (8:11–15). Verse 10 thus becomes one of the preparatory remarks that the Lukan Jesus finds necessary.[60] Its content is the division of the nation of Israel. The proverb reflects the sociological isolation of the Christians ("to you," ὑμῖν) within Israel, and later among the Gentiles ("to the others," τοῖς δὲ λοιποῖς). This painful failure is made comprehensible through biblical tradition, and is overcome by means of a strong awareness of self-identity among the young community. The Christian church should remember the gift ("it has been given," δέδοται) of God, that is, the revelation of the mysteries of the kingdom of God.[61] Without claiming to uncover an antignostic tendency,[62] I would note that the evangelist avoids concepts such as γνῶναι ("to know") and μυστήρια ("secrets") in the redactional parts of his work, particularly in the book of Acts.[63] In Paul's footsteps he prefers the terminology of faith over that of knowledge, and the Jewish apocalyptic vocabulary concerning the mysteries of God is foreign to him. He retains the saying of Jesus about the μυστήρια of God only out of faithfulness to tradition, which probably prescribed the plural form (shared with Matthew against Mark) for him. According to this primitive Christian tradition, Jesus' preaching of the kingdom of God belongs to the genre of apocalyptic. The Christians are the recipients of a self-disclosing, supernaturally communicated revelation. As with visions or dreams, the parables uncover the hidden but still real power of God over the world for them. The μυστήρια are both the "signifier" and the "referent" of the parables, which are understood as "signifying." What Luke finds already in the tradition

is, on the one hand, the privileged position of Christians (the emphatic "to you," ὑμῖν), and on the other, their passive ("it has been given," δέδοται) and active ("to know," γνῶναι) behavior vis-à-vis this revelation.

Over against them stand the others: τοῖς δὲ λοιποῖς ("to the others") sounds deprecatory. Their fate is tragic, and will be mentioned again several times before the end of Acts (28:25–28). For they have heard and not understood, have had it before their eyes but not seen. The rich content of the message has remained empty and closed for them. Thus the parables stand before them like unsolved riddles.

The Semitic languages do not differentiate exactly between consequence and purpose. This could also be said, mutatis mutandis, for Greek, since ἵνα can introduce either a purpose or a result clause. The tradition thus initially states only that the majority have rejected the gospel. But then an explanation follows: this negative decision is part of the long story of the hardening of Israel's heart, and can be expressed in the same words (seeing and not seeing, hearing and not understanding). In the last analysis, God has not only foreseen this situation but has actively brought it to pass. Human responsibility stands alongside divine power, which here in this biblical citation takes the form of an indictment.

In this context Mark, and especially Matthew, have drawn from Isa 6:9–10. Luke reserves this citation for the end of the book of Acts, where he wishes to paint vividly the separaton between believers and unbelievers.[64] Here he toes the line with biblical tradition: Israel did not want to hear their God. The accusation in v. 10b, shortened from Mark, simply calls to mind a prophetic saying. Thus he underlines precisely the division of Israel: the Christians have heard and understood (8:10a), and for this reason are called again and again (8:8b) to stay true to the

59   See Joachim Gnilka, *Die Verstockung Israels: Isaias 6,9–10 in der Theologie der Synoptiker* (SANT 3; Munich: Kösel, 1961) 120.

60   In comparison with Mark, Luke upsets the balance between Luke 8:10a and 8:10b when he shortens the second member (see Gnilka, *Verstockung*, 123).

61   The mss. that omit τῆς βασιλείας ("the kingdom," as does Eusebius) probably do so for stylistic reasons, in order to avoid a double genitive.

62   With W. C. van Unnik, "Die Apostelgeschichte und die Häresien," *ZNW* 58 (1967) 240–46 (now in idem, *Sparsa Collecta*, 1.402–9) against Charles H. Talbert, *Luke and the Gnostics* (Nashville: Abingdon, 1966).

63   Luke nowhere explicitly mentions an esoteric teaching, but tends to remove the barrier between the disciples and the people that he finds in Mark and Q (see Gnilka, *Verstockung*, 124). Luke also softens Mark's text by deleting τὰ πάντα, as well as the last part of the quotation from Isa 6:9–10, which states the impossibility of reform and forgiveness.

64   See François Bovon, "'How Well the Holy Spirit Spoke Through the Prophet Isaiah to Your Ancestors!' (Acts 28:25)," in idem, *New Testament Traditions and Apocryphal Narratives* (trans. J. Happiseva-Hunter; PTMS 36; Allison Park, Pa.: Pickwick, 1995) 43–50.

word (8:15), while the "rest" have seen and heard in vain (8:10b). Luke 8:10b is a negative response to 8:8b. Christian existence is one that hears. But the consequences of this are centered in concrete life: the theology (word of God and chosen status) and the sociology of Christianity (differentiation of the Christian "sect") are seen as a complete whole.

Luke omits the last words of the Markan citation from Isaiah (μήποτε ἐπιστρέψωσιν καὶ ἀφεθῇ αὐτοῖς, "so that they may not turn again and be forgiven"). Does he intend to avoid the problem of the consequences of the hardening of hearts and lay the chief responsibility to the devil's account (ἵνα μὴ πιστεύσαντες σωθῶσιν, "so that they may not believe and be saved," 8:12)?[65] Does he want to leave open the possibility of the repentance of Israel until the time of the apostles, and only then draw the line? Does he transmit words so reminiscent of predestination with conviction? In naïve paradox, he emphasizes both the successful completion of God's plan and the decisive responsibility of the human will.

The Radiance of the Word (vv. 16–18)

■ **16** Both in content and in sequence, Luke remains true to Mark in v. 16. In his formulation, however, he is influenced by the version of this logion in Q, which, despite his antipathy toward the double inclusion of similar or parallel logia, he cites again in 11:33.[66] The lamp is first lit because of the guests that are to arrive. These two details come from Q. Why Luke avoids the foreign word μόδιος here and replaces it with the banal σκεῦος ("jar") is unclear.[67] Luke's preference for the version in Q is comprehensible, however, since it is formulated in much more fluent language than the clumsy Markan version.[68]

The logion is formally an antithetical wisdom saying, since wise behavior (8:16b) is contrasted to the foolish behavior that everyone avoids (8:16a). But the wisdom is found not in the literary character but in the metaphorical sense of the saying. The image, which would have been easily understood then, must be explained today: a λύχνος is a small lamp usually made of clay, filled with oil, and lit with a wick. It could be set on its stand (λυχνία) or hung from it. The stand could be portable or fastened to the wall. With σκεῦος, Luke has in mind a vase the form of which is similar to a bushel.

It is self-evident that no one would hide a burning lamp. There are three possible answers to the question of why Jesus nevertheless speaks about a vessel or a bed: (1) One could use an overturned bowl to extinguish a lamp, without dirtying one's fingers. The saying would then be contrasting "lighting" with "extinguishing" as opposites.[69] (2) The image may contrast "showing" with "hiding": a bowl and a bed would be two possible hiding places. Where the bed is unexplained in the first solution, in this solution the bowl remains unclear. (3) The lamp is a ritual object, comparable to, for example, the constantly burning lamp of Hanukkah. Since one is not allowed to extinguish it, when one wishes darkness[70] one can only hide it while it continues to burn.[71] One could also suggest a fourth interpretation: the hollow of the bowl could extinguish the lamp, but the bed, especially a straw mattress, could catch fire. The lamp fulfills the function proper to its nature only in the middle station between too little light and too much fire.

Luke has written up to this point about the acceptance of the word (8:4–15), but now turns to its radiance. He does not necessarily intend to name Jesus allegorically with ἅψας. But in the guests he surely sees the individuals attracted by the present-day Christian

---

65   So Gnilka, *Verstockung*, 125.

66   Two differences between Luke 8:16 and 11:33 may be mentioned: two different expressions for "hiding"; and the bushel is missing in 8:16 but present in 11:33.

67   *Μόδιος* is a loanword from Latin. Luke avoids such foreign words. But why does he leave it in Luke 11:33?

68   According to Schrage (*Thomas-Evangelium*, 81–85), the version in *Gos. Thom.* 33b appears to be dependent on that of Luke (Luke 8:16 and esp. 11:33). *Gos. Thom.* 33b adds "and all who come out."

69   See Joachim Jeremias, "Die Lampe unter dem

Scheffel," *ZNW* 39 (1940) 237–40 (reprinted in idem, *Abba: Studien zur neutestamentlichen Theologie und Zeitgeschichte* [Göttingen: Vandenhoeck & Ruprecht, 1966] 99–102) 101–2 (cited according to the latter).

70   According to the Law, a married couple should embrace one another in the dark (see J. Duncan M. Derrett, "The Lamp Which Must Not Be Hidden [Mk IV,21]," in idem, *Law in the New Testament* [London: Darton, Longman and Todd, 1970] 189–207, esp. 192).

71   See ibid.

mission. Verse 16 calls, in the language of wisdom, for the execution of the mission, first in word, but also in deed. Luke takes from Mark the connection between word and light, but he intensifies it: the light does not only assist in seeing reality, much more it is in itself the reality that must be considered ($\mathring{\iota}\nu\alpha \ldots \beta\lambda\acute{\epsilon}\pi\omega\sigma\iota\nu \ \tau\grave{o} \ \varphi\hat{\omega}\varsigma$, "that [they] may see the light"): the light of the gospel streams forth into the world of darkness. The popular interpretation, according to which one should not be too humble, is foreign to this text. Origen is closer to its intention, when he calls those who light the lamps $o\mathring{\iota} \ \varphi\omega\tau\acute{\iota}\zeta o\nu\tau\epsilon\varsigma \ \mathring{\epsilon}\alpha\upsilon\tau o\hat{\iota}\varsigma \ \varphi\hat{\omega}\varsigma \ \gamma\nu\acute{\omega}\sigma\epsilon\omega\varsigma$ ("those who illumine themselves with the light of knowledge").[72]

■ **17** The second saying is transmitted by both Q (Luke 12:2) and *Gos. Thom.* 5 (even in Greek).[73] Perhaps the transformation of Mark's final clauses into relative clauses can be explained from the variant in Q (Luke 12:2; Matt 10:26). The proverb consists of a strict parallelism of clauses. Because of the $\mathring{o}$, Luke brings the Markan $\varphi\alpha\nu\epsilon\rho\acute{o}\nu$ ("evident") forward in the sentence (he could just as well have written $\varphi\alpha\nu\epsilon\rho\omega\vartheta\acute{\eta}\sigma\epsilon\tau\alpha\iota$). He tries to soften the repetition of $\varphi\alpha\nu\epsilon\rho\acute{o}\nu$ with the help of the version in Q by introducing $\gamma\iota\nu\acute{\omega}\sigma\kappa\omega$ ("to know"). Thus in his version the second half of the proverb has a double conclusion ($o\mathring{\upsilon} \ \mu\grave{\eta} \ \gamma\nu\omega\sigma\vartheta\hat{\eta}$ and $\kappa\alpha\grave{\iota} \ \epsilon\mathring{\iota}\varsigma \ \varphi\alpha\nu\epsilon\rho\grave{o}\nu \ \mathring{\epsilon}\lambda\vartheta\eta$, "that will not become known," "and come to light"), which could also have been his intention stylistically, since many proverbs or speeches have a rhetorical broadening at the end (as can be seen in the Beatitudes, Luke 6:22).

Where 8:16 underscores the responsibility of the light-bearer, 8:17 could signify an *inner* necessity and represent an immanent self-revelation.[74] Just because $\kappa\rho\upsilon\pi\tau\acute{o}\nu$ ("hidden") and $\mathring{\alpha}\pi\acute{o}\kappa\rho\upsilon\varphi o\nu$ ("disclosed") are the grammatical subjects does not mean that they are such in terms of content. They are rather a reality that someone else brings into the light from outside. Should not this discreet other person receive light? He can only be God. But what is "hidden" and "covered over"? According to Jewish views, a number of divine and eschatological realities remain hidden until the time of fulfillment. It is thus not a question of an esoteric teaching. According to this Jewish theological topos, the final divine revelation occurs simultaneously with the complete and total manifestation of the human deeds and thoughts that have, until then, remained hidden.[75] But as in Mark, in this context $\kappa\rho\acute{\upsilon}\pi\tau o\nu$ and $\mathring{\alpha}\pi\acute{o}\kappa\rho\upsilon\varphi o\nu$ mean only the divine purpose. According to 8:10, the Christian community receives these secrets of the kingdom of God by receiving the revelation of the true meaning of these $\mu\upsilon\sigma\tau\acute{\eta}\rho\iota\alpha$ ("the secrets"). The privilege of the Christians consists in this (8:17). The futuristic-eschatological force, however, should not be missed. Despite the certainty of its conviction, in regard to the word, the church is still living prior to the final manifestation (cf. 1 Cor 13:12).

■ **18a** Luke takes from Mark 4:23–24 only the reinterpreted summons ($\pi\hat{\omega}\varsigma$, "how," and no longer $\tau\acute{\iota}$, "what") to hear correctly.[76] The verbs $\mathring{\alpha}\kappa o\acute{\upsilon}\epsilon\tau\epsilon$ ("hear") and $\beta\lambda\acute{\epsilon}\pi\epsilon\tau\epsilon$ ("see") thus confirm the organic relationship between the *preaching* of Jesus in the parable that is to be heard and its correctly understood *interpretation* by the church in the commentary. The two proverbs (8:16–17) reflect the same structure, but expand it in view of the present, where the kerygma (8:16) and its narrative, parenetic, or theological development (8:17) mutually strengthen one another. Since the summons to hear correctly surprisingly occurs *after* the message is given (as in 8:8b), this indicates that "hearing" is not an outer, acoustic activity, but an inner, consensual attitude.

---

72 See Origen, frg. 95.1 in *Matthäuserklärung*, vol. 3.1: *Fragmente und Indices* (ed. E. Klostermann; GCS; Origenes Werke 12; Berlin: Akademie-Verlag, 1968–76) 53; Schrage, *Thomas-Evangelium*, 84.

73 See P. Oxy. 654, no. 4 (cited in Aland, *Synopsis*, 180). Note the introduction: "Recognize what is before you, and what is hidden from you will be revealed to you."

74 In the sense of God's self-revelation in history.

75 On the revelation of the eschatological blessings of salvation, see the commentary on 2:30–32 above; see also 1 Cor 3:12–13 on the laying bare of all human works.

76 Luke deletes Mark 4:23 ("he who has ears . . .") in order to avoid a repetition of 8:8, and he deletes Mark 4:24b (concerning the measure), since he has already made use of it in the Q version at Luke 6:38.

■ **18b** Like Mark, Luke here inserts the controversial saying about possession and loss. Luke received it from two different sources: from Mark (this passage) and from Q (Luke 19:26). As with the logion in 8:16 and 11:33, Luke preserved both variants.[77] The original meaning remains a riddle. It could have been a realistic observation of wisdom that the rich become ever richer and the poor ever poorer, or it could reflect pedagogical or religious experience, by which the teacher or the divinity prefers to give his wisdom to those disciples who know how to nurture this received knowledge. In the Synoptic tradition, especially in Luke, it clearly concerns the relationship to the word of God ($\gamma \acute{\alpha} \rho$, "for"). Whoever has entered into a living relationship with God through the Christian message will also be enriched by living affective bonds within the community, and all the more so at the eschatological banquet. He is "blessed" both now and later (cf. 6:20–22 in view of the present, and 14:15, originally an independently transmitted logion, in view of future salvation).

Aside from a stylistic alteration, Luke modifies the Markan text at only one point: to the extent that it is not "what they have" that is taken from the punished individuals, but "what they think they have" ($\mathring{o}$ $\delta o \kappa \epsilon \hat{\imath}$ $\mathring{\epsilon} \chi \epsilon \iota \nu$). This explication is not only logical but also confirmed by experience. As in the parables about the self-righteous (15:7; 18:9), Luke has in mind pious individuals who believe they possess a sort of personal capital with God and to be able tranquilly to depend on this. But this is a possession in appearance only, as Luke emphasizes, in good Pauline tradition.[78]

Elective Kinship (vv. 19–21)

■ **19–21** Does Luke pass over the next three pericopes in Mark (4:26–34) because he does not have our present text of Mark? Since this hypothesized shorter version of Mark is nowhere indicated in the manuscript tradition, one can probably eliminate this hypothesis. Does Luke omit the parable of the seed that grows by itself (Mark 4:26–29) (1) because it identifies the kingdom of God with the sower; (2) because the various types of soil are reduced to one (good soil?); (3) because the earth produces automatically and thus human responsibility is either given too much or too little weight; (4) because Luke did not understand the point of the parable? The term $\alpha \mathring{\upsilon} \tau \acute{o} \mu \alpha \tau o \varsigma$ bothers him as it does Matthew, who symptomatically "replaces" the parable with that of the tares among the wheat (Matt 13:24–30). The parable of the mustard seed (Mark 4:30–32) is not eliminated by Luke but transmitted later (13:18–19). And the reflection over parables (Mark 4:33–34) is not expunged because Luke dislikes it, but because, according to his understanding, it is only a repetition of the previously explicated theory of parables (Luke 8:9–10).

Thus Luke rounds out his compositional unit with the apothegm about Jesus' true family, which appears in Mark 3:31–35 *before* the parable of the sower and the verses attached to it. This confirms a rule of Lukan composition: as soon as he drops or resumes the narrative thread in Mark, he changes the sequence of the pericopes, apparently for reasons of content.[79] In form this is an apothegm.[80] In a particular situation (the successful Jesus spending time together with the crowds) an event (the arrival of Jesus' family) gives the teacher, gifted with presence of mind, the opportunity to formulate an appropriate and instructive proverb.[81]

Though Luke is using the Markan version, his editorial hand is unmistakable: he reformulates it stylistically and shortens it drastically, especially at the end.[82] In the Catholic tradition, one sees in this the theological inten-

---

77 The saying has also found its way into the *Gos. Thom.* 41, which states that he who has, has it "in his hand," and that he who does not have, shall have even the "little" that he does have taken from him.

78 Cf. the polemical picture of Abraham that Paul draws in Rom 4:1–2: Abraham has not "discovered" the $\kappa \alpha \acute{\upsilon} \chi \eta \mu \alpha$ ("grounds for boasting") that Jewish theologians ascribe to him and so did not "possess" ($\mathring{\epsilon} \chi \epsilon \iota$) it.

79 Cf. Luke 6:12–19.

80 Schramm (*Markus-Stoff*, 123) notes that the "deviations from Mark 3:31–35 . . . [are] specifically Lukan" (in n. 3 he enumerates a series of examples,

esp. the "wanting to see" passages in Luke 9:9; 19:3–4; 23:8 and the phrase "the word of God"). It is therefore not necessary to presuppose a source other than Mark.

81 See Schneider, "Antworten."

82 *Gos. Thom.* 99 shares this brevity with Luke, but uses vocabulary that is closer to Mark and Matthew (e.g., it has "the will of my father" instead of "the word of God"). *Gos. Thom.* 99 adds an explanation as the conclusion: "It is they who will enter into my Father's kingdom."

tion to omit Jesus' provocative question and to avoid the juxtaposition between "outer" and "inner," in order to spare Jesus' family and make a place for them within the circle of believers.[83] This corresponds to the birth narrative, and "saves" the faith of the virgin Mary.

In the sequence of the Lukan version,[84] there is a first scene telling the arrival of Jesus' mother and brothers,[85] who cannot achieve their goal, that is, to meet with him (v. 19),[86] to see him (v. 20), because of the crowds. Two groups are thus juxtaposed. In the second scene, an anonymous voice[87] informs Jesus of the news that the readers know already. But where the narrative (v. 19) underscores the external obstacles, the message (v. 20) emphasizes the inner purpose. Thus v. 20 does not merely repeat v. 19, but presents the two possible attitudes with which people can crowd around Jesus. The first is characterized by "seeing" (v. 20), and the second by "hearing" (v. 21). The first contents itself with the visible figure of the man Jesus on the level of human kinship, and the second recognizes, in the figure of Jesus, a God (or the Word of God) who has graciously approached humankind. Thus a new definition of family is developed, for this elective kinship depends on both divine initiative and on human willingness ($\dot{\alpha}\kappa o\acute{u}o\nu\tau\epsilon\varsigma$, "those who hear") and perseverance ($\pi o\iota o\hat{u}\nu\tau\epsilon\varsigma$, "those who do"). The countours of the opposition between spirit and flesh are here illustrated narratively.

How does Luke bring this position into consonance with the birth narrative? Through the concept of faith. Mary becomes part of the circle of disciples only after Easter, not because of her motherhood, but because of the faith she demonstrates there (Luke 1:38; 2:19, 51). It is certain that, in Luke's version, the possibility of discipleship for the mother and brothers of Jesus is not excluded, while Mark and Matthew limit the proverb to the disciples or audience that Jesus has in view. Yet the point of the apothegm remains that the strongest human relationships (mother and child) can be put into question by the gospel. This anthropological rupture can be a saving event, as long as it is achieved by and grounded in christology. For the new family that one dreams of, then as now, receives its beginning in a relationship with the bearer of the word of God ("*my* mother and *my* brothers," v. 21). Only then does it develop interpersonally. The sequence of Luke's narrative (from vv. 19 to 21) illustrates this.[88] One indeed finds in Luke a softening of the harshness of this apothegm, not because of Mariology, but because of his concept of faith.

Conclusion

In the unit 8:4–21, Luke is reflecting on the relationship between the word of God and its appropriation by humankind. The readers learn that the word of God itself comes to them in parables and mysteries. According to Luke, Jesus takes care in communicating it, and his role as mediator is fully recognized. The expected acceptance of it by humanity is ostentatiously pushed into the foreground. The reception of the word of God proves itself in faithfulness and in ethics. These ethics are not limited to duties as such, but are rather developed in the congregation, which is understood as the family of Jesus.

---

83 Josef Blinzler (*Die Brüder und Schwestern Jesu* [SBS 21; Stuttgart: Katholisches Bibelwerk, 1967] 88) and Raymond E. Brown (*Mary in the New Testament* [Philadelphia: Fortress Press, 1978] 167–70) call attention to the brevity of the Lukan text in relation to Mark.

84 In Luke 8:19–21 one encounters various variants of about equal worth that, however, do not affect the sense (e.g., in some mss. v. 19 has the verb "arrive" in the singular, in others it is in the plural).

85 For Luke, they must be real brothers (see the denominational discussion at this point). Why have the "sisters" disappeared? Probably because in Mark they are only present in the mouth of the crowd (Mark 3:32).

86 $\Sigma\upsilon\nu\tau\upsilon\gamma\chi\acute{\alpha}\nu\omega$ ("to encounter," "to meet") occurs only here in Luke.

87 One observes the passive wording: $\dot{\alpha}\pi\eta\gamma\gamma\acute{\epsilon}\lambda\eta$ ("he was told"). The verb is indeed typically Lukan (45 times in the NT, of which 23 are in Luke), but only here among his writings is it found in the passive form.

88 See Brown, *Mary*, 169–70.

The Stilling of the Storm (8:22–25)

Bibliography

Birdsall, James Neville, "Khanmeti Fragments of the Synoptic Gospels from Ms. Vind. Georg. 2," *OrChr* 55 (1971) 62–63, 86–89.

Bornkamm, Günther, "The Stilling of the Storm in Matthew," in idem, Gerhard Barth, and Heinz Joachim Held, *Tradition and Interpretation in Matthew* (trans. P. Scott; NTL; Philadelphia: Westminster, 1963) 52–57.

Busse, *Wunder*, 196–205.

Fuchs, Albert, "Die 'Seesturmperikope' Mk 4:35–41 parr. im Wandel der urkirchlichen Verkündigung," in idem, ed., SNTU 15 (Linz: Albert Fuchs, 1990) 101–33.

Goldammer, Kurt, "*Navis Ecclesiae*: Eine unbekannte altchristliche Darstellung der Schiffsallegorie," *ZNW* 40 (1941) 76–86.

Harlé, P.-A., "La tempête apaisée: notes exégétiques sur cette péricope synoptique à trois témoins [Matt 8:23-27; Mk 4:35-41; Lk 8:22-25]," *FV* 65 (1966) 81–88.

Hilgert, Earle, "Symbolismus und Heilsgeschichte in den Evangelien: Ein Beitrag zu den Seesturm- und Gerasenererzählungen," in F. Christ, ed., *Oikonomia: Heilsgeschichte als Thema der Theologie: Oscar Cullmann zum 65. Geburtstag* (Hamburg/Bergstedt: Reich, 1967) 51–56.

Kertelge, *Wunder*, 91–100.

Léon-Dufour, "Tempête."

Pokorný, Petr, "Die Romfahrt des Paulus und der antike Roman," *ZNW* 64 (1973) 233–44.

Schenke, *Wundererzählungen*, 1–93.

Schramm, *Markus-Stoff*, 124–25.

Theissen, *Miracle Stories*, 99–103.

van der Loos, *Miracles*, 638–49.

22 It happened on one day that he got into a boat with his disciples, and he said to them, "Let us go across to the other side of the lake." So they put out. 23/ But while they were sailing he fell asleep, and a windstorm swept down on the lake, and the boat was filling with water, and they came into danger. 24/ They went to him and woke him up, and said, "Master, Master, we are lost!" But he, when he woke up, rebuked the wind and the raging waves; they ceased, and there was a calm. 25/ He said to them, "Where is your faith?" They were afraid and amazed, and said to one another, "Who then is this, that he commands even the winds and the water, and they obey him?"

Analysis

Whereas the stilling of the storm in Mark is still part of the same day on which the parables were spoken (Mark 4:35), Luke places it later, since for him that day concludes with the pericope concerning the family of Jesus (Luke 8:19–21). The coming of dusk is thus absent from his account, and, correspondingly, the symbolism of the absence of God associated with it. The transition into this pericope, and thus from word to deed, is indicated only by the usual redactional introductory formula ($\dot{\epsilon}\gamma\acute{\epsilon}\nu\epsilon\tau o$ $\delta\grave{\epsilon}$ $\dot{\epsilon}\nu$ $\mu\iota\mathring{\alpha}$ $\tau\hat{\omega}\nu$ $\dot{\eta}\mu\epsilon\rho\hat{\omega}\nu$, "it happened on one day," 8:22).[1]

After his transposition of the Markan source ("relatives of Jesus"—"parables"), from here onward Luke follows the Markan sequence (Mark 4:35ff.). Since Jesus did not teach from a boat (see above on 8:4), the evangelist must add that he boards one now (8:22). Mark is surely the source here. There are indeed Semitisms, none of which, however, have an un-Lukan character,[2] and minor agreements with Matthew,[3] which vary in significance. The mention of boarding the boat and of the presence of the disciples (v. 22) is necessary in both the first and the third Gospels because of the context.[4] After 8:1–3 it is unlikely that Luke would have written $o\acute{\iota}$ $\delta\acute{\omega}\delta\epsilon\kappa\alpha$ ("the Twelve") if he were not influenced by a tradition other than Mark.[5] The other agreements with Matthew are striking, but can probably be explained through oral tradition.

Luke cleans up his Markan source both in language and content. Mark's colloquial historical present disappears. Luke omits Jesus' departure from the crowds in v. 22, as well as the mention of the other boats (Mark

---

1   Fitzmyer (1.726) places too much weight on the caesura when he says that a new section begins here. A clear break must be recognized at 8:1.

2   Cf. $\dot{\epsilon}\gamma\acute{\epsilon}\nu\epsilon\tau o$ ("it happened") to introduce a sentence; $\dot{\epsilon}\nu$ $\mu\iota\mathring{\alpha}$ $\tau\hat{\omega}\nu$ $\dot{\eta}\mu\epsilon\rho\hat{\omega}\nu$ ("on one day") and $\kappa\alpha\grave{\iota}$ $\alpha\dot{\upsilon}\tau\acute{o}\varsigma$ ("and he"); see Schramm, *Markus-Stoff*, 125.

3   In addition to what is cited in the text, observe the common word order of Luke and Matthew in v. 24: $\pi\rho o\sigma\epsilon\lambda\vartheta\acute{o}\nu\tau\epsilon\varsigma$ . . . $\delta\iota\acute{\eta}\gamma\epsilon\iota\rho\alpha\nu$ ($\mathring{\eta}\gamma\epsilon\iota\rho\alpha\nu$) $\alpha\dot{\upsilon}\tau\grave{o}\nu$ $\lambda\acute{\epsilon}\gamma o\nu\tau\epsilon\varsigma$. The astonishment ($\dot{\epsilon}\vartheta\alpha\acute{\upsilon}\mu\alpha\sigma\alpha\nu$) mentioned at the end of such a miracle in v. 25 is hardly surprising: Matthew and Luke may have chosen the verb independently of one another.

4   Mark (at 4:35), on the other hand, may simply be referring back to the context of Mark 4:1.

5   See Schramm, *Markus-Stoff*, 124.

4:36), and uses the appropriate language of seafarers (e.g., ἀνάγω, πλέω, and συμπληρόω[6] in vv. 22–23). In v. 23 he improves the narrative sequence: he mentions Jesus' being asleep[7] before the storm breaks out. Though he considers the concrete details in Mark (the stern of the ship, the pillow) to be superfluous, the express mention of the danger (κινδυνεύω) is very important to him. In the cry for help (v. 24),[8] (1) the ἐπιστάτης ("master," "foreman") in Luke suits the situation better than the Markan διδάσκαλος ("teacher"); (2) the repetition of the vocative ἐπίστατα underscores the greatness of the danger;[9] and (3) the criticism of Jesus present in the cry of the disciples in Mark ("doesn't it bother you?") is omitted. The words of rebuke in Mark 4:39 are also not quoted, only mentioned, presumably since Luke does not personify wind and water. Everything happens very fast: Jesus rebukes, the wind and water become still, everything is tranquil. Jesus' critical question (v. 25) is formulated more strictly and its content is different. Jesus does not reproach the disciples for cowardice, nor for an absolute lack of faith—only for a relative lack. According to Luke, as in Matthew, the disciples' final reaction, the question that sounds almost like a confession, is the result not just of fear (φοβηθέντες, Mark 4:41) but of awe (ἐθαύμασαν; cf. Matt 8:27). As everywhere, Luke knows that the body of water is a lake, not an ocean (vv. 22–25).

This story belongs to the genre of the miraculous victory of the hero over the elements, for example, a rescue miracle.[10] The distance from an exorcism is not great, especially where the elements are personified, as in Mark. Ἐπιτιμάω ("to rebuke") is attested both in exorcisms[11] and in rescue miracles. This pericope also has a close relationship to another genre, the epiphany, for in its present form (already in Mark) it has two points: the rescue of the disciples, and the cryptic behavior of the Lord. In waking up and showing his active authority, Jesus reveals something of his identity. One can thus speak of a christological rescue miracle, or a soteriological epiphany.

The following structural elements are present: (1) within a normal situation (v. 22), a catastrophe (v. 23) suddenly threatens; (2) a call for help to a higher power (v. 24a) remains the only possibility of assistance; (3) the hero abruptly triumphs over the elements (v. 24b). After this first conclusion, however, the story develops in two further directions: (4) the critical questioning of the victor (v. 25a); and (5) the questioning awe of the rescued (v. 25b).[12] Especially points 4 and 5 indicate the present function of the narrative within the church: the faith of the members of the congregation will be tested in analogous situations, and the identity of Jesus should be comprehended in a confessional manner. As points 1–3 show, the original function of the episode was to testify to the saving power that God offers through Jesus. There is as little reflection on the separation between the material and physical world in this story as in the Hebrew Bible testimonies about the crossing of the Reed Sea. As a sym-

---

6   The plural συνεπληροῦντο ("they were filling with water") is surprising, since it is the boat that becomes full and not the passengers. How can such awkwardness be explained? Through an assimilation to the—correct—plural ἐκινδύνευον ("they came into danger") or through the identification of the person with his means of transportation? On the nautical vocabulary of these verses, see Plummer (225–26), who also calls attention to the contrast between the imperfect of these two verbs and the aorist κατέβη ("[it] swept down").

7   Luke's "he fell asleep" (ἀφύπνωσεν) is more vivid than Mark's "he slept" (καθεύδων; Mark 4:38). In classical Greek ἀφυπνόω means "to awake"; "to fall asleep" is καθυπνόω. At the time of the Gospels, however, other authors also used ἀφυπνόω in the meaning "to fall asleep"; see Godet, *Commentaire*, 1.526; and Lagrange, 246; *Hermas* 1.3 (*Vis.* 1.1.3).

8   Luke uses διεγείρω ("to awaken") twice (v. 24a and b), while in Mark (4:38–39) both the simple and the compound verb appear once each (though in Mark 4:38 the ms. tradition is not uniform). Matt 8:25–26 uses the simple verb twice.

9   This rhetorical figure of repetition is called *epanadiplosis* (see BDF §493.1). According to Lagrange (246), the repetition of ἐπίστατα ("master") in their address to Jesus, which is to be ascribed to their emotions rather than to Luke's style, carries no reproach. Rather, it underscores the urgency of a request directed toward a friend.

10   See Theissen, *Miracle Stories*, 99–103; and van der Loos, *Miracles*, 641–44.

11   See 4:35 and 9:42.

12   Fitzmyer (1.728) also mentions these five elements, although he combines my nos. 4 and 5 into one, and divides my no. 3 into two (Christ's command and its effect).

13   With Ernst, 274. Ludger Schenke is even of the opinion that such an allegorical interpretation of

bol—with this, participation in reality is described in the linguistic consciouness of that time—this narrative is a witness both to the salvation of the disciples and to the salvation of the hearers addressed by the story.[13]

The description of trouble at sea pertains to many genres in antiquity: epic, history, the ancient novel, biography, educational literature.[14] Jews feared the element of the sea, so foreign to them, and understood it as a cipher of the originary element of the chaotic powers (the symbolism of storm and shipwreck).[15] For this reason, they expressed their confession of faith as a trust in the God who is victorious over the sea[16] and the storm. The prayer in the midst of trouble at sea is thus the appropriate expression of this faith.[17]

In contrast with the Jewish parallels, in which *God* uses, for example, shipwreck as a punishment (Jonah), or miraculously hears the prayer of a child (*y. Ber.* 9.13b) or a righteous person (*b. B. Mes.* 59b) at sea, Jesus himself works the miracle here. To make possible the assignment of this power to the Messiah, this episode adopts the Hellenistic motif of the rescuing or protecting passenger.[18] The dramatic tension of such stories is often effected by presenting the passenger first as powerless,

as a child (*y. Ber.* 9.13b), as a prisoner (Paul in Acts 27:14–44), or asleep (as here). It is also christologically important that Jesus achieves victory *without praying*. Thus he is exalted into the sphere of God himself, and his victories are part of the catalogue of the saving acts of YHWH.[19]

Luke's literary technique is interesting: in his accentuation of the conciseness of this narrative, already present because of its genre, the evangelist confirms his tendency to preserve as many of these episodes as possible.

Commentary

The readers recognize three trajectories in this story: Jesus, his disciples, and the storm. Its meaning develops from the interaction of these mobile trajectories. During the trip, Jesus shows three types of behavior: toward himself (sleep), toward the elements (command), and toward his disciples (critical question). The elements, wind and water, also act in three phases: they begin and end in a normal state, and briefly enter into crisis. Aside from their presence, the disciples are not mentioned in the first stage; in the second it is not their feelings but

the story was still possible before the redaction by Mark (*Die Wundererzählungen des Markusevangeliums* [SBB; Stuttgart: Katholisches Bibelwerk, 1974] 77–78).

14 See Theissen, *Miracle Stories*, 99. Xavier Léon-Dufour ("La tempête apaisée," in idem, *Études*, 149–82, esp. 155) and Schenke (*Wundererzählungen*, 60–69) examine ancient stories about controlling the raging sea. One also finds stories about storms and shipwrecks as well as stories of miraculous rescue in the Apocryphal Acts, for example the *Acts of Timothy* 9.24–28 (ed. H. Usener [Bonn: Carolus Georgus, 1877]), the *Acts of John* by Pseudo-Prochorus 5–14 (T. Zahn, ed., *Acta Joannis: unter Benutzung von C. v. Tischendorfs Nachlass* [1880; reprinted Hildesheim: Gerstenberg, 1975]), and also the *Acts of Philip* 3.10–15 (33–34); see Junod and Kaestli, *Acta Iohannis*, 2.738–40; François Bovon, Betrand Bouvier, and Frédéric Amsler, *Acta Philippi: Textus* (CCSA 11; Turnhout: Brepols, 1999) 94–107.

15 On the symbolism of water, see Philippe Reymond, *L'eau, sa vie et sa signification dans l'Ancien Testament* (VTSup 6; Leiden: Brill, 1958).

16 See Ps 18(LXX 17):16; 29(LXX 28):3; 65:7 (LXX 64:8); 89:9 (LXX 88:10); 104(LXX 103):6–7; 106(LXX 105):9; and esp. 107(LXX 106):23–32 (according to Fitzmyer, 1.728).

17 See *T. Naph.* 6 (stilling of the storm, shipwreck, and prayer); see Theissen (*Miracle Stories*, 100) and van der Loos (*Miracles*, 643–46), who cites further examples. According to Schenke (*Wundererzählungen*, 60) the bearers of the tradition knew about the story of the stilling of the storm in the Jonah narrative (he believes there are close similarities with Jonah 1:4–16), though the core of the story—the mighty act of Jesus and his control over demonic powers—have no corresponding features there.

18 See Theissen, *Miracle Stories*, 101–2; and Schenke, *Wundererzählungen*, 63: The healing gods Asklepios, Serapis, and the Dioscuri rescue from the dangers of the sea.

19 See Léon-Dufour, "Tempête," 174. One thinks immediately of the passage through the Reed Sea (Exod 14:15–31), which the early Christian wall paintings of the Via Latina connect typologically with the raising of Lazarus (see Lieselotte Kötzsche-Breitenbruch, *Die neue Katakombe an der Via Latina in Rom: Untersuchungen zur Ikonographie der alttestamentlichen Wandmalereien* [JAC Ergänzungsband 4; Münster: Aschendorff, 1976] 79–83). On the invective in 2 Macc 9:8 against Antiochus IV Epiphanes, the enemy of God, who claims to command the waves of the sea, see Fitzmyer, 1.728.

their actions (they wake Jesus and implore him); whereas in the third, their inner attitude comes to expression.[20]

■ **22** Luke introduces the episode with the ἐγένετο ("it happened") of the LXX and the formulaic ἐν μιᾷ τῶν ἡμερῶν ("on one day") as a signal of the beginning. Jesus (indicated by the christological καὶ αὐτός, "and he") boards a boat, of course to go away (this is confirmed at the end of the sentence with ἀνήχθησαν, "so they put out"). Purposely, nothing is said about the helmsman, but mention is made of Jesus' companions, the disciples: according to 8:1–3, they comprise at least the twelve disciples and the women.[21] The responsibility for the voyage lies in their hands and in Jesus' hands. The destination is also indicated, by Jesus himself: "the other shore." It is both a *common* journey (διέλθωμεν, "let us go across," first person plural) and a journey *across* (διά in διέλθωμεν, εἰς τὸ πέραν, "over," "to the other side"). Luke is, of course, describing an actual historical voyage, but he is also aware of the literary and rhetorical comparison between human life and a precarious sea voyage.

■ **23** In v. 23 two additional dangers become apparent: Jesus' sleeping and the sudden onset of the storm. Jesus' sleeping fulfills a number of narrative functions: it expresses the confidence of the hero,[22] sets up a contrast with his powerful intervention, and makes possible a storm that Jesus otherwise would have seen. But sleep also receives a theological function: the image of sleep in the Hebrew Bible expresses the inactivity and the putative absence of God.[23] There are indeed times when Jesus is "sleeping," or in which his congregation believes

this to be the case. Especially in the period after Easter, his absence is hard to understand.[24] It is comparable to sleep, since a sleeping person is both present and absent. The episode is encouraging the proper interpretation of this sleep: the *doubting* disciples see only the visible, and encounter Christ's unseen authority first with blindness and then with hesitation. The *believing* readers are expected to become conscious of the power of the Lord despite his absence. Doubt sees and wavers, but faith stands firm, even when it sees nothing.

The storm winds come crashing down (καταβαίνω). Luke has in mind the mountains and gorges of the west side of the lake, from which the wind can suddenly descend.[25] A λαῖλαψ is a whirlwind that rises from below to above, or a violent falling wind.[26] It is a wind (one often encounters this word near ἄνεμος or πνεῦμα, "wind") that destroys everything. As an image, λαῖλαψ helps to visualize a danger that suddenly befalls humanity. In Jer 25:32 (LXX 32:32) λαῖλαψ μεγάλη ("a great windstorm") is the eschatological testing. In Philo one finds a rhetorical description of such a storm with the wise advice that a ship should stay in the harbor in such weather. Only a fool or a drunk would attempt to set sail in a λαῖλαψ. "For whoever wishes to sail without danger should, whenever possible, wait for a peaceful, favorable, and smooth wind."[27]

Jesus is thus comparable to a careless sailor. He falls asleep instead of paying attention, and continues sailing when he should rather have stayed in harbor. Thus water fills[28] the ship and puts all those traveling with him in danger. The feeling of powerlessness that grips the

---

20 Léon-Dufour ("Tempête," 164) concludes: "In Luke more attention is focused on the disciples than on the event."

21 Far too many commentators think exclusively of the male disciples and forget that female disciples are also present.

22 See Caesar's example, who (according to Plutarch *Caes.* 38.5), in the midst of a storm, is said to have called out: "'Go, my good man,' he said, 'Be fearless! Don't be afraid! You are carrying Caesar on board and with him his fate!'" Similarly, Dio Cassius 41.46.

23 See Pss 7:6 (LXX 7:7); 35(LXX 34):23 ; 44:23 (LXX 43:24); 59(LXX 58):5–6; 80(LXX 79):3; Isa 51:9 (God is called that he should awaken, i.e., to champion the cause of his people); Ps 78(LXX 77):65 (God has awoke and has beaten the enemies); Ps 121(LXX 120):4 (the God of Israel does not sleep, he watches over his people). See Thomas H.

McAlpine, *Sleep, Divine and Human, in the Old Testament* (JSOTSup 38; Sheffield: JSOT Press, 1987).

24 On the problem of the absence of the Risen One in the book of Acts, see Bovon, *Lukas,* 83.

25 Much has already been written on the storms on Lake Gennesaret; see Jack Finegan, *The Archeology of the New Testament: The Life of Jesus and the Beginning of the Early Church* (Princeton: Princeton University Press, 1969) 47–48.

26 See Job 21:18; Wis 5:14, 23; Sir 48:9, 12 (the rapture of Elijah); *T. Naph.* 6:4; 2 Pet 2:17. In the LXX and the other Greek translations of the HB, the word is used both in its original and in its figurative meaning (to indicate the actual or apocalyptic visitation); see Hatch and Redpath *s.v.;* and BAGD *s.v.*

27 *Somn.* 2.85–86.

28 On the odd use of the plural verb here, see n. 6 above.

disciples also overcomes the first Christians, who feel themselves abandoned by God and Christ in the predicament of the world.

■ **24** A single deed of the disciples is described with three verbs: they seek refuge in their Lord by going to him,[29] waking him, and speaking to him. Verse 24a therefore analyzes three aspects of prayer: the motion toward God, the address, and the request. The prayer itself (v. 24b) is extremely concise: there are only a doubled address and a situation of need presented in a single verb.

Ἐπιστάτης means "foreman," "master." The disciples thus recognize in Jesus less a teacher (as in Mark) than a carrier of authority and power. In the juxtaposition of this title and the dramatic situation ("we are lost"), Christian hope comes to expression. The ἐπιστάτης is now no longer asleep (διεγερθείς, "he woke up"). On the contrary, the disciples experience how he is also the Lord of the elements and how they obey him. Through his word,[30] he prepares an end to the raging of the wind and water.[31] What happens thereafter is not the quiet of death, but the tranquility of peace.[32]

■ **25** The disciples for their part must not fall asleep in this re-achieved pleasant situation. The rescuing but also ruling Messiah takes care of this with the question (v. 25): Ποῦ ἡ πίστις ὑμῶν; (lit. "Where your faith?"). This nominal sentence broadens the perspective, especially toward the future. It does not read, "Where *was* your faith?" or "Where *is* your faith?"[33] but "*Where your faith?*" It is the hope of the Lukan Jesus "to find faith on earth" at his return (18:8).

The reaction of the disciples is not ethical but christological. They encounter the *power* of the ἐπιστάτης ("master") with the double feelings of fear and amazement, and they ask about the *identity* of Jesus. They know from Scripture that only God has a word that is effective to this extent (Ps 104[LXX 103]:6–9; Nah 1:4).[34] This christological question foreshadows the question of Herod Antipas in 9:9 and the messianic discussion in 9:18–22. The readers already know from the story of the centurion from Capernaum (7:7–8) that the Christian faith is to be identified with trust in a Messiah who commands. But the range of messianic power is broadened here: the lord of the congregation is even (καί) Lord of the cosmos.[35]

Conclusion

This pericope deftly harmonizes the concept of Christ and the concept of faith, and indicates that there is no christological definition without the language of faith and no active faith without a relationship to the exalted Jesus.[36]

---

29 One should probably not think of the rocking boat so much as the affective (as if liturgical?) movement of the disciples toward Christ.

30 On ἐπιτιμάω ("to rebuke"), see 4:35 and the notes to the commentary on it above.

31 Κλύδων means a violent billow; see Antoniadis, *Évangile,* 101.

32 Γαλήνη signifies a calm on the sea (a list of occurrences if found in BAGD *s.v.,* which states that γαλήνη can also be used in figurative sense). Unlike Mark and Matthew, Luke does not think it is necessary to emphasize the γαλήνη by adding μεγάλη. He is even less interested in the source of the evil (the storm). What most concerns him is the overcoming of that evil, through the intervention of Christ and the faith of his people.

33 Not a few mss. read: "Where is (ἐστίν) your faith?" (see here the critical apparatus in Nestle-Aland). Roloff (*Kerygma,* 165) notes that, in contrast to the other miracle stories, the question about πίστις occurs here only after salvation. This "faith" is not a general trust in God, but rather the particular trust that had grown while the community lived with Jesus: the disciples should have believed that Jesus would not leave them all alone even in sleep.

34 Fitzmyer (1.730) mentions these two instances.

35 The first καί must be translated with "even" ("even the winds . . . and the water"). Léon-Dufour ("Tempête," 153, 182) takes up the patristic analogy between the ship shaken by the storm and the church threatened by the world; see Tertullian *Bapt.* 12; and Kurt Goldammer, "*Navis Ecclesiae*: Eine unbekannte altchristliche Darstellung der Schiffsallegorie," *ZNW* 40 (1941) 6–86. Additional literature can be found in Léon-Dufour, "Tempête," 179 n. 13.

36 Starting points for a modern history of research are found in Godet, *Commentaire,* 1.529; and van der Loos, *Miracles,* 639–40. The latter attempts to steer a middle course between fundamentalism and rationalism. He underscores the conflict of the two powers: the power of the storm and the power of Christ (*Miracles,* 647–48).

The Gergesene Demoniac (8:26–39)

Bibliography

Annen, *Heil.*

Baarda, Tjitze, "Gadarenes, Gerasenes, Gergesenes and the 'Diatessaron' Traditions," in E. E. Ellis and M. Wilcox, eds., *Neotestamentica et Semitica: Festschrift Matthew Black* (Edinburgh: Clark, 1969) 181–97.

Bligh, John, "The Gerasene Demoniac and the Resurrection of Christ," *CBQ* 31 (1969) 383–90.

Böcher, Otto, *Christus Exorcista* (BWANT 96; Stuttgart: Kohlhammer, 1972).

idem, *Dämonenfurcht.*

Bultmann, *History*, 210-11, 423.

Busse, *Wunder*, 205–18.

Cave, Cyrill Hayward, "The Obedience of Unclean Spirits," *NTS* 11 (1964–65) 93–97.

Craghan, John F., "The Gerasene Demoniac," *CBQ* 30 (1968) 522–36.

de Burgos, M., "El poseso de Gerasa (Mc 5,1–20): Jesús portador de una existencia liberadora," *Communio* 6 (1973) 103–18.

Dibelius, *Tradition*, 66–103.

Féliers, J., "L'exégèse de la péricope des porcs de Gérasa dans la patristique latine," in F. L. Cross, ed., *Papers Presented to the Fifth International Conference on Patristic Studies 1967* (StPatr 10, part 1; TU 107; Berlin: Akademie-Verlag, 1970) 225–29.

Haenchen, *Weg*, 189–204.

Jülicher, *Gleichnisreden*, 2.218.

Karris, Robert J., "Luke 8:26–39: Jesus, the Pigs and Human Transformation," *New Theology Review* 4 (1991) 39–51.

Kertelge, *Wunder*, 101–10.

Kleist, James A., "The Gadarene Demoniacs," *CBQ* 9 (1947) 101–5.

Koch, Dietrich-Alex, *Die Bedeutung der Wundererzählungen für die Christologie des Markusevangeliums* (BZNW 42; Berlin/New York: de Gruyter, 1975) 55–64.

Lamarche, Paul, "Le possédé de Gérasa (Mt 8,28–34; Mc 5,1–20; Lc 8,26–39)," *NRTh* 90 (1968) 581–97.

Masson, Charles, "Le démoniaque de Gérasa (Marc 5,1–20; Mt 8,28–34; Lc 8,26–39)," in idem, *Vers les Sources*, 20–37.

Pesch, *Besessene.*

Robinson, James M., *Das Geschichtsverständnis des Markus-Evangeliums* (AThANT 30; Zurich: Zwingli-Verlag, 1956) 42–54.

Sahlin, Harald, "Die Perikope vom gerasenischen Besessenen und der Plan des Markusevangeliums," *StTh* 18 (1964) 159–72.

Schenke, *Wundererzählungen*, 173–95.

Schramm, *Markus-Stoff*, 126.

Smith, Morton, *Jesus the Magician* (San Francisco: Harper & Row, 1978).

Starobinski, Jean, "The Gerasene Demoniac: A Literary Analysis of Mark 5:1–20," in F. Bovon, ed., *Structural Analysis and Biblical Exegesis: Interpretational Essays* (trans. A. M. Johnson Jr.; PTMS 3; Pittsburgh: Pickwick, 1974) 57–84.

Theissen, *Miracle Stories*, 85–94.

26 Then they traveled to the country of the Gergesenes, which is opposite Galilee. 27/ As he stepped out on land, a man of the city who had demons ran to meet him. For a long time he had worn no clothes, and he did not live in a house but in the tombs. 28/ When he saw Jesus, he cried out, fell down before him, and shouted at the top of his voice, "What do I have to do with you, Jesus, Son of the Most High God? I beg you, do not torment me" — 29/ for Jesus had commanded the unclean spirit to come out of the man. For many times it had seized him; he was kept tied up, and bound with chains and shackles. And when he would break the bonds, he would be driven by the demon into the wilds. 30/ But Jesus asked him, "What is your name?" He said, "Legion"; for many demons had entered him. 31/ And they implored him that he may not order them to go out into the abyss. 32/ Now there on the mountainside a large herd of swine was feeding; and the demons implored Jesus to let them enter these. So he gave them permission. 33/ And when the demons came out of the man, they entered the swine, and the herd rushed down the steep bank into the lake and drowned.

34 When the swineherds saw what had happened, they ran off and brought the news to the city and to the country. 35/ Then they came out to see what had happened, and came to Jesus, and found the man from whom the demons had gone out sitting at the feet of Jesus, clothed and in his right mind. And they were afraid. 36/ Those who had seen it told them how the one who had been possessed by demons had been saved. 37/ Then all the people of the surrounding country of the Gergesenes asked Jesus to leave them; for they were seized with great fear. So after he got into the boat, he returned. 38/ The man from whom the demons had gone begged him that he might be with him; but Jesus sent him away and said, 39/ "Return to your home, and declare everything that God has done for you." So he went away, proclaiming throughout the city everything that Jesus had done for him.

Analysis

The Context

Luke retains the connection found in Mark between the stilling of the storm and the healing of the demoniac. In 8:22 he has Jesus express clearly his intent to travel over to the far side of the sea.[1] Now that the primal elements of wind and water[2] have obeyed him, the Lord can sail over quietly.[3] What awaits him there, in this land of "difference," ἀντιπέρα τῆς Γαλιλαίας (the "opposite of Galilee," 8:26), as Luke alone writes, is narrated in an alienating fashion (8:26–39). It is a single story, so that Jesus' journey has the form of a concise advance into a strange land. It also does not last long, since the crowds are waiting for him and receive him again at his return (8:40). Many details already in Mark indicate that the action takes place in non-Jewish territory: the number and name of the demons, the impure life in the presence of the dead, the presence of the pigs, and the epithet ὕψιστος ("most high") for God.[4] Too much emphasis should not be placed on the story as an allusion to the salvation-historical calling of the Gentiles, since Luke omits the journey of Jesus to Tyre and Sidon found in Mark (Mark 7:24–37).

The Adopted Structure

Although the text of Mark is not without discrepancies, Luke accepts its structure nearly without change: the encounter is actually described twice (8:27–28), the command to be exorcised (8:28a) takes place before the conversation with the demon (8:30–32), the request of the demon is repeated (8:31–32b). The conclusion of the episode also remains in Luke (8:34–39) as convoluted, clumsy, and opaque as it is in Mark: this concerns the flight of the shepherds, the arrival of the inhabitants, the spread of the news about the events (by those who saw the healing?), the inhabitants' request of Jesus to leave their territory, Jesus' refusal of the healed man's request, and his command to tell others. Luke's only departure is the division in two and the partial postponement of Mark's long description of the demoniac (Mark 5:3–5): Luke leaves the first short description in its original place (8:27b), whereas he places the longer description between Jesus' two commands (8:29b; see Mark 5:8–9). The reason for this transposition may be the caesura between the two consecutive addresses of Jesus to the demons in Mark. The description (8:29b) serves to justify (γάρ, "for") the saving power of Jesus (8:29a, 30).

Luke Rewrites the Text

Verse 26: Since Jesus is traveling by boat, καταπλέω ("to travel") is more suitable than ἔρχομαι ("to go"). Luke avoids the repetition of the direction (εἰς τὸ πέραν . . . and εἰς τὴν χώραν) by replacing the first expression with a relative sentence (ἥτις).

Verse 27: In Mark the encounter takes place as soon as Jesus lands.[5] A comparison between the two Gospels shows the following: Luke's preference for ἀνήρ ("a man"), adaptation to the number of the demons (reformulation as ἔχων δαιμόνια, "to have demons"),[6] the deletion of a repetition (Mark's ἐκ τῶν μνημείων, "out of the tombs," is skillfully replaced by "out of the city"), the redactional mention of nakedness foreshadowing 8:35, and the short (when compared with Mark) indication of the demoniac's place of residence.

Verse 28: Luke improves the narrative part stylistically (δέ instead of καί, abolition of the pleonasm κράξας φωνῇ μεγάλῃ, "calling out with a loud voice"). He works out his intentions in the content: since the

---

1 The parallel in Mark 4:35 has simply "to the other side." The lake is not mentioned.

2 See Luke 8:25. Luke avoids the word "sea" (θάλασσα), for he knows the size and the nature of this "lake" (λίμνη, Luke 8:22, 23, 33).

3 For a report on the discovery and preservation of a boat sunk in Lake Gennesaret that most likely comes from the time of Jesus, see Shelley Wachsmann, "The Galilee Boat," *BARev* 14.5 (1988) 18–33. On the symbolism of the ship, see Earle Hilgert, *The Ship and Related Symbolism in the New Testament* (Assen: Royal Vangorcum, 1962).

4 This is a frequent title in the LXX and in the writings of Hellenistic Judaism. It is used particularly by non-Israelites as the designation for the supreme deity or the God of Israel: see Gen 14:19–20 (in the mouth of Melchizedek) and Josephus *Ant.* 16.6.2 §163 (Augustus calls Hyrcanus II a "high priest of the ὕψιστος God"). See Georg Bertram, "ὕψος, κτλ.," *TDNT* 8 (1972) 614–20.

5 As he does so often, Luke here deletes the εὐθύς ("immediately") of Mark (Mark 5:2).

6 In an inconsistent manner, Luke later uses the singular in v. 29.

encounter has already taken place, the Markan "from afar" and "he ran" disappear; and since only God, or at the most Christ *after* Easter, can be worshiped, προσπίπτω ("to fall down before") replaces προσκυνέω ("to bend the knee before," "to worship"). The correction of ὁρκίζω ("I invoke you") to δέομαι ("I ask you") heads in the same direction. In v. 29a παραγγέλλω ("to command") is better than the simple λέγω ("to say"). The transition from direct (Mark) to indirect speech (Luke) coordinates Jesus' two statements (8:29, 30) better.

Verse 29b adapts the convoluted description in Mark 5:3–5 into Lukan language. While Mark describes the superiority of the demoniac over his guards, Luke places the overwhelming power of the demons over the demoniac in the foreground (συναρπάζω, "to seize," and ἐλαύνω, "to drive," are Lukan).[7]

Verse 30 contains three Lukan peculiarities: (1) the aorist ἐπηρώτησεν ("[Jesus] asked") after the imperfect (v. 29); (2) two δέs instead of two καίs as in Mark; (3) the causal clause (ὅτι) that becomes a remark of the author rather than the answer of the demons.

Verse 31: The first, negative request of the demon contains, in addition to linguistic improvements,[8] a theological hint by Luke about a possible exorcism of the demons into hell (ἄβυσσος, "the abyss"). Although the deviations from Mark are minute in v. 32, they become

more numerous in v. 33 in the word δαιμόνιον ("demon"), beloved by Luke, and in "lake" (not "sea").[9] Like Matthew, Luke omits the fantastic and popular number (2,000) of pigs.

Luke narrates the shepherds' reaction (vv. 34–35) in Mark's words. He makes only a few improvements: δέ twice for καί; the addition of ἰδόντες ("when they saw") to explain the flight; the omission of the unnecessary αὐτούς; ἐξῆλθον ("to go out") instead of ἦλθον (εἰς, "to," twice in v. 34); the harmonization of the tenses;[10] the more lively aorist εὗρον instead of θεωροῦσιν (both "they saw"); "patchwork" to remove the Markan impression that the man is not yet healed.[11] The only theologically relevant correction is the addition of the words παρὰ τοὺς πόδας ("at the feet"). Luke uses this to underscore the discipleship of the healed man.[12]

The reaction of the inhabitants is surprising (vv. 36–37), since Luke repeats the verbs ἀπήγγειλαν ("they brought the news") and ἰδόντες ("when they saw") from v. 34, and he additionally mentions the amazement of the people over "the way that the demoniac[13] was saved" (ἐσώθη, 8:36), for theological reasons. Additionally, v. 37 is reformulated with a designation of location and the motive for the fear.[14] Luke's reasons for transforming a dependent clause into an independent sentence are unclear, all the more since the aorist ὑπέστρεψεν ("he returned") cannot yet express the

---

7   Another small difference is the place to which the wretch is driven by the demons: in Mark he is forced to live among the graves and in the hills; in Luke he is driven into the desert. Luke thus avoids the repetition of the word "graves" and at the same time can allude to the commonly held belief that the desert was the place where demons live.

8   In view of the multiplicity of demons, Luke prefers the plural (παρεκάλουν, "they implored [him]") over the singular (Mark 5:10). With the deletion of πολλά ("many"), he avoids repeating it and at the same time refrains from using a colloquial expression. The request of the demons is expressed in a more amiable manner in Luke than in Mark.

9   See also ἀποπνίγω (Mark has πνίγω). Luke is fond of compound verbs. In addition, ἀποπνίγω is used in the passive particularly to indicate "asphyxiation in the water" (see Bailly, *Dictionnaire*, s.v.).

10   Luke chooses the aorist, thereby eliminating the historical present of Mark (Mark 5:15a).

11   Mark writes τὸν δαιμονιζόμενον . . . τὸν ἐσχηκότα τὸν λεγιῶνα ("the demoniac . . . the

one having the legion"), Luke τὸν ἄνθρωπον ἀφ' οὗ τὰ δαιμόνια ἐξῆλθεν ("the man from whom the demons had gone out").

12   Luke prefers here ἄνθρωπος over ἀνήρ, although he generally uses the latter. Perhaps he uses ἄνθρωπος because he wants to deemphasize gender and stress the humanity that the healed man has now regained.

13   Ὁ δαιμονισθείς (aorist passive participle) stands in the place of the ambiguous ὁ δαιμονιζόμενος (Mark 5:16).

14   Ὅτι φόβῳ μεγάλῳ συνείχοντο ("for they were seized with great fear") is a Lukan expression. "Great fear" is also found in Luke 2:9 and Acts 5:5, 11. The verb συνέχω (esp. in the middle and passive) turns up nine times in Luke's two-volume work (the first and only occurrence until now was Luke 4:38), but it is used only three times in the rest of the NT.

realization of the return because of vv. 38–39. Beyond what is said in Mark, Luke wants to show that Jesus (αὐτὸς δέ, "and he," has a christological character)[15] takes human fear into consideration. The return of the healed man does not signify defeat.

The concluding scene (vv. 38–39) is more strongly redactional. Δέομαι ("to beg") describes the position of the man with regard to Jesus better than παρακαλέω. Since Luke has pulled ὁ δαιμονισθείς ("the one who had been possessed by demons," Mark) further forward (8:36), as is his habit, he makes recourse to a paraphrase that he has indeed already used in 8:35.[16] Luke prefers σύν to the Markan μετά because of his stylistic sensibilities. Ἀπολύω ("dismiss") suits the context better than ἀφίημι ("abandon"). Luke achieves a dramatic effect with ὑπόστρεφε ("return!" Markan ὑπάγε): just like Jesus ("he returned," ὑπέστρεψεν, 8:37), the healed individual must return.[17] Now Luke can use the verb διηγέομαι ("to set out in detail") that he avoided in v. 36. He simplifies the end of the scene and thereby creates a parallelism between the work of God in commanding (v. 39a) and the work of Jesus in executing it (v. 39b). After v. 37, he no longer gives any indications of location. Perhaps he is playing down a rash mission into foreign lands, since the hour of the mission to the Gentiles has not yet struck. The renunciation of God's compassion (καὶ ἠλέησέν σε, "and what mercy he has

shown you," Mark 5:19) has a linguistic justification, since ἐλεέω cannot take ὅσα as an object.[18] He leaves out the final reaction of the inhabitants (καὶ πάντες ἐθαύμαζον, "and everyone was amazed," Mark 5:20). Thus Luke's last sentence emphasizes the work of the Father and the Son.[19]

This comparison shows unequivocally that Luke had only Mark as a source.[20] The Griesbach hypothesis, which has been put forward anew,[21] runs aground for linguistic reasons, since Matthew's influence on Luke cannot be demonstrated, and the question as to why, in this case, Mark would have used his main source—Luke—so carelessly cannot be answered.

In the prehistory of this narrative,[22] the effect of Markan redaction on the tradition he inherited is an unsettled issue. The secondary character of the last section (the healed man as a witness for Christ)[23] has generally been acknowledged. It is not necessary for the genre, and reflects ecclesiastical concerns. The episode with the pigs is often considered secondary, first because of the doublet, and then because of the end of the narrative (Luke 8:34–39), where it plays no further role.[24] It is, however, constitutive of the story, although the conclusion of the narrative has indeed been lengthened in the successive redactions.[25]

In its written version, the story belongs to the genre of the exorcism,[26] which is to be distinguished from

---

15   One can connect this expression with καὶ αὐτός ("and he"), which Jeremias examines (*Sprache*, 37–38).

16   The pluperfect (ἐξεληλύθει) agrees better with the sequence of tenses here than would the aorist (ἐξῆλθεν) used earlier in v. 35, unless this aorist were understood in the sense of a pluperfect.

17   Luke deletes the words "to your family" (Mark 5:19), since he regards them as superfluous after the expression "to your home."

18   The accusative following ἐλεέω indicates the person receiving compassion.

19   Why does Luke dispense with the verb ἄρχομαι ("to begin") twice in this section (see Mark 5:17, 20), although he readily uses it elsewhere?

20   Schramm (*Markus-Stoff*, 126) and Franz Annen (*Heil für die Heiden: Zur Bedeutung und Geschichte der Tradition vom besessenen Gerasener [Mk 5,1–20 parr.]* [FTS 20; Frankfurt am Main: Knecht, 1976] 22) are of the same opinion.

21   See the notes to the analysis of the Sermon on the Plain above.

22   Annen (*Heil*, 11–19) summarizes the older works.

23   Even Matthew was conscious of the secondary character of Mark 5:18–20. He concludes with the demand for Jesus to leave the country (Matt 8:34).

24   The words καὶ περὶ τῶν χοίρων ("and about the swine," Mark 5:16) appear as an awkward addition.

25   Rudolf Pesch argues that a report about an exorcism underlies this section, which report was expanded by the characteristic formal elements of the healing miracle and by elements drawn from the ritual of exorcism (*Der Besessene von Gerasa: Entstehung und Überlieferung einer Wundergeschichte* [SBS 56; Stuttgart: Katholisches Bibelwerk, 1972] 21–49). Annen (*Heil*, 70–71), on the other hand, sees here a traditional form with its various elements, which has been considerably edited by Mark.

26   On the literary form of this exorcism and of exorcisms in general, see Theissen, *Miracle Stories*, 85–90; Otto Böcher, *Dämonenfurcht und Dämonenabwehr: Ein Beitrag zur Vorgeschichte der christlichen Taufe* (BWANT 90; Stuttgart: Kohlhammer, 1970); idem, *Christus Exorcista* (BWANT 96; Stuttgart:

healing. The former concerns the existence of the demon, the latter its effects (sickness). In an exorcism the hero attacks the demon itself, whereas in a healing the sick person and his or her suffering are the focus. The method used by the thaumaturg is also different for both. The conclusion of an exorcism can only be the expulsion of the demon and the liberation of the demoniac connected with this. Five structural elements of the genre of exorcism can be found here: (1) the encounter; (2) the defense of the demon and his discussion with the exorcist; (3) the *apopompe* ("sending away");[27] (4) the *epipompe* ("sending upon"); (5) the impression the exorcism leaves on the audience. The manner in which Jesus introduces the miraculous healing is what is unusual and impressive in this case: he demands to know the name of the demon in order to achieve power over it. Both of the concessive requests of the demon correspond to the usual development of an exorcism. The *epipompe* (new residence of the demon) is not unusual.[28] Only the abundance of the elements is unusual here.

Luke does not narrate many exorcisms. The first one, told more soberly, is in 4:33–37, and the next in 11:14.[29] But he firmly believes in the existence and the power of demons (see, e.g., 11:14–26). Behind the demons is the devil himself, who still exercises his power over the earth and its inhabitants.[30]

Commentary

In precritical exegesis, the questions were always the same: did Jesus heal one (Mark and Luke) or two (Matthew) demoniacs? What was the name of the place where the miracle took place, and was there a steep cliff there? How can Jesus be absolved for the loss of the pigs? What degree of historicity does the report possess, and how should such cases of exorcism be evaluated?[31] Such questions detract attention from Luke's true concern. His interest is to emphasize the manifestation of Jesus' divine authority on the one hand, and the decline in the power of the demons on the other. Both things take place neither in the familiar homeland nor in a protected "city," but "over there," on the other side of the fearful water, in the unprotected "country."[32] Both things also occur in an *encounter*.

The Encounter (vv. 26–28)

■ **26–28** As a Greek, Luke would understand geographical space as a system of cities with the hinterland that belongs to them.[33] He does not explicitly emphasize that Jesus has progressed into the *Gentile* world, although he is aware of the geopolitical situation (3:1–2), and, along with the tradition before him, of the Jewish symbolism surrounding Jesus' enterprise. He underscores the dangerous aspect of this journey with the traditional sea voyage, and the bizarre aspect with an encounter outside the city.

The manuscripts attest three names for the region in which the action takes place: the region of the Gerasenes (agreeing with Mark), that of the Gadarenes (Matthean influence), and that of the Gergesenes (Origen would locate the miracle there).[34] Gerasa (today's Jerash) lies more than 50 kilometers southeast of the

---

Kohlhammer, 1972); Klaus Thraede, "Exorzismus," *RAC* 7 (1969) 44–117.

27   The Greek *apopompe* ("sending away") is the command for the demons to come out and, as a performative expression, also means the expulsion itself. The Greek *epipompe* ("sending over") occurs when the demons pass over to another victim (e.g., an animal, an object, something in nature). This consequence is unavoidable, since a demon cannot be killed.

28   There is a Babylonian text in which a demon is expelled and driven into a pig (see Pesch, *Besessene*, 37–38).

29   Cf. the reference to various exorcisms in Luke 8:2.

30   See the excursus on the devil in the commentary on Luke 4:1–13 above.

31   I take these various questions from Paul Lamarche ("Le possédé de Gérasa [Mt 8,28–34; Mc 5,1–20; Lc

8,26–39]," *NRTh* 90 [1968] 581–97, esp. 581), who approaches the problem from a different perspective.

32   In contrast to today, when one must flee the city to find a peaceful landscape, in antiquity the area between cities was perceived as a place full of peril (see Maurice Aymard, "Espaces," in F. Braudel, ed., *La Méditerranée: L'espace et l'histoire* [Paris: Arts et métiers graphiques, 1977] 179–218, esp. 185).

33   See Busse, *Wunder*, 215.

34   See Origen *Comm. in Joh.* 6.41 (24 = §§208–11; in E. Klostermann, ed., *Origenes Werke 4* [GCS 10; Leipzig: Hinrichs, 1899] 4.150); and idem, *Commentaire sur saint Jean: Livres VI et X* (ed. C. Blanc; SC 157; Paris: Cerf, 1970) 2.288–91.

lake. There were several Gadaras at the time, the nearest of which (today's Umm Qeis) is located on the south side of Wadi Yarmuk, about 10 kilometers southeast of the lake. It is uncertain whether the Gergesa in Origen and the manuscripts should be identified with the place on the east shore of the lake near Wadi es-Samak.[35] The old reading "Gergesenes" could be an accommodation to a local Christian tradition according to which the people of that locality kept the memory of the event, and thus is suspect. But Gadara is also suspicious, since it suits the narrative better geographically than the more famous Gerasa. The only location left is the one farthest from the lake, Gerasa. Thus what proves itself to be false geographically could nonetheless be the original reading. But since Gerasa was a well-known city, it could also be a correction of the lesser-known location. Thus "Gergesenes" is chosen here as the best reading.[36]

As soon as Jesus is on terra firma, the demoniac runs up to him. His first words seem to indicate a polite inhabitant of the city. Thus he has not lost all trace of humanity despite demonic domination. His politeness and human identity are a narrative hint of his theological desire for salvation. After this, however, the present miserable condition of the demoniac is painted in vivid colors.[37] The numerousness of the demons has robbed him (cf. 8:2) of two signs of humanity: a clothed condition and community with fellow humans. That he lives among the graves indicates that he is closer to the dead than the living. Cemeteries in general are impure for ancient sensibilities, particularly those of the Jews. Existence that has become inhuman without God is here vividly characterized. Synoptic tradition is certainly the product of reflection on the symbolism of such a situation, and it connected the elements midrashically with Scripture, particularly Isaiah 65 (LXX).[38] It is an open question whether Luke was conscious of this biblical passage, but the symbolic connotations were familiar to him anyway (cf. Acts 26:18).

In v. 28 the voice that speaks through the demoniac is that of the demons, and these immediately recognize Jesus' superior power, as the title "Son of the Most High God" attests. There is no real battle, only a bargaining about the most painless possible capitulation.[39] Ὁ ὕψιστος ("the most high") might be an additional hint at the Gentile world, since non-Jews call God this in the LXX.[40] By changing the invocation (ὁρκίζω, "I adjure")[41] to a request (δέομαι, "I beg"), does Luke intend to show that the authority of Jesus is recognized from the start,[42] to exclude Jesus from the magical power of the demons, or to characterize Jesus' answer to the request as an act of grace?[43]

A Look at the Author (v. 29)

■ **29** Jesus' reaction is not expressed narratively until v. 30. Luke speaks in v. 29. According to the variant one chooses for παραγγέλλω ("to command," imperfect or aorist), the text concerns Jesus' healing purpose, the beginning or the entire sequence of events, or the exorcism in general.[44] More important here is the intervention of the author, which allows his intentions in structuring this narrative to be expressed (esp. in γάρ, "for").

---

35 See the historical-archaeological map ("Blatt Nord") enclosed in vol. 4 of *BHH*. Today this place bears the name Korsi or Kersa. On the whole question, see Félix-Marie Abel, *Géographie de la Palestine* (2 vols.; 1933–38; EtB; reprinted Paris: Gabalda, 1967) 1.323–25; 2.300, 332.

36 On this question see Fitzmyer, 1.736–37, who in the end decides with Nestle-Aland and Gottfried Schille ("Γερασηνὸς, κτλ.," *EDNT* 1 [1990] 245) in favor of "Gerasenes."

37 On ἱκανός, which in Luke can mean "considerable," see Cadbury, *Style*, 196; and Karl Heinrich Rengstorf, "ἱκανός," *TDNT* 3 (1965) 293–96.

38 See John F. Craghan, "The Gerasene Demoniac," *CBQ* 30 (1968) 522–36; and Cyrill Hayward Cave, "The Obedience of Unclean Spirits," *NTS* 11 (1964–65) 93–97. For additional proponents of this connection to the HB, see Annen, *Heil*, 92. The LXX text in Isa 65:3 identifies the idols with demons, and in Isa 65:4 refers to heathen cults in tombs and caves (cf. Rom 10:20–21).

39 On the christological knowledge of the demons see the commentary on 4:34 above; see further the commentary on 4:33–37.

40 See Plummer, 229. See n. 4 above.

41 Luke uses ὁρκίζω in an exorcism formula only in Acts 19:13.

42 See Grundmann, 181.

43 Statements connected with δέομαι are sometimes directed to a person (Acts 8:34; 26:3), usually, however, to God (Luke 10:2) or to Jesus (Luke 5:12; 9:38).

44 It is very difficult to choose between παρήγγελλεν (imperfect), the reading, e.g., of ℵ, and

In this description of possession, the human and demonic are first mixed together. The demons are the unexpressed subject of συνηρπάκει ("[it] had seized"), whereas only the man can be the subject of the next verb, ἐδεσμεύτο ("he was tied up," v. 29b). In the healing itself,[45] Luke separates the human and the demons and reduces the number of the demons to a single number, in order to command them better. Whereas v. 27 concisely portrays the dehumanization of the victim; vv. 28–29 illustrate his helplessness against the repeated attacks[46] of the demon. Συναρπάζω ("to grasp violently," "to grab," "to seize") and ἐλαύνω ("to drive") could in those days be applied to supernatural powers, and also to the natural elements if they attacked a boat.[47] The ineffectual fetters that the careful but powerless fellow humans apply to him[48] only show that the poor demoniac suffers[49] from a far more dangerous power.[50]

The Unconcluded Conversation (vv. 30–31)

■ **30–31** From a form-critical perspective, inquiring about the name belongs to magical exorcism, not the Christian variety. Nevertheless, since it occurs here, it fulfills another function. Regarding the admission of the demons in v. 28b, the narrative concern is not how to achieve domination over them, but to achieve "a maximum of demonic concentration."[51] The singular ("unclean spirit" and "demon," v. 29) should not give the wrong impression: many demons (ἔχων δαιμόνια, "who had demons," 8:27; δαιμόνια πολλά, "many demons," 8:30) rule this man, indeed a huge number: a legion (cf. the numerous pigs). The name is vivid: just like the hosts of angels (Matt 26:53), the demons are also organized in military fashion (cf. the opposed battle forces in the War Scroll at Qumran).[52] If one looks down from the acropolis at Masada to the ruins of the camp of the Roman legions, one can form an idea of the metaphorical value

---

παρήγγειλεν (aorist) found, e.g., in P[75]. Does the imperfect here mean "he commanded," "he was commanding," or "he had commanded"? Does the aorist mean "he commanded," "he started to command," or "he had commanded"? See BDF §§318, 325–28, 331–32; James A. Kleist, "The Gadarene Demoniacs," *CBQ* 9 (1947) 101–5, esp. 103; and Charles Masson, "Le démoniaque de Gérasa (Marc 5,1–20; Mt 8,28–34; Lc 8,26–39)," in idem, *Vers les Sources*, 20–37, esp. 24–25 (regarding the imperfect in the parallel at Mark 5:8).

45 Influenced by Mark 5:8, the bilingual Codex Bezae (D) and the Latin Codex Palatinus (e) insert direct speech once again: "Come out!" (ἔξελθε).

46 Πολλοῖς . . . χρόνοις is not clear: "on many occasions" (Plummer, 230), "for many times," is to be preferred here rather than "for a long time" (BDF §201). The use of the dative instead of the accusative is contrary to classical usage.

47 On these two verbs see BAGD *s.v.* The use of the pluperfect for συναρπάζω alone shows that the tormenting took place before Jesus' command. In the NT only Luke uses the verb συναρπάζω (see Acts 6:12; 19:29; 27:15).

48 The verb δεσμεύω means "to bind" in the sense of "to tie together two parts that would otherwise fall apart." Ἅλυσις (a "chain" to bind together the hands) and πέδη (a "shackle" for the feet) are terms that often appear together in the writings of this period (see BAGD *s.v.*) The more general term τὰ δεσμά comprises the two more specific terms (see Tob 8:3). The bonds are meant to protect him (φυλασσόμενος). On this meaning of φυλάσσω

("to guard"), see BAGD *s.v.* φυλάσσω (lc), even though Bauer places this passage under definition 1b ("to guard someone to prevent him fr. escaping"). Both meanings probably coincide here: one protects another by preventing a dangerous person from escaping.

49 The present participle διαρρήσσων (from διαρρήσσω, "to break," a later form of διαρρήγνυμι) and the imperfect ἠλαύνετο ("he would be driven") convey an iterative nuance.

50 He is driven into the desert. On the desert (one must understand χώρα with the adjective ἔρημος) as the preferred place of residence for demons (another was water), see Böcher, *Dämonenfurcht*, 50–53. It is less important to ask whether demons exist than it is to determine what content fills that which is expressed in a particular linguistic formulation in a particular culture (see Jean Starobinski, "The Gerasene Demoniac: A Literary Analysis of Mark 5:1–20," in F. Bovon, ed., *Structural Analysis and Biblical Exegesis: Interpretational Essays* [trans. A. M. Johnson Jr.; PTMS 3; Pittsburgh: Pickwick, 1974] 57–84, esp. 82–84).

51 Haenchen, *Weg*, 193.

52 The scribal variation can be traced back to the fact that there are two spellings in Greek for "legion": λεγιών and λεγεών. On this term see Franz Annen, "λεγιών," *EDNT* 2 (1991) 345–46. As in v. 29, Luke also here intervenes in the story. He alters Mark's ὅτι clause (Mark 5:9) and comments on the incident like a reporter. The aorist εἰσῆλθεν "they entered") has the meaning of a pluperfect.

of this description. A further request from the demons[53] comes next. Luke remains under the impression that there are many demons and uses the third person plural, contrary to the usual rules of grammar. Now that Jesus has entered into conversation with the demons, they dare to "implore" him ($\pi\alpha\rho\alpha\kappa\alpha\lambda\acute{\epsilon}\omega$, v. 31, rather than $\delta\acute{\epsilon}o\mu\alpha\iota$, "to beg," v. 28). With the word $\mathring{\alpha}\beta\upsilon\sigma\sigma\sigma\varsigma$ ("the abyss") Luke[54] clarifies Mark's formulation, in which the demons merely ask not to be sent out of the region.[55] The concept carries theological weight, since it describes the underworld, a place of punishment where, according to Jewish apocalyptic,[56] the enemies of God will be kept in confinement, beginning with the devil (Rev 20:1, 3). It is a place that, in Jewish symbolism, awakens associations with the negative connotation of the sea. In Luke's time it was "thought of as a 'prison for spirits,'" in which its inmates, especially the Antichrist, would stay "until their release in the tribulation before the end."[57] $\mathring{\alpha}\beta\upsilon\sigma\sigma\sigma\varsigma$, however, also sounds vivid to the Greek ear.

The Concession (vv. 32–33)

■ **32–33** The mention of a large[58] herd of pigs foreshadows the leap off the cliff that comes next. Since pigs are unclean animals (Lev 11:7), this is most likely a pagan or semi-pagan environment (cf. Luke 15:15).[59] "For both contemporary Judaism as well as for the early Jewish

Christians, the pig was the signboard of the Gentiles. It comes as no surprise that the Gentile power with which the Jews were then most in conflict, the Romans, were given the title of pig. It is an irony of history that the Romans themselves actually encouraged this not exactly flattering identification by means of the military standard of the Legion X Fretensis stationed in Syria-Palestine."[60]

Since the demons also belong to the unclean world, they suggest that they be transferred to the pigs. In v. 31 they have made several (imperfect) general requests; here in v. 32 they give a concrete proposal (aorist). In v. 31 they want to evade a command ($\acute{\epsilon}\pi\iota\tau\acute{\alpha}\sigma\sigma\omega$, "to order") by Jesus. Now, they ask for permission from Jesus (twice $\acute{\epsilon}\pi\iota\tau\rho\acute{\epsilon}\pi\omega$). When Jesus expresses his agreement with this, the exorcism occurs. We have already heard of the demons' restlessness (v. 29b). As they once entered the demoniac, they now enter the pigs, and, together with their involuntary hosts, leap off the cliff[61] into the water. While the pigs drown and perish (lit. "suffocate"),[62] it is assumed that the demons remain imprisoned in the $\mathring{\alpha}\beta\upsilon\sigma\sigma\sigma\varsigma$ ("the abyss"). The fall of the pigs illustrates not only the narrative confirmation of the successful exorcism,[63] but also the power of the Lord Jesus over the demonic world, which power awakens trust and hope in the reader. According to Luke, Jesus is not guilty of the death of the animals. The demons made

---

53 There is an earlier request in v. 28b.

54 They do not want to go into the underworld (v. 31). On $\mathring{\iota}\nu\alpha\ \mu\acute{\eta}$ ("lest"), see BDF §369.

55 One observes here that the demons are holding on to their prey and do not want to leave it ($\mathring{\alpha}\pi\epsilon\lambda\vartheta\epsilon\mathring{\iota}\nu$, "to go out").

56 See Joachim Jeremias, "$\mathring{\alpha}\beta\upsilon\sigma\sigma\sigma\varsigma$," *TDNT* 1 (1964) 9–10: "under the influence of Persian and Hellenistic conceptions, [the abyss becomes] the place in which apostate spirits are confined (Jub. 5:6ff.; Eth. En. 10:4ff., 11ff.; 18:11ff. etc.; Jd. 6; 2 Pt. 2:4)." In the LXX the word was used to translate תְּהוֹם ("primeval waters"), and in Hellenistic Greece it could signify Hades.

57 Jeremias, "$\mathring{\alpha}\beta\upsilon\sigma\sigma\sigma\varsigma$," *TDNT* 1 (1964) 10. More literature can be found in K. Schneider, "Abyssos," *RAC* 1 (1941) 60–62; Paul Hoffmann, *Die Toten in Christus: Eine religionsgeschichtliche und exegetische Untersuchung zur paulinischen Eschatologie* (NTAbh n.s. 2; Münster: Aschendorff, 1966) 176–80; Otto Böcher, "$\mathring{\alpha}\beta\upsilon\sigma\sigma\sigma\varsigma$," *EDNT* 1 (1990) 4.

58 The adjective $\mathring{\iota}\kappa\alpha\nuο\acute{\iota}$ (of which Luke is so fond)—

used here in the sense of "many" (see n. 37 above)—replaces the word $\mu\epsilon\gamma\acute{\alpha}\lambda\eta$ and the expression "approximately two thousand" added a little later by Mark (Mark 5:13).

59 Greek has several words for swine: $\acute{ο}\ \mathring{υ}\varsigma$ or $\sigma\mathring{υ}\varsigma$ ("wild boar," "hog," "pig") and $\acute{ο}\ \chi o\acute{\iota}\rho o\varsigma$ (properly "a piglet," but later "a pig" in general; from it comes the diminutive $\tau\grave{ο}\ \chi o\iota\rho\acute{\iota}o\nu$). Since Hellenistic times $\acute{ο}\ \chi o\acute{\iota}\rho o\varsigma$ has been the predominant term. On the pig in Judaism, see Str-B 1.448–50, 492–93; Roland de Vaux, "The Sacrifice of Pigs in Palestine and in the Ancient East," in idem, *The Bible and the Ancient Near East* (trans. D. McHugh; Garden City, N.Y.: Doubleday, 1971) 252–69; Annen, *Heil*, 162–73.

60 Annen, *Heil*, 173.

61 $\acute{Ο}\ \kappa\rho\eta\mu\nuό\varsigma$: "a steep place," "embankment," "precipice," "cliff." This word, which appears only here in Luke, is firmly rooted in the tradition, for it is found in all three Synoptic accounts.

62 On $\mathring{\alpha}\pi o\pi\nu\acute{\iota}\gamma\omega$ ("to drown"), see n. 9 above.

63 Not completely satisfied with a successful exorcism, Apollonius of Tyana required a visible sign from

the proposal and thus carry the full responsibility. It is possible that a popular legend about tricking the devil is behind this episode.[64]

The Reaction to the Miracle (vv. 34–39)

■ **34–39** The narrative assumes the proximity between Jesus and the shepherds, who witness the event, and also the relationship between the demoniac and the pigs. It is possible that Luke thinks that the (probably) flying demons could have been seen. The shepherds[65] do not dare to complain to Jesus. They flee before the holy and find relief in telling of their misfortune ($\dot{\alpha}\pi\alpha\gamma\gamma\dot{\epsilon}\lambda\lambda\omega$ means "to come back with a message," "to bring news"). "In the city and in the country" means "everywhere." As Mark did already, Luke also conceives of the geography as including a city in the region. The fertile ($o\dot{\iota}\ \dot{\alpha}\gamma\rho o\dot{\iota}$, "the country," 8:34) and the unfertile ($\alpha\dot{\iota}\ \ddot{\epsilon}\rho\eta\mu o\iota$, "the wilds," 8:29) zones belong to its hinterland, as do the mountains ($\tau\dot{o}\ \ddot{o}\rho o\varsigma$, 8:32) and their meadows. The lake ($\dot{\eta}\ \lambda\dot{\iota}\mu\nu\eta$, 8:22) serves as a natural boundary on one side. $\dot{H}\ \pi\epsilon\rho\dot{\iota}\chi\omega\rho o\varsigma$ ("the surrounding country," 8:37) could indicate the areas that bound this region on the other side. But it more likely means the region of the Gergesenes itself; $\pi\epsilon\rho\iota$- indicates the environs, not neighboring regions. The final episode (vv. 34–39) is not as descriptively narrated; Luke hardly improves the banal prose of his source here.[66]

The function of vv. 34–35 is the public confirmation of the events. The shepherds and those who are informed by them "see what had happened." Indeed, they do not all see the same thing, but at least the obvious result of the entire affair: the healed man. He is described antithetically to vv. 27 and 29: he sits peacefully, instead of raving about;[67] he is wearing clothes, thus no longer naked;[68] he looks reasonable, and no longer like a demoniac.[69] Normality and salvation are not mutually exclusive, since Jesus wants to have people with him in their re-achieved humanity. Salvation is not, however, reduced to normality: as explicated in the redactional phrase $\pi\alpha\rho\dot{\alpha}\ \tau o\dot{\upsilon}\varsigma\ \pi\dot{o}\delta\alpha\varsigma\ \tau o\hat{\upsilon}\ \dot{I}\eta\sigma o\hat{\upsilon}$ ("at the feet of Jesus"), the healed individual has become a disciple and has entered the phase of his education for the kingdom of God. The effect on the spectators is not yet faith, but rather fear,[70] since the message has been, up until now, pure narrative without interpretation ($\dot{\alpha}\pi\alpha\gamma\gamma\dot{\epsilon}\lambda\lambda\omega$, "to bring good news"). A Christian witness that results in bringing people to faith is only possible once the healed and newly believing individual begins to "proclaim" ($\kappa\eta\rho\dot{\upsilon}\sigma\sigma\omega$, v. 39) the work of God that is concealed within the work of Jesus.

The identity of the next recipients of the news ($\alpha\dot{\upsilon}\tau o\hat{\iota}\varsigma$, "to them") remains unclear, since the evangelist is concerned only that the information is spread. What is still missing, the interpretation of the news, is communi-

---

the expelled demon. The demon obliged by knocking over a statue (see Philostratus *Vit. Ap.* 4.20). The mention here of the $\ddot{\alpha}\beta\upsilon\sigma\sigma o\varsigma$ ("abyss," peculiar to Luke, v. 31) may well recall the myth of Eubuleus: the earth swallows the pig-herder Eubuleus along with his herd as it yawns open during the abduction of Kore (= Persephone). The abduction of Demeter's daughter was celebrated in Athens during the Thesmophoria. See Dibelius, *Tradition*, 88 (in the 3d ed., however, he wonders how much weight can be given to this comparison).

64   On the deceived devil see Bultmann, *History*, 210 n. 3.

65    $O\dot{\iota}\ \beta\dot{o}\sigma\kappa o\nu\tau\epsilon\varsigma$ (lit. "the feeders," "those who tend to grazing"): those who watch over pigs and are responsible for them. Observe that the participle is in the present tense: "They were in the act of feeding the pigs." Cf. $\pi o\iota\mu\dot{\epsilon}\nu\epsilon\varsigma$ ("shepherds") in Luke 2:8 and "feed ($\beta\dot{o}\sigma\kappa\epsilon$) my sheep" in John 21:15, 17.

66   Note the repetitions: $\dot{\epsilon}\xi\hat{\eta}\lambda\vartheta o\nu$ and $\hat{\eta}\lambda\vartheta o\nu$ in v. 35, $\dot{\alpha}\pi\dot{\eta}\gamma\gamma\epsilon\iota\lambda\alpha\nu$ in vv. 34 and 36.

67   "Sitting" is esp. the position of a student (cf. Acts

22:3, where Paul learns "at the feet of Gamaliel"). Now healed, the demoniac is sitting, dressed and in his right mind, at the feet of Jesus.

68   In any society clothing is a mark of identity, and proper dress a sign of normalcy. In Scripture, clothing also takes on a spiritual dimension. See Edgar Haulotte, *Symbolique du vêtement selon la Bible* (Théologie 65; Paris: Aubier, 1966).

69   In Greece the word $\sigma\omega\phi\rho o\sigma\dot{\upsilon}\nu\eta$ means first a state of normality, and then a moral quality. The vocabulary of $\sigma\omega\phi\rho o\sigma\dot{\upsilon}\nu\eta$ found its way into Hellenistic Judaism and then into Christianity. See Spicq, *Lexicon*, 3.359–65; and Dieter Zeller, "$\sigma\omega\phi\rho o\sigma\dot{\upsilon}\nu\eta$, $\kappa\tau\lambda$.," *EDNT* 3 (1993) 329–30.

70   On the fear before the numinous, see Horst Balz, "$\phi o\beta\dot{\epsilon}\omega$," *TDNT* 9 (1974) 209–10.

cated to the readers, in accordance with Luke's kerygmatic purpose. In v. 36 it is again the evangelist speaking, and he strongly emphasizes his own concern: he underscores that the spectators have seen (ἰδόντες) how a demoniac was healed. Both the former state of possession and the final exorcism of the demons are for him past facts (aorist). Mere knowlege of this is not sufficient, however; it is thus possible to see the facts of salvation without yet achieving the faith that Jesus hopes for. Only on the basis of a Christian interpretation of history can the presentation or proclamation of these facts become a gospel that brings faith and salvation in its train.

The concept of σῴζω means first "to liberate," "to rescue" from a tragic imprisonment (from sickness, possession, death). Luke often writes about the present reality of salvation in this sense. The Lukan Jesus attests this in his proclamation, and in his deeds in the name of God; for this reason Luke calls believers in Acts 2:47 simply οἱ σῳζόμενοι ("those who are saved"). This present nature of salvation, which neither replaces nor excludes its future fulfillment, is typical of Lukan soteriology.[71] Without the kerygmatic explanation of the events, the spectators remain oppressed by fear.[72] Thus they all[73] decide to request of Jesus that, in view of his power, he guarantee the necessary distance from them by departing.[74] Jesus answers concretely by boarding the boat to return to Galilee.[75]

In vv. 34–39 physical distance expresses an inner attitude. The fear of the shepherds and inhabitants demands spatial removal, while the healed man desires community (εἶναι σὺν αὐτῷ, "to be with him," v. 38) with Jesus.[76] Jesus does not accede to this wish, since such a discipleship would be too cheap in his eyes. A childish dependence would replace the ethical responsibility of being a Christian. To be healed (v. 36) means for Luke to assume a duty, which indeed is not formulated as a law: this disciple is to return to his family, whereas others must leave their families (9:59–60; 14:26; 18:28). He had been excluded from society because of his possessed state, so his return home is a symbol of his healing. The return, which is not only a social reintegration (itself not a small thing), is connected by Jesus to the assignment to tell what God has done for him (v. 39a; cf. 1:1). Only by a mature separation from his savior can he grow in his faith. The healed individual obeys (v. 39b) and proclaims (κηρύσσω) what has happened to him. He rightly interprets the act of God (v. 39a) christologically (v. 39b). Not only his house (v. 39a) but also the whole city (v. 39b) learns what has happened, and this proclamation makes possible the step from fear to faith.

Conclusion

Luke describes a double epiphany in this vivid exorcism. The saving power of the Son of God is revealed in it, as is the fall of the evil powers. This double epiphany, which occurs together with a triumph of Christ, is not claimed abstractly, but occurs in an encounter and develops in the recovery of health. Thus the readers feel themselves addressed by the story and take their place alongside the hearers as the first witnesses of the miracle.

---

71 On salvation in Luke see Bovon, *Theologian*, 239–66.

72 Συνέχω is "to hold together," "to press together"; in the passive "to be pressed," "squeezed," "suppressed" (see Euripides *Herac.* 634).

73 On this point they are all in agreement: ἅπαν τὸ πλῆθος κτλ. ("all the people").

74 Note the redundancy and the alliteration in ἀπελθεῖν ἀπ᾽ αὐτῶν ("to leave them"). Most likely it underscores the distance.

75 Even though Jesus speaks once more with the healed man in vv. 38–39, the aorist here (ὑπέστρεψεν, subject = Jesus) may actually be understood to conclude the story, as far as Jesus is concerned. For the healed man, the story ends at v. 39. It is also possible, however, that the aorist ὑπέστρεψεν has an ingressive meaning ("he started to leave"). See BDF §331.

76 Ἐδεῖτο (v. 38) means "he asked," "he made a request," "he begged" (but one should not forget the original meaning of δέομαι, "to be in need of"). Ἐπερωτάω in v. 30 and also ἐρωτάω in v. 37, however, have different shades of meaning: "to ask in order to learn something," in other words, "to inquire." Παρακαλέω in v. 31 and v. 32, on the other hand, means "to request," "to call," " to appeal for help," "to implore." As one can see, the vocabulary for asking in this section has a wealth of nuances.

History of Interpretation

According to the exegesis of the Latin fathers,[77] this story illustrates the salvation of lost humanity. Life among the graves means a life far from God, and nakedness signifies the absence of faith or sinful shamelessness. In view of Christ's victory, the demons would like to remain outside hell until the day of the Lord. They request to move from the Gentiles into the heretics, the proud, and the idolatrous. The shepherds are equated with the responsible officials of either the synagogue or the heresies, and the population of this region with the Jews who rejected Jesus. In the missionary command (vv. 38–39), the Latin fathers recognize an invitation (expressed in Pauline terms; cf. Phil 1:22) to remain in the flesh for the sake of the salvation of their brothers and sisters. Today's exegete may criticize the details of this allegorical exegesis, but must agree to the extent that the Synoptic accounts turn attention to a broader interpretation beyond mere historical reminiscence.

77   The interested reader will find in J. Féliers's article references to the church fathers, and to the passages in which individual issues related to this story are discussed, such as the confession of the demons, the request of the demons, the death of the pigs ("L'exégèse de la péricope des porcs de Gérasa dans la patristique latine," in F. L. Cross, ed. *Papers Presented to the Fifth International Conference on Patristic Studies 1967* [StPatr 10, part 1; TU 107; Berlin: Akademie-Verlag, 1970] 225–29). On the wooden ceiling of the Church of St. Martin at Zillis (Graubünden, Switzerland), fields 107 and 108 depict scenes from the story of the Gerasene demoniac.

Jairus's Daughter and the Woman with the Discharge of Blood (8:40–56)

Bibliography

Bultmann, *History*, 214–15, 424.

Busse, *Wunder*, 219–31.

Dambrine, Liliane, "Guérison de la femme hémor-roïsse et résurrection de la fille de Jaïre: Un aspect de la lecture d'un texte: Marc 5,21–43; Matthieu 9,18–26; Luc 8,40–56," *CBFV* (1971) 75–81.

Dokka, Trond S., "En fortolkning av Mk 5:21–43 med synoptisk sammenlikning," *NTT* 93 (1992) 149–62.

Kertelge, *Wunder*, 110–20.

Kreyenbühl, Johannes, "Ursprung und Stammbaum eines biblischen Wunders," *ZNW* 10 (1909) 265–76.

Marxsen, "Bibelarbeit."

Pesch, "Jairus (Mk 5,22 / Lk 8,41)," *BZ* n.s. 14 (1970) 252–56.

Potin, Jacques, "L'Évangile (Mt 9,18–26): Guérison d'une hémorroïsse et résurrection de la fille de Jaïre," *AsSeign* 78 (1965) 25–36.

Robbins, Vernon K., "The Woman Who Touched Jesus' Garment: Socio-Rhetorical Analysis of the Synoptic Accounts," *NTS* 33 (1987) 502–15.

Roloff, *Kerygma*, 153–55.

Schenke, *Wundererzählungen*, 196–216.

Schmithals, Walter, *Wunder und Glaube: Eine Ausle-gung von Markus 4,35–6,6a* (BibS [N] 59; Neukirchen-Vluyn: Neukirchener Verlag, 1970) 69–91.

Schramm, *Markus-Stoff*, 126–27.

van der Loos, *Miracles*, 509–19, 567–73.

Verweyen, Hansjürgen, "Einheit und Vielfalt der Evangelien am Beispiel der Redaktion von Wundergeschichten (insbesondere Mk 5,25–34 parr.)," *Didaskalia* 11 (1981) 3–24.

40 Now when Jesus returned, the crowd welcomed him, for they were all there and waiting for him. 41/ Just then there came a man named Jairus, who was a leader of the synagogue. And when he fell at Jesus' feet, he begged him to come to his house, 42/ for he had an only daughter, about twelve years old, and she was dying. But as he went, the crowds almost crushed him. 43/ Now a woman who had been suffering from a discharge of blood for twelve years, who had spent all she had on physicians and could not be healed by anyone, 44/ came up to him and touched the fringe of his clothes from behind, and immediately her discharge of blood stopped. 45/ Then Jesus asked, "Who is it that touched me?" When all denied it, Peter said, "Master, the crowds surround you and press in on you." 46/ But Jesus said, "Someone touched me; for I noticed that power went out from me." 47/ But when the woman saw that she could not remain hidden, she came trembling; and falling down before him, she declared in the presence of all the people the reason she had touched him, and how she had been immediately healed. 48/ He said to her, "Daughter, your faith has saved you; go in peace."

49 While he was still speaking, someone came from the leader's house to say, "Your daughter is dead; do not trouble the teacher any longer." 50/ But when Jesus heard this, he replied to him, "Do not fear. Only believe, and she will be saved." 51/ When he came to the house, he did not allow anyone to enter with him, except Peter, John, and James, and the child's father and mother. 52/ They were all weeping and wailing for her; but he said, "Do not weep; for she is not dead but sleeping." 53/ And they laughed at him, knowing that she was dead. 54/ But he took her by the hand, called out and said, "Child, get up!" 55/ And her spirit returned, and she got up at once. Then he ordered that she be given something to eat. 56/ Her parents were astounded; but he ordered them to tell no one what had happened.

Analysis

Markan priority in relation to the other Synoptics is so obvious in this pericope, despite minor agreements between Matthew and Luke,[1] that no secondary tradition need be assumed here.[2] The similarity in form and content between Luke 8:44 and Matt 9:20 is nevertheless puzzling. Did both independently use Mark 6:56b in advance? Or is the mention of κράσπεδον ("fringe") in Luke 8:44 secondary (D and *it* do not have it)? Most likely, the weight of oral tradition, still alive during Matthew and Luke's era, is the motive force here.

---

1 Ἰδού . . . ἄρχων ("just then . . . a leader," v. 41), θυγάτηρ ("daughter," v. 42), προσελθοῦσα ὄπισθεν ἤψατο τοῦ κρασπέδου τοῦ ἱματίου αὐτοῦ ("came up to him and touched the fringe of his clothes from behind," v. 44), εἰς τὴν οἰκίαν ("to the house," v. 51).

2 Contra Marie-Emile Boismard, in idem, P. E. Benoit, and A. Lamouille, eds., *Synopse des quatre Évangiles en français* (3 vols.; Paris: Cerf, 1965–77) 2.194–211. Also Schramm (*Markus-Stoff*, 126–27) does not presuppose any supplementary tradition here.

Luke never uses his sources, particularly Mark, without rewriting. Although the content remains the same,[3] the language and style are always more narrative, fluent, and elegant, and in a word, easier to read.[4] In the narrative frame, it is clear that Luke mentions Jesus' departure already in v. 37, and takes up the intervening time by narrating the return of the healed man to his home (vv. 38–39), in order to make the length of the voyage more perceptible to his audience. So everyone returns (ὑποστρέφω, "to return," three times, vv. 37, 39, 40). At the end (v. 56), Luke skips over the preaching in Nazareth (Mark 6:1–6a), which he has already narrated at length (4:16–30), and continues with the commissioning of the disciples. The transition thereby becomes a bit rough, but Luke produces a connection between the two pericopes through the addition of the word δύναμις ("power") in 9:1 (cf. 8:46 par. Mark 5:30).[5]

In his introduction to the pericope, Luke neglects many of the matters of lesser importance (cf. v. 37b) in order to concentrate on the emotions of the crowd. As often, this is illustrated narratively: the crowd waits for Jesus and receives him warmly.[6] Luke thereby creates a small transitional summary passage. Thus, in the rest of its development, the course of the narrative becomes tighter, smoother, and slightly altered. According to Jairus's request,[7] the daughter is his only child (μονογενής), and her age (twelve years) is given here already (cf. Mark 5:42). Why does Luke omit the laying on of hands, differently than he does in 4:40? The hope for healing remains unexpressed (Luke 8:42), in contrast to

Mark 5:23, since Luke connects salvation with faith (cf. Luke 8:12, 25a, 50).[8]

Luke simplifies the account of the woman's illness, and her hope and miraculous healing, in order to emphasize the dialogue that follows.[9] Jesus' question (v. 45; cf. v. 46a) is rhetorical, since he knows who has touched him (v. 46b–47a). The "reproachful undertone of the answer"[10] of the disciples (Mark 5:31) disappears in Peter's polite response.[11] Jesus' omniscience is juxtaposed to the disciples' lack of knowledge. Luke contrasts the general denial (Luke adds ἀρνουμένων δὲ πάντων, "when all denied it," to his source in Mark) with the woman's later confession before the crowd (ἀπήγγειλεν ἐνώπιον παντὸς τοῦ λαοῦ, "she declared in the presence of all the people," which is different from Mark 5:33b, "she told him the whole truth"). Since the woman has already been healed, Luke deletes the command, "be healed from your illness" (Mark 5:34).

Uncharacteristically,[12] Luke retains the historical present (ἔρχεται, "he comes," v. 49) for the sake of drama. But he alters the present imperative into an aorist (πίστευσον, "believe," v. 50), probably because, for him, Jairus does not yet believe. The accompaniment of the three disciples, the entry into the house that is mentioned twice, and the entry into the room (Mark 5:37–40) are summarized in a single sentence.[13] The disadvantage of this shortening is that one is no longer sure exactly who is both mourning the girl and mocking Jesus (vv. 52–53). In any case, Jesus stands alone against all who know that the girl has died. This temporary cer-

---

3   See Schlatter, 89.

4   Klostermann (101–3) and Busse (*Wunder*, 219–26) have examined Luke's version down to the last detail. According to Schramm (*Markus-Stoff*, 127) two features in 8:40–56 are not typical for Luke: the use of ὑπάγω ("to return," "to go") in v. 42 and the use of direct speech in v. 46b. One should note that the direct speech—influenced by the text of Mark—actually begins earlier in v. 46a (ἥψατό μού τις, "someone touched me"). Though the verb ὑπάγω never occurs in the book of Acts, a similar use of its infinitive can be found in Luke 17:14.

5   See Busse, *Wunder*, 220.

6   Luke also uses προσδοκάω ("to wait") in Luke 1:21; 3:15; 7:19–20; 12:46. It is usually the crowds who are waiting. In the NT only Luke uses ἀποδέχομαι ("to welcome," "to receive," elsewhere in Luke 9:11; Acts 2:41; 18:27; 21:17; 24:3; 28:30). The word always indicates a positive acceptance or reception.

7   See Busse (*Wunder*, 221): "Partially in indirect speech, partially in an objective report with the transformation of the necessary information."

8   See Busse, *Wunder*, 221.

9   Luke does not indicate the woman's motive for touching Jesus (Mark 5:28). In this way he can more easily emphasize her faith in v. 48. The power that emanates from Jesus is described in the dialogue (v. 46) rather than the narrative (Mark 5:30).

10   Busse, *Wunder*, 222.

11   See Klostermann, 102–3.

12   Out of ninety instances, this is the only time that Luke does not change the historic present in Mark (see Busse, *Wunder*, 222 n. 1).

13   See Klostermann, 103.

tainty increases the dramatic tension. As in v. 40, Luke prefers inner intensity to external commotion ($\vartheta\acute{o}\rho\upsilon\beta\sigma\varsigma$ vs. $\vartheta\rho\rho\upsilon\beta\epsilon\hat{\iota}\sigma\vartheta\epsilon$, Mark 5:38–39). Does he delete $\tau\alpha\lambda\iota\vartheta\grave{\alpha}$ $\kappa\sigma\hat{\upsilon}\mu$ ("arise, little girl") because he generally avoids foreign words, or because this $\beta\alpha\rho\beta\alpha\rho\iota\kappa\grave{\eta}\ \lambda\acute{\epsilon}\xi\iota\varsigma$ ("barbarian phrase") sounds like a magical spell in the ears of a Greek reader?[14] For Luke it is important that the girl's spirit returns before she arises. He simplifies the command to be silent (v. 56), and the command to bring something to eat is moved forward, logically, as a demonstration of the efficacy of the healing (v. 55).

The summary passage (v. 40) serves form-critically both as a transition and as an introduction. The miracle account begins with $\kappa\alpha\grave{\iota}\ \iota\delta\sigma\acute{\upsilon}$ ("and see," "just then"), for which vv. 41–42a form the introduction and exposition.[15] The sick girl does not appear, but rather her father, who justifies his request.[16] The accompaniment of the crowd (v. 42b) makes possible the second miracle story, which prolongs the drama, and shows the main elements of the genre[17] in a different order (vv. 43–48). Since, contrary to the usual structure, a representative (the father) and then an envoy (the servant) appear, an intermezzo is needed to allow time for the sick girl to die. Either oral tradition or Mark himself used this need cleverly and intercalated two miracle stories in "sandwich" fashion.[18] The second story suits the first both narratively and theologically, because two women, a younger and an older one, are healed and accepted by Jesus; twelve years also plays a role for both. In both cases, as well, a weak faith grows stronger.

The first miracle story is interrupted in the middle of its exposition. It only continues dramatically with the news of the girl's death (v. 49). After a word of encouragement (v. 50), the actual description of the miracle follows: (1) an introductory depiction of the scene (v. 51); (2) misunderstanding and ridicule, which usually belong in the exposition (vv. 52–53); (3) the touch and the miracle-working word (v. 54); (4) the miracle itself[19] and its ascertainment (v. 55). Verse 56 forms the conclusion of the entire composition with the awe expressed at the miracle that has been performed and the command to remain silent.[20]

This pericope is important to Luke not only because he found it in his Markan source, but also because of the sociology of its functional setting. It is usually claimed that this is the context of missionary preaching in the Hellenistic world.[21] But even in the oral tradition, Jesus the wonder-worker did not play the only significant role. Both the women are relevant, especially in their relationship with Jesus. Sociologically, the account does not concern merely the crescendo from healing to resurrection,[22] but also Jesus' acceptance of two women, that is, their acceptance by the early Christian community. The first, the older one, receives healing despite her halakhic

---

14   Busse opts for the second solution (*Wunder*, 223): Luke wants to avoid the misconception that Jesus' miracle has anything to do with magic.

15   See Theissen, *Miracle Stories*, 72–74.

16   Numbers 1, 2, 4, 8, 10, and 12 of Theissen's table (*Miracle Stories*, 73–74).

17   The structure of the intervening miracle (vv. 43–48) consists of three parts: (1) an introduction (focusing on the woman) and exposition (v. 43); (2) the miracle itself (v. 44); and (3) an even longer conclusion in the form of a dialogue, in which Jesus turns first to his disciples and then to the woman (vv. 45–48).

18   See Theissen (*Miracle Stories*, 50): "The most attractive narrative use of the motif of delay."

19   The indication that the girl's life breath returns (v. 55a) signifies a development of Mark's text. This return of the life breath is not a confirmation of the miracle, but rather the miracle itself, which is generally not described in the NT.

20   Numbers 18, 21, 13, 14, 22, 24, 26, 30, and 29 of Theissen's table (*Miracle Stories*, 73–74).

21   See Gnilka, *Markus*, 1.213. Kertelge distinguishes sharply between the pre-Markan tradition and Mark's redaction (*Wunder*, 110–20). He attributes to Mark the secrecy motif, and the hermeneutical function of Jesus' resurrection for the interpretation of the two miracles. Besides the characteristic outline of the Hellenistic miracle story, he also mentions elements borrowed from the HB. He wonders whether to assign the healing of the woman with the discharge of blood to the trajectory of Moses (during the exodus there was no sickness) and the resuscitation of the girl to the trajectory of Elijah and Elisha.

22   If one turns back a page, one finds that an exorcism immediately precedes the healing (Luke 8:26–39).

impurity. Does this not mean that the early community administered forgiveness and acceptance into the church just as Jesus did, in clear distancing from synagogue regulations? If one is aware of the extent to which the vocabulary of resurrection was used in the early church to describe Christian existence,[23] could one not see in the daughter of Jairus the experience of young Christian women? Sociologically, Jairus, the head of the synagogue, could reflect the attraction of the synagogue to early Christianity. In this respect, faith could also be considered, historically, an expression of the success of early Christian preaching.[24]

The manuscript tradition is unstable at many points. The phrase "who spent all she had on doctors" (v. 43) is missing in some important manuscripts.[25] It still represents, however, a good stylistic reworking of Mark 5:26 by Luke;[26] but every decision in this case remains hypothetical in the final analysis. In v. 44 the words "touched the fringe of his clothes" is probably original in view of the weight of the manuscripts in question,[27] whereas the mention of the disciples alongside Peter ($\kappa\alpha\grave{\iota}$ $o\acute{\iota}$ $\sigma\grave{\nu}\nu$ $\alpha\grave{\upsilon}\tau\hat{\wp}$, "and those with him," v. 45) is a post-Lukan harmonizing addition. The same is true for the words $\kappa\alpha\grave{\iota}$ $\lambda\acute{\epsilon}\gamma\epsilon\iota\varsigma$ · $\tau\acute{\iota}\varsigma$ o $\grave{\alpha}\psi\acute{\alpha}\mu\epsilon\nu\acute{o}\varsigma$ $\mu o\upsilon$ ("and you say: who touched me?") attested at the end of v. 45 in numerous manuscripts. The variant versions of this particular reading and the shorter text in important manuscripts such as P[75], ℵ, and B speak against its originality. Although the well-attested $\mu\eta\kappa\acute{\epsilon}\tau\iota$ ("no longer") in v. 49 is a hapax legomenon, Luke apparently used it here under the influence of Mark 5:35 ($\tau\acute{\iota}$ $\acute{\epsilon}\tau\iota$) and of the $\acute{\epsilon}\tau\iota$ that he already used. The sequence of the apostles (Peter, John, and James) in v. 51 is most probably that in Acts 1:13, rather than that in Luke 6:14. James before John is well attested, but influenced by Mark 5:37. In v. 54 one per-

ceives the weight of the Markan text in the manuscripts that add $\grave{\epsilon}\kappa\beta\alpha\lambda\grave{\omega}\nu$ $\acute{\epsilon}\xi\omega$ $\pi\acute{\alpha}\nu\tau\alpha\varsigma$ $\kappa\alpha\acute{\iota}$ ("he threw out everyone and"). Although corruptions can enter the text accidentally in the process of transmission (the shorter text in v. 43 could reflect the loss of a line), the great number of variants can be explained on the basis of known tendencies, above all from harmonization with other Gospels.

Commentary

■ **40** The crowds have accompanied Jesus since 8:4, but several days have likely elapsed (8:22). Jesus has left his country to make a stop on the other side of the lake (8:26–27). After working a miracle, he returns[28] and is welcomed by the crowds.

In Jewish eschatology one "awaits" ($\pi\rho o\sigma\delta o\kappa\acute{\alpha}\omega$) the Messiah (7:19–20), and in Luke's time Christians are awaiting his parousia (2 Pet 3:12–14).[29] The waiting in v. 40 is thus hardly neutral, as also $\acute{o}\chi\lambda o\varsigma$ is not any sort of crowd, but should be viewed as an image of the people of God (cf. 8:47). Luke is thus adding a theological significance to information provided by Mark. The crowd's reception is thus connected with joy.[30] Like the Christians in Luke's time, the people experience the absence and renewed presence of the Lord. Theology and experience are inseparably connected with one another. Verse 42 shows that the crowds play no secondary role in Luke[31] (in contrast especially to Matthew), and still have to learn how to go to meet someone.

■ **41** Verse 41 prosaically transmits a series of details, a few of which are actually unnecessary. Those exegetes

---

23 See the baptismal hymn in Eph 5:14.

24 I first became aware of this sociological perspective through the papers of Roy Bowen Ward and Howard Clark Kee at the 1983 Society for New Testament Studies seminar held in Canterbury.

25 According to Nestle-Aland. See the apparatus there as well as that in the *New Testament in Greek*, and also the remarks of Metzger, *Textual Commentary*, 145.

26 The verb $\pi\rho o\sigma\alpha\nu\alpha\lambda\acute{\iota}\sigma\kappa\omega$ ("to spend") is a hapax legomenon in the NT. Luke also uses the simple verb $\grave{\alpha}\nu\alpha\lambda\acute{\iota}\sigma\kappa\omega$ in its literal sense (Luke 9:54), in a statement taken from the HB. Luke is also familiar

with the meaning "material goods" for $\acute{o}$ $\beta\acute{\iota}o\varsigma$ (e.g., Luke 21:4, where he writes $\pi\acute{\alpha}\nu\tau\alpha$—and not $\acute{o}\lambda o\nu$ as here—$\tau\grave{o}\nu$ $\beta\acute{\iota}o\nu$, "all she had to live on").

27 See Metzger, *Textual Commentary*, 145–46.

28 $\Upsilon\pi o\sigma\tau\rho\acute{\epsilon}\varphi\omega$ ("to return") is used exclusively in the NT by Luke, e.g., for the happy return from a missionary trip (Luke 10:17).

29 Or they are no longer expecting it (see Luke 12:46; Matt 24:50).

30 See Plummer, 234. In Luke 9:11 Jesus welcomes the crowd.

31 By "crowd" Luke indicates the totality of those who are overwhelmed by God's love in Christ. The

who lay weight on the Hebrew meaning of the name Jairus[32] believe that it existed in the earliest form of the story. But this is probably a feature from the novelizing tendencies of later transmission, as is his position as head of synagogue.[33] No reader can mistake Jesus' greatness, when this holder of high office bows down before him and petitions him. The Christian affair is thus not a merely incidental and dubious sect.[34]

■ **42** Verse 42 contains both the indispensable elements of the "skeleton" of the narrative as well as hints about its "flesh." Many passages from antiquity describe fatherly love for a daughter. Luke describes this exclusive relationship with $\mu o \nu o \gamma \epsilon \nu \eta \varsigma$ ("only [daughter]"),[35] in a world that, in contrast to our own, values a multiple number of children. The tragedy is intensified by the fact that the daughter who lies dying[36] has just become nubile, and is thus at an age at which she can give life to others. Jesus' agreement to go to the house, which is of course important, is only mentioned, since the narrative now takes a twist. It turns toward the crowd.[37] Their pressing in around Jesus allows the entrance of the second woman.

■ **43–48** Her condition is all the more dramatic because

her discharge of blood renders her ritually unclean and thus socially isolated. Contact with her is forbidden by the Law. Thus the word $\ddot{\alpha}\pi\tau o\mu\alpha\iota$ ("to touch") is key here.

Discharges of blood in women are treated in Lev 15:25–30. After stating that a woman is ritually impure, it lists the objects and people that become impure through contact with her. Last, it describes the offering to be made upon recovery. Lev 15:31 is valid for all the cases described: the impure person must be kept separate, and any contact with the sanctuary for her is strongly prohibited.[38] The Mishnah tractate *Zabim* treats Leviticus 15, but more from the perspective of the man who has an emission of semen than from that of the woman with a discharge of blood, who is to be treated analogously. Great emphasis is placed on the possibility of contagion and the degree of impurity. The reason for the impurity is that the flow of semen comes from a dead member, in contrast to an ejaculation of semen, which comes from living flesh.[39] It is difficult to say how broadly distributed this complicated regulation already was at the time of Jesus.[40] The LXX seems to have read Leviticus 15 less ritualistically (cf. Lev 15:31 LXX). It

crowd remains a loose collection of people, even though they have already been following Jesus for some time. As an assembly called out and preferred over Jesus' own family, the crowd can also be dismissed again. Will they turn against Jesus? See Rudolf Meyer, "ὄχλος," *TDNT* 5 (1967) 586–88.

32 More likely "illumined by God" rather than "awakened by God." Those exegetes who give more weight to etymology opt, of course, for the second possibility. Gnilka (*Markus*, 1.211, esp. n. 12) urges against such excessive etymologizing. On the various individuals with the name Jairus in the Bible and in contemporary sources, see Fitzmyer, 1.745.

33 In v. 41 Luke corrects εἷς τῶν ἀρχισυναγώγων (Mark 5:22) to "the head of the synagogue." In v. 49 (= Mark 5:35) he retains the title, and in v. 51 he omits it along with all of Mark 5:38. This procedure can be explained by Luke's concern to clarify an uncommon word (even though according to BAGD *s.v.* the title ἀρχισυνάγωγος was used in other religious communities besides Judaism) and to avoid repetition. On the organization of the synagogue at that time, see Romano Penna, "Les Juifs à Rome au temps de l'apôtre Paul," *NTS* 28 (1981–82) 321–47, esp. 328–30. The title ἄρχοντες, as the designation for the executive committee of the council of elders, appears quite frequently (at least fifty times) in literary attestations and inscriptions that refer to the Jewish community of Rome. Ἀρχισυνάγωγος occurs five times and indicates the individual responsible for the buildings, the worship services, and formal governance.

34 See Acts 26:26.

35 The adjective μονογενής ("only [daughter]") is missing in Matthew and Mark.

36 One notes the imperfect ἀπέθνῃσκεν ("she was dying").

37 To underscore that Jesus is being pressed from every side, Luke writes "crowd" in the plural (v. 42). Συμπνίγω means "to smother," "to choke" (see Luke 8:14, the parable of the seed).

38 The MT of Lev 15:31 can be understood in different ways: as an offense committed by the impure person, or as a protection of the pure person from the impure. The text of the LXX differs markedly from this: the impure Israelites shall be careful and devout by turning away from their impurities (καὶ εὐλαβεῖς ποιήσετε τοὺς υἱοὺς Ἰσραὴλ ἀπὸ τῶν ἀκαθαρσιῶν αὐτῶν, "and you shall make the sons of Israel acceptable from their impurities").

39 See *t. Zabim* 2.4; also the preface to the tractate *Zabim* (*Mischnajot: Die sechs Ordnungen der Mischna* [Basel: V. Goldschmidt, 1968] 6.588).

40 See Jacob Neusner, *A History of the Mishnaic Law of*

may suffice simply to mention the structure of purity and impurity as a hermeneutical aid.

A discharge of blood during or apart from menstruation belongs to the sphere of death and impurity, in contrast to living blood, the gift of God and carrier of life (Lev 17:11). Like illness, impurity is contagious. God's Law and human traditions intend to preserve life, to determine with the utmost seriousness the extent and degree of impurification that has already taken place, and to guard against further evil. Both the sick individual and the rest of the people of God must be protected.

According to the Law and its interpretation at that time, the unclean woman was not supposed to enter into a crowd. If she touches someone (v. 44), this is a sin and renders that person impure for a day. But in v. 48, on the contrary, Jesus interprets this action on the part of the woman as faith. Verse 43 vividly expresses her previous useless attempts to be healed. She has spent her entire fortune on doctors,[41] but none could heal her. Her misery is thus threefold: she has no more possessions, she has lost her health, and her ritual impurity has separated her from God and from other people. In this condition she nevertheless dares to hope and to trust in Jesus. The stereotypical formula, "your faith has saved you," has a sociological functional setting in the early Christian church: the woman with the discharge of blood is the symbol of people who would like to be accepted by the church. With this formula, and with the telling of such miracle stories, the early church, in contrast to the synagogue, emphasizes its conviction that God will not keep such people at a distance. Unlike God's law regarding the sanctuary (Lev 15:31), Jesus as the representative of God does not subject such people with discharges of blood to the danger of death. On the contrary, a healing power streams forth from him that restores life (v. 46). The instant healing ($\pi\alpha\rho\alpha\chi\rho\hat{\eta}\mu\alpha$, "immediately," v. 44, is repeated in the conclusion in

v. 47) shows divine agreement and the new definition of faith.

This unrestrained power seems magical to us. But Luke reports such miracles through direct contact in other passages (7:14; Acts 5:14; 19:11–12). Here he wishes only to emphasize God's new saving intention through his sent messenger. Despite the easily misunderstood wording of the formula, it is not faith that heals but the power of God. This new economy of salvation, however, demands a certain human attitude: $\pi\iota\sigma\tau\iota\varsigma$ ("faith"). This is far different from magic. Death and life, perdition and salvation are placed next to one another and after one another in this story: the flow of blood is vividly stanched[42] by the exercise of divine power.

Despite the criticism of the Law contained in this story, Jesus is presented as a Jew. He wears on his garment the fringe demanded by Moses (Num 15:37–39; Deut 22:12). This was braided from four individual threads of virgin wool, of which three (later two) were white, and one (later two) were bluish purple, to indicate heaven. These were sewed and knotted in the four corners of the garment, but not right on the edges.[43] The outer garment, worn as a shawl would be today, would not fall completely to the ground. Thus it is understandable that the afflicted woman would be able to touch Jesus' garment from behind, even in the crowd.[44] The main passage about the fringe (Num 15:37–39) states that it will be a sign to people to remind them to run not after their own sinful thoughts ($\dot{o}\pi\iota\sigma\omega$, "after," occurs twice), but after the commands of God. Does the text thus discreetly indicate that the woman who stands behind Jesus and touches his fringe wishes to keep the commands of God in mind, and not her own sinful thoughts? Then the juxtaposition of law and gospel would be even more deeply rooted in the narrative, and the woman would be presented as a model not only of faith but of the new obedience.

Purities (SJLA 6; Leiden: Brill, 1977) 16.194–211.

41 This statement sounds like a detail from a romance. Cf. *Acts Phil.* 4:4–6 (40–44): the apostle Philip is successful in healing the daughter of Nikokleides, for whom no doctor could procure relief.

42 The change from $\xi\eta\rho\alpha\dot{\iota}\nu\omega$ ("to dry up," Mark) to $\ddot{\iota}\sigma\tau\eta\mu\iota$ ("to stop," Luke) is more likely a result of Luke's literary sensibilities rather than his alleged medical knowledge. On the intransitive use of $\ddot{\iota}\sigma\tau\eta\mu\iota$ (e.g., to express that a discharge of blood

has come to an end), see BAGD *s.v.* $\ddot{\iota}\sigma\tau\eta\mu\iota$ (II.1a).

43 See Str-B 4.1.277–92. The Greek word $\tau\dot{o}\ \kappa\rho\dot{\alpha}\sigma\pi\epsilon-\delta o\nu$ signifies the edge, the hem, or the border of something. In the LXX the term is used five times (of which four are in the plural), three times for צִיצִת, and twice for כָּנָף.

44 See Godet, 1.390–91.

The end of the story begins for Jesus with a double obstacle, first the crowd (v. 42b) and then the woman with the discharge of blood. Jesus first has a normal reaction (v. 45a) that draws out an answer from the suspects. All defend themselves,[45] and Peter defends the crowd, including the woman, politely and extensively (v. 45b).[46] Jesus is not, however, satisfied with this answer, and retorts (v. 46). The verb "to notice"[47] has the effect of a threat. The woman, whose story is described in full detail (v. 47), gives her confession. When she sees that nothing can remain hidden from the Lord, she comes forward trembling and throws herself down at his feet. She describes the two phases of the event, that is, the reason for her action and its final result. The reader now anxiously awaits the conclusion. The climax is not the miracle itself, but the word of Jesus, which is not a word of punishment but a word of acceptance. This is the point of the episode. The woman need have no fear; her touching Jesus was a sign of her faith, unlike the pressing of the crowd. And God affirms such faith.[48] Jesus' address of $\vartheta υγάτηρ$ ("daughter"), to a woman who is likely older than he, is astonishing. One must see in it both the customary address of a Jewish teacher,[49] and at the same time, the authority of the Christian Messiah.[50]

This insertion into the other miracle story "expresses even more clearly the element of lateness."[51] True faith proves itself above all when, in the face of certain events, everything is too late, humanly speaking. The last test of faith is death. "On faith without limits"[52] is the title that best corresponds to the content of the Markan and Lukan versions of this pericope, this in contrast to the Matthean version, which praises the miracle of resurrection and neglects the issue of faith. The episode of the woman with the discharge of blood forces Jesus to arrive at the house of the sick girl too late.[53] Does the coupling of both stories indicate the problem of discrimination? If one takes time to help a needy person,[54] will not then other poor, sick, and, above all, dead people be neglected? The Thessalonians ask this question.[55] Is not this tragedy of the love of one's neighbor unavoidable? In his use of the Markan version, Luke emphasizes, almost in Pauline fashion but with Johannine accents, that it is never too late for God, because God uses even situations in which—humanly speaking—everything is far too late, in order to reveal the glory of his Son.

■ **49** The story first seems to affirm that the faint hope in v. 42 is now extinguished. This occurs through the message of one of Jairus's domestic servants,[56] who declares in the form of a nearly insolent piece of advice

---

45 One can touch another person either as a result of being pushed in a throng or as a deliberate act. Either way, whoever denies touching another person denies doing it consciously.

46 On $\dot{ε}πιστάτης$ ("master"), see the commentary on Luke 5:5 above. $\dot{Α}ποϑλίβω$ means "to press," "squeeze," "press out" "press in" (cf. Num 22:25 LXX). Peter means that the crowd was pushing and pressing against Jesus.

47 The aorist $\ddot{ε}γνων$ refers to the moment when Jesus perceives and determines that power has gone out from him.

48 Roloff (*Kerygma*,153–55) emphasizes the $πίστις$ ("faith") of the woman. He rightly considers v. 48 as the climax of the intervening story. This faith has nothing to do with magic or with autosuggestion. According to Roloff, it is not this faith motif that caused these two stories to be linked together.

49 The vocative "daughter" is used already in the HB to refer to a relationship beyond family ties. This form of address can be employed when speaking to a woman who is either younger or holds a lower

position (e.g., Ps 45:11 [LXX 44:12]; Zeph 3:14; Lam 4:21–22). See J. Kühlewein, "בַּ‎," *TLOT* 1.241.

50 Cf. Luke 13:16.

51 Willi Marxsen, "Bibelarbeit über Mk 5,21–43 / Mt 9,18–26," in idem, *Der Exeget als Theologe: Vorträge zum Neuen Testament* (Gütersloh: Mohn, 1968) 175.

52 Marxsen, "Bibelarbeit," 180. In Matthew the girl is already dead at beginning of the story. The faith of the father is not being tested: Mark 5:36 par. Luke 8:50 has no parallel in Matthew.

53 Marxsen ("Bibelarbeit"), however, does not explain why a story like that of the woman with a discharge of blood would be chosen to serve this purpose.

54 Note that the expression $\ddot{ε}τι αὐτοῦ λαλοῦντος$ ("while he was still speaking") is typical of Luke (cf. 22:47).

55 Marxsen ("Bibelarbeit," 176–77) mentions 1 Thess 4:13–18, though without drawing this conclusion.

56 Lit. "one from beside the head of the synagogue"; in contrast to v. 41, Luke here retains the title regularly used by Mark, $\dot{α}ρχισυνάγωγος$ ("leader of the synagogue"; see the notes to v. 41 above).

to his master, "Do not trouble[57] the teacher any longer." Jesus' title of "teacher" comes from Mark.

■ **50** Verse 50 is narratively somewhat inept, but nevertheless extremely relevant theologically: despite all the grammatical ambiguity, αὐτῷ designates the father.[58] The reason that he should not "fear" stems from the context of revelation,[59] for the whole story is coming to its climax. The divine messenger becomes active. He first asks for trust.[60] The author connects with the last word of Jesus in the interpolated story, which already related faith and healing (v. 48). Here faith is not ascertained after the miracle, but is demanded beforehand. The account neglects to mention again the prior faith of the father; in its earlier transmission, the narrative first described Jesus as wonder-worker, and then picked up the theme of faith, that is, the attitude of the father. The significance of πιστεύω ("to believe") and σῴζω ("to save") are initially limited to the case of the girl who has died, but the reader sees beyond this to understand that it also means everyone's death and resurrection, and the Christian faith as such.

■ **51** Verse 51 follows one of the rules of the genre: the miracle is prepared, that is, the scene is set. The mystery of it is indicated in that only a few privileged individuals should be present: the same group of three from among the disciples who are otherwise there at particularly important stages of Jesus' life (cf. 9:28), the child's[61] father, and, in last place, the mother.

■ **52–53** Although it is not clear in Luke, the people in v. 52 are most likely other people, friends, and mourners. One knows the rites of mourning fairly well from the Hebrew Bible.[62] Luke economically limits the description to crying and breast-beating. The ceremony of mourning develops more quietly and normally than in Mark. In order to create the necessary calm to perform the miracle, Jesus requests those present to interrupt the mourning ritual, "for she is not dead but sleeping."[63] The laughter of these people who are, in part, professionals, is reminiscent of the doubt typically expressed in the genre of miracle accounts[64] as well as of pagan laughter at Christian preaching of the resurrection (Acts 17:32). The apparently rational people (v. 53) and Jesus, who rests in God, are emphatically contrasted to one another.

■ **54** "To take by the hand" is an expression of help in the Bible.[65] Through words and gestures, verbal and nonverbal, Jesus effects the resuscitation of the girl.[66] Ἐφώνησεν ("he called out") describes (differently than λέγων, "he said") the role of the voice, and foreshadows the active power of the word.[67] Ἔγειρε is an imperative with the intransitive meaning "wake up" or "stand up."[68]

■ **55–56** The expression "and her spirit returned" is unique to Luke. Behind this is the idea that the spirit or soul of a dead person remains for a while (the Jews usually thought of three days) in the vicinity of the corpse, before it departs forever for the world of the dead. The

---

57 Σκύλλω means lit. "to flay," "to skin." Did the cultivated public of Luke's day regard its use in the figurative sense, "to weary," "to annoy," as vulgar? In Luke 7:6 the middle voice is used (μὴ σκύλλου).

58 The αὐτῷ in v. 50 is somewhat awkward: Luke intends it to indicate the father who is present, while the reader probably thinks first of the servant who has just spoken.

59 On μὴ φοβοῦ ("do not fear") in connection with the "numinous," see the commentary on 1:13 and 1:30 above.

60 Mark uses the present imperative (πίστευε), which expresses duration and generality. Luke (8:50) employs the aorist imperative (πίστευσον), which calls for a quick response in a particular context.

61 Luke here calls the girl ἡ παῖς (v. 51). He puts the same expression in Jesus' mouth (v. 54). Mark uses τὸ παιδίον four times and τὸ κοράσιον twice.

62 See Eva Osswald, "Trauer," *BHH* 3 (1966) 2021–23.

63 Καθεύδω means "to lie down," "to lie down to sleep," "to sleep." Κοιμάω is often used in the NT

in either the passive or middle voice, but its active sense is "to lie on a bed," "to stretch out."

64 See Theissen, *Miracle Stories*, 56.

65 See Peter von der Osten-Sacken, "κρατέω," *EDNT* 2 (1991) 314–15. In order to express a rescue by God, the HB occasionally uses the expression "God takes someone by the hand" (see Ps 73 [LXX 72]:23, ἐκράτησας τῆς χειρὸς τῆς δεξιᾶς μου, "you hold my right hand").

66 The nominative ὁ or ἡ παῖς is frequently used in the place of the vocative (the vocative παῖ appears to be either avoided or no longer known).

67 On the role that the word itself played in ancient medicine, see Pedro Laín Entralgo, *La Curación por la Palabra en la Antigüedad Clásica* (Madrid: Revista de Occidente, 1958).

68 See BAGD *s.v.* ἐγείρω (1b).

miracle is greater in 7:12–13, where the young man is already lying in the coffin, and still greater in John 11, where Lazarus was laid in his grave four days before. The second miracle (καὶ ἀνέστη παραχρῆμα, "and she got up at once") occurs in symmetry to the first (καὶ παραχρῆμα ἔστη ἡ ῥύσις τοῦ αἵματος αὐτῆς, "and immediately [her] discharge stopped," 8:44). Luke is here able to use, as does Mark, the two usual verbs for resurrection, ἐγείρω (v. 54) and ἀνίσταμαι (v. 55). The story has reached its climax. The miracle is confirmed in that the girl eats something (v. 55) and the parents are amazed (v. 56); both statements have the function of lending credence to this unbelievable event. The lack of any reaction on the part of the three disciples shows that mention of them should be judged a secondary addition to the original story.

The command to remain silent is not an expression of Luke's christology, but is part of the genre of a miracle account. It underscores the mysterious atmosphere and the humble attitude of the miracle-worker, who wants neither money (cf. v. 43) nor fame.

Conclusion

In the midst of an expectant crowd, Jesus accepts the contact forbidden by the Law with the ritually impure and with death. Despite their suffering, indeed, even though everything seems to speak against it, the trust that the father of the girl and the afflicted woman show in Jesus has no limits. In their faith in God and trust in Jesus, the woman and the girl experience the healing power of God, and become a paradigm for the Jewish Christian and Gentile Christian communities.

The Commissioning of the Twelve (9:1–6)

Bibliography

Beare, Francis W., "The Mission of the Disciples and the Mission Charge: Matthew 10 and Parallels," *JBL* 89 (1970) 1–13.

Bultmann, *History*, 145, 332, 408.

Degenhardt, Hans-Joachim, *Lukas, Evangelist der Armen: Besitz and Besitzverzicht in den lukanischen Schriften: Eine traditions- und redaktionsgeschichtliche Untersuchung* (Stuttgart: Katholisches Bibelwerk, 1965) 60–68.

Delebecque, Edouard, "'Secouez la poussière de vos pieds': Sur l'hellénisme de Luc IX,5," *RB* 89 (1982) 177–84.

Ford, Josephine Massyngberde, "Money 'bags' in the Temple (Mk 11,16)," *Bib* 57 (1976) 249–53.

Frizzi, Giuseppe, "Mandare-inviare in Luca-Atti, una chiave importante per la comprensione dell'escatologia di Luca," *RivB* 24 (1976) 359–401.

idem, "La 'missione' in Luca-Atti," *RivB* 32 (1984) 395–423.

Fuchs, Albert, "Die synoptische Aussendungsrede in quellenkritischer und traditionsgeschichtlicher Sicht," in SNTU 17 (Linz: Albert Fuchs, 1992) 5–53.

Goulder, Michael D., "From Ministry to Passion in John and Luke," *NTS* 29 (1983) 561–68.

Goulet, "Vies."

Haenchen, *Weg*, 220–34.

Hahn, *Mission*, 41–46.

Hengel, *Charismatic Leader*, 73–80.

Hoffmann, *Logienquelle*, 245–48.

Kaestli, Jean-Daniel, "Les scènes d'attribution des champs de mission et de départ de l'apôtre dans les Actes apocryphes," in Bovon, *Actes apocryphes*, 249–64.

Kasting, Heinrich, *Die Anfänge der urchristlichen Mission* (BEvTh 55; Munich: Kaiser, 1969) 110–14.

Leo, F., "Diogenes bei Plautus," *Hermes* 41 (1906) 441–46.

Lührmann, *Logienquelle*, 59.

Manson, Thomas Walter, *The Sayings of Jesus as Recorded in the Gospels according to St. Matthew and St. Luke* (London: SCM, 1949) 179–82.

Miyoshi, Michi, *Der Anfang des Reiseberichtes Lk 9.51–10.24: Eine redaktionsgeschichtliche Untersuchung* (AnBib 60; Rome: Pontifical Biblical Institute Press, 1974) 59–94.

Moessner, David P., "Luke 9:1–50: Luke's Preview of the Journey of the Prophet Like Moses of Deuteronomy," *JBL* 102 (1983) 575–605.

O'Toole, Robert F., "Luke's Message in Luke 9:1–50," *CBQ* 49 (1987) 74–89.

Røsaeg, N. A., "Hus og vei: En ny eksegese av 'utsendelsestalen' i evangeliene (Lk 10:2–12p; 9:1–6p)," *Tidsskrift for Teologi og Kirke* 63 (1992) 161–79.

Schott, E., "Die Aussendungsrede Mk 10. Mc 6. Lc 9.10," *ZNW* 7 (1906) 140–50.

Schramm, *Markus-Stoff*, 26–28, 128 n. 1, 186.

Schulz, *Q*, 404–19.

Schürmann, Heinz, "Mt 10,5b–6 und die Vorgeschichte des synoptischen Aussendungsberichtes," in J. Blinzler et al., eds., *Neutestamentliche Aufsätze: Festschrift J. Schmid* (Regensburg: F. Pustet, 1963) 270–82 (= Schürmann, *Untersuchungen*, 137–49).

Testa, Emmanuele, "I 'discorsi di missione' di Gesù," *SBFLA* 29 (1979) 7–41.

1 **Then Jesus called the Twelve together and gave them power and authority over all demons and to cure diseases, 2/ and he sent them out to proclaim the kingdom of God and to heal the sick. 3/ And he said to them, "Take nothing for your journey, no staff, nor bag, nor bread, nor silver—not even an extra undergarment. 4/ Whatever house you enter, stay there, and leave from there. 5/ Wherever they do not accept you, leave that town and shake the dust off your feet as a testimony about them." 6/ They departed and went from village to village, proclaiming the good news and curing diseases everywhere.**

Analysis

In chap. 9 Luke continues to follow Mark as his source, which he has been doing since 8:4. He nevertheless skips over various Markan pericopes. Because of the programmatic composition in 4:16–30 (Jesus' preaching in Nazareth), Luke omits Mark 6:1–6a, which would fall between Luke 8 and 9. After reporting Herod's question and the opinion of the masses (9:7–9), Luke leaves out the narration of the death of John (Mark 6:17–29), which he considers to be an anecdotal diversion. Between 9:17 and 9:18, an astonishing series of pericopes is lacking: Jesus walking on the sea, the healing of the sick on the western shore, the dialogue about clean and unclean, the Syrophoenician woman, the healing of a deaf mute, the feeding of the four thousand, the demand for a sign, the leaven of the Pharisees, and the healing of the blind man outside Bethsaida (Mark 6:45–8:26). By doing this, Luke places the remaining Markan material in a new light. Luke 9:1–50 has a christological concentration, and, because the Twelve are actively involved, also an ecclesiological one (Herod's question, Peter's confession, the two predictions of the passion, the transfiguration of Jesus).

The commissioning of the Twelve is told very similarly in Mark and Q,[1] to the extent that one can postulate a single original literary unit.[2] "To the basic form there belong, first the sending out, then the ruling about equipment, further the instruction about behaviour in houses, and finally that about behaviour in towns."[3] This original form is probably a post-Easter composition with archaic elements that had been transmitted independently (see the commentary on v. 3 below). Matthew has blended both accounts in his chap. 10, whereas Luke preserves them separately, transforming the Q account into an extensive description of the commissioning of the seventy (10:1–16), in contrast to this account in 9:1–6. The two commissioning accounts correspond to the two phases of the Christian proclamation, as well as the double origin of the church from Jews and Gentiles, which will leave its imprint on the structure of the book of Acts.

Already in chap. 9, Luke is looking ahead to the material of chap. 10.[4] This is hardly surprising, since the Q account assumes a commissioning of the *Twelve*. The healing of diseases (v. 1), the kingdom of God (and not repentance, Mark 6:9) as the content of the proclamation (v. 2), the proscription of walking sticks (v. 3), and the formulation of the shaking of the dust from one's feet (v. 5) all come from Q. That Luke and Matthew do not describe the disciples being sent out in twos (Mark 6:7) or mention their sandals (Mark 6:12) could also be understood as the influence of Q. The new introductions (Mark 6:8, 10), which leave little trace in Luke (only 9:3) and even less in Matthew, show the original independence of the sayings of Jesus, and their composition into a collection here: the first saying explains the conditions of travel (v. 3), the second, behavior during stays with hosts (vv. 4–5).

The doubling of the commissioning account provides an important index for the function that Luke accords his literary work. He transmits the commissioning of the Twelve; but for his time, his church, and his understanding of the practice of mission, he also needs a mission to the Gentiles proleptically anchored in the life of Jesus. This second account is especially transparent, and betrays the concerns and responsibilities of the Christian mission in Lukan times. In all this, Luke does not produce a completely new composition, since the commissioning of the Twelve already possessed this double character for both Mark and Q.[5] Luke has merely drawn out their intentions to the logical conclusion, in the sense of both past and future salvation history.

The functional setting of this tradition is surely the missionary practice of the earliest communities;[6] despite the usual heading, "The Commissioning of the Twelve,"[7] the account lays less weight on the mission of the disciples than on the commands of the Lord. Structurally, we have a narrative frame (vv. 1–2, 6) in which is embedded a speech of *Jesus* (vv. 3–5, introduced with, "And he said to them"). The latter of course retains a much more lasting value for the church than a few hagiographic tales of the missionary successes of the Twelve. Even the first part of the frame (vv. 1–2) describes the initiative and activity of the Lord, not the disciples. But as an installation of the Twelve, this pericope, like the calling of the Twelve (6:12–16), has a deeper ecclesiological significance. The earliest communities, and then Luke, see in it the legitimizing justification of mission as the normative structure of their practical activity.

Luke is, however, aware that contemporary practice cannot simply adopt the earliest methods slavishly; Jesus was still present as a human being then, and is no longer. In addition, it is now important to proclaim the resurrection of the Son, and not just generally the kingdom of God. Finally, the details of the preparations are no longer applicable in Luke's time (cf. 22:35–38).

---

1   On Mark 6:6b–13 and the material common to Matthew and Luke, see Ferdinand Hahn, *Mission in the New Testament* (trans. F. Clarke; SBT 1.47; Naperville, Ill.: Allenson, 1965) 41–46.

2   See Bultmann, *History*, 145.

3   Hahn, *Mission*, 43.

4   See Schramm, *Markus-Stoff*, 186; and Schneider, 1.200.

5   See Haenchen, *Weg*, 221, 226.

6   Loisy (261) finds in this pericope an expression of the dual function of the first missionaries: preaching and driving out spirits. Luke's effort to bring the story home to his readers also explains why he had to omit Matt 10:5–6, since it prohibits going to the Samaritans and to the Gentiles. On this omission see Godet, 1.399–400.

7   See Aland, *Synopsis*, 200.

Despite this, the narratives in Acts show a relationship between the missionary practice described in the pre-Easter and experienced in the post-Easter periods: (1) Both here and there, the missionary receives power and authority from the Lord (Acts 26:15–18); (2) preaching and healing occur together (Acts 3:1–26); (3) the missionary experiences acceptance or rejection: he or she should use the hospitable house as the center of activity (e.g., Acts 18:7), but in the case of resistance (Acts 13:51; 18:6), continue on and shake the dust from his or her shoes. One can wonder whether the commissioning account in Numbers 13 and Joshua 2 have influenced the New Testament form. Aside from the vocabulary of the commissioning (Num 13:3, 16, 17; Josh 2:1), the number of twelve delegates in Numbers 13 ("one from each tribe," Num 13:2), and a report upon return (διηγήσαντο αὐτῷ, "[they] told [him]," Num 13:27 LXX; cf. Luke 9:10), the goal of the mission and the structure of the accounts differ.

Commentary

The Installation and Commissioning (vv. 1–2)

■ **1** The Twelve[8] appear for the third time in the Gospel of Luke as a closed group: after their calling (6:12–16), they accompany Jesus together with a group of women (8:1–3). Now they are to participate in Jesus' mission, which was already announced beforehand (6:13).[9] Jesus first calls them and gathers them around himself.[10] He then gives them a share in his authority[11] and sends them out. Without receiving this power, the mission would not be fulfillable, but "he gives what he requires." For this reason, the evangelist transposes the Markan sequence (ἀποστέλλω – δίδωμι, "I send—I give").[12] The δύναμις ("power") that makes possible the healings and the ἐξουσία ("authority") that makes possible the exorcisms are assigned to these miracles in chiastic arrangement.[13]

■ **2** If one does not read "the sick" after "heal,"[14] the reference to the twofold task breaks off abruptly. In contrast to Matthew, and probably to Q, the kingdom of God is no longer described by its proximity (Matt 10:7; Luke 10:9). The redactional expression "to proclaim the kingdom of God" (cf. Acts 28:31) comprises the content of Jesus' preaching and the pre-Easter gospel (cf. 4:43).[15] Luke here attributes to the concept "the kingdom of God" more christological weight than eschatological.[16] Just as the Lukan Messiah has been a healing figure until now, his emissaries are also supposed to heal people. They will bring soteriological benefits by word and deed, in the name of Jesus, who has come in the name of God. That which characterizes the activity of Jesus will also determine the Twelve and the seventy (i.e., the church).

8   Some good mss. add the title "Apostles" to "the Twelve." See Metzger (*Textual Commentary*, 146), who speaks too critically of "later copyists."

9   According to Godet (1.396–97), Jesus brings his operations in Galilee to a close by multiplying his influence through the work of the Twelve.

10 While Mark and Matthew use the verb προσκαλέω, Luke employs συγκαλεσάμενος. Note, first, the middle form (he calls them to himself); second, the συν- in συγκαλέω (he calls them together).

11 Luke chooses the punctiliar aorist ἔδωκεν; Mark, however, the imperfect ἐδίδου. In contrast to Schneider (1.201) and Marshall (351), I do not conclude from this that Jesus has given his disciples power and authority only for this one time.

12 Luke, though fond of the vocabulary of "beginning," here deletes Mark's ἤρξατο (Mark 6:7; is it in order to avoid the ambiguity of the Markan expression ἤρξατο αὐτοὺς ἀποστέλλειν, "he began to send them out"?).

13 The parallel in Matthew shows that the topic of healing diseases comes from Q. In order to inte-grate it, Luke inserts the word δύναμις ("power"; on δύναμις see the commentary on 5:17, n. 23). That Luke is using two sources explains the awkwardness in the grammar. Yet Plummer (239) is of the opinion that there are no grammatical problems here: "νόσους θεραπεύειν ['to cure diseases'] depends on δύναμιν καὶ ἐξουσίαν ['power and authority'], and is co-ordinate with ἐπὶ πάντα τὰ δαιμόνια ['over all demons']."

14 The words "the sick" are well attested in the form τοὺς ἀσθενεῖς or τοὺς ἀσθενοῦντας (see Matt 10:8).

15 On κηρύσσω ("to proclaim"), see the commentary on 3:3. According to Godet (1.397–98), the forceful proclamation (the preaching of God's kingdom) is more important than the miracles. It involves telling others about what Jesus has done, calling to mind what he has taught, and proclaiming the crucial significance of his actions and teachings.

16 See Conzelmann, *Theology*, 114 n. 3.

The Preparation for the Journey (vv. 3–5)

■ **3** After the basic assignment come the practical rules for the trip (εἰς τὴν ὁδόν, "on the way") and its individual stages (in the houses). The travel rules contain archaic materials that Christian tradition passes on with respect and very few editorial changes. Verse 3 is constructed logically: (1) the general rule is first given (take nothing); then (2) four forbidden items (walking stick, travel bag, bread, and money[17]), each linked with μήτε; (3) in the conclusion, a fifth basic item, that one can wear but not take along extra (undergarment).[18] Such radical gospel injunctions were most likely followed literally by itinerant preachers in the early days of the church, and probably reflect the eschatological and polemical requirements of the historical Jesus. In Luke's time they were regarded with respect, but are no longer all currently in use, as one sees in the book of Acts. The list describes minimalist preparations for a journey, perhaps in critical engagement with the preparations of pilgrims traveling to Jerusalem.[19] Jesus would then be radically transvaluing the goal, the content, and the conditions of traditional pilgrimage: instead of going up to Jerusalem, one goes to the dispersed children of Israel; instead of fulfilling one's own religious duty, one brings the new message to others. Instead of a pilgrim's equipment, one wears the minimalist outfit of the last days. If this hypothesis were true, missionary travel would achieve a liturgical significance. The missionary would sanctify the profane sphere of the house by his or her activity. The quality of the holy would reach humanity in its worldliness, and people would no longer enter the holy temple. The presupposition of this radical transvaluation would be a meditation on the *location* of the holy presence of God, which would depend no longer on the temple but on the person of the divine messenger. The transfer of the holy from the temple to the person corresponds to Jesus' conviction, and is part of his own self-understanding. Such a shift, however, is also typical of late antiquity.[20] Luke perhaps no longer understands the polemical and apocalyptic import of Jesus' speech, though he does perceive that Jesus sends out the Twelve without human resources, but with divine help. What was originally concrete and literal is now metaphorically true. Later, in 22:35–38, Luke has in mind this change that takes place after the passion and understands divine aid as coming through human intermediaries, without denying the metaphorical language (the image of the sword). Perhaps Luke also wants to distinguish the Christian missionary from the traveling Cynic philosopher, who brings his wisdom to the market with travel bag, walking stick, and coat.[21] The Markan statement about the "staff"[22] sounds complicated, and is a first attempt at accommodation to new circumstances, whereas Luke and Matthew transmit the original version. The prohibition of a pilgrim's staff would be an element in the criticism of Jewish pilgrimage mentioned above.

The renunciation of possessions by the disciples was probably originally an adoption of the Levitical practice (cf. Num 18:31). This is not in opposition to a worker's being worth his or her hire in Luke 10:7 (this appears in Paul in 1 Cor 9:4, 14 as a command of the Lord). What Luke says about being received in the houses is in agreement with this saying. Since 1 Tim 5:18 justifies a salary by referring to Num 18:31 (a Levitical regulation), the Levitical renunciation of possessions and income has probably been applied to the first Christian missionaries. The harmonization of these two commands intends (as in the tradition of manna) the simple survival of the believers, which excludes the possibility of any human hope of the accumulation of possessions. Without per-

---

17 Mark 6:8 reads χαλκόν ("copper coin"; the Greek drachma was worth six oboli, and one obolus was worth eight χαλκοί). Luke prefers ἀργύριον ("silver piece"; ἄργυρος signifies silver as a metal and then also as a minted coin). Ἀργύριον occurs frequently in the LXX (see Baruch Kanael and Ernst Höhne, "Münzen," *BHH* 2 [1964] 1249–56).

18 Two undergarments are implied: the one that is being worn is permitted, the other that is kept in reserve is forbidden. On the distributive ἀνά, see BDF §248.1.

19 See Str-B 1.565 (on Matt 10:9).

20 See Brown, *Antiquity*, 1–26.

21 See F. Leo, "Diogenes bei Plautus," *Hermes* 41 (1906) 441–46; Schürmann, 1.502 n. 24; Schneider, 1.201. On the multilayered ancient image of the philosopher, see Goulet, "Vies."

22 See further the interesting remarks of Marshall, 352.

haps understanding all the Hebrew Bible connotations of these regulations, Luke comprehended the basic pattern of behavior and appropriated it.

■ **4** The saying about the houses is odd (v. 4).[23] The parallel in 10:7 affords some illumination: the congregation should grow out of the first house that converts to the faith. A transfer to another house would cause jealousy and give the impression that the missionary had favorite converts. The natural human tendency to prefer greater comfort is also attacked here. Additionally, the existence of several churches in the same location is also not acceptable. The house becomes the place in which the local congregation assembles, which is clear in Rom 16:5, 1 Cor 16:19, and the book of Acts. "Leave from there" means leave this *house* and this *town*.[24]

■ **5** Verse 5 describes the negative possibility: the rejection of the messengers and their message.[25] This gesture is well known in the ancient Near East. It does not express anger or a desire for revenge, but symbolizes the rupture of human relations and the fear of impurity. The Pharisees shook the dust from their feet upon return to Judea from Gentile regions.[26] We perceive the gesture as lack of love for a neighbor, but it is not the same as a curse.[27] Love of one's neighbor sometimes requires that one leave others alone to be responsible for themselves, for love that tries to force is no longer love. According to Luke, this symbolic behavior was still alive in the time of Paul (Acts 13:51).[28] The nonverbal action speaks louder than words; it constitutes a "testimony about them" (rather than "against them"),[29] that other people—and above all, God—should hear.

The Realization of the Journey (v. 6)

■ **6** Verse 6 says at the same time both little and much;[30] little, because one would like details about this first mission, and much, because Luke soberly and yet emphatically communicates the decisive fact: the disciples obediently follow the command of their Lord. The Apocryphal Acts of the Apostles, on the other hand, mention the first impediments and the initial hesitation of the apostles sent out by the resurrected Lord, and in this way reflect the dangers of travel at that time and the difficulties of the early Christian mission.[31]

Διήρχοντο ("to go through") describes the entire journey through (δια-) the countryside, and κατὰ τὰς κώμας ("from village to village") the various stops along

23 See James Reiling and Jan Lodewijk Swellengrebel, *A Translator's Handbook on the Gospel of Luke* (Helps for Translators 10; Leiden: Brill, 1971) 365: "The clause appears to mean that in each place the disciples are to stay in the very first house which offers them hospitality."

24 See Lagrange, 259. The missionary situation that is presupposed here (new communities are emerging) differs from that described later in the *Didache*, since *Did.* 11.3–6 regulates the brief stay of itinerant apostles in already existing communities. See Haenchen, *Weg*, 222–23; and Willy Rordorf and André Tuilier, *La doctrine des douze apôtres (Didachè)* (SC 248; Paris: Cerf, 1978) 51–63, 184–85.

25 Luke states that they are to go "outside this city" (the expression is missing in Mark 6:11, but is given in Matt 10:14 in even more detail). Luke does not appear to know the words "and if someone does not listen to you" (Mark 6:11), although they are found in Matt 10:14.

26 See Plummer, 240; and Str-B 1.571.

27 Luke reads ἀποτινάσσω, Mark and Matthew ἐκτινάσσω (the two verbs are practically synonyms). Otherwise, Luke's language in v. 5 is closer to that of Matthew, and thus to that of Q.

28 The wording of Acts 13:51 is not identical but similar: the verb is ἐκτινάσσω (see the preceding note), the "dust" is followed by a simple genitive ("of the feet"), and there is also the expression "at them," but not "as a testimony." In my opinion the meaning of this gesture is the same as that in Luke 9:5. See also Acts 18:6, where Paul shakes out his clothes, and Acts 22:23, where the Jews who are plotting against Paul fling their coats into the air and throw up dust.

29 In this gesture, which signals separation, one senses a certain aggressive attitude and detects a judgmental undertone.

30 V. 6 bears a strong Lukan imprint. The adverb πανταχοῦ ("everywhere"), though rare in the Gospel, is customary in Acts (Acts 17:30; 24:3; 28:22), which is not surprising, since Luke is developing his concept of universalism in that book. For his part Schürmann (1.504) understands πανταχοῦ more in an intensive rather than an extensive sense.

31 See Jean-Daniel Kaestli, "Les scènes d'attribution des champs de mission et de départ de l'apôtre dans les Actes apocryphes," in Bovon, *Actes apocryphes*, 249–64. During the exciting time of the beginning, it was enough for Christians to know that Jesus had sent out his disciples (Luke 9:1–6); in later, less euphoric times, actual depictions of how the mission began became necessary (see the Apocryphal Acts of the Apostles).

346

the way. The choice of the word "village" is conscious:[32] Luke sees Jesus himself working in the *cities*. He perceives the *villages* to be the appropriate testing ground for the inexperienced Twelve.

He summarizes the content of the mission with its twofold structure briefly but fittingly: Jesus' disciples bring the gospel in word and deed.[33] Luke thereby achieves a literary *inclusio* with the beginning of the pericope (vv. 1–2).

Only Luke uses πανταχοῦ ("everywhere") for the mission of the Twelve. He thinks universalistically and understands this first mission as a prolepsis of the future mission of the apostles (Acts 1:8).[34]

Conclusion

The disciples have not only become believers (5:1–11; 6:12–16) but also witnesses of Jesus by following him (8:1; Acts 1:21–22), and finally here, witnesses of the kingdom of God (cf. already Luke 6:13). In this way Jesus makes concrete an unavoidable aspect of faith, the sending forth. The gospel sends us "away" again and again.[35] God already demanded this of Abraham. Here, however, the disciples return to their Lord immediately afterward (9:10a). But the account nevertheless anticipates the final separation at the ascension.[36] At the conclusion (v. 5), it mentions a further and very different separation: the rupture of human relations with the hardhearted listeners. The Twelve thus stand in a double isolation: they are sent forth by their Lord (vv. 1–2) and rejected by people (v. 5). But the account does not leave them in complete isolation. They also enter hospitable houses and there experience the productive exchange of material and spiritual goods of which Paul speaks.

The emphasis on the renunciation of material goods in the account (v. 3) is in symmetrical relationship to that which Jesus says about personal separations in other passages (see 14:26; 18:28–30). In renouncing private property, the disciples make themselves dependent on the congregation. In speaking about the first mission here, Luke mentions the most important components of common life in the church. This cannot happen without defining the structure of faith as a double response to the call and sending forth by Jesus.

The most important aspect is still the relationship between the disciples and their Lord, for the disciples are given authority through their commissioning, and participate in the ministry of Jesus. This participatory work of the Twelve perhaps explains why Luke does not tell us whether they went forth to fulfill their task two by two, alone, or all together. What is decisive is that they have assumed a shared responsibility with Jesus.[37]

---

32 See Grundmann, 185. Ernst (286) represents another opinion.

33 The occurrence of the verb θεραπεύω ("to cure") in v. 6 resumes that of v. 1, thus bracketing the enclosed material. It is surprising that Luke does not follow Mark in differentiating between healings and exorcisms here (Mark 6:12–13), for he does distinguish them earlier (Luke 9:1).

34 According to Lagrange (260), Jesus wants everyone in Galilee to know that the kingdom of God is coming. Among the evangelists, Matthew bases the mission on Jesus' compassion for the people, Mark, on his concern to instruct the disciples, and Luke "takes the middle ground between Matthew and Mark."

35 In a personal conversation, Joseph Moingt has brought to my attention that this urgent invitation to go constitutes a fundamental requirement of the gospel.

36 The second account of the ascension (Acts 1:9–11) deals with this separation (see Gerhard Lohfink, *Die Himmelfahrt Jesu: Untersuchungen zu den Himmelfahrts- und Erhöhungstexten bei Lukas* [SANT 26; Munich: Kösel, 1971] 251–75; and Bovon, *Theologian*, 176–77).

37 Schürmann (1.501) is of the opinion that in Luke's view the kerygma of the apostles is based on the kerygma proclaimed by Jesus.

Bibliography

Berger, Klaus, *Die Auferstehung des Propheten und die Erhöhung des Menschensohnes: Traditions-geschichtliche Untersuchungen zur Deutung des Geschickes Jesu in frühchristlichen Texten* (SUNT 13; Göttingen: Vandenhoeck & Ruprecht, 1976) 18–21.

Conzelmann, *Theology*, 51.

Fitzmyer, Joseph A., "The Composition of Luke, Chapter 9," in Talbert, *Perspectives*, 139–52.

Gils, *Jésus prophète*, 20–21.

Haenchen, *Weg*, 234–37.

Hengel, *Charismatic Leader*, 36–37.

Hoehner, *Herod*, 110, 113, 123, 127, 149, 159, 184–97, 215.

Pesch, Rudolf, "Das Messiasbekenntnis des Petrus," *BZ* n.s. 17 (1973) 178–95; 18 (1974) 20–31.

idem, "Zur Entstehung des Glaubens an die Auferstehung Jesu," *ThQ* 153 (1973) 201–28.

Ravens, D. A. S., "Luke 9:7–62 and the Prophetic Role of Jesus," *NTS* 36 (1990) 119–29.

Rese, Martin, "Einige Überlegungen zu Lukas XIII,31–33," in Dupont, *Christologie*, 201–25.

Schnackenburg, Rudolf, "Die Erwartung des 'Propheten' nach dem Neuen Testament und den Qumran-Texten," *StEv* 1 (1959) 622–39 (= TU 73).

Schramm, *Markus-Stoff*, 128–29.

Wilkens, Wilhelm, "Die Auslassung von Mark. 6,45–8,26 bei Lukas im Licht der Komposition Luk. 9,1–50," *ThZ* 32 (1976) 193–200.

7 **And Herod the tetrarch heard about all that had taken place, and he was perplexed, because it was said by some that John had been raised from the dead, 8/ by some that Elijah had appeared, and by others that one of the ancient prophets had arisen. 9/ But Herod said, "John I beheaded; but who is this about whom I hear such things?" And he tried to see him.**

Analysis

Luke's account contains two words in common with Matthew (ὁ τετρααάρχης, "the tetrarch," and ἠγέρθη,

"he arose," v. 7), and otherwise mostly agrees with Mark, except for Herod's doubt (v. 7b and 9b) and his wish to see Jesus (v. 9c).[1] One should not accord too much significance to the two minor agreements between Matthew and Luke.[2] Both of them corrected Mark with the same tendency. Ὁ τετρααάρχης was Herod's correct title; "king" was too colloquial or politically suspect.

What is peculiar to Luke's account comes from his own redactional activity.[3] In v. 7 stylistic smoothing of his source predominates, because ἤκουσεν ("he heard") requires an object. Luke writes τὰ γινόμενα πάντα ("all that had taken place"),[4] but the expression remains vague and probably concerns the missionary work of the Twelve and the ministry of Jesus. In the next sentence Luke employs an elegant new formulation (καὶ διηπόρει διὰ τὸ λέγεσθαι ὑπό τινων . . . , "and he was perplexed, because it was said by some . . .") to avoid Mark's ambiguous αὐτοῦ and his unfortunate double subject (ἐγένετο τὸ ὄνομα and ἔλεγον). The correction of ἐγήγερται to ἠγέρθη is perhaps influenced by Mark 6:16 (οὗτος ἠγέρθη). As elsewhere, Luke denies the Baptist his title (ὁ βαπτίζων), probably for stylistic rather than theological reasons.[5] His reason for deleting the mention of Jesus' powerful deeds (Mark 6:14b) is not clear.

Herod is the sole subject of Luke's account. The opinions of the masses[6] are not described separately as in Mark, but are integrated into the personal doubts of the tetrarch in a stylistically elegant formulation (ὑπό τινων . . . ὑπό τινων . . . ἄλλων δέ). The second and third[7] opinions have a content that differs from that in Mark (see the commentary below).

The Markan sequence is retained. After Herod has become aware of the various opinions about Jesus, he himself speaks. Luke then uses this statement to express his own purposes, since he changes it significantly. Only the historical result remains the same (the execution of John). In place of a judgment, Luke has a question, which refers to the present situation (ἤκουσεν . . . τὰ γινόμενα πάντα, "he heard about all that had taken

---

1   See Lagrange, 260.
2   See Schramm, *Markus-Stoff*, 128–29.
3   See ibid., 128.
4   In the expression τὰ γινόμενα πάντα, the word πάντα ("all") is emphasized. While πάντα occurs frequently in Luke (see 12:30; 16:14; 18:21), he only rarely uses γινόμενον as a verb or substantive, in

the singular or in the plural (see Luke 21:31; 23:8; Acts 12:9; 28:6).
5   It seems that Luke considers it incorrect to use the participle ὁ βαπτίζων as a title.
6   Haenchen (*Weg*, 237) points out correctly that the ms. of Mark that Luke was using had the plural

place," v. 7) with the phrase ἀκούω τοιαῦτα ("I hear such things").[8] Both the monarch and the reader await a christological answer. But Luke is not yet satisfied. He himself has the last word, not Herod; the evangelist adds a narrative and psychologizing consequence of the prince's doubt, namely the desire to see Jesus (v. 9c), which prepares the scene in 23:6–12.[9]

Commentary

■ **7a** Herod's fate unfolds itself discreetly and sporadically in the background of the drama of the chosen people of God: his father was ruling (1:5) when the story began, and he himself was tetrarch of Galilee when God sent forth his call to John (3:1–2). Because of Herod, the Baptist lost his freedom (3:19–20) and finally his life (9:9). Herod wished to know Jesus' identity (9:7–9), to kill him (13:31–33) or to manipulate him (23:6–12). In the face of Jesus' resistance, Herod finally took Pilate's side (23:12; Acts 4:27) and ridiculed Jesus (Luke 23:11). Herod's nephew suffered the death that a persecutor deserves (Acts 12). The course of Herod's fate can be understood only from the standpoint of the chosen people. The resulting portrait works in the interest of salvation history: Luke describes political power not in a popular and hagiographical style, but as a historian would, in its reality and limitations. But this is not Luke's deepest concern, either; he is most interested in

the relationship of Herod and his family to the early Jesus movement and to Jesus' disciples. The prince is not condemned ipso facto.[10] On the contrary, Luke wishes to draw the attention of contemporary rulers to the matter of the gospel. Herod is a bad example, but his portrait is not drawn purely negatively. His perplexity is the necessary first step toward the gospel (9:7).[11] He consequently *questions* (9:9; 23:9).[12] Above all, he wants to *see* (9:9; 23:8). Luke does not condemn this interest in Jesus, rather the contrary. But the intention behind it is evil (9:9; 23:8), for Herod would like to marvel at a sign that Jesus performs (23:8) not in order to come to faith, but rather to be confirmed in his regal identity. According to Luke, a ruler is also able to react differently and to consider faith as a possible conclusion for his existential dilemma (Acts 26:28). Luke expects much for the future of the church from this quarter. His whole work, especially Luke 23:6–12, is a key to the interpretation of this pericope, along with Mark 6:14–16.

■ **7b–9** The three possible identifications (vv. 7b–8) are not important in themselves. Only the christological question is important in the structure of chap. 9: Τίς δέ ἐστιν οὗτος . . . ; ("Who is this . . . ?"). It foreshadows Jesus' question and Peter's confession, which Jesus interprets through the suffering of the Messiah (9:18–22). In contrast to Mark,[13] who presents Herod as believing

---

ἔλεγον in Mark 6:14 and not the well-attested singular ἔλεγεν.

7   With the words τῶν ἀρχαίων ("of the old prophets" or "of the old times") Luke avoids the unfortunate repetition of the word "prophet" in Mark 6:15.

8   The uneasiness of Herod already mentioned in v. 7 (διηπόρει, "he was perplexed") sets the stage for the attitude that the monarch finally assumes: he remains unsatisfied with his question (v. 9). One observes the change from the punctiliar aorist ἤκουσεν to the durative imperfect διηπόρει (see Plummer, 241). The verb διαπορέω is missing in the LXX and appears in the NT only in Luke, who is fond of compound verbs with δια- (Acts 2:12; 5:24; 10:17, always in the imperfect). Luke certainly uses this verb because he encounters the simple verb ἀπορέω (in the form ἠπόρει) in the report about the death of the Baptist (Mark 6:20), which he himself does not incorporate into his Gospel.

9   Conzelmann (*Theology*, 51) correctly underscores

the connection that Herod Antipas has with all three segments of Jesus' life: Galilee, the journey, and Jerusalem.

10   Martin Rese holds a different view ("Einige Überlegungen zu Lukas XIII,31–33," in Dupont, *Christologie*, 201–25, esp. 212–15). In his opinion Luke tends to disparage Herod.

11   According to Grundmann (185), Herod regards the problem of "John the Baptist" as being solved, but he still faces the problem of "Jesus."

12   Walter Schmithals (*Das Evangelium nach Lukas* [Zürcher Bibelkommentare NT 3.1; Zurich: Theologischer Verlag, 1980] 109) thinks that Herod simply asks this question out of curiosity, whereas, of course, it was "a question of genuine perplexity . . . an important step on the way to the truth."

13   This is underscored esp. by Loisy (263) and Grundmann (185).

Jesus to be John redivivus, Luke describes a greedy and novelty-hungry personality, who is from the outset certain of only one thing: John is not Jesus.[14]

Luke thus presents his own portrait of Herod. He is a man who knows how to ask questions, legitimately wishes to see, but who treats first John and then Jesus wrongly, because of his lack of faith. This could be a construction of the author, although some think that Luke the historian interviewed people like Chuza (Luke 8:3) or Menachem (Acts 13:1), who knew Herod personally.[15]

There are thus three opinions about Jesus. First, Jesus is John redivivus. The Synoptics presuppose a belief in the resurrection of a dead prophet,[16] without limiting this to the group of John's disciples. This belief was probably widespread at the time,[17] since the ancient world attests varied anthropological conceptions (the continuity of one's person after death, people coming back to life, etc.). Among the population of Galilee, which was not free of syncretistic traditions, the conviction of a new appearance of the Baptist could have developed, whereby the expression "raised from the dead" is perhaps a Christian formulation.

Second, Jesus is Elijah redivivus. Luke knows that neither Elijah nor Enoch have died. The prophesied return of Elijah thus cannot be described as a resurrection, but rather, for substantive and scriptural reasons, only as an "appearance"[18] (the question of how deeply ingrained the expectation of an Elijah redivivus was in the Judaism of that time must remain open).[19] Luke allows the Baptist to walk in the spirit of Elijah (1:17), and Jesus carries prophetic traits of Elijah (9:54);[20] but, in contrast to Mark 9:11–13, Luke does not describe the Baptist as Elijah redivivus.[21]

Third, Jesus is a Hebrew Bible prophet redivivus. Mark only emphasized the similarity ($\pi\rho o\varphi\acute{\eta}\tau\eta\varsigma\ \acute{\omega}\varsigma$ . . . , "a prophet like . . ."), but Luke describes public opinion as identifying Jesus with a resurrected ($\grave{\alpha}\nu\acute{\epsilon}\sigma\tau\eta$) prophet. The possibility of this popular belief thus does not bother him.

Common to these three possibilities is the prophetic element and the possibility of a redivivus. Everyone is surprised at the new efflorescence of the prophecy[22] that they had believed extinguished, and everyone measures it against the standard of the past. Only what is known is possible. Luke does not evaluate these opinions. They are for him probably half-truths. Jesus indeed has something to do with Hebrew Bible prophecy, but not in the fashion that these people imagine. What is historically important is the prophetic impression that Jesus left on the masses, which the combined Synoptic tradition attests. Neither messianic characteristics nor hypothetical priestly aspects impressed them, as emphasized in 9:19, where the same sequence occurs (John, Elijah, a prophet). Thus it is likely that the Christians simplified Jewish popular traditions about Jesus. Despite the Christian impress, the emphasis on the prophetic aspect is striking.[23] Miracles (cf. Mark 6:14b) are more often the sign of a prophet than the works of a messiah. In Jewish sources, Jesus the miracle-worker was soon branded a magician.[24]

---

14 Klostermann (104) and James Reiling and Jan Lodewijk Swellengrebel (*A Translator's Handbook on the Gospel of Luke* [Helps for Translators 10; Leiden: Brill, 1971] 368) point to the emphatic ἐγώ ("I") of Herod: since I have killed him, I know that it cannot be John the Baptist. Lagrange (261) speaks of the impudent nonchalance with which the tyrant here expresses himself.

15 See perhaps Godet, 1.402; and Zahn, 21, 370.

16 On the heated debate over the matter of the belief in resurrection among Jews in that period, see Ulrich Wilckens, *Auferstehung: Das biblische Auferstehungszeugnis historisch untersucht und erklärt* (Themen der Theologie 4; Stuttgart/Berlin: Kreuz, 1970) 137–43; Rudolf Pesch, "Zur Entstehung des Glaubens an die Auferstehung Jesu," *ThQ* 153 (1973) 201–28, esp. 222–26; Gnilka, *Markus*, 1.247–48. In this connection the following texts are often cited: CD 6.10–11; Rev 11:3–12; *Apoc. Elijah* 4:14–15; 5:32. Lagrange (261) has already noted that the resurrection of the just is to be placed more likely in the hereafter and therefore after the messianic age.

17 Thus the belief in a Nero redivivus, to which Rev 17:11 seems to allude.

18 See Mal 3:23–24 (*NRSV* 4:5–6); Sir 48:10.

19 On the expectation of Elijah in ancient Judaism, see Hahn, *Titles*, 354–65.

20 See Dubois, "Elie."

21 See Conzelmann, *Theology*, 24–25.

22 See 1 Macc 14:41; Rengstorf, *Concordance*, 116.

23 On Jesus as a prophet, see Luke 4:24; 7:16; 13:33; 24:19; and Gils, *Jésus prophète*, 25–29.

24 See Morton Smith, *Jesus the Magician* (New York: Harper & Row, 1978).

Conclusion

The passage 9:1–6 shifts the reader's attention from Jesus to his disciples, and through them to the whole country. Now the issue is the ruler of the region, and the opinions of the masses about Jesus (9:7–9). Exceptionally, the political ruler is at the center of the narrative, half in his function as a judicial power, half as an interested individual. Herod knows neither what he should do nor what he should think. How will this hesitating ruler finally react? Along with the Christians of the earliest times, Luke's conclusion about Herod is negative.

The Feeding of the Five Thousand (9:10–17)

Bibliography

Bagatti, Bellarmino, "Dove avvenne la moltiplicazione dei pani?" *Salmanticensis* 28 (1981) 293–98.

Becker, Ulrich, "Die wunderbare Speisung," in idem and Siegfried Wibbing, *Wundergeschichten* (Gütersloh: Gütersloher Verlaghaus Gerd Mohn, 1965) 55–74.

Brock, Sebastian P., "A Note on Luke IX.16 (D)," *JTS* 14 (1963) 391–92.

Busse, *Wunder*, 232–48.

Farrer, "Loaves."

Fowler, Robert M., *Loaves and Fishes: The Function of the Feeding Stories in the Gospel of Mark* (SBLDS 54; Chico, Calif.: Scholars Press, 1981).

Friedrich, Gerhard, "Die beiden Erzählungen von der Speisung in Mark 6,31–44; 8,1–9," *ThZ* 20 (1964) 10–22.

Hebert, "Feeding."

Heising, *Die Botschaft der Brotvermehrung: Zur Geschichte und Bedeutung eines Christusbekenntnisses im Neuen Testament* (2d ed.; SBS 15; Stuttgart: Katholisches Bibelwerk, 1967).

idem, "Exegese."

Kertelge, *Wunder*, 129–45.

Knackstedt, J., "Die beiden Brotvermehrungen im Evangelium," *NTS* 10 (1963–64) 309–35.

Körtner, Ulrich H. I., "Das Fischmotiv im Speisungswunder," *ZNW* 75 (1984) 24–35.

Magne, Jean, "Les récits de la multiplication des pains à la lumière de la solution nouvelle du problème synoptique proposée par Philippe Rolland," *Ephemerides Liturgicae* 106 (1992) 477–525.

Müller-Pozzi, Heinz, "Die Speisung der Fünftausend als Ansatz eines psycho-analytischen Verständnisses der Person und Verkündigung Jesu," in Y. Spiegel, ed., *Doppeldeutlich: Tiefendimensionen biblischer Texte* (Munich: Kaiser, 1978) 13–23.

Neirynck, Frans, "The Matthew-Luke Agreements in Mt 14,13–14 / Lk 9,10–11 (par. Mk 6,30–34): The Two-Source Theory Beyond the Impasse," *EThL* 60 (1984) 25–44.

Patsch, "Abendmahlsterminologie."

Petersen, Karen, "Zu den Speisungs- und Abendmahlsberichten," *ZNW* 32 (1933) 217–18.

Pettem, Michel, "Le premier récit de la multiplication des pains et le problème synoptique," *SR* 14 (1985) 73–84.

Richardson, Alan, "The Feeding of the Five Thousand," *Int* 9 (1955) 144–49.

Rolland, Philippe, "La question synoptique demande-t-elle une réponse compliquée?" *Bib* 70 (1989) 217–23.

Stegner, William Richard, "Lucan Priority in the Feeding of the Five Thousand," *BibRev* 21 (1976) 19–28.

Theissen, *Miracle Stories*, 103–6, 169, 208–9.

van Cangh, "Multiplication."

idem, *La multiplication des pains et l'eucharistie* (LD 86; Paris: Cerf, 1975), esp. 148–55.

idem, "Thème."

van der Loos, *Miracles*, 619–37.

van Iersel, Bastiaan Martinus Franciscus, "Die wunderbare Speisung und das Abendmahl in der synoptischen Tradition," *NovT* 7 (1964–65) 167–94.

Wehr, Gerhard, "Wunder," in Y. Spiegel, ed., *Doppeldeutlich: Tiefendimensionen biblischer Texte* (Munich: Kaiser, 1978) 74–82.

Ziener, "Brotwunder."

10 And after their return the apostles told Jesus all they had done. And he took them with him and withdrew away from there in the direction of a city called Bethsaida. 11/ But the crowds found out about it and followed him; and he welcomed them, and spoke to them about the kingdom of God, and healed those who needed to be cured. 12/ The day was drawing to a close, and the twelve, who had come to him, said, "Send the crowd away, so that they may go into the surrounding villages and farms, to lodge and get provisions; for we are here in a deserted place." 13/ And he said to them, "You give them something to eat." They said, "We have no more than five loaves and two fish—unless we are to go and buy food for all these people." 14/ For there were about five thousand men. And he said to his disciples, "Make them settle down in groups of about fifty each." 15/ They did so and made them all settle down. 16/ And taking the five loaves and the two fish, he looked up to heaven, and said the blessing over them and broke them, and gave them to the disciples to set before the crowd. 17/ And they ate and all were filled. What was left over of the pieces of bread was gathered up, twelve baskets full.

Analysis

The Context

The introduction to this pericope also concludes a previous episode:[1] the commissioning of the Twelve (9:1–6).

---

1   Luke has interrupted it with Herod's reaction to Jesus' activity. Mark goes a step further by inserting an additional interlude: the report of the death of John the Baptist (Mark 6:17–29).

Luke is not able to narrate anything more specific about their missionary activity, and thus does not describe the content of their report to Jesus upon their return. This introduction of the pericope is connected to Jesus' intention to withdraw in private with his disciples (9:10b). After the work directed outward, it is now time for some reflection within the community. The distribution of the bread (this is more suitable than "the multiplication of the bread"), which takes place in seclusion, has the same relationship to the missionary activity of the apostles as the Eucharist—which in antiquity was celebrated secretly—has with public preaching.

In both the mission (9:1–6) and the distribution of the bread (9:10–17), the twelve apostles play an important role. Luke's "great omission" (which falls between 9:17 and 18)[2] results in the brusque presentation of Peter's confession (9:18–22), which, thematically, provides an impressive answer to Herod's question (9:7–9). Thus this section has two pairs of corresponding units that alternate with one another: the mission and distribution of bread on the one hand, and the christological question and its answer on the other.

The Tradition

The four Gospels transmit six reports of a miraculous feeding: the feeding of the five thousand in Mark 6:31–44 (par. Matt 14:13–21 and Luke 9:10–17), of the four thousand in Mark 8:1–10 (par. Matt 15:32–39), and of the five thousand in John 6:1–15, where the Johannine version shows peculiarities found in both the Synoptic variants. The situation is not the usual one, in which Mark and Q transmit a doublet, different versions of the same saying. The second version in Mark is, in Luke, a victim of the "great omission." This is surprising, since both the setting of this version in a Gentile region and the symbolic number of seven baskets of leftover pieces point to the Gentile church, which is a special concern of Luke. But Luke generally avoids doublets.[3] Nevertheless, no influence of the second

Markan version of the distribution of bread can be detected in 9:10–17. Even the Johannine version has only two incidental points of contact with the Lukan narrative.[4]

Luke 9:10–17 reworks the first Markan account, retaining its order and showing the influence of its content. The major or minor agreements between Matthew and Luke against Mark do not really show the influence of a version in Q.[5] None of the items cited in favor of this provide sufficient proof: the drastic shortening of the transition in Mark 6:31 (Luke 9:10), the deletion of the scriptural allusion to sheep without a shepherd and the introduction of healings (Luke 9:11), the deletion of the part of the dialogue that falls between "You give them something to eat," and the calculation of the five loaves and two fish (Luke 9:13), ὡσεί (cf. Matt 14:21) and εἶπεν (Luke 9:14), and the omission of the distribution of the fish (Luke 9:16). For Luke reworks the introduction differently than Matthew (e.g., the ship disappears in Luke). Matthew omits Num 27:17 (or 1 Kgs [LXX 3 Kgdms] 22:17), because he has already used this quotation (Matt 9:36). True to his technique of shortening, Matthew even finds the reply of the disciples (Mark 6:37b) superfluous, whereas Luke just transposes it (v. 13b). The only item that is still surprising is the mention of the healings of Jesus in Luke 9:11 (par. Matt 14:14), but one could lay this to the account of the continuing effect of oral tradition.[6]

The Peculiarities of the Lukan Redaction

1. *The introduction* (vv. 10–11a): as usual, the evangelist perceives more liberty to rework the frame of the traditional narrative than he does in the narrative proper. The repeated mention of the wilderness and the juxtaposition of "by ship" and "by foot" disappear; the concept of retreating into seclusion is underscored by ὑποχωρέω ("to withdraw"). Is Bethsaida (attested in both Mark 6:45 and 8:22) an indication that Luke knew Mark 6:45–8:26, although he did not reproduce this unit as

---

2   See the analysis of Luke 9:18–22 below.

3   See Fitzmyer, 1.81–82, and 102–3 (with bibliography).

4   See Fitzmyer, 1.762: "These points are the crowds following Jesus (9:11; cf. John 6:2) and the mention of the five thousand present prior to the miracle itself (9:14; cf. John 6:10)."

5   William Richard Stegner even goes so far as to affirm that Luke's report represents the oldest version ("Lucan Priority in the Feeding of the Five Thousand," *BibRev* 21 [1976] 19–28).

6   See Marshall, 358.

such?[7] Εἰς ("to") most likely gives the direction rather than the destination, since Jesus, the disciples, and the crowds are "in a deserted place" according to v. 12. The accompaniment of the knowing[8] crowd is a vague paraphrase of the Markan scenario.

2. *The beginning* (v. 11b): Instead of an expression of compassion and the allusion to Scripture, Luke writes καὶ ἀποδεξάμενος αὐτούς ("and he welcomed them"). He thus replaces the biblical style[9] with a Greek expression of hospitality. As in 9:1–2, Luke avoids the imprecise ἤρξατο with infinitive, and names the content of Jesus' teaching: the kingdom of God (not its nearness). As in 9:1–2, Jesus' healing activity occurs in parallel with his preaching.

3. *The approach of the disciples* (v. 12): In comparison to Mark, Luke inserts the reason for the disciples' approach later (the ὅτι-clause) and avoids mentioning twice the lateness of the hour. He writes, more elegantly than his source, "the day was drawing to a close." He speaks of "the Twelve" to avoid a further repetition (cf. τοῖς μαθηταῖς, "the disciples," v. 16). He describes in a manner more to the point than Mark why it is that the disciples urge their Lord to send the crowds to the surrounding villages and farms: they need lodging, which Luke adds to Mark 6:36, and provisions, which he describes with precisely the right term, ἐπισιτισμός.[10]

4. *The dialogue* (vv. 13–15): The dialogue between Jesus and his disciples is shortened from Mark's version into a single reply of Jesus and then of the disciples. Did Mark expand the dialogue of the oral tradition narratively, almost apocryphally? The mention of 200 denarii in John 6:7 would seem to indicate an expansion already in oral tradition, which Mark accepts but which disturbs Matthew and Luke. Luke adds the content of the omitted reaction of the disciples (Mark 6:37b) at the end of their next replay (v. 13b). Formally, favorite Lukan words such as πᾶς ("all") and λαός ("people") occur. He can use ἀγοράζω ("to buy") here, which he replaced with εὑρίσκω ("to find") in v. 12. He moves forward the conclusion of the Markan account (v. 14a), so that the great number of people[11] can provide a dramatic accentuation of the miracle that follows. The injunction to settle down is reworked: he does not mention the green grass (like the concept of the shepherd above), but just the groups of fifty.[12] The Semitic syntax of συμπόσια συμπόσια and πρασιαί πρασιαί is replaced.[13]

5. *The central action* (v. 16): Because of the conservative character of the obvious liturgical language, Luke is closest to Mark here.[14] Of six Markan verbs, five of them recur in Luke.[15] As 9:17 confirms, his interest in the fish wanes.

6. *The exit* (v. 17): The first sentence is identical with Mark's, except for the emphatic placement of the word πάντες ("all") at the end. The satiety, not the multiplica-

---

7   The text here at the end of v. 10 is uncertain. On the different readings see Godet, 1.403–4; and Marshall, 359. Godet represents the outdated thesis that there were two places with the name Bethsaida. But there is only one: a city in Gaulanitis, on the northern shore of Lake Gennesaret, east of the Jordan. Etymologically the name means "place of provisions" or "house of fishing" (see Grundmann, 186; Xavier Léon-Dufour, *Dictionary of the New Testament* [trans. T. Prendergast; San Francisco: Harper & Row, 1980] 113; and Heinz-Wolfgang Kuhn, "Zum neuen Stand der Grabungen auf et-Tell [Bethsaida-Julias]," *Welt und Umwelt der Bibel* 4 [1998] 78–80).

8   The absolute use of γινώσκω ("to know"; γνόντες without an object = "having been informed of it") can also be found elsewhere, but rather with the meaning "to be sensible," "to comprehend," "to be right" (see Bailly, *Dictionnaire, s.v.* γινώσκω, 2.1).

9   See the verb σπλαγχνίζομαι ("to have compassion") and the biblical quotation in Mark 6:34.

10 See Plummer, 243. It is interesting to note that the translation of the word צֵידָה ("provision," which

together with בַּיִת, "house," comprises the word Bethsaida) in the LXX is ἐπισιτισμός ("provision"), a word that Luke uses in v. 12.

11 See v. 14: Ὡσεὶ ἄνδρες πεντακισχίλιοι ("about five thousand men"; Matt 14:21 adds "not counting women and children"); ὡσεί, "about," is Lukan.

12 The groups of a hundred are missing. Ἀνά has a distributive meaning (as in 9:3).

13 The vivid Greek word συμπόσιον is also lost thereby. Luke prefers to use κατακλίνω over ἀνακλίνω.

14 Luke and Mark have the imperfect ἐδίδου ("he was giving," stressing that the action lasted for some time because of the large number of people), while Matthew and John have the aorist (emphasizing the uniqueness of the action). According to Godet (1.407), the imperfect means "He gave, and kept on giving." In the rest of the sentence, Luke replaces the final clause of Mark with an infinitive of purpose (παραθεῖναι, "to set").

15 Luke adds αὐτούς ("them") after εὐλόγησεν ("he blessed") and erases—in contrast to Mark—the repe-

tion—that is, the ecclesiological stress rather than the thaumaturgical—is more important to Luke. He simplifies the description of the surplus (all the evangelists emphasize the number twelve) by omitting the fish. Luke has already mentioned the number of those present at the beginning of the account (v. 14a).

The Genre

To describe this as a nature miracle is imprecise and outmoded.[16] In more recent classification, this narrative belongs to the category of the miraculous gift:[17] the miracle-worker grants *material* gifts by means of a miracle, often foodstuffs or meals. He takes the initiative in working a miracle that is neither hoped for nor requested. The actions are not important, only the result. The miracle itself is not described, and the gift seems to be normal and natural. Such narratives emphasize the abundance of the gift. The narratives have no institutional connection, nor do they have the function of explaining a practice or of polemically justifying an alternative; for this reason, they do not place any weight on thaumaturgy as such. They rather encourage pious imagination (on the affective level) and faith to work "allegorically," that is, to see the true benefit behind the material gift (on the cognitive level).

The history of this genre extends back to the oldest layers of the Hebrew Bible, to the tradition about manna (Exod 16; Num 11) and to the narratives about Elijah and Elisha (1 Kgs [LXX 3 Kgdms] 17 and 2 Kgs [LXX 4 Kgdms] 4:42–44). Rabbinic literature knows stories about the pious poor, whom God nourishes miraculously during a famine.[18] And the genre is attested into Byzantine times, in which an apocryphal legend about an apostle describes a miracle about foodstuffs that are never exhausted.[19] The functional setting of these mirac-

ulous feedings in the New Testament differs from that of the texts about the Last Supper. According to Hermann Patsch, the setting of the latter is the liturgical ceremony; of the former, the instruction of the congregation or missionary preaching.[20] In my opinion missionary preaching as the functional setting of these miraculous feedings is rather unlikely, so that the instruction of the congregation would be the best possibility. I am aware, however, that even this is too general in the final analysis, although it is difficult to find a more concrete situation. The theology that is presupposed in this account could perhaps provide a further index, for it points to the conviction transmitted in popular belief that God never abandons his people, and again and again feeds them in situations of distress. In sociological terms, such accounts are circulated among people who are threatened and whose wisdom is supported by the faith of their fathers (cf. 1 Kgs [LXX 3 Kgdms] 17:14);[21] each concrete narrative actualizes the traditional faith.

One must, however, take into account a possible contamination with the texts concerning the Last Supper, the setting, function, and genre of which are quite different.[22] Because of this, in this account the sequence of the gestures acted out by the miracle-worker deserves attention, as it would not in a normal exponent of its genre. The gestures are indeed central and should be taken as a common basic element of all the versions of the feeding story. As far as its genre, this pericope becomes ever more a cult legend over time.

Commentary

■ **10–11** The return of the Twelve is narrated briefly. It achieves significance only when compared with the commissioning account (9:1–6). Jesus, who has called the

---

tition of the bread and fish. One encounters another blessing of bread in Luke at 24:30, but a blessing of fish is mentioned here only (v. 16). In Luke it is the people who bless God (Luke 1:64; 2:28; 24:53), or it is God, Christ, or a man of God who blesses the people (Luke 2:34; 6:28; 24:50, 51; Acts 3:26; passive voice in Luke 1:28 [variant], 42; 13:35; 19:38; Acts 3:25).

16 Though one can still find this explanation in Fitzmyer, 1.763.

17 See perhaps Theissen, *Miracle Stories*, 103–6.

18 See the story of the miraculously filled oven of Ḥaninah ben Dosa (b. Ta'anit 24b–25a, cited in

Theissen, *Miracle Stories*, 104).

19 See *Acts Phil.* 15.5 according to ms. Athos, Xenophontos 32, folio 90, verso.

20 See Hermann Patsch, "Abendmahlsterminologie außerhalb der Einsetzungsberichte: Erwägungen zur Traditionsgeschichte der Abendmahlsworte," *ZNW* 62 (1971) 210–31, esp. 210–11, 231.

21 See the commentary on v. 17 below.

22 These contexts are examined with great care by Patsch, "Abendmahlsterminologie." Karen Petersen sees in the participle λαβών ("taking") the influence of Eucharist liturgy, which tends to replace ἔλαβεν ("he took") with λαβών ("Zu den

Twelve to a task requiring responsibility (9:1), now takes them back again into his care (9:10). Then, the concern was to preach, to engage with the outside world, but now the apostles wish to tell their experiences and to turn inward in the intimacy of the congregation. Luke juxtaposes the private retreat of Jesus to his public ministry,[23] so that, as before, strenuous restlessness (9:6) is contrasted to the eventual rest (9:10).

Unlike Mark, in Luke a deserted place is significant as the location not for secret teachings by Jesus[24] but rather for prayer (5:16) or for an intimate conversation (Acts 23:19). It is clear that Jesus wishes to pray with his disciples and have quiet conversation; the Lukan redaction of the next episode (9:18) will show precisely this. As in 4:42, the press of the crowds prevents him from his objective. This time, the Lord allows this disturbance, or rather, this success, and puts off his intention until later (until 9:18). The verb ἀποδέχομαι ("to welcome") here has the meaning of a friendly reception by a person of higher rank.[25] Jesus then fulfills his usual saving mission

in word and healing, formulated in the durative imperfect tense.[26]

■ **12** After this refrainlike summary passage, the actual story begins with the coming night.[27] The Twelve take the initiative now,[28] as already in v. 10, since they are concerned about the lodgings[29] of the crowd and their provisions.[30] Jesus and his disciples, as well as the crowd, stand on a threshold from one place to another, and between day and night. In this dangerous time of transition, Jesus takes care of their provisions, but, as it will be in the time of the church, he does this through the mediation of the Twelve.[31]

■ **13–15** The disciples react in both a wise and foolish fashion at the same time (9:13b):[32] wise from the perspective of those outside the faith, and foolish if one knows the story already. The numbers (five loaves and two fish) are deeply rooted in gospel tradition, although I find in them no symbolic meaning.[33] Bread and "something on it" (here, fish) is a usual meal (cf. John 21:9).[34] Jesus does not respond to the rational objection of his

Speisungs- und Abendmahlsberichten," *ZNW* 32 [1933] 217–18). This liturgy has thus influenced the Synoptic tradition, the scribes of the NT, and early Christian writers.

23 Against his own wishes, Luke follows the Synoptic tradition in placing the διήγησις ("report") of the Twelve (9:10a) before their private retreat (9:10b). Ὑποχωρέω means "to withdraw to oneself," "to abandon the field," "to retreat" (the location can be indicated by εἰς following the verb, as here; see BAGD *s.v.*).

24 Cf. Mark 4:34; 6:31–32; 7:33; 9:2, 28; 13:3.

25 See Plummer, 242. Jesus welcomes the crowd, although it robs him and his disciples of their peace.

26 On the βασιλεία ("kingdom"), see Fitzmyer, 1.153–57. Λαλέω περὶ κτλ. ("to speak about") recalls the activity of the philosophers. On λαλέω in Luke, see Helmut Jaschke, "Λαλεῖν bei Lukas: Ein Beitrag zur lukanischen Theologie," *BZ* n.s. 15 (1971) 109–14.

27 Cf. "at sunset" in Luke 4:40; "at night" in 2:8.

28 According to Lagrange (262), v. 12 is a very carefully constructed sentence (ἰᾶτο "he healed," in v. 11 is an imperfect).

29 On κατάλυμα ("lodging"), see the commentary on 2:7b above. On κώμη ("village") see the commentary on 4:43 and the analysis of 5:17–26 above. Ἀγρός, which first means "a field" and then "an estate," could indicate here a farm.

30 On ἐπισιτισμός ("provisions," "food"), see Plummer, 243.

31 The placement of ὑμεῖς ("you") at the end of the sentence here (v. 13a) lends it emphasis (see Plummer, 244).

32 The proposal of the disciples in v. 13b is more of a veiled refusal than it is a serious suggestion (see Loisy, 265).

33 Against Austin M. Farrer ("Loaves and Thousands," *JTS* 4 [1953] 1–14), who maintains that there is a connection in Mark between the five loaves of bread and the five thousand people, just as there was between the twelve loaves of the bread of the Presence (Lev 24:8) and the twelve tribes: "Seven thousands have still to receive their loaves" (p. 4). On p. 12 he claims that Luke appropriated this symbolism from Mark.

34 The modern Greek word for "fish," ψάρι, comes from the ancient Greek word ὀψάριον (the diminutive of ὄψον), which means, first, "something roasted" or "grilled" (from ὀπτάω, "to roast," "bake"); second, the roasted thing that—along with bread—makes an entire meal; third, it can refer to (baked) fish (cf. Luke 24:42, ἰχθύος ὀπτοῦ μέρος, "a portion of fried fish").

disciples and instead requests their cooperation. Why do the κλισίαι ("groups") each number fifty people? Because there are five thousand? Or does the word have an ecclesiological meaning, as in the Hebrew Bible or at Qumran?[35] The book of Acts does not confirm this. Ἡ κλισία is in this case a dining group.[36] The reader should thus imagine one hundred such groups, which are served by the twelve disciples.

■ **16** In the center of the story, the people and the disciples recede into the background. Now Jesus acts alone. He takes the loaves and fish, fulfills a gesture of prayer with his eyes[37] (in this way, he speaks not only to God but also to the spectators). After the two participles that describe the preparation of his action come the two main verbs: Jesus blesses and breaks the bread. A blessing said over the bread and salt is part of the beginning of every Jewish meal, for which only a piece of bread is necessary. Jesus' gesture here is reminiscent of the Last Supper (22:19), at which he took the entire loaf in his hand. Luke avoids the Markan repetition of τοὺς ἄρτους ("the loaves") with αὐτούς ("them") after "bless";[38] neither he nor Mark mentions the fish. Since he does not place αὐτούς after κατέκλασεν ("break"), he does not have in mind a blessing of God, as do the other evangelists, but rather a blessing of the elements. Blessing is of course a relational concept.[39] God can bless people, just as people may bless God. Jesus' glance alone is already a prayer here. It is, however, not a request for God's power but a prayer of thanks. By his blessing he transfers his power to the bread and the fish; as in the healings (5:17; 6:19; 8:46), a δύναμις ("power") goes forth from him and

makes the miracle possible. Despite the reminiscence of the Last Supper in v. 16, Luke does not use his own words of institution,[40] since the ancient Christian faithfulness to traditional materials does not necessarily result in the slavish repetition of untouchable formulas.

Despite ἐμέρισεν in Mark 6:41, and διαμερίσατε in Luke 22:17 (both "distribute"), Luke uses παρατίθημι ("lay before," "set before"), a verb that is used especially in contexts of eating[41] (cf. 10:8). It is unlikely that the meaning "hand over," "entrust" plays a role here; symbolically, a παραθήκη ("entrusting") could refer only to the disciples, not to the crowd.

■ **17** Anyone who has never experienced hunger will have difficulty understanding the meaning of the elementary aorist ἔφαγον ("they ate") and the joy of satiety. Eating in those times meant to experience continued life, joy in the meal, and fellowship. The text tries to portray the abundance vividly: five thousand people receive food, and all are sated; great quantities of bread and fish are even left over. It would be desirable to write a theology of "abundance," the bulk of which would treat Pauline texts, for περισσεύω ("to be in surplus") is attested in Luke in only a handful of passages.[42] Luke 12:21 could provide the key to the theological use of περισσεύω.

There are four individual points to elaborate, before presenting a summary interpretation: (1) John 6:12–13 explains the Synoptic verb αἴρω ("gather up," v. 17). The surplus must not be wasted, but brought along with them. (2) Περισσεύω ("to be in surplus") and τὰ κλάσματα ("broken pieces") are deeply rooted in the tradi-

35 See Exod 18:21, 25; 1QS 2.21–22; 1QSa 1.14–15; 1QM 4.1–5; also 3.16–17; and CD 13:1 (cf. Fitzmyer, 1.767; and Schürmann, 1.516).

36 According to Godet (*Commentaire*, 1.570), this word signifies a "camp," the "tent" of shepherds and soldiers, the "bed," the "divan," and finally persons seated or reclining at table, a "dinner party" (see 3 Macc 6:31).

37 In the HB this gesture can also be a sign of idolatry: the eyes are lifted up to heaven in order to worship the stars (Deut 4:19). Especially later, however, it is a gesture of prayer (see Job 22:26).

38 Sebastian P. Brock rightly refutes the argument that the variant εὐλόγησεν ἐπ᾽ αὐτούς is a Semitism and is thus original ("A Note on Luke IX.16 [D]," *JTS* 14 [1963] 391–92). The wording corresponds to the Hellenistic Jewish mode of expression.

39 See n. 15 above.

40 Καὶ λαβὼν ἄρτον εὐχαριστήσας ἔκλασεν καὶ ἔδωκεν αὐτοῖς λέγων ("Then he took a loaf of bread, and when he had given thanks, he broke it and gave it to them, saying, . . ." Luke 22:19). On the relationship between the five loaves of bread in our story here and the bread of Lord's Supper, see Farrer, "Loaves," 5–6; and Arthur G. Hebert, "History in the Feeding of the Five Thousand," *StEv* 2 (1964) 65–72 (= TU 87).

41 See BAGD *s.v.*

42 Luke 9:17; 12:15; 15:17; 21:4; and Acts 16:5, where abundance in God is differentiated from earthly surplus.

tion (despite Mark 6:43, but see Mark 8:8), as are the number of loaves and fish. The leftovers are not entire loaves or fish, but pieces that were part of the first five loaves and two fish blessed by the Lord. (3) Ὁ κόφινος (the large, sturdy basket, a "carrying basket") is mentioned in all four accounts of the feeding of the five thousand, whereas Mark and Matthew use ἡ σπυρίς (the smaller "basket," used especially for foodstuffs) for the feeding of the four thousand.[43] The redactional consideration in Mark 8:19–20 (par. Matt 16:9–10) respects this probably important difference, just as no one dares to change anything about the number of baskets. Perhaps the Jews rather use the κόφινοι, whereas for Greeks σπυρίδες belong to daily life.[44] The twelve carrying baskets would then stand symbolically for the twelve apostles and Israel, and the seven baskets for the seventy Gentile nations (Mark 8:1–9, 14–21 mention the disciples, not the Twelve). (4) The symbolism of beverages plays no role here, in contrast to the Last Supper. Jesus' words of blessing are omitted, and there is no "chorus," for example, an expression of joy on the part of the crowd.[45]

God's messenger gives to the people of Israel, whom he has attracted to himself, more than their daily portion of comestible provisions, in miraculous fashion. The Lord cares for the entire life of a person. The term "bread" is rich in connotations; when it is consecrated and eaten with the faith of the congregation, it is near to the Word of God. Here it should be associated with the bread of the "Our Father" (11:3), and not with the demonic miraculous bread of the temptation (4:3–4).[46]

Every Christian of that time who knew the Scriptures would not miss the typological meaning of this pericope. In the prophetic tradition, God is the Lord of famine as well as abundance. Next to 1 Kgs (LXX 3 Kgdms) 17:8–16, the story of Elisha in 2 Kgs (LXX 4 Kgdms) 4:42–44 should be compared.[47] Both of these Hebrew Bible texts contain, along with this pericope, the following components: (1) the encounter with a divine miracle-worker; (2) the realization of the lack of bread; (3) the presence of students or disciples of the man of God; (4) his command to distribute the meal; (5) the resistance of the students or disciples; (6) the execution of the command; (7) the miraculous feeding and the mention of the surplus. Jesus stands in this biblical tradition and nourishes the hungry people even better than the prophets did. Thus the Israelite belief is realized: "We will receive food to eat, and there will be some left over." It is clear from a Hebrew Bible proverb that this belief was already traditional at that time and part of Hebrew wisdom: "The jar of meal will not be emptied and the jug of oil will not fail until the day that the Lord sends rain on the earth" (1 Kgs [LXX 3 Kgdms] 17:14). The Lord is thus faithful; he nourishes his people naturally with rain and soil, but also miraculously in times of crisis. The food is indeed of the material sort, but since its origin is either directly or indirectly divine, bread is close to spiritual nourishment and the Word of God.

The origins of Israelite faith in the exodus remained vital through the prophets, especially Elijah and Elisha;[48] John sees in this miracle the fulfillment of the prophecy of a new Moses (Deut 15:15, 18). The setting of the

---

43 If one were to follow this distinction, one would expect both Luke and Paul to have used κόφινος to describe the escape from Damascus. But Luke uses the word σπυρίς (Acts 9:25), while Paul employs the term σαργάνη (2 Cor 11:33).

44 Juvenal (3.14; 6.542) mentions a Jew and a Jewess, respectively, carrying a *cophinus* (cf. Fitzmyer, 1.769).

45 Both Lagrange (265) and Fitzmyer (1.769) have noticed this. Cf., however, John 6:14.

46 Hebert ("Feeding," 68) compares the multiplication of the loaves here with Jesus' refusal in the temptation story to transform the stone into bread (Luke 4:1–4), and contrasts the two episodes with each other.

47 See Jean-Marie van Cangh, "Le thème des poissons dans les récits évangéliques de la multiplication des pains," *RB* 78 (1971) 71–83, esp. 71; and Alkuin

Heising, "Exegese und Theologie der alt- und neutestamentlichen Speisewunder," *ZKTh* 86 (1964) 80–96, esp. 90–96. Heising ("Exegese," 91 n. 39) is of the opinion that John 6:1–15 is related to 2 Kgs (LXX 4 Kgdms) 4:2–44, since one finds barley loaves in both texts.

48 On Elisha see *TOB* at 2 Kgs 4:1, n. e (p. 681).

episode in the wilderness reminds Israel of their origins as a lost and wandering people, and of God's protection. God took their hunger seriously, and responded to the need at that time, but not in a natural way: he gave his people "earthly" goods through a "heavenly" gift: manna and quails. The symbolism of manna leads to the concept of bread in the New Testament, and the fish can be explained as a reference to the quails, which indeed "fell from heaven," but had beforehand "risen up" (Exod 16:13), even from the direction of the "sea." In this context they are like flying fish.[49] Jesus is thus not only a prophet like Elisha or Elijah, but also the last prophet like Moses.[50]

The development of the story takes place in five stages.[51] At the beginning is a typological account: Jesus brings an end to the hunger of the people, and realizes, indeed fulfills, the biblical faith. In the wasteland, in the space of transition, he plays the role of the prophet and the new Moses. He saves the people from their misery.

The first interpretation of the story presupposes a connection with the Last Supper. The interest in the "unliturgical" fish recedes, and the action is structured by the words of institution. Only there and here do the four verbs occur that concern the bread: take, bless, break, and give.

The action is also oriented to the two main centers of early Christianity: in Mark 6 toward Jerusalem, and in Mark 8 toward Antioch. Indications of each are, on the one hand, the number twelve (Mark 6:43), the words κόφινοι ("carrying baskets," 6:43) and εὐλογέω ("to bless"), which one finds in the "Aramaic" tradition of the institution of the Last Supper (Mark 14:22); on the other hand, there is the number seven (like the seven leaders of the Hellenists, Acts 6, and the seventy missionaries, Luke 10), the Greek σπυρίς ("small basket") and εὐχαριστέω ("to give thanks"), which are found in the words of institution among the Hellenists (1 Cor 11:24; Luke 22:19).

Mark uses both traditions: the first version (6:32–44) takes place on the west, that is, the Jewish, side of the lake; and the second (8:1–9) on the east, that is, the Gentile, side. Luke employs only one version, the "Aramaic," not the "Hellenistic" version more familiar to him through oral tradition, because this second version is part of the "great omission." At the same time, he tries to void doublets when possible.[52]

Conclusion

Christologically, Jesus appears as a prophet like Elijah, and as the last prophet like Moses. It is no coincidence that exactly these two figures appear in the pericope of the transfiguration of Jesus (9:28–36), standing next to the transfigured Jesus. In the time between Herod's

---

49 Cf. Wis 19:10–12.

50 The texts cited by Jean-Marie van Cangh about the eschatological banquet where Behemoth and Leviathan are eaten (*2 Bar.* 29:3–8; *1 Enoch* 60:24 [meaning disputed]) are a less convincing parallel ("La multiplication des pains dans l'évangile de Marc: Essai d'exégèse globale," in M. Sabbe, ed., *L'Évangile selon Marc: Tradition et rédaction* [BETL 34; Gembloux: Duculot, 1974] 309–46, esp. 336). On the other hand, one should not forget that Moses replies to God reproachfully that all the fish of the sea would not be enough to satisfy Israel (see Num 11:22). Cf. also *Sipre Numbers* 11.22, where fish are swimming in the water that flows from the rock that Moses struck with his staff (see Jean-Marie van Cangh, *La multiplication des pains et l'eucharistie* [LD 86; Paris: Cerf, 1975] 106–7). However, further attempts to explain the presence of fish in the multiplication stories must be rejected (see idem, "Thème," 73–76).

51 Heising ("Exegese") reconstructs another history of tradition. There are two traditions behind our sto-

ries: The first, Tradition A (Jesus as the merciful shepherd), is known only to the Synoptics, and the other, Tradition B (Jesus as a prophet greater than Elijah and Elisha), is used by John but is also known to Mark. Georg Ziener refers to an interpretation of a single event that is always being required anew by the circumstances ("Die Brotwunder im Markusevangelium," *BZ* n.s. 4 [1960] 282–85): behind all the stories lies a single event. The more time passes, the farther removed one becomes from this event, until finally a person—like Mark—believes that it originally involved two separate events. My own explanation is closer to that of van Cangh ("Multiplication," 345–46), although I am unable to recognize the fading and later restrengthening of the fish motif in the course of the pre-Markan tradition.

52 Matthew preserves both Markan versions (Matt 14:13–21; 15:32–39).

question and Peter's answer (you are "the Messiah of God," 9:20), Jesus acts out his identity:[53] through preaching and healing, and then through the feeding, where in each case the christological concern is also soteriological.

Ecclesiologically, Jesus expects the cooperation of the disciples, although before Easter they do not completely understand what is actually happening here. The mediating role of the Twelve anticipates their later, post-Easter responsibilities of office,[54] although Christ understands this office not in the sense of ruling over others, but as service to himself and thereby for the individuals who belong to him.[55] Additionally, it is not the person of the officeholder who justifies his or her calling to this service, but far more the God who has chosen and sent him

or her. The function of the officeholder is not static and set for all time, but is oriented toward the needs of the church, as it develops outward (9:1–10a) and inward (9:10b–17), that is, in its existence in secular daily life, and in the establishment of the holy congregation.[56]

The people of God are thus on a journey: between day and night, country and city, in the wilderness. The Lord loves them, provides for them, nourishes them, although perhaps differently than they would like. In any case, God graciously grants his gifts through his son and through those he commissions, and in surplus. This surplus does not, however, belong to his people, but is intended for others. God's love communicates itself not in a power that excludes, but in a dynamic that integrates.[57]

---

53 See Marshall, 357; and the fine piece by Alan Richardson, who argues that the various accounts of the multiplication reveal the identity of Jesus, the universality of salvation, the satisfying nature of the Eucharist, and the eschatological expectation ("The Feeding of the Five Thousand," *Int* 9 [1955] 144–49). According to Hebert ("Feeding," 72), the multiplication of the loaves is "a case in which an incident of the ministry of Jesus has been meditated upon and preached upon in the church, in order to focus all the light upon Jesus himself, and show who he is." The subject of Hebert's article is the historicity of the event, which he opposes on critical grounds. Godet (1.403) underscores the historicity of this miracle, one of the most apparent and undeniable of all Jesus' miracles.

54 See Ziener, "Brotwunder," 284; Schürmann, 1.514.

55 Marshall (357) emphasizes that the powerless disciples obtain from Christ the strength that they had lacked up to now.

56 For this reason they are called "apostles" by the world around them (9:10), but "the Twelve" among themselves (9:12). Perhaps Luke speaks of

"disciples" in v. 16 because the task has now extended beyond the "Twelve" to the church of the present age.

57 Heinz Müller-Pozzi is not so much interested in a psychoanalytic exegesis of the text as he is in trying to understand Jesus' psyche ("Die Speisung der Fünftausend als Ansatz eines psycho-analytischen Verständnisses der Person und Verkündigung Jesu," in Y. Spiegel, ed., *Doppeldeutlich: Tiefendimensionen biblischer Texte* [Munich: Kaiser, 1978] 13–23). For him, the text reveals a "motherly" Jesus who offers beneficial unity with the source of all good (cf. Freud's "oral phase"). Along with the nourishment Jesus provides more than just mere material property. He imparts well-being and protection. He satisfies a need. As a myth, the story resolves a conflict: restoration of the original unity that was lost in individuation.

Peter's Confession of the Messiah (9:18–22)

Bibliography

Bastin, Marcel, *Jésus devant sa Passion* (LD 92; Paris: Cerf, 1976) 123–42.

Baum, Armin Daniel, *Lukas als Historiker der letzten Jesusreise* (Wuppertal: Brockhaus, 1993).

Brown, R. E., K. P. Donfried, and J. Reumann, eds., *Peter in the New Testament* (Minneapolis: Augsburg, 1973) 64–69, 111–12.

Bultmann, Rudolf, "Die Frage nach dem messianischen Bewußtsein Jesu und das Petrus-Bekenntnis," *ZNW* 19 (1919–20) 165–74 (= idem, *Exegetica* [ed. E. Dinkler; Tübingen: Mohr-Siebeck, 1967] 1–9).

Conzelmann, *Theology*, 55–57.

Cullmann, Oscar, "L'Apôtre Pierre instrument du diable et instrument de Dieu: La place de Matt. 16,16–19 dans la tradition primitive," in A. J. B. Higgins, ed., *New Testament Essays: Studies in Memory of T. W. Manson* (Manchester: Manchester University Press, 1959) 94–105.

idem, *Peter: Disciple, Apostle, Martyr: A Historical and Theological Study* (trans. F. V. Filson; London: SCM, 1962).

Dietrich, *Petrusbild*, 94–104.

Dinkler, Erich, "Petrusbekenntnis und Satanswort: Das Problem der Messianität Jesu," in Dinkler, *Zeit und Geschichte*, 127–53 (= idem, *Signum Crucis* [Tübingen: Mohr-Siebeck, 1967] 283–312).

Flender, *Heil*, 46–48.

Haenchen, Ernst, "Leidensnachfolge: Eine Studie zu Mk 8,27–9,1 und den kanonischen Parallelen," in idem, *Die Bibel und Wir: Gesammelte Aufsätze II* (Tübingen: Mohr-Siebeck, 1968) 102–34.

Hahn, *Titles*, 223–28.

Miller, Donald E., "Luke 9:18–24," *Int* 37 (1983) 64–67.

Mundle, W., "Die Geschichtlichkeit des messianischen Bewusstseins Jesu," *ZNW* 21 (1922) 299–311.

Schramm, *Markus-Stoff*, 130–36.

Schütz, Frieder, *Der leidende Christus: Die angefochtene Gemeinde und das Christuskerygma der lukanischen Schriften* (BWANT 89; Stuttgart: Kohlhammer, 1969).

Vögtle, Anton, "Messiasbekenntnis und Petrusverheißung: Zur Komposition Mt 16,13–23 par.," *BZ* n.s. 1 (1957) 252–72; 2 (1958) 85–103 (= idem, *Evangelium*, 137–70).

18 And it happened once when Jesus was praying alone that his disciples were near him. And he asked them, "Who do the crowds say that I am?" 19/ They answered, "John the Baptist; but others, Elijah; and still others, that a prophet, one of the ancient ones, has arisen." 20/ He said to them, "But who do you say that I am?" Peter answered, "The Messiah of God." 21/ But he sternly ordered and commanded them not to tell that to anyone, 22/ saying, "The Son of Man must suffer greatly, and be rejected by the elders, chief priests, and scribes, and be killed, and on the third day be raised."

Analysis

Luke skips over a great number of pericopes in Mark (Mark 6:45–8:26), and the reason for this remains unclear. A few indications suggest that he indeed knew this section, such as the location Bethsaida (9:10; cf. Mark 6:45 and 8:22).[1] A mistake similar to the scribal error of *homoioteleuton* cannot account for the omission, since the Lukan text eliminates more than just the materials that Mark narrates between the two accounts of the multiplication of the bread. Would the reason for this truncation be Luke's intention to avoid writing too long a work, alongside his preference for his special source, which he would like to incorporate a little later into his travel account? Does he also wish to avoid doublets? Jesus' walking on the water (Mark 6:45–52) is, however, not a true doublet to the stilling of the storm (Mark 4:35–41 par. Luke 8:22–25). The woman with the discharge of blood (Mark 5:25–34 par. Luke 8:43–48) similarly does not form a parallel with the Syrophoenician woman (Mark 7:24–30). Only the two feedings (Mark 6:31–44 par. Luke 9:10–17; and Mark 8:1–10) can count as true doublets. It is an open question whether Luke took offense at the Pharisaic questions about the Law and tradition (Mark 7:1–23), since Mark's solution is not opposed to Luke's ethics. And it is improbable that he is avoiding the narration of the Messiah's journey to for-

---

1   Godet (1.412–17), who summarizes the state of research at the end of the 19th century, is of the opinion that Luke has available neither Mark nor Matthew, but rather a number of narrative cycles in the stage of their initial draft, which is still stylistically awkward. At this point, Godet thinks, Luke has omitted an entire cycle. An excursus on this question can be found in Schürmann, 1.525–27; and an overview of the more recent explanations in Fitzmyer, 1.770–71.

eign countries (Tyre and Sidon, Mark 7:24, 31), since Jesus has already been to the Decapolis (Luke 8:26–39).

After the "great omission," then, Luke (9:18) resumes the Markan narrative sequence at Mark 8:27. He does, however, introduce a detail about Jesus' prayer in v. 18a that he found in a different passage: in Mark 6:31–32 Jesus is also seeking a quiet place with his disciples,[2] and retreats to be alone after the feeding of the five thousand (Mark 6:46). Since Luke shows the same structure and uses the same verb ($\pi\rho o\sigma\epsilon\acute{u}\chi o\mu\alpha\iota$, "to pray"), 9:18a reflects Mark 6:46, which is a verse *within* the "great omission," which Luke accordingly knew. The tension between Jesus' being alone (9:18a) and the presence of the disciples (9:18b) can be explained by means of this doubled Markan origin in both Mark 6:46 on the one hand, and in Mark 6:31–32 and Mark 8:27 on the other. Luke takes from Mark 8:27a only the presence of the disciples, which he expresses with a verb peculiar to him, $\sigma\acute{u}\nu\epsilon\iota\mu\iota$ ("to be with"),[3] but not the location ("in the villages of Caesarea Philippi"); this occurs probably because the solitude is important to him, he finds the Markan expression artless, and he has already decided to use Bethsaida (9:10).

From v. 18b to v. 22, he follows Mark closely, since the pericope contains words of Jesus. There are some deviations, however: "on the way" (Mark 8:27) disappears, since for Luke the journey has already ended. He also avoids repeating "his disciples," and replaces "people" (Mark 8:27) with a favorite word, "crowds." The three popular statements are similar to Luke 9:7–8,[4] especially the third, $\H{o}\tau\iota$ $\pi\rho o\phi\acute{\eta}\tau\eta\varsigma$ $\tau\iota\varsigma$ $\tau\hat{\omega}\nu$ $\dot{a}\rho\chi\alpha\acute{\iota}\omega\nu$ $\dot{a}\nu\acute{\epsilon}\sigma\tau\eta$

("that a prophet, one of the ancient ones, has arisen," 9:19). Peter's[5] exclamation is more literary in Luke than in Mark: the accusative in Peter's statement corresponds to Jesus' question.[6] Luke did not read the title "son" in his manuscript of Mark; this variant is only weakly attested.[7] The stylistic improvement on Mark 8:30 in v. 21 lies in the Lukan verb $\pi\alpha\rho\alpha\gamma\gamma\acute{\epsilon}\lambda\lambda\omega$ ("to command"), where the present formulation is reminiscent of 5:14 and 8:56. The close relationship that Luke establishes between the command to silence and the first prediction of the passion is important (vv. 21–22). Where Mark begins a new sentence (in Nestle-Aland even a new paragraph), Luke unites the two themes in a single sentence.[8] The beginning ($\H{\eta}\rho\xi\alpha\tau o$, "he began") and the teaching ($\delta\iota\delta\acute{a}\sigma\kappa\epsilon\iota\nu$, "to teach," Mark 8:31) thereby disappear. Differently than Mark, Luke understands Jesus' opponents as a group, and surely thinks of the Sanhedrin (22:66), for which reason he only uses the article $\tau\hat{\omega}\nu$ for the Jewish authorities once, in front of the first-named group, the elders.[9] Together with Matthew, Luke uses the phrase—in contrast to Mark—$\kappa\alpha\iota$ $\tau\hat{\eta}$ $\tau\rho\acute{\iota}\tau\eta$ $\H{\eta}\mu\acute{\epsilon}\rho\alpha$ $\dot{\epsilon}\gamma\epsilon\rho\vartheta\hat{\eta}\nu\alpha\iota$ ("and on the third day be raised"). Where Mark consistently uses "after three days,"[10] Luke writes exclusively "on the third day" (also at 18:33; 24:7, 46). Luke thus skips over the short summary passage, and the conversation between Jesus and Peter in Mark 8:32–33, because he does not see the sense of a sermon in this context, and because the tone and severity of this not entirely transparent dialogue are intolerable to him.

---

2 Note in Mark $\kappa\alpha\tau$ $\dot{\iota}\delta\acute{\iota}\alpha\nu$ twice; cf. Luke 9:10, $\kappa\alpha\tau$ $\dot{\iota}\delta\acute{\iota}\alpha\nu$ and Luke 9:18a, $\kappa\alpha\tau\grave{a}$ $\mu\acute{o}\nu\alpha\varsigma$ ("alone").

3 In the NT $\sigma\acute{u}\nu\epsilon\iota\mu\iota$ ("to be together") is only found twice, both times in Luke—here and in Acts 22:11. Some mss., most notably B*, read $\sigma\upsilon\nu\acute{\eta}\nu\tau\eta\sigma\alpha\nu$ ("they met").

4 As for John and Elijah in 9:19, Luke follows as his source Mark 8:28: John is called $\dot{o}$ $\beta\alpha\pi\tau\iota\sigma\tau\acute{\eta}\varsigma$ ("the baptist"), and Elijah receives no additional designation. In the case of the prophets, the third possibility being considered by the crowds, Luke deviates from Mark and goes back to Luke 9:8.

5 Why, in contrast to Mark, does Luke drop the article before $\Pi\acute{\epsilon}\tau\rho o\varsigma$ ("Peter")? According to BDF §260, "The use of the article with proper names was colloquial." But Lukan usage in this respect is not consistent, as 9:32 shows clearly.

6 Jesus' question "Who do you say I am?" had become

so deeply imprinted on the Christian consciousness that it retains the same form in all three Synoptic accounts.

7 On the variants $\upsilon\acute{\iota}\acute{o}\nu$ ("son") or $\tau\grave{o}\nu$ $\upsilon\acute{\iota}\acute{o}\nu$ after $\tau\grave{o}\nu$ $\chi\rho\iota\sigma\tau\acute{o}\nu$ ("the anointed one," "the Messiah"), see *New Testament in Greek*, 197, as well as the apparatus in Nestle-Aland.

8 The empty space in Nestle-Aland between v. 21 and v. 22 is uncalled for. Even less justified is the period placed after v. 21 in Aland, *Synopsis*, 231.

9 Luke's use of $\dot{a}\pi\acute{o}$ to replace Mark's $\dot{u}\pi\acute{o}$ can be explained by the presence of the verb $\dot{a}\pi o\delta o\kappa\iota$-$\mu\alpha\sigma\vartheta\hat{\eta}\nu\alpha\iota$.

10 Mark 8:31; 9:31; 10:34.

Commentary

■ **18–20** Luke places Peter's confession in a different context than does Mark. He has prepared his readers from the beginning of his account for Jesus' messianic identity. Until this point, indeed, the focus has been faith, but never the messianic confession of a disciple. Luke has structured artfully the sublime scene of the calling of disciples in 5:1–11. Somewhat later he presents the choosing of the Twelve and their appointment as apostles (6:12–16), among whom Peter is chosen as the first, and receives his new name (6:14). Then the Twelve appear in the service of the mission (9:1–6) and the gathering (9:10–17). Where the questioning Herod remains alone and uncertain when faced with the various popular opinions (9:7–9), Jesus begins a conversation with Peter in the form of a question, which leads to the disclosure of the christological identity of the questioner. By structuring his narrative in this way, Luke wants to prove that the disciples, through Peter's statement, recognized their Lord while he was still in Galilee, that is, long before his passion, and knew him with christological correctness. In contrast to Mark, Luke places no emphasis on the disciples' lack of comprehension of Jesus' suffering (but see 9:45 and 18:34). This does not mean, however, that the cross will not make them stumble. Peter himself will betray Jesus (22:31–34, 54–62), but that will be a single and provisional act of weakness. After his tears (22:62), his repentance (22:32b), and Jesus' resurrection, Peter will recognize him again with christological correctness, and will take the stage as the spokesman of the Twelve. Luke is thus concerned both with ecclesiology and christology here. The reader learns that Peter answered the Lord correctly: the church's confession has its roots in the pre-Easter period.

■ **21** How does Luke understand the command to silence? There are two possible interpretations: (1) either the title of Christ is dangerous without the correction that follows it (v. 22), the prediction of the passion; or (2) the leaders of the people cannot believe in Jesus' messianism; therefore, the ministry of the Lord may come to an end too early through their powerful intervention (cf. 22:66–71).

Peter's confession (v. 20b) is at the same time also a conclusion of the first part of the Gospel. But a saying from Jesus himself, the first prediction of the Passion, now anticipates the continuation and the conclusion of the Gospel of Luke (v. 22). In conversation with the Lord, the faith of the disciples deepens: the disciples (and the readers) should turn their attention to the suffering Christ.

■ **22** Luke adopts two theological points from Mark with special avidity: δεῖ ("it is necessary") and παθεῖν ("to suffer"). God has a plan (cf. Acts 2:23). Between divine fate and human freedom runs the path of the living God, who foresees the suffering of the Son of Man and integrates it. According to Luke, not only death but suffering is a characteristic of Christian messianism (cf. Acts 26:23). Παθεῖν, then, encompasses both the rejection and dying of Jesus. The highest authority in Judaism will be deceived and reject the divine message. Ἀποδοκιμάζω means "to declare unusable after a test," "to reject." The greater the consciousness of mission, the greater is the disappointment, normally, in the face of incomprehension. But the Lukan Jesus is not expressing his feelings; Luke simply transmits the liturgical, hard, and naked formula. Jesus will not only die like everyone else (ἀποθνήσκω), but he will be killed (ἀποκτείνω). The sentence of the Sanhedrin (there is no mention of Pilate here) will be transformed into a murder. The Lukan Peter in the book of Acts uses the same verb, even in the active tense (Acts 3:15: ἀπεκτείνατε, "you killed"). But human beings can kill no more than the body (Luke 12:4–5). God will continue to work, will integrate the murder into his plan, and will grant it an entirely new meaning through Jesus' resurrection.

Conclusion

Not only Good Friday comes into view here for the first time, but also Easter. Although the entire Christian message in Luke has its foundation in the resurrection, this pericope is reticent about the decisive event. The meaning of the suffering and the implications of the resurrection remain obscure.

About Following Jesus (9:23–27)

Bibliography

Bultmann, *History,* passim.

Dautzenberg, *Leben,* 51–82.

Dinkler, Erich, "Jesu Wort vom Kreuztragen," in W. Eltester, ed., *Neutestamentliche Studien: Festschrift Rudolf Bultmann* (BZNW 21; Berlin: Töpelmann, 1954) 110–29 (= Dinkler, *Signum Crucis* [Tübingen: Mohr-Siebeck, 1967] 77–98).

Grässer, Erich, *Das Problem der Parusieverzögerung in den synoptischen Evangelien und in der Apostelgeschichte* (3d ed.; BZNW 22; Berlin: de Gruyter, 1977) 131–37.

Green, Michael P., "The Meaning of Cross-Bearing," *BSac* 140 (1983) 117–33.

Griffiths, J. G., "The Disciple's Cross," *NTS* 16 (1969–70) 358–64.

Ha Fong, Maria Ko, *Crucem tollendo Christum sequi: Untersuchung zum Verständnis eines Logions Jesu in der alten Kirche* (Münster: Aschendorff, 1984).

Künzi, Martin, *Das Naherwartungslogion Markus 9,1 par.: Geschichte seiner Auslegung* (BGBE 21; Tübingen: Mohr-Siebeck, 1977).

Lindeskog, Gösta, "Das Rätsel des Menschensohnes," *StTh* 22 (1968) 149–76.

O'Callaghan, José, "Nota crítica a Mc 8,36," *Bib* 64 (1983) 116–17.

Roosen, Anton, "'Quand il viendra dans la gloire des saints anges' (Lc 9,26) . . . ," in M. Benzerath et al., eds., *La Pâque du Christ, Mystère du salut: Festschrift F.-X. Durrel* (LD 112; Paris: Cerf, 1982) 147–58.

Schneider, Gerhard, *Parusiegleichnisse im Lukas-Evangelium* (SBB 74; Stuttgart: Katholisches Bibelwerk, 1975) 66–69.

Schulz, *Nachfolgen,* 82–90, 97, 162–65, 267.

idem, "Wer mein Jünger sein will, der nehme TÄGLICH sein Kreuz auf sich!" *BK* 24 (1969) 9.

Wijngaards, John N. M., "Let Him Take Up His Cross . . . ," *Vidyajyoti* 47 (1983) 106–17.

23 Then he said to them all, "If any want to become my followers, let them deny themselves and take up their cross daily and follow me. 24/ For those who want to save their life will lose it, and those who lose their life for my sake will save it. 25/ For does it profit people if they gain the whole world, but lose or forfeit themselves? 26/ For those who are ashamed of me and my words, of them the Son of Man will also be ashamed when he comes in his glory and that of the Father and of the holy angels. 27/ But truly I tell you, there are some standing here who will not taste death before they see the kingdom of God."

Analysis

According to Luke, Jesus was alone with the disciples during Peter's confession and the first prediction of the passion (v. 18a), but it is possible that the crowds may have remained present in the background (differently than in Mark 8:34a, where Jesus calls to the crowds to come), so that Jesus can now direct his speech to everyone (v. 23a). In v. 23b Luke extends the saying beyond what he finds in Mark 8:34b, by connecting the carrying of the cross with daily life ($\kappa\alpha\vartheta$' $\dot{\eta}\mu\acute{\epsilon}\rho\alpha\nu$, "daily," and the change from $\dot{\epsilon}\lambda\vartheta\epsilon\hat{\iota}\nu$ to $\ddot{\epsilon}\rho\chi\epsilon\sigma\vartheta\alpha\iota$, the aorist to the present tense). At a single point (v. 24), Luke, agreeing with Matthew, follows the traditional, probably oral version about "losing one's life" (Mark 8:35): he retains only the christological emphasis of the saying ($\ddot{\epsilon}\nu\epsilon\kappa\epsilon\nu$ $\dot{\epsilon}\mu\hat{o}\hat{\upsilon}$, "for my sake"), and omits the kerygmatic expansion in Mark ($\kappa\alpha\grave{\iota}$ $\tau\hat{o}\hat{\upsilon}$ $\epsilon\dot{\upsilon}\alpha\gamma\gamma\epsilon\lambda\acute{\iota}o\upsilon$, "and for the sake of the gospel"). In the saying about "gaining the whole world" (Mark 8:36–37), Luke is the only one of the Synoptics who deletes (v. 25) the rationalizing justification ("for what would someone give in exchange for his soul?"). Although he begins the verse in exactly the same manner as Mark ($\tau\acute{\iota}$ $\gamma\acute{\alpha}\rho$, Mark 8:36, 37), his deletion is not a mistake but a conscious omission, probably in order to strengthen the connection between the loss of one's life (v. 24) and the saying about gaining the world (v. 25). The causal function of the various $\gamma\acute{\alpha}\rho$s ("for," vv. 24, 25, 26) is not certain. The saying about "being ashamed" (Mark 8:38) is corrected in both Matt 16:27 and Luke 9:26, more emphatically in Matthew, where the matter of the final judgment is mentioned explicitly, and more weakly in Luke, who deletes the probably secondary addition of the sinful generation in Mark (who repeats a deuteronomistic topos),[1] in favor of an oral version of the saying. Luke does indeed retain the saying in Mark 9:1 (about the people who will not die before the parousia, 9:27), despite its opposition to his theological concerns, thus demonstrating himself to be a true tradent; he does, however, interpret it in the sense of his own eschatological scheme (see below).

---

1   See Deut 1:35; 32:5, 20.

With regard to form criticism, this unit is a series of individual sayings that probably developed and were transmitted independently of the prediction of the passion, as their distribution throughout Q demonstrates,[2] where a number of them are also attested (14:27; 17:33; 12:9). They were added here because of their thematic relationship to the prediction of the passion.

Verse 23 is a summons part in the style of casuistry, part in the style of parenesis. The three imperatives originally reflected three stages of discipleship. With the addition of "daily," they are on the way to becoming synonymous. Luke, who usually does not like to include doublets, also gives the Q version of this logion in 14:27.

Verse 24 is a double saying with an antithetical character, in the wisdom tradition. Thematically, the teaching of the two ways stands in the background, and perhaps also texts like Deut 30:15–18, which could also explain the dualism of the parable of the two houses (Luke 6:47–49). As Luke 17:33 and John 12:25 show, the christological, pre-Markan interpretation ($\H{\epsilon}\nu\epsilon\kappa\epsilon\nu$ $\H{\epsilon}\mu o\hat{v}$, "for my sake") is secondary and disturbs the strict parallel structure. The appearance of the word "want" only in the negative clause probably has theological significance.

Verse 25 is a rhetorical question, which wise people would naturally answer negatively. The subject of the verb is not the individual Christian but, as in the wisdom tradition, the individual taken as part of the nation. The exaggeration ("to gain the whole world") also attests the wisdom character of the saying (as in 18:25).

Verse 26 reflects the concept of retribution known from the Hebrew Bible. The image is of Jesus as a teacher, who instructs ("my words"), and not of a reigning or suffering Messiah. The clause beginning with $\H{o}\tau\alpha\nu$ ("when") disturbs the symmetry and can be understood as a Christian interpretation: the apocalyptic content presumably provoked the insertion of the title "Son of Man" in the main clause (cf. 12:9, where it is lacking).

The saying in v. 27, which is not attested in Q, is more likely to be influenced by apocalyptic rather than wisdom tradition. Jesus foresees the dawn of the kingdom of God. Jesus' position within the vision is not expressed, but he is more likely on the side of the coming kingdom than of the contemporary audience who survives until that point: the saying thus presupposes the death of Jesus.

This small collection brings together wisdom sayings of Jesus about proper living and gives them a christological coloring ("cross," "for my sake," etc.), as well as an apocalyptic impact (especially in the last saying, which does not treat the theme of decision at all). Their present context, in immediate proximity to the first prediction of the passion (9:22), gives the sayings a Christian interpretation. Life in the faith is possible only by following the crucified Messiah Jesus. Conversely, the presence of this small collection lends the christology of Peter's confession (9:18–21) an exemplary character.[3]

Q knew most of these sayings as individual units. Citations in early Christian literature show that they continued to be transmitted as isolated units in parallel to the Markan tradition. Some of these citations are more likely taken from oral tradition than from a written gospel.[4]

Luke thus follows Mark in connecting these sayings to the prediction of the passion, in the sequence of the sayings, and in the broader audience. Here and there, he allows the voice of oral tradition to be heard, or expresses his own concerns. His redactional deletion of the hard words between Peter and Jesus (Mark 8:32–33) is especially important.

---

2   Since Matt 10:38–39—taken from Q—has already combined the logia about carrying one's cross and losing one's life, one can assume that the two sayings were associated in this context quite early, certainly earlier than Mark (see Gnilka, *Markus*, 2.22).

3   See Voss, *Christologie*, 171.

4   Various parallels are collected in the notes to Mark 8:34—9:1 and its parallels in Aland, *Synopsis*, 236. 2 Tim 2:12 (a parallel for Luke 9:26) certainly derives from oral tradition, as also probably *2 Clem.* 6.2 and Justin *1 Apol.* 15.12 (a parallel for Luke 9:25, but even closer to Matt 16:26). *Gos. Thom.* 55 is closer to the Q version of carrying one's cross (Luke 14:27 and par.) than it is to Mark's (Luke 9:23 and par.). *Gos. Thom.* 67 is a gnostic modification of the Synoptic version of the logion concerning losing one's life (Luke 9:25 and par.).

Commentary

In the Lukan understanding of these sayings,[5] the crowds have experienced the gracious favor of God in the feeding (vv. 10–17). It is now time to teach them how one exists before God (vv. 23–27). The imperative thus in no wise takes first place here. But there is also no christological knowledge (vv. 18–22) that does not end in a turning back to God (vv. 23–27). For this reason, the crowds do not yet have the capacity to make a confession like that of Peter.

■ **23** Now begins a speech to the entire people, that is, directed at the same time to the entire reading or hearing audience, that is in part informative, and in part exhortative (v. 23a).

Faith is not simply an assent that something is true. It is a personal movement toward the person who is God's representative. Verse 23 does not insist as much on this movement as vv. 10–17, but requires mature ethical cooperation, for Christian existence in Luke is walking (ἔρχεσθαι, "to go") in the accompaniment (ἀκολουθείτω μοι, "let them follow me") and under the leadership of Jesus (ὀπίσω μου, "after me"). In the post-Easter situation, this means to live in the midst of the world, under the kerygma, under baptism, and in community—what Paul describes with the term "imitate." Without the break with one's self (ἀρνησάσθω ἑαυτόν, "let them deny themselves"), repentance has no consequences. "To deny oneself" does not mean to hate oneself (cf. 10:27), but, expressed in modern terms, to deny one's inauthentic manner of existence, to deconstruct the proud façade of one's identity, and to bring to view one's genuine, plain, fragile "I" in relationship to Christ. The tax collector of the parable (18:13) exemplifies this saying.

Where ἀρνησάσθω ἑαυτόν ("let them deny themselves") indicates the moment of separation from one's own past, καὶ ἀράτω τὸν σταυρὸν αὐτοῦ καθ᾽ ἡμέραν ("let them . . . take up their cross daily") describes the

direction of personal ethics. Faithfulness in the faith points to suffering and following Jesus. Luke writes, "It is through many persecutions that we must enter the kingdom of God" (Acts 14:22). Jesus does not require suffering as such, but foresees that love of God and one's neighbor (Luke 10:27) cannot be made concrete without self-sacrifice and shared suffering. The imminent expectation of Christ's return is no longer dominant, but there is an expectation of rest in God, either after death or after the parousia. The first saying is structured so that following Jesus is expressed twice, at the beginning and the end, and is interpreted in two ways in the middle of the saying, through the idea of a rupture with one's sinful past, and through the description of an obedient present and future.

■ **24** The verb θέλω ("to will," "to want") perhaps serves as the link between v. 23 and v. 24. In the tradition, the connection was in the decision of the will: in v. 23 the will to affirm, and in v. 24 the will to deny. The Lukan theology of relationship is concerned with both of these possible answers by the human will to the divine initiative (vv. 10–17).

The paradox of the expression itself (v. 24) describes what the catastrophic attempt to save one's own life constitutes: one fails to save one's life, precisely when one wants to save it. "To save one's life" is not a negative expression in itself. On the contrary, God wants us to save our own lives. What Luke's Christ condemns is a saving of one's self in which people try to realize their legitimate hopes through their own actions, their own efforts, their own thoughts. People miss what they are aiming to do, then, when they try to save up their lives for themselves. God gives us a life that belongs to us only when we give it to someone else. This remarkable characteristic of human life can be explained theologically because God is the foundation and result of this life. The failure of self-justification can be perceived even on the psychological level of interpersonal experience, because an existence that is purely concerned with

---

5   On the meaning of these sayings in Mark and in the tradition, see Gnilka, *Markus*, 2.23–27. On v. 23 see Schulz, *Nachfolgen;* and idem, "Wer mein Jünger sein will, der nehme TÄGLICH sein Kreuz auf sich!" *BK* 24 (1969) 9. On v. 24 see Dautzenberg, *Leben;* on v. 25 see José O'Callaghan, "Nota crítica a Mc 8,36," *Bib* 64 (1983) 116–17; on v. 26 see Gösta Lindeskog, "Das Rätsel des Menschensohnes," *StTh*

22 (1968) 149–76; and on v. 27 see Erich Grässer, *Das Problem der Parusieverzögerung in den synoptischen Evangelien und in der Apostelgeschichte* (3d ed.; BZNW 22; Berlin: de Gruyter, 1977) 131–37.

oneself is a ruined existence, so long as it lacks the quality and warmth of human communication.

In the second half, "to lose one's life" should be placed in quotation marks, because it only seems to be a lost life. Christian existence in the second century was evaluated in this way by many pagans: miserable, without enjoyment, sad, full of suffering.[6] "For my sake" makes Jesus' purpose explicit. The christological referent means that the Christian life is not a life under a new law, but a life in fellowship with the Lord. God will, in the end, save such a life.

■ **25** In his Gospel, Luke symbolizes unbelief not with the Hebrew Bible image of promiscuity, but with that of greed.[7] The Semitic-sounding saying in v. 25 didactically places possession of everything next to losing oneself.[8] The drive to save oneself is here made more precise in the impulse to gain possessions, where "to gain the world"[9] also includes power. The consequence of this mirage would be the deprivation of all the rest from possessions, and their inexorable desire for revenge. To express it positively, community of goods results in a successful life: one receives by giving.[10]

Current psychology and even solid common sense tell us that no one can live without a structured ego and a few possessions as symbols of this identity. Luke's Christ is surely not advocating such a denial of life. What he requires is located in the midst of a lively and life-giving relationship between God and people. Only from this communication is it even possible in the first place to understand oneself other than as self-righteous, and to understand "having" as something other than private possession. Church history provides many figures that only "found themselves" by "losing themselves." For Western Christendom, Francis of Assisi is the embodiment of this gospel requirement.[11]

■ **26** I will comment on v. 26 extensively in the context of interpreting the parallel Q version of this saying in Luke 12:8–9, merely indicating here some of the characteristics specific to v. 26. Instead of a formula with two halves of equal weight (12:8–9), only the danger of betrayal is named here, parallel to v. 25. It is not only the "confession" (cf. 12:8) that disappears here; Luke also writes, in contrast to 12:9, an emotionally intense word taken from Mark 8:38: ἐπαισχύνομαι ("to be ashamed"). Faith and witness are thus not just matters of intelligence, but also of the heart. It requires inner determination and maturity not to behave like all the rest, to speak one's own opinion and to have public courage. One can easily be ashamed of certain relationships that are not part of the general consensus. Christians had to overcome this embarrassment in both the world of Judaism and in the urban centers of Hellenism.[12] Both the person (με, "me") and the teaching (τοὺς ἐμοὺς λόγους, "and . . . my words") could be offensive. Paul attests this feeling and the overcoming of it: "For I am not ashamed of the gospel" (Rom 1:16). But ἐπαισχύνομαι ("to be ashamed") does not stand for just a feeling, but a complete behavior. Shame paralyzes people and determines them both internally and externally. The saying intends to remain in the realm of images, and for this reason speaks of the shame of the Son of Man with a grain of salt.

---

6   On the Gentiles' contempt for the Christian way of life, see Pierre de Labriolle, *La réaction païenne: Étude sur la polémique antichrétienne du Iᵉʳ au VIᵉ siècle* (10th ed.; Paris: L'Artisan du Livre, 1950) 117–24 (on Celsus).

7   See Bovon, *Lukas*, 110–12.

8   Luke adds ἀπολέσας (the aorist participle of ἀπόλλυμι, "to lose," "to destroy") in v. 25 as a contrast to σώσει ("to save"), which plays an essential role in the preceding verse (v. 24), in order to strengthen the connection between the two verses.

9   Κερδαίνω means "to gain," "to profit," "to derive benefit from," " to gain money, time, prestige, etc." (see LSJ *s.v.*). The ὅλος ("whole") modifying ὁ κόσμος ("the world") clarifies the matter: even the world in its entirety.

10   Luke invests the sentence with elegance by replacing Mark's καί with δέ and by converting the structure into a chiasm: κερδήσας (A) τὸν κόσμον ὅλον (B) ἑαυτὸν δὲ (B') ἀπολέσας ἢ ζημιωθείς (A'). Why does Luke everywhere replace the Markan "his soul" with "himself"? Surely Luke regards the two expressions as synonymous. D* and a few other mss. have infinitives instead of participles—undoubtedly a result of Mark's influence.

11   See Werner Goez, "Franciscus von Assisi (1181/82–1226)," *TRE* 11 (1983) 299–307.

12   On shame in the HB, see Fritz Stolz, "בוש," *TLOT* 1.204–7, who points out two aspects that in complementarity, one objective (misery, decay, disgrace) and the other subjective (shame, disgrace). However, the author underestimates the subjective aspect of this verb in the religious context. On ἐπαισχύνομαι ("to be ashamed") in the NT, see Rudolf Bultmann, "αἰσχύνω, κτλ.," *TDNT* 1 (1964) 189–91, who refers to the great influence of the

■ **27** Mark 9:1 transmits a saying that indicates the parousia, especially in its Matthean parallel version (16:28).[13] Luke, for his part, gives the logion a sense that is bearable in his own time by deleting the words "has come with power" from his Markan source. His view no longer spans the time from the present to the eschaton, for the end for him is no longer in the imminent future. What he takes away from the imminent apocalyptic parousia, he gives to salvation history:[14] the kingdom of God is already present in Jesus, even if not "in power." Luke allows himself to be inspired by this logion in chaps. 1–2, in order to structure the now fulfilled promise in the figure of Simeon (2:26):[15] the old man can now die, for he has seen God's salvation (2:30). In the same way, Jesus' contemporaries may die, for they have seen him (9:27). But Luke nevertheless retains the thought of a span of time between the formulation of the logion and the final "seeing of the kingdom" in that he leaves the form of the saying as untouched as possible. When will Luke's contemporaries see the kingdom of God? He gives no unequivocal answer, since his faithfulness to the tradition answers "later," while his faith believes "already now." Since the ascension (beginning of Acts) marks the second greatest caesura after the incarnation (beginning of the Gospel), the envisaged span of time reaches from now until the resurrection and ascension.[16] We thus are in the period of time of the disciples, who are contemporaries and witnesses, and whose lives will last until after the passion. According to Luke, the τινές ("some") of v. 27 are the believers who are addressed in vv. 23–26, especially the Twelve. One thinks immediately of the Lukan definition of apostle (Acts 1:21–22), which encompasses the same period of time, and presupposes the same presence of the witnesses here (in the life of Jesus) and there (in the time of the church). Luke interprets the saying in a radically new sense, but does so with the conscious purpose of finding the intention of Jesus in the tradition, since the saying spoke of the kingdom of God and not of the parousia of the Son of Man. According to Luke, Jesus himself represents the link between his coming and the kingdom of God (11:20).

Conclusion

Luke 9:23–27 is Jesus' fourth sermon. It follows the Sermon on the Plain (6:20–49), the sermon of parables (8:4–21), and the directives for mission (9:3–5), and it stands in a christological context. This context highlights two things. First, there is no way of assenting to the teaching present in the first three sermons without a personal relationship to Christ. What 6:47 already said is all the more true here: anyone who listens to Jesus' teaching is at the same time a person who is bound to him affectively (πᾶς ὁ ἐρχόμενος πρός με, "everyone who comes to me," 6:47). To "be ashamed" of the other describes here in v. 26 the opposite of this attitude. Second, the consequence of this mutual adherence is fellowship in suffering; the cross, so feared in antiquity, is the first sign along this common way. The Lukan theology of joy does not mean to obscure this serious fact. But the disciples, who "will taste death," can rejoice as did Simeon, for they "see the kingdom of God" already (v. 27).

LXX. "Shame" is not so much a feeling as it is a reality, the experience of God's judgment (see A. Horstmann, "αἰσχύνομαι," *EDNT* 1 (1990) 42–43.

13   On the history the interpretation of this verse (Luke 9:27), see Martin Künzi, *Das Naherwartungslogion Markus 9,1 par.: Geschichte seiner Auslegung* (BGBE 21; Tübingen: Mohr-Siebeck, 1977).

14   See Conzelmann, *Theology*, 104–5 (I refer to the same redactional changes as does Conzelmann; I would, however, represent them somewhat differently than he does).

15   See the commentary on 2:25–28 above.

16   See Bovon, *Theologian*, 12–14, 22–23, 35–38, 424 n. 45.

The Transfiguration (9:28–36)

Bibliography

Autret, Gérard et al., "Le récit de la transfiguration selon Saint Marc: Proposition de lecture," *Sémiotique et Bible* 9 (1978) 36–58.

Baldacci, P. R., "The Significance of the Transfiguration Narrative in the Gospel of Luke: A Redactional Investigation" (diss., Marquette University, 1974); see *DissAb* 36 (1975) 1591-A.

Baltensweiler, *Verklärung*.

Best, Thomas F., "The Transfiguration: A Select Bibliography," *JETS* 24 (1981) 157–61.

Bovon, *Theologian*, 91–93, 439–40 n. 52.

Caird, George Bradford, "The Transfiguration," *ExpTim* 67 (1955–56) 291–94.

Conzelmann, *Theology*, 57–59.

Coune, Michael, "Saint Luc et le mystère de la Transfiguration," *NRTh* 108 (1986) 3–12.

Dietrich, *Petrusbild*, 104–16.

Eichinger, Matthias, *Die Verklärung Christi bei Origenes: Die Bedeutung des Menschen Jesus in seiner Christologie* (Vienna: Herder, 1969).

Feuillet, A., "Les perspectives propres à chaque évangéliste dans les récits de la transfiguration," *Bib* 39 (1958) 281–301.

Garrett, Susan R., "Exodus from Bondage: Luke 9:31 and Acts 12:1–24," *CBQ* 52 (1990) 656–80.

Gause, R. Hollis, "The Lukan Transfiguration Account: Luke's Pre-Crucifixion Presentation of the Exalted Lord in the Glory of the Kingdom of God" (diss., Emory University, 1975); see *DissAb* 36 (1976) 4569-A.

George, Augustin, "La transfiguration (Luc 9,28–36)," *BVC* 33 (1960) 21–25.

Gerber, Wolfgang, "Die Metamorphose Jesu, Mk 9,2f. par.," *ThZ* 23 (1967) 385–95.

Glombitza, "Titel."

Haulotte, *Vêtement*.

Junod, Éric, "Polymorphie du Dieu Sauveur," in J. Ries, ed., *Gnosticisme et monde hellénistique* (Publications de l'Institut orientaliste de Louvain 27; Louvain-La-Neuve: Université catholique de Louvain, 1982) 38–46.

Junod and Kaestli, *Acta Iohannis*, 1.192–97; 2.466–93.

Léon-Dufour, "Transfiguration."

McGuckin, John A., "Jesus Transfigured: A Question of Christology," *Clergy Review* 69 (1984) 271–79.

Miquel, "Mystère."

Neirynck, "Minor Agreements."

Nützel, *Verklärungserzählung*.

Orbe, *Cristología*, 2.96–141.

Pamment, Margaret, "Moses and Elijah in the Story of the Transfiguration," *ExpTim* 92 (1981) 338–39.

Ramsey, Arthur Michael, *The Glory of God and the Transfiguration of Christ* (London/New York: Longmans, Green, 1949).

Reid, Barbara, *The Transfiguration: A Source- and Redaction-Critical Study of Luke 9:28–36* (Paris: Gabalda, 1993).

Riesenfeld, *Jésus transfiguré*.

Ringe, Sharon H., "Luke 9:28–36: The Beginning of an Exodus," *Semeia* 28 (1983) 83–99.

Sabbe, Maurits, "La rédaction du récit de la transfiguration," in E. Massaux et al., *La venue du Messie: Messianisme et eschatologie* (RechBib 6; Paris/Bruges: Desclée de Brouwer, 1962) 65–100.

Schramm, *Markus-Stoff*, 136–39.

Stroumsa, Gedaliahu, "Polymorphie divine et transformation d'un mythologème: L'Apocryphon de Jean et ses sources," *VC* 35 (1981) 412–34.

Trites, Allison A., "The Transfiguration in the Theology of Luke: Some Redactional Links," in L. D. Hurst and N. T. Wright, eds., *The Glory of Christ in the New Testament: Festschrift George Bradford Caird* (Oxford: Clarendon, 1987) 71–82.

Wild, R., *His Face Shone Like the Sun: Encountering the Transfigured Christ in Scripture* (New York: Alba House, 1986).

28 Now it happened about eight days after these words that Jesus took with him Peter and John and James, and went up on the mountain to pray. 29/ And it happened that while he was praying that the appearance of his face changed, and his clothes became dazzling white. 30/ Suddenly they saw two men talking to him, who were Moses and Elijah. 31/ They appeared in glory and were speaking of his departure, which he was to fulfill in Jerusalem. 32/ Now Peter and his companions were weighed down with sleep; but since they had stayed awake, they saw his glory and the two men who stood with him. 33/ And it happened that as they were leaving him, Peter said to Jesus, "Master, it is good for us to be here; let us make three huts, one for you, one for Moses, and one for Elijah"—not knowing what he was saying. 34/ While he was saying this, a cloud came and overshadowed them; and they were terrified as they entered the cloud. 35/ Then from the cloud came a voice that said, "This is my Son, the Chosen One; listen to him!" 36/ When the voice had spoken, Jesus was found alone. And they kept silent and in those days told no one any of the things they had seen.

Analysis

Synoptic Comparison

The transfiguration appears in Luke in the same sequence of pericopes as in Mark and Matthew. Its proximity to Peter's confession (9:18–22) is especially important. As in 9:23–27, Luke uses Mark as his source, but shows some independence (e.g., vv. 31–33), displaying at the same time many small similarities to Matthew.[1] Luke may have known a special source in addition to Mark,[2] or he may have known a pre-Markan text that diverges from the present form of Mark.[3] But both Luke's own peculiarities as well as the similarities to Matthew can be more convincingly explained on the basis of redactional tendencies.[4] If 9:28–36 diverges further from Mark than 9:23–27, this is because Luke treats the narrative passages with greater freedom than the sayings of Jesus. Mark is not canonical Holy Scripture for Luke, but rather a respectable attempt to narrate events, though one that is entirely in need of revision (cf. 1:1–4). In contrast to Matthew, Luke deletes the ending of the Markan pericope (the dialogue during the descent from the mountain, Mark 9:9–13), because he does not equate the Baptist with Elijah.[5]

Luke clearly rewrites the Markan version. After making a connection to the preceding pericope with "after these words," he uses his favorite construction twice, a formulation with ἐγένετο (not as skillfully in v. 28, and with ἐν τῷ and the infinitive in v. 29). As for content, he corrects the date (eight, not six, days) and the sequence of the disciples (John before James). He replaces the verb μεταμορφόω ("to be transfigured") with τὸ εἶδος ... ἕτερον ("the appearance ... changed"); he omits the too prosaic, naïve, or rustic remark about the fuller (Mark 9:3b) and insists (v. 31) on the conversation of Moses and Elijah[6] with Jesus, where οἳ ὀφθέντες ἐν δόξῃ ("they appeared in glory") may be inspired by the Markan ὤφθη ("he appeared," 9:4). He emphasizes the glory of the two men and of Jesus (vv. 31–32), and introduces the theme of the sleepiness of the disciples (v. 32) from the Gethsemane pericope (Mark 14:37–42 par. Luke 22:45–46). He anticipates Jesus' solitude (Mark 9:8; Luke 9:36) in v. 33a,[7] and he lets Jesus' companions leave him here already. Ἐπιστάτα ("master") can be attributed to Luke's antipathy for foreign words. He mentions the disciples' fear (Mark 9:6b) only after describing the cloud, and explains it with the ambiguous expression ἐν τῷ εἰσελθεῖν αὐτοὺς εἰς τὴν νεφέλην ("as they entered the cloud"). The voice of God follows the Markan version with the exception of a single word (ἀγαπητός, "beloved," in Mark, ἐκλελεγμένος, "chosen," in Luke). Verse 36, a free rendering of Mark, serves as an ending, in which v. 36a is an accommodation to Mark 9:8, and v. 36b (the silence of the disciples) shows Luke's redactional peculiarities. Common to Matthew and Luke is the interest in Jesus' face. Both use the word πρόσωπον ("face," Luke 9:29; Matt 17:2). In Matthew it is one of the repetitions that he likes (cf. 28:3), whereas Luke, in contrast, replaces μεταμορφόω ("to be transformed") with a biblical expression (e.g., Dan 3:19 LXX). This minor agreement is as much a matter of chance[8] as the other in v. 34 (ταῦτα δὲ αὐτοῦ λέγοντος; Matt 17:5, ἔτι αὐτοῦ λαλοῦντος), where both expressions are neither identical nor have the same function. The Lukan genitive, redactional in its form (cf. 13:17), serves as the beginning of a new paragraph.[9] Luke thus does not have a second source for this pericope. The account of the transfiguration was also told orally.[10]

---

1   See Frans Neirynck, "Minor Agreements: Matthew-Luke in the Transfiguration Story," in Hoffmann, *Orientierung*, 253–66.

2   Thus, e.g., Schramm in *Markus-Stoff*, 136–39. For further examples see Neirynck, "Minor Agreements," 253–56.

3   Thus, e.g., Marie-Emile Boismard, in idem, P. E. Benoit and A. Lamouille, eds., *Synopse des quatre Évangiles en français* (3 vols.; Paris: Cerf, 1965–77) 2.30–32, 251–52.

4   Neirynck comes to this hypothesis after a detailed examination ("Minor Agreements").

5   See Conzelmann, *Theology*, 24–25, 196.

6   "Elijah with Moses" in Mark (Mark 9:4; in Mark 9:5, however, Moses is mentioned first) becomes "Moses and Elijah" in Luke. Luke places Moses first, which corresponds to the course of salvation history and the overall scheme of the Scriptures (see Luke 24:27, 44).

7   Also typical for Luke is the use of πρός after εἶπεν (v. 33; note that Mark uses the dative).

8   See Neirynck, "Minor Agreements," 256–60.

9   See ibid., 260–64.

10   Dietrich (*Petrusbild*, 106–9) is of the opinion that vv. 28–33a come from another source.

Structure of the Unit

The elements that structure the pericope[11] are ἐγένετο ("it happened," vv. 28, 29, 33), καὶ ἰδού ("suddenly," v. 30), and the genitive absolute (v. 34). They delimit from one another the various episodes that follow sequentially. Verse 28 narrates the ascent up the mountain, v. 29 the transfiguration, vv. 30–31 the conversation, whereas v. 32 tells of the disciples' condition, and v. 33, Peter's suggestion. Verse 34 describes the coming of the cloud, and v. 35, the content of the voice; the reaction of the disciples (v. 36) fills out the last verse. The various episodes, however, do form a literary unit, which is signaled by the symmetrical initial and concluding verses (vv. 28, 36). The first part of the event, the transfiguration and the conversation with Moses and Elijah (vv. 29–31), is to be *seen;* but the second part, with the divine voice (vv. 34–35), is to be *heard.* The group of three disciples sees the glory of the other group of three, and hears the heavenly voice; both of the disciples' reactions (vv. 32, 36) are structured symmetrically. The only individual episode that has no symmetrical counterpart is Peter's odd suggestion (v. 33). The structure that results should not be seen as a static chiasm, but as a dynamic process from a supernatural sign (vv. 29–31) to its divine interpretation (vv. 34–35).

v. 28	frame
vv. 29–31	divine sign
v. 32	human reaction (general)
v. 33	human reaction (concrete)
vv. 34–35	divine interpretation
v. 36	human reaction and frame

Genre and Context in the History of Religions

Various interpretations, which reflect discomfort on the part of the exegetes, have attempted to determine the genre of the account: an enthronement scene (Harald Riesenfeld), a prophetic (Félix Gils) or apocalyptic (Maurits Sabbe) vision, a divine epiphany (R. Silva), a midrash (L. F. Rivera), or a cult narrative (R. Hollis Gause).[12] But the question of genre cannot be separated from the context of the narrative within the history of religions.[13] Various paths cross here. The Sinai tradition (Exod 24)[14] and the transfiguration of Moses as mediator (Exod 34:29–35)[15] are in the background, as is the royal and messianic ideology of the Hebrew Bible in the divine pronouncement. Both can take on an apocalyptic coloration. The reference to Jewish tradition is not sufficient, however, for unlocking the genre and content.[16] The theme of polymorphism comprises "simultaneous or serial appearances of the same being in various forms that are meant to be held in awe."[17] A thorough mono-

---

11 See Godet, 1.423–24; Gnilka, *Markus,* 2.30–32; Fitzmyer, 1.795–96; and Johannes M. Nützel, *Die Verklärungserzählung im Markusevangelium: Eine redaktionsgeschichtliche Untersuchung* (FB 6; Würzburg: Echter, 1973) esp. 46, 296. An examination of these various scholarly treatments makes clear how much the issue of the text's composition has been fused with its interpretation.

12 Nützel (*Verklärungserzählung,* 17, 50, 27, 68, 38) presents, along with other points of view, the dissertation by R. Hollis Gause, "The Lukan Transfiguration Account: Luke's Pre-Crucifixion Presentation of the Exalted Lord in the Glory of the Kingdom of God" (diss., Emory University, 1975); see *DissAb* 36 (1976) 4569-A.

13 This text has been examined from the history-of-religions approach to see, in particular, whether it may have been influenced by HB and Jewish traditions. See Nützel, *Verklärungserzählung,* 75, who cites Wolfgang Gerber, "Die Metamorphose Jesu, Mk 9,2f. par.," *ThZ* 23 (1967) 385–95. Gerber argues that in the background lies an apocalyptic or even a mystical Jewish tradition.

14 Moses climbs up the mountain with three relatives

and seventy elders. Also mentioned are a cloud and a divine voice (see Gnilka, *Markus,* 2.32).

15 Fitzmyer (1.799) is not sure whether one can detect here any influence from Exod 34:29–35.

16 Must one cite Jewish mysticism with its speculations about "little" Yahweh and the "Metatron," and its connection of this heavenly being with Cant 5 and Dan 7, as does Gedaliahu Stroumsa ("Polymorphie divine et transformation d'un mythologème: L'Apocryphon de Jean et ses sources," *VC* 35 [1981] 412–34)? Pierre Miquel shows that exegesis during the Middle Ages also compared the Transfigured One with the lover of the Song of Songs ("Le mystère de la Transfiguration," *Questions liturgiques et paroissiales* [Louvain] 42 [1961] 194–223, esp. 197).

17 Éric Junod, "Polymorphie du Dieu Sauveur," in J. Ries, ed., *Gnosticisme et monde hellénistique* (Publications de l'Institut orientaliste de Louvain 27; Louvain-La-Neuve: Université catholique de Louvain, 1982) 38–46, esp. 39.

graph on this topic unfortunately still does not exist, so that both the origin and genres of this theme remain unclear. It is manifest, however, that the various types of polymorphism must be distinguished from one another, and that they do not necessarily presuppose Docetism. Polymorphism explains the transfiguration of Jesus (his human and divine form), the trio Moses–Elijah–Jesus, and the epiphanic nature of the scene.

As a human leader, Jesus stands in the Jewish tradition of the transfigured Moses and the various messianic expectations, but as a divine messenger he is on the alien level of the polymorphic divinities. In the Jewish tradition the chosen one is lifted up into the heavenly sphere, but in the Hellenistic tradition the compassionate divinity appears and lowers himself. These two movements, exaltation and revelation, narratively attest a two-level christology that is not yet clearly stated and that also occurs in the genre of homology (cf. Rom 1:3b–4). The account of Jesus' baptism (3:21–22) betrays the same christological concerns, as well as a similar genre (with sign and interpretation). The complicated christological background shows that such an account is not a type generated by popular curiosity, but that it belongs to learned reflection. Since, however, theology is at the same time doxology, the functional setting of this unit presupposes not the study chamber of an isolated theologian but the worship space of a Hellenistic Jewish Christian congregation.[18]

The story of Jesus' transfiguration was well known in the second century. The account in 2 Pet 1:17–18 stands within the tradition of the Matthean version.[19] The *Apocalypse of Peter* describes the transfiguration in its own words. Its dialogue format allows Jesus to answer Peter's questions (e.g., about the identity of Moses and Elijah, or about the other righteous individuals from the old covenant). The author inserts a description of paradise between two of the questions, and after the statement of the divine voice, Peter narrates how a crowd of people greet the three figures and then enter into a second heaven (Ps 24[LXX 23]:6 is the prophecy that is said to be fulfilled). Since the author speaks explicitly of the closing of heaven at the end, he understands the scene as an apocalyptic vision, with Jesus as the *angelus interpres*.[20]

In the *Acts of Peter,* one finds a sermon by Peter about the transfiguration, which presupposes its reading in the liturgy. The apostle first defends the common appeal of the Scriptures, because the Lord appears to his followers according to the ability of each one: "the Lord in his mercy was moved to show himself in another shape and to be seen in the form of a human being."[21] The author understands the account as a christophany, and completely forgets Moses and Elijah. The interest is in the relationship of the frightened disciple to his Lord as he reveals himself. The accommodation of the figure of Jesus to the human ability to perceive the divine is presupposed here.

In the *Acts of John,* the favorite disciple mentions in a sermon the various forms that Jesus assumed in order to accommodate himself to his disciples. In this context John briefly mentions the transfiguration account, which he understands as an indescribable theophany (Moses and Elijah are not mentioned, *Acts John* 90). He then describes a more extensive scene in which he could marvel at the polymorphy of Jesus (*Acts John* 90). He then narrates in addition (*Acts John* 91) the impression that this second transfiguration of Jesus made on James and Peter, for these disciples saw another image.

These testimonies about the various forms of Jesus, and about his only apparent corporeality, are meant to effect a response of faith after the final words of the sermon.[22] In the later *Acts of Philip* the readers experience a transfiguration of the apostle himself in the circle of his disciples; and when they, trembling with fear, are unable

---

18   On the prehistory of the Markan text, esp. on the unlikely hypothesis of an Easter appearance transferred to another place, see Fitzmyer, 1.795–96.

19   See Éric Fuchs and Pierre Reymond, *La deuxième épître de saint Pierre* (CNT 13b; Neuchâtel: Delachaux et Niestlé, 1980) 68–71.

20   See *Apoc. Pet.* 15–17 (4–20) in Hennecke-Schneemelcher, 2.680–83. This work is extant in an Ethiopic translation and partly in a Greek text, and is not to be confused with another work bearing the same name from Nag Hammadi (NHC VII.3). See

C. Detlef G. Müller, "Apocalypse of Peter," in Hennecke-Schneemelcher, 2.620–25.

21   *Acts Pet.* 20; translation by Wilhelm Schneemelcher in Hennecke-Schneemelcher, 2.303; see Gérard Poupon, "Les Actes de Pierre," in Bovon, *Actes apocryphes,* 299–301.

22   See Junod and Kaestli, *Acta Iohannis,* 1.192–97 (text and translation) and 2.466–93 (commentary). Note the silence that ensues after such revelations, such as *Acts John* 93, similarly at Luke 9:36. Lukan influ-

to bear the intensity of the light, he reminds them of Jesus (probably in the transfiguration account in the Gospels), transforms back to his original form, and calms the audience.[23]

The revelations of Jesus to three figures[24] are perhaps influenced by the transfiguration scenes in the Gospels, but the motif of the three figures is probably pre-Christian[25] and left its traces already in the Gospels. All the apocryphal passages emphasize, on the one hand, an understanding of the transfiguration as a theophany, and, on the other, an interpretation of the multiplicity of the figures as a pedagogical method and as the appropriate expression of the indescribable divinity.[26]

Commentary

Although the transfiguration best expressed for many ancient Christians and Gnostics their christology and their understanding of reality, it causes difficulties for readers in the present day. Its historicity seems impossible, and the doctrine of the incarnation of Jesus seems to be threatened by the account. At the same time, modern readers cannot close their eyes to the beauty of the narrative. If they also know something of orthodox theology, they will perceive that Jesus is not taking on an alien nature provisionally, but rather uncovering his true identity.[27]

The Frame (v. 28)

■ **28** In just a few words, a lot is said, or rather, hinted at. The transfiguration pericope answers the question of the preceding discussion ("after these words"). Through it, especially through the heavenly voice, God confirms Jesus' prediction (9:22). But where Jesus places his messianic suffering in first place, the glory of the Son manifests itself here. Expressed differently: the concise, restrained formulation εὑρέθη Ἰησοῦς μόνος ("Jesus was found alone," 9:36) is a negative counterpart to the short, magnificent ending in v. 22, the reference to Jesus' resurrection (καὶ τῇ τρίτῃ ἡμέρᾳ ἐγερθῆναι, "and on the third day be raised").

After this *christological* link with the previous pericope, there is also an *anthropological* or *ecclesiological* reference to the context: immediately after Peter's confession, the disciples and, through them, the congregation (and the readers) have learned of the necessity of the suffering of the Messiah (9:22) and his followers (9:23–24). The transfiguration possesses a parenetic and comforting function.[28]

Is this pericope meant to form a conclusion to the Galilean period, in symmetry to the baptismal account? The account of the journey indeed only begins in 9:51, but the redactional conversation of the three figures (9:31) already points to the future passion. One can probably assume a formal relationship to the baptism account (an *inclusio* of the first part of the Gospel), but the first prediction of the passion, like the transfiguration, primarily foreshadows what is to follow, indeed announces it.[29]

The Lukan indication of time presents two questions: Why is it in the nominative (cf. Josh 1:11 LXX as a parallel)?[30] Is the evangelist consciously correcting Mark's

ence also becomes visible in the motif of the prayer that accompanies the ascent up the mountain in *Acts John* 90. In the rest of the *Acts of John* one can see that the author has taken considerable freedom in appropriating material from the narrative of Luke's Gospel.

23 *Acts Phil.* 5.22–23 (60–61). See François Bovon, "Les Actes de Philippe," in Bovon, *Actes apocryphes*, 301–4.

24 See, e.g., the Apocryphon of John, NHC 2.1.1.30–2.9.

25 Perhaps reminiscent of the three phases of Horus as the sun god (in the morning a child, at noon an adult, and in the evening an old man) or of the deities in the Palmyric triad.

26 For further details on its reception, see the passage on the history of interpretation at the end of this section.

27 See Olivier Clément, *Transfigurer le temps: Notes sur*

le temps à la lumière de la tradition orthodoxe (Neuchâtel: Delachaux et Niestlé, 1959) 97–121.

28 Heinrich Baltensweiler (*Die Verklärung Jesu: Historisches Ereignis und synoptische Berichte* [AThANT 33; Zurich: Zwingli-Verlag, 1959] 55–56) and George Bradford Caird (*The Gospel of St. Luke* [PNTC; Harmondsworth: Penguin, 1963] 132) emphasize that the transfiguration must have corresponded with a crisis situation in Jesus' life. According to Baltensweiler, Jesus confronts the temptation to become a political messiah for the last time (see Nützel, *Verklärungserzählung*, 23, 48).

29 On the literary function of the proleptic "announcement of future topics," see Albert Vanhoye, *La structure littéraire de l'Épître aux Hébreux* (Paris: Desclée de Brouwer, 1963) 37.

30 BDF §144 remarks that Luke 9:28 mixes the construction of ἐγένετο δὲ . . . καί ("it happened . . .

mention of six days, or is he trying to indicate the same span of time by including in his reckoning, as was done in antiquity, the previous day (Peter's confession) and the following day (the transfiguration)? The number eight more likely has a special significance for Luke. The eighth day, the day after the week, the resurrection, the new creation, or eternal rest could all be described eschatologically with this number.[31] But did the number eight already have this patristic meaning?[32] In addition, the text does not read "on the eighth day." Might the number eight even refer to the Feast of Booths (Sukkot, Lev 23:36), the eighth day of which, in various Jewish circles, had a significance greater than that of a simple celebration of the return to everyday life?[33] Luke is thus not speaking simply of a week.[34] This indication of time is the only one in the life of Jesus, if one excludes the passion narrative.[35]

That Jesus chooses only Peter, John, and James as his companions (cf. 8:51 and Mark 14:33; differently in Luke 22:39) characterizes the event that follows as particularly important. Luke often places John after Peter, in second place (cf. 8:51; Acts 4:13; 8:14). In accordance with his concept of the church, he has little interest in James (cf. Acts 12:2). Luke's fidelity to tradition (here Mark) demands James's presence, but Luke's theological concerns place James last.

The motif of the mountain[36] intimates an encounter with the divine, which is also the goal of prayer, mentioned in the text. At the decisive points of his life, the Lukan Jesus wants to remain in prayerful contact with his Father.[37]

Jewish readers will not miss the "quotation" of the Hebrew Bible here in the scenery, and will immediately think of Moses, his three companions, the mountain, and the nearness of God (Exod 24). But the quotation becomes a "mixed quotation," since the pericope narrates a transfiguration (Exod 34:29–35). Moreover, this reception of the Hebrew Bible does not occur slavishly, but with creative power: the New Testament scene produces an original image from the free "citations" and the new elements.

Luke does not say that Jesus himself worked the miracle of the transfiguration. He probably means rather that Jesus has met the "entrance requirements" (v. 28) and that God is the one who acts (v. 29).

---

and"; see §442.5) with the date in the nominative. Luke inserts another participial phrase ($\pi\alpha\rho\alpha$-$\lambda\alpha\beta\grave{\omega}\nu$ $\kappa\tau\lambda$., "taking with") between the $\kappa\alpha\acute{\iota}$ and the main verb ($\grave{\alpha}\nu\acute{\epsilon}\beta\eta$: "he went up") which only overloads the whole sentence, making it sound awkward.

31 On the eighth day see *2 Enoch* 33:1–2. This is a passage from the longer recension of *2 Enoch* (a redactional addition? See André Vaillant, *Le livre des secrets d'Hénoch: Texte slave et traduction française* [Paris: Institut d'études slaves, 1952] 102–5; F. I. Andersen, "2 [Slavonic Apocalypse of] Enoch," in *OTP* 1.156, also 93–94. See as well *Barn.* 15.8–9; cf. Pierre Prigent and Robert A. Kraft, *Épître de Barnabé* [SC 172; Paris: Cerf, 1971] 186–88; Auguste Luneau, *L'histoire du salut chez les Pères de l'Église: La doctrine des âges du monde* [ThH 2; Paris: Beauchesne, 1964] 438 [in the index *s.v.* "Jour, huitième"]).

32 Edward Earle Ellis thinks it did (*The Gospel of Luke* [2d ed.; NCB; reprinted Grand Rapids: Eerdmans, 1981] 142, 276), and Grundmann (192) also affirms it but with some caution. However, Marshall (382) is not convinced.

33 See *Jub.* 32:27–29; Robert Martin-Achard, *Essai biblique sur les fêtes d'Israël* (Geneva: Labor et Fides, 1974) 83–88.

34 According to Karl Ludwig Schmidt, Luke wanted to say the same thing as Mark: it had been a week (*Der Rahmen der Geschichte Jesu: Literarkritische Untersuchungen zur ältesten Jesusüberlieferung* [1919; reprinted Darmstadt: Wissenschaftliche Buchgesellschaft, 1964] 223–24). He would have done this in the manner of the Romans, for whom "eight days" was synonymous with "one week."

35 See Fitzmyer, 1.797. One also notes that Luke is fond of using $\acute{\omega}\sigma\epsilon\acute{\iota}$ ("about") before a number.

36 Why has Luke omitted the adjective "high"? On the location of this mountain, see Harald Riesenfeld, *Jésus transfiguré: L'arrière plan du récit évangélique de la transfiguration de Notre-Seigneur* (ASNU 16; Copenhagen: Munksgaard, 1947) 217, 244, 293. The mountain identified as "Tabor" in *Gos. Heb.* frg. 3 (see Hennecke-Schneemelcher, 1.177) is the mountain of the temptation. Fitzmyer (1.798) is of the opinion that Tabor is equated with the Mount of Transfiguration for the first time in a text attributed to Origen (or Pseudo-Origen), *Exegetica in Psalmos*, Ps 88:13 (*PG* 12.1548). This identification is no longer questioned by the time of Cyril of Jerusalem (*Cat. Myst.* 12.16).

37 Luke prefers "in order to pray" over Mark's formulation, $\kappa\alpha\tau$ '$\grave{\iota}\delta\acute{\iota}\alpha\nu$ $\mu\acute{o}\nu o \upsilon\varsigma$ ("by themselves alone," Mark 9:2; the Markan expression underscores the

The Divine Sign (v. 29)

■ **29** While praying, the εἶδος ("form") of Jesus' face changes, and his garment also begins to shine. Τὸ πρόσωπον here means "face," but could also describe the entire "figure." What becomes "different" is not the identity, which is envisaged in τὸ πρόσωπον, but its appearance, which is expressed by τὸ εἶδος ("form").[38] The word ἕτερον ("other" of two) expresses a change not in essence but in the relationship of Jesus to the others, and of the others to him. According to Luke, Jesus does not become different from what he was before, but for a moment his appearance becomes a divine sign to humanity, the sign of his true identity. In Luke this christological observation remains embedded in the doctrine of God; "the different appearance" does not express Jesus' divine nature, but a relationship of God to him, just as he stands, now in prayer, in the right relationship to God. Indeed, in contrast to the theophanies (esp. that in Exod 24:9–11), the transfiguration of Jesus' appearance[39] is in the center of the account, which, differently from that of Moses (Exod 34:29–35), is not a mere mirror of the glory he has just received, but is a window onto the father-son relationship, which the voice will explain.

Jesus' garment[40] also changes, and becomes λευκός ("white," "brilliant"). Ἐξαστράπτω ("to shine forth," "to flash") is rare; Luke probably took it from biblical vision accounts (Ezek 1:4, 7; Nah 3:3). Shining garments and figures are part and parcel of apocalyptic materials.[41] If one is aware that the garment is an expression of status, and, more broadly, of identity, the hint is clear: Jesus belongs to the divine realm. It is not impossible that behind this image is also the supersession of Adam's natural clothing, the sign of his fall; Jesus is clothed in glory here, just as Adam was before his fall.[42] Church fathers (e.g., Anastasius of Sinai) saw this connection.[43]

Jesus' Journey (vv. 30–31)

■ **30–31** A new episode begins with καὶ ἰδού ("behold," "suddenly"). The main figure is still present, but he is suddenly flanked by two men (probably one on each side). Luke assumes the role of the *angelus interpres* and gives us their names. Mark's odd formulation is put in chronological sequence: Moses and Elijah. The reason for their appearance and presence is not given.[44] It is not because they had never truly died (Enoch would be the

---

aspect of community). Monloubou is of the opinion that Luke mentions the prayers of Jesus to encourage Christians to communicate with God (*Prière*, 57–61). Luke mentions Jesus' prayer once again in v. 29.

38 On the terms πρόσωπον and εἶδος, see the extensive citations in BAGD *s.v.*

39 On the transformation see Str-B 1.752; Johannes Behm, "μορφή," *TDNT* 4 (1967) 755–59; Gnilka (*Markus*, 2.33); and Fitzmyer (1.798–99), who cites a text from Qumran (lQapGen 2.16–17). A number of exegetes maintain that Luke has avoided Mark's verb μεταμορφόω ("to change form," Mark 9:2) in order to preclude any confusion with the pagan notion of metamorphosis, but I doubt it. Luke also uses similar words when he describes the transfiguring of Stephen's face (Acts 6:15). Paul, on the other hand, speaks of the present transfiguration of the face of believers from one degree of glory to another in 2 Cor 3:18, and in the same chapter he shows that he is aware of the motif of Moses' shining face.

40 Although ὁ ἱματισμός ("dress," "clothing") is a singular, it corresponds exactly to the plural τὰ ἱμάτια in Mark 9:3 and indicates the visible outer clothes, in contrast to the χιτών (a garment worn next to the skin), which here is deliberately avoided.

41 See Dan 10:5–6; Rev 1:12–16; Str-B 1.752–53.

42 Haulotte (*Vêtement*, 186–90) refers to *Gen. Rab.* 20.12, *Pirqe R. El.* 14–20 (before the fall, Adam as king and priest wore a shining, seamless garment), and the Greek writing *Apoc. Mos.* 20–21 (Adam loses the garment of glory and of righteousness after the fall). See Riesenfeld, *Jésus transfiguré*, 115, 246; also Gnilka, *Markus*, 2.33.

43 Σήμερον ἐπὶ τοῦ ὄρους ὁ τοὺς στυγνοὺς ἐκείνους καὶ κατηφεῖς περιβληθεὶς δερματίνους χιτῶνας ἀμπεχόνην ὑπέδυ θεότευκτον, ἀναβαλλόμενος φῶς ὡς ἱμάτιον ("Today on the mountain he who was clothed in those dreadful and detestable animal hides has put on a garment made by God, and he is wrapped in light as with a robe," Ps 104[LXX 103]:2). This is from a homily on the transfiguration by Anastasius of Mt. Sinai, edited by André Guillou ("Le Monastère de la Théotokos au Sinaï," *Mélanges d'archéologie et d'histoire* 67 [1955] 217–58, esp. 239). See also Xavier Léon-Dufour, "La transfiguration de Jésus," in idem, *Études*, 83–122, esp. 97–99, who emphasizes that in the transfigured Jesus the expected eschatological glory is anticipated.

44 The appearances here of Moses and Elijah make many exegetes uncomfortable. See Riesenfeld, *Jésus transfiguré*, 253; Gnilka, *Markus*, 2.32–34; and

main character in this case), but because they represent the Law and the Prophets, who had foreseen Christ's fate, above all his suffering. Luke is familiar with a division of Scripture into three parts (24:44) alongside the division into two (24:27; Acts 26:22).

The redactional v. 31 confirms this: the content of the conversation is the "departure of Jesus." According to the plan of salvation, the realization of which is imminent (ἤμελλεν), this event will take place in Jerusalem (Ἰερουσαλήμ in the Semitic, holy, and salvation-historical orthography). In the verb πληροῦν ("to fulfill"), Luke sees a "fulfillment"[45] of God's will. Ἔξοδος ("departure") is ambiguous. In Luke clarity is appropriate to historical narrative, while a cryptic phrase characterizes the form of an oracle.[46] Verse 31 thus discreetly indicates the near future, like the saying of the twelve-year-old Jesus (2:49) or the promise of the resurrected one (24:49). Ἔξοδος is thus a euphemism for death, but Luke knows that this is not God's last word. Jesus' journey leads from Good Friday to Easter, and finally to the ascension, which Luke will narrate like a separation and an ἔξοδος ("exodus," "departure"; see Luke 24:50–51, ἐξήγαγεν . . . ἔξω, "he led them out"; and Acts 1:9–11). It is entirely possible that he also has in mind the fundamental experience of Israel, the exodus from Egypt.[47]

The Audience (vv. 32–33)

■ **32** The author's view now moves from the extraordinary scene to the chosen spectators. But even their description still serves the majesty of the event. Their stunned reaction communicates to the reader something of the unbearable brightness of the transfiguration. Luke could have had the disciples fall to the ground (like Paul in Acts 9:4), or cry out in fear (like John in Rev 19:10), or suddenly become blind (like Paul in Acts 9:8). These are typical consequences of a theophany. Here, in contrast, the tradition has Peter expressing his contentment about what has happened; too great a reaction of shock would have thus been mistaken here.

For this reason, Luke chooses the motif of sleep, which is also familiar, and was perhaps suggested to him by the Markan Gethsemane account (14:37–42). Thus in the numinous transfiguration, it is less the *tremendum* of the mystery than the *fascinosum* that is expressed. The unusual event has hypnotized them, as it were. People in antiquity believed themselves to be near to the divine while sleeping or dreaming.[48] Jesus' miraculous transfiguration effects a sort of ἔξοδος ("departure") by the disciples. Usually scholars think of two phases: the disciples are first overcome by sleep and may only observe the glory after they awaken. This is psychologically and

---

Nützel, *Verklärungserzählung*, 43–46, 79–82. In order to explain their presence, the biblical principle of needing two witnesses has been cited; one also recalls the two witnesses in Rev 11. Already Mal 4:4–5 (LXX 3:22–24) mentions the names of Moses and Elijah in the same context. Luke does not say here that these two figures have also been transfigured, but rather that they appear in eschatological glory.

45   Though Luke has a predilection for using πληρόω in the passive, he uses the active voice here, as in similar contexts and statements, e.g., Acts 3:18 and esp. 13:25.

46   See François Bovon, "Effet de réel et flou prophétique dans l'œuvre de Luc," in *À cause*, 349–59.

47   On the word ἔξοδος see Riesenfeld, *Jésus transfiguré*, 261, 277, who is reminded of Isaac; Marshall, 384–85; Fitzmyer, 1.800; and Dietrich, *Petrusbild*, 106–7. A. Feuillet emphasizes that Luke connects the transfiguration with the final drama in his Gospel ("Les perspectives propres à chaque évangéliste dans les récits de la transfiguration," *Bib* 39 [1958] 281–301, esp. 290). In Acts 13:24 Luke uses εἴσοδος ("entry") to signify the beginning of Jesus' ministry. Ἔξοδος was also used at that time

as a euphemism for "death" (see 2 Pet 1:15; Wis 3:2; 7:6; Josephus *Ant.* 4.8.2 §189). In the LXX the word signifies a "going out" in various repects: leaving a house, the exodus from Egypt, the emergence from the body of one's mother, or departure from this life. In biblical texts it is sometimes used with "entrance" to express the totality of something, e.g., 1 Sam (LXX 1 Kgdms) 29:6 ("your entrance and your exit"), or 1 Kgs (LXX 3 Kgdms) 3:7.

48   See Albrecht Oepke, "καθεύδω," *TDNT* 3 (1965) 431–33. For literature on sleep in antiquity, see Horst Balz, "ὕπνος," *TDNT* 8 (1972) 545; and the supplementary bibliography in *ThWNT* 10.2 (1979) 1287. While κοιμάω originally means "to lay someone on a bed" and καθεύδω "to lay oneself down to go to sleep," ὑπνόω (intransitive in both the active and passive forms) signifies "sleep" itself. See the commentary on 8:23 above, n. 23.

narratively improbable. In contrast to the guilty disciples of Gethsemane (Mark 14:37–42), the disciples have not fallen asleep, but are almost weighed down with sleep (βεβαρημένοι).[49] Διαγρηγορήσαντες δέ ("but since they had stayed awake," probably adversative) tells the readers that the disciples have nevertheless remained awake (one should not overlook δια-; at no moment do they lose their consciousness).[50] The Lukan formulation also suggests that their condition should not be described either as sleep or being awake,[51] but a "second" consciousness that the Hebrew Bible attributes, for example,[52] to Abraham (Gen 15:12) and Daniel (Dan 8:18; 10:9), when God communicates with them. The transfiguration is just as real as the advent of the Spirit σωματικῷ εἴδει ("in bodily form") at Jesus' baptism (Luke 3:22). The three disciples saw the glory of the three figures and were, in some way, taken into this divine world; thus Peter emphasizes that it is good here (v. 33). Something of the ambiguity of 2 Cor 3:18 also comes to play in this passage: the disciples see the glory but also reflect it. The symmetry between the three figures above and the three disciples below underscores the human participation in the glory of God.

Luke is responsible for the introduction of the word δόξα ("glory," vv. 31–32). He uses it, however, not in the Greek sense ("opinion," "appearance"), but in the biblical sense (divine "glory," the LXX word for כָּבוֹד). The meaning "brilliance" may have already taken up residence in the Hellenistic courtly language of that time. The image has thus shifted: from the original Hebrew meaning of "weight," one progresses to the image of "light" (brightness of light) and "brilliance" (powerful brightness), which has already begun in Hebrew (esp. in Third Isaiah; cf. Isa 60:1–2).[53] The connection of δόξα ("glory") to the temple belongs in the past. In Luke δόξα belongs to God and God's world. For human beings it is now tied to the resurrection; to this extent its eschatological dimension cannot be separated from christology. Jesus alone, through his resurrection, has entered into his δόξα, that is, into the glory of God that is now promised to him (24:26). As the Son of God, Jesus is the prophesied carrier of the divine glory, but with the exception of the transfiguration, he will assume it only after his suffering. Only in his parousia will it finally be manifest to all humanity (9:26; 21:27).[54]

Peter is the central figure here; only his personal reaction is narrated. The usual Lukan address of Jesus as "master" (ἐπιστάτα)[55] suits this context. Two things are contained in καλόν ἐστιν ("it is good"):[56] Peter feels good as a subject, and, at the same time, dresses this feeling in an objective form, by emphasizing: it is appropriate that we may be here too; indeed, it corresponds to the divine will.

---

49 When Luke here writes βεβαρημένοι, is he being inspired by Mark's καταβαρυνόμενοι in Mark 14:40, which Matthew likewise renders with βεβαρημένοι?

50 Other exegetes see no distinction between δια-γρηγορέω here and γρηγορέω, claiming that the δια- has now lost its specific meaning. LSJ offers yet another interpretation: to "start into full wakefulness."

51 The tractate from NHC 1 concerning the resurrection (*Letter to Rheginus*, NHC 1.3 48.3–19) mentions that Elijah and "Moses with him" (the wording is more reminiscent of Mark 9:4 than of Matt 17:3 or Luke 9:30) were present at the transfiguration of Jesus. If this reference to the Gospel is intended to prove that the resurrection is no illusion, then it does so because the author of the tractate regarded both Elijah and Moses as having been resurrected.

52 Against the views of the Montanists and the other religious enthusiasts, the orthodox theologians of Christian antiquity affirmed that the biblical heroes did not lose their ability to see clearly, even in ecstasy (see François Bovon, *De vocatione gentium: Histoire de l'interprétation d'Act. 10,1–11,18 dans les six premiers siècles* [BGBE 8; Tübingen: Mohr-Siebeck, 1967] 145–47, 167–71).

53 See Claus Westermann, "כבד," *TLOT* 2.599. On δόξα in general and in the LXX in particular, see Harald Hegermann, "δόξα," *EDNT* 1 (1990) 344–48.

54 On δόξα in Luke see Riesenfeld, *Jésus tranfiguré*, 98, 245–47, 294; Schürmann, 1.554; Fitzmyer, 1.794; and Léon-Dufour, "Transfiguration," 98–99.

55 Luke uses foreign words only reluctantly. Moreover, ῥαββί ("rabbi," Mark 9:5) in the present context is rather colorless, as Matthew himself recognizes, substituting κύριε ("lord"). On ἐπιστάτης in Luke see Glombitza, "Titel."

56 The expression καλόν ἐστιν followed by the infinitive is common in Greek (see Gnilka, *Markus*, 2.34 n. 27). On the interpretation of Peter's proposal in patristic and medieval writers, see Miquel, "Mystère," 203–5.

■ 33 Verse 33a prepares Peter's speech. He is responding not only to the revelation of glory but, with a slight anxiety, to the danger of its transitoriness: as Jesus separates from the other two figures, the curtain in front of the "play" begins to fall. This sensitively portrayed anxiety replaces the Markan aversion before the divine, which Luke deletes.

Peter's offer is not clear. It would be comprehensible if the disciples wanted tents for all those participating (and thus also for themselves), in order to be able to enjoy the moment longer. But why only three tents, for Jesus, Moses, and Elijah? According to both Luke and Mark, the apostle did not understand what he was saying, thus incorrectly appraising the situation. But in what sense? The tents allude to the Israelites' period of wandering in the wilderness, which the Israelites commemorated during the Feast of Booths (Sukkot) by living for a week in tents. According to the principle of correspondence between originary and eschatological time, the hope would also be for an eschatological existence under the tent (cf. Luke 16:9).[57] The Festival of Booths at that time had assumed this eschatological perspective, and the glory of God was celebrated with special joy, being symbolized by an abundance of lamps.[58] Judaism made a connection between the tents for the faithful and the tent of the presence of God.[59] Luke was perhaps alluding to this festival with the reference to eight days (v. 28). Peter's misinterpretation thus does not concern the motif of the tents, but probably the characteristics of the tent. He did not understand that Jesus himself becomes the place of divine presence and glory for the new,

eschatological time. Peter experienced Jesus' transfiguration, but did not understand it.[60] The next episode has its own meaning, but it can also be read as an answer to Peter's suggestion: none of these three figures has need of these tents, which are ridiculous for them, because they would have been set up by human beings.

The Cloud and the Voice (vv. 34–35)

■ 34 Luke's view now turns away from the audience and toward the "play" again. Instead of reading about "glory," one reads three times here the word "cloud" (the word "shadow" is in the word ἐπισκιάζω, "overshadow"). Light and cloud, lightning and smoke are motifs that accompany theophanies.[61] In the wilderness the people of Israel were accompanied by a column of fire during the night, and by a column of cloud during the day (Exod 13:21–22). Νεφέλη ("cloud") describes the presence of God in the wilderness (Exod 33:9–10; 40:38), and then the coming of the Shekinah to the temple on the day of its dedication (1 Kgs [LXX 3 Kgdms] 8:10). The νεφέλη proclaims, "Pay attention, God is about to appear." In the first phase God is active in the visible transfiguration, and in the second, in the audible voice. The νεφέλη is thus not at all a means for God to hide, or a symbol of Christ's suffering, but shows God's presence. The disciples understand this, and are fearful before God. Luke thus has shifted the Markan motif (9:6–8) and explicated it. The passage of Lev 23:42–43 in *Targum Neofiti*, concerning the Festival of Booths, supports this natural understanding of the unclear αὐτούς ("them," v. 34b).[62]

57 See Rev 12:12 (σκηνόω in the sense "to dwell").
58 See the literature cited at n. 33 above. On the connection between the tents in Luke 9:33 (and its parallels in Matthew and Mark) and Sukkot, see Riesenfeld, *Jésus transfiguré*, 256, 297; and Jan-Adolf Bühner, "σκηνή," *EDNT* 2 (1991) 251.
59 See *Tg. Neof.* Lev 23:42–43 (text given below at the commentary on v. 34).
60 According to Dietrich (*Petrusbild*, 112–16), Peter shows his ignorance of salvation history with his proposal. Even the one who confessed Jesus as the Messiah (Luke 9:20) has not comprehended that the suffering of the Christ is necessary.
61 According to Riesenfeld (*Jésus transfiguré*, 130–45), the cloud indicates God's presence and protection (see Exod 13:21–22; 1 Kgs [LXX 3 Kgdms] 8:10; Ezek 10:3). In my opinion, however, the images of the shadow and of the tent point to divine protec-

tion (see Ps 60[LXX 61]:5), while the cloud can be thought of as God's presence. Fitzmyer (1.802) cites Josephus *Ant.* 3.12.5 §290; 3.14.4 §310. In the first passage, according to the priests and the Levites in the desert, the cloud stands for God's presence. In the second passage, the text states explicitly that the cloud stands for "the epiphany of God."
62 P75 deletes the troublesome αὐτούς ("them"), thus expressing quite clearly that the disciples were afraid as they entered the cloud. On the basis of external evidence, the reading ἐκείνους εἰσελθεῖν should be preferred since it is attested by the great majority of mss., including most of the best witnesses, and it is the reading of the textus receptus (cf. *New Testament in Greek*, 204, which takes it as its basic text). But on the basis of internal evidence, εἰσελθεῖν αὐτούς should be preferred since it is the more difficult reading (*lectio difficilior*), thus the

Lev 23:43	*Neofiti* 1.3
so that your generations	so that your generations
may know	may know
that I made the people	that I made the children
of Israel live	of Israel live
in booths	in the brilliant cloud
	of my Shekinah
when I brought them out	in the time that I let them leave
of the land of Egypt;	the land of Egypt free,
I am the Lord your God.	I, the Lord, your God.

■ **35** The divine voice uses a formula of identification. By portraying the removal of Moses and Elijah (v. 33a), Luke elegantly avoids any ambiguity, for οὗτος can only describe Jesus. Since, in pre-Christian Judaism, "son" was not a messianic title,[63] the messianic interpretation of the transfiguration as an enthronement of the Messiah Jesus is unlikely.[64] If the voice describes Jesus as "son," it refers to the preexistent son in the Christian sense of the father-son relationship.[65]

The symbolism of the scene does not point in the direction of the Davidic tradition, but rather of the Sinai tradition, and is less concerned with the Messiah than with the place of God's presence. The answer does not indicate the holy past or the liturgical present, but rather the person of Jesus. The transfiguration has the same mighty significance for the life of Jesus that the resurrection has for his death: we should recognize this man, who is neither priest nor king, who is from Nazareth and not Jerusalem, as the last and final revelation of God. God has only given a few legitimizing signs, but, in addition to the voice at the baptism, the voice at the transfiguration provides the strongest proof. Behind

the development and function of this text is the matter of how the Christians could explain Jesus' failure among Israel.

The description of Jesus as ὁ ἐκλελεγμένος ("the chosen one"), where Mark and Matthew have ὁ ἀγαπητός ("the beloved one"), is a striking departure.[66] Luke has a preference for the verb ἐκλέγω ("to single out," "to choose"), especially the middle form ἐκλέγομαι ("to choose," "to elect"; half of the occurrences of this word in the NT are in Luke), but not the verbal adjective ἐκλεκτός, which he uses only in Luke 18:7 and 23:35. But this does not explain the hapax legomenon ἐκλελεγμένος, which probably has the same meaning.[67] As a result of the songs about the servant of God (Isa 42:1 LXX: ὁ ἐκλεκτός), a title "the chosen one of God" developed within Judaism, a title that is not to be interpreted in an exclusively messianic way.[68] The Lukan text is probably based on this Semitic tradition, and likely follows an oral tradition that has translated an Aramaic or Hebrew theological expression into Greek ("the chosen one"), in a redactional acceptance of a traditional substantive (as a title) or adjective, that is competing with the Markan text (ὁ ἀγαπητός, "the beloved one").

Ὁ ἐκλελεγμένος is a welcome addition in terms of its content, because "my Son" connects Jesus to his Father, and "the Chosen One," with his mission and his people. The background of ὁ ἐκλελεγμένος in the Hebrew Bible (cf. Isa 42:1), as well as αὐτοῦ ἀκούετε ("listen to him"; cf. Deut 18:15), goes in the direction of Jesus' prophetic mission. The transfiguration is thus true to the Sinai tradition, and links Jesus with Moses in

---

one more likely to be altered by a scribe. This is the reading of Nestle-Aland, with which I agree.

63 See Riesenfeld, *Jésus transfiguré*, passim; similarly Baltensweiler, *Verklärung*, 116–18.

64 See Fitzmyer, 1.802–3, 485–86.

65 Luke shows that a new stage of revelation has begun. In Luke 3:22 (the baptismal scene), it is Jesus who is addressed and who learns that he is God's Son (using the second person singular, "You are my Son"); here the voice addresses the three main disciples, and reveals the mystery of divine sonship (using the third person singular, "This is my Son").

66 2 Pet 1:17 reports what the voice said at the transfiguration as follows: ὁ υἱός μου ὁ ἀγαπητός μου οὗτός ἐστιν, εἰς ὃν ἐγὼ εὐδόκησα ("This is my Son, my Beloved, with whom I am well pleased"; with minor variants). Several mss. also read ἀγαπη-

τός here in Luke, but this reading can be explained as a scribal assimilation to the text of the other two Synoptic accounts. A few mss. also add ἐν ᾧ ηὐδόκησα (or εὐδόκησα, "in whom I am pleased"), probably due to contamination from the Matthean parallel and from the text of the baptismal scene. Some mss. read ἐκλεκτός instead of ἐκλελεγμένος (see the apparatus in *New Testament in Greek*, 205).

67 One cannot find a single occurrence of this participle in either the LXX or Josephus.

68 See Fitzmyer, 1.803; and Gottlob Schrenk, "λέγω, κτλ.," *TDNT* 4 (1967) 184–85.

his role as a prophetic mediator. But in contrast to what the people heard from Moses, the people shall hear not the words of the Law but those of salvation, from the Son (from Luke 3:6 to Acts 28:28). The immediate context and the parallel at 23:35 show that Luke connects the chosen status with the *suffering* mission of Jesus.

The baptism account has a christological function in Luke's total composition (Jesus himself is addressed directly by God: "You are my beloved Son . . ."), and the transfiguration has an ecclesiological role (God is here instructing the disciples). Jesus' true identity is revealed to the disciples.[69] A decision (αὐτοῦ ἀκούετε, "listen to him") is demanded from them.

With the words αὐτοῦ ἀκούετε, the Lukan text goes its own way, perhaps again on the basis of oral tradition. The sequence of the words corresponds to Deut 18:15, where the LXX indeed uses a future middle (αὐτοῦ ἀκούσεσθε). Thus Luke is not attempting an exact quotation. In ἀκούω the later meaning, "to obey," is already present.[70]

The Final Act (v. 36)

■ **36** The voice at the transfiguration is both climax and end of the revelation. With the simultaneity of the voice of God and Jesus' solitude, Luke expresses the same idea as the Markan "suddenly." The subjective aspect of the Markan parallel (the gaze of the disciples) is missing in Luke. He mentions only silence as a reaction of the disciples. In Luke the disciples do not tell anything about Jesus' divinity until Pentecost, just as they understand

nothing of his suffering until Easter. Salvation history has its own rhythm.

History of Interpretation and Conclusion

Since the transfiguration appeals to the senses, the fine arts play a significant role in the history of interpretation for this passage: consider only the mosaic in the monastery at Sinai, the painting of Raphael, miniatures in codices, and stained-glass windows. The interpretation of the transfiguration was already vigorously debated in the second century, above all the metamorphosis itself and the nature of its perception by the disciples. It contributed both to schism and to edification in the church:[71] Marcion read in the scene a radical critique by the divine Christ of the Hebrew Bible's economy of salvation.[72] Gnostics believed that the transfiguration supported their Docetism.[73] During the christological controversies, the orthodox fathers meditated on the incarnation and the two natures of Jesus by considering the transfigured Christ.[74] The history of interpretation of the transfiguration is largely still to be written.[75]

The Lukan transfiguration brings the glory and the lowliness of Jesus close together, his δόξα ("glory") and his ἔξοδος ("departure"). God's loving care is so concrete that God has entered into human history in the mission of his Son. The movement of salvation history leads the Son through suffering into glory. The light and darkness of the transfiguration summarize the entire divine economy. A Byzantine theologian imagines that

---

69 See n. 65 above.

70 On "listen to him" see Riesenfeld, *Jésus transfiguré*, 270, 298; and Gnilka, *Markus*, 2.36. Notice the use of the present imperative (expressing the enduring validity of the command) and how αὐτοῦ ("him") is placed first for emphasis.

71 On the historical impact of this pericope, see Antonio Orbe, *Cristología gnóstica: Introducción a la soteriología de los siglos II y III* (2 vols.; BAC 384–85; Madrid: La Editorial Catolica, 1976) 2.96–141; Miquel, "Mystère"; and Gnilka, *Markus*, 2.37–39.

72 See Tertullian *Adv. Marc.* 4.22.2. According to Tertullian, Marcion omitted Jesus' conversation with these HB figures concerning his ἔξοδος. According to Epiphanius *Adv. haer.* 42.11.6, scholia 17, however, Marcion included the conversation of the three figures "in glory," but excluded the subject of the ἔξοδος.

73 See Orbe, *Cristología*, 2.139.

74 See also *Sermo 38* (51) on the transfiguration by Leo the Great (*Léon le Grand, Sermons*, vol. 3 [trans. R. Dolle; SC 74; Paris: Cerf, 1961] 14–21). In this sermon Leo argues in §2 that Luke 9:27 and its parallels refer to the three disciples who later behold the transfigured one ("there are some standing here who will not taste death before they see the kingdom of God"). This event does not show them his divinity, which still remains hidden to those living in corrupted flesh, but it does reveal to them the royal glory of the Son of Man.

75 On Origen see Matthias Eichinger, *Die Verklärung Christi bei Origenes: Die Bedeutung des Menschen Jesus in seiner Christologie* (Vienna: Herder, 1969). Oddly enough, the Feast of the Transfiguration gained acceptance only at a rather late date (see K. Dienst, *RGG* 6 [3d ed.; 1962] 1358; Maurice Sachot, *L'homélie pseudo-chrysostomienne sur la Transfiguration: CPG 4724, BHG 1975* [EHS, Theologie 151;

the discussion of the three figures happened like this: Moses perhaps said, "You are the one, whose passion I prefigured through the slaughtered lamb and the completed Pesach [Passover]." Elijah perhaps said the words, "I prefigured your resurrection by raising the widow's son."[76]

The divine reality shines through human reality like lightning: in the annunciation to Mary (1:35), at the baptism (3:22), at the transfiguration (9:35), and at Easter (24:36–40). Not only salvation history, a category of time, but also the divine sphere, a category of space, becomes accessible. The miracle, however, is not founded solely in divine glory (it is clear that God is *God*), but also in Jesus' lowliness (in his ἔξοδος, "departure," v. 31), and in his solitude (Ἰησοῦς μόνος, "Jesus alone," v. 36).[77]

Luke does not give the disciples a passive role in this scene. He especially emphasizes that they see (εἶδον τὴν δόξαν αὐτοῦ . . . "they saw his glory," v. 32; ὧν ἑώρακαν, "the things they had seen," v. 36). They do not understand everything now—especially the suffering of the Messiah remains hidden from them. What they see, however, is more than a merely external miracle:

they suddenly understand the Son's true identity. The transfiguration happens especially for them[78] and among them. Without exaggerating, one could say that, in the final analysis, it is they who are transfigured. Luke expresses the transfiguration of the disciples with the ecstasy that he ascribes to them (v. 32). This special form of consciousness was believed in the time of the church to take place when an individual was illuminated by the Holy Spirit. An anthropological expectation (from lowliness to the glory of the resurrection) corresponds to the christological content of faith (from divine glory to lowliness). "Christ was transfigured, not by taking what he was not, but by revealing to his companions, the disciples, what he was, by opening their eyes and causing the blind to see."[79] The mystery of the transfiguration was not a miracle, but the end of miracle.[80] "Just as Christ's baptism illuminated the mystery of the first rebirth, the transfiguration is the sacrament of the second rebirth. For this reason, the entire trinity revealed itself there: the Father in his voice, the Son in his humanity, and the Holy Spirit in the bright cloud."[81]

Frankfurt am Main: Peter Lang, 1981] 22–37).

76 Theophylactus *Enarratio Matt.* 17.3 (*PG* 123.328c).

77 See Clement of Alexandria *Strom.* 6.16 (140.3).

78 See Clement of Alexandria *Exc. Theod.* 4.1: "And when he appeared to his apostles on the mountain in glory, he did not do this for his own sake but because of the church, which represents the chosen race, so that the church may recognize the progress (προκοπή) which he achieved after his exodus (ἔξοδος) from the flesh." François Sagnard, the editor of this fragment (Clement of Alexandria, *Excerpta ex Theodoto* [SC 23; Paris: Cerf, 1970]), ascribes this section (pp. 58–59) to Clement him-

self, but Orbe (*Cristología*, 2.136–39) disputes this attribution.

79 See John of Damascus *Hom. in Transfigurationem* 12 (*PG* 96.564c), cited in Miquel, "Mystère," 220.

80 See Miquel, "Mystère," 218, who refers to Francis of Sales and Cajetano.

81 Thomas Aquinas *Summa theologiae* 3.45.4–2.

The Healing of the Possessed Son (9:37–43a)

Bibliography

Achtemeier, "Lukan Perspective."

Aichinger, Hermann, "Zur Traditionsgeschichte der Epileptiker-Perikope Mk 9,14–29 par Mt 17,14–21 par Lk 9,37–43a," in A. Fuchs, ed., *Probleme der Forschung* (SNTU A.3; Vienna/Munich: Herold, 1978) 114–43.

idem, "Miracles."

Bornkamm, "Πνεῦμα."

Bultmann, *History*, 211–12, 419–20.

Busse, *Wunder*, 249–67.

Conzelmann, *Theology*, 59–60.

Fitzmyer, Joseph A., "The Composition of Luke, Chapter 9," in Talbert, *Perpectives*, 139–52.

Howard, Virgil P., *Das Ego Jesu in den synoptischen Evangelien: Untersuchungen zum Sprachgebrauch Jesu* (Marburger theologische Studien 14; Marburg: Elwert, 1975) 86–97.

Kertelge, *Wunder*, 174–79.

Léon-Dufour, "Épisode."

Lesky and Waszink, "Epilepsie."

Rist, John M., *On the Independence of Matthew and Mark* (SNTSMS 32; Cambridge: Cambridge University Press, 1968) 61–62.

Roloff, *Kerygma*, 143–52.

Schenk, Wolfgang, "Tradition und Redaktion in der Epileptiker-Perikope Mk 9,14–29," *ZNW* 63 (1972) 76–94.

Schenke, L., *Die Wundererzählungen des Markusevangeliums* (SBB; Stuttgart: Katholisches Bibelwerk, 1977) 314–49.

Schmithals, Walter, "Die Heilung des Epileptischen (Mk 9,14–29): Ein Beitrag zur notwendigen Revision der Formgeschichte," *ThViat* 13 (1975–76) 211–33.

Schramm, *Markus-Stoff*, 139–40.

Sterling, Gregory E., "Jesus as Exorcist: An Analysis of Matthew 17:14–20; Mark 9:14–29; Luke 9:37–43a," *CBQ* 55 (1993) 467–93.

Talbert, *Patterns*, 26, 28.

Theissen, *Miracle Stories*, 136–37, 177–78.

Vaganay, Léon, "Les accords négatifs de Matthieu-Luc contre Marc: L'épisode de l'enfant épileptique (Mt 17,14–21; Mc 9,14–29; Lc 9,37–43a)," in idem, *Le problème synoptique: Une hypothèse de travail* (Bibliothèque de théologie 3.1; Tournai: Desclée, 1954) 405–25.

van der Loos, *Miracles*, 397–405.

Wilkinson, John, "The Case of the Epileptic Boy," *ExpTim* 79 (1967) 38–42.

37 **But it happened that on the next day, when they came down from the mountain, a great crowd met him. 38/ Just then a man from the crowd shouted, "Teacher, I beg you to take a look at my son, for he is my only one. 39/ Suddenly a spirit seizes him, and all at once it shrieks and convulses him, with foam at the mouth, and it will scarcely leave him, when it mauls him. 40/ And I begged your disciples to cast it out, but they could not." 41/ But Jesus answered, "You faithless and perverse generation, how much longer must I be with you and bear with you? Bring your son here." 42/ But while he was still coming, the demon dashed him to the ground in convulsions. And Jesus rebuked the unclean spirit, healed the boy, and gave him back to his father. 43a/ And all were astounded at the majesty of God.**

Synchronic Analysis

This small pericope is located between the proclamation of Jesus' glory (9:28–36) and the second prediction of the passion (9:43b–45).[1] Who is Jesus? Who is he for humanity? These questions dominate chap. 9, along with the question that results from them: What is the human reaction to Jesus?

The unit 9:37–43a forms a complete healing miracle.[2] The time and place are given at the beginning (v. 37a), in relation to the transfiguration that precedes it. After a concise description of the situation (v. 37b),[3] the story begins with the well-known signal καὶ ἰδού ("just then," v. 38a). A man approaches from out of the crowd[4] and asks for help in the style typical for this genre.[5] The father's speech, which takes up nearly half the account, comprises a cry for help along with a justification for it

---

1 On the structure of Luke 9, see the analysis of Luke 9:1–6 and the conclusion to Luke 9:10–17 above; and Joseph A. Fitzmyer, "The Composition of Luke, Chapter 9," in Talbert, *Perpectives*, 139–52.

2 See Xavier Léon-Dufour, "L'épisode de l'enfant épileptique," in *Études*, 183–227, esp. 208–10 (reprinted from J. Cambier et al., *La formation des Évangiles: Problème synoptique et Formgeschichte* [Recherches bibliques 2; Bruges/Paris: Desclée de Brouwer, 1957] 85–115). I do not see why Busse (*Wunder*, 252–53) views the entire passage (Luke 9:37–50) as a unity.

3 Here the aorist is used, not, as expected for a summary, the imperfect, but the mention of the crowd gives a generalizing aspect to the sentence.

4 Observe the special position that Luke assigns to the crowd by mentioning it twice (vv. 37 and 38).

5 The attention of the reader is directed toward the

(v. 38b); an extended description of the illness, which is understood as demon possession (v. 39); and the mention of an unsuccessful attempt at healing by Jesus' disciples (v. 40). The father describes the constantly recurring attacks in a colloquial style.[6] The group of disciples around Jesus must be imagined in juxtaposition to the crowd, out of which the man is speaking. Jesus' answer is short. It is not an accident that the people at whom his answer is directed are not specifically mentioned (v. 41a), since the first part is a complaint directed at "you" (plural, v. 41b), and the second, a short command to the father (v. 41c), which addresses his request (v. 38b). Jesus' initiative awakens an act of resistance from the evil demon (v. 42a), so that his command to the demon seems like a counterattack (v. 42b). Jesus' last reaction (v. 42b) is described three times, depending on the person concerned—the unclean spirit, the boy, or the father. Then follows the predictable and typical amazed response from the crowd (v. 43a).

    A. Approach of the crowd (v. 37)
      B. The father's call for his son (v. 38)
        C. Description of the attacks of the evil spirit (v. 39)
          D. The disciples' failure (v. 40)
          D.' Critique of this generation (v. 41ab)
      B.' Command to the father (v. 41c)
        C.' Resistance of the evil spirit (v. 42a)
      B.'' Healing of the son by Jesus' word (v. 42b)
    A.'' Amazement of the crowd (v. 43a)

This simplified scheme clarifies the following aspects of the pericope: (1) Jesus' surprising complaint (D' = v. 41ab) relates to the disciples' failure (D = v. 40).[7] These two elements are dispensable in the narrative; at the end, the disciples play no role. (2) Jesus' first command (B' = v. 41c) is a delaying motif. The purpose of the command is not to effect the healing, but to create the prerequisites for it. Thus the father does not immediately receive what he wants. The narrative nevertheless falls into two parts: the victorious restoration by Jesus of the son, and his return to his father corresponds to the presentation of the evil spirit and its loss.[8]

From a form-critical perspective, this is an exorcism, not a healing.[9] The requisite motifs and themes of this genre are all present.[10]

Diachronic Analysis

Both in the gist of the story and in its vocabulary, this episode is reminiscent of the resurrection of the son of the widow in Nain (7:10–17) and of the daughter of Jairus (8:40–56), to such an extent that we perceive the redactional hand of the evangelist.[11] But Luke is not writing in the absence of tradition (cf. Matt 17:14–21 and Mark 9:14–29). Although this pericope is located in a "Markan section," a number of considerations weigh against the use of the Markan parallel (9:14–29) as a source. Mark has a complicated structure, with additional conversations with the father about the beginning of the possession (9:21–24), and with the disciples about the exorcism (9:28–29). These additions can almost be described form-critically as "apocryphal," since they answer questions left open in the tradition. If one separates tradition from redaction in the Markan parallel, it

---

expectation of help, not only by the man's cry but also by his request that Jesus look at his son.

6   Note the *present* indicative that Luke uses to describe the seizures that happen over and over again.

7   Plummer (255), in contrast, understands that Jesus criticizes the father and the crowd. For additional opinions, see Godet, 1.434–36.

8   If one follows Theissen (*Miracle Stories*, 72–74), one recognizes four parts: introduction, v. 37; exposition, vv. 38–40; the middle, vv. 41–42; and the end, v. 43a.

9   It is obvious from v. 39 that this is a case of demon possession: Jesus threatens the impure spirit (v. 42b). The *apopompe* itself ("sending away" of the demon) is not related. In its place one finds a refer-

ence to the healing of the young man (v. 43a). This is, however, the only place in the story where it approximates a healing miracle.

10   See Theissen, *Miracle Stories,* 47–72. On succumbing to a demon and the exorcist's struggle with a spirit, see ibid., 87–89.

11   There are similarities with the resurrection story of the boy at Nain: there is the crowd (7:11), of whose presence we are reminded yet one more time (7:12), the only son (7:12), and the return of the son to his nearest relative, his mother (7:15). There are also similarities with the resurrection story of Jairus's daughter: There is the expectant crowd (8:40), the expression "just then . . . a man . . ." (8:41), the only child (8:42), who at the end (8:51, 54) is called a παῖς.

would seem that the result is a traditional unit[12] that is similar to the Lukan version of the miracle.

Some interpreters, however, propose that either Mark or the tradition before him was working with two parallel traditions, in the first of which the disciples and their teacher discuss the problem of the power to work miracles, and in the second of which, the father and Jesus discuss the matter of faith.[13] Yet others are of the opinion that the issue of the father's faith was added to an original account of Jesus' triumph over the inability of his disciples.[14] But one must recall that oral transmission did not cease at Mark's first fixation of the story in writing. Luke, like Matthew, knows a divergent form[15] and is influenced by it, although he respects the Markan sequence. It is the pressure of the oral tradition that causes Luke to reject the redactional addition in Mark (the private conversation in 9:28–29). He is thus able, at the same time, to spare the disciples this criticism. The second, perhaps pre-Markan addition (Mark 9:21–24, the conversation with the father) is unnecessary for Luke, since he avoids repetitions (such as the description of the sickness, Mark 9:21–22); his concern is not human faith (Mark 9:23–24), but divine power (Luke 9:43a).

In its original function, the account helped answer the question of how such a miracle can happen.[16] The original version emphasized the *power of the miracle-worker* (Mark 9:18). As time passed, another answer was necessary: the miracle only became possible through the *faith of the one who asks* (Mark 9:21–24); the weight is transferred to the recipient of the miracle. Mark manages to keep both of these traditional perspectives together, whereas Luke is primarily influenced by the first version of the miracle, although with a derived significance: the miracle occurs less through the power of the miracle-worker, and more through the divine power of the Messiah (Luke 9:43a). Luke thus adopts his Markan source only in a weakened form; the theological reasons for this are his faithfulness to oral tradition and his intent to create a strong global composition (chap. 9).

Luke also omits the dialogue between the transfiguration and the miracle that is transmitted by Mark (9:11–13), less because of the noneschatological character of the Baptist than because of the hope for the restoration of all things that Luke connects with the

---

12 On the pre-Markan form of the story, see Günther Bornkamm, "Πνεῦμα ἄλαλον: Eine Studie zum Markusevangelium," in idem, *Gesammelte Aufsätze,* vol. 4, *Geschichte und Glaube II* (BevTh 53; Munich: Kaiser, 1971) 21–36, esp. 25 (reprinted from K. Gaiser, ed., *Das Altertum und jedes neue Gute: Festschrift W. Schadewaldt* [Stuttgart: Kohlhammer, 1970] 369–85).

13 See Bultmann, *History*, 211–12; Loisy, 276–77; Bornkamm, "Πνεῦμα," 24; and Paul J. Achtemeier, "Miracles and the Historical Jesus: A Study of Mk 9,14–29," *CBQ* 37 (1975) 471–91, esp. 482, who writes: "In that way, a miracle story previously uninterpreted (vss. 17–18, 20?, 26b–27), and a miracle story (vss. 20–22, 25–26a) previously unacceptably interpreted (vss. 23–24) were given a new interpretation by their combination, and by the addition of a new statement about faith (vs. 19) which turned the point from Jesus' faith to the lack of faith of the disciples, thus also throwing new emphasis on the ambiguous faith of the father." Bornkamm ("Πνεῦμα," 24, 28–30) believes that he has found in the double illness of the boy (epilepsy and muteness) further evidence of two originally separate reports.

14 See, e.g., Roloff, *Kerygma*, 148, who ascribes vv. (14–17a,) 17b–19a, 19c–20, 25–27 to the tradition. Without taking into consideration the agreement between Matthew and Luke, Wolfgang Schenk sees behind Mark's report only a single story ("Tradition und Redaktion in der Epileptiker-Perikope Mk 9,14–29," *ZNW* 63 [1972] 76–94). For Kertelge (*Wunder*) vv. 14–19 and 28–29 of Mark's account are redactional, while vv. 20–27 are considered to contain the core of traditional material. Unaware of the works of Léon Vaganay and Paul J. Achtemeier, Hermann Aichinger ("Traditionsgeschichte") conjectures the priority of Mark, but assumes that both Matthew and Luke had to have used a deutero-Mark, in order to account for their agreements with each other ("Zur Traditionsgeschichte der Epileptiker-Perikope Mk 9,14–29 par Mt 17,14–21 par Lk 9,37–43a," in A. Fuchs, ed., *Probleme der Forschung* [SNTU A.3; Vienna/Munich: Herold, 1978] 114–43).

15 Even though I disagree with Léon Vaganay's thesis that the original version was a Greek proto-Matthew, I find his masterful analysis compelling. Also in the direction of a non-Markan tradition is Schramm (*Markus-Stoff*, 139–40), who is unaware of Vaganay's essay. Busse (*Wunder*, 256) maintains that Mark is the sole source for Luke 9:37–43a. Léon-Dufour ("Épisode," 210–27) speaks only of literary contacts between the three versions, against any direct dependence of Luke on Mark.

16 The verbs "can" and "cannot" turn up in connec-

Messiah (Acts 3:19–20). The fulfillment of the prophecy about Elijah is to be in Jesus, not in the Baptist. Despite this, the Baptist does not belong to the old covenant,[17] but stands on the threshold of the new era, as the birth narrative attests.

Commentary

Introduction and Exposition (vv. 37–40)

■ **37** The nocturnal experience of the small circle is over. It is day now, "the next day."[18] Jesus and his three disciples have come down off the mountain as they did after the selection of the Twelve (6:17). Similarly also, the crowd[19] is waiting, more precisely, they run up to him; συναντάω ("to meet") describes a significant encounter full of expectation.[20] At a corresponding passage in 6:17–19, Luke expressly mentions the hope of the crowds, who want to hear Jesus and experience his

healing power. Here only the latter expectation is mentioned, in the words of a single person, the father.

■ **38** The man[21] calls out.[22] In Luke βοάω ("to shout") expresses either a cry for help (as here), or a cry of anger (as in Acts 25:24). He asks Jesus for a "look" (δέομαι often means "to pray" in Luke).[23] Ἐπιβλέπω ("to take a look")[24] here means the helpful and powerful gaze of the miracle-worker;[25] the direction is indicated by the repetition of ἐπί ("to," "at"): at his only son. The possession of his son by demons would not only cause the father emotional suffering, but would also stigmatize him in ancient society. It endangers both his descendants and his current reputation. His suffering is rooted in his fear of the unpredictable attacks,[26] in his grieving over his son, and in his own shame (cf. the similar ὄνειδος, "shame," of Elizabeth in Luke 1:25).[27]

■ **39** The description of the illness consists in a short narration (καὶ ἰδού, "suddenly") of the recurring

---

17 Thus, the well-known thesis of Conzelmann (*Theology*, 167 n. 1).

18 Ἐξῆς ("the following") occurs five times in the NT, all of them in Luke. The *New Testament in Greek* (205–6), besides giving the reading of the textus receptus, ἐν τῇ ἑξῆς ἡμέρᾳ, mentions other variants including διὰ τῆς ἡμέρας.

19 Ὄχλος πολύς ("a great crowd") comes from Mark 9:14, while the comment about climbing down the mountain is taken from Mark 9:9a. Mark respects the logic of the action and specifies more exactly than either Matthew or Luke that Jesus and the three chosen disciples first met the remaining disciples. The oral tradition available to Matthew and Luke, in addition to their copy of Mark, was unaware of the connection of this passage with the transfiguration, as can be shown by comparison of Luke 9:37 with Matt 17:14.

20 This is a Lukan verb: four of its six occurrences in the NT are found in Luke (Luke 9:37; 22:10; Acts 10:25; 20:22). The other two instances are found in the context of Abraham's meeting with Melchizedek (Heb 7:1, 10).

21 Like v. 37, v. 38 also attests genuine Lukan vocabulary: καὶ ἰδού, ἀνήρ, and βοάω. There is a slight difference in meaning between Luke's ἀπὸ τοῦ ὄχλου (*"from* the crowd") and Mark's ἐκ τοῦ ὄχλου (*"of* the crowd"), but Luke's wording fits the context better since it is not the father's location (ἐκ) that is important but the distance (ἀπό) that he dares to put between himself and the crowd.

tion with the disciples (Mark 9:18, 28–29) as well as with the father (Mark 9:23).

22 Both Matthew and Luke attest the father's request, but they do so in different ways. In Matthew he falls on his knees before Jesus (Matt 17:14); in Luke he cries out and makes his request (Luke 9:38; cf. 18:38).

23 Δέομαί σου ("I beg you") occurs four times in Luke: Luke 8:28; 9:38; Acts 8:34; 21:39. Since one would expect an imperative to follow, one is inclined to read here the proparoxytone ἐπιβλέψαι (aorist middle imperative), though ἐπιβλέπω is hardly ever used in the middle voice. I therefore hold to the aorist active infinitive accented on the penult, but I hasten to point out that not a few mss. have the aorist active imperative ἐπίβλεψον. It would be interesting to know how the minuscule mss. accent ἐπιβλέψαι. Unfortunately, this information is not reported in the apparatus of the *New Testament in Greek* (206), which simply prints the textus receptus, ἐπίβλεψον.

24 Ἐπιβλέπω is used for the look of pity in 1 Sam (LXX 1 Kgdms) 1:11; 9:16.

25 Luke retains Mark's title διδάσκαλε ("teacher"), which in a plea for a miracle should surprise no one, since there were indeed certain rabbis in antiquity who possessed thaumaturgical powers (see Geza Vermes, *Jesus the Jew: A Historian's Reading of the Gospels* [2d ed.; New York: Macmillan, 1976] 69–82).

26 Those who have come in contact with epilepsy know all about the fears that grip this young man's family.

27 See Erna Lesky in idem and Jan Hendrik Waszink, "Epilepsie," *RAC* 5 (1962) 819–31, esp. 829 (bottom)–830 (top).

attacks. The reason for these crises is a spirit (v. 39), an unclean spirit (v. 42), who, in contrast to the one in Mark 9:17, can scream (κράζει). A few words, but not the sentence structure, are reminiscent of Mark: λαμβάνει αὐτόν ("it seizes him," cf. αὐτὸν καταλάβῃ in Mark 9:18), σπαράσσει ("it convulses [him]," cf. συνεσπάραξεν in Mark 9:20 and σπαράξας in Mark 9:26), μετὰ ἀφροῦ ("with foam"; cf. ἀφρίζει in Mark 9:18). The gnashing of teeth and the parching in Mark 9:18a, the endangerment by fire and water (Mark 9:22; the main characteristics of the "moon sickness" according to the Matthean version [17:15]), as well as the symptom of apparent death (Mark 9:26), have no counterpart in Luke 9:37–43a. The items that Luke adopts correspond to objective observation: the attack "seizes" the sick man, and the observer is disturbed by the "suddenness," by the "scream" (or better, "sighing"), and by the "foam at the mouth." The slow subduing of the attack and the exhaustion after it (v. 39b) also correspond to clinical observation.[28]

An educated ancient reader of the Synoptic accounts would interpret this description of the illness as the ἱερὴ νοῦσος ("sacred disease," *morbus sacer*). For ancient scientific medicine recognized the main characteristics of an epileptic attack, distinguished among the three phases of a crisis, mentioned the signs that would appear before an attack, and also described the scream as the victim fell to the ground.[29] The main contribution of the Hippocratic tractate περὶ ἱερῆς νούσου ("about the sacred disease") is to see its origins no longer in the irrational realm of gods and demons. But according to the original understanding of the disease, which of course lived on in popular culture and in magical lore until late antiquity, the origin of the evil is not to be seen in nature. The sickness was called "holy" because it

was attributed to the power of a divinity, especially the mood goddess Selene (cf. Matt 17:15), or to a demon; this attribution was linked in Judaism to a corresponding doctrine of sin. Even the so-called doctor, Luke, is not aware of the scientific explanation of epilepsy. Origen shares this demonological presupposition and transmits it to Christendom for the next several centuries:

> Let physicians, then, discuss the physiology of the matter, inasmuch as they think that there is no impure spirit in the case, but a bodily disorder, and inquiring into the nature of things let them say, that the moist humours which are in the head are moved by a certain sympathy which they have with the light of the moon, which has a moist nature; but as for us, who also believe the Gospel that this sickness is viewed as having been effected by an impure dumb and deaf spirit.[30]

Even though the Christians at that time did not accept the scientific explanation, they also did not share the popular resignation or the various suggestions of the magical arts, despite sharing the same demonological explanation.[31] According to their viewpoint, only the word of the healing Messiah could liberate the boy. Jesus does not examine the father's guilt—which would have corresponded to a possible doctrine of retribution in contemporary Judaism—but has only the future of the possessed boy in view. He shows no fear of pollution, and does not shy from contact with the demonic world.[32]

■ **40** Verse 40 mentions a failed attempt at exorcism on the part of the disciples.[33] Luke stays close to Mark here,[34] but is not much interested in this failure. In Luke the victorious Lord stands alone at the center of the scene.

---

28 The mss. vary in v. 39b between the two synonyms μόλις and μόγις ("scarcely").

29 See Lesky in idem and Waszink, "Epilepsie," 826 (bottom). In cols. 824–29 the author defines epilepsy, gives its pathology, and discusses the various clinical and therapeutic aspects of epilepsy from the standpoint of ancient medical knowlege. See also John Wilkinson, "The Case of the Epileptic Boy," *ExpTim* 79 (1967) 38–42.

30 *Comm. in Matt.* 13.6, on Matt 17:15 (E. Klostermann, ed., *Origenes Werke* [GCS 11; Leipzig: Hinrichs, 1899] 10.193). Translation by J. Patrick, ANF 10.478.

31 See Lesky in idem and Waszink, "Epilepsie," 821–24; and van der Loos, *Miracles*, 402–5.

32 Gentiles attempted to keep the demon of epilepsy at a distance by spitting (see Lesky in idem and Waszink, "Epilepsie," 829).

33 See in addition the precedent of Gehasi in 2 Kgs (LXX 4 Kgdms) 4:31.

34 With the exception of Luke's ἐδεήθην ("I begged," redactional) and οὐκ ἠδυνήθησαν ("they could not"), which he shares with Matthew.

Middle and Conclusion (vv. 41–43a)

■ **41** At the beginning, Jesus speaks like the Jewish figure of rejected wisdom.[35] The quotation-like nature of his words explains the slight discrepancy with the context (e.g., that Jesus attacks the disciples with a critique of "this generation"). Independently from one another, or under the influence of the same oral variant, Luke and Matthew have harmonized the criticism with Scripture:[36] the generation[37] that is addressed is not only ἄπιστος ("faithless"), but also διεστραμμένη ("perverse," "corrupt"). It presently embodies the complete guilt of Israel. Like the figure of wisdom, the messenger of God confronts all alone the refractory nation, and asks how long he can continue to endure this situation.[38] We read such a judgment of "this generation" in 11:29–32 (the sign of Jonah); 11:49–51 (the blood of the prophets); 17:25 (the prediction of the passion); Acts 2:40 (the rescue from this generation). After the second prediction of the passion (Luke 9:43b–45), Luke will indicate the disciples' lack of comprehension. The saying in 9:41 already heads in this direction.[39]

With a change in address from the plural to the singular, Jesus requests the father to bring his son (προσάγαγε for the Markan φέρετε, "bring"). It is assumed that the father is in agreement with this command.

■ **42** On the way to Jesus, the demon perceives the danger that threatens, and defends itself (in a form-critically typical way).[40] The demon does not employ speech as a weapon, but causes an attack in the sick boy. This results in the healing power of the Messiah being manifested all the more impressively. The concept ἔτι ("still") appears to be important, since the demon fights back before the child has even arrived at Jesus. Luke expresses with two verbs a thought that Mark suggests to him:[41] the demon tugs at the child and convulses him (συνεσπάραξεν).

Jesus' rebuke, in the content of which Luke has no interest, in contrast to Mark 9:25, suffices metonymically for the exorcism itself;[42] ἐπιτιμάω ("to rebuke") occurs frequently in the exorcisms in the Synoptic Gospels. The father receives his son back healthy; this is, for him, like a return of something lost.

■ **43a** Luke ends the miracle story in typical style with a choral conclusion (9:43a: "astounded" is possibly inspired by the poorly placed ἐξεθαμβήθησαν, Mark 9:15). The numerous crowd (Luke 9:37) as well as "all" (9:43) marvel at God's greatness. Behind the person of Jesus who acts, they see God at work. Ἡ μεγαλειότης is not exactly τὸ μέγεθος ("the greatness"), but rather "the sublimeness," "the highness," "the splendor," "the majesty."[43]

Conclusion

In chap. 9 Luke places Jesus alternately in public episodes and private conversations. In the scenes that are hidden from the masses, the reader receives a hermeneutical key for the deeds of the Lord that are visible for all to see; and through the visible deeds, they receive again a confirmation of the revealed teaching. What the disciples have learned first concerns the identity of Jesus, and then his mission. The relationship of Jesus to God, and his healing power, the origins of

35   See Dibelius, *Tradition*, 278; and Bornkamm, "Πνεῦμα," 26–27, who cites *1 Enoch* 42:1–3 and Prov 1:20–33. Also Busse, *Wunder*, 265–66.

36   See Num 14:27; Deut 32:5, 20; Isa 6:11; 65:2. Schürmann (1.570) thinks that Jesus employs the language not only of the disillusioned prophets but also of God when he is enraged at his people.

37   On this "generation" see Odil Hannes Steck, *Israel und das gewaltsame Geschick der Propheten: Untersuchungen zur Überlieferung des deuteronomistischen Geschichtsbildes im Alten Testament* (WMANT 23; Neukirchen-Vluyn: Neukirchener Verlag, 1967) 32 n. 1, 39 n. 1, and 162 n. 1.

38   According to Godet (1.434–35), Jesus feels like a foreigner on earth; the previous evening's celebration, his transfiguration, has awakened in him a longing for home.

39   Luke's wording here is no closer to Matthew's than it is to Mark's. Note that Luke has put πρὸς ὑμᾶς ("with you") after the verb ἔσομαι ("I will be") and has deleted the second ἕως πότε ("how long," "until when"), replacing it with a καί.

40   Theissen classifies it as his sixteenth motif in *Miracle Stories*, 57, 79.

41   See ῥήσσω ("dash," "tug," a later form of ῥήγνυμι) in Mark 9:18 and συσπαράσσω ("convulse") in Mark 9:20.

42   In Mark 9:25–27 this scene is portrayed dramatically.

43   According to BAGD *s.v.*, Luke uses the word again in Acts 19:27, where he puts it in the mouth of a pagan defending the majesty of Artemis. In the NT the word appears again only in 2 Pet 1:16, where it describes the glory of Christ at the transfiguration.

which were illuminated like lightning in the transfiguration (9:28–36), were confirmed in the victory over the evil spirit.[44]

The condition that we today call epilepsy is one of the most cryptic of diseases. The loss of consciousness for a time would have meant in antiquity that the afflicted person was possessed by a superhuman power. What could anyone, either the shocked spectator or the sick person, do to stop it? The text names the healing word of the divine Son as the solution, which completely overshadows the limited results of contemporary medicine and the counterfeit successes of magic.[45]

Can we as Christians today have more than a hope in God's victory over death and disease? We would take an epileptic son to the doctor, who indeed would perhaps not be able to heal the "holy" sickness, but could stabilize it at least. On the other hand, is not the nice formulation of Ambroise Paré a bit cheap for the Christian faith ("Je le pansay, Dieu le guarit" ["I bandage him, God healed him]")? Should we limit the work of God today exclusively to the interiority of a human being? As interpreters, we should not project our culturally specific conception of reality into the first century and explain that the healing of this boy would have been "impossible."[46] But we are also in no position to prove the historical truth of the miracle through the theological relevance of the miracle story.[47] Jesus had many contemporaries who also claimed a similar ability to work miracles.[48] The definition of a "miracle" varies from one age to another. Thus the "essence" of a miracle varies as well: what would be for many of our contemporaries an impossible trespassing of natural law would have been in antiquity an astonishing and powerful proof of divine origin, for the divine was not excluded from nature. The evidentiary power of a miracle for a religious idea was neither zero nor total. Jesus himself exercised the abilities of an exorcist, and the first Christians found in this miracle story a testimony, but not a proof that would take its place alongside the word.

---

44 Busse writes (*Wunder,* 260): "Luke gives this episode the form of a messianic epiphany account."

45 Agreeing with Bornkamm, "Πνεῦμα," 30–31.

46 See Achtemeier, "Miracles," 488.

47 See ibid., 489.

48 See ibid., 489–90.

The Second Prediction of the Passion
The Disciples' Conflict about Rank
The Strange Exorcist (9:43b–50)

Bibliography

On Luke 9:43b–45
Bastin, "Annonce."
idem, *Jésus devant sa Passion* (LD 92; Paris: Cerf, 1976) 123–42.
Dömer, *Heil*, 83–85.
Gamba, "Senso."
Hooker, *Jesus and the Servant.*

On Luke 9:46–48
Kodell, Jerome, "Luke and the Children: The Beginning and End of the Great Interpolation (Luke 9:46–56; 18:9–23)," *CBQ* 49 (1987) 415–30.
Leaney, Robert, "Jesus and the Symbol of the Child (Luke ix. 46–48)," *ExpTim* 66 (1954–55) 91–92.
Légasse, *Jésus et l'enfant.*
Lindeskog, Gösta, "Logia-Studien," *StTh* 4 (1950) 129–89, esp. 171–77.
Robbins, Vernon K., "Pronouncement Stories and Jesus' Blessing of the Children: A Rhetorical Approach," *Semeia* 29 (1983) 43–74.
Schnackenburg, "Mark."
Schramm, *Markus-Stoff*, 140–41.
Vaganay, "Schématisme."
Weber, *Jesus and the Children.*

On Luke 9:49–50
Baltensweiler, Heinrich, "'Wer nicht gegen uns (euch) ist, ist für uns (euch)!' Bemerkungen zu Mk 9,40 und Lk 9,50," in *Festschrift Bo Reicke = ThZ* 40, no. 2 (1984) 130–36.
Fridrichsen, Heinrich, "Wer nicht mit mir ist, ist wider mich," *ZNW* 13 (1912) 273–80.
Nestle, Wilhelm, "'Wer nicht mit mir ist, der ist wider mich,'" *ZNW* 13 (1912) 84–87.
Roloff, *Kerygma*, 185–86.
Wilhelms, Eino, "Der fremde Exorzist: Eine Studie über Mark. 9,38ff," *StTh* 3 (1949) 162–71.

43b Since everyone was amazed at all that he was doing, he said to his disciples, 44/ "Let these words sink into your ears: the Son of Man is going to be betrayed into human hands." 45/ But they did not understand this saying; and it was hidden from them, so that they could not perceive it. And they were afraid to ask him about this saying. 46/ A question, however, arose among them as to which one of them was the greatest. 47/ And Jesus knew the question of their hearts, and took a little child and put him by his side, 48/ and said to them, "Whoever welcomes this child in my name welcomes me, and whoever welcomes me welcomes the one who sent me; for whoever is the least among all of you, he or she is great." 49/ But John answered, "Master, we saw someone casting out demons in your name, and we tried to forbid him, because he does not follow with us." 50/ And Jesus said to him, "Do not forbid it; for whoever is not against you is for you."

Analysis

After the surprising shift from the transfiguration (9:28–36) to the crisis of the "epileptic" (9:37–43a), the first part of the Gospel (1:1–9:50) ends even more cryptically (9:43b–50). Against the background of the miracle performed successfully in front of the crowd,[1] the Lukan Jesus now chooses the tone of parenesis (9:44a) and the style of prophecy (9:44b). Compared with the emphatic success of Jesus' deed (9:43ab),[2] these words encounter incomprehension (9:45a) and silent fear (9:45b) from the disciples. The paradox of the situation becomes clear in that the *crowd* applauds the divine power that has been demonstrated, while the suffering of the divine representative proclaimed to the disciples leaves them speechless.[3] Then a discussion erupts within the circle of the disciples (9:46): the conflict about rank. Without waiting to be asked, Jesus intervenes on the basis of his supernatural knowledge (9:47a). As often, Luke sketches the image of a wise teacher, who dispenses a teaching, which at the same time represents the solution to the disagreement, by employing a parabolic action: taking a child to his side (9:47b). But the saying that corresponds to the action is not the very next thing he says, but rather the wisdom saying about the smaller one, who is indeed "great" (9:48b). At first glance, the saying that comes in between (9:48a) seems to treat a dif-

---

1 Observe how Luke connects the crowd's excitement over the healing (9:43a) with their general amazement at Jesus' deeds (9:43b).

2 At v. 43b, Loisy (279) also refers back to v. 43a.

3 Giuseppe Gamba is of the opinion that vv. 43b–45 are carefully constructed ("Senso e significato funzionale di Luca 9,43b–45," in *Il messianismo* [ASB 18; Brescia: Paidea, 1966] 233–67, esp. 234–35): there are two antithetical strophes; Jesus is subject of the first (vv. 43b–44), and the disciples the subject of the second (v. 45).

ferent theme: the theological appurtenance of the messenger to the divine author, and the decisive ethical behavior in response to them. But the sequence within the saying (the child—I [= Jesus]—the one who sends [= God]) forms the basis of the theocentric saying about the child. Thus it also alludes to the disagreement, as is shown by the manner in which Jesus' gesture (taking a child to his side, 9:47b) and the first saying (allusion to the child, 9:48a) fit together.

In working through these materials, Luke also tries to form a link to the next, the last, episode, which is evident in the detail that John's question (9:49) appears as a reaction (ἀποκριθεὶς δέ, "but John answered"). In concluding the episode, Jesus gives a double answer. In the first part he demands tolerance for the concrete case (9:50a), and in the second part he gives a general justification in proverbial style (9:50b). After this sapiental conclusion, Luke solemnly begins the travel narrative (9:51ff.). Detailed exegesis will make clear whether this pericope consists of three units (9:43b–45, 46–48, 49–50),[4] two units (9:43b–45, 46–50), or just one unit (9:43b–50).

Luke again accepts the Markan sequence: after the second prediction of the passion (Mark 9:30–32 par. Luke 9:43b–45) comes the disciples' conflict about rank (Mark 9:33–37 par. Luke 9:46–48), as well as the strange exorcist (Mark 9:38–40 par. Luke 9:49–50).[5] He does,

however, ignore Mark 9:42–50.[6] Both evangelists indeed begin their travel narrative at the same point (Mark 10:1 par. Luke 9:51), but with a complete divergence in substance. The various hypotheses about the preliterary origins of this pericope develop in totally different directions.[7] The most convincing solution is that the functional setting for the smaller units was the oral instruction of the earliest community, and that the present proximity of these episodes and floating sayings to one another can be explained on the basis of catchwords and conceptual association.[8] In any case, Mark's is the first available written version, not that of Matthew or Luke. Despite this, the manner in which this unit came together (second prediction of the passion, the disciples' conflict about rank, and the strange exorcist) remains a puzzle. Luke retained both the sequence and the content of his Markan source here.

Synoptic Comparison
Luke omits the Markan transition at the beginning of this pericope, that is, Jesus' roving travels with his group through Galilee and his desire to remain incognito (Mark 9:30).[9] In its place he repeats, in a paraphrase (9:43b), the spreading effect of Jesus' miracles (9:43a). The amazement at them remains (ἐκπλήσσομαι, "to be astounded," there; θαυμάζω, "to amaze," here), and remains universal (πάντες, "all," there; ἐπὶ πᾶσιν, "at

---

4   Gamba (ibid., 251–54) proposes the following structure: the three scenes of vv. 43b–50 conclude the teaching theme found in the three-part section (4:14–6:49; 7:1–23; 7:24–9:50). This section is devoted to the witness that Scripture, miracles, and teaching give for Jesus. In Gamba's opinion, 9:43b–45 refers to the torment of the cross, which must be overcome; 9:46–48 refers to the Father, and 9:49–50 to his followers.

5   The sequence in Matthew is slightly different: the evangelist inserts the question about the temple tax (Matt 17:24–27) between Matt 17:22–23 (the second prediction of the passion) and Matt 18:1–5 (the rivalry among the disciples). Moreover, Matthew does not know about the episode involving the strange exorcist (Mark 9:38–40 par. Luke 9:49–50), and he moves the logion about the glass of water (Mark 9:41) to another location (Matt 10:42).

6   Mark 9:42 (the logion of the millstone) is adopted by Luke, but at another location, 17:1–2.

7   There is another possibility, in addition to the construction of Léon Vaganay and the astonishing solu-

tion of William Bussmann, who finds the origin of Mark 9:33–40 in a shorter text that is practically identical with Luke 9:46–50. Vaganay maintains the thesis that a sermon had concluded the fourth part of a version of Matthew that had been translated from Aramaic into Greek ("Le schématisme du discours communautaire," *RB* 60 [1953] 203–44 [= idem, *Le problème synoptique: Une hypothèse de travail* (Bibliothèque de théologie 1; Tournai: Desclée, 1954) 361–404]): various elements of it survive in Matt 18:1–35, Mark 9:33–50, and Luke 9:46–50. I know of William Bussmann, *Synoptische Studien* (3 vols.; Halle: Buchhandlung des Waisenhauses, 1925–31) 1.171–72, 215–16, only via Rudolf Schnackenburg, "Mk 9,33–50," in J. Schmid and A. Vögtle, eds., *Synoptische Studien: Festschrift A. Wikenhauser* (Munich: Zink, 1953) 184–206, esp. 190–92.

8   See Schnackenburg, "Mark," 184–206.

9   Matthew, on the other hand, intervenes decisively in this transition (Matt 17:22).

all," here). The only difference is that, in comparison with the brief notice of amazement in 9:43a, the introductory formula of 9:43b expands the perspective by using a generalizing formulation (ἐπὶ πᾶσιν οἷς ἐποίει, "at all that he was doing"–imperfect). And whereas 9:43a refers to the greatness of God, 9:43b varies the theme by emphasizing the role of the intermediary.[10] In 9:48, however, one is again made aware of the complementarity between God and his messenger. At the end of v. 43, Luke again approximates Mark,[11] for example, in the mention of the disciples. At the beginning of v. 44, he introduces a call to attention, the origins of which are redactional.[12] He ends abruptly with the mention of the betrayal of the Son of Man into human hands.[13] Given his great respect for the sayings of Jesus, this is amazing, for he thus deletes from Mark 9:31 the explicit mention of Jesus' death and resurrection.[14] But he does manage to avoid any formal repetition of the first prediction of the passion (9:22), and he emphasizes with this saying, as he formulates it,[15] an interpretation of Jesus' death that is close to his heart: the fact of being betrayed, and thus Jesus' coming suffering.[16]

Whereas Matthew 17:23b goes its own way, with its phrase about the grieving of the disciples, Luke remains faithful to his source (Mark), but in v. 45 he expands both parts of Mark 9:32 with the mention of the disciples' incomprehension[17] and the content of the question they suppress.[18]

As often, Luke greatly modifies the Markan beginning of the next paragraph.[19] He shortens the topo-

---

10 Even though it is not explicit, Jesus alone must be the subject of ἐποίει ("he was doing") in Luke 9:43b. Note the transition from the greatness of God (9:43a) to the actions of Jesus (9:43b).

11 But Luke has changed the verb: Luke has εἶπεν ("he said") with πρός ("to"), while Mark 9:31 has ἐδίδασκεν ("he taught") with the accusative.

12 Even though a few exegetes (like Marshall, 393) assert that τίθημι εἰς τὰ ὦτα ("to place in the ears") is a Semitism. One sees here Luke's characteristic complementarity of "doing" (v. 43b) and "saying" (v. 44), where action is more significant than speaking, or at least precedes it (see Acts 1:1).

13 Like Matthew, Luke makes his wording more precise than Mark's by adding μέλλει ("to be about to") to the infinitive παραδίδοσθαι ("to be betrayed"), thus replacing Mark's present tense with a future. This minor agreement between Matthew and Luke should be attributed to oral tradition. Matt 17:22-23 follows Mark from this point onward, ending with the prophetic statements of Jesus' death and resurrection, while Luke breaks off after the statement about the Son of Man's betrayal into human hands. Various explanations are given for the γάρ ("for") in Luke 9:44: first, formally, it could represent a somewhat unfortunate adaptation of the Markan ὅτι; or second, thematically, the issue of prophecy (9:44b) justifies the call to be watchful (9:44a). On this γάρ see Gamba, "Senso," 243. Marcel Bastin believes with great optimism that the Lukan wording of this prophecy (9:44b) comes nearest to being the original, authentic form of Jesus' own words ("L'annonce de la passion et les critères de l'historicité," RevScRel 50 [1976] 289-329, esp. 329; 51 [1977] 187-213).

14 The parallel of Mark 9:31 at Matt 17:23 proves that Mark's text indeed contained these words, but that Luke has omitted them.

15 It seems obvious to me—pace Gamba ("Senso," 239-48)—that what the disciples are supposed to put into their ears (v. 44a) is the contents of v. 44b (the prophetic statement).

16 See the predictions in Luke, which are particularly Lukan in this respect: Luke 17:25 and 24:46 (in regard to content), and 24:7 (in regard to form); see also 18:32-33 (dependent on Mark).

17 I think the words ἵνα μὴ αἴσθωνται αὐτό ("so that they could not perceive it") are redactional, but in the opinions of Zahn (391 n. 14) and Marshall (393), they were already in the tradition.

18 By repeating the word ῥῆμα ("word"), Luke creates an inclusio, thus either betraying his pedantry or proving his literary sensitivity. One should also observe that all the words of Mark 9:32 appear in Luke 9:45 with one exception: Mark has ἐπερωτῆσαι, while Luke has ἐρωτῆσαι (though in each passage there are some mss. which have the other reading). This situation is surprising, since Luke normally prefers compound verbs. It is possible that Luke wants to make a distinction between the use of ἐρωτῆσαι with the accusative (= "to ask someone") and ἐπερωτῆσαι (= "to ask someone about something"). Yet both verbs can be used with a double accusative, and the expression ἐρωτάω with the accusative of the person questioned and περί with the genitive of the thing asked is common and correct.

19 Lagrange (281) observes correctly that Luke presents the teaching given in connection with the child (in vv. 46-48) as the answer to the dispute among the disciples, whereas Mark merely juxtaposes both elements.

graphical information[20] and omits the dialogue that introduces it in Mark 9:33. He thus arrives at a better connection between the two episodes (prediction of the passion and the conflict about rank), which now take place on the same occasion. The comparison of Luke 9:46 with 9:47a shows that Luke also wants to express Jesus' supernatural wisdom; this was indeed already the purpose of Mark 9:33–35, though in a somewhat different manner. Is it for the purpose of shortening the account that Luke also omits Mark 9:35?[21] It is more likely that he knows a saying with similar content that he wants to insert at the end of this unit (Luke 9:48b),[22] and leaves out Mark 9:35 (as does Matthew) to avoid creating a doublet with Luke 22:26.[23] But indeed it is not possible to achieve absolute clarity about the omission of Mark 9:35 in Luke.[24]

After the redactional description of Jesus' knowledge (9:47a), Luke describes his gestures toward the child in a form that diverges slightly but significantly from Mark (9:47b): Jesus takes the child to his side (Mark: "into their midst" and "into his arms").[25] The reason for this is not a rejection of Jesus' expression of emotion,[26] but rather that Luke is describing a child who can stand, not an infant who must be carried (as in Mark).[27] The accompanying saying (9:48a) is extremely close to the Markan source (9:37),[28] whereas Luke probably himself composed the last saying in the scene (9:48b).[29]

The reader can detect the skillful hand of the author in 9:49–50, for Luke again connects the episode more integrally than does Mark with the previous scene (with ἀποκριθεὶς δέ, "but [John] answered,"), avoids the repetition (here the "follow" from Mark 9:38, although this repetition is not text-critically secure in Mark), and corrects theological inaccuracies (one does not follow the disciples themselves as in Mark 9:38, but Jesus "with" his disciples, μεθ' ἡμῶν). His love of the title ἐπιστάτης ("master," in contrast to the Markan διδάσκαλος, "teacher") is well known. Given this form of address, John expects a command, not a teaching. The reason for deleting Mark 9:39, 41–50 is unclear. Luke is probably in a hurry to arrive finally at the travel narrative (Luke 9:51ff.). So he concludes the paragraph with the statement, "whoever is not against you is for you" (9:50b par. Mark 9:40), which has an only apparently contradictory counterpart in 11:23: "Whoever is not with me is against me, and whoever does not gather with me scatters."[30]

---

20 See also perhaps v. 43b.

21 Luke does not know the sayings in Matt 18:3–4 ("become like children"), and so he continues to follow Mark. Schramm (*Markus-Stoff*, 130–36, 140–41) does not find Mark behind Luke 9:43b–45, as he does with Luke 9:46–50. He postulates that Luke 9:43b–45 depends on a special source.

22 Luke 9:48b ("the least is the greatest") remains in the semantic field of greatness with which the pericope began (Luke 9:46). Simon Légasse (*Jésus et l'enfant: 'Enfants,' 'Petits' et 'Simples' dans la tradition synoptique* [EtB; Paris: Gabalda, 1969] 27–32, 72–75, esp. 29) points out the *inclusio* μείζων ("greater," "greatest," v. 46)–μέγας ("great," v. 48).

23 See Luke 13:30 ("the last—the first") and 22:24–27 (the concept of greatness is defined in terms of service).

24 See Schnackenburg ("Mark," 199), who represents the view that Luke 9:48b (the lesser is great) is a parallel to Mark 9:35, which Luke has accommodated to the setting of the rivalry among the disciples and the presence of the child (note the Lukan ὁ μικρότερος, "the smallest," for ἔσχατος ["the least," Mark 9:35] and the absence of διάκονος ["servant," Mark 9:35] in Luke).

25 Along with Léon Vaganay ("Schématisme," 377), I ascribe ἐπιλαβόμενος ("taking") and παρ' ἑαυτῷ ("by his side") to Luke.

26 Marshall (396) is mistaken when he thinks that Luke has omitted the statement about Jesus' holding the child in his arms in order to avoid mentioning the human feelings of Jesus.

27 See Luke 2:28, where Simeon takes the infant Jesus into his arms.

28 Two small differences are worth mentioning: (1) Luke has "this child," Mark has "one of the children," while Matthew, who appends Matt 18:5 to some additional logia in 18:3–4, gives v. 5 a completely different form. (2) Luke makes the logion more concise.

29 According to Vaganay ("Schématisme," 372) ἐν ("among"), ὑμῖν ("you"), and μέγας ("great") at the end of v. 48 belong to an old layer, while πᾶσιν ("all") and ὑπάρχων ("is") come from Luke's pen. For Schnackenburg's view, see n. 24 above.

30 In my opinion 9:50 and 11:23 are two versions of the same original saying. The former comes from Mark, and the latter comes from Q (Matt 12:30 preserves only Q's version). Luke overcomes the apparent contradiction between these two statements by addressing the well-meaning outsiders in 9:50, but in 11:23 he rebukes the lukewarm (from the inner circle, as Marshall believes [399]?), who do not want to make a decision. Perhaps because of the verb κακολογῆσαι ("to speak evil"), which occurs in Mark 9:39 in a logion that Luke omits, both Eino

In conclusion, one can say that in Luke 9:43b–50 the evangelist adopts three shorter units from Mark—indeed not without shortening and reinterpreting them—that had been linked together with other units (Mark 9:41–50) for reasons hard to understand.

Commentary

The Riddle of the Betrayal (vv. 43b-45)

In Luke 9 christological questions alternate with questions about church office; parts of it concern Jesus, and other parts his disciples. The account of the healing of the possessed boy even alludes to the contrast between Jesus' power and the preliminary powerlessness of the disciples.

■ **43b–44** This juxtaposition between the teacher and his "followers" is sharpened in the second prediction of the passion. In comparison with the generally shared awe about Jesus (9:43b),[31] the silence of Jesus' closest companions in view of his prophecy (9:44b), and despite his parenetic encouragement (9:44a), is all the more embarrassing.

The advice, or the command, to come to terms with the necessary betrayal of the Son of Man is especially Lukan. On the level of metacommunication, Jesus wants to convince his disciples to hear and understand (9:44a).

In this half-verse, the intention of the entire Lukan composition becomes comprehensible, or rather, "audible," for being a Christian is an existence concerned with hearing, whereby one needs to receive not just any words, but explicitly these words (τοὺς λόγους τού-τους), which should be retained in memory, and which concern christology and, within christology, the passion narrative.

The incomprehension of the disciples in v. 45 is perhaps the most important reason for the deletion of the reference to the death and resurrection: in its Lukan form, Jesus' prophecy (9:44b) remains more cryptic than the first prediction of the passion (9:22). The mysterious Son of Man shall or should be betrayed into human hands.[32] Which human beings? Why the betrayal? What sort of suffering is meant?

■ **45** The disciples' discomfort at this saying[33] is purposely emphasized by Luke. Not only do they not understand it (ἠγνόουν), its meaning is also hidden from them.[34] As if this did not suffice, Luke also adds, "so that they could not perceive it." Behind the encoded meaning of this saying is God, who predestines (final ἵνα), but, on the other side, also human beings in their blindness to salvation history (consecutive ἵνα).[35] If the truth sounds so shocking, it is understandable that the interested parties do not dare, from fear, to ask. In con-

---

Wilhelms ("Der fremde Exorzist: Eine Studie über Mark. 9,38ff," *StTh* 3 [1949] 162–71, esp. 166) and Schürmann (1.799) understand that the saying here in Luke 9:50 presupposes a situation of persecution. See also Godet, *Commentaire,* 1.622.

31 On θαυμάζω ("to be amazed") see Gamba, "Senso," 236. The basic meaning is "to marvel," "to stand in astonishment before a θαῦμα," i.e., before something visible. In its figurative sense, the word means "to be surprised," "to admire" in an approving way (only rarely in an unfavorable sense).

32 The literature on παραδίδωμι ("to betray") is too vast to survey. According to Morna D. Hooker (*Jesus and the Servant: The Influence of the Servant Concept of Deutero-Isaiah in the New Testament* [London: SPCK, 1959] 92–95), the verb occurs approximately 250 times in the LXX and primarily indicates an action of God (only 20 times referring to a human action). Hooker regards this instance as an action of God, but she rules out here any influence from Isa 53:12; see also Bastin, "Annonce," 313–22.

33 Ῥῆμα ("word," "saying," Mark 9:32) was in the tradition and was already part of the pre-Markan layers of the prediction of the passion. The redactional

contribution of Luke to v. 45 consists of his repetition of the term ῥῆμα. Also redactional is the plural οἱ λόγοι οὗτοι ("these words," v. 44a). Morna D. Hooker (*Jesus and the Servant,* 95) points out that one finds often three motifs side by side in the predictions of the passion: the title "Son of Man," the theme of necessity, and the theme of suffering.

34 The use and nuances of παρακαλύπτω ("to hide") deserve a more detailed investigation. According to Marshall (394) παρακαλύπτω with ἀπό is a Hebraism. On ἀγνοέω ("to fail to understand"), see Gamba, "Senso," 255–57. Like Paul (1 Cor 1:30; 2:6–9), Luke believes that human beings were not able to recognize the mystery—in spite of their desire for the revelation of Jesus and God—before it was finally realized (for this reason Gamba understands the ἵνα in a consecutive rather than a final sense). The same misunderstanding on the part of the disciples is encountered again in Luke 18:34.

35 According to Godet (1.437), the clause introduced with ἵνα explains that God in his providence permits this blindness. On ἵνα see Gamba, "Senso,"

trast to the enthusiastic beginning (9:43b), there is only incomprehension at the end (9:45); between the two (9:44) is the cryptic statement about the betrayal of the Son of Man. Is this not the entire relationship between the first (1:5–9:50) and the second (9:51–19:27) parts of the Gospel, a relationship that one can already detect in the transfiguration (9:28–36)?

True Greatness (vv. 46–48)

■ **46** Διαλογισμός ("thought," "question," "discussion")[36] is better understood as a discussion rather than an argument. The word usually has a negative connotation in Luke, and locates the issue within the heart. Just as the devil works on human beings from the outside (cf. 22:3), the discussion here approaches (εἰσῆλθεν, "enters among") the disciples from outside, as an objective, almost personalized being, as it were. It is an unavoidable event, but also an internal matter, since human beings share responsibility for its effect on them.

The content of the discussion is summarized in an elegant dependent clause, with a verb in the optative, a mood that had become rare by New Testament times.[37]

The subject was who would be the greatest[38] among the disciples,[39] not who would be greater than the disciples, as the answer in v. 48b finally makes clear.

■ **47** Verse 47 makes the reader aware of two things. The author first stresses, in a participial phrase, that Jesus—like God himself—knows the secrets of the heart;[40] then he attaches Jesus' symbolic gestures in two phases: Jesus takes[41] a child[42] and places it by his side. As the contrast with Mark shows, this proximity to Jesus has a particular meaning, since it expresses a choice and a privilege, just as being a Christian does in itself (cf. 10:21–22).

■ **48a** Without words, a symbolic action nevertheless remains multivalent. For this reason, Jesus adds an interpretation to it, as did the prophets formerly. Oddly, the interpretive saying stands in a certain tension with the introductory question about greatness, since the child is not immediately introduced as an adult, that is, as the "great one," in accordance with the expected paradox. The content of the saying in v. 48a does not aim at the child's "greatness," but at the child's receptivity.[43] The readers thus find themselves confronted with a double

255–57 (cf. n. 34 above). Loisy (280) notes that while the stubbornness of the disciples is a distinctive feature of Mark's Gospel, it is not in Luke. Luke gives an explanation for their misunderstanding: God has willed it.

36 On διαλογισμός see the commentary on 2:35b above. Some expositors, such as Légasse (*Jésus et l'enfant*, 28) and Hans Ruedi Weber (*Jesus and the Children: Biblical Resources for Study and Preaching* [Geneva : World Council of Churches, 1980] 45), argue that this dialogue only took place within the mind of each of the disciples, so that Jesus had to know their thoughts, and thus appears even more miraculous. I rather think that there is some tension between v. 46 and v. 47a: since the evangelist has attempted to combine the prediction of the passion (vv. 43b–45) with the rivalry among the disciples (vv. 46–48), Jesus has now become a witness of their altercation so that the need for his miraculous knowledge has been lessened. On the miraculous knowledge of hidden thoughts, see Bieler, ΘΕΙΟΣ ANHP, 1.87–90. Godet (*Commentaire*, 1.617) understands the διαλογισμός in v. 46 as a "conversation" and in v. 47a as an "altercation."

37 Vaganay ("Schématisme," 369–70) notes how elegantly Luke has expressed a possibility in the present time.

38 Regarding the form, the comparative was often used instead of the superlative in the Greek of that day (see Vaganay, "Schématisme," 369, and BDF §60 and §244). Regarding the content, Str-B 1.249–50 notes that the rabbis asked who—in the world to come—would be the greatest.

39 According to Plummer (257) one must construe αὐτῶν with τίς: "Who of them is the greatest?" But the same sense results if one construes αὐτῶν with the comparative: "Who is the greatest of them?" (and not, as Grundmann argues [197], "Who is greater than they [i.e., the disciples]?").

40 God searches the heart (see 1 Chr 28:9; Ps 138[139]:23; Rom 8:27; Rev 2:33). See also n. 36 above.

41 In ἐπιλαβόμενος ("taking") I recognize the hand of Jesus resting on (ἐπί) the chosen child: by this act of Jesus, the child is honored (so Plummer, 257, and Marshall, 396). For Lagrange (281) it is merely a symbolic action.

42 Of course, παιδίον ("child") is a diminutive, but this does not mean that the child is an infant. On the image of the children and their upbringing in antiquity, one may read the accomplished accounts in Légasse, *Jésus et l'enfant*, 276–87; and Weber, *Jesus and the Children*, 65–78.

43 Plummer (258) additionally notes that here it is not the child who is the true disciple, but the one who welcomes such a child.

394

transmutation of the words: within the proof that the little one (v. 47) is truly the great one (v. 48b), the viewpoint also changes—the debate no longer concerns *whom* the Lord considers to be the "great one," but first the question of *who* accepts God and his ambassador. Righteousness thus has two sides: it concerns the acceptance of the chosen person by God, symbolized in the acceptance of the little one by Jesus (vv. 47 and 48b), as well as the acceptance, by the believer, of the Father (ὁ ἀποστείλας με, "the one who sent me"), the Son (ἐμέ, "me"), and the undervalued fellow human being (v. 48a).[44]

Verses 46–48 can thus be divided in the following manner:

A. Question (v. 46)
   B. Nonverbal (i.e., ambiguous) answer (v. 47)
   B.' First, indirect answer (v. 48a)
A.' Second, direct answer (v. 48b)

These two sides of righteousness are also two sides of faith: the passive experience of being accepted, and active service.[45] Both structural elements of the essence of being Christian are also attested in the saying at 22:26.

In considering receptivity (v. 48a), one should note that there is no gap between the level of historical existence and that of the eschatological reality of the kingdom of God,[46] but rather, as the similar saying in Luke 12:8–9 proves, a close bracketing of the two: to accept God or Christ by faith is the consequence of the ethical reception of the little one by the individual believer, or by the congregation.

The expression "in my name," which was already in Luke's source at Mark 9:37, is frequently encountered in the Third Gospel.[47] I connect it grammatically with the verb "welcome" and not with the phrase "this child."[48] One could also connect the expression "in my name" both to the child and to the one who welcomes it. This would agree with one of Luke's literary devices, and with his theology of relationship

■ **48b** Being "great"[49] will not realize itself only in eschatological time, but also already in the here and now.[50] Despite their close relationship, the two steps must also be distinguished. Thus the Baptist is "great" within the historical economy of salvation (1:15), but remains the "smallest" according to the criteria of the kingdom of God (7:28). Church and kingdom, mission and salvation should be distinguished, even if the verbs ἐπιλαμβάνομαι ("to lay hold of," "to obtain," "to take") and δέχομαι ("to receive," "to welcome") express the reciprocal exchange evident in love and in the experience of faith. Christ accepts us (v. 47), as we also may accept him. How could the "smallest"[51] fail to become "great" through such mutual acceptance?

---

44   The child accordingly represents Jesus, and at the same time, both of them, in their insignificance and suffering, represent God's presence. According to Weber (*Jesus and the Children*, 78–92), Jesus' statement here in v. 48 stands in direct contradiction to the ancient—also Jewish—way of thinking. As Schürmann (1.576) has explained, the statement is rather a continuation of a HB tradition that puts God on the side of the poor. Légasse (*Jésus et l'enfant*, 30) notes that honor is not due to the child simply because he is a child, but it is due to him for Jesus' sake. Légasse here underscores that the reversal of values implied in this logion corresponds to the manner in which God deals with humans, humbling the rich and exalting the poor. In his opinion Luke does not demand that everyone must become small, but that the smallest must also be honored in the community.

45   See Schürmann, 1.576: "Δέχεσθαι means here a caring 'acceptance,' perhaps even an enduring 'welcome,' because both Jesus and God want to be 'welcomed.'"

46   In historical time "the smallest," in eschatological time "great." Matthew especially has recognized this eschatological aspect when he asks the question of the disciples in this setting by specifying: "Who is the greatest *in the kingdom of heaven*?" (Matt 18:1).

47   See the list in Plummer, 258.

48   As does Godet, 1.439.

49   This greatness is expressed in the Christian system by service, as seen from Luke 22:26.

50   The expression "in my name," which was already in Luke's source at Mark 9:37, is frequently encountered in the third Gospel (see the list in Plummer, 258). I connect it grammatically (as does Godet, 1.618) with the verb "welcome" and not with the phrase "this child." One could also connect the expression "in my name" both to the child and to the one who welcomes it. This would agree with one of Luke's literary devices, and with his theology of relationship.

51   According to Marshall (396), the last sentence of v. 48 represents the climax of the pericope. Marshall gives three possible interpretations for ὁ

The Strange Exorcist (vv. 49–50)

■ **49–50** Structurally, the small dialogue[52] between John[53] and Jesus (9:49–50) is similar to the longer story of Eldad and Medad in Num 11:24–30. Joshua, the favorite disciple of Moses, asks him to "hinder" (κώλυσον αὐτούς, Num 11:28 LXX) in their work the two chosen men who were absent at the official bestowal of the Spirit on the tent of meeting. But the leader of Israel does not acquiesce to his demand.

It is undeniable that this Hebrew Bible episode exercised a literary influence on Luke 9:49–50. Although it is not the only key to the meaning of this verse, it does help one to understand the situation. For one thing, the name John becomes comprehensible. The son of Zebedee relates to the inner circle of Jesus' disciples as does Joshua to Moses. The strange exorcist exercises the same function as the disciples (9:1). The divine power at his disposal is not used for some extravagant purpose. Like Eldad and Medad, he is both "in" and "out" at the same time: out, because he is outside the group around Jesus,[54] and in, because he knows the christological roots of divine power (ἐν τῷ ὀνόματί σου, "in your name"). The strange exorcist is an outsider, not a usurper, in contrast to the sons of Sceva (Acts 19:13–17). In the background of this episode, which is divided after the manner of the model from the Hebrew Bible, is the confessional pluralism in earliest Christianity.[55] Jesus' spontaneous reaction,[56] which is similar to Moses' answer (μὴ κωλύετε, "do not forbid"), solves a burning problem: the recognition of competing missions.

It is true that the text does not discuss the details of such a recognition. Jesus' general and, at the same time, positive answer is sufficient. The Christian mission of other groups must not be sabotaged. This also connects with the theme of greatness, since the work of a missionary is "great" not in its uniqueness but in its adequacy to the purpose. So there are no "greatest" missionaries, only Christians who, as long as they are true Christians, are "great." The greatness of the strange exorcist casts no shadow on the ordinary missionary, who also qualifies as "great." To hinder the stranger would mean to work for the group, that is, for the church, and not for the central figure, that is, for the Lord.

μικρότερος: (1) the "smallest" is Jesus; (2) the "smallest" is the one who chooses to be like this child; and (3) the "smallest" is the one who really is the "smallest." In this context (ἐν πᾶσιν ὑμῖν, "among all of you") the comparative ὁ μικρότερος must have a superlative meaning. Both Godet (1.437–38) and Plummer (p. 258) emphasize that Luke says "great" and not "the greatest," which they then moralize: Jesus wants to protect the disciples from the sin of pride.

52 According to Plummer (257–58), 9:46–48 and 49–50 represent two examples of humility; the second indicates the humility of tolerance. According to Schürmann (1.574), 9:46–48 deals with an internal problem within the Christian community, while 9:49–50 deals with an external problem between the Christian community and the outside world.

53 As Godet writes (*Commentaire*, 1.616, 620): a John "who has gone over the top," as the disciples have done in v. 46.

54 On the verb ἀκολουθέω ("to follow") in Luke, see the commentary on 5:27–28 above. The journey to Jerusalem—and to the cross—begins soon. The disciples will also follow their master; they will suffer and be "the least," like him. The verb "to follow" connects that which precedes (discipleship, 9:43b–50) with that which follows, where outsiders (9:51–56)—who like the strange exorcist should not be rebuked—as well as the disciples (9:57–62) are now called to follow.

55 Note the Gospel fragment of P. Oxy. 1224, fol. 2ʳ, col. 1 (p. 176), above in the commentary on 6:27–28 (n. 29).

56 The text of this verse has been transmitted rather poorly. The textual critic is here faced with three problems. First, is there an article ὁ before Ἰησοῦς ("Jesus") in v. 50a or not? Luke normally has the article, and the ms. tradition also points into this direction. Second, some witnesses read after μὴ κωλύετε ("do not forbid it," v. 50a) "for he is not against you." This is certainly a gloss. P⁴⁵ (Chester Beatty 1) reads: "for he is neither against you nor for you." Third, through the influence of the Synoptic parallels and of itacism (ὑμῶν, "you," and ἡμῶν "us," are pronounced alike), there are in the ms. tradition major variations for the concluding statement in v. 50b. There are four solutions to choose from: (a) "He who is not against you is for you" (Nestle-Aland). (b) "He who is not against us is for us" (= Mark 9:40). (c) "He who is not against you is for us." And (d) "He who is not against us is for you." Solution (d) is poorly attested; (c) is attested by few but good witnesses; it yields a parenetic sense; (b) is too dependent on Mark 9:40. Nestle-

For this reason, the wisdom saying expresses a truth in this situation: "whoever is not against you is for you."[57] Of course, the same rule must apply to the strange exorcist, that is, for competing groups, as applies to Jesus' closest disciples: missionary work (here exorcism) must serve the glory of God, not one's own reputation. Only in this way is the stranger not "against you." But if this is so, then he is for us, that is, for the mission and the salvation of humanity. A further observation is important in this context: the power of Jesus' name, which is equivalent to the freedom of the Holy Spirit, works within the institution, though it is not solely at the disposal of its officials.[58]

Conclusion

Despite the formal differences, and the colorful profusion of the various themes, an impressive coherence dominates 9:43b–50: How does church leadership live with the double message of success and suffering (vv. 43b–45)? What is the true greatness of church officials, and, more generally, of every believer (vv. 46–48)? How can the competition that so often erupts be transformed into cooperation (vv. 49–50)?

Aland has certainly made the right decision in choosing the remaining possibility, (a) (a conclusion already reached by Godet, 1.440–41).

57 Since the 17th century (see Anton Fridrichsen, "Wer nicht mit mir ist, ist wider mich," *ZNW* 13 [1912] 273–80, esp. 273 n. 1 and 280 n. 2), expositors have cited a Latin parallel (to both Luke 9:50 and 11:23), found in Cicero's defense of Q. Ligarius (46 BCE), the exiled supporter of Pompey (*Lig.* 33): "Valeat tua vox illa, quae vicit. Te enim dicere audiebamus nos omnes adversarios putare, nisi qui nobiscum essent; te omnes, qui contra te non essent, tuos" ("May what you have said that has led to victory prevail! For we have heard you to say that we think everyone is an adversary except those who have been with us, while you think everyone who has not been against you is yours"). Wilhelm Nestle concludes from this pre-Christian parallel text that

this saying did not come from Jesus but that it has been scripted for him ("'Wer nicht mit mir ist, der ist wider mich,'" *ZNW* 13 [1912] 84–87). Anton Fridrichsen contradicts Nestle: a pre-Christian parallel does not exclude a priori the authenticity of this saying. It was probably a situation in which Jesus picked up a wisdom saying that was already in common use and then adapted it for his own purpose.

58 Godet makes two important observations (1.440): Jesus here is opposing the monopoly of the disciples, and he is opposing their attempt to limit God's power. Schürmann (1.578–79) rightly points out that in vv. 49–50 an ecclesiological question is being debated, and, in the answer, it is confirmed that the grace of Jesus is also effective outside the circle of the disciples.

1:59-61	67	1:72b	74	2:4-5	83, 84, 86[45]
1:59	70, 71	1:73	67, 74	2:4	58, 84, 137[22]
1:60	48	1:73a	74	2:5-7	44[4]
1:62-63	24[83], 67, 71	1:73b-74a	74, 75[74]	2:6-20	81
1:62	39, 39[84], 50[72], 102[42]	1:74	67, 72	2:6-7	69[21], 85, 88, 91
1:63-67	92	1:74b-75	75, 75[74]	2:6-7a	82, 85, 86
1:63	70	1:74b-75a	78	2:6	69, 69[20], 81, 85, 88[65], 96
1:64	67, 71, 72, 72[41], 159[4], 355[15]	1:75	47[34], 67, 68	2:7	86, 88[65], 89[74], 90
1:65-67	72[41]	1:76-79	67, 68, 68[6], 69, 74, 104	2:7b	81, 356[29]
1:65-66a	67	1:76-77	67[1], 68, 68[13], 69, 75, 75[80], 76	2:8-20	81, 87
1:65	70, 77, 273[54], 273[52]	1:76	47[34], 67, 68, 69, 71, 76, 78, 103, 281	2:8-14	93, 94
1:66	70, 71			2:8-12	81, 86
1:66a	67, 72	1:77	67, 128, 182	2:8	81, 86, 87, 87[53], 91, 330[65], 356[27]
1:66b	67, 77	1:78-79	76, 90[83]		
1:67-80	29	1:78	67, 67[1], 72[49], 76	2:9	87, 88, 90, 324[14]
1:67	36[57], 71, 84, 100, 151	1:78a	67, 76	2:10-12	88, 90
1:68-79	7, 72[41], 77, 103[48], 109[1]	1:78b-79	68	2:10-11	91
1:68-75	74	1:78b	67, 76	2:10	35[40], 36[48], 88, 88[66], 103[48], 106
1:68-71	75	1:79	67, 76		
1:68-75	67, 68, 75	1:79b	76	2:11	44[4], 46, 81, 86, 88, 88[65], 88[66], 89[72], 125[52], 129[76], 154
1:68-69	68, 69, 73, 74	1:80	67, 71, 77, 81, 96, 106, 118, 283[38]		
1:68	35, 67, 68, 72[45], 78, 102, 274[58], 274[59]	2	22, 49, 57, 82, 104, 115[59], 118	2:12	38[77], 71, 89, 89[74], 90, 93
1:68a	67, 72	2:1-40	29	2:13-14	35[37], 81, 88, 90
1:68b-69	72	2:1-21	29, 79	2:13	90, 92
1:68b	67	2:1-20	48, 81	2:14	90, 91, 91[88], 93, 111
1:69	67, 68, 74	2:1-14	93	2:15-20	81, 91, 92, 93, 94
1:70	67, 68, 73, 73[56], 74, 75[74]	2:1-7	94	2:15	87[54], 91, 92
1:71-73a	73	2:1-5	81, 82, 83, 93, 96, 112	2:15c	187
1:71	67, 72, 73, 74, 74[70], 75[74]	2:1-3	83	2:16	71, 89[74], 90, 92
1:72-73	74	2:1-2	83	2:16b	92
1:72-73a	74	2:1	3, 81, 83, 120, 143[40]	2:17-20	92
1:72	67, 71, 74[65], 74[70]	2:2	83	2:17-18	92
1:72a	74	2:3	83, 84		
1:72b-73a	67, 75[74]	2:4-7	82[13]		

412

4:37	151, 159, 165, 167[4], 175	4:44	49[52], 158, 161, 165, 213, 273[52], 274[64]	5:12-16	173, 176, 267
4:38-39	163, 164, 175	5	168, 207	5:12-14	157[43], 174[15]
4:38	159, 163, 210, 324[14]	5:1—6:19	171[26]	5:12-13	175
4:38a	163[35]	5:1-11	6[6], 77[7], 158, 166, 167, 167[1], 171, 173, 176, 190, 216, 266, 347, 363	5:12	167, 174, 176, 176[23], 178, 178[1], 327[43]
4:38b	163[35]			5:12a	173, 174
4:39	3, 112, 159, 163, 170, 175, 301			5:12b-14	174
4:40-44	177[29]	5:1-3	167, 187	5:13	173, 175, 176[23]
4:40-41	159, 163, 164, 176, 177[29], 213[14], 301[18], 301[19]	5:1-2	4, 172[29]	5:13a	177
		5:1	167, 174[8], 178, 299, 299[2], 305	5:13b	177
4:40	159, 160, 164, 165, 175, 179, 190[22], 334, 356[27]	5:2	168, 169, 170	5:14	99, 173, 174, 176, 176[24], 176[26], 362
		5:3-7	172[29]	5:15-16	157[43], 173, 176
4:40a	160	5:3	167, 169	5:15	151, 174, 176, 301[18]
4:40b	160	5:3b	169[14]		
4:41	160, 160[5], 162[23], 163, 164, 212, 213	5:4-9	167	5:15a	173, 176[27]
		5:4-5	169, 179	5:15b-16	173
4:41a	160	5:4	167, 169	5:16	160, 173, 174, 356
4:41b	160	5:5	102[39], 169, 170[16], 274, 339[46]		
4:42-44	178, 214, 257			5:17-39	173
		5:6-7	170	5:17-26	174, 178, 194, 202, 202[18], 267, 356[29]
4:42-43	164, 177	5:7	40[95]		
4:42	159, 160, 160[9], 160[10], 160[11], 164, 177[30], 356	5:8-11	170, 172[29], 186		
		5:8	169, 170, 187	5:17-19	181
4:42b	160[8]	5:9-10a	170	5:17	165[44], 167, 178, 181, 181[23], 201, 203, 213[17], 262, 272[46], 284[53], 300[14], 344[13], 357
4:43-44	167, 173, 203, 299[2]	5:9	167, 171		
		5:10-11	167		
4:43	33[17], 158, 161, 164, 165, 174, 179[2], 300[14], 307[19], 344, 356[29]	5:10	35[40], 167, 169, 210		
		5:10a	171	5:17a	179[3]
		5:10b	167, 169[14], 170	5:17c	179[3]
		5:10c	170, 171[21]	5:18	179, 179[7], 181
		5:11	167, 171, 187	5:18b	178, 179
				5:19	179
				5:19a	178
		5:12—6:19	167	5:20-24	293

417

Reference	Pages
8:26	323
8:27-28	323
8:27	323, 328, 330
8:27b	323
8:28-29	328
8:28	323, 327, 329, 385[23]
8:28a	323
8:28b	328, 329[53]
8:29	323[6], 324, 328, 327, 328[52], 330
8:29a	323. 324
8:29b	323, 324, 328, 329
8:30-32	323
8:30-31	328
8:30	323, 324, 328
8:31-32b	323
8:31	127[61], 324, 329, 329[54], 330[63], 331[76]
8:32-33	329
8:32	127[61], 324, 329, 330, 331[76]
8:33	323[2], 324
8:34-39	323, 325, 330, 331
8:34-35	324
8:34-35	330
8:34	324, 330, 330[66]
8:35	205[43], 324, 325, 330[66]
8:36-37	324
8:36	205[43], 324, 325, 330[66], 331
8:37	273[54], 324, 325, 329[58], 330, 331[76], 334
8:37b	334
8:38-39	325, 331[75], 332, 334
8:38	331, 331[76]
8:39	92[98], 330, 331[75], 334
8:39a	325, 331
8:39b	325, 331
8:40-56	333, 334[4], 383
8:40	323, 334, 335, 336, 383[11]
8:41-42a	335
8:41	127[61], 8:41 333[1], 336, 337[33], 339[56], 383[11]
8:42	111[16], 268[13], 333, 333[1], 334, 334[4], 336, 337, 337[37], 339, 383[11]
8:42b	335, 339
8:43-48	335, 335[17], 337, 361
8:43	335[17], 336, 338, 341, 338
8:44	333, 333[1], 335[17], 336, 338, 341
8:45-48	335[17]
8:45	334, 336
8:45a	339
8:45b	339
8:46	181[23], 272[46], 334[9], 338, 339, 357
8:46a	334, 334[4]
8:46b-47a	334
8:46b	334[4]
8:47	336, 338, 339
8:48	293, 298, 298[60], 334[9], 338, 339[48], 340
8:49	262[34], 334, 335, 336, 337[33], 339
8:50	35[40], 334, 335, 339[52], 340, 340[58], 340[60]
8:51	211, 333[1], 335, 336, 337[33], 340, 340[61], 374, 383[11]
8:52-53	334, 335, 340
8:52	340
8:53	340
8:54	113, 204, 335, 336, 340, 340[61], 341, 383[11]
8:55-56	340
8:55	335, 341
8:56	334, 335, 341, 362
9	342, 343, 382, 384, 387, 393
9:1-50	342
9:1-10a	360
9:1-6	209, 300, 342, 343, 346[31], 351, 352, 353, 355, 363, 382[1]
9:1-2	343, 344, 347, 354
9:1	161[18], 162, 181[23], 334, 344, 347[33], 356, 396
9:2	171[24], 343, 344
9:3-5	343, 345, 368

6:14	358[45]	21:9	356	2:16	100[23], 144
6:15	145[49], 209[16]	21:15	330[65]	2:17	106, 106[78], 128, 128
6:26-34	145[49]	21:17	330[65]	2:23	2, 11, 285, 363
6:42	155	21:22	100[30]	2:33	126
6:69	162[28]	21:23	100[30]	2:36	23[77]
7:1-4	145[49]	21:24-25	17, 17[17]	2:37-47	125
7:30	157[43]	21:24	17	2:37	123
7:42	87[51]			2:38	182
7:53—8:11	296[52]	**Acts**		2:40	127[61], 387
8:16	114[45]	1:1-11	11	2:41	168[8], 203[24], 334[6]
8:59	157[43]	1:1	17, 21, 22[54], 24, 25, 152, 277, 391[12]	2:43	203[24], 273[54]
9:3	34[25]			2:44-45	225
9:14	203	1:2-3	25	2:46	200[27], 227
9:22	227[49]	1:2	25, 209	2:47	168[8], 331
10:20-21	287[80]	1:3-8	25	3:1-26	344
10:30	114[45]	1:3	19[22], 140	3:1	101[31], 200[27], 211[33]
10:39	157[43]	1:4	36[59]	3:10	202
11	341	1:5-22	118[2]	3:11	101[31], 112[33], 211[33]
11:16	211[36]	1:5	36[59], 126	3:12	104[58]
11:49	120[16]	1:7	39[88]	3:13	21[42]
12:1-8	291	1:8	25, 36[59], 52, 52[81], 53, 347	3:15	363
12:3	294	1:9-11	128[70], 179[11], 347[36], 376	3:17	204[37]
12:25	365	1:9	192	3:18	376[45]
12:42	227[49]	1:11	103	3:19-20	385
13:13	254[57]	1:13	207, 207[4], 210, 210[25], 210[26], 299[5], 336	3:20-21	68
13:16	249	1:14	49, 208	3:20	39[88]
14:22	114	1:21-22	22, 136, 136[16], 166, 347, 368	3:21	73[56]
15:20a	249	1:22-23	21, 209	3:21b	68
15:27	21[44]	1:24	209	3:22	63[80]
16:2	227[49]	1:26	21[42]	3:24	22[62]
18:6	157[43]	2	261	3:25	74[65], 74[71], 355[15]
18:13	120[16]	2:3-4	126	3:26	355[15]
18:19	120[16]	2:4	36[59]	4:4	168[8]
18:28—19:16	34[33]	2:5	100[26]	4:6	120[16]
19:25-27	30	2:7	155, 155[30]	4:12	142
19:26-27	274	2:11	61[63]	4:13	112, 211[33], 374
20:13	59	2:12	349[8]	4:14	293[13]
20:24-29	281	2:14-36	123	4:19	211[33]
20:28	59			4:24-31	208
20:29	39[85], 265, 281				
20:30-31	17, 17[17]				
20:31	17				
21	17, 29, 171				
21:1-11	167				
21:4	170				

Revelation (*cont.*)

18:19	222[11]
19:1-8	226[37]
19:1-2	56[6]
19:5b	56[6]
19:6b-8a	56[6]
19:9	222[11]
19:10	376
20:1	329
20:3	329
20:6	222[11]
21:2	191[34]
21:4	226[37]
21:9	191[34]
22:7	222[11]
22:14	222[11]
22:16	134[4]
22:17	191[34]
22:18-19	17[17]

c / Deuterocanonical Books and Pseudepigrapha

Apocalypse of Elijah

4.14-15	350[16]
5:32	350[16]

Apocalypse of Moses

20-21	375[42]

Aristeas, Epistle of

8	19[29]
148	20[39]
196	20[39]
227	234[18]
322	19[29]

2 Baruch

10:6—12:4	55[6]
29:3-8	359[50]
54:10	59[42]
85:1	73[56]

3 Baruch

1–2	103[51]
4:13	103[51]
4:14	103[51]
11:7	103[51]
17:4	103[51]

1 Enoch

10:11ff.	329[56]
18:11ff.	329[56]
40:9	39[81]
42:1-3	387[35]
60:24	359[50]
90:6-7	37[68]

2 Enoch

23	45[15]
33:1-2	374[31]
42:6-12	222
50:3	234[18]
52	222

1 Esdras

5:38	70[28]
8:91(LXX 88)	106[79]

2 Esdras (4 Ezra)

2:61	70[28]
4:28-32	309[34]
9:31	308[26]
9:45	61[55]
10:6	59[42]
10:16	70[28]
10:20-24	55[6]
14:11	137
14:24	71[36]

Joseph and Aseneth

23.9	234[18]
28.14	234[18]
29.3	234[18]

Jubilees

5:6ff.	329[56]
11:11	308[27]
23:26	37[68]
32:27-29	374[33]

Judith

4:6-7	71
4:7	58[29]
6	329[56]
6:6	105
8:1-2	105[73]
8:4-6	106[76]
9:8	87[59]
10:9	59[47]
13:18	59[42]
15:13	189[16]

1 Maccabees

2:1-2	71[33]
2:7-13	55[6]
4:24	118[3]
4:46	129[71]
7:17	118[3]
9:21	118[3]
9:27	129[71]
9:41	118[3]
11:33	237[38]
14:41	129[71], 350[22]

2 Maccabees

2:32	19[29]
3:29	39[84]
6:7	272[43]
6:8	272[43]
6:17	19[29]
6:21	272[43]
7:6	118[3]
7:9	102[38]
7:42	272[43]
8:36	189[16]
9:8	319[19]
12:4	170[16]
15:12	311[53]
15:24	180[15]

3 Maccabees

6:31	357[36]
7:21	124[47]

4 Maccabees

4:1	311[53]

Psalms of Solomon

2:1	56
2:2	56

70.9-34 192[36]
71.3-21 192[36]
72.17-29 192[36]
74.21-22 192[36]
75.25-76.9 192[36]
78.13-24 192[36]
78.26-79.13 192[36]
81.28-82.26 192[36]
84.22-23 192[36]
85.32-86.7 192[36]

Gospel of Thomas
5 314
9 306[13]
26 247[7]
31 155
33b 313[68]
34 247[7]
41 315[77]
45 247, 247[7], 247[8]
46 284[50]
47 186[1], 188, 188[10], 188[11]
54 221
55 365[4]
58 221
67 365[4]
68-69 221
68 221, 221[2]
69a 221[2]
69b 221, 221[2], 221[3]
78 278[10]
99 315[82]
104 186[1]

Gospel of Pseudo-Matthew
15.2 100[24]
31.1-2 110[11]
38.1 110[11]

Hermas
Visions
1.3 (1.1.3) 318[7]
7 (2.3.2) 309[42]
9.6 (3.1.6) 87[57]
13.4 (3.5.4) 237[38]
15 (3.7.3) 311[51]
17.5 (3.9.5) 237[38]
19 (3.11.3) 310[49], 310[51]
23 (4.2.4-5) 310[49], 310[51]
Similitudes
51 (2.5-7) 310-11[51]
74 (8.8.5) 311[51]
75 (8.9.1) 309[42]
75 (8.9.4) 311[51]
95.1-2 (9.18.1) 237[38]
97 (9.20.1-2) 311[51]
105.6-8 (9.28.6-8) 221[5]

Hippolytus of Rome
Apostolic Tradition
16 124[41]

Hippolytus
Refutatio omnium haeresium
5.8.45 (5.3.45) 46[26]

Ignatius
Letter to the Trallians
9.1 288[86]

Infancy Gospel of Pseudo-Thomas
(6, 14) 110[11]

Irenaeus
Adversus haereses
1.7.4-5 263[46]
1.20.2 113
1.26.1 131[91]
1.30.11-14 131[91]
3.1.1 9[11]
3.11.1 131[91]
4.31.2 288[91]
5.12.2 288[91]

Jerome
Adversus Pelagium
3.2 131[88]
Commentarii in Isaiam prophetam
4 (on Isa 11:2) 131[89]
Epistles
46.13 271[33]
52.8 196[2]
58.3 90[78]
108.13 271[33]
De viris illustribus
7 10[13]

John Chrysostom
Hom. in Act.
30.4 297[58]

John of Damascus
Hom. in Transfigurationem
12 381[79]

Justin
1 Apologia
1.15.9-10 234[16]
14.3 232[8]
15.8 190[24]
15.9-10 232[8]
15.9 232
15.12 365[4]
16.1 232[8]
16:10 247
Dialogus cum Tryphone
49:4-5 118[5]
78 90[78]

Origen
De Principiis
19[31]
In Johannem Commentarius
6.41 326[34]
In Mattheum Commentarius
13.6 (on Matt 17:15) 386[30]
frg 95.1 314[72]
Homiliae in Evangelium secundum Lucam
13.1-3 91[93]
14-17 99[15]
15.3 101[35]

h / Other Greek and Latin Literature

Strabo
    17.1.17   269[18]
    17.1.43   97[8]

Suetonius
Augustus
    28.1   83[20]

Sylloge inscriptionum graecarum[3]
    3.1168.37   87[57]

Tacitus
Annals
    1.11.7   83[20]
    15.44   233[12]

Theophrastus
Characteres
    5   23[67]

Thucydides
    2.47-52   175[17]
    6.54.7   71[37]

Titulus Tibertinus
(CIL 14:3613 and
ILS 918)
        84, 84[24]

Virgil
Eclogues
    4.49   45[12]

Xenophon
Anabasis
    2.6.10   87[55]
    3.2.10   62[75]
Cyropaedia
    7.5.50   101[33]
Historia graeca
    6.4.23   62[75]

Xenophon Ephesius
Ephesiaca
    1.7.1   93[104]

Zenobius
Paroemiographus
    1.73   287[81]

Designer's Notes

In the design of the visual aspects of *Hermeneia,* consideration has been given to relating the form to the content by symbolic means.

The letters of the logotype *Hermeneia* are a fusion of forms alluding simultaneously to Hebrew (dotted vowel markings) and Greek (geometric round shapes) letter forms. In their modern treatment they remind us of the electronic age as well, the vantage point from which this investigation of the past begins.

The Lion of Judah used as visual identification for the series is based on the Seal of Shema. The version for *Hermeneia* is again a fusion of Hebrew calligraphic forms, especially the legs of the lion, and Greek elements characterized by the geometric. In the sequence of arcs, which can be understood as scroll-like images, the first is the lion's mouth. It is reasserted and accelerated in the whorl and returns in the aggressively arched tail: tradition is passed from one age to the next, rediscovered and re-formed.

"Who is worthy to open the scroll and break its seals. . . ."
Then one of the elders said to me
"weep not; lo, the Lion of the tribe of David,
the Root of David, has conquered,
so that he can open the scroll and
its seven seals."
Rev. 5:2, 5

To celebrate the signal achievement in biblical scholarship which *Hermeneia* represents, the entire series will by its color constitute a signal on the theologian's bookshelf: the Old Testament will be bound in yellow and the New Testament in red, traceable to a commonly used color coding for synagogue and church in medieval painting; in pure color terms, varying degrees of intensity of the warm segment of the color spectrum. The colors interpenetrate when the binding color for the Old Testament is used to imprint volumes from the New and vice versa.

Wherever possible, a photograph of the oldest extant manuscript, or a historically significant document pertaining to the biblical sources, will be displayed on the end papers of each volume to give a feel for the tangible reality and beauty of the source material.

The title-page motifs are expressive derivations from the Hermeneia logotype, repeated seven times to form a matrix and debossed on the cover of each volume. These sifted-out elements will be seen to be in their exact positions within the parent matrix.

Horizontal markings at gradated levels on the spine will assist in grouping the volumes according to these conventional categories.

The type has been set with unjustified right margins so as to preserve the internal consistency of word spacing. This is a major factor in both legibility and aesthetic quality; the resultant uneven line endings are only slight impairments to legibility by comparison. In this respect the type resembles the hand-written manuscripts where the quality of the calligraphic writing is dependent on establishing and holding to integral spacing patterns.

All of the type faces in common use today have been designed between AD 1500 and the present. For the biblical text a face was chosen which does not arbitrarily date the text, but rather one which is uncompromisingly modern and unembellished so that its feel is of the universal. The type style is Univers 65 by Adrian Frutiger.

The expository texts and footnotes are set in Baskerville, chosen for its compatibility with the many brief Greek and Hebrew insertions. The double-column format and the shorter line length facilitate speed reading and the wide margins to the left of footnotes provide for the scholar's own notations.

Kenneth Hiebert

Category of biblical writing,
key symbolic characteristic,
and volumes so identified.

1
Law
(boundaries described)
   Genesis
   Exodus
   Leviticus
   Numbers
   Deuteronomy

2
History
(trek through time and space)
   Joshua
   Judges
   Ruth
   1 Samuel
   2 Samuel
   1 Kings
   2 Kings
   1 Chronicles
   2 Chronicles
   Ezra
   Nehemiah
   Esther

3
Poetry
(lyric emotional expression)
   Job
   Psalms
   Proverbs
   Ecclesiastes
   Song of Songs

4
Prophets
(inspired seers)
   Isaiah
   Jeremiah
   Lamentations
   Ezekiel
   Daniel
   Hosea
   Joel
   Amos
   Obadiah
   Jonah
   Micah
   Nahum
   Habakkuk
   Zephaniah
   Haggai
   Zechariah
   Malachi

5
New Testament Narrative
(focus on One)
   Matthew
   Mark
   Luke
   John
   Acts

6
Epistles
(directed instruction)
   Romans
   1 Corinthians
   2 Corinthians
   Galatians
   Ephesians
   Philippians
   Colossians
   1 Thessalonians
   2 Thessalonians
   1 Timothy
   2 Timothy
   Titus
   Philemon
   Hebrews
   James
   1 Peter
   2 Peter
   1 John
   2 John
   3 John
   Jude

7
Apocalypse
(vision of the future)
   Revelation

8
Extracanonical Writings
(peripheral records)

ΚΑΙ ΕΓΕΝΕΤΟ ΕΝ ΤΩ ΕΥΛΟΓΕΙΝ ΑΥΤΟΝ ΑΥ
ΔΙΕΣΤΗ ΑΠ ΑΥΤΩΝ ΚΑΙ ΑΝΕΦΕΡΕΤΟ ΕΙΣ ΤΟΝ
ΟΥΡΑΝΟΝ ΚΑΙ ΑΥΤΟΙ ΠΡΟΣΚΥΝΗΣΑΝΤΕΣ ΑΥ
ΤΟΝ ΥΠΕΣΤΡΕΨΑΝ ΕΙ ΙΗΛΜ ΜΕΤΑ ΧΑΡΑC
ΜΕΓΑΛΗC ΚΑΙ ΗCΑΝ ΔΙΑ ΠΑΝΤΟC ΕΝ ΤΩ
ΙΕΡΩ ΕΥΛΟΓΟΥΝΤΕC ΤΟΝ ΘΝ ⳨

EΥΑΓΓΕΛΙΟΝ
ΚΑΤΑ
ΛΟΥΚΑΝ

EΥΑΓΓΕΛΙΟΝ
ΚΑΤΑ ΙΩΑΝΗΝ

ΕΝ ΑΡΧΗ ΗΝ Ο ΛΟΓΟC ΚΑΙ Ο ΛΟΓΟC ΗΝ ΠΡΟC ΤΟΝ
ΘΝ ΚΑΙ ΘC ΗΝ Ο ΛΟΓΟC ΟΥΤΟC ΗΝ ΕΝ ΑΡΧΗ ΠΡΟC
ΤΟΝ ΘΝ ΠΑΝΤΑ ΔΙ ΑΥΤΟΥ ΕΓΕΝΕΤΟ ΚΑΙ ΧΩΡΙC
ΑΥΤΟΥ ΕΓΕΝΕΤΟ ΟΥΔΕ ΕΝ Ο ΓΕΓΟΝΕΝ ΕΝ ΑΥΤΩ
ΖΩΗ ΗΝ ΚΑΙ Η ΖΩΗ ΗΝ ΤΟ ΦΩC ΤΩΝ ΑΝΩΝ
ΚΑΙ ΤΟ ΦΩC ΕΝ ΤΗ CΚΟΤΕΙΑ ΦΑΙΝΕΙ ΚΑΙ Η CΚΟ
ΤΕΙΑ ΑΥΤΟ ΟΥ ΚΑΤΕΛΑΒΕΝ ΕΓΕΝΕΤΟ ΑΝΘΡΩ
ΠΟC ΑΠΕCΤΑΛΜΕΝΟC ΠΑΡΑ ΘΥ ΟΝΟΜΑ ΑΥΤΩ
ΙΩΑΝΗC ΟΥΤΟC ΗΛΘΕΝ ΕΙC ΜΑΡΤΥΡΙΟΝ ΙΝΑ
ΜΑΡΤΥΡΗCΗ ΠΕΡΙ ΤΟΥ ΦΩΤΟC ΙΝΑ ΠΑΝΤΕC
ΠΙCΤΕΥCΩCΙΝ ΔΙ ΑΥΤΟΥ ΟΥΚ ΗΝ ΕΚΕΙ
ΝΟC ΤΟ ΦΩC ΑΛΛ ΙΝΑ ΜΑΡΤΥΡΗCΗ ΠΕΡΙ ΤΟΥ
ΦΩΤΟC ΗΝ ΤΟ ΦΩC ΤΟ ΑΛΗΘΙΝΟΝ Ο ΦΩΤΙ
ΖΕΙ ΠΑΝΤΑ ΑΝΟΝ ΕΡΧΟΜΕΝΟΝ ΕΙC ΤΟΝ ΚΟ
CΜΟΝ ΕΝ ΤΩ ΚΟCΜΩ ΗΝ ΚΑΙ Ο ΚΟCΜΟC ΔΙ
ΑΥΤΟΥ ΕΓΕΝΕΤΟ ΚΑΙ Ο ΚΟCΜΟC ΑΥΤΟΝ ΟΥΚ
ΕΓΝΩ ΕΙC ΤΑ ΙΔΙΑ ΗΛΘΕΝ ΚΑΙ ΟΙ ΙΔΙΟΙ ΑΥ
ΤΟΝ ΟΥ ΠΑΡΕΛΑΒΟΝ ΟCΟΙ ΔΕ ΕΛΑΒΟΝ ΑΥΤΟΝ
ΕΔΩΚΕΝ ΑΥΤΟΙC ΕΞΟΥCΙΑΝ ΤΕΚΝΑ ΘΥ ΓΕ
ΝΕCΘΑΙ ΤΟΙC ΠΙCΤΕΥΟΥCΙΝ ΕΙC ΤΟ ΟΝΟΜΑ ΑΥ
ΤΟΥ ΟΙ ΟΥΚ ΕΞ ΑΙΜΑΤΩΝ ΟΥΔΕ ΕΚ ΘΕΛΗΜΑ
ΤΟC CΑΡΚΟC ΟΥΔΕ ΕΚ ΘΕΛΗΜΑΤΟC ΑΝΔΡΟC
ΑΛΛ ΕΚ ΘΥ ΕΓΕΝΝΗΘΗCΑΝ ΚΑΙ Ο ΛΟΓΟC CΑΡΞ Ε
ΓΕΝΕΤΟ ΚΑΙ ΕCΚΗΝΩCΕΝ ΕΝ ΗΜΙΝ ΚΑΙ Ε
ΘΕΑCΑΜΕΘΑ ΤΗΝ ΔΟΞΑΝ ΑΥΤΟΥ ΔΟΞΑΝ ΩC ΜΟ
ΝΟΓΕΝΟΥC ΠΑΡΑ ΠΑΤΡΟC ΠΛΗΡΗC ΧΑΡΙΤΟC
ΚΑΙ ΑΛΗΘΕΙΑC ΙΩΑΝΗC ΜΑΡΤΥΡΕΙ ΠΕΡΙ ΑΥΤΟΥ
ΚΑΙ ΚΕΚΡΑΓΕΝ ΟΥΤΟC ΗΝ ΟΝ ΕΙΠΟΝ
Ο ΟΠΙCΩ ΜΟΥ ΕΡΧΟΜΕΝΟC ΕΜΠΡΟCΘΕΝ ΜΟΥ
ΓΕΓΟΝΕΝ ΟΤΙ ΠΡΩΤΟC ΜΟΥ ΗΝ ΟΤΙ ΕΚ ΤΟΥ